Lecture Notes in Computer Science 11736

More information about this series at http://www.springer.com/series/7410

Kazue Sako · Steve Schneider ·
Peter Y. A. Ryan (Eds.)

Computer Security – ESORICS 2019

24th European Symposium
on Research in Computer Security
Luxembourg, September 23–27, 2019
Proceedings, Part II

 Springer

Editors
Kazue Sako
NEC Corporation
Kawasaki, Japan

Steve Schneider 🆔
University of Surrey
Guildford, UK

Peter Y. A. Ryan 🆔
University of Luxembourg
Esch-sur-Alzette, Luxembourg

ISSN 0302-9743   ISSN 1611-3349   (electronic)
Lecture Notes in Computer Science
ISBN 978-3-030-29961-3   ISBN 978-3-030-29962-0   (eBook)
https://doi.org/10.1007/978-3-030-29962-0

LNCS Sublibrary: SL4 – Security and Cryptology

This Springer imprint is published by the registered company Springer Nature Switzerland AG
The registered company address is: Gewerbestrasse 11, 6330 Cham, Switzerland

Preface

This book contains the papers that were selected for presentation and publication at the 24th European Symposium on Research in Computer Security (ESORICS 2019) which was held together with affiliated workshops in Luxembourg, September 23–27, 2019. The aim of ESORICS is to further the progress of research in computer, information, and cyber security, as well as in privacy, by establishing a European forum for bringing together researchers in these areas, by promoting the exchange of ideas with system developers, and by encouraging links with researchers in related fields.

In response to the call for papers, 344 papers were submitted to the conference. These papers were evaluated on the basis of their significance, novelty, and technical quality. Each paper was reviewed by at least three members of the Program Committee and external reviewers, and papers authored by Program Committee members had four reviewers. The reviewing process was single-blind. The Program Committee had intensive discussions which were held via EasyChair. Finally, 67 papers were selected for presentation at the conference, giving an acceptance rate of 19.5%. We were also delighted to welcome keynote talks from Adi Shamir, Véronique Cortier, and Bart Preneel.

Following the reviews, two papers were selected for joint Best Paper Award, to share the 1,000 EUR prize generously provided by Springer: "A Frame-work for Evaluating Security in the Presence of Signal Injection Attacks," by Ilias Giechaskiel, Youqian Zhang, and Kasper Rasmussen; and "Breakdown Resilience of Key Exchange Protocols: NewHope, TLS 1.3, and Hybrids," by Jacqueline Brendel, Marc Fischlin, and Felix Günther.

The Program Committee consisted of 95 members across 24 countries. There were submissions from a total of 1,071 authors across 46 countries, with 23 countries represented among the accepted papers.

ESORICS 2019 would not have been possible without the contributions of the many volunteers who freely gave their time and expertise. We would like to thank the members of the Program Committee and the external reviewers for their substantial work in evaluating the papers. We would also like to thank the organization chair, Peter B. Roenne, the workshop chair, Joaquin Garcia-Alfaro, and all workshop co-chairs, the posters chair, Alfredo Rial, the publicity chair, Cristina Alcaraz, and the ESORICS Steering Committee and its chair, Sokratis Katsikas.

Finally, we would like to express our thanks to the authors who submitted papers to ESORICS. They, more than anyone else, are what makes this conference possible.

We hope that you found the program to be stimulating and a source of inspiration for future research.

July 2019

Kazue Sako
Steve Schneider
Peter Y. A. Ryan

Organization

ESORICS Steering Committee

Sokratis Katsikas (Chair)	NTNU, Norway
Michael Backes	Saarland University, Germany
Joachim Biskup	TU Dortmund, Germany
Frederic Cuppens	IMT Atlantique, France
Sabrina De Capitani di Vimercati	Università degli Studi di Milano, Italy
Dieter Gollmann	Hamburg University of Technology, Germany
Mirek Kutylowski	Wroclaw University of Technology, Poland
Javier Lopez	University of Malaga, Spain
Jean-Jacques Quisquater	University of Louvain, Belgium
Peter Y. A. Ryan	University of Luxembourg, Luxembourg
Pierangela Samarati	Università degli Studi di Milano, Italy
Einar Snekkenes	NTNU, Norway
Michael Waidner	Fraunhofer, Germany

Program Committee

Mitsuaki Akiyama	NTT, Japan
Cristina Alcaraz	University of Malaga, Spain
Elli Androulaki	IBM Research - Zurich, Switzerland
Frederik Armknecht	Universität Mannheim, Germany
Vijay Atluri	Rutgers University, USA
Marina Blanton	University at Buffalo, USA
Carlo Blundo	Università degli Studi di Salerno, Italy
Christian Cachin	University of Bern, Switzerland
Alvaro Cardenas	The University of Texas at Dallas, USA
Aldar C-F. Chan	University of Hong Kong, Hong Kong, China
Yan Chen	Northwestern University, USA
Sherman S. M. Chow	The Chinese University of Hong Kong, Hong Kong, China
Mauro Conti	University of Padua, Italy
Jorge Cuellar	Siemens AG, Germany
Frédéric Cuppens	Telecom Bretagne, France
Nora Cuppens-Boulahia	IMT Atlantique, France
Marc Dacier	EURECOM, France
Sabrina De Capitani di Vimercati	Università degli Studi di Milano, Italy
Hervé Debar	Telecom SudParis, France
Stéphanie Delaune	CNRS, France

Olivier Pereira	UCLouvain, Belgium
Günther Pernul	Universität Regensburg, Germany
Joachim Posegga	University of Passau, Germany
Bart Preneel	Katholieke Universiteit Leuven, Belgium
Christina Pöpper	New York University, USA
Indrajit Ray	Colorado State University, USA
Giovanni Russello	The University of Auckland, New Zealand
Mark Ryan	University of Birmingham, UK
Reyhaneh Safavi-Naini	University of Calgary, Canada
Kazue Sako	NEC, Japan
Pierangela Samarati	Università degli Studi di Milano, Italy
Damien Sauveron	XLIM – University of Limoges, UMR CNRS 7252, France
Steve Schneider	University of Surrey, UK
Einar Snekkenes	NTNU, Norway
Willy Susilo	University of Wollongong, Australia
Pawel Szalachowski	SUTD, Singapore
Qiang Tang	Luxembourg Institute of Science and Technology, Luxembourg
Qiang Tang	New Jersey Institute of Technology, USA
Juan Tapiador	Universidad Carlos III de Madrid, Spain
Nils Ole Tippenhauer	CISPA, Germany
Helen Treharne	University of Surrey, UK
Aggeliki Tsohou	Ionian University, Greece
Jaideep Vaidya	Rutgers University, USA
Luca Viganö	King's College London, UK
Michael Waidner	Fraunhofer, Germany
Cong Wang	City University of Hong Kong, Hong Kong, China
Lingyu Wang	Concordia University, Canada
Edgar Weippl	SBA Research, Austria
Christos Xenakis	University of Piraeus, Greece
Zhe Xia	Wuhan University of Technology, China
Kehuan Zhang	The Chinese University of Hong Kong, Hong Kong, China
Sencun Zhu	The Pennsylvania State University, USA

Additional Reviewers

Abidin, Aysajan	Al-Mallah, Ranwa	Bamiloshin, Michael
Abusalah, Hamza	Andriotis, Panagiotis	Bampatsikos, Michail
Aggelogianni, Anna	Anglès-Tafalla, Carles	Batra, Gunjan
Ahmed, Chuadhry Mujeeb	Anikeev, Maxim	Belgacem, Boutheyna
Akand, Mamunur	Asif, Hafiz	Belles, Marta
Al Maqbali Fatma	Avizheh, Sepideh	Berger, Christian

Bezawada, Bruhadeshwar
Bkakria, Anis
Blanco-Justicia, Alberto
Blazy, Olivier
Bolgouras, Vaios
Bountakas, Panagiotis
Boureanu, Ioana
Brandt, Markus
Böhm, Fabian
Cao, Chen
Catuogno, Luigi
Cetinkaya, Orhan
Chadha, Rohit
Chan, Mun Choon
Chawla, Gagandeep
Chen, Haixia
Chen, Jianjun
Chen, Liqun
Chen, Long
Chen, Xihui
Chen, Yueqi
Chothia, Tom
Ciampi, Michele
Cook, Andrew
Cortier, Véronique
Costa, Nüria
Cui, Shujie
Dang, Hung
Dargahi, Tooska
Dashevskyi, Stanislav
de Miceli, Jean-Yves
De Salve, Andrea
Debant, Alexandre
Deo, Amit
Diamantopoulou, Vasiliki
Dietz, Marietheres
Divakaran, Dinil Mon
Dominguez Trujillo,
   Antonio
Dryja, Tadge
Du, Minxin
Du, Xuechao
Dufour Sans, Edouard
Duman, Onur
Duong, Dung
Elkhiyaoui, Kaoutar

Englbrecht, Ludwig
Espes, David
Fan, Xiong
Farao, Aristeidis
Farhang, Sadegh
Fdhila, Walid
Fenghao, Xu
Ferreira Torres, Christof
Gangwal, Ankit
Ge, Chunpeng
Geneiatakis, Dimitris
Georgiopoulou,
   Zafeiroula
Giorgi, Giacomo
Groll, Sebastian
Gupta, Maanak
Gusenbauer, Matthias
Han, Jinguang
Hassan, Fadi
Hermans, Jens
Hicks, Christopher
Hirschi, Lucca
Hlavacek, Tomas
Homoliak, Ivan
Horne, Ross
Hu, Kexin
Iliou, Christos
Jacomme, Charlie
Jeitner, Philipp
Jiongyi, Chen
Jonker, Hugo
Judmayer, Aljosha
Kalloniatis, Christos
Kambourakis, Georgios
Karamchandani, Neeraj
Kasinathan, Prabhakaran
Kavousi, Mohammad
Kern, Sascha
Khan, Muhammad Hassan
Kim, Jongkil
Klaedtke, Felix
Kohls, Katharina
Kostoulas, Theodoros
Koutroumpouxos,
   Nikolaos
Kuchta, Veronika

Köstler, Johannes
La Marra, Antonio
Labani, Hasan
Lakshmanan, Sudershan
Lal, Chhagan
Lazzeretti, Riccardo
Lee, Jehyun
Leng, Xue
León, Olga
Li, Li
Li, Shujun
Li, Wanpeng
Li, Wenjuan
Li, Xing
Li, Xusheng
Li, Yanan
Li, Zengpeng
Li, Zhenyuan
Libert, Benoît
Lin, Chengjun
Lin, Yan
Liu, Ximing
Lobe Kome, Ivan Marco
Losiouk, Eleonora
Loukas, George
Lu, Yang
Lu, Yuan
Lyvas, Christos
Ma, Haoyu
Ma, Jack P. K.
Maene, Pieter
Majumdar, Suryadipta
Malliaros, Stefanos
Mardziel, Piotr
Marin, Eduard
Marson, Giorgia
Martinez, Sergio
Matyunin, Nikolay
Menges, Florian
Menghan, Sun
Michailidou, Christina
Milani, Simone
Minaud, Brice
Minematsu, Kazuhiko
Mizera, Andrzej
Moch, Alexander

Moessner, Klaus
Mohamady, Meisam
Mohammadi, Farnaz
Moisan, Frederic
Moreau, Solène
Moreira, Josè
Murayama, Yuko
Murmann, Patrick
Muñoz, Jose L.
Mykoniati, Maria
Ng, Lucien K. L.
Ngamboe, Mikaela
Nguyen, Quoc Phong
Ning, Jianting
Niu, Liang
Nomikos, Nikolaos
Ntantogian, Christoforos
Oqaily, Alaa
Oqaily, Momen
Ouattara, Jean-Yves
Oya, Simon
Panaousis, Manos
Papaioannou, Thanos
Parra Rodriguez, Juan D.
Parra-Arnau, Javier
Pasa, Luca
Paspatis, Ioannis
Peeters, Roel
Pelosi, Gerardo
Petrovic, Slobodan
Pfeffer, Katharina
Pitropakis, Nikolaos
Poh, Geong Sen
Polian, Ilia
Prestwich, Steve
Puchta, Alexander
Putz, Benedikt
Pöhls, Henrich C.
Qiu, Tian
Ramírez-Cruz, Yunior
Ray, Indrani
Reuben, Jenni

Rezk, Tamara
Rios, Ruben
Rizos, Athanasios
Román-García, Fernando
Rozic, Vladimir
Rupprecht, David
Sakuma, Jun
Saracino, Andrea
Schindler, Philipp
Schmidt, Carsten
Schnitzler, Theodor
Schumi, Richard
Sempreboni, Diego
Sengupta, Binanda
Sentanoe, Stewart
Sepideh Avizheh,
    Shuai Li
Shikfa, Abdullatif
Shioji, Eitaro
Shirani, Paria
Shrishak, Kris
Shuaike, Dong
Simo, Hervais
Singelée, Dave
Siniscalchi, Luisa
Situ, Lingyun
Smith, Zach
Smyth, Ben
Song, Yongcheng
Soriente, Claudio
Soumelidou, Aikaterini
Stifter, Nicholas
Sun, Yuanyi
Sundararajan, Vaishnavi
Tabiban, Azadeh
Tajan, Louis
Taubmann, Benjamin
Thomasset, Corentin
Tian, Yangguang
Tripathi, Nikhil
Tueno, Anselme
Ullrich, Johanna

Vanhoef, Mathy
Venugopalan, Sarad
Veroni, Eleni
Vielberth, Manfred
Viet Xuan Phuong, Tran
Walzer, Stefan
Wang, Daibin
Wang, Hongbing
Wang, Jiafan
Wang, Tielei
Wang, Xiaolei
Wang, Xiuhua
Wang, Zhi
Wattiau, Gaetan
Wesemeyer, Stephan
Wong, Harry W. H.
Wu, Daoyuan
Wu, Huangting
Xu, Jia
Xu, Jiayun
Xu, Ke
Xu, Shengmin
Xu, Yanhong
Yang, Kang
Yang, Shaojun
Yang, Wenjie
Yautsiukhin, Artsiom
Yuan, Chen
Zalonis, Jasmin
Zamyatin, Alexei
Zavatteri, Matteo
Zhang, Chao
Zhang, Liang Feng
Zhang, Yuexin
Zhao, Guannan
Zhao, Yongjun
Zheng, Yu
Zhou, Dehua
Zhou, Wei
Zhu, Tiantian
Zou, Qingtian
Zuo, Cong

Abstracts of Keynote Talks

The Insecurity of Machine Learning: Problems and Solutions

Adi Shamir

Computer Science Department, The Weizmann Institute of Science, Israel

Abstract. The development of deep neural networks in the last decade had revolutionized machine learning and led to major improvements in the precision with which we can perform many computational tasks. However, the discovery five years ago of adversarial examples in which tiny changes in the input can fool well trained neural networks makes it difficult to trust such results when the input can be manipulated by an adversary. This problem has many applications and implications in object recognition, autonomous driving, cyber security, etc, but it is still far from being understood. In particular, there had been no convincing explanations why such adversarial examples exist, and which parameters determine the number of input coordinates one has to change in order to mislead the network. In this talk I will describe a simple mathematical framework which enables us to think about this problem from a fresh perspective, turning the existence of adversarial examples in deep neural networks from a baffling phenomenon into an unavoidable consequence of the geometry of R^n under the Hamming distance, which can be quantitatively analyzed.

Electronic Voting: A Journey to Verifiability and Vote Privacy

Véronique Cortier

CNRS, LORIA, UMR 7503, 54506, Vandoeuvre-lès-Nancy, France

Abstract. Electronic voting aims to achieve the same properties as traditional paper based voting. Even when voters vote from their home, they should be given the same guarantees, without having to trust the election authorities, the voting infrastructure, and/or the Internet network. The two main security goals are vote privacy: no one should know how I voted; and verifiability: a voter should be able to check that the votes have been properly counted. In this talk, we will explore the subtle relationships between these properties and we will see how they can be realized and proved.

First, verifiability and privacy are often seen as antagonistic and some national agencies even impose a hierarchy between them: first privacy, and then verifiability as an additional feature. Verifiability typically includes individual verifiability (a voter can check that her ballot is counted); universal verifiability (anyone can check that the result corresponds to the published ballots); and eligibility verifiability (only legitimate voters may vote). Actually, we will see that privacy implies individual verifiability. In other words, systems without individual verifiability cannot achieve privacy (under the same trust assumptions).

Moreover, it has been recently realised that all existing definitions of vote privacy in a computational setting implicitly assume an honest voting server: an adversary cannot tamper with the bulletin board. As a consequence, voting schemes are proved secure only against an honest voting server while they are designed and claimed to resist a dishonest voting server. Not only are the security guarantees too weak, but attacks are missed. We propose a novel notion of ballot privacy against a malicious bulletin board. The notion is flexible in that it captures various capabilities of the attacker to tamper with the ballots, yielding different flavours of security.

Finally, once the security definitions are set, we need to carefully establish when a scheme satisfies verifiability and vote privacy. We have developed a framework in EasyCrypt for proving both verifiability and privacy, yielding machine-checked security proof. We have applied our framework to two existing schemes, namely Helios and Belenios, and many of their variants.

Cryptocurrencies and Distributed Consensus: Hype and Science

Bart Preneel

COSIC, an imec lab at KU Leuven, Belgium

Abstract. This talk will offer a perspective on the fast rise of cryptocurrencies based on proof of work, with Bitcoin as most prominent example. In about a decade, a white paper of nine pages has resulted in massive capital investments, a global ecosystem with a market capitalization of several hundreds of billions of dollars and the redefinition of the term crypto (which now means cryptocurrencies). We will briefly describe the history of electronic currencies and clarify the main principles behind Nakamoto Consensus. Next, we explain how several variants attempt to improve the complex tradeoffs between public verifiability, robustness, privacy and performance. We describe how Markov Decision processes can be used to compare in an objective way the proposed improvements in terms of chain quality, censorship resistance and robustness against selfish mining and double spending attacks. We conclude with a discussion of open problems.

Contents – Part II

Software Security

Automatically Identifying Security Checks for Detecting Kernel
Semantic Bugs   3
    Kangjie Lu, Aditya Pakki, and Qiushi Wu

Uncovering Information Flow Policy Violations in C Programs
(Extended Abstract).   26
    Darion Cassel, Yan Huang, and Limin Jia

BinEye: Towards Efficient Binary Authorship Characterization
Using Deep Learning.   47
    *Saed Alrabaee, ElMouatez Billah Karbab, Lingyu Wang,
    and Mourad Debbabi*

Static Detection of Uninitialized Stack Variables in Binary Code   68
    Behrad Garmany, Martin Stoffel, Robert Gawlik, and Thorsten Holz

Towards Automated Application-Specific Software Stacks   88
    Nicolai Davidsson, Andre Pawlowski, and Thorsten Holz

Cryptographic Protocols

Identity-Based Encryption with Security Against the KGC:
A Formal Model and Its Instantiation from Lattices.   113
    Keita Emura, Shuichi Katsumata, and Yohei Watanabe

Forward-Secure Puncturable Identity-Based Encryption for Securing
Cloud Emails   134
    *Jianghong Wei, Xiaofeng Chen, Jianfeng Wang, Xuexian Hu,
    and Jianfeng Ma*

Feistel Structures for MPC, and More   151
    *Martin R. Albrecht, Lorenzo Grassi, Léo Perrin, Sebastian Ramacher,
    Christian Rechberger, Dragos Rotaru, Arnab Roy,
    and Markus Schofnegger*

Arithmetic Garbling from Bilinear Maps   172
    Nils Fleischhacker, Giulio Malavolta, and Dominique Schröder

Security Models

SEPD: An Access Control Model for Resource Sharing
in an IoT Environment.   195
     Henrique G. G. Pereira and Philip W. L. Fong

Nighthawk: Transparent System Introspection from Ring -3   217
     Lei Zhou, Jidong Xiao, Kevin Leach, Westley Weimer, Fengwei Zhang,
     and Guojun Wang

Proactivizer: Transforming Existing Verification Tools into Efficient
Solutions for Runtime Security Enforcement.   239
     Suryadipta Majumdar, Azadeh Tabiban, Meisam Mohammady,
     Alaa Oqaily, Yosr Jarraya, Makan Pourzandi, Lingyu Wang,
     and Mourad Debbabi

Enhancing Security and Dependability of Industrial Networks
with Opinion Dynamics   263
     Juan E. Rubio, Mark Manulis, Cristina Alcaraz, and Javier Lopez

Searchable Encryption

Dynamic Searchable Symmetric Encryption with Forward
and Stronger Backward Privacy   283
     Cong Zuo, Shi-Feng Sun, Joseph K. Liu, Jun Shao, and Josef Pieprzyk

Towards Efficient Verifiable Forward Secure Searchable
Symmetric Encryption   304
     Zhongjun Zhang, Jianfeng Wang, Yunling Wang, Yaping Su,
     and Xiaofeng Chen

Generic Multi-keyword Ranked Search on Encrypted Cloud Data   322
     Shabnam Kasra Kermanshahi, Joseph K. Liu, Ron Steinfeld,
     and Surya Nepal

An Efficiently Searchable Encrypted Data Structure for Range Queries   344
     Florian Kerschbaum and Anselme Tueno

Privacy

GDPiRated – Stealing Personal Information On- and Offline   367
     Matteo Cagnazzo, Thorsten Holz, and Norbert Pohlmann

Location Privacy-Preserving Mobile Crowd Sensing
with Anonymous Reputation   387
     Xun Yi, Kwok-Yan Lam, Elisa Bertino, and Fang-Yu Rao

OCRAM-Assisted Sensitive Data Protection on ARM-Based Platform   412
  Dawei Chu, Yuewu Wang, Lingguang Lei, Yanchu Li, Jiwu Jing,
  and Kun Sun

Privacy-Preserving Collaborative Medical Time Series Analysis
Based on Dynamic Time Warping.   439
  Xiaoning Liu and Xun Yi

Key Exchange Protocols

IoT-Friendly AKE: Forward Secrecy and Session Resumption Meet
Symmetric-Key Cryptography.   463
  Gildas Avoine, Sébastien Canard, and Loïc Ferreira

Strongly Secure Identity-Based Key Exchange with Single
Pairing Operation   484
  Junichi Tomida, Atsushi Fujioka, Akira Nagai, and Koutarou Suzuki

A Complete and Optimized Key Mismatch Attack on NIST
Candidate NewHope   504
  Yue Qin, Chi Cheng, and Jintai Ding

Breakdown Resilience of Key Exchange Protocols: NewHope,
TLS 1.3, and Hybrids   521
  Jacqueline Brendel, Marc Fischlin, and Felix Günther

Web Security

The Risks of WebGL: Analysis, Evaluation and Detection   545
  Alex Belkin, Nethanel Gelernter, and Israel Cidon

Mime Artist: Bypassing Whitelisting for the Web with JavaScript
Mimicry Attacks.   565
  Stefanos Chaliasos, George Metaxopoulos, George Argyros,
  and Dimitris Mitropoulos

Fingerprint Surface-Based Detection of Web Bot Detectors   586
  Hugo Jonker, Benjamin Krumnow, and Gabry Vlot

Testing for Integrity Flaws in Web Sessions.   606
  Stefano Calzavara, Alvise Rabitti, Alessio Ragazzo,
  and Michele Bugliesi

Author Index   625

Contents – Part I

Machine Learning

Privacy-Enhanced Machine Learning with Functional Encryption   3
  Tilen Marc, Miha Stopar, Jan Hartman, Manca Bizjak,
  and Jolanda Modic

Towards Secure and Efficient Outsourcing of Machine
Learning Classification   22
  Yifeng Zheng, Huayi Duan, and Cong Wang

Confidential Boosting with Random Linear Classifiers for Outsourced
User-Generated Data   41
  Sagar Sharma and Keke Chen

BDPL: A Boundary Differentially Private Layer Against Machine
Learning Model Extraction Attacks   66
  Huadi Zheng, Qingqing Ye, Haibo Hu, Chengfang Fang, and Jie Shi

Information Leakage

The Leakage-Resilience Dilemma   87
  Bryan C. Ward, Richard Skowyra, Chad Spensky, Jason Martin,
  and Hamed Okhravi

A Taxonomy of Attacks Using BGP Blackholing 107
  Loïc Miller and Cristel Pelsser

Local Obfuscation Mechanisms for Hiding Probability Distributions 128
  Yusuke Kawamoto and Takao Murakami

A First Look into Privacy Leakage in 3D Mixed Reality Data 149
  Jaybie A. de Guzman, Kanchana Thilakarathna, and Aruna Seneviratne

Signatures and Re-encryption

Flexible Signatures: Making Authentication Suitable
for Real-Time Environments 173
  Duc V. Le, Mahimna Kelkar, and Aniket Kate

DGM: A Dynamic and Revocable Group Merkle Signature 194
  Maxime Buser, Joseph K. Liu, Ron Steinfeld, Amin Sakzad,
  and Shi-Feng Sun

Puncturable Proxy Re-Encryption Supporting to Group Messaging Service. . .   215
Tran Viet Xuan Phuong, Willy Susilo, Jongkil Kim, Guomin Yang,
and Dongxi Liu

Generic Traceable Proxy Re-encryption and Accountable Extension
in Consensus Network   234
Hui Guo, Zhenfeng Zhang, Jing Xu, and Mingyuan Xia

Side Channels

Side-Channel Aware Fuzzing   259
Philip Sperl and Konstantin Böttinger

NetSpectre: Read Arbitrary Memory over Network   279
Michael Schwarz, Martin Schwarzl, Moritz Lipp, Jon Masters,
and Daniel Gruss

maskVerif: Automated Verification of Higher-Order Masking
in Presence of Physical Defaults   300
Gilles Barthe, Sonia Belaïd, Gaëtan Cassiers, Pierre-Alain Fouque,
Benjamin Grégoire, and Francois-Xavier Standaert

Automated Formal Analysis of Side-Channel Attacks
on Probabilistic Systems   319
Chris Novakovic and David Parker

Formal Modelling and Verification

A Formal Model for Checking Cryptographic API Usage in JavaScript   341
Duncan Mitchell and Johannes Kinder

Contingent Payments on a Public Ledger: Models and Reductions
for Automated Verification   361
Sergiu Bursuc and Steve Kremer

Symbolic Analysis of Terrorist Fraud Resistance   383
Alexandre Debant, Stéphanie Delaune, and Cyrille Wiedling

Secure Communication Channel Establishment: TLS 1.3
(over TCP Fast Open) vs. QUIC   404
Shan Chen, Samuel Jero, Matthew Jagielski, Alexandra Boldyreva,
and Cristina Nita-Rotaru

Attacks

Where to Look for *What You See Is What You Sign?* User Confusion
in Transaction Security   429
    Vincent Haupert and Stephan Gabert

On the Security and Applicability of Fragile Camera Fingerprints   450
    Erwin Quiring, Matthias Kirchner, and Konrad Rieck

Attacking Speaker Recognition Systems with Phoneme Morphing.   471
    Henry Turner, Giulio Lovisotto, and Ivan Martinovic

Practical Bayesian Poisoning Attacks on Challenge-Based Collaborative
Intrusion Detection Networks   493
    *Weizhi Meng, Wenjuan Li, Lijun Jiang, Kim-Kwang Raymond Choo,
    and Chunhua Su*

A Framework for Evaluating Security in the Presence of Signal
Injection Attacks.   512
    Ilias Giechaskiel, Youqian Zhang, and Kasper B. Rasmussen

Secure Protocols

Formalizing and Proving Privacy Properties of Voting Protocols
Using Alpha-Beta Privacy   535
    Sébastien Gondron and Sebastian Mödersheim

ProCSA: Protecting Privacy in Crowdsourced Spectrum Allocation   556
    *Max Curran, Xiao Liang, Himanshu Gupta, Omkant Pandey,
    and Samir R. Das*

Breaking Unlinkability of the ICAO 9303 Standard for e-Passports
Using Bisimilarity.   577
    Ihor Filimonov, Ross Horne, Sjouke Mauw, and Zach Smith

Symmetric-Key Corruption Detection: When XOR-MACs Meet
Combinatorial Group Testing   595
    Kazuhiko Minematsu and Norifumi Kamiya

Useful Tools

Finding Flaws from Password Authentication Code in Android Apps   619
    *Siqi Ma, Elisa Bertino, Surya Nepal, Juanru Li, Diethelm Ostry,
    Robert H. Deng, and Sanjay Jha*

Identifying Privilege Separation Vulnerabilities in IoT Firmware
with Symbolic Execution   638
    Yao Yao, Wei Zhou, Yan Jia, Lipeng Zhu, Peng Liu, and Yuqing Zhang

iCAT: An Interactive Customizable Anonymization Tool   658
    Momen Oqaily, Yosr Jarraya, Mengyuan Zhang, Lingyu Wang,
    Makan Pourzandi, and Mourad Debbabi

Monitoring the GDPR   681
    Emma Arfelt, David Basin, and Søren Debois

Blockchain and Smart Contracts

Incentives for Harvesting Attack in Proof of Work Mining Pools   703
    Yevhen Zolotavkin and Veronika Kuchta

A Lattice-Based Linkable Ring Signature Supporting Stealth Addresses   726
    Zhen Liu, Khoa Nguyen, Guomin Yang, Huaxiong Wang,
    and Duncan S. Wong

Annotary: A Concolic Execution System for Developing Secure
Smart Contracts   747
    Konrad Weiss and Julian Schütte

PDFS: Practical Data Feed Service for Smart Contracts   767
    Juan Guarnizo and Pawel Szalachowski

Towards a Marketplace for Secure Outsourced Computations   790
    Hung Dang, Dat Le Tien, and Ee-Chien Chang

Author Index   809

Software Security

Automatically Identifying Security Checks for Detecting Kernel Semantic Bugs

Kangjie Lu[✉], Aditya Pakki, and Qiushi Wu

University of Minnesota, Minneapolis, USA
kjlu@umn.edu

Abstract. OS kernels enforce a large number of security checks to validate system states. We observe that security checks are in fact very informative in inferring critical semantics in OS kernels. Specifically, security checks can reveal (1) whether an operation or a variable is critical but can be erroneous, (2) what particular errors may occur, and (3) constraints that should be enforced for the uses of a variable or a function. Such information is particularly valuable for detecting kernel semantic bugs because the detection typically requires understanding critical semantics. However, identifying security checks is challenging due to not only the lack of clear criteria but also the diversity of security checks.

In this paper, we first systematically study security checks and propose a mostly-automated approach to identify security checks in OS kernels. Based on the information offered by the identified security checks, we then develop multiple analyzers that detect three classes of common yet critical semantic bugs in OS kernels, including NULL-pointer dereferencing, missing error handling, and double fetching. We implemented both the identification and the analyzers as LLVM passes and evaluated them using the Linux kernel and the FreeBSD kernel. Evaluation results show that our security-check identification has very low false-negative and false-positive rates. We also have found 164 new semantic bugs in both kernels, 88 of which have been fixed with our patches. The evaluation results confirm that our system can accurately identify security checks, which helps effectively identify numerous critical semantic bugs in complex OS kernels.

Keywords: OS kernel · Semantic bug · Security check · Missing check · Error handling

1 Introduction

OS kernels not only process inputs from both arbitrary user-space programs and underlying hardware, but also manage resources and perform complicated operations that are often error-prone. To ensure the security, OS kernels carry out a large number of `if` and `switch` statements (we refer to them as *conditional statements* [33] hereafter for simplicity) to validate system states. A conditional statement becomes a security check when it is used to capture errors. That is,

© Springer Nature Switzerland AG 2019
K. Sako et al. (Eds.): ESORICS 2019, LNCS 11736, pp. 3–25, 2019.
https://doi.org/10.1007/978-3-030-29962-0_1

a security check is a conditional statement that sanitizes erroneous states, such as lines 4 and 9 in Fig. 1. By contrast, normal conditional statements do not capture errors but are used to select normal execution paths, such as line 2 in Fig. 1. We will present the definition of security checks in Sect. 2.1.

While security checks are intended to prevent erroneous states, they are in fact very informative in understanding critical semantics. In particular, security checks reveal at least three kinds of code semantics: (1) whether an operation or a variable is security-critical but can be erroneous, (2) what particular errors the code may have, and (3) what constraints should be enforced for the uses of a variable or a function. For example, the security check at line 4 of Fig. 1 reveals that the variable addr is critical but erroneous— its value can be out of the valid boundary. Further, we can infer that addr might be used for memory accesses, and to avoid potential out-of-bound accesses, the "within-boundary" con-

```
1  int ret = -EINVAL;
2  if (flags & VM_SHARED) {
3      page = vmf->page;
4      if (addr < vm_end)
5          ret = 0;
6  }
7  else {
8      page = vmf->cow_page;
9      if (!page_count(page))
10         // error handling
11         // or fixing
12         BUG();
13     ret = put_page(page);
14  }
15  // error-code returning
16  return ret;
```

Fig. 1. Two security checks (lines 4 and 9, but not 2).

straint should be enforced before using addr. Such information is valuable for detecting critical semantic bugs. By identifying which variables are critical but can be erroneous, we can inspect whether they are thoroughly validated before being used and whether the errors are handled properly. On the other hand, security checks themselves are problematic, e.g., a security check can be invalidated by race conditions, or a security check may target a wrong condition.

It is worth noting that identifying security checks is also useful for fuzzing and system hardening. Fuzzing techniques [10] are often inefficient in exploring deep paths because of the barriers set by checks [3,9,20]. By specifically solving the constraints from security checks and focusing fuzzing on checked variables, one can efficiently guide the fuzzing to pass through the security checks and have a better chance to trigger critical issues. On the other hand, existing system-hardening techniques such as memory safety [18,24] and fault/memory isolation [1,11,16,27,36] tend to have a high performance overhead. Identifying critical semantics would allow researchers to selectively focus on a small set of protection targets and thus improve performance.

While the identification of security checks presents rich opportunities for detecting critical semantic bugs and hardening systems, it is a challenging task. First, whether a conditional statement is a security check depends on its context. To decide if a conditional statement is a security check, one must consider multiple aspects: where the checked variable comes from, how it is checked, what it is used for, how and where it is used, what the potential reliability and security impact is, etc. All these aspects depend on the context of the code and developers' logic. Further, security checks can be highly diverse in form—we have neither clear criteria for identifying security checks nor even definition of them. Therefore, it is a challenge to automatically identify security checks.

In this paper, we aim to automate the identification of security checks in complex and large OS kernels, and use the identified security checks to detect various classes of common and critical kernel semantic bugs, including NULL-pointer dereferencing, missing error handling, and double fetching. We first carry out a study on security checks to understand their characteristics. Based on the study, we then develop CHEQ (security-check magnifier), an automated tool for identifying security checks in OS kernels. The key insight behind CHEQ is that security checks validate erroneous states, hence checking failures require *handling*. The hard problem of reasoning about the context and properties of conditional statements is therefore transformed into the one of identifying failure-handling (FH for short) code, which can be automated because FH has clear patterns. According to our study, FH patterns include (1) returning an error code, (2) stopping the current execution, (3) fixing the erroneous state (typically the checked variable), and (4) issuing error messages. We call them *FH primitives*.

After identifying security checks, we further use them to detect three classes of common and critical semantic bugs: NULL-pointer dereferencing, missing error handling, and double fetching. Specifically, NULL-pointer dereferencing is that a pointer can be NULL but is dereferenced without any NULL check. Missing error handling is that a returned error code is not handled, e.g., being ignored. Double-fetch bugs are cases in which an external variable is copied into the kernel space and security-checked; however, the buggy code copies the variable in again and uses it without a further check. As shown in prior works [2,6–8,12,25,31,35], all these classes of bugs are common and may cause critical security issues including system crashes, data losses, information leaks, and even privilege escalation. Unlike prior works, our detection focuses on security-checked variables that can cause critical impacts, thereby eliminating overwhelming false-positive and non-critical cases, as shown in Sect. 6.2.

We implemented CHEQ and semantic-bug detection as multiple LLVM analysis passes. We then extensively evaluated both of them. Evaluation results show that CHEQ successfully identifies 97.5% ground-truth security checks we collected from patches for recent missing-check bugs and that 98.3% of identified security checks are real. These results show that CHEQ is accurate in identifying security checks. We have also applied our bug detection to both the Linux kernel and the FreeBSD kernel and found 164 new bugs. Specifically, we found 24 NULL-pointer dereferencing bugs, 128 missing error handling bugs, and 12 double-fetch bugs. We have reported the bugs in the Linux kernel to maintainers, and patches for 88 bugs have been accepted. The promising detection results mainly benefit from CHEQ's accurate identification of security checks because security checks help identify critical variables and functions that can be erroneous and reveal the constraints that should be enforced when they are used.

We make the following contributions in this paper:

- **A study of security checks.** We conduct a study of security checks to find intrinsic differences between security checks and normal conditional statements, and to classify how errors are typically handled.

- **Automatic identification of security checks.** We propose a mostly-automated approach to identify security checks in OS kernels. The approach incorporates multiple techniques such as identifying custom error codes and constructing a control-flow graph marked with FH primitives.
- **Detection of three classes of semantic bugs.** We harness CHEQ for the detection of three classes of common and critical semantic bugs: NULL-pointer dereferencing, missing error handling, and double-fetching. We have found 164 new semantic bugs in the Linux kernel and the FreeBSD kernel. Many of these bugs have been fixed with our reported patches.
- **A new, open-source tool.** We implement CHEQ as an easy-to-use LLVM pass and open-source[1] it to facilitate future research on semantic-bug detection and fuzzing.

2   A Study of Security Checks

OS kernels have prevalent conditional statements such as `if` and `switch` statements. The majority of conditional statements are normal *selectors* but not security checks, as will be shown in our evaluation (Sect. 6.1). In the code sample shown in Fig. 1, line 2 is an example of selectors that sets `page` and continues normal execution. Lines 4 and 9 are instead security checks because they are intended to capture errors. To differentiate security checks from normal selectors, we need a definition of security checks. To this end, we investigated a set of ground-truth security checks. Previous papers and Linux maintainers reported and fixed numerous missing-check bugs. Intuitively, these bugs were typically fixed by inserting security checks. Therefore, we can collect ground-truth security checks from fixes for previous missing-check bugs. Specifically, we collected 40 security checks from previous papers [15,31,32,34,35]; 50 and 20 security checks from the `git` patch history of the Linux kernel and the FreeBSD kernel, respectively. Based on the intrinsic features of the security checks, we provide the definition of security checks, which does not adhere to any specific program. With the generic definition, we further manually collected 490 security checks from the source code of different modules in both kernels, and characterized FH primitives.

2.1   Definition of Security Checks

We first define security checks based on their intrinsic features that do not adhere to any specific programs. We observe that security checks are intended to capture errors, so their conditions (in the `if` or `switch` statements) indicate erroneous states. Once an error is captured, at least one branches will handle it, and at least one branches will continue the normal execution.

To formally define security checks, we suppose that B_C is a basic block that contains a conditional statement. B_C has multiple successor basic blocks, B_S. B_{Si}, where i is an integer index, represents the "ith" successor basic block. B_R

---

[1] https://github.com/umnsec/cheq.

is a basic block that contains a return instruction in the current function. We define sequence S_i as $[B_C, B_{Si}, ..., B_R]$, which represents all code paths that start from B_C, contain B_{Si}, and end with B_R. Note that, since there could be multiple sub-paths between B_{Si} and B_R, S_i may cover multiple code paths that contain B_C, B_{Si}, and B_R. With these terms, we use S_i to represent branch "i" of B_C and define the FH property P of S_i as follows.

$$P(S_i) = \begin{cases} \text{MUST-FH if all of its following code paths have FH primitives} \\ \text{NO-FH if none of its following code paths has FH primitives} \\ \text{MAY-FH otherwise} \end{cases} \quad (1)$$

We then identify the conditional statement in B_C as a security check if:

$$\exists S_i \text{ such that } P(S_i) = \text{MUST-FH}$$
$$and \quad (2)$$
$$\exists S_j, \text{ where } i \neq j, \text{ such that } P(S_j) = \text{MAY-FH or NO-FH}$$

In other words, we identify a conditional statement as a security check if it has at least one MUST-FH branches and at least one MAY-FH or NO-FH branches.

2.2 Handling Security-Check Failures

In this section, we study the common ways of handling checking failures.

Returning Error Codes. The most common strategy for handling a checking failure is to return an error code upstream, and callers will take care of handling the erroneous states based on the error codes. Error codes can be *standard* or *custom*. OS kernels usually define standard error codes in a uniform manner. For example, the Linux kernel defines 150 standard macro error codes (e.g., EINVAL) in errno.h and errno-base.h. In addition, -1 and NULL, when used as a return value, are also standard error codes. However, false is often used to represent a normal Boolean value instead of an error. In subsystems, developers may define custom error codes to represent module-specific errors. For example, VM_FAULT_* are custom error codes used in the memory-management module. Unlike standard error codes, custom error codes are diverse and defined in different files, which makes the identification of custom error codes challenging.

Issuing Error Messages. In many cases, developers are aware of the failure scenarios of their code. While production code is never released with assert() turned on, a failure is notified via an error message. Although most kernel drivers and file systems have custom error-message functions to log failures, such functions have clear patterns. Taking the Linux kernel as an example, such functions often have a name ending with a log level (e.g., ERR) and take a variable number of arguments.

Stopping Execution. Another common strategy for handling failures is to abort the execution of the offending process. In this case, when the system enters an erroneous state that fails a security check, the process takes a safe route to terminate itself. Termination is a safer alternative to avoid harmful side effects such as memory corruption, inconsistent states, and many others. In the kernel, termination is achieved by calling functions such as panic() and BUG(). Such functions typically have patterns such as dumping the contents of the stack, printing the trace, and self-crashing.

Fixing Errors Instantly. In the event of failure, a few shallow errors are handled locally in the current function by instantly fixing the erroneous value. After the instant fix, the execution can continue without termination or error handling. Such an instant fix is uncommon and is usually limited to simple cases such as assigning a previously cached value to a potentially changed variable or resetting a variable to a boundary value.

3 CHEQ: Identifying Security Checks

Since checking failures requires handling which has clear patterns as summarized in Sect. 2, CHEQ automatically identifies security checks through identifying FH. In this section, we present the approach of CHEQ and the design of its key components.

3.1 A Motivating Example

We first use the example shown in Fig. 1 to illustrate how to identify security checks through FH primitives. The goal is to identify which conditional statements (lines 2, 4, and 9) are security checks. Each conditional statement has two branches. The key challenge is to decide whether their branches have FH primitives. Since the code is straightforward, we can quickly analyze the code to identify FH primitives and security checks. Specifically, one branch of the conditional statement at line 9 calls BUG(), an error-handling function, thus is marked as MUST-FH. However, its other branch assigns the return value of put_page() to ret, which may or may not be an error code. Therefore, this branch is marked as MAY-FH. Figure 2 shows the control-flow edges marked with the corresponding FH properties. Based on the definition of security checks, the conditional statement at line 9 is identified as a security check. Similarly, the conditional statement at line 4 is a security check. However, the conditional statement at line 2 is not a security check because neither of the branches is marked as MUST-FH.

While identifying the security checks in the given example is easy, it becomes challenging when the code is complicated. We identify two main challenges as follows.

- **C1:** Comprehensively identifying FH primitives. OS kernels have many custom error codes and error-handling functions. Automatically identifying them is challenging.
- **C2:** Interactively marking FH properties for error returning. Since error codes are often propagated and changed along code paths across functions. Deciding whether a branch finally ends with returning an error code can be complicated.

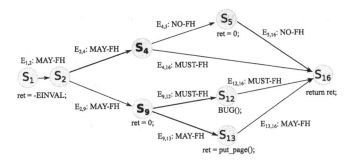

Fig. 2. The corresponding FH graph of the code in Fig. 1. S: statement; E: edge connecting two statements. Each edge is marked with an FH property. Conditional statementsS4 and S9 are identified as security checks based on the definition; however, S2 is not a security check.

Fig. 3. The workflow of CHEQ. CHEQ takes as inputs the source code of the target kernel and an initial list of basic error-handling functions, and then automatically identifies security checks.

3.2 Approach Overview

Figure 3 shows the workflow of CHEQ. CHEQ takes as inputs the source code of an OS kernel and a list of *basic* error-handling functions of the kernel as a priori knowledge. Note that error-handling functions include both the ones for stopping the execution and the ones for issuing error messages. The first step of CHEQ is to comprehensively identify error-handling functions and error codes. Based on the provided list of basic error-handling functions, CHEQ employs two automated approaches to augment the lists of error-handling functions and error codes. With the lists, CHEQ moves to the second step to identify FH primitives in basic blocks. Although instant error fixes in the current function are uncommon, CHEQ also identifies them with the patterns described in Sect. 2.2. After identifying all basic blocks with FH primitives, CHEQ constructs the FH graph with edges marked with properties MUST-FH, MAY-FH, and NO-FH. At last, CHEQ queries the graph to identify security checks.

3.3   Finding Error-Handling Functions and Error Codes

The first step of CHEQ is to augment the lists of error-handling functions (functions for stopping execution and issuing error messages) and error codes.

Collecting Error-Handling Functions. We present two heuristic-based approaches for automatically collecting more error-handling functions based on the provided basic

```
1   /* VM_FAULT_ERROR is a custom error code */
2   if (unlikely(fault & VM_FAULT_ERROR))
3       /* Call error-handling function BUG() */
4       BUG();
5   if (ret < sizeof(*reply)) {
6       /* Call error-handling function */
7       pr_err("bad size %d \n", ret);
8       /* EINVAL is a standard error code */
9       return -EINVAL;
10  }
```

Fig. 4. Two ways of associating error codes to the calls of error-handling functions.

ones. These two approaches are complementary to each other. Also, they are general and applicable to other system software. (1) *Wrapper-based approach.* An OS kernel has only a small number of basic error-handling functions because they are critical and are often implemented in assembly. For example, BUG(), panic(), and dump_stack() in Unix-like OS kernels are functions for terminating the offending process. Moreover, basic functions printk() and fprintf() are used for issuing error messages. Developers often write wrappers of such functions to have module-specific error-handling functions. Therefore, by identifying wrappers of the provided list of basic error-handling functions, we can find general error-handling functions. We will present the identification of wrappers in Sect. 5.1. (2) *Pattern-based approach.* The wrapper-based approach has a limitation in identifying error-message functions. Functions printk() and fprintf() become error-message functions only when their arguments have certain patterns (e.g., containing KERN_ERR and stderr). To complement the wrapper-based approach, we also use patterns. OS kernels provide severity levels for logging messages. For example, with the Linux convention, error-handling functions typically have a name or an argument with a severity level. Specifically, levels 0-4 (KERN_EMERG, KERN_ALERT, KERN_CRIT, and KERN_ERR) indicate critical issues. Further, such functions take a variable number of arguments. Detecting these patterns is straightforward for a static analysis tool. We present the details in Sect. 5.1.

Collecting Error Codes. To identify error returning, we need to decide if the returned value is an error code, which requires us to first know defined error codes. While standard error codes are defined in dedicated header files (e.g., errno.h), custom error codes scatter across numerous files over different modules. Manually collecting custom error codes is impractical; we thus propose a general approach to automatically find both standard and custom error codes. We observe that error codes are macro constants and often appear together with calls of error-handling functions. Figure 4 shows two ways of how error codes and error-handling functions are associated. In the first case, if a macro constant (e.g., VM_FAULT_ERROR) is checked in a conditional statement, and a branch calls an error-handling function (e.g., BUG()), the macro constant is an error code. This is sensible because the macro constant acts as an error indicator. In the second case, if a macro constant is returned in a basic block that calls an error-handling function (e.g., `pr_err()`), the macro constant is also an error code. This is because the basic block is in an error path for handling the error. Using these associations, we can automatically find both standard and custom error codes based on error-handling functions.

3.4   Identifying FH Primitives

After collecting the lists of error-handling functions and error codes, CHEQ moves to the second step to identify FH primitives. In this step, CHEQ analyzes the bitcode files of the target kernel and identifies LLVM basic blocks that have FH primitives.

Identifying Error-Code Returning. Even with the list of error codes, identifying error-returning primitives can be complicated. Not every error code used in a function will be returned, and whether a value is an error code depends on some context. For example, NULL in an assignment instruction is an error code only when the assignment targets a return value of the function. More importantly, error codes can be propagated and changed across functions. To precisely identify error-returning primitives, a data-flow analysis is required to decide whether a return instruction finally returns an error code.

CHEQ begins the data-flow analysis by identifying return instructions in each function F of the kernel. To decide whether the return value RV_F of a return instruction is an error code, CHEQ backwardly analyzes values propagating to it. Specifically, CHEQ identifies all sources of RV_F. The sources can be a constant, a local variable, a global variable, or an argument of F. If a source is a constant error code, CHEQ determines that the basic block that contains the instruction (e.g., store) assigning the error code to the return value has an error-returning primitive. Because the returned value is decided by the last assignment, CHEQ stops the backward data-flow analysis once a source is found. CHEQ's analysis is inter-procedural. That is, error codes coming from called functions will also be covered.

In our current implementation, we chose *not* to use alias analysis [5] for the data-flow analysis because we observed that error-code propagation is straightforward and typically does not involve complicated point-to relationships. For instance, we did not see any example in our study in which an error code is stored to memory through a pointer and later loaded through a different pointer. If we experience non-negligible false reports due to aliasing, we can include alias analysis in the future, which is orthogonal to CHEQ.

Identifying Error Handling and Fixing. Identifying error-handling primitives that issue error messages or stop the execution is straightforward with identifying the calls of corresponding functions. In this section, we present how to identify instant error-fixing cases that do not return an error code or call an error-handling function. The insight we use to identify instant error fixes is that such fixes are usually limited to simple cases such as resetting a variable with an old value or a boundary value. Based on our observation in Sect. 2, in these cases, two variables are compared in a conditional statement, and then one is assigned to the other. Therefore, if a conditional statement compares two variables a and b, and $a = b$ or $b = a$ occurs in the basic block following the conditional statement, we identify it as an instant error fix. Note that such an analysis is by no means complete but can only cover most error-fixing cases we observed in our study.

3.5 Constructing FH Graph

After collecting all basic blocks that have FH primitives, the next step is to analyze the branches of a conditional statement to see if they satisfy the definition of security check. To facilitate the analysis of the FH properties of all branches, we propose to construct FH graphs—augmented control-flow graphs whose edges are marked with FH properties. Figure 2 shows an illustrating example of the FH graph. The graph is constructed using an iterative algorithm. Initially, all edges are marked as NO-FH. The algorithm then traverses the control-flow graph from the function entry. When reaching a basic block with FH primitives, the algorithm updates the properties of forwardly and backwardly reachable edges based on the following policy.

- For error-fixing and error-handling primitives, since they do not "propagate", we update properties of only the incoming and outgoing edges of the current basic block.
- For error-code returning primitives, since error codes propagate, we iteratively update properties of *all* edges reachable to and from the current basic block. Properties are merged upon branches based on Eq. 1. Note that, we have a dedicated flag to differentiate error handling and error returning.

3.6 Identifying Security Checks

With the FH graph, identifying security checks is simplified as querying the FH properties of the outgoing edges of conditional statements. A conditional statement that has at least one MUST-FH outgoing edges and at least one MAY-FH or NO-FH outgoing edges is identified as a security check. In the example in Fig. 2, by checking the properties of $E_{4,5}$, $E_{4,16}$, $E_{9,12}$, and $E_{9,13}$, we identify conditional statements S_4 and S_9 as security checks. However, S_2 is not a security check because neither of its branches is MUST-FH.

4   Detecting Critical Kernel Semantic Bugs

Security checks are very informative in revealing critical semantics. Without such information, a bug detected by previous approaches [2,6–8,12,25,31,35] may not be critical at all or is unlikely to be triggered. In this section, we will present how to use this information to effectively detect critical semantic bugs involving NULL-pointer dereferencing, missing error handling, and double fetching, in the OS kernels.

Categorizing Security Checks. Before we identify semantic bugs, we first categorize security checks into three classes: NULL check (checking a pointer against NULL), error-code check (checking a variable against an error code), and value check (all other cases). To identify if the condition in a security check is an error code, we will further analyze the source of the checked variable to ensure that it may come from an error code. After categorizing security checks, we use them to detect each class of semantic bugs.

4.1   Detecting Null-Pointer Dereferencing

NULL-pointer dereferencing is a case in which a pointer that is potentially NULL is dereferenced without a NULL check. NULL-pointer dereferencing will typically result in crashes of a program. In OS kernels, NULL-pointer dereferencing will at least result in the termination of the offending process, leading to Denial-of-Service.

Detection Approach. We observe that NULL pointers, in most cases, come from the return values of functions (e.g., memory allocators). Our detection for NULL-pointer dereferencing consists of three steps: (1) identifying functions that may return NULL pointers, (2) identifying cases where the returned pointers of the callsites of such functions are directly dereferenced without a NULL check, and (3) ranking the cases based on the likelihood of the functions returning a NULL pointer.

Analyzing NULL Pointers. An input of the detection is the NULL checks identified by CHEQ. By backwardly tracking (i.e., backward data-flow analysis) the sources of the checked pointers, we first identify which functions return the NULL pointers. With this analysis, we collect a list of functions that may return NULL pointers. After that, we thoroughly identify all the callsites of these functions and forwardly track their return values (pointers) to decide whether they are NULL-checked and dereferenced. Note that all the analyses are inter-procedural.

Ranking Based on Statistics. After the analysis, our detection generates two global maps for these functions. One map records how many callsites of a function do not have NULL checks, and the other map records how many callsites of the function do have NULL checks. With these two maps, we generate the "no-check" ratio for each function. To generate the bug report, we rank the callsites that do not have NULL checks in an ascending order, based on the ratio. Cases with a lower no-check ratio are more likely to be real bugs. Functions with a 100% or zero ratio are excluded from the ranked list.

```
1  /* drivers/target/target_core_rd.c */      1  /* File: drivers/scsi/sg.c */
2  static ssize_t rd_set_configfs_dev_params() {  2  /* First data fetch from buf to opcode */
3    int arg;                                   3  __get_user(opcode, buf);
4    /* arg is uninitialized if match_int fails*/  4
5    match_int(args, &arg);                     5  /* Security check against opcode */
6    /* ERROR: page refcount can be undefined */  6  if ((opcode >= 0xc0)
7    rd_dev->rd_page_count = arg;               7       && old_hdr.twelve_byte)
8  }                                            8      cmd_size = 12;
9  int match_int(substring_t *s, int *result) { 9
10   buf = match_strdup(s);                    10  /* Second data fetch from buf to cmnd */
11   if (!buf) return -ENOMEM;                 11  if (__copy_from_user(cmnd, buf, cmd_size))
12   val = simple_strtol(buf, &endp, base);    12      return -EFAULT;
13   if (endp == buf) return -EINVAL;          13  /* First byte in cmnd could have been
14   *result = (int) val;                      14   * changed in user space */
15 }                                           15  sg_common_write(..., cmnd, ...);
```

Fig. 5. A new missing error handling bug.

Fig. 6. A new double-fetch bug.

4.2   Detecting Missing Error Handling

We next detect missing error handling. Figure 5 shows an example of such bugs. Line 5 incorrectly assumes the success of match_int(), by not checking its return value. However, this function has multiple ways to fail (line 11 and 13) and returns different error codes. When match_int() fails, arg is not touched and left uninitialized, which may contain random or even malicious value [13]. Using arg as a refcount (line 7) will result in memory exhaustion or denial-of-service attacks [14]. In fact, since such bugs completely miss the intended security checks, they may result in many other critical issues such as data losses, information leaks, or even privilege escalation [15,25,35].

Detection Approach. Similar to detecting NULL-pointer dereferencing, we identify functions that might return error codes (both standard and custom error codes) and use data-flow analysis to determine whether these returned error codes are handled. We mark a returned error code as "handled" when it is both security-checked and handled with at least one of the FH primitives described in Sect. 2.2. Similarly, we record how many returned error codes of a function are handled and how many are not handled, and rank the unhandled cases based on the ratio.

4.3   Detecting Double-Fetch Bugs

In addition to checking critical function calls, security checks also reveal the constraints that should be enforced to the uses of a variable. We further exploit such information to detect double-fetch bugs [6,23,31,32,34]. Figure 6 shows a new double-fetch bug found with CHEQ. The first byte in buf is fetched twice and checked in between. If a malicious multi-threaded user-space program races to change the byte, line 15 may use a value smaller than 0xc0, thus invalidating the security check.

Detection Approach. We detect double-fetch bugs in three steps: (1) identifying the sources of checked variables; (2) if the sources are data fetches (e.g., `copy_from_user()`) from the user space, analyzing whether the source data is fetched again, and (3) deciding that the constraints (i.e., security checks) are not enforced before the newly fetched data is used. Compared to existing detection [31,34], a unique strength of our detection is that it uses CHEQ to target only cases in which the fetched data is critical. That is, invalid values of fetched data may result in critical errors. Such detection eliminates non-critical cases which are very common, as reported by both Deadline [34] and Wang et al. [31].

5   Implementation

We have implemented CHEQ and bug detection as LLVM (of version 8.0.0) passes. We also have an LLVM pass for constructing a global call-graph for all kernel modules. Error-handling functions and error codes are collected through both Python script code and LLVM data-flow analysis, and saved to the configuration file of CHEQ. The report of CHEQ includes details about the identified security checks, including the conditional statement and its source code, the corresponding source line, and the FH primitives and their source code. We now present some interesting implementation details.

5.1   Collecting Error-Handling Functions

We implement two heuristic-based approaches to augment the list of error-handling functions. In the current implementation, the initial list contains only 10 basic error-handling functions such as `BUG()` and `panic()`, and our following two approaches substantially found additional 531 in the Linux kernel and 93 in the FreeBSD kernel.

Finding Wrappers. First, we identify functions that internally call the provided basic error-handling functions. Second, we ignore non-functional code such as message-printing code. Third, if a function does not call other functions but just basic error-handling functions, we identify it as a wrapper. The wrapper-based approach is mainly for identifying error-handling functions that stop the current execution.

Finding Patterns. We also rely on patterns to find custom error-message functions. We collect all the functions that have a name ending with the error level (0-4) and a variable number of parameters. To minimize false positives, we further rely on the call-graph to ensure that general printing functions `printk` and `fprintf` are internally called.

5.2   Preparing LLVM IR for CHEQ

Compiling Source Code. Compiling the OS kernels like the Linux kernel into LLVM IR often has compatibility issues. Since CHEQ is a code-analysis tool instead of a code-instrumentation tool, we choose to discard modules that cannot be compiled successfully. For the Linux kernel, we compiled 17,343 modules (source-code files) with the `allyesconfig` option; only 7 modules failed. For the FreeBSD kernel, we compiled 1,483 modules, without any failure case, with the `GENERIC` configuration. To preserve the original code patterns in the LLVM IR as much as possible, which is useful for debugging purposes and understanding how functions are called, we compiled the source code using the `-O0` optimization and completely disabled inlining by modifying Clang. We use debug information to differentiate macro constants from general integers in LLVM IR. To find targets of an indirect call, we use the signature-based approach [19, 30] to map address-taken functions to indirect callsites. We unroll loops once. That is, we treat `while` and `for` statements as `if` statements. Such simplification would not affect the accuracy of CHEQ because the FH properties are independent irrespective of the number of iterations.

6   Evaluation

In this section, we evaluate CHEQ and our bug detection by applying them to the Linux kernel of version 4.20.0-rc5 with the top git commit number `b72f711a4efa` and the FreeBSD-13 kernel with the top git commit number `d2e46ebc0d4`.

6.1   Evaluating Security-Check Identification

Statistical Results. Before presenting the evaluation results, we first present some interesting statistical numbers in Table 1. The analysis covered 10.2 and 1.2 million lines of code for the Linux kernel and the FreeBSD kernel respectively, reported by the tool `cloc`. For Linux, CHEQ identified 447K security checks from 1.6 million general conditional statements. 137K (28%) security checks are identified through error-handling functions or error-fixing code. Instant error fixing is uncommon; CHEQ found only 3,350 security checks via error fixes. The combination is larger than the total number because a security check may have multiple FH primitives. For FreeBSD, CHEQ identified 25K security checks from 139K conditional statements, 9K (35%) of which were identified through error-handling functions or error-fixing code. Such security checks cannot be identified through error-code returning.

Table 1. Some security check–related statistical numbers reported by CHEQ.

Kernel	SLOC	Files	Conditional statements	Security checks	Through error codes	Through EH function	Through error fixing
Linux	10.2M	17K	1.6M	447K	362K	137K	3,350
FreeBSD	1.2M	1.5K	139K	25K	17K	9K	536

False Negatives. CHEQ identifies security checks via the existences of FH primitives. CHEQ may have false negatives if not all FH primitives are precisely identified. To find false negatives, we used the ground-truth set of security checks collected in Sect. 2. The set consists of 600 security checks in total. All of the corresponding conditional statements are present in the Linux kernel of the version in our experiments. We used a script to match the ground-truth security checks with the ones reported by CHEQ, through source-code line numbers. If one cannot be matched, we mark it as a false negative, and then analyze the causes manually.

In total, CHEQ identified 585 (97.5%) security checks and missed 15 (5 are from previous missing-check patches, and 10 are from the set we manually collected). We analyzed the causes of false negatives. The main cause is that the FH primitives used in CHEQ failed to cover some special cases. Specifically, eight cases handle failures by just returning "`void`" or `false` instead of an error code. Five cases just release the system resources (e.g., calling `release_mem_region()`) upon failures and do not return an error or issue an error message. The last two cases store the error code to a global variable or an argument instead of the return value. CHEQ can be improved to eliminate the last two cases by including arguments and globals as error-code propagation channels.

False Positives. CHEQ identified 447K and 25K security checks for Linux and FreeBSD kernels. To evaluate false positive, we randomly selected 500 and 100 security checks reported by CHEQ for each kernel, and confirmed whether they are real security checks based on the definition of security checks (Sect. 2.1). Note that our definition of security checks does not adhere to any specific program, so the confirmation would not suffer from overfitting problems. The results show that 590 (98.3%) of them are true positives.

We then analyzed the causes of the 10 false positives. Specifically, the most common cause (five cases) is misidentifying custom error codes. Another common cause (three cases) is that some conditions are always true. For example, `WARN_ON(cond)` logs an error when `cond` is evaluated to be true. Therefore, `WARN_ON(1)` is not a security check, but will be a false positive in CHEQ when the target program is compiled with the `O0` optimization level. This is an easy-to-fix problem in CHEQ because we can identify such conditions with compiler optimization. The remaining cases are caused by inaccurate identification of indirect-call targets. As described in Sect. 3.4, CHEQ identifies external error codes by inter-procedurally tracking external functions. We may eliminate such false positives by not tracking indirect calls; however, it will introduce false negatives.

Scalability. The experiments were performed on Ubuntu 16.04 LTS with LLVM version 8.0 installed. The machine has a 64 GB RAM and an Intel CPU (Xeon R CPU E5-1660 v4, 3.20 GHz) with 8 cores. CHEQ is fast—it finished the whole analysis for either Linux or FreeBSD within three minutes: two and half minutes are for loading bitcode files and constructing call-graph, and only half minute is for the identification of security checks.

Generality. CHEQ requires only the LLVM-compilable source code and the initial list of basic error-handling functions (Sect. 3.3) in the target program. Since OS kernels typically have clear patterns for error-handling functions, we expect that the manual effort for collecting error-handling functions in new system software is small. To confirm this, we manually investigated Unix-like kernels including OpenBSD, and NetBSD, Darwin-XNU (MacOS), ReactOS (Windows-like), and Chromium browser. We found that all these systems have clear patterns for error-handling functions. Specifically, Unix-like kernels and Darwin-XNU have the same patterns as the Linux kernel, so CHEQ can be directly used to find their error-handling functions. ReactOS and Chromium browser have different but clear patterns of error-handling functions (e.g., `FIXME()` and `LOG(ERROR)`) and thus require only limited manual effort for collecting them. We also found that all these programs have dedicated header files that define standard error codes.

6.2   Evaluating Semantic-Bug Detection

To demonstrate the usefulness of security checks, we describe the results of our bug detection on both the Linux and FreeBSD kernels. Due to limited space, we will primarily focus on the details for the Linux kernel.

NULL-Pointer Dereferencing Bugs. To balance false positives and false negatives, we carefully use a threshold of 10% for the "no-check" ratio to report potential bugs (without the threshold, CHEQ reported in total 3,400 cases). This returns us the top 280 entries in the list. We manually confirmed these entries and found 21 new bugs, as shown in Table 3. False positives are mainly caused by aliasing issues and "can't fail" cases such as using the `__GFP_NOFAIL` flag in allocations, so that they will not fail. We reported all bugs by submitting patches, and Linux maintainers have fixed 7 bugs with our patches.

Missing Error Handling Bugs. To evaluate CHEQ's effectiveness in detecting error-handling bugs, we again set 10% as the no-check ratio, which returns us 682 potential bugs. We manually analyzed them and have confirmed 125 new error-handling bugs. We have submitted the patches for these 125 bugs, and Linux maintainers have accepted 78 (applied 70 and confirmed 8) of them. The main cause of false positives is that the errors are unlikely to occur in the given contexts. In comparison, when we disable CHEQ and generally detect cases where a returned error code is not checked or handled, the detection reports 507,043 cases (the number is only 8,744 when CHEQ is enabled), making bug-confirmation infeasible, which shows the usefulness of CHEQ in eliminating false reports by focusing on erroneous and critical cases only.

Table 4 indicates that drivers code contains about 80% of the bugs. From our interaction with the maintainers, we have some interesting findings. First, the interaction between the kernel and hardware is highly unreliable, thus requiring frequent security checks. Second, if failures occur in an `exiting` stage such as powering down of a device, maintainers believe the security checks for failures are unnecessary. Further, bug fixing resembles the existing error handling protocol. For example, developers inaccurately handle bugs in protocol functions having the void-type return values. This is probably because developers could not return an error code in such functions and instead log these with the corresponding driver. These results confirm the viability of CHEQ to find critical and common semantic bugs in OS kernels.

Double-Fetch Bugs. Although double-fetch bugs have been extensively detected recently, our detector still reports 66 potential double-fetch cases in the Linux kernel; 12 of them have been confirmed as real bugs, and three has been fixed. We did not find any double-fetch cases in the FreeBSD kernel. The details of the new bugs are shown in Table 2. Most false positives are caused by inaccuracy in identifying overlapping in the two fetches. Such false positives can be eliminated with symbolic execution, as shown in [34]. The unique strength of our detection is that it employs CHEQ to find the checked "first" fetches, so the checked variables must be critical. This way, it significantly narrows down the analysis scope and simplifies the detection. We further reverted the patches for 40 double-fetch bugs reported in [31,32,34]; some of them are still not patched yet. Our detection successfully reported all these bugs, confirming the detection effectiveness.

We believe that the promising bug-detection results mainly benefit from CHEQ's identification of security checks, which helps automatically infer what are critical and erroneous, and thus eliminate overwhelming false reports.

7   Related Work

To the best of our knowledge, CHEQ is the first to identify security checks. We identify two research lines that are related to CHEQ: analyzing error-code propagation and handling, and detecting missing-check bugs.

Error-Code Propagation and Handling. A handful of research works have investigated bugs in error-code propagation and handling. EIO [4] and Rubio-González et al. [21] proposed static analysis techniques to detect incorrect error code propagation in Linux file and storage systems. EPEx [7] and APEx [8] identify code paths in a callee function that may return error codes and check if the error codes are handled in callers. These tools conservatively identify a return value as an error code as long as it falls in the specified range of error codes. For example, they consider any value $\leqslant 0$ an error code in OpenSSL. ErrDoc [29] relies on EPEx [7] to find potential error-handling bugs, and then further diagnose and fix them. Hector [22] finds error-returning paths based on standard or user-specified error codes, and detects resource-release bugs along with the paths.

CHEQ has a different research goal from these tools—identifying security checks that can be used for detecting various classes of semantic bugs. Detecting error-handling bugs is just one application of CHEQ. Even for the part of detecting error-handling bugs, CHEQ differentiates itself from these tools. First, these tools check only error-code returning and propagation, but not calls to error-handling functions or error-fixing code which are covered in CHEQ. Our evaluation (Sect. 6.1) shows that about 30% of security checks cannot be identified through error-code returning. Second, they do not have an accurate way of identifying custom error codes, which is an important challenge overcome in CHEQ. Last but not least, CHEQ can specifically identify which conditional statement results in the error-code returning, which can be challenging when error-codes are propagated and changed along the code paths across functions.

Missing-Check Detection. Vanguard [25] detects missing checks for only four specified critical operations such as arithmetical division. Our bug detection is agnostic about the operations and can detect missing checks for all functions across the kernel. LRSan [32] detects lacking-recheck bugs. It however uses only standard error codes to find checks without considering custom error codes or other FH primitives; therefore, it identified only 131K security checks in the Linux kernel. In comparison, CHEQ is comprehensive and precise in identifying various classes of FH primitives. Juxta [15] utilizes cross-checking to detect semantic bugs such as missing checks in the Linux file systems. It requires multiple implementations of the same standard, such as POSIX for file operations; therefore, it cannot detect security checks in modules containing unique implementations. CHEQ helps address the limitation by automatically identifying security checks.

There are also a few complementary detection tools to our bug detection. Specifically, Chucky [35] combines static analysis and machine learning techniques to uncover missing checks by considering the context of the code. AutoISES [28] generates custom security specifications relying on the similarity of data structures for a given security check across C libraries. Rolecast [26] finds new missing security bugs in PHP scripts by detecting rule violations. MACE [17] finds missing authorization checks in web applications by checking authorization state consistency.

8   Conclusion

We presented our study on security checks and CHEQ, an automated tool for precisely identifying security checks in OS kernels. We also presented that, with identified security checks, we can effectively detect semantic bugs. CHEQ identifies security checks by detecting FH primitives using multiple new techniques such as custom error-code identification and FH graph. Evaluation results show that CHEQ has very low false-positive and false-negative rates. CHEQ also offers opportunities for improving the security of OS kernels by significantly narrowing down the analysis scope to enable expensive and precise analysis techniques. With CHEQ, we detected three classes of critical and common semantic bugs: NULL-pointer dereferencing, missing error handling, and double fetching. We have found 164 new bugs in the Linux and FreeBSD kernels, most of which have been fixed with our patches by maintainers. We believe that the identification of security checks could facilitate future research on semantic-bug detection.

Acknowledgment. We would like to thank the anonymous reviewers for their helpful suggestions and comments. This research was supported in part by the NSF award CNS-1815621. Any opinions, findings, conclusions, or recommendations expressed in this material are those of the authors and do not necessarily reflect the views of NSF.

A   Appendix

Table 2. New double-fetch bugs detected with CHEQ. S: Submitted, A: Applied, C: Confirmed.

Subsystem	File	Function	Fetched and checked variable	#Bugs	Status
x86	wmi.c	wmi_ioctl	buf->length	1	S
stm	core.c	stm_char_policy_set_ioctl	size	1	S
scsi	sg.c	sg_write	opcode	1	A
	sg.c	sg_read	old_hdr	1	A
	megaraid.c	mega_m_to_n	signature	1	S
	commctrl.c	aac_send_raw_srb	fibsize	1	S
	dpt_i2o.c	adpt_i2o_passthru	size	2	S
acpi	custom_method.c	cm_write	max_size	1	S
coda	psdev.c	coda_psdev_write	hdr.opcode	2	C
sched	core.c	sched_copy_attr	size	1	A

Table 3. List of new NULL-pointer dereferencing bugs detected with CHEQ. In column S, S, C, and A are Submitted, Confirmed, and Applied patches, respectively. In column K, L, F are the Linux and FreeBSD kernels.

Filename	Called function	S	K
ci_hdrc_msm.c	of_get_next_available_child	A	L
coh901318_lli.c	dma_pool_create	S	L
fsl-edma-common.c	dma_pool_create	S	L
virtgpu_kms.c	idr_alloc	S	L
virtgpu_vq.c	idr_alloc	S	L
qedr_iw_cm.c	idr_find	A	L
message.c	api_parse	A	L
cx231xx-input.c	i2c_new_device	S	L
cxgb3_offload.c	alloc_skb	S	L
mvpp2_main.c	acpi_match_device	A	L
lag_conf.c	kmalloc_array	S	L

Filename	Called function	S	K
rx.c	kcalloc	S(2)	L
pcie-designware-host.c	alloc_page	S	L
qcom-ngd-ctrl.c	platform_device_alloc	S	L
fw.c	netdev_alloc_skb	S	L
mmal-vchiq.c	vmalloc	S	L
nf_tables_api.c	nla_nest_start	A	L
conntrack.c	nla_nest_start	S	L
rpc_rdma.c	xdr_inline_decode	C	L
netlink_compat.c	genlmsg_put	A	L
iir.c	cam_sim_alloc	S	F
crypto.c	crypto_checkdriver	S	F
ocs_mgmt.c	ocs_malloc	S	F

Table 4. List of new missing error handling bugs detected with CHEQ. A number in column S indicates multiple bugs in the module, and S: Submitted, A: Applied, C: Confirmed. In column K, L and F indicate Linux and FreeBSD, respectively.

Filename	Called function	S	K
sfi.c	intel_scu_devices_create	S	L
sfi.c	sfi_handle_ipc_dev	S	L
clock_ops.c	pm_clk_acquire	A	L
hci_bcm.c	bcm_init	S	L
hci_intel.c	intel_init	S	L
core.c	devm_hwrng_unregister	A	L
clk-versaclock5.c	vc5_pll_recalc_rate	S	L
sh_cmt.c	sh_cmt_clock_event_resume	S	L
mv_xor.c	mv_xor_channel_add	A	L
hidma_mgmt.c	hidma_mgmt_init	A	L
stm32-mdma.c	stm32_mdma_probe	A	L
memconsole-coreboot.c	memconsole_coreboot_read	S	L
amdgpu_ucode.c	amdgpu_ucode_create_bo	S	L
analogix-anx78xx.c	anx78xx_poweron	S(2)	L
hid-lenovo.c	lenovo_probe_tpkbd	A(2)	L
lm80.c	lm80_probe	A(2)	L
lm80.c	set_fan_div	A	L
xilinx-xadc-core.c	xadc_probe	A	L
ad9523.c	ad9523_setup	A	L
addr.c	ib_nl_ip_send_msg	C	L
sa_query.c	ib_nl_set_path_rec_attrs	S(6)	L
qplib_sp.c	bnxt_qplib_map_tc2cos	A	L
samsung-keypad.c	samsung_keypad_probe	S	L
ad7879.c	ad7879_irq	A	L
elants_i2c.c	elants_i2c_calibrate	C(2)	L
leds-lp5523.c	lp5523_init_program_engine	A	L
drxj.c	drxj_dap_atomic_read_write_block	S	L
drxd_hard.c	InitCC	A(5)	L
drxd_hard.c	SC_ProcStartCommand	A(3)	L
drxd_hard.c	SC_SendCommand	A	L
drxk_hard.c	drxk_get_stats	S	L
lgdt3306a.c	lgdt3306a_read_signal_strength	A(2)	L
mt312.c	mt312_set_frontend	S	L
si2165.c	si2165_wait_init_done	A	L
sp8870.c	sp8870_set_frontend_parameters	A	L
mxl111sf-phy.c	mxl111sf_config_mpeg_in	S	L
cpia1.c	do_command	S(2)	L
cpia1.c	sd_config	S	L
m5602_mt9m111.c	mt9m111_probe	A	L
m5602_po1030.c	po1030_probe	A	L
mc13xxx-core.c	mc13xxx_adc_do_conversion	A	L
sm501.c	sm501_base_init	S	L
atmel-ssc.c	ssc_request	S	L
ics932s401.c	ics932s401_update_device	S	L
bcm_sf2.c	bcm_sf2_sw_mdio_write	A	L
atl1e_main.c	atl1e_mdio_write	A	L
cudbg_lib.c	cudbg_collect_hw_sched	A	L
80003es2lan.c	e1000_init_hw_80003es2lan	A(2)	L
80003es2lan.c	e1000_reset_hw_80003es2lan	A	L
netxen_nic_init.c	netxen_validate_firmware	A	L
mcdi.c	efx_mcdi_set_id_led	A	L
dwmac-sunxi.c	sun7i_gmac_init	A	L

Filename	Called function	S	K
niu.c	niu_pci_vpd_scan_props	A(2)	L
cpts.c	cpts_create	A	L
phy.c	phy_mii_ioctl	S	L
xilinx_gmii2rgmii.c	xgmiitorgmii_read_status	C	L
slic_ds26522.c	slic_read	C	L
wmi.c	ath6kl_wmi_set_roam_lrssi_cmd	A	L
usb.c	brcmf_usb_register	A	L
mesh.c	lbs_persist_config_init	A(2)	L
pci-exynos.c	exynos_pcie_assert_reset	S	L
alienware-wmi.c	alienware_zone_init	S	L
twl4030_charger.c	twl4030_bci_get_property	A	L
palmas-regulator.c	palmas_set_mode_smps	A	L
tps65910-regulator.c	tps65910_probe	A	L
rtc-coh901331.c	coh901331_resume	A	L
rtc-hym8563.c	hym8563_rtc_read_time	A	L
rtc-rv8803.c	rv8803_handle_irq	S(2)	L
dpcsup.c	aac_aif_callback	S	L
qcom-ngd-ctrl.c	qcom_slim_ngd_ctrl_probe	S	L
qcom-ngd-ctrl.c	of_qcom_slim_ngd_register	S	L
hal_init.c	rtl871x_load_fw_cb	S	L
ioctl_linux.c	rtw_wps_start	A	L
ms.c	mspro_rw_multi_sector	C	L
ms.c	ms_copy_page	A(2)	L
ms.c	mspro_stop_seq_mode	S	L
sd.c	reset_sd	S	L
sd.c	sd_execute_write_data	A	L
target_core_rd.c	rd_set_configfs_dev_params	A(2)	L
max310x.c	max310x_uart_init	S	L
adp8870_bl.c	adp8870_bl_ambient_light_zone_store	S	L
sysfs.c	btrfs_sysfs_feature_update	A	L
root.c	proc_root_init	S	L
xfs_super.c	xfs_fs_dirty_inode	S	L
verifier.c	check_func_call	C	L
verifier.c	check_helper_call	C	L
verifier.c	check_ld_abs	C	L
alarmtimer.c	alarmtimer_suspend	S	L
compaction.c	sysctl_extfrag_handler	A	L
hmm.c	hmm_devmem_pages_remove	A	L
main.c	batadv_init	S	L
net_namespace.c	net_ns_init	A	L
route.c	ipv6_sysctl_rtcache_flush	A	L
ip_set_core.c	call_ad	A	L
netlink_compat.c	tipc_nl_compat_sk_dump	A	L
gus_main.c	snd_gus_init_control	S	L
sb16_main.c	snd_sb16dsp_pcm	A	L
ews.c	snd_ice1712_6fire_read_pca	A	L
rt5663.c	rt5663_parse_dp	S	L
sst-mfld-platform-pcm.c	sst_media_hw_params	A	L
pod.c	pod_startup4	A	L
variax.c	variax_startup6	S	L
netback.c	ether_ifattach	S	F
kern_umtx.c	umtxq_check_susp	S	F
scsi_enc.c	cam_periph_runccb	S	F

References

1. Dautenhahn, N., Kasampalis, T., Dietz, W., Criswell, J., Adve, V.: Nested kernel: an operating system architecture for intra-kernel privilege separation. In: ACM SIGPLAN Notices, vol. 50, pp. 191–206. ACM (2015)
2. Dillig, I., Dillig, T., Aiken, A.: Static error detection using semantic inconsistency inference. In: Proceedings of the 28th ACM SIGPLAN Conference on Programming Language Design and Implementation, PLDI 2007 (2007)
3. Gan, S., et al.: CollAFL: path sensitive fuzzing. In: 2018 IEEE Symposium on Security and Privacy (SP), pp. 679–696. IEEE (2018)
4. Gunawi, H.S., Rubio-González, C., Arpaci-Dusseau, A.C., Arpaci-Dusseau, R.H., Liblit, B.: EIO: error handling is occasionally correct. In: FAST, vol. 8, pp. 1–16 (2008)
5. Hardekopf, B., Lin, C.: The ant and the grasshopper: fast and accurate pointer analysis for millions of lines of code. In: ACM SIGPLAN Notices, vol. 42, pp. 290–299. ACM (2007)
6. InfoSec Institute: Exploiting Windows Drivers: Double-fetch Race Condition Vulnerability (2016). http://resources.infosecinstitute.com/exploiting-windows-drivers-double-fetch-race-condition-vulnerability
7. Jana, S., Kang, Y.J., Roth, S., Ray, B.: Automatically detecting error handling bugs using error specifications. In: USENIX Security Symposium, pp. 345–362 (2016)
8. Kang, Y., Ray, B., Jana, S.: APEx: automated inference of error specifications for C APIs. In: Proceedings of the 31st IEEE/ACM International Conference on Automated Software Engineering, pp. 472–482. ACM (2016)
9. Kim, S.Y., et al.: CAB-FUZZ: practical concolic testing techniques for COTS operating systems. In: 2017 USENIX Annual Technical Conference (USENIX ATC 2017), pp. 689–701 (2017)
10. Klees, G., Ruef, A., Cooper, B., Wei, S., Hicks, M.: Evaluating fuzz testing. In: Proceedings of the 2018 ACM SIGSAC Conference on Computer and Communications Security, pp. 2123–2138. ACM (2018)
11. Koning, K., Chen, X., Bos, H., Giuffrida, C., Athanasopoulos, E.: No need to hide: protecting safe regions on commodity hardware. In: Proceedings of the Twelfth European Conference on Computer Systems, pp. 437–452. ACM (2017)
12. Kremenek, T., Twohey, P., Back, G., Ng, A., Engler, D.: From uncertainty to belief: inferring the specification within. In: Proceedings of the 7th Symposium on Operating Systems Design and Implementation, OSDI 2006 (2006)
13. Lu, K., Walter, M.T., Pfaff, D., Nümberger, S., Lee, W., Backes, M.: Unleashing use-before-initialization vulnerabilities in the Linux kernel using targeted stack spraying. In: NDSS (2017)
14. Mao, J., Chen, Y., Xiao, Q., Shi, Y.: RID: finding reference count bugs with inconsistent path pair checking. ACM SIGARCH Comput. Archit. News **44**(2), 531–544 (2016)
15. Min, C., Kashyap, S., Lee, B., Song, C., Kim, T.: Cross-checking semantic correctness: the case of finding file system bugs. In: Proceedings of the 25th Symposium on Operating Systems Principles, pp. 361–377. ACM (2015)
16. Mogosanu, L., Rane, A., Dautenhahn, N.: MicroStache: a lightweight execution context for in-process safe region isolation. In: Bailey, M., Holz, T., Stamatogiannakis, M., Ioannidis, S. (eds.) RAID 2018. LNCS, vol. 11050, pp. 359–379. Springer, Cham (2018). https://doi.org/10.1007/978-3-030-00470-5_17

17. Monshizadeh, M., Naldurg, P., Venkatakrishnan, V.: MACE: detecting privilege escalation vulnerabilities in web applications. In: Proceedings of the 2014 ACM SIGSAC Conference on Computer and Communications Security, pp. 690–701. ACM (2014)
18. Nagarakatte, S., Zhao, J., Martin, M.M., Zdancewic, S.: SoftBound: highly compatible and complete spatial memory safety for C. ACM SIGPLAN Not. **44**(6), 245–258 (2009)
19. Niu, B., Tan, G.: Modular control-flow integrity. In: ACM SIGPLAN Notices, vol. 49, pp. 577–587. ACM (2014)
20. Peng, H., Shoshitaishvili, Y., Payer, M.: T-FUZZ: fuzzing by program transformation. In: 2018 IEEE Symposium on Security and Privacy (SP), pp. 697–710. IEEE (2018)
21. Rubio-González, C., Gunawi, H.S., Liblit, B., Arpaci-Dusseau, R.H., Arpaci-Dusseau, A.C.: Error propagation analysis for file systems. In: ACM SIGPLAN Notices, vol. 44, pp. 270–280. ACM (2009)
22. Saha, S., Lozi, J.P., Thomas, G., Lawall, J.L., Muller, G.: Hector: detecting resource-release omission faults in error-handling code for systems software. In: 2013 43rd Annual IEEE/IFIP International Conference on Dependable Systems and Networks (DSN), pp. 1–12. IEEE (2013)
23. Schwarz, M., et al.: Automated detection, exploitation, and elimination of double-fetch bugs using modern CPU features. In: Proceedings of the 2018 on Asia Conference on Computer and Communications Security, pp. 587–600. ACM (2018)
24. Serebryany, K., Bruening, D., Potapenko, A., Vyukov, D.: AddressSanitizer: a fast address sanity checker. Presented as part of the 2012 USENIX Annual Technical Conference (USENIX ATC 2012), pp. 309–318 (2012)
25. Situ, L., Wang, L., Liu, Y., Mao, B., Li, X.: Vanguard: detecting missing checks for prognosing potential vulnerabilities. In: Proceedings of the Tenth Asia-Pacific Symposium on Internetware, p. 5. ACM (2018)
26. Son, S., McKinley, K.S., Shmatikov, V.: RoleCast: finding missing security checks when you do not know what checks are. In: ACM SIGPLAN Notices, vol. 46, pp. 1069–1084. ACM (2011)
27. Song, C., Lee, B., Lu, K., Harris, W., Kim, T., Lee, W.: Enforcing kernel security invariants with data flow integrity. In: NDSS (2016)
28. Tan, L., Zhang, X., Ma, X., Xiong, W., Zhou, Y.: AutoISES: automatically inferring security specification and detecting violations. In: USENIX Security Symposium, pp. 379–394 (2008)
29. Tian, Y., Ray, B.: Automatically diagnosing and repairing error handling bugs in C. In: Proceedings of the 2017 11th Joint Meeting on Foundations of Software Engineering, pp. 752–762. ACM (2017)
30. Van Der Veen, V., et al.: A tough call: mitigating advanced code-reuse attacks at the binary level. In: 2016 IEEE Symposium on Security and Privacy (SP), pp. 934–953. IEEE (2016)
31. Wang, P., Krinke, J., Lu, K., Li, G., Dodier-Lazaro, S.: How double-fetch situations turn into double-fetch vulnerabilities: a study of double fetches in the Linux kernel. In: 26th USENIX Security Symposium (USENIX Security 2017), pp. 1–16 (2017)
32. Wang, W., Lu, K., Yew, P.C.: Check it again: detecting lacking-recheck bugs in OS kernels. In: Proceedings of the 2018 ACM SIGSAC Conference on Computer and Communications Security, pp. 1899–1913. ACM (2018)
33. Wikibooks: C Programming/Program flow control (2017). https://en.wikibooks.org/wiki/C_Programming/Program_flow_control

34. Xu, M., Qian, C., Lu, K., Backes, M., Kim, T.: Precise and scalable detection of double-fetch bugs in OS kernels. In: 2018 IEEE Symposium on Security and Privacy (SP), pp. 661–678. IEEE (2018)
35. Yamaguchi, F., Wressnegger, C., Gascon, H., Rieck, K.: Chucky: exposing missing checks in source code for vulnerability discovery. In: Proceedings of the 2013 ACM SIGSAC Conference on Computer & Communications Security, pp. 499–510. ACM (2013)
36. Yee, B., et al.: Native client: a sandbox for portable, untrusted x86 native code. In: 2009 30th IEEE Symposium on Security and Privacy, pp. 79–93. IEEE (2009)

Uncovering Information Flow Policy Violations in C Programs (Extended Abstract)

Darion Cassel[1]([⊠]), Yan Huang[2], and Limin Jia[1]

[1] Carnegie Mellon University, Pittsburgh, PA 15213, USA
{darioncassel,liminjia}@cmu.edu
[2] Indiana University, Bloomington, IN 47405, USA
yh33@indiana.edu

Abstract. Programmers of cryptographic applications written in C need to avoid common mistakes such as sending private data over public channels or improperly ordering protocol steps. These secrecy, integrity, and sequencing policies can be cumbersome to check with existing general-purpose tools. We have developed a novel means of specifying and uncovering violations of these policies that allows for a much lighter-weight approach than previous tools. We embed the policy annotations in C's type system via a source-to-source translation and leverage existing C compilers to check for policy violations, achieving high performance and scalability. We show through case studies of recent cryptographic libraries and applications that our work is able to express detailed policies for large bodies of C code and can find subtle policy violations. We show formal connections between the policy annotations and an information flow type system and prove a noninterference guarantee of our design.

Keywords: Information flow · Type systems · Security

1 Introduction

Programs often have complex data invariants and API usage policies written in their documentation or comments. The ability to detect violations of these invariants and policies is key to the correctness and security of programs. This is particularly important for cryptographic protocols and libraries, which the security of large systems depend on. There has been much interest in checking implementations of cryptographic protocols [3,12–15,25,28,41]. These verification systems, while comprehensive in their scope, require expert knowledge of both the cryptographic protocols and the verification tool to be used effectively.

What remains missing is a lightweight, developer-friendly, compile-time tool to help programmers identify errors that violate high-level policies on C programs. Particularly important policies are secrecy (e.g., sensitive data is not

© Springer Nature Switzerland AG 2019
K. Sako et al. (Eds.): ESORICS 2019, LNCS 11736, pp. 26–46, 2019.
https://doi.org/10.1007/978-3-030-29962-0_2

given to untrusted functions), integrity (e.g., trusted data is not modified by untrusted functions), and API call sequencing (e.g., the ordering of cryptographic protocol steps is maintained), all of which are information flow policies.

In this paper, we present a framework called `FlowNotation` where C programmers can add lightweight annotations to their programs to express policy specifications. These policies are then automatically checked by C compiler, potentially revealing policy violations in the implementation. Our annotations are in the same family as *type qualifiers* (e.g. CQual [22,37,57]), where qualifiers such as *tainted* and *trusted* are used to identify violations of integrity properties of C programs; supplying tainted inputs to a function that requires a trusted argument will cause a type error. Our work extends previous results to support more complex and refined sequencing properties. Consider the following policy: a data object is initially tainted, then it is sanitized using an `encodeURI` API, then serialized using a `serialize` API, and finally written to disk using a `fileWrite` API. Such API sequencing patterns are quite common, but cannot be straightforwardly captured using previous type qualifier systems. `FlowNotation` extends type qualifiers to include a sequence of labels for specifying such policies. However, rather than implementing a new type system, `FlowNotation` translates an annotated C program to another C program, which is then checked by a C compiler for policy violations. The key insight is that qualified C types can be translated to C structures whose fields are the original C types. Consequently, we leverage performant C type checkers for checking large codebases.

To gain a formal understanding of the type of errors that we can uncover with this system, we model the annotated types as *information flow types*, which augment ordinary types with security labels. We define a core language *polC* and prove that its information flow type system enforces noninterference. The novelty of *polC*'s type system is that the security labels are sequences of secrecy and integrity labels, specifying the path under which data can be relabeled. Relabeling corresponds to *declassification* (marking secrets as public) and *endorsement* (marking data from untrusted source as trusted). The type system ensures that relabeling functions are called in the correct order. We also define μC, a core imperative language with nominal types but without information flow labels in order to model a fragment of C. We then formally define our translation algorithm based on *polC* and μC and prove the algorithm correct. The formalism not only makes explicit assumptions made by our algorithm, but also provides a formal account of the properties being checked by the annotations.

To demonstrate the effectiveness of `FlowNotation`, we implement a prototype for a subset of C and evaluate the prototype on several cryptographic libraries. Our evaluation shows that we are able to check useful information flow policies in a modular way and uncover subtle program flaws. Our full paper can be found at [21] and the source code of `FlowNotation` can be downloaded from the following URL: https://github.com/flownotation.

2   Overview and Motivating Examples

System Overview. The left side of Fig. 1 illustrates how `FlowNotation` works. First, a programmer annotates policies. `FlowNotation` takes the annotated program and produces a translated C program, which is then type-checked using an off-the-shelf C compiler. A type error implies a policy violation. Once free of violations, the unannotated, pre-translation program is used.

Checking Secrecy Policies. Suppose developers are working on a C project that uses customers' financial data. This project integrates a secure two-party computation component that allows Alice and Bob to find out which of the two is wealthier without revealing their wealth to the other or relying on a trusted third party. Let us assume that the program obtains Alice's balance using the function `get_alice_balance`, then calls function `wealthierA` to see whether Alice is wealthier than Bob. `wealthierA`'s implementation uses a library that provides APIs for secure computation primitives.

```
int bankHandler() { int balA; balA = get_alice_balance(); ...
    wealthierA(balA); }
```

The variable `balA` contains Alice's balance, so it should be handled with care; in particular, the secrecy of `balA` is maintained. One way is to use information flow types (e.g. [51]) to assign `balA` the type (**int AlicePriv**), indicating that it is an integer containing an `AlicePriv` type of secret. In contrast, the type (**int Public**) can be given to variables that do not contain secrets. The type system then makes sure that read and write operations involving `balA` are consistent with its secrecy label. For instance, if a function `postBalance`(**int Public**), which is meant to post the balance publicly, is called with `balA` as the argument, the type system will reject this program for violating the secrecy policy.

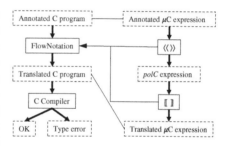

Fig. 1. Overview of `FlowNotation`.

`FlowNotation`'s annotations are *information flow labels*, each of which has a *secrecy* component and an *integrity* component. Programmers can provide these annotations above the declaration of `balA` to specify the secrecy policy as follows.

```
#requires AlicePriv:secrecy
int balA;
```

Here, `#requires` is a directive to help parse this annotation (in practice, `#pragma` prefaces it). `AlicePriv` is a secrecy label. `secrecy` indicates only the secrecy component is of concern and `balA`'s integrity component is automatically assigned `bot`, the lowest integrity. This annotation can be used to check P_1 below:

P_1: `balA` should never be given as input to an untrusted function.

The corresponding information flow type of `balA` is **int**(`AlicePriv`, `bot`). Trusted functions are those trusted by the programmer not to leak `balA`. Let us assume our programmer trusts the following APIs. The API `encodeA` converts an integer argument into a bit representation similar to what is used in Obliv-C [54] for use with a garbled circuit. The API yao_execA takes a pointer to a function f and an argument for f, and runs f as a circuit with Yao's protocol [52]. API reveal gives the result to both parties. The following code is for Alice (Bob's program is symmetric, which we omit):

```
int compare(int a, int b) { return a > b; }
int wealthierA(int balA) {
    int res = yao_execA(&compare, encodeA(balA));
    reveal(&res, ALICE); }
```

This program first encodes Alice's balance, and then calls yao_execA with the comparison function and Alice's encoded balance as arguments, and finally calls reveal. The code as it stands will not type-check after being translated, unless the programmer annotates the secure computation APIs.

```
#param AlicePriv:secrecy
int encodeA(int balA);
#param(2) AlicePriv:secrecy
int yao_execA(void* compare, int balA);
```

These two annotations state that the functions must accept parameters with the label AlicePriv. In the second annotation, #param(2) specifies that the annotation should only apply to the second parameter. A violation of P_1 will be detected, when balA is given to a function that does not have this kind of annotation; e.g. that is not allowed to accept AlicePriv-labeled data.

Checking Integrity and Sequencing Policies. FlowNotation can also be used to check for violations of the following, more refined, policy:

$$P_2 : \text{balA should be used by the encoding function}$$
$$\text{and then by the Yao protocol execution.}$$

The annotation for balA is:

```
#requires AlicePriv:secrecy then EncodedBal:integrity
int balA;
```

The keyword then allows for the sequencing of labels. Corresponding changes are made to the other annotations:

```
#param AlicePriv:secrecy
#return EncodedBal:integrity
int encodeA(int balA);
#param(2) EncodedBal:integrity
int yao_execA(void* compare, int balA);
```

The encodeA function, as before, requires the argument to have the AlicePriv secrecy label. In addition, the return value from encodeA will have the integrity label EncodedBal, stating that it is endorsed by the encodeA function to be properly encoded. The yao_execA function requires the argument to have the same integrity label. If only encodeA is annotated with EncodedBal at its return value, the type system will check that an appropriate API call sequence (encodeA followed by yao_execA) is applied to the value stored in balA.

3   A Core Calculus for Staged Release

We formally define *polC*, which models annotated C programs that
FlowNotation takes as input. We show that *polC*'s type system can enforce not
only secrecy and integrity policies, but also staged information release and data
endorsement policies. We prove that our type system enforces noninterference,
from which the property of staged information release is a corollary.

3.1   Syntax and Operational Semantics

The syntax of *polC* is summarized in Fig. 2. We write ℓ to denote security labels,
which consist of a secrecy tag s and an integrity tag ι. We assume there is a
security lattice $(S, \sqsubseteq_S)$ for secrecy tags and a security lattice $(I, \sqsubseteq_I)$ for integrity
tags. The security lattice $\mathcal{L} = (L, \sqsubseteq)$ is the product of the above two lattices.
The top element of the lattice is $(\top_S, \bot_I)$ (abbreviated $\top$), denoting data that
do not contain any secret and come from the most trusted source; and the
bottom element is $(\bot_S, \top_I)$ (abbreviated $\bot$), denoting data that contain the
most secretive information and come from the least trusted source.

A policy, denoted ρ is a sequence of labels specifying the precise sequence
of relabeling (declassification and endorsement) of the data. The example from
Sect. 2 uses the following policy: $(AlicePrivate, \bot_I)::(\bot_S, EncodedBal)::\bot$. A policy always ends with either the top element, indicating no further relabeling is
allowed, or the bottom element, indicating arbitrary relabeling is allowed. For
our application domain, the labels are distinct points in the lattice that are not
connected by any partial order relations except $\top$ and $\bot$.

Labels	$\ell ::= (s, \iota)$	
Policies	$\rho ::= \bot \mid \top \mid \ell :: \rho$	
1st order types	$b ::= \text{int} \mid \text{ptr}(s) \mid T$	
Simple sec. types	$t ::= b\,\rho \mid \text{unit}$	
Security types	$s ::= t \mid [pc](t \to t)^\rho$	
Values	$v ::= x \mid n \mid () \mid f \mid T\{v_1, \cdots, v_k\} \mid loc$	
Expressions	$e ::= v \mid e_1 \, \text{bop} \, e_2 \mid v\,e \mid \text{let } x = e_1 \text{ in } e_2$	
	$\mid v.i \mid \text{if } v_1 \text{ then } e_2 \text{ else } e_3 \mid v := e$	
	$\mid \text{new } e \mid *v \mid \text{reLab}(\ell'::\bot \leftarrow \ell::\top)\,v$	

Fig. 2. Syntax of *polC*

A simple (first-order)
security type, denoted t,
is obtained by adding
policies to ordinary types.
Our core language sup-
ports integers, unit, pointers, and record types
(struct T $\{t_1, \cdots, t_k\}$ to
model C structs). Here T
is the defined name for
a record type. To sim-
plify our formalism, we
assume that defined type
T is always a record type named T. Our information flow types use the policy ρ,
rather than a single label ℓ. The meaning of an expression of type int ρ is that this
expression is evaluated to an integer and it induces a sequence of declassification
(endorsement) operations according to the sequence of labels specified by ρ. For
instance, $e : \text{int } H::L::\bot$ means that e initially is of int H, then it can be given
to a declassification function to be downgraded to int L, the resulting expression
can be further downgraded to bottom. $e : \text{int } H::L::\top$ is similar except that the

last expression cannot be declassified further; i.e.. it stays at L security level. The annotated type for balA in Sect. 2 can be similarly interpreted.

The unit type is inhabited by one element (), so it does not need a label. A function type is of the form $[pc](t_1 \rightarrow t_2)^\rho$, where t_1 is the argument's type, t_2 is the return type, ρ is the security label of the function indicating who can receive this function, and pc, called the program counter, is the security label representing where this function can be called. A function f of type $[L::\bot](t_1 \rightarrow t_2)^{H::\bot}$ cannot be called in an if branch that branches on a value with label $H::\bot$ and the function itself cannot be given to an attacker whose label is $L::\bot$.

Our expressions are reminiscent of A-normal forms (ANF): all elimination forms use only values (e.g., $v.i$, instead of $e.i$). This not only simplifies our proofs, but also the translation rules (presented in Sect. 4). The fragment of C that is checked in our case studies is quite similar to this form. Values can be variables, integers, unit, functions, records, and store locations. Since we are modeling an imperative language, all functions are predefined, and stored in the context Ψ. Expressions include function calls, if statements, let bindings, and store operations. One special expression is the relabeling (declassification) operation, written $\mathsf{reLab}(\ell'::\bot \leftarrow \ell::\top)\, v$. This operation changes the label of v from $\ell::\top$ to $\ell'::\bot$. Such an expression should only appear in trusted declassification functions. For our applications, we further restrict the relabeling to be between two labels; from one ending with the top element to one ending with bottom element. We will explain this later when we explain the typing rules.

$polC$'s small step semantic rules are denoted $\Psi \vdash \sigma\, /\, e \longrightarrow \sigma'\, /\, e'$, where Ψ stores all the functions, σ maps locations to values and e is the expression to be evaluated. The rules are standard and can be found in our full paper.

3.2   Typing Rules

The type system makes use of several typing contexts. We write D to denote the context for all the type definitions. We only consider type definitions of record (struct) types, written $T \mapsto \mathsf{struct}\ T\ \{t_1, \cdots, t_k\}$. The typing context for functions is denoted F. We distinguish two types of functions: ordinary functions, and declassification/endorsement functions whose bodies are allowed to contain relabeling operations, written $f{:}(\mathsf{d\&e})[pc]t_1 \rightarrow t_2$. F does not dictate the label of a function f. Instead, the context in which f is used decides f's label.

$$\begin{aligned}
&\textit{Type def. ctx} &&D ::= \cdot \mid D, T \mapsto \mathsf{struct}\ T\ \{t_1, \cdots, t_k\} \\
&\textit{Func typing ctx}\ F ::= \cdot \mid F, f{:}[pc]t_1 \rightarrow t_2 \mid F, f{:}(\mathsf{d\&e})[pc]t_1 \rightarrow t_2 \\
&\textit{Store Typing} &&\Sigma ::= \cdot \mid \Sigma, loc : s
\end{aligned}$$

We write Σ to denote the typing context for pointers. It maps a pointer to the type of its content. Γ is the typing context for variables, and pc is the security label representing the program counter. Typing judgment: $D; F; \Sigma; \Gamma \vdash v : t$ types values, and $D; F; \Sigma; \Gamma; pc \vdash e : t$ types expressions. The typing rules for $polC$ are summarized in the full paper.

Most of these typing rules are standard. These rules carefully arrange the constraints on policies and the program counter so that the noninterference theorem can be proven. We explain the rule P-T-E-DE, which types the application of a declassification/endorsement function and is unique to our system.

$$\frac{D; F; \Sigma; \Gamma \vdash v_f : (\mathsf{d\&e})[pc'](b\ \ell_1 :: \top \to b\ \ell_2 :: \bot)^{\rho_f} \quad}{D; F; \Sigma; \Gamma; pc \vdash e_a : b\ \rho \quad \rho = \ell_1 :: \ell_2 :: \rho' \quad \rho_f \sqcup pc \sqsubseteq pc'}{D; F; \Sigma; \Gamma; pc \vdash v_f\ e_a : b\ \ell_2 :: \rho'} \ \text{P-T-E-DE}$$

We first define when a policy ρ_1 is less strict than another, ρ_2, written $\rho_1 \sqsubseteq \rho_2$, as the point-wise lifting of the label operation $\ell_1 \sqsubseteq \ell_2$. When one policy reaches its end, we use $\bot \sqsubseteq \rho$ or $\rho \sqsubseteq \top$. $\bot$ represents a policy that can be arbitrarily reclassified and thus is a subtype of any policy ρ. $\top$ is the strictest policy that forbids any reclassification; so any policy is less strict than $\top$.

The first premise checks that v_f relabels data from ℓ_1 to ℓ_2. The second premise checks that e_a's type matches that of the argument of v_f; further, e_a's policy ρ has ℓ_1 and ℓ_2 as the first two labels, indicating that e_a is currently at security level ℓ_1 and the result of processing e_a has label ℓ_2. Finally, the return type of the function application has the tail of the policy ρ. The policy of e_a does not change; instead, the policy of the result of the relabeling function inherits the tail of e_a's policy. Therefore, our type system is not enforcing type states of variables as found in the Typestate system [48]. These declassification and endorsement functions only rewrite one label, not a sequence of labels. This allows us to have finer-grained control over the stages of relabeling.

$$\frac{D; F; \Sigma; \Gamma \vdash v : b\ \rho \quad pc \sqsubseteq \rho'}{D; F; \Sigma; \Gamma; pc \vdash \mathsf{reLab}(\rho' \Leftarrow \rho)\ v : b\ \rho'} \ \text{P-T-E-Relabel}$$

$$\frac{D; F; \Sigma; \Gamma; pc \vdash e : s' \quad s' \leq s}{D; F; \Sigma; \Gamma; pc \vdash e : s} \ \text{P-T-E-Sub}$$

The typing rule for relabeling ensures that the pc label is lower than or equal to the resulting label. We have the standard subtyping rule, which uses the same notion of label subtyping introduced above.

3.3   Noninterference

We prove a noninterference theorem for $polC$'s type system by adapting the proof technique used in FlowML [45]. We extend our language to include pairs of expressions and pairs of values to simulate two executions that differ in "high" values. We only explain the key definitions for the theorem.

We first define equivalences of expressions in terms of an attacker's observation. We assume that the attacker knows the program and can observe expressions at the security level ℓ_A. To be consistent, when ℓ_A is not $\top$ or $\bot$, the attacker's policy is written $\ell_A::\top$. Intuitively, an expression of type $b\ \rho$ should not be visible to the attacker if existing declassification functions cannot relabel data with label ρ down to $\ell_A::\top$. For instance, if $\rho = H::L::\bot$ and there is no declassification function from H to L, then an attacker at L cannot distinguish between two different integers v_1 and v_2 of type int ρ. On the other hand, if there is a function f :$_{d\&e}$ int $H::\top \rightarrow L::\bot$, then v_1 and v_2 are distinguishable by the attacker. We define when a policy ρ is in H w.r.t. the attacker's label, the function context, and the relabeling operations (when values of type $b\ \rho$ are not observable to the attacker) as follows. $\rho \in H$ if ρ cannot be *rewritten* to be a policy that is lower or equal to the attackers' policy. Here $F; R \vdash \rho \rightsquigarrow \rho'$ holds when $\rho = \ell_1::\cdots::\ell_i::\rho'$ and there is a sequence of relabeling operations in F and R, using which ρ can be rewritten to ρ'. For instance, when $\ell_A = \bot$

$$F_1 = \texttt{encodeA} : (\text{d\&e})\text{int}\ (AlicePrivate, \bot_I) :: \top \rightarrow \text{int}\ (\bot_S, EncodedBal) :: \bot$$
$$F_2 = F_1, \texttt{yao\_execA} : (\text{d\&e})\text{int}\ (\bot_S, EncodedBal) :: \top \rightarrow \text{int}\ \bot$$
$$\ell_A; \cdot; \cdot \vdash\ (AlicePrivate, \bot_I) \in H \qquad \ell_A; F_1; \cdot \vdash\ (\bot_S, EncodedBal) \in H$$
$$\ell_A; F_2; \cdot \nvdash\ (\bot_S, EncodedBal) \in H$$

Our noninterference theorem (defined below) states that given an expression e that is observable by the attacker, and two equivalent substitutions δ_1 and δ_2 for free variables in e (denoted $\delta_1 \approx_H \delta_2$), and both $e\delta_1$ and $e\delta_2$ terminate, then they must evaluate to the same value. In other words, the values of sub-expressions that are not observable by the attacker do not influence the value of observable expressions.

Theorem 1 (Noninterference). *If* $D; F; \Gamma; \bot \vdash e : s$, e *does not contain any relabeling operations, given attacker's label* ℓ, *and substitution* δ_1, δ_2 *s.t.* $F \vdash \delta_1 \approx_H \delta_2 : \Gamma$, *and* $\ell; F; \cdot \vdash labOf(s) \notin H$ *and* $\Psi \vdash \emptyset\ /\ e\delta_1 \longrightarrow^* \sigma_1\ /\ v_1$ *and* $\Psi \vdash \emptyset\ /\ e\delta_2 \longrightarrow^* \sigma_2\ /\ v_2$, *then* $v_1 = v_2$.

It follows from Noninterference that given $D; F; x{:}\text{int}\ \ell_1::\cdots::\ell_n::\bot \vdash e :$ int $\ell_n::\top$ where the attacker's label is ℓ_n, the attacker can only gain knowledge about the value for x if there is a sequence of declassification/endorsement functions f_is that remove label ℓ_i from the policy to reach $\ell_n::\top$. If $\ell_i \nsubseteq \ell_{i+1}$, the f_is have to be applied in the correct order, as dictated by the typing rules.

4   Embedding in a Nominal Type System

The type system of *polC* can encode interesting security policies and help programmers identify subtle bugs during development. However, implementing a feature-rich language with *polC*'s type system requires non-trivial effort. Moreover, only programmers who are willing to rewrite their codebase in this new language can benefit from it. Rather than create a new language, FlowNotation leverages C's type system to enforce policies specified by *polC*'s types.

The mapping between the concrete workflow of FlowNotation, *polC* and μC, and the algorithms defined here is shown in Fig. 1. We first define a simple imperative language μC with nominal types and annotations, which models

the fragment of C that FlowNotation works within. We show how the anno-
tated types and expressions can be mapped to types and expressions in *polC* in
Sect. 4.1. Then in Sect. 4.2, we show how to translate *polC* programs back to μC.
These two algorithms combined describe the core algorithm of FlowNotation.
We prove our translation correct in Sect. 4.3.

4.1 μC and Annotated μC

Expressions and the typing context names of μC are the same as those in *polC*.
The types in μC do not have information flow policies.

Expressions	$e ::= \cdots \mid \text{let } x : \beta = e_1 \text{ in } e_2$	*Typ. Annot.* $\beta ::= a \mid a_1 \to a_2$
Basic types	$\pi ::= T \mid \text{int} \mid \text{unit} \mid \text{ptr}(\tau)$	*Types* $\tau ::= \pi \mid \pi_1 \to \pi_2$
Annotation	$a ::= \pi \mid T \text{ at } \rho \mid \text{int at } \rho \mid \text{ptr}(\beta) \text{ at } \rho$	
Annot. typedef $D_a ::= \cdot \mid D_a, T \mapsto \text{struct } T\{a_1, \cdots, a_k\}$		
Annot. Func. $F_a ::= \cdot \mid F_a, f : a_1 \to a_2 \mid F_a, f : (\text{d\&e})a_1 \to a_2$		

Programmers will provide policy annotations, denoted β, which are very
similar to labeled types s. We keep them separate, as programmers do not need
to write out the fully labeled types. A programmer can annotate defined record
types T at ρ, integers int at ρ, both the content and the pointer itself $\text{ptr}(\beta)$ at ρ,
or the record type struct $T\{\beta_1, \cdots, \beta_k\}$. The last case is used to annotate type
declarations in the context D. We extend expressions with annotated expressions;
let $x : a = e_1$ in e_2. We assume that let bindings, type declarations, and function
types are the only places where programmers provide annotations.

4.2 Translating Annotated Programs to μC

Instead of defining an algorithm to translate an annotated μC program e_a to
another μC program, we first define an algorithm that maps e_a into a program
e_l in *polC*; then an algorithm that translates e_l to a μC program.

Mapping from Annotated μC to *polC*. This mapping helps make explicit
all the assumptions and necessary declassification and endorsement operations
needed to interpret those annotations as proper *polC* types and programs.

We write $\langle\!\langle \beta \rangle\!\rangle$ to denote the mapping of unannotated and annotated μC types
to *polC* types. Unannotated types are given a special label U (unlabeled, defined
as $(\bot_S, \bot_I)$); annotated types are translated as labeled types. All function types
are given the pc label $\bot$, so the function body can be typed with few restrictions.
The mapping is straightforwardly defined over the structure of the annotated
types and we show a few rules below.

$$\frac{\pi \in \{\text{int}, T\}}{\langle\!\langle \pi \rangle\!\rangle = \pi \ U} \qquad \frac{\pi \in \{\text{int}, T\}}{\langle\!\langle \pi \text{ at } \rho \rangle\!\rangle = \pi \ \rho} \qquad \frac{\forall i \in [1,2], \langle\!\langle a_i \rangle\!\rangle = t_i}{\langle\!\langle a_1 \to a_2 \rangle\!\rangle = [\bot](t_1 \to t_2)}$$

$$\frac{\begin{array}{c} D_a; F_a; \Gamma_a \vdash \langle\!\langle v \rangle\!\rangle \Rightarrow lv \qquad tpOf(lv) = T\ \rho \\ D_a(T) = (\text{struct } T\{\beta_1, \cdots, \beta_n\}) \qquad \forall i \in [1, n], \rho = labOf(\langle\!\langle \beta_i \rangle\!\rangle) \end{array}}{D_a; F_a; \Gamma_a; t \vdash \langle\!\langle v.i \rangle\!\rangle \Rightarrow lv.i} \text{ L-FIELD-U}$$

$$\frac{\begin{array}{c} D_a; F_a; \Gamma_a \vdash \langle\!\langle v \rangle\!\rangle \Rightarrow lv \qquad tpOf(lv) = T\ \rho \\ D_a(T) = (\text{struct } T\{\beta_1, \cdots, \beta_n\}) \qquad \exists i \in [1, n], \rho \neq labOf(\langle\!\langle \beta_i \rangle\!\rangle) \end{array}}{D_a; F_a; \Gamma_a; t \vdash \langle\!\langle v.i \rangle\!\rangle \Rightarrow \text{let } y : T \perp = \text{reLab}(\perp \Leftarrow \rho)\ lv \text{ in } (y@T \perp).i} \text{ L-FIELD}$$

$$\frac{\begin{array}{c} D_a; F_a; \Gamma_a \vdash \langle\!\langle v_1 \rangle\!\rangle \Rightarrow lv_1 \qquad tpOf(lv_1) = \text{int } \rho \\ D_a; F_a; \Gamma_a; t \vdash \langle\!\langle e_2 \rangle\!\rangle \Rightarrow le_2 \qquad D_a; F_a; \Gamma_a; t \vdash \langle\!\langle e_3 \rangle\!\rangle \Rightarrow le_3 \end{array}}{\begin{array}{c} D_a; F_a; \Gamma_a; t \vdash \langle\!\langle \text{if } v_1 \text{ then } e_2 \text{ else } e_3 \rangle\!\rangle \\ \Rightarrow \text{let } x : \text{int } \perp = (\text{reLab}(\perp \Leftarrow \rho)\ lv_1) \text{ in if } x@\text{int } \perp \text{ then } le_2 \text{ else } le_3 \end{array}} \text{ L-IF}$$

Fig. 3. Mapping of expressions (selected rules)

Expressions have two sets of mapping rules: $D_a; F_a; \Gamma_a; s \vdash \langle\!\langle e \rangle\!\rangle \Rightarrow le$ and $D_a; F_a; \Gamma_a \vdash \langle\!\langle v \rangle\!\rangle \Rightarrow lv$. The mapping rules use the annotated typing contexts: D_a, F_a, and Γ_a. The reading of the first judgement is that an annotated expression e is mapped to a labeled expression le given annotated typing contexts D_a, F_a, Γ_a, and e's *polC* type s. The second judgment is similar, except that it only applies to values and the type of v is not given. Here le and lv are expressions with additional type annotations of form @s to ease the translation process from *polC* to μC. For instance, $n@\text{int } U$ means that n is an integer and it is supposed to have the type int U. This way, we can give the same integer different types, depending on the context under which they are used: $n@\text{int } U$ and $n@\text{int } \rho$ are translated into different terms.

A value is mapped to itself with its type annotated. For example, integers are given int U type, since they are unlabeled. Selected expression mapping rules are listed in Fig. 3. The tricky part is mapping expressions whose typing rules in *polC* require label comparison and join operations. Obviously, the μC type system cannot enforce such complex rules. Instead, we add explicit relabeling to certain parts of the expression to ensure that the types of the translated μC program enforce the same property as types in the corresponding *polC* program.

There are two rules for record field access: one without explicit relabeling (L-FIELD) and one with (L-FIELD-U). Rule L-FIELD applies when all the elements in the record have the same label as the record itself. Rule L-FIELD-U explicitly relabels the record first, so the record type changes from $T\ \rho$ to $T \perp$, resulting in the field access having the same label as the element. This is because when the labels of the elements are not the same as the record, the typing rule P-T-E-FIELD will join the type of the field with the label of the record. However, this involves label operations, which μC's type system cannot handle. L-DEREF and L-ASSIGN are similar. The mapping of if statements (L-IF) relabels the conditional v_1 to have int $\perp$ type, so the branches are typed under the same program counter as the if expression. We write $\text{reLab}(\perp \Leftarrow \rho)$ as a short hand for a sequence of relabeling operations $\mathsf{reLab}(\ell::\bot \Leftarrow \ell_n::\top) \cdots \mathsf{reLab}(\ell_i::\bot \Leftarrow \ell_{i-1}::\top) \cdots \mathsf{reLab}(\ell_2::\bot \Leftarrow \ell_1::\top)$ where $\rho = \ell_1:: \cdots ::\ell_n::\ell$ and ℓ is either $\top$ or $\bot$. The implications of relabeling operations are discussed at the end of this section.

Translation from *polC* to μC. The translation of types is shown below. It returns a μC type and a set of new type definitions. We use a function $genName(t, \rho)$ to deterministically generate a string based on t and ρ as the identifier for a record type. It can simply be the concatenation of the string representation of t and ρ, which is indeed what we implemented for C (Sect. 5).

$$\frac{\rho \in \{U, \bot\}}{[\![\mathsf{int}\ \rho]\!]_D = (\mathsf{int}, \cdot)} \qquad \frac{\rho \notin \{U, \bot\} \qquad T = genName(\mathsf{int}, \rho)}{[\![\mathsf{int}\ \rho]\!]_D = (T, T \mapsto \mathsf{struct}\ T\ \{\mathsf{int}\})}$$

$$\frac{\rho \notin \{U, \bot\} \qquad T' = genName(T, \rho) \qquad T \mapsto \mathsf{struct}\ T\ \{\tau_1, \cdots, \tau_n\} \in D}{[\![T\ \rho]\!]_D = (T', T' \mapsto \mathsf{struct}\ T'\ \{\tau_1, \cdots, \tau_n\})}$$

We distinguish between a type with a label that is U or $\bot$ and a meaningful label. The translation of the type $b\ U$ is simply b. This is because $b\ U$ is mapped from an unannotated type b to begin with, so the translation returns its original type. Similarly $b\ \bot$ is generated by our relabeling operations during the mapping process, and should be translated to its original type b. A type annotated with a meaningful policy ρ is translated into a record type to take advantage of nominal typing. The translation also returns the new type definition. This would also prevent label subtyping based on the security lattice. However, this is acceptable given our application domain because the labels provided by programmers are distinct points in the lattice that are not connected by any partial order relations except the $\top$ and $\bot$ elements. Record types are translated to record types and the fields of the labeled record type $T\ \rho$ have the same type as those for T, stored in the translated context D. This works because we assume that all labeled instances of the record type T (i.e., all $T\ \rho$) share the same definition.

Expression translation recursively translates the sub-expressions. The μC type system does not have complex label checking, so rule T-APP-DE has to insert label conversions. The argument label is cast from $\ell_1::\ell_2::\rho$ to $\ell_1::\top$, as required by f, and the result of the function is cast from $\ell_2::\bot$ to $\ell_2::\rho'$.

$$\frac{\begin{array}{c} tpOf(lv_f) = (\mathsf{d\&e})[pc](t_1 \to t_2)^{\rho_f} \\ [\![lv_f]\!]_D = (v_f, D_f) \qquad tpOf(lv_a) = b\ \rho \\ \rho = \ell_1::\ell_2::\rho' \qquad [\![\mathsf{reLab}(\ell_1::\top \Leftarrow \rho)lv_a]\!]_D = (e', D_1) \\ [\![\mathsf{reLab}(\ell_2::\rho' \Leftarrow \ell_2::\bot)(z@b\ \ell_2::\bot)]\!]_D = (e'', D_2) \\ [\![t_1]\!]_D = (\tau_1, D_3) \qquad [\![t_2]\!]_D = (\tau_2, D_4) \end{array}}{\begin{array}{c} [\![lv_f\ lv_a]\!]_D = (\mathsf{let}\ y : \tau_1 = e'\ \mathsf{in}\ \mathsf{let}\ z : \tau_2 = v_f\ y \\ \mathsf{in}\ e'', D_f \cup D_1 \cup D_2 \cup D_3 \cup D_4) \end{array}}\ \text{T-APP-DE}$$

These operations are different from the ones inserted during the mapping process because they only exist to help μC simulate the E-APP-DE typing rule in *polC*, but do not really have declassification or endorsement effects. The relabeling operations are translated to record operations, as shown in Fig. 4.

$$tpOf(lv_f) = (\text{d\&e})[pc](t_1 \rightarrow t_2)^{\rho_f}$$

$$\frac{\begin{array}{c} [\![lv_f]\!]_D = (v_f, D_f) \qquad tpOf(lv_a) = b\ \rho \\ \rho = \ell_1 :: \ell_2 :: \rho' \qquad [\![\text{reLab}(\ell_1 :: \top \Leftarrow \rho)lv_a]\!]_D = (e', D_1) \\ [\![\text{reLab}(\ell_2 :: \rho' \Leftarrow \ell_2 :: \bot)(z@b\ \ell_2 :: \bot)]\!]_D = (e'', D_2) \\ [\![t_1]\!]_D = (\tau_1, D_3) \qquad [\![t_2]\!]_D = (\tau_2, D_4) \end{array}}{\begin{array}{c} [\![lv_f\ lv_a]\!]_D = (\text{let}\ y : \tau_1 = e'\ \text{in let}\ z : \tau_2 = v_f\ y \\ \text{in}\ e'', D_f \cup D_1 \cup D_2 \cup D_3 \cup D_4) \end{array}} \quad \text{T-App-DE}$$

$$\frac{\begin{array}{c} [\![lv]\!]_D = (v, D_1) \quad tpOf(lv) = b\ \rho\ (b\ \text{is not a struct type}) \\ \rho' \notin \{\bot, U\} \qquad \rho \notin \{\bot, U\} \qquad [\![b\ \rho']\!]_D = (T, D_2) \end{array}}{[\![\text{reLab}(\rho' \Leftarrow \rho)lv]\!]_D = (\text{let}\ x = v.1\ \text{in}\ (T)\{x\}, D_1 \cup D_2)} \quad \text{T-ReLab-N1}$$

$$\frac{\begin{array}{c} [\![lv]\!]_D = (v, D_1) \quad tpOf(lv) = b\ \rho\ (b\ \text{is not a struct type}) \\ \rho' \notin \{\bot, U\} \qquad \rho \in \{\bot, U\} \qquad [\![b\ \rho']\!]_D = (T, D_2) \end{array}}{[\![\text{reLab}(\rho' \Leftarrow \rho)lv]\!]_D = ((T)\{v\}, D_1 \cup D_2)} \quad \text{T-ReLab-N2}$$

$$\frac{\begin{array}{c} [\![lv]\!]_D = (v, D_1) \qquad tpOf(lv) = b\ \rho \\ b\ \text{is not a struct type} \qquad \rho \notin \{\bot, U\} \qquad \rho' \in \{\bot, U\} \end{array}}{[\![\text{reLab}(\rho' \Leftarrow \rho)lv]\!]_D = (v.1D_1)} \quad \text{T-ReLab-N3}$$

$$\frac{[\![lv]\!]_D = (v, D_1) \qquad labOf(lv) = b\ \rho \qquad \rho, \rho' \in \{U, \bot\}}{[\![\text{reLab}(\rho' \Leftarrow \rho)lv]\!]_D = (v, D_1)} \quad \text{T-ReLab-SAME}$$

$$\frac{\begin{array}{c} \rho \notin \{\bot, U\}\ \text{or}\ \rho' \notin \{\bot, U\} \\ tpOf(lv) = T\ \rho \qquad [\![T\ \rho']\!]_D = (T', D_1) \qquad [\![lv]\!]_D = (v, D_2) \end{array}}{\begin{array}{c} [\![\text{reLab}(\rho' \Leftarrow \rho)lv]\!]_D = \text{let}\ x_1 = v.1\ \text{in}\ \cdots \text{let}\ x_n = v.n \\ \text{in}\ (T')\{x_1, \cdots, x_n\}, D_1 \cup D_2) \end{array}} \quad \text{T-ReLab-Struct}$$

Fig. 4. Selected relabeling rules

Rule T-ReLab-N1 relabels a value with a labeled type. The translated expression is a reassembled record using the fields of the original record. Rule T-ReLab-N2 relabels an expression with a U and $\bot$ label to a meaningful label. In this case, the translated expression is a record. Rule T-ReLab-N3 translates an expression relabeled from a meaningful label to a U or $\bot$ label to a projection of the record. The next rule, T-ReLab-SAME, does not change the value itself, because we are just relabeling between U and $\bot$ labels. The final relabeling rule, T-ReLab-Struct, deals with records. In this case, we simply return the reassembled record because record types that only differ in labels have the same types for the fields.

4.3 Correctness

We prove a correctness theorem, which states that if our translated nominal type system declares an expression e well-typed, then the labeled expression e_l, where e is translated from, is well-typed under $polC$'s type system. Formally:

Theorem 2 (Translation Soundness (Typing)). *If $D_a; F_a; \Gamma_a; s \vdash \langle\!\langle e \rangle\!\rangle = le$, $\langle\!\langle D_a \rangle\!\rangle = D_l$, $\langle\!\langle F_a \rangle\!\rangle = F_l$, $\langle\!\langle \Gamma_a \rangle\!\rangle = \Gamma_l$, $[\![D_l]\!] = D$, $[\![\Gamma_l]\!]_D = (\Gamma, D_1)$, $[\![F_l]\!]_D = (F, D_2)$, $[\![le]\!]_D = (e', D_3)$, and $D \cup D_1 \cup D_2 \cup D_3; F; \cdot; \Gamma \vdash e' : \tau$ implies $D_l; F_l; \cdot; \Gamma_l \vdash tmOf(le) : s$ and $[\![s]\!] = (\tau, \_)$*

Here, $tmOf(le)$ denotes an expression that is the same as le, with labels (e.g., @int U) removed. The proof is by induction over the derivation of $D_a; F_a; \Gamma_a; s \vdash \langle\!\langle e \rangle\!\rangle \Rightarrow le$. It is not hard to see that the translated program has the same behavior as the original program, as they only differ in that the translated program has many indirect record constructions and field accesses.

Relabeling Precision. It is clear from the mapping algorithm that a number of powerful relabeling operations are added. In all cases (except the if statement) we could do better by not relabeling all the way to bottom, but to the label of the sub-expressions. However, that would require a heavy-weight translation algorithm that essentially does full type-checking.

Implicit Flows. The security guarantees of programs that require relabeling operations to be inserted are weakened in the sense that in addition to the special declassification and endorsement functions, these relabeling operations allow additional observation by the attacker. This means that the resulting program can implicitly leak information via branches, de-referencing, and record field access. However, for our application domain we aim to check simple data usage and function call patterns which, as seen in our case studies, manifest errors with explicit flows. These policy violations are still detected if we don't have recursive types (See the full paper for explanations and our case studies are not affected).

5   Implementation

We explain how the annotations and translation algorithms of `FlowNotation` are implemented for C.

Translation of Annotations for Simple Types. Utilizing C's nominal typing via the **typedef** mechanism is key to realizing $polC$ type system within the bounds of C's type system. The declaration of the $polC$ type t ρ in C will be **typedef struct** $\{t$ d; $\}$ ρ@t;. Here ρ@t is a string representing the type t ρ and it is simply a concatenation of the string representation of the policy ρ and the type t. Consider the annotated code snippet. `#requires l1:secrecy` `then l2:secrecy` **int** x; In $polC$, the type of x is int $(l1, \bot_I)::(l2, \bot_I)::\bot$. The generated C typedef is **typedef struct** $\{$**int** d;$\}$ `l1S_l2S_int`; This definition contains the original type, which allows access to the original data stored in x in the transformed program.

Structures and Unions. We allow programmers to annotate structures in two ways: an instance of a structure can be annotated with a particular policy, or individual fields of an instance of a structure can be given annotations. The names of structures hold a particular significance within C since they are nominal types, and thus, they need to be properly handled. Unions are treated in a parallel manner, so we omit the details.

A policy on an instance of a structure is annotated and translated following the same formula as annotations on simple C types. Suppose we have the following annotation and code: `#requires l1:secrecy then l2:secrecy` **struct** `foo x;`. FlowNotation will produce the following generated type definition: **typedef struct** `{`**struct** `foo d;} l1S_l2S_foo;` This is different from the algorithm in Sect. 4, where structures are not nested and annotations are applied to structure definitions rather than instances. This is done in the implementation because the definition of `foo` might be external and therefore may not be known to the translation algorithm, so we simply nest the entire structure.

Finally, we explain how member accesses are handled. Suppose a struct `foo` contains members `f1` and `f2`, and an annotation of policy p has been placed on member `f1`, but no annotation has been placed on member `f2`. The generated type definition for the structure is as follows: **typedef struct** `{ p_int f1;` `foo d; } p_foo;`. Assume x has type `p_foo`. Access to `f1` is still `x.f1`, since there is a copy of it in x. Access to `f2` is rewritten to `x.d.f2`. The field initialization is rewritten similarly. `foo x={.f1=1,.f2=2};` is transformed to this: `foo x={.f1=1,.d={.f2=2}};`.

Pointers. We provide limited support for pointers. Here is an example of how annotations on pointers are handled: `#requires AlicePriv:secrecy` **int**`*` `x;` The translated code is below; a type definition of struct `AlivePrivS_int` is generated: `AlicePrivS_int* x;`. The following function can receive x as an argument because the annotation for its parameter matches that of x: `#param` `AlicePriv:secrecy` **int** `f(`**int**`* x){...}`.

The annotation for pointers only annotates the content of the pointer. Even though *polC* allows policies on the pointer themselves, we did not implement that feature. We also do not support pointer arithmetic, which is difficult to handle for many static analysis tools, especially lightweight ones like ours. However, our system will flag aliasing of pointers across mismatched annotated types. Our system will also flag pointer arithmetic operations on annotated types as errors. Programmers can encapsulate those operations in trusted functions and annotate them to avoid such errors.

Typecasts. The C type system permits typecasts, allowing one to redefine the type of a variable in unsound ways. Casting of non-pointer annotated types will be flagged as an error by `FlowNotation`. This is because our types are realized as C structures; type checkers do not allow arbitrary casting of structures. However, our tool cannot catch typecasts made on annotated pointers; a policy on a pointer will be lost if a typecast is performed.

Limitations. As previously mentioned, we do not handle pointer arithmetic. We only provide limited support for function pointers. We do not support C's builtin operators, such as the unary ++. We do not support typecasts on pointers, nor can we flag violations due to implicit void pointer conversion. We provide partial support for variadic functions. Finally, we do not support using `#return` with a function that has a **void** return type. These are careful design choices we made so our tool is lightweight and remains practical; we emphasize that our tool is not meant for verification. Further explanations can be found in our full paper, and limitations of our type system can be found in Sect. 4.3.

6   Case Studies

We evaluate the effectiveness of `FlowNotation` at discovering violations of secrecy, integrity, and sequencing API usage policies on several open-source cryptographic libraries. Our results are summarized in Fig. 5. We examine: Obliv-C, a compiler for dialect of C directed at secure computation [54,55]; SCD-toObliv, a set of floating point circuits synthesized into C code [56]; the Absent-minded Crypto Kit, a library of Secure Computation protocols and primitives [33,34]; Secure Mux, a secure multiplexer application [59]; the Pool Framework, a secure computation memory management library [58,59]; Pantaloons RSA, the top GitHub result for an RSA implementation in C [43]; MiniAES, an AES multiparty computation implementation [30,31]; Bellare-Micali OT, an implementation of the Bellare-Micali oblivious transfer protocol [6]; Kerberos ASN.1 Encoder, the ASN.1 encoder module of Kerberos [1]; Gnuk OpenPGP-do, a portion of the OpenPGP module from gnuk [53]; Tiny SHA3, a reference implementation of SHA3 [46]. We determine application-specific policies and implement them with our annotations. Representative cases are explained next; additional cases are in the full paper.

Library	# Pol	Sec	Int	Seq	LoA	~ LoC	Issues	RT(s)
Obliv-C Library	2	1	1	0	11	80	0	0.04
SCDtoObliv FP Circuits	4	4	0	0	10	43,000	1	5.55
ACK Oqueue	7	7	7	2	19	700	0	0.17
Secure Mux Application	4	3	4	0	11	150	0	0.06
Pool Framework	4	2	4	0	8	500	1	0.16
Pantaloons RSA	5	2	3	0	12	300	1	0.11
MiniAES	9	4	4	1	13	2000	0	0.08
Bellare-Micali OT	5	3	2	0	12	100	2	0.05
Kerberos ASN.1 Encoder	2	2	0	1	8	300	0	0.12
Gnuk OpenPGP-do	5	0	5	1	11	250	1	0.10
Tiny SHA3	3	3	0	1	6	200	0	0.10

Fig. 5. Evaluation Results. #Pol is the number of policies. Sec, int, seq are secrecy, integrity, and sequencing policies. LoA, LoC are lines of annotations, code. RT(s) is runtime in seconds.

SCDtoObliv Floating Point Circuits. First, we show that `FlowNotation` can be used to discover flaws in large, automatically generated segments of code that would be very difficult for a programmer to manually analyze.

SCDtoObliv [56] synthesizes floating point circuit in C via calls to boolean gate primitives implemented in C. While this approach produces performant floating point circuits for secure computation applications, the resulting circuit files are hard to interpret and debug. The smallest of these generated circuit files is around 4000 lines of C code while the largest is over 14,000 lines. We annotate particular wires based on the circuit function to check that particular invariants such as which bits should be used in the output and which bits should be flipped are maintained.

`FlowNotation` uncovered a flaw in the subtraction circuit. The Obliv-C subtraction circuit actually uses an addition circuit to compute $A + (-B)$. The function that does the sign bit flipping, `__obliv_c__flipBit`, is annotated so that it can only accept an input with the *needsFlipping* label as follows.

```
#param needsFlipping:secrecy
void __obliv_c__flipBit(OblivBit* src)
```

Our tool reports an error; rather than the sign bit of the second operand being given to `__obliv_c__flipBit` the sign bit of the *first* operand was given to `__obliv_c__flipBit`. Instead of computing $A + (-B)$ the circuit computes $(-A) + B$; the result of evaluating the circuit is negated with respect to the correct answer.

Gnuk OpenPGP-DO. The last case study shows that `FlowNotation` can uncover a known null-pointer dereferencing bug and another potential bug in the gnuk OpenPGP-DO file, which handles OpenPGP Smart Card Data Objects (DO). We present the latter in the full paper.

The function `w_kdf` handles the reading or writing of DOs that support encryption via a Key Derivation Function (KDF) in the OpenPGP-DO file.

```
static int rw_kdf (uint16_t tag, int with_tag,
    const uint8_t *data, int len, int is_write)
```

If the data is being read, it is copied to a buffer via the function `copy_do_1`: `static void copy_do_1(uint16_t tag, const uint8_t *do_data,` `int with_tag)`. One invariant is that the `do_data` pointer must point to a valid segment of data; it must not be null. We provide the following annotation:

```
#param(2) check-valid-ptr:integrity
static void copy_do_1(uint16_t tag, const uint8_t *do_data, int
    with_tag)
```

This annotation states that the second parameter will only be accepted if it has been endorsed by a function that returns data annotated with the *check_valid_ptr* label. We provide such a function and rewrite all nullity checks to use it.

```
#return check_valid_ptr:integrity
const uint8_t *check_do_ptr(const uint8_t *do_ptr)
```

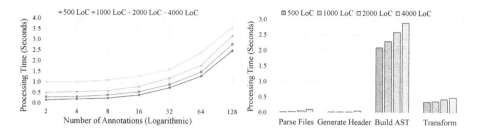

Fig. 6. Processing time vs Number of annotations and time per processing stage

Returning back to the `rw_kdf` function, when data is being read, the following call of `copy_do_1` occurs: `copy_do_1(tag, do_ptr[NR_DO_KDF], with_tag);` The issue is `copy_do_1` is annotated to require a null-pointer check for parameter two, but that check was not performed.

Performance Evaluation. We evaluate the performance of `FlowNotation` on synthetically generated C programs and annotations. To elicit worse-case behavior, the generated annotations are predominantly sequencing annotations constructed from a set of templates representative of common API patterns from our case studies.

We evaluate how the runtime of `FlowNotation` is affected by the program size and the number of annotations (Fig. 6). We evaluate the runtime of four C programs, with 500, 1000, 2000, and 4000 lines of code respectively. For each program, we increase the number of annotations, up to 128. `FlowNotation` is efficient: all experiments finish within 4 s. `FlowNotation` is intended to be run on individual modules (libraries) that rarely exceed a couple thousand lines of code unless they are automatically generated, like the SCDtoObliv circuit file (14,000 LoC). Even then, it finishes within 6 s.

To better understand how each component of `FlowNotation` contributes to the processing time, we profile execution time for each part. The results are summarized in Fig. 6, which shows a cross-section of Fig. 6 with only the samples with 128 annotations. The four stages of `FlowNotation` are: "Parse Files", where annotations are retrieved; "Generate Header", where the header file with definitions for the transformed types is generated; "Build AST", where the C parsing library, pycparser [7] builds an AST; "Transform", where the implementation of the translation algorithm of `FlowNotation` runs. The majority of the overhead is due to the C parsing library we use.

7   Related Work

Tools for Analyzing C Programs. Many vulnerabilities stem from poorly written C programs. As a result, many C program analysis tools have been built. Several C model checkers (e.g. [4,10,11,24,38]) and program analysis tools [20, 27,29,42] are open source and readily downloadable. Our policies can be encoded as state machines and checked by some of the tools mentioned above, which are general purpose and more powerful than ours but are not tuned for analyzing API usage patterns like ours.

Closest to our work is CQual [36]. Both theoretical foundations and practical applications of type qualifiers have been investigated [17,22,35,37,57]. Our annotations are type qualifiers and our work and prior work on type qualifiers share the goal of producing a lightweight tool to check simple secrecy and integrity properties. We additionally support sequencing of atomic qualifiers, which is a novel contribution. Both our's and prior work do not handle implicit flows. We prove noninterference of our core calculus, which other systems did not. Another difference is that CQual relies on a custom type checker, while our policies are checked using C's type system. Finally, CQual supports qualifier inference, which can reduce the annotation burden on programmers. We do not have general qualifier inference because we rely on existing C compiler's type checkers.

Information Flow Type Systems. Information flow type systems is a well-studied field. Several projects have extended existing languages to include information flow types (e.g., [44,45]). Sabelfeld et al. provided a comprehensive summary in their survey paper [47]. Most information flow type systems do not deal with declassification. At most, they will include a "declassify" primitive to allow information downgrade, similar to our relabel operations. However, we have not seen work where the sequence of labels is part of the information flow type like ours, except for JRIF [39]. As a result, we are able to prove a noninterference theorem that implies API sequencing. JRIF uses finite state automata to enforce sequencing policies, which can entail a large runtime overhead.

Other projects that target enforcement of sequencing policies similar to those we have presented rely on runtime monitoring, not types [5,9,18,19,23,50].

Linear Types and Typestate. Our sequencing policies are tangentially related to other type systems that aim to enforce API contracts. This line of work includes typestate and linear types [2,32,48]. The idea is that by using typestate/linear types one can model and check behaviors such as files being opened and closed in a balanced manner [2]. However, unlike in typestate the types on variables don't change in our system; when a part of a policy is fulfilled there is a new variable that "takes on" the rest of the policy.

Cryptographic Protocol Verification. Several projects have proposed languages to make verification of cryptographic programs more feasible: Jasmine, Cryptol, Vale, Dafny, F*, and Idris [3,15,16,40,41,49], to name a few. There are also general tools for verifying cryptographic protocols [8,12–14,25,26,28]. These languages and tools are general purpose and more powerful than ours. However, none of these tools directly support checking properties of C implementations of cryptographic libraries like we do. Bhargavan et al.'s work uses refinement types to achieve similar goals as ours [13]. The annotated types can be viewed as refinement types: $\{x : \tau \mid \rho\}$, where the policy is encoded as a predicate. Their system is more powerful, however it only supports F# code.

Acknowledgement. This work is supported in part by the National Science Foundation via grants CNS1704542 and CNS1464113, and by the National Institutes of Health via award 1U01EB023685-01.

References

1. Kerberos ASN.1 encoder. https://github.com/krb5/krb5/tree/master/src/lib/krb5/asn.1. Accessed 2018
2. Aldrich, J., Sunshine, J., Saini, D., Sparks, Z.: Typestate-oriented programming. In: Proceedings of OOPSLA (2009)
3. Almeida, J.B., et al.: Jasmin: high-assurance and high-speed cryptography. In: Proceedings of CCS (2017)
4. Ball, T., Rajamani, S.K.: The SLAM project: debugging system software via static analysis. In: Proceedings of POPL (2002)
5. Barany, G., Signoles, J.: Hybrid information flow analysis for real-world C code. In: Gabmeyer, S., Johnsen, E.B. (eds.) TAP 2017. LNCS, vol. 10375, pp. 23–40. Springer, Cham (2017). https://doi.org/10.1007/978-3-319-61467-0_2
6. Bellare, M., Micali, S.: Non-interactive oblivious transfer and applications. In: Brassard, G. (ed.) CRYPTO 1989. LNCS, vol. 435, pp. 547–557. Springer, New York (1990). https://doi.org/10.1007/0-387-34805-0_48
7. Bendersky, E.: pycparser. https://github.com/eliben/pycparser. Accessed 2017
8. Bengtson, J., Bhargavan, K., Fournet, C., Gordon, A.D., Maffeis, S.: Refinement types for secure implementations. ACM Trans. Program. Lang. Syst. (TOPLAS) **33**(2), 8 (2011)
9. Beringer, L.: End-to-end multilevel hybrid information flow control. In: Jhala, R., Igarashi, A. (eds.) APLAS 2012. LNCS, vol. 7705, pp. 50–65. Springer, Heidelberg (2012). https://doi.org/10.1007/978-3-642-35182-2_5
10. Beyer, D., Henzinger, T.A., Jhala, R., Majumdar, R.: The software model checker blast. Int. J. Softw. Tools Technol. Transfer **9**, 505–525 (2007)
11. Beyer, D., Keremoglu, M.E.: CPACHECKER: a tool for configurable software verification. In: Gopalakrishnan, G., Qadeer, S. (eds.) CAV 2011. LNCS, vol. 6806, pp. 184–190. Springer, Heidelberg (2011). https://doi.org/10.1007/978-3-642-22110-1_16
12. Bhargavan, K., Fournet, C., Corin, R., Zalinescu, E.: Cryptographically verified implementations for TLS. In: Proceedings of CCS (2008)
13. Bhargavan, K., Fournet, C., Gordon, A.D.: Modular verification of security protocol code by typing. In: Proceedings of POPL (2010)
14. Blanchet, B.: An efficient cryptographic protocol verifier based on prolog rules. In: Proceedings of CSFW (2001)
15. Bond, B., et al.: Vale: verifying high-performance cryptographic assembly code. In: Proceedings of USENIX (2017)
16. Brady, E.: Idris, a general-purpose dependently typed programming language: design and implementation. J. Functional Program. **23**, 552–593 (2013)
17. Broadwell, P., Harren, M., Sastry, N.: Scrash: a system for generating secure crash information. In: Proceedings of SSYM (2003)
18. Broberg, N., van Delft, B., Sands, D.: Paragon for practical programming with information-flow control. In: Shan, C. (ed.) APLAS 2013. LNCS, vol. 8301, pp. 217–232. Springer, Cham (2013). https://doi.org/10.1007/978-3-319-03542-0_16
19. Broberg, N., Sands, D.: Paralocks: role-based information flow control and beyond. In: Proceedings of POPL (2010)

20. Cadar, C., Dunbar, D., Engler, D.: KLEE: unassisted and automatic generation of high-coverage tests for complex systems programs. In: Proceedings of OSDI (2008)
21. Cassel, D., Huang, Y., Jia, L.: FlowNotation technical report. https://arxiv.org/abs/1907.01727 (2019)
22. Chin, B., Markstrum, S., Millstein, T.: Semantic type qualifiers. In: Proceedings of PLDI (2005)
23. Chong, S., Myers, A.C.: End-to-end enforcement of erasure and declassification. In: Proceedings of CSF (2008)
24. Clarke, E., Kroening, D., Lerda, F.: A tool for checking ANSI-C programs. In: Jensen, K., Podelski, A. (eds.) TACAS 2004. LNCS, vol. 2988, pp. 168–176. Springer, Heidelberg (2004). https://doi.org/10.1007/978-3-540-24730-2_15
25. Cortier, V., Warinschi, B.: Computationally sound, automated proofs for security protocols. In: Sagiv, M. (ed.) ESOP 2005. LNCS, vol. 3444, pp. 157–171. Springer, Heidelberg (2005). https://doi.org/10.1007/978-3-540-31987-0_12
26. Costanzo, D., Shao, Z., Gu, R.: End-to-end verification of information-flow security for C and assembly programs. In: Proceedings of PLDI (2016)
27. Cousot, P., et al.: The ASTREÉ analyzer. In: Sagiv, M. (ed.) ESOP 2005. LNCS, vol. 3444, pp. 21–30. Springer, Heidelberg (2005). https://doi.org/10.1007/978-3-540-31987-0_3
28. Cremers, C.J.F.: The scyther tool: verification, falsification, and analysis of security protocols. In: Gupta, A., Malik, S. (eds.) CAV 2008. LNCS, vol. 5123, pp. 414–418. Springer, Heidelberg (2008). https://doi.org/10.1007/978-3-540-70545-1_38
29. Cuoq, P., Kirchner, F., Kosmatov, N., Prevosto, V., Signoles, J., Yakobowski, B.: Frama-C. In: Eleftherakis, G., Hinchey, M., Holcombe, M. (eds.) SEFM 2012. LNCS, vol. 7504, pp. 233–247. Springer, Heidelberg (2012). https://doi.org/10.1007/978-3-642-33826-7_16
30. Damgård, I., Zakarias, R.: MiniAES repository. https://github.com/AarhusCrypto/MiniAES. Accessed 2017
31. Damgård, I., Zakarias, R.: Fast oblivious AES a dedicated application of the MiniMac protocol. In: Pointcheval, D., Nitaj, A., Rachidi, T. (eds.) AFRICACRYPT 2016. LNCS, vol. 9646, pp. 245–264. Springer, Cham (2016). https://doi.org/10.1007/978-3-319-31517-1_13
32. DeLine, R., Fähndrich, M.: Enforcing high-level protocols in low-level software. In: Proceedings of PLDI (2001)
33. Doerner, J.: Absentminded crypto kit repository. https://bitbucket.org/jackdoerner/absentminded-crypto-kit/. Accessed 2017
34. Doerner, J., Shelat, A.: Scaling ORAM for secure computation. In: Proceedings of CCS (2017)
35. Evans, D.: Static detection of dynamic memory errors. In: Proceedings of PLDI (1996)
36. Foster, J.S., Fähndrich, M., Aiken, A.: A theory of type qualifiers. In: Proceedings of PLDI (1999)
37. Foster, J.S., Aiken, A.S.: Type qualifiers: lightweight specifications to improve software quality. Ph.D. thesis, University of California, Berkeley (2002)
38. Gurfinkel, A., Kahsai, T., Komuravelli, A., Navas, J.A.: The SeaHorn verification framework. In: Kroening, D., Păsăreanu, C.S. (eds.) CAV 2015. LNCS, vol. 9206, pp. 343–361. Springer, Cham (2015). https://doi.org/10.1007/978-3-319-21690-4_20
39. Kozyri, E., Arden, O., Myers, A.C., Schneider, F.B.: JRIF: Reactive Information Flow Control for Java (2016). http://hdl.handle.net/1813/41194

40. Leino, K.R.M.: Dafny: an automatic program verifier for functional correctness. In: Clarke, E.M., Voronkov, A. (eds.) LPAR 2010. LNCS (LNAI), vol. 6355, pp. 348–370. Springer, Heidelberg (2010). https://doi.org/10.1007/978-3-642-17511-4_20

41. Lewis, J.R., Martin, B.: Cryptol: high assurance, retargetable crypto development and validation. In: Proceedings of MILCOM (2003)

42. Machiry, A., Spensky, C., Corina, J., Stephens, N., Kruegel, C., Vigna, G.: DR. CHECKER: a soundy analysis for Linux kernel drivers. In: Proceedings of USENIX (2017)

43. McGee, M.: Pantaloons/RSA repository. https://github.com/pantaloons/RSA/. Accessed 2017

44. Myers, A.C.: JFlow: practical mostly-static information flow control. In: Proceedings of POPL (1999)

45. Pottier, F., Simonet, V.: Information flow inference for ML. In: Proceedings of POPL (2002)

46. Saarinen, M.J.O.: Tiny SHA3. https://github.com/mjosaarinen/tiny_sha3. Accessed 2017

47. Sabelfeld, A., Myers, A.C.: Language-based information-flow security. IEEE J. Sel. Areas Commun. **21**, 5–19 (2003)

48. Strom, R.E., Yemini, S.: Typestate: a programming language concept for enhancing software reliability. IEEE Trans. Softw. Eng. **SE-12**, 157–171 (1986)

49. Swamy, N., Chen, J., Fournet, C., Strub, P., Bhargavan, K., Yang, J.: Secure distributed programming with value-dependent types. In: Proceedings of ICFP (2011)

50. Vachharajani, N., et al.: RIFLE: an architectural framework for user-centric information-flow security. In: Proceedings of MICRO (2004)

51. Volpano, D., Smith, G.: A type-based approach to program security. In: Bidoit, M., Dauchet, M. (eds.) CAAP 1997. LNCS, vol. 1214, pp. 607–621. Springer, Heidelberg (1997). https://doi.org/10.1007/BFb0030629

52. Yao, A.C.C.: How to generate and exchange secrets. In: Proceedings of SFCS (1986)

53. Yutaka, N.: Gnuk. https://www.fsij.org/category/gnuk.html. Accessed 2018

54. Zahur, S., David, E.: Obliv-C: a language for extensible data-oblivious computation (2015)

55. Zahur, S.: Obliv-C repository. https://github.com/samee/obliv-c/. Accessed 2017

56. Zahur, S., Cassel, D.: SCDtoObliv repository. https://github.com/samee/obliv-c/tree/obliv-c/SCDtoObliv. Accessed 2017

57. Zhang, X., Edwards, A., Jaeger, T.: Using CQUAL for static analysis of authorization hook placement. In: Proceedings of USENIX (2002)

58. Zhu, R., Huang, Y., Cassel, D.: Pool framework repository. https://github.com/jimu-pool/PoolFramework/. Accessed 2017

59. Zhu, R., Huang, Y., Cassel, D.: Pool: Scalable on-demand secure computation service against malicious adversaries. In: Proceedings of CCS (2017)

BinEye: Towards Efficient Binary Authorship Characterization Using Deep Learning

Saed Alrabaee[1,2(✉)], ElMouatez Billah Karbab[2], Lingyu Wang[2], and Mourad Debbabi[2]

[1] United Arab Emirates University, Al Ain, Abu Dhabi, UAE
salrabaee@uaeu.ac.ae
[2] CIISE, Concordia University, Montreal, QC, Canada
{s_alraba,e_karbab,wang,debbabi}@encs.concordia.ca

Abstract. In this paper, we present BinEye, an innovative tool which trains a system of three convolutional neural networks to characterize the authors of program binaries based on novel sets of features. The first set of features is obtained by converting an executable binary code into a gray image; the second by transforming each executable into a series of bytecode; and the third by representing each function in terms of its opcodes. By leveraging advances in deep learning, we are then able to characterize a large set of authors. This is accomplished even without the missing features and despite the complications arising from compilation. In fact, BinEye does not require any prior knowledge of the target binary. More important, an analysis of the model provides a satisfying explanation of the results obtained: BinEye is able to auto-learn each author's coding style and thus characterize the authors of program binaries. We evaluated BinEye on large datasets extracted from selected open-source C++ projects in GitHub, Google Code Jam events, and several programming projects, comparing it wiexperimental results demonstrate that BinEye characterizes a larger number of authors with a significantly higher accuracy (above 90%). We also employed it in the context of several case studies. When applied to Zeus and Citadel, BinEye found that this pair might be associated with common authors. For other packages, BinEye demonstrated its ability to identify the presence of multiple authors in binary code.

1 Introduction

When analyzing malware binaries, reverse engineers often pay particular attention to malware author style characteristics for several reasons [1]. First, reports from anti-malware companies indicate that finding the similarities among malware code styles can aid in developing profiles for malware families [2]. Second, recently released reports by Citizen Lab [3,4] show that malware binaries written by authors having the same origin share similar styles. Third, many malware

© Springer Nature Switzerland AG 2019
K. Sako et al. (Eds.): ESORICS 2019, LNCS 11736, pp. 47–67, 2019.
https://doi.org/10.1007/978-3-030-29962-0_3

packages might have been written only by authors with the specialized knowledge required for dealing with particular resources, for example, the malware targeting the SCADA system; thus, this insight provides a critical clue for establishing the level of expertise of an author. Last, clustering binary functions based on common style characteristics or author origin may help reverse engineers to identify the group of functions that belong to a particular malware family or to decompose the binary based on the origin of its functions.

The ability to conduct these analyses at the binary level is especially important for security applications such as malware analysis because the source code for malware is not always available. However, in automating binary authorship attribution, two challenges are typically encountered: the binary code lacks many abstractions (e.g., variable names) that are present in the source code; and the time and space complexities of analyzing binary code are greater than those for the corresponding source code. Although significant efforts have been made to develop automated approaches for source code authorship attribution [5,6], these often rely on identifying features that will likely be lost in the strings of bytes representing binary code after the compilation process; these features include variable and function naming, comments, and space layout.

To this end, there have been a few attempts at binary authorship attribution. Typically, they employ machine learning methods to extract unique features for each author and then match a given binary against such features to identify the author [7–10]. These approaches are affected by refactoring techniques, compilers, compilation settings, or code transformation methods. Further, these approaches are not applied to real malware binaries. Recently, the feasibility of authorship attribution for malware binaries was discussed at the BlackHat conference [3]. It was concluded that it is possible to group malware binaries according to authorship styles based on a set of features. However, the process is not automated and requires considerable human intervention.

Problem Statement. We address the characterization of the author of a binary code based on its style and assume that the reverse engineer has access to a set of binary code samples each of which is attributed to one of a set of candidate authors. The reverse engineer may proceed by converting each labeled sample into a feature vector and training a classifier from these vectors using machine learning techniques. The classifier can then be used to assign the unknown binary code to the most likely author. Since we have a repository of known authors, we treat this part of the problem as a closed-world [9] supervised machine learning task. It can also be viewed as a multi-class problem in which the classifier calculates the most likely author for the unknown binary. A complication arises when the binary code is written by multiple authors, as is common for malware binaries [3] or projects in GitHub. In such instances, the reverse engineer is interested in clustering the functions written by the same author.

Solution Overview. To address the aforementioned issues, this paper presents BinEye, an innovative framework that leverages recent advances in deep neural networks to build a framework robust to changes in the compiler or to code transformation. We used large collections of sample binary code from each author compiled with different compilers/compilation settings to train a deep learning network to attribute the authors in a robust way.

BinEye encompasses three deep learning networks, so its input comprises three sets of features. The first are the opcode sequences, which make it possible to detect the styles of programmers according to their coding traits. The second are the function invocations extracted from assembly files, such as open-file and close-file. The underlying intuition is that one author may rely on a set of API functions, but another may use a different set of APIs. Specifically, we map each API call in the sequence invocation to a fixed length high-dimensional vector that semantically represents the method invocation and replace the sequence of the assembly API calls by a sequence of vectors. Afterward, we feed the sequence of vectors to a deep neural network (i.e., a convolutional neural network) with multiple layers. A similar approach is applied to the opcodes. The third set of features is obtained by converting the binary file into a gray scale image and then leveraging past efforts to identify transformed image features [11, 12]. The latter features are based on both the executable structure and the binary content of the executable. The intuition is that binary files produced by authors with similar style characteristics will generate similar image texture patterns. Compared to existing features such as N-grams, the image processing-based features are less vulnerable to the changes introduced by refactoring tools or code transformation [11]. We note some attractive characteristics of convolutional neural networks. For example, the nodes of CNNs can act as filters over the input space and can reveal strong correlations in the binary code. Also, in the classification process, a CNN is considered a fast neural network compared to other neural networks such as recurrent neural networks [13].

Having different votes from our three neural networks might be a sign of a binary code written by multiple authors. In this case, we perform authorship clustering comply with the following steps: First, the binaries are disassembled using IDA Pro [14]. However, since IDA fails to identify the boundaries of functions, we employ Nucleus [15] to perform compiler-agnostic function detection. Next, compiler-related functions and library-related functions are filtered out. After that, we extract opcode sequences from the user-related functions using a sliding window with a size of at most b opcodes, where b is a user-specified threshold. The resulting opcode sequences are then ranked based on mutual information, and finally, the ranked opcodes are used to cluster functions according to similarities in the author style characteristics. A standard clustering algorithm, k-means [16], is used for this purpose.

Contributions. Our contributions are summarized below.

- We design BinEye, a novel approach for authorship characterization. Based on deep learning, our approach discovers patterns that are related to author styles. BinEye is the first attempt to investigate the power of CNNs for binary authorship attribution.
- We evaluate BinEye on a set of binaries by more than 1,500 authors compiled with different compilers and compilation settings. The results show that

BinEye achieves high precision: 98%. Moreover, it is also robust in its ability to tolerate the noise injected by refactoring tools, code transformation methods, and other code transformations arising from the use of different compilers and optimization speed levels.

- Finally, **BinEye** is among the first approaches toward applying automated authorship characterization to real malware binaries. The results provide evidence and insights about malware authorship characterization that match the findings of domain experts obtained through manual analyses.

2   System Overview

The architecture of **BinEye** is illustrated in Fig. 1.

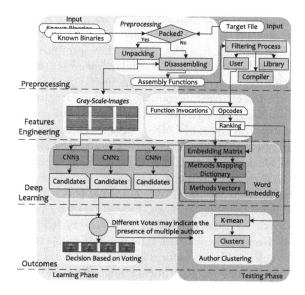

Fig. 1. BinEye architecture

As shown, the four main components are: (i) Preprocessing component where PEfile [17] is employed to check if the binary file is packed. If it is packed, the corresponding unpacker, such as UPX, is used to unpack the binary file and pass the unpacked binary file to the disassembler tools such as IDA Pro [14]. (ii) Feature engineering which deals with a different set of features that are related to the authorship attribution. This component is able to accept either an executable file or an assembly file as input. In the case of executable file, *BinEye* converts executable file to a gray-scale images. These images are passed to CNN3 that does automatically features engineering. In the case of assembly file, BinEye extracts the following features: (1) opcode sequences that are ranked through mutual information; (2) function invocations. Subsequently, we map each opcode in the sequence to a fixed length high-dimensional vector that semantically represents the opcode and replace the sequence of the binary function by a sequence of vectors. Afterward, we feed the sequence of vectors to a neural network with multiple layers. Then, it is passed to CNN1 while we apply the same to function invocations and passed the engineered features to CNN2. The three CNNs are trained by these sets of features. Once we have a target binary, each CNN will return a set of candidates according to the training features. These candidates are passed to decision component that decides based on the majority voting of three CNNs. In case of equal votes, we perform the following steps for clustering process: (1) Filtration task is performed on the assembly functions that filters out compiler-related functions and library-related function. (2) Opcode sequences are then extracted from the user-related functions using a sliding window with a size of at most b opcodes, where b is a user-specified threshold. (3) These opcode sequences are ranked through mutual information. Finally, (4) the ranked opcodes are used to cluster functions according to the similarity of the author's style characteristics of the binary code. Standard clustering algorithm (k-means) [16] is used for this purpose.

3 BinEye: Design Overview

3.1 Features Processing

Opcode Sequences. BinEye workflow starts by extracting the sequences of opcode. Our goal is to discover patterns that might discover the author style such as the preference in using keywords, compilers, resources, etc. It also captures the author's preference of using different keywords or resources. We only consider groups of such preferences with equivalent or similar functionality in order to avoid functionality-dependent features. For instance, keyword type preferences for inputs (e.g., using cin, scanf), preferences of using particular resources or a specific compiler, and the manner in which certain keywords are used can serve as further indications of an author's habits.

Function Invocations. BinEye starts by extracting the sequences of API calls from user-related functions. Our goal is to formalize the assembly to keep the maximum raw information with minimum noise. We require a manual categorization of APIs to correlate them to author style. For this reason, we treat assembly functions as a sequence of API calls. We consider all the API calls with no filtering, where the order is part of the information we use to characterize the author.

Binary Image Features Extraction. We take the binary file content as a vector of bytes. This vector is transferred into a two-dimensional matrix of fixed width d. In other words, the first d bytes go to the first row of the matrix, and the nth group of d bytes goes to the nth row of the matrix. This approach is similar to the malware visualization techniques proposed in [11,18]. The two-dimensional matrix, after a necessary padding, is now considered as a digital gray-scale image, which is "resized" into a square image of width s for efficient computation. We use a fixed width transformation as proposed in [11] to maintain the consistency in the texture produced as a result of this transformation. As long as the same width is used for each binary file, the choice of the width does not affect the similarity of the texture produced among similar executables. The methodology for computing the texture-based features is described as follows: We compute the features based on GIST descriptors [12]. The descriptors are computed by first filtering the image in various frequency sub-bands and then computing local block statistics on the filtered images. In image processing terminology, the functions modeling the filters are often referred to as Gabor Wavelets [19]. The image is then filtered using this filter bank to produce k filtered images. Each filtered image is further divided into BxB sub-blocks and the average value of a sub-block is computed and stored as a vector of length $L = B^2$. For more details we refer the reader to [11]. We test the intuition of using image features for binary authorship by modeling such images in a controlled experiment with source code (ground truth). We observe that different image regions usually represent the binary sections: .text, .rdata, .data, and .rsrc. Also, images could reveal ASCII text, initialized data, uninitialized data, etc. Moreover, we observe in our experiment that the image width varies according to the file size but the image texture remains same in case of different variants of the same binary file. Further, we test the image features against packed binaries. We observe through our experiment that when the binary is packed, there are two types of compression: low and high compression. The image-related features still do a good job if the binary compression is low, such as with Winupack packing tool; however, when binary compression is high, such as with UPX, the images texture will look different. It is worthy to mention that when unpacked author binaries with several similar variants are packed with a specific packer, then the images of the newly packed binaries (of the same author) are also similar. We will add such details in the final version of our research to further clarify this point.

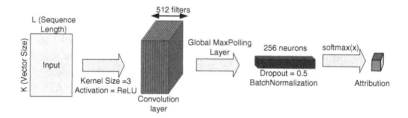

Fig. 2. BinEye neural network architecture

3.2   Deep Learning Process

We follow the same process in [20].

1- Discretization of Opcode/Function Invocations Sequences. In this step, we discretize the sequences of opcodes/function invocations (e.g., API) sequences that are in a binary code (Algorithm 1). More precisely, we replace each API keyword with an identifier, resulting in a sequence of numbers. We also build a dictionary that maps each API call to its identifier. Notice that in the current implementation, the mapping dictionary is deployed with the learning model to map the API calls of the analyzed binaries. In the deployment, we consider a big dataset that covers most of the API calls. Also, if we have unknown API calls, we replace them with fixed identifiers.

Algorithm 1. Discretization

    Input : $OSeq$: Opcode Sequence
              $MapDict$: Mapping Dict
    Output: $DSeq$: Discrete Sequence

1 **begin**
2     $DSeq = \texttt{EmptyList}();$
3   **foreach** $P \in OSeq$ **do**
4   **if** $m \in MapDict.Keys()$ **then**
5             $Dvalue \leftarrow MapDict[P];$
6             $DSeq.Add(Dvalue);$
7   **else**
8             $length = size(MapDict);$
9             $Dvalue \leftarrow length + 1;$
10            $MapDict[m] = Dvalue;$
11            $DSeq.Add(Dvalue);$

12   **return** $DSeq, MapDict;$

2- Unification of the Sequences' Size. The length of the sequences varies from one binary to another. Hence, it is important to unify the length of the sequences. There are two cases depending on the length of the sequence and the hyper-parameter. We choose a uniform sequence size as follows: (i) If the length of a given sequence is greater than the uniform sequence size L, we take only the first L items to represent the binary. (ii) In case the length of the sequence is less than L, we pad the sequence with zeros. It is important to mention that the uniform sequence size hyper-parameter has an influence on the accuracy of BinEye. A simple rule is that the larger is the size, the better is, but this will require a lot of computation power and a long time to train the neural network.

3- Generation of the Semantic Vectors. The identifier in the sequences needs to be shaped to fit as input to our neural network. This could be solved by representing each identifier by a vector. The question that arises is *how are such vectors produced?* A straightforward solution is to use one-hot vectors, where a vector has one in the interface value row, and zero in the rest. Such a vector is very sparse because its size is equal to the number of API calls, which makes it impractically and computationally prohibitive for the training and the deployment. To address this issue, we resort to a dense vector that uses a continuous space. These vectors are semantically related, and we could express their relation by computing a distance. The smaller the distance is, the more related the vectors are (i.e., the API calls). We describe word embedding in later Section. The output of this step is sequences of vectors for each binary file that keeps the order of the original API calls; each vector has a fixed size M (hyper-parameter).

4- Prediction using a Neural Network. The neural network is composed of several layers. The number of layers and the complexity of the model are hyper-parameters. However, we aim to keep the neural network model as simple as possible to gain in the execution time during its deployment. In our design, we rely on the convolution layers [21] to automatically discover the pattern in the assembly functions. The input to the neural network is a sequence of vectors, i.e., a matrix of $L \times M$ shape. In the training phase, we train the neural network parameters (layers weight) based on the binary vector sequence and its labels. In the deployment phase, we extract the sequence of bytes and use the embedding model to produce the vector sequence. Finally, the neural network takes the vector sequence to decide about the given binary code.

3.3   Embedding Method

The neural network takes vectors as input. Therefore, we represent opcode/function invocation sequences as vectors. As a result, we formalize a binary file as a sequence of vectors with fixed size (L). We could use one-hot vector. However, its size is the number of unique patterns in our dataset. This makes such a solution not scalable to large-scale training. Also, the word embedding technique outperforms the results of the one-hot vector technique in our case [22–24]. Therefore, we seek a compact vector, which also has a semantic value. To fulfill these requirements, we choose the word embedding techniques, namely, word2vec [23] and GloVe [24]. Our primary goal is to have a dense vector for each sequence that keeps track of its contexts in a large dataset of binary code. Thus, in contrast with one-hot vectors, each word embedding vector contains a numerical summary of the opcode/function invocation sequences representation. Moreover, we could apply geometric techniques on the pattern vectors to measure the semantic relationship between their characteristics, i.e., developers tend to use certain API calls in the same context.

In our context, we learn these vectors from our dataset that contains different labels by using word2vec [23]. The latter is a computationally efficient predictive model from learning word embedding vectors, which are applied on the binary code. The output obtained from training the embedding word model is a matrix $K \times A$, where K is the size of the embedding vector, and A is the number of unique patterns. Both K and A are hyper-parameters; we use $K = 64$ in all our models. In contrast, the hyper-parameter A is a major factor in the accuracy of *BinEye*. The more unique patterns we consider, the more accurate and robust our model is. Notice that, our word embedding is trained along with the neural network, where we tune both of them for a given task such as detection. Despite that, it can be trained separately to generate the embedding word vector independently of the detection task. In the deployment phase, *BinEye* uses the word embedding model and looks up for each API call identifier to find the corresponding embedding vector.

4   BinEye Neural Network

Our proposed neural network is inspired by [22]. They employ a neural network for sentence classification task. The proposed architecture defenestrates high results and outperforms state-of-the-art works with a relatively simple neural network design. In this paper, we investigate the following questions: *Why could such a Natural Language Processing (NLP) model be efficient in Binary Authorship Characterization? And why do we choose to build it on top of this design* [22]? We formulate our answers as follows: (i) Analyzing the text by employing NLP is a challenging field since there is an enormous number of vocabularies. We also have the same semantics with many combinations of words, which we call the *natural language obfuscation*. In our context, we deal with sequences of opcode and API method calls (e.g., function convocation) and want to find the combination of patterns of opcode/method calls, which indicate the author style characteristics. We use the API method calls as they appear in the binary, i.e., there is a temporal relationship between API methods in basic blocks but we ignore the order among these blocks. By analogy to NLP, the basic blocks are the sentences and the API method calls are the words. It applies to the opcode sequences in assembly file. Further, the function (paragraph) is a list of basic blocks (unordered sentences). This task looks easier compared to the NLP one because of the huge difference in the vocabulary, i.e., the number of API method calls is significantly less than the number of words in natural language. Also, the combination in the NLP is much complex compared to API calls/opcode. (ii) We choose to use this model due to its efficiency. Table 1 depicts the neural network architecture of BinEye attribution task.

Table 1. BinEye neural network

1	Layers	Options	Active
2	Convolution	Filter $= 512$, FilterSize $= 3$	ReLU
3	MaxPooling	-	-
4	FC	#Neurons $= 256$, Dropout $= 0.5$	ReLU
5	FC	#Neurons $= 1$, # of authors in the training dataset	Softmax

There are multiple neurons, one for each author. As presented in Fig. 2, the first layer is a convolution layer [22] with rectified linear unit (ReLU) activation function ($f(x) = max(0, x)$). Afterward, we use global max pool [22] and connect it to a fully-connected layer. Notice that in addition to Dropout [21] used to prevent over-fitting, we also utilize batch-normalization [21] to improve our results. Finally, we have an output layer, where the number of neurons depends on the attribution task.

4.1   Clustering Similar Functions

We use a standard clustering algorithm (k-means) [16] to group functions with similar author styles attributes $(v_{n_1}, \ldots, v_{n_z})$ into k clusters $S = S_1, \ldots, S_k$ and $(k \leq |F_{P_1}| + |F_{P_2}|)$ to minimize the intra-cluster sum of squares. In the following equation, μ_i denotes the mean of the feature values of each cluster.

$$\underset{S}{\arg\min} \sum_{i=1}^{k} \sum_{v_j \in S_i} \|v_j - \mu_i\|^2 \tag{1}$$

The parameter k may be estimated either by following standard practices in k-means clustering [16], or by beginning with one cluster and continually dividing the clusters until the points assigned to each cluster have a Gaussian distribution as described in [25].

5   Evaluation

In this section, we present the evaluation results for the possible use cases described earlier in this paper. Section 5.1 shows the setup of our experiments and provides an overview of the data we collected. The main results on authorship attribution are then presented. Subsequently, we evaluate the identification of the presence of multiple authors as well as the scalability of *BinEye*. Also, we have studied the impact of different CNN parameters on the *BinEye* accuracy. The impact of evading techniques is then studied. Finally, *BinEye* is applied to real malware binaries and the results are discussed.

5.1   Implementation Environment

The described binary feature extractions are implemented using separate python scripts for modularity purposes, which altogether form our analytical system. A subset of the python scripts in our evaluation system is used in tandem with IDA Pro disassembler [14]. The Neo4j [26] graph database is utilized to perform complex graph operations such as k-graph (ACFG) extraction. Gephi [27] is used for all graph analysis functions (e.g., page rank) that are not provided by Neo4j. The MongoDB database is used to store extracted features according to its efficiency and scalability. For the sake of usability, a graphical user interface in which binaries can be uploaded and analyzed is implemented. For CNN setup, we first use a convolution with 16 output channels is performed on the input feature vectors before the first dense block. We use kernel size 3×3 for convolutional layers. We follow zero-padded for inputs to keep the feature-map size fixed [21]. We use 3×3 convolution followed by 4×4 average pooling as transition layers between two contiguous blocks. At the end of the last block, a global average pooling is performed and then a softmax classifier is attached. The feature-map sizes in the two blocks are 128×128, and 64×64, respectively. The initial convolution layer comprises 2k convolutions of size 7×7 with stride 2; the number of feature-maps in all other layers also follow from setting k. The GPU is TITAN X, RAM is 128 GB, and the CPU is Intel E5-2630.

5.2   Dataset

The utilized dataset is composed of several files from different sources, as described below: (i) GitHub [28], where a considerable amount of real open-source projects are available; (ii) Google Code Jam [29]; and (iii) a set of known malware files representing a mixture of different families including the nine families provided in Microsoft Malware Classification Challenge [3]. Statistics about the dataset are provided in Table 2. To construct our experimental datasets, we compile the source code with different compilers and compilation settings to measure the effects of such variations. We use GNU Compiler Collection's gcc, g++, Clang, ICC, as well as Microsoft Visual Studio (VS) 2010, with different optimization levels.

Table 2. Statistics about the dataset used in the evaluation

Source	# of authors	# of prog.	# of func.
GitHub	600	9,650	1,900,000
Google Jam	1,300	21,500	2,165,120
Total	1,900	31,150	4,065,120

5.3   Evaluation Methodology

We have used the datasets introduced in Table 2 in our evaluation process. For each program in the datasets, we have author label. To construct a data representation suitable for learning and evaluation, we process the binaries in each corpus with the IDA Pro, ParseAPI in Paradyn, and Jakstab to obtain features that are related to characteristics. We eliminate statically linked library functions, compiler related functions, and other known binary code snippets or borrowed that are unrelated to the author styles. Our evaluation methodology involves both standard ten-fold cross-validation and random subset testing, depending on the experiment: For classification of the entire data set, we use ten-fold cross-validation. When evaluating how classification accuracy behaves as a function of the number of authors represented in the data, we randomly draw a subset of authors and use their programs in the test. The evaluation results are presented under the following metrics:

- *True positives* (TP): This metric measures the number of binaries that the system successfully able to identify their correct authors.
- *False negatives* (FN): This metric measures the number of binaries that the system incorrectly assigned to wrong authors.
- *False positives* (FP): This metric measures the number of binaries that the system incorrectly assigned to an author.
- *Precision* (P): It is the percentage of positive prediction, i.e., the percentage of the correct identified author out of all samples. $P = \frac{TP}{TP+FP}$
- *Recall* (R): It is the percentage of authors identified out of all samples. $R = \frac{TP}{TP+FN}$

5.4   Accuracy

The purpose of this experiment is to evaluate the accuracy of characterizing the author of in program binaries.

Table 3. F-result

	Precision	Recall	F_1
CNN3	0.95	0.87	0.91
CNN2	0.89	0.86	0.87
CNN1	0.84	0.79	0.81
BinEye	0.98	0.91	0.94

Evaluation Settings. The evaluation of *BinEye* system is conducted using the datasets described in Sect. 5.2. The data is randomly split into 10 sets, where one set is reserved as a testing set, and the remaining sets are used as training sets. The process is then repeated 15 times. To evaluate *BinEye* and to compare it with existing methods, precision P and recall R measures are applied. Furthermore, since the application domain targeted by *BinEye* is much more sensitive to false positives than false negatives, we employ an F1-measure.

BinEye Accuracy. We first investigate the accuracy of our proposed system in attributing the author of program binaries based on author styles. The results are reported in Table 3. The highest accuracy obtained by our tool is 0.94 when all features are together. Further, we can observe that the CNN3 (image features) returns the highest accuracy of 0.91. This is due to the fact that the author's knowledge, expertise, and styles may together form a unique image patterns. The second highest precision is 0.89 that obtained through CNN2. This is due to the fact that the author may use his expertise to implement a specific task

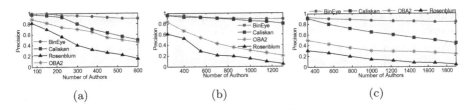

(a)   (b)   (c)

Fig. 3. Accuracy results of authorship attribution obtained by *BinEye*, Caliskan-Islam et al. [9], Rosenblum et al. [10], and OBA2 [7], on (a) Github, (b) Google Code Jam, and (c) Mixed.

by using specific API call and then leave a clue behind it. This clue might be captured through function invocations.

Results Comparison. First, we compare *BinEye* with the existing authorship attribution methods [7,9,10]. We evaluate the authorship classification technique presented by Rosenblum et al. [10], whose source code is available at [30], although the dataset is not available. The source code of the proposed technique as well as the dataset by Caliskan-Islam et al. [9] are available at [31]. We have contacted the author of OBA2 [7] for getting the both dataset and the source code and we have them. Caliskan-Islam et al. present the largest scale evaluation of binary authorship attribution in the literature, which contains *600* authors with *8* training programs per author. Rosenblum et al. present a large-scale evaluation of *190* authors with at least *8* training programs, while Alrabaee et al. present a small scale evaluation of 5 authors with *10* programs for each. We compare our results with these methods by using the datasets mentioned in Table 2 except the malware dataset since the aforementioned methods are not designed for malware binaries. Figure 3 details the results of comparing the accuracy between *BinEye* and all other existing methods.

It shows the relationship between the accuracy (*precision*) and the number of authors present in all datasets, where the accuracy decreases as the size of author population increases. The results show that *BinEye* achieves better accuracy in determining the author of binaries based on authorship attribution in the case of GitHub dataset and mixed dataset. Taking all four approaches into consideration, the highest precision of authorship attribution is close to *100%* on the Github dataset with less than *200* authors, while the lowest accuracy is *2%* when *1900* authors are involved. *BinEye* also identifies the author of Google dataset with an average precision of *91%* while an average accuracy of *96%* when the dataset is GitHub. The main reason for this is due to the fact that the authors of projects in Github have no restrictions when developing projects. In addition, the advanced programmers of such projects usually design their own class or template to be used in the projects. This makes the attribution process for such kind of authors are effective to identify them. The lower precision obtained by *BinEye* is approximately *84%* on a mixed dataset with *1900* authors. As shown in Fig. 3(b), Caliskan-Islam et al. [9] approach achieves highes accuracy among all. We believe that the reason behind Caliskan-Islam et al. approach superiority on Google Jam Code is that this dataset is simple and can be easily decompiled to source code.

We find that the accuracy of existing methods [9,10] depends heavily on the application's domain. For example, in Fig. 3, a good level of accuracy is observed for the Google data set, where the average accuracy is *90%* while the average accuracy is *70%* when the GitHub dataset is applied. Further, existing methods use disassembler and decompilers to extract features from binaries. Caliskan-Islam et al. [9] use a decompiler to translate the program into C-like pseudo code via Hex-Ray [32]. They pass the code to a fuzzy parser for C, thus obtaining an abstract syntax tree from which features can be extracted. In addition to Hex-Ray limitations [32], the C-like pseudo code is different from the original code to the extent that the variables, branches, and keywords are different.

For instance, we find that a function in the source code consists of the following keywords: (1-do, 1-switch, 3-case, 3-break, 2-while, 1-if) and the number of variables is two. Once we check the same function after decompiling its binary, we find that the function consists of the following keywords: (1-do, 1-else/if, 2-goto, 2-while, 4-if) and the number of variables is four. This will evidently lead to misleading features, thus increasing the rate of false positives.

5.5   False Positive Rate

We investigated the false positives to understand situations in which *BinEye* is likely to make incorrect attribution decisions. The average false positive rate of 0.02% is very low and could be neglected. The reason for this low false positive rate is that *BinEye* uses a multi CNNs networks that is based on majority votes. We observed that the Google dataset has the highest false positive rate; we believe the reason is that each programmer follows standard coding instructions, which limits individual coding traits.

5.6   Run-Time Performance

In this section, we evaluate the efficiency of `BinEye`, i.e., the runtime during the deployment phase. We divide the runtime into two parts: (i) *Preprocessing time*: the required time to extract and pre-process the features. (ii) *Detection time:* time needed to make the prediction about a given feature vectors. We analyze the detection time on the model complexity of different hardware. Table 4 depicts the average preprocessing and detection time, related to each hardware. The server machines spend, on average, 7 s in the preprocessing time, which is very acceptable for production. It is worthy to mention that we do not optimize the current preprocessing workflow. Further, Table 4 presents the detection time on average that is related to each hardware.

As shown, the detection time is almost close to each other in all hardware. Also, the detection time is very low for all the hardware. As for the Desktop, the detection time is 5.15 s. Moreover, the pre-process time takes 25% more than the prediction time in case of server GPU. Here, we ask the following question:

Table 4. Run-time vs. Hardware

	Preprocess			Prediction		
	Server GPU	Server CPU	Desktop	Server GPU	Server CPU	Desktop
Time (s)	7.25	9.4	18.6	1.75	2.35	3.85

Which part in the preprocessing needs optimization? To answer this question, we measure the preprocessing time for the following tasks: (I) the disassembly time using IDA Pro; (II) the filtration time; (III) the features extraction; (IV) the embedding generation time from the extracted features. The average processing time for each task is shown in Table 5.

Table 5. Processing time for different tasks

Task	Preprocess		
	Server GPU	Server CPU	Desktop
Disassembly	1.5	1.8	2.6
Filtration	1.75	1.9	3.0
Extraction	2.5	3.3	7.3
Embedding	1.5	2.4	6.7

As shown in Table 5, it is clear that the preprocessing time for disassembly and filtration tasks could be neglected. It is also the embedding task could be neglected. We observe that the feature extraction task takes the most time.

5.7 Impact of Compilers and Compilation Settings

We are further interested to study the impact of different compilers and compilation settings on the precision of our proposed system. We perform the following tasks: (i) testing the ability of *BinEye* when identifying the author from binaries compiled with the same compiler, but different compiler optimization levels. Specifically, we use binaries that were compiled with GCC/VS on x86 architecture using optimization levels O2 and O3. In this test, the average precision remains same (93%). (ii) We use a different configuration to identify the author of program compiled with both a different compiler and different compiler optimization levels. Specifically, we use programs compiled for x86 with VS −O2 and GCC −O3. In this test, the average precision is 91.9%. We also redo the test for the same binaries compiled with ICC and Clang compilers. The average precision remains almost the same 92.8%.

5.8 Impact of Evading Techniques

The adversary may use existing evading techniques to prevent authorship attribution systems. Hence, we consider a random set of *250* files from our dataset that belong to 50 authors. Those files are used for the evading techniques experiments as described below.

Refactoring Techniques. First, we use the C++ refactoring tools [33,34]. These tools may perform the following methods: (i) renaming a variable (RV); (ii) moving a method from a superclass to its subclasses (MM); and (iii) extracting a few statements and placing them into a new method (NM). We obtain a precision of *93%* in correctly characterizing authors, which is only a mild drop in comparison to the *92%* precision observed without applying refactoring techniques. More specifically, the accuracy remains the same when the RV technique is applied, whereas the accuracy drops slightly when MM and NM are applied. Since some of the features used in *BinEye* are based on semantic features, they are not significantly affected by these techniques.

Impact of Source Obfuscation. Second, we use some existing tools (e.g., Trigress [35]) to obfuscate the source code by applying the following methods: (i) Virtualization which transforms a function into an interpreter whose bytecode language is specialized for this function; (ii) Jitting which transforms a function into one that generates its machine code at runtime; and (iii) Dynamic which transforms a function into one that continuously modifies its machine code at runtime. Our system is able to deal with such binaries. In our system, we have dynamic features that can tackle such evading techniques. However, almost other features fail with the binaries resulted after such obfuscations. Additionally, we use LLVM framework to perform CFG flattening at source level. These methods affect the accuracy by about 1.5%. The main reason behind this small drop is that the compiler can reduce the effect of those methods when the executable is created.

Impact of Obfuscation. We are interested in determining how *BinEye* handles simple binary obfuscation techniques intended for evading detection, as implemented by tools such as Obfuscator-LLVM [36]. These obfuscators replace instructions by other semantically equivalent instructions, introduce spurious control flow, and can even completely flatten control flow graphs. Obfuscation techniques implemented by Obfuscator-LLVM are applied to the samples prior to classifying the authors. We apply *BinEye* directly on the obfuscated samples. We obtain an accuracy of *93%* in correctly classifying authors, which is only a slight drop in comparison to the *90%* accuracy observed without obfuscation. We combine the refactoring process, source obfuscation, with the binary obfuscation. More specifically, we first apply the refactoring techniques on the selected dataset (*250* files), then apply obfuscation methods at the source level, after which they are compiled using Visual Studio 2010. We apply the binary obfuscation techniques, the accuracy drops from *93%* to *89%*. For the advanced obfuscation, we choose: (i) CFG Obfuscation (push/jmp), (ii) Instruction Aliasing, (iii) Hardware Breakpoint and (iv) Instruction Counting., and (v) Encryption Packer. To test our system against the aforementioned techniques, we choose 10 representative obfuscated samples from [37]. The results show that our system precision drops from 93% to 81%.

5.9 Discussion

Through our experiments, we find the following observations:

Feature Pre-processing. With those existing methods, we have encountered top-ranked features related to the compiler (e.g., stack frame setup operation). It is thus necessary to filter irrelevant functions (e.g., compiler functions) in order to better identify author-related portions of code. To this end, we utilize a more elaborate method for filtration based on FLIRT technology for library identification as well as our proposed system for the filtration of compiler functions. Successful distinction between these two groups of functions leads to considerable time savings and helps shift the focus of analysis to more relevant functions.

Source of Features. Existing methods use disassembler and decompilers to extract features from binaries. Caliskan-Islam et al. [9] use a decompiler to translate the program into C-like pseudo code via Hex-Ray [32]. They pass the code to a fuzzy parser for C, thus obtaining an abstract syntax tree from which features can be extracted. In addition to Hex-Ray limitations [32], the C-like pseudo code is different from the original code to the extent that the variables, branches, and keywords are different.

Function Inlining: In practice, the compiler may sometimes inline a small function into its caller code as an optimization. This may introduce additional complexity. We notice that function inlining can drop the precision of our system by 5%. While the precision of OBA2 and Caliskan-Islam et al. approach are not affected.

Privacy Concerns: Our tool could be misused to violate privacy of the coders. Therefore, we have to consider the privacy implications of *BinEye* in the future work.

6 Multi-authorship Attribution Problem

In this section we carry out an experiment to demonstrate that it is possible to perform multi-author authorship attribution by applying BinEye to discover the presence of multiple authors.

Synthetic Dataset. The first dataset we use for multi-authorship attribution originates from the Google Code Jam 2010–2017. It consists of single-authored programs and for each author there are multiple programs because it is a multi-round programming contest. We focus on participants from the final round (a total of 400 participants) who have at least 15 C++ programs. To evaluate multi-authorship attribution, we synthetically generate multi-author programs by merging randomly selected files from different authors. For example, consider two authors A and B. We merge two programs (F_A, F_B) written by these authors to form a multi-author program. Using the same approach, we generate multiple executables by merging files from two, three, four, five, and six different authors. We perform the following setup: first training each network in our model based on single-authorship dataset, then we test each of them based on the merged dataset (i.e., files that we create with merging multi-authors). We report the accuracy in Table 6.

Table 6. Evaluation result for identifying the presence of multiple authors in synthetic dataset

Network	Opt.	Metrics	# of Authors Per File						
			2	3	4	5	6	7	8
CNN1 (Opcode)	O0	Prec.	0.95	0.96	0.96	0.97	0.96	0.98	0.97
		Rec.	0.91	0.92	0.93	0.92	0.95	0.95	0.94
	O1	Prec.	0.95	0.96	0.96	0.96	0.96	0.97	0.97
		Rec.	0.90	0.90	0.91	0.91	0.90	0.92	0.91
	O2	Prec.	0.94	0.95	0.96	0.96	0.96	0.95	0.96
		Rec.	0.90	0.91	0.90	0.91	0.91	0.92	0.92
	O3	Prec.	0.93	0.94	0.93	0.93	0.94	0.95	0.95
		Rec.	0.91	0.91	0.90	0.90	0.92	0.92	0.92
CNN2 (Images)	O0	Prec.	0.98	0.99	0.98	0.98	0.98	0.99	0.99
		Rec.	0.96	0.96	0.95	0.95	0.97	0.96	0.95
	O1	Prec.	0.97	0.98	0.98	0.97	0.97	0.98	0.97
		Rec.	0.96	0.96	0.95	0.95	0.95	0.95	0.95
	O2	Prec.	0.97	0.96	0.98	0.97	0.97	0.97	0.97
		Rec.	0.96	0.96	0.95	0.96	0.96	0.95	0.95
	O3	Prec.	0.97	0.97	0.96	0.98	0.96	0.97	0.97
		Rec.	0.96	0.96	0.97	0.95	0.96	0.96	0.96
CNN3 (API calls)	O0	Prec.	0.91	0.92	0.92	0.92	0.91	0.93	0.93
		Rec.	0.89	0.90	0.90	0.89	0.89	0.89	0.89
	O1	Prec.	0.91	0.91	0.90	0.90	0.91	0.91	0.91
		Rec.	0.88	0.89	0.89	0.89	0.89	0.89	0.89
	O2	Prec.	0.90	0.91	0.90	0.89	0.89	0.89	0.89
		Rec.	0.89	0.89	0.88	0.89	0.89	0.89	0.90
	O3	Prec.	0.91	0.92	0.92	0.92	0.92	0.92	0.92
		Rec.	0.88	0.89	0.88	0.88	0.88	0.88	0.89

GitHub Dataset. We manually collect a set of GitHub projects and check the contributors who have written the code of these projects. We limit our system to programs written in C/C++ and we ignore authors whose contribution is merely adding lines. For this purpose, we collect 50 projects (for the sake of privacy, we removed the details of these projects such as project names) to which 50–1500 authors contributed. We report the accuracy in Table 7. It is worthy to mention that the filtration process to isolate external library code from the code written by their users, it is very important and it increases the precision significantly. In this experiment, we find about 10%–23% of the functions are related to STL and Boost code. We learn our proposed method in Sect. 3.1 to determine such functions.

Table 7. Evaluation result for identifying the presence of multiple authors in GitHub dataset

Network	Opt.	Metrics	# of Authors Per Project						
			50	100	150	200	250	300	350
CNN1 (Opcode)	O0	Prec.	0.93	0.92	0.90	0.90	0.90	0.89	0.89
		Rec.	0.90	0.88	0.88	0.87	0.86	0.85	0.94
	O1	Prec.	0.92	0.91	0.90	0.89	0.88	0.88	0.97
		Rec	0.91	0.90	0.90	0.88	0.88	0.87	0.91
	O2	Prec.	0.91	0.91	0.90	0.89	0.89	0.88	0.96
		Rec	0.90	0.89	0.88	0.87	0.87	0.86	0.92
	O3	Prec.	0.91	0.90	0.90	0.89	0.89	0.88	0.95
		Rec	0.92	0.91	0.91	0.89	0.89	0.89	0.92
CNN2 (Images)	O0	Prec.	0.99	0.99	0.99	0.99	0.99	0.99	0.99
		Rec	0.98	0.97	0.97	0.95	0.95	0.96	0.96
	O1	Prec	0.99	0.99	0.98	0.98	0.97	0.97	0.97
		Rec.	0.97	0.97	0.96	0.95	0.94	0.94	0.95
	O2	Prec.	0.97	0.97	0.96	0.96	0.96	0.96	0.97
		Rec	0.96	0.96	0.96	0.95	0.95	0.94	0.95
	O3	Prec.	0.95	0.95	0.94	0.94	0.94	0.94	0.97
		Rec	0.96	0.95	0.95	0.95	0.95	0.94	0.96
CNN3 (API calls)	O0	Prec.	0.93	0.93	0.92	0.92	0.92	0.91	0.93
		Rec	0.91	0.91	0.91	0.90	0.90	0.90	0.89
	O1	Prec.	0.92	0.92	0.91	0.91	0.91	0.91	0.91
		Rec	0.91	0.91	0.90	0.89	0.89	0.89	0.89
	O2	Prec.	0.90	0.90	0.90	0.90	0.89	0.89	0.89
		Rec	0.90	0.90	0.89	0.89	0.89	0.88	0.90
	O3	Prec.	0.91	0.91	0.91	0.90	0.90	0.90	0.90
		Rec	0.89	0.89	0.88	0.87	0.87	0.87	0.87

7 Conclusion

To conclude, we have presented the first known effort on characterizing the author of binary code based on personnel characteristics. Previous research has applied machine learning techniques to extract stylometry styles and can distinguish between *5–800* authors, whereas we can handle up to *19500* authors.

In addition, existing works have only employed artificial datasets, whereas we included more realistic datasets. We also applied our system to known malware (e.g., `Zeus` and `Citadel`). Our findings indicated that the accuracy of these techniques drops dramatically to approximately *45%* at a scale of more than *150* authors. It is easier to attribute authors with advanced expertise or authors of realistic datasets than it is to attribute authors of less expertise or authors of artificial datasets. For example, in the GitHub dataset, the authors of a sample can be identified with greater than *90%* accuracy. In summary, our system demonstrates superior results on more realistic datasets and real malware and can detect the presence of multiple authors.

References

1. Alrabaee, S., Shirani, P., Wang, L., Debbabi, M.: Fossil: a resilient and efficient system for identifying foss functions in malware binaries. ACM Trans. Priv. Secur. (TOPS) **21**(2), 8 (2018)
2. Techniqal report, Resource 207: Kaspersky Lab Research proves that Stuxnet and Flame developers are connected. http://www.kaspersky.com/about/news/virus/2012/
3. Big Game Hunting: Nation-state malware research, BlackHat (2015). https://www.blackhat.com/docs/us-15/materials/us-15-MarquisBoire-Big-Game-Hunting-The-Peculiarities-Of-Nation-State-Malware-Research.pdf
4. Citizen Lab. University of Toronto, Canada (2015). https://citizenlab.org/
5. Caliskan-Islam, A., et al.: De-anonymizing programmers via code stylometry. In: USENIX (2015)
6. Frantzeskou, G.: Source code authorship analysis for supporting the cybercrime investigation process, pp. 470–495 (2004)
7. Alrabaee, S., Saleem, N., Preda, S., Wang, L., Debbabi, M.: Oba2: an onion approach to binary code authorship attribution. Digit. Invest. **11**, S94–S103 (2014)
8. Alrabaee, S., Wang, L., Debbabi, M.: On the feasibility of binary authorship characterization. Digit. Invest. **28**, S3–S11 (2019)
9. Caliskan-Islam, A., et al.: When coding style survives compilation: de-anonymizing programmers from executable binaries, arXiv preprint arXiv:1512.08546 (2015)
10. Rosenblum, N., Zhu, X., Miller, B.P.: Who wrote this code? Identifying the authors of program binaries. In: Atluri, V., Diaz, C. (eds.) ESORICS 2011. LNCS, vol. 6879, pp. 172–189. Springer, Heidelberg (2011). https://doi.org/10.1007/978-3-642-23822-2_10
11. Kirat, D., Nataraj, L., Vigna, G., Manjunath, B.: Sigmal: a static signal processing based malware triage. In: Proceedings of the 29th Annual Computer Security Applications Conference, pp. 89–98. ACM (2013)
12. Oliva, A., Torralba, A.: Modeling the shape of the scene: a holistic representation of the spatial envelope. Int. J. Comput. Vis. **42**(3), 145–175 (2001)
13. Wei, Y., et al.: HCP: a flexible CNN framework for multi-label image classification. IEEE Trans. Pattern Anal. Mach. Intell. **38**(9), 1901–1907 (2016)
14. HexRays: IDA Pro (2011). https://www.hex-rays.com/products/ida/index.shtml. Accessed Feb 2016
15. Andriesse, D., Slowinska, A., Bos, H.: Compiler-agnostic function detection in binaries. In: IEEE Euro S&P (2017)

16. Farnstrom, F., Lewis, J., Elkan, C.: Scalability for clustering algorithms revisited. ACM SIGKDD Explor. Newsl. **2**(1), 51–57 (2000)
17. PEfile (2012). http://code.google.com/p/pefile/. Accessed Nov 2016
18. Nataraj, L., Karthikeyan, S., Jacob, G., Manjunath, B.: Malware images: visualization and automatic classification. In: Proceedings of the 8th International Symposium on Visualization for Cyber Security, p. 4. ACM (2011)
19. Daugman, J.G.: Complete discrete 2-D gabor transforms by neural networks for image analysis and compression. IEEE Trans. Acoust. Speech Signal Process. **36**(7), 1169–1179 (1988)
20. Karbab, E.B., Debbabi, M., Derhab, A., Mouheb, D.: MalDozer: automatic framework for android malware detection using deep learning. Digit. Invest. **24**, S48–S59 (2018)
21. Huang, G., Liu, Z., Weinberger, K.Q., van der Maaten, L.: Densely connected convolutional networks, arXiv preprint arXiv:1608.06993 (2016)
22. Kim, Y.: Convolutional neural networks for sentence classification, CoRR (2014)
23. Mikolov, T., Sutskever, I., et al.: Distributed representations of words and phrases and their compositionality. In: NIPS Neural Information Processing Systems (2013)
24. Pennington, J., Socher, R., et al.: GloVe: global vectors for word representation. In: Conference on Empirical Methods in Natural Language Processing (2014)
25. Hamerly, G., Elkan, C., et al.: Learning the k in k-means. In: NIPS, vol. 3, pp. 281–288 (2003)
26. The Scalable Native Graph Database (2015). http://neo4j.com/
27. The Gephi plugin for nneo4j (2015). https://marketplace.gephi.org/plugin/neo4j-graph-database-support/
28. The GitHub repository (2016). https://github.com/
29. The Google Code Jam (2008–2015). http://code.google.com/codejam/
30. The materials supplement for the paper. Who Wrote This Code? Identifying the Authors of Program Binaries. http://pages.cs.wisc.edu/~dnater/esorics-supp/
31. Programmer De-anonymization from Binary Executables (2015). https://github.com/calaylin/bda
32. Hex-Ray decompiler (2015). https://www.hex-rays.com/products/decompiler/
33. Refactoring tool (2016). https://www.devexpress.com/Products/CodeRush/. Accessed Feb 2017
34. C++ refactoring tools for visual studio (2016). http://www.wholetomato.com/. Accessed Feb 2016
35. Tigress is a diversifying virtualizer/obfuscator for the C language (2016). http://tigress.cs.arizona.edu/
36. Junod, P., Rinaldini, J., Wehrli, J., Michielin, J.: Obfuscator-LLVM: software protection for the masses. In: Proceedings of the 1st International Workshop on Software Protection, pp. 3–9. IEEE Press (2015)
37. Branco, R.R., Barbosa, G.N., Neto, P.D.: Scientific but not academical overview of malware anti-debugging, anti-disassembly and Anti-VM technologies (2012)

Static Detection of Uninitialized Stack Variables in Binary Code

Behrad Garmany[(⊠)], Martin Stoffel[(⊠)], Robert Gawlik[(⊠)], and Thorsten Holz[(⊠)]

Horst Görtz Institute for IT-Security (HGI),
Ruhr-Universität Bochum, Bochum, Germany
{behrad.garmany,martin.stoffel,robert.gawlik,thorsten.holz}@rub.de

Abstract. More than two decades after the first stack smashing attacks, memory corruption vulnerabilities utilizing stack anomalies are still prevalent and play an important role in practice. Among such vulnerabilities, uninitialized variables play an exceptional role due to their unpleasant property of unpredictability: as compilers are tailored to operate fast, costly interprocedural analysis procedures are not used in practice to detect such vulnerabilities. As a result, complex relationships that expose uninitialized memory reads remain undiscovered in binary code. Recent vulnerability reports show the versatility on how uninitialized memory reads are utilized in practice, especially for memory disclosure and code execution. Research in recent years proposed detection and prevention techniques tailored to source code. To date, however, there has not been much attention for these types of software bugs within binary executables.

In this paper, we present a static analysis framework to find uninitialized variables in binary executables. We developed methods to lift the binaries into a knowledge representation which builds the base for specifically crafted algorithms to detect uninitialized reads. Our prototype implementation is capable of detecting uninitialized memory errors in complex binaries such as web browsers and OS kernels, and we detected 7 novel bugs.

1 Introduction

Memory corruption vulnerabilities are prevalent in programs developed in type-unsafe languages such as C and C++. These types of software faults are known since many years and discovering memory corruption bugs in binary executables has received a lot of attention for decades. Nevertheless, it is still an open research problem to efficiently detect vulnerabilities in binary code in an automated and scalable fashion. Especially *temporal* bugs seem to be a common problem in complex programs, an observation that the steady stream of reported vulnerabilities confirms [12–14,43]. In practice, especially web browsers are often affected by temporal bugs and these programs suffer from use-after-free vulnerabilities, race

© Springer Nature Switzerland AG 2019
K. Sako et al. (Eds.): ESORICS 2019, LNCS 11736, pp. 68–87, 2019.
https://doi.org/10.1007/978-3-030-29962-0_4

conditions, uninitialized memory corruptions, and similar kinds of software vulnerabilities.

One specific challenge is the efficient detection of uninitialized memory errors, such as uninitialized stack variables. While such vulnerabilities got into the focus of several real-world attacks [4, 9–11, 14, 21], they still represent an attack vector that is not studied well and often overlooked in practice. The basic principle of such vulnerabilities is straightforward: if a variable is declared but not defined (i.e., not initialized properly) and used later on in a given program, then an attacker may abuse such a software fault as an attack primitive. The uninitialized variable may for example contain left-over information from prior variables in stale stack frames used during prior function calls. This information can be used to disclose memory and leak sensitive information, which can then be used by an attacker to bypass *Address Space Layout Randomization* (ASLR) or other defenses. In the worst case, an attacker can control the content of an uninitialized variable and use it to execute arbitrary code of her choice, hence fully compromising the program. Uninitialized memory errors represent a vulnerability class that often affects complex, real-world programs: for example, at the 2016 edition of the annual *pwn2own* contest, Microsoft's *Edge* web browser fell victim to an uninitialized stack variable [4]. As a result, this vulnerability was enough to exploit the memory corruption vulnerability and gain full control over the whole program. Similarly, an uninitialized structure on the stack was used in the *pwn2own* contest 2017 to perform a guest-to-host privilege escalation in VMware [21].

The detection of uninitialized variables in an automated way has been studied for software whose source code is available [17, 22, 24]. The urge for such systems, especially targeting the stack, is also addressed by recent research through tools like SAFEINIT [30] or UNISAN[27]. These systems set their main focus on prevention and also rely on source code.

In practice, however, a lot of popular software is unfortunately proprietary and only available in binary format. Hence, if source code is unavailable, we need to resort to binary analysis. The analysis of binary code, on the other hand, is much more challenging since some of the context information gets lost during the compilation phase. The loss of data and context information (e.g, names, types, and structures of data are no longer available) hampers analysis and their reconstruction is difficult [20, 23, 39]. Thus, the development of precise analysis methods is more complicated without this information. Addressing this issue, we are compelled to consider every statement in the assembly code as it might relate to uninitialized memory of stack variables.

In this paper, we address this challenge and propose an automated analysis system to statically detect uninitialized stack variables in binary code. Since dynamic analysis methods typically lack comprehensive coverage of all possible paths, we introduce a novel static analysis approach which provides full coverage, at the cost of potentially unsound results (i.e., potential false positive and false negatives). However, unveiling potential spots of uninitialized reads and covering the whole binary poses a more attractive trade-off given the high value of detecting novel vulnerabilities. Note that the information obtained by our approach can further serve in a dynamic approach, e.g., to automatically verify each warning generated by our method.

Our analysis is performed in two phases: First, we designed a framework to lift binary software into an intermediate representation, which is further transformed into a knowledge base that serves our *Datalog* programs. We opted for Datalog given that this declarative logic programming language enables us to efficiently query our deductive database that contains facts about the binary code. Based on Datalog, we then devised a points-to analysis which is both flow- and field-sensitive. More specifically, with points-to information we have explicit information on indirect writes and reads that are connected to passed pointers. This allows us to track the indirect read or write back to the specific calling context where the points-to information is further propagated and incorporated in our knowledge base. This analysis step builds up the conceptual structure on which our dataflow algorithms operate to detect uninitialized variables.

To demonstrate the practical feasibility of the proposed method, we implemented a prototype which is tailored to detect uninitialized stack variables. Our results show that we can successfully find all uninitialized stack vulnerabilities in the Cyber Grand Challenge (CGC) binaries. In addition, we detected several real-world vulnerabilities in complex software such as web browsers and OS kernel binaries. Finally, our prototype is able to detect and pinpoint new and previously unknown bugs in programs such as *objdump*, and *gprof.*

In summary, our main contributions in this paper are:

- We design and implement an automated static analysis approach and introduce several processing steps which enable us to encode the complex data flow within a given binary executable to unveil unsafe zones in the control flow graph (i.e., basic blocks in which potential uninitialized reads might occur).
- We present a flow-, context- and field-sensitive analysis approach built on top of these processing steps, suitable for large-scale analysis of binary executables to detect uninitialized reads in a given binary executable.
- We evaluate and demonstrate that our analysis framework can detect both vulnerabilities in synthetic binary executables and complex, real-world programs. Our results show that the framework is capable of finding new bugs.

2   Uninitialized Stack Variables

Stack variables are local variables stored in the stack frame of a given function. A function usually allocates a new stack frame during its prologue by decreasing the stack pointer and setting up a new frame pointer that points to the beginning of the frame. Depending on the calling convention, either the caller or callee take care of freeing the stack frame by increasing the stack pointer and restoring the old frame pointer. For example, in the `stdcall` calling convention, the callee is responsible for cleaning up the stack during the epilogue. It is important to note that data from deallocated stack frames are *not* automatically overwritten during a function's prologue or epilogue. This, in particular, means that old (and thus stale) data can still be present in a newly allocated stack frame. A stack variable that is not initialized properly hence contains old data from earlier, deallocated stack frames. Such a variable is also called *uninitialized*. An uninitialized stack variable can lead to undefined behavior, not at least due to its unpleasant property that the program does not necessarily crash upon such inputs. In practice, uninitialized variables can be exploited in various ways and pose a serious problem [4,9–11,14,28]. They usually contain junk data, but if an attacker can control these memory cells with data of her choice, the software vulnerability might enable arbitrary code execution.

To tackle this problem, the compiler can report uninitialized stack variables at compile time for intraprocedural cases. Unfortunately, interprocedural cases are usually not taken into account by compilers. This lies in the nature of compilers which need to be fast and cannot afford costly analysis procedures. Even for optimization purposes, past research reveals that the benefits of extensive interprocedural analyses are not large enough to be taken account of in compilers [35].

3   Design

In the following, we provide a comprehensive overview of our static analysis framework to detect uninitialized stack variables in binary executables. Our analysis is divided into two processing stages. In a pre-processing step, we lift the binary into an IL and transform each function into SSA with respect to registers. The transformed functions are translated into Datalog facts which serve as our extensional database or *knowledge base.*

Based on this database, we then perform an interprocedural points-to analysis with respect to stack pointers. The analysis also results in information about pointers that are passed as arguments to functions and hence we can determine those pointers that enter a new function context. The reconstructed information about indirect definitions and uses of stack locations is used in a post-processing state in which we determine *safe zones* for each stack access. Safe zones consist of *safe basic blocks*, i.e., a use in these blocks with respect to the specific variable is covered by a definition on all paths. Stack accesses outside their corresponding safe zone produce warnings. For each variable, we determine a safe zone in its corresponding function context.

Our dataflow algorithms propagate information about safe zones from callers to callees and vice versa. If a path exists from the entry of a function to the use of a variable, which avoids the basic blocks of its safe zone, then the stack access is flagged *unsafe*. If a potentially uninitialized parameter is passed to a function, we check if the exit node of the function belongs to its safe zone. This in particular means that each path from the entry point of the function to the leaf node is covered by a definition (i.e., initialization) of the variable.

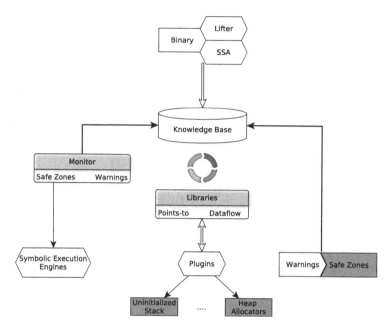

Fig. 1. Architecture implemented by our prototype.

We propagate this information back to the call sites, i.e., the fallthrough basic block at the call site is added to the safe zone of the variable in the context of the caller. This information in turn is further propagated and used at other call sites. Figure 1 shows the architecture implemented by our prototype. Our design allows to attach different checker plugins into the system that work and enrich the same knowledge base with valuable information. Each plugin can be run in parallel. Whenever a new information enters the knowledge base, the plugins adapt to it.

Warnings and safe zones are outputs of the analysis phase and put into the knowledge base. A monitor observes changes made to safe zones and warnings to either spawn the Datalog algorithms or a symbolic execution engine. The symbolic execution engine tackles the path sensitivity and is fed with safe zones of each stack variable. The aim of the symbolic execution engine is to reach the warning, i.e., a potential uninitialized read, by avoiding the safe zone of that variable. The whole procedures cycle, i.e., each component contributes to the knowledge base which in turn is consumed by other components to adapt.

Our current prototype is tailored towards uninitialized stack variables. However, as the plugin system suggests, we are able to enrich the analyses with heap information (see Sect. 5.3). In the next sections, we explain the individual analysis steps in detail and present examples to illustrate each step.

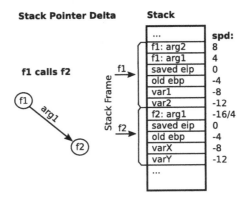

Fig. 2. Stack pointer delta (spd) addressing.

3.1 Stack Pointer Delta

On Intel x86 and many other instruction set architectures, the stack pointer is used to keep a reference to the top of the stack. The stack is usually accessed in relation to the current stack pointer. On Intel x86, the frame pointer is additionally linked to the stack pointer and keeps a reference to the beginning of the current stack frame. A function stack frame can, therefore, be located on different stack addresses depending on its stack pointer value. Because of this, we can not refer to a stack address directly. Instead, we use a delta value depending on the stack pointer. We refer to this addressing type as *stack pointer delta addressing*. A stack frame always starts at delta zero and grows towards negative values. Therefore, local variables are located at negative offsets, while passed arguments through the stack reside at positive offsets. We handle arguments passed through the *fastcall* calling convention for both x64 and x86 architectures in a generic way by means of Datalog rules. To simplify the analysis, we rebase all memory accesses on the stack to be relative to the stack pointer instead of using the frame pointer.

Definition 1. *Let S be the set of all stack variables. Each $s \in S$ is a tuple of the form (spd_s, fld_s) where spd_s is the stack pointer delta of s and fld an optional field value added to the base address of the underlying memory object.*

Figure 2 illustrates this concept. Function f1 calls f2. The resulting stack is shown on the right-hand side. In each stack frame the saved EIP value is mapped to the delta value zero. A direct access to var1 inside function f1 is associated with $(-8, 0)$, since it is at delta -8. Variable $varX$ is also at delta value -8 but inside function f2. Each delta value is associated with the corresponding function in which the access occurs.

3.2 Points-To Analysis for Binaries

Analyzing binary machine code poses many challenges to overcome. The lack of type information forces us to analyze each IL statement. To overcome the

Input: EDB
Output: Points-To Facts

① VPtsTo(V1, SPD, Addr, Ctx) : −
   StackPointer(V1, Addr, SPD).

② VPtsTo(V1, SPD, Addr, Ctx) : −
   Assign(V1,V2, Addr),
   VptsTo(V2, SPD, _, Ctx).

③ VPtsTo(V1, SPD2, Addr, Ctx) : −
   Load(V1, V2, Disp, Addr, Ctx),
   VPtsTo(V2, SPD, Addr2, Ctx),
   CanReach(Addr, Addr2, Ctx),
   PointerPtsTo(SPD, Disp, SPD2).

④ PointerPtsTo(SPD,Disp,SPD, Ctx) : −
   Store(V1, Disp, V2, Addr, Ctx),
   VPtsTo(V1, SPD, _, Ctx),
   VptsTo(V2, SPD, _, Ctx).

⑤ VPtsTo(Res, SPD+Value, Addr, Ctx) : −
   BinOp(Op, Res, V1, V2, Addr, Ctx),
   VPtsTo(V1, SPD, _, Ctx),
   Constant(V2, Value, Addr).

⑥ VPtsTo(V2, SPD2, CalleeAddr, Callee) : −
   Param(V1, Arg, Addr, Caller,
              V2, CalleeAddr, Callee),
   TranslateSPD(Arg, Callee, SPD2),
   VptsTo(V1, _, _, Caller).

⑦ VPtsTo(V1, SPD, Addr, Ctx) : −
   Phi(V1, PhiReg, Addr, Ctx),
   VptsTo(V1, SPD, _, Ctx).

⑧ IndirectDef(V1, SPD, Addr) : −
   Store(V1, Disp, V2, Addr, Ctx),
   VptsTo(V1, SPD, _, Ctx).

⑨ IndirectUse(V1, SPD, Addr) : −
   Load(V1, V2, Disp, Addr, Ctx),
   VptsTo(V1, SPD, _, Ctx).

Algorithm 1. Points-To Analysis.

Variables:

$Addr$	Instruction address
V_i	Register or memory expression
SPD	Stack pointer delta value (spd) of the corresponding stack location
Ctx	Function name/context
Arg	Part of Param facts; describes which parameter we are dealing with ($1st, 2nd, \ldots$)

EDB Facts:

StackPointer	A fact that unifies V1 with the register that holds a pointer. The Addr of the instruction and the spd value of the stack location are stored in the corresponding variables, respectively.
Assign	Corresponds to a **mov** instruction in assembly
Load	Dereference from $V_2 + Disp$ and store it into V_1
Store	Store content of V_2 into memory at $V_1 + Disp$
Param	Describes a parameter pass at the call site ($Addr$) from actual V_1 in the caller context to a formal V_2 in the callee context
TranslateSPD	Translates the spd value of the parameters in the context of the callee and vice versa. In x86 first parameter has spd value 4, second has 8 etc.
BinOp	Describes a binary operation where Op is applied on V_1 and V_2 and the result is stored in Res.
Constant	Describes a constant value used in a binary operation
Phi	Corresponds to an SSA phi assignment. $PhiReg$ is bound to registers in the phi expression

Fig. 3. Variables and EDB facts.

complicated arrangement of work list algorithms, we decided to opt for a declarative approach. Rather than solving the problem by an imperative algorithm, we describe the problem and let the solver perform the evaluation strategy. Therefore, we utilize an Andersen-style algorithm [1] in Datalog which is flow- and field-sensitive. Our algorithm is inspired by recent research done by Smaragdakis et al. [40,41]. They show how context, flow, and field sensitivity can be achieved in large-scale through a Datalog-based approach. We adapted their approach and tailored our algorithms for binary analysis.

Each information about memory loads, stores, assignments, arithmetic operations, control flow, and parameter passes which is expressed in terms of the IL, is extracted into an extensional database (*EDB*). For each binary, an EDB is produced which represents a knowledge base of a priori facts.

A simplified version of our approach delivers the idea and is presented by Algorithm 1. The Datalog algorithm is fed with the EDB which builds the base for Datalog rules to derive new facts. These new facts build the intensional database (*IDB*). The *IDB* and *EBD* form our *knowledge base*. In Fig. 3, we summarize the facts and variables used in Algorithm 1. Some rules are left-out for the sake of brevity.

Datalog. Datalog is a declarative logic programming language that has its roots in the database field [5] and its general purpose is to serve as a query language for large, complex databases. Datalog programs run in polynomial time and are guaranteed to terminate. Conventional Datalog uses a Prolog-like notation, but with simpler semantics and without the data structures that Prolog provides. Its approach to resolve new facts is close to what dataflow algorithms do with arrangements of worklist algorithms. It strives a set-oriented approach which we require, rather than a goal-oriented approach as done in Prolog. A Datalog program consists of facts and rules which are represented as *Horn clauses* of the form: $P_0 : - P_1, \ldots, P_n$, where P_i is a literal of the form $p(x_1, \ldots, x_k)$ such that p is a predicate and the x_j are terms. The left-hand side of the clause is called *head*; the right-hand side is called *body*. A clause is true when each of its literals in the body are true.

Rules. Refer to Algorithm 1. The predicate VPtsTo stands for the points-to set of a variable. Rule ② specifies the following: Given an assignment from V2 to V1 at a specific address, include the points-to set of V2 into that of V1. Rule ⑤ specifies a case of derived pointers: Given a binary operation such that Res = V1 + V2, where V1 is a pointer, check if V2 is a constant. If the conditions hold, then Res points to a stack location with a stack pointer delta of SPD+Value. Variable Value is grounded by the third fact in the body of this rule. With rule ⑤ we deduce a new points-to set that corresponds to a new stack location, which in turn is again used to derive new points-to set information by the recursive chain of rules. This procedure is performed on all rules until the process saturates, i.e., a fixpoint is reached where we do not gain additional facts. Another rule that deserves attention is rule ⑥. Here points-to information is tracked into the context of the callee. The rule specifies that if a stack pointer is passed as a parameter, then a new points-to set is created for that parameter in the context of the callee. If, for example, a stack pointer is passed as an argument, then TranslateSPD in the body of the rule gives us its stack pointer delta value in the context of the callee. A new points-to set is created for this argument which is basically a new derived fact. This fact, in turn, falls into the recursive chain to serve for deducing new facts. The procedure provides an on-demand approach to track arguments of a function, only when they are passed by reference. We achieve context-sensitivity by introducing tags at each call sites. These tags are linked with the parameters. To illustrate the approach, let's assume that our analyzer runs over the following piece of code:

```
foo:                                    main:
0x8049000 mov eax, [esp+4]              ...
0x8049004 mov dword [eax], 0xff         0x80490f0: lea ebx, [esp-0x30]
0x804900a mov [eax+4], eax              0x80490f4: push ebx
                                        0x80490f5: call foo
```

At 0x80490f0–0x80490f4 a stack pointer is pushed onto the stack with a delta of -0x30 which resides in [esp+4] in the context of foo. As the result of the preprocessing step, we have Param and TranslateSPD facts extracted into our EDB (see Fig. 3). For this example, we have the facts Param([esp_17], 1, 0x80490f5, ''main'', [esp+4], ''foo''), and TranslateSPD(1, ''foo'', 4), where [esp_17] corresponds to the location the stack pointer is pushed to at 0x80490f4. Since we are dealing with a passed stack pointer, our analysis derives VptsTo([esp_17], -0x30, 0x80490f4. ''main''). By using rule ⑥, the points-to analysis can now deduce the fact VPtsTo([esp+4], 4, 0x8049000, ''foo''). Note that the pointer is now considered to have a delta of 4 in the *new context*. We do this to keep track of pointers that are parameters, otherwise we lose focus on where the pointer might *originate* from.

With rule ②, we get the connection to eax, and with rule ③, ④ the connection of [eax+4] to the underlying memory object, i.e., a pointer to itself. By Definition 1, we refer to [eax+4] as $(4, 4)$ since the base points to a location with delta 4 and we are accessing the location that is 4 bytes apart from the base.

3.3   Safe Zones

In this section we describe our approach to determine if a given stack read is safe. With *safe* we refer to the property that a read is covered by its definitions on all paths. Each basic block where a *safe* read occurs is considered a *safe basic block*. Since we are dealing with different memory objects, the set of safe basic blocks is different for each object/variable. More formally, we define it as follows.

Definition 2. *Let* $CFG = (V, E)$ *be the control flow graph,* S *the set of all stack variables, and let* $Defs = \{(spd, fld, bb_s) \mid bb_s \in V, (spd, fld) \in S\}$ *be the set of all stack accesses that define the stack location* (spd, fld) *at* bb_s. bb_s *is called a safe basic block. Each edge that originates from* bb_s *is called a safe edge with respect to* (spd, fld). *Each safe edge is a tuple of the form* (spd, fld, bb_s, bb_t) *with* $(bb_s, bb_t) \in E$. *The set of all safe basic blocks with respect to* (spd, fld) *is called the safe zone of* (spd, fld).

Apparently, if all incoming edges to a basic block are *safe edges* with respect to some variable (spd,fld) then that basic block is a *safe basic blocks* for that variable. To determine *safe zones* of each variable we proceed as sketched in Algorithm 2. An unsafe read occurs if a path exists that avoids the safe zone, i.e., a path from the entry of the function to the *use* location which does not go through safe edges. Lines 17–21 generalize this procedure for all stack accesses. If such a path does not exist, we flag the basic block as safe.

In its essence the algorithm does a reaching definition analysis for each stack variable and labels the basic blocks and edges accordingly. The initial process for building safe zones is achieved through lines 7–13. From each definition node with respect to the specific stack variable, the information about its definition is propagated further along its path in the control flow graph.

Each stack variable is associated with its own safe zone. Note that we do not use memory SSA as it introduces conflicts and complicates the points-to analysis. Hence, benefits of SSA in this manner are marginal.

```
1: Input: CFG = (V, E), Defs, Uses
2:        DOM (dominator sets)
3: Outputs: SafeZone, E (SafeEdges)
4: Let E' = SafeEdges = {}
5: Let SafeZone = Defs
6: Let Vars =          ⋃          (spd, fld)
              (spd,fld,bb) ∈ Defs ∪ Uses
7: for each (spd, fld, bb) ∈ SafeZone do
8:     E' = E' ∪ {(spd, fld, bb, bbₓ) | (bb, bbₓ) ∈ E}
9:     for each bb_d ∈ DOM(bb) do
10:        E' = E' ∪ {(spd, fld, bb_d, bbₓ) | (bb_d, bbₓ) ∈ E}
11:        SafeZone = SafeZone ∪ {(spd, fld, bb_d)}
12:    end for
13: end for
14: Let Unsafe = {}
15: for each (spd, fld, bb) ∈ Vars do
16:    if ∃p =< bb_{start}, . . . , bb_i, bb_j, . . . , bb > with
17:        (spd, fld, bb_i, bb_j) ∉ E', ∀bb_i, bb_j ∈ p, i ≠ j
18:        then Unsafe = Unsafe ∪ {(spd, fld, bb)}
19:        else SafeZone = SafeZone ∪ {(spd, fld, bb)}
20: end for
```

Algorithm 2. Sketch: Computation of Safe Zones

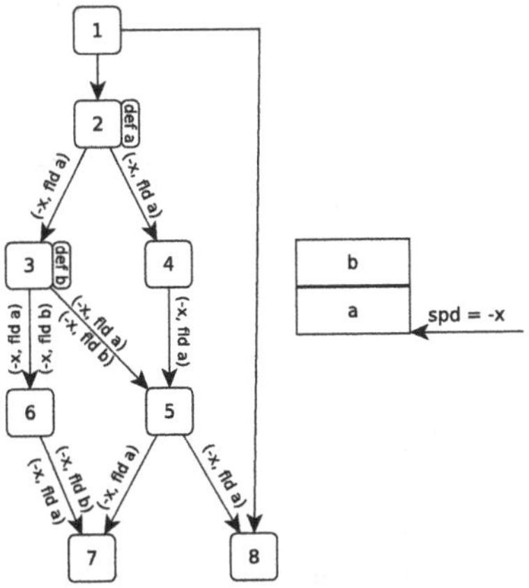

Fig. 4. Graphical representation of labeling safe edges.

Example 31. *Figure 4 illustrates the labeling of safe edges. Basic blocks 2 and 3 define variables a and b, respectively. Each use of the variable in these basic blocks is considered safe. Accordingly, each use of variable b in {3, 6} is considered safe. At a stack pointer delta of −x an access to variable a is possible. Its field/offset (fld a) is zero. For an access to variable b, fld b is added. Safe Zone with respect to (−x, fld a) consists of basic basic blocks {2, 3, 4, 6, 5, 7}. For (−x, fld b) we have {3, 6}. Each use of the variable in these basic blocks is considered safe.*

3.4 Interprocedural Flow Analysis

During the data flow analysis, we propagate state information that concerns the initialization of passed arguments between caller and callee. Information about pointers is passed back and forth by the points-to analysis. We use this information to determine indirect accesses (see rule ⑧, ⑨ in Algorithm 1). If a leaf node in the callee context is flagged *safe* with respect to a stack access, we flag the corresponding call sites as safe. This procedure propagates information back to the caller, extending the safe zone in the caller context. In turn, Algorithm 2 needs another run by using the new information and distinguish between unsafe and safe accesses to the stack. Previously unsafe accesses might turn to safe accesses through this process. This procedure is repeated until it saturates, i.e., no changes to the set of safe basic blocks.

Summaries: A common technique used in interprocedural static analysis is the use of summaries [37]. These summaries can be block summaries which gather the effects of a basic block, or function summaries that gather the effects of the whole function with respect to the variables of interest. Whenever a function call is encountered, these summaries are utilized and applied. The facts in Datalogs EDB and its deduced facts through rules in the IDB can be seen as such summaries. Whenever a function call is encountered, the analysis uses facts about the function that concern the variables of interest.

Multiple Analyses Plugins: As shown in Fig. 1, our design has a plugin mechanism. All plugins operate on the same knowledge base. Plugins deduce and incorporate knowledge into the knowledge base which can transparently be tapped by other plugins and library routines. This, for instance, allows the *Uninitialized Stack* plugin to operate on information deduced by the *Heap Allocators* plugin. Each plugin can be run in parallel and whenever new information enter the knowledge base, the plugins adapt to it. Each change to the knowledge base with respect to warnings and safe zones is monitored.

Detecting Uninitialized Accesses: When the analysis reaches its fixpoint, all information about safe and unsafe zones with respect to all stack accesses is present. A stack access outside its safe zone causes a warning. Additionally, we track each use to its origin, i.e., in the case of a stack pointer, we track it to the call site where the pointer originates from.

3.5   Symbolic Execution

For each warning, we need to check if a satisfiable path exists to the use of the variable by avoiding its safe zone. We therefore need a mechanism for path-sensitivity in our analysis process. To tackle path sensitivity, we utilize under-constrained symbolic execution [32]. Under-constrained symbolic execution immensely improves the scalability by checking each function directly, rather than the whole program. Due to the lack of context before the call of the function under analysis some register/memory values are unconstrained, hence the under-constrained term.

For each variable that caused a warning, we feed the symbolic execution engine with information about its safe zones. Satisfiability is checked from the function entry to the flagged variable by avoiding the basic blocks in its safe zone. We start at each origin, i.e., the function where the stack variable originates from. To improve the scalability of the symbolic execution, we initially skip each function call. If a path is satisfiable then we might have an overapproximation, since some skipped function might have made a constraint become unsatisfiable.

For unsatisfiable paths, we look at the *unsat-core*, i.e. those constraints which have caused the path become unsatisfiable. A function that alters one of these variables in those constraints is then set free to be processed by the engine; again in a similar fashion by first skipping calls in the new function context until we eventually reach a satisfiable state. The only difference is that we now force the engine to run into basic blocks that modify the variables that made our constraints become unsatisfiable. As a result, we basically overapproximate the set of satisfiable paths. Filtered warnings are removed as such in the knowledge base.

4   Implementation

Our prototype is implemented on top of the Amoco framework [44]. The decision for Amoco is favored due to its flexible IL. It allows us to extend its set of expressions. Each new expression transparently integrates and interplays with the standard set of expressions.

We retrieve the control-flow graph from the disassembler IDA Pro which is shown to be the most accurate [2]. Each basic block is transformed into an Amoco basic block. We extended Amoco to support SSA and implemented the algorithm proposed by Cytron et al. [15]. In particular, we adapted the concept of *collectors* that are described in Van Emmerik's work on decompilers [45]. Collectors can be seen as an instrumentation of the SSA algorithm. The algorithm proposed by Cytron et al. uses a stack of live definitions whenever a basic block is processed. This information is valuable to put into a knowledge base. For instance, we can instrument the algorithm to write a set of live definitions at call sites into our knowledge base which we use to translate SSA subscripted expressions back and forth between caller and callees. Due to SSA with respect to registers, we obtain partial flow sensitivity.

We built the symbolic execution on top of angr [38], a platform agnostic binary analysis framework. As Fig. 1 indicates, we plan to attach more engines to our framework. This is motivated by the fact that each engine comes with advantages and its shortcomings, which we hope to compensate by combining different engines. The points-to analysis results are saved into a separate database. If extensions are needed, we can reuse this database and let Datalog evaluate new facts based on the new extensions.

5   Evaluation

In this section, we evaluate the prototype implementation of our analysis framework and discuss empircal results. Note that the analysis framework is by design OS independent. Our analyses were performed on a machine running with Intel Xeon CPUs E5-2667@2.90GHZ and 128GB RAM. The programs presented in Tables 1 and 2 are compiled for *x86-64*. Our prototype is not limited to 64 bit, but also supports 32 bit binaries.

Table 1. Analysis results for the relevant CGC binaries that contain an uninitialized memory vulnerability.

Binary	Functions	Facts	Pointer facts	Stack accesses	Unique warnings
Hackman	70	46k	545	943	9
Accel	185	109k	2179	2057	33
TFTTP	58	30k	175	600	3
MCS	122	156k	860	2498	11
NOPE	105	57k	568	1378	8
Textsearch	90	50k	290	597	2
SSO	64	26k	204	650	4
BitBlaster	10	4k	42	95	1

5.1 CGC Test Corpus

As a first step to obtain a measurement on how our approach copes with realistic, real-world scenarios, we evaluated our prototype over a set of Cyber Grand Challenge (CGC) binaries which, in particular, contain a known uninitialized stack vulnerability. These CGC binaries are built to imitate real-world exploit scenarios and deliver enough complexity to stress out automated analysis frameworks. Patches of the vulnerabilities ease the effort to find the states of true positives and hence these binaries can serve as a ground truth for our evaluation. We picked those binaries from the whole CGC corpus that are documented to contain an uninitialized use of a stack variable as an exploit primitive and we evaluate our prototype with these eight binaries.

Table 1 shows our results for this CGC test setup. The third column of the table depicts the number of facts extracted from the binary building up the EDB. The fourth column shows the number of deduced pointer facts. The fifth column depicts the total number of stack accesses. The sixth column denotes the number of potential uninitialized stack variables grouped by their stack pointer delta value and their origin. This approach is similar to *fuzzy stack hashing* as proposed by Molnar et al. [31] to group together instances of the same bug.

For each of the eight binaries, we successfully detected the vulnerability. Each detected use of an uninitialized stack variable is registered, among which some might stem from the same origin. Therefore, we group those warnings by the stack pointer delta values of those stack variables from which they originate. The individual columns of Table 1 depict this process in numbers. We double-checked our results with the patched binaries to validate that our analysis process does not produce erroneous warnings for patched cases. For each patched binary, our analysis does not generate a warning for the vulnerabilities anymore.

Table 2. Analysis results for binutils-2.30, ImageMagick-6.0.8, gnuplot 5.2 patchlevel 4. Number in parentheses denotes the number of verified bugs.

Binary	Functions	Facts	Pointer facts	Stack accesses	Unique warnings
objdump	2.5k	>4M	>19k	23k	42 (2)
ar	2.4k	>3.2M	>16k	19k	24
as-new	2.2k	>2.9M	>9k	15k	29
gprof	2.3k	>3.8M	>16k	20k	34 (1)
cxxfilt	2.2k	>3.1M	>15k	18k	22
ld-new	2.8k	>3.8M	>16k	22k	15
strings	2.2k	>3.5M	>15k	19k	11
size	1.9k	>3.1M	>15k	19k	20
readelf	115	>107k	>5k	543	4
gnuplot	3k	>7.2M	>12k	23k	54 (2)
Image Magick	6.5k	>24M	>31k	150k	168 (2)

5.2 Real-World Binaries

Beyond the synthetic CGC test cases, we also applied our analysis framework on real-world binaries. Table 2 summarizes our results for *binutils gnuplot*, and *ImageMagick*. The values in parentheses are manually verified bugs. Note that the number of warnings pinpointing the root cause and the potential flaw through an uninitialized variable is comparatively *small* to the number of all accesses. Additionally, our symbolic execution filter was able to reduce the warning rate by a factor of eight in our experiments. Despite the false positive rates which we discuss in the next sections, we strongly believe that the output of our prototype is a valuable asset for an analyst and the time spent to investigate is worth the effort. The numbers are given in column 6 of Table 2. Overall, we found two recently reported vulnerabilities in *ImageMagick*, two previously unknown bugs in *objdump*, one unknown bug in *gprof*, and two bugs in *gnuplot*. A manual analysis revealed that the bugs in objdump and gprof are not security critical. The two bugs in gnuplot were fixed with the latest patchlevel at the time of writing.

Our analysis can also cope with complex programs such as web browsers, interpreters and even OS kernels in a platform-agnostic manner. We tested our framework on *MSHTML (Internet Explorer 8, CVE-2011-1346), Samba (CVE-2015-0240), ntoskrnl.exe (Windows kernel, CVE-2016-0040), PHP (CVE-2016-7480)*, and *Chakra (Microsoft Edge, CVE-2016-0191)*. In each case, we successfully detected the vulnerability in accordance to the CVE case.

Error Handling Code: Our study on hundreds of warnings shows that many warnings are internally handled by the programs itself through error handling code. To address this problem, we implemented a plugin that checks—starting from the corresponding call site—if a return value might go into a sanitization process. We track the dataflow into a jump condition and measure the distance to the leaf node. If it is smaller than a threshold value of 3, we assume that the return value is sanitized and handled. This simple procedure works surprisingly well in most cases to shift the focus away from paths that run into error handling code.

5.3 Heap Allocations

User space programs use a variation of `malloc` for allocating memory dynamically. Performance-critical applications like browsers even come with their own custom memory allocators. To enable tracking of dynamic memory objects, we use a list of known memory allocators and enriched the knowledge base with pointer information. The points-to analysis grabs this information and deduces new facts. As a consequence we can observe a coherence between stack locations and heap. While this is an experimental feature of our framework, it has proven itself valuable by pinpointing three uninitialized bugs in `gprof` and `objdump` which originate from the heap.

6 Discussion

The discovery of vulnerabilities for both the CGC binaries and real-world binaries demonstrates that our approach can successfully detect and pinpoint various kinds of uninitialized memory vulnerabilities. Our analysis is tailored to stack variables, with a design that is well-aligned with the intended purpose of a bug-detecting static analysis. However, it also comes with some limitations that are not currently tackled by our prototype and we discuss potential drawbacks of our approach in the following.

Heap: It is well known that analyzing the data flow on the heap is harder than data flow on the stack and in registers. To address this problem, for example Rinetzky and Sagiv proposed an approach to infer shape predicates for heap objects [36]. More recently, the topic of separation logic has garnered more attention as a general purpose shape analysis tool [34]. This is—among other reasons—due to the fact that aliasing analysis becomes much more difficult for real-world code that makes use of the heap as compared to the data flow that arises from stack usage. We account for all stack accesses under the reconstructed CFG. Hence, a stack variable which is initialized through a heap variable is supported by our approach. A points-to analysis needs to account for this interplay. Therefore, we implemented a component that adapts to the given set of points-to facts and tracks heap pointers originating from known heap allocators (see Sect. 5.3). This procedure is by design not sound, however the discovered bugs which originated from the heap were found by using this approach.

Many performance-critical applications like browsers have their own custom memory allocators which poses a problem to address. However, there is work on this field with promising results as shown in recent research done by Chen et al. [6,8].

False Positives/False Negatives: Many analyzers come with a set of strategies to deal with the number of warnings by, for instance, checking the feasibility of paths. Each strategy is usually tied to certain aspects of the problem, an approach which we adapted and discussed in the last sections to tackle false positives. However, we are dealing with many *undecidable* problems here, i.e., the perfect disassembly and the fact that detection of uninitialized variables itself is *undecidable* in general.

Aggressive compiler optimizations can also pose a burden on the disassembly process as they can facilitate the problem of unpredictable control flow. Even for a state-of-the-art tool like IDA Pro, control-flow analysis is hampered by unpredictability and indirect jumps. Points-to information can resolve some of these indirect jumps [16]. However, its demand for context sensitivity is expensive for large applications. Programs that contain recursion further restrict the capabilities of static analysis, as shown by Reps [33]. A combination with dynamic approaches might prove itself valuable and information derived by them can be incorporated into our knowledge base. Recall, that each change in the knowledge base is adapted transparently, i.e., facts are removed, added and deduced constantly by adding or removing information from it.

A valuable feature for any analyzer is the question of *soundness*. A fully sound analysis is hard to achieve in practice due to code that we cannot analyze (e.g., libraries which are not modeled or dynamically dispatched code where we might loose sight). A sound analysis needs a perfect disassembly resulting in a perfect CFG, which is an *undecidable* problem. Therefore, false negatives are not avoidable. Similar source code based systems use the term *soundiness* [26] as they can guarantee soundness for specific parts of the code under analysis only [29].

We strongly believe that if an analyzer finds enough errors to repay the cost of studying its output, then the analyzer will be a valuable and cost-effective instrument in practice.

7   Related Work

The development of methods for static analysis spans a wide variety of techniques. Modern compilers like the GNU-Compiler, MSVC, or Clang can report uninitialized variables during compile time. They utilize the underlying compiler framework to implement an intraprocedural analysis to detect potential uninitialized variables. As discussed earlier, compilers are trimmed to run fast, and the analysis time for costly interprocedural algorithms is not desired. For optimization purposes, the benefits of extensive interprocedural analyses might not be desirable to apply [35].

Flake was one of the first to discuss attacks against overlapping data [18], an attack vector closely related to our work on uninitialized memory reads. His presentation focuses on finding paths that have overlapping stack frames with a target (uninitialized) variable.

Wang et al. present case studies about undefined behavior [46] among which are induced by the use of uninitialized variables. In a more recent work, Lee et al.

introduce several methods to address undefined behavior in the LLVM compiler with a small performance overhead [25].

A popular attempt to tackle the problem of uninitialized memory reads is binary hardening. STACKARMOR [7] represents a hardening technique that is tailored to protect against stack-based vulnerabilities. To determine functions that might be prone to uninitialized reads, static analysis is used to identify stack locations which cannot proven to be safe. The system can protect against uninitialized reads but cannot detect them. SAFEINIT [30] extended this idea and represents a hardening technique specifically designed to mitigate uninitialized read vulnerabilities. The authors approach the problem from source code: based on Clang and LLVM, the general idea is to initialize all values on the allocations site of heaps and stacks. In order to keep the overhead low, several strategies are applied to identify suitable spots. They modify the compiler to insert their initialization procedures. By leveraging a multi-variant execution approach, uninitialized reads can be detected. This, however, needs a corpus of proper inputs that can trigger those spots. UNISAN [27] represents a similar approach to protect operating system kernels. Based on LLVM, the authors propose a compiler-based approach to eliminate information leaks caused by uninitialized data that utilizes dataflow analysis to trace execution paths that lead to possible leaking spots. UNISAN checks for allocations to be fully initialized when they leave the kernel space, and instruments the kernel in order to initialize allocations with zeros, if the check is violated.

Another recent approach by Lu et al. [28] targets uninitialized reads in the Linux kernel. They propose techniques for stack spraying to enforce an overlap of the sprayed data with uninitialized memory. With a combination of symbolic execution and fuzzing, they present a deterministic way to find execution paths which prepare data that overlaps with data of a vulnerability.

Giuffrida et al. [19] present a monitoring infrastructure to detect different kinds of vulnerabilities, among them uninitialized reads. They perform static analysis at compile time to index program state invariants and identify typed memory objects. The invariants represent safety constraints which are instrumented as metadata into the final binary. Their approach also allows to update and manage metadata dynamically. The proposed framework monitors the application in realtime and checks for invariant violations. Ye et al. propose a static value-flow analysis [47]. They analyze the source and construct a value flow graph which serves to deduce a measure of definedness for variables. The analysis results are used to optimize the instrumentation process of binaries.

Other systems which instrument binaries either at compile or execution time to detect uninitialized reads at runtime are proposed in the literature [3, 42]. These systems can be used in combination with a fuzzer or a test suite to detect uninitialized variables. One advantage of these dynamic systems is that for each detected uninitialized bug an input vector can be derived. On the other hand, only executed paths will be detected and hence the code coverage is typically low. In addition, an appropriate corpus of input data is needed. In contrast, our static approach is capable of analyzing binary executables in a scalable way that provides high code coverage.

In summary, the wealth of work in recent research, most of which rely on source code, is tailored to instrumentation purposes to aid dynamic analysis in a monitoring environment. In contrast, our approach follows a purely large-scale static analysis that addresses the proactive detection of bugs in binary executables.

8   Conclusion

Uninitialized memory reads in an application can be utilized by an attacker for a variety of possibilities, the typical use case being an information leak that allows an attacker to subsequently bypass information hiding schemes. In this paper, we proposed a novel static analysis approach to detect such vulnerabilities, with a focus on uninitialized stack variables. The modularity of our framework enables flexibility. We have built a prototype of the proposed approach that is capable of doing large-scale analyses to detect uninitialized memory reads in both synthetic examples as well as complex, real-world binaries. We believe that our system delivers new impulses to other researchers.

Acknowledgements. We thank the anonymous reviewers for their valuable feedback. This work was supported by the German Research Foundation (DFG) within the framework of the Excellence Strategy of the Federal Government and the States – EXC 2092 CaSa – 39078197. In addition, this work was supported by the European Research Council (ERC) under the European Union's Horizon 2020 research and innovation programme (ERC Starting Grant No. 640110 (BASTION)).

References

1. Andersen, L.O.: Program analysis and specialization for the C programming language. Ph.D. thesis (1994)
2. Andriesse, D., Chen, X., van der Veen, V., Slowinska, A., Bos, H.: An in-depth analysis of disassembly on full-scale x86/x64 binaries. In: USENIX Security Symposium (2016)
3. Bruening, D., Zhao, Q.: Practical memory checking with Dr. Memory. In: Proceedings of the 9th Annual IEEE/ACM International Symposium on Code Generation and Optimization (2011)
4. Budd, C.: Pwn2Own: Day 2 and Event Wrap-Up, March 2016. http://blog.trendmicro.com/pwn2own-day-2-event-wrap/
5. Ceri, S., Gottlob, G., Tanca, L.: What you always wanted to know about datalog (and never dared to ask). IEEE Trans. Knowl. Data Eng. 1(1), 146–166 (1989)
6. Chen, X., Slowinska, A., Bos, H.: Who allocated my memory? Detecting custom memory allocators in c binaries. In: 2013 20th Working Conference on Reverse Engineering (WCRE) (2013)
7. Chen, X., Slowinska, A., Andriesse, D., Bos, H., Giuffrida, C.: StackArmor: comprehensive protection from stack-based memory error vulnerabilities for binaries. In: Symposium on Network and Distributed System Security (NDSS) (2015)

8. Chen, X., Slowinska, A., Bos, H.: On the detection of custom memory allocators in c binaries. Empirical Softw. Eng. **21**(3), 753–777 (2016)
9. CVE-2012-1889: Vulnerability in microsoft xml core services. http://www.cve.mitre.org/cgi-bin/cvename.cgi?name=cve-2012-1889
10. CVE-2014-6355: Graphics component information disclosure vulnerability. http://www.cve.mitre.org/cgi-bin/cvename.cgi?name=CVE-2014-6355
11. CVE-2015-0061: Tiff processing information disclosure vulnerability. http://www.cve.mitre.org/cgi-bin/cvename.cgi?name=CVE-2015-0061
12. CVE-Statistics-Chrome: Google Chrome Vulnerability Statistics (2014). http://www.cvedetails.com/product/15031/Google-Chrome.html
13. CVE-Statistics-Firefox: Mozilla Firefox Vulnerability Statistics (2014). http://www.cvedetails.com/product/3264/Mozilla-Firefox.html
14. CVE-Statistics-IE: Microsoft Internet Explorer Vulnerability Statistics (2014). http://www.cvedetails.com/product/9900/Microsoft-Internet-Explorer.html
15. Cytron, R., Ferrante, J., Rosen, B.K., Wegman, M.N., Zadeck, F.K.: Efficiently computing static single assignment form and the control dependence graph. ACM Trans. Program. Lang. Syst. (TOPLAS) **13**(4), 451–490 (1991)
16. Evans, I., et al.: Control jujutsu: on the weaknesses of fine-grained control flow integrity. In: ACM Conference on Computer and Communications Security (CCS) (2015)
17. Fehnker, A., Huuck, R., Jayet, P., Lussenburg, M., Rauch, F.: Goanna—a static model checker. In: Brim, L., Haverkort, B., Leucker, M., van de Pol, J. (eds.) FMICS 2006. LNCS, vol. 4346, pp. 297–300. Springer, Heidelberg (2007). https://doi.org/10.1007/978-3-540-70952-7_20
18. Flake, H.: Attacks on uninitialized local variables (2006)
19. Giuffrida, C., Cavallaro, L., Tanenbaum, A.S.: Practical automated vulnerability monitoring using program state invariants. In: Conference on Dependable Systems and Networks (DSN) (2013)
20. Haller, I., Slowinska, A., Bos, H.: MemPick: data structure detection in C/C++ binaries. In: Proceedings of the 20th Working Conference on Reverse Engineering (WCRE) (2013)
21. Hariri, A.A.: VMware Exploitation through Uninitialized Buffers, March 2018. https://www.thezdi.com/blog/2018/3/1/vmware-exploitation-through-uninitialized-buffers
22. Horwitz, S., Reps, T., Sagiv, M.: Demand interprocedural dataflow analysis, vol. 20. ACM (1995)
23. Jin, W., et al.: Recovering C++ objects from binaries using inter-procedural data-flow analysis. In: Proceedings of ACM SIGPLAN on Program Protection and Reverse Engineering Workshop 2014 (2014)
24. Khurshid, S., PǍsǍreanu, C.S., Visser, W.: Generalized symbolic execution for model checking and testing. In: Garavel, H., Hatcliff, J. (eds.) TACAS 2003. LNCS, vol. 2619, pp. 553–568. Springer, Heidelberg (2003). https://doi.org/10.1007/3-540-36577-X_40
25. Lee, J., et al.: Taming undefined behavior in LLVM. In: ACM SIGPLAN Conference on Programming Language Design and Implementation (PLDI) (2017)
26. Livshits, B., et al.: In defense of soundiness: a manifesto. Commun. ACM **58**(2), 44–46 (2015)
27. Lu, K., Song, C., Kim, T., Lee, W.: Unisan: proactive kernel memory initialization to eliminate data leakages. In: ACM Conference on Computer and Communications Security (CCS) (2016)

28. Lu, K., Walter, M.T., Pfaff, D., Nürnberger, S., Lee, W., Backes, M.: Unleashing use-before-initialization vulnerabilities in the Linux kernel using targeted stack spraying. In: Symposium on Network and Distributed System Security (NDSS) (2017)

29. Machiry, A., Spensky, C., Corina, J., Stephens, N., Kruegel, C., Vigna, G.: DR. CHECKER: a soundy analysis for Linux kernel drivers. In: USENIX Security Symposium (2017)

30. Milburn, A., Bos, H., Giuffrida, C.: SafeInit: comprehensive and practical mitigation of uninitialized read vulnerabilities. In: Symposium on Network and Distributed System Security (NDSS) (2017)

31. Molnar, D., Li, X.C., Wagner, D.A.: Dynamic test generation to find integer bugs in x86 binary Linux programs. In: USENIX Security Symposium (2009)

32. Ramos, D.A., Engler, D.: Under-constrained symbolic execution: Correctness checking for real code. In: USENIX Security Symposium (2015)

33. Reps, T.: Undecidability of context-sensitive data-dependence analysis. ACM Trans. Program. Lang. Syst. 22(1), 162–186 (2000)

34. Reynolds, J.C.: Separation logic: a logic for shared mutable data structures. In: Proceedings of the 17th Annual IEEE Symposium on Logic in Computer Science, pp. 55–74. IEEE (2002)

35. Richardson, S., Ganapathi, M.: Interprocedural analysis useless for code optimization. Technical report, Stanford, CA, USA (1987)

36. Rinetzky, N., Sagiv, M.: Interprocedural shape analysis for recursive programs. In: Wilhelm, R. (ed.) CC 2001. LNCS, vol. 2027, pp. 133–149. Springer, Heidelberg (2001). https://doi.org/10.1007/3-540-45306-7_10

37. Sharir, M., Pnueli, A.: Two approaches to interprocedural data flow analysis. Computer Science Department, New York University, New York, NY (1978)

38. Shoshitaishvili, Y., et al.: SOK: (state of) the art of war: offensive techniques in binary analysis. In: IEEE Symposium on Security and Privacy (2016)

39. Slowinska, A., Stancescu, T., Bos, H.: Howard: a dynamic excavator for reverse engineering data structures. In: Symposium on Network and Distributed System Security (NDSS), San Diego, CA (2011)

40. Smaragdakis, Y., Balatsouras, G.: Pointer analysis. Found. Trends Program. Lang. 2(1), 1–69 (2015)

41. Smaragdakis, Y., Bravenboer, M.: Using datalog for fast and easy program analysis. In: de Moor, O., Gottlob, G., Furche, T., Sellers, A. (eds.) Datalog 2.0 2010. LNCS, vol. 6702, pp. 245–251. Springer, Heidelberg (2011). https://doi.org/10.1007/978-3-642-24206-9_14

42. Stepanov, E., Serebryany, K.: MemorySanitizer: fast detector of uninitialized memory use in C++. In: 2015 IEEE/ACM International Symposium on Code Generation and Optimization (CGO) (2015)

43. Szekeres, L., Payer, M., Wei, T., Song, D.: SoK: eternal war in memory. In: IEEE Symposium on Security and Privacy (2013)

44. Tillequin, A.: Amoco (2016). https://github.com/bdcht/amoco

45. Van Emmerik, M.J.: Static single assignment for decompilation. Ph.D. thesis, The University of Queensland (2007)

46. Wang, X., Chen, H., Cheung, A., Jia, Z., Zeldovich, N., Kaashoek, M.F.: Undefined behavior: what happened to my code? In: Proceedings of the Asia-Pacific Workshop on Systems (2012)

47. Ye, D., Sui, Y., Xue, J.: Accelerating dynamic detection of uses of undefined values with static value-flow analysis. In: Proceedings of Annual IEEE/ACM International Symposium on Code Generation and Optimization (2014)

Towards Automated Application-Specific Software Stacks

Nicolai Davidsson[1], Andre Pawlowski[2(⊠)], and Thorsten Holz[2]

[1] Google, Zürich, Switzerland
ndavidsson@google.com
[2] Horst Görtz Institute (HGI), Ruhr-Universität Bochum, Bochum, Germany
{andre.pawlowski,thorsten.holz}@rub.de

Abstract. Software complexity has increased over the years. One common way to tackle this complexity during development is to encapsulate features into a shared library. This allows developers to reuse already implemented features instead of reimplementing them over and over again. However, not all features provided by a shared library are actually used by an application. As a result, an application using shared libraries loads unused code into memory, which an attacker can use to perform code-reuse and similar types of attacks. The same holds for applications written in a scripting language such as PHP or Ruby: The interpreter typically offers much more functionality than is actually required by the application and hence provides a larger overall attack surface.

In this paper, we tackle this problem and propose a first step towards automated application-specific software stacks. We present a compiler extension capable of removing unneeded code from shared libraries and—with the help of domain knowledge—also capable of removing unused functionalities from an interpreter's code base during the compilation process. Our evaluation against a diverse set of real-world applications, among others *Nginx*, *Lighttpd*, and the PHP interpreter, removes on average 71.3% of the code in *musl-libc*, a popular libc implementation. The evaluation on web applications show that a tailored PHP interpreter can mitigate entire vulnerability classes, as is the case for *OpenConf*. We demonstrate the applicability of our debloating approach by creating an application-specific software stack for a Wordpress web application: we tailor the libc library to the Nginx web server and PHP interpreter, whereas the PHP interpreter is tailored to the Wordpress web application. In this real-world scenario, the code of the libc is decreased by 65.1% in total, thereby reducing the available code for code-reuse attacks.

1 Introduction

To reduce complexity of software and provide low-level features in a consistent manner, the concept of shared libraries was developed. This gives developers the possibility to focus solely on the user-facing application rather than re-implementing common functionality such as memory management or string processing functions over and over again. However, since not all code of a given

K. Sako et al. (Eds.): ESORICS 2019, LNCS 11736, pp. 88–109, 2019.
https://doi.org/10.1007/978-3-030-29962-0_5

shared library is used in a given program, the downside of this concept is that unnecessary code is loaded into memory: a recent study finds that only 5% of the *libc*, the standard library for the C programming language, is used on average across 2,016 applications of the Ubuntu Desktop environment [32].

From an attacker's perspective, the typical way to exploit an existing vulnerability is to reuse existing code (e. g., ret2libc [39] or return-oriented programming [35] (ROP)) to execute shellcode and bypass existing mitigation systems such as W⊕R and address space layout randomization (ASLR). Since shared libraries offer a plethora of (mostly) unused code, the attacker has a large variety of existing functions or code parts to choose from. The same holds for applications written in interpreted languages, such as PHP, Python, or Ruby: the interpreter is a complex piece of software and offers more functionality than the application actually requires [31]. Hence, an attacker that is able to inject her own script code into the application can leverage these provided but unused methods to execute her exploit.

One way to remove the unused code of a shared library is to statically link it against the target application. This allows the linker to remove the unnecessary code and thus reduce the availability of code snippets an attacker can choose from for a code-reuse attack. However, this increases the complexity in managing software updates: since each application has to be compiled statically linked with all used libraries, each has to be updated when a vulnerability is found in the code of *any* used library. To tackle this problem, Quach et al. [32] presented the concept of *piece-wise compilation and loading*. It allows to compile an application and shared libraries with additional metadata to have a customized loader only load the needed code into memory. Unfortunately, the concept of this approach only works with shared libraries and does not apply to applications written in interpreted languages.

In this paper, we present a first step towards *automatic application-specific software stacks*. Our goal is to customize the software stack for a given application (e. g., a web application or server application) such that only the actually required library code and underlying execution environment is contained within the software stack, hence *debloating* the software stack. To achieve this goal, we introduce a compiler extension capable of removing unused code from shared libraries, written in C. With information about which exported functions the target application uses, the compiler pass can omit functions at compile time from the shared library that are not used by the application or library itself. As a result, a shared library specifically tailored to the target application is created. To enhance usability, our approach is able to create shared libraries that are tailored to more than one application (e. g., a script interpreter and a web server). In contrast to a statically linked library, tailoring to a group of applications provides the same flexibility as a dynamically shared library given that only the shared library has to be re-compiled if a vulnerability in its code was discovered. When deployed with other existing defenses, such as Control-Flow Integrity (CFI) [11], an application-specific software stack further restricts the wiggle room an attacker can exploit to perform a successful attack.

Moreover, we show that—with the help of domain knowledge—this approach is also capable of removing unused functionalities in script interpreters when targeting an application written in an interpreted language (such as PHP or Ruby). Consider for example a Wordpress installation. With our approach, a PHP interpreter can be tailored to the concrete Wordpress web application. Since all unused functionalities are removed from the interpreter, an attacker that is able to inject script code (e. g., by uploading a script file) is no longer able to leverage them for their attack. Moreover, instead of removing unused functionalities in the interpreter, our approach allows to replace them with *booby traps* [16], i. e., dormant code that when executed triggers an alarm. This way, an ongoing attack can be detected when a functionality that was removed is executed. Note that the Wordpress-specific PHP interpreter and the web server can be compiled with our debloating approach for libraries, leading to an application-specific software stack. Regarding the recent trend to separate services into container (such as Docker [1]) to provide a better security in case of a vulnerability, this makes tailoring shared libraries to specific server applications real-world deployable.

An application-specific script interpreter also allows to reduce the attack surface significantly in environments in which untrusted scripts are executed (such as Google App Engine [4]). Normally, unwanted functionalities are disabled in configuration files. However, since the code that provides these functionalities is still available in the script interpreter, an attacker might be able to bypass the restrictions and escape the interpreter's internal sandbox [29]. When compiling the script interpreter in an application-specific way, the code for the unneeded functionalities are completely removed, which prevents an attacker from using them entirely.

We evaluated our prototype compiler pass for LLVM by tailoring two libc implementations (*musl-libc* and *uClibc*) to a diverse set of applications. The results show that on average the code for the *musl-libc* tailored to an application is reduced by 71.3%. A previous study on libc utilization [32] concluded that only 5% of code on average is used in the library. However, their evaluation set consists of mostly small applications, which explains the significant difference in comparison to our results. Additionally, we show that by using domain knowledge, our prototype is able to mitigate possible attacks on web applications: starting from *seven* security-critical PHP functions that might be used for *remote command execution* (according to the RIPS code analyzer [7]) in the interpreter, a PHP interpreter tailored to *OpenConf* or *FluxBB* only contains *one* sensitive PHP function. This significantly raises the bar for an attacker able to execute own PHP code since using a removed PHP functionality triggers a booby trap and hence raises an alarm. In fact, in case of *OpenConf*, our approach removes the possibility to execute shell commands from the interpreter in most system configurations due to the nature of the remaining sensitive PHP function. Additionally, we show the real-world applicability of our approach by creating a Docker container consisting of an application-specific software stack for a *Wordpress* installation. Our evaluation shows that the code of the libc used by the web server and PHP interpreter in this container is reduced by 65.1% in total, hence demonstrating that our debloating approach removes a signification fraction of unused code.

Contributions. In summary, we provide the following contributions:

- We present the design and implementation of an LLVM compiler pass capable of removing unused code from shared libraries and script interpreters written in C that effectively reduces the available code snippets for reuse attacks by debloating the software stack used by a given application.
- Our evaluation shows that on average 71.3% of the code in the *musl-libc* is removed when tailoring it to a target application. Moreover, when applying our approach to the PHP interpreter by targeting specific web applications, it is capable of eliminating entire vulnerability classes, such as *command execution*.

To foster research on this topic, we release the code of our LLVM compiler pass as open-source software under https://github.com/RUB-SysSec/ASSS.

2   Background

Shared libraries offer developers a way to reuse already implemented functionalities in their program. These functionalities can either be *code* in the form of functions or *data* (e.g., global variables). For example, libc provides the developer with a variety of low-level functionalities (e.g., memory allocation and string processing). During compilation, there are two ways to couple the external functionalities with the own application: *static linking* and *dynamic linking*. In case of static linking, the external functionalities are resolved and plainly copied into the application during compilation. This means that no shared library is needed to execute the application since all library-provided functionalities are part of the program itself and hence available in memory. In case of dynamic linking, the external functionalities are replaced with a symbol which is resolved during the execution of the program. Hence, the shared libraries that provide the functionalities have to be present in memory to execute the application.

In practice, dynamic linking is used in most deployment scenarios. This allows the system to use the same shared library for multiple applications. Furthermore, having only one copy of the shared library improves usability during software patching: if a vulnerability is found in a function offered by a shared library, the user only needs to update the corresponding shared library. Since all dependent applications use this shared library, the vulnerability is fixed for all of them. In case of static linking, all applications using this functionality have to be updated to fix the vulnerability. As explained earlier, the main downside of using dynamic linking is the fact that this approach increases the amount of unused code that is mapped into the memory of the application. Therefore, sensible operations in functionalities not used by the application itself are also present in memory.

3 High-Level Overview

The idea behind application-specific software stacks is based on the observation
that applications do not use every functionality provided by their underlying
software stack (e. g., interpreters or libraries). Therefore, it is safe to remove
code of these unused functionalities to debloat the application without affecting
it. Furthermore, by removing code snippets or whole functions that can potentially be used by an attacker in code-reuse attacks narrows down the options
an attacker has. This also holds for scripting languages, for example, in a web
application context: the script interpreter offers more functionality than the web
application uses. Stripping the interpreter from these functionalities debloats the
interpreter, but does not interfere with the given web application. Moreover, in
cases an attacker is able to insert her own script code (e. g., by uploading a script
file to a web server), she is limited in the interpreter functionalities she can use.

    We define two layers for a software stack: the *application layer* and the *sup-
port layer*. The application itself resides on the application layer. This can either
be a native code application or an application written in an interpreted language
(e. g., web application). In a web application context, the application layer also
includes the web framework the application uses. The libraries and script interpreter are located on the support layer. This layer provides functionalities that
are used by the application. However, it also contains additional code and functionalities that are not used by the application. Underneath the support layer
resides the operating system (OS). Functionalities provided by the OS are usually accessed via the support layer through low-level libraries such as the libc.

    Our goal is to debloat the software stack by removing unneeded code from the
support layer. This is done by analyzing the application and retrieving control
transfers from the application layer into the support layer. This information is
then used to recompile the support layer without the unused code. The result
is a software stack tailored to the application. However, this approach is not
limited to tailoring the support layer to only one application, thus increasing its
usability. Consider for example a Wordpress installation. The libraries used by
the web server and PHP interpreter can be specifically tailored to support both.
Moreover, the PHP interpreter can be customized to only contain functionalities
used by Wordpress. Hence, the debloating is achieved throughout the whole
software stack by preserving the usability of shared libraries.

    In the case of native code applications, the same code reduction can be
achieved by using static linking during the compilation and linking process. As
a result, the functionalities provided by the libraries and used by the application are directly inserted into the code of the program. This moves part of the
support layer directly into the application layer. However, this also means that
the advantages of sharing libraries between multiple applications are also lost.
As a result, as soon as a vulnerability is discovered in a library functionality,
all applications using this library have to be updated. Application-specific software stacks, on the other hand, still provide the advantages of shared libraries.
It is possible to group different applications to use one shared library tailored

to them (as in our example a web server and script interpreter). Hence, our approach offers a middle ground between code reduction and usability.

4   Approach

In this section, we describe our approach for application-specific software stacks. We start by describing the basic method of our LLVM pass and refining it step-by-step throughout this section until each challenge encountered is tackled. The final goal in this paper is to create a Wordpress installation with a tailored PHP interpreter and a libc implementation application-specific to the interpreter and web server. Hence, the described method focuses only on tailoring the libraries to a target application first. Afterwards, domain knowledge is used to enhance our approach to also support specific script interpreters. However, due to space constraints we only describe the modifications to support the PHP interpreter and refer to our Technical Report [19] for the modifications made to support the Ruby interpreter and to see the full algorithm.

4.1   Libraries

The control-flow transfer from the application layer into the support layer can be performed in multiple ways. In the easiest form, it is a direct call of a function. However, more complicated constructs such as indirect calls via function pointers are also possible. An analysis tailoring libraries to a specific application at compile time must not miss any of these, since one missing functionality leads to an uncompilable library in the best case, and a broken application in the worst. Next, we describe a method for LLVM capable of handling all these cases.

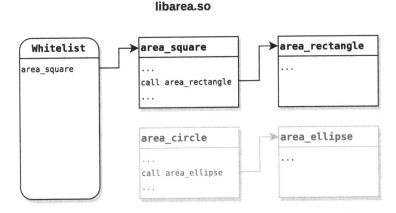

Fig. 1. Example of the basic idea of the analysis. A target application uses the function area_square. Hence, the function area_rectangle is also added to the whitelist.

Base Method. We start with a whitelist of functions, which initially contains all exported functions of the library used by the target application. The exported functions can be obtained by reading the metadata of the target application (e. g., with the help of the binutils tool `readelf`). Consider the example shown in Fig. 1. The target application uses the function `area_square` of the library. During compilation, each currently processed function is checked if it resides in the whitelist. If the function `area_square` is processed, all direct control-flow transfers are also explored. Each new function that is reachable by the direct control-flow transfer is added to the whitelist and further explored. In this example, the function `area_rectangle` is added to the whitelist. This phase of searching for new reachable functions is called *function exploration*. Since this phase uses a depth-first search (DFS) approach, it is guaranteed to visit all functions that are reachable by an initial given function. Hence, all functions in the whitelist after the analysis is finished are necessary for the application to work. All other functions can be safely removed. In the given example, `area_circle` and `area_ellipse` are dismissed.

Indirect Control-Flow Transfers. Unfortunately, the compiler cannot always determine the target of a control-flow transfer. Often control-flow transfers are handled with the help of function pointers, i. e., through indirect call instructions. Therefore, we have to consider them during our analysis. Hence, we have to extend our approach to work with instructions handling function pointers. We found that the following LLVM intermediate representation (IR) instructions are capable of handling function pointers:

- `store`: storing data in a variable.
- `return`: returning data at the end of a function.
- `select`: chooses between two distinct values depending on a boolean condition.
- `phi`: merging multiple variables into a single variable for Single Static Assignment (SSA) form [17].

Since all these instructions can work with a function pointer, our analysis has to be able to process them. Therefore, we extend the *function exploration* phase to extract the data handled by these instructions to find all indirect control-flow transfers. If the extracted data is a function pointer, we continue the exploration at the pointer target.

This refined method handles all possible function pointers that are set inside the used code. However, since the semantics of the code are not considered, this analysis can overestimate the actually used functions. Consider for example a `select` instruction that chooses between two function pointers. When the boolean condition evaluates always to true, then only one function is ever reached by this code construct. Yet, our analysis considers both functions as reachable and thus overestimates the actually used functions. Note that this conservative overestimation guarantees us to not break the application.

Global Variables. Although function pointers set directly in the code are already handled by our analysis, function pointers can also reside in global variables. Since the current form of our analysis is not able to find these function pointers in global variables, a valid call using a function pointer from a global variable would break the application. To handle global variables, we add a *global exploration* phase to our analysis. In this phase, all global variables are processed and checked for function pointers. If they contain a function pointer, the target is added to the whitelist as well. The *global exploration* phase is executed before the *function exploration* phase to guarantee that the newly whitelisted functions are also explored.

A discussion about limitations of our function pointer analysis is given in Sect. 7.

4.2   Script Interpreters

Often applications written in scripting languages like PHP, Ruby, or Python are not translated into native code, but interpreted by the corresponding script interpreter. As a result, the interpreter itself is a part of the support layer for these applications. However, in contrast to the method described in Sect. 4.1 for native code libraries, the analysis cannot just remove code from the interpreter since it cannot distinguish which code belongs to a certain interpreter functionality. Hence, to build an application-specific interpreter, our analysis has to leverage domain knowledge about the internals of the target interpreter. More specifically, the analysis has to know the mapping of script functions to native code functions. To achieve our goal of running a Wordpress installation with an application-specific interpreter, we modify our analysis to work with the PHP interpreter in the following. We refer to our Technical Report [19] for modifications on our analysis to work with the Ruby interpreter.

PHP stores information for each registered PHP function in global *function entries*, which are basically a map of structs [8]. The structs contain, among others, the pointer to the native code function and the name of the PHP function. During execution, they are used to handle the transition from PHP to native code. The interpreter uses these function entries to look up the native code function that is eventually executed to perform the application's desired functionality. Hence, modifying these function entries during the compilation of the PHP interpreter to remove the code from it is the best way to keep our approach as generic as possible. Since the function entries are part of the architecture of PHP, they are less likely to change between different PHP versions and hence our approach should be compatible with upcoming PHP releases.

To enable our analysis to remove PHP functionalities from the interpreter at compile time, we introduce a whitelist of PHP functions and modify the *global exploration* phase. The modification extracts the PHP function names from the PHP global *function entries* and checks if they are on the PHP whitelist. If they are, the corresponding native function is stored for processing during the *function exploration* phase. As a result, the native code corresponding to the functionality only remains in the interpreter when it is on the PHP whitelist.

PHP supports the paradigm of object-oriented programming, i. e., functions can be associated to classes. An example of a class and its member function directly provided by the PHP interpreter is the `Directory` class and its function `read` [3]. However, the PHP function name does not contain any information about the associated class. Hence, if multiple classes register a PHP function with the same name, our analysis is not able to distinguish between them. Consider an example where classes `A` and `B` both register a function with the name `read`. If the application only uses `A::read`, our analysis will still whitelist the `read` function of both classes. This loss in precision results in the PHP interpreter still containing functionality that is not needed, however, it guarantees to not break the application.

5 Implementation

Our prototype implementation resides inside the compiler itself since it has to be able to modify the code and data structures directly (e. g., for the PHP interpreter). Hence, to build a tailored software stack for a given software, the whole support layer has to be re-compiled using our compiler pass. The support layer consists of the libraries (and script interpreter) of the target application, and all libraries used by the libraries. Eventually, an application-specific software stack is created for the given software. For native code applications, the used exported functions have to be extracted as initial information for the compiler pass (e. g., with the help of the binutils tool `readelf`). For applications using script languages, the analysis to get all used interpreter functionalities has to be done by external tools like Parse [6] for PHP.

We built the prototype of our approach as compiler pass for LLVM 5.0.1. In total, our implementation consists of around 1,000 lines of C++ and 100 lines of Python code. To prevent possible dependency issues, each created module by LLVM is merged into one. This gives our compiler pass a global view of all existing code and data. Since our pass works on the LLVM IR, it is completely architecture and platform independent. Hence, each architecture that is supported by LLVM is also supported by our approach (e. g., ARM or MIPS).

To integrate it into the build process of an application as seamlessly as possible, we created a compiler wrapper script. This script is used as compiler for the application and handles all steps needed to perform our analysis.

A detailed discussion on limitations of our approach is given in Sect. 7.

5.1 Manual Configuration

Although our approach aims to automate the process in creating an application-specific software stack, a user might want to preserve certain functionality in the libraries. This can have various reasons, e. g., using the same library by multiple applications. Hence, the user is able to modify the configuration file for the library and add additional function names to the whitelist. Furthermore, a library could need an additional whitelisted function which is not referenced directly from the application. This is the case for C entry functions (e. g., `_start`) which are directly called by the loader during load time.

Since LLVM does not lift assembly instructions into its IR, control-flow transfers to functions done in assembly are not detected by our analysis. We encountered five such cases in which assembly instructions in the code call a function not referenced in the rest of the code base (three in *musl-libc* and two in *uClibc*). Since we did not encounter any cases outside of the libc, we believe such cases more common in libraries providing low-level functionalities such as memory management and hence an exception.

Another case for manual configuration are functions that are resolved dynamically via loader functionalities such as `dlsym`. Since these functions do not have a reference in the code (either a direct reference or an indirect via a function pointer), our current prototype is not able to detect them. However, since we only encountered one case of dynamically resolved functions during our evaluation (`__dls3` in *musl-libc*), we believe this feature to be rarely used in practice. Furthermore, this function was not resolved by loader functionalities, but by a self-implemented version of `dlsym` inside the *musl-libc*. This shows further how difficult it is to fully automate the process of creating an application-specific software stack and the reason for allowing manual configuration. A detailed discussion on how to address these cases in an automated way is given in Sect. 7.

5.2   Booby Trapping Script Interpreters

Most scripting languages offer ways to list all registered functions. An attacker able to execute script commands is therefore able to use this functionality as information leak to circumvent removed functionality. For example, the PHP function `get_defined_functions` returns all functions registered to the interpreter. To thwart these attempts, our approach is not only able to remove functionality from the script interpreter, but to replace its native code implementation with a booby trap [16]. A booby trap contains code that when executed warns from an attack. Since this code lies dormant in memory and is never executed by the benign application, an execution of this code detects an altered control flow and hence an ongoing attack. When the native code implementation of a script function is replaced by this code, an attacker executing interpreter functionality that is not used by the application otherwise is detected. Furthermore, this removes any leak regarding the information about functions registered to the interpreter. If the attacker does not have access to the source code of the application (e. g., a proprietary application), this removes the possibility to circumvent booby traps.

6   Evaluation

As a target for our applications, we use Linux on the Intel x86-64 architecture because of its popularity as a server system. In this section, we first evaluate the effect of an application-specific software stack on the used shared libraries, afterwards a PHP interpreter tailored to specific web applications is measured. Subsequently, we study the code reduction of our approach on our running example: an application-specific software stack for a Wordpress installation. Finally, we perform a security evaluation of our approach on the basis of several CVEs and discuss the performance overhead.

6.1   Libraries

To evaluate the effect of our approach on native code applications, we compile different libc versions as an application-specific software stack. Unfortunately, the most common implementation *glibc* is written in GNU C, an extension of the C programming language which is not supported by LLVM [28]. Therefore, we resort to two other popular libc implementations: *musl-libc* (1.1.18) and *uClibc* (0.9.34). The *musl-libc* focuses on speed, feature-completeness, and simplicity [5]. It is used, for instance, by the Alpine Linux distribution, which is the distribution used for official Docker containers [15]. The *uClibc* implementation targets microcontrollers and therefore focuses mainly on size [10] (e. g., it is used by the buildroot project [2]). We compile both libc implementations without any changes by our transformation to have a complete shared library to compare against as an upper boundary. As a lower boundary, we compile both implementations using our approach with a minimal configuration which contains the least amount of functions necessary in the initial whitelist to compile the library (5 functions for *musl-libc* and 12 functions for *uClibc*).

To show the effect of an application-specific shared library, we compile the libc implementation for different applications: *Micro-Lisp*, *Nginx* (1.13.8), *Lighttpd* (1.4.48), *Busybox* (1.28), *PHP* (7.3.0-dev) for different web applications, and *Miniruby* (2.6.0-dev). To have a small basic PHP interpreter that supports all base features of our used web applications, we enabled support for Mysqli and zlib and disabled support for XML, iconv, PEAR, and DOM. Additionally, the PHP interpreter is also compiled in a minimal configuration (the least amount of functions necessary to run it) and in a complete configuration to better show the impact of an application-specific library. The *Ruby* interpreter has the option to build a smaller version of itself called *Miniruby*. This interpreter only contains the core functionalities (YARV instruction set [34]) of the *Ruby* interpreter. Since the difference between a complete *Miniruby* interpreter and a minimal *Miniruby* are smaller, it is more suited to show the impact of our approach than the full-fledged *Ruby* interpreter. For *Busybox*, we had to disable the coreutil functionalities: `date`, `echo`, `ls`, `mknod`, `mktemp`, `nl`, `stat`, `sync`, `test` and `usleep`. We were not able to compile *uClibc* with LLVM when these features were activated because of the dependency on buildroot. Hence, we had to modify the toolchain for *uClibc* to work without buildroot.

Code Reduction. Table 1 depicts the results of our measurements. As evident from the table, the complete *musl-libc* has 2,603 functions, whereas a minimal configuration only needs 358 functions (13.8%) to be compilable. These configurations provide an upper and lower boundary of the code reduction that

Table 1. Results of the remaining code for *musl-libc* and *uClibc*. On top for each library, the table shows the number of functions and code size for the complete and minimal library. The minimal library shows the remaining code for a configuration which contains the minimal number of functions to compile the library. Following the same metrics for the library tailored to a specific application.

Application	# Funcs	%	Code Size	%	Application	# Funcs	%	Code Size	%
musl-libc (complete)	2,603		1,007 kB		uClibc (complete)	891		450 kB	
musl-libc (minimal)	358	13.8	116 kB	11.5	uClibc (minimal)	164	18.4	108 kB	23.9
Micro-lisp	366	14.1	118 kB	11.7	*Micro-lisp*	168	18.9	115 kB	25.5
Busybox	893	34.3	345 kB	34.2	*Busybox*	388	43.6	329 kB	73.2
Nginx	762	29.3	276 kB	27.4					
Lighttpd	745	28.6	260 kB	25.9					
PHP (Complete)	1,014	39.0	390 kB	38.8					
PHP (FluxBB)	817	31.4	296 kB	29.4					
PHP (OpenConf)	839	32.2	326 kB	32.3					
PHP (Wordpress)	874	33.6	336 kB	33.4					
PHP (Minimal)	768	29.5	280 kB	27.8					
Miniruby (Complete)	907	34.8	325 kB	32.3					
Miniruby (Minimal)	684	26.3	221 kB	21.9					

is possible for a target application. When tailoring the *musl-libc* to a specific application, *Micro-lisp* needs the fewest functions from the library with 14.1% remaining. In fact, this configuration needs only eight functions more than the minimal configuration which is necessary to compile the library. A complete *PHP* interpreter needs the most with 39.0%. On average, 30.3% of the functions remain in the *musl-libc* when tailored to an application. Since *uClibc* focuses on being as small as possible to work on microcontrollers, it does not have all features that the libc provides. Therefore, only *Busybox* and *Micro-Lisp* of our evaluation set work with this library. The complete library has 891 functions, whereas the minimal configuration only has 164 (18.4%). A *uClibc* tailored to *Micro-lisp* has 168, which are 18.9% of all functions and only four functions more than the minimal configuration possible. The *Busybox* configuration has 43.6% functions remaining after its compilation. This shows that even a library focusing on being as small as possible can be further reduced by our approach. The code size confirms that the libraries did not only lose small wrapper-like functions, but that the code is reduced in a proportional way to the number of functions present.

Removing PHP functionalities from the interpreter also influences the code required in the underlying libc. A complete PHP interpreter has 39.0% of the functions available in the *musl-libc* remaining, whereas a minimal PHP interpreter only needs 29.5% of the functions in the library. A PHP interpreter tailored to the *Wordpress* web application, the largest web application of our evaluation set, needs only 33.6% of the functions of the *musl-libc*. On average, a PHP interpreter tailored to a web application needs only 32.4% of the functions. This shows that for software debloating it is imperative to not only focus on the shared libraries itself, but to take into account the actual application running when an interpreted language is used.

Table 2. Results of our gadget evaluation for *musl-libc* and *uClibc*. On top for each library, the table shows the number of unique ROP gadgets, jump-oriented programming (JOP) gadgets, call-oriented programming (COP) gadgets, call-preceding (CP) gadgets, and syscall gadgets for the complete and minimal library. The minimal library shows the remaining gadgets for a configuration which contains the minimal number of functions to compile the library. Following the same metrics for the library tailored to a specific application.

Application	# unique	%	# JOP	%	# COP	%	# CP	%	syscall	%
musl-libc (complete)	9,692		332		324		581		157	
musl-libc (minimal)	1,578	16.3	40	12.1	106	32.7	108	18.6	81	51.6
Micro-lisp	1,581	16.3	36	10.8	113	34.9	110	18.9	81	51.6
Busybox	3,203	33.1	152	45.8	204	62.7	252	43.4	103	65.6
Nginx	3,196	33.0	105	31.6	166	51.2	209	36.0	106	67.5
Lighttpd	2,694	27.8	97	29.2	163	50.3	224	38.6	101	64.3
PHP (Complete)	4,012	41.4	130	39.2	235	72.5	281	48.4	106	67.5
PHP (FluxBB)	2,950	30.4	99	29.8	210	64.8	222	38.2	100	63.7
PHP (OpenConf)	3,387	35.0	101	30.4	201	62.0	226	38.9	97	61.8
PHP (Wordpress)	3,518	36.3	133	40.1	184	56.8	223	38.4	97	61.8
PHP (Minimal)	2,794	28.8	85	25.6	187	57.7	195	33.6	96	61.2
Miniruby (Complete)	3,533	36.5	97	29.2	181	55.9	237	40.8	112	71.3
Miniruby (Minimal)	2,578	26.6	59	17.8	176	54.3	181	31.2	104	66.2
uClibc (complete)	6,101		663		285		546		733	
uClibc (minimal)	1,736	28.5	87	13.1	75	26.3	142	26.0	150	20.5
Micro-lisp	1,724	28.3	82	12.4	77	27.0	146	26.7	150	20.5
Busybox	3,896	63.9	315	47.5	129	45.3	312	57.1	325	44.3

Code-Reuse Attacks. A modern way for an attacker to exploit a vulnerability in an application is to reuse existing code. One way for an attacker is to transfer the control flow to an existing function in a library with crafted arguments and therefore execute the behavior the attacker desires (e. g., ret2libc attack [39]). However, since the number of existing functions in the library is significantly reduced, an attacker may not be able to find a function that executes the behavior she needs. For example, in all configurations listed in Table 1, except for *Busybox* for *uClibc*, the function `system` which is usually used to execute shell commands in an exploit is removed from the code.

Another way to reuse existing code for an attack is called return-oriented programming (ROP) [35]. For this exploiting technique, small code snippets called *gadgets* are combined by the attacker to build the shellcode. Since an attacker needs a variety of different ROP gadgets to obtain the shellcode she needs, we measured the reduction of gadgets in the library with the tool *ROPgadget* [33] in version 5.6. While a tailored software stack alone does not prevent code-reuse attacks, this metric gives an estimate on the limitation an application-specific software stack imposes on ROP attacks. Besides measuring the number of unique ROP gadgets remaining, we also measured security-sensitive gadgets such as

Table 3. Results for PHP. The categories show the number of sensitive functions remaining in the PHP interpreter for each configuration. The special configurations *complete* and *minimal* give the numbers of sensitive functions for an unmodified PHP interpreter and a PHP interpreter containing the least number of functions to be executable.

	Base interpreter		Application-specific interpreter		
	Complete	Minimal	FluxBB	OpenConf	Wordpress
Code execution	5	0	3	2	3
Command execution	7	0	1	1	4

jump-oriented programming (JOP) [12], call-oriented programming (COP) [13], call-preceding gadgets (CP) [13], and syscall gadgets [35].

A minimal configuration of *musl-libc* and *uClibc* has only 16.3% and 28.5% of the unique ROP gadgets the complete library has. A tailored *musl-libc* has in the worst case 41.4% of unique ROP gadgets remaining for the complete PHP interpreter and in the best case 16.3% for *Micro-lisp*. For a tailored *uClibc*, 28.3% of the unique ROP gadgets remain for *Micro-lisp* and 63.9% for *Busybox*. Since *uClibc* is already optimized in regard to code size, the gadget reduction was to be expected less than the one for *musl-libc*. A full overview of all remaining gadgets is given in Table 2.

Overall, our evaluation shows that an application-specific library loses most of its code. The code size reduces proportionally to the number of functions removed. Furthermore, the number of unique ROP gadgets is reduced significantly, which narrows down the choices an attacker has when exploiting a vulnerability. While an application-specific software stack alone does not prevent code-reuse attacks, the combination of a tailored software stack with other defenses (e. g., CFI) might restrict an attacker sufficiently to prevent exploitation.

6.2   Web Applications

To show the applicability of an application-specific software stack for applications using a script interpreter, we measure the impact of our approach on web applications, namely FluxBB (version 1.5.10, 21,295 LOC), OpenConf (version 6.80, 21,232 LOC), and Wordpress (version 4.9.1, 183,820 LOC). We focus on web applications for PHP and use the same interpreter as compiled for the evaluation in Sect. 6.1. To give a realistic overview, we have chosen web applications of different categories and sizes. To generate the initial whitelist of PHP functions as described in Sect. 4.2, we use the static analysis tool Parse [6]. Unfortunately, Parse does not support the paradigm of object-oriented programming, which leads to the necessity to add two additional functions to the initial whitelist for *FluxBB* (`dir` and `read`) and one for *Wordpress* (`mysqli_connect`).

Although modern web applications often provide a way to install additional plugins, we only evaluate our approach on the basic web applications to give a base line of removable functionalities. If someone wants to use specific plugins, these plugins only have to be included into the extraction of PHP functions for the initial whitelist to work with the resulting customized interpreter.

To evaluate the quality of the removed code, we measure the number of remaining sensitive functions in the script interpreter. We use the categories provided by the open source version of RIPS, a static PHP security scanner [9]. Since the goal of an application-specific script interpreter is to reduce the impact of an attacker executing arbitrary PHP code (e. g., by uploading an attacker controlled script file), we focus on the categories *Code Execution* and *Command Execution*. *Code Execution* contains all functions that allow an attacker to execute arbitrary PHP functionality and *Command Execution* contains all functions that allow an attacker to execute shell commands on the host. Table 3 shows the full results, in the following we provide a high-level overview.

The base interpreter without any functions removed has five PHP functions in the *Code Execution* category (`assert`, `create_function`, `preg_filter`, `preg_replace`, and `preg_replace_callback`). In contrast, a minimal configuration of the interpreter (least amount of PHP functions necessary to run the interpreter itself) does not have any such function. This shows that it is possible to remove this functionality completely from the interpreter as long as the target web application does not use one of the sensitive functions. Unfortunately, all projects use some *Code Execution* functionality and hence our approach is not able to remove it completely from the script interpreter with *FluxBB* using three different PHP functions, *OpenConf* two, and *Wordpress* three.

PHP functions that provide the ability to execute arbitrary shell commands on the host system are in the category *Command Execution*. A complete PHP interpreter provides seven such functions (`exec`, `passthru`, `popen`, `proc_open`, `shell_exec`, `system`, and `mail`) and a minimal configuration none. Unfortunately, each of the web applications of our evaluation set again uses at least one sensitive function from the category. For a *FluxBB* installation, the only PHP function allowing arbitrary shell command execution remaining is `exec`. However, since `exec` is only used to display the system's uptime in the administration control panel, removing it from the code would allow to remove the ability to execute shell commands completely from the script interpreter. Hence, an attacker that is able to upload her own script file to a web server is no longer able to execute shell commands. An *OpenConf* configuration has also only one PHP function remaining in the *Command Execution* category, the function `mail`. However, there are multiple limiting factors to consider before an attacker is able to execute shell commands with the help of `mail` which we discuss in Sect. 6.4 in detail. Hence, a tailored script interpreter for *OpenConf* removes the attack vector of *Command Execution* in most cases completely. A configuration for *Wordpress* has still four PHP functions that allow shell command execution. Here, the functionality still remains in the script interpreter and a malicious usage is only mitigated by the insertion of booby traps as explained in Sect. 5.2.

An attacker not knowing about the tailored PHP interpreter that gains arbitrary PHP function execution could trigger a booby trap by executing a removed functionality.

In summary, an application-specific script interpreter reduces the available options for executing code or shell commands. Furthermore, it is also able to remove certain functionalities altogether and leave the attacker with no possibility to perform such an attack. In cases where the functionality still remains in the interpreter, it mitigates its malicious effects by inserting booby traps (which are especially effective in case of proprietary web applications) that can be triggered by an attacker using a removed functionality.

6.3 Use Case: Wordpress Container

To evaluate the debloating effect for a real-world scenario, we created a Docker container for our running example, an application-specific *Wordpress* installation. This container comprises of a PHP interpreter tailored to *Wordpress*, as well as a *musl-libc* tailored to the *Nginx* web server and PHP interpreter. Since the web server has to interact with the interpreter directly, PHP is additionally compiled with the FastCGI Process Manager (FPM). This scenario comprises a setting for which our approach was designed. One shared library tailored to multiple applications to keep the usability benefits of dynamic linking and a script interpreter customized for a web application.

The code reduction for the script interpreter is as discussed in Sect. 6.2. However, the reduction in the library is different since it is now tailored to two applications. The code of the *musl-libc* is reduced to 351 kB (34.9% of its original size). To put things in perspective, the *musl-libc* tailored solely to a *Wordpress* customized PHP interpreter has only 33.4% of its code remaining and a *Nginx*-specific library 27.4%. This suggests that most of the library functions are shared by PHP and *Nginx*. Only 2.958 unique ROP gadgets were found (41.2% of the original amount). Even when comparing to a library specific to a complete PHP interpreter, this shared *musl-libc* setup results in a smaller library with less code.

In summary, this real-world setting shows a significant code reduction even with a library tailored to multiple applications. Since this code reduction restricts the options for an attacker performing an attack (e. g., whole function reuse, ROP, or PHP code execution), it is an important additional piece for a security-in-depth environment already providing other forms of defenses (e. g., CFI).

6.4 Security Evaluation

OpenConf 5.30 had multiple vulnerabilities that could be chained together to gain remote code execution [18]. This was achieved by injecting PHP code into an uploaded file and executing it. In an application-specific script interpreter for *OpenConf*, the attacker's possibilities are limited after gaining PHP code execution. The only remaining way to execute shell commands is by using the mail function which allows control over the arguments passed to the underlying sendmail command. However, before the arguments are passed to sendmail by the PHP interpreter, they are escaped internally. As a result, it is exploited by creating a file that can be abused as PHP shell and thus gain PHP code execution [21]. However, again the only remaining way for the attacker to execute shell commands with her created PHP shell is with the mail function. Hence, it is not possible for the attacker to execute any shell commands with the tailored PHP interpreter. The only exception is a system that uses the Exim mail server which allows a direct shell command execution with the mail function. Therefore, depending on the system configuration, an application-specific script interpreter would mitigate such an attack.

CVE-2016-5771 and CVE-2016-5773 in the PHP interpreter were found for Pornhub's bug bounty program in 2016 [22]. The penetration testers used it to exploit the unserialize function and gain remote code execution on the server. In their ROP shellcode, they used the function zend_eval_string to interpret a given string as PHP code. Although an application-specific PHP interpreter would not have eliminated this vulnerability (since the code was used by the web application), the exploiting could be made more difficult with it. For example, the native code function zend_eval_string is not present in any of our tailored interpreter instances (except the complete PHP interpreter). Additionally, when interpreting a string as PHP code, it might use a removed functionality and thus trigger a booby trap. Hence, depending on the used web application, the range of suitable candidates to use for an exploit can be limited.

6.5   Performance

Since our approach only removes unnecessary code from the support layer of the target application, it does not induce a performance penalty. However, it does not have a performance gain either, because only code is removed that is not executed by the application anyways. The memory consumption of an application-specific library is smaller than the consumption of the complete library, since code is removed from the binary and therefore not loaded into memory. Nonetheless, since each group of applications need their own tailored library, the overall memory consumption of the system is increased. However, since using containers for each service (which also increase the memory consumption for each used library) gains more popularity, we deem it acceptable for practical deployments.

7   Discussion

Scripting languages often offer the possibility to dynamically evaluate code (such as eval in PHP). When used by the application, it makes the initial analysis to gather all necessary interpreter functionalities much harder. Our approach relies on the accuracy of specialized analysis tools for this. However, if the analysis tool is not able to provide accurate data, the tailored interpreter could break the application. Furthermore, if a user-provided input is directly passed to an evaluation function, stripping down the interpreter becomes impossible since the user can provide any programming construct she likes. However, such flawed code constructs allow direct access to the system anyway and trying to prevent it can be regarded as a losing battle.

As evident from our evaluation, an application-specific interpreter reduces the options an attacker has if she is able to execute own code in a targeted web application. Furthermore, it is able to remove certain vulnerability classes completely. However, if a web application uses a certain interpreter functionality that can also be used for an attack, our approach is not able to thwart this. To be more precise, if a web application relies on the PHP function exec to execute commands directly on the system (like in the case of *FluxBB*), our approach cannot remove it. To mitigate attacks using this functionality, approaches to monitor such remaining functions can be deployed additionally [37].

We showed that the concept of our approach is capable of working with script interpreters such as PHP and Ruby. However, as script interpreters have different internal structures, our approach cannot be used directly with another interpreter such as Python. To support it, domain knowledge of the interpreter's internal workings has to be integrated (i.e., the mapping of script functions to native code functions). As this merely means that additional engineering effort is needed to support other interpreters, it does not constitute a limitation of the general concept of our approach.

Another limitation is that each application needs its own customized libraries. As a result, when running multiple services like a web application in combination with a database server, both need their own tailored libc (or combine their analysis results to create one libc for both applications). On first glance, this seems infeasible for a real-world scenario. However, the recent trend to separate each part of a service into a container, such as Docker [1] (which uses Alpine Linux with *musl-libc* for official containers), makes our approach applicable for real-world scenarios. When running a web application, one container can contain the web server as well as a script interpreter (e.g., PHP) with a shared application-specific software stack and another container the database server with its own tailored software stack. Thus, enhancing the security mechanism of separating services with reduced options for an attacker to reuse existing code.

As the evaluation in Sect. 6 has shown, minor manual configuration is still necessary in some cases. For web applications these were cases where the used static analysis tool Parse was not able to process object-oriented programming constructs. However, this is not a shortcoming of our approach, but just a limitation of the used analysis tool. Using a different analysis tool that is capable of handling object-oriented programming like RIPS [7] solves this problem. Minor manual configuration was also necessary for both tested libc versions. These were either cases that LLVM could not handle due to assembly, functions that are called by the loader, or functions that were resolved dynamically during runtime by the loader as explained in Sect. 5.1. These cases require more engineering work and do not constitute conceptual limitations of our approach. Assembly directly used in the source code can either be lifted to LLVM IR with tools such as McSema [38] or processed separately. Entry point functions called directly by the loader can be whitelisted initially by just adding the names of the C specific starting functions (e. g., `_start`). We did not do this to have a complete evaluation. Dynamically resolved functions can be addressed by integrating a data-flow analysis which ends in the corresponding library functions (e. g., `dlsym`). However, solving this in general is hard since the only case we encountered used a self-implemented function of the `dlsym` functionality to resolve the function pointer. Hence, our approach can be seen as a first step to an automated way to create application-specific software stacks.

Our current prototype focuses on removing unused code from shared libraries and script interpreters written in C, however, support for C++ is subject of future work. To work with C++, our approach has to be able to handle virtual function tables (vtables) which are used on a low-level to implement polymorphism. A naive approach would be to whitelist all functions that are part of a vtable. However, this would decrease the precision of the code debloating and heavily overestimates the used functions. A better way would be to improve the static analysis to only keep functions in the vtable that are actually used. For this to work correctly, our approach has to track the data flow of vtables precisely to identify all used functions and must be able to modify entries in the vtables to remove unused ones [30].

Our approach uses a flow-insensitive analysis to find function pointer targets with which we did not encounter any misses during our evaluation. However, the C programming language allows constructs that do not provide sufficient meaningful information in LLVM to determine the possible targets. In these edge cases, a more sophisticated points-to analysis has to be implemented like the one developed by Emami et al. [20].

8   Related Work

Debloating software is an appealing approach to thwart attacks and we now discuss works closely related to ours. Based on the observation that an application only uses a small part of the code provided by a shared library, Quach et al. [32] presented a debloating approach. They developed a compiler extension that adds metadata to an ELF binary (application and shared libraries) about the location of functions and their dependencies. On execution of an application, the loader writes the shared library into memory and then removes all functions that are not used by the application by overwriting them. However, though the analysis is similar to the presented one, their approach is only applicable to native code applications and does not work with applications written for a script interpreter.

JRed [24] is an automated approach to remove unused code from Java applications. It analyzes the bytecode of an application and removes unused code in the application itself and core libraries of the JRE. However, it is only capable of handling Java bytecode and ignores native code libraries during its analysis. Since JRed only targets Java bytecode, it does not tackle challenges like indirect control-flow transfers through function pointers as done by our approach.

Landsborough et al. [27] presented an approach to remove unwanted functionalities from binary code by using a genetic algorithm. Since it works on traces obtained via dynamic analysis, it needs test cases that execute every functionality the target application should keep. If the set of test cases is not complete, the code corresponding to a needed but not tested functionality is removed and thus breaks the application. Additionally, it does not scale and did not even terminate when removing a feature from the *echo* application of coreutils. *Chisel* [23] aims to support programmers to debloat programs. It needs the source code and a high-level specification of its functionalities to remove unwanted features with the help of delta debugging. A similar goal is pursued by Sharif et al. [36] and their prototype implementation *TRIMMER*, a LLVM compiler extension. With the help of a user-provided manifest about the desired features, it tries to remove unwanted functionalities to debloat the application. A binary-only approach targeting specifically applications using a client-server architecture is presented by Chen et al. [14]. Their approach uses binary-rewriting techniques and a user-provided list of features with corresponding test cases to execute those to customize the target application. *BinRec* [25] also aims at debloating already compiled applications. It is based on LLVM and needs to lift the target binary into the LLVM IR before it can perform its transformations. Since automatically removing features from an application on the binary level is prone to errors, *BinRec* also provides a fallback mechanism to use removed code from the original binary. In contrast to our approach, these approaches focus on removing features from a target application itself, while we aim to remove unused functionalities from libraries and script interpreters.

An approach to debloat the Linux kernel was presented by Kurmus et al. [26]. Their approach focuses on optimizing the configuration for the Linux kernel to remove unnecessary features at compile time. This work is orthogonal to ours and can further improve the security of the system by not only tailoring the userspace software stack in an application-specific way, but also optimizing the Linux kernel to target a specific application.

9   Conclusion

In this paper, we presented an approach to compile shared libraries tailored to a specific application by removing unused code from them. Since complex applications, such as the PHP interpreter, do not even use half of the provided functions in a shared library, we showed that this debloating significantly reduces the choices an attacker has for code-reuse attacks. Furthermore, we demonstrated that with the help of domain knowledge, our approach is also capable of tailoring a script interpreter to a script application (e. g., a web application).

We demonstrated an application-specific software stack tailored to a *Wordpress* installation (customized PHP interpreter, *libc* tailored to web server and interpreter), and showed a significant code reduction.

Acknowledgements. This work was supported by the German Research Foundation (DFG) within the framework of the Excellence Strategy of the Federal Government and the States – EXC 2092 CaSa – 39078197. In addition, this work was supported by the European Research Council (ERC) under the European Union's Horizon 2020 research and innovation programme (ERC Starting Grant No. 640110 (BASTION)).

References

1. Docker - Build, Ship, and Run Any App, Anywhere. https://www.docker.com/
2. Buildroot - Making Embedded Linux Easy (2018). https://buildroot.org
3. Directory::read (2018). http://php.net/manual/en/directory.read.php
4. Google Cloud: App Engine - Build Scalable Web & Mobile Backends in Any Language (2018). https://cloud.google.com/appengine/
5. musl libc (2018). https://www.musl-libc.org
6. Parse: A PHP Security Scanner (2018). https://github.com/psecio/parse
7. PHP Security Analysis - RIPS (2018). https://www.ripstech.com/
8. Registering and using PHP functions (2018). http://www.phpinternalsbook.com/php7/extensions_design/php_functions.html
9. RIPS Sensitive Sinks (2018). https://github.com/ripsscanner/rips/blob/master/config/sinks.php
10. uClibc (2018). https://www.uclibc.org
11. Abadi, M., Budiu, M., Erlingsson, U., Ligatti, J.: Control-flow integrity. In: ACM Conference on Computer and Communications Security (CCS) (2005)
12. Bletsch, T., Jiang, X., Freeh, V.W., Liang, Z.: Jump-oriented programming: a new class of code-reuse attack. In: ACM Conference on Computer and Communications Security (CCS) (2011)
13. Carlini, N., Wagner, D.: ROP is still dangerous: breaking modern defenses. In: USENIX Security Symposium (2014)
14. Chen, Y., Sun, S., Lan, T., Venkataramani, G.: TOSS: tailoring online server systems through binary feature customization. In: Workshop on Forming an Ecosystem Around Software Transformation (FEAST) (2018)
15. Christner, B.: Docker Official Images are Moving to Alpine Linux (2016). https://www.brianchristner.io/docker-is-moving-to-alpine-linux/
16. Crane, S., Larsen, P., Brunthaler, S., Franz, M.: Booby trapping software. In: ACM New Security Paradigms Workshop (NSPW) (2013)
17. Cytron, R., Ferrante, J., Rosen, B.K., Wegman, M.N., Zadeck, F.K.: Efficiently computing static single assignment form and the control dependence graph. In: ACM Transactions on Programming Languages and Systems (TOPLAS) (1991)
18. Dahse, J.: OpenConf 5.30 - Multi-Step Remote Command Execution (2016). https://blog.ripstech.com/2016/openconf-multi-step-remote-command-execution/
19. Davidsson, N., Pawlowski, A., Holz, T.: Towards automated application-specific software stacks. Technical report, arXiv:1907.01933 (2019)
20. Emami, M., Ghiya, R., Hendren, L.J.: Context-sensitive interprocedural points-to analysis in the presence of function pointers. In: ACM SIGPLAN Conference on Programming Language Design and Implementation (PLDI) (1994)
21. Golunski, D.: Pwning PHP mail() function For Fun And RCE - New Exploitation Techniques and Vectors - Release 1.0 (2017). https://exploitbox.io/paper/Pwning-PHP-Mail-Function-For-Fun-And-RCE.html
22. Habalov, R.: How we broke PHP, hacked Pornhub and earned $20,000 (2016). https://www.evonide.com/how-we-broke-php-hacked-pornhub-and-earned-20000-dollar/

23. Heo, K., Lee, W., Pashakhanloo, P., Naik, M.: Effective program debloating via reinforcement learning. In: ACM Conference on Computer and Communications Security (CCS) (2018)
24. Jiang, Y., Wu, D., Liu, P.: JRed: program customization and bloatware mitigation based on static analysis. In: Computer Software and Applications Conference (COMPSAC) (2016)
25. Kroes, T., et al.: BinRec: attack surface reduction through dynamic binary recovery. In: Workshop on Forming an Ecosystem Around Software Transformation (FEAST) (2018)
26. Kurmus, A., et al.: Attack surface metrics and automated compile-time OS kernel tailoring. In: Symposium on Network and Distributed System Security (NDSS) (2013)
27. Landsborough, J., Harding, S., Fugate, S.: Removing the kitchen sink from software. In: Conference on Genetic and Evolutionary Computation (GECCO) (2015)
28. Muench, M., Pagani, F., Shoshitaishvili, Y., Kruegel, C., Vigna, G., Balzarotti, D.: Taming transactions: towards hardware-assisted control flow integrity using transactional memory. In: Monrose, F., Dacier, M., Blanc, G., Garcia-Alfaro, J. (eds.) RAID 2016. LNCS, vol. 9854, pp. 24–48. Springer, Cham (2016). https://doi.org/10.1007/978-3-319-45719-2_2
29. Park, T., Lettner, J., Na, Y., Volckaert, S., Franz, M.: Bytecode corruption attacks are real-and how to defend against them. In: Conference on Detection of Intrusions and Malware & Vulnerability Assessment (DIMVA) (2018)
30. Pawlowski, A., et al.: MARX: uncovering class hierarchies in C++ programs. In: Symposium on Network and Distributed System Security (NDSS) (2017)
31. Quach, A., Erinfolami, R., Demicco, D., Prakash, A.: A multi-OS cross-layer study of bloating in user programs, kernel and managed execution environments. In: Workshop on Forming an Ecosystem Around Software Transformation (FEAST) (2017)
32. Quach, A., Prakash, A., Yan, L.K.: Debloating software through piece-wise compilation and loading. In: USENIX Security Symposium (2018)
33. Salwan, J.: ROPgadget (2018). https://github.com/JonathanSalwan/ROPgadget
34. Sasada, K.: YARV: yet another RubyVM: innovating the ruby interpreter. In: Conference on Object-oriented Programming, Systems, Languages, and Applications (OOPSLA) (2005)
35. Shacham, H.: The geometry of innocent flesh on the bone: return-into-libc without function calls (on the x86). In: ACM Conference on Computer and Communications Security (CCS) (2007)
36. Sharif, H., Abubakar, M., Gehani, A., Zaffar, F.: TRIMMER: application specialization for code debloating. In: International Conference on Automated Software Engineering (ASE) (2018)
37. Staicu, C.A., Pradel, M., Livshits, B.: Synode: understanding and automatically preventing injection attacks on node.js. In: Symposium on Network and Distributed System Security (NDSS) (2018)
38. Trail of Bits: McSema (2018). https://github.com/trailofbits/mcsema
39. Tran, M., Etheridge, M., Bletsch, T., Jiang, X., Freeh, V., Ning, P.: On the expressiveness of return-into-libc attacks. In: International Symposium on Research in Attacks, Intrusions, and Defenses (RAID) (2011)

Cryptographic Protocols

Identity-Based Encryption with Security Against the KGC: A Formal Model and Its Instantiation from Lattices

Keita Emura[1](✉), Shuichi Katsumata[2], and Yohei Watanabe[1]

[1] National Institute of Information and Communications Technology (NICT), Tokyo, Japan
{k-emura,yohei.watanabe}@nict.go.jp
[2] National Institute of Advanced Industrial Science and Technology (AIST), Tokyo, Japan
shuichi.katsumata@aist.go.jp

Abstract. The *key escrow problem* is one of the main barriers to the widespread real-world use of identity-based encryption (IBE). Specifically, a key generation center (KGC), which generates secret keys for a given identity, has the power to decrypt all ciphertexts. At PKC 2009, Chow defined a notion of security against the KGC, that relies on assuming that it cannot discover the underlying identities behind ciphertexts. However, this is not a realistic assumption since, in practice, the KGC manages an identity list and hence it can easily guess the identities corresponding to given ciphertexts. Chow later closed the gap between theory and practice by introducing a new entity called an identity-certifying authority (ICA) and proposed an *anonymous key-issuing protocol*. Essentially, this allows the users, KGC, and ICA to interactively generate secret keys without users ever having to reveal their identities to the KGC. Unfortunately, the proposed protocol did not include a concrete security definition, meaning that all of the subsequent works following Chow lack the formal proofs needed to determine whether or not it delivers a secure solution to the key escrow problem.

In this paper, based on Chow's work, we formally define an IBE scheme that resolves the key escrow problem and provide formal definitions of security against corrupted users, KGC, and ICA. Along the way, we observe that if we are allowed to assume a fully trusted ICA, as in Chow's work, then we can construct a trivial (and meaningless) IBE scheme that is secure against the KGC. Finally, we present a lattice-based construction in our new security model based on the Gentry–Peikert–Vaikuntanathan (GPV) IBE scheme (STOC 2008) and Rückert's lattice-based blind signature scheme (ASIACRYPT 2010).

1 Introduction

1.1 Identity-Based Encryption

Public key cryptography has long been in widespread real-world use, but it has the issue that public keys look like random strings. Consequently, public key

© Springer Nature Switzerland AG 2019
K. Sako et al. (Eds.): ESORICS 2019, LNCS 11736, pp. 113–133, 2019.
https://doi.org/10.1007/978-3-030-29962-0_6

infrastructure (PKI) has also been developed to prove the validity of public keys. *Identity-based encryption* (IBE) [27] can reduce the costs associated with PKI systems by enabling users to select arbitrary strings (such as e-mail addresses or bio-information) as public keys. A special entity called the key-generation center (KGC) maintains a master public/secret key pair (mpk, msk). The KGC (implicitly) confirms the validity of each user ID and then issues an associated secret key sk_{ID} using the master secret key msk. Once the master public key mpk has been downloaded from the KGC, anyone can encrypt messages if they know the recipient's ID. IBE is standardized by ISO/IEC 18033-5 and IEEE P1363.3.

1.2 Key Escrow Problem and Current Solutions

The *key escrow problem* is a significant barrier to the widespread real-world use of IBE, and is a serious concern for communication privacy. Specifically, the KGC potentially has the power to decrypt all ciphertexts, since it can generate secret keys for any ID. Several attempts have already been made to deal with this issue by reducing the amount of trust we put in the KGC.

One line of research is to make users participate in the secret key-generation process. In certificateless encryption (CE) [3], in addition to the secret key sk_{ID} generated by the KGC, each user also needs to generate their own public/secret key pair (pk, sk). Here, both the ID and pk are required to encrypt messages, so decryption involves both sk_{ID} and sk. This means that the KGC can no longer decrypt ciphertexts, since it does not know sk. However, the PKI now has to certify the pk as well, as they are required for encryption. Garg et al. [12,13] improved the CE approach by having the KGC aggregate and compress all users' public keys. Instead of generating a secret key sk_{ID} for each user, the KGC updates and maintains mpk using the pair (ID, pk) for each user ID. As in IBE, encryption and decryption only require (mpk, ID) and sk, respectively. However, one drawback when implementing this in practice is that mpk must be periodically updated.

Another approach is to define an independent notion of security against the KGC for *standard* IBEs. Here, we call an IBE standard if encryption requires only a (static) mpk and ID, and decryption requires only sk_{ID}, as originally defined in [27]. Here, the essential idea is to capture some notion of anonymity [1,6] with respect to the KGC, specifically to guarantee that ciphertexts reveal no information about the underlying identities, and hence that the KGC cannot determine the correct identity needed to decrypt a given ciphertext. Based on this design criterion, Izabachène and Pointcheval [17] formalized anonymity with respect to the KGC for identity-based key encapsulation mechanisms (IB-KEMs). However, as Chow [10] pointed out, their definition is incomplete, since it considers the situation where an adversary can only obtain the challenge ciphertext, whereas in a standard IB-KEM, adversaries can obtain both the challenge ciphertext and the corresponding session key. In order to define a more stringent notion of security against the KGC, Chow [10] introduced the notion of KGC anonymous ciphertext indistinguishability (ACI-KGC), which guarantees that the KGC cannot obtain any information about the corresponding plaintext from a ciphertext *if the author's identity is chosen randomly and unknown to the KGC.* However, as he noted, requiring ACI-KGC is still insufficient in practice: the KGC typically manage lists of issued identity/secret key pairs, so it could decrypt any ciphertext via brute force by running the decryption algorithm against all the secret keys issued so far. In other words, even though ACI-KGC is a well-motivated security definition, it would be impossible to satisfy in practice. To resolve this gap between the security notion and practical implementation, Chow also introduced, in the same paper, a new entity called an *identity-certifying authority* (ICA) and defined an *anonymous key-issuing protocol.* In this protocol, the ICA authenticates the user's identity ID by providing them certificates. The user can then use this certificate to interact with the KGC and obtain sk_{ID} without revealing their identity ID, an idea reminiscent of blind IBEs [8,15].[1] Since the KGC is now outsourcing the work of authenticating users to the ICA, it will no longer know which identities it has generated secret keys for.

Chow's work [10] was a significant step toward defining a standard IBE scheme that can resolve the key escrow problem. However, in this research, we identify some deficiencies in this formulation and show that the definition must be refined. First, as explained above, Chow introduced a new entity called the ICA and proposed an anonymous key-issuing protocol involving the user, the KGC, and the ICA to close the gap between the ACI-KGC security notion for standard IBEs and practical KGC implementations. However, unfortunately, Chow defined ACI-KGC only between the user and the KGC and did not provide any formal treatment when the ICA is used to authenticate the users. He does provide some informal argument suggesting that something similar to ACI-KGC should hold for a standard IBE scheme where the ICA authenticates the users, however, on closer look, ACI-KGC is not a notion which can be naturally extended to such scenarios. Considering the relevance of key escrow problems for IBE in the real world, the definition which we base our security on must properly formalize ACI-KGC in the presence of an ICA. Second, in Chow's definition, the ICA is fully trusted. We observe that this extra (strong) assumption makes the definition completely void and trivial to achieve. In particular, consider the following IBE scheme, defined between the users, the KGC, and the fully trusted ICA: the ICA plays the role of the KGC in a standard IBE scheme and the KGC does nothing. It is easy to see that this construction achieves ACI-KGC security, since the KGC holds no secret information and standard anonymous IBE readily implies ACI-KGC. In other words, we have simply transferred all the trust from the KGC to the ICA and also deferred the key escrow problem to it. This shows that, if we are to make this a well-defined and well-motivated security notion, we cannot fully trust the ICA.

Finally, all subsequent works [23,28] have followed Chow's general outline and in particular, they are all pairing-based constructions and insecure in the face of quantum computing. It is therefore, an interesting question to ask whether we

---

[1] Note that without an ICA this can never be secure since a malicious user can obtain sk_{ID} for any ID without identification. Recall that in practice KGC implicitly authenticates the users to which it provides sk_{ID}.

can construct a *provably secure* post-quantum IBE under any sensible security notion that resolves the key escrow problem.

1.3   Our Contribution

In this paper, we formalize a standard IBE scheme that captures the key escrow problem and provide a candidate construction. Our formalization is inspired by Chow's original work and is based on the idea of creating an ICA to authenticate the system's users. We describe this scheme as *blind IBE with certified identities* to differentiate between prior formalizations. This terminology follows from the fact that the proposed secret key-generation process can be seen as a blind IBE combined with an ICA to certify user identities. We also propose a lattice-based approach to constructing such a blind IBE based on the Learning with Errors (LWE) assumption in the random oracle model. As far as we are aware, this is the first post-quantum IBE to resolve the key escrow problem based on Chow's work.[2] Our contributions can be summarized in more detail as follows.

Formalization of a Blind IBE with Certified Identities. We formalize a standard IBE scheme (which we call blind IBE with certified identities) that resolves the key escrow problem based on Chow's work [10]. Our definition involves three entities: the users, the KGC, and the ICA. The ICA is responsible for authenticating users by issuing certificates, while the KGC is responsible for (blindly) generating secret keys for users. We define three security notions, one for each of the three entities involved. Specifically, we define indistinguishability and anonymity against chosen plaintext attacks for the users (IND-ANON-CPA), the KGC (IND-ANON-KGC), and the ICA (IND-ANON-ICA). The first of these, IND-ANON-CPA, captures the standard concept of IBE security, while the second and third model cases where the KGC or the ICA is malicious. Our IBE formalization takes all the aforementioned issues into account: the syntax captures anonymous key-issuing via IND-ANON-KGC security, and the ICA is no longer fully trusted due to our additional definition of IND-ANON-ICA security. Our formalization can be seen as a natural and formal extension of Chow's idea of combining ACI-KGC security with an anonymous key-issuing protocol.

Lattice-Based Instantiation. We also provide a concrete instantiation of a blind IBE with certified identities, based on the LWE problem in the random oracle model. Our construction is based on the standard lattice-based IBE scheme by Gentry–Peikert–Vaikuntanathan (GPV-IBE) [14], which is arguably the most efficient IBE scheme based on standard lattice assumptions. The two main technical hurdles involved in developing our construction are as follows.

(a) *Realizing Anonymous Key Issuing.* Unlike standard IBE, where the KGC knows (i.e., authorizes via some certification mechanism) which ID it is issuing

---

[2] We note that another potential path to resolving the key escrow problem may be to consider distributed KGCs. Specifically, it may be possible to use the threshold variant of GPV IBE scheme by Bendlin et al. [4] to obtain a lattice-based IBE scheme secure against the key escrow problem. We leave this as potential future direction.

secret keys to, IBE schemes that deal with the key escrow problem cannot allow the KGC to know the IDs corresponding to the secret keys. This is the main reason why the ICA was introduced: it authorizes users by providing them with certificates that do not leak their ID, which they can then use to obtain secret keys from the KGC. The main problem here is thus figuring out what the certificate should look like and how to combine it with GPV-IBE's key-generation process.

Our main observation is that the secret keys of GPV-IBE is only a short vector over $\mathbb{Z}^m$ and the key-generation process of GPV-IBE can be viewed as a signing algorithm through the Naor transformation [5]. Concretely, a secret key for ID, which is a short vector over $\mathbb{Z}^m$, can be seen as a signature for some message (related to ID) over $\mathbb{Z}_q^n$. At a high level, the user in our construction will end up receiving two certificates: one from the ICA and another from the KGC, and then the user will combine them together to form a secret key for the GPV-IBE. However, the two certificates must be related to one specific ID in some meaningful way or otherwise the user can simply mix-and-match different certificates together. To this end, we build on the lattice-based blind signature scheme proposed by Rückert [25] and use it in a way so that the KGC can blindly sign to a vector over $\mathbb{Z}_q^n$ which implicitly commits to an ID. We note that Rückert [26] later mentions that the blind signature scheme in [25] is vulnerable in some use cases, however, the way we use it avoids this problem.

(b) *Satisfying IND-ANON-KGC Security.* Informally, IND-ANON-KGC security stipulates that even if the KGC receives polynomially many ciphertexts for the same ID, as long as the ID is sampled from a sufficiently high min-entropy source, then it cannot tell whether the ciphertexts are real or sampled uniformly at random from the ciphertext space. In other words, even though the KGC can construct secret keys for any ID, it should not be able to identify the right ID corresponding to the ciphertexts with more than negligible probability. Below we recall the ciphertext of GPV-IBE: $c_0 = \mathbf{u}_{\mathsf{ID}}^\top \mathbf{s} + x + \mathsf{M}\lfloor q/2 \rceil$ and $\mathbf{c}_1 = \mathbf{A}^\top \mathbf{s} + \mathbf{x}$, where $\mathsf{M} \in \{0, 1\}$ is the plaintext, $\mathbf{A} \in \mathbb{Z}_q^{n \times m}$ is included in mpk, $\mathbf{u}_{\mathsf{ID}} = \mathsf{H}(\mathsf{ID}) \in \mathbb{Z}_q^n$ is a hash value (derived from the random oracle), $\mathbf{s} \in \mathbb{Z}_q^n$ is a uniformly random vector over $\mathbb{Z}_q^n$, and $\mathbf{x}, x$ are small "noise" terms.

At first glance, IND-ANON-KGC security seems highly related to IBE in the multi-challenge setting [16] where an adversary can obtain polynomially many challenge ciphertexts, and therefore, may seem that the security proof of IND-ANON-KGC follows from a simple hybrid argument. However, this intuition is inaccurate. The key difference between the two security notions is that in IND-ANON-KGC the KGC holds the master secret key to the IBE scheme, i.e., the trapdoor for the lattice generated by $\mathbf{A}$. In particular, the adversary for IND-ANON-KGC (which is the KGC) has the power to fully recover the randomness $\mathbf{s}$ from $\mathbf{c}_1$ in the ciphertext. This prevents us from using an entropy-based argument on the vector $\mathbf{s}$ to argue uniformness of c_0, as was done in previous proofs for GPV-IBE in the multi-challenge setting [19]. We therefore depart from previous proof techniques for GPV-IBE to prove IND-ANON-KGC of our proposed IBE scheme. We take advantage of the fact that the adversary does not have knowledge of the ID corresponding to the challenge ciphertext. Note that to the contrary, in the multi-challenge setting, the adversary was able to specify the ID that is being encrypted. In our security proof, we use the fact that $\mathbf{u}_{\mathsf{ID}} = \mathsf{H}(\mathsf{ID}) \in \mathbb{Z}_q^n$ is distributed as a uniformly random vector from the view of the adversary in the random oracle model and embed $\mathbf{u}_{\mathsf{ID}}$ as the LWE secret, rather than embedding the encryption randomness $\mathbf{s}$ as in previous proofs.

2   Preliminaries

Notations. For a distribution or random variable X we write $x \leftarrow X$ to denote the operation of sampling a random x according to X. For a set S, we write $s \leftarrow S$ as a shorthand for $s \leftarrow U(S)$. For a vector $\mathbf{v} \in \mathbb{R}^n$, denote $\|\mathbf{v}\|$ as the standard Euclidean norm. For a matrix $\mathbf{R} \in \mathbb{R}^{n \times n}$, denote $\|\mathbf{R}\|$ as the length of the longest column and $\|\mathbf{R}\|_{\mathrm{GS}}$ as the longest column of the Gram-Schmidt orthogonalization of $\mathbf{R}$. We denote $s_1(\mathbf{R})$ as the largest singular value of $\mathbf{R}$. Finally, denote $\langle A, B \rangle$ as an interactive protocol between two PPT algorithms A and B.

Lattices and Gaussian Measures. A (full-rank-integer) m-dimensional lattice Λ in $\mathbb{Z}^m$ is a set of the form $\{\sum_{i \in [m]} x_i \mathbf{b}_i | x_i \in \mathbb{Z}\}$, where $\mathbf{B} = \{\mathbf{b}_1, \cdots, \mathbf{b}_m\}$ are m linearly independent vectors in $\mathbb{Z}^m$. We call $\mathbf{B}$ the basis of the lattice Λ. For any positive integers n, m and $q \geq 2$, a matrix $\mathbf{A} \in \mathbb{Z}_q^{n \times m}$ and a vector $\mathbf{u} \in \mathbb{Z}_q^n$, we define the lattices $\Lambda^\perp(\mathbf{A}) = \{\mathbf{z} \in \mathbb{Z}^m | \mathbf{Az} = \mathbf{0} \mod q\}$ and $\Lambda_{\mathbf{u}}^\perp(\mathbf{A}) = \{\mathbf{z} \in \mathbb{Z}^m | \mathbf{Az} = \mathbf{u} \mod q\}$.

Lemma 1 ([14]). *Let n, m, q be positive integers such that $m \geq 2n \log q$. Let σ be any positive real such that $\sigma \geq \omega(\sqrt{\log n})$. Then for $\mathbf{A} \leftarrow \mathbb{Z}_q^{n \times m}$ and $\mathbf{e} \leftarrow D_{\mathbb{Z}^m, \sigma}$, the distribution of $\mathbf{u} = \mathbf{Ae} \mod q$ is statistically close to uniform over $\mathbb{Z}_q^n$.*

Furthermore, fix $\mathbf{u} \in \mathbb{Z}_q^n$. Then the conditional distribution of $\mathbf{e} \leftarrow D_{\mathbb{Z}^m, \sigma}$ given $\mathbf{Ae} = \mathbf{u} \mod q$ for a uniformly random $\mathbf{A}$ in $\mathbb{Z}_q^{n \times m}$ is statistically close to $D_{\Lambda_{\mathbf{u}}^\perp(\mathbf{A}), \sigma}$.

Lemma 2 ([14]). *Let n, m, q be positive integers with $m \geq 2n \log q$, $\sigma \geq \omega(\sqrt{\log m})$, and $\mathbf{u}$ be an arbitrary vector in $\mathbb{Z}_q^n$. Then, for all but a q^{-n} fraction of $\mathbf{A} \in \mathbb{Z}_q^{n \times m}$, if we sample a vector $\mathbf{x} \leftarrow D_{\Lambda_{\mathbf{u}}^\perp(\mathbf{A}), \sigma}$, we have $\Pr[\|\mathbf{x}\| > \sqrt{m}\sigma] < \mathsf{negl}(n)$.*

Lemma 3 (Noise Rerandomization, [18]). *Let q, ℓ, m be positive integers and r a positive real satisfying $r > \max\{\omega(\sqrt{\log m}), \omega(\sqrt{\log \ell})\}$. Let $\mathbf{b} \in \mathbb{Z}_q^m$ be arbitrary and $\mathbf{z}$ chosen from $D_{\mathbb{Z}^m, r}$. Then there exists a PPT algorithm ReRand such that for any $\mathbf{V} \in \mathbb{Z}^{m \times \ell}$ and positive real $\sigma > s_1(\mathbf{V})$, $\mathsf{ReRand}(\mathbf{V}, \mathbf{b} + \mathbf{z}, r, \sigma)$ outputs $\mathbf{b}'^\top = \mathbf{b}^\top \mathbf{V} + \mathbf{z}'^\top \in \mathbb{Z}_q^\ell$, where $\mathbf{z}'$ is distributed statistically close to $D_{\mathbb{Z}^\ell, 2r\sigma}$.*

Sampling Algorithms. The following lemma states useful algorithms for sampling short vectors from lattices.

Lemma 4 ([14,20]). *Let $n, m, q > 0$ be integers with $m \geq 2n \log q$.*

- TrapGen$(1^n, 1^m, q) \rightarrow (\mathbf{A}, \mathbf{T_A})$: *There exists a randomized algorithm that outputs a matrix $\mathbf{A} \in \mathbb{Z}_q^{n \times m}$ and a full-rank matrix $\mathbf{T_A} \in \mathbb{Z}^{m \times m}$, where $\mathbf{T_A}$ is a basis for $\Lambda^{\perp}(\mathbf{A})$, $\mathbf{A}$ is statistically close to uniform and $\|\mathbf{T_A}\|_{\mathsf{GS}} = O(\sqrt{n \log q})$.*
- SamplePre$(\mathbf{A}, \mathbf{u}, \mathbf{T_A}, \sigma) \rightarrow \mathbf{e}$: *There exists a randomized algorithm that, given a matrix $\mathbf{A} \in \mathbb{Z}_q^{n \times m}$, a vector $\mathbf{u} \in \mathbb{Z}_q^n$, a basis $\mathbf{T_A}$ for $\Lambda^{\perp}(\mathbf{A})$, and a Gaussian parameter $\sigma > \|\mathbf{T_A}\|_{\mathsf{GS}} \cdot \omega(\sqrt{\log m})$, outputs a vector $\mathbf{e} \in \mathbb{Z}^m$ sampled from a distribution which is $\mathsf{negl}(n)$-close to $D_{\Lambda_{\mathbf{u}}^{\perp}(\mathbf{A}), \sigma}$.*

Hardness Assumption. We define the Learning with Errors (LWE) problem introduced by Regev [24].

Definition 1 (Learning with Errors). *For integers $n = n(\lambda)$, $m = m(\lambda)$, $q = q(n) > 2$, an error distribution $\chi = \chi(n)$ over $\mathbb{Z}^m$, and a PPT algorithm $\mathcal{A}$, the advantage for the learning with errors problem $\mathsf{LWE}_{n,m,q,\chi}$ of $\mathcal{A}$ is defined as $\mathsf{Adv}_{\mathcal{A}}^{\mathsf{LWE}_{n,m,q,\chi}} = \left| \Pr\left[\mathcal{A}(\mathbf{A}, \mathbf{A}^{\top}\mathbf{s} + \mathbf{z}) = 1 \right] - \Pr\left[\mathcal{A}(\mathbf{A}, \mathbf{w} + \mathbf{z}) = 1 \right] \right|$ where $\mathbf{A} \leftarrow \mathbb{Z}_q^{n \times m}$, $\mathbf{s} \leftarrow \mathbb{Z}_q^n$, $\mathbf{w} \leftarrow \mathbb{Z}_q^m$, and $\mathbf{z} \leftarrow \chi$. We say that the LWE assumption holds if $\mathsf{Adv}_{\mathcal{A}}^{\mathsf{LWE}_{n,m,q,\chi}}$ is negligible for all PPT algorithm $\mathcal{A}$.*

We note adding the noise term $\mathbf{z} \leftarrow \chi$ to the uniform element in $\mathbf{w} \leftarrow \mathbb{Z}_q^m$ is done intentional. This is only a syntactical change to make the proof using Lemma 3 during the security proof easier as done in prior works [18,19].

For prime q and $\alpha \in (0, 1)$, the (decisional) $\mathsf{LWE}_{n,m,q,D_{\mathbb{Z},\alpha q}}$ for $\alpha q > 2\sqrt{n}$ has been shown by Regev [24] via a quantum reduction to be as hard as approximating the worst-case SIVP and GapSVP problems to within $\tilde{O}(n/\alpha)$ factors in the ℓ_2-norm in the worst case. In the subsequent works, (partial) dequantumization of the reduction were achieved [7,21].

3 Blind Identity-Based Encryption with Certified Identities

In this section, we present a new and secure IBE formalization that resolves the key escrow problem. As mentioned in the introduction, we refer to this primitive as *blind IBE with certified identities*, since the secret key-generation process can be seen as blind IBE [8,15] with an ICA to certify users' identities. For simplicity, we occasionally call it "IBE" for simplicity.

In our scheme, users first authenticate themselves with the ICA to obtain certificates, which they then use to run an interactive protocol with the KGC and construct secret keys $\mathsf{sk_{ID}}$ for use as in standard IBE. Here, the KGC never knows which user ID it is interacting with, and in particular, this implies that it does not know the $\mathsf{sk_{ID}}$. We assume that users communicate with the ICA and the KGC via secure channels. Note that we use the same encryption and decryption algorithms as in standard IBE.

Definition 2 (Blind IBE with Certified Identities). *A blind IBE scheme with certified identities* Π_{IBE} *consists of the following PPT algorithms:*

$\mathsf{Setup}(1^\lambda) \to$ params*: The setup algorithm takes as input a security parameter* 1^λ*, and outputs a public parameter* params*. We assume the identity space* $\mathcal{ID}$ *and the message space* $\mathcal{M}$ *are defined by* params*. Moreover, we assume* params *are implicitly provided as input to all algorithms.*

$\mathsf{KGC.KeyGen}($params$) \to ($mpk, msk$)$*: The setup algorithm run by KGC takes as input* params*, and outputs a master public key* mpk *and a master secret key* msk*.*

$\mathsf{ICA.KeyGen}($params$) \to ($vk, ik$)$*: The key-generation algorithm run by ICA takes as input* params*, and outputs a certificate verification key* vk *and a certificate-issuing key* ik*.*

$\mathsf{ICA.Cert}($vk, ik, ID$) \to ($cert, td$)$*: The certificate-issuing algorithm run by ICA takes as inputs a certificate verification key* vk*, certificate-issuing key* ik *and an identity* ID $\in \mathcal{ID}$*, and outputs a certificate* cert *and a trapdoor information* td*.*

$\mathsf{IBE.Enc}($mpk, ID, M$) \to$ ct*: The encryption algorithm run by a user takes as inputs the master public key* mpk*, an identity* ID $\in \mathcal{ID}$ *and a message* M $\in \mathcal{M}$*, and outputs a ciphertext* ct*.*

$\mathsf{IBE.Dec}($mpk, sk$_{\mathsf{ID}},$ ct$) \to$ M *or* $\perp$*: The decryption algorithm run by a user takes as input the master public key* mpk*, a secret key* sk$_{\mathsf{ID}}$ *and a ciphertext* ct*, and outputs* M *or* $\perp$*.*

$\langle\mathsf{ObtainKey}($mpk, ID, cert, td$), \mathsf{IssueKey}(mpk, msk, vk)\rangle$*:   The   interactive   key-issuing protocol between a user and the KGC involves two interactive algorithms* ObtainKey *and* IssueKey*. The user and the KGC interactively run the* ObtainKey *algorithm and the* IssueKey *algorithm, respectively, as follows.*

    User: *The user takes as input* (mpk, ID, cert, td) *as specified by the input of* ObtainKey*, and sends a first-round message* M$_{\mathsf{user}}$ *to KGC.*

    KGC: *The KGC takes as input* (mpk, msk, vk) *as specified by the input of* IssueKey *along with the message* M$_{\mathsf{user}}$ *sent by the user, and returns a second-round message* M$_{\mathsf{KGC}}$ *to the user.*

    User: *On input the message* M$_{\mathsf{KGC}}$ *from the KGC, the user (locally) outputs either* sk$_{\mathsf{ID}}$ *or* $\perp$*.*

We denote (sk, ϵ) $\leftarrow \langle\mathsf{ObtainKey}($mpk, ID, cert, td$), \mathsf{IssueKey}(mpk, msk, vk)\rangle$ *to indicate that the final output obtained by the user and the KGC are the secret key* sk$_{\mathsf{ID}}$ *and an empty string* ϵ*, respectively. Note that depending on what the KGC responds as the second message* M$_{\mathsf{KGC}}$*,* sk$_{\mathsf{ID}}$ *may be set to* $\perp$*. Furthermore, we call* (M$_{\mathsf{user}}$, M$_{\mathsf{KGC}}$) *as the* transcript *of the protocol.*

Correctness. For all $\lambda \in \mathbb{N}$, all ID $\in \mathcal{ID}$, and all M $\in \mathcal{M}$, IBE.Dec (mpk, sk$_{\mathsf{ID}}$, ct) $=$ M holds with overwhelming probability where it is taken over the randomness used in running params $\leftarrow$ Setup(1^λ), (mpk, msk) $\leftarrow$ KGC.KeyGen(params), (vk, ik) $\leftarrow$ ICA.KeyGen(params), (cert, td) $\leftarrow$ ICA.Cert (vk, ik, ID), (sk$_{\mathsf{ID}}$, ϵ) $\leftarrow \langle\mathsf{ObtainKey}($mpk, ID, cert, td$), \mathsf{IssueKey}(mpk, msk, vk)\rangle$, and ct $\leftarrow$ IBE.Enc(mpk, ID, M).

Remark 1 (On the round complexity of key issuing). The above definition only considers a two-move key-issuing protocol. One can easily generalize the definition to a multi-move protocol, however, we restricted it to a two-move protocol for simplicity. Indeed, the instantiation we provide in Sect. 4 will be two-move.

Security Against Users. As in standard IBE, we consider the notion of security against corrupted users and define indistinguishability against chosen plaintext attacks. We call this IND-ANON-CPA, to explicitly indicate that it implies anonymity. Broadly speaking, this differs from other similar definitions or standard IBE in that an adversary $\mathcal{A}$ can access the certifying oracle, that will output certificates for any ID (except the challenge identity ID*), and can also supply the certificates obtained to the key-generation oracle. Note that we do not consider an adversary $\mathcal{A}$ that can obtain a certificate for ID*, since this will allow $\mathcal{A}$ to trivially break security. This corresponds to the assumption that, in practice, an adversary cannot obtain a certificate for the challenge identity ID*.

Definition 3 (IND-ANON-CPA). *We define IND-ANON-CPA security by the following game between a challenger and a PPT adversary $\mathcal{A}$. Below, let* CTSamp *be a sampling algorithm that takes a master public key as input and outputs an element in the ciphertext space.*

- Setup. *At the outset of the game, the challenger runs* params $\leftarrow$ Setup(1^λ), (mpk, msk) $\leftarrow$ KGC.KeyGen(params), (vk, ik) $\leftarrow$ ICA.KeyGen(params), *and initializes an empty list* IDList := $\emptyset$. *The challenger further picks a random coin* coin $\leftarrow$ $\{0,1\}$ *and keeps it secret. The challenger gives* (params, mpk, vk) *to $\mathcal{A}$. After this, $\mathcal{A}$ can adaptively make the following three types of queries to the challenger in arbitrary order: certificate, secret key, and challenge queries. $\mathcal{A}$ can query the first two arbitrarily polynomially many times and the third only once.*

    Certificate Query: *If $\mathcal{A}$ submits* ID $\in \mathcal{ID}$ *to the challenger, the challenger computes* (cert, td) $\leftarrow$ ICA.Cert(vk, ik, ID) *and returns* (cert, td) *to $\mathcal{A}$. It then stores* ID *to* IDList.

    Secret Key Query: *If $\mathcal{A}$ submits a first-round message* M_{user} *to the challenger, the challenger runs the* IssueKey *algorithm taking as inputs* (mpk, msk, vk) *and the message* M_{user}, *and obtains a second-round message* M_{KGC}. *It then returns* M_{KGC} *to $\mathcal{A}$.*

    Challenge Query: *If $\mathcal{A}$ submits* (ID*, M*) *to the challenger where* ID* $\in$ $\mathcal{ID}$, ID* $\notin$ IDList, *and* M* $\in \mathcal{M}$, *the challenger proceeds as follows: If* coin $= 0$, *the challenger returns* ct* $\leftarrow$ IBE.Enc(mpk, ID*, M*). *Otherwise, if* coin $= 1$, *the challenger returns* ct* $\leftarrow$ CTSamp(mpk).

- Guess. *$\mathcal{A}$ outputs a guess* $\widehat{\text{coin}} \in \{0,1\}$ *for* coin. *We say that* Π_{IBE} *is IND-ANON-CPA secure if the advantage*

$$\text{Adv}_{\text{IBE},\mathcal{A}}^{\text{IND-ANON-CPA}}(\lambda) = \left| \Pr[\text{coin} = \widehat{\text{coin}}] - 1/2 \right|$$

is negligible for any PPT adversary $\mathcal{A}$.

Security Against the KGC. We also consider the notion of security against the honest-but-curious KGC, which follows the protocol but attempts to obtain information about the underlying plaintexts from the observed ciphertexts. This is a more stringent and practical security notion than the corresponding notion informally stated in [10]. A more detailed explanation on the difference between prior works is provided in Remark 2. In brief, our definition guarantees that if the KGC runs, i.e., generates secret keys as specified, it cannot obtain any information about the corresponding identities or plaintexts from ciphertexts, even if it uses knowledge obtained via the key-issuing protocol.

At the start of the security game, the adversary $\mathcal{A}$ is given the master secret key msk along with all public information (mpk, params, vk). In addition, $\mathcal{A}$ is allowed to access two oracles, namely, the key-generation and encryption oracles. First, $\mathcal{A}$ obtains the secret key $\mathsf{sk_{ID}}$ for a randomly chosen identity ID from the key-generation oracle. This captures the scenario where an unknown user ID generates their secret key $\mathsf{sk_{ID}}$ via executing $\langle \mathsf{ObtainKey}, \mathsf{IssueKey} \rangle$ with the KGC. The identities sent to the key-generation oracle are stored in an identity list IDList. In addition, for any plaintext M and any ID in IDList, $\mathcal{A}$ can ask for a ciphertext ct from the encryption oracle. This captures the scenario where the KGC can observe ciphertexts for all users to whom it has issued secret keys. In the challenge phase, $\mathcal{A}$ specifies the challenge identity ID^* from IDList (and submits an arbitrary message M^*) to obtain the challenge ciphertext ct^*. Note that $\mathcal{A}$ does not specify ID nor ID^* itself, but simply specifies the indices in IDList. It is clear that if ciphertexts reveal any information about the corresponding identities, $\mathcal{A}$ could easily win the game by creating $\mathsf{sk_{ID^*}}$. In particular, our definition captures both indistinguishability and anonymity.

Definition 4 (IND-ANON-KGC). *We define IND-ANON-KGC security by the following game between a challenger and a PPT adversary $\mathcal{A}$. Below, let* CTSamp *be a sampling algorithm that takes a master public key as input and outputs an element in the ciphertext space.*[3]

- Setup. *At the outset of the game, the challenger runs* params $\leftarrow$ Setup(1^λ), (mpk, msk) $\leftarrow$ KGC.KeyGen(params), (vk, ik) $\leftarrow$ ICA.KeyGen(params) *and initializes an empty set* IDList $:= \emptyset$ *and an integer* $Q_{\mathsf{key}} := 0$. *The challenger further picks a random coin* coin $\leftarrow \{0, 1\}$ *and keeps it secret. The challenger gives* (params, mpk, msk, vk) *to* $\mathcal{A}$. *After this,* $\mathcal{A}$ *can adaptively make the following three types of queries to the challenger in an arbitrary order: encryption, issue key, and challenge queries.* $\mathcal{A}$ *can query the first two arbitrarily polynomial many times and the third only once.*

  Encryption Query: *If* $\mathcal{A}$ *submits an index i and a message* M $\in \mathcal{M}$ *to the challenger, the challenger first checks if $i \in [Q_{\mathsf{key}}]$ where $[0]$ is defined as the empty set. If not, the challenger forces* $\mathcal{A}$ *to output a random coin* $\widehat{\mathsf{coin}}$

---

[3] We note that the sampling algorithm CTSamp does not necessarily have to be identical to the one we defined in the IND-ANON-CPA security. This is true for the subsequent IND-ANON-ICA security.

in $\{0,1\}$. *Otherwise, the challenger retrieves the i-th entry* ID *of* IDList *and returns* ct ← IBE.Enc(mpk, ID, M).

IssueKey Query: *If* $\mathcal{A}$ *makes an IssueKey query, the challenger first randomly samples* ID ← $\mathcal{ID}$ *and computes* (cert, td) ← ICA.Cert(vk, ik, ID). *It then runs* ObtainKey *on inputs* (mpk, ID, cert, td) *to obtain the first-round message* M_{user} *and returns* M_{user} *to* $\mathcal{A}$. *Finally, the challenger stores* ID *to* IDList *and updates* Q_{key} ← $Q_{key} + 1$.

Challenge Query: *If* $\mathcal{A}$ *submits* (M^*, i^*) *to the challenger where* $M^* \in \mathcal{M}$, *the challenger first checks if* $i^* \in [Q_{key}]$. *If not, the challenger forces* $\mathcal{A}$ *to output a random coin* $\widehat{coin}$ *in* $\{0,1\}$. *Otherwise, the challenger proceeds as follows: The challenger first retrieves the* i^*-*th entry* ID^* *of* IDList. *Then, if* coin = 0, *the challenger returns* ct^* ← IBE.Enc(mpk, ID^*, M^*). *Otherwise, if* coin = 1, *the challenger returns* ct^* ← CTSamp(mpk).

– *Guess.* $\mathcal{A}$ *outputs a guess* $\widehat{coin}$ ∈ $\{0,1\}$ *for* coin. *We say that* Π_{IBE} *is IND-ANON-KGC secure if the advantage*

$$\mathsf{Adv}_{IBE,\mathcal{A}}^{IND\text{-}ANON\text{-}KGC}(\lambda) = \left| \Pr[coin = \widehat{coin}] - 1/2 \right|$$

is negligible for any PPT adversary $\mathcal{A}$.

Remark 2 (Differences from the existing definition). As described above, our idea is based on Chow's work [10]. However, Chow's notion of security against the KGC (ACI-KGC) is defined for standard IBE under the assumption that the KGC does not know the identities used in the system. However, this assumption is generally invalid since, in practice, the KGC manages identity lists in order to identify users before generating their keys.[4] By contrast, IND-ANON-KGC is defined for a version of IBE where the KGC generates secret keys without having access to such an identity list, meaning that the key-generation process does not violate the real-world usage.

Security Against the ICA. Unlike Chow's work [10] that only considered a fully trusted ICA, we aim to define security against a potentially malicious ICA. However, such a definition is difficult. A malicious ICA can generate certificates for any identity ID and thereby obtain the corresponding secret keys by impersonating the user and interacting with the KGC. Therefore, in principle, we cannot allow the ICA to have arbitrary access to the key-generation oracle (i.e., interacting with the KGC). Given this, we model the malicious ICA that generates a potentially malicious key pair (vk, ik) Given this, we model the malicious ICA to have the capability of generating a potentially malicious key pair (vk, ik) [5] while disallowing it to have access to the key-generation oracle. Unlike Chow's definition, our definition prevents to construct a trivial IBE

---

[4] In the same paper [10], Chow acknowledged this issue and introduced an anonymous key-issuing protocol to close the gap between the assumption and reality, however, he did not give any formal definition of ACI-KGC for IBE where secret keys are generated with this protocol.

[5] Looking ahead, this will be implicit in our definition since the IBE.Enc algorithm is independent of (vk, ik).

scheme secure against the KGC mentioned in the introduction; the ICA plays the role of the KGC in a standard IBE scheme and the KGC does nothing.

Definition 5 (IND-ANON-ICA). *We define IND-ANON-ICA security by the following game between a challenger and an PPT adversary $\mathcal{A}$. Below, let* CTSamp *be a sampling algorithm that takes a master public key as input and outputs an element in the ciphertext space.*

- Setup. *At the outset of the game, the challenger runs* params $\leftarrow$ Setup(1^λ) *and* (mpk, msk) $\leftarrow$ KGC.KeyGen(params). *The challenger picks a random coin* coin $\leftarrow$ $\{0, 1\}$ *and keeps it secret. The challenger gives* (params, mpk) *to* $\mathcal{A}$. *Then,* $\mathcal{A}$ *can make the following challenge query once.*

    Challenge Query: *If* $\mathcal{A}$ *submits* (ID*, M*) *to the challenger where* ID* $\in$ $\mathcal{ID}$ *and* M* $\in$ $\mathcal{M}$, *the challenger proceeds as follows: If* coin $= 0$, *the challenger returns* ct* $\leftarrow$ IBE.Enc(mpk, ID*, M*). *Otherwise, if* coin $= 1$, *the challenger returns* ct* $\leftarrow$ CTSamp(mpk).

- Guess. $\mathcal{A}$ *outputs a guess* $\widehat{\text{coin}}$ $\in$ $\{0, 1\}$ *for* coin. *We say that* Π_{IBE} *is IND-ANON-ICA secure if the advantage*

$$\mathsf{Adv}_{\mathsf{IBE},\mathcal{A}}^{\text{IND-ANON-ICA}}(\lambda) = \left| \Pr[\text{coin} = \widehat{\text{coin}}] - 1/2 \right|$$

is negligible for any PPT adversary $\mathcal{A}$.

Remark 3. One can consider a stronger definition than what we define above; the malicious ICA is allowed to get secret keys for any ID ($\neq$ ID*) during the game. The reason why we do not define this stronger notion is that, compared to our weaker definition, it seems to only capture some additional unnatural scenarios. In practice, if the ICA can impersonate any user ID ($\neq$ ID*) and interact with the KGC, it is only fair to assume that it is also able to impersonate ID*, and hence, obtain a secret key for ID* by interacting with the KGC. Nonetheless, we like to point out that our construction appearing in the next section can in fact be proven to satisfy such a stronger definition.

4   Proposed IBE Scheme

In this section, we present our proposed scheme. This combines the GPV IBE scheme [14] with Rückert's full-domain hash style lattice-based blind signature scheme [25]. Although Rückert [26] later found [25] that his signature scheme is vulnerable (to an attack we will explain later), fortunately, this vulnerability does not affect our scheme, where the ICA issues a certificate and the KGC issues a secret key only if the certificate is valid.

Construction. Let the identity space $\mathcal{ID}$ of the IBE scheme Π_{IBE} be $\mathcal{ID} = \{0, 1\}^*$. In practice, by using collusion resistant hash functions, we can set $\mathcal{ID} = \{0, 1\}^\ell$ for $\ell = O(\lambda)$. Here, we occasionally treat elements in $\mathbb{Z}_q^n$ as binary strings over $\{0, 1\}^{n \log q}$ through some fixed canonical embedding. Let PRF : $\mathcal{K} \times \mathcal{X} \to$

$\mathcal{Y}$ be any pseudorandom function with appropriate domain $\mathcal{X}$ and range $\mathcal{Y}$. I.e., let $\mathcal{X}$ include $\mathcal{ID}$ and the set of all the first-round messages M_{user}, and let range $\mathcal{Y}$ include an appropriate length of randomness used by algorithms ICA.Cert and IssueKey. Finally, let Π_{Sig} : (Sig.KeyGen, Sig.Sign, Sig.Verify) be a deterministic digital signature scheme with message space $\{0,1\}^{n \log q}$ where the randomness used to sign a message is derived deterministically from the signing key and the message. Using PRFs, any digital signature scheme can be derandomized. We assume that Π_{Sig} provides the standard security notion of existential unforgeability under an adaptive chosen message attack (eu-cma).

Setup(1^λ): Choose positive integers n, m and prime q, and output params = $(1^\lambda, 1^n, 1^m, q, \alpha', \sigma, H)$, where $H : \{0,1\}^* \to \mathbb{Z}_q^n$ is a hash function modeled as a random oracle.

KGC.KeyGen(params): Run $(\mathbf{A}, \mathbf{T_A}) \leftarrow$ TrapGen($1^n, 1^m, q$) and sample a PRF key $s_{KGC} \leftarrow \mathcal{K}$. Then, output a master pubic key mpk $= \mathbf{A} \in \mathbb{Z}_q^{n \times m}$ and a master secret key msk $= (\mathbf{T_A}, s_{KGC})$.

ICA.KeyGen(params): Run $(vk_{Sig}, sk_{Sig}) \leftarrow$ Sig.KeyGen(1^λ) and sample a PRF key $s_{ICA} \leftarrow \mathcal{K}$. Then, output a certificate verification key vk $= vk_{Sig}$ and a certificate issuing key ik $= (sk_{Sig}, s_{ICA})$.

ICA.Cert(vk, ik, ID): Parse ik $= (sk_{Sig}, s_{ICA})$ and compute $\mathbf{u}_{ID} = H(ID)$. Then, sample a short vector $\mathbf{y}_{ID,1} \leftarrow \{0,1\}^m$ and compute $\mathbf{u}_{ID,1} = \mathbf{A}\mathbf{y}_{ID,1}$. Furthermore, compute $\mathbf{u}_{ID,2} = \mathbf{u}_{ID} - \mathbf{u}_{ID,1} \in \mathbb{Z}_q^n$ and $\sigma_{Sig} \leftarrow$ Sig.Sign($sk_{Sig}, \mathbf{u}_{ID,2}$). Finally, output a certificate cert $= (\mathbf{u}_{ID,2}, \sigma_{Sig})$ and trapdoor information td $= \mathbf{y}_{ID,1}$. Here, we assume all the randomness used in this algorithm is derived from $r_{ID} \leftarrow$ PRF(s_{ICA}, ID).

IBE.Enc(mpk, ID, M): Compute $\mathbf{u}_{ID} = H(ID)$. To encrypt a message M $\in \{0,1\}$, sample $\mathbf{s} \leftarrow \mathbb{Z}_q^n$, $\mathbf{x} \leftarrow D_{\mathbb{Z}^m, \alpha' q}$, and $x \leftarrow D_{\mathbb{Z}, \alpha' q}$, and compute $c_0 = \mathbf{u}_{ID}^\top \mathbf{s} + x + M\lfloor q/2 \rceil$ and $\mathbf{c}_1 = \mathbf{A}^\top \mathbf{s} + \mathbf{x}$. Finally, output a ciphertext ct $= (c_0, \mathbf{c}_1)$.

IBE.Dec(mpk, sk_{ID}, ct): Parse $sk_{ID} = \mathbf{e}_{ID}$ and ct $= (c_0, \mathbf{c}_1)$. Compute $w = c_0 - \mathbf{e}_{ID}^\top \mathbf{c}_1$. Output 0 if w is closer to 0 than to $\lfloor q/2 \rceil$ modulo q, and 1, otherwise.

⟨ObtainKey(mpk, ID, cert, td), IssueKey(mpk, msk, vk)⟩: The user and the KGC interactively runs ObtainKey and IssueKey, respectively.

User: On input (mpk, ID, cert, td), set the first-round message M_{user} = cert and send M_{user} to the KGC. Here, cert $= (\mathbf{u}_{ID,2}, \sigma_{Sig})$.

KGC: On input (mpk, msk, vk) and the first-round message M_{user}, parse vk $= vk_{Sig}$ and $M_{user} = (\mathbf{u}_{ID,2}, \sigma_{Sig})$. If Sig.Verify($vk_{Sig}, \mathbf{u}_{ID,2}, \sigma_{Sig}$) $= \bot$, then set $M_{KGC} = \bot$ and send M_{KGC} to the user. Otherwise, parse mpk $= \mathbf{A}$ and msk $= (\mathbf{T_A}, s_{KGC})$. Then, sample a short vector $\mathbf{y}_{ID,2} \leftarrow$ SamplePre($\mathbf{A}, \mathbf{u}_{ID,2}, \mathbf{T_A}, \sigma$), set $M_{KGC} = \mathbf{y}_{ID,2}$, and send M_{KGC} to the user. Here, we assume all the randomness used in this algorithm is derived from $r_{M_{user}} \leftarrow$ PRF(s_{KGC}, M_{user}).

User: If $M_{KGC} = \bot$, then output $\bot$. Otherwise, parse td $= \mathbf{y}_{ID,1}$ and $M_{KGC} = \mathbf{y}_{ID,2}$, set $\mathbf{e}_{ID} = \mathbf{y}_{ID,1} + \mathbf{y}_{ID,2}$ and (locally) output the secret key $sk_{ID} = \mathbf{e}_{ID}$.

Remark 4 (Generating randomness via PRFs). Here, we generate the randomness used by the ICA.Cert and IssueKey algorithms via PRFs. This has the effect of only allowing the adversary to obtain one valid certificate cert per identity ID and one valid second-round message M_{KGC} per first-round message $M_{user}(= cert)$. We require this condition during the security proof for reasons similar to those for other lattice-based IBE schemes [2,9,14].

Remark 5 (Role of certificates). If the validity of cert is not checked, then users can obtain information about the master secret key as follows. First, the user samples y_1 from $\mathbb{Z}_q^m$, computes $u' = Ay_1$, and then sends u' directly to the KGC, which returns e_{ID} such that $Ae_{ID} = u'$. If we let $e = y_1 - e_{ID}$, then $Ae = A(y_1 - e_{ID}) = 0$. This means that the user has obtained an e satisfying $Ae = 0$. If enough users collude together, than we can recover a trapdoor T_A for A such that $AT_A = 0$. Thus, for the security proof, we must require that users cannot obtain such an e. This attack has been identified by Rückert [26] as an issue in constructing a full-domain-hash style lattice-based blind signature scheme. In our scheme, users have no choice but to use the u'_{ID} issued by the ICA unless they can forge cert, and this issue does not appear.

Correctness. The following lemma states the correctness of our blind IBE scheme with certified identity.

Lemma 5 (Correctness). *Suppose the parameters q, σ and α' satisfy $\sigma > \omega(\sqrt{n \log m \log q})$ and $\alpha' < 1/(8\sigma\sqrt{m})$. Then our scheme is correct with overwhelming probability.*

Proof. If the key issuing protocol between the user and the KGC is run correctly, then any user ID will obtain a secret key $sk_{ID} = e_{ID}$ such that $Ae_{ID} = A(y_{ID,1} + y_{ID,2}) = u_{ID,1} + u_{ID,2} = u_{ID}$. Let $ct \leftarrow IBE.Enc(mpk, ID.M)$. Then when we run IBE.Dec with sk_{ID}, we obtain $w = c_0 - e_{ID}^\top c_1 = M\lfloor q/2 \rceil + x + (y_{ID,1} + y_{ID,2})^\top x$. By Lemma 4, we have that $y_{ID,2}$ is distributed negligibly close to $D_{\Lambda_{u_{ID,2}}^\perp(A),\sigma}$. Then, by Lemma 2, we have $\|y_{ID,2}\| \leq \sigma\sqrt{m}$ with overwhelming probability. Since, $x \leftarrow D_{\mathbb{Z},\alpha'q}$ and $x \leftarrow D_{\mathbb{Z}^m,\alpha'q}$ and $y_{ID,1} \in \{0,1\}^m$ the error term w can be bounded by $\|x + (y_{ID,1} + y_{ID,2})^\top x\| \leq 2\alpha'q\sigma\sqrt{m}$, where we used the subgaussian property to make a finer analysis of the noise bound on $y_{ID,1}^\top x$ (See for example [14,22]). Hence, for the error term to have absolute value less than $q/4$, it suffices to choose the parameters as in the statement. □

Parameter Selection. For the system to satisfy correctness and make the security proof work, we need the following restrictions. Note that we will prove the security of the scheme under the LWE assumption whose noise rate is α, which is lower than α' that is used in the encryption algorithm.

- The error term is less than $q/4$ (i.e., $\alpha' < 1/8\sigma\sqrt{m}$ by Lemma 5)
- TrapGen operates properly (i.e., $m > 3n \log q$ by Lemma 4)
- Samplable from $D_{\Lambda_u^\perp(A),\sigma}$ (i.e., $\sigma > \|T_A\|_{GS} \cdot \omega(\sqrt{\log m}) = O(\sqrt{n \log m \log q})$ by Lemma 4),
- σ is sufficiently large so that we can apply Lemma 1 (i.e., $\sigma > \omega(\log n)$),
- We can apply Lemma 3 (i.e., $\alpha'/2\alpha > \sqrt{(\sigma + 1)^2 m + 1}$),
- $LWE_{n,m,q,D_{\mathbb{Z},\alpha q}}$ is hard (e.g., $\alpha q > 2\sqrt{n}$ for prime q).

To satisfy these requirements, for example, we can set the parameters $m, q, \sigma, \alpha, \alpha'$ as: $m = n^{1+\kappa}$, $q = n^{2+3.5\kappa}$, $\sigma = n^{0.5+\kappa}$, $\alpha'q = n^{1.5+2\kappa}$, and $\alpha q = 2 \cdot n^{0.5}$, where $\kappa > 0$ is a constant that can be set arbitrarily small. In the above, we round up m to the nearest integer and q to the nearest largest prime.

Multi-bit Encryption. Although the above scheme only provides 1-bit encryption, we can extend it to provide k-bit encryption without incurring a factor k blow up of the ciphertext size. We change the range of the hash function as $H : \{0,1\}^* \to \mathbb{Z}_q^{n \times k}$. Then, a plaintext vector $M \in \mathbb{Z}_q^k$ is encrypted as $c_0 = u_{ID}^\top s + x' + M\lfloor q/2 \rceil \in \mathbb{Z}_q^k$ where $s \leftarrow \mathbb{Z}_q^{n \times k}$ and $x' \leftarrow D_{\mathbb{Z}^k, \alpha'q}$ (c_1 is the same). Note that the secret key is now required to be a matrix $e_{ID} \in \mathbb{Z}^{m \times k}$.

5   Security Analysis

Theorem 1. *Our blind IBE scheme with certified identity Π_{IBE} is IND-ANON-CPA secure in the random oracle model if the underlying signature scheme Π_{Sig} is eu-cma secure, the PRF is pseudorandom, and assuming the hardness of $LWE_{n,m,q,D_{\mathbb{Z},\alpha q}}$. Alternatively, we can get rid of the second requirement by replacing the PRF by the random oracle.*

Proof Overview. Here, we give an overview of the proof and the proof is provided in the full version of this paper due to page limitation. The high level structure of the proof follows the original GPV IBE security proof. That is, for a random oracle query ID, the challenger first samples e_{ID} from $D_{\mathbb{Z}^m, \sigma}$ and sets $u_{ID} = Ae_{ID}$, instead of sampling e_{ID} from $D_{\Lambda_{u_{ID}}^\perp(A), \sigma}$. Since our key-issuing protocol is 2-move, and $u_{ID,2}$ contained in $u_{ID,2}$ depends on the key issuing, we employ this idea twice: the challenger samples $y_{ID,1}$ from $\{0,1\}^m$ and $y_{ID,2}$ from $D_{\Lambda_u^\perp(A), \sigma}$, and sets $u_{ID} = A(y_{ID,1} + y_{ID,2})$, and also sets $u_{ID,2} = u_{ID} - Ay_{ID,1}$. We remark that the distribution of $Ay_{ID,2}$ is statistically close to uniform over $\mathbb{Z}_q^n$ [14], and thus $u_{ID} \leftarrow \mathbb{Z}_q^n$ and $u_{ID} = A(y_{ID,1} + y_{ID,2})$ are identical from $\mathcal{A}$'s view. We also remark that we adopt the proof strategy of Katsumata et al. [19]. In the original GPV-IBE scheme the so-called partitioning technique was used to prove security; the simulator divides the identity space into two in such a way that for one partition it can only construct secret keys and for the other it can only construct challenge ciphertexts. However, this proof strategy was notorious for having a loose reduction. Recently, Katsumata et al. [19] provided a much tighter reduction by following the proof technique of the Cramer-Shoup encryption scheme [11]. Since our proof follows the strategy of [19], it enjoys tight security as well.

Theorem 2. *Our blind IBE scheme with certified identity Π_{IBE} is IND-ANON-KGC secure in the random oracle model if the PRF is pseudorandom and assuming the hardness of the $LWE_{n,m,q,D_{\mathbb{Z},\alpha q}}$ problem. Alternatively, we can get rid of the first requirement by replacing the PRF by the random oracle.*

Proof Overview. In our security proof, we use the fact that $\mathbf{u}_{\mathsf{ID}} = \mathsf{H}(\mathsf{ID}) \in \mathbb{Z}_q^n$ is distributed as a uniformly random vector from the view of the adversary in the random oracle model and embed $\mathbf{u}_{\mathsf{ID}}$ as the LWE secret, rather than embedding the encryption randomness $\mathbf{s}$ as in previous proofs. Recall that the LWE assumption informally states the following: given a uniformly random matrix $\mathbf{B} \leftarrow \mathbb{Z}_q^{n \times \ell}$ and some vector $\mathbf{v} \in \mathbb{Z}_q^{\ell}$, there is no PPT algorithm that can decide with non-negligible probability whether $\mathbf{v}$ is of the form $\mathbf{B}^{\top}\mathbf{d} + \mathbf{x}$ for some secret vector $\mathbf{d} \leftarrow \mathbb{Z}_q^n$ and noise $\mathbf{x}$, or a uniformly random vector over $\mathbb{Z}_q^{\ell}$. To restate, while in prior proofs encryption randomness $\mathbf{s}$ was set as the LWE secret $\mathbf{d}$, during our security proof, we set $\mathbf{u}_{\mathsf{ID}} = \mathsf{H}(\mathsf{ID})$ as $\mathbf{d}$ instead. Moreover, since the encryption randomness $\mathbf{s}$ of each ciphertext is completely known to the adversary in the IND-ANON-KGC setting, we set each of the $\mathbf{s}$ as the columns of the LWE matrix $\mathbf{B}$.

Proof. Let $\mathcal{A}$ be a PPT adversary against the IND-ANON-KGC security game with advantage ϵ. We assume $\mathcal{A}$ makes at most Q' random oracle queries, Q IssueKey queries, and N encryption queries, where $Q'(\lambda), Q(\lambda)$ and $N(\lambda)$ can be arbitrary large polynomials. We also define the sampling algorithm CTSamp as an algorithm which takes any $\mathsf{mpk} = \mathbf{A} \in \mathbb{Z}_q^{n \times m}$ as input and outputs $(t, \mathbf{A}^{\top}\mathbf{s} + \mathbf{x}) \in \mathbb{Z}_q \times \mathbb{Z}_q^m$, where $t \leftarrow \mathbb{Z}_q$, $\mathbf{s} \leftarrow \mathbb{Z}_q^n$, and $\mathbf{x} \leftarrow D_{\mathbb{Z}^m, \alpha' q}$. In the following let X_i denote the event that $\mathcal{A}$ wins in Game_i. We modify the games so that in the final game, the adversary will have no winning advantage.

Game_0: This is the original security game. At the beginning of the game the challenger prepares params, $(\mathsf{mpk}, \mathsf{msk})$, and $(\mathsf{vk}, \mathsf{ik})$ as specified by the game and gives $(\mathsf{params}, \mathsf{mpk}, \mathsf{msk}, \mathsf{vk})$ to $\mathcal{A}$. The challenger also prepares two empty lists IDList and HList, and an integer $Q_{\mathsf{key}} := 0$. Here, the list HList is absent in the security definition and only introduced to be used throughout this proof. Moreover, throughout this proof, for clarity we adopt the notation $\mathsf{IDList}[i] = \mathsf{ID}$ to indicate that the i-th index of the list IDList is set to ID. Initially, we have $\mathsf{IDList}[i] = \perp$ for all $i \in [Q]$. The challenger also picks a random coin $\mathsf{coin} \leftarrow \{0, 1\}$ which it keeps secret. Finally, the challenger answers to the queries made by the adversary $\mathcal{A}$ as follows:

- When $\mathcal{A}$ makes a random oracle query on ID, the challenger first checks if $(\mathsf{ID}, \star) \in \mathsf{HList}$. If so, it retrieves the (unique) tuple $(\mathsf{ID}, \mathbf{u}_{\mathsf{ID}})$ and returns $\mathbf{u}_{\mathsf{ID}}$ to $\mathcal{A}$. Otherwise, it samples a random $\mathbf{u}_{\mathsf{ID}} \leftarrow \mathbb{Z}_q^n$ and updates $\mathsf{HList} \leftarrow \mathsf{HList} \cup \{(\mathsf{ID}, \mathbf{u}_{\mathsf{ID}})\}$. Then, it returns $\mathbf{u}_{\mathsf{ID}}$ to $\mathcal{A}$. Here, the challenger can query the random oracle similarly to $\mathcal{A}$ (See the following item on IssueKey query).
- When $\mathcal{A}$ makes the j-th ($j \in [N]$) encryption query on index i and a message M_j, the challenger checks $i \in [Q_{\mathsf{key}}]$. If not, the challenger forces $\mathcal{A}$ to output a random coin $\widehat{\mathsf{coin}} \leftarrow \{0, 1\}$. Otherwise, it retrieves $\mathsf{ID}_i = \mathsf{IDList}[i]$ and the unique tuple $(\mathsf{ID}_i, \mathbf{u}_{\mathsf{ID}_i}) \in \mathsf{HList}$ (which is guaranteed to exist). Then, it computes $c_0^{(j)} = \mathbf{u}_{\mathsf{ID}_i}^{\top}\mathbf{s}_j + x_j + \mathsf{M}_j \lfloor q/2 \rceil$ and $\mathbf{c}_1^{(j)} = \mathbf{A}^{\top}\mathbf{s}_j + \mathbf{x}_j$ as specified by the scheme and returns the ciphertext $\mathsf{ct} = (c_0^{(j)}, \mathbf{c}_1^{(j)})$ to $\mathcal{A}$.
- When $\mathcal{A}$ makes an IssueKey query, the challenger first samples $\mathsf{ID} \leftarrow \mathcal{ID}$. It then queries the random oracle on input ID and receives back

u_{ID}. Then, it proceeds with generating (cert, td) as specified by algorithm ICA.Cert$(\text{vk}, \text{ik}, \text{ID})$ (i.e., runs the algorithm after the receiving $u_{ID} = H(\text{ID})$ back from the random oracle), and sets the first-round message $M_{user} = \text{cert}$. It then returns M_{user} to $\mathcal{A}$. Finally, the challenger updates $Q_{key} \leftarrow Q_{key} + 1$ and then sets $\text{IDList}[Q_{key}] = \text{ID}$. Here, as in the real scheme, the randomness used to compute M_{user} is generated by $r_{ID} \leftarrow \text{PRF}(s_{ICA}, \text{ID})$, where the PRF key s_{ICA} is included in the certificate issuing key ik which the challenger generates at the beginning of the game.

- When $\mathcal{A}$ queries for a challenge ciphertext on index i^* and a message M^*, the challenger checks $i^* \in [Q_{key}]$. If not, the challenger forces $\mathcal{A}$ to output a random coin $\widehat{\text{coin}} \leftarrow \{0,1\}$. Otherwise, it retrieves $\text{ID}_{i^*} = \text{IDList}[i^*]$ and the unique tuple $(\text{ID}_{i^*}, u_{\text{ID}_{i^*}}) \in \text{HList}$. It returns $\text{ct}^* \leftarrow \text{CTSamp}(\text{mpk})$ if $\text{coin} = 1$. Otherwise, if $\text{coin} = 0$, it proceeds the same as it does for the encryption queries and returns $\text{ct}^* = (c_0, \mathbf{c}_1) = (u_{\text{ID}_{i^*}}^\top \mathbf{s} + x + M^* \lfloor q/2 \rceil, \mathbf{A}^\top \mathbf{s} + \mathbf{x})$ to $\mathcal{A}$.

At the end of the game, $\mathcal{A}$ outputs a guess $\widehat{\text{coin}}$ for coin. Finally, the challenger outputs $\widehat{\text{coin}}$. By definition, we have $\left| \Pr[X_0] - \frac{1}{2} \right| = \left| \Pr[\widehat{\text{coin}} = \text{coin}] - \frac{1}{2} \right| = \text{Adv}_{\text{IBE}, \mathcal{A}}^{\text{IND-ANON-KGC}}(\lambda)$.

Game$_1$: In this game, we change how the challenger generates the randomness used for answering the IssueKey query. In particular, the challenger always samples fresh randomness to be used when made an IssueKey query. Notably, even if the challenger happens to sample the same ID on two different IssueKey queries, it will use an independently sampled randomness. The only difference in the view of the adversary $\mathcal{A}$ in Game$_0$ and Game$_1$, is how the randomness are generated to answer the IssueKey query. Since the identity space $\mathcal{ID}$ is exponentially large and $\mathcal{A}$ only makes $Q = \text{poly}(\lambda)$ many queries, the probability of sampling the same ID for two different IssueKey queries is negligible. Conditioned on this fact, the view of $\mathcal{A}$ is negligibly close assuming the pseudorandomness of the PRF. Therefore, combing the two arguments, we have $|\Pr[X_0] - \Pr[X_1]| = \text{negl}(\lambda)$. In the following games, we will no longer explicitly mention the used randomness for simplicity and assume $\text{ik} = \text{sk}_{\text{Sig}}$.

Game$_2$: In this game, we change how the challenger responds to the IssueKey queries. In particular, the challenger responds as follows for an IssueKey query:

- When $\mathcal{A}$ queries for an IssueKey query, the challenger first samples $\text{ID} \leftarrow \mathcal{ID}$. The challenger then queries the random oracle on input ID and receives back u_{ID}. Then, it samples $\mathbf{u}_{\text{ID},2} \leftarrow \mathbb{Z}_q^n$ (independent of ID) and signs $\sigma_{\text{Sig}} \leftarrow \text{Sig.Sign}(\text{sk}_{\text{Sig}}, \mathbf{u}_{\text{ID},2})$, where sk_{Sig} is included in the certificate issuing key ik. It then sets $M_{user} = \text{cert} = (\mathbf{u}_{\text{ID},2}, \sigma_{\text{Sig}})$, and returns M_{user} to $\mathcal{A}$. Finally, the challenger updates $Q_{key} \leftarrow Q_{key} + 1$ and sets $\text{IDList}[Q_{key}] = \text{ID}$.

From the view of the adversary $\mathcal{A}$, the only difference between the two games are in how the vector $\mathbf{u}_{\text{ID},2}$ is created. In the previous game, the challenger first sampled $\mathbf{y}_{\text{ID},1} \leftarrow \{0,1\}^m$ and set $\mathbf{u}_{\text{ID},2} = \mathbf{u}_{\text{ID}} - \mathbf{A}\mathbf{y}_{\text{ID},1}$ where $\mathbf{u}_{\text{ID}} = H(\text{ID})$

was obtained via a random oracle query. Here, combining the three facts; $\mathsf{td} = y_{\mathsf{ID},1} \leftarrow \{0,1\}^m$ is information theoretically hidden from $\mathcal{A}$; $\mathbf{A}$ is statistically close to uniform (Lemma 4); and by the left-over-hash lemma, we have that $\mathbf{u}_{\mathsf{ID},2}$ is distributed uniformly close to random over $\mathbb{Z}_q^n$ regardless of the value taken by $\mathbf{u}_{\mathsf{ID}}$. Therefore, since the distribution of $\mathbf{u}_{\mathsf{ID},2}$ is statistically close in Game_1 and Game_2, we have $|\Pr[X_1] - \Pr[X_2]| = \mathsf{negl}(\lambda)$.

Game_3: In this game, we change when the challenger queries each identity ID sampled during the IssueKey query to the random oracle. Namely, we make the following changes:

- When $\mathcal{A}$ queries for an IssueKey query the challenger directly samples $\mathbf{u} \leftarrow \mathbb{Z}_q^n$ and signs $\sigma_{\mathsf{Sig}} \leftarrow \mathsf{Sig.Sign}(\mathsf{sk}_{\mathsf{Sig}}, \mathbf{u})$. It then sets $\mathsf{M}_{\mathsf{user}} = \mathsf{cert} = (\mathbf{u}, \sigma_{\mathsf{Sig}})$, and returns $\mathsf{M}_{\mathsf{user}}$ to $\mathcal{A}$. Finally, the challenger updates $Q_{\mathsf{key}} \leftarrow Q_{\mathsf{key}} + 1$.
- When $\mathcal{A}$ makes the j-th ($j \in [N]$) encryption query on index i and a message M_j, the challenger first checks $i \in [Q_{\mathsf{key}}]$. If not, the challenger forces $\mathcal{A}$ to output a random coin $\widehat{\mathsf{coin}} \leftarrow \{0,1\}$. It then further checks if $\mathsf{IDList}[i] = \bot$. If so, the challenger samples $\mathsf{ID}_i \leftarrow \mathcal{ID}$ and sets $\mathsf{IDList}[i] = \mathsf{ID}_i$. Otherwise, it retrieves $\mathsf{ID}_i = \mathsf{IDList}[i]$. Then, the challenger queries the random oracle on input ID_i and receives back $\mathbf{u}_{\mathsf{ID}_i}$. Finally, it computes $c_0^{(j)} = \mathbf{u}_{\mathsf{ID}_i}^\top \mathbf{s}_j + x_j + \mathsf{M}_j \lfloor q/2 \rfloor$ and $\mathbf{c}_1^{(j)} = \mathbf{A}^\top \mathbf{s}_j + \mathbf{x}_j$ as specified by the scheme and returns the ciphertext $\mathsf{ct} = (c_0^{(j)}, \mathbf{c}_1^{(j)})$ to $\mathcal{A}$.
- When $\mathcal{A}$ queries for a challenge ciphertext on index i^* and message M^*, it proceeds as it did to answer the encryption query.

The only difference between the previous game is the timing on which ID is sampled by the challenger, and hence, when the random oracle is queried on input ID which the challenger samples. However, since in Game_2 the challenger never required ID to answer to the IssueKey query anymore due to the modification we made, it is easy to see that the view of $\mathcal{A}$ is identical in both games. Here, note that the randomness used by the challenger to answer the IssueKey queries were no longer tied to ID due to the modification we made in Game_1. In particular, the challenger is only required to check whether the i-th identity ID_i was sampled or not when it is queried on the i-th index for the encryption or challenge ciphertext query. Therefore we have $\Pr[X_2] = \Pr[X_3]$.

Game_4: In this game, at the outset of the game, the challenger samples a random index $I \leftarrow [Q]$ and keeps it secret. It then checks whether the index i^* submitted by $\mathcal{A}$ as the challenge ciphertext satisfies $i^* = I$. If not, it forces $\mathcal{A}$ to output a random coin $\widehat{\mathsf{coin}} \leftarrow \{0,1\}$. We will call this event abort. Otherwise, it proceeds in the same was as in the previous game. We have $|\Pr[X_4] - 1/2| = |\Pr[X_3|\neg\mathsf{abort}] \cdot \Pr[\neg\mathsf{abort}] + (1/2) \cdot \Pr[\mathsf{abort}] - 1/2| = (1/Q) \cdot |\Pr[X_3] - 1/2|$, where we used the fact that event X_3 occurs independently of event abort, and when abort occurs the challenger outputs a random coin $\widehat{\mathsf{coin}}$ on behalf of $\mathcal{A}$.

Game_5: In this game, we modify how the challenger answers the encryption and challenge ciphertext query on $I \in [Q]$. In particular, we make the following modification:

- When $\mathcal{A}$ makes the j-th ($j \in [N]$) encryption query on index i and a message M_j, if $i \neq I$, then it proceeds as in the previous game. Otherwise, if $i = I$, then the challenger samples $ct^{(j)} \leftarrow$ CTSamp(mpk) and returns $ct^{(j)}$ to $\mathcal{A}$.
- When $\mathcal{A}$ queries for a challenge ciphertext on index i^* and message M^*, it checks whether $i^* = I$ and forces $\mathcal{A}$ to output a random coin $\widehat{coin} \leftarrow \{0,1\}$ if not satisfied. Otherwise, it returns $ct^* \leftarrow$ CTSamp(mpk) to $\mathcal{A}$ regardless of the value of coin $\in \{0,1\}$.

Lemma 6 shows that $|\Pr[X_4] - \Pr[X_5]| = $ negl(λ) assuming the hardness of the LWE problem. We omit the proof of the lemma due to the page limitation and it appears in the full version of this paper.

Lemma 6. *If the* LWE$_{n,m,q,D_{\mathbb{Z},\alpha q}}$ *assumption holds, then* $|\Pr[X_4] - \Pr[X_5]| = $ negl(λ).

Let we conclude the proof of Theorem 2. Observe that since the challenge ciphertext is sampled in the same way for both coin $= 0$ and 1, we have $\Pr[X_5] = 1/2$. Therefore, combining everything together, we have Adv$_{\text{IBE},\mathcal{A}}^{\text{IND-ANON-KGC}}(\lambda) = |\Pr[X_0] - 1/2| = Q \cdot$ negl(λ). Thus, we conclude that Adv$_{\text{IBE},\mathcal{A}}^{\text{IND-ANON-KGC}}(\lambda)$ is negligible for all PPT adversary $\mathcal{A}$ since $Q = $ poly(λ). $\square$

Theorem 3. *Our blind IBE scheme with certified identity* Π_{IBE} *is IND-ANON-ICA secure in the random oracle model if the* PRF *is pseudorandom and assuming the hardness of the* LWE$_{n,m,q,D_{\mathbb{Z},\alpha q}}$ *problem. Alternatively, we can get rid of the first requirement by replacing the* PRF *by the random oracle.*

Proof. The IND-ANON-ICA game played between the adversary and the challenger is a strictly weaker variant of the IND-ANON-CPA game. In other words, any adversary with non-negligible advantage against the IND-ANON-ICA game also has non-negligible advantage against the IND-ANON-CPA game. Therefore, Theorem 1 proves Theorem 3. We point out that since the challenger never requires to answer a certificate query in the IND-ANON-ICA game, we do not additionally require the eu-cma security for the signature scheme Π_{Sig}. $\square$

Acknowledgments. This work was supported by JSPS KAKENHI Grant Numbers JP16K00198, JP17K12697, and JP17J05603, and was supported by JST CREST Grant Number JPMJCR19F6, Japan.

References

1. Abdalla, M., et al.: Searchable encryption revisited: consistency properties, relation to anonymous IBE, and extensions. J. Cryptology **21**(3), 350–391 (2008)
2. Agrawal, S., Boneh, D., Boyen, X.: Efficient lattice (H)IBE in the standard model. In: Gilbert, H. (ed.) EUROCRYPT 2010. LNCS, vol. 6110, pp. 553–572. Springer, Heidelberg (2010). https://doi.org/10.1007/978-3-642-13190-5_28
3. Al-Riyami, S.S., Paterson, K.G.: Certificateless public key cryptography. In: Laih, C.-S. (ed.) ASIACRYPT 2003. LNCS, vol. 2894, pp. 452–473. Springer, Heidelberg (2003). https://doi.org/10.1007/978-3-540-40061-5_29

4. Bendlin, R., Krehbiel, S., Peikert, C.: How to share a lattice trapdoor: threshold protocols for signatures and (H)IBE. In: Jacobson, M., Locasto, M., Mohassel, P., Safavi-Naini, R. (eds.) ACNS 2013. LNCS, vol. 7954, pp. 218–236. Springer, Heidelberg (2013). https://doi.org/10.1007/978-3-642-38980-1_14

5. Boneh, D., Franklin, M.: Identity-based encryption from the weil pairing. In: Kilian, J. (ed.) CRYPTO 2001. LNCS, vol. 2139, pp. 213–229. Springer, Heidelberg (2001). https://doi.org/10.1007/3-540-44647-8_13

6. Boyen, X., Waters, B.: Anonymous hierarchical identity-based encryption (without random oracles). In: Dwork, C. (ed.) CRYPTO 2006. LNCS, vol. 4117, pp. 290–307. Springer, Heidelberg (2006). https://doi.org/10.1007/11818175_17

7. Brakerski, Z., Langlois, A., Peikert, C., Regev, O., Stehlé, D.: Classical hardness of learning with errors. In: STOC, pp. 575–584 (2013)

8. Camenisch, J., Kohlweiss, M., Rial, A., Sheedy, C.: Blind and anonymous identity-based encryption and authorised private searches on public key encrypted data. In: Jarecki, S., Tsudik, G. (eds.) PKC 2009. LNCS, vol. 5443, pp. 196–214. Springer, Heidelberg (2009). https://doi.org/10.1007/978-3-642-00468-1_12

9. Cash, D., Hofheinz, D., Kiltz, E., Peikert, C.: Bonsai trees, or how to delegate a lattice basis. In: Gilbert, H. (ed.) EUROCRYPT 2010. LNCS, vol. 6110, pp. 523–552. Springer, Heidelberg (2010). https://doi.org/10.1007/978-3-642-13190-5_27

10. Chow, S.S.M.: Removing escrow from identity-based encryption. In: Jarecki, S., Tsudik, G. (eds.) PKC 2009. LNCS, vol. 5443, pp. 256–276. Springer, Heidelberg (2009). https://doi.org/10.1007/978-3-642-00468-1_15

11. Cramer, R., Shoup, V.: A practical public key cryptosystem provably secure against adaptive chosen ciphertext attack. In: Krawczyk, H. (ed.) CRYPTO 1998. LNCS, vol. 1462, pp. 13–25. Springer, Heidelberg (1998). https://doi.org/10.1007/BFb0055717

12. Garg, S., Hajiabadi, M., Mahmoody, M., Rahimi, A.: Registration-based encryption: removing private-key generator from IBE. In: Beimel, A., Dziembowski, S. (eds.) TCC 2018. LNCS, vol. 11239, pp. 689–718. Springer, Cham (2018). https://doi.org/10.1007/978-3-030-03807-6_25

13. Garg, S., Hajiabadi, M., Mahmoody, M., Rahimi, A., Sekar, S.: Registration-based encryption from standard assumptions. In: Lin, D., Sako, K. (eds.) PKC 2019. LNCS, vol. 11443, pp. 63–93. Springer, Cham (2019). https://doi.org/10.1007/978-3-030-17259-6_3

14. Gentry, C., Peikert, C., Vaikuntanathan, V.: Trapdoors for hard lattices and new cryptographic constructions. In: STOC, pp. 197–206 (2008)

15. Green, M., Hohenberger, S.: Blind identity-based encryption and simulatable oblivious transfer. In: Kurosawa, K. (ed.) ASIACRYPT 2007. LNCS, vol. 4833, pp. 265–282. Springer, Heidelberg (2007). https://doi.org/10.1007/978-3-540-76900-2_16

16. Hofheinz, D., Koch, J., Striecks, C.: Identity-based encryption with (almost) tight security in the multi-instance, multi-ciphertext setting. In: Katz, J. (ed.) PKC 2015. LNCS, vol. 9020, pp. 799–822. Springer, Heidelberg (2015). https://doi.org/10.1007/978-3-662-46447-2_36

17. Izabachène, M., Pointcheval, D.: New anonymity notions for identity-based encryption. In: SCN, pp. 375–391 (2008)

18. Katsumata, S., Yamada, S.: Partitioning via non-linear polynomial functions: more compact IBEs from ideal lattices and bilinear maps. In: Cheon, J.H., Takagi, T. (eds.) ASIACRYPT 2016. LNCS, vol. 10032, pp. 682–712. Springer, Heidelberg (2016). https://doi.org/10.1007/978-3-662-53890-6_23

19. Katsumata, S., Yamada, S., Yamakawa, T.: Tighter security proofs for GPV-IBE in the quantum random oracle model. In: Peyrin, T., Galbraith, S. (eds.) ASIACRYPT 2018. LNCS, vol. 11273, pp. 253–282. Springer, Cham (2018). https://doi.org/10.1007/978-3-030-03329-3_9

20. Micciancio, D., Peikert, C.: Trapdoors for lattices: simpler, tighter, faster, smaller. In: Pointcheval, D., Johansson, T. (eds.) EUROCRYPT 2012. LNCS, vol. 7237, pp. 700–718. Springer, Heidelberg (2012). https://doi.org/10.1007/978-3-642-29011-4_41

21. Peikert, C.: Public-key cryptosystems from the worst-case shortest vector problem. In: STOC, pp. 333–342. ACM (2009)

22. Peikert, C.: An efficient and parallel gaussian sampler for lattices. In: Rabin, T. (ed.) CRYPTO 2010. LNCS, vol. 6223, pp. 80–97. Springer, Heidelberg (2010). https://doi.org/10.1007/978-3-642-14623-7_5

23. Qi, F., Tang, X., Wei, Q.: New escrow-free scheme for hierarchical identity-based encryption. In: Wang, G., Zomaya, A., Perez, G.M., Li, K. (eds.) ICA3PP 2015. LNCS, vol. 9532, pp. 701–713. Springer, Cham (2015). https://doi.org/10.1007/978-3-319-27161-3_64

24. Regev, O.: On lattices, learning with errors, random linear codes, and cryptography. In: STOC, pp. 84–93. ACM Press (2005)

25. Rückert, M.: Lattice-based blind signatures - preliminary version -. In: Algorithms and Number Theory (2009)

26. Rückert, M.: Lattice-based blind signatures. In: Abe, M. (ed.) ASIACRYPT 2010. LNCS, vol. 6477, pp. 413–430. Springer, Heidelberg (2010). https://doi.org/10.1007/978-3-642-17373-8_24

27. Shamir, A.: Identity-based cryptosystems and signature schemes. In: Blakley, G.R., Chaum, D. (eds.) CRYPTO 1984. LNCS, vol. 196, pp. 47–53. Springer, Heidelberg (1985). https://doi.org/10.1007/3-540-39568-7_5

28. Wei, Q., Qi, F., Tang, Z.: Remove key escrow from the BF and Gentry identity-based encryption with non-interactive key generation. Telecommun. Syst. **69**(2), 253–262 (2018)

Forward-Secure Puncturable Identity-Based Encryption for Securing Cloud Emails

Jianghong Wei[1,2,3], Xiaofeng Chen[1,2(✉)], Jianfeng Wang[1,2], Xuexian Hu[3], and Jianfeng Ma[1]

[1] State Key Laboratory of Integrated Service Networks, Xidian University, Xi'an, China
`jianghong.wei.xxgc@gmail.com`, {`xfchen,jfwang`}`@xidian.edu.cn`, `jfma@mail.xidian.edu.cn`
[2] State Key Laboratory of Cryptology, P. O. Box 5159, Beijing 100878, China
[3] State Key Laboratory of Mathematical Engineering and Advanced Computing, PLA Strategic Force Information Engineering University, Zhengzhou, China
`xuexian_hu@hotmail.com`

Abstract. As one of the most important manners of personal and business communications, cloud emails have been widely employed due to its advantages of low-cost and convenience. However, with the occurrence of large-scale email leakage events and the revelation of long-term monitoring of personal communications, customers are increasingly worried about the security and privacy of their sensitive emails. In this paper, we first formalize a new cryptographic primitive named forward-secure puncturable identity-based encryption (fs-PIBE) for enhancing the security and privacy of cloud email systems. This primitive enables an email receiver to individually revoke the decryption capacity of a received email that was encrypted, while retaining the decryption capacity of those unreceived ones. Consequently, those received emails remain secure even if the secret key is comprised. Thus, it provides more practical forward secrecy than traditional forward-secure public key encryption, in which the decryption capacity of those received and unreceived emails is revoked simultaneously. Besides, we propose a concrete construction of fs-PIBE with constant size of ciphertext, and prove its security in the standard model. We present the performance analysis to demonstrate its merits.

Keywords: Identity-based encryption · Puncturable encryption · Forward secrecy · Encrypted cloud emails

1 Introduction

Though instant messaging systems are increasingly and widely used, email continues to be one of the mainstream methods to deliver information and data. At

© Springer Nature Switzerland AG 2019
K. Sako et al. (Eds.): ESORICS 2019, LNCS 11736, pp. 134–150, 2019.
https://doi.org/10.1007/978-3-030-29962-0_7

the same time, the advantages of cloud computing enable more enterprises and organizations to deploy their own cloud email systems over third-party cloud servers in a cheap and scalable way. The Radicati Group [29] reported that, in 2019, the total number of emails sent and received per day will exceed 293 billion, and the worldwide revenue of cloud business email will roughly achieve $35 billion. On the other hand, the contents of emails usually involve some sensitive information, such as personal credit card bills and the enterprise's business contracts. Thus, ensuring the privacy and security of email messages has become customers' primary requirement. Worse, in recent years, there have been various reports of massive leakage of email messages [32, 33]. This further aggravates customers' concerns about email security. To this end, it has been strongly suggested that cloud emails should be sent in the encrypted form, and the cloud email server just needs to provide transportation service of delivering encrypted emails that can only be decrypted by those intended receivers.

OpenPGP [6] and S/MIME [24] are two main standards for encrypting emails with the public key encryption based on public key infrastructures (PKIs). These two protocols have co-existed more than two decades, and numerous efforts have been made to improve them in terms of security and efficiency [13, 19]. However, they still have failed to be widely adopted [1]. As pointed out by Ryan [25], this is mainly because that none of them can simultaneously meet the requirements of practicability and security. The major issue comes from that they both require an additional trusted certificate authority to manage all users' certificates, e.g., certificate creation, storage and revocation.

The emergence of identity-based encryption (IBE) [27] eliminates the mandatory requirement for PKIs. It allows a user to derive his/her public key from any string, such as telephone number and email address. Consequently, a email sender just needs to maintain registered email addressees, rather than storing and verifying the certificate of the intended receiver. This greatly facilitates the use of encrypted emails, because customers are more accustomed to the idea that the intended email receiver is identified with a string easy to read and remember (e.g., email address), rather than a public key (e.g., certificate). Due to these advantages, IBE is considered to be an attractive solution for securing email communications. There have been some commercial encrypted cloud email systems that are built upon IBE, such as Proofpoint Email Protection [23] and DataMotion SecureEmail [9].

In practice, due to wide and mixed use of multiple mobile devices (e.g, smartphone, tablet and PC), customers' long-term secret keys are more likely to get revealed than expected. For example, the malware might extract secret keys from mobile devices, customers might be lawfully enforced to submit their secret keys to law enforcement agencies, the cloud server might occasionally backup customers' secret keys, and so on. Therefore, *forward secrecy*, which guarantees the security of those previously encrypted emails in the case that customers' current secret keys are occasionally compromised, is vital for preserving customer confidentiality. It is considered to be an indispensable security property of encrypted email systems [30]. However, none of the above encrypted email systems have provided a mechanism of achieving forward secrecy.

Addressing the above problem is not trivial. Some early works [5,26] tired to provide forward secrecy of encrypted email systems by periodically issuing short-time public/private key pairs for all users. This manner seriously relies on a highly-available communication channel to issue fresh secret keys, and thus is not robust. On the other hand, there have been some secure email protocols [8,28] that employ Diffie-Hellman key exchange to capture forward secrecy. But they mandatorily require either the email sender/receiver and the email server or the email sender and receiver to be online simultaneously. This obviously does not match practical email communication scenario of *store-and-forward*, in which emails are firstly sent to the email server and cached, and then are delivered to the intended receiver when he/she is online.

Forward secure public key encryption [7,35] enables us to capture the forward secrecy of encrypted email systems without interactions and frequent key distributions. With this kind of encryption scheme, each customer can evolve the secret key unidirectionally and periodically, and uses different secret keys during each time interval, while the public key remains unchanged. As a result, even if the current secret key is disclosed, those previously encrypted emails still remain secure. However, this method also has not been broadly approved. This is mainly because that it sacrifices usability for achieving forward secrecy. More precisely, when a customer's secret key is updated to next time interval, he/she losses decryption capacity of all those unreceived encrypted emails. But, in practice, it is very common for customers to receive emails that were sent in previous time intervals due to unexpected reasons, such as network failure, whitelist in email and anonymous mixnets. Thus, how to achieve forward secrecy of encrypted cloud email systems without sacrificing practicality is still a challenging problem.

1.1 Our Contribution

In this paper, we focus on forward secure identity-based encryption scheme that can yield encrypted cloud email systems with practical forward secrecy. Specifically, our contribution is as follows:

- We introduce a new cryptographic primitive named forward-secure puncturable identity-based encryption (fs-PIBE), and define its syntax and security notion. This primitive allows a customer to individually revoke the decryption capacity of those encrypted emails that have been received, while retaining the decryption capacity of those unreceived ones. Therefore, it is more practical than traditional forward secure IBE.
- We propose a concrete construction of fs-PIBE scheme. Our scheme is proved to be secure under a well-studied complexity assumption in the standard model, and achieves constant size of ciphertext. Furthermore, we introduce a framework of encrypted cloud email systems based on fs-PIBE. It features of practical forward secrecy.
- We present a theoretical analysis of the proposed fs-PIBE scheme in terms of computation cost and communication overhead. The analysis results indicate

that, at the cost of acceptable storage cost, the proposed fs-PIBE construction captures desirable security guarantees without trading off usability.

1.2 Related Work

OpenPGP [6] and S/MIME [24] are the two most widely known encrypted email protocols, and are both built upon PKIs. That is, each customer's public key is associated with a signed certificate, and customers' software clients need to maintain and verify certificates of email servers and intended email receivers. It is too complicated for common customers to understand and use them. This is the main reason why they have failed to take off. Nonetheless, some efforts have made to improve their security, such as adding forward secrecy to OpenPGP [5], enhancing certificate transparency [25], fixing security pitfalls of encryption model [22], and so on.

Shamir [27] introduced the notion of IBE to avoid the issue of certificate management. It offers the possibility of using any string that can identify customers' identities (e.g., email addresses) as their public keys, and was first instantiated by Boneh and Franklin [3]. Since then, a large number of IBE schemes have been proposed to improve its security, efficiency and scalability, such as fully secure IBE [31], tightly secure IBE [16] and hierarchical IBE [2]. Now there have been many commercial softwares [9,23] that use these IBE schemes to build encrypted cloud email systems without PKIs. In addition, motivated by some specific application requirements of email communication, several new cryptographic primitives have been proposed for encrypted cloud email systems, such as identity-based broadcast proxy re-encryption [34] and public key encryption with keyword search [20].

To achieve the forward secrecy of encrypted email systems, early works focused on designing particular Diffie-Hellman key exchange protocols, and utilized the resulted session key to secure email communications. For example, Sun et al. [28] proposed two secure email protocols providing perfect forward secrecy. Their first protocol essentially is an ephemeral version of traditional Diffie-Hellman key exchange, and the second one was indicated to be flawed [10]. There are some other similar forward secure email protocols [8,18]. Unfortunately, they either fail against active attacks, or require an interactive message exchange before securely transmitting emails.

In Eurocrypt 2003, Canetti et al. [7] proposed a forward secure public key encryption, and made it possible to achieve the forward secrecy of encrypted emails without interactions. In their scheme, the whole lifetime of the system is divided into multiple discrete time intervals, and each customer him/herself updates the secret key unidirectionally at the end of each time interval, while the public key remains unchanged. Consequently, each customer uses different secret keys during each time interval, and the disclosure of the current secret key does not affect the security of those previously encrypted emails. Their method is widely used to achieve forward secrecy of various other public key cryptographic primitives like forward secure IBE [35] and ring signature [17].

However, Green and Miers [14] recently pointed out that Canetti et al.'s [7] method is relatively blunt and not practical enough. Specifically, by updating the secret key, a customer can revoke the decryption capacity for a given time interval. But this also means that he/she losses access to all emails that were encrypted yet unreceived in this time interval. In other words, their manner fails to achieve revocation of decryption capacity of individual encrypted emails. They further proposed puncture encryption to overcome this problem. In their scheme, after a receiver decrypting a ciphertext, she/he immediately punctures the secret key with tags associated with the ciphertext. As a result, the punctured secret key will no longer be able to decrypt any ciphertext including these tags. By combining with a hierarchical IBE scheme [2], they presented a puncturable forward secure encryption scheme that captures fine-grained forward secrecy. But the ciphertext size of their scheme is linear with the size of attached tags, its security proof was conducted in the random oracle model. Their idea of achieving forward secrecy is quickly used to construct other forward secure cryptographic primitives, including forward secure proxy re-encryption [12], zero round-trip time key exchange with full forward secrecy [11,15]. These forward secure puncturable encryption schemes naturally yield encrypted cloud email systems with more practical forward secrecy than previous ones, while all of them still require the support of PKIs.

1.3   Organization

The remainder of this paper is structured as follows: Sect. 2 reviews preliminaries. In Sect. 3, we formalize the syntax and security notion of fs-PIBE. Section 4 provides a concrete construction of fs-PIBE, and gives the security and efficiency analysis. In Sect. 5, we introduce a framework of encrypted cloud email systems based on fs-PIBE. Finally, we conclude this paper in Sect. 6.

2   Preliminaries

2.1   Notation

We use bold lowercase letters like u to represent vectors, and denote by $[m]$ the positive integer set $\{1, \ldots, m\}$. For a binary string w, let $|w|$ be its length and $w[j]$ its j-th bit. Given a group $\mathbb{G}_T$, let $R \stackrel{\$}{\leftarrow} \mathbb{G}_T$ indicate uniformly sampling an element R from $\mathbb{G}_T$ at random. PPT standards for probabilistic polynomial time.

2.2   Bilinear Map

Given a security parameter $\kappa \in \mathbb{N}$, denote by $\mathbb{G}$ and $\mathbb{G}_T$ two multiplicative cyclic groups with a large prime order p in size of κ. Let g be a random generator of $\mathbb{G}$. These two groups $\mathbb{G}$ and $\mathbb{G}_T$ are said to be bilinear provided that there exists a map $e : \mathbb{G} \times \mathbb{G} \to \mathbb{G}_T$ satisfying the following conditions:

- *Bilinearity.* For any group elements $h, w \in \mathbb{G}$ and integers $x, y \in \mathbb{Z}_p$, it holds that $e(h^x, w^y) = e(h, w)^{xy}$.
- *Non-degeneracy.* It is required that $e(g, g) \neq 1_{\mathbb{G}_T}$, where $1_{\mathbb{G}_T}$ is the unit element of $\mathbb{G}_T$.
- *Computability.* Given any group elements $h, w \in \mathbb{G}$, there exists an algorithm to efficiently compute $e(h, w)$.

For convenience of description, denote by $(\mathbb{G}, \mathbb{G}_T, e, p, g)$ the bilinear groups defined as above.

2.3 Complexity Assumption

Given bilinear groups $(\mathbb{G}, \mathbb{G}_T, e, p, g)$, let a, s be two integers randomly sampled from $\mathbb{Z}_p$. The decisional q-BDHE problem defined over $(\mathbb{G}, \mathbb{G}_T, e, p, g)$ is stated as follows: given $\boldsymbol{g} = (g, g^a, \ldots, g^{a^q}, g^{a^{q+2}}, \ldots, g^{a^{2q}}, g^s, R) \in \mathbb{G}^{2q+1} \times \mathbb{G}_T$, decide either $R = e(g, g)^{a^{q+1}s}$ or $R \xleftarrow{\$} \mathbb{G}_T$. The advantage of an algorithm $\mathcal{C}$ solving the decisional q-BDHE problem by outputting a bit $\beta \in \{0, 1\}$ is captured as

$$\mathsf{Adv}_{\mathcal{C}}^{q\text{-BDHE}}(\kappa) = \left| \Pr\left[\mathcal{C}(\boldsymbol{g}, R = e(g, g)^{a^{q+1}s}) = 0\right] - \Pr\left[\mathcal{C}(\boldsymbol{g}, R \xleftarrow{\$} \mathbb{G}_2) = 0\right] \right|.$$

Definition 1 (Decisional q-BDHE Assumption [4]). *The decisional q-BDHE assumption holds over $(\mathbb{G}, \mathbb{G}_T, g, p, e)$ provided that for any PPT algorithm, its advantage of solving the decisional q-BDHE problem is a negligible function $\mathsf{negl}(\kappa)$ of the security parameter κ.*

3 Forward-Secure Puncturable Identity-Based Encryption

3.1 Syntax of fs-PIBE

A forward-secure puncturable identity-based encryption scheme is a tuple of the following six PPT algorithms:

- $\mathsf{Setup}(\kappa, \tau_{max}, n)$: On input a security parameter κ, the maximum number of time intervals τ_{max} and the maximum number of tags allowed to attach to a ciphertext n, this algorithm outputs the public parameter PP and the master secret key MSK.
- $\mathsf{KeyGen}(\mathsf{PP}, \mathsf{MSK}, \mathsf{ID})$: On input the public parameter PP, the master secret key MSK and an identity ID, this algorithm outputs an initial secret key $\mathsf{SK}_{0,\emptyset}$ for ID.
- $\mathsf{Puncture}(\mathsf{PP}, \mathsf{SK}_{\tau, \mathcal{P}_{i-1}}, \hat{t}_i)$: On input the public parameter PP, a punctured secret key $\mathsf{SK}_{\tau, \mathcal{P}_{i-1}}$ on time interval τ and a tag $\hat{t}_i$, this algorithm outputs a new punctured secret key $\mathsf{SK}_{\tau, \mathcal{P}_i}$.
- $\mathsf{Update}(\mathsf{PP}, \mathsf{SK}_{\tau, \mathcal{P}_i}, \tau')$: On input the public parameter PP, a punctured secret key $\mathsf{SK}_{\tau, \mathcal{P}_i}$ on time interval τ and a new time interval $\tau' > \tau$ ($\tau' \leq \tau_{max}$), this algorithm outputs a new updated secret key $\mathsf{SK}_{\tau', \mathcal{P}_i}$.

- Encrypt($\mathsf{PP}, \mathsf{ID}, S, M, \tau$): On input the public parameter PP, a receiver's identity ID, a tag set $S = \{t_1, \ldots, t_d\}$ $(d \leq n)$, a message M to encrypt and a time interval τ, this algorithm outputs a ciphertext CT, which is implicitly associated with S and τ.
- Decrypt($\mathsf{PP}, \mathsf{SK}_{\tau, \mathcal{P}_i}, \mathsf{CT}$): On input the public parameter PP, a punctured secret key $\mathsf{SK}_{\tau, \mathcal{P}_i}$ on time interval τ and a ciphertext CT, this algorithm outputs the message M or a symbol $\perp$ indicating a decryption failure.

CORRECTNESS. The correctness of fs-PIBE requires that, for any public parameter and master secret key $(\mathsf{PP}, \mathsf{MSK}) \leftarrow \mathsf{Setup}(\kappa, \tau_{max}, n)$, any secret key $\mathsf{SK}_{0,\emptyset} \leftarrow \mathsf{KeyGen}(\mathsf{PP}, \mathsf{MSK}, \mathsf{ID})$, any tag sets $S = \{t_1, \ldots, t_d\}$ and $\mathcal{P} = \{\hat{t}_1, \ldots, \hat{t}_i\}$, any time interval τ, and any message M, it holds that

$$\mathsf{Decrypt}\big(\mathsf{PP}, \mathsf{SK}_{\tau,\emptyset}, \mathsf{Encrypt}(\mathsf{PP}, \mathsf{ID}, S, M, \tau)\big) = M,$$

$$\mathsf{Decrypt}\big(\mathsf{PP}, \mathsf{SK}_{\tau,\mathcal{P}_j}, \mathsf{Encrypt}(\mathsf{PP}, \mathsf{ID}, S, M, \tau)\big) = M, \text{ if } S \cap \mathcal{P}_j = \emptyset,$$

$$\mathsf{Decrypt}\big(\mathsf{PP}, \mathsf{SK}_{\tau,\mathcal{P}_j}, \mathsf{Encrypt}(\mathsf{PP}, \mathsf{ID}, S, M, \tau)\big) = \perp, \text{ if } S \cap \mathcal{P}_j \neq \emptyset,$$

where $\mathsf{SK}_{\tau,\emptyset} \leftarrow \mathsf{Update}(\mathsf{PP}, \mathsf{SK}_{0,\emptyset}, \tau)$, and for each index j belonging to $\{1, \ldots, i\}$, $\mathsf{SK}_{\tau,\mathcal{P}_j} \leftarrow \mathsf{Puncture}(\mathsf{PP}, \mathsf{SK}_{\tau,\mathcal{P}_{j-1}}, \hat{t}_j)$ and $\mathcal{P}_j = \{\hat{t}_1, \ldots, \hat{t}_j\}$.

The above correctness mandates that a non-punctured secret key $\mathsf{SK}_{\tau,\emptyset}$ can decrypt any correct ciphertext. However, if it was punctured with tags belonging to $\mathcal{P}_j$, then it cannot decrypt any ciphertext containing any tag in $\mathcal{P}_j$.

3.2   Security Definition of fs-PIBE

Security for fs-PIBE is defined via the $\mathsf{IND\text{-}PUN\text{-}ID\text{-}CPA}$ game played between a challenger $\mathcal{C}$ and an adversary $\mathcal{A}$. We consider selective tag security of fs-PIBE, where the adversary $\mathcal{A}$ is required to specify the challenge tag set before seeing the public parameter. The game has the following six phases.

Initialization. The adversary $\mathcal{A}$ chooses a challenge tag set $S^* = \{t_1^*, \ldots, t_d^*\}$ and submits it to the challenger $\mathcal{C}$.

Setup. In this phase, on input the security parameter κ, a total number of time intervals τ_{max} and a maximum number of tags n, the challenger $\mathcal{C}$ performs the setup algorithm $\mathsf{Setup}(\kappa, \tau_{max}, n) \to (\mathsf{PP}, \mathsf{MSK})$, and forwards the public parameter PP to the adversary $\mathcal{A}$. In addition, for each identity ID, the challenger $\mathcal{C}$ maintain a tuple $(\mathsf{ID}, \mathsf{SK}_{\tau,\mathcal{P}_i}, \mathcal{P}_{\mathsf{ID}}, \tau)$ recording the state of ID's secret key. That is, the secret key $\mathsf{SK}_{\tau,\mathcal{P}_i}$ is now on time interval τ, and has been punctured with tags in $\mathcal{P}_{\mathsf{ID}}$.

Query phase 1. The adversary $\mathcal{A}$ is allowed to adaptively issue the following queries:

- $\mathcal{Q}_{punc}(\mathsf{ID}, \hat{t})$: Given an identity ID and a tag $\hat{t}$, the challenger $\mathcal{C}$ checks if there exists a tuple $(\mathsf{ID}, \mathsf{SK}_{\tau,\mathcal{P}_{i-1}}, \mathcal{P}_{\mathsf{ID}}, \tau)$. If yes, it directly performs the algorithm $\mathsf{Puncture}(\mathsf{PP}, \mathsf{SK}_{\tau,\mathcal{P}_{i-1}}, \hat{t}) \to \mathsf{SK}_{\tau,\mathcal{P}_i}$, and replaces the original tuple with $(\mathsf{ID}, \mathsf{SK}_{\tau,\mathcal{P}_i}, \mathcal{P}_{\mathsf{ID}} \cup \{\hat{t}\}, \tau)$. Otherwise, it successively runs the algorithms $\mathsf{KeyGen}(\mathsf{PP}, \mathsf{MSK}, \mathsf{ID}) \to \mathsf{SK}_{0,\emptyset}$ and $\mathsf{Puncture}(\mathsf{PP}, \mathsf{SK}_{0,\emptyset}, \hat{t}) \to \mathsf{SK}_{0,\mathcal{P}_1}$, and further creates a new tuple $(\mathsf{ID}, \mathsf{SK}_{0,\mathcal{P}_1}, \{\hat{t}\}, 0)$.

- $\mathcal{Q}_{update}(\text{ID}, \tau')$: Given an identity ID and a time interval τ', the challenger $\mathcal{C}$ checks if there exists a tuple $(\text{ID}, \text{SK}_{\tau, \mathcal{P}_i}, \mathcal{P}_{\text{ID}}, \tau)$ $(\tau < \tau')$. If yes, it directly runs the algorithm $\text{Update}(\text{PP}, \text{SK}_{\tau, \mathcal{P}_i}, \tau') \rightarrow \text{SK}_{\tau', \mathcal{P}_i}$, and replaces the original tuple with $(\text{ID}, \text{SK}_{\tau', \mathcal{P}_i}, \mathcal{P}_{\text{ID}}, \tau')$. Otherwise, it successively runs the algorithms $\text{KeyGen}(\text{PP}, \text{MSK}, \text{ID}) \rightarrow \text{SK}_{0, \emptyset}$ and $\text{Update}(\text{PP}, \text{SK}_{0, \emptyset}, \tau) \rightarrow \text{SK}_{\tau, \emptyset}$, and creates a new tuple $(\text{ID}, \text{SK}_{\tau, \emptyset}, \emptyset, \tau)$.
- $\mathcal{Q}_{corrupt}(\text{ID})$: Given an identity ID, the challenger $\mathcal{C}$ checks if there exists a tuple $(\text{ID}, \text{SK}_{\tau, \mathcal{P}_i}, \mathcal{P}_{\text{ID}}, \tau)$. If yes, it directly returns $\text{SK}_{\tau, \mathcal{P}_i}$ to the adversary $\mathcal{A}$. Otherwise, it runs the algorithm $\text{KeyGen}(\text{PP}, \text{MSK}, \text{ID}) \rightarrow \text{SK}_{0, \emptyset}$, and returns $\text{SK}_{0, \emptyset}$ to the adversary $\mathcal{A}$. In addition, it creates a new tuple $(\text{ID}, \text{SK}_{0, \emptyset}, \emptyset, 0)$.

Challenge. The adversary $\mathcal{A}$ selects two messages M_0 and M_1, a time interval τ^* as well as an identity ID^*, and submits them to the challenger $\mathcal{C}$. If the adversary $\mathcal{A}$ has issued a corruption query with respect to $(\text{ID}^*, \text{SK}_{\tau, \mathcal{P}_i}, \mathcal{P}_{\text{ID}^*}, \tau)$ such that $\mathcal{P}_{\text{ID}^*} \cap S^* = \emptyset$ and $\tau < \tau^*$, then the challenger $\mathcal{C}$ rejects the challenge. Otherwise, it picks a random bit $\beta \in \{0, 1\}$, and returns the challenge ciphertext $\text{CT}^* \leftarrow \text{Encrypt}(\text{PP}, \text{ID}^*, S^*, M_\beta, \tau^*)$ to the adversary $\mathcal{A}$.

Query phase 2. This phase is identical to the query phase 1, except that the adversary $\mathcal{A}$ cannot issue a corruption query with respect to $(\text{ID}^*, \text{SK}_{\tau, \mathcal{P}_i}, \mathcal{P}_{\text{ID}^*}, \tau)$ such that $\mathcal{P}_{\text{ID}^*} \cap S^* = \emptyset$ and $\tau < \tau^*$.

Guess. The adversary $\mathcal{A}$ outputs a guess bit $\beta' \in \{0, 1\}$. The adversary $\mathcal{A}$ wins if $\beta' = \beta$. Its advantage in the IND-PUN-ID-CPA game is defined as

$$\text{Adv}_{\mathcal{A}, \text{fs-PIBE}}^{\text{IND-PUN-ID-CPA}}(\kappa) = \left| \Pr[\beta' = \beta] - \frac{1}{2} \right|.$$

Definition 2 (IND-PUN-ID-CPA Security of fs-PIBE). *We say that a forward-secure puncturable identity-based encryption scheme is IND-PUN-ID-CPA secure if for any PPT adversary $\mathcal{A}$, its advantage $\text{Adv}_{\mathcal{A}, \text{fs-PIBE}}^{\text{IND-PUN-ID-CPA}}(\kappa)$ in the above game is negligible for sufficiently large security parameter κ.*

To capture fine-grained forward secrecy of IBE, we allow an adversary $\mathcal{A}$ to obtain a secret key $\text{SK}_{\tau, \mathcal{P}_i}$ of the challenge identity ID^* via a corruption query $\mathcal{Q}_{corrupt}(\text{ID}^*)$. But it is restricted that either $\text{SK}_{\tau, \mathcal{P}_i}$ has been punctured with a tag $t_j^* \in S^*$ via a puncture query $\mathcal{Q}_{punc}(\text{ID}^*, t_j^*)$, or $\text{SK}_{\tau, \mathcal{P}_i}$ has been updated to a time interval τ that is larger than τ^* via an update query $\mathcal{Q}_{update}(\text{ID}^*, \tau)$.

4 The fs-PIBE Construction

4.1 High Description

We first describe some notations used below. We use a binary tree $\mathcal{BT}$ to manage time intervals as in Canetti et al.'s [7] scheme. That is, if the total number of time intervals is τ_{max}, then we select a binary tree of depth ℓ such that $\tau_{max} \leq 2^\ell$. Each time interval τ is assigned to a leaf node η_τ of $\mathcal{BT}$ in order from left to right. For a node η of $\mathcal{BT}$, denote by w_η the binary string that represents the path from the root node ϵ to η, in which 0 implies that the path passes through the left child node and 1 the right child node. In the absence of ambiguity, for each time interval τ, we directly rewrite w_{η_τ} with w_τ for simpling descriptions. Given a node η, let $\mathcal{R}(\eta)$ be its right child node[1], and $\mathsf{Path}(\eta)$ be the collection of all nodes on the path from ϵ to η. Then, for each time interval τ, we define a node set $\mathcal{N}_\tau = \{\mathcal{R}(\eta) | \eta \in \mathsf{Path}(\eta)\}$. Such a definition enjoys the following property: *Given two time intervals $\tau < \tau'$, for each node $\eta' \in \mathcal{N}_{\tau'}$, there exists a node $\eta \in \mathcal{N}_\tau$ such that w_η is a prefix of $w_{\eta'}$.*

Our construction is motivated by Green and Miers' puncture encryption scheme [14], and built upon Waters' IBE scheme [31]. Specifically, we divide the whole lifetime of the system into multiple time intervals, and each user uses different secrete keys during each time interval. For a time interval τ, we produce a secret key component $\boldsymbol{sk}_{\tau,\eta}$ for each node $\eta \in \mathcal{N}_\tau$. Then, at the end of τ, by the above property of $\mathcal{N}_\tau$, we can unidirectionally derive a secret key component $\boldsymbol{sk}_{\tau+1,\eta'}$ from $\boldsymbol{sk}_{\tau+1,\eta}$ for each node $\eta' \in \mathcal{N}_{\tau+1}$, where w_η is a prefix of $w_{\eta'}$. At this point, we only captures general forward secrecy as in Canetti et al.'s scheme [7]. Furthermore, we embed a set S of descriptive tags into each ciphertext by introducing a polynomial defined over them, which enables the size of ciphertext in our construction to achieve constant, rather than being linear with the size of attached tags as in Green and Miers' scheme [14]. Upon receiving and decrypting a ciphertext associated with the tag set S, we puncture the secret key with each tag belonging to S such that the punctured secret key will no longer be able to decrypt any ciphertext that is embedded with any tag in S. This procedure is similar to produce a secret key component for a negated attribute in [21]. Now, we achieve fine-grained forward secrecy. That is, the decryption capacity of those encrypted messages that have been received is revoked, while the decryption capacity of those unreceived ones is still reserved. Moreover, maintaining secret keys for multiple time intervals allow the user to retain the decryption capacity of more unreceived messages.

4.2   The Proposed Construction

The proposed fs-PIBE construction consists of a tuple of algorithms (Setup, KeyGen, Puncture, Update, Encrypt, Decrypt), which are specified as follows:

- Setup(κ, τ_{max}, n): The setup algorithm is performed by a private key generator (PKG). Given a security parameter κ, the total number of time intervals τ_{max} and the maximum number of tags allowed to attach to a ciphertext n, this algorithm generates bilinear groups $(\mathbb{G}, \mathbb{G}_T, e, p, g)$, chooses a random exponent $\alpha \in \mathbb{Z}_p$ and lets $Z = e(g, g)^\alpha$. Let the message space be $\mathcal{M} \subseteq \mathbb{G}_T$, the tag space be $\mathcal{T} \subseteq \mathbb{Z}_p$ and the identity space be $\mathcal{ID} = \{0,1\}^l$. Particularly, let $\hat{t}_0 \in \mathcal{T}$ be a distinctive tag not used in normal encryption and puncture operations. Then, it initializes a binary tree $\mathcal{BT}$ of depth ℓ to manage all time intervals $\{0, \ldots, \tau_{max} - 1\}$ such that $\tau_{max} \leq 2^\ell$. Moreover, this algorithm chooses random vectors $\boldsymbol{u} = (u_0, \ldots, u_l) \in \mathbb{G}^{l+1}$, $\boldsymbol{v} = (v_0, \ldots, v_\ell) \in \mathbb{G}^{\ell+1}$ and

---

[1] For a leaf node η_τ, we assume that $\mathcal{R}(\eta_\tau) = \eta_\tau$.

$\boldsymbol{h} = (h_1, \ldots, h_n) \in \mathbb{G}^n$. To simplify subsequent descriptions, for each identity $\text{ID} \in \mathcal{ID}$ and binary string $w \in \{0,1\}^{\leq \ell}$, we define two functions $H(\text{ID}) = u_0 \cdot \prod_{j=1}^{l}(u_j)^{\text{ID}[j]}$ and $V(w) = v_0 \cdot \prod_{j=1}^{|w|}(v_j)^{w[j]}$. Finally, the algorithm outputs the master secret key as $\text{MSK} = g^{\alpha}$, and publishes the public parameter as $\text{PP} = \{(\mathbb{G}, \mathbb{G}_T, e, p, g), Z, \boldsymbol{u}, \boldsymbol{v}, \boldsymbol{h}\}$.

- KeyGen(PP, MSK, ID): The secret key generation algorithm is also run by the PKG. Given the public parameter PP, the master secret key MSK and an identity ID, this algorithm first chooses random exponents $r_{id}, r_0, r_0' \in \mathbb{Z}_p$, and computes

$$\boldsymbol{sk}_{\emptyset} = (sk_{\emptyset,1}, sk_{\emptyset,2}, sk_{\emptyset,3}, \boldsymbol{sk}_{\emptyset,4}) = (g^{r_0}, g^{r_{id}}, \hat{t}_0, \boldsymbol{sk}_{\emptyset,4}),$$

$$\boldsymbol{sk}_{\emptyset,4} = (k_{\emptyset,2}, k_{\emptyset,3}, \ldots, k_{\emptyset,n}) = ((h_1^{-\hat{t}_0} \cdot h_2)^{r_0}, (h_1^{-\hat{t}_0^2} \cdot h_3)^{r_0}, \ldots, (h_1^{-\hat{t}_0^{n-1}} \cdot h_n)^{r_0}).$$

Furthermore, for each node $\eta \in \mathcal{N}_0$, this algorithm calculates

$$\boldsymbol{sk}_{0,\eta} = (sk_{0,0}, sk_{0,1}, sk_{0,|w_\eta|+1}, \ldots, sk_{0,\ell})$$
$$= (g^{\alpha} \cdot h_1^{r_0} \cdot H(\text{ID})^{r_{id}} \cdot V(w_\eta)^{r_0'}, g^{r_0'}, (v_{|w_\eta|+1})^{r_0'}, \ldots, (v_\ell)^{r_0'}).$$

Finally, this algorithm outputs an initial secret key $\text{SK}_{0,\emptyset} = \{\boldsymbol{sk}_{\emptyset}, \{\boldsymbol{sk}_{0,\eta}\}_{\eta \in \mathcal{N}_0}\}$ for identity ID.

- Puncture(PP, $\text{SK}_{\tau, \mathcal{P}_{i-1}}, \hat{t}_i$): The puncture algorithm is performed locally by a user without interactions. Given the public parameter PP, a punctured secret key $\text{SK}_{\tau, \mathcal{P}_{i-1}}$ on time interval τ and a tag $\hat{t}_i$, this algorithm first parses $\text{SK}_{\tau, \mathcal{P}_{i-1}}$ as $\{\boldsymbol{sk}_{\emptyset}, \boldsymbol{sk}_{\mathcal{P}_1}, \ldots, \boldsymbol{sk}_{\mathcal{P}_{i-1}}, \{\boldsymbol{sk}_{\tau,\eta}\}_{\eta \in \mathcal{N}_\tau}\}$, where $\boldsymbol{sk}_{\emptyset} = (sk_{\emptyset,1}, sk_{\emptyset,2}, sk_{\emptyset,3}, \boldsymbol{sk}_{\emptyset,4})$, $\boldsymbol{sk}_{\emptyset,4} = (k_{\emptyset,2}, \ldots, k_{\emptyset,n})$ and $\boldsymbol{sk}_{\tau,\eta} = (sk_{\tau,0}, sk_{\tau,1}, sk_{\tau,|w_\eta|+1}, \ldots, sk_{\tau,\ell})$. Then, it randomly picks exponents $\lambda_i, r_i, r_i' \in \mathbb{Z}_p$, and computes

$$\boldsymbol{sk}_{\emptyset}' = (sk_{\emptyset,1}', sk_{\emptyset,2}', sk_{\emptyset,3}', \boldsymbol{sk}_{\emptyset,4}') = (sk_{\emptyset,1} \cdot g^{r_i'}, sk_{\emptyset,2}, sk_{\emptyset,3}, \boldsymbol{sk}_{\emptyset,4}'),$$

$$\boldsymbol{sk}_{\emptyset,4}' = (k_{\emptyset,2}', \ldots, k_{\emptyset,n}') = (k_{\emptyset,2} \cdot (h_1^{-\hat{t}_0} h_2)^{r_i'}, \ldots, k_{\emptyset,n} \cdot (h_1^{-\hat{t}_0^{n-1}} h_n)^{r_i'}),$$

$$\boldsymbol{sk}_{\mathcal{P}_i} = (sk_{\mathcal{P}_i,1}, sk_{\mathcal{P}_i,2}, sk_{\mathcal{P}_i,3}, \boldsymbol{sk}_{\mathcal{P}_i,4}) = (g^{\lambda_i} \cdot h_1^{r_i}, g^{r_i}, \hat{t}_i, \boldsymbol{sk}_{\mathcal{P}_i,4}),$$

$$\boldsymbol{sk}_{\mathcal{P}_i,4} = (k_{\mathcal{P}_i,2}, \ldots, k_{\mathcal{P}_i,n}) = ((h_1^{-\hat{t}_i} \cdot h_2)^{r_i}, \ldots, (h_1^{-\hat{t}_i^{n-1}} \cdot h_n)^{r_i}),$$

$$\boldsymbol{sk}_{\tau,\eta}' = (sk_{\tau,0} \cdot g^{-\lambda_i} \cdot h_1^{r_i'}, sk_{\tau,1}, sk_{\tau,|w_\eta|+1}, \ldots, sk_{\tau,\ell}).$$

Finally, this algorithm outputs a new punctured secret key $\text{SK}_{\tau, \mathcal{P}_i}$ in the form of $\{\boldsymbol{sk}_{\emptyset}', \boldsymbol{sk}_{\mathcal{P}_1}, \ldots, \boldsymbol{sk}_{\mathcal{P}_{i-1}}, \boldsymbol{sk}_{\mathcal{P}_i}, \{\boldsymbol{sk}_{\tau,\eta}'\}_{\eta \in \mathcal{N}_\tau}\}$.

- Update(PP, $\text{SK}_{\tau, \mathcal{P}_i}, \tau'$): The secret key update algorithm is also run locally by a user without interactions. Given the public parameter PP, a punctured secret key $\text{SK}_{\tau, \mathcal{P}_i}$ on time interval τ and a new time interval $\tau' > \tau$, this algorithm first parses the secret key $\text{SK}_{\tau, \mathcal{P}_i} = \{\boldsymbol{sk}_{\emptyset}, \boldsymbol{sk}_{\mathcal{P}_1}, \ldots, \boldsymbol{sk}_{\mathcal{P}_i}, \{\boldsymbol{sk}_{\tau,\eta}\}_{\eta \in \mathcal{N}_\tau}\}$, where $\boldsymbol{sk}_{\tau,\eta} = (sk_{\tau,0}, sk_{\tau,1}, sk_{\tau,|w_\eta|+1}, \ldots, sk_{\tau,\ell})$. Then, for each $\eta' \in \mathcal{N}_{\tau'}$ it finds out a node $\eta \in \mathcal{N}_\tau$ such that w_η is a prefix of $w_{\eta'}$, and further computes

$$\boldsymbol{sk}_{\tau',\eta'} = \left(sk_{\tau,0} \cdot V(w_{\tau'})^{r_{\tau'}} \cdot \prod_{j=|w_\eta|+1}^{|w_{\eta'}|} (sk_{\tau,j})^{w_{\eta'}[j]}, sk_{\tau,1} \cdot g^{r_{\tau'}}, \right.$$

$$\left. sk_{\tau,|w_{\eta'}|+1} \cdot (v_{|w_{\eta'}|+1})^{r_{\tau'}}, \dots, sk_{\tau,\ell} \cdot (v_\ell)^{r_{\tau'}} \right),$$

where $r_{\tau'}$ is an exponent randomly sampled from $\mathbb{Z}_p$. Finally, this algorithm outputs an updated secret key $\text{SK}_{\tau',\mathcal{P}_i} = \{\boldsymbol{sk}_\emptyset, \boldsymbol{sk}_{\mathcal{P}_1}, \dots, \boldsymbol{sk}_{\mathcal{P}_i}, \{\boldsymbol{sk}_{\tau',\eta'}\}_{\eta' \in \mathcal{N}_{\tau'}}\}$ for time interval τ'.

- Encrypt($\text{PP}, \text{ID}, S, M, \tau$): This algorithm is performed by a sender intending to send a message to a receiver with identity ID. Given the public parameter PP, a receiver's identity ID, a tag set $S = \{t_1, \dots, t_d\}$ $(d \leq n)$, a message M to encrypt and a time interval τ, this algorithm first defines a coefficient vector $\boldsymbol{z} = (z_1, \dots, z_n)$ form the polynomial $f(x) = \prod_{t \in S}(x - t) = \sum_{j=1}^{n} z_j x^{j-1}$, where $z_j = 0$ for $d + 1 < j \leq n$. Then, it picks a random integer $s \in \mathbb{Z}_p$ and computes

$$\text{CT} = (c_0, c_1, c_2, c_3, c_4) = \left(Z^s \cdot M, g^s, H(\text{ID})^s, V(w_\tau)^s, (h_1^{z_1} \cdots h_n^{z_n})^s \right).$$

Finally, this algorithm outputs a ciphertext CT, along with S and τ.

- Decrypt($\text{PP}, \text{SK}_{\tau,\mathcal{P}_i}, \text{CT}$): This algorithm is run by a receiver with identity ID. Given the public parameter PP, a punctured secret key $\text{SK}_{\tau,\mathcal{P}_i}$ on time interval τ and a ciphertext CT, this algorithm first uses the tag set S to compute a coefficient vector $\boldsymbol{z} = (z_1, \dots, z_n)$ as in the encryption algorithm. Then, it parses the secret key $\text{SK}_{\tau,\mathcal{P}_i}$ as $\{\boldsymbol{sk}_\emptyset, \boldsymbol{sk}_{\mathcal{P}_1}, \dots, \boldsymbol{sk}_{\mathcal{P}_i}, \{\boldsymbol{sk}_{\tau,\eta}\}_{\eta \in \mathcal{N}_\tau}\}$, where $\boldsymbol{sk}_\emptyset = (sk_{\emptyset,1}, sk_{\emptyset,2}, sk_{\emptyset,3}, \boldsymbol{sk}_{\emptyset,4})$, $\boldsymbol{sk}_{\emptyset,4} = (k_{\emptyset,2}, \dots, k_{\emptyset,n})$. For $m = 1$ to i, let $\boldsymbol{sk}_{\mathcal{P}_m} = (sk_{\mathcal{P}_m,1}, sk_{\mathcal{P}_m,2}, sk_{\mathcal{P}_m,3}, \boldsymbol{sk}_{\mathcal{P}_m,4})$, $\boldsymbol{sk}_{\mathcal{P}_m,4} = (k_{\mathcal{P}_m,2}, k_{\mathcal{P}_m,3}, \dots, k_{\mathcal{P}_m,n})$. Let $\boldsymbol{sk}_{\tau,\eta_\tau} = (sk_{\tau,0}, sk_{\tau,1})$. Next, the algorithm successively computes

$$k_0 = \prod_{j=2}^{n} (k_{\emptyset,j})^{z_j}, \quad k_m = \prod_{j=2}^{n} (k_{\mathcal{P}_m,j})^{z_j} \quad \text{for } m = 1 \text{ to } i,$$

$$C_0 = \left(\frac{e(k_0, c_1)}{e(k_{\emptyset,1}, c_4)} \right)^{\frac{-1}{f(t_0)}} \cdot \frac{e(sk_{\emptyset,2}, c_2) \cdot e(sk_{\tau,1}, c_3)}{e(sk_{\tau,0}, c_1)},$$

$$C_m = \left(\frac{e(k_m, c_1)}{e(k_{\mathcal{P}_m,2}, c_4)} \right)^{\frac{-1}{f(\hat{t}_m)}} \cdot \frac{1}{e(sk_{\mathcal{P}_m,1}, c_1)} \quad \text{for } m = 1 \text{ to } i.$$

Finally, this algorithm outputs the message $M = c_0 \cdot \prod_{j=0}^{i} C_j$.

CORRECTNESS. Now we demonstrate the correctness of the above construction. First, for each $m \in [i]$, note that

$$k_m = \prod_{j=2}^{n} (k_{\mathcal{P}_m,j})^{z_j} = \prod_{j=2}^{n} \left(h_1^{-\hat{t}_m^{j-1}} \cdot h_j \right)^{r_m z_j} = (h_1)^{-r_m \cdot \sum_{j=2}^{n} z_j \hat{t}_m^{j-1}} \cdot \prod_{j=2}^{n} h_j^{r_m z_j}$$

$$= (h_1)^{r_m \cdot (z_1 - f(\hat{t}_m))} \cdot \prod_{j=2}^{n} h_j^{r_m z_j} = (h_1)^{-r_m \cdot f(\hat{t}_m)} \cdot \left(\prod_{j=1}^{n} h_j^{z_j} \right)^{r_m}.$$

Similarly, we have that $k_0 = (h_1)^{-r_0 \cdot f(\hat{t}_0)} \cdot \left(\prod_{j=1}^{n} h_j^{z_j} \right)^{r_0}$, where r_0 is reassigned as $r_0 \leftarrow r_0 + \sum_{j=1}^{i} r'_j$.

Second, observe that

$$C_0 = \left(\frac{e\left((h_1)^{-r_0 \cdot f(\hat{t}_0)} \cdot \left(\prod_{j=1}^{n} h_j^{z_j} \right)^{r_0}, g^s\right)}{e\left(g^{r_0}, (h_1^{z_1} \cdots h_n^{z_n})^s\right)} \right)^{\frac{-1}{f(\hat{t}_0)}} \cdot \frac{e(g^{r_{id}}, H(\text{ID})^s) \cdot e(g^{r_\tau}, V(w_\tau)^s)}{e\left(g^{\alpha'} \cdot h_1^{r_0} \cdot H(\text{ID})^{r_{id}} \cdot V(w_\tau)^{r_\tau}, g^s\right)}$$

$$= e(h_1^{r_0}, g^s) \cdot e(g, g)^{-\alpha' s} \cdot e(h_1^{r_0}, g^s)^{-1} = e(g, g)^{-\alpha' s},$$

where $\alpha' = \alpha - \sum_{m=1}^{i} \lambda_m$. Similarly, we have that $C_m = e(g, g)^{-\lambda_m \cdot s}$ for $m \in [i]$. Thus, we conclude that

$$c_0 \cdot \prod_{m=0}^{i} C_m = M \cdot e(g, g)^{\alpha s} \cdot e(g, g)^{(\sum_{m=1}^{i} \lambda_m - \alpha) \cdot s} \cdot \prod_{m=1}^{i} e(g, g)^{-\lambda_m \cdot s} = M.$$

4.3 Security Analysis

The security of the proposed fs-PIBE scheme is captured as follows:

Theorem 1. *If the decisional q-BDHE assumption holds over bilinear groups* $\mathbb{G}$ *and* $\mathbb{G}_T$, *then the proposed fs-PIBE scheme is IND–PUN–ID–CPA secure. Formally, we have that*

$$\text{Adv}_{\mathcal{C}}^{q\text{-BDHE}}(\kappa) \geq \frac{1}{64(l+1) \cdot q_{id} \cdot \tau_{max}} \cdot \text{Adv}_{\mathcal{A}, \text{fs-PIBE}}^{\text{IND-PUN-ID-CPA}}(\kappa),$$

where l *is the length of identity,* q_{id} *is the number of generated secret keys for answering queries, and* τ_{max} *is the total number of time intervals.*

Due to space constraints, we will provide the detailed proof in our full version.

4.4 Efficiency Analysis

In this subsection, we theoretically discuss the performance of the proposed fs-PIBE scheme, by comparing it with the underlying Waters' IBE scheme [31] and the FSPE scheme of Green and Miers' [14][2]. For ease of notation, we denote by $|\mathbb{G}|$, $|\mathbb{G}_T|$ and $|\mathbb{Z}_p|$ the size of an element from $\mathbb{G}$, $\mathbb{G}_T$ and $\mathbb{Z}_p$, respectively. Let $|\mathcal{P}|$ be the number of punctured tags. $\texttt{Exp}$ means one exponentiation operation and $\texttt{Pair}$ one pairing operation.

In Table 1 we provide the sizes of public parameter, secret key and ciphertext in these listed schemes. Compared with the original Waters' IBE scheme [31] and the FSPE scheme of Green and Miers [14], the sizes of public parameter and secret key in the proposed fs-PIBE scheme increase a lot. However, it is bounded by the maximum number n of allowed tags and the depth ℓ of the binary tree used to manage time intervals. At the cost of acceptable storage space, the

---

[2] We exclude the FSPE scheme in [15] from comparisons since it is a generic one.

Table 1. Comparisons with previous works in terms of storage and communication cost

Schemes	#Public parameter	#Secret key	#Ciphertext
Waters IBE [31]	$(l+4)|G|+|G_T|$	$2|G|$	$3|G|+|G_T|$
FSPE [14]	$(n+\ell+4)|G|+|G_T|$	$(3|\mathcal{P}|+2(\ell-|w_\eta|)+4)|G|$	$(n+2)|G|+|G_T|$
fs-PIBE	$(n+\ell+l+3)|G|+|G_T|$	$((n+1)|\mathcal{P}|+\sum_{\eta\in\mathcal{N}_\tau}(\ell-|w_\eta|+1))|G|$	$4|G|+|G_T|$

ciphertext size in the proposed scheme achieves constant as in Waters' IBE scheme [31]. In fact, we can obtain a natural construction of fs-PIBE scheme by simultaneously running Waters' IBE scheme [31] and the FSPE scheme of Green and Miers [14] as follows: Select a random element R when needing to encrypt a message M, then encrypt $M \cdot R$ with IBE and R with FSPE. Although this construction achieves practical forward secrecy in the setting of IBE, it still needs PKIs to support the usage of FSPE, and brings redundancy of public parameter and ciphertext. It can be seen that the proposed fs-PIBE scheme is more compact.

Table 2 summaries the computation complexity of main algorithms in these listed schemes, in which we only consider the dominant operations: exponentiation and pairing. Similar to Green and Miers' puncture encryption scheme [14], the computation cost of the proposed fs-PIBE scheme is determined by the number $|\mathcal{P}|$ of punctured tags and the maximum number n of tags allowed to attach to each ciphertext. But the difference is that the number of attached tags in the proposed fs-PIBE scheme is allowed to dynamically range from 1 to n, but the number in Green and Miers' scheme is fixed to be n. Thus, our scheme is more flexible. In addition, the computation complexity of the encryption algorithm in our proposal is independent of any parameter. Focusing on the security of these schemes, our fs-PIBE scheme and Waters' IBE scheme are secure in the standard model, while the FSPE scheme is secure in the random oracle model.

Table 2. Comparisons with previous works in terms of computation overhead

Schemes	KeyGen	Puncture	Update	Encrypt	Decrypt
Waters IBE [31]	$O(1)\texttt{Exp}$	–	–	$O(1)\texttt{Exp}+O(1)\texttt{Pair}$	$O(1)\texttt{Pair}$
FSPE [14]	$O(\ell)\texttt{Exp}$	$O(1)\texttt{Exp}$	$O(\ell)\texttt{Exp}$	$O(n)\texttt{Exp}+O(1)\texttt{Pair}$	$O(n+|\mathcal{P}|)\texttt{Exp}+O(|\mathcal{P}|)\texttt{Pair}$
fs-PIBE	$O(n+\ell)\texttt{Exp}$	$O(n)\texttt{Exp}$	$O(\ell)\texttt{Exp}$	$O(1)\texttt{Exp}+O(1)\texttt{Pair}$	$O(n+|\mathcal{P}|)\texttt{Exp}+O(|\mathcal{P}|)\texttt{Pair}$

5   Encrypted Cloud Email Systems from fs-PIBE

In this section, we introduce a framework of encrypted cloud email systems based on fs-PIBE. In our framework, there are four types of participants: PKG, email sender, email receiver and cloud email server.

Specifically, our framework employs a fs-PIBE scheme fs-PIBE = (Setup, KeyGen, Puncture, Update, Encrypt, Decrypt) and a symmetric encryption scheme SE = (Encrypt, Decrypt), and utilizes a hybrid encryption fashion to secure cloud email communications. Its workflow is comprised of the following phases:

① **Initialization**: In this phase, the PKG selects necessary parameters, and runs the algorithm fs-PIBE.Setup$(\kappa, \tau_{max}, n) \to$ (PP, MSK). Then, it publishes the public parameter PP.

② **Customer Registration**: In this phase, each customer selects his/her email address ID (i.e., his/her public key), and then registers with the PKG. That is, the PKG issues an initial secret key $SK_{0,\emptyset} \leftarrow$ fs-PIBE.KeyGen(PP, MSK, ID) to the customer.

③ **Send Encrypted Cloud Emails**: In this phase, when an email sender wants to send an email message M to an receiver with address ID, he/she first picks an encryption key K for SE, and respectively produces ciphertexts fs-PIBE.Encrypt$(PP, ID, S, K, \tau) \to$ Header and SE.Encrypt$(K, M) \to$ CT. The encrypted email (Header, CT) is then sent to the cloud email server.

④ **Cache and Deliver Encrypted Emails**: In this phase, the cloud email server takes charge of caching and delivering encrypted emails. That is, when the intended receiver is online, it forwards (Header, CT) to him/her.

⑤ **Decrypt Encrypted Emails**: In this phase, upon receiving the encrypted email, the receiver first utilizes the current secret key to decrypt the encryption key fs-PIBE.Decrypt$(PP, SK_{\tau, \mathcal{P}_i}, \text{Header}) \to$ K, and further recovers the email message SE.Decrypt$(K, CT) \to M$.

⑥ **Puncture and Update Secret Key**: In this phase, the receiver punctures the current secret key by running fs-PIBE.Puncture$(PP, SK_{\tau, \mathcal{P}_{i-1}}, \hat{t}_i)$ for each $\hat{t}_i \in S$. In addition, at the end of time interval τ, he/she derives the secret key for next time interval $SK_{\tau', \mathcal{P}_i} \leftarrow$ fs-PIBE.Update$(PP, SK_{\tau, \mathcal{P}_i}, \tau')$. Depending on the receiver's security policy configuration, he/she can preserve secret keys for multiple time intervals simultaneously.

The correctness of our framework comes from the correctness of the underlying fs-PIBE scheme and symmetric encryption scheme. By correctly implementing the hybrid encryption fashion, its security can be reduced to the security of fs-PIBE and SE. Compared with previous encrypted email systems, our framework provides stronger security guarantee without sacrificing usability.

6   Conclusion

In this paper, focusing on how to achieve the forward secrecy of encrypted cloud email systems without requiring PKIs and sacrificing the usability, we introduce the notion of forward-secure puncturable identity-based encryption. Specifically, we formalize its syntax and security notion, and also propose a concrete construction. The proposed fs-PIBE scheme has constant size of ciphertext, and is proved to be secure in the standard model. The efficiency analysis indicates that the proposed fs-PIBE captures practical forward secrecy at the cost of acceptable storage overhead, and thus is desirable for encrypted cloud email systems.

Acknowledgement. This work is supported in part by the National Nature Science Foundation of China under Grants 61702549, 61572382 and 61702401, and in part by the National Cryptography Development Fund (No. MMJJ20180110), and in part by the Open Foundation of State Key Laboratory of Integrated Services Networks (Xidian University) under Grant ISN19-12.

References

1. Abu-Salma, R., Sasse, M.A., Bonneau, J., Danilova, A., Naiakshina, A., Smith, M.: Obstacles to the adoption of secure communication tools. In: IEEE S&P 2017, pp. 137–153. IEEE (2017)
2. Boneh, D., Boyen, X., Goh, E.-J.: Hierarchical identity based encryption with constant size ciphertext. In: Cramer, R. (ed.) EUROCRYPT 2005. LNCS, vol. 3494, pp. 440–456. Springer, Heidelberg (2005). https://doi.org/10.1007/11426639_26
3. Boneh, D., Franklin, M.: Identity-based encryption from the weil pairing. In: Kilian, J. (ed.) CRYPTO 2001. LNCS, vol. 2139, pp. 213–229. Springer, Heidelberg (2001). https://doi.org/10.1007/3-540-44647-8_13
4. Boneh, D., Gentry, C., Waters, B.: Collusion resistant broadcast encryption with short ciphertexts and private keys. In: Shoup, V. (ed.) CRYPTO 2005. LNCS, vol. 3621, pp. 258–275. Springer, Heidelberg (2005). https://doi.org/10.1007/11535218_16
5. Brown, I., Back, A., Laurie, B.: Forward secrecy extensions for OpenPGP, April 2002. https://tools.ietf.org/html/draft-brown-pgp-pfs-03
6. Callas, J., Donnerhacke, L., Finney, H., Shaw, D., Thayer, R.: OpenPGP Message Format, November 2007, RFC 4880. https://tools.ietf.org/html/rfc4880
7. Canetti, R., Halevi, S., Katz, J.: A forward-secure public-key encryption scheme. In: Biham, E. (ed.) EUROCRYPT 2003. LNCS, vol. 2656, pp. 255–271. Springer, Heidelberg (2003). https://doi.org/10.1007/3-540-39200-9_16
8. Chen, H.C.: Secure multicast key protocol for electronic mail systems with providing perfect forward secrecy. Secur. Commun. Netw. **6**(1), 100–107 (2013)
9. DataMotion: DataMotion SecureMail (2013). https://www.proofpoint.com/us/products/email-protection. Accessed 18 April 2019
10. Dent, A.W.: Flaws in an e-mail protocol. IEEE Commun. Lett. **9**(8), 718–719 (2005)
11. Derler, D., Jager, T., Slamanig, D., Striecks, C.: Bloom filter encryption and applications to efficient forward-secret 0-RTT key exchange. In: Nielsen, J.B., Rijmen, V. (eds.) EUROCRYPT 2018. LNCS, vol. 10822, pp. 425–455. Springer, Cham (2018). https://doi.org/10.1007/978-3-319-78372-7_14
12. Derler, D., Krenn, S., Lorünser, T., Ramacher, S., Slamanig, D., Striecks, C.: Revisiting proxy re-encryption: forward secrecy, improved security, and applications. In: Abdalla, M., Dahab, R. (eds.) PKC 2018. LNCS, vol. 10769, pp. 219–250. Springer, Cham (2018). https://doi.org/10.1007/978-3-319-76578-5_8
13. Garfinkel, S.L., Miller, R.C.: Johnny 2: a user test of key continuity management with S/MIME and outlook express. In: Proceedings of the 2005 Symposium on Usable Privacy and Security, pp. 13–24. ACM (2005)

14. Green, M., Miers, I.: Forward secure asynchronous messaging from puncturable encryption. In: 2015 IEEE Symposium on Security and Privacy-S&P 2015, pp. 305–320 (2015)

15. Günther, F., Hale, B., Jager, T., Lauer, S.: 0-RTT key exchange with full forward secrecy. In: Coron, J.-S., Nielsen, J.B. (eds.) EUROCRYPT 2017. LNCS, vol. 10212, pp. 519–548. Springer, Cham (2017). https://doi.org/10.1007/978-3-319-56617-7_18

16. Hofheinz, D., Jia, D., Pan, J.: Identity-based encryption tightly secure under chosen-ciphertext attacks. In: Peyrin, T., Galbraith, S. (eds.) ASIACRYPT 2018. LNCS, vol. 11273, pp. 190–220. Springer, Cham (2018). https://doi.org/10.1007/978-3-030-03329-3_7

17. Huang, X., et al.: Cost-effective authentic and anonymous data sharing with forward security. IEEE Trans. Comput. **64**(4), 971–983 (2015)

18. Kim, B.H., Koo, J.H., Lee, D.H.: Robust e-mail protocols with perfect forward secrecy. IEEE Commun. Lett. **10**(6), 510–512 (2006)

19. Laurie, B., Langley, A., Kasper, E.: Certificate Transparency, June 2013, RFC 6962. http://www.rfc-editor.org/info/rfc6962

20. Li, H., Huang, Q., Shen, J., Yang, G., Susilo, W.: Designated-server identity-based authenticated encryption with keyword search for encrypted emails. Inf. Sci. **481**, 330–343 (2019)

21. Ostrovsky, R., Sahai, A., Waters, B.: Attribute-based encryption with non-monotonic access structures. In: CCS 2007, pp. 195–203. ACM (2007)

22. Poddebniak, D., et al.: Efail: breaking S/MIME and OpenPGP email encryption using exfiltration channels. In: USENIX Security Symposium, pp. 549–566 (2018)

23. Proofpoint: Proofpoint Email Protection (2005). https://www.proofpoint.com/us/products/email-protection. Accessed 18 Apr 2019

24. Ramsdell, B., Turner, S.: Secure/Multipurpose Internet Mail Extensions (S/MIME) Version 3.2 Message Specification, January 2010, RFC 5751 (Proposed Standard). https://tools.ietf.org/html/rfc5751

25. Ryan, M.D.: Enhanced certificate transparency and end-to-end encrypted mail. In: NDSS, pp. 1–14 (2014)

26. Schneier, B., Hall, C.: An improved e-mail security protocol. In: Proceedings 13th Annual Computer Security Applications Conference, pp. 227–230. IEEE (1997)

27. Shamir, A.: Identity-based cryptosystems and signature schemes. In: Blakley, G.R., Chaum, D. (eds.) CRYPTO 1984. LNCS, vol. 196, pp. 47–53. Springer, Heidelberg (1985). https://doi.org/10.1007/3-540-39568-7_5

28. Sun, H.M., Hsieh, B.T., Hwang, H.J.: Secure e-mail protocols providing perfect forward secrecy. IEEE Commun. Lett. **9**(1), 58–60 (2005)

29. The Radicati Group Inc.: Cloud Email and Collaboration-Market Quadrant 2019, March 2019. https://www.radicati.com/wp/wp-content/uploads/2019/03/Cloud-Email-and-Collaboration-Market-Quadrant-2019-Brochure.pdf. Accessed 8 Apr 2019

30. Unger, N., et al.: SoK: secure messaging. In: 2015 IEEE Symposium on Security and Privacy, pp. 232–249. IEEE (2015)

31. Waters, B.: Efficient identity-based encryption without random oracles. In: Cramer, R. (ed.) EUROCRYPT 2005. LNCS, vol. 3494, pp. 114–127. Springer, Heidelberg (2005). https://doi.org/10.1007/11426639_7

32. Wikileaks: Hillary Clinton Email Archive, March 2016. https://wikileaks.org/clinton-emails/. Accessed 8 Apr 2019

33. Wikileaks: The Podesta Emails, March 2016. https://wikileaks.org/podesta-emails/. Accessed 8 Apr 2019

34. Xu, P., Jiao, T., Wu, Q., Wang, W., Jin, H.: Conditional identity-based broadcast proxy re-encryption and its application to cloud email. IEEE Trans. Comput. **65**(1), 66–79 (2016)
35. Yao, D., Fazio, N., Dodis, Y., Lysyanskaya, A.: ID-based encryption for complex hierarchies with applications to forward security and broadcast encryption. In: Proceedings of the 11th ACM Conference on Computer and Communications Security, pp. 354–363. ACM (2004)

Feistel Structures for MPC, and More

Martin R. Albrecht[1], Lorenzo Grassi[2,3], Léo Perrin[4], Sebastian Ramacher[2], Christian Rechberger[2], Dragos Rotaru[5,6], Arnab Roy[5(✉)], and Markus Schofnegger[2]

[1] Royal Holloway, University of London, Egham, UK
[2] IAIK, Graz University of Technology, Graz, Austria
[3] Know-Center GmbH, Graz, Austria
[4] Inria, Paris, France
[5] University of Bristol, Bristol, UK
arnab.roy@bristol.ac.uk
[6] imec-Cosic, Department of Electrical Engineering, KU Leuven, Leuven, Belgium

Abstract. Efficient PRP/PRFs are instrumental to the design of cryptographic protocols. We investigate the design of dedicated PRP/PRFs for three application areas - secure multiparty computation (MPC), ZKSNARK and zero-knowledge (ZK) based PQ signature schemes. In particular, we explore a family of PRFs which are generalizations of the well-known Feistel design approach followed in a previously proposed application specific design - MiMC. Attributing to this approach we call our family of PRP/PRFs GMiMC.

In MPC applications, our construction shows improvements (over MiMC) in throughput by a factor of more than 4 and simultaneously a 5-fold reduction of preprocessing effort, albeit at the cost of a higher latency. Another use-case where MiMC outperforms other designs, in SNARK applications, our design GMiMCHash shows moderate improvement. Additionally, in this case our design benefits from the flexibility of using smaller (prime) fields. In the area of recently proposed ZK-based PQ signature schemes where MiMC was not competitive at all, our new design has 30 times smaller signature size than MiMC.

1 Introduction

Computing on Encrypted Data. Due to an increasing maturity of secure multi-party computation, there are a couple of companies such as Partisia [48],

L. Grassi has been partialy supported by EU H2020 project Safe-DEED, grant agreement n°825225. S. Ramacher has been partially supported by the Austrian Research Promotion Agency (FFG) within the ICT of the future grants program, grant agreement n°863129 (project IoT4CPS), of the Federal Ministry for Transport, Innovation and Technology (BMVIT) and by A-SIT Secure Information Technology Center Austria. D. Rotaru was supported by the Defense Advanced Research Projects Agency (DARPA) and Space and Naval Warfare Systems Center, Pacific (SSC Pacific) under contract No. N66001-15-C-4070. Arnab Roy is supported by the EPSRC funding under grant No. EPSRC EP/N011635/1.

ⓒ Springer Nature Switzerland AG 2019
K. Sako et al. (Eds.): ESORICS 2019, LNCS 11736, pp. 151–171, 2019.
https://doi.org/10.1007/978-3-030-29962-0_8

Sepior [51], Sharemind [16], Unbound [56] which try to incorporate MPC frameworks into large projects to offer services where the companies do not need to know the user inputs to be able to compute on them [10]. Since the complexity of these systems grows, one must be able to incorporate encrypted databases with an MPC system to deal with data in transit or at rest.

For example, the trivial way of storing outputs to be used later is each party in the MPC engine to encrypts the respective share using a (different) symmetric key and posts it to the database. Later on, when the parties have decided to carry further computations on these shares they simply decrypt the ciphertexts using their corresponding keys. Notice that for a given shared secret there are N ciphertexts where N is the number of parties. This is where cryptographic primitives such as block ciphers play an important role in storing outputs from the MPC engine into an encrypted database: parties can engage in an MPC protocol to compute an encryption of the share using a shared key. In this way, parties jointly produce a single ciphertext rather than having N ciphertexts per stored share.

If one chooses AES as the underlying primitive for the encryption scheme then the share conversions become the bottleneck of MPC procedures when the underlying engine performs arithmetic modulo p. This is indeed the case for most of the frameworks such as MP-SPDZ [7], SCALE-MAMBA [6], BDOZa [13], VIFF [27] and conversion to their boolean counterpart with same security properties is an expensive task. Hence, for efficient and secure computation of algorithms modulo p we would like a blockcipher over the same field. Grassi et al. [35] give several constructions for lightweight pseudorandom functions (PRFs) when evaluated in a *prime field* of large characteristic and concluded that among various other options MiMC [4] is competitive, which is the starting point of our design as well.

Besides database storage, MPC-friendly PRFs can cover other use-cases as well explored in [18,35]. These include searchable encryption, authenticated encryption, oblivious RAM done in a distributed fashion using MPC and an efficient PRF.

(ZK)SNARK. The most well-known use of (ZK)SNARK is in the area of privacy/anonymity providing cryptocurrency. Zcash [11] is the most popular cryptocurrency which uses this protocol. Zcoin, Zencash are examples of cryptocurrencies based on the (ZK)SNARK protocol. One of the performance bottle-neck in these applications is the lack of "efficient" hash function over suitable (prime) field. In cryptocurrency protocols such hash functions are typically used to insert the (hashed) coin values in a Merkle hash tree. In [4] it was shown for the first time that a hash function designed over prime field are significantly faster than SHA2 or SHA3 in SNARK setting. This almost directly speeds up the performance of (ZK)SNARK-based protocols which use SHA2.

ZK-Based Signature. Finally, we consider signature schemes based on zero-knowledge proofs of a preimage of a one-way function. It was recently shown that such schemes can be viable alternatives [22,23] when instantiated with symmetric primitives (to construct a one-way function) that have a low number of multiplications. Public and private keys are minimized and only consist of a plaintext-ciphertext pair and the secret key, respectively. On top of the post-quantum security of the zero-knowledge proof system (see [21,32] for recent improvenets of its security analysis), the only hardness assumption required to prove security is the one-wayness of the underlying function. Signature sizes strongly depend on the product of the number of multiplications of the OWF and the size of the field in which the multiplications are performed. The signature and verification times depend on the details of the scheme in a less straight-forward way. The block size of the instantiations we are interested in is around 256 bits.

Our Results. In this article, we continue exploring the construction strategies of symmetric cryptography which benefit MPC, (ZK)SNARK and PQ signa-ture applications. We generalize the design approach used in MiMC [4]. More specifically, we use the unpopular design strategy (in symmetric cryptography) – unbalanced Feistel network, and a new balanced Feistel network, for construct-ing a new family of block ciphers – GMiMC (in Sect. 2.1) and use it to construct the hash function GMiMCHash (in Sect. 2.2).

We show the performance of GMiMC in MPC applications based on secret sharing techniques such as BDOZa [13], SPDZ [28] or VIFF [27]. Previous works [35,49] did not take into account how to optimize the number of multiplications per encrypted share and treated the PRF as a black-box when extending to more inputs. We show that using our construction one can choose to encrypt multiple shares at once thus amortizing the number of multiplications per share and results in a more efficient preprocessing phase. We consider our work to be beneficial when there is a large number of blocks to encrypt. From a theoretical point of view two of our constructions are the first to avoid the linear increase of time and data sent across the parties in the preprocessing phase with the number of encrypted blocks (in $\mathbb{F}_p$). Namely, the cost per encrypted share if we encrypt more shares in one go. Details can be found in Sect. 6.1.

For (ZK)SNARK applications our design GMiMCHash provides the flexibil-ity of using prime field for smaller primes. For example, GMiMC can be used to obtain a permutation of input size ≈1024-bit over 128 bit prime field. In MiMC, this permutation could only be constructed using 1024 or 512-bit primes. Additionally, GMiMCHash shows moderate improvement in performance (see Sect. 6.2) compared to MiMC.

In the case of the PQ signature scheme, LowMC [2,5] was considered to be clearly the best choice for small signatures and runtimes. MiMC resulted in 10 times larger and hence unpractical signature sizes. As we have shown in Sect. 6.3, GMiMC is competitive with LowMC and far more efficient than MiMC. This performance is due the flexibility of GMiMC in providing many different field sizes by choosing different branch numbers.

Related Work. Recently, Agrawal et al. [1] considered the problem of parties jointly computing a symmetric-key encryption using a distributed PRF with implications to systems dealing with secret management [47] or enterprise net-work authentication. Our approach is slightly different since it evaluates the block-cipher inside the MPC engine. Our result is useful when clients can use it as a standalone tool to encrypt data on their own to then make the encryption compatible with the MPC storage as well.

Secure cryptographic primitives that require a low number of multiplications have many applications. These primitives can reduce the cost of countermeasures against various side-channel attacks [26,36], eliminate the ciphertext expansion in homomorphic encryption schemes [5,20,34,44,45], help dealing with encrypted data in secure multi-party computation systems [5,35,49], increase throughput or latency in SNARKs [4], and reduce the signature size of signature schemes and (privacy-preserving) variants, e.g. ring and EPID group signature schemes, based on one-way functions from symmetric-key primitives and non-interactive zero-knowledge proofs [17,22,29,30,38]. Research efforts in this area are manifold and cover questions on finding circuits for concrete mappings such as S-Boxes [19], foundational theoretical results on the complexity of PRGs, PRFs, and cryptographic hashes [8,9], and new ad-hoc designs of permutations, ciphers and hash functions tailored for various multiplication-related metrics [4,5,20,44].

2   Description of Generalized MiMC

Notation. In a Feistel network, X_{i-1} denotes the input to the branch i, where $1 \leq i \leq t$. X_{t-1} and X_0 denote the inputs to the leftmost and rightmost branches respectively. $X_i \in \mathbb{F}$ for a finite field $\mathbb{F}$. The block size (in bits) of the keyed Feistel permutation is denoted by N, while $n = \lceil \log_2 |\mathbb{F}| \rceil$ denotes the branch size (in bits). $\mathbb{F}_p$ denotes the finite field of prime order p. $\mathbb{F}_{2^m}$ denotes a finite field of order 2^m. The length of the key of a block cipher is given in number of bits and is denoted by κ. In particular, throughout this article we work with two different cases (depending on the practical implementation), denoted as:

- the *univariate* case, for which the key-size is $\kappa = n = \lceil \log_2 |\mathbb{F}| \rceil$;
- the *multivariate* case, for which the key-size is $\kappa = N = n \cdot t = \lceil \log_2 |\mathbb{F}| \rceil \cdot t$.

2.1   The Block Cipher GMiMC

We construct *"Generalized Feistel MiMC"* (GMiMC) variants from three generalized Feistel networks, e.g., with contracting round function (CRF), expanding round function (ERF), which are unbalanced Feistel networks and a new balanced Fiestel network which we call Multi-Rotating (MR). Each of the following constructions is a keyed permutation over $\mathbb{F}_{2^n}$ or $\mathbb{F}_p$. The three main parameters of the block ciphers are denoted by $[\kappa, t, n]$. For example, GMiMC$_{\text{crf}}[4n, 4, n]$ denotes the permutation GMiMC with CRF which has branch size n, key size $4n$ and number of branches 4. The descriptions of each block cipher over $\mathbb{F}_p$ are obtained by replacing the XOR-sum $\oplus$ with the corresponding sum $+$ modulo p. We recall that S-Box$(x) = x^3$ is a permutation in $GF(2^n)$ iff n is odd, while it is a permutation in $GF(p)$ iff $p \neq 1 \mod 3$ (see "Hermite's criterion" for more details).

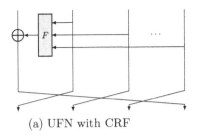

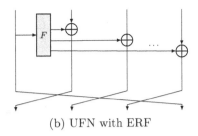

(a) UFN with CRF   (b) UFN with ERF

Fig. 1. UFN with ERF

GMiMC$_{\text{crf}}$. An unbalanced Feistel network (UFN) with a contracting round function (CRF) can be written as

$$(X_{t-1}, \ldots, X_0) \leftarrow (X_{t-2}, \ldots, X_0, X_{t-1} \oplus F(X_{t-2}, \ldots, X_0))$$

where X_i is the input to the i-th branch of the Feistel network and $F(\cdot)$ is a key-dependent function in round j, cf. Fig. 1a. In GMiMC$_{\text{crf}}$ we define the j-th round function as

$$F(x_{t-2}, \ldots, x_0) := \left(\bigoplus_i x_i \oplus k_j \oplus c_j \right)^3$$

where c_j and k_j are respectively the round constant and the key of the round j (for $1 \leq j \leq r$).

GMiMC$_{\text{erf}}$. An unbalanced Feistel network with an expanding round function (ERF) can be written as

$$(X_{t-1}, \ldots, X_0) \leftarrow (X_{t-2} \oplus F(X_{t-1}), \ldots, X_0 \oplus F(X_{t-1}), X_{t-1})$$

where X_i is the input to the i-th branch of the Feistel network and $F(\cdot)$ is a key-dependent function in round j, cf. Fig. 1b. In GMiMC$_{\text{erf}}$ the j-th round function is defined as

$$F(x) := (x \oplus k_j \oplus c_j)^3$$

where k_j and c_j are as in GMiMC$_{\text{crf}}$.

GMiMC$_{\text{mrf}}$. In [54], Suzaki and Minematsu introduced new variants of the GFN structure where the linear mixing applied after the Feistel functions is a complex permutation rather than a simple rotation. This allowed them to build GFNs operating on $t = 2^b$ branches such that full diffusion is achieved in $2b$ rounds rather than the $2t$ rounds needed by a Nyberg-style construction [46]. They later used this approach to build the lightweight block cipher TWINE [55].

Here, we introduce the Multi-Rotating structure for generalized Feistel networks, which provides full diffusion as quickly as a TWINE-like structure without the constraint that the number of branches is a power of 2. It is also conceptually much simpler and thus easier in practice to apply to a larger number of branches.

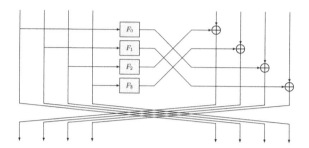

Fig. 2. One round $\mathcal{R}_s$ of an 8-branch Multi-Rotating Feistel network with a rotation by $s = 2$.

These improvements come at the cost of the use of a *different mixing layer in each round* which, to the best of our knowledge, has not been considered for a Feistel or generalized Feistel structure so far. However, we note that previously, the Serpent designers (of SPN type) considered using different mixing layers in each round in their design. In particular, they considered using a different linear transformation for even and odd rounds (see [15, App. A.6]), before settling for their current design.

To introduce the Multi-Rotating Feistel network structure, we first give a general expression of its round function. A *rotated Feistel round* is a permutation $\mathcal{R}_s$ parameterized by a rotation amount s which operates on an even number of branches and works as follows:

$$\big(X_{t-1}, \ldots, X_0\big) \leftarrow \big(X_{t/2-1} + F_{-s}(X_{t-1-g(s,0)}), \ldots,$$
$$X_0 \oplus F_{t/2-1-s}(X_{t-1-g(s,t/2-1)}), X_{t-1}, \ldots, X_{t/2}\big),$$

where the index of the function $F(\cdot)$ is taken modulo $t/2$ and $g(s, i) = s + i$ mod $t/2$. This process is summarized in Fig. 2. Like in GMiMC$_{\mathsf{Nyb}}$, each F_i in the j-th round of GMiMC$_{\mathsf{mrf}}$ is defined as

$$F_i(x) := \big(x \oplus k_{i+j\cdot t/2} \oplus c_{i+j\cdot t/2}\big)^3,$$

where $c_{i+j\cdot t/2}$ are distinct constants in round j and $k_{i+j\cdot t/2}$ are round keys. By iterating such rounds $\mathcal{R}_s$ for varying values of s we obtain a block cipher. An instance of such an r-round block cipher is specified using the sequence $\{s_0, \ldots, s_{r-1}\}$ of the r rotation amounts used. As explained in [3, App. B], it is possible to build a GFN with optimal diffusion by choosing the sequence $\{s_j\}_{j<r}$ carefully. We build a GMiMC$_{\mathsf{mrf}}$ instance operating on t branches using a sequence of rotations $\{s_j\}_{0\leq j<r}$ where

$$s_{2\ell} = 0 \quad \text{and} \quad s_{2\ell+1} = 2^{\ell \pmod{\lceil \log_2(t/2)\rceil}}. \tag{1}$$

For instance, if $t = 32$, then $\log_2(t/2) = 4$ and this sequence can be written as $\{0, 1, 0, 2, 0, 4, 0, 8, 0, 1, 0, 2, 0, 4, 0, 8, 0, 1, \ldots\}$, i.e. it consists in as many repetitions as needed of the pattern $\{0, 1, 0, 2, 0, 4, 0, 8\}$ of length $2\log_2(t/2) = 8$.

To better understand the security of GMiMC$_{mrf}$, we now investigate its *diffusion*. We borrow our definition of diffusion from [54]: if a variable y intervenes in the expression of an internal state word X then we say that X *depends* on y. If all output words of a (round-reduced) block cipher depend on all input words, we say that this primitive provides *full diffusion*.

The diffusion provided by GMiMC$_{mrf}$ using the sequence of rotations from Eq. (1) is quantified by the following Theorem, proved in [3, App. B].

Theorem 1. *Let X_j^i denote the word with index j at the input of round i, so that for example X_j^0 denotes a plaintext word. Consider a GMiMC$_{mrf}$ instance operating on t branches with the rotation sequence in Eq. 1. If $i \geq 2\lceil \log_2(t) \rceil$, then X_j^i depends on $X_{j'}^0$ for any j, j'. The same is true in the backwards direction. In other words, GMiMC$_{mrf}$ provides full diffusion after $2\lceil \log_2(t) \rceil$ rounds.*

Key Schedule. When $|k| = n$ (i.e. the univariate case), then $k_i = k \ \forall i$. The key schedule for the multivariate case $|k| = t \times n$ is a little more complicated. Let $k = k_0||k_1|| \ldots ||k_{t-1}$, and let M be an *invertible* $t \times t$ matrix with elements in $\mathbb{F}_{2^n}$ or $\mathbb{F}_p$ that satisfies the following condition:

- $\forall i : 1 \leq i \leq \lceil R/t \rceil$ where R is the number of rounds:[1]

$$M^i[j,l] \equiv (\underbrace{M \times M \times .... \times M}_{i\text{-th times}})[j,l] \neq 0$$

for all $0 \leq j, l < t$, where $X[j,l]$ denotes the coefficient in row j and column l of the matrix X.

For each $1 \leq i \leq \lceil R/t \rceil$ let

$$[k_{i \cdot t}||k_{i \cdot t+1}|| \ldots ||k_{(i+1) \cdot t-2}||k_{(i+1) \cdot t-1}]^T =$$
$$M \times [k_{(i-1) \cdot t}||k_{(i-1) \cdot t+1}|| \ldots ||k_{i \cdot t-2}||k_{i \cdot t-1}]^T.$$

The second condition on M guarantees that *each subkey depends linearly on all the first t subkeys*. This fact has an important consequence. Consider GMiMC$_{crf}$ and/or GMiMC$_{erf}$ instantiated with a key schedule that uses the subkeys cyclically, i.e. $k_{i,j} = \hat{k}_{j \cdot t/2 + i \pmod t}$. If the attacker guesses $t - 1$ subkeys, then she can *potentially* skip both the first and the last $t - 1$ rounds. Instead, in the case in which each subkey depends linearly on all the first t subkeys, this strategy simply does not apply. As a result, the proposed key schedule allows to save a certain number of rounds (approximately $t - 1$) w.r.t. a key schedule that uses the subkeys cyclically. Similar argumentation holds for GMiMC$_{mrf}$.

---

[1] If no matrix exists that satisfies such condition, choose a matrix M for which the total number of zero coefficients for each M^i is minimum.

Round Constants and Number of Rounds. For all the above constructions the round constants are generated randomly over the suitable field and fixed. The number of rounds for each of the above block ciphers is chosen to thwart the cryptanalytic attacks mentioned in Sect. 4. In this article we only provide the number of rounds for the variants which are used in the target applications in Sect. 6. For the generic formulae of the number of rounds (depending on t, n or p) we refer to the [3].

2.2   Hash Function

To construct the hash function GMiMCHash (over $\mathbb{F}_p$), we use one of the structures, e.g. the GMiMC$_{\mathrm{erf}}$, with fixed (arbitrary) subkeys.[2] Denoting the fixed key permutation as GMiMC$^{\pi}_{\mathrm{erf}}[\kappa, t, n]$, GMiMCHash is constructed by instantiating a sponge construction [14] with GMiMC$^{\pi}_{\mathrm{erf}}[\kappa, t, n]$. The number of rounds of the permutation GMiMC is chosen according to the *univariate* case $2^{\kappa} = 2^n \approx p$.

When the internal permutation $\mathcal{P}$ of an N-bit sponge function (composed of c-bit capacity and r-bit bitrate – $N = c + r$) is modeled as a randomly chosen permutation, it has been proven by Bertoni et al. [14] to be indifferentiable from a random oracle up to $2^{c/2}$ calls to $\mathcal{P}$. In other words, a sponge with a capacity of c provides $2^{c/2}$ collision and $2^{c/2}$ (second) preimage resistance. Given a permutation of size N and a desired security level s, we can hash $r = N - 2s$ bits per call to the permutation.

As usual, the message is first padded according to the sponge specification so that the number of message blocks is a multiple of r, where r is the rate in sponge mode. For GMiMCHash-l we use a GMiMC permutation where $N = n{\cdot}t = 4{\cdot}l+1$ and $s = 2 \cdot l$. For GMiMCHash-256 we thus use a GMiMC permutation with $N = n \cdot t = 1024$ or 1025. The rate and the capacity are chosen as 512 and 513 respectively. This choice allows for processing the same amount of input bits as SHA-256 (512 bits) while at the same time offering collision security nd preimage security of 256 bits.

We highlight that while we could use any of the GMiMC constructions, GMiMC$_{\mathrm{erf}}$ turns out to be the most efficient choice in several settings as shown in Sect. 6.2.

3   Security Analysis

We have performed an in-depth security analysis of the GMiMC family of block ciphers (and hash function). In this article we only provide ideas of the most important attacks (in Sect. 4) which are decisive to the design. Due to the page constraint we refer to the extended version [3] of this article for the details of the analyses.

---

[2] We emphasize that no key schedule is required in this case, since there is no secret-key material.

Important Remark. *Due to our target applications, here we limit ourselves to provide the number of rounds to guarantee security* **only** *in the following two scenarios:*

- *GMiMC instantiated over* $\mathbb{F}_p$ with prime size 128 or more (used in SNARKs and MPC applications);
- *GMiMC instantiated over* $\mathbb{F}_{2^n}$ *in the low-data scenario* (used for application like PQ-Signature Scheme).

We stress that this choice is motivated by the fact that we focus only on the scenarios that are useful for our applications.

For some applications like PQ-Signature scheme, the attacker has a limited access to data (e.g. 1 or 2 (plaintext, ciphertext) pairs) as a result, only few attacks (e.g. the GCD one) apply to this case. The security analysis for this particular case is over $\mathbb{F}_{2^n}$ and proposed in [3, Sect. 5]. As the attacker can have access to few (plaintext, ciphertext) pairs, only few attacks (e.g. the GCD one) apply to this case.

Analysis of GMiMCHash over $\mathbb{F}_p$. For the hash function GMiMCHash case, the number of rounds of the inner permutation is chosen according to the corresponding univariate case. This is due to the following considerations. First, as we just recalled in the previous section, when the internal permutation $\mathcal{P}$ of an $N = c+r$ bit sponge function is modeled as a randomly chosen permutation, the sponge hash function is indifferentiable from a random oracle up to $2^{c/2}$ calls to $\mathcal{P}$. The numbers of rounds of the univariate case is sufficient to guarantee security against any (secret-/known-/chosen-) distinguisher which is independent of the key. Equivalently, this means that such number of rounds guarantee that $\mathcal{P}$ does not present any non-random/structural property (among the ones known in the literature). It follows that the previous assumption is satisfied. These and the fact that every key-recovery attack is meaningless in the hash scenario support our choice to consider the univariate case in order to determine the number of rounds of the inner permutation.

4 Security Analysis of GMiMC (over $\mathbb{F}_p$)

Almost all the attacks are independent of the fact that (a) the size of the key is equal to the branch size $\kappa = n$ (equivalently, $2^\kappa \simeq p$ for the $\mathbb{F}_p$ case) or (b) equal to $\kappa = N = t \cdot n$ (equivalently, $2^\kappa \simeq p^t$ for the $\mathbb{F}_p$ case). Since the cryptanalysis strategy of the three designs are very similar, in the following we give a complete analysis only for GMiMC$_{\mathsf{crf}}$, while we refer to [3, App. C - D] for the analysis of the other proposals.

4.1 Algebraic Attacks

In this section, we consider algebraic attacks against GMiMC. These attacks are particularly relevant for applications in which the attacker has access only to a limited number of (plaintext, ciphertext) pairs available to the attacker.

A main element in all these attacks is the degree reached in each of our constructions after r rounds. Here we give an idea of the analysis for the GMiMC$_{\mathsf{crf}}$ (similar for all other constructions). For all (algebraic) attacks in the following, we only care about the minimum degree after round r on the $t-1$ branch:

$$d_{t-1,t-1} = 3^{r-2t+2}.$$

The degree of each word of the plaintext in the t-branch is given by a similar formula ([3, Sect. 4.1]) both for the univariate and multivariate cases.

GCD Attack. As for the original MiMC [4], an attack strategy against GMiMC is to compute the Greatest Common Divisors (GCD). In particular, given more than one known (plaintext, ciphertext) pair or even working on the output of different branches of a single known (plaintext, ciphertext) pair, one can construct their polynomial representations and compute their polynomial GCD to recover a multiple of the key.[3] Note that this is a known-plaintext attack, and not a chosen-plaintext one, and it is one of the few attacks that applies in the low-data scenario. *Since interpolation attack is more efficient than GCD attack (from the attacker point of view)*, we discuss all details of this attack in [3, Sec. 5.1 - App. C.4], together with other low-data attacks.

Gröbner Bases. The natural generalization of GCDs to the multivariate case is the notion of a Gröbner basis [25]. The attack proceeds like the GCD attack with the final GCD computation replaced by a Gröbner basis computation. Due to the Feistel structure, we highlight that it is possible to construct multivariate "meet-in-the-middle" polynomials. Here we only give the summary of the attack. The details of the attack is given in the extended version [3] of this article.

GMiMC$_{\mathsf{crf}}$ *(Case: $2^\kappa \simeq p^t$).* To prevent the Gröbner basis attack, the minimum number of rounds r must satisfy $p^\varphi \cdot \binom{t-\varphi+d-1}{d-1}^\omega \geq p^t$, for all $\varphi \in \{0, \ldots, t-2\}$, where the degree d is a function of the number of rounds r, that is, $d = d(r)$ and $2 \leq \omega < 3$ is the linear algebra constant. For our parameter choices, this expression is minimized for $\varphi = 0$. We thus require

$$\binom{t+d}{d}^\omega = \left(\frac{t + 3^{r-2t+2}}{3^{r-2t+2}}\right)^\omega \approx p^t.$$

By setting $\omega = 2$ and after simplifying [3, Sec. 4.1] the above expression we obtain

$$r = \lceil 2t + 1/2 \log_2(p) \cdot \log_3 2 - 2 + \log_3 t \rceil.$$

To thwart Meet-in-the-Middle attacks, this value is doubled.

---

[3] Improving the computational complexity of this attack using more pairs is an open problem. Since the cost is dominated by the size of the polynomials involved, it is not clear if significant improvements are possible.

Interpolation Attack. As for the original MiMC, one of the most powerful attacks against the GMiMC family is the interpolation attack, introduced by Jakobsen and Knudsen [37] in 1997. This method can be extended to a key-recovery attack.

GMiMC$_{crf}$ is secure against interpolation attack if $(3^{r-2t+2})^t \approx 2^N \simeq p^t$. Hence, $r = \frac{\log_2(p)}{\log_2 3} + (2t - 2)$ rounds will be secure against the above-mentioned attacks. Conservatively, $2r + 2$ rounds will be secure against meet-in-the-middle attacks/distinguishers for the case $2^\kappa \simeq p$, while $2r + t + 1$ rounds will be secure against meet-in-the-middle attacks/distinguishers for the case $2^\kappa \simeq p^t$.

Higher-Order Differential. Let $\mathcal{A}$ be an affine space. Higher-order differential attacks [41] exploit the fact that $\bigoplus_{x \in \mathcal{A}} P(x) = 0$ if the dimension of $\mathcal{A}$ is higher than the degree of $P(\cdot)$. To thwart higher-order differential attacks, the number of rounds must be chosen in order to ensure that the algebraic degree of the GMiMC family of block ciphers is bigger than the biggest subspace in $\mathbb{F}$.

Due to the strategy exploited by the higher-order differential attack, there is a crucial difference between the cases $\mathbb{F}_{2^N}$ and $\mathbb{F}_p$. In particular, while $\mathbb{F}_{2^m}$ is always a subspace of $\mathbb{F}_{2^n}$ for each $m \leq n$, the only subspaces of $\mathbb{F}_p$ are $\{0\}$ and $\mathbb{F}_p$. It follows that the biggest subspace of $(\mathbb{F}_p)^t$ has dimension t, with respect to the biggest subspace of $(\mathbb{F}_{2^n})^t$, which has dimension $n \cdot t = N$. As shown in details in [3], the number of rounds previously given (necessary to protect GMiMC w.r.t. previous attacks) guarantees security against this attack.

4.2 Statistical Attacks

All the statistical attacks which we have considered can be carried out in the same way over $\mathbb{F}_p$ or/and over $\mathbb{F}_{2^n}$ against reduced round GMiMC. We analyzed the security of GMiMC against *classical and truncated differential, linear,* and *impossible differential* attacks. Since this type of attacks does not provide more advantage compared to the algebraic attacks, we skip the details. We refer the interested readers to the extended version of this article [3] for the details of the aforementioned analyses.

4.3 Other Attacks

We claim that GMiMC instantiated using the number of rounds of the univariate case[4] is secure in the known- and chosen-key model. In particular, such permutation is used in order to construct the hash function using the sponge construction. We recall that the (required) indifferentiable of the internal permutation of a sponge function from a random oracle - for a fixed key - is equivalent to the security of GMiMC in the known- and chosen-key model.

---

[4] The number of rounds in this case is given considering the number of rounds of any possible distinguisher - which is independent of the secret key - in the MitM scenario plus a secure margin. Since the key is fixed in the known- and chosen-key model, this number of rounds provides the security in these scenarios.

Finally we explicitly state that we do not have claims in the related-key model as we do not consider it to be relevant for the intended use case.

Quantum Improvements. In a post-quantum setting, the cost of exhaustive key search is square rooted by Grovers' algorithm. Statistical attacks remain unchanged (except perhaps their computational part). The quantum interpolation attack gives no significant advantage to the adversary since the attack requires $d/2$ queries, where d is the degree of the polynomial [24]. It is not clear that Grover's algorithm can help to improve the GCD attack. The attack cost $\mathcal{O}(d \cdot \log^2 d)$ operations on inputs of size d. Thus, even with the square root reduction the attacker will still need to write the inputs of size d as classically; a similar argument holds for Gröbner basis attacks.

Finally, since we are here interested in post-quantum security of classical schemes and not in the security of symmetric primitives running on a quantum computer themselves, better attacks are known using Simon's algorithm [33].

5   Parameter-Space Exploration

We compared the effects of different parameters in our Feistel-based constructions with block size N. We compared the parameters of the GMiMC within the range of the values in the three different applications e.g. length of the prime or n, number of branches t and number of rounds R. The main purpose of this comparison is to identify the optimal range of values for these parameters when the block size is fixed.

Both GMiMC$_\mathsf{crf}$ and GMiMC$_\mathsf{erf}$ have only one multiplication at each round while GMiMC$_\mathsf{mrf}$ has $t/2$ multiplications per round. By our analysis, it turns out that GMiMC$_\mathsf{erf}$ is always more efficient than GMiMC$_\mathsf{crf}$ and GMiMC$_\mathsf{mrf}$, since it always requires a lower number of rounds to be secure. In this article we only provide the performance of the best candidate for the target applications. For a more generic discussion of the different parameters and their effect on the multiplicative complexity we refer to the [3, Sect. 6].

6   Implementation Results

6.1   MPC Setting

Security Model. Our protocols are built to support the SPDZ-family protocols which guarantee security even when there is a dishonest majority of parties involved in the computation [13,28]. This means that we support an arbitrary number of computing parties, say, N_c and an adversary can corrupt up to $N_c - 1$ parties.

The implementation is written in a high-level language similar to Python [40] and is compatible with MP-SPDZ [7] and SCALE-MAMBA [6]. We have benchmarked the protocols using the SPDZ framework[5], which provides active security against multiple malicious parties.

To compute a circuit with secret shared inputs in SPDZ, there are two generic phases. The first step is to produce random Beaver triples, also called the preprocessing phase, which is independent of the inputs and can be done in advance. The second step is the online phase, which consumes a triple whenever there is a multiplication between shared values. Additions of secret values and scalar multiplications are (almost) for free in SPDZ. The protocols ran across two computers with Intel i7-4790 CPUs at 3.60 GHz and 16 GB of RAM connected via a 1 GB/s LAN network and an average round-trip time of 0.3 ms (see Table 1). In our setting, both keys and messages are secret shared between the two parties and each experiment was averaged among five executions with at least 1000 block cipher calls.

Table 1. Two-party costs for MiMC and GMiMC over a 1 Gb/s LAN network with an average ping time of 0.3 ms. The variable t denotes the number of branches for GMiMC and no. of blocks for MiMC, whereas R is the number of cipher rounds.

Mode	(t,R)	Online cost				Prep (ms)
		# Comm. rounds	Openings	Latency (ms)/$\mathbb{F}_p$	Throughput $\mathbb{F}_p$/s	
GMiMC$_{crf}$	4	178	534	3.65	15026	2.96
GMiMC$_{erf}$		172	516	3.55	15669	2.86
GMiMC$_{mrf}$		175	525	3.62	8194	5.83
MiMC	4 blocks	73	876	1.58	9965	4.86
GMiMC$_{crf}$	16	238	714	1.21	39247	0.99
GMiMC$_{erf}$		208	624	1.06	49006	0.86
GMiMC$_{mrf}$		183	549	1.02	8440	6.1
MiMC	16 blocks	73	3504	0.47	10780	4.86

For a complete measurement of an MPC protocol, one needs to have in mind both preprocessing and online phases. The preprocessing phase cost is determined by the number of secret shared multiplications. Performance of the online phase is given by the multiplicative depth of the circuit to be evaluated as well as the number of openings (whenever a party reveals a secret value). For the online phase we give measurements in terms of *latency* and *throughput*. Latency indicates the minimum time spent for computing one encrypted $\mathbb{F}_p$ block, whereas throughput shows the maximum $\mathbb{F}_p$ objects that can be encrypted in parallel per second. Since the only non-linear operation we use in our block ciphers is $x \mapsto x^3$, this is done with three openings and two Beaver triples (for details see [49]). We instantiate each block cipher with 8 and 64 input blocks/branches, where each block lies in $\mathbb{F}_p$ and $p \approx 2^{128}$. Note that for GMiMC

---

[5] https://github.com/bristolcrypto/SPDZ-2.

constructions in MPC we have used an n-bit key. For a fair comparison with previous evaluations of MiMC in SPDZ, the online phase runs on a single thread.

The preprocessing column (Prep, Table 1) denotes the amount of time required to generate the triples for a single block cipher evaluation (4 or 16 encrypted blocks/branches) in a two party SPDZ protocol. The figures for this column were estimated using the recent protocol by Keller et al. [39] which is the fastest known protocol for SPDZ triples. We used the LowGear protocol with computational security 128 and 64 bit statistical security.

Experiments (Table 1) show that $GMiMC_{crf}$ and $GMiMC_{erf}$ have a very fast preprocessing phase because they perform a low number of multiplications. A big advantage of these two is how well they scale in terms of triples used, since they require one multiplication per cipher iteration. This is in contrast with MiMC, where increasing the number of blocks to be encrypted by a factor of c results in c times more multiplications. We stress that these two constructions are first to our knowledge which avoid the linear increase of pre-processing data with the number of blocks. As an example of this behavior consider the case of 16 blocks for the preprocessing column (Table 1). Here $GMiMC_{erf}$ is 5.5 times smaller than MiMC: 0.86 ms vs. 4.86 ms. We can see that $GMiMC_{crf}$ and $GMiMC_{erf}$ have a higher online throughput compared to the rest of the variants, although they have a larger number of communication rounds. The reason is that fewer openings - or multiplications in our case mean less data sent between the parties so we can batch more executions in parallel. Thus in a LAN network the number of rounds has a minor impact. As for the WAN results, as expected MiMC preprocessing phase induces a large cost but the online phase is slightly faster than our proposed ciphers. The interested reader can find the experiments on a slow network in the full version of our paper [3].

6.2   SNARKs

The rank-1 constraints (r1cs) in SNARK is defined in [12] as a system of bilinear equations over a field $\mathbb{F}$. The number of *rank-1 constraints* (r1cs) for a function contributes to the efficiency of the SNARK algorithm [4]. In this setting we count the number of multiplications required to generate the values of *witness variables* defined in [12]. We describe the r1cs for $GMiMC_{crf}$ in Appendix A. For the other two construction it can be constructed similarly.

We implemented all three constructions in a SNARK setting using NTL [52] for the permutations and hash functions. $GMiMC_{erf}$ shows the best performance among the 3 constructions and we only show its performance result in Table 2. We also compared the performance with MiMC. For $N \approx 1024$-bit (prime) block size $GMiMC_{erf}$, with $t = 8$, we observe an improvement over MiMC-1025. For hashing a single message block (e.g. 512 bit), GMiMCHash-256 is more than 1.2 times faster than MiMCHash-256 and is significantly (>12 times) faster than SHA-256. We stress that in comparison with MiMCHash the primary advantage of $GMiMC_{erf}$Hash is that it can be used over 256 bit or smaller field size. For all the field operations we have used the NTL together with the gf2x library. All the computations were performed on a system having an Intel Core i7-4790 with

3.6 GHz processor with 16 GB memory. We took the average time over ≈2000 iterations. The last column in the Table 2 is mainly to demonstrate the performance of the design in a smaller field (below 128 bit prime).

Table 2. Comparison of MiMC with GMiMC$_{erf}$ (with different numbers of branches) in SNARK in $\mathbb{F}_p$ when the block size is 1024 bits.

$(t, \log_2(p), R)$	MiMC [4]		GMiMC$_{erf}$		
	$(1, 1024, 646)$	$(2, 513, 647)$	$(4, 256, 332)$	$(8, 128, 178)$	$(16, 64, 141)$
Constraint generation	4.553 ms	5.077 ms	4.735 ms	4.732 ms	8.057 ms
Witness generation	1.079 ms	0.639 ms	0.388 ms	0.296 ms	0.449 ms
Total time	5.632 ms	5.716 ms	5.123 ms	5.028 ms	8.507 ms
#additions	646	1293	996	1246	2115
#multiplications	1293	1293	664	356	282

Note that the number of constraints for GMiMCHash-256 is only one more than the number of constraints for GMiMC$_{erf}$. Hence the time taken by the hash function and the permutation with fixed key are the same (in Table 2).

6.3 Post-quantum Signatures

Picnic [22] is a new class of digital signature schemes which derive their security entirely from the security of symmetric-key primitives, have extremely small key pairs, and are highly parameterizable. The construction is based on a one-way function f, where for the secret key x the image $y = f(x)$ is published as the public key. A signature on a message is then obtained from a non-interactive zero-knowledge proof of the relation $y = f(x)$, that incorporates the message in the challenge generation. This proof uses ZKB++, a Σ-protocol for statements over general circuits made non-interactive. When instantiating f with LowMC [2,5], reducing the signature size by reducing the number of multiplication gates comes at the cost of a more expensive linear layer, which leads to a runtime vs. signature size trade-off. Since the security proofs in [22] only require a block cipher with a reduced data complexity of 1, the overall performance can be greatly improved as this fact allows to choose instances with less rounds. For the 128-bit PQ security level (i.e., 256-bit block size and key size) a good trade-off can be found by using 10 S-Boxes and 38 rounds, resulting in a view size of 1140 bits.

We implemented the signature scheme using GMiMC$_{erf}$ with key size and block size of ≈256 bits to build the one-way function. We consider instances with a data complexity of 1. The reduction steps of the modular multiplications were accelerated by using special prime moduli and irreducible polynomials of special form for prime fields and binary fields, respectively: generalized Mersenne

Table 3. Comparison of MiMC with GMiMC$_{erf}$ and LowMC [5] when the block size is ≈ 256 bits in the context of ZKB++. In LowMC-(N, m, R), N denotes the block size, m is the number of S-Boxes, and R denotes the number of rounds. Runtimes given for Sign and Verify are for the circuit computations only.

Scheme	(n, t, R)	Sign	Verify	View size
MiMC [4]	$(256, 1, 162)$	333.97 ms	166.28 ms	83456 bits
	$(272, 1, 172)$	92.45 ms	46.32 ms	94112 bits
GMiMC$_{erf}$ over $\mathbb{F}_p$	$(3, 86, 261)$	97.32 ms	72.06 ms	1566 bits
	$(4, 64, 196)$	62.35 ms	45.16 ms	1568 bits
	$(32, 8, 55)$	4.95 ms	3.05 ms	3520 bits
	$(136, 2, 163)$	67.51 ms	35.21 ms	44336 bits
GMiMC$_{erf}$ over $\mathbb{F}_{2^n}$	$(3, 86, 261)$	16.06 ms	10.76 ms	**783 bits**
	$(17, 16, 63)$	3.73 ms	2.30 ms	1071 bits
	$(33, 8, 56)$	**3.34 ms**	**2.29 ms**	1848 bits
LowMC-$(256, 10, 38)$	-	3.74 ms	3.52 ms	1140 bits
LowMC-$(256, 1, 363)$	-	9.55 ms	7.12 ms	1089 bits

primes [53] were used for prime fields and trinomials and pentanomials with middle terms close to each other [50] were used for binary fields.

In Table 3, we compare the circuit runtimes (i.e., runtimes without protocol overheads such as pseudo-random number sampling and the computation of commitments) of MiMC and GMiMC$_{erf}$ with different numbers of branches benchmarked on an Intel Core i7-4790 with 3.6 GHz. We also include the view size required per repetition of ZKB++, and numbers for two instances of LowMC using optimizations for the round key computations and linear layer [31]. Measuring only the circuit runtimes allows us to obtain a more accurate comparison in terms of computation time, which directly relates to the total runtime of the protocol, whereas the view sizes directly related and to the signature size.

Instantiations using $\mathbb{F}_{2^n}$ tend to perform better than the comparable parameterizations in $\mathbb{F}_p$ for mainly two reasons: in $\mathbb{F}_{2^n}$ additions do not require reductions, the cubing operation can be implemented with only one multiplication. In any case, even for very small fields with slower runtime, GMiMC$_{erf}$ performs significantly better in terms of view size and runtime than MiMC. Compared to LowMC, choosing an instance over $\mathbb{F}_{2^3}$ allows us to beat the smallest signatures sizes obtainable using LowMC with one S-Box by 306 bits in terms of view size. We also note that both signing and verification times are smaller when using instances providing a good trade-off (i.e., setting $n = 17$ or $n = 33$), and view sizes can be kept small too.

7   Discussion and Open Problems

One key take-away of this work is that, when it comes to building structures in symmetric cryptography with MPC and related applications in mind, there are old and prematurely discarded ideas that are worthwhile to revisit.

Unbalanced Feistel networks appeared in the late 1980s and have rarely been used in recent designs. As an illustration, consider that among all the lightweight block cipher designs listed on the CryptoLux lightweight block cipher wiki,[6] 7 are Type-II GFNs and 10 are balanced Feistel networks, whereas *none* is of the UFN or ERF type. And yet exactly those types turn out to be the best in our setting. The structure of MiMC is strongly related to a design from the mid 1990s, which in recent textbooks [42, Sect. 8.4] was even shown as an example of how not to design a cipher. However, it has turned out to be very good in many applications where multiplicative complexity matters. It may well be that the Cryptographers had lost interest in the UBF or never considered it a reasonable option and yet it is the best in several of our specific use cases. This naturally raises the question: What are other known but out-of-fashion structures which might be very suitable for MPC, SNARKs, PQ signatures or related applications?

In this paper our focus was on constructions that can natively deal with elements of fields in large characteristic. For other use-cases, binary extension fields may be interesting. For this, we leave a general security analysis (especially concerning higher-order differential attacks) as an open future problem.[7]

A   R1CS for GMiMC$_{crf}$

For GMiMC$_{crf}$ the rank-1 constraints are as follows:

$$\sum_{i=0}^{t-1} X_i + U + k_r + C_r = 0, \ U \cdot U = Y, \ U \cdot Y + X_{t-1} = Z,$$

where k_r and C_r are round keys and round constants respectively. For GMiMC$_{crf}$ Hash the round keys are fixed to a constant. The number of multiplication for GMiMC$_{crf}$ Hash is 2 per round. Therefore the total number of multiplications is $2R$ where R is the number of rounds in the block cipher GMiMC$_{crf}$. Each round also requires $t - 1$ field additions.

References

1. Agrawal, S., Mohassel, P., Mukherjee, P., Rindal, P.: DiSE: distributed symmetric-key encryption. In: Lie et al. [43], pp. 1993–2010 (2018)

---

[6] https://www.cryptolux.org/index.php/Lightweight_Block_Ciphers.
[7] Our ZKBoo use-case uses such fields, but the analysis we provide is rather specific to the needed low data-complexity security requirements.

2. Albrecht, M., Rechberger, C., Schneider, T., Tiessen, T., Zohner, M.: Ciphers for MPC and FHE. Cryptology ePrint Archive, Report 2016/687 (2016). http://eprint.iacr.org/2016/687

3. Albrecht, M.R., et al.: Feistel structures for MPC, and more. Cryptology ePrint Archive, Report 2019/397 (2019). https://eprint.iacr.org/2019/397

4. Albrecht, M., Grassi, L., Rechberger, C., Roy, A., Tiessen, T.: MiMC: efficient encryption and cryptographic hashing with minimal multiplicative complexity. In: Cheon, J.H., Takagi, T. (eds.) ASIACRYPT 2016. LNCS, vol. 10031, pp. 191–219. Springer, Heidelberg (2016). https://doi.org/10.1007/978-3-662-53887-6_7

5. Albrecht, M.R., Rechberger, C., Schneider, T., Tiessen, T., Zohner, M.: Ciphers for MPC and FHE. In: Oswald, E., Fischlin, M. (eds.) EUROCRYPT 2015. LNCS, vol. 9056, pp. 430–454. Springer, Heidelberg (2015). https://doi.org/10.1007/978-3-662-46800-5_17

6. Aly, A., et al.: Scale-mamba v1.3: Documentation (2018). https://homes.esat.kuleuven.be/~nsmart/SCALE/

7. N. Analytics. MP-SPDZ (2019). https://github.com/n1analytics/MP-SPDZ

8. Applebaum, B., Haramaty, N., Ishai, Y., Kushilevitz, E., Vaikuntanathan, V.: Low-complexity cryptographic hash functions. In: 8th Innovations in Theoretical Computer Science Conference - ITCS 2017. LIPIcs, vol. 67, pp. 7:1–7:31. Schloss Dagstuhl - Leibniz-Zentrum fuer Informatik (2017)

9. Applebaum, B., Ishai, Y., Kushilevitz, E.: Cryptography in NC^0. SIAM J. Comput. **36**(4), 845–888 (2006)

10. Archer, D.W., et al.: From keys to databases - real-world applications of secure multi-party computation. Cryptology ePrint Archive, Report 2018/450 (2018). https://eprint.iacr.org/2018/450

11. Ben-Sasson, E., et al.: Decentralized anonymous payments from bitcoin. In: 2014 IEEE Symposium on Security and Privacy, pp. 459–474. IEEE Computer Society Press, May 2014

12. Ben-Sasson, E., Chiesa, A., Genkin, D., Tromer, E., Virza, M.: SNARKs for C: verifying program executions succinctly and in zero knowledge. In: Canetti, R., Garay, J.A. (eds.) CRYPTO 2013. LNCS, vol. 8043, pp. 90–108. Springer, Heidelberg (2013). https://doi.org/10.1007/978-3-642-40084-1_6

13. Bendlin, R., Damgård, I., Orlandi, C., Zakarias, S.: Semi-homomorphic encryption and multiparty computation. In: Paterson, K.G. (ed.) EUROCRYPT 2011. LNCS, vol. 6632, pp. 169–188. Springer, Heidelberg (2011). https://doi.org/10.1007/978-3-642-20465-4_11

14. Bertoni, G., Daemen, J., Peeters, M., Van Assche, G.: On the indifferentiability of the sponge construction. In: Smart, N. (ed.) EUROCRYPT 2008. LNCS, vol. 4965, pp. 181–197. Springer, Heidelberg (2008). https://doi.org/10.1007/978-3-540-78967-3_11

15. Biham, E., Anderson, R., Knudsen, L.: Serpent: a new block cipher proposal. In: Vaudenay, S. (ed.) FSE 1998. LNCS, vol. 1372, pp. 222–238. Springer, Heidelberg (1998). https://doi.org/10.1007/3-540-69710-1_15

16. Bogdanov, D., Laur, S., Willemson, J.: Sharemind: a framework for fast privacy-preserving computations. In: Jajodia, S., Lopez, J. (eds.) ESORICS 2008. LNCS, vol. 5283, pp. 192–206. Springer, Heidelberg (2008). https://doi.org/10.1007/978-3-540-88313-5_13

17. Boneh, D., Eskandarian, S., Fisch, B.: Post-quantum EPID signatures from symmetric primitives. In: Matsui, M. (ed.) CT-RSA 2019. LNCS, vol. 11405, pp. 251–271. Springer, Cham (2019). https://doi.org/10.1007/978-3-030-12612-4_13

18. Boneh, D., Ishai, Y., Passelègue, A., Sahai, A., Wu, D.J.: Exploring crypto dark matter. In: Beimel, A., Dziembowski, S. (eds.) TCC 2018. LNCS, vol. 11240, pp. 699–729. Springer, Cham (2018). https://doi.org/10.1007/978-3-030-03810-6_25

19. Boyar, J., Peralta, R., Pochuev, D.: On the multiplicative complexity of Boolean functions over the basis (cap, +, 1). Theor. Comput. Sci. **235**, 43–57 (2000)

20. Canteaut, A., et al.: Stream ciphers: a practical solution for efficient homomorphic-ciphertext compression. In: Peyrin, T. (ed.) FSE 2016. LNCS, vol. 9783, pp. 313–333. Springer, Heidelberg (2016). https://doi.org/10.1007/978-3-662-52993-5_16

21. Chailloux, A.: Quantum security of the Fiat-Shamir transform of commit and open protocols. IACR Cryptology ePrint Archive 2019:699 (2019)

22. Chase, M., et al.: Post-quantum zero-knowledge and signatures from symmetric-key primitives. In: Thuraisingham, B.M., Evans, D., Malkin, T., Xu, D. (eds.) ACM CCS 17, pp. 1825–1842. ACM Press, October 2017

23. Chase, M., et al.: The Picnic Signature Algorithm Specification (2017). https://github.com/Microsoft/Picnic/blob/master/spec.pdf

24. Childs, A.M., van Dam, W., Hung, S., Shparlinski, I.E.: Optimal quantum algorithm for polynomial interpolation. In: ICALP. LIPIcs, vol. 55, pp. 16:1–16:13. Schloss Dagstuhl - Leibniz-Zentrum fuer Informatik (2016)

25. Cox, D.A., Little, J., O'Shea, D.: Ideals, Varieties, and Algorithms - An Introduction to Computational Algebraic Geometry and Commutative Algebra. Undergraduate Texts in Mathematics, 2 edn. Springer, Heidelberg (1997)

26. Daemen, J., Peeters, M., Van Assche, G., Rijmen, V.: Nessie Proposal: NOEKEON (2000). http://gro.noekeon.org/Noekeon-spec.pdf

27. Damgård, I., Geisler, M., Krøigaard, M., Nielsen, J.B.: Asynchronous multiparty computation: theory and implementation. In: Jarecki, S., Tsudik, G. (eds.) PKC 2009. LNCS, vol. 5443, pp. 160–179. Springer, Heidelberg (2009). https://doi.org/10.1007/978-3-642-00468-1_10

28. Damgård, I., Pastro, V., Smart, N., Zakarias, S.: Multiparty computation from somewhat homomorphic encryption. In: Safavi-Naini, R., Canetti, R. (eds.) CRYPTO 2012. LNCS, vol. 7417, pp. 643–662. Springer, Heidelberg (2012). https://doi.org/10.1007/978-3-642-32009-5_38

29. Derler, D., Ramacher, S., Slamanig, D.: Generic double-authentication preventing signatures and a post-quantum instantiation. In: Baek, J., Susilo, W., Kim, J. (eds.) ProvSec 2018. LNCS, vol. 11192, pp. 258–276. Springer, Cham (2018). https://doi.org/10.1007/978-3-030-01446-9_15

30. Derler, D., Ramacher, S., Slamanig, D.: Post-quantum zero-knowledge proofs for accumulators with applications to ring signatures from symmetric-key primitives. In: Lange, T., Steinwandt, R. (eds.) PQCrypto 2018. LNCS, vol. 10786, pp. 419–440. Springer, Cham (2018). https://doi.org/10.1007/978-3-319-79063-3_20

31. Dinur, I., Kales, D., Promitzer, A., Ramacher, S., Rechberger, C.: Linear equivalence of block ciphers with partial non-linear layers: application to lowMC. In: Ishai, Y., Rijmen, V. (eds.) EUROCRYPT 2019. LNCS, vol. 11476, pp. 343–372. Springer, Cham (2019). https://doi.org/10.1007/978-3-030-17653-2_12

32. Don, J., Fehr, S., Majenz, C., Schaffner, C.: Security of the Fiat-Shamir transformation in the quantum random-oracle model. IACR Cryptology ePrint Archive 2019:190 (2019)

33. Dong, X., Li, Z., Wang, X.: Quantum cryptanalysis on some generalized Feistel schemes. Cryptology ePrint Archive, Report 2017/1249 (2017). https://eprint.iacr.org/2017/1249

34. Doröz, Y., Shahverdi, A., Eisenbarth, T., Sunar, B.: Toward practical homomorphic evaluation of block ciphers using prince. In: Böhme, R., Brenner, M., Moore, T., Smith, M. (eds.) FC 2014. LNCS, vol. 8438, pp. 208–220. Springer, Heidelberg (2014). https://doi.org/10.1007/978-3-662-44774-1_17

35. Grassi, L., Rechberger, C., Rotaru, D., Scholl, P., Smart, N.P.: MPC-friendly symmetric key primitives. In: Weippl, E.R., Katzenbeisser, S., Kruegel, C., Myers, A.C., Halevi, S. (eds.) ACM CCS 2016, pp. 430–443. ACM Press, October 2016

36. Grosso, V., Leurent, G., Standaert, F.-X., Varıcı, K.: LS-designs: bitslice encryption for efficient masked software implementations. In: Cid, C., Rechberger, C. (eds.) FSE 2014. LNCS, vol. 8540, pp. 18–37. Springer, Heidelberg (2015). https://doi.org/10.1007/978-3-662-46706-0_2

37. Jakobsen, T., Knudsen, L.R.: The interpolation attack on block ciphers. In: Biham, E. (ed.) FSE 1997. LNCS, vol. 1267, pp. 28–40. Springer, Heidelberg (1997). https://doi.org/10.1007/BFb0052332

38. Katz, J., Kolesnikov, V., Wang, X.: Improved non-interactive zero knowledge with applications to post-quantum signatures. In: Lie et al. [43], pp. 525–537 (2018)

39. Keller, M., Pastro, V., Rotaru, D.: Overdrive: making SPDZ great again. In: Nielsen, J.B., Rijmen, V. (eds.) EUROCRYPT 2018. LNCS, vol. 10822, pp. 158–189. Springer, Cham (2018). https://doi.org/10.1007/978-3-319-78372-7_6

40. Keller, M., Scholl, P., Smart, N.P.: An architecture for practical actively secure MPC with dishonest majority. In: Sadeghi, A.-R., Gligor, V.D., Yung, M. (eds.) ACM CCS 2013, pp. 549–560. ACM Press, November 2013

41. Knudsen, L.R.: Truncated and higher order differentials. In: Preneel, B. (ed.) FSE 1994. LNCS, vol. 1008, pp. 196–211. Springer, Heidelberg (1995). https://doi.org/10.1007/3-540-60590-8_16

42. Knudsen, L.R., Robshaw, M.J.B.: The Block Cipher Companion. Springer, Heidelberg (2011). https://doi.org/10.1007/978-3-642-17342-4

43. Lie, D., Mannan, M., Backes, M., Wang, X. (eds.): ACM CCS 2018. ACM Press, October 2018

44. Méaux, P., Journault, A., Standaert, F.-X., Carlet, C.: Towards stream ciphers for efficient FHE with low-noise ciphertexts. In: Fischlin, M., Coron, J.-S. (eds.) EUROCRYPT 2016. LNCS, vol. 9665, pp. 311–343. Springer, Heidelberg (2016). https://doi.org/10.1007/978-3-662-49890-3_13

45. Naehrig, M., Lauter, K.E., Vaikuntanathan, V.: Can homomorphic encryption be practical? In: Proceedings of the 3rd ACM Cloud Computing Security Workshop, CCSW 2011, pp. 113–124 (2011)

46. Nyberg, K.: Generalized Feistel networks. In: Kim, K., Matsumoto, T. (eds.) ASIACRYPT 1996. LNCS, vol. 1163, pp. 91–104. Springer, Heidelberg (1996). https://doi.org/10.1007/BFb0034838

47. Infrastructure Secret Management Software Overview. https://gist.github.com/maxvt/bb49a6c7243163b8120625fc8ae3f3cd

48. Partisia. https://partisia.com/

49. Rotaru, D., Smart, N.P., Stam, M.: Modes of operation suitable for computing on encrypted data. IACR Trans. Symm. Cryptol. **2017**(3), 294–324 (2017)

50. Scott, M.: Optimal irreducible polynomials for GF(2^m) arithmetic. Cryptology ePrint Archive, Report 2007/192 (2007). http://eprint.iacr.org/2007/192

51. Sepior. https://sepior.com/

52. Shoup, V.: Number Theory Library 5.5.2 (NTL). http://www.shoup.net/ntl/

53. Solinas, J.A.: Generalized mersenne numbers. Technical report, NSA (1999)

54. Suzaki, T., Minematsu, K.: Improving the generalized Feistel. In: Hong, S., Iwata, T. (eds.) FSE 2010. LNCS, vol. 6147, pp. 19–39. Springer, Heidelberg (2010). https://doi.org/10.1007/978-3-642-13858-4_2

55. Suzaki, T., Minematsu, K., Morioka, S., Kobayashi, E.: *twine*: a lightweight block cipher for multiple platforms. In: Knudsen, L.R., Wu, H. (eds.) SAC 2012. LNCS, vol. 7707, pp. 339–354. Springer, Heidelberg (2013)

56. Unbound. https://www.unboundtech.com/

Arithmetic Garbling from Bilinear Maps

Nils Fleischhacker[1], Giulio Malavolta[2(✉)], and Dominique Schröder[3]

[1] Ruhr University Bochum, Bochum, Germany
[2] Carnegie Mellon University, Pittsburgh, USA
giulio.malavolta@hotmail.it
[3] Friedrich Alexander Universität Erlangen-Nürnberg, Erlangen, Germany

Abstract. We consider the problem of garbling arithmetic circuits and present a garbling scheme for inner-product predicates over exponentially large fields. Our construction stems from a generic transformation from predicate encryption which makes only blackbox calls to the underlying primitive. The resulting garbling scheme has practical efficiency and can be used as a garbling gadget to securely compute common arithmetic subroutines. We also show that inner-product predicates are complete by generically bootstrapping our construction to arithmetic garbling for polynomial-size circuits, albeit with a loss of concrete efficiency.

In the process of instantiating our construction we propose two new predicate encryption schemes, which might be of independent interest. More specifically, we construct (i) the first pairing-free (weakly) attribute-hiding non-zero inner-product predicate encryption scheme, and (ii) a key-homomorphic encryption scheme for linear functions from bilinear maps. Both schemes feature constant-size keys and practical efficiency.

1 Introduction

Garbled circuits were introduced by Yao in an oral presentation about secure function evaluation [40]. Given a function f and an input x, Yao's machinery generates a garbled circuit $\tilde{f}$ and an encoded input $\tilde{x}$. Anyone holding $\tilde{x}$ can then evaluate the garbled circuit $\tilde{f}$ to recover the output $f(x)$ and nothing beyond that. Garbled circuits have been cast in the more generic framework of randomized encodings [26] and were first recognized as a cryptographic primitives on its own in the work of Bellare, Hoang, and Rogaway [11]. Since their introduction, garbled circuits have found an enormous range of application to problems such as computation over encrypted data [14], parallel cryptography [5], functional encryption [36], and many others.

Yao's classical construction assumes a binary encoding of the inputs and operates over boolean gates. Since arithmetic computation appear often in real-life scenarios, a natural question to ask is whether one can garble arithmetic circuits over fields of exponential size. This is motivated by efficiency constraints, as operating directly on the arithmetic representation of the input avoids the costly bit decomposition step. Furthermore, certain cryptographic models [4]

© Springer Nature Switzerland AG 2019
K. Sako et al. (Eds.): ESORICS 2019, LNCS 11736, pp. 172–192, 2019.
https://doi.org/10.1007/978-3-030-29962-0_9

only admit access to inputs as atomic ring elements. Consider an input encrypted under a linearly homomorphic encryption scheme [17], in this case there is no efficient (non-interactive) algorithm to decompose it to its binary representation and the only admissible operations are field addition and scalar multiplication.

The first milestone in this regard was set by Applebaum, Ishai, and Kushilevitz [6] when they proposed the first non-trivial garbling scheme for arithmetic computations over the integers. The scheme is based on the hardness of the learning with errors (LWE) problem [35]. They also show several information-theoretic garbling gadgets for arithmetic branching programs (or, equivalently, arithmetic formulae). The price to pay for perfect security is a quadratic blowup in the input encodings, i.e., to evaluate a circuit of size s one needs $O(s^2)$ space to encode its inputs. In this sense the former construction has better asymptotics.

1.1 Our Results

In this work we continue the study of arithmetic garbling and we propose a simple construction from number-theoretic assumptions. Specifically, we construct a garbling scheme for inner-product predicates over exponentially large fields, assuming the hardness of standard problems in bilinear groups. We shall note that, in general, input vectors are linear in the size of the predicate being computed so the cost of evaluating the encoding function might be comparable to evaluating the function itself. There are however two important differences that make the problem of garbling inner-products non-trivial: (i) Part of the input vector might be fixed in advance, in which case some steps of the encoding circuit can be precomputed, and (ii) the encoding function does not depend on the garbled function. This means that the garbling algorithm and the encoding algorithm can be executed non-interactively by two different parties.

Our construction (Sect. 3) consists of a compiler that transforms a predicate encryption scheme into an arithmetic garbling scheme for inner products. The garbling algorithm makes only blackbox use of the underlying primitives and thus has practical efficiency. In contrast with information-theoretic garbling schemes, the size of the encoding depends exclusively on the decryption keys of the predicate encryption. To instantiate our construction we propose a zero (ZIPE) and a non-zero (NIPE) inner-product predicate encryption scheme from standard assumptions, more specifically:

- A NIPE scheme from DDH or LWE with constant-size keys (Sect. 4).
- A ZIPE scheme with small keys (2 group elements) and with ciphertexts consisting of exactly n group elements (where n is the length of the vectors) from standard assumptions in bilinear groups (Sect. 5).

Combined with the DDH-based NIPE, the input encodings of our garbling scheme add only two group elements and two integers (in $\mathbb{Z}_p$) to the size of the original vector, regardless of the vector length. This is asymptotically optimal and it is comparable with the work of Applebaum et al. [7], where they construct short encodings for classical boolean garbling. Finally we show that arithmetic garbling for inner-product predicates is complete in the sense that it can be generically bootstrapped to the evaluation of polynomial-size circuits (Sect. 6), albeit with a loss in efficiency.

1.2   Applications

Our garbling scheme for inner-products is motivated by practical scenarios where one needs to efficiently garble simple arithmetic circuits. Such a garbling gadget can also be used as a building block within a larger protocol to boost the efficiency of certain arithmetic subroutines while retaining all of the advantages of garbling schemes (e.g., low latency). Here we highlight some tasks of interest which can be solved with a garbling scheme for inner-product predicates.

FHE Decryption. Most recent fully-homomorphic encryption schemes, (e.g., [22]) feature a decryption algorithm of the form

$$\langle sk, c \rangle \in \left[\frac{p}{2} - N, \frac{p}{2} + N \right] \quad (\bmod\ p)$$

where sk and c are vectors in $\mathbb{Z}_p^n$, and N is a polynomially large noise range. The decryption algorithm returns 1 if the above condition is satisfied and 0 otherwise. This relation can be easily encoded as an inner-product predicate by the so called lazy-OR trick [24]

$$\exists \eta \in \left[\frac{p}{2} - N, \frac{p}{2} + N \right] : \langle sk, c \rangle - \eta \equiv 0 \quad (\bmod\ p).$$

It is clear that whenever c encrypts a 0 the garbling scheme returns 0 in all position, whereas if c is an encryption of 1 then the garbling gadget will return 0 everywhere except in exactly one position where it returns 1. To hide the exact position of the 1 – as this would leak the value of η – we can randomly permute the order in which the inner-product relation is tested against each η.

Private Set Intersection Predicate. A private set intersection predicate refers to the problem of securely computing whether two vectors $(x, y) \in \mathbb{Z}_p^{2n}$ have a common element, i.e., whether there exists an i such that $x_i = y_i$. A standard approach to perform this task is to encode y as an n degree polynomial p_y with roots in $(y_1, \ldots, y_n)$ and evaluate

$$\exists i \in \{1, \ldots, n\} : p_y(x_i) \equiv 0 \quad (\bmod\ p).$$

If we consider the vector of coefficients of p_y and the n vectors $(x_i, x_i^2, \ldots, x_i^n)$, then this reduces to the computation of inner-product predicates, which we can efficiently garble.

Matrix Multiplication. It is easy to see that the multiplication of an $n \times n$ matrix with an n size vector reduces to n instances of inner-products. It follows that matrix multiplication predicates (and in general secure linear algebra computations) can be generically reduced to the task of computing inner-products. Our scheme can garble predicates of the form $A \cdot B = C$, where $A \in \mathbb{Z}_p^{n \times m}$, $B \in \mathbb{Z}_p^{m \times n}$, and C is a publicly known $\mathbb{Z}_p^{n \times n}$ matrix.

Statistics on Private Data. Our scheme can also be used to garble several interesting measures over a private dataset x. Among others, we can securely check whether the weighted mean x is equal to a certain known value μ by garbling the vector $(x\| -1)$ and issuing encoding for the vector $\left(\frac{w_1}{n}, \ldots, \frac{w_n}{n}, \mu\right)$. Then we have

$$\left\langle (x\| -1), \left(\frac{w_1}{n}, \ldots, \frac{w_n}{n}, \mu\right)\right\rangle = \frac{\sum_{i=1}^{n} w_i x_i}{n} - \mu = 0,$$

where $(w_1, \ldots, w_n)$ is a vector of weights. As a further example, we can garble the square Euclidean distance between two vectors $\boldsymbol{x}$ and $\boldsymbol{y}$ by expanding the equation

$$d_{\boldsymbol{x},\boldsymbol{y}} = (x_1 - y_1)^2 + \ldots + (x_n - y_n)^2$$

and encoding the mixed terms as inner-products.

1.3 Concrete Efficiency

In the following we discuss the concrete efficiency of our garbling scheme for inner-product predicates, when instantiated with our ZIPE and the DDH-based NIPE. We measure the computational efficiency of our main algorithms in terms of number of modular exponentiations and pairings and we omit routine calculations such as additions and multiplications. The costs for an inner-product predicate over $\mathbb{F}^n$ are detailed below.

- *Garbling*: The cost of the garbling algorithm is dominated by a call of the setup and encryption algorithm of the NIPE and ZIPE scheme, for a total of $(5n+11)$ exponentiations. The size of the garbled circuit is $(n+2)$ elements of the source group $\mathbb{G}_1$, an element of the target group $\mathbb{G}_T$, and $(n+3)$ elements of a DDH-hard group $\mathbb{G}$.
- *Encoding*: The encoding algorithm runs in time comparable to that of $(n+2)$ exponentiations. The size of the encoded input is two element of source group $\mathbb{G}_2$ and two integers in $\mathbb{Z}_p$.
- *Evaluation*: The circuit evaluation consists of one call each to the decryption algorithms of the NIPE and ZIPE scheme. This accounts for $(2n + 4)$ exponentiations and 2 pairings. Note that the number of pairings (the most expensive operation) is independent of the vector length.

When compared with information-theoretic constructions, our scheme brings down the size of the encodings from quadratic to independent of the circuit size. This is an asymptotic improvement. The efficiency comparison with the construction of [6] is less clear since it is lattice-based. A concrete comparison would require an implementation of their scheme, which is beyond the scope of this work. Regardless, we believe that broadening the set of assumptions that suffice to construct arithmetic garbling with non-trivial efficiency is an interesting goal on its own. Finally we remark that there exist tailor-made protocols to solve each individual task, among the applications that we suggested above, which are highly optimized for the goal and in practice outperform our solution. However our construction gives a unified and generic approach to securely compute a large family of functions and inherits all the distinguishing features of garbling schemes, such as the low round complexity.

1.4 Our Techniques

In this section we outline the main ideas behind our work and we give an overview of the techniques developed throughout the paper.

Arithmetic Garbling from Predicate Encryption. Our initial observation is an interesting connection between garbling schemes and predicate encryption for inner-products. A predicate encryption scheme allows one to encrypt a message m under a vector $x \in \mathbb{Z}_p^n$ and issue decryption keys for vectors $y \in \mathbb{Z}_p^n$. The decrypter can recover m if and only if $\langle x, y \rangle = 0$. Furthermore, no information about x is leaked beyond the fact that it is orthogonal to y. Given such a predicate encryption, we can construct an arithmetic garbling scheme for inner-product predicates in a very natural way: Garbling a vector x corresponds to encrypting a fixed message m^* under x, whereas encoding an input y consists of generating a key for y. The evaluator can test whether the decryption algorithm returns m^* and learn whether $\langle x, y \rangle = 0$. Since the predicate encryption is attribute-hiding, this does not reveal any further information about x.

However a garbling scheme must satisfy some additional properties. Among others, the scheme must guarantee the authenticity of its output, i.e., the evaluator can efficiently show a proof of the result of the computation. This property has proven useful in the context of zero-knowledge protocols [27] and verifiable computation [21]. A naive approach would be to substitute m^* with a random message r^* which constitutes a valid proof that $\langle x, y \rangle = 0$, as otherwise the decryption would have failed. However for the complementary case ($\langle x, y \rangle \neq 0$) the evaluator is left with nothing. Standard techniques, such as garbling the complement of x, do not seem to apply here since we would need to find a vector $\bar{x}$ orthogonal to any y such that $\langle x, y \rangle \neq 0$, which may not exist.

We resolve this issue by shifting the complement to the cryptographic primitive: We additionally deploy a non-zero inner-product predicate encryption scheme, which returns the encrypted message if $\langle x, y \rangle \neq 0$. Given such a scheme, the solution consists in encrypting another random message under the same x, which can be used to certify that the two vectors are not orthogonal. Since our garbling algorithm makes only blackbox use of the underlying primitives, the resulting instantiations are simple and practical.

Arithmetic Garbling for Circuits. The connection between garbling and predicate encryption is not limited to inner-products predicates but generalizes to polynomial-size circuits using universal encodings [38]. However, current instantiations of attribute-hiding predicate encryption for circuits [20] are not yet in the domain of practicality and are based on newly crafted assumptions.

Fortunately inner-product predicates are a very powerful tool and we show that our garbling scheme for inner-product predicates can be generically bootstrapped into an arithmetic garbling scheme for poly-size circuit with small (poly-size) domain. If we assume a relaxed model on the arithmetic representation of the inputs, then we can leverage standard techniques to extend our scheme to an exponentially large input domain. The remainder of this work focuses on constructing efficient inner-product encryption schemes to instantiate our arithmetic garbling scheme. Our schemes aim at minimizing the size of the decryption keys, as their size determines the size of the input encodings.

Non-zero Inner-Product Encryption. We propose an efficient predicate encryption scheme for non-zero inner-products with small keys. The construction consists of a generic transformation from inner-product functional encryption, a primitive introduced by Abdalla et al. [1]. Our transformation makes only two calls to the encryption (resp. decryption) algorithm of the inner-product functional encryption scheme and preserves all the properties of the underlying construction. This transformation yields:

- the first pairing-free (weakly) attribute-hiding predicate encryption for non-zero inner-products,
- the first (weakly) attribute-hiding scheme based on the DDH assumption, and
- the first adaptively payload hiding scheme with a tight security reduction.

In the DDH-based instance, a key for a vector of any length corresponds to the vector itself and 2 elements of $\mathbb{Z}_p$.

Zero Inner-Product Encryption. To construct a zero inner-product predicate encryption scheme, we start from the same design paradigm as the lattice-based scheme of Boneh et al. [13]. In [13] the authors propose a fully key-homomorphic public-key encryption scheme. Such a primitive allows anyone to transform an encryption under attribute x into an encryption under $(f(x), [f])$, where $f(x) \in \mathbb{F}$ and $[f]$ is an encoding of the circuit computing f. Predicate encryption can then be instantiated in a very natural way: On input a predicate f, one can issue a key for $(1, [f])$ and the decrypter can publicly apply the transformation from above to any ciphertext and decrypt if and only if $f(x) = 1$. The advantage of this class of schemes is that the complex operations are pushed to public algorithms and therefore the resulting decryption keys are typically small.

We apply the same idea to the bilinear maps settings: Our scheme can be seen as a key-homomorphic encryption for *linear functions*. The private key of a vector consists of two group elements, regardless of the vector length. For a vector of length n, a ciphertext consists of exactly n group elements. In contrast, previous solutions with similar key sizes (such as [10, 15, 32]), require at least $2n$ elements. A crucial difference with respect to prior work [13, 18, 39] is that our scheme achieves some notion of attribute hiding even for keys that correctly decrypt ciphertexts.

1.5   Related Work

The first formal treatment of arithmetic garbling is due to Applebaum, Ishai, and Kushilevitz [6]. They proposed (i) a construction for any circuit based on lattices and (ii) an information-theoretic construction for branching programs (or, equivalently, NC1 circuits). A shortcoming of the latter scheme is that the input encoding grows quadratically with the circuit size, i.e., the encodings for a circuit of size s have length $O(s^2)$. A followup work of Ball, Malkin, and Rosulek [9] investigates the concrete efficiency of arithmetic garbling gadgets in the context of secure computation. Their constructions generalize the free-XOR technique [30], however the size of their garbled circuit grows linearly with the size of the modulus. They show how to circumvent this and compute arithmetic operations modulo large smooth integers (via Chinese remaindering) but their techniques do not extend to exponentially large prime moduli.

Attribute-Based Encryption (ABE) was first introduced in the seminal work of Goyal et al. [37] and refined in [25,33]. Predicate encryption (PE) is a special case of ABE where ciphertexts hide the encoded policy, in addition to the message. This notion was proposed by Katz, Sahai and Waters in [29] where they constructed a scheme for inner-products: The owner of a key for a vector x can decrypt a ciphertext generated over a vector y only if $\langle x, y \rangle = 0$. ZIPE and NIPE schemes have been first identified in the work of Attrapadung and Libert [8] where the authors also showed the utility of public-index inner-product PE. The efficiency of inner-product-based schemes was improved by Chen, Gay and Wee in [15] and the first NIPE with constant-size ciphertexts has been recently proposed in [16].

In a different line of research Abdalla et al. [1] suggested a functional encryption scheme for inner-products (IPFE) where ciphertexts encode some vector x and users with keys for a vector y can learn the inner-product $\langle x, y \rangle$. This result has been extended to achieve full security [3], function privacy [12], and support quadratic functions [10]. In the latter work, Baltico et al. also proposed a generic transformation to predicate encryption for bilinear map evaluation. However, such a transformation retains security only for those vectors x and y such that $\langle x, y \rangle \in \{0, 1\}$. In particular, this is insufficient to instantiate a fully-fledged NIPE, where the range of the inner-product spans the whole $\mathbb{Z}_p$. Following a similar paradigm, a trace-and-revoke scheme has been recently proposed by Agrawal et al. [2]. A related work by Parno et al. [34] identifies a surprising connection between ABE and verifiable computation. The main idea is the following: The server is given a ciphertext under the attribute x and a key for a function f, then it is clear that the server will be able to decrypt only if $f(x) = 1$. In this work we push this observation even further: If the ABE scheme has some weak attribute-hiding properties, then it can be bootstrapped to a fully-fledged garbling scheme.

Concurrent Work. In concurrent and independent work, Katsumata and Yamada [28] show a similar compiler from inner-product functional encryption to NIPE, thus also obtaining a NIPE from the DDH assumption. However, the crucial difference with respect to our work is that their NIPE does not achieve any form of attribute-hiding, which is necessary to instantiate our construction of arithmetic garbling for inner-product predicates.

2   Preliminaries

In this section we introduce the notation and some basic definitions that we will use throughout our work. We denote by $\lambda \in \mathbb{N}$ the security parameter and by $\mathsf{poly}(\lambda)$ any function that is bounded by a polynomial in λ We call a function $\mathsf{negl}(\lambda)$ negligible if for every $c \in \mathbb{Z}$, there exists some $N \in \mathbb{Z}$ such that for all $\lambda > N$ it holds that $\mathsf{negl}(\lambda) < \frac{1}{\lambda^c}$ We say that an algorithm is PPT if it is modeled as a probabilistic Turing machine whose running time is bounded by some function $\mathsf{poly}(\lambda)$ Given a set S, we denote by $x \leftarrow_\$ S$ the sampling of an element uniformly at random from S. Vectors $(x_1, \ldots, x_n)$ are written as $\boldsymbol{x}$ and $\langle \boldsymbol{x}, \boldsymbol{y} \rangle$ denotes the inner product of $\boldsymbol{x}$ and $\boldsymbol{y}$.

2.1   Garbling Schemes

We recall the notion of garbling schemes as presented in [11].

Definition 1 (Garbling Scheme). *A garbling scheme* $\mathsf{GC} = (\mathsf{GC.Garble},$ $\mathsf{GC.Enc}, \mathsf{GC.Dec}, \mathsf{GC.Eval}, \mathsf{GC.ev})$ *is a tuple of algorithms, where C describes the circuit* $\mathsf{GC.ev}(C, \cdot) : \mathbb{F}^n \mapsto \mathbb{F}^m$ *that we want to garble and where the remaining algorithms follow.*

$(\tilde{C}, e, d) \leftarrow \mathsf{GC.Garble}(1^\lambda, C) :$ *On input 1^λ and C, the probabilistic garbling algorithm outputs a garbled circuit description $\tilde{C}$, the input encoding information e, and the output decoding information d.*

$\tilde{X} \leftarrow \mathsf{GC.Enc}(e, x) :$ *The (possibly) probabilistic encoding algorithm takes the encoding information e as input, and an initial input $x \in \mathbb{F}^n$, and outputs a garbled input $\tilde{X}$.*

$\tilde{Y} \leftarrow \mathsf{GC.Eval}(\tilde{C}, \tilde{X}) :$ *On input a garbled circuit $\tilde{C}$ and a garbled input $\tilde{X}$, evaluate $\tilde{C}$ on $\tilde{X}$ to produce a deterministic garbled output $\tilde{Y}$.*

$y \leftarrow \mathsf{GC.Dec}(d, \tilde{Y}) :$ *The deterministic decoding algorithm takes as input the decoding information d, and a garbled output $\tilde{Y}$, and outputs a final output $y \in \mathbb{F}^m$.*

The security notions that we consider are *privacy, obliviousness*, and *authenticity*. Privacy means that seeing the garbled circuit $\tilde{C}$ with a garbled input $\tilde{X}$ and decoding information d does not reveal more about C and x than $C(x)$. We denote by $\Phi(C)$ some side information that the garbled circuit leaks about the original circuit C, such as its size and topology. To define this formally, we resort to the simulation-based definition, which can be shown to be equivalent to the game-based one via a standard argument (see [11]).

Definition 2 (Φ-Privacy). *Let* GC $=$ (GC.Garble, GC.Enc, GC.Dec, GC.Eval, GC.ev) *be a garbling scheme and Φ a side information function.* GC *achieves Φ-privacy if there exists a* PPT *simulator $\mathcal{S}$ such that for all* PPT *adversaries $\mathcal{A}$ there exists a negligible function* negl *such that*

$$2 \cdot \Pr[\mathsf{ExpPriv}_{\mathsf{GC},\Phi}^{\mathcal{A}}(1^{\lambda}) = 1] - 1 \leq \mathsf{negl}(\lambda),$$

where $\mathsf{ExpPriv}_{\mathsf{GC},\Phi}^{\mathcal{A}}(1^{\lambda})$ *is defined below.*

1. *On input 1^{λ}, $\mathcal{A}$ outputs a circuit C and an input $x \in \mathbb{F}^{n}$.*
2. *The challenger samples a bit $b \leftarrow_{\$} \{0,1\}$ and computes:*
   (a) *$(\tilde{C}, e, d) \leftarrow$ GC.Garble$(1^{\lambda}, C)$ and $\tilde{X} \leftarrow$ GC.Enc(e, x) if $b = 0$.*
   (b) *$y \leftarrow$ GC.ev(C, x) and $(\tilde{C}, \tilde{X}, d) \leftarrow \mathcal{S}(1^{\lambda}, y, \Phi(C))$ if $b = 1$.*
3. *The adversary is given $(\tilde{C}, \tilde{X}, d)$, outputs a bit b' and succeeds if $b = b'$.*

Authenticity prevents the adversary from learning any output labels other than the ones it can learn itself from evaluating the circuit. This prevents a malicious adversary from claiming the evaluation yielded a different result.

Definition 3 (Authenticity). *Let* GC $=$ (GC.Garble, GC.Enc, GC.Dec, GC.Eval, GC.ev) *be a garbling scheme.* GC *achieves authenticity if for all* PPT *adversaries $\mathcal{A}$ there exists a negligible function* negl *such that*

$$\Pr[\mathsf{ExpAuth}_{\mathsf{GC}}^{\mathcal{A}}(1^{\lambda}) = 1] \leq \mathsf{negl}(\lambda),$$

where $\mathsf{ExpAuth}_{\mathsf{GC}}^{\mathcal{A}}(1^{\lambda})$ *is defined below.*

1. *On input 1^{λ}, $\mathcal{A}$ outputs a circuit C and an input $x \in \mathbb{F}^{n}$.*
2. *The challenger computes $(\tilde{C}, e, d) \leftarrow$ GC.Garble$(1^{\lambda}, C)$ and $\tilde{X} \leftarrow$ GC.Enc(e, x).*
3. *The adversary is given $(\tilde{C}, \tilde{X})$ and outputs an encoding $\tilde{Y}$.*
4. *The adversary succeeds if $\tilde{Y} \neq$ GC.Eval$(\tilde{C}, \tilde{X})$ and GC.Dec$(d, \tilde{Y}) \neq \perp$.*

Obliviousness says that the adversary should not learn any information about the output of the computation if not given the decoding information d. For a formal definition we refer the reader to [11].

2.2   Predicate Encryption

We recall the concept of *predicate encryption* (PE) [29]. A PE scheme allows to encrypt messages for certain attributes and to encode Boolean predicates in the decryption keys. We denote by Σ an arbitrary set of attributes and by $\mathcal{F}$ an arbitrary family of predicates over Σ, which may depend on the security parameter λ and/or on the public parameters of the scheme. We denote the message space by $\mathbb{M}$.

Definition 4 (Predicate Encryption). *A predicate encryption scheme* PE *for a class of predicates* $\mathcal{F}$ *over the set of attributes* Σ *consists of four* PPT *algorithms* $(\mathsf{Setup}_{\mathsf{PE}}, \mathsf{KGen}_{\mathsf{PE}}, \mathsf{Enc}_{\mathsf{PE}}, \mathsf{Dec}_{\mathsf{PE}})$ *such that:*

$\mathsf{Setup}_{\mathsf{PE}}(1^\lambda)$: *The setup algorithm outputs a master public key* ek *and a corresponding master secret key* msk.

$\mathsf{KGen}_{\mathsf{PE}}(\mathsf{msk}, f)$: *The key generation algorithm takes as input the master secret key and a predicate* $f \in \mathcal{F}$. *It outputs a key* dk_f.

$\mathsf{Enc}_{\mathsf{PE}}(\mathsf{ek}, \mathsf{A}, m)$: *The encryption takes as input the public key* ek, *an attribute* $\mathsf{A} \in \Sigma$, *and a message* $m \in \mathbb{M}$. *It returns a ciphertext* c.

$\mathsf{Dec}_{\mathsf{PE}}(\mathsf{dk}_f, c)$: *The decryption algorithm takes as input a secret key* dk_f *and a ciphertext* c. *It outputs either a message* m *or a special symbol* $\perp$.

For correctness, we require that for all $\lambda \in \mathbb{N}$ all $(\mathsf{ek}, \mathsf{msk}) \in \mathsf{Setup}_{\mathsf{PE}}(1^\lambda)$, all $f \in \mathcal{F}$, all $\mathsf{dk}_f \in \mathsf{KGen}_{\mathsf{PE}}(\mathsf{msk}, f)$, all $m \in \mathbb{M}$, and all $\mathsf{A} \in \Sigma$:

If $f(\mathsf{A}) = 1$ then $\mathsf{Dec}_{\mathsf{PE}}(\mathsf{dk}_f, \mathsf{Enc}_{\mathsf{PE}}(\mathsf{ek}, \mathsf{A}, m)) = m$.

A predicate encryption is *attribute-hiding* if the ciphertexts hide the payload and the attribute. In this work we only consider a very weak version of this property, which is however sufficient for our purposes. In our game, the adversary must specify the challenge attributes $(\mathsf{A}^0, \mathsf{A}^1)$ together with the queries to the $\mathsf{KGen}_{\mathsf{PE}}$ oracle before being provided with the public parameters. Furthermore, the adversary can request only one key to the $\mathsf{KGen}_{\mathsf{PE}}$ oracle. We call this property *static attribute-hiding* and provide a formal definition below.

Definition 5 (Static Attribute-Hiding). *A predicate encryption scheme* PE *is* statically attribute-hiding *with respect to* $\mathcal{F}$ *if for all* PPT *adversaries* $\mathcal{A}$ *there exists a negligible function* negl *such that*

$$2 \cdot \Pr[\mathsf{ExpAH}_{\mathsf{PE}}^{\mathcal{A}}(1^\lambda) = 1] - 1 \leq \mathsf{negl}(\lambda),$$

where $\mathsf{ExpAH}_{\mathsf{PE}}^{\mathcal{A}}(1^\lambda)$ *is defined below.*

1. *On input* 1^λ, $\mathcal{A}$ *outputs a pair of attributes* $(\mathsf{A}^0, \mathsf{A}^1) \in \Sigma^2$ *and a predicate* $f \in \mathcal{F}$. *If* $f(\mathsf{A}^0) \neq f(\mathsf{A}^1)$ *then the challenger aborts.*
2. $\mathsf{Setup}_{\mathsf{PE}}(1^\lambda)$ *is run to generate* ek *and* msk *and the adversary is given* ek *and* $\mathsf{KGen}_{\mathsf{PE}}(\mathsf{msk}, f)$.
3. $\mathcal{A}$ *outputs two equal-length messages* (m_0, m_1). *If* $f(\mathsf{A}^0) = f(\mathsf{A}^1) = 1$, *then it is required that* $m_0 = m_1$. *A random bit* b *is chosen and* $\mathcal{A}$ *is given the ciphertext* $c \leftarrow \mathsf{Enc}_{\mathsf{PE}}(\mathsf{ek}, \mathsf{A}^b, m_b)$.
4. $\mathcal{A}$ *outputs a bit* b' *and succeeds if* $b = b'$.

A predicate encryption scheme achieves *payload-hiding* if the message of a ciphertext is hidden from users whose predicate does not satisfy the encoded vector $\boldsymbol{x}$. Both zero inner-product encryption (ZIPE) [29] and non-zero inner-product encryption (NIPE) [8] can be seen as a special case of what presented above. For the missing formal definitions we refer the reader to the full version [19].

2.3   Inner-Product Functional Encryption

Here we provide a formal definition of an Inner-Product Functional Encryption (IPFE) scheme. This primitive was introduced in the work of Abdalla et. al [1]. Such a scheme allows one to encode a vector field elements $v \in \mathbb{F}^n$ in a ciphertext and to produce decryption keys for a vector u of the same family.

Definition 6 (Inner-Product Functional Encryption). *Let* $\mathbb{F}$ *be a field. An* inner-product functional encryption *scheme* IPFE *consists of four* PPT *algorithms* $(\mathsf{Setup}_{\mathsf{IPFE}}, \mathsf{KGen}_{\mathsf{IPFE}}, \mathsf{Enc}_{\mathsf{IPFE}}, \mathsf{Dec}_{\mathsf{IPFE}})$ *such that:*

$\underline{\mathsf{Setup}_{\mathsf{IPFE}}(1^\lambda)}$: *The setup algorithm outputs a master public key* ek *and a corresponding private key* msk.

$\underline{\mathsf{KGen}_{\mathsf{IPFE}}(\mathsf{msk}, y)}$: *The key generation algorithm takes as input the master secret key and a vector* $y \in \mathbb{F}^n$. *It outputs a key* dk_y.

$\underline{\mathsf{Enc}_{\mathsf{IPFE}}(\mathsf{ek}, x)}$: *The encryption takes as input the public key* ek *and a vector* $x \in \mathbb{F}^n$. *It returns a ciphertext* c.

$\underline{\mathsf{Dec}_{\mathsf{IPFE}}(\mathsf{dk}_y, c)}$: *The decryption algorithm takes as input a secret key* dk_y *and a ciphertext* c. *It outputs either a message* $m \in \mathbb{F}$ *or a special symbol* $\bot$.

We define correctness as: for all λ all $(\mathsf{ek}, \mathsf{msk}) \leftarrow \mathsf{Setup}_{\mathsf{IPFE}}(1^\lambda)$, all $y \in \mathbb{F}^n$, all $\mathsf{dk}_y \leftarrow \mathsf{KGen}_{\mathsf{IPFE}}(\mathsf{msk}, y)$, and all $x \in \mathbb{F}^n$ it holds that $\mathsf{Dec}_{\mathsf{IPFE}}(\mathsf{dk}_y, \mathsf{Enc}_{\mathsf{IPFE}}(\mathsf{ek}, x)) = \langle x, y \rangle$. An IPFE scheme is semantically secure if an adversary holding a key for a vector y and a ciphertext under a vector x does not learn anything except for $\langle x, y \rangle$. The formal definition is given below.

Definition 7 (Semantic Security). *An inner-product functional encryption scheme* IPFE *is semantically secure if for all* PPT *adversaries* $\mathcal{A}$ *there exists a negligible function* negl *such that*

$$2 \cdot \Pr[\mathsf{ExpSec}^{\mathcal{A}}_{\mathsf{IPFE}}(1^\lambda) = 1] - 1 \leq \mathsf{negl}(\lambda),$$

where $\mathsf{ExpSec}^{\mathcal{A}}_{\mathsf{IPFE}}(1^\lambda)$ *is defined below.*

1. $\mathsf{Setup}_{\mathsf{IPFE}}(1^\lambda)$ *is run to generate* ek *and* msk *and the adversary* $\mathcal{A}$ *is given the pair* $(1^\lambda, \mathsf{ek})$.
2. $\mathcal{A}$ *may adaptively request keys for vectors* $y_1, \ldots, y_q \in \mathbb{F}^n$. *In response,* $\mathcal{A}$ *is given the corresponding keys* $\mathsf{dk}_{y_i} \leftarrow \mathsf{KGen}_{\mathsf{IPFE}}(\mathsf{msk}, y_i)$.
3. $\mathcal{A}$ *outputs two equal-length messages* $(x_0, x_1) \in \mathbb{F}^{2n}$. *If there is an* i *such that* $\langle y_i, x_0 \rangle \neq \langle y_i, x_1 \rangle$, *then the challenger aborts.* $\mathcal{A}$ *random bit* b *is chosen and* $\mathcal{A}$ *is given the ciphertext* $c \leftarrow \mathsf{Enc}_{\mathsf{IPFE}}(\mathsf{ek}, x_b)$.
4. *The adversary may continue to request keys for additional vectors, subject to the same restrictions as above.*
5. $\mathcal{A}$ *outputs a bit* b' *and succeeds if* $b = b'$.

2.4 Bilinear Maps and Complexity Assumptions

Here we recall the notion of bilinear maps and introduce our complexity assumptions. Let $\mathbb{G}_1$ and $\mathbb{G}_2$ be two cyclic groups of prime order p and let $g_1 \in \mathbb{G}_1$ and $g_2 \in \mathbb{G}_2$ be the respective generators. Let $e : \mathbb{G}_1 \times \mathbb{G}_2 \to \mathbb{G}_T$ be a function that maps pairs of elements in $(\mathbb{G}_1, \mathbb{G}_2)$ to elements of some cyclic group $\mathbb{G}_T$ of order p. Throughout the following sections we write all of the group operations multiplicatively, with identity elements denoted by 1. We require that:

- The map e and all the group operations in $\mathbb{G}_1$, $\mathbb{G}_2$, and $\mathbb{G}_T$ are efficiently computable.
- The map e is non degenerate, i.e., $e(g_1, g_2) \neq 1$.
- The map e is bilinear, i.e., $\forall u \in \mathbb{G}_1, \forall v \in \mathbb{G}_2, \forall (a, b) \in \mathbb{Z}^2, e(u^a, v^b) = e(u, v)^{ab}$.

We introduce the External Diffie-Hellman (XDH) assumption below.

Definition 8 (XDH Assumption). *The XDH assumption holds in $\mathbb{G}_1$ if, for all* PPT *algorithms $\mathcal{A}$, there exists a negligible function* negl *such that*

$$\left| \Pr\left[1 \leftarrow \mathcal{A}\left(g_1, g_1^a, g_1^b, g_1^{ab} \right) \right] - \Pr\left[1 \leftarrow \mathcal{A}\left(g_1, g_1^a, g_1^b, g_1^c \right) \right] \right| \leq \mathsf{negl}(\lambda)$$

where the probability is taken over the random choice of the generator $g_1 \in \mathbb{G}_1$, the random choice of $(a, b, c) \in (\mathbb{Z}_p^*)^3$, and the random coins of $\mathcal{A}$.

3 Arithmetic Garbling for Inner-Product Predicates

In this section we present our compiler that turns predicate encryption schemes into garbling schemes for inner-product predicates. Our first observation is that the ciphertext of an inner-product predicate encryption scheme can already be seen as a garbled circuit if it satisfies some mild attribute-hiding properties. However, to achieve authenticity one needs to encrypt a predicate f and its complement $\bar{f}$. For inner-product predicates, the complement of the predicate defined by a vector $\boldsymbol{x}$ is a vector $\boldsymbol{y}$ such that for all $\boldsymbol{z}$ it holds that $\langle \boldsymbol{x}, \boldsymbol{z} \rangle = 0 \implies \langle \boldsymbol{y}, \boldsymbol{z} \rangle \neq 0$ and vice versa. Thus $\boldsymbol{y}$ is not always efficiently computable. We resolve this issue by lifting the complement to the encryption scheme. Our construction (Fig. 1) garbles the family of predicates $\mathcal{F} = \{ f_{\boldsymbol{y}} \mid \boldsymbol{y} \in \mathbb{F}^n \}$ where $f_{\boldsymbol{y}} : \mathbb{F}^n \to \{0, 1\}$ is defined as

$$f_{\boldsymbol{y}}(\boldsymbol{x}) := \begin{cases} 0 & \text{if } \langle \boldsymbol{y}, \boldsymbol{x} \rangle = 0 \\ 1 & \text{otherwise.} \end{cases}$$

Our scheme uses a $\mathsf{NIPE} = (\mathsf{Setup}_{\mathsf{NIPE}}, \mathsf{KGen}_{\mathsf{NIPE}}, \mathsf{Enc}_{\mathsf{NIPE}}, \mathsf{Dec}_{\mathsf{NIPE}})$ and $\mathsf{ZIPE} = (\mathsf{Setup}_{\mathsf{ZIPE}}, \mathsf{KGen}_{\mathsf{ZIPE}}, \mathsf{Enc}_{\mathsf{ZIPE}}, \mathsf{Dec}_{\mathsf{ZIPE}})$ for inner products of vectors in $\mathbb{F}^{n+1}$ in a blackbox way.

GC.Garble$(1^\lambda, \boldsymbol{y})$	GC.Eval$(\tilde{C}, \tilde{X})$
$\boldsymbol{r} \leftarrow_\$ \mathbb{F}^n$	**parse** $\tilde{C}$ **as** $\left(c_1^0, c_1^1\right)$
$\left(r^0, r^1\right) \leftarrow_\$ \{0,1\}^{2\lambda}$	**parse** $\tilde{X}$ **as** $(\mathsf{dk}_{\mathsf{ZIPE}}, \mathsf{dk}_{\mathsf{NIPE}})$
$(\mathsf{ek}_{\mathsf{ZIPE}}, \mathsf{msk}_{\mathsf{ZIPE}}) \leftarrow \mathsf{Setup}_{\mathsf{ZIPE}}(1^\lambda)$	$\tilde{r}^0 \leftarrow \mathsf{Dec}_{\mathsf{ZIPE}}(\mathsf{dk}_{\mathsf{ZIPE}}, c^0)$
$(\mathsf{ek}_{\mathsf{NIPE}}, \mathsf{msk}_{\mathsf{NIPE}}) \leftarrow \mathsf{Setup}_{\mathsf{NIPE}}(1^\lambda)$	$\tilde{r}^1 \leftarrow \mathsf{Dec}_{\mathsf{NIPE}}(\mathsf{dk}_{\mathsf{NIPE}}, c^1)$
$c^0 \leftarrow \mathsf{Enc}_{\mathsf{ZIPE}}\left(\mathsf{ek}_{\mathsf{ZIPE}}, \boldsymbol{y}\| - \langle \boldsymbol{y}, \boldsymbol{r} \rangle, r^0\right)$	$\tilde{Y} := \left(\tilde{r}^0, \tilde{r}^1\right)$
$c^1 \leftarrow \mathsf{Enc}_{\mathsf{NIPE}}\left(\mathsf{ek}_{\mathsf{NIPE}}, \boldsymbol{y}\| - \langle \boldsymbol{y}, \boldsymbol{r} \rangle, r^1\right)$	**return** $\tilde{Y}$
$\tilde{C} := \left(c^0, c^1\right)$	
$e := (\mathsf{msk}_{\mathsf{ZIPE}}, \mathsf{msk}_{\mathsf{NIPE}}, \boldsymbol{r})$	GC.ev$(\boldsymbol{y}, \boldsymbol{x})$
$d := \left(r^0, r^1\right)$	**return** $f_{\boldsymbol{y}}(\boldsymbol{x})$
return $(\tilde{C}, e, d)$	
GC.Enc$(e, \boldsymbol{x})$	GC.Dec$(d, \tilde{Y})$
parse e **as** $(\mathsf{msk}_{\mathsf{ZIPE}}, \mathsf{msk}_{\mathsf{NIPE}}, \boldsymbol{r})$	**parse** d **as** $\left(r^0, r^1\right)$
$\mathsf{dk}_{\mathsf{ZIPE}} \leftarrow \mathsf{KGen}_{\mathsf{ZIPE}}(\mathsf{msk}_{\mathsf{ZIPE}}, \boldsymbol{x} + \boldsymbol{r}\|1)$	**parse** $\tilde{Y}$ **as** $\left(\tilde{r}^0, \tilde{r}^1\right)$
$\mathsf{dk}_{\mathsf{NIPE}} \leftarrow \mathsf{KGen}_{\mathsf{NIPE}}(\mathsf{msk}_{\mathsf{NIPE}}, \boldsymbol{x} + \boldsymbol{r}\|1)$	**if** $\tilde{r}^0 = r^0$ **then return** 0
$\tilde{X} := (\mathsf{dk}_{\mathsf{ZIPE}}, \mathsf{dk}_{\mathsf{NIPE}})$	**elseif** $\tilde{r}^1 = r^1$ **then return** 1
return $\tilde{X}$	**else return** $\perp$

Fig. 1. An arithmetic garbling scheme for inner product predicates.

Theorem 1. *Let Φ be the function that takes as input an inner-product predicate and returns the length of its vector. Let* NIPE *be a statically attribute-hiding NIPE scheme and let* ZIPE *be a statically attribute-hiding ZIPE scheme, then the garbling scheme* GC *as described in Fig. 1 achieves Φ-privacy and authenticity.*

Due to space constraints, the proof of the above theorem is deferred to the full version of this work [19]. In the full version it is also shown how to achieve obliviousness by modifying the garbling algorithm in a non-blackbox way.

Input Encoding. The core property of arithmetic garbled circuits is to reduce the task to evaluate a circuit to evaluating an *affine* function over the inputs that depends only on some randomness (and in particular not on the input itself). This corresponds to the encoding function, which in our construction consists of the evaluation of the key generation of the NIPE and ZIPE schemes. Concerning our instantiations, the NIPE's key generation (see Sect. 4) is identical to the algorithm of the underlying IPFE scheme which in turn, for all the schemes proposed by Agrawal et al. [3], evaluates an affine function over the inputs. For the case of the ZIPE (see Sect. 5), the key generation corresponds to the computation of an affine function "in the exponent". Both classes of functions are well studied in the context of secure arithmetic computation and admit efficient secure evaluation protocols [31].

4   Non-zero Inner Product Encryption

Our construction of NIPE is a simple transformation based on inner product functional encryption (IPFE). The basic idea is to encrypt the attribute vector $\boldsymbol{x}$ multiplied by the message m with an IPFE scheme. Clearly, trying to decrypt with a vector $\boldsymbol{y}$ such that $\langle \boldsymbol{x}, \boldsymbol{y} \rangle = 0$, will destroy all information about m, since the decryption algorithm will output $\langle m\boldsymbol{x}, \boldsymbol{y} \rangle = m \langle \boldsymbol{x}, \boldsymbol{y} \rangle = 0$. On the other hand, decrypting with any vector such that $\langle \boldsymbol{x}, \boldsymbol{y} \rangle \neq 0$ yields a blinded version of the message, where the mask is $\langle \boldsymbol{x}, \boldsymbol{y} \rangle$. Since $\boldsymbol{x}$ is unknown to the eyes of the decryptor, to enable correctness, we should add a second IPFE ciphertext, of the vector $\boldsymbol{x}$, which decrypted with the same vector $\boldsymbol{y}$ will reveal the blinding factor. However, this simple version does not achieve any form of attribute-hiding, since the decryptor can learn non-trivial information about $\boldsymbol{x}$, in case of correct decryption. To counter this issue, we blind the inner product $\langle \boldsymbol{x}, \boldsymbol{y} \rangle$ with an additional random scalar r. In the security analysis, this additional degree of freedom will allow us to equivocate the attributes. The scheme is formally described in Fig. 2.

$\mathsf{Setup}_{\mathsf{NIPE}}(1^\lambda)$	$\mathsf{KGen}_{\mathsf{NIPE}}(\mathsf{msk}, \boldsymbol{y})$
$(\mathsf{ek}, \mathsf{msk}) \leftarrow \mathsf{Setup}_{\mathsf{IPFE}}(1^\lambda)$	$\mathsf{dk} \leftarrow \mathsf{KGen}_{\mathsf{IPFE}}(\mathsf{msk}, \boldsymbol{y})$
return $(\mathsf{ek}, \mathsf{msk})$	**return** dk
$\mathsf{Enc}_{\mathsf{NIPE}}(\mathsf{ek}, \boldsymbol{x}, m)$	$\mathsf{Dec}_{\mathsf{NIPE}}(\mathsf{dk}, c)$
$r \leftarrow_\$ \mathbb{F}$	**parse** c **as** (c_1, c_2)
$c_1 \leftarrow \mathsf{Enc}_{\mathsf{IPFE}}(\mathsf{ek}, mr \cdot \boldsymbol{x})$	$s \leftarrow \mathsf{Dec}_{\mathsf{IPFE}}(\mathsf{dk}, c_1)$
$c_2 \leftarrow \mathsf{Enc}_{\mathsf{IPFE}}(\mathsf{ek}, r \cdot \boldsymbol{x})$	$t \leftarrow \mathsf{Dec}_{\mathsf{IPFE}}(\mathsf{dk}, c_2)$
return (c_1, c_2)	**if** $t \neq 0$ **then return** st^{-1}
	return $\perp$

Fig. 2. Construction of non-zero inner product encryption.

It is easy to see that NIPE is correct. By the correctness of IPFE, it holds that $s = \langle mr\boldsymbol{x}, \boldsymbol{y} \rangle = mr \langle \boldsymbol{x}, \boldsymbol{y} \rangle$ and $t = \langle r\boldsymbol{x}, \boldsymbol{y} \rangle = r \langle \boldsymbol{x}, \boldsymbol{y} \rangle$. If $\langle \boldsymbol{x}, \boldsymbol{y} \rangle \neq 0$ we therefore have $st^{-1} = \frac{mr \langle \boldsymbol{x}, \boldsymbol{y} \rangle}{r \langle \boldsymbol{x}, \boldsymbol{y} \rangle} = m$. If on the other hand $\langle \boldsymbol{x}, \boldsymbol{y} \rangle = 0$ then $t = 0$ and the decryption algorithm will always output $\perp$.

Theorem 2. *Let* IPFE *be a semantically secure inner product functional encryption scheme, then the non-zero inner product encryption scheme* NIPE *shown in Fig. 2 is adaptively payload-hiding.*

The proof is given in the full version of this work [19]. In [19] it is also shown that the same scheme achieves the standard notion of adaptive payload hiding.

4.1 Instantiations

Our transformation relies on a very powerful abstraction of inner-product functional encryption: We require that the inner product of keys and messages is computed over a finite field and that the scheme supports messages from an exponentially large domain. Recent proposals for an adaptively-secure inner-product functional encryption [3] include:

1. A scheme from DDH for small messages for inner product computations over $\mathbb{Z}_p$. The key size is that of two integers in $\mathbb{Z}_p$.
2. A construction from LWE for inner products over $\mathbb{Z}_p$ with a stateful key generation algorithm, where keys are of size $\mathbb{Z}_p^\mu$, where μ depends on the security parameter but not on the vector length n.

A direct application of our transformation to the first scheme would yield a NIPE with an inefficient decryption algorithm: The output of the original scheme is of the form g^m, that in our construction would translate into two elements $(g^r, g^{mr}) \in \mathbb{G}^2$, for a randomly distributed r. To retrieve m one would then compute two discrete logarithms. However we can easily solve this, for messages m from a small domain, via a nonblack-box modification of our decryption algorithm. To retrieve m one can compute the discrete logarithm of g^{mr} to base g^r. Assuming a message space sufficiently small, this gives us the first full-fledged NIPE from the DDH assumption. Note that the attribute space is still exponentially large.

We stress that a small message space does not hinder the applicability of a NIPE to our garbling scheme (Sect. 3), which requires one to encrypt a large message $r^1 \in \{0,1\}^\lambda$. We suggest two possible solutions to bypass this problem:

1. Encrypt r^1 bit-by-bit using fresh random coins for each encryption. The scheme remains secure by a standard hybrid argument.
2. Modify the garbling scheme in a non-black box way to set the decoding label corresponding to 1 to $H(g^r \| g^{r^1 r})$, where $H : \mathbb{G}^2 \to \{0,1\}^\lambda$ is any collision-resistant hash function. Note that the garbling algorithm has access to the random coins of the encryption, and therefore the pair $(g^r, g^{r^1 r})$ is efficiently computable. This allows the evaluation algorithm to recover the correct label without computing any discrete logarithm.

For the second instantiations, our NIPE scheme inherits the stateful key generation algorithm. This is not an issue in the context of garbling schemes since our construction issues only a single decryption key.

5   Zero Inner Product Encryption

Our ZIPE scheme is inspired by the work of Boneh et al. [13] and can be seen as a key-homomorphic public-key encryption for linear functions. Recall that a key-homomorphic public key encryption allows anyone to transform an encryption under attribute x into an encryption under $(f(x), [f])$, where $f(x) \in \mathbb{F}$ and $[f]$ is an encoding of the circuit computing f. This design paradigm offers a very natural way to instantiate an attribute-based encryption scheme: One can simply issue a key for $(1, [f])$ and the decrypter can publicly apply the transformation of above to any ciphertext and decrypt if and only if $f(x) = 1$. The advantage of this class of schemes is that the computational burden is pushed to public operation and therefore the resulting decryption keys are typically small.

We exploit the same idea to construct a predicate encryption with small keys from bilinear maps. Since our public evaluation happens in the exponent, our scheme is key-homomorphic for linear functions only. However, a crucial difference with respect to the work of Boneh et al. [13] is that the structure of bilinear groups allows us to hide the attributes even to the eyes of the evaluator, which applies the function f *obliviously* over x. Our scheme can be seen as a lightweight version of prior pairing-based constructions [18,39], with a different notion of security which is tailored for our purposes. The formal description of our construction is shown in Fig. 3.

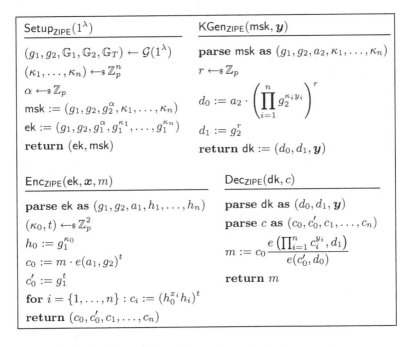

Fig. 3. Construction of zero inner product encryption.

For correctness, evaluating the decryption algorithm we get the following:

$$
c_0 \frac{e\left(\prod_{i=1}^{n} c_i^{y_i}, d_1\right)}{e(c_0', d_0)} = m \cdot e(a_1, g_2)^t \frac{e\left(\prod_{i=1}^{n}(h_0^{x_i} h_i)^{ty_i}, g_2^r\right)}{e\left(g_1^t, a_2 \cdot \left(\prod_{i=1}^{n} g_2^{\kappa_i y_i}\right)^r\right)}
$$

$$
= m \cdot e(g_1, g_2)^{\alpha t} \frac{e\left(\prod_{i=1}^{n}(h_0^{x_i} h_i)^{y_i}, g_2\right)^{rt}}{e(g_1, g_2)^{\alpha t} e(g_1, \prod_{i=1}^{n} g_2^{\kappa_i y_i})^{rt}}
$$

$$
= m \cdot \frac{e\left(\prod_{i=1}^{n} g_1^{y_i(\kappa_0 x_i + \kappa_i)}, g_2\right)^{rt}}{e(g_1, \prod_{i=1}^{n} g_2^{\kappa_i y_i})^{rt}}
$$

$$
= m \cdot \frac{e\left(g_1^{\kappa_0 \langle y, x \rangle + \sum_{i=1}^{n} \kappa_i y_i}, g_2\right)^{rt}}{e(g_1, g_2^{\sum_{i=1}^{n} \kappa_i y_i})^{rt}}
$$

$$
= m \cdot \frac{e(g_1, g_2)^{rt\kappa_0 \langle y, x \rangle + rt \sum_{i=1}^{n} \kappa_i y_i}}{e(g_1, g_2)^{rt \sum_{i=1}^{n} \kappa_i y_i}}
$$

$$
= m \cdot e(g_1, g_2)^{rt\kappa_0 \langle y, x \rangle} \tag{1}
$$

Clearly, if $\langle y, x \rangle = 0$, then Eq. 1 is equal to m. On the other hand, if $\langle y, x \rangle \neq 0$ then Eq. 1 would only be equal to m if $rt\kappa_0 \langle y, x \rangle$ happens to be equal to 0 which will happen only with negligible probability.

Theorem 3. *If the XDH assumption holds in $(\mathbb{G}_1, \mathbb{G}_2)$, then the zero inner product encryption scheme ZIPE shown in Fig. 3 is statically attribute-hiding.*

The security proof of the following theorem is shown in the full version [19]. Additionally, in [19] we also prove that the same scheme satisfies the notion of selective payload hiding against standard assumptions in bilinear groups.

6   Bootstrapping to P/poly

We discuss several bootstrapping techniques to extend the domain of a garbling scheme for inner-products. As previously discussed, the main difference between arithmetic and standard garbling is that the former does not have access to the binary representation of the input x. Instead, the encoding algorithm must operate directly on the algebraic representation of x as a field element. Here we consider two variants of such a model:

1. The encoding algorithm has access to the algebraic representation of the first n powers of the input $(x, x^2, \ldots, x^n) \in \mathbb{F}^n$ This relaxed model is motivated by the scenario when the input is encrypted under a multiplicatively-homomorphic encryption scheme (such as ElGamal [17]).
2. In the (standard) more restrictive version, the encoding algorithm operates only on $x \in \mathbb{F}$

Depending on which model we consider, we describe a different bootstrapping technique to compile an arithmetic garbling scheme for inner-product predicates to a fully-fledged arithmetic garbling scheme for P/poly. For the latter case, the transformation is limited to circuits with small (poly-size) input domain.

Loose Arithmetic Representation. As already observed by Katz, Sahai, and Waters [29], inner-product predicates are sufficient to encode the evaluation of bounded-degree polynomials: Garbling the evaluation of a polynomial $p(\mathfrak{x}) = c_0 + c_1\mathfrak{x} + \ldots, c_n\mathfrak{x}^n$ is done by evaluating $\mathsf{GC.Garble}(1^\lambda, \boldsymbol{c})$, where $\boldsymbol{c} := (c_0, c_1, \ldots, c_n)$. Then, the encoding of the input x is obtained by running the encoding algorithm on the vector $\boldsymbol{x} := (1, x, x^2, \ldots, x^n)$. Then, the resulting garbled circuit securely evaluates the predicate $\langle \boldsymbol{c}, \boldsymbol{x} \rangle = p(x) = 0$, which corresponds to a polynomial predicate of degree-n.

It is a well known fact that any NC1 circuit can be represented by a polynomial with polynomial degree [23], which immediately implies that our garbling scheme supports log-depth circuits. Since NC1 circuits have a boolean output space, then polynomial predicates suffice. Given this garbling gadget for NC1 circuits, the final step of the transformation consists in applying the Chinese Remainder Theorem-based compiler of Applebaum, Ishai, and, Kushilevitz [6], which yields an arithmetic garbling scheme for P/poly.

Restrictive Arithmetic Representation. The main ingredient of the transformation is a classical projective garbling scheme.[1] Let $\{1, \ldots, n\}$, for some polynomially-bounded n, be the input space. To garble a function f one first runs a classical garbling scheme on the following (boolean) circuit

$\Gamma(x)$

parse $x = x_1 \| \ldots \| x_n$

for $i \in \{1 \ldots, n\}$:   **if** $x_i = 1$ **then** $y := i$

return $f(y)$

and obtains the vector of labels $(X_1^0, X_1^1, \ldots, X_n^0, X_n^1)$ together with the encoded circuit $\tilde{\Gamma}$. Then for each $i \in \{1, \ldots, n\}$ run the arithmetic garbling scheme for inner products for the following predicate

$$\Upsilon_i(x) := \ x - i = 0$$

using X_i^0 and X_i^1 as the random coins (i.e., the values of r^0 and r^1 in Fig. 1). The final garbled circuit consists of the elements $(\tilde{\Gamma}, \tilde{\Upsilon}_1, \ldots, \tilde{\Upsilon}_n)$. Inputs are then encoded using the corresponding algorithm $\tilde{X} \leftarrow \mathsf{GC.Enc}(e, x)$, as defined in Fig. 1. Given $\tilde{X}$, one can evaluate all the circuits $(\tilde{\Upsilon}_1, \ldots, \tilde{\Upsilon}_n)$, which return the set of labels $(X_1^0, \ldots, X_{x-1}^0, X_x^1, X_{x+1}^0, \ldots, X_n^0)$. That is, the evaluator recovers the 0 label on all bits except for the position corresponding to the value x. Such a set of labels constitutes a valid encoding for $\tilde{\Gamma}$ so the evaluator can recover the result of the computation $f(x)$.

Acknowledgements. Research supported in part by a gift from Ripple, a gift from DoS Networks, a grant from Northrop Grumman, a Cylab seed funding award, and

---

[1] A garbling scheme is said to be projective if the encoding information is in the form of a list of labels $(X_1^0, X_1^1, \ldots, X_n^0, X_n^1)$, which are selected according to the binary representation of the input.

a JP Morgan Faculty Fellowship. Research based upon work supported by the German research foundation (DFG) through the collaborative research center 1223 and the training school 2475 and by the state of Bavaria at the Nuremberg Campus of Technology (NCT). NCT is a research cooperation between the Friedrich-Alexander-Universität Erlangen-Nürnberg (FAU) and the Technische Hochschule Nürnberg Georg Simon Ohm (THN).

References

1. Abdalla, M., Bourse, F., De Caro, A., Pointcheval, D.: Simple functional encryption schemes for inner products. In: Katz, J. (ed.) PKC 2015. LNCS, vol. 9020, pp. 733–751. Springer, Heidelberg (2015). https://doi.org/10.1007/978-3-662-46447-2_33

2. Agrawal, S., Bhattacherjee, S., Phan, D.H., Stehlé, D., Yamada, S.: Efficient public trace and revoke from standard assumptions: extended abstract. In: ACM CCS 2017, pp. 2277–2293 (2017)

3. Agrawal, S., Libert, B., Stehlé, D.: Fully secure functional encryption for inner products, from standard assumptions. In: Robshaw, M., Katz, J. (eds.) CRYPTO 2016. LNCS, vol. 9816, pp. 333–362. Springer, Heidelberg (2016). https://doi.org/10.1007/978-3-662-53015-3_12

4. Applebaum, B., Avron, J., Brzuska, C.: Arithmetic cryptography: extended abstract. In: ITCS 2015, pp. 143–151 (2015)

5. Applebaum, B., Ishai, Y., Kushilevitz, E.: Cryptography in NC^0. In: 45th FOCS, pp. 166–175 (2004)

6. Applebaum, B., Ishai, Y., Kushilevitz, E.: How to garble arithmetic circuits. In: 52nd FOCS, pp. 120–129 (2011)

7. Applebaum, B., Ishai, Y., Kushilevitz, E., Waters, B.: Encoding functions with constant online rate or how to compress garbled circuits keys. In: Canetti, R., Garay, J.A. (eds.) CRYPTO 2013. LNCS, vol. 8043, pp. 166–184. Springer, Heidelberg (2013). https://doi.org/10.1007/978-3-642-40084-1_10

8. Attrapadung, N., Libert, B.: Functional encryption for inner product: achieving constant-size ciphertexts with adaptive security or support for negation. In: Nguyen, P.Q., Pointcheval, D. (eds.) PKC 2010. LNCS, vol. 6056, pp. 384–402. Springer, Heidelberg (2010). https://doi.org/10.1007/978-3-642-13013-7_23

9. Ball, M., Malkin, T., Rosulek, M.: Garbling gadgets for Boolean and arithmetic circuits. In: ACM CCS 2016, pp. 565–577 (2016)

10. Baltico, C.E.Z., Catalano, D., Fiore, D., Gay, R.: Practical functional encryption for quadratic functions with applications to predicate encryption. In: Katz, J., Shacham, H. (eds.) CRYPTO 2017. LNCS, vol. 10401, pp. 67–98. Springer, Cham (2017). https://doi.org/10.1007/978-3-319-63688-7_3

11. Bellare, M., Hoang, V.T., Rogaway, P.: Foundations of garbled circuits. In: ACM CCS 2012, pp. 784–796 (2012)

12. Bishop, A., Jain, A., Kowalczyk, L.: Function-hiding inner product encryption. In: Iwata, T., Cheon, J.H. (eds.) ASIACRYPT 2015. LNCS, vol. 9452, pp. 470–491. Springer, Heidelberg (2015). https://doi.org/10.1007/978-3-662-48797-6_20

13. Boneh, D., et al.: Fully key-homomorphic encryption, arithmetic circuit ABE and compact garbled circuits. In: Nguyen, P.Q., Oswald, E. (eds.) EUROCRYPT 2014. LNCS, vol. 8441, pp. 533–556. Springer, Heidelberg (2014). https://doi.org/10.1007/978-3-642-55220-5_30

14. Cachin, C., Camenisch, J., Kilian, J., Müller, J.: One-round secure computation and secure autonomous mobile agents. In: Montanari, U., Rolim, J.D.P., Welzl, E. (eds.) ICALP 2000. LNCS, vol. 1853, pp. 512–523. Springer, Heidelberg (2000). https://doi.org/10.1007/3-540-45022-X_43

15. Chen, J., Gay, R., Wee, H.: Improved dual system ABE in prime-order groups via predicate encodings. In: Oswald, E., Fischlin, M. (eds.) EUROCRYPT 2015. LNCS, vol. 9057, pp. 595–624. Springer, Heidelberg (2015). https://doi.org/10.1007/978-3-662-46803-6_20

16. Chen, J., Libert, B., Ramanna, S.C.: Non-zero inner product encryption with short ciphertexts and private keys. In: Zikas, V., De Prisco, R. (eds.) SCN 2016. LNCS, vol. 9841, pp. 23–41. Springer, Cham (2016). https://doi.org/10.1007/978-3-319-44618-9_2

17. ElGamal, T.: A public key cryptosystem and a signature scheme based on discrete logarithms. In: Blakley, G.R., Chaum, D. (eds.) CRYPTO 1984. LNCS, vol. 196, pp. 10–18. Springer, Heidelberg (1985). https://doi.org/10.1007/3-540-39568-7_2

18. Escala, A., Herranz, J., Libert, B., Ràfols, C.: Identity-based lossy trapdoor functions: new definitions, hierarchical extensions, and implications. In: Krawczyk, H. (ed.) PKC 2014. LNCS, vol. 8383, pp. 239–256. Springer, Heidelberg (2014). https://doi.org/10.1007/978-3-642-54631-0_14

19. Fleischhacker, N., Malavolta, G., Schröder, D.: Arithmetic garbling from bilinear maps. Cryptology ePrint Archive, Report 2019/082 (2019). https://eprint.iacr.org/2019/082

20. Garg, S., Gentry, C., Halevi, S., Raykova, M., Sahai, A., Waters, B.: Candidate indistinguishability obfuscation and functional encryption for all circuits. In: 54th FOCS, pp. 40–49 (2013)

21. Gennaro, R., Gentry, C., Parno, B.: Non-interactive verifiable computing: outsourcing computation to untrusted workers. In: Rabin, T. (ed.) CRYPTO 2010. LNCS, vol. 6223, pp. 465–482. Springer, Heidelberg (2010). https://doi.org/10.1007/978-3-642-14623-7_25

22. Gentry, C., Sahai, A., Waters, B.: Homomorphic encryption from learning with errors: conceptually-simpler, asymptotically-faster, attribute-based. In: Canetti, R., Garay, J.A. (eds.) CRYPTO 2013. LNCS, vol. 8042, pp. 75–92. Springer, Heidelberg (2013). https://doi.org/10.1007/978-3-642-40041-4_5

23. Gorbunov, S., Vaikuntanathan, V., Wee, H.: Functional encryption with bounded collusions via multi-party computation. In: Safavi-Naini, R., Canetti, R. (eds.) CRYPTO 2012. LNCS, vol. 7417, pp. 162–179. Springer, Heidelberg (2012). https://doi.org/10.1007/978-3-642-32009-5_11

24. Gorbunov, S., Vaikuntanathan, V., Wee, H.: Predicate encryption for circuits from LWE. In: Gennaro, R., Robshaw, M. (eds.) CRYPTO 2015. LNCS, vol. 9216, pp. 503–523. Springer, Heidelberg (2015). https://doi.org/10.1007/978-3-662-48000-7_25

25. Goyal, V., Pandey, O., Sahai, A., Waters, B.: Attribute-based encryption for fine-grained access control of encrypted data. In: ACM CCS 2006, pp. 89–98 (2006). Available as Cryptology ePrint Archive Report 2006/309

26. Ishai, Y., Kushilevitz, E.: Randomizing polynomials: a new representation with applications to round-efficient secure computation. In: 41st FOCS, pp. 294–304 (2000)

27. Jawurek, M., Kerschbaum, F., Orlandi, C.: Zero-knowledge using garbled circuits: how to prove non-algebraic statements efficiently. In: ACM CCS 2013, pp. 955–966 (2013)

28. Katsumata, S., Yamada, S.: Non-zero inner product encryption schemes from various assumptions: LWE, DDH and DCR. In: Lin, D., Sako, K. (eds.) PKC 2019. LNCS, vol. 11443, pp. 158–188. Springer, Cham (2019). https://doi.org/10.1007/978-3-030-17259-6_6

29. Katz, J., Sahai, A., Waters, B.: Predicate encryption supporting disjunctions, polynomial equations, and inner products. In: Smart, N. (ed.) EUROCRYPT 2008. LNCS, vol. 4965, pp. 146–162. Springer, Heidelberg (2008). https://doi.org/10.1007/978-3-540-78967-3_9

30. Kolesnikov, V., Schneider, T.: Improved garbled circuit: free XOR gates and applications. In: Aceto, L., Damgård, I., Goldberg, L.A., Halldórsson, M.M., Ingólfsdóttir, A., Walukiewicz, I. (eds.) ICALP 2008. LNCS, vol. 5126, pp. 486–498. Springer, Heidelberg (2008). https://doi.org/10.1007/978-3-540-70583-3_40

31. Naor, M., Pinkas, B.: Oblivious transfer and polynomial evaluation. In: 31st ACM STOC, pp. 245–254 (1999)

32. Okamoto, T., Takashima, K.: Achieving short ciphertexts or short secret-keys for adaptively secure general inner-product encryption. In: Lin, D., Tsudik, G., Wang, X. (eds.) CANS 2011. LNCS, vol. 7092, pp. 138–159. Springer, Heidelberg (2011). https://doi.org/10.1007/978-3-642-25513-7_11

33. Ostrovsky, R., Sahai, A., Waters, B.: Attribute-based encryption with non-monotonic access structures. In: ACM CCS 2007, pp. 195–203 (2007)

34. Parno, B., Raykova, M., Vaikuntanathan, V.: How to delegate and verify in public: verifiable computation from attribute-based encryption. In: Cramer, R. (ed.) TCC 2012. LNCS, vol. 7194, pp. 422–439. Springer, Heidelberg (2012). https://doi.org/10.1007/978-3-642-28914-9_24

35. Regev, O.: On lattices, learning with errors, random linear codes, and cryptography. In: 37th ACM STOC, pp. 84–93 (2005)

36. Sahai, A., Seyalioglu, H.: Worry-free encryption: functional encryption with public keys. In: ACM CCS 2010, pp. 463–472 (2010)

37. Sahai, A., Waters, B.: Fuzzy identity-based encryption. In: Cramer, R. (ed.) EUROCRYPT 2005. LNCS, vol. 3494, pp. 457–473. Springer, Heidelberg (2005). https://doi.org/10.1007/11426639_27

38. Valiant, L.G.: Universal circuits (preliminary report). In: ACM STOC, pp. 196–203. ACM (1976)

39. Wee, H.: Attribute-hiding predicate encryption in bilinear groups, revisited. In: Kalai, Y., Reyzin, L. (eds.) TCC 2017. LNCS, vol. 10677, pp. 206–233. Springer, Cham (2017). https://doi.org/10.1007/978-3-319-70500-2_8

40. Yao, A.C.-C.: How to generate and exchange secrets (extended abstract). In: 27th FOCS, pp. 162–167 (1986)

Security Models

SEPD: An Access Control Model for Resource Sharing in an IoT Environment

Henrique G. G. Pereira and Philip W. L. Fong[(⊠)]

Department of Computer Science, University of Calgary, Calgary, Alberta, Canada
{henrique.pereira,pwlfong}@ucalgary.ca

Abstract. In an open Internet-of-Things (IoT) environment, the chance encounters of smart devices have made it difficult to articulate access control policies for complete strangers. Based on the metaphor of public sphere, the access control model SEPD is proposed to ease policy administration and facilitate trust inspiration for IoT devices. We articulate a system architecture for SEPD, and offer an in-depth study of its access control policies, known as presence policies. In particular, we characterize when presence policies are resilient against half-truth attacks, devise a policy language based on Temporal Constraint Networks, and empirically profile the efficiency of constructing proofs of compliance for presence policies.

Keywords: Internet of Things · Access control model ·
Public sphere · Presence policy · Half-truth attacks ·
Temporal Constraint Networks · Distributed trust management

1 Introduction

This work attempts to address two access control challenges in Internet-of-Things (IoT) environments [4,32,37,38]. The first challenge is that of ***policy administration***. As the number of devices proliferates, and as chance encounters between unfamiliar devices become the norm, manual specification of access control policies becomes unscalable. The second challenge is that of ***trust inspiration***, especially between devices who do not know one another previously. We want to provide means for complete strangers to gain the trust of one another without resorting to the use of a global identity management framework.

Take, for example, a smart home owned by John. In John's living room is a smart TV, a smart stereo system, as well as other gadgets. If John wants to specify access control policies for these fixtures, so that his family members (a relatively small and stable set of users) can access the resources in the smart devices he owns, then standard access control paradigms apply readily [15,18, 21,28]. However, imagine John now hosts a party in his living room. Visitors want to make music, videos, and sensor data streams available for access by one another. Worst still, although they know John either directly or through friends, they may not know one another. In fact, no one, not even John, knows everyone

© Springer Nature Switzerland AG 2019
K. Sako et al. (Eds.): ESORICS 2019, LNCS 11736, pp. 195–216, 2019.
https://doi.org/10.1007/978-3-030-29962-0_10

in the party. Policy administration and trust inspiration become particularly challenging.

Public Spheres. The challenges in the previous example arise from the fact that John turns his living room into a public sphere. A ***public sphere*** has four qualities [22]: (1) It is not "gated," and is therefore accessible by everyone. (2) It is used for diverse purposes, even at the same time. (3) It promotes the sharing of experiences. (4) Participants are aware of sharing expectations. As an example, we do not limit who can enter a park or a mall (Quality 1). Those who enter know full well that they will meet people, and their appearances and actions will be observable by others (Quality 4). Yet, these interactions are exactly what people look for when they enter that space (Quality 3), although they congregate not for a single purpose (Quality 2). A public sphere is therefore different from a private space, in that it is not intimate (participants do not know one another), it is unprotected (interactions are not centrally mediated), and it is unfamiliar (who or what you interact with may change relatively frequently). The goal of this work is *to use the public sphere as a controlling metaphor for regulating the sharing of digital resources during the chance encounters of smart devices.* Though a worthy goal in its own right, protecting infrastructure resources is not our main focus.

The SEPD Model. We propose an access control model ***SEPD***, for supporting the sharing of resources in public spheres. SEPD offers four features. (1) Well-defined **S**paces serve as arenas for resource sharing. Entering a space is a physical gesture for a user to signal that she consents to make a limited subset of her resources sharable with other visitors of that space. (2) The owner of a space will configure and announce access control policies that regulate resource sharing among visitors of the space. Users now enter the space with an explicitly articulated **E**xpectation of what is to be shared and what kind of person will have access. (3) Access control policies are formulated in terms of users' history of **P**resence in the space. The "familiar faces" will earn higher levels of access. (4) The authorization system is structured in the style of a **D**istributed trust management system [9]. The authorization system does not track the location history of the users. Instead, location verifiers are in place to issue presence certificates to the users. To access a resource currently in the space, the user must construct a proof of compliance using the presence certificates, demonstrating to the resource-bearing device that her history of visitation satisfies the access control policy issued by the space owner. Features (1) and (2) ease policy administration: Users are relieved from formulating and updating access control policies, as such responsibilities are now delegated to the space owner. Features (3) and (4) support the establishment of trust without resorting to a global identity management solution. Historical presence data become a ground for inspiring trust, as people have done in the physical world for millennia.

Contributions. This work (a) proposes a system architecture for SEPD (Sect. 3), (b) characterizes when a presence policy is resilient against half-truth attacks (Sect. 4), (c) devises a policy language for specifying presence policies using Temporal Constraint Networks (Sect. 5), and (d) evaluates the efficiency of constructing a proof of compliance using Mixed Integer Programming (Sect. 6).

Notations. We write $dom(f)$ and $ran(f)$ respectively for the domain and range of a function f. If $S \subseteq dom(f)$, then $f|_S$ denotes the restriction of f to the smaller domain S. K_A and K_A^{-1} denotes respectively the public and private key of principal A.

2   Related Work

Location-based Access Control (LBAC) takes into account the location of the requestor when authorization decisions are made [3,5,12,30]. For example, a nurse is allowed to access the medical record of a patient only if she is in the premise of the hospital [12]. The location of a principal is inferred through sensor readings, and the authorization decision is a function of this location information [10]. In the physical world, physical interactions are possible only because of the physical presence of an actor: e.g., to turn on or off the lights in a room requires someone to use the switch, so the design of the switch itself embodies the access control policy [30]. To be present at a particular location may already be the result of some positive authorization decisions, as access to this location could be protected by conventional methods such as guards, fences or locked doors [12]. Extensions to Role-Based Access Control (RBAC) [5,11,27] and to Relationship-Based Access Control (ReBAC) [34] have been proposed to support location awareness. For example, a combination of RBAC and physical access control (keypad locks, smart-cards on doors) was presented in [5], where users would be assigned a spatial-role after interacting with one of the physical components of the system. LBAC policies are envisioned to take into account conditions that are position-based (conditions that involve having the user present at a specified location), movement-based (conditions that involve having the user moving in a specific direction or at a certain speed), or interaction-based (conditions involving relationships between multiple users or entities) [3]. Our work is unique in that SEPD policies take into account of the requester's history of presence (Sect. 4.1), on top of whether the requester is currently present, thereby giving it a flavour of History-Based Access Control (HBAC) [14,25,31].

Attribute-Based Access Control (ABAC) has been advocated to ease policy administration in IoT environments. An example is NIST's Next Generation Access Control (NGAC), in which automated device registration facilities the introduction of new devices [6]. Users, however, are known principals in the authorization system. Proposed for protecting messages sent to smart vehicles, the dynamic groups of Gupta *et al.* are induced by attributes, some of which are location related [19]. In both works, users and/or resources are known entities to the authorization system. SEPD, however, supports resource sharing among resource-requesting and resource-bearing devices that neither know one another nor are known to the authorization system. This is achieved by structuring the authorization scheme as a distributed trust management framework [9] (Sect. 3).

Policy administration is facilitated by having the space owner specify policies in an intensional policy language (Sects. 4–5).[1]

HCAP is a history-based capability system designed to support the enforcement of history-based access control policies in an IoT environment, in order to impose workflow-induced or spatially-induced order of accesses [33]. Authorization in HCAP depends on the history of access, while authorization in SEPD is dependent on the history of presence (Sect. 4.1). The chief security challenge of HCAP is to prevent the replay of security tokens, while the main security challenge of SEPD are half-truth attacks (Sect. 4.2). HCAP policies are specified as Security Automata [31], while SEPD policies are specified via Temporal Constraint Networks (Sect. 5).

3   System Overview

3.1   System Participants and Trust Assumptions

SEPD assumes the existence of a public key infrastructure (PKI). When two parties communicate, they know the public key of the other party. It is assumed that mutual authentication is performed prior to all communications, which occur through secure channels. In SEPD are three types of participants.

(1) **Public Space.** The first participant is a *public space* (or simply *space*), which is a real-world environment with physical boundaries and accessible to users. A space provides an arena for strangers to interact and share experiences. Each space is operationally defined by one or more *location verifier (LV)*. A user agent may prove to an LV that she is present at the space, and the LV will issue a presence certificate attesting to that fact. Further details concerning presence certificates are given in Sect. 3.2.

While a location proof system can be realized using different approaches [16,29,36,39], an implementation of the LV can make use of secure Distance-Bounding (DB), where a prover tries to convince a verifier that they are within a certain physical distance, by solving a challenge within a limited amount of time [7,8,13]. Multiple DB protocols have been proposed, including public-key based protocols that do not assume an online connection to a trusted server nor a shared secret between the prover and the verifier [20]. Using a public-key DB protocol would allow the LV to be a self-contained entity, and require little additional computing capabilities to issue the presence certificates. This technology is currently available for consumers, with commercial solutions available from different vendors, such as 3db-Access. A study on different DB protocols, possible attacks, and their security properties is presented in [1].

To simplify discussion, we assume that each space has exactly one LV. We assume that the LV is physically secure, so that other participants (including the

---

[1] Policy specification can be *extensional* (enumerating all possible authorizations, as in access control matrices [18]), or *intensional* (articulating the abstract condition of authorization, as in ABAC [21], ReBAC [15], and distributed trust management [9]). Intensional policy specifications are preferred in IoT applications, as intensional specifications offer better scalability than extensional ones.

space owner) may not tamper with the private key of the LV as well as its software configuration. We assume that the LV is not equipped with general-purpose communication capability for Internet access, but is equipped only with enough communication capability to perform distance bounding. The LV does not track location history of users. The LV can be seen as part of the infrastructure of the environment, like a street light.

(2) Space Owner. Another participant is the *owner* of the space, whose responsibility is to specify and publicize access control policies that govern how resources are to be shared when users enter into the space. Doing so establishes a publicly aware expectation of sharing for that space (the **E** in SEPD). The owner defines a number of *resource identifiers*, such as "radio," "pictures for meditation," etc. Each resource identifier names a group of resources that a visitor may want to share when she enters into the space. Resource identifiers are therefore akin to the standard profile items in social media platforms. The space owner also specifies an access control policy for each resource identifier. These access control policies are then published by a *policy and authorization server (PAS)*, who acts as an agent of the space owner. User agents (i.e., devices, see below) obtain the latest policies from the PAS. Section 3.3 gives an overview of such policies.

In our design, presence certificates are never passed to the PAS, and the PAS is not aware of users' access history. The PAS is not required to track user state: there is no notion of a user having to "log on" prior to access. There is not even a need for the user to "register for an account" with the PAS, just like we do not ask a citizen to register before entering a park. All these contribute to scalability, privacy, and openness.

(3) Users. A third group of participants are *users*, who bring along *user agents*, which are devices such as smartphones, wearables, hearables, etc. Each user agent encapsulates resources named by resource identifiers. By entering the space, the users physically gesture that they are willing to share those resources under policies set out by the space owner. The authorization scheme is described in Sect. 3.4. As we shall see, the authorization scheme takes the form of a distributed trust management system, and thus authorization checks are performed by user agents when they receive access requests from one another (rather than conducted centrally in a cloud). Consequently, the space owner's policies are merely recommendations. A user agent may still choose not to honor those policies, or choose to impose additional authorization checks.

The space owner may install fixture devices in the public space. For example, a smart wall may probe nearby users, and project a sample of their "pictures for meditation" to the wall. A smart jukebox may play a sample of songs streamed by the "radio" resources of nearby users. These devices are just like any other user agents, and thus subject to the same access control as others. Since fixture devices are always present in the space, they would eventually acquire the status of "familiar faces" after installation.

3.2   Establishing a History of Presence

Access control policies in SEPD are formulated in terms of the requestor's history of presence at the space. This provides a means for complete strangers to build trust. When a user U visits a space S, her user agent A will prove to the LV of S that U is currently present. The LV will in turn issue **presence certificates** to U to testify for her presence. We write $Presence_{LV}(U, t_1, t_2)$ to denote the presence certificate issued by the LV (i.e., signed by the private key K_{LV}^{-1}) to assert that user U (more precisely, the public key K_U) was present in some time interval $[t_1, t_2]$.

Obviously, U cannot prove her presence in a continuous manner. If U proves her presence at successive time points $t_1, t_2, \ldots, t_n$, where $t_{i+1} - t_i \leq \delta$ for some small δ, then we accept that U is present continuous during the interval $[t_1, t_n]$. There is still a risk that U lies by exiting S momentarily. The smaller δ is, the less risk we have to bear. Choosing δ to be, say, 15 min would result in a manageable risk for a university campus spanning hundreds of acres of land. More specifically, when U first arrives at S at time t, she will request the LV to *initiate a visitation*, and the latter will issue the presence certificate $Presence_{LV}(U, t, t + \delta)$. Once U has been issued a presence certificate $Presence_{LV}(U, t_1, t_2)$, she may request to *extend a visitation* at any time t before the clock reaches t_2 (i.e., $t \in [t_1, t_2]$), by (a) sending to LV the existing certificate $Presence_{LV}(U, t_1, t_2)$, and (b) obtaining from the LV a new presence certificate $Presence_{LV}(U, t_1, t+\delta)$. When the visitation terminates, U simply does not further extend her visitation. Consequently, the LV does not need to track the state of users.

As a result, user U ends up receiving a series of presence certificates after a single visitation:

$$Presence_{LV}(U, t_1, t_2), Presence_{LV}(U, t_1, t_3), \ldots Presence_{LV}(U, t_1, t_n). \quad (1)$$

Note that the presence certificates that testify to only parts of a visitation (e.g., $Presence_{LV}(U, t_1, t_3)$) are not revoked. Here, we have adopted the monotonic interpretation of certificates as advocated by Li and Feigenbaum [24]. All presence certificates are valid; they just do not necessarily tell the whole truth. Adopting a monotonic interpretation of presence certificates allows us to avoid dealing with inefficient revocation schemes involving, for example, Certificate Revocation Lists (CRLs) and Merkle hash trees [23]. Designed for devices that are not computationally well endowed, our scheme reduces both communications and complexity. The downside is that our design leads to the possibility of half-truth attacks, a problem to be addressed in Sects. 4.2–4.3.

3.3   Publishing Presence Policies

The SEPD model shifts the responsibilities of crafting and maintaining access control policies from the individual users to the space owner. Access control policies are authored by the space owner and published by the PAS. In particular, the owner assigns a policy to each resource identifier r she wants to support. These policies are called **presence policies**, as the requestors are required to demonstrate physical presence in order for access to be granted. The simplest policy is this: *"Grant access if the requestor is currently present."* A more demanding policy $\mathcal{P}$ may also require the requestor to have been present in the past, so as to privilege the "known faces": *"Grant access if the requestor is currently present, and had visited this space on at least three different days in the previous week."* Note that the operational meaning of $\mathcal{P}$ is dependent on the current time. For example, at noon on April 29, 2019, the requirement of $\mathcal{P}$ is operationalized into the following **presence predicate** ($P_{2019\text{-}04\text{-}29\text{-}12\text{-}00}$): *"Access may be granted if the requestor is present in the interval [2019-04-29-12-00, 2019-04-29-12-30], and had visited this space on at least three different days during the interval [2019-04-22-00-00, 2019-04-28-23-59]."* Presence policies and presence predicates are formally defined in Sect. 4. Each presence predicate P_t is encoded in some machine-readable format Q to facilitate processing by user agents. The design of this machine-readable policy language is the topic of Sect. 5.

If a user is interested in accessing resources in devices currently present in the space, she will request the PAS to issue a **policy certificate** for the current time t. We write $Policy_{\text{PAS}}(r, t, \Delta, Q)$ to denote the policy certificate issued by the PAS (i.e., signed by the private key K_{PAS}^{-1}) to assert that resource r can be accessed within the time window $[t, t + \Delta]$ on the condition that the requestor satisfies the presence predicate specified in Q. The user may reuse the same policy certificate repeatedly during the time interval $[t, t + \Delta]$.

Note that the presence predicate in the example above ($P_{2019\text{-}04\text{-}29\text{-}12\text{-}00}$) grants access only for a limited time window (12:00–12:30). There are a few reasons for this design: (1) This supports the evolution of policies. (2) Different access requirements can be imposed at a different time of the day (or a different day of the week, etc.). (3) Again, this design is influenced by Li and Feigenbaum [24], so that we do not need to revoke policy certificates.

3.4   Authorizing Access Requests

SEPD authorization is performed in a distributed manner, rather than mediated by a centralized Policy Decision Point (PDP). When the user agent A_1 of user U_1 requests to access resource r in the user agent A_2 of user U_2, the following events occur.

1. User agent A_1 would have already contacted the PAS to obtain a policy certificate $Policy_{\text{PAS}}(r, t, \Delta, Q)$. In addition, A_1 would have already constructed a proof of compliance Π, which is a subset of the presence certificates issued by the LV for U_1 in the past. The set Π provides sufficient evidence that U_1 satisfies the conditions specified in Q. The construction of Π also produces a short explanation m of why Π satisfies Q.
2. A_1 now sends to A_2 an access request consisting of: (a) the resource identifier r, (b) the policy certificate $Policy_{\text{PAS}}(r, t, \Delta, Q)$, (c) the proof of compliance Π, and (d) the explanation m.

3. A_2 now validates the following before granting access: (i) the current time is within the time interval $[t, t + \Delta]$, (ii) the policy certificate is issued by the PAS, and is about the accessibility of resource r, (iii) every presence certificate in Π is issued by the LV, and is about U_1 (more precisely, about K_{U_1}), (iv) m properly explains how Π satisfies Q.

As we shall see, the validation of Π and m in Step 3 can be conducted efficiently (Sect. 5.3); their construction (Step 1), even though a computationally hard problem (Sect. 5.3), has acceptable performance in practice (Sect. 6).

Again, even if the authorization checks are satisfied, user agent A_2 may still choose to refuse the request of A_1 or impose additional checks on top of the requirements of SEPD.

4   Presence Policies

4.1   Presence Policies and Proofs of Compliance

Neither the LV nor the PAS track location history. Users are responsible for storing their own presence certificates. When the client requests a device to grant access, it presents to the latter a **proof of compliance**, which is made up of presence certificates issued by the LV in the past. The resource-bearing device will authorize access only if the proof of compliance satisfies the **presence policy** announced by the PAS. We make these notions formal in the following.

Definition 1. A **time interval** I is a bounded and closed interval $[x, y] = \{z \in \mathbb{R} \mid x \leq z \leq y\}$, where $x, y \in \mathbb{R}$ and $x \leq y$. We write $min(I)$ and $max(I)$ for x and y respectively, $len(I)$ for $y - x$, and Int for the family of all time intervals.

In the following we do not differentiate a presence certificate and the time interval it asserts, unless such a differentiation is necessary.

Definition 2. A **proof of compliance** Π is a finite set of time intervals. We write PoC for the family of all proofs of compliance.

A presence policy specifies when a client has presented enough evidence to be granted access. Such evidence takes the form of a proof of compliance Π.

Definition 3. A **presence predicate** $P : \mathsf{PoC} \to \mathbb{B}$ maps a proof of compliance to a boolean authorization decision. A **presence policy** $\mathcal{P}$ is an indexed family of presence predicates, $\{P_t\}_{t \in \mathbb{R}}$, such that for every time point $t \in \mathbb{R}$, $P_t(\Pi)$ is true only if there exists $I \in \Pi$ such that $t \in I$.

Since the semantics of a presence policy is parameterized by the current time (e.g., "grant access if the requestor is present now as well as one week ago"), the time index t informs the presence predicate P_t of the current time. In addition, the requestor is required to be currently present in order to be granted access. Of course, a presence predicate may impose further presence requirements on top of this minimum requirement.

In a public sphere, users are not necessarily known by one another, nor by the space owner. We, therefore, use past presence as a criterion of trust.

Example 1. We list in the following several ways by which past presence could be employed to inspire trust. In each of the following presence policies, we assume the implicit requirement that the client must be present currently, and list the additional criterion required by that policy.

1. **Heavy user** $(\mathcal{P}_1)$. *"The total amount of time in which the requestor was present last week exceeds T hours."* We do not care if the requestor visits one time or a hundred times. So long as the total duration of stay is long enough, we consider her a heavy user, and thus deserved to be trusted.
2. **Long stay** $(\mathcal{P}_2)$. *"The requestor has made at least one continuous stay of over T hours last week."* Unlike the previous example, we want the T hours to constitute a single, continuous visitation. A long stay reflects the requestor's commitment, which forms the basis of trust in this type of policy.
3. **Spread** $(\mathcal{P}_3)$. *"The requestor has made at least 3 separate visitations last month, each in a different week."* The requestor is required to distribute her stay over multiple visitations across a wide spread of time. Spread demonstrates another form of commitment.
4. **Frequency** $(\mathcal{P}_4)$. *"The requestor has made k separate visitations, all within last week, and no two consecutive visitations are apart by more than T hours."* Frequent visits are yet another demonstration of commitment.
5. **Regularity** (P_5). *"There is a day in the week for which the requestor always makes a visit every week during the last month."* The requestor has formed a habit of visiting.
6. **Non-monotonicity** $(\mathcal{P}_6)$. *"The requestor only visits in the morning during the last year (i.e., never visits in the afternoon)."* Again, this policy is about visitation habits. What is unique about his policy is that it uses negative information ("never").

All the policies above require the user to demonstrate past "commitments," while the sorts of commitment required are different for different policies.

4.2   Resiliency Against Half-Truth Attacks

Since neither the PAS nor the LV tracks the location history of the users, a resource-bearing device relies on the proof of compliance presented by the requestor to determine if authorization is granted. The requestor may withhold information (e.g., omitting a certificate) in order to gain access. Consider, for example, policy $\mathcal{P}_6$ ("visits only in the morning") in Example 1. No set of certificates can give conclusive evidence that the requestor has never visited in the afternoon, for the client may withhold certificates that testify to afternoon visits. Policies that are resilient to the malicious withholding of information by the clients must be monotonic in nature: such policies consume only positive information. While the inability to support presence policies that consume negative information can be seen as a limitation of SEPD, this requirement of monotonicity is commonplace in distributed trust management systems [9].

Recall that a user may present a presence certificate to the LV and request that the latter issues a new presence certificate that testifies to a longer stay.

By the end of a visitation, the user ends up collecting the series of presence certificates displayed in (1). Such a feature necessitates a unique requirement for monotonicity. Consider, for example, policy $\mathcal{P}_4$ in Example 1. The policy requires that consecutive stays to be apart for T hours. The client receives certificates that testify to longer and longer stays, but it could choose to present only the shorter ones to give the impression that the stays are very far apart, but in reality, a new visit starts only seconds after a former visit finishes. Such malicious disclosure of only a part of a longer stay is what we call **half-truth attacks**. Preventing half-truth attacks is a unique challenge of our authorization system.

Not all presence policies are resilient to the withholding of information in general, and the selective presentation of half-truth in particular. We characterize in the following presence policies that are resilient to half-truth attacks.

Definition 4. *(1) Given $\Pi \in \mathsf{PoC}$, we write $\cup\Pi$ for the set $\bigcup_{I \in \Pi} I$. (2) An interval I_2 is a* **right extension** *of interval I_1, written $I_1 \subseteq_R I_2$, whenever $I_1 \subseteq I_2$ and $min(I_1) = min(I_2)$. (3) Given $\Pi_1, \Pi_2 \in \mathsf{PoC}$, we say that Π_2* **R-subsumes** *Π_1, written $\Pi_1 \sqsubseteq_R \Pi_2$, whenever there exists a function $f : \Pi_1 \to \Pi_2$ such that for every $I \in \Pi_1$, $I \subseteq_R f(I)$.*

(It is easy to check that both $\subseteq_R$ and $\sqsubseteq_R$ are partial orderings.) Suppose a proof of compliance Π_1 contains an interval I_1, and a presence predicate P authorizes access for Π_1 (the reader may find it helpful to think of P as corresponding to $\mathcal{P}_2$ in Example 1). But it turns out that I_1 is a half-truth, meaning that the actual stay is captured by another certificate I_2, where $I_1 \subseteq_R I_2$. Intuitively, the presence predicate P is resilient to half-truth attacks if P still authorizes access when it is presented with another proof of compliance Π_2 that is obtained from Π_1 by replacing I_1 with I_2. This is a special case of $\Pi_1 \sqsubseteq_R \Pi_2$.

The definition below enumerates four candidate notions that can be used for capturing the idea of resiliency against half-truth attacks. Their relationships are outlined in the following theorem (see Appendix B.1 for a proof).

Definition 5. *Suppose $P : \mathsf{PoC} \to \mathbb{B}$ is a presence predicate. (1) P is* **semantically monotonic** *if and only if, for every $\Pi, \Pi' \in \mathsf{PoC}$, $\cup\Pi \subseteq \cup\Pi'$ implies that $P(\Pi) \to P(\Pi')$. (2) P is* **syntactically monotonic** *if and only if, for every $\Pi, \Pi' \in \mathsf{PoC}$, $\Pi \subseteq \Pi'$ implies that $P(\Pi) \to P(\Pi')$. (3) P is* **R-reducible** *if and only if, for every $\Pi \in \mathsf{PoC}$, if there exists distinct intervals $I_1, I_2 \in \Pi$ such that $I_1 \subseteq_R I_2$, then $P(\Pi) \to P(\Pi \setminus \{I_1\})$. (4) P is* **R-resilient** *if and only if, for every $\Pi, \Pi' \in PoC$, $\Pi \sqsubseteq_R \Pi'$ implies that $P(\Pi) \to P(\Pi')$*
A presence policy $\mathcal{P} = \{P_t\}_{t \in \mathbb{R}}$ is semantically monotonic (resp. syntactically monotonic, R-reducible, R-resilient) if and only if P_t is semantically monotonic (resp. syntactically monotonic, R-reducible, R-resilient) for every $t \in \mathbb{R}$.

Theorem 1. *Suppose P is a presence predicate. (1) If P is semantically monotonic, then P is R-resilient. (2) P is R-resilient if and only if P is both syntactically monotonic and R-reducible. The same can be said about presence policies.*

Among the four notions in Definition 5, R-resiliency best captures the idea of resiliency against half-truth attacks. Semantic monotonicity is too stringent. It ignores the notion of a visitation. Of all the policies in Example 1, only $\mathcal{P}_1$ is semantically monotonic. Specifically, $\mathcal{P}_2$, which is intuitively resilient to half-truth attacks, is R-resilient but not semantically monotonic. Theorem 1 tells us that R-resiliency can be factorized into two requirements: syntactic monotonicity and R-reducibility. R-resiliency is thus weaker than semantic monotonicity but stronger than syntactic monotonicity. R-reducibility implies that the client needs to store only one presence certificate for each visitation: i.e., the one with the longest duration. Hereafter, we use the terms "resiliency against half-truth attacks" and "R-resiliency" interchangeably.

4.3   A Policy Idiom to Ensure R-Resiliency

Some presence policies are not resilient to half-truth attacks: e.g., $\mathcal{P}_3$, $\mathcal{P}_4$, and $\mathcal{P}_5$ from Example 1. Yet the notions of spread, frequency, and regularity exemplified by these policies are valuable ways to inspire trust. We would like to craft presence policies that on the one hand approximate these notions, and on the other hand guarantee resiliency against half-truth attacks.

A careful analysis of Example 1 would reveal that the notions of spread ($\mathcal{P}_3$), frequency ($\mathcal{P}_4$), and regularity ($\mathcal{P}_5$) are not R-resilient because they are framed in terms of "separate visitations." Extending an interval to the right could potentially cause it to overlap with other existing intervals, and thus visitations are no longer "separate." We, therefore, outline below a policy idiom that can be used for crafting an R-resilient policy while allowing notions such as spread, frequency, and regularity to be approximated. The key is to work with "time windows" rather than "separate visitations."

Definition 6. *An **admissible-window scheme** is a triple $\chi = (\mathsf{wd}, \mathsf{ad}, \mathsf{ag})$, where:*

- *The **windowing function** $\mathsf{wd} : \mathbb{R} \to 2^{\mathsf{Int}}$ divides the timeline into intervals called **windows**. The argument to the windowing function is the current time. The window set $\mathsf{wd}(t)$ satisfies the following three properties. (1) The set $\mathsf{wd}(t)$ is finite. (2) For every $W \in \mathsf{wd}(t)$, $max(W) \leq t$. In other words, given the current time t, the windowing function defines windows over the past timeline. (3) For intervals $W_1, W_2 \in \mathsf{wd}(t)$, exactly one of the following holds: (a) $W_1 \cap W_2 = \emptyset$, (b) $W_1 = W_2$, or (c) $W_1 \cap W_2$ is a singleton set. In other words, the windows returned by wd do not overlap with one another except perhaps at the borders. Lastly, the windows returned by wd are not necessarily of the same size, but uniform window size is a typical case.*
- *The **admissibility predicate** $\mathsf{ad} : \mathsf{PoC} \to \mathbb{B}$ is an R-resilient presence predicate. The intention is to use ad to classify the windows as either **admissible** or not. More precisely, given a window $W \in \mathsf{Int}$ and a proof of compliance $\Pi \in \mathsf{PoC}$, we define Π/W to be the set $\{I \cap W \mid I \in \Pi, I \cap W \neq \emptyset\}$. A window W is admissible whenever $\mathsf{ad}(\Pi/W)$ is true.*
- *The **aggregation predicate** $\mathsf{ag} : \mathsf{PoC} \to \mathbb{B}$ is a syntactically monotonic presence predicate. The intention is to use ag to capture notions such as*

frequency, spread, and *regularity (which are syntactically monotonic but not necessarily R-resilient).*

The presence policy $\mathcal{P}_\chi$ is the family of presence predicates $\{P_t\}_{t \in \mathbb{R}}$ such that:

$$P_t(\Pi) = \mathsf{ag}(admissible(\Pi, t))$$

where $admissible(\Pi, t) = \{W \in \mathsf{wd}(t) \mid \mathsf{ad}(\Pi/W)\}$.

The next theorem ensures that the policy constructed from an admissible-window scheme is resilient to half-truth attacks (see Appendix B.2 for a proof).

Theorem 2. *Suppose χ is an admissible-window scheme. Then the presence policy $\mathcal{P}_\chi$ is R-resilient.*

Example 2. $\mathcal{P}_5$ from Example 1, which is not R-resilient, can be approximated by the R-resistant policy $\mathcal{P}_5^\star$: *"There is a day of the week such that for every week in last month, there is a continuous visitation that intersects with that day of the week for at least T hours."* This approximation is obtained by the admissible-window scheme $\chi = (\mathsf{wd}, \mathsf{ad}, \mathsf{ag})$ defined as follows. The windowing function $\mathsf{wd}(t)$ returns a set of windows, one for each day in the last month (relative to the current time t). The admissibility predicate $\mathsf{ad}(\Pi)$ returns true if and only if Π contains an interval I such that $len(I) \geq T$. It is easy to check that ad is R-resilient. The aggregation predicate $\mathsf{ag}(\Pi)$ returns true when there exists a day of the week D and a month M in the timeline, such that all the day-windows in M that correspond to D are members of Π. It is easy to check that ag is syntactically monotonic (but not R-resilient). $\mathcal{P}_5^\star$ is actually the presence policy $\mathcal{P}_\chi$ induced by the admissible-window scheme $\chi = (\mathsf{wd}, \mathsf{ad}, \mathsf{ag})$. According to Theorem 2, $\mathcal{P}_5^\star$ is R-resilient.

Similarly, $\mathcal{P}_3$ and $\mathcal{P}_4$ can also be approximated by the admissible-window policy idiom. There is no need to pretend that $\mathcal{P}_5^\star$ is equivalent to $\mathcal{P}_5$. They are not. Nevertheless, the admissible-window policy idiom allows one to translate notions such as frequency, spread, and regularity, which are not resilient to half-truth, to R-resilient policies that approximate their meanings.

5   A Policy Language

The owner of a public space needs a policy language for specifying presence policies. Such a language should (a) offer enough expressiveness to capture a wide range of presence policies, (b) provide efficient means for the authorization server to verify a proof of compliance, and (c) support the authoring of policies that are resilient against half-truth attacks. We have based our design of such a policy language on the **temporal constraint network (TCN)** [2,26,35], and augmented TCN with a number of extensions. Knowledge of TCNs is assumed in the rest of the paper. Readers who are new to TCNs and Allen's algebra are directed to Appendix A for a brief introduction.

5.1   Presence Predicate Specifiers

Recall that a TCN is a graph structure in which every node is a placeholder for a time interval, and every directed edge prescribes a temporal relation that must hold between the time intervals represented by the two ends of the directed edge (Appendix A). An **extended temporal constraint network (ETCN)** essentially is a TCN augmented with two additional types of nodes. A **floating node** can only be instantiated to a time interval with a specific duration. An **anchored node** can only be instantiated to a pre-selected time interval.

Definition 7. *An **extended temporal constraint network (ETCN)** Θ is a tuple (N, R, F, A, C, L, M), where the components are described as follows. The pair (N, C) is a TCN. The node set $N = R \uplus A \uplus F$ is partitioned into three disjoint sets: R is the set of **regular nodes**, F is the set of **floating nodes**, and A is the set of **anchored nodes**. $L : F \to \mathbb{R}$ maps each floating node to a duration. $M : A \to \mathsf{Int}$ maps each anchored node to a time interval. We write N_Θ, R_Θ, F_Θ, A_Θ, C_Θ, L_Θ, and M_Θ for the components of Θ.*

*An **instantiation** of an ETCN Θ is a function $m : N_\Theta \to \mathsf{Int}$. Instantiation m **satisfies** Θ if and only if (a) m satisfies the TCN (N_Θ, C_Θ), (b) $len(m(v)) = L_\Theta(v)$ for every $v \in F_\Theta$, and (c) $m(v) = M_\Theta(v)$ for every $v \in A_\Theta$.*

Definition 8. *A **presence predicate specifier (PPS)** Q is a syntactic means for specifying a presence predicate. It is defined inductively as follows, together with the functions $nodes(Q)$ and $regulars(Q)$.*

- *An ETCN Θ is a PPS, with $nodes(\Theta) = N_\Theta$ and $regulars(\Theta) = R_\Theta$.*
- *If $Q_1, \ldots, Q_n$ are PPSs, such that $nodes(Q_1), \ldots, nodes(Q_n)$ are pairwise disjoint, and $1 \leq m \leq n$, then the **threshold construct** $Q = (Q_1, \ldots, Q_n)_{\geq m}$ is a PPS. In addition, $nodes(Q) = \cup_{1 \leq i \leq n} nodes(Q_i)$, and $regulars(Q) = \cup_{1 \leq i \leq n} regulars(Q_i)$.*

Function $m : X \to \mathsf{Int}$ is an instantiation of Q if $X \subseteq nodes(Q)$. Instantiation m satisfies Q if and only if the following holds:

- *If Q is an ETCN Θ, then $dom(m) = N_\Theta$, and m satisfies Θ as an ETCN.*
- *If Q is a threshold construct $(Q_1, \ldots, Q_n)_{\geq m}$, then there exists at least m distinct PPSs Q_i among $\{Q_1, \ldots, Q_n\}$ such that $m|_{nodes(Q_i)}$ satisfies Q_i.*

*The **disjunction** $Q_1 \vee Q_2$ and the **conjunction** $Q_1 \wedge Q_2$ denote $(Q_1, Q_2)_{\geq 1}$ and $(Q_1, Q_2)_{\geq 2}$ respectively.*

*We say that a PPS Q **represents** a presence predicate P if and only if, for every $\Pi \in \mathsf{PoC}$, $P(\Pi)$ is true whenever Q is satisfied by an instantiation m such that for every $v \in dom(m)$, either $v \notin regulars(Q)$ or $m(v) \in \Pi$.*

Checking if a given instantiation m satisfies a predicate specifier Q takes time polynomial to the size of Q.

Example 3. Suppose the presence policy $\mathcal{P}_2$ in Example 1 is $\{P_t\}_{t \in \mathbb{R}}$. Then P_t can be represented by the PPS Θ defined as follows. (1) $R_\Theta = \{u\}$. (2) $F_\Theta = \{v\}$. (3) $A_\Theta = \{w\}$. (4) $L_\Theta(v)$ corresponds to T hours. (5) $A_\Theta(w)$ is the time interval that spans the last week (relative to the current time t). (6) $C_\Theta(v, u) = C_\Theta(v, w) = \{s, d, f, eq\}$.

5.2   Supporting the Admissible-Window Policy Idiom

One of the benefits of basing presence policy specification on ETCNs is that the latter supports the authoring of R-resilient policies. The admissible-window policy idiom defined in Sect. 4.3 can be captured by a PPS in which every component ETCN $\Theta = (N, R, F, A, C, L, M)$ has the following structural properties (the disjunctive relation $\mathbf{B}$ is the universal relation defined in Appendix A):

- If $u, v \in R$, or $u, v \in A$, then $C(u, v) = C(v, u) = \mathbf{B}$. If $u, v \in F$, then $C(u, v)$ and $C(v, u)$ can be any disjunctive relations.
- There is an injective function $flt : R \to F$, such that for every $u \in R$, $C(flt(u), u) = \{s, d, f, eq\}$ and $C(u, flt(u)) = \{si, di, fi, eq\}$. For $u \in R$ and $v \in F$, if $v \neq flt(u)$, then $C(u, v) = C(v, u) = \mathbf{B}$.
- There is a surjective function $anc : F \to A$. For every $u \in F$, $C(u, anc(u)) = \{s, d, f, eq\}$ and $C(anc(u), u) = \{si, di, fi, eq\}$. For $v \in F$ and $w \in A$, if $w \neq anc(v)$, then $C(v, w) = C(w, v) = \mathbf{B}$.

Intuitively, each anchored node encodes a window. Contained within each window is a set of floating nodes. The floating nodes can be related to one another via any temporal relations. It is required that each regular node u "covers" a distinct floating node $flt(u)$, meaning that the regular node u is required to intersect with the window $anc(flt(u))$ for at least a duration of $L(flt(u))$. The duration requirements encode an R-resilient admissibility condition, while the threshold constructs encode a syntactically monotonic aggregation condition. Therefore, the presence predicate represented by such a PPS is R-resilient.

An ETCN Θ that satisfies the above structural properties is said to be **idiomatic**. Every idiomatic ETCN Θ with m anchored nodes represents the same presence predicate as the conjunction of m idiomatic ETCNs, each with only one anchored node. From now on we only consider idiomatic ETCNs with one anchored node.

Example 4. Consider $\mathcal{P}_5^* = \{P_t\}_{t \in \mathbb{R}}$ from Example 2. The presence predicate P_t is represented by the disjunction $Q_{Mon} \vee Q_{Tue} \vee \ldots \vee Q_{Sun}$. The PPS Q_{Mon} is the conjunction $Q_{1st\text{-}Mon} \wedge \ldots \wedge Q_{4th\text{-}Mon}$ (assuming there are four Mondays in the previous month). $Q_{1st\text{-}Mon}$ is the ETCN Θ defined as follows. (1) $A_\Theta = \{w\}$ contains a single window w where $M_\Theta(w)$ is the interval spanning the first Monday of the previous month (relative to the current time t). (2) $F_\Theta = \{v\}$ contains a floating node v with duration $L_\Theta(v)$ corresponding to T hours. (3) $R_\Theta = \{u\}$ contains a regular node u. (4) C_Θ is formulated according to the structural properties above. The rest of the PPS can be formulated in an analogous manner.

5.3   Constructing a Proof of Compliance

A second benefit of adopting an ETCN-based policy language is that a proof of compliance can be validated to satisfy a presence predicate in a very efficient manner (with the help of a short witness). Note that constructing a proof of compliance is computationally hard, as the corresponding decision problem is NP-complete (see Appendix B.3 for a proof).

Problem: PPS-SAT
Instance: A PPS Q and a finite set DB of time intervals (previously issued by the location verifier).
Question: Is there an instantiation m of Q such that (a) m satisfies Q, and (b) for every $v \in dom(m)$, $v \in regulars(Q)$ implies $m(v) \in DB$?

Theorem 3. PPS-SAT *is* NP-*complete.*

In the above, the proof of compliance Π is essentially $ran(m|_{regulars(Q)})$, and m provides a "witness" explaining how Π satisfies the policy predicate represented by Q. While constructing Π and m is hard, checking if Π satisfies the presence predicate represented by Q when m is given is very efficient.

Although the requestor must now solve an NP-complete problem (Sect. 3.4), the task is less formidable than it appears. First, according to Sect. 3.3 a policy certificate is effective for a duration of Δ, meaning that m can be reused before the policy certificate expires. Second, since the presence predicate represented by Q is R-reducible (Theorem 1), the client does not need to store all the presence certificates ever issued to her, but only the one corresponding to the longest interval of each visitation. That means DB has a manageable size. Third, the construction of a satisfying instantiation for Q can be modularized by solving one idiomatic ETCN at a time. For each idiomatic ETCN Θ, we do not need to consider all the intervals in DB, but only those intervals that intersect with the anchored node of Θ. For typical window sizes like days, weeks, and months, the number of intersecting intervals is at best moderate if not small.

PPS-SAT instances can be solved by using a **Mixed Integer Programming (MIP)** solver. Mature implementations of MIP solvers are available (e.g., the Google CP-SAT Solver). We sketch below a Karp reduction that takes as input a PPS-SAT instance consisting of (a) an idiomatic ETCN Θ, and (b) a finite set DB of time intervals (previously certified by the location verifier), and returns an equivalent MIP instance. Suppose $DB = \{I_1, \ldots, I_p\}$, $R_\Theta = \{u_1, \ldots, u_m\}$, $F_\Theta = \{v_1, \ldots, v_n\}$, and $A_\Theta = \{w\}$. A disjunctive relation **R** is **restrictive** if it does not contain all the 13 basic relations. For each restrictive $C_\Theta(v_i, v_j)$, we enumerate its members as $\{\mathbf{r}_1^{i,j}, \ldots, \mathbf{r}_{q(i,j)}^{i,j}\}$, where $q(i,j) = |C_\Theta(v_i, v_j)|$. The output MIP instance consists of the following set of variables:

1. For $1 \le i \le m$ and $1 \le j \le p$, the boolean variable $b_{i,j}$ indicates whether the regular node u_i is instantiated with time interval I_j.
2. For each restrictive $C_\Theta(v_i, v_j)$, and $1 \le k \le q(i,j)$, the boolean variable $c_{i,j,k}$ indicates whether the time interval assigned to v_i and the one assigned to v_j are related by the basic relation $\mathbf{r}_k^{i,j}$.
3. For $1 \le i \le n$, real variables x_i^r and y_i^r are the two boundary points of the time interval that is assigned to regular node u_i. Similarly, real variables x_i^f, y_i^f, x^w, y^w are boundary points of the floating and anchored intervals.

The output MIP instance contains the following constraints:

- For $1 \le i \le m$, impose constraints (a) $\Sigma_{j=1}^p b_{i,j} = 1$, (b) $x_i^r = \Sigma_{j=1}^p min(I_j) \times b_{i,j}$, and (c) $y_i^r = \Sigma_{j=1}^p max(I_j) \times b_{i,j}$.

- For $1 \leq i \leq m$ and $v_j = flt(u_i)$, impose (a) $x_i^r \leq x_j^f$, and (b) $y_j^f \leq y_i^r$.
- For $1 \leq i \leq n$, impose (a) $x^w \leq x_i^f$, (b) $y_i^f \leq y^w$, and (c) $y_i^f - x_i^f = L(v_i)$.
- Impose constraints $x^w = min(M(w))$ and $y^w = max(M(w))$.
- For each restrictive $C_\Theta(v_i, v_j)$, impose constraint $\Sigma_{k=1}^{q(i,j)} c_{i,j,k} = 1$.
- For each basic relation $\mathbf{r}_k^{i,j}$ in a restrictive $C_\Theta(v_i, v_j)$, impose a constraint to simulate the semantics of $\mathbf{r}_k^{i,j}$ when $c_{i,j,k} = 1$. For example, if $\mathbf{r}_k^{i,j}$ is the basic relation p (precedes), then impose the constraint $c_{i,j,k} \times y_i^f < c_{i,j,k} \times x_j^f + (1 - c_{i,j,k})$. If $c_{i,j,k} = 1$, then the constraint requires $y_i^f < x_j^f$ (i.e., the interval assigned to v_i precedes the interval assigned to v_j). Otherwise, $c_{i,j,k} = 0$, and the constraint is trivially satisfied. The other 12 basic relations can be simulated in a similar manner.

Given a solution to the output MIP instance, one can construct a satisfying instantiation m of Θ by consulting x_i^r, y_i^r, x_i^f, y_i^f, x^w, and y^w.

6   Performance Evaluation

An apparent challenge to our proposed authorization scheme is whether the requestor can efficiently construct a proof of compliance out of the set of presence certificates issued by the LV in the past. We conducted controlled experiments to demonstrate that constructing proofs of compliance using the MIP reduction in Sect. 5.3 can be performed with acceptable efficiency. All experiments were executed on an Intel Core i5 6200U 2.4 GHz PC with 8 GB DDR3 RAM, 512 GB SSD, running Windows 10 64-Bit. We used Python 3.6 to implement the MIP reduction (Sect. 5.3), and the Google CP-SAT Solver to solve the MIP instances and to collect timing statistics.

Experiment 1 - Increasing Policy Size: The first experiment was designed to assess the performance impact of different policy sizes. To that end, we fixed the number of presence certificates used for constructing proofs of compliance. Recall that the PPS can be solved modularly, one idiomatic ETCN at a time. The presence certificates considered for each idiomatic ETCN are only those that intersect with the anchored node. This number, in practice, is much smaller than the total number of presence certificates owned by the user. Suppose the window is a year, and the client visits her workplace once per day for 50 weeks during that year, we would expect her to accumulate approximately $50 \times 5 = 250$ presence certificates that intersect with the window (by R-resiliency, only one presence certificate needs to be kept for each visitation). We, therefore, constructed a timeline of 23 discrete time points and generated an interval set DB containing all the $\binom{23}{2} = 253 \approx 250$ distinct intervals on that timeline.

For each n from 5 to 50, in increments of 5, we generated 100 ETCNs. Each ETCN Θ is generated according to the admissible-window structural properties (Sect. 5.2), with n regular nodes, n floating nodes $(v_1, \ldots, v_n)$, and one anchored node (w). We set $M_\Theta(w)$ to an interval covering all the 23 discrete time points. Then n intervals $(I_1, \ldots, I_n)$ are randomly sampled from DB, with each sampled

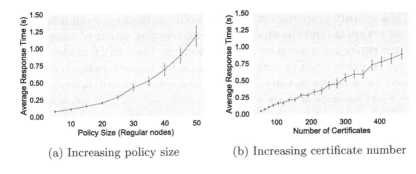

(a) Increasing policy size   (b) Increasing certificate number

Fig. 1. Results: (a) Experiment 1; (b) Experiment 2

interval I_i corresponding to a floating node v_i. We set $L_\Theta(v_i) = len(I_i)$. For $v_i, v_j \in F_\Theta$, we set $C_\Theta(v_i, v_j) = \{\mathbf{r}\}$, where $\mathbf{r}$ is the basic relation relating I_i to I_j. The resulting PPS-SAT instance (Θ, DB) is thus satisfiable.

The 1,000 PPS-SAT instances are reduced to MIP instances (Sect. 5.3). Each MIP instance is solved, and the solving time is recorded. If the MIP solver fails to obtain a solution within 2 s, we terminate the constraint-solving session. For only 5 out of the 1,000 MIP instances (0.5%) did the solver fail to complete within 2 s. We compute the average constraint-solving time for those completed instances. Figure 1a shows that policy size has a direct impact on the running time of the solver: the bigger n is, the more variables and constraints will there be in the MIP instance. Nevertheless, even with $n = 50$ (and with 253 presence certificates to consider), the running time is still within 1.5 s, which is quite acceptable as the computed instantiation can be reused throughout the period $[t, t + \Delta]$ (Sect. 3.3 gives an example Δ of 30 min).

Experiment 2 - Increasing Certificate Number: This experiment was designed to evaluate the performance impact of increasing the number of presence certificates. Let DB_m be the set of all $\binom{m}{2}$ intervals from a timeline consisting of m discrete time points. For each integer m from 11 to 32, we generated 100 ETCNs in the same way we did in Experiment 1, but fixed $n = 30$. Again, the 2,200 MIP instances are solved, and the average constraint-solving time for each m is computed, excluding 3 of the 2,200 times (0.14%) in which the MIP solver fails to complete in 2 seconds. See Fig. 1b. Increasing the number of certificates had a smaller effect than increasing the policy size, as the number of constraints added to the MIP instance when more certificates are used is much lower than the number of constraints added when the ETCN size is increased.

7   Conclusion and Future Work

A new access control model, SEPD, has been proposed for easing policy administration and facilitate trust inspiration in an open IoT environment. The architecture of the SEPD model is based on the metaphor of public spheres. We studied the security properties of presence policies, their expression in temporal constraint networks, and the efficiency of constructing proofs of compliance.

We are exploring a number of extensions to the SEPD model. First, we would like to extend SEPD with mechanisms for bootstrapping trust, so that newcomers (who have never been present) to a space can still inspire some level of trust when accompanied by a trusted escort. Second, we are working on a decentralized approach to resource discovery in a public sphere. Third, we are examining how reputation and presence history can be combined in a single distributed trust management framework.

Acknowledgements. This work is supported in part by an NSERC Discovery Grant (RGPIN-2014-06611) and a Canada Research Chair (950-229712).

A   Temporal Constraint Networks

Allen identifies 13 **basic relations** between any two time intervals [2,26]. Those relations are **precedes (p), meets (m), overlaps (o), starts (s), during (d), finishes (f)**, and their respective converse relations (i.e., **preceded by [si], met by [mi], overlapped by [o], started by [si], contains [di]**, and **finished by [fi]**), as well as **equality (eq)**. Table 1 gives the definition of these relations. These 13 basic relations capture all the possible relations between two intervals.

Let $\mathbf{B} = \{p, pi, m, mi, o, oi, s, si, d, di, f, fi, eq\}$ be the set of all basic relations. $\mathbf{B}$ is called the **universal relation**. We write $X\mathbf{r}Y$ to assert that interval X is related to interval Y in the basic relation $\mathbf{r}$. Given $X, Y \in \mathsf{Int}$, there exists exactly one basic relation $\mathbf{r} \in \mathbf{B}$ such that $X\mathbf{r}Y$. Given $\mathbf{R} \subseteq \mathbf{B}$, we write $X\mathbf{R}Y$ to assert that there exists $\mathbf{r} \in \mathbf{R}$ such that $X\mathbf{r}Y$. The set $\mathbf{R}$ is called a **disjunctive relation**.

A **temporal constraint network (TCN)** is an edge-labeled, complete, directed graph $\Theta = (N, C)$, so that each directed edge $(u, v) \in N \times N$ is associated with a disjunctive relation $C(u, v) \subseteq \mathbf{B}$. An **instantiation** of Θ is a function $m : N \to \mathsf{Int}$. Instantiation m **satisfies** Θ if and only if $m(u)\,C(u, v)\,m(v)$ for every edge $(u, v) \in N \times N$. We say that Θ is **consistent** if and only if there exists an instantiation that satisfies Θ.

Table 1. Allen's 13 basic relations between intervals $X = [x_1, x_2]$ and $Y = [y_1, y_2]$.

Relation	r	X r Y	r^{-1}	Relation	r	X r Y	r^{-1}
Precedes	p	$x_1 < x_2 < y_1 < y_2$	pi	Starts	s	$x_1 = y_1 < x_2 < y_2$	si
Meets	m	$x_1 < x_2 = y_1 < y_2$	mi	During	d	$y_1 < x_1 < x_2 < y_2$	di
Overlaps	o	$x_1 < y_1 < x_2 < y_2$	oi	Finishes	f	$y_1 < x_1 < x_2 = y_2$	fi
				Equals	eq	$x_1 = y_1 \wedge x_2 = y_2$	eq

B   Proofs

B.1   Proof of Theorem 1

Statement (1): Suppose P is semantically monotonic. Consider $\Pi, \Pi' \in \mathsf{PoC}$ and $t \in \mathbb{R}$. If $\Pi \sqsubseteq_R \Pi'$ via the function $f : \Pi \to \Pi'$, then we have the following containment:

$$\cup \Pi = \bigcup_{I \in \Pi} I \subseteq \bigcup_{I \in \Pi} f(I) \subseteq \bigcup_{I' \in \Pi'} I' \subseteq \cup \Pi'$$

which, by semantic monotonicity, implies $P(\Pi) \to P(\Pi')$. P is therefore R-resilient.

Statement (2): We begin by proving that R-resiliency implies syntactic monotonicity. Suppose P is R-resilient. Consider $\Pi, \Pi' \in \mathsf{PoC}$ where $\Pi \subseteq \Pi'$. Construct $f : \Pi \to \Pi'$ so that $f(I) = I$. Thus $\Pi \sqsubseteq_R \Pi'$. By the R-resiliency of P, we have $P(\Pi) \to P(\Pi')$ as required by syntactic monotonicity.

Next, we demonstrate that R-resiliency implies R-reducibility. Suppose P is R-resilient. Consider $\Pi \in \mathsf{PoC}$ where there exists distinct intervals $I_1, I_2 \in \Pi$ such that $I_1 \subseteq_R I_2$. Construct $f : \Pi \to \Pi \setminus \{I_1\}$ so that:

$$f(I) = \begin{cases} I_2 & \text{if } I = I_1 \\ I & \text{otherwise} \end{cases}$$

Function f thus witnesses to the fact that $\Pi \sqsubseteq_R \Pi \setminus \{I_1\}$. By R-resiliency, we know that $P(\Pi) \to P(\Pi \setminus \{I_1\})$.

So far, we have demonstrated that R-resiliency implies the conjunction of syntactic monotonicity and R-reducibility. We complete the proof of Statement (1) by showing that syntactic monotonicity and R-reducibility jointly imply R-resiliency. Suppose P is both syntactically monotonic and R-reducible. Consider $\Pi, \Pi' \in \mathsf{PoC}$. If $\Pi \sqsubseteq_R \Pi'$ via the function $f : \Pi \to \Pi'$, then the following implication holds:

$$\begin{aligned} P(\Pi) &\to P(\Pi \cup \Pi') && \text{by syntactic monotonicity} \\ &\to P(\Pi') && \text{by R-reducibility} \end{aligned}$$

B.2   Proof of Theorem 2

Let $\chi = (\mathsf{wd}, \mathsf{ad}, \mathsf{ag})$, and $\mathcal{P}^\chi = \{P_t\}_{t \in \mathbb{R}}$. Suppose $\Pi \sqsubseteq_R \Pi'$ via the function $f : \Pi \to \Pi'$. We show in the three steps below that $P_t(\Pi) \to P_t(\Pi')$.

Step 1. We show that $\Pi/W \sqsubseteq_R \Pi'/W$ for every $W \in \mathsf{Int}$. To this end, we construct a function $g : \Pi/W \to \Pi'/W$ so that $X \subseteq_R g(X)$ for every $X \in \Pi/W$.

Consider an interval $I \in \Pi$. Since $I \subseteq_R f(I)$, we know the following two facts: (1) If $I \cap W \neq \emptyset$, then $f(I) \cap W \neq \emptyset$. (2) $I \cap W \subseteq_R f(I) \cap W$. Therefore, by having g maps $I \cap W$ to $f(I) \cap W$ when $I \cap W \neq \emptyset$, the requirement of $X \subseteq_R g(X)$ will be satisfied.

The problem with the above construction is that the resulting mapping g may not be functional. The latter happens when there are distinct intervals $I_1, I_2 \in \Pi$ for which $I_1 \cap W = I_2 \cap W$. To correct this, observe that if $X \subseteq_R Y_1$ and $X \subseteq_R Y_2$, then either $Y_1 \subseteq_R Y_2$ or $Y_2 \subseteq_R Y_1$, and thus we have (a) $X \subseteq_R Y_1 \cup Y_2$, and (b) either $Y_1 = Y_1 \cup Y_2$ or $Y_2 = Y_1 \cup Y_2$. We therefore define g as follows:

$$g(X) = \bigcup_{I \in \Pi,\, I \cap W = X} f(I) \cap W$$

The function g witnesses to the fact that $\Pi/W \sqsubseteq_R \Pi'/W$.

Step 2. We demonstrate that $admissible(\Pi, t) \subseteq admissible(\Pi', t)$. By definition, a window W belongs to $admissible(\Pi, t)$ whenever $\mathsf{ad}(\Pi/W)$. But we showed in **Step 1** that $\Pi/W \sqsubseteq_R \Pi'/W$. Therefore, by the R-resiliency of ad, we also have $\mathsf{ad}(\Pi'/W)$ as a result, meaning $W \in admissible(\Pi', t)$. Consequently, every member of $admissible(\Pi, t)$ is also a member of $admissible(\Pi', t)$.

Step 3. We can now conclude that $P_t(\Pi) \rightarrow P_t(\Pi')$, because the syntactic monotonicity of ag guarantees that $\mathsf{ag}(admissible(\Pi, t)) \rightarrow \mathsf{ag}(admissible(\Pi', t))$.

B.3   Proof of Theorem 3

That PPS-SAT is in NP is obvious. We demonstrate NP-hardness by a reduction from graph k-colorability [17]. Given an instance $G = (V, E)$ of graph k-colorability, the reduction produces an instance (Θ, DB) of PPS-SAT, where DB contains k distinct intervals, and Θ is the ETCN $(V, V, \emptyset, \emptyset, C, \emptyset, \emptyset)$, such that $C(u, v) = \mathbf{B} \setminus \{eq\}$ if $uv \in E$, but $C(u, v) = \mathbf{B}$ if $uv \notin E$. It is easy to see that G is k-colorable if and only if $(\Theta, DB) \in$ PPS-SAT.

References

1. Ahmadi, A., Safavi-Naini, R.: Directional distance-bounding identification. In: Mori, P., Furnell, S., Camp, O. (eds.) ICISSP 2017. CCIS, vol. 867, pp. 197–221. Springer, Cham (2018). https://doi.org/10.1007/978-3-319-93354-2_10

2. Allen, J.F.: Maintaining knowledge about temporal intervals. Commun. ACM **26**(11), 832–843 (1983)

3. Ardagna, C.A., Cremonini, M., Damiani, E., di Vimercati, S.D.C., Samarati, P.: Supporting location-based conditions in access control policies. In: Proceedings of ASIACCS 2006, pp. 212–222. ACM, Taipei (2006)

4. Bertin, E., Hussein, D., Sengul, C., Frey, V.: Access control in the internet of things: a survey of existing approaches and open research questions. Ann. Telecommun. J. **74**(7–8), 375–388 (2019)

5. Bertino, E., Kirkpatrick, M.S.: Location-based access control systems for mobile users: concepts and research directions. In: Proceedings of ACM SIGSPATIAL SPRINGL 2011, pp. 49–52. ACM, Chicago (2011)

6. Bezawada, B., Haefner, K., Ray, I.: Securing home IoT environments with attribute-based access control. In: Proceedings of ABAC 2018, Tempe, AZ, USA, pp. 43–53 (2018)

7. Brands, S., Chaum, D.: Distance-bounding protocols. In: Helleseth, T. (ed.) EURO-CRYPT 1993. LNCS, vol. 765, pp. 344–359. Springer, Heidelberg (1994). https://doi.org/10.1007/3-540-48285-7_30

8. Bussard, L., Bagga, W.: Distance-bounding proof of knowledge to avoid real-time attacks. In: Sasaki, R., Qing, S., Okamoto, E., Yoshiura, H. (eds.) SEC 2005. IAICT, vol. 181, pp. 223–238. Springer, Boston, MA (2005). https://doi.org/10.1007/0-387-25660-1_15

9. Chapin, P.C., Skalka, C., Wang, X.S.: Authorization in trust management: features and foundations. ACM Comput. Surv. **40**(3), 1–48 (2008). Article no. 9

10. v. Cleeff, A., Pieters, W., Wieringa, R.: Benefits of location-based access control: a literature study. In: Proceedings of IEEE/ACM CPSCom 2010, pp. 739–746. IEEE, Hangzhou, December 2010

11. Damiani, M.L., Bertino, E., Catania, B., Perlasca, P.: GEO-RBAC: a spatially aware RBAC. ACM Trans. Inf. Syst. Secur. **10**(1), 1–42 (2007). Article no. 2

12. Decker, M.: Requirements for a location-based access control model. In: Proceedings of MoMM 2008, pp. 346–349. ACM, Linz (2008)

13. Fischlin, M., Onete, C.: Subtle kinks in distance-bounding: an analysis of prominent protocols. In: Proceedings of WiSec 2013, pp. 195–206. ACM, Budapest (2013)

14. Fong, P.W.L.: Access control by tracking shallow execution history. In: Proceedings of the 2004 IEEE Symposium on Security and Privacy (S&P 2004), Berkeley, CA, USA, pp. 43–55, May 2004

15. Fong, P.W.: Relationship-based access control: protection model and policy language. In: Proceedings of CODASPY 2011, pp. 191–202. ACM, San Antonio (2011)

16. Gambs, S., Killijian, M.O., Roy, M., Traoré, M.: PROPS: a PRivacy-preserving lOcation proof system. In: Proceedings of the 33rd IEEE International Symposium on Reliable Distributed Systems (SRDS 2014), Nara, Japan, pp. 1–10, October 2014

17. Garey, M.R., Johnson, D.S.: Computers and Intractability: A Guide to the Theory of NP-Completeness. W. H. Freeman & Co., New York (1990)

18. Graham, G.S., Denning, P.J.: Protection: principles and practice. In: AFIPS Conference Proceedings 1971 (Fall). ACM, Las Vegas (1971). https://doi.org/10.1145/1478873.1478928

19. Gupta, M., Benson, J., Patwa, F., Sandhu, R.: Dynamic groups and attribute-based access control for next-generation smart cars. In: Proceedings of CODASPY 2019, pp. 61–72. ACM, Richardson (2019)

20. Hermans, J., Peeters, R., Onete, C.: Efficient, secure, private distance bounding without key updates. In: Proceedings of WiSec 2013, pp. 207–218. ACM, Budapest (2013)

21. Hu, V.C., et al.: Guide to Attribute Based Access Control (ABAC) Definition and Considerations. National Institute of Standards and Technology (2014). https://doi.org/10.6028/nist.sp.800-162

22. Kang, J., Cuff, D.: Pervasive computing: embedding the public sphere. Washington Lee Law Rev. **65**, 93–146 (2005)

23. Kocher, P.C.: On certificate revocation and validation. In: Hirchfeld, R. (ed.) Financial Cryptography 1998, pp. 172–177. Springer, Heidelberg (1998)

24. Li, N., Feigenbaum, J.: Nonmonotonicity, user interfaces, and risk assessment in certificate revocation. In: Syverson, P. (ed.) FC 2001. LNCS, vol. 2339, pp. 166–177. Springer, Heidelberg (2002). https://doi.org/10.1007/3-540-46088-8_16

25. Ligatti, J., Bauer, L., Walker, D.: Run-time enforcement of nonsafety policies. ACM Trans. Inf. Syst. Secur. **12**(3), 1–39 (2009). Article no. 19

26. Ligozat, G.: Qualitative Spatial and Temporal Reasoning. Wiley, Hoboken (2013)
27. Ray, I., Kumar, M., Yu, L.: LRBAC: a location-aware role-based access control model. In: Bagchi, A., Atluri, V. (eds.) ICISS 2006. LNCS, vol. 4332, pp. 147–161. Springer, Heidelberg (2006). https://doi.org/10.1007/11961635_10
28. Sandhu, R.S., Coyne, E.J., Feinstein, H.L., Youman, C.E.: Role-based access control models. Computer **29**(2), 38–47 (1996)
29. Saroiu, S., Wolman, A.: Enabling new mobile applications with location proofs. In: Proceedings of HotMobile 2009. ACM, Santa Cruz (2009)
30. Sastry, N., Shankar, U., Wagner, D.: Secure verification of location claims. In: Proceedings of WiSe 2003, pp. 1–10. ACM, San Diego (2003)
31. Schneider, F.B.: Enforceable security policies. ACM Trans. Inf. Syst. Secur. **3**(1), 30–50 (2000)
32. Sicari, S., Rizzardi, A., Grieco, L., Coen-Porisini, A.: Security, privacy and trust in internet of things: the road ahead. Elsevir Comput. Netw. J. **76**, 146–164 (2015)
33. Tandon, L., Fong, P.W.L., Safavi-Naini, R.: HCAP: a history-based capability system for IoT devices. In: Proceedings of SACMAT 2018. ACM, Indianapolis (2018)
34. Tarameshloo, E., Fong, P.W.L.: Access control models for geo-social computing systems. In: Proceedings of the 19th ACM Symposium on Access Control Models and Technologies (SACMAT 2014), London, Ontario, Canada, pp. 115–126, June 2014
35. Vilain, M., Kautz, H.: Constraint propagation algorithms for temporal reasoning. In: Proceedings of AAAI 1986, pp. 377–382. AAAI Press, Philadelphia (1986)
36. Wang, X., Pande, A., Zhu, J., Mohapatra, P.: STAMP: enabling privacy-preserving location proofs for mobile users. IEEE/ACM Trans. Netw. **24**(6), 3276–3289 (2016)
37. Yang, Y., Wu, L., Yin, G., Li, L., Zhao, H.: A survey on security and privacy issues in internet-of-things. IEEE Internet Things J. **4**(5), 1250–1258 (2017)
38. Zhang, Y., Wu, X.: Access control in internet of things: a survey. In: Proceedings of APTEC 2017, pp. 1544–1557. DEStech, Kuala Lumpur (2017)
39. Zhu, Z., Cao, G.: Applaus: a privacy-preserving location proof updating system for location-based services. In: Proceedings IEEE INFOCOM 2011, pp. 1889–1897 (2011)

Nighthawk: Transparent System Introspection from Ring -3

Lei Zhou[1,2], Jidong Xiao[3], Kevin Leach[4], Westley Weimer[4],
Fengwei Zhang[2,5(✉)], and Guojun Wang[6]

[1] Central South University, Changsha, China
[2] Wayne State University, Detroit, USA
{gn6392,fengwei}@wayne.edu
[3] Boise State University, Boise, USA
jidongxiao@boisestate.edu
[4] University of Michigan, Ann Arbor, USA
{kjleach,weimerw}@umich.edu
[5] SUSTech, Shenzhen, China
[6] Guangzhou University, Guangzhou, China
csgjwang@gzhu.edu.cn

Abstract. During the past decade, virtualization-based (e.g., virtual machine introspection) and hardware-assisted approaches (e.g., x86 SMM and ARM TrustZone) have been used to defend against low-level malware such as rootkits. However, these approaches either require a large Trusted Computing Base (TCB) or they must share CPU time with the operating system, disrupting normal execution. In this paper, we propose an introspection framework called NIGHTHAWK that transparently checks system integrity at runtime. NIGHTHAWK leverages the Intel Management Engine (IME), a co-processor that runs in isolation from the main CPU. By using the IME, our approach has a minimal TCB and incurs negligible overhead on the host system on a suite of indicative benchmarks. We use NIGHTHAWK to check the integrity of the system software and firmware of a host system at runtime. The experimental results show that NIGHTHAWK can detect real-world attacks against the OS, hypervisors, and System Management Mode while mitigating several classes of evasive attacks.

1 Introduction

Security vulnerabilities [28] that enable unauthorized access to computer systems are discovered and reported on a regular basis. Upon gaining access, attackers frequently install various low-level malware or rootkits [2] on the system to retain control and hide malicious activities. While many solutions target different specific threats, the key ideas are similar: the defensive technique or analysis

---

L. Zhou—Work was done while visiting COMPASS lab at Wayne State University.

K. Sako et al. (Eds.): ESORICS 2019, LNCS 11736, pp. 217–238, 2019.
https://doi.org/10.1007/978-3-030-29962-0_11

gains an advantage over the attacker by executing in a more privileged context. More specifically, to detect low-level malware, virtualization-based defensive approaches [20, 21] and hardware-assisted defensive approaches [5, 27, 32, 46] have been proposed. However, both approaches come with inherent limitations.

Limitations in Virtualization. Virtualization-based approaches require an additional software layer (i.e., the hypervisor) to be introduced into the system, resulting in two problems. First, virtualization can incur significant performance overhead. While CPU vendors and hypervisor developers have worked to improve the performance of CPU and memory virtualization, the cost of I/O virtualization remains high [25]. Second, and more importantly, mainstream hypervisors have a large trusted computing base (TCB). Hypervisors such as Xen or KVM contain many thousands of lines of code in addition to the millions of lines present in the control domain. Thus, while virtualization has facilitated significant defensive advances in monitoring the integrity of a target operating system, attackers in such systems can target the hypervisor itself. By exploiting vulnerabilities in the large TCB of the hypervisor, attackers can escape the virtualized environment and wreak havoc on the underlying system.

Limitations in Hardware. Hardware-assisted approaches are not burdened by large TCBs. However, to provide a trustworthy execution environment, hardware-assisted approaches typically require either (1) an external monitoring device or (2) specialized CPU support for examining state such as Intel System Management Mode (SMM). The former, seen in Copilot [32], Vigilare [27], and LO-PHI [37], typically use a co-processor (on a PCI card or an SoC) that runs outside of the main CPU. Such a requirement increases costs and precludes large-scale deployment. The latter, seen in HyperSentry [5], HyperCheck [48] runs code in SMM and monitors the target host system. While it does not require any external devices, code running in SMM can disrupt the flow of execution in the system. Running code in SMM requires the CPU to perform an expensive context switch from the OS environment to SMM. This switch suspends the OS and application execution until the SMM code completes, that is benefit for static analyzing the current host running state. But this suspension of execution results in abnormalities (e.g., lost clock cycles) that are detectable from the OS context. Attackers can measure and exploit such abnormalities so as to escape detection or hide malicious activities.

To address the limitations of current approaches, we present NIGHTHAWK, a framework leveraging the Intel Management Engine (IME). While the IME is intended as an advanced system management feature (e.g., for remote system administration of power and state), in this work, we leverage the IME to construct a system introspection framework which is capable of efficiently checking the integrity of critical kernel and hypervisor structures and system firmware. To the best of our knowledge, this is the first paper to consider using the IME for such application. Our proposed framework offers the following advantages in comparison to previous work:

- **No extra hardware required.** The IME has been integrated in virtually every Intel processor chipset since 2008. Therefore, the proposed framework can be deployed in most current commercially-available Intel-based computer systems without requiring external peripheral support.
- **High privilege.** As a co-processor running independently from the main CPU, the IME has a high privilege level in a computer system.[1] The IME has unrestricted access to the host system's resources, making it suitable for analyzing the integrity of the underlying operating system, hypervisor, or firmware.
- **Small TCB.** The IME runs a small independent Minix 3 OS distribution. As Minix 3 uses a microkernel architecture, it contains only thousands of lines of kernel code (cf. millions of lines of code in modern hybrid architecture systems like Linux or Windows). The reduced size of code results in a decreased trusted code base.
- **Low overhead.** Since the IME runs in an isolated co-processor, executing code in the IME does not disrupt the normally-executing tasks on the main CPU and does not compete for resources with the underlying OS. Thus, code executing in the IME incurs very little overhead on the target system.[2]
- **Transparency.** In addition to low overhead, the isolation of the IME means that the host OS are not aware of code executing in the IME. This allows transparent analysis of the host system from the IME.

We apply our prototype to several indicative experiments in which we verify the integrity of (1) kernel code, (2) virtualization system core code, and (3) System Management RAM. Our experimental results show that NIGHTHAWK is able to detect real-world rootkits, including kernel-level rootkits and SMM rootkits, and incurs minimum performance overhead on the target system. Our main contributions are:

- We present NIGHTHAWK, a novel introspection framework that transparently checks the integrity of the host system at runtime. We leverage the Intel Management Engine, an extant co-processor that runs alongside the main CPU, enabling a minimal TCB and detection of low-level system software attacks while incurring negligible overhead.
- We demonstrate a prototype of NIGHTHAWK that can detect real-world attacks against operating system kernels, Xen and KVM hypervisors, and System Management RAM. Furthermore, NIGHTHAWK is robust against page table manipulation attacks and transient attacks.
- NIGHTHAWK causes low latency to verify the integrity of critical data structures. Our results show that NIGHTHAWK takes 0.502 s to verify the integrity of the system call table (4 KB) of the host operating system. This low latency results in a small system overhead on the host.

---

[1] Expanding on Intel's privilege rings, userspace applications are said to have ring 3 privilege while the kernel has ring 0 privilege. The IME is said to have ring -3 privilege [12,40].

[2] Cache contention and bus bandwidth limits may incur overhead.

2   Background

We introduce the Intel Management Engine and System Management Mode.

Intel Management Engine: The Intel Management Engine is a subsystem which includes a separate microprocessor, its own memory, and an isolated operating system [13]. The IME has been integrated into Intel x86 motherboards since 2008 and was frequently used for remote system administration. Once the system is powered on, the IME runs in isolation, and its execution is not influenced by the host system on the same physical machine. To contact with isolated IME from host system, Intel designed the Host Embedded Controller Interface (HECI, also called Management Engine Interface) to secure exchange data between host memory and IME. Note that some other chipsets integrated co-processors, like the Intel Innovation Engine [16], also have the similar features, but are designed for special platforms (e.g., Data Center Servers) rather than for ordinary computers. Thus, in this paper, we build our introspection framework based on the IME rather than the Innovation Engine.

System Management Mode: System Management Mode (SMM) is a highly privileged execution mode included in all current x86 devices since the 386. It is used to handle system-wide functions such as power management or vendor-specific system control. SMM is used by the system firmware, but not by applications or normal system software. The code and data used in SMM are stored in a hardware-protected memory region named SMRAM. Under normal operation, SMRAM is inaccessible from outside of SMM unless configured otherwise (i.e., if SMRAM is unlocked). SMM code is executed by the CPU upon receiving a system management interrupt (SMI), causing the CPU to switch modes to SMM (e.g., from protected mode). The hardware automatically saves the CPU state, including control registers like CR3, in a dedicated region in SMRAM. After executing SMM code, the CPU state is restored and it resumes execution as normal. We use SMM in tandem with the IME to transparently gather accurate data from a system, even when it is compromised.

3   Threat Model and Assumptions

In this work, we assume the operating system, the hypervisor, and even SMM are not trusted. In contrast, due to its isolation and small TCB, we favor deploying security-critical software in the IME. We use this environment to run our code and introspect activities occurring in the operating system, the hypervisor, and SMM. Additionally, we assume an attacker does not have physical access to the machine. We assume that we start with a trustworthy firmware image (i.e., BIOS) so that we can reliably insert our IME introspection code. We assume the booting process of the Intel TXT [18] is trusted. We assume SMM could be compromised via a software vulnerability at runtime. However, attacks against SMM due to architectural bugs like cache poisoning [44] are out of scope because such attacks can be mitigated with official patch [45]. We assume the hardware can be trusted to function normally (e.g., hardware trojans are out of scope).

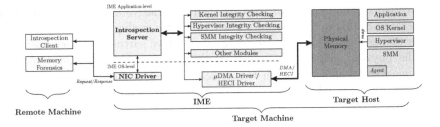

Fig. 1. High level architecture of the NIGHTHAWK. The user operates a Remote Machine to interact with the Target Machine. We place custom IME code on the Target Machine, consisting of an Introspection server and several Integrity Checking Modules. When the user invokes an integrity checking command, the server dispatches the corresponding Integrity Checking Module, which in turn creates a communication channel with the Target Host's physical memory using either μDMA or HECI. We place custom SMM "Agent" code on the Target Host. The SMM Agent is capable of basic introspection to recover critical data structures, which can be transmitted to the IME using the same μDMA/HECI channel. The Introspection Server can transmit the resulting data back to the Remote Machine for analysis or forensics.

4 System Architecture

In NIGHTHAWK, we leverage the IME to transparently monitor the integrity of the target system's memory (i.e., code and data) belonging to the kernel, any hypervisor present, and SMRAM. When an integrity violation is detected, our IME code asserts that an attack has occurred. Our system consists of a *Target Machine*, which we seek to protect, and a *Remote Machine*, which is used to interact with the Target Machine. An overview of NIGHTHAWK is shown in Fig. 1, we then describe those key roles in more detail.

Target Machine: It represents the potentially vulnerable system we want to analyze and protect. The Target Machine contains both the IME and an underlying Target Host (e.g., operating system or hypervisor). We use the IME as the key component in NIGHTHAWK to transparently introspect the Target Machine's physical memory. An Introspection Client, which is deployed on the Remote Machine, allows the user to send introspection commands to the Target Machine's IME. An Introspection Server on the Target Machine's IME then processes these commands. The Introspection Server invokes an analysis module on behalf of the Remote Machine. In this paper, we implemented three integrity checking modules: (1) kernel, (2) hypervisor, and (3) SMM. Each module corresponds to a particular class of attack that may occur against the Target Machine.

When the Introspection Server processes a command from the Client, we initialize the corresponding module and acquire the Target Host's memory. We use μDMA to access the host's memory. By design, μDMA only understands physical addresses, so we bridge the semantic gap to understand the Host's high-level abstractions (i.e., virtual memory addresses). We perform some initial reconnaissance on the Target Host's memory—we collect virtual memory addresses of some critical kernel/hypervisor data structures to derive a mapping to physical addresses. In SMM, we first build a SMRAM static configuration map for comparison at runtime. This map allows us to retrieve virtual memory addresses from the physical memory regions we acquire via μDMA. Next, we create a communication channel between the Target Machine's physical memory space and the IME's external memory space by using μDMA and HECI. This channel enables transferring critical data structures (e.g., the system call table, a hypervisor's kernel text, and saved architectural state) to the IME. Afterwards, each integrity checking module is able to locate relevant data structures in the IME's external memory space and perform integrity checking.

Remote Machine: It serves as a way for a user to remotely access the Target Machine and assess its integrity transparently. More specifically, the Remote Machine implements a simple Introspection Client that allows access to the Target Machine's IME remotely. Users can issue commands using the Introspection Client, and receive results from the Target Machine's IME. We implement several commands that are usable by the Introspection Client, including fetching segments of kernel memory for verification. We also implement a Memory Forensics Helper for dumping memory images to the Remote Machine for offline analysis. Due to the resource-constrained nature of the IME processor, it is more efficient to dump memory from the Target Machine and use the Remote Machine to perform more computationally-expensive analyses. Users can develop more complex memory forensic analysis helper based on their needs.

Both the Introspection Client and the Memory Forensics Helper work in tandem to communicate with the IME on the Target Machine. Rather than developing a custom communication protocol, we rely on the existing IME remote management protocol [42], which is a RESTful HTTPS protocol for remote management tasks. We reverse-engineered the protocol to augment it with custom commands used by our integrity checking code.

Integration: To summarize, we seek to protect a Target Machine from malicious attacks using the IME. We use custom IME code to implement integrity checking for the Target Machine's kernel, hypervisor, and SMM code and data. A user can interact with an Introspection Client to perform various integrity checking tasks. Because the IME enables transparent and low-overhead access to the Target Machine's physical memory, we can detect the presence of advanced attacks by leveraging a combination of integrity checks and introspection.

5 Implementation

In this section, we describe implementation details pertinent to our prototype of NIGHTHAWK. We embedded custom IME firmware on the Target Machine to transparently acquire the Target Host memory with low overhead. Loosely, there are two main parts of the implementation: (1) preparing the Target Machine with custom IME firmware, and (2) interacting with the Target Machine's IME at runtime (Fig. 2).

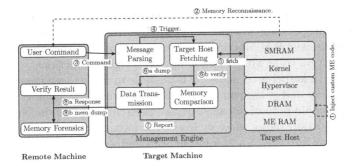

Fig. 2. High-level overview of the implementation. Following the numbered arrows, we (1) inject custom code into the IME on the Target Machine, and (2) acquire physical addresses of critical data structures. Next, the user (3) issues commands to the Introspection Server, which (4) triggers the corresponding command. (5) the IME uses μDMA and a modified HECI channel to fetch the target data from the Target Host and SMM memory. Depending on the command, the resulting memory is either (6a) dumped to the Remote Machine or (6b) checked locally for integrity. If applicable, (7) the integrity is checked with respect to a clean version of memory. Finally, the result is (8) transmitted back to the Remote Machine.

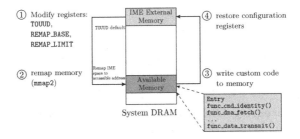

Fig. 3. Custom IME code injection. First, we configure system registers (TOUUD, top of upper usable memory, REMAP_BASE, and REMAP_LIMIT in step 1) to map the IME external memory to a userspace-accessible region of memory (step 2). We write custom instructions to that region (step 3), then restore the configuration registers (step 4).

5.1   Preparing the Target Machine

The Intel Management Engine is a secret system developed by Intel, one except vendors expanding IME functions should be a hard challenge. With several previous ME related research works [12,31,40], we adopt the memory-remapping approach taken by Tereshkin and Wojtczuk [40]: essentially, the external IME RAM is configured to be accessible by the Target Host by configuring several system registers that influence memory mapping. The workflow is shown in Fig. 3. In practice, developers can work with vendors to deploy custom IME code that does not require such a workaround. SMM can be protected in a similar way.

Since we directly get the runtime IME memory data but not open-source of IME code, we first reverse engineer the ME code with assembly instruction set (chipset-dependent, and ARCompact [39] in testbed). Next, we trigger the remote command to run related thread in the target machine's IME, we then debug each corresponding functions and analyze the branch instructions (i.e., *bl*) to address the suitable functions and positions for introspection. Finally, we insert introspection code while maintaining the original functions.

However, with kernel-level access, it is possible to reuse those memory control registers to remap and subsequently alter the IME-reserved memory region and SMRAM. This could potentially allow attackers to compromise the NIGHTHAWK. To close the injection vector after we insert the introspection code into the IME and SMRAM, we implement a lock mechanism on those memory control register by leveraging Intel TXT [18] with the follow operations.

1. We pre-install Trusted Boot [41] (TBoot), a booting module based on Intel TXT Technology to perform a measured and verified launch of an OS kernel/VMM. We can configure the TBoot to lock the memory control registers.
2. We configure the bootloader to use TBoot to boot the Linux kernel, then restart the target machine from remote server with an IME based remotely reboot instruction.

After rebooting, the custom IME and SMM code remains intact because booting into TXT mode prevents memory control registers from being modified.

5.2 Target Host Reconnaissance

In this subsection, we describe challenges associated with verifying the integrity of kernel, hypervisor, and SMM code and data, the solutions we chose, and how these solutions mitigate certain attacks.

Static Kernel Integrity Checking. The static kernel segments include both OS and Hypervisor kernel code and data. Typically, kernel code and several key data structures such as the system call table and the interrupt descriptor table do not change during runtime, but attackers might modify these structures, violating the kernel's integrity. To monitor kernel integrity, we use the system symbol table like System.map to gather crucial virtual addresses. System.map is a map from kernel symbols to virtual addresses. We can then obtain that symbol's physical address, which resides at a fixed offset away from its virtual address.[3] We use this approach to find physical addresses of several critical structures, including the system call table, the interrupt descriptor table, the kernel code and data segments, and (when applicable) hypervisor modules.

SMM Integrity Checking. Unlike the kernel or the hypervisor, accessing SMM memory is less straightforward. SMM code is stored in and executes from the System Management RAM (SMRAM), which is an isolated address space. This isolation feature can be locked or unlocked through configuring special register in the BIOS to protect access after booting. If SMRAM is unlocked, we can measure the integrity directly via the μDMA channel. However, even if SMRAM

---

[3] While this offset can be system-dependent, in most Linux setups, kernel virtual addresses are 0xc0000000 bytes from the corresponding physical address.

is locked, we implement a secure communication channel between the IME and SMM. Since HECI is an unique interface designed to communicate between the IME and host, we reuse the related HECI registers to create a channel between the IME and SMM. Atop this channel, we add code to check the integrity of both SMM-related code and register values. We can communicate this information from SMM over the HECI channel, at which point we can verify results within the IME. This approach enables transparent and rapid evaluation of SMM code and data even when the target machine is compromised.

Mitigating Attacks. NIGHTHAWK is co-processor based approach that suffers from the address translation redirection attack (ATRA) [19] and transient attacks [27,48]. However, NIGHTHAWK is able to detect these attacks. For ATRA attacks, first, we store a clean copy of kernel page table by accessing the symbol `swapper_pg_dir` at kernel initialization stage. Second, we obtain the CR3 register value by leveraging SMM (SMRAM is protected by SMM integrity checking). Thus, the binding between the virtual and physical memory addresses can be verified in the IME subsystem. For transient attacks, NIGHTHAWK works in an independently environment with little introspecting trace. Compared to the SMM-based monitoring approaches like HyperCheck [48] and HyperSentry [5], introspection interval of NIGHTHAWK becomes more harder to be gleaned by attackers. Moreover, the code in the IME can run *continuously* without halting the target OS, and thus attackers cannot predict when a memory page will be checked.

5.3   Measuring Integrity via Custom IME

Next, we discuss the introspection workflow in NIGHTHAWK. As the IME is intended for remote administration, it contains basic networking code. We reverse-engineered our IME firmware to find these networking functions that could be reused by our injected IME code. The injected code is composed with list of introspected object structures and checking functions. Essentially, we modified the IME code to perform introspection activities in response to requests sent from the Introspection Client on the remote machine. The workflow consists of four steps, shown in Fig. 4.

1. When the target machine receives a network command, it is received by the remote machine in the `recv_cmd()` function. Then, `msg_parse()` determines which integrity checking operation it needs to perform.
2. Next, we fetch the specified target data. We use a μDMA channel between the Target Host and the IME to fetch the specified data from memory. If the target data is from locked SMRAM, `data_fetch()` creates the HECI channel between the IME and SMM.
3. After fetching, NIGHTHAWK compares the hash value of the fetched memory with the original version established during boot in the IME system.
4. After comparison, `data_transmit()` transfer the results to the remote machine for continue analyzing.

Next, we discuss key aspects of the introspection workflow.

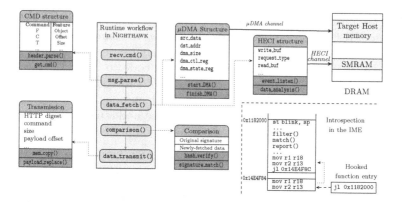

Fig. 4. The introspection workflow in the IME. We reverse-engineered the locations of several network-related functions in the existing IME code on our Target Machine. We added code to include custom commands to support our main goal of checking the integrity of the Target Host.

μDMA based Memory Fetching. NIGHTHAWK uses the μDMA engine to access the Target Host's physical memory from the IME. Our prototype's chipset [17] supports configuration of four μDMA channels (i.e., we can have four memory requests in-flight simultaneously). We use a number of auxiliary registers to control the size, direction, and other properties of the μDMA request. First, we write certain structures (e.g., the source and destination addresses) to auxiliary registers so as to engage the μDMA engine to automatically retrieve portions of the Target Host's physical memory. Then, the μDMA engine automatically stores the requested memory content in an IME-designated location. Once the function has acquired the specified amount of data, the μDMA request stops. Note that, in some special case like ATRA attack defense, we get the CR3 value first by leveraging SMM, and then fetch the corresponding memory page.

Checking Runtime SMRAM. For unlocked SMRAM, we directly access the memory through μDMA and check the integrity in the IME. For locked SMRAM, NIGHTHAWK introspects the SMRAM through the cooperative HECI channel. In the IME, we add a static SMRAM configuration during the initialization stage, which includes the SMM code and the original value for each SMM register (e.g., SMBASE – 0xa0000). In SMM, we add two main functions: First, we use the SDBM hash algorithm [29] to calculate the integrity of SMRAM code, and we check the values of SMM-related registers at runtime. This helps us defend against attacks that attempt to change the SMM configuration or otherwise alter SMRAM. Second, we establish a communication channel between the IME and SMM by configuring a number of HECI Host registers: H_CBRW (Host Circular Buffer Read Window), H_IG (Host Interrupt Generate), and H_CSR (Host Control Status). In particular, writing to H_IG generates an interrupt to the IME. This HECI-based communication channel can pass data from SMM to the IME to check SMM code and data.

5.4   Remote Machine

We discuss how the Introspection Client interacts with the Target Host. There are two main functions implemented on the remote machine: information collection and transparent introspection of Target Host. The remote machine initiates a request over the network to begin introspecting the Target Host. Once the Target Host is initialized, a communication channel is established to collect memory address information, including symbol names, addresses, sizes, etc. from the target machine. The collected information is transmitted to the remote machine for later use. After this initiation, the introspection session can begin. The remote machine interacts with the target machine in three scenarios:

- First, system administrators set the IME username and password for secure login. The remote machine supplies credentials for user authentication to create a secure channel with target machine.
- Second, remote machine sends the introspection command following the developed small custom protocol, shown in Table 6 in Appendix. Moreover, the communication is encrypted via a session key established at runtime.
- Third, the remote machine receives responses to commands from the target machine. There are two types of response: integrity verification and forensic analyses. Integrity verification is processed in the IME system, thus the response would be a Boolean result indicating whether the integrity was violated. Memory forensic analyses are offloaded to the remote machine, so the response contains a large memory dump.

6   Evaluation

Our experimental environment consists of two physical machines: the target machine, with a 3.0 GHz Intel E8400 CPU, ICH9D0 I/O Controller Hub, and 2 GB RAM. An Intel e1000e Gigabit network card is integrated in the Intel DQ35JO motherboard. The BIOS version is JOQ3510J.86A.0933. For kernel integrity testing, the target machine runs Ubuntu with Linux kernel versions 2.6.x to 4.x. For hypervisor integrity testing, both Xen 4.4 and KVM 2.0 are used. The remote machine runs Microsoft Windows 10 with WireShark [7] installed for network packet monitoring. In this section, we evaluate NIGHTHAWK from two aspects: *effectiveness* (i.e., does our system detect the presence of real-world threats?) and *efficiency* (i.e., does our system incur a low overhead?).

6.1   Effectiveness

We measure effectiveness by introspecting the Linux kernel, hypervisor, and SMM, as well as detecting ATRA and transient attacks.

Kernel Integrity Verification. We consider 5 real-world kernel rootkits, shown in Table 1, which fall into two categories:

Table 1. The effectiveness of NIGHTHAWK introspection.

Type	Attacked object	Attacks [1,2,9]	Detected
OS kernel	system call table	benign	✗
	kernel _text	*pusezk*	✓
	kernel _data	*Diamorphine*	✓
	IDT_table		
	page directory entry	*kbeast*	✓
	page table entry	*amark*	✓
		adore-ng	✓
		manual modification	✓
Hypervisor	kvm.ko	benign	✗
	kvm_intel.ko	*pusezk*	✓
	Xen kernel _text	*Diamorphine*	✓
	_stext _etext	*kbeast*	✓
	hypercall_page		
	IDT_table	*amark*	✓
	page directory entry	*adore-ng*	✓
	page table entry	manual modification	✓
SMM	SMRAM	benign	✗
		SMM reloaded	✓
		manual modification	✓

- System call table modification. Rootkits with kernel-level privilege can write to this table by manipulating the control register CR0. 4 of our 5 rootkits belong to this category: **Pusezk**, **Diamorphine**, **amark**, and **Kbeast** [2].
- Function pointer modification. For this category, we choose **adore-ng** [1]. **adore-ng** hooks the virtual file system interface to subvert normal detection. For example, to hide a malicious process, it redirects the iterate pointer in a kernel data structure `proc_root_operations` so that the malicious process will not be displayed in the `/proc` file system.

In addition to these real-world kernel rootkits, we also manually and randomly modify kernel memory pages in the kernel text and data segments.

Hypervisor Integrity Verification. In addition to installing our 5 rootkits in a Xen system, we also emulate hypervisor attacks in two ways. First, we modify the IDT, hypercall, and exception tables in a Xen system to represent a compromised Xen hypervisor. Second, we manually modify bytes in system memory of a KVM guest. In particular, we identify base addresses of KVM modules (`kvm.ko` and `kvm-intel.ko`), then randomly modify 5 bytes in these regions. These two approaches allow us to simulate an attacker that compromises the integrity of a Xen or KVM hypervisor.

SMM Integrity Verification. To demonstrate SMM integrity verification, we employ existing SMM attacks (i.e., the SMM Reload program [9]) to maliciously modify the SMI handler. We statically identify the RSM instruction that ends the SMI handler, and insert malicious instructions (e.g., `mov $x, %addr`) to simulate an attack that can modify arbitrary memory addresses. To detect these attacks, we verify memory pages in SMRAM (see Sect. 5.2 for details on acquiring this memory). We then compare their runtime states with their clean states, and we consider any discrepancy as an integrity violation. We can thus detect the existing and simulated SMM attacks described above.

ATRA Detection. We keep a clean copy of the kernel page table at system initialization stage through searching the *swapper_pg_dir* symbol. We use the CR3 value (acquired relying on SMM) to search for the corresponding physical page directory entry and page table entry via physical memory. In addition, we test the experiment when Page Global Directory and CR3 changed under Kernel Page Table Isolation (KPTI) mechanism and IDT based attack [19]. Finally, we compare the search data to determine if a change has been made. Our comparison results show that NIGHTHAWK can detect the trace of ATRA.

Transient Attack Detection. To detect transient attacks, we continuously scan kernel pages in the IME system. We install a rootkit based on toorkit [15], the rootkit is able to timing change the pointer address of the system call table which leads to attacker-controller system calls. The rootkit emulates a transient attack by quickly invoking `insmod` and `rmmod` in the Linux OS. We also modify the code to parameterize the attack time (i.e., the time elapsed between `insmod` and `rmmod`). We sweep the attack time from 3 ms to 700 ms, and run each configuration 20 times. Our results in Table 2 show that NIGHTHAWK can detect transient attacks if the attacking time is more than 700 ms. However, if the attacking time is less than 400 ms, the detection rate decreases linearly because NIGHTHAWK requires a certain amount of execution time. That said, our approach can detect many real transient system attacks [24,43], which remain in memory for seconds at a time. While attacks such as bus snooping [23] are fast enough to evade detection, they require physical access to the machine and are thus out of scope.

Table 1 shows our experimental results for kernel-, hypervisor-, and SMM-level attacks. The results indicate that the rootkits as well as our manual modification are detected by NIGHTHAWK. This demonstrates that NIGHTHAWK is effective in monitoring the integrity of the OS kernel, the hypervisor, and SMM code. In addition, our experimental results also show that NIGHTHAWK detects ATRA and transient attacks.

6.2   Efficiency

The efficiency of NIGHTHAWK is mainly determined by the time cost of three logical operations: (1) data fetching, (2) integrity checking, and (3) data transmission. We measure the time consumed by each operation. For data fetching, we also measure its memory overhead, so that we can ascertain that NIGHTHAWK does not have noticeable impact on the target system.

Table 2. Transient attack detection.   **Table 3.** Time consumed by DMA.

Execution time (ms)	Attacks detected rate
< 8	<2.5%
12	7.5%
63	8.3%
123	22.5%
218	33.3%
437	68.3%
515	81.4%
643	92.1%
>700	100%

Object	Size (KB)	Time (s)
(General data)	1	0.258 ± 0.010
	4	0.261 ± 0.010
	64	0.267 ± 0.010
	256	0.387 ± 0.120
	2,048	3.06 ± 0.350
	3,096	4.67 ± 0.430
System call table	4	0.261 ± 0.010
Linux kernel	6,466	9.75 ± 1.300
Hypervisor	336	1.31 ± 0.130
IDT	1	0.258 ± 0.010
Swapper_pg_dir	4	0.263 ± 0.010
SMRAM (unlocked)	128	0.383 ± 0.120
Random	10,240	15.4 ± 3.920

6.2.1   DMA Fetching Overhead

We first measure the DMA data fetching operation. Regardless of whether introspection is performed on the IME or on the remote machine, each Target Host memory segment must first be fetched into the IME space via μDMA.

Table 3 illustrates the time consumed by using DMA fetching. When the size of DMA-transmitted memory is smaller than 64 KB, the time consumed is approximately 0.26 s. This is due to the DMA channel using 16 lines to access the DRAM in parallel, allowing 2^{16} bytes of data each time. When the size is larger than 64 KB, the time consumed is linear to the amount of DMA operations. To improve the DMA effectiveness, we enable 4 μDMA channels to parallelly fetch at most 256 KB target physical memory one time. The bottom half of Table 3 shows the time consumed retrieving specific segments.

Figure 5 shows the wall clock time to perform different memory dump fetching. While system_call_table, PDE, and PTE pages are all 4 KB blocks of memory, the overhead is lower for system_call_table analysis because it requires only one fixed-address request. In contrast, the overhead is higher for page table analysis because acquiring page tables requires resolving additional indirection (i.e., fetching CR3 and separate requests to follow PDEs and PTEs) which needs multiple μDMA operations. In our tests, we found that it took 0.815 s to fetch the PTE entries and 1.28 s to verify the page table.

Since the DMA operations from the IME and the Target Host share the same RAM, concurrent RAM accesses are inevitable in our system. During DMA transfer, the CPU is idle and has no control of the memory buses. We use the STREAM benchmark [26] to measure the performance degradation imposed on the target machine. We use the memcpy function in an infinite loop to keep the DMA fetching operation running. Figure 6 shows there are minimum differences in memory bandwidth with and without NIGHTHAWK introspection: most of the

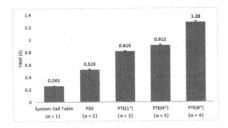

Fig. 5. Time consumed by fetching data. * represents the number of PTEs. α represents accessing times.

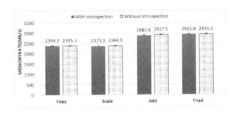

Fig. 6. Memory throughput degradation due to introspection.

time, the performance degradation is less than 0.2%, and even in the worst case (i.e., in the *Add* function test), the degradation is only 1.47%.

6.2.2 Integrity Checking Overhead

The second operation we measure is integrity checking. For each memory segment in question, we compute a hash value, and compare it with a pre-computed value supplied by the remote machine representing the clean state. Therefore, the time cost depends on the hash algorithm we choose. Recall for simplicity we chose to implement SDBM hashing [29]. Our test result shows that, to compute a hash value for a 4 KB memory page, the algorithm takes 7.3 ms. To verify the page table address, we simply compare each entry item in the table by value.

We only check the kernel page table, and at most 257 4 KB-size pages we need to compare—however, in practice about 10 pages suffice. Thus, compared to the fetching stage, the overhead for comparison is much lower—less than 2 ms each time.

6.2.3 Transmission Overhead

The third operation we measure is data transmission. In general, we send an introspection command from the remote machine and receive the verification result. We use one small message to pass the data ($< 1\,KB$), taking 228 ms on average. When considering a memory dump (i.e., $> 64\,KB$) to the remote machine, we divide the data into multiple packets and transmit them into multiple messages. We find that transmitting 64 KB data takes 4.9 s and that this duration grows linearly with the transmit size.

6.2.4 Efficiency Evaluation Summary

Overall, a typical introspection cycle contains the above three logical operations. Table 4 summarizes the time spent in each operation and in total. For instance, the system call table or the SMRAM (unlocked[4]), the introspection takes less than 1.5 s to acquire the integrity status.

---

[4] Even when SMRAM is locked, using our HECI-based communication channel, we incur roughly 17 ms to perform end-to-end integrity checking.

Table 4. The performance of the complete introspection about NIGHTHAWK.

Object	Size (KB)	Data fetching time (s)	Comparison time (s)	Data transmission time (s)	Total time (s)
System call table	4	0.26 ± 0.010	0.007 ± 0.001	0.224 ± 0.030	0.50 ± 0.030
kvm_intel.ko	336	1.31 ± 0.130	0.601 ± 0.010	0.231 ± 0.030	2.14 ± 0.150
PDE	4	0.52 ± 0.010	0.007 ± 0.001	0.230 ± 0.030	0.76 ± 0.040
SMRAM (unlocked)	128	0.39 ± 0.150	0.320 ± 0.005	0.228 ± 0.030	0.94 ± 0.200

7   Related Work

In this section, we survey the related work. Our research is mainly related to two categories of work: trusted execution environments, Intel ME.

Trusted Execution Environment. Trusted execution environments (TEEs) are intended to provide a safe haven for programs to execute sensitive tasks. We can use software- or hardware-based approaches to create TEEs.

Typically, software-based approaches leverage virtualization. Terra [14] runs applications with diverse security requirements in different virtual machines managed by a trusted Virtual Machine Monitor so that compromised applications do not interfere with others. Some hypervisor-based introspection approaches like SecVisor [34] can also provide a small TCB, but still incurs significant overhead, whereas NIGHTHAWK does not. In contrast, hardware-based approaches rely on different hardware features. KI-Mon [23] is a hardware-based DMA module and hash accelerator on the external SoC component used as an event-triggered kernel integrity monitor. GRIM [22] uses GPUs to check the kernel's integrity at high speed. TZ-RKP [4] is the representative work using ARM TrustZone to construct a TEE for OS kernel protection. HyperCheck [48] and HyperSentry [5] both employs Intel SMM to build a TEE and monitor hypervisor integrity. Chevalier *et al.* [6] proposed using a co-processor to monitor SMM code behavior, but it requires modifying the SMM code for instrumentation which is implemented with QEMU and simulation. In this paper, we build our TEE using the IME, and use it to monitor the host system.

Works on Intel ME. By design [33], the IME has full access to the system's memory, peripheral devices, and networks. Because of this high privilege, the IME has attracted attention from security researchers [35,36,38]. For example, to analyze the code in the IME, Sklyarov [35] proposed an SPI-based approach to fetch the IME firmware from the storage flash chip. In other work, Sklyarov [36] presented a static analysis approach in which he was able to distinguish the different functions in the IME via matching the signature of each code module. In addition, security vulnerabilities in the IME were also discovered [12,40]. Tereshkin *et al.* [40] proposed a memory remapping approach which enables the host CPU to access the IME memory. Ermolov *et al.* [12] revealed multiple buffer overflow vulnerabilities in the IME, which allows local users to perform a privilege-escalation attack and run arbitrary code. Due to the powerful but uncontrolled function in IME, some researchers [8,10,11,31] tried to disable the IME or confine its ability to interact with the host system, yet do not cause any disruption to the normal operation in the host system. In this paper, we demonstrate that defenders can leverage IME to introspect the host system.

8 Discussion

Security Issues: In our prototype, we implement NIGHTHAWK via code injection into the IME. It is possible to be compromised by new attacks despite mitigating the interface for code injection. The security arms race will persist, however the IME has a reasonably small TCB. NIGHTHAWK is able to defense the SMM attacks which intend to access the locked SMRAM by reconfiguring the SMM related registers. However, if the SMM code can be manipulated directly by attackers, SMM based functions like CR3 reading operation may not be trusted but we can defense it by integrating the work [6].

Other Kernel-Level Attacks: In our evaluation, if an attacker operates faster than the checking time required by NIGHTHAWK, we may not be able to detect it. To reduce the risk of transient attacks, we can reduce the integrity checking time. There are several optimizations we could make with additional engineering effort. Other kernel-level attacks like Direct Kernel Object Manipulation (DKOM) can also be detected by NIGHTHAWK by using similar approaches like Perkins *et al.* [30] with additional effort.

DMA Access: The introspection workflow in NIGHTHAWK leverages μDMA to fetch host memory. If the μDMA channel from the IME is blocked (e.g., by I/OMMU [3]), it will prevent NIGHTHAWK from reading the Target Host memory. Fortunately, I/OMMU can be configured to allow this access in the BIOS. Moreover, NIGHTHAWK is able to check the I/OMMU configuration similar to IOCheck [47]. Note that the IME accessing reserved 16MB memory at the top of DRAM does not go through the Intel VT-d remapping (i.e., I/OMMU implementation of Intel) [17], thus, I/OMMU cannot block IME from accessing its inner memory.

Performance: The performance of NIGHTHAWK heavily depends on the hardware design of the IME. In this paper, our testbed's IME suffered from low performance (Sect. 6.2) mainly due to a slow ME processor speed. However, this situation can be improved with a powerful chipset [12]. In addition, we reverse engineered our testbed's IME to inject code. This approach may not have resulted in the best performance (i.e., there may have been a higher-performance method of customizing IME code).

9 Conclusions

In this paper, we presented NIGHTHAWK, a transparent introspection framework for verifying the memory integrity of a Target Machine. It leverages Intel ME, an existing co-processor running aside with the main CPU with ring -3 privilege, so that our approach has a minimal TCB, is capable to detect low-level system software attacks, and introduces minimal overhead. To demonstrate the effectiveness of our system, we implemented a prototype of NIGHTHAWK with two physical machines. The experimental results show that NIGHTHAWK is able to detect real-world attacks against OS kernels, Xen- and KVM-based hypervisors, and System Management RAM. The experimental results show NIGHTHAWK verifies the integrity of target host system with a low performance overhead.

Acknowledgments. Lei Zhou was supported by the China Scholarship Council at Wayne State University. This work is supported in part by the National Natural Science Foundation of China under Grant Number 61632009, the Guangdong Provincial Natural Science Foundation under Grant Number 2017A030308006.

A   Appendix: Intel ME

An overview of system components and the IME is shown in Fig. 7.

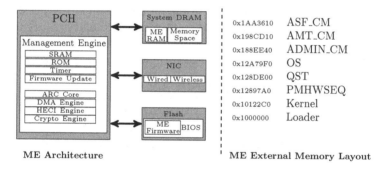

ME Architecture   ME External Memory Layout

Fig. 7. Overview of the IME. We use its isolation features to provide transparent system introspection capabilities. The left shows the IME in relation to other parts of a host system. The right shows the IME's memory layout on our prototype. Adapted from Ruan [33]

B   Appendix: Code added in Intel IME

Properties of our custom IME added code are shown in Table 5. All told, we wrote 400 lines of new C code and 270 lines of new assembly code, all of which fit in an IME firmware image less than 2 KB in size.

C   Appendix: Remote Communication Protocol

Here we present the details about remote communication protocol between remote server and IME in target machine.

Table 5. Introspection code added in custom IME firmware

Code section	Language	Size (# lines)
DMA fetching	C	210
Integrity checking	C	70
Introspection Server	C	120
IME injection	ASM	270

Table 6. Communication commands in NIGHTHAWK, each consisting of an operation and corresponding object. Any Command can be combined with any Object.

Command	Description	Object	Description
F	Fetch the physical memory from Target Host to the IME	SCT	The information about System Call Table
C	Compare the Target Host memory in the IME system	LK	The information about Linux Kernel
T	Transmit the introspection results from the IME to Remote Machine	HYP	The information about Hypervisor
D	Dump the Target Host memory from the IME to Remote Machine	SMM	The information about SMRAM

D   Appendix: Performance of the IME Core

We run experiments to investigate the computational capabilities of the IME. In particular, we develop a CPU speed testing benchmark, which we inject into the memcpy function in the IME. That is, this benchmark executes every time memcpy is invoked. The testing program is a nested-loop (inner loop: n, outer loop: m) function with 15 instructions in the inner loop such that $n \times m = 10^6$. We read the time stamp counter at the beginning and the end of the benchmark—denoted as T_1 and T_2, and thus approximate the average speed of the IME CPU using the formula $v \approx \frac{15 \times 10^6 \times (n \times m)}{(T_2 - T_1)}$. We sweep $n = 100, 200, ..., 10000$ and $m = 100, 200, 1000$; the experimental result shows that the IME CPU executes approximately 15 million instructions each second. Compared to the target system's main CPU (which can execute billions of instructions per second), the IME CPU has a significantly lower performance.

References

1. Adore-ng (2018). https://github.com/trimpsyw/adore-ng/
2. RootKits List (2018). https://github.com/d30sa1/RootKits-List-Download
3. Abramson, D., et al.: Intel virtualization technology for directed I/O. Intel Technol. J. **10**(3), 179–192 (2006)

4. Azab, A.M., et al.: Hypervision across worlds: real-time kernel protection from the arm trustzone secure world. In: Proceedings of the 2014 ACM SIGSAC Conference on Computer and Communications Security (CCS) (2014)
5. Azab, A.M., Ning, P., Wang, Z., Jiang, X., Zhang, X., Skalsky, N.C.: HyperSentry: enabling stealthy in-context measurement of hypervisor integrity. In: Proceedings of the 17th ACM Conference on Computer and Communications Security (CCS) (2010)
6. Chevalier, R., Villatel, M., Plaquin, D., Hiet, G.: Co-processor-based behavior monitoring: application to the detection of attacks against the system management mode. In: Proceedings of the 33rd Annual Computer Security Applications Conference (2017)
7. Combs, G.: Wireshark (2019). https://www.wireshark.org
8. Corna, N.: ME cleaner: tool for partial deblobbing of Intel ME/TXE firmware images (2017). https://github.com/corna/me_cleaner
9. Duflot, L., Levillain, O., Morin, B., Grumelard, O.: Getting into the SMRAM: SMM Reloaded. CanSecWest (2009)
10. Erica, P., Peter, E.: Intel's Management Engine is a security hazard, and users need a way to disable it (2017). https://www.eff.org/deeplinks/2017/05/intels-management-engine-security-hazard-and-users-need-way-disable-it
11. Ermolov, M., Goryachy, M.: Disabling Intel ME 11 via undocumented mode (2017). http://blog.ptsecurity.com/2017/08/disabling-intel-me.html
12. Ermolov, M., Goryachy, M.: How to Hack a Turned-Off Computer, or Running Unsigned Code in Intel Management Engine. Black Hat Europe (2017)
13. Gael, H.I.: Intel AMT and the Intel ME (2009). https://intel.com/en-us/blogs/2011/12/14/intelr-amt-and-the-intelr-me
14. Garfinkel, T., Pfaff, B., Chow, J., Rosenblum, M., Boneh, D.: Terra: a virtual machine-based platform for trusted computing. In: ACM SIGOPS Operating Systems Review (2003)
15. Github: ToorKit (2015). https://github.com/deb0ch/toorkit
16. Intel: Innovation Engine (2015). https://en.wikichip.org/wiki/intel/innovation_engine
17. Intel Corporation: Intel 3 Series Express Chipset Family (2007). https://www.intel.com/Assets/PDF/datasheet/316966.pdf
18. Intel Corporation: Intel Trusted Execution Technology (Intel TXT): Software Development Guide (2017). https://www.intel.com/content/dam/www/public/us/en/documents/guides/intel-txt-software-development-guide.pdf
19. Jang, D., Lee, H., Kim, M., Kim, D., et al.: Atra: address translation redirection attack against hardware-based external monitors. In: Proceedings of the 2014 ACM SIGSAC Conference on Computer and Communications Security (2014)
20. Jiang, X., Wang, X., Xu, D.: Stealthy malware detection through VMM-based out-of-the-box semantic view reconstruction. In: Proceedings of the 14th ACM conference on Computer and Communications Security (CCS) (2007)
21. Jones, S.T., Arpaci-Dusseau, A.C., Arpaci-Dusseau, R.H.: VMM-based hidden process detection and identification using Lycosid. In: Proceedings of the fourth ACM SIGPLAN/SIGOPS International Conference on Virtual Execution Environments (VEE) (2008)
22. Koromilas, L., Vasiliadis, G., Athanasopoulos, E., Ioannidis, S.: GRIM: leveraging GPUs for kernel integrity monitoring. In: Monrose, F., Dacier, M., Blanc, G., Garcia-Alfaro, J. (eds.) RAID 2016. LNCS, vol. 9854, pp. 3–23. Springer, Cham (2016). https://doi.org/10.1007/978-3-319-45719-2_1

23. Lee, H., et al.: KI-Mon: a hardware-assisted event-triggered monitoring platform for mutable kernel object. In: USENIX Security Symposium (2013)
24. Lipp, M., Schwarz, M., Gruss, D., Prescher, T., Haas, W., Fogh, A., et al.: Meltdown: reading kernel memory from user space. In: Proceedings of the 27th Conference on USENIX Security Symposium (2018)
25. Malka, M., Amit, N., Ben-Yehuda, M., Tsafrir, D.: rIOMMU: efficient IOMMU for I/O devices that employ ring buffers. In: ACM SIGPLAN Notices (2015)
26. McCalpin, J.D.: STREAM (2018). http://www.cs.virginia.edu/stream/ref.html
27. Moon, H., Lee, H., Lee, J., Kim, K., Paek, Y., Kang, B.B.: Vigilare: toward snoop-based kernel integrity monitor. In: Proceedings of the 2012 ACM Conference on Computer and Communications Security (CCS) (2012)
28. National Institute of Standards, NIST: National Vulnerability Database (2018). http://nvd.nist.gov
29. Partow, A.: General Purpose Hash Function Algorithms (2018). http://www.partow.net/programming/hashfunctions
30. Perkins, J.H., et al.: Automatically patching errors in deployed software. In: Proceedings of the ACM SIGOPS 22nd Symposium on Operating Systems Principles (2009)
31. Persmule: Neutralize ME firmware on SandyBridge and IvyBridge platforms (2016). https://hardenedlinux.github.io/firmware/2016/11/17/neutralize_ME_firmware_on_sandybridge_and_ivybridge.html
32. Petroni Jr, N.L., Fraser, T., Molina, J., Arbaugh, W.A.: Copilot-a Coprocessor-based Kernel Runtime Integrity Monitor. In: USENIX Security Symposium (2004)
33. Ruan, X.: Platform Embedded Security Technology Revealed: Safeguarding the Future of Computing with Intel Embedded Security and Management Engine. Apress (2014)
34. Seshadri, A., Luk, M., Qu, N., Perrig, A.: SecVisor: a tiny hypervisor to provide lifetime kernel code integrity for commodity OSes. In: Proceedings of the 21st ACM Symposium on Operating Systems Principles (SOSP) (2007)
35. Sklyarov, D.: Intel ME: flash file system explained. Black Hat Europe (2017)
36. Sklyarov, D.O.: ME: The Way of the Static Analysis. TROOPERS17 (2017)
37. Spensky, C., Hu, H., Leach, K.: LO-PHI: low-observable physical host instrumentation for malware analysis. In: NDSS (2016)
38. Stewin, P., Bystrov, I.: Understanding DMA malware. In: Flegel, U., Markatos, E., Robertson, W. (eds.) DIMVA 2012. LNCS, vol. 7591, pp. 21–41. Springer, Heidelberg (2013). https://doi.org/10.1007/978-3-642-37300-8_2
39. Synopsys: embARC (2019). https://embarc.org/embarc_osp/doc/build/html/arc/arc.html
40. Tereshkin, A., Wojtczuk, R.: Introducing ring-3 rootkits. Black Hat USA (2009)
41. The Fedora Project: TBoot (2018). https://sourceforge.net/projects/tboot
42. UPnP Forum: MeshCommander (2018). http://www.meshcommander.com/
43. Wei, J., Payne, B.D., Giffin, J., Pu, C.: Soft-timer driven transient kernel control flow attacks and defense. In: 2008 Annual Computer Security Applications Conference (ACSAC) (2008)
44. Wojtczuk, R., Rutkowska, J.: Attacking SMM memory via Intel CPU cache poisoning. Invisible Things Lab (2009)
45. Yao, J.: SMM Protection in EDK II (2017). https://uefi.org/sites/default/files/resources/Jiewen
46. Zhang, F., Leach, K., Stavrou, A., Wang, H., Sun, K.: Using hardware features for increased debugging transparency. In: 2015 IEEE Symposium on Security and Privacy (SP) (2015)

47. Zhang, F., Wang, H., Leach, K., Stavrou, A.: A framework to secure peripherals at runtime. In: Kutyłowski, M., Vaidya, J. (eds.) ESORICS 2014. LNCS, vol. 8712, pp. 219–238. Springer, Cham (2014). https://doi.org/10.1007/978-3-319-11203-9_13
48. Zhang, F., Wang, J., Sun, K., Stavrou, A.: Hypercheck: A hardware-assistedintegrity monitor (2014)

Proactivizer: Transforming Existing Verification Tools into Efficient Solutions for Runtime Security Enforcement

Suryadipta Majumdar[1](✉), Azadeh Tabiban[2], Meisam Mohammady[2],
Alaa Oqaily[2], Yosr Jarraya[3], Makan Pourzandi[3], Lingyu Wang[2],
and Mourad Debbabi[2]

[1] Information Security and Digital Forensics, University at Albany, Albany, USA
smajumdar@albany.edu
[2] Concordia Institute for Information Systems Engineering, Concordia University,
Montreal, Canada
{a_tabiba,m_ohamma,a_oqaily,wang,debbabi}@encs.concordia.ca
[3] Ericsson Security Research, Ericsson Canada, Montreal, Canada
{yosr.jarraya,makan.pourzandi}@ericsson.com

Abstract. Security verification plays a vital role in providing users the needed security assurance in many applications. However, applying existing verification tools for runtime security enforcement may suffer from a common limitation, i.e., causing significant delay to user requests. The key reason to this limitation is that these tools are not specifically designed for runtime enforcement, especially in a dynamic and large-scale environment like clouds. In this paper, we address this issue by proposing a proactive framework, namely, *Proactivizer*, to transform existing verification tools into efficient solutions for runtime security enforcement. Our main idea is to leverage existing verification tools as black boxes and to proactively trigger the verification process based on dependency relationships among the events. As a proof of concept, we apply Proactivizer to several existing verification tools and integrate it with OpenStack, a popular cloud platform. We perform extensive experiments in both simulated and real cloud environments and the results demonstrate the effectiveness of Proactivizer in reducing the response time significantly (e.g., within 9 ms to verify a cloud of 100,000 VMs and up to 99.9% reduction in response time).

Keywords: Proactive framework · Runtime security enforcement · Security verification

1 Introduction

Security verification has been playing an important role in protecting a wide-range of IT infrastructures mainly due to its capability of providing security guarantee in diverse environments (e.g., networking [13], cyber physical systems [42] and software programs [29]). However, there is a paradigm shift in the

© Springer Nature Switzerland AG 2019
K. Sako et al. (Eds.): ESORICS 2019, LNCS 11736, pp. 239–262, 2019.
https://doi.org/10.1007/978-3-030-29962-0_12

concept of security solutions especially after the wide-adoption of clouds [1,33]; where it is now essential to prevent a security breach to avoid its potentially unrecoverable damages and ensure continuous security guarantee; both of which can only be achieved through runtime security enforcement.

To that end, most existing security verification tools (e.g., [6,8,20,22,25,30, 39]) for the cloud fall short in dealing with the dynamic and large-scale nature of clouds and offering runtime security enforcement. Specifically, those tools may cause significant delay in responses at runtime. This is not surprising since those tools are not specifically designed for runtime security enforcement of a large-scale dynamic environment like clouds; which also implies that modifying those tools for this purpose can be difficult.

We further illustrate this limitation through a motivating example.

Motivating Example. The upper part of Fig. 1 shows the typical response time when several existing verification tools (e.g., declarative logic programming (Datalog) [19,30] and boolean satisfiability problem (SAT) [26], graph theory [6] and access control [20]) are utilized for runtime security policy enforcement, and highlights their common limitation. The lower part of the figure illustrates our key ideas to overcome that limitation, as detailed in the following.

- Even though these tools have been successful in diverse security applications, such as verifying virtual infrastructure [6,30] and virtual network [19,30], and enforcing access control policies [20,26] in the cloud, all of them may suffer from a common limitation, i.e., causing a significant delay (e.g., 15 s to four minutes), when applied to continuously protecting the cloud through runtime security enforcement [6,19,20,26,30].
- The complexity of those tools and the fact that they were not initially designed for runtime enforcement imply that it could require tremendous amounts of time and effort to modify those tools for efficient runtime enforcement.
- Alternatively, our key idea is to take a blackbox approach, and proactively trigger those tools based on predicted events, such that we will already have the verification results ready, when the actual events arrive (e.g., conducting verification of the `add network` event in advance as soon as the `create VM` event occurs).

More specifically, we propose a proactive verification framework, which considers those verification tools as blackboxes and transforms them into efficient solutions for runtime security enforcement. First, we develop a predictive model to capture various dependency relationships (e.g., probabilistic and temporal) to anticipate future events. Second, we design our proactive verification framework, namely, *Proactivizer*, with detailed methodology and algorithms. Third, as a proof of concept, we apply Proactivizer to several existing verification tools (i.e., Congress [30], Sugar [38], Weatherman [6] and Patron [20]), which adopt diverse verification methods, i.e., Datalog, SAT, graph-theoretic and access control, respectively. Fourth, we detail our implementation of the proposed framework based on OpenStack [31], and demonstrate how our system may be easily

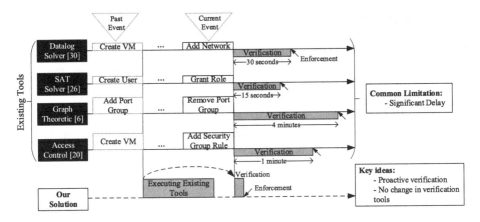

Fig. 1. Identifying the common issue in existing verification tools to offer runtime security enforcement and positioning our solution

ported to other cloud platforms (e.g., Amazon EC2 [2] and Google GCP [12]). Finally, we evaluate our solution through extensive experiments with both synthetic and real data. The results confirm our framework can reduce the response time of those verification tools to a practical level (e.g., within nine milliseconds for 85.8% of the time).

In summary, our main contributions are as follows.

– As per our knowledge, we are the first to propose a generic proactive framework to transform existing verification tools into efficient solutions for runtime security enforcement. The main benefit of this framework is that it requires little modification to those tools.
– By applying the Proactivizer framework to a diverse collection of existing verification tools (e.g., Datalog, Satisfiability solver, access control and graph theoretic solution), we demonstrate its potential as a low cost solution for improving the efficiency of other existing verification tools in a wide range of applications (e.g., IoTGuard [7] and TopoGuard [15,36]).
– As a proof of concept, we integrate our solution into OpenStack [31], a major cloud platform, and evaluate the effectiveness of our predictive model (e.g., up to 93% prediction accuracy) and the efficiency of our runtime security enforcement system (e.g., responding in maximum few milliseconds) using both synthetic and real data.

The remainder of the paper is organized as follows. Section 2 provides preliminaries. Section 3 presents our framework. Sections 5 and 6 provide the implementation details and experimental results, respectively. Section 7 discusses different aspects of this work. Section 8 summarizes related works. Section 9 concludes the paper.

2   Preliminaries

This section provides a background on dependency relationships (which will later be used to build predictive models in Sect. 3.2) and defines our threat model.

2.1   Dependency Relationships

We mainly consider three types of dependency relationships: structural, probabilistic and temporal. In the following, we explain them by taking cloud events as examples.

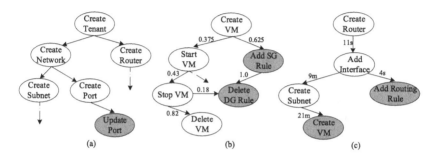

Fig. 2. Examples of (a) structural, (b) probabilistic, and (c) temporal dependency relationships among cloud events

Structural Dependencies. Figure 2(a) shows an example of structural dependencies in the cloud based on [23]. The structural dependency represents the relationships among cloud events, which are imposed by the cloud management platform (e.g., OpenStack [31]), e.g., a descendent node (or event) cannot occur before any of its ancestors.

Probabilistic Dependencies. Figure 2(b) shows an example of the probabilistic dependencies as proposed in [24]. The probabilistic dependency indicates the behavioral pattern of cloud events, e.g., the probability of occurrences of a descendent node depends on the occurrences of its ancestors.

Temporal Dependencies. Figure 2(c) shows an example of temporal dependencies. This dependency indicates the time intervals between occurrences of different events, e.g., a descendent node occurs with an average interval from the occurrences of its ancestors.

2.2   Threat Model

In the remainder of this paper, we will focus on cloud platforms. We assume that the cloud management platforms: (a) may be trusted for the integrity of the API calls, event notifications, and database records (existing techniques on trusted computing and remote attestation may be applied to establish a chain of trust from TPM chips embedded inside the cloud hardware, e.g., [3,16,34]), and (b) may have implementation flaws, misconfigurations and vulnerabilities that can be potentially exploited by malicious entities to violate security policies specified by cloud tenants. The cloud users including cloud operators and agents (on behalf of a human) may be malicious. Any threats directing from the cloud management operations is within the scope of this work. Therefore, any violation bypassing the cloud management interface is beyond the scope of this work. Also, our focus is not to detect specific attacks or intrusions, even though our framework may catch violations of specified security policies due to either misconfigurations or vulnerabilities. We assume that before our runtime approach, an initial verification is performed and potential violations are resolved. However, if our solution is added from the commencement of a cloud, obviously no prior security verification is required.

3   The Proactivizer Framework

This section presents the methodology of the Proactivizer framework.

3.1   Proactivizer Overview

Figure 3 shows an overview of our framework. There are three major steps of the Proactivizer framework: prediction, proactive verification and runtime enforcement. In Step 1 (detailed in Sect. 3.2), Proactivizer first extracts dependency relationships among cloud events from the historical data (e.g., logs), then builds a predictive model leveraging those dependencies and finally predicts future events utilizing the predictive model. In Step 2 (detailed in Sect. 3.3), to conduct proactive verification on the predicted future event, Proactivizer first prepares inputs related to that event for different verification tools, then executes those tools for verification and finally interprets the obtained verification results to prepare a watchlist (which is a list of allowed parameters for that future event). In step 3 (detailed in Sect. 3.4), for runtime security enforcement, Proactivizer intercepts critical events (which may cause potential violation of a security policy), then checks its parameters against the prepared watchlist and finally enforces the decision (e.g., allow or deny). In the following, we detail each step.

3.2   Prediction

This section illustrates the prediction steps using an example and then elaborates them.

Example 1. Figure 4 shows an example of three major steps of building the predictive model. First, Proactivizer extracts dependencies (e.g., transitions, frequencies and intervals) from the cloud logs. The transition, E1-E2, indicates that event E1 occurs before event E2. The corresponding frequency, 5, means

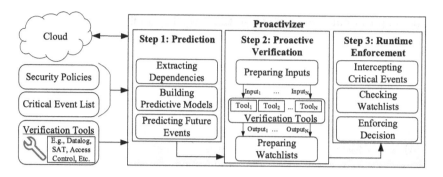

Fig. 3. A high-level overview of Proactivizer

that transition E1-E2 has appeared five times. The following interval, 553, says that event E2 occurs on average 553 s after the occurrence of event E1. Second, it builds the predictive model from those transitions; where the edge between events E1 and E2 indicates transition E1-E2, and the label on that edge, $f(p_1, t_1)$, is the prediction score (discussed later in this section) from the frequency (p_1) and interval (t_1). Third, it predicts critical events (E4 or E5) using this model. From the current event, E1, it predicts event E4 as a potential future event, because its prediction score, f_1, is greater than that of event E5 (f_2). In *Example 2*, we show how to conduct the proactive verification of event E4.

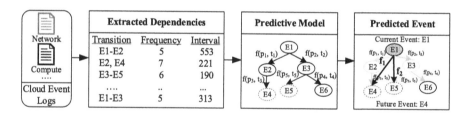

Fig. 4. An example of different steps of the Proactivizer prediction

Log Processing. The processing of logs is mainly to prepare the data to build the predictive model. We describe its major steps (which are mostly inspired by LeaPS+ [27]) as follows. First, we parse raw cloud logs and label all fields of each log entry. Second, we identify the event type (i.e., generic operation name) based on the cloud-platform API documentation. Third, we prepare the whole chain of identified events partitioned into transitions. Fourth, we obtain their frequencies and intervals. Finally, those transitions and their frequencies are utilized to obtain a probabilistic model (e.g., Bayesian network), which is then forwarded to build the predictive model. Note that Proactivizer periodically re-evaluates this Bayesian network for subsequent intervals.

Building the Predictive Model. Figure 5 shows the inputs and output of our time-series predictor [14]. The inputs are mainly the Bayesian networks obtained from the previous steps for different time periods, and the time intervals between event transitions. Then, we feed these intervals and the corresponding Bayesian network for a certain period to the time-series predictor for training. After the $(k-1)$th (where k is an integer number) step of training, we predict the conditional probability, $P_t(B|A)$, between events B and A at a given time t in the future. Thus, the predictor also measures the conditional probability for non-immediate transitions (e.g., $P_t(D|A)$). Our predictor follows a continuous training, part of which may update the value of $P_t(D|A)$ at the step $k+1$, and progressively updates the model. The effectiveness of our predictive model is evaluated in Sect. 6. We utilize this model to conduct the proactive verification as follows.

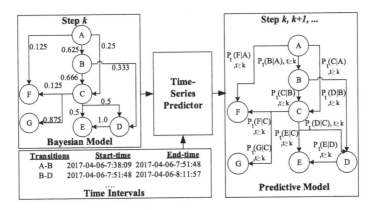

Fig. 5. An excerpt input/output of the time-series predictor

3.3 Proactive Verification

This section illustrates the proactive steps using an example and then elaborates them.

Example 2. Figure 6 shows different steps of our proactive verification for the predicted event (E4) in *Example 1*. First, Proactivizer prepares the inputs for different verification tools to verify the predicted event, E4, with the current event parameter, S1. To that end, it identifies policy P2 as one of the affected policies by critical event (CE) E4. Then, the input for tool $Tool_1$ is prepared to verify event E4 with parameter S1 against policy P2. Similarly, policies, $P3$ and $P27$, are prepared for tools, $Tool_2$ and $Tool_N$. Second, it executes verification tools, $Tool_1$, $Tool_2$ and $Tool_N$, to verify those policies (note that, while Proactivizer can support different tools at the same time, integrating many tools may inadvertently increase the system's complexity, which is why this feature is optional). Third, after the verification, Proactivizer interprets their outputs,

and conclude that none of these policies will be breached, if the E4 event with
the S1 parameter really occurs. Therefore, we add the parameters, S1, to the
watchlist of the event E4. Similarly, we can show that for another parameter
set, S3, the event E4 violates the policy P3 and hence, S3 is not added to the
watchlist; which is further illustrated in *Example 3*.

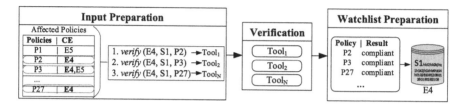

Fig. 6. An example of different steps of our proactive verification (where the predicted
critical event (CE) is E4 and current event parameter is S1)

Figure 7 shows the major steps of our proactive verification. The figure also
indicates the common steps for all verification tools that are integrated with the
Proactivizer framework, and tool-specific unique steps.

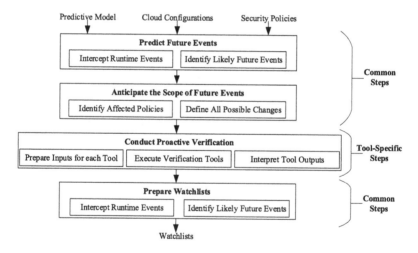

Fig. 7. The major steps of the proactive verification by the Proactivizer framework

Common Verification Steps. We elaborate on three major common steps as
follows.

– *Predicting Future Events.* This step is to predict the future events from the
current event using the predictive model (obtained in Sect. 2). To this end,
Proactivizer first intercepts each event request sent to the cloud platform and

obtains the detailed information (e.g., event type and its parameters). Second, it obtains the prediction scores (as discussed in Sect. 3.2) for each critical event from the intercepted event type. Third, it shortlists the predicted events which have greater prediction scores than the threshold (which is set by the users of Proactivizer).

- *Anticipating the Scope of Future Events.* This step is to anticipate the possible changes related to the predicted future event, as the event specifics (such as exact parameter values) are unknown at this point of time. To this end, Proactivizer first identifies the affected policies by that event from the list of security policies and corresponding critical events (as shown in Fig. 6). Second, it anticipates the possible parameters for the future events by considering all available values of those parameters from the current cloud configurations. These anticipated information will be later used by the tool-specific steps in Sect. 4.
- *Preparing Watchlists.* After the tool-specific steps (in Sect. 4), Proactivizer prepares the watchlist(s) from the verification results. Specifically, Proactivizer identifies the set of parameters for which a security violation is reported by any of the tools, and, includes the remaining anticipated parameters in the watchlist of the predicted event.

The tool-specific verification steps will be discussed in Sect. 4.

3.4   Runtime Security Enforcement

This step enforces security policies using the watchlists (obtained from the previous step) at runtime as follows. (a) It holds the event execution whenever a critical event has occurred. (b) It checks the parameters of the current event against its watchlists. (c) Proactivizer only allows (or recommends to pass) the execution of the current event, if the parameters are in the watchlists. Otherwise, it denies the request.

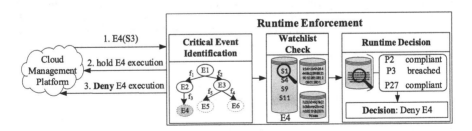

Fig. 8. An example of different steps of the Proactivizer runtime security enforcement

Example 3. Figure 8 shows an example of this step; where Proactivizer intercepts the critical event E4 with the parameter set, S3. First, Proactivizer identifies that E4 is a critical event, and hence, requests the cloud platform to hold the execution of the E4 event request. Second, it searches S3 in the watchlist of E4. The parameter set, S3, is not found in the watchlist, specifically, because S3 breached policy P3 in the previous step in *Example 2*. Finally, Proactivizer denies the current event request E4.

4   Proactivizer Applications

This section details the Proactivizer integration steps for three candidate applications.

4.1   Datalog-Based Security Verification

This section first provides the background on a Datalog-based security verification tool, namely, Congress [30], and then describes how we integrate Congress with Proactivizer.

Background. Congress [30] is an OpenStack [31] project to verify security policies for cloud infrastructures. Congress leverages declarative logical programming language (a.k.a. Datalog). We discuss its integration with Proactivizer as follows.

The Details of Congress Integration. The major steps of this integration are to prepare Congress inputs and interpret its verification results. To prepare its inputs, our one-time efforts are to express policies in the Datalog format and identify required data and their sources for each security policy. Then, the runtime efforts are to populate the policy with the current event parameters and execute Congress with the prepared inputs. After Congress finishes the verification, Proactivizer analyzes Congress outputs to identify the parameter values for which a policy will be breached before preparing the watchlist (as in Sect. 3.3). We further show the Congress integration using an example as follows.

Example 4. In this example, we consider a security policy (provided by Congress [30]), which states that *"every network connected to a VM must be either public or private and owned by someone in the same group as the VM owner"*. For this policy, the **add network** event is one of the critical events, and we store the allowed network ID for each VM on the watchlist. We first express this policy as in Congress's format:

$$\text{error}(\text{vm}) : -\text{nova} : \text{instance}(\text{vm}), \text{nova} : \text{network}(\text{vm}, \text{network}), \qquad (1)$$
$$\text{notneutron} : \text{public}(\text{network}), \text{nova} : \text{owner}(\text{vm}, \text{vmowner}),$$
$$\text{neutron} : \text{owner}(\text{network}, \text{netowner}), \text{notsame\_group}(\text{vmowner}, \text{netowner})$$
$$\text{same\_group}(x, y) : -\text{group}(x, g), \text{group}(y, g)$$
$$\text{group}(x, g) : -\text{keystone} : \text{group}(x, g)$$
$$\text{group}(x, g) : -\text{ad} : \text{group}(x, g)$$

For the explanation of this expression, we refer the readers to [30]. The data sources are the configurations from different services (e.g., Nova and Neutron) of OpenStack.

At runtime, the common steps in Sect. 3.3 provides the predicted event add network, the parameter of current event, VM1, and all the network IDs, N1, N2 and N3, for that tenant. As a part of the Congress-specific effort, Proactivizer updates the nova:network table on the simulated environment of Congress as if these three networks are added to the VM1 VM, and executes Congress to verify the above-mentioned policy. The result of Congress is formatted as error(VM1,N3), which indicates that adding network N3 to VM VM1 will violate the policy. Using this interpretation, the final common step (in Sect. 3.3) prepares the watchlist.

4.2   SAT-Based Security Verification

This section first provides the background on a satisfiability (SAT) solver, namely, Sugar [38], and then describes how we integrate Sugar with Proactivizer.

Background. Sugar [38] is a SAT solver, which expresses policies as a constraint satisfaction problem (CSP). If all constraints are satisfied, then Sugar returns SAT (which indicates a policy violation). We discuss its integration with Proactivizer as follows.

The Details of Sugar Integration. To prepare Sugar inputs, our one-time efforts are to express policies in the CSP format and identify the required data and their sources. Then, our runtime efforts are to populate that CSP policy with both current and predicted event parameters and execute Sugar to verify that policy. After the verification, Proactivizer interprets Sugar's outputs to prepare the watchlist to avoid any policy violation. We further show the Congress integration using an example as follows.

Example 5. For this example, we consider a security policy (provided by [26]), which states that *"a user must not hold any role from another domain"* (where domain is a collection of tenants). Here, the grant role event is a critical event, and the allowed roles are in the watchlist for each domain. Proactivizer first expresses the policy as:

$$(\text{and}\quad \text{BelongsToD}(u, d)\ \text{AuthorizedR}(u, t, r) \tag{2}$$
$$(\text{not}\quad \text{TenantRoleDom}(t, r, d)))$$

Here, u is the user, d is the domain, t is the tenant and r is the role. For the explanation of each constraint, we refer the readers to [26]. For this policy, we collect user, role, tenant and domain, from the identity management service (Keystone) of OpenStack.

At runtime, similarly as in *Example 4*, the predicted event is grant role, the current event parameter is u1 user ID and possible roles are r1, r2 and r3. Then, Proactivizer instantiates the policy in *Equation (2)* with each user-role pair, e.g., (u1, r1), (u1, r2) and (u1, r3), and executes Sugar to verify the policy. The result of Sugar provides the pair, (u1, r3), for which it gets a SAT result; which means that granting role r3 to user u1 will violate the policy, and hence, role r3 will not be added to the watchlist.

4.3   Access Control Policy Verification

This section first provides the background on an access control tool, namely, Patron [20], and then describes how we integrate Patron with Proactivizer.

Background. Patron [20] is an access control policy verification solution for clouds. To that end, Patron verifies each runtime event request against a list of access control policies defined by tenants. We discuss its integration with Proactivizer as follows.

The Details of Patron Integration. At runtime, Proactivizer expresses the predicted event in Patron's format, which includes event type, caller of an event and requested resources, and executes Patron to verify that event. After Patron's verification, Proactivizer checks Patron's decision to prepare the watchlist. We further explain this step using an example as follows.

Example 6. In this example, we consider a security policy stating that *"a tenant admin only can add security group rules to the VMs of the same tenant"*. At runtime, the predicted event is `add security group rule` and the caller of the current event is `tenant1-admin`. Proactivizer prepares the Patron inputs as: {input 1: {`add security group rule`, user: `tenant1-admin`, VM1} and input 2: {`add security group rule`, user: `tenant1-admin`, VM2}}. The results of Patron are {input 1: `allow`} and {input 2: `deny`}, respectively. Therefore, it only adds the VM1 to the watchlist.

5   Implementation

This section presents the high-level architecture of Proactivizer, and then details its integration into OpenStack [31], a popular cloud platform.

Architecture. There are five major components in our solution (Fig. 9). (i) The data collector collects logs and configurations from the cloud platform. (ii) The predictive model builder is mainly to build the predictive model using Bayesian network and time-series. (iii) The interceptor interacts with the cloud platform at runtime. (iv) The proactive verifier mainly provides the interface to plug various verification tools and builds watchlists. (v) The policy enforcement module enforces the runtime decision on the cloud platform. Algorithm 1 shows the functionalities of these modules.

Implementation Details. In the predictive model builder, to process raw logs, we first use Logstash [10], a data processing engine, and then utilize our own scripts to further obtain event sequences and their corresponding frequency and intervals. The resulted set of sequences is the input dataset to a Python Bayesian Network toolbox[1]. Afterwards, the obtained Bayesian networks are provided to a time-series predictor, ARMAX [14], which is a widely used method in prediction of stochastic processes in various fields.

---

[1] https://pypi.org/project/pgmpy/.

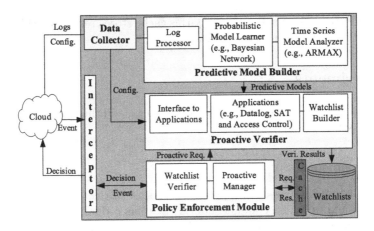

Fig. 9. A high-level architecture of our solution

Algorithm 1: Proactivize (*CloudOS, Policies, Tools*)

1: **procedure** BUILDPREDICTIVEMODEL(*Logs*)
2:    **for** each timePeriod $t_i \in T$ **do**
3:       $Sequence[]$ = identifySequence($Logs_{t_i}$)
4:       $bayesianNetwork$ = prepareBN($Sequence[]$)
5:       $predictiveModel$ = buildTimeSeriesModel($bayesianNetwork, Sequence[].interval$)

6: **procedure** INTERCEPTEVENT(*interceptedEvent , Policies*)
7:    **for** each policy $p_i \in Policies$ **do**
8:       **if** $interceptedEvent \in Policy.critical\text{-}events$ **then**
9:          $decision$ = verifyWL($interceptedEvent$)
10:          **return** $decision$
11:       **else**
12:          manageProactive($interceptedEvent$)

13: **procedure** VERIFYWL(*critical-event*)
14:    **if** $critical\text{-}event.params \in critical\text{-}events.WL$ **then**
15:       $decision=$ "allow"
16:    **else**
17:       $decision=$ "deny"
18: **procedure** MANAGEPROACTIVE(*interceptedEvent*)
19:    **for** each critical-event $c_i \in Policies.critical\text{-}events$ **do**
20:       $distance$ = measureDistance($predictiveModel, c_i, interceptedEvent$)
21:       **if** $distance = c_i.threshold$ **then**
22:          $policy[]=$affectPolicy(c_i)
23:          verifyProactive($c_i, interceptedEvent.params, policy[]$)

24: **procedure** VERIFYPROACTIVE(*critical-event, params, Policies*)
25:    **for** each policy $p_i \in Policies$ **do**
26:       $input$ = prepareInput (*Tools, p_i, critical-event, params*)
27:       $result$ = interpretResult(verify (*Tools, input*))

The interceptor is implemented as a middleware so that it intercepts each request to the OpenStack services (similarly as in [20,37]). The proactive verifier currently integrates three candidate applications (Congress [30], Patron [20] and Sugar [38]) with Proactivizer. The watchlists are mainly stored in a MySQL database. In addition, we implement a cache as memory-mapped file system (mmap) in Python (similarly as in [20]); this cache stores recent watchlist queries to accelerate the decision mechanisms.

6   Experiments

This section first explains our experimental settings, and then presents the results using both synthetic and real data.

6.1   Experimental Settings

Our testbed cloud is based on OpenStack version Mitaka. There are one controller node and up to 80 compute nodes, each has a dual-core CPU and 2 GB memory with the Ubuntu 16.04 server. Based on a recent survey [32] on Open-Stack, we simulate an environment with maximum 1,000 tenants and 100,000 VMs. There are four synthetic datasets, DS1–DS4, where we vary the number of VMs from 10,000 to 100,000 and number of tenants from 1,000 to 10,000, simultaneously. The synthetic dataset includes over 4.5 millions records. We further utilize data collected from a real community cloud hosted at one of the largest telecommunication vendors; which contains 1.6 GB text-based logs with 128,264 relevant entries (and 400 uniques records after processing) for the period of 500 days. We repeat each experiment at least 100 times.

6.2   Experimental Results

In the following, we present our experimental results.

Efficiency Improvement in Proactivizer Applications. The objective of the first set of experiments is to demonstrate the efficiency improvement resulted from the Proactivizer integration with different applications. Table 1 summarizes the response time of three candidate applications (i.e., Congress [30] (a Datalog solution), Patron [20] (an access control tool) and Sugar [38] (SAT solver)) before and after the integration with Proactivizer for four different datasets (DS1–DS4) and four different policies (P1–P4). The response time of those applications without the Proactivizer integrations results from five seconds to 103 s. On the other hand, after the Proactivizer framework integration, the response time of these tools remains within nine milliseconds. In summary, our framework significantly improves the response time of these tools (e.g., around 99.9% reduction on average). Furthermore, in Fig. 10, we compare the response time of incremental implementations of both Sugar [26] (Inc-Sugar) and Patron [20] (Inc-Patron) for different events with and without the integration of Proactivizer. Specifically, Fig. 10(a) shows that the response time of Sugar has been reduced to around 8 ms from 200 ms as an effect of Proactivizer. Figure 10(b) shows the similar nature of response time improvement in Patron. On average, Proactivizer reduces the response time of Inc-Sugar and Inc-Patron by 93.74% and 94.64%, respectively. We further check the effect of our cache implementation, and observe that the

Table 1. The response time before (in seconds) and after (in milliseconds) the integration of Proactivizer to Sugar (a SAT solver), Congress (a Datalog-based tool), and Patron (an access control tool) for the runtime security enforcement of different policies (P1, P2, P3 and P4) for different datasets, DS1-DS4. Here, P1: Common Ownership, P2: Minimum Exposure, P3: No Cross-Tenant Port and P4: No Bypass policies

Dataset	Proactivizer	Sugar[38]			Patron[20]		Congress[30]		
		P1	P2	P3	P1	P2	P2	P3	P4
DS1	Without (in s)	5.3	6.6	96.5	12.3	60.1	20.1	27.2	30
	With (in ms)	5.6	8.1	7.5	5.6	8.1	8.1	7.5	7.1
DS2	Without (in s)	6.5	7.2	102.3	15.9	67.1	21.1	29.2	35
	With (in ms)	5.8	8.2	7.8	5.8	8.2	8.2	7.8	7.4
DS3	Without (in s)	9.4	10.5	109.5	21.9	75.3	25.4	31.9	35.7
	With (in ms)	6.6	8.3	8.1	6.6	8.3	8.3	8.1	7.4
DS4	Without (in s)	15.3	16.4	118.7	29.5	87.9	30	34.2	39.1
	With (in ms)	6.8	8.3	8.2	6.8	8.3	8.3	8.2	7.4
Average improvement (%)		**99.93**			**99.97**		**99.96**		

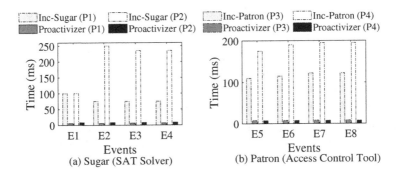

Fig. 10. The response time (in milliseconds) before and after the integration of Proactivizer for verifying (a) the Common Ownership (P1) and Minimum Exposure (P2) policies by Inc-Sugar (using SAT) and (b) the No Cross-Tenant Port (P3) and No Bypass (P4) policies by Inc-Patron (using access control) for different events and our largest dataset. Here, E1: grant role, E2: delete role, E3: delete user, E4: delete tenant, E5: create VM, E6: start VM, E7: add security group rule and E8: delete security group rule

response time can be reduced to even less than one millisecond (which is shown in Appendix B for the space constraint).

Effectiveness of our Predictive Model. The second set of experiments is to show the effectiveness of our predictive model in terms of prediction match/error and fitting to the real observation. Figure 11 shows a comparison between our predictive model (based on the ARMAX function) and the state-of-art dependency model (based on Bayesian network (BN)) [24] for different threshold values. Here, the prediction match rate refers to the percentage of time proactive

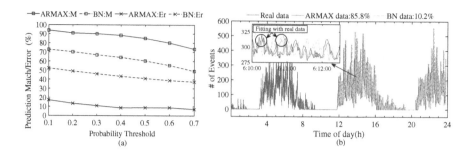

Fig. 11. Comparison between our predictive model using ARMAX and state-of-art dependency model (based on Bayesian network (BN)) [24] in terms of (a) the percentage of prediction match(M)/error(Er) (b) the percentage of fitting with the real data

verification results are useful, and the prediction error rate is its inverse. Specifically, Fig. 11(a) shows that our model ensures the best response time on average 85.8% of the time. In the best case, it can reach up to 93% of prediction match with selective threshold values. Figure 11(b) shows the superior fitting capability of ARMAX over BN; where we train the ARMAX model for 24 h and the resulted model is used in prediction for the next 24 h. As illustrated in the magnified window, both measurements in BN (dashed yellow lines) are lagging behind the real dataset (in blue). On the other hand, our trained ARMAX model (in red) can predict the time series more accurately (85% fit). These results strongly support the effectiveness of our ARMAX model.

Experiments with Real Cloud. We conduct similar experiments on the real data (Table 2). Due to the significantly smaller number of observations (i.e., 400 unique records), the ARMAX model shows less superiority (up to 65%) over Bayesian network and in few cases is inferior. The real effectiveness of our prediction model is shown through the relatively larger datasets (in Fig. 11).

Table 2. Effectiveness of ARMAX vs. Bayesian network for real data (with 400 records)

Probability threshold	0.4	0.45	0.5	0.55	0.6	0.65	0.7	0.75	0.8
ARMAX prediction match (%)	97.36	96.5	96.5	88.6	82.45	82.4	73.7	68.4	66.6
Bayesian network prediction match (%)	65	65.8	65.8	65.8	65.78	65.8	65.8	65.8	65.8
Improvement ratio (%)	48	46.6	46.6	65.8	34.6	25.3	12	4	1.3
ARMAX prediction error (%)	80.6	77.41	64.5	54.8	42	42	32.2	25.8	25.8
Bayesian network prediction error (%)	74.2	74.2	74.2	74.2	74.2	74.2	74.2	74.2	74.2
Improvement ratio (%)	−8.7	−4.3	13	26	43.5	56.5	65.2	65.2	78.2

Overall these results show that the response time with our framework can be less than one millisecond in the best case (with cache), and in the worst case (for an incorrect prediction), Proactivizer will have no effect on those applications.

However, for most cases (around 85.8% time), Proactivizer can keep the response time of these applications within nine milliseconds.

7   Discussion

Additional Efforts to Add a New Verification Tool. Proactivizer is a framework to plug different verification tools. Therefore, we design the Proactivizer framework in a manner that most steps remain tool-agnostic (as shown in Sect. 3.3). As a result, to add a new tool with Proactivizer, the main efforts are to prepare the inputs specific to that tool and interpret its results (as shown in Sect. 4).

Choosing the Value of the Threshold. As described in Sect. 3 and evaluated in Sect. 6, our solution schedules the computation based on a threshold probability. As shown in Fig. 11, lower values of threshold result in better prediction match. However, the prediction error also increases in such cases. Therefore, an optimal threshold value has to be chosen based on the tenant's need and experiences.

Reliance on the List of Critical Events. Like other existing solutions (e.g., Congress [30] and Weatherman [6]), our solution currently relies on manual identification of a list of critical events as inputs. However, our preliminary study shows that this identification process can be at least semi-automated by adopting a feedback module, which progressively can update and complete this list leveraging retroactive auditing tools (e.g., [22,25]). We report the detailed results of the study in our future work.

Choice of Prediction Function. Proactivizer leverages the predictive model to proactively trigger those verification tools. Therefore, the accuracy of our prediction function might be critical in achieving the best performance of Proactivizer. In this paper, we explore Bayesian network and ARMAX time series function and show the superiority of ARMAX function for our purpose (through experimental results in Sect. 6).

Supported Security Policies. Proactivizer is a general framework in which various verification tools can be plugged to verify a wide range of security policies. Therefore, potentially Proactivizer could support a wide range of security policies. To demonstrate this generality, we have so far integrated three verification tools with three totally different policy languages and specifications. In the near future, we intend to extend applying Proactivizer beyond the cloud environment, such as, in SDN and IoT.

Adapting to Other Cloud Platforms. Even though our current implementation is for OpenStack, the Proactivizer design is platform-agnostic. Therefore, Proactivizer can be adapted to other cloud platforms (e.g., Amazon EC2 [2] and Google GCP [12]) with a one-time effort for implementing a platform-specific interface. To this end, we provide a concrete guideline to adapt Proactivizer for other cloud platforms in Appendix A.

8   Related Work

Table 3 summarizes the comparison between existing works and Proactivizer. The first and second columns list existing works and their verification methods. The next three columns indicate different cloud layers, such as user-level, virtual infrastructure at the tenant level (T) and virtual network at the cloud service provider (CSP) level. The next three columns compare these works based on the adopted approaches. The next columns compare them according to different features, i.e., runtime enforcement capability, considering verification tools as blackboxes, serving as a general-purpose solution, supporting expressive policy languages and offering automated inputs. Note that the (○) symbol is for the Run. Enforcement column indicates that the corresponding work offers runtime enforcement with significant delay, and an (N/A) in the Blackbox column means that the corresponding solution is not utilizing any so-called verification tool.

Table 3. Comparing existing works with Proactivizer. The symbols (•), (-) and N/A mean supported, not supported, and not applicable, respectively. Note that, symbol ○ is used for the solutions which support runtime enforcement with significant delay.

Proposals	Methods	Layers			Approaches			Features				
		User-level	Virtual Infr. (T)	Virtual Net. (CSP)	Retroactive	Intercept-and-Check	Proactive	Run. Enforcement	Blackbox	General purpose	Expressive	Automated
Patron [20]	Access Control	•	-	-	-	•	-	○	N/A	-	-	•
Majumdar et al. [26]	SAT Solver	•	-	-	-	•	-	-	•	-	•	•
Madi et al. [21]	SAT Solver	-	•	•	•	-	-	-	•	-	•	•
Weatherman (V1) [6]	Graph-theoretic	-	•	-	-	•	-	○	-	-	•	•
Weatherman (V2) [6]	Graph-theoretic	-	•	-	-	-	•	•	-	-	•	-
Congress (V1) [30]	Datalog	•	•	•	-	•	-	○	-	-	•	•
Congress (V2) [30]	Datalog	•	•	•	-	-	•	•	-	-	•	-
NoD [19]	Datalog	-	-	•	•	-	-	-	•	-	•	•
LeaPS [24]	Custom + Bayesian	•	•	•	-	-	•	•	N/A	-	-	•
Proactivizer	-	•	•	•	-	-	•	•	•	•	•	•

In summary, Proactivizer differs from the existing works as follows. Firstly, Proactivizer is the first proactive framework, which leverages existing tools as a blackbox and transforms them into efficient solutions for runtime security enforcement. Secondly, Proactivizer can potentially support a wide range of security policies due to its inherited expressiveness from the integrated tools, and serve as a general-purpose framework.

Retroactive and Intercept-and-Check Approach. Unlike our work, retroactive verification approach (e.g., [8,19,22,25,39–41]) can detect violations only after they occur, which may expose the system to high risks. Existing intercept-and-check approaches (e.g., [6,20,26,30]) perform major verification tasks while holding the event instances blocked. As a result, these works tend to cause significant delay to the user requests; e.g., Weatherman [6] reports a four-minute delay to verify a mid-sized cloud. In contrast, our framework transforms these intercept-and-check approaches into an efficient solution for runtime security enforcement (as reported in Sect. 6). There exist other intercept-and-check solutions (e.g., TopoGuard [15], TopoGuard+ [36] and IoTGuard [7]) for SDN and IoT environments. These works can potentially be the applications of the Proactivizer framework to further improve their response time.

Proactive Approach. There exist few proactive works (e.g., [6,23,24,30,44]) for clouds. Weatherman [6] and Congress [30] verify security policies on a future change plan using the graph-based and Datalog-based model proposed in [4,5], respectively. Unlike our automated predictive model, those works rely on manual inputs of future plan. PVSC [23] proactively verifies security compliance by utilizing the static patterns in dependency models. PVSC [23] and LeaPS [24] are both customized for specific security policies and environment. Whereas, Proactivizer is designed to support a wide-range of security policies in diverse environments. In addition, Foley et al. [11] propose an algebra for anomaly-free firewall policies for OpenStack. Many state-based formal models (e.g., [9,17,18,35]) are proposed for program monitoring. Our work differs from them as we target in providing a generic proactive framework for plugging various verification tools, and these works potentially can be the applications of Proactivizer.

9 Conclusion

In this paper, we proposed Proactivizer, a generic proactive framework to transform existing verification tools into efficient solutions for runtime security enforcement. To this end, we leveraged the existing tools as blackboxes and proactively triggered the verification process based on the dependency relationships among the events. As a proof of concept, we applied Proactivizer to several existing verification tools (e.g., SAT solver, Datalog-based tool and access control tool) and integrated it with OpenStack, a widely used cloud platform. Through our extensive experiments in both simulated and real cloud environments, we demonstrated the effectiveness of our framework in reducing response time significantly (e.g., within nine milliseconds for 85.8% of the time). As future work, we intend to conduct a cost analysis of our proactive verification for different threshold values to help users in choosing more appropriate threshold value. Also, we plan to explore other time series functions to identify the best option.

Acknowledgement. We thank the anonymous reviewers for their insightful comments. This work is partially supported by the Natural Sciences and Engineering Research Council of Canada and Ericsson Canada under CRD Grant N01823 and by PROMPT Quebec.

A   Guideline to Adapt to Other Cloud Platforms

Our solution interacts with the cloud platform (e.g., while collecting logs and intercepting runtime events) through two modules: pre-processor and interceptor. These two modules require to interpret implementation- specific event instances, and intercept runtime events. First, to interpret platform-specific event instances to generic event types, we currently maintain a mapping of the APIs from different platforms. Table 4 enlists some examples of such mappings. Second, the interception mechanism may require to be implemented for each cloud platform. In OpenStack, we leverage WSGI middleware to intercept and enforce the proactive auditing results so that compliance can be preserved. Through our preliminary study, we identified that almost all major platforms provide an option to intercept cloud events. In Amazon using AWS Lambda functions, developers can write their own code to intercept and monitor events. Google GCP introduces GCP Metrics to configure charting or alerting different critical situations. Our understanding is that our solution can be integrated to GCP as one of the metrics similarly as the *dos_intercept_count* metric, which intends to prevent DoS attacks. The Azure Event Grid is an event managing service from Azure to monitor and control event routing which is quite similar as our interception mechanism. Therefore, we believe that our solution can be an extension of the Azure Event Grid to proactively audit cloud events. Tables 4 and 5 represent the necessary mapping to be used for extending our approach from OpenStack to other cloud platforms. The rest modules of our solution deal with the platform-independent data, and hence, the next steps in our solution are platform-agnostic.

Table 4. Mapping event APIs from different cloud platforms to generic event types

Generic event type	OpenStack [31]	Amazon EC2-VPC [2]	Google GCP [12]	Microsoft Azure [28]
Create VM	POST/servers	aws opsworks --region create-instance	gcloud compute instances create	az vm create 1
Delete VM	DELETE/servers	aws opsworks --region delete-instance --instance-id	gcloud compute instances delete	az vm delete
Update VM	PUT/servers	aws opsworks --region update-instance --instance-id	gcloud compute instances add-tags	az vm update
Create security group	POST/v2.0/ security- groups	aws ec2 create-security-group	N/A	az network nsg create
Delete security group	DELETE/v2.0/ security- groups/{security_ group_id}	aws ec2 delete-security -group --group-name	N/A	az network nsg delete

Table 5. Interception supports to adopt our solution in major cloud platforms

Cloud platform	Interception support
OpenStack	*WSGI Middleware* [43]
Amazon EC2-VPC	*AWS Lambda Function* [2]
Google GCP	*GCP Metrics* [12]
Microsoft Azure	*Azure Event Grid* [28]

B   Performance of the Cache Implementation

Figure 12 illustrates the response time in case there is a cache hit (when runtime parameters is found in the implemented cache memory) and the additional
delay for a cache miss (when requested parameters is not in the cache memory)
for Patron and Congress, respectively. In Fig. 12(a), for different sizes of cache,
we observe a quasi constant response time (which is less than one millisecond)
for Patron with our framework, and an additional delay for a cache miss of
up to four milliseconds. Figure 12(b) shows the results of similar experiment for
Congress with our framework; where a cache hit causes further improvement on
the response time, but a cache miss may cause up to 137 ms of delay. Overall
the results show the response time can be even less than one millisecond at the
best case, and at the worst case (when the prediction is incorrect), Proactivizer
will have no effect on those applications. However, for most cases (around 85.5%
time), Proactivizer can keep their response time within ten milliseconds.

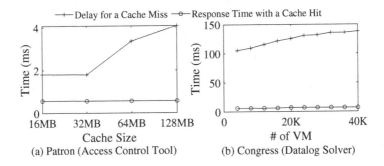

Fig. 12. The average response time for a cache hit and delay for a cache miss for (a)
Patron (access control tool) and (b) Congress (Datalog solver), while varying the size
of the cache and number of VMs, respectively

References

1. Aikat, J., et al.: Rethinking security in the era of cloud computing. IEEE Secur.
   Priv. **15**(3), 60–69 (2017)

2. Amazon. Amazon virtual private cloud. https://aws.amazon.com/vpc. Accessed 14 Feb 2018

3. Bellare, M., Yee, B.: Forward integrity for secure audit logs. Technical report, Citeseer (1997)

4. Bleikertz, S., Groß, T., Schunter, M., Eriksson, K.: Automated information flow analysis of virtualized infrastructures. In: Atluri, V., Diaz, C. (eds.) ESORICS 2011. LNCS, vol. 6879, pp. 392–415. Springer, Heidelberg (2011). https://doi.org/10.1007/978-3-642-23822-2_22

5. Bleikertz, S., Vogel, C., Groß, T.: Cloud radar: near real-time detection of security failures in dynamic virtualized infrastructures. In: Proceedings of the 30th Annual Computer Security Applications Conference (ACSAC), pp. 26–35. ACM (2014)

6. Bleikertz, S., Vogel, C., Groß, T., Mödersheim, S.: Proactive security analysis of changes in virtualized infrastructures. In: Proceedings of the 31st Annual Computer Security Applications Conference (ACSAC), pp. 51–60. ACM (2015)

7. Celik, Z.B., Tan, G., McDaniel, P.: IoTGuard: dynamic enforcement of security and safety policy in commodity IoT. In: Proceedings of 2019 Annual Network and Distributed System Security Symposium (NDSS 2019), February 2019

8. Doelitzscher, F., Fischer, C., Moskal, D., Reich, C., Knahl, M., Clarke, N.: Validating cloud infrastructure changes by cloud audits. In: Eighth World Congress on Services (SERVICES), pp. 377–384. IEEE (2012)

9. Dolzhenko, E., Ligatti, J., Reddy, S.: Modeling runtime enforcement with mandatory results automata. Int. J. Inf. Secur. **14**(1), 47–60 (2015)

10. Elasticsearch. Logstash. https://www.elastic.co/products/logstash. Accessed 14 Feb 2018

11. Foley, S.N., Neville, U.: A firewall algebra for OpenStack. In: Conference on Communications and Network Security (CNS), pp. 541–549. IEEE (2015)

12. Google. Google cloud platform. https://cloud.google.com. Accessed 14 Feb 2018

13. Hamed, H., Al-Shaer, E., Marrero, W.: Modeling and verification of IPSEC and VPN security policies. In: 13th IEEE International Conference on Network Protocols (ICNP 2005), pp. 10–pp. IEEE (2005)

14. Hamilton, J.D.: Time series analysis. Economic Theory. II, pp. 625–630. Princeton University Press, USA (1995)

15. Hong, S., Xu, L., Wang, H., Gu, G.: Poisoning network visibility in software-defined networks: new attacks and countermeasures. In: Proceedings of 2015 Annual Network and Distributed System Security Symposium (NDSS 2015), February 2015

16. Li, M., Zang, W., Bai, K., Yu, M., Liu, P.: Mycloud: supporting user-configured privacy protection in cloud computing. In: Proceedings of the 29th Annual Computer Security Applications Conference (ACSAC), pp. 59–68. ACM (2013)

17. Ligatti, J., Bauer, L., Walker, D.: Run-time enforcement of nonsafety policies. ACM Trans. Inf. Syst. Secur. (TISSEC) **12**(3), 19 (2009)

18. Ligatti, J., Reddy, S.: A theory of runtime enforcement, with results. In: Gritzalis, D., Preneel, B., Theoharidou, M. (eds.) ESORICS 2010. LNCS, vol. 6345, pp. 87–100. Springer, Heidelberg (2010). https://doi.org/10.1007/978-3-642-15497-3_6

19. Lopes, N.P., Bjørner, N., Godefroid, P., Jayaraman, K., Varghese, G.: Checking beliefs in dynamic networks. In: 12th USENIX Symposium on Networked Systems Design and Implementation (NSDI 2015), pp. 499–512 (2015)

20. Luo, Y., Luo, W., Puyang, T., Shen, Q., Ruan, A., Wu, Z.: OpenStack security modules: a least-invasive access control framework for the cloud. In: IEEE 9th International Conference on Cloud Computing (CLOUD) (2016)

21. Madi, T., et al.: ISOTOP: auditing virtual networks isolation across cloud layers in OpenStack. ACM Trans. Priv. Secur. (TOPS) **22**(1), 1 (2018)

22. Madi, T., Majumdar, S., Wang, Y., Jarraya, Y., Pourzandi, M., Wang, L.: Auditing security compliance of the virtualized infrastructure in the cloud: application to OpenStack. In: Proceedings of the Sixth ACM Conference on Data and Application Security and Privacy (CODASPY), pp. 195–206. ACM (2016)

23. Majumdar, S., et al.: Proactive verification of security compliance for clouds through pre-computation: application to OpenStack. In: Askoxylakis, I., Ioannidis, S., Katsikas, S., Meadows, C. (eds.) ESORICS 2016. LNCS, vol. 9878, pp. 47–66. Springer, Cham (2016). https://doi.org/10.1007/978-3-319-45744-4_3

24. Majumdar, S., et al.: LeaPS: learning-based proactive security auditing for clouds. In: Foley, S.N., Gollmann, D., Snekkenes, E. (eds.) ESORICS 2017. LNCS, vol. 10493, pp. 265–285. Springer, Cham (2017). https://doi.org/10.1007/978-3-319-66399-9_15

25. Majumdar, S., et al.: Security compliance auditing of identity and access management in the cloud: application to OpenStack. In: 7th International Conference on Cloud Computing Technology and Science (CloudCom), pp. 58–65. IEEE (2015)

26. Majumdar, S., et al.: User-level runtime security auditing for the cloud. IEEE Trans. Inf. Forensics Secur. 13(5), 1185–1199 (2018)

27. Majumdar, S., et al.: Learning probabilistic dependencies among events for proactive security auditing in clouds. J. Comput. Secur. 27(2), 165–202 (2019)

28. Microsoft. Microsoft Azure virtual network. https://azure.microsoft.com. Accessed 14 Feb 2018

29. Nitta, N., Takata, Y., Seki, H.: An efficient security verification method for programs with stack inspection. In: Proceedings of the 8th ACM Conference on Computer and Communications Security, pp. 68–77. ACM (2001)

30. OpenStack. OpenStack Congress (2015). https://wiki.openstack.org/wiki/Congress. Accessed 14 Feb 2018

31. OpenStack. OpenStack open source cloud computing software (2015). http://www.openstack.org. Accessed 14 Feb 2018

32. OpenStack. OpenStack user survey (2018). https://www.openstack.org/user-survey/2018-user-survey-report/. Accessed 24 Apr 2019

33. Ren, K., Wang, C., Wang, Q.: Security challenges for the public cloud. IEEE Internet Comput. 16(1), 69–73 (2012)

34. Schear, N., Cable II, P.T., Moyer, T.M., Richard, B., Rudd, R.: Bootstrapping and maintaining trust in the cloud. In: Proceedings of the 32nd Annual Conference on Computer Security Applications. ACM (2016)

35. Schneider, F.B.: Enforceable security policies. Trans. Inf. Syst. Secur. (TISSEC) 3(1), 30–50 (2000)

36. Skowyra, R., et al.: Effective topology tampering attacks and defenses in software-defined networks. In: Proceedings of the 48th Annual IEEE/IFIP International Conference on Dependable Systems and Networks (DSN 2018), June 2018

37. Tabiban, A., Majumdar, S., Wang, L., Debbabi, M.: Permon: an openstack middleware for runtime security policy enforcement in clouds. In: Proceedings of the 4th IEEE Workshop on Security and Privacy in the Cloud (SPC 2018), June 2018

38. Tamura, N., Banbara, M.: Sugar: a CSP to SAT translator based on order encoding. In: Proceedings of the Second International CSP Solver Competition, pp. 65–69 (2008)

39. Ullah, K.W., Ahmed, A.S., Ylitalo, J.: Towards building an automated security compliance tool for the cloud. In: 12th International Conference on Trust, Security and Privacy in Computing and Communications (TrustCom), pp. 1587–1593. IEEE (2013)

40. Wang, C., Chow, S.S., Wang, Q., Ren, K., Lou, W.: Privacy-preserving public auditing for secure cloud storage. IEEE Trans. Comput. **62**(2), 362–375 (2013)
41. Wang, Y., Wu, Q., Qin, B., Shi, W., Deng, R.H., Hu, J.: Identity-based data outsourcing with comprehensive auditing in clouds. IEEE Trans. Inf. Forensics Secur. **12**(4), 940–952 (2017)
42. Wardell, D.C., Mills, R.F., Peterson, G.L., Oxley, M.E.: A method for revealing and addressing security vulnerabilities in cyber-physical systems by modeling malicious agent interactions with formal verification. Procedia Comput. Sci. **95**, 24–31 (2016)
43. WSGI. Middleware and libraries for WSGI (2016). http://wsgi.readthedocs.io/en/latest/libraries.html. Accessed 15 Feb 2018
44. Yau, S.S. Buduru, A.B., Nagaraja, V.: Protecting critical cloud infrastructures with predictive capability. In: 8th International Conference on Cloud Computing (CLOUD), pp. 1119–1124. IEEE (2015)

Enhancing Security and Dependability of Industrial Networks with Opinion Dynamics

Juan E. Rubio[1(✉)], Mark Manulis[2], Cristina Alcaraz[1], and Javier Lopez[1]

[1] Department of Computer Science, University of Malaga, Campus de Teatinos s/n, 29071 Malaga, Spain
{rubio,alcaraz,jlm}@lcc.uma.es
[2] Surrey Centre for Cyber Security (SCCS), University of Surrey, Guildford, UK
m.manulis@surrey.ac.uk

Abstract. Opinion Dynamics poses a novel technique to accurately locate the patterns of an advanced attack against an industrial infrastructure, compared to traditional intrusion detection systems. This distributed solution provides profitable information to identify the most affected areas within the network, which can be leveraged to design and deploy tailored response mechanisms that ensure the continuity of the service. In this work, we base on this multi-agent collaborative approach to propose a response technique that permits the secure delivery of messages across the network. For such goal, our contribution is twofold: firstly, we redefine the existing algorithm to assess not only the compromise of nodes, but also the security and quality of service of communication links; secondly, we develop a routing protocol that prioritizes the secure paths throughout the topology considering the information obtained from the detection system.

Keywords: Advanced · Persistent · Threat · Opinion dynamics · Quality · Service · Routing · Protocol

1 Introduction

Today, most critical infrastructures of all industrial sectors (such as transport or the Smart Grid) are controlled by SCADA systems (Supervisory Control and Data Acquisition), which access in real time to the devices that govern the production chain. As far as cybersecurity is concerned, these devices have traditionally lacked protection, since industrial networks had to function in isolation from other environments. However, there is currently a growing interconnection of control systems with other networks (such as the Internet) for the outsourcing of services or the storage of data, which is caused by the decrease in cost and standardization of hardware and software. As a result, there has also been a growth of reported security threats, as industrial systems are now also victims of the problems suffered by information technologies [1, 2].

© Springer Nature Switzerland AG 2019
K. Sako et al. (Eds.): ESORICS 2019, LNCS 11736, pp. 263–280, 2019.
https://doi.org/10.1007/978-3-030-29962-0_13

In this regard, the **Advanced Persistent Threats (APT)** represent the most critical hazard in recent years. These are sophisticated attacks perpetrated against a specific organization, where the attacker has considerable experience and resources to penetrate the victim's network, using a multitude of vulnerabilities and attack vectors [3]. They use stealthy techniques to go undetected for a prolonged period of time, from the initial intrusion to the subsequent propagation movements (a.k.a. lateral movements) within the APT life-cycle. Stuxnet was the first APT reported (in 2010), although many others APTs have appeared later, such as Duqu, DragonFly, BlackEnergy, and ExPetr [4].

Diverse security services must be applied to detect and deter the effects of these threats and minimize the impact on the infrastructure, combining cutting-edge technologies for accurately monitoring these threats. Traditional security solutions like firewalls or antivirus software must be coupled with advanced services (e.g., data loss prevention, advanced detection of malware, trusted computing) and security awareness procedures to protect the industrial systems from a holistic point of view, during their entire life-cycle. In this sense, Intrusion Detection Systems (IDS) represent a first line of defense against the wide range of cyber-threats leveraged by an APT. Numerous mechanisms have been proposed in the industry and academia that make use of machine learning techniques [5] or propose advanced services that analyze the internal traffic to detect specific attacks [6]. However, they only address security in precise points of the infrastructure or they do not consider the persistence of attacks over time. Consequently, there is still a need to find other defense solutions that enable the traceability of APTs throughout the control network, beyond the initial intrusion.

For this goal, authors in [7] propose a distributed consensus algorithm based on *Opinion Dynamics* [8], making use of graph theory. They demonstrate the feasibility of this novel approach to keep track of the anomalies suffered by devices over the entire network, potentially caused by an APT. This information can be used to put in place accurate mechanisms aiming to prevent the propagation of the APT or to minimize their impact. However, the initial approach from [7] does not take into account anomaly indicators concerning the Quality of Service (QoS) of the communication links. As a consequence, it has limitations in the monitoring of the network health and in the choice of countermeasures to ensure best-possible connectivity in the presence of APT. The previously proposed response technique for the maintenance of network paths does not sufficiently apply to traditional industrial scenarios. By improving the original approach we are able to design a more realistic response technique, showing the effectiveness of the Opinion Dynamics to ensure the continuity of communications in the presence of an APT. More concretely, we present a routing protocol that ensures the delivery of messages with a low probability of interception, while ensuring a decent level of QoS, resulting in a combined approach. Our contributions in this article can be summarized as follows:

– Improved Opinion Dynamics model based on anomaly indicators related to the QoS of the communication links and the security of hosts.

– Enhanced routing approach for reliable connectivity in presence of APT based on the improved Opinion Dynamics model.

The remainder of this paper is organized as follows: Sect. 2 introduces the preliminary concepts related to the Quality of Service indicators used in this work and the original APT-related anomaly detection approach based on Opinion Dynamics. The improved approach based on QoS indicators is proposed in Sect. 3 and the enhanced routing approach is presented in Sect. 4. Section 5 provides simulations and evaluation of our results. Section 6 draws conclusions.

2   Preliminary Concepts and Related Work

2.1   Quality of Service Indicators for Routing Protocols

Critical infrastructures governed by industrial networks require to work at all times, even in the presence of intruders; for this goal, we propose the use of a routing protocol as a response technique that uses the security information provided by a distributed detection system. However, in order to guarantee the delivery performance, this protocol must also make resource reservation and excise network control, in order to respond in a timely manner.

In traditional data networks, routing protocols simply use shortest path algorithms for the path computation, based on a single metric like hop-count or delay. In turn, QoS-aware routing protocols take into account further metrics to addressing the Quality of Service, in particular [9,10]:

– **Delay time.** It measures the time taken to transfer data across the network from one node to another. This value is often used to establish allowance limits for the communication links, in order to select the fastest route. In real-time operations, jitter or packet delay variations are used, measured with a sliding window of fractions of seconds. This is due to the dependence on the application (e.g., isolated environment of sensors, Internet connection to the SCADA system) or the network congestion, which could potentially slow down the communications.
– **Bandwidth.** It holds the maximum rate of data that can be transferred from a source to a destination per time unit. In order for the industrial devices to measure it, it is reasonable to determine the maximum bandwidth available at a given time. However, the computation of this value (along with delay) for routing purposes is a challenging problem since it can frequently change, as well as delay [11]. Also, in presence of an APT, there could not be any centralized control for allocating bandwidth among the nodes. For this reason, most existing QoS-aware routing protocols in the literature assume that the available bandwidth is known [12]. There are some others that estimate this value with carrier-sense capability of the underlying protocols (e.g., IEEE 802.11) to measure the idle and busy time ratio, and then adding this information to the route control packets.

– **Packet loss.** Packet loss can be used to measure availability, which represents the probability that some recipient is reachable with the claimed quality at a given moment of time. The packet loss is usually calculated as the ratio of lost packets or dropped connections in connection-oriented systems (e.g., upon retrieval of information from sensors).

Based on the set of adequate metrics, QoS-aware routing protocols perform resource estimation at each node and proceed with the route selection [13–15]. Routes are usually chosen to maximize the available bandwidth while minimizing the delay and the loss probability. However, finding a path that simultaneously satisfies more than one constraint is a NP-Problem. For this reason, heuristic approaches resulting in more efficient algorithms are often used in the literature. For instance, [16] adopts three different criteria for the Optimized Link State Routing Protocol [17]. Another efficient scalable heuristic applied in [18] is based on Lagrangian relaxation. Another approach is based on the shortest-widest path algorithm [19], where a path with maximum bandwidth is found using a variant of the Dijkstra shortest-path algorithm and if there exists more than one such path then the one with the lowest delay is chosen.

Apart from these approaches, it is also possible to generate a single QoS metric from multiple parameters of the communication links. For the sake of simplicity and with the aim of aggregating different metrics (i.e., delay, bandwidth, packet loss ratio) our approach utilizes the following QoS function [20]:

$$S(c) = \frac{B(c)}{D(c) \times L(c)} \tag{1}$$

where for a given communication link c, the metrics applied are the link's bandwidth B, delay D and packet loss L. Due to the reasons discussed before, the estimation of these metrics at each node is out of the scope of this article.

The output of $S(c)$, when evaluated for a given communication link, is directly proportional to the quality of service that it experiences. This information can already be used for establishing a priority when selecting the routes along the network. However, besides the QoS measures applied to communication links, we will also introduce a security-based criterion for the selection of nodes that are traversed by our routing protocol. This additional information is provided by the Opinion Dynamics based detection system, explained in the following.

2.2   Using Opinion Dynamics for APT Detection

Compared to traditional defense solutions, Opinion Dynamics [8] has been demonstrated to be a suitable technique for APT detection, as originally described in [7]. In a later publication, its authors extend this work to enable the traceability of attacks along their whole life-cycle by analyzing the movements and anomalies suffered across the affected network [21].

From a general perspective, this distributed cooperative algorithm models the behavior of a group of individuals in a society: each one (which we will refer to as 'agent') holds his/her own opinion, which is, to a certain extent, influenced by the rest (and so does his/her opinion). After some time, the entire society is fragmented into formed consensus of distinct spectra of opinions, belonging to agents who are closer in their posture. Applied in the context of intrusion detection (with multiple of these agents deployed over the infrastructure), Opinion Dynamics can help to identify the portions of the network which are subject of an attack (and their criticality degree), by correlating the anomalies (subtle or evident) sensed by agents. At the same time, it is possible to trace events occurred in the network from the very first moment the intruder breaks in.

The formal description of the algorithm and how to apply consensus to this particular context is explained in the following. Suppose a network architecture given by the graph $G(V, E)$, where V represents the set of devices within the production chain (e.g., controllers, sensors or actuators) and E refers to the communication links that connect these nodes. Let A be the set of agents such that $A = a_1, a_2, ..., a_n$, being $|A| = |V|$. According to Opinion Dynamics, $x_i(t)$ represents the individual opinion of agent a_i in the iteration t, which can be valued from zero to one (where one means the highest anomaly). To represent the influence between agents, each agent i assigns a weight to each neighbor j, which is denoted by w_{ij}. We assume that $\sum_{k=1}^{n} w_{ik} = 1$, in such a way that all agents account for their own opinion.

Altogether, for a single execution of the algorithm at any given time of the control system cycle, the formation of the new opinion for agent i in the next iteration $t + 1$ is described with this expression: $x_i(t + 1) = \sum_{j=1}^{n} w_{ij}x_j(t)$. This formula models the opinion as a weighted average of the rest of agents' opinions. If we successively calculate this value for many iterations, different clusters of opinions are formed when t tends to infinity, which can also be visualized in a graph. Then, this information can be used to accurately identify different attacked areas within the network, which are potentially monitored by large sets of agents that exhibit the same anomaly pattern. The more affected areas will be those which comprise a greater number of agents with a high opinion value. At this point, in terms of adapting this multi-agent algorithm to our particular scenario, two questions appear:

(1) **The representation of the initial opinion $x_i(0)$ for every agent i,** that in practice holds the degree of anomaly detected by them. Authors of the original publication [7] arbitrarily select a set of hierarchically connected nodes within the network that play the role of agents to perform the detection; then, they model their initial opinion by computing the deviation in the *betweenness centrality* score [22] with respect to its value in normal conditions. This indicator holds the level of connectivity that every node within the topology experiences. However, as it will be analyzed later in Sect. 3 and mentioned in [21], Opinion Dynamics is open to include new anomaly indicators that serve as an input to agents. In our case, we are interested in representing anomalies caused by the compromise of both devices and communication links.

(2) **The representation of the weight given by each agent to its respective neighbors,** in order to consider their influence on the opinion about the severity of the incidence detected. The original approach is based on a simple

criterion to choose the weight assigned among agents: the closer two opinions of two connected nodes are (their values), the higher the weight assigned between them will be. This means that, for every agent, the weight given to its neighbors is uniformly divided into those agents whose opinion is very similar to its own, considering an ε threshold for the difference between both values. Intuitively, this simulates the fact that agents located nearby with the same degree of anomaly sensed are prone to detect the same threat in their surroundings. Again, although this may be a valid criterion to model the weight, it could be enhanced to realistically reflect other environmental conditions involved (e.g., Quality of Service), as discussed in Sect. 3.

After assessing the security of the network with Opinion Dynamics, we can use this information to execute defense procedures. Authors in [7] leverage a simple message routing algorithm to ensure the reachability of nodes in presence of an attack. However, more techniques can be combined and deployed dynamically, either proactive (e.g., placing honeypots over the affected zones to gain knowledge from the adversary or using redundancy of links between agents) or reactive (e.g., recovery of nodes or links to reduce the impact on the infrastructure). In this sense, a potential study could be conducted to find an effective defense strategy (e.g., through specific validation approaches like game theory). In this paper, we show the weaknesses of the original proposal and illustrate the utility of the detection with an alternative solution that addresses those issues. This will be described later in Sect. 4.

3   Modified Opinion Dynamics Approach: Analysis of Communication Links

As argued in Sect. 2.2, the original approach based on Opinion Dynamics for the APT detection [7] requires further improvement. First, the aforementioned approach only focuses on the detection of topological changes over a graph-defined network, where a subset of nodes of V (called the *Dominating Set*) are in charge of exchanging their opinions, which are represented with the ratio of change in their *betweenness centrality* indicator. Accordingly, the attacker model just contemplates the compromise of nodes to perform a removal of links. Even though this is valid to show the applicability of the algorithm using graph theory, we must go beyond and come up with different ways to model such opinion value in a real industrial ecosystem. The reason is that APTs comprise a wide range of attack vectors besides the mere denial of service, which pose a source of different anomalies (mostly subtle), that are potentially measured and correlated by the agent associated with the affected node. Therefore, the aim is to realistically analyze the security state of each node and its neighborhood, in order to create a quantitative value that would serve as an input to the Opinion Dynamics. In general, two (possibly simultaneous) approaches can be suggested for this task:

– Use an IDS to retrieve events and alerts based on which the security state of the node in question can be analyzed. This may also include events triggered by vulnerability scanners or antivirus software.

– Analyse the incoming and outgoing network traffic and perform comparison with the normal behavior, for example, by applying machine learning techniques and assessing anomalies with regard to the traffic volume, delays, network connections and protocols used.

With this, we assume that the agent would have enough input data to compute a single opinion value for the security state of its monitored device. At this point, the effectiveness from the use of specific ways to derive such value could be compared, which would strongly depend on the actual network setup (e.g., topology, technologies, communication protocols) and it is not in the scope of this paper; instead, we point out that the novelty and effectiveness of the Opinion Dynamics approach resides in the ability to correlate anomalies throughout the network and thereby get insight into the location and severity of attacks; the way to uptake the individual anomaly detection is customizable and reliant on the security scenario that we want to achieve, thereby working as a framework.

One related issue is the implementation of this mechanism in an industrial infrastructure. As discussed in [21], these agents can be either logical or physical. On the one hand, we can assume that the status of individual devices can be retrieved from a centralized entity, which consists of a computationally powerful node in charge of correlating the anomalies from all agents. Ideally, this node would then apply protection measures (e.g., honeypots, data recovery, backup servers) based on the security state of the network. In practice, this can be easily implemented by using switches in port-mirroring mode, so that all traffic from the nodes is relayed to a central correlator system, for instance. On the other hand, we could also consider that these agents can be physically deployed over the network, in form of monitoring devices or integrated with the software of the industrial assets. However, this option is not as feasible, since manufacturers and operators of critical infrastructures are reluctant to introduce modifications in their hardware and software (mainly due to computational limitations and use of privative software).

Regardless of the method used for the anomaly detection, we especially look into the security of the opinion exchange in this paper. In this regard, the original approach does not provide details about how the agents transfer their opinions between them or to a central correlator. If the same communication channels are used to deliver the Opinion Dynamics values, we must prevent against an attacker being able to compromise these links and potentially forge malicious opinions. At the same time, besides assessing the security of each node, the algorithm should also take the QoS of the communication links into consideration to safely send this information, as well as to route other messages (e.g., commands or data) between the devices. In the following, we propose a modification of the weight calculation mechanism to consider the QoS of the communication links and the confidence assigned to neighbors for the opinion transmission. This poses a solution to the second issue raised in Sect. 2.2.

To begin with, let's consider the original model: each agent i determines the weight given to every neighbor j in its neighborhood N_i through this expression:

$$w_{ij} = 1/N_i' \tag{2}$$

where N_i' is the subset of neighbors of N_i, whose difference in opinion with agent i is below ε. Otherwise, w_{ij} becomes zero. Even though this is just a criterion to reflect the degree of similitude between agents, it lacks much accuracy since it leaves behind several other aspects involved; in this case, we want to introduce an additional factor to regulate this weight through considering the QoS of the channel in the neighborhood.

Let $\mathcal{S}: E \to \mathcal{R}$ be a function that assigns QoS scores to communication links in the network defined by $G(V, E)$, as presented in Sect. 2.1. The higher the score of S for a given link is, the more QoS it provides. For a given i, we aim to fairly distribute w_{ij} by giving a higher value to those agents j whose $\mathcal{S}(e_{ij})$ is greater, where $e_{ij} \in E$ represents the bidirectional communication link between i and j. This methodology complies with the following three conditions:

- **C1.** The sum of weights given by agent i to the neighbors in N_i' must be 1, also considering threshold ε. $\sum_{j=1}^{N_i'} w_{ij} = 1$.
- **C2.** The own agent i must have a sensitive fixed weight assigned to itself. For instance, we can assume $w_{ii} = 0.5$; the reason is that it is not fair that it associates a higher level of confidence to any other agent, whose link of communication can be minimally compromised.
- **C3.** The rest of weight ($1/2$ in this case) assigned by agent i is distributed among neighbors in N_i' proportionally to the quality of their communication links. If we define $q = \sum_{j}^{N'i} \mathcal{S}(e_{ij})$, then the resulting weight value is defined by $w_{ij} = (1 - w_{ii}) * \mathcal{S}(e_{ij})/q$.

Example. Table in Fig. 1 shows the calculation of w_{ij} for the node C in the example graph (where $i = C$) following the proposed methodology, compared to the original one. The weight value that is computed using the new methodology is denoted by w_{ij}'. In both cases, a value of $\varepsilon = 0.35$ has been considered. As we can see, the new distribution of weight results more equitable, where node C assigns a higher weight to nodes A and D, since their links show a better quality and security (which is represented by the $\mathcal{S}(e_{Cj})$ column).

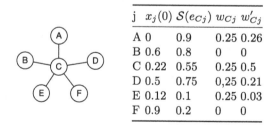

j	$x_j(0)$	$\mathcal{S}(e_{Cj})$	w_{Cj}	w_{Cj}'
A	0	0.9	0.25	0.26
B	0.6	0.8	0	0
C	0.22	0.55	0.25	0.5
D	0.5	0.75	0,25	0.21
E	0.12	0.1	0.25	0.03
F	0.9	0.2	0	0

Fig. 1. Example of weight calculation by agent C

4   QoS-Aware Routing Based on Opinion Dynamics

In response to an APT, the combined opinions determined by the monitoring agents on the industrial network with regard to the security of its nodes and the QoS aspects of their communication links can subsequently be used to enhance network routing. Here we present a novel approach aiming to enhance routing algorithms used in industrial networks such that the probability of packets being intercepted by potentially compromised network nodes is minimized while the Quality of Service of paths through which these packets are routed is maximized. This way, we can ensure the confidentiality and reliability of the network until the threat is completely eradicated from the infrastructure.

Note that our approach can also replace the initial response mechanism proposed in [7] which aims to enhance delivery of messages in presence of APT by relying on a redundant non-compromised part of the network topology and using secret sharing to split packets into chunks that are randomly dispatched over multiple paths. Their approach has a number of shortcomings as discussed in the following. First, their attack model is based on a complete removal of communication links by compromised nodes and does not consider a more realistic scenario where such links may experience varying QoS levels as a result of an attack. As observed in the recent years, many APT usually rely on zero-day vulnerabilities and make use of stealthy techniques to go unnoticed for a prolonged period of time, until they finally exfiltrate information or destroy the physical equipment. Therefore, it is necessary to consider a more subtle behavior of the attacker who may not wish to fully disrupt the communication and be detected. Second, the assumption on the existence of a redundant non-compromised topology in industrial control networks is not realistic. The architecture of such networks very frequently responds to a fixed configuration where all resources are rigidly connected with each other and so installation of a separate network topology might require significant investment and modifications of existing hardware devices. Third, their approach relies on the shortest-path estimation for which sending network nodes are assumed to know the entire network topology and has therefore limitations when used in combination with existing routing protocols that may not require nodes to have this knowledge.

Our approach is more general and realistic in that it aims at enhancing available routing algorithms to take into account the anomalies determined by the monitoring agents for the QoS levels of communication links and the security of network nodes when making routing decisions rather than selecting an optimal route based on the shortest path only. In order to set the background for our approach, we consider a typical architecture of an industrial network following the ISA-95 standard [23]. In practice, due to the modernization of industrial technologies in recent years, these networks have evolved towards a more distributed model. Control devices (i.e., PLCs or RTUs) govern the production cycle by retrieving data from field devices (i.e., sensors and actuators), according to the information exchanged with SCADA systems. These are evolving towards cloud-based solutions, that interconnect other services within the organization. This way, we see how the network is divided into two main sections: the industrial assets (which we will refer to as 'operational technologies', OT) and the IT (Information Technologies). This is the base that authors assume to extend the topology used in [7], used now to show the feasibility of our routing protocol.

Let $G(E, V)$ be a graph that describes the overall network topology. This graph is composed of the two subgraphs $G(V_{IT}, E_{IT})$ and $G(V_{OT}, E_{OT})$, which are interconnected by a set of intermediate firewalls V_{FW} so that $V = V_{IT} \cup V_{OT} \cup V_{FW}$. More specifically, both are joined by the firewalls V_{FW}, that have connections with the nodes of V_{IT} and V_{OT} that belong to the Power Dominating Set (PDS) of those subnetworks. This concept refers to a set of hierarchically selected nodes that have the maximum dominance over the entire network [24]. With respect to the network topology, we note that each of these subnetworks has a different configuration. On the one hand, $G(V_{OT}, E_{OT})$ follows a power-law distribution of the type $y \propto x^{-\alpha}$ [25], which models the hierarchical topology of an electric power grid and its high-level substations, which are subsequently connected to nodes with less connectivity (e.g., sensors and actuators). On the other hand, $G(V_{IT}, E_{IT})$ presents a small-world distribution, that models the traditional topology of TCP/IP networks on the Internet [26].

Over this distribution of nodes, there are two types of communication flows: information about the production chain delivered from the lower layers to the managerial IT network and, in reverse way, control commands issued from that section (e.g., the SCADA system) to the industrial process. For both types of the communication flows we base our approach on the Bellman-Ford algorithm [27] that is at the core of the Distance Vector Routing (DVR) [28] protocol, which determines the path to remote nodes using hop count as a metric. Each node holds a table that contains the distance to each node and the next hop in the route. This information is exchanged periodically with the neighbors, to ultimately compute the path using the Bellman-Ford algorithm. This contrasts to the Dijkstra's path-finding algorithm [29] used in [7], that finds the shortest path by requiring all nodes to have overall knowledge of the network topology and is at the core of the Link-State Routing (LSR) protocol [30]. In this protocol routers periodically flood the entire network to ensure that each node holds a synchronized copy of the routing table. By choosing DVR over LSR we can compute paths locally without involvement centralized routers as communicating with such nodes in presence of APT would impose additional risks.

The Bellman-Ford algorithm uses a weighted directed graph $G(V, E)$. The shortest distance from a node to the rest is determined by overestimating the true distance, following the principle of relaxation. In our case, since we want to prioritize QoS and security for the chosen path over the distance, we represent the weight assigned to each link $e_{ij} \in E$ as

$$W(e_{ij}) = \frac{X_t(j)}{S(e_{ij})} \tag{3}$$

where $X_t(j)$ is the final anomaly value of node j after executing the Opinion Dynamics as specified in Sect. 3. We select j instead of i since we want to prevent the messages against propagating to a node that is potentially compromised. On the other hand, $S(e_{ij})$ refers to the QoS score of the communication channel e_{ij}, as specified in Sect. 2.1. The higher the anomaly sensed by the agent in node j is, the greater the weight assigned to that link will be. Correspondingly, the S score is inversely proportional to that value. By this means, we take into consideration the security of devices and the Quality of Service of their links when deploying our response technique in form of routing protocol.

Such DVR-based routing approach can be executed at any time of the production chain, paired with a previous execution of the Opinion Dynamics algorithm for adapting the network to the current security level, thereby achieving resilience. Therefore, we assume the process to update the routes can be executed as frequently as the security scenario imposes, which would not imply additional computing costs for the devices if we consider that the detection algorithm is executed in a central correlator system separated from the industrial network, as suggested in [7]. In the following, we prove the effectiveness of our technique by simulating successive attacks against a network. Note that this approach can be validated in the future with game theory to consider dynamic attack behaviors and additional defense solutions.

5 Simulation and Evaluation

In this section, our primary aim is to prove that the proposed QoS-aware routing approach based on Opinion Dynamics can effectively minimize the interception of messages, avoiding paths that contain compromised nodes while ensuring an acceptable level of quality. First, we define the attack model used in our simulation that determines how the anomalies are generated over the network and measured by the agents. Then, we execute the technique (i.e., the delivery of messages and the QoS analysis) with different parametrization of the topology and attacks performed. Finally, we evaluate the simulation findings.

5.1 Attack Model: Simulation of Attacks and Anomalies

In order to define a more realistic attack model for our response technique, we assume an attacker can break into the infrastructure by leveraging zero-day vulnerabilities and then use stealthy techniques to propagate over the network, until information is filtered or disruption to the infrastructure is caused.

Therefore, contrary to the approach based on the alteration of links, we consider an attack model based on a succession of lateral movements over the network nodes, aiming to infect as many devices as possible so that the security when delivering messages is jeopardized. Let *attackSet* be this sorted set of attack stages that an APT can perform against the industrial network, which is defined by $G(V, E)$ and is composed by the IT and OT sections, as explained in Sect. 4. This set comprises a finite number of elements of the following kind:

- **attackITnode**: the adversary initializes the APT or propagates the attack to a device in the IT subnetwork.

- **attackFWnode**: the attacker compromises a firewall (when the previously compromised node has connection with it), in order to propagate to the other section of the control network.
- **attackOTnode**: the intruder compromises a node in the industrial section of the network.

Every time the attacker takes over a new device, two main variables change:

1. From the **security** perspective, the agent associated with the compromised node notices an increase in the anomaly level, that ranges from zero to one, as described before. If we define x as the initial opinion vector for all agents, then x_i^t is updated in the simulation after attack number t. For simplicity, we assign a value that is randomly generated according to a uniform distribution over $(0, 1)$, simulating the existence of both subtle and evident anomalies.
2. From the perspective of **Quality of Service**, the agent also senses a potential alteration in the QoS experienced in the incoming or outgoing connections, as a consequence of the attack. The value of $S(e_{ik})$ for all $e_{ik} \in E$ in the simulations is originally chosen from a uniform distribution over $(0, 1)$, to represent the presence of channels with different QoS levels. In the event of an attack, the value of $S(e_{ik})$ and $S(e_{ki})$ scores decreases (being zero the minimum), where i is the attacked node and k refers to all neighbors of i such that there exists $e_{ik} \in E$ (since each connection is bidirectional). This decrease is represented by δ. Since the attacker can leverage stealthy techniques to go unnoticed without affecting the communications, this value is also chosen uniformly at random from $(0, 1)$.

Algorithm 1. APT life cycle

---

output: X representing the final opinion value for all agents, S representing the QoS scores of links
local: Graph $G(V, E)$ representing the network, where $V = V_{IT} \cup V_{OT} \cup V_{FW}$
input: attackSet $\leftarrow$ attackStage$_{APT_x}$, representing the APT chain of attacks

$x \leftarrow zeros(|V|)$ (initial opinion vector)
$\{attack \leftarrow first\ attack\ from\ attackSet\}$
while attackSet $\neq \oslash$ **do**
    $x(attackNode) \leftarrow U(0, 1), \delta \leftarrow U(0, 1)$
    for neighbour **in** neighbours(attackNode) **do**
        $S(attackNode, neighbour) \leftarrow S(attackNode, neighbour) - \delta$
        $S(neighbour, attackNode) \leftarrow S(neighbour, attackNode) - \delta$
    end for

    $X \leftarrow \text{COMPUTEOPINIONDYNAMICS}(x, S)$
    $attackSet \leftarrow attackSet \setminus attack$
end while

Algorithm 1 describes the proposed APT life cycle. For all the attack stages in the provided *attackSet* parameter, the security of agents and the QoS score of the links is reevaluated, as described before: firstly, the attacked node (specified with *attackNode*) is assigned with a random value of anomaly (i.e., the opinion of its agent) in the uniform (0,1) distribution. Then, each of its ingoing and outgoing links are updated with a diminished QoS score, according to the value of δ. Afterwards, Opinion Dynamics is executed to aggregate all opinions and calculate their final values, which eases the identification of zones under the effect of the APT following the algorithm explained in Sect. 3. Finally, this information can be input to the routing protocol.

5.2   Reliable Message Delivery

Once the attack model has been defined, we can execute the defender's code based on the routing protocol in presence of an APT to firstly show that messages are successfully delivered in a way that the probability of traversing a compromised node (i.e., with an opinion value greater than zero) is lower than using the previously proposed approach in [7]. To simulate this, a set of 100 different messages are randomly generated, whose sender and recipient belong to the graph $G(V, E)$, making sure that more than one path exists between both nodes. Half of these messages are control commands (i.e., sent from the IT section to one device in the lowest levels of the infrastructure), while the other half are data packets, generated in the production chain and dispatched to the IT subnetwork. Therefore, messages are delivered in both ways based on the industrial topology defined in Sect. 4.

In order to compare the level of security experienced by the response technique and consequently compare it with other solutions, we define the *compromise level* indicator for each of the messages sent. This holds the sum of anomaly values (i.e., opinions calculated with the Opinion Dynamics algorithm, represented with X in Algorithm 1), which are measured by the set of nodes that compose the path described by the message, in the route from the recipient to the destination. The greater this value is, the highest probability for the message to be intercepted will be. For a given number N of messages transmitted, we can determine the *average compromise level* as

$$\frac{\sum_{i=1}^{N} \sum_{j=1}^{|R|} X_j}{N} \tag{4}$$

where X_j is the opinion of agent j, $1 \leq j \leq |R|$, and R is the set of nodes that each message i traverses. This overall value is calculated for our custom routing protocol and will be compared with two other approaches: on the one hand, **(a)** **the previously proposed mechanism in [7]**, that is based on the Dijkstra's shortest-path algorithm, without considering the opinions of the agents; on the other hand, **(b)** **the Dijkstra's path-finding algorithm parametrized with the opinion of agents** as weights for the search of the optimal path (i.e., the route with a minimal compromise level). In other words, for the computation of the path from sender to recipient in $G(V, E)$, (a) uses a weighting function W for each edge $e_{ij} \in$ such that $W(e_{ij}) = 1$ if e_{ij} simply exists (so that the destination is reached in the minimum number of hops). As for (b), $W(e_{ij}) = X_j$, hence prioritizing not to hop to a compromised node. Our aim is to show how (c) **our approach based on Bellman-Ford algorithm**, that uses the weighting function defined in Eq. 3, achieves better security (i.e., the value of compromise level) than (a), with closer results to (b).

In this experiment (carried out in Matlab), we have generated a random industrial network of 50, 100 and 200 nodes following the topology described in Sect. 4 (where the two halves of nodes are respectively used for the IT and OT subnetworks and an extra firewall node is used to merge them). Over these topologies, we have simulated the effect of an APT (according to Algorithm 1) composed by 50, 100 and 200 attack actions, respectively. We have represented the overall behavior of Stuxnet (since it is one of the most documented attacks) at a basic level: the APT begins by compromising one node from the IT network (originally using malicious USB flash drives) and then spreads through the entire subnetwork until it finally breaks into the OT section, where the threat propagates until it infects the target device (the uranium enriching centrifuges).

By making sure the number of attacks reaches the number of nodes, we represent the most critical scenario when the APT takes over the entire network, thereby showing the effectiveness of the algorithm at all times (although this validation process could be further optimized if attacker and defender were part of a dynamically confronted competition with specific action rules, by means of game theory). After each attack phase, the Opinion Dynamics algorithm is executed and the set of 100 random messages are delivered, putting into play the three aforementioned routing algorithms. Finally, the average of compromise is calculated. The plot in Fig. 2 shows the evolution of this value over the entire set of attacks for the three assessed solutions.

As we can see, the Dijkstra's algorithm that uses the opinion of agents as weights to compute the path serves as the baseline of the minimum compromise level that can be achieved. However, our approach based on Bellman-Ford algorithm presents a similar result with a slight increment of anomaly experienced, that still remains far from the high value experienced by the Dijkstra's scheme proposed in [7], as we wanted to demonstrate. We will now prove that our approach also provides better Quality of Service requirements.

5.3   Quality of Service Experienced

After analyzing how our solution effectively experiences a lower level of compromise when routing the messages, it is also necessary to prove that the paths generated by the protocol also achieve an adequate Quality of Service, which is the main contribution of this paper. This would ensure a fast and reliable communication, especially necessary when the computed paths impose several hops to reach the recipient as a consequence of avoiding the effect of the attack.

Following the previous methodology, we aim to deliver a set of 100 messages over the graph $G(V, E)$ in such a way that the number of hops is minimized and the Quality of Service experienced is maximized. This time, we define the *QoS level* indicator for each message sent as the sum of individual QoS scores for all the successive edges that belong to the path (as explained in Sect. 2.1) divided by the number of hops that this message performs. The greater this value is, the better quality of service with a lower number of nodes traversed will be. Given N messages transmitted, we can determine the *average QoS level* as

$$\frac{\sum_{i=1}^{N} \frac{\sum_{j=1}^{|R|} S(e^j)}{hops_i}}{N} \tag{5}$$

where S is the QoS score function from Eq. 1, e^j refers to edges from the route R which is taken by message i, and $hops_i$ is the number of intermediate hops. This average QoS value is calculated for our routing approach in presence of APT using the same topology and attack scenarios as in the previous test case, and is compared with the two other approaches: **(a) the previously proposed mechanism in** [7], that is based on the Dijkstra's shortest-path algorithm without accounting for any QoS implications; and **(b) the Dijkstra's path-finding algorithm parametrized with the QoS score of the edges** as weights for the search of the optimal path (i.e., the route with a maximum quality). Thus, (a) uses an W weighting function for each edge e_{ij} such that $W(e_{ij}) = 1$ if e_{ij} simply exists, while in (b) it uses $W(e_{ij}) = 1/S(e_{ij})$, hence prioritizing the path with maximum Quality of Service. In this case, our aim is now to show how **(c) our approach based on Bellman-Ford algorithm**, that uses the weighting function defined in Eq. 3, achieves a better QoS level than (a), with closer results to (b).

The plot in Fig. 3 represents the evolution in the average QoS levels. As the previous test case, the QoS-aware Distance Vector Routing presents a QoS level per hop ratio similar to the Dijkstra's algorithm weighted with the QoS scores. As we can see, the three routing approaches have their QoS levels diminished as the APT evolves (due to the attacks and consequent decrease of the S scores, as explained in Algorithm 1), but our approach shows a higher QoS level, close to the one experienced by the optimal Dijkstra's solution. Therefore, we have demonstrated our reliable routing approach behaves in a nearly optimal way, more efficiently than the original response technique [7]. Figures 2 and 3 prove that QoS- or security anomaly-based routing alone are not sufficient, since both criteria must be complied to ensure a delivery of messages balanced with a decent level of security and QoS. In addition, table-driven routing algorithms like DVR with the Bellman-Ford algorithm also ensure an ad-hoc selection of routes without any central entities involved in the communications, which can help achieving a higher level of security while alleviating the large amount of traffic that route updates like the original protocol can imply.

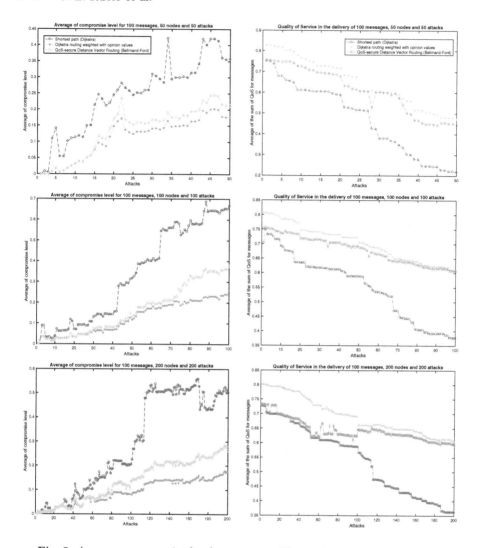

Fig. 2. Average compromise level   **Fig. 3.** Average QoS level

6   Conclusions and Future Work

Nowadays, APTs impose a major problem for the security of Industrial Control Networks, for which the Opinion Dynamics approach has been shown to represent a promising solution. In this work, we have revisited the original approach to analyze its applicability and enhance the algorithm with the aim of enabling reliable communications. We have defined an aggregated Quality of Service score that permits to prioritize the opinions of agents transmitted through trustworthy links and made the detection system account for anomalies in the communication channels besides anomalies sensed on the nodes. We have further developed an alternative routing approach that uses the anomaly information measured by the agents in relation to the security of nodes and the QoS indicators of the communication links to choose paths with an almost optimal degree of security and QoS. Finally, the superiority of our approach over prior work has been demonstrated with an extended attack model and simulations using modern industrial network topologies. Our ongoing work involves defining an extended set of response solutions coupled with a more realistic attack model, with the aim of finding an adaptable defensive strategy using game theory. This is being addressed in TI&TO, a two-player game where the defender leverages multiple protection measures based on the Opinion Dynamics detection approach.

Acknowledgments. This work has been partially supported by the research project SealedGRID (H2020-MSCA-RISE-2017), financed from the European Unions Horizon 2020 research and innovation programme under the Marie Sklodowska-Curie grant agreement No. 777996, as well as by the project DISS-IIoT, financed by the University of Malaga (UMA) through the "I Plan Propio de Investigación y Transferencia". Likewise, the work of the first author has been partially financed by the Spanish Ministry of Education under the FPU program (FPU15/03213).

References

1. ICS-CERT: Overview of Cyber Vulnerabilities (2018). http://ics-cert.us-cert.gov/content/overview-cyber-vulnerabilities. Accessed July 2018
2. Da Li, X., He, W., Li, S.: Internet of things in industries: a survey. IEEE Trans. Ind. Inform. **10**(4), 2233–2243 (2014)
3. Singh, S., Sharma, P.K., Moon, S.Y., Moon, D., Park, J.H.: A comprehensive study on apt attacks and countermeasures for future networks and communications: challenges and solutions. J. Supercomput. 1–32 (2016)
4. Lemay, A., Calvet, J., Menet, F., Fernandez, J.: Survey of publicly available reports on advanced persistent threat actors. Comput. Secur. **72**, 26–59 (2018)
5. Mitchell, R., Chen, I.-R.: A survey of intrusion detection techniques for cyber-physical systems. ACM Comput. Surv. (CSUR) **46**(4), 55 (2014)
6. Marchetti, M., Pierazzi, F., Colajanni, M., Guido, A.: Analysis of high volumes of network traffic for advanced persistent threat detection. Comput. Netw. **109**, 127–141 (2016)
7. Rubio, J.E., Alcaraz, C., Lopez, J.: Preventing advanced persistent threats in complex control networks. In: Foley, S.N., Gollmann, D., Snekkenes, E. (eds.) ESORICS 2017. LNCS, vol. 10493, pp. 402–418. Springer, Cham (2017). https://doi.org/10.1007/978-3-319-66399-9_22
8. Hegselmann, R., Krause, U., et al.: Opinion dynamics and bounded confidence models, analysis, and simulation. J. Artif. Soc. Soc. Simul. **5**(3) (2002)
9. Badis, H., Al Agha, K.: QOLSR, QOS routing for ad hoc wireless networks using OLSR. Eur. Trans. Telecommun. **16**(5), 427–442 (2005)
10. Crawley, E., Nair, R., Rajagopalan, B., Sandick, H.: A framework for QoS-based routing in the internet. Technical report (1998)
11. Lin, C.R., Liu, J.-S.: QoS routing in ad hoc wireless networks. IEEE J. Sel. Areas Commun. **17**(8), 1426–1438 (1999)
12. Chen, L., Heinzelman, W.B.: A survey of routing protocols that support QoS in mobile ad hoc networks. IEEE Netw. **21**(6), 30–38 (2007)

13. Ogwu, F.J., Talib, M., Aderounmu, G.A., Adetoye, A.: A framework for quality of service in mobile ad hoc networks. Int. Arab J. Inf. Technol. **4**(1), 33–40 (2007)
14. Chen, S., Nahrstedt, K.: An overview of quality of service routing for next-generation high-speed networks: problems and solutions. IEEE Netw. **12**(6), 64–79 (1998)
15. Sana, A.B., Iqbal, F., Mohammad, A.A.K.: Quality of service routing for multipath manets. In: 2015 International Conference on Signal Processing And Communication Engineering Systems (SPACES), pp. 426–431. IEEE (2015)
16. Ge, Y., Kunz, T., Lamont, L.: Quality of service routing in ad-hoc networks using OLSR. In: Proceedings of the 36th Annual Hawaii International Conference on System Sciences, 9 p. IEEE (2003)
17. Clausen, T., Jacquet, P.: Optimized link state routing protocol (OLSR). Technical report (2003)
18. Badis, H., Agha, K.A.: A distributed algorithm for multiple-metric link state QoS routing problem. In: Mobile And Wireless Communications Networks: (With CD-ROM), pp. 141–144. World Scientific (2003)
19. Badis, H., Agha, K.A.: Quality of service for the ad hoc optimized link state routing protocol (QOLSR) (2005)
20. Wang, Z., Crowcroft, J.: Quality-of-service routing for supporting multimedia applications. IEEE J. Sel. Areas Commun. **14**(7), 1228–1234 (1996)
21. Rubio, J.E., Roman, R., Alcaraz, C., Zhang, Y.: Tracking advanced persistent threats in critical infrastructures through opinion dynamics. In: Lopez, J., Zhou, J., Soriano, M. (eds.) ESORICS 2018. LNCS, vol. 11098, pp. 555–574. Springer, Cham (2018). https://doi.org/10.1007/978-3-319-99073-6_27
22. Nie, S., Wang, X., Zhang, H., Li, Q., Wang, B.: Robustness of controllability for networks based on edge-attack. PloS One **9**(2), e89066 (2014)
23. International Society of Automation: ISA-95 standard (2017). https://www.isa.org/isa95/. Accessed Dec 2017
24. Haynes, T.W., Hedetniemi, S.M., Hedetniemi, S.T., Henning, M.A.: Domination in graphs applied to electric power networks. SIAM J. Discret. Math. **15**(4), 519–529 (2002)
25. Pagani, G.A., Aiello, M.: The power grid as a complex network: a survey. Phys. A: Stat. Mech. Appl. **392**(11), 2688–2700 (2013)
26. Watts, D.J., Strogatz, S.H.: Collective dynamics of 'small-world' networks. Nature **393**(6684), 440 (1998)
27. Bellman, R.: On a routing problem. Q. Appl. Math. **16**(1), 87–90 (1958)
28. Marina, M.K., Das, S.R.: On-demand multipath distance vector routing in ad hoc networks. In: Ninth International Conference on Network Protocols, pp. 14–23. IEEE (2001)
29. Dijkstra, E.W.: A note on two problems in connexion with graphs. Numerische mathematik **1**(1), 269–271 (1959)
30. Fortz, B., Thorup, M.: Optimizing OSPF/IS-IS weights in a changing world. IEEE J. Sel. Areas Commun. **20**(4), 756–767 (2002)

Searchable Encryption

Dynamic Searchable Symmetric Encryption with Forward and Stronger Backward Privacy

Cong Zuo[1,2], Shi-Feng Sun[1,2(✉)], Joseph K. Liu[1(✉)], Jun Shao[3], and Josef Pieprzyk[2,4]

[1] Faculty of Information Technology, Monash University, Clayton 3168, Australia
{cong.zuo1,shifeng.sun,joseph.liu}@monash.edu
[2] Data61, CSIRO, Melbourne/Sydney, Australia
josef.pieprzyk@data61.csiro.au
[3] School of Computer and Information Engineering, Zhejiang Gongshang University, Hangzhou 310018, Zhejiang, China
chn.junshao@gmail.com
[4] Institute of Computer Science, Polish Academy of Sciences, 01-248 Warsaw, Poland

Abstract. Dynamic Searchable Symmetric Encryption (DSSE) enables a client to perform updates and searches on encrypted data which makes it very useful in practice. To protect DSSE from the leakage of updates (leading to break query or data privacy), two new security notions, forward and backward privacy, have been proposed recently. Although extensive attention has been paid to forward privacy, this is not the case for backward privacy. Backward privacy, first formally introduced by Bost et al., is classified into three types from weak to strong, exactly Type-III to Type-I. To the best of our knowledge, however, no practical DSSE schemes without trusted hardware (e.g. SGX) have been proposed so far, in terms of the strong backward privacy and constant roundtrips between the client and the server.

In this work, we present a new DSSE scheme by leveraging simple symmetric encryption with homomorphic addition and bitmap index. The new scheme can achieve both forward and backward privacy with one roundtrip. In particular, the backward privacy we achieve in our scheme (denoted by Type-I$^-$) is stronger than Type-I. Moreover, our scheme is very practical as it involves only lightweight cryptographic operations. To make it scalable for supporting billions of files, we further extend it to a multi-block setting. Finally, we give the corresponding security proofs and experimental evaluation which demonstrate both security and practicality of our schemes, respectively.

Keywords: Dynamic Searchable Symmetric Encryption ·
Forward privacy · Backward privacy

© Springer Nature Switzerland AG 2019
K. Sako et al. (Eds.): ESORICS 2019, LNCS 11736, pp. 283–303, 2019.
https://doi.org/10.1007/978-3-030-29962-0_14

1   Introduction

Cloud storage solutions become increasingly popular and economically attractive for users who need to handle large volumes of data. To protect the data stored on the cloud, users normally encrypt the data before sending it to the cloud. Unfortunately, encryption destroys the natural structure of data and consequently, data needs to be decrypted before processing. To solve this dilemma, searchable symmetric encryption (SSE) has been proposed [6,8,16]. SSE not only protects confidentiality of data but also permits searching over encrypted data without a need for decryption. Furthermore, SSE is much more efficient compared to other cryptographic techniques such as oblivious RAM (ORAM) that attract a punishing computational overhead [11,20].

Early SSE solutions were designed for a static setting, i.e., an encrypted database cannot be updated. This feature of SSE severely restricts their applications. To overcome this limitation and make SSE practical, dynamic searchable symmetric encryption (DSSE) was proposed (see [5,13]). DSSE allows both searching and updating. However, security analysis becomes more complicated as an adversary can observe the behavior of the database during the updates (addition and deletion of data). For instance, an adversary can find out if an added/deleted file contains previously searched keywords. Cash et al. [4] argued that updates can leak information about the contents of database as well as about search queries and keywords involved. For example, file-injection attacks can reveal user queries by adding to a database a small number of carefully designed files [21].

Consequently, two new security notions called forward and backward privacy were proposed to deal with the leakages mentioned above. They were informally introduced by Stefanov et al. in 2014 [17]. Roughly speaking, for any adversary who may continuously observe the interactions between the server and the client, forward privacy is satisfied if addition of new files does not leak any information about previously queried keywords. In a similar vein, backward privacy holds if files that previously added and later deleted do not leak "too much" information within any period that two search queries on the same keyword happened[1]. Bost [2] formally defined forward privacy and designed a forward-private DSSE scheme, which is resistant against file-injection attacks [21]. The scheme has been extended by Zuo et al. [23] so it supports range queries. In contrast, backward privacy attracted less attention. Recently, Bost et al. [3] defined three variants of backward privacy in order from strong to weak. They are:

- Type-I – backward privacy with insertion pattern. Given a keyword w and a time interval between two search queries on w, then Type-I leaks information about when new files containing w were inserted and the total number of updates on w.

---

[1] The files are leaked if the second search query is issued after the files are added but before they are deleted. This is unavoidable, since the adversary can easily tell the difference of the search results before and after the same search query.

– Type-II – backward privacy with update pattern. Apart from the leakages of Type-I, it additionally leaks when all updates (including deletion) related to w occurred.
– Type-III – weak backward privacy. It leaks information of Type-II and it also leaks exactly when a previous addition has been canceled by which deletion.

For example, assume that a query has the following form {time, operation, (keyword, file)}. Given the following queries: $\{1, search, w\}$, $\{2, add, (w, f_1)\}$, $\{3, add, (w, f_2)\}$, $\{4, add, (w, f_3)\}$, $\{5, del, (w, f_2)\}$ and $\{6, search, w\}$. Then after time 6, Type-I leaks that there are 4 updates, the files f_1 and f_3 match the keyword w and these two files were added at time 2 and 4, respectively. Type-II additionally leaks time 3 and 5 when the updates related to keyword w occurred. Type-III leaks also the fact that the addition at time 3 has been canceled by the deletion at time 5[2].

Bost et al. [3] gave several constructions with different security/efficiency trade-offs. Their FIDES scheme achieves Type-II backward privacy. Their schemes DIANA$_{del}$ and Janus provide better performance at the expense of security (they are Type-III backward-private). Their scheme MONETA, which is based on the recent TWORAM construction of Garg et al. [11], achieves Type-I backward privacy. Ghareh Chamani et al. [12], however, argued that the MONETA scheme is highly impractical due to the fact that it is based on TWORAM, and it serves mostly as a theoretical result for the feasibility of Type-I schemes. Sun et al. [19] proposed a new DSSE scheme named Janus++. It is more efficient than Janus as it is based on symmetric puncturable encryption. Janus++ can only achieve the same security level as Janus (Type-III).

Very recently, Ghareh Chamani et al. [12] designed three DSSE schemes. The first scheme MITRA achieves Type-II backward privacy and it is based on symmetric key encryption getting better performance than FIDES [3]. The second scheme ORION achieves Type-I backward privacy. It requires $O(logN)$ rounds of interaction and applies ORAM [20], where N is the total number of keyword/file-identifier pairs. The third design is HORUS. The number of interactions is reduced to $O(d_w)$ at the expense of lower security guarantees (Type-III backward privacy), where d_w is the number of deleted entries for w. Zuo et al. [23] also constructed two DSSE schemes supporting range queries. Their first scheme achieves forward privacy. Their second scheme (called SchemeB) uses bit string representation and the Paillier cryptosystem which achieves backward privacy. However, they did not provide any formal analysis for the backward privacy of their scheme. To the best of our knowledge, no practical DSSE schemes achieve both the high-level backward privacy and constant interactions between the client and the server.

---

[2] In this example, there is only one addition/deletion pair. For Type-II, the server knows which addition has been canceled by which deletion easily. However, there may have many addition/deletion pairs, then the server cannot know which deletion cancels which addition.

Table 1. Comparison with previous works

Scheme	Roundtrips bet. client and server	Client storage	Forward privacy	Backward privacy	Without ORAM
FIDES [3]	2	$O(|\mathbf{W}|log|D|)$	✓	Type-II	✓
DIANA$_{del}$ [3]	2	$O(|\mathbf{W}|log|D|)$	✓	Type-III	✓
Janus [3]	1	$O(|\mathbf{W}|log|D|)$	✓	Type-III	✓
Janus++ [19]	1	$O(|\mathbf{W}|log|D|)$	✓	Type-III	✓
MITRA [12]	2	$O(|\mathbf{W}|log|D|)$	✓	Type-II	✓
HORUS [12]	$O(log d_w)$	$O(|\mathbf{W}|log|D|)$	✓	Type-III	✗
SchemeB [23]	2	$O(2|\mathbf{W}|log|D|)$	✗	Unknown	✓
MONETA [3]	3	$O(1)$	✓	Type-I	✗
ORION [12]	$O(logN)$	$O(1)$	✓	Type-I	✗
Our schemes	1	$O(|\mathbf{W}|log|D|)$	✓	Type-I$^-$	✓

N is the number of keyword/file-identifier pairs, d_w is the number of deleted entries for keyword w. $|\mathbf{W}|$ is the collection of distinct keywords, $|D|$ is the total number of files.

Our Contributions. In this paper, we propose an efficient DSSE scheme (named FB-DSSE) with a stronger backward privacy (denoted as Type-I$^-$ backward privacy) and one roundtrip (without considering the retrieval of actual files), which also achieves forward privacy. This scheme is based on a bitmap index and a simple symmetric encryption with homomorphic addition. Later, we extend it to a multi-block setting (named MB-FB-DSSE). Table 1 compares our schemes (FB-DSSE and MB-FB-DSSE) with other designs supporting backward privacy. In particular, our contributions are as follows:

- We formally introduce a new type of backward privacy, named Type-I$^-$ backward privacy, which leaks less information than Type-I. More precisely, for a query with a keyword w, it only leaks the number of previous updates associated with w, time when these updates happened, and files that currently match w. Type-I$^-$ leaks no information about when each file was inserted. For our example, Type-I$^-$ only leaks that there are 4 updates and f_1, f_3 currently matching keyword w^3. Although it is not clear the impact of leaking the insertion time in practice, it is believed that the less information the scheme leaks, the higher security it guarantees, since the leakage might be leveraged by the adversary to launch some potential attacks.
- We design a Type-I$^-$ backward-private DSSE FB-DSSE by leveraging the bitmap index and the simple symmetric encryption with homomorphic addition. FB-DSSE also achieves forward privacy, which is based on the framework of [2]. In the scheme, we achieve forward privacy through a new technique

---

[3] Note that, it does not leak the insertion time of f_1 and f_3.

which deploys symmetric primitive instead of the public primitive [2] (one-way trapdoor permutation), which makes our scheme more efficient.

- To support an even larger number of files with improved efficiency, we extend our first scheme to the multi-block setting. We call it MB-FB-DSSE. In our experimental analysis, for the MB-FB-DSSE scheme with 1 billion files, the search and update time are 5.84 s and 46.41 ms, respectively, where the number of blocks is 10^3 and the bit length of each block is 10^6. For the same number of files, the FB-DSSE scheme consumes 9.07 s for search and 125.23 ms for update (note that, bit length is 10^9). Finally, the security analyses are given to show that our schemes are forward and Type-I^- backward private.

1.1 Related Works

Song et al. [16] showed how to perform keyword search over encrypted data using symmetric encryption. To search for a keyword w, the server compares every encrypted keyword in a file with a token (issued by the client). The search time is linear with the number of keyword/file-identifier pairs, which is not efficient. Later, Curtmola et al. [8] designed an efficient SSE based on inverted index, which achieves sub-linear search time. The authors also quantified the leakage of an SSE and gave a formal security definition for SSE. Cash et al. [6] proposed a highly scalable SSE, which supports large databases. Following this work, many SSE schemes have been proposed addressing different aspects. For example, Sun et al. [18] focused on the usage of SSE in a multi-client setting. Zuo et al. [22] proposed an SSE scheme, which supports more general Boolean queries. To support database updates, dynamic SSE schemes are introduced in [2,3,5,13].

Early schemes have been designed under the assumption that the encrypted database is static, i.e., it cannot be updated. Dynamic SSE schemes were introduced in [5,13]. For DSSE schemes, it is assumed that an encrypted database can be updated, i.e. new files can be added and some existing files can be removed. However, a dynamic nature of databases brings new security problems. Two security notions, namely, forward and backward privacy, have been informally introduced in [17]. Further works concentrates on refinements of the privacy notions for DSSE schemes [2,3,12,19].

There is also a line of investigation that concentrates on the design of SSE schemes that can handle a richer (complex) queries. Cash et al. [6] proposed an SSE scheme that handles Boolean queries. Faber et al. [9] extended the scheme so it can handle more complex queries about ranges, substrings and wild cards. A majority of forward private DSSE schemes support single keyword queries only. Zuo et al. [23] proposed a forward private DSSE scheme supporting range queries. Recently, SGX has been used to instantiate hardware-based SSE. We refer readers to [1,10] for more details.

1.2 Organization

The remaining sections of this paper are organized as follows. In Sect. 2, we give the necessary background information and describe building blocks that are used in this paper. In Sect. 3, we define DSSE and its security notions. In Sect. 4, we present our DSSE schemes. Their security and experimental analyses are given in Sects. 5 and 6, respectively. Finally, Sect. 7 concludes this work.

2   Preliminaries

In this paper, λ denotes the security parameter, $\|$ stands for the concatenation and $|m|$ denotes the bit length of m. We use bitmap index[4] to represent file identifiers [15]. More precisely, there is a bit string bs of the length ℓ, where ℓ is the maximum number of files that a scheme can support. The i-th bit of bs is set to 1 if there exists file f_i, and 0 otherwise. Figure 1 illustrates an instance for 6 files, i.e. $\ell = 6$. Assume that there exists file f_2 and f_3 (see Fig. 1(a)). If we want to add file f_1, we need to generate the bit string $2^1 = 000010$ and add it to the original bit string (see Fig. 1(b)). Now, if we want to delete file f_2, we need to generate the bit string $-2^2 = -4 = -000100$. As our index computation is done modulo 2^6, we can convert $-4 = 2^6 - 2^2 = 60 \pmod{2^6}$, which is 111100 in binary. The string 111100 is added to the original bit string (see Fig. 1(c)). Note that manipulation on bitmap indexes for addition and deletion can be done by modulo addition. In other words, the bitmap index can be (homomorphicly) encrypted and updated (to reflect addition or deletion of files) using encryption with homomorphic property.

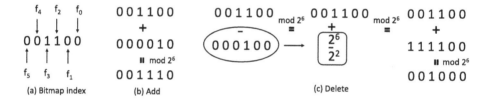

Fig. 1. An example of our bitmap index

2.1   Simple Symmetric Encryption with Homomorphic Addition

A simple symmetric encryption with homomorphic addition Π [7] consists of the following four algorithms Setup, Enc, Dec and Add as described below:

- $n \leftarrow$ Setup(1^λ): For the security parameter λ, it outputs a public parameter n, where $n = 2^\ell$ is the message space and ℓ is the maximum number of files a scheme can support.
- $c \leftarrow$ Enc(sk, m, n): For a message m, the public parameter n and a random secret key sk ($0 \le sk < n$), it computes a ciphertext $c = sk + m \bmod n$, where m is the message $0 \le m < n$. Note that, for every encryption, the secret key sk needs to be stored, and it can only be used once.

---

[4] A special kind of data structure which has been widely used in database community.

- $m \leftarrow \mathsf{Dec}(sk, c, n)$: For the ciphertext c, the public parameter n and the secret key sk, it recovers the message $m = c - sk \bmod n$.
- $\hat{c} \leftarrow \mathsf{Add}(c_0, c_1, n)$: For two ciphertexts c_0, c_1 and the public parameter n, it computes $\hat{c} = c_0 + c_1 \bmod n$, where $c_0 \leftarrow \mathsf{Enc}(sk_0, m_0, n)$, $c_1 \leftarrow \mathsf{Enc}(sk_1, m_1, n)$, $n \leftarrow \mathsf{Setup}(1^\lambda)$ and $0 \le sk_0, sk_1 < n$.

Correctness. For the correctness of this scheme, it is required that sum of two ciphertexts $\hat{c} = c_0 + c_1 \bmod n$ decrypts to $m_0 + m_1 \bmod n$ under the $\hat{sk} = sk_0 + sk_1 \bmod n$ or in other words

$$\mathsf{Dec}(\hat{sk}, \hat{c}, n) = \hat{c} - \hat{sk} \bmod n = m_0 + m_1 \bmod n.$$

It is easy to check that this requirement holds.

Remark. For the encryption and decryption algorithms of Π, the secret key sk can only be used once.

Perfectly Security [7]. We say Π is perfectly secure if for any PPT adversary $\mathcal{A}$, their advantage in the perfectly-security game is negligible or

$$\mathbf{Adv}^{\mathsf{PS}}_{\Pi, \mathcal{A}}(\lambda) = |\Pr[\mathcal{A}(\mathsf{Enc}(sk, m_0, n)) = 1] - \Pr[\mathcal{A}(\mathsf{Enc}(sk, m_1, n)) = 1]| \le \epsilon,$$

where $n \leftarrow \mathsf{Setup}(1^\lambda)$, the secret key sk $(0 \le sk < n)$ is kept secret and $\mathcal{A}$ chooses m_0, m_1 s.t. $0 \le m_0, m_1 < n$.

2.2   Notations

Notations used in the work are given in Table 2.

3   DSSE Definition and Security Model

A database DB is a list of file-identifier/keyword-set pairs, which is denoted as $\mathsf{DB} = (f_i, \mathbf{W}_i)_{i=1}^\ell$. The file identifier is $f_i \in \{0, 1\}^\lambda$, $\mathbf{W}_i \subseteq \{0, 1\}^*$ is a set of all keywords contained in the file f_i and ℓ is the total number of files in DB. We also denote $\mathbf{W} = \cup_{i=1}^\ell \mathbf{W}_i$ as all keywords in DB. We identify $\mathbf{W}$ as a collection of all distinct keywords that occur in DB. Note that, $|\mathbf{W}|$ is the total number of keywords and $N = \sum_{i=1}^\ell |\mathbf{W}_i|$ is denoted as the total number of file-identifier/keyword pairs. A set of files that satisfy a query q is denoted by $\mathsf{DB}(q)$. Note that, in this paper, we use bitmap index to represent the file identifiers. For a search query q, the result is a bit string bs, which represents a list of file identifiers in $\mathsf{DB}(q)$. For an update query u, a bit string bs is used to update a list of file identifiers. Moreover, we isolate the actual files from the metadata (e.g. file identifiers). We only focus on the search of the metadata. The ways we can retrieve the encrypted files are not described in this paper.

Table 2. Notations (used in our schemes)

Notation	Description
DB	A database
λ	The security parameter
ST_c	The current search token for a keyword w
EDB	The encrypted database EDB which is a map
F	A secure PRF
W	The set of all keywords of the database DB
CT	A map stores the current search token ST_c and counter c for every keyword in **W**
f_i	The i-th file
bs	The bit string which is used to represent the existence of files
ℓ	The length of bs
e	The encrypted bit string
Sum_e	The sum of the encrypted bit strings
sk	The one time secret key
Sum_{sk}	The sum of the one time secret keys
B	The number of blocks
bs	The bit string array with length B
e	The encrypted bit string array with length B
Sum$_e$	The sum of the encrypted bit string arrays with length B
sk	The one time secret key array with length B
Sum$_{sk}$	The sum of the one time secret key arrays with length B

3.1 DSSE Definition

A DSSE scheme consists of an algorithm **Setup** and two protocols **Search** and **Update** that are executed between a client and a server. They are described as follows:

- (EDB, σ) ← **Setup**(1^λ, DB): For a security parameter λ and a database DB, the algorithm outputs a pair: an encrypted database EDB and a state σ. EDB is stored by the server and σ is kept by the client.
- ($\mathcal{I}$, $\perp$) ← **Search**(q, σ; EDB): For a state σ, the client issues a query q and interacts with the server who holds EDB. At the end of the protocol, the client outputs a set of file identifiers $\mathcal{I}$ that match q and the server outputs nothing.
- (σ', EDB') ← **Update**(σ, op, in; EDB): For a state σ, the operation $op \in \{add, del\}$ and a collection of $in = (f, \mathbf{w})$ pairs, the client requests the server (who holds EDB) to update database by adding/deleting files specified by the collection in. Finally, the protocol returns an updated state σ' to the client and an updated encrypted database EDB' to the server.

Remark. There are two variants of result model for SSE schemes. In the first one (considered in the work [6]), the server returns encrypted file identifiers $\mathcal{I}$ so the client needs to decrypt them. In the second one (studied in the work [2]), the server returns the file identifiers to the client directly. In our work, we consider the first variant, where the protocol returns encrypted file identifiers.

3.2 Security Model

DSSE security is modeled by interaction between the Real and Ideal worlds called DSSEREAL and DSSEIDEAL, respectively. The behavior of DSSEREAL is exactly the same as the original DSSE. However, DSSEIDEAL reflects a behavior of a simulator $\mathcal{S}$, which takes the leakage of the original DSSE as input. The leakage is defined by a function $\mathcal{L} = (\mathcal{L}^{Setup}, \mathcal{L}^{Search}, \mathcal{L}^{Update})$, which details what information the adversary $\mathcal{A}$ can learn during execution of the **Setup** algorithm, **Search** and **Update** protocols.

If the adversary $\mathcal{A}$ can distinguish DSSEREAL from DSSEIDEAL with a negligible advantage, the information leakage is limited to $\mathcal{L}$ only. More formally, we consider the following security game. The adversary $\mathcal{A}$ interacts with one of the two worlds DSSEREAL or DSSEIDEAL and would like to guess it.

- DSSEREAL$_{\mathcal{A}}(\lambda)$: First **Setup**(λ, DB) is run and the adversary gets EDB. $\mathcal{A}$ performs search queries q (or update queries (op, in)). Eventually, $\mathcal{A}$ outputs a bit b, where $b \in \{0, 1\}$.
- DSSEIDEAL$_{\mathcal{A},\mathcal{S}}(\lambda)$: Simulator $\mathcal{S}$ with the input $\mathcal{L}^{Setup}(\lambda, DB)$ is executed. For search queries q (or update queries (op, in)) generated by the adversary $\mathcal{A}$, the simulator $\mathcal{S}$ replies by using the leakage function $\mathcal{L}^{Search}(q)$ (or $\mathcal{L}^{Update}(op, in)$). Eventually, $\mathcal{A}$ outputs a bit b, where $b \in \{0, 1\}$.

Definition 1. *Given a DSSE scheme and the security game described above. The scheme is $\mathcal{L}$-adaptively-secure if for every PPT adversary $\mathcal{A}$, there exists an efficient simulator $\mathcal{S}$ (with the input $\mathcal{L}$) such that,*

$$|\Pr[\text{DSSEREAL}_{\mathcal{A}}(\lambda) = 1] - \Pr[\text{DSSEIDEAL}_{\mathcal{A},\mathcal{S}}(\lambda) = 1]| \leq negl(\lambda).$$

Leakage Function. Before define the leakage function, we define a search query $q = (t, w)$ and an update query $u = (t, op, (w, bs))$, where t is the timestamp, w is the keyword to be searched (or updated), op is the update operation and bs denotes a list of file identifiers to be updated. For a list of search queries Q, we define a search pattern $\mathbf{sp}(w) = \{t : (t, w) \in Q\}$, where t is a timestamp. The search pattern leaks the repetition of search queries on w. Result pattern $\mathbf{rp}(w) = \overline{bs}$, $\overline{bs}$ represents all file identifiers that currently matching w. Note that, after a search query, we implicitly assume that the server knows the final result $\overline{bs}^5$.

---

[5] After getting $\overline{bs}$, the client may retrieve the file identifiers represented by $\overline{bs}$ which is not described in this paper.

3.3   Forward Privacy

Informally, for any adversary who may continuously observe the interactions between the server and the client, forward privacy guarantees that an update does not leak information about the newly added files that match the previously issued queries. The definition given below is taken from [2]:

Definition 2. *A $\mathcal{L}$-adaptively-secure DSSE scheme is forward-private if the update leakage function $\mathcal{L}^{Update}$ can be written as*

$$\mathcal{L}^{Update}(op, in) = \mathcal{L}'(op, \{(f_i, \mu_i)\}),$$

where $\{(f_i, \mu_i)\}$ is the set of modified file-identifier/keywords pairs, μ_i is the number of keywords corresponding to the updated file f_i.

Remark. In this paper, the leakage function will be $\mathcal{L}^{Update}(op, w, bs) = \mathcal{L}'(op, bs)$.

3.4   Backward Privacy

Similarly, within any period that two search queries on the same keyword happened, backward privacy ensures that it does not leak information about the files that have been previously added and later deleted. Note that, information about files is leaked if the second search query is issued after the files are added but before they are deleted. In 2017, Bost et al. [3] formulated three different levels of backward privacy from Type-I to Type-III in decreasing level of privacy. In our construction, we use a new data structure (see Fig. 1), which achieves a stronger level of backward privacy. We call it Type-I$^-$, which leaks less information than Type-I. We refer readers to [3] for more details. Type-I$^-$ and Type-I definitions are given below.

- Type-I$^-$: Given a time interval between two search queries for a keyword w, then it leaks the files that currently match w and the total number of updates for w.
- Type-I: Given a time interval between two search queries for a keyword w, then it leaks not only files that currently match w and the total number of updates for w (Type-I$^-$) but additionally when the files were inserted.

To define Type-I$^-$ formally, we need a new leakage functions Time. For a search query on keyword w, Time(w) lists the timestamp t of all updates corresponding to w. Formally, for a sequence of update queries Q':

$$\text{Time}(w) = \{t : (t, op, (w, bs)) \in Q'\}.$$

Definition 3. *A $\mathcal{L}$-adaptively-secure DSSE scheme is Type-I$^-$ backward-private iff the search and update leakage function $\mathcal{L}^{Search}, \mathcal{L}^{Update}$ can be written as:*

$$\mathcal{L}^{Update}(op, w, bs) = \mathcal{L}'(op), \mathcal{L}^{Search}(w) = \mathcal{L}''(sp(w), rp(w), \text{Time}(w)),$$

where $\mathcal{L}'$ and $\mathcal{L}''$ are stateless.

4   Our Construction

In this section, we give our Type-I$^-$ backward private DSSE scheme. To achieve forward privacy, we follow the framework of the forward-private DSSE from [2]. To improve the efficiency of the underlying forward-private DSSE, we use a hash function that replaces a public key primitive (i.e. one-way function in [2]) to achieve forward privacy. See Sect. 4.2 for more details.

4.1   Overview

To achieve backward privacy, the DSSE schemes from [3,19] used puncturable encryption, which can be used to "puncture" the deleted file identifiers. Then the deleted file identifiers cannot be decrypted (searched). The schemes achieve Type-III backward privacy only. In our construction, instead of encrypting file identifiers independently, we use a new data structure, the bitmap index (as illustrated in Fig. 1(a)), where all file identifiers are represented by a single bit string. To add or delete a file identifier, the bit string is modified as shown in Fig. 1(b) and (c), respectively. Besides, our scheme does not leak the update type since both addition and deletion are done by one modulo addition[6]. To securely update the encrypted database, our scheme requires an additive homomorphic encryption as the underlying encryption primitive.

The most popular additive homomorphic encryption is the Paillier cryptosystem [14]. Unfortunately, the Paillier cryptosystem attracts a very large computation overhead and can support a limited number of files (up to the number of bits in a message/ciphertext space, e.g. 1024 bits). After observing our bitmap index, we notice that we only need the addition of ciphertexts (the bit strings). Also, we do not need to use one key for all encryption and decryption. Therefore we can use a simple symmetric encryption (the key can be only used once) with homomorphic addition (Sect. 2.1) to add the ciphertexts (and the keys) simultaneously. To save the client storage, we can use a hash function with a secret key K to generate all the one time keys. E.g. $H(K, c)$, where c is a counter. It is worth nothing that this technique has been used in [7] in the context of wireless sensor networks.

4.2   DSSE with Forward and Stronger Backward Privacy

Now we are ready to give our forward and stronger backward private DSSE construction FB-DSSE – see Algorithm 1. Our scheme is based on the framework of the forward private DSSE from [2], a simple symmetric encryption with homomorphic addition $\Pi = (\textsf{Setup}, \textsf{Enc}, \textsf{Dec}, \textsf{Add})$, and a keyed PRF F_K with key K. The scheme is defined by the following algorithms:

- $(\textsf{EDB}, \sigma = (n, K, \mathbf{CT})) \leftarrow \textsf{Setup}(1^\lambda)$: The algorithm is run by a client. It takes the security parameter λ as input. Then it chooses a secret key K and

---

[6] Deletion is by adding a negative number.

an integer n, where $n = 2^\ell$ and ℓ is the maximum number of files that this scheme can support. Moreover, it initializes two empty maps EDB and **CT**, which are used to store the encrypted database as well as the current search token ST_c and the current counter c (the number of updates) for each keyword $w \in \mathbf{W}$, respectively. Finally, it outputs encrypted database EDB and the state $\sigma = (n, K, \mathbf{CT})$, and the client keeps $(K, \mathbf{CT})$ secret.

Algorithm 1. FB-DSSE

Setup(1^λ)

1: $K \xleftarrow{\$} \{0,1\}^\lambda$, $n \leftarrow$ **Setup**(1^λ)
2: **CT**, EDB $\leftarrow$ empty map
3: **return** (EDB, $\sigma = (n, K, \mathbf{CT})$)

Update$(w, bs, \sigma; \text{EDB})$
Client:
1: $K_w \| K'_w \leftarrow F_K(w)$, $(ST_c, c) \leftarrow \mathbf{CT}[w]$
2: **if** $(ST_c, c) = \perp$ **then**
3:     $c \leftarrow -1$, $ST_c \leftarrow \{0,1\}^\lambda$
4: **end if**
5: $ST_{c+1} \leftarrow \{0,1\}^\lambda$
6: $\mathbf{CT}[w] \leftarrow (ST_{c+1}, c+1)$
7: $UT_{c+1} \leftarrow H_1(K_w, ST_{c+1})$
8: $C_{ST_c} \leftarrow H_2(K_w, ST_{c+1}) \oplus ST_c$
9: $sk_{c+1} \leftarrow H_3(K'_w, c+1)$
10: $e_{c+1} \leftarrow \text{Enc}(sk_{c+1}, bs, n)$
11: Send $(UT_{c+1}, (e_{c+1}, C_{ST_c}))$ to server.
Server:
12: $\text{EDB}[UT_{c+1}] \leftarrow (e_{c+1}, C_{ST_c})$

Search$(w, \sigma; \text{EDB})$
Client:
1: $K_w \| K'_w \leftarrow F_K(w)$, $(ST_c, c) \leftarrow \mathbf{CT}[w]$
2: **if** $(ST_c, c) = \perp$ **then**
3:     **return** $\varnothing$

4: **end if**
5: Send (K_w, ST_c, c) to server.
Server:
6: $Sum_e \leftarrow 0$
7: **for** $i = c$ to 0 **do**
8:     $UT_i \leftarrow H_1(K_w, ST_i)$
9:     $(e_i, C_{ST_{i-1}}) \leftarrow \text{EDB}[UT_i]$
10:     $Sum_e \leftarrow \text{Add}(Sum_e, e_i, n)$
11:     Remove $\text{EDB}[UT_i]$
12:     **if** $C_{ST_{i-1}} = \perp$ **then**
13:         $Break$
14:     **end if**
15:     $ST_{i-1} \leftarrow H_2(K_w, ST_i) \oplus C_{ST_{i-1}}$
16: **end for**
17: $\text{EDB}[UT_c] \leftarrow (Sum_e, \perp)$
18: Send Sum_e to client.
Client:
19: $Sum_{sk} \leftarrow 0$
20: **for** $i = c$ to 0 **do**
21:     $sk_i \leftarrow H_3(K'_w, i)$
22:     $Sum_{sk} \leftarrow Sum_{sk} + sk_i \bmod n$
23: **end for**
24: $bs \leftarrow \text{Dec}(Sum_{sk}, Sum_e, n)$
25: **return** bs

- $(\sigma', \text{EDB}') \leftarrow \mathbf{Update}(w, bs, \sigma; \text{EDB})$: The algorithm runs between a client and a server. The client inputs a keyword w, a state σ and a bit string bs[7]. Next the client encrypts the bit string bs by using the simple symmetric encryption with homomorphic addition to get the encrypted bit string e. To save the client storage, the one time key sk_c is generated by a hash function $H_3(K'_w, c)$, where c is the counter. Then he/she chooses a random search token and use a hash function to get the update token. He/She also uses another hash function to mask the previous search token. After that, the client sends

---

[7] Note that, we can update many file identifiers through one update query by using bit string representation bs.

the update token, e and the masked previous search token C to the server and update **CT** to get a new state σ'. Finally, the server outputs an updated encrypted database EDB'.

- $bs \leftarrow$ **Search**$(w, \sigma; \text{EDB})$: The protocol runs between a client and a server. The client inputs a keyword w and a state σ, and the server inputs EDB. Firstly, the client gets the search token corresponding to the keyword w from **CT** and generates the K_w. Then he/she sends them to the server. The server retrieves all the encrypted bit strings e corresponding to w. To reduce the communication overhead, the server adds them together by using the homomorphic addition (**Add**) of the simple symmetric encryption to get the final result Sum_e and sends it to the client. Finally, the client decrypts it and outputs the final bit string bs which can be used to retrieve the matching files. Note that, in order to save the server storage, for every search, the server can remove all entries corresponding to w and store the final result Sum_e corresponding to the current search token ST_c to the EDB.

4.3 Multi-block Extension for Large Number of Files

The number of files supported by FB-DSSE is determined by the length of the public parameter $n = 2^\ell$, which is the modulus. Theoretically, it can be of an arbitrary length but a larger n (e.g. $\ell = 2^{23}$) will significantly slow down modular operations. Efficiency analysis and experiments will be given in Sect. 6. However, there are many applications that require a system able to manage up to a billion of files. Therefore, we still need to find an efficient solution for such applications.

In this section, we extend our basic scheme to multi-block setting in order to handle a larger number of files efficiently. The idea is to split the long bit sequence ℓ into multiple smaller blocks and have multiple (e.g. B) blocks **bs** instead of one block bs. For every block of **bs**, the operations are exactly the same as FB-DSSE. We denote the extension of FB-DSSE as MB-FB-DSSE, which is shown in Algorithm 2. This scheme consists of following algorithms:

- $(\text{EDB}, \sigma = (n, K, \mathbf{CT})) \leftarrow$ **Setup**(1^λ): The algorithm is exactly same as the one in FB-DSSE.
- $(\sigma', \text{EDB}') \leftarrow$ **Update**$(w, \mathbf{bs}, \sigma; \text{EDB})$ and $\mathbf{bs} \leftarrow$ **Search**$(w, \sigma; \text{EDB})$: The two protocols are similar to the ones in FB-DSSE. The difference is that we use multiple blocks **bs** rather than one block bs to support large number of files, where **bs** is an array with length B and it stores all the bit strings bs. For each block, the operations are exactly same as the ones in FB-DSSE. Correspondingly, we have **e**, **sk**, $\mathbf{Sum_e}$ and $\mathbf{Sum_{sk}}$ which are arrays with the length of B. $\mathbf{Sum_e}$ and $\mathbf{Sum_{sk}}$ are used to store the sum of all encrypted bit string arrays **e** and secret keys **sk**, respectively. The length of the bit string bs will be reduced and the computation time of these blocks will be shorter.

Algorithm 2. Multi-block extension MB-FB-DSSE (Difference in red)

Setup(1^λ)
1: Same as the one in FB-DSSE.
Update$(w, \mathbf{bs}, \sigma; \text{EDB})$
Client:
1: Same as the one in FB-DSSE.
2: **for** $j = 0$ to B **do**
3:    $\text{sk}_{c+1}[j] \leftarrow H_3(K'_w, c+1\|j)$
4:    $\text{e}_{c+1}[j] \leftarrow \text{Enc}(\text{sk}_{c+1}[j], \mathbf{bs}[j], n)$
5: **end for**
6: Send $(ST_{c+1}, (\text{e}_{c+1}, C_{ST_c}))$ to the server.
Server:
7: $\text{EDB}[ST_{c+1}] \leftarrow (\text{e}_{c+1}, C_{ST_c})$
Search$(w, \sigma; \text{EDB})$
Client:
1: Same as the one in FB-DSSE.
Server:

2: $\text{Sum}_\text{e} \leftarrow 0$
3: **for** $i = c$ to 0, $j = 0$ to B **do**
4:    $(\text{e}_i, C_{ST_{i-1}}) \leftarrow \text{EDB}[ST_i]$
5:    $\text{Sum}_\text{e}[j] \leftarrow \text{Add}(\text{Sum}_\text{e}[j], \text{e}_i[j], n)$
6:    Same as the one in FB-DSSE.
7: **end for**
8: $\text{EDB}[ST_c] \leftarrow (\text{Sum}_\text{e}, \bot)$
9: Send Sum_e to the client.
Client:
10: $\text{Sum}_\text{sk} \leftarrow 0$
11: **for** $i = c$ to 0, $j = 0$ to B **do**
12:    $\text{sk}_i[j] \leftarrow H_3(K'_w, i\|j)$
13:    $\text{Sum}_\text{sk}[j] \leftarrow \text{Sum}_\text{sk}[j] + \text{sk}_i[j] \bmod n$
14: **end for**
15: **for** $j = 0$ to B **do**
16:    $\mathbf{bs}[j] \leftarrow \text{Dec}(\text{Sum}_\text{sk}[j], \text{Sum}_\text{e}[j], n)$
17: **end for**
18: **return** $\mathbf{bs}$

5   Security Analysis

In this section, we give the security analysis of our schemes.

Theorem 1. *(Adaptive security of FB-DSSE). Let F be a secure PRF, $\Pi = (\text{Setup}, \text{Enc}, \text{Dec}, \text{Add})$ be a perfectly secure simple symmetric encryption with homomorphic addition, and H_1, H_2 and H_3 be random oracles. We define $\mathcal{L}_{\text{FB-DSSE}} = (\mathcal{L}_{\text{FB-DSSE}}^{Search}, \mathcal{L}_{\text{FB-DSSE}}^{Update})$, where $\mathcal{L}_{\text{FB-DSSE}}^{Search}(w) = (\mathbf{sp}(w), \mathbf{rp}(w), \mathbf{Time}(w))$ and $\mathcal{L}_{\text{FB-DSSE}}^{Update}(op, w, \mathbf{bs}) = \bot$. Then FB-DSSE is $\mathcal{L}_{\text{FB-DSSE}}$-adaptively secure.*

Similar to [2], we will set a set of games from DSSEREAL to DSSEIDEAL, and we will show that every two consecutive games is indistinguishable. Finally, we will simulate DSSEIDEAL with the leakage functions defined in Theorem 1. Due to the page limitation, we move the full proof to the Appendix.

Corollary 1. *(Adaptive forward privacy of FB-DSSE). FB-DSSE is forward-private.*

From Theorem 1, we can infer that FB-DSSE achieves forward privacy, since the leakage function $\mathcal{L}^{Update}$ of FB-DSSE does not leak the keyword during update as defined in Definition 2.

Corollary 2. *(Adaptive Type-I^- backward privacy of FB-DSSE). FB-DSSE is Type-I^- backward-private.*

From Theorem 1, we can infer that FB-DSSE achieves Type-I$^-$ backward privacy, since the leakage functions of FB-DSSE leak less information than the leakage functions in Definition 3.

Remark. For the multi-block extension MB-FB-DSSE, the underlying construction is almost same as FB-DSSE except that it encrypts multi-block bit string **bs** rather than one bit string bs. Hence, it inherits the forward privacy and Type-I$^-$ backward privacy of FB-DSSE.

6   Experimental Analysis

Our schemes deploy simple symmetric primitives to achieve strong backward privacy, which are more efficient than the schemes in [3,12] because the authors of [3,12] deploy ORAM [11,20] to achieve strong backward privacy. The scheme Janus++ in [19] is the most efficient backward-private scheme which is based on the scheme Janus in [3]. However, Janus++ only achieves Type-III backward privacy. Table 3 compares the results.

Table 3. Comparison of computing overhead

Scheme	Search	Update
Janus [3]	$O(n_w + d_w) \cdot t_{\text{PE.Dec}}$	$O(1) \cdot (t_{\text{PE.Enc}}$ or $t_{\text{PE.Punc}})$
Janus++ [19]	$O(n_w + d_w) \cdot t_{\text{SPE.Dec}}$	$O(1) \cdot (t_{\text{SPE.Enc}}$ or $t_{\text{SPE.Punc}})$
MONETA [3]	$\hat{O}(a_w log N + log^3 N) \cdot t_{\text{SKE}}$	$\hat{O}(log^2 N) \cdot t_{\text{SKE}}$
ORION [12]	$O(n_w log^2 N) \cdot t_{\text{SKE}}$	$O(log^2 N) \cdot t_{\text{SKE}}$
FB-DSSE [Sect. 4.2]	$O(a_w) \cdot t_{ma}$	$O(1) \cdot t_{ma}$
MB-FB-DSSE [Sect. 4.3]	$O(a_w) \cdot t_{ma} \cdot B$	$O(1) \cdot t_{ma} \cdot B$

N is the number of keyword/file-identifier pairs, n_w is the number of files currently matching keyword w, d_w is the number of deleted entries for keyword w, and a_w is the total number of updates corresponding to keyword w. $t_{\text{PE.Enc}}$, $t_{\text{PE.Dec}}$ and $t_{\text{PE.Punc}}$ are the encryption, decryption and puncture time of a public puncturable encryption. $t_{\text{SPE.Enc}}$, $t_{\text{SPE.Dec}}$ and $t_{\text{SPE.Punc}}$ are the encryption, decryption and puncture time of a symmetric puncturable encryption. t_{SKE} is the encryption and decryption time of a symmetric key encryption. t_{ma} is the computational time of a modular addition, and B is the number of blocks. $\hat{O}$ notation hides polylogarithmic factors.

In this section, we evaluate the performance of our schemes in a test bed of one workstation. This machine plays the roles of client and server. The hardware and software of this machine are as follows: Mac Book Pro, Intel Core i7 CPU @ 2.8GHz RAM 16GB, Java Programming Language, and macOS 10.13.2. Note that, we use the bitmap index to denote file identifiers and we tested the search and update time for one keyword. We use the "BigInteger" with different bit length to denote the bitmap index with different size which acts as the database with different number of files. The relation between the i-th bit and the actual file is out of our scope.

For every keyword, we run the update operation **Update** for this keyword 20 times. In other words, every keyword has 20 entries. The update time includes the client token generation time and server update time, and the search time includes the token generation time, the server search time and the client decryption time. Note that the result only depends on the maximum number of files supported by the system (the bit length), but not the actual number of files in the server.

First, we give the search and update time of FB-DSSE with different bit length in Fig. 2(a). The bit length refers to ℓ, which is equal to the maximum number of files supported by the system. From Fig. 2(a), we can see that the update and search time grow with the increasing of bit length. We also can observe that the update time with the bit length from 10^5 to 10^6 does not increase a lot. This is because the addition and modular have not contribute too much when the bit length is less than 10^6.

In Fig. 2(b), we evaluate the search and update time of MB-FB-DSSE with different number of blocks, where the total bit length is 10^9. When we divide one bit string (10^9) into different blocks, we can see that the running time is lesser than one block in Fig. 2(a). For the number of blocks from 10 to 10^3, it can be seen that the update and search time decrease. However, when the number of blocks is 10^4, the update and search time increase, due to the fact that when the bit string decreases to a certain length, the addition and modular time are not decreased too much.

To support an extreme large number of files (such as 1 billion), MB-FB-DSSE may be preferred than FB-DSSE. For example, the search and update time of MB-FB-DSSE are 5.84 s and 46.41 ms, respectively, where the number of blocks is 10^3 and the bit length of each block is 10^6. However, the search and update time of FB-DSSE supporting 1 billion files (bit length $= 10^9$) are 9.07 s and 125.23 ms, respectively.

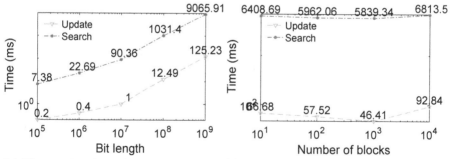

(a) The running time of FB-DSSE with different bit length

(b) The running time of MB-FB-DSSE with different number of blocks for 10^9 bits

Fig. 2. The running time of our schemes

7   Conclusion

In this paper, we gave a DSSE scheme with stronger (named Type-I⁻) backward privacy which also achieves forward privacy efficiently. Moreover, to make it scalable for supporting billions of files with high efficiency, we extended our first scheme to the multi-block setting. From the experimental analysis, we can see that the efficiency of the first scheme with extreme large bit length can be improved by splitting a long bit string into multiple short bit strings. Currently, our schemes only support single keyword queries. In the future, we will make our schemes support multiple keywords queries.

Acknowledgment. The authors thank the anonymous reviewers for the valuable comments. This work was supported by the Natural Science Foundation of Zhejiang Province [grant number LZ18F020003] and the Australian Research Council (ARC) Grant DP180102199. Josef Pieprzyk has been supported by the Australian Research Council grant DP180102199 and Polish National Science Center grant 2018/31/B/ST6/03003.

Appendix

Theorem 1. (Adaptive security of *FB-DSSE*). Let F be a secure PRF, $\Pi = (Setup, Enc, Dec, Add)$ be a perfectly secure simple symmetric encryption with homomorphic addition, and H_1, H_2 and H_3 be random oracles and output λ bits. We define $\mathcal{L}_{FB\text{-}DSSE} = (\mathcal{L}_{FB\text{-}DSSE}^{Search}, \mathcal{L}_{FB\text{-}DSSE}^{Update})$, where $\mathcal{L}_{FB\text{-}DSSE}^{Search}(w) = (sp(w), rp(w), Time(w))$ and $\mathcal{L}_{FB\text{-}DSSE}^{Update}(op, w, bs) = \perp$. Then *FB-DSSE* is $\mathcal{L}_{FB\text{-}DSSE}$-adaptively secure.

Proof. In this proof, the server is the adversary $\mathcal{A}$ who tries to break the security of our FB-DSSE. The challenger $\mathcal{C}$ is responsible for generating the search tokens and ciphertexts, and the simulator $\mathcal{S}$ simulates the transcripts between $\mathcal{A}$ and $\mathcal{C}$ at the end.

Game G_0: G_0 is exactly same as the real world game $\text{DSSEREAL}_{\mathcal{A}}^{FB\text{-}DSSE}(\lambda)$, such that

$$\Pr[\text{DSSEREAL}_{\mathcal{A}}^{FB\text{-}DSSE}(\lambda) = 1] = \Pr[G_0 = 1].$$

Game G_1: In G_1, when querying F to generate a key for a keyword w, the challenger $\mathcal{C}$ chooses a new random key if the keyword w is never queried before, and stores it in a table Key. Otherwise return the key corresponding to w in the table Key. If an adversary $\mathcal{A}$ is able to distinguish between G_0 and G_1, we can then build an adversary $\mathcal{B}_1$ to distinguish between F and a truly random function. More formally,

$$\Pr[G_0 = 1] - \Pr[G_1 = 1] \leq \mathbf{Adv}_{F, \mathcal{B}_1}^{\text{prf}}(\lambda).$$

Game G_2: In G_2, as depicted in Algorithm 3, in the **Update** protocol, we pick random strings for the update token UT and store it in table UT. Then, in the

Search protocol, we program these random strings to the output of the random oracle H_1 where $H_1(K_w, ST_c) = \text{UT}[w, c]$. When $\mathcal{A}$ queries H_1 with the input (K_w, ST_c), $\mathcal{C}$ will output $\text{UT}[w, c]$ to $\mathcal{A}$ and store this entry in table H_1 for future queries. If the entry (K_w, ST_{c+1}) already in table H_1, $\text{UT}[w, c+1]$ cannot be programed to the output of $H_1(K_w, ST_{c+1})$ and this game aborts. Now, we will show that the possibility of the game aborts is negligible. The search token is chosen randomly by the challenger $\mathcal{C}$, then the possibility that the adversary guesses the right search token ST_{c+1} is $1/2^\lambda$. Assume $\mathcal{A}$ makes polynomial p queries, then the possibility is $p/2^\lambda$. So we have

$$\Pr[G_1 = 1] - \Pr[G_2 = 1] \leq p/2^\lambda$$

Algorithm 3. G_2

Setup(1^λ)

1: $K \xleftarrow{\$} \{0,1\}^\lambda$, $n \leftarrow$ Setup(1^λ)
2: **CT**, EDB $\leftarrow$ empty map
3: **return** (EDB, $\sigma = (n, K, \textbf{CT})$)

Update(w, bs, σ; EDB)

Client:

1: $K_w || K'_w \leftarrow$ Key(w)
2: $(ST_0, \cdots, ST_c, c) \leftarrow \textbf{CT}[w]$
3: **if** $(ST_c, c) = \perp$ **then**
4:     $c \leftarrow -1$, $ST_c \leftarrow \{0,1\}^\lambda$
5: **end if**
6: $ST_{c+1} \leftarrow \{0,1\}^\lambda$
7: $\textbf{CT}[w] \leftarrow (ST_0, \cdots, ST_{c+1}, c+1)$
8: $UT_{c+1} \leftarrow \{0,1\}^\lambda$
9: $\text{UT}[w, c+1] \leftarrow UT_{c+1}$
10: $C_{ST_c} \leftarrow H_2(K_w, ST_{c+1}) \oplus ST_c$
11: $sk_{c+1} \leftarrow H_3(K'_w, c+1)$
12: $e_{c+1} \leftarrow$ Enc(sk_{c+1}, bs, n)
13: Send $(UT_{c+1}, (e_{c+1}, C_{ST_c}))$ to server.

Server:

14: EDB$[UT_{c+1}] \leftarrow (e_{c+1}, C_{ST_c})$

Search(w, σ; EDB)

Client:

1: $K_w || K'_w \leftarrow$ Key(w)
2: $(ST_0, \cdots, ST_c, c) \leftarrow \textbf{CT}[w]$
3: **if** $(ST_c, c) = \perp$ **then**
4:     **return** $\varnothing$
5: **end if**
6: **for** $i = 0$ to c **do**
7:     $H_1(K_w, ST_i) \leftarrow \text{UT}[w, i]$
8: **end for**
9: Send (K_w, ST_c, c) to server.

Server:

10: $Sum_e \leftarrow 0$
11: **for** $i = c$ to 0 **do**
12:     $UT_i \leftarrow H_1(K_w, ST_i)$
13:     $(e_i, C_{ST_{i-1}}) \leftarrow$ EDB$[UT_i]$
14:     $Sum_e \leftarrow$ Add(Sum_e, e_i, n)
15:     Remove EDB$[UT_i]$
16:     **if** $C_{ST_{i-1}} = \perp$ **then**
17:         *Break*
18:     **end if**
19:     $ST_{i-1} \leftarrow H_2(K_w, ST_i) \oplus C_{ST_{i-1}}$
20: **end for**
21: EDB$[UT_c] \leftarrow (Sum_e, \perp)$
22: Send Sum_e to client.

Client:

23: $Sum_{sk} \leftarrow 0$
24: **for** $i = c$ to 0 **do**
25:     $sk_i \leftarrow H_3(K'_w, i)$
26:     $Sum_{sk} \leftarrow Sum_{sk} + sk_i$ mod n
27: **end for**
28: $bs \leftarrow$ Dec(Sum_{sk}, Sum_e, n)
29: **return** bs

Game G_3: In G_3, we model the H_2 as a random oracle which is similar to H_1 in G_2. Then we have

$$\Pr[G_2 = 1] - \Pr[G_3 = 1] \leq p/2^\lambda$$

Game G_4: In G_4, similar to G_2, we model the H_3 as a random oracle. $\mathcal{A}$ does not know the key K'_w, then the possibility that he guesses the right key is $1/2^\lambda$ (we set the length of K'_w to λ). Assume $\mathcal{A}$ makes polynomial p queries, the possibility is $p/2^\lambda$. So we have

$$\Pr[G_3 = 1] - \Pr[G_4 = 1] \leq p/2^\lambda$$

Game G_5: In G_5, we replace the bit string bs with an all 0 bit string, and the length of the all 0 bit string is ℓ. If an adversary $\mathcal{A}$ is able to distinguish between G_5 and G_4, then we can build a reduction $\mathcal{B}_2$ to break the perfectly security of the simple symmetric encryption with homomorphic addition Π. So we have

$$\Pr[G_4 = 1] - \Pr[G_5 = 1] \leq \mathbf{Adv}^{\mathrm{PS}}_{\Pi,\mathcal{B}_2}(\lambda).$$

Simulator. Now we can replace the searched keyword w with $\mathbf{sp}(w)$ in G_5 to simulate the simulator $\mathcal{S}$ in Algorithm 4, $\mathcal{S}$ uses the first timestamp $\hat{w} \leftarrow \min \mathbf{sp}(w)$ for the keyword w. We remove the useless part of Algorithm 3 which will not influence the view of $\mathcal{A}$.

Now we are ready to show that G_5 and **Simulator** are indistinguishable. For **Update**, it is obvious since we choose new random strings for each update in G_5. For **Search**, $\mathcal{S}$ starts from the current search token ST_c and choose a random string for previous search token. Then $\mathcal{S}$ embeds it to the ciphertext C through H_2. Moreover, $\mathcal{S}$ embeds the $\overline{bs}$ to the ST_c and all 0s to the remaining search tokens through H_3. Finally, we map the pairs (w, i) to the globe update count t. Then we can map the values in table UT, C and sk that we chose randomly in **Update** to the corresponding values for the pair (w, i) in the **Search**. Hence,

$$\Pr[G_5 = 1] = \Pr[\mathrm{DSSEIDEAL}^{\mathrm{FB\text{-}DSSE}}_{\mathcal{A},\mathcal{S}}(\lambda) = 1]$$

Finally,

$$\Pr[\mathrm{DSSEREAL}^{\mathrm{FB\text{-}DSSE}}_{\mathcal{A}}(\lambda) = 1] - \Pr[\mathrm{DSSEIDEAL}^{\mathrm{FB\text{-}DSSE}}_{\mathcal{A},\mathcal{S}}(\lambda) = 1]$$

$$\leq \mathbf{Adv}^{\mathrm{prf}}_{F,\mathcal{B}_1}(\lambda) + \mathbf{Adv}^{\mathrm{PS}}_{\Pi,\mathcal{B}_2}(\lambda) + 3p/2^\lambda$$

which completes the proof.

Algorithm 4. Simulator $\mathcal{S}$

$\mathcal{S}.\mathbf{Setup}(1^\lambda)$

1: $n \leftarrow \mathtt{Setup}(1^\lambda)$
2: $\mathbf{CT}, \mathtt{EDB} \leftarrow$ empty map
3: **return** $(\mathtt{EDB}, \mathbf{CT}, n)$

$\mathcal{S}.\mathbf{Update}()$

Client:

1: $\mathtt{UT}[t] \leftarrow \{0,1\}^\lambda$
2: $\mathtt{C}[t] \leftarrow \{0,1\}^\lambda$
3: $\mathtt{sk}[t] \leftarrow \{0,1\}^\lambda$
4: $\mathtt{e}[t] \leftarrow \mathtt{Enc}(\mathtt{sk}[t], 0s, n)$
5: Send $\mathtt{UT}[t], (\mathtt{e}[t], \mathtt{C}[t]))$ to the server.
6: $t \leftarrow t + 1$

$\mathcal{S}.\mathbf{Search}(\mathtt{sp}(w), \mathtt{rp}(w), \mathtt{Time}(w))$

Client:

1: $\hat{w} \leftarrow \min \mathtt{sp}(w)$
2: $K_{\hat{w}} || K'_{\hat{w}} \leftarrow \mathtt{Key}(\hat{w})$
3: $(ST_c, c) \leftarrow \mathbf{CT}[\hat{w}]$
4: parse $\mathtt{rp}(w)$ as $\overline{bs}$.

5: Parse $\mathtt{Time}(w)$ as $(t_0, \cdots, t_c)$.
6: **if** $(ST_c, c) = \perp$ **then**
7:     **return** $\varnothing$
8: **end if**
9: **for** $i = c$ to 0 **do**
10:     $ST_{i-1} \leftarrow \{0,1\}^\lambda$
11:     Program $H_1(K_{\hat{w}}, ST_i) \leftarrow \mathtt{UT}[t_i]$
12:     Program $H_2(K_{\hat{w}}, ST_i) \leftarrow \mathtt{C}[t_i] \oplus ST_{i-1}$
13:     **if** $i = c$ **then**
14:         Program $H_3(K'_{\hat{w}}, i) \leftarrow \mathtt{sk}[t_i] - \overline{bs}$
15:     **else**
16:         Program $H_3(K'_{\hat{w}}, i) \leftarrow \mathtt{sk}[t_i]$
17:     **end if**
18: **end for**
19: Send $(K_{\hat{w}}, ST_c, c)$ to the server.

References

1. Amjad, G., Kamara, S., Moataz, T.: Forward and backward private searchable encryption with SGX. In: Proceedings of the 12th European Workshop on Systems Security, p. 4. ACM (2019)
2. Bost, R.: Σοφος: forward secure searchable encryption. In: CCS 2016, pp. 1143–1154. ACM (2016)
3. Bost, R., Minaud, B., Ohrimenko, O.: Forward and backward private searchable encryption from constrained cryptographic primitives. In: CCS 2017, pp. 1465–1482. ACM (2017)
4. Cash, D., Grubbs, P., Perry, J., Ristenpart, T.: Leakage-abuse attacks against searchable encryption. In: CCS 2015, pp. 668–679. ACM (2015)
5. Cash, D., et al.: Dynamic searchable encryption in very-large databases: data structures and implementation. In: NDSS 2014, vol. 14, pp. 23–26. Citeseer (2014)
6. Cash, D., Jarecki, S., Jutla, C., Krawczyk, H., Roşu, M.-C., Steiner, M.: Highly-scalable searchable symmetric encryption with support for Boolean queries. In: Canetti, R., Garay, J.A. (eds.) CRYPTO 2013. LNCS, vol. 8042, pp. 353–373. Springer, Heidelberg (2013). https://doi.org/10.1007/978-3-642-40041-4_20
7. Castelluccia, C., Mykletun, E., Tsudik, G.: Efficient aggregation of encrypted data in wireless sensor networks. In: 3rd Intlernational Symposium on Modeling and Optimization in Mobile, Ad Hoc, and Wireless Sensor Networks, Italy (2005)
8. Curtmola, R., Garay, J., Kamara, S., Ostrovsky, R.: Searchable symmetric encryption: improved definitions and efficient constructions. In: CCS 2006, pp. 79–88. ACM (2006)
9. Faber, S., Jarecki, S., Krawczyk, H., Nguyen, Q., Rosu, M., Steiner, M.: Rich queries on encrypted data: beyond exact matches. In: Pernul, G., Ryan, P.Y.A.,

Weippl, E. (eds.) ESORICS 2015. LNCS, vol. 9327, pp. 123–145. Springer, Cham (2015). https://doi.org/10.1007/978-3-319-24177-7_7

10. Fuhry, B., Bahmani, R., Brasser, F., Hahn, F., Kerschbaum, F., Sadeghi, A.-R.: HardIDX: practical and secure index with SGX. In: Livraga, G., Zhu, S. (eds.) DBSec 2017. LNCS, vol. 10359, pp. 386–408. Springer, Cham (2017). https://doi.org/10.1007/978-3-319-61176-1_22

11. Garg, S., Mohassel, P., Papamanthou, C.: TWORAM: efficient oblivious RAM in two rounds with applications to searchable encryption. In: Robshaw, M., Katz, J. (eds.) CRYPTO 2016. LNCS, vol. 9816, pp. 563–592. Springer, Heidelberg (2016). https://doi.org/10.1007/978-3-662-53015-3_20

12. Ghareh Chamani, J., Papadopoulos, D., Papamanthou, C., Jalili, R.: New constructions for forward and backward private symmetric searchable encryption. In: CCS 2018, pp. 1038–1055. ACM (2018)

13. Kamara, S., Papamanthou, C., Roeder, T.: Dynamic searchable symmetric encryption. In: CCS 2012, pp. 965–976. ACM (2012)

14. Paillier, P.: Public-key cryptosystems based on composite degree residuosity classes. In: Stern, J. (ed.) EUROCRYPT 1999. LNCS, vol. 1592, pp. 223–238. Springer, Heidelberg (1999). https://doi.org/10.1007/3-540-48910-X_16

15. Sharma, V.: Bitmap index vs. b-tree index: Which and when? Oracle Technical Network (2005). http://www.oracle.com/technetwork/articles/sharma-indexes-093638.html

16. Song, D.X., Wagner, D., Perrig, A.: Practical techniques for searches on encrypted data. In: S&P 2000, pp. 44–55. IEEE (2000)

17. Stefanov, E., Papamanthou, C., Shi, E.: Practical dynamic searchable encryption with small leakage. In: NDSS 2014, vol. 71, pp. 72–75 (2014)

18. Sun, S.-F., Liu, J.K., Sakzad, A., Steinfeld, R., Yuen, T.H.: An efficient non-interactive multi-client searchable encryption with support for Boolean queries. In: Askoxylakis, I., Ioannidis, S., Katsikas, S., Meadows, C. (eds.) ESORICS 2016. LNCS, vol. 9878, pp. 154–172. Springer, Cham (2016). https://doi.org/10.1007/978-3-319-45744-4_8

19. Sun, S.F., et al.: Practical backward-secure searchable encryption from symmetric puncturable encryption. In: CCS 2018, pp. 763–780. ACM (2018)

20. Wang, X.S., et al.: Oblivious data structures. In: CCS 2014, pp. 215–226. ACM (2014)

21. Zhang, Y., Katz, J., Papamanthou, C.: All your queries are belong to us: the power of file-injection attacks on searchable encryption. In: USENIX Security Symposium, pp. 707–720 (2016)

22. Zuo, C., Macindoe, J., Yang, S., Steinfeld, R., Liu, J.K.: Trusted Boolean search on cloud using searchable symmetric encryption. In: Trustcom 2016, pp. 113–120. IEEE (2016)

23. Zuo, C., Sun, S.-F., Liu, J.K., Shao, J., Pieprzyk, J.: Dynamic searchable symmetric encryption schemes supporting range queries with forward (and backward) security. In: Lopez, J., Zhou, J., Soriano, M. (eds.) ESORICS 2018. LNCS, vol. 11099, pp. 228–246. Springer, Cham (2018). https://doi.org/10.1007/978-3-319-98989-1_12

Towards Efficient Verifiable Forward Secure Searchable Symmetric Encryption

Zhongjun Zhang[1,2], Jianfeng Wang[1,2(✉)], Yunling Wang[1],
Yaping Su[1], and Xiaofeng Chen[1,2]

[1] State Key Laboratory of Integrated Service Networks (ISN), Xidian University,
Xi'an 710071, China
zhong_jun@163.com, {jfwang,xfchen}@xidian.edu.cn,
ylwang0304@163.com, ypingsu@126.com
[2] State Key Laboratory of Cryptology, P. O. Box 5159, Beijing 100878, China

Abstract. Searchable Symmetric Encryption (SSE) allows a server to perform search directly over encrypted data outsourced by user. Recently, the primitive of forward secure SSE has attracted significant attention due to its favorable property for dynamic data searching. That is, it can prevent the linkability from newly update data to previously searched keyword. However, the server is assumed to be honest-but-curious in the existing work. How to achieve verifiable forward secure SSE in malicious server model remains a challenging problem. In this paper, we propose an efficient verifiable forward secure SSE scheme, which can simultaneously achieve verifiability of search result and forward security property. In particular, we propose a new verifiable data structure based on the primitive of multiset hash functions, which enables efficient verifiable data update by incrementally hash operation. Compared with the state-of-the-art solution, our proposed scheme is superior in search and update efficiency while providing verifiability of search result. Finally, we present a formal security analysis and implement our scheme, which demonstrates that our proposed scheme is equipped with the desired security properties with practical efficiency.

Keywords: Searchable encryption · Forward security ·
Verifiable search

1 Introduction

Cloud computing enables convenient and on-demand network access to a centralized pool of configurable computing resources, which offers seemly unlimited storage and computation sources. With the rapid development of cloud computing, resource-constraint users prefer to outsource their data to the server. Despite its tremendous benefits, the outsourced data suffers from the security and privacy concerns. According to a recent report, Facebook has leaked over 540 million records including users' IDs, account names, and their activities [15].

© Springer Nature Switzerland AG 2019
K. Sako et al. (Eds.): ESORICS 2019, LNCS 11736, pp. 304–321, 2019.
https://doi.org/10.1007/978-3-030-29962-0_15

One possible solution is to encrypt data with traditional encryption techniques before outsourcing. However, it is intractable to perform search over the encrypted data.

Searchable Symmetric Encryption (SSE) enables the server to search directly over the encrypted data, which has been well studied in both academic and industrial community [5,8,13,21]. More specifically, a user outsources the encrypted documents along with a search index to the cloud server. When the user is interested in a keyword, he generates a search token and submits it to the server. Then the server performs search and returns the matched documents. Recently, the notion of dynamic SSE has aroused wide concern, which can support efficient data update in practical application. However, most of the existing dynamic SSE schemes leak some useful information in data search and update phases. Zhang et al. [27] introduced an effective attack that can fully recover the client's queried keywords by injecting a small number of documents.

To resist the above attack, Bost et al. [2] presented a novel forward secure SSE scheme, where each keyword is attached with a state at local. More specifically, the state is used to update the encrypted index when the document that contains the corresponding keyword is inserted. That is, a new state can be derived from the current state, which can be used to locate the updated document identifier. Note that all the previous states can be derived from the current state. It means that the server can match all the corresponding documents with the given state. According to one-way property of trapdoor permutation, anyone cannot infer the future state from the current state. That implies any adversary cannot obtain the relation between the newly inserted document and the previously searched keyword without the latest state. Thus, the forward security can be achieved. Very recently, Song et al. [22] proposed a more efficient forward secure SSE scheme named FAST based on symmetric primitive. We argue that all the above-mentioned schemes are constructed with the honest-but-curious server model. That is, the server is assumed to perform honestly all the search operations. However, the server may be not fully trust and returns a part of the matched documents due to its selfish behavior. To fight against the malicious server, verifiable SSE has received considerable attention [1,6,20,25,26]. Bost et al. [3] proposed a verifiable forward secure SSE scheme called $\Sigma o\phi o\varsigma$-ϵ based on Verifiable Hash Tables (VHT). However, the VHT must be reconstructed each time an update occurs, which causes low update efficiency and high communication cost. To our best knowledge, how to construct an efficient verifiable SSE scheme with forward security remains a great challenge.

1.1   Our Contribution

In this paper, we further study on verifiable forward secure SSE. Our contributions can be summarized as follows:

- We propose an efficient verifiable forward secure SSE scheme based on the primitive of multiset hash functions, which can achieve verifiability of the search result while maintaining forward security. Our proposed construction supports efficient verification of search by adopting only symmetric cryptographic primitives.

- Compared with the state-of-the-art solution FAST [22], our proposed scheme can generate a new state in a random fashion instead of the (symmetric) encryption operations in the phase of data updating. Furthermore, it achieves optimized search efficiency without involving the corresponding decryption operations.
- We present the formal security proof of our proposed scheme and provide a thorough implementation of it. The experiment results demonstrate that our construction enjoys a good search and update efficiency.

1.2 Related Work

Song et al. [21] introduced the concept of symmetric searchable encryption (SSE). Subsequently, plenty of research have been exploited in [4,5,8,13,17,23,24]. Goh [13] presented the first index-based SSE scheme to enhance the search efficiency. Curtmola et al. [8] presented the formal security definition of SSE. Cash et al. [5] designed the first sublinear SSE scheme that support boolean queries. Recently, several attacks on SSE have been devised [12,16,27], where the leakage information of data update can be used to recover the client's query. To resist the mentioned attack, several forward secure SSE schemes have been designed to protect the linkability from newly update data to previously searched keyword. Setfanov et al. [23] first formalized the notion of forward security for SSE. Bost [2] presented an efficient forward secure SSE scheme based on the work of [23]. Nevertheless, the computation cost of trapdoor permutation become the primary performance bottleneck. Very recently, Song et al. [22] proposed two more practical forward secure SSE schemes (i.e. FAST and FASTIO) by using only symmetric cryptographic primitives.

Another privacy concern about SSE is the correctness and completeness of search result. Chai et al. proposed the notation of verifiable SSE and constructed the first verifiable SSE scheme based on the character tree [6]. Kurosawa and Ohtaki [18] proposed the first verifiable SSE scheme against the active adversary in 2012 and later extended their scheme to support update operation [19]. Wang et al. [26] proposed a verifiable SSE scheme supporting conjunctive keyword search based on the accumulator. Note that all the existing verifiable SSE can only work in the static SSE setting. In [3], Bost et al. proposed the first verifiable forward secure SSE scheme based on the primitive of Verifiable Hash Tables (VHT). We argue that the Bost's scheme suffers from low data update efficiency and high communication cost due to the reconstruction of VHT. In this work, we will further study how to design a practical forward secure SSE in dynamic SSE application.

1.3 Organization

The rest of this paper is organized as follows. In Sect. 2, we present some preliminaries and the security definitions of our scheme. Section 3 gives the details of our proposed scheme. The formal security and efficiency analysis are given in Sect. 4. The performance evaluation and the conclusion are given in Sects. 4.2 and 6 respectively.

Table 1. Notations and Descriptions

Notations	Descriptions
λ	Security parameter
Σ	The map stored on the client side
T	The map stored on the server side
ind	The identifier of document
l	The length of identifier
op	The update operation taken from the set $\{add, del\}$
st_i	The i-th state
DB	The representation of the whole database
DB(w)	All identifiers of documents containing keyword w
DB$_i(w)$	All identifiers of documents containing w under state st_i
d	The number of keyword-document pairs in DB
H	The representation of hash function
F	The representation of pseudo random function
$\mathcal{H}$	The representation of multiset hash functions
$hash$	The output of multiset hash functions
m	The length of $hash$
R	The representation of search result
$proof$	The representation of proof

2 Preliminaries

In this section, we first describe the notations used in this work, as shown in Table 1. Then we give a brief introduction of the multiset hash functions, which is exploited to construct our scheme. After that, we present a formal security definition.

2.1 Multiset Hash Functions

Clarke et al. [7] introduced an efficient cryptographic primitive named Multiset hash functions, which can map a multiset of arbitrary finite size to a string of fixed length. The difference from the standard hash functions is that the input is a multiset rather than a string. The most attractive property of multiset hash functions is incremental. That is, when a new member is added to the multiset, we can quickly update the result without recalculating over the entire new input.

Given a multiset M, a triple of probabilistic polynomial time algorithms $(\mathcal{H}, +_{\mathcal{H}}, \equiv_{\mathcal{H}})$ is a multiset hash functions if it satisfies the following properties:

- **Compression:** $\mathcal{H}$ is a probabilistic algorithm which can map a multiset to a byte array (a byte array of length m). We call the output of $\mathcal{H}$ as *hash*.
- **Incrementality:** If a new element e is added into M, $\mathcal{H}(M)$ can be incrementally calculated on the basis of the previous *hash* without recalculating. Formally, $\mathcal{H}(M \cup \{e\}) \equiv_{\mathcal{H}} \mathcal{H}(M) +_{\mathcal{H}} \mathcal{H}(\{e\})$.
- **Comparability:** For the same input, $\mathcal{H}$ may output different *hashes* since it is a probabilistic algorithm. Therefore, we need $\equiv_{\mathcal{H}}$ to check whether two *hashes* are equal. Formally, the relation $\mathcal{H}(M) \equiv_{\mathcal{H}} \mathcal{H}(M)$ must hold for all multisets M.

In [7], Clarke et al. introduced four constructions of multiset hash functions, which are MSet-Mu-Hash, MSet-Add-Hash, MSet-VAdd-Hash and MSet-XOR-Hash. Specifically, MSet-Mu-Hash is based on multiplication in a finite field, which results in poor efficiency. MSet-Add-Hash and MSet-VAdd-Hash improve the efficiency by replacing the multiplication with addition and vector addition modular a large integer respectively. All the constructions above are multiset-collision resistant (it is difficult to find two multisets to produce the same *hash*). MSet-XOR-Hash is the most efficient one for only using the XOR operation. Besides, it is set-collision resistant (it is difficult to find a set and a multiset to produce the same *hash*). Considering the efficiency and sufficiency of set-collision resistant property in our scheme, we use the MSet-XOR-Hash construction. we present the definition of the MSet-XOR-Hash as follows:

$$
\begin{cases}
\mathcal{H}(r, M) = H(0, r) \oplus \bigoplus_{m \in M} H(1, m) \\
\mathcal{H}(r, M \cup \{x\}) \equiv_{\mathcal{H}} \mathcal{H}(r, M) +_{\mathcal{H}} \mathcal{H}(r, \{x\}) \equiv_{\mathcal{H}} \mathcal{H}(r, M) \oplus H(1, x) \\
\mathcal{H}(r, M \setminus \{x\}) \equiv_{\mathcal{H}} \mathcal{H}(r, M) -_{\mathcal{H}} \mathcal{H}(r, \{x\}) \equiv_{\mathcal{H}} \mathcal{H}(r, M) \oplus H(1, x)
\end{cases}
$$

2.2 Verifiable Dynamic Searchable Symmetric Encryption

Searchable symmetric encryption (SSE) scheme allows a client to encrypt his data before outsourcing them to the server while preserving the ability to search on it. Furthermore, a verifiable dynamic SSE scheme allows a client to update in the outsourced database and to verify the integrity of search result. A verifiable dynamic SSE scheme $\Pi = (\mathbf{Setup}, \mathbf{Search}, \mathbf{Update}, \mathbf{Verify})$ consists of three protocols and one algorithm.

- $(K, \sigma; \text{EDB}) \leftarrow \mathbf{Setup}(\lambda, \text{DB}; \perp)$: In this protocol, the client takes a security parameter λ and a database DB as input and outputs (K, σ), where K is the secret key, σ is the client's state. The server outputs EDB which is the encrypted database stored in the server.

- $(\sigma', \text{R}, proof; \text{EDB}') \leftarrow \textbf{Search}(K, \sigma, w; \text{EDB})$: This is a protocol between a client with input (K, σ, w) and a server with input EDB. After this protocol, the server returns the matched result R and corresponding $proof$ to the client. The client's state σ may be updated to σ' and the encrypted database EDB may be updated to EDB'.
- $(\sigma'; \text{EDB}') \leftarrow \textbf{Update}(K, \sigma, ind, w, op; \text{EDB})$: For the update protocol, the client's input is (K, σ, ind, w, op), where ind is the identifier, w is the keyword and op is the operation. Notice that $op = add$ or $op = del$ indicates adding or deleting a keyword-document pair. The server's input is the encrypted database EDB. After this protocol, σ and EDB may be updated.
- $(Accept \text{ or } Reject) \leftarrow \textbf{Verify}(K, \sigma, \text{R}, proof)$: This algorithm takes $(K, \sigma, \text{R}, proof)$ as input, where R and $proof$ are returned by the server. The algorithm is used to check whether R is both correct and complete. If yes, the algorithm outputs $Accept$. Otherwise, it outputs $Reject$.

2.3   Security Definitions

All SSE schemes inevitably leak information to the server as the result of communication between the client and the server. Hence, we can give the security definition of our scheme by describing the leakage information. Corresponding to $\Pi = (\textbf{Setup}, \textbf{Search}, \textbf{Update}, \textbf{Verify})$, the leakage function can be defined as $\mathcal{L} = \{\mathcal{L}_{\textbf{Setup}}, \mathcal{L}_{\textbf{Search}}, \mathcal{L}_{\textbf{Update}}, \mathcal{L}_{\textbf{Verify}}\}$. Let $\mathcal{A}$ be an adversary and $\mathcal{S}$ be a simulator. We can define the following two probabilistic experiments:

- $\textbf{Real}_{\mathcal{A}}^{\Pi}(\lambda)$: $\mathcal{A}$ chooses a security parameter λ, then the experiment runs $\textbf{Setup}(\lambda, \perp; \perp)$ and returns initialized data structure Σ and T to $\mathcal{A}$. $\mathcal{A}$ adaptively chooses a keyword w and generates a query by running the client phase of search protocol. The experiment answers the query by performing $\textbf{Search}(k_s, w, \Sigma; \text{T})$ and $\textbf{Verify}(w, \Sigma, \text{R}, proof)$, then gives all client outputs to $\mathcal{A}$. As for update operation, $\mathcal{A}$ generates a query and then the experiment answers the query by running $\textbf{Update}(k_s, ind, w, op, \Sigma; \text{T})$ and returns all outputs to the adversary $\mathcal{A}$. Finally, $\mathcal{A}$ outputs a bit $b \in \{0, 1\}$ as the output of the experiment.
- $\textbf{Ideal}_{\mathcal{A},\mathcal{S}}^{\Pi}(\lambda)$: $\mathcal{A}$ chooses a security parameter λ. Given the leakage function $\mathcal{L}_{\textbf{Setup}}(\lambda)$, the simulator $\mathcal{S}$ generates the empty data structures Σ and T by running $\mathcal{S}(\mathcal{L}_{\textbf{setup}}(\lambda))$ and returns them to $\mathcal{A}$. Then $\mathcal{A}$ adaptively chooses a search or verify query q. The simulator answers the query by performing $\mathcal{S}(\mathcal{L}_{\textbf{Search}}(q))$ or $\mathcal{S}(\mathcal{L}_{\textbf{Verify}}(q))$. As for update operation, the simulator answers the update query by running $\mathcal{S}(\mathcal{L}_{\textbf{Update}}(q))$. Finally, the adversary $\mathcal{A}$ outputs a bit $b \in \{0, 1\}$ as the output of the experiment.

We say Π is $\mathcal{L}$-adaptively-secure searchable symmetric encryption scheme if for any probabilistic polynomial time adversary $\mathcal{A}$, there exists a simulator $\mathcal{S}$ such that:

$$\left| Pr(\textbf{Real}_{\mathcal{A}}^{\Pi}(\lambda) = 1) - Pr(\textbf{Ideal}_{\mathcal{A},\mathcal{S}}^{\Pi}(\lambda) = 1) \right| \leq \textbf{negl}(\lambda)$$

2.4   Leakage Functions

The design philosophy of SSE schemes is to allow users to search over encrypted data efficiently while revealing as little information as possible. Similar to [2,22], we will describe the security of our scheme with leakage functions $\mathcal{L}$. We suppose that $\mathcal{L}$ keeps the query history Hist $= (\mathrm{DB_i}, q_i)_{i=0}^{Q}$ which contains all queries issued so far and the snapshots of the database corresponding to q_i. The entries are $q_i = (i, w)$ for a search query on keyword w, or $q_i = (i, ind, w, op)$ for a update query, or $q_i = (i, w, \mathrm{R}, proof)$ for a verify query where R and $proof$ are returned by the server. The integer i is the counter of all queries. The access pattern $\mathbf{ap}$ is defined as $\mathbf{ap}(\mathrm{Hist}) = (t_1, \ldots, t_Q)$. The entries of $\mathbf{ap}(\mathrm{Hist})$ are $t_i = (i, \mathrm{DB}_i(w_i), proof_i)$ for a search query, or $t_i = (i, op_i, ind_i, proof_i)$ for a update query. The query pattern $\mathbf{qp}$ is defined as $\mathbf{qp}(w) = \{i \mid q_i \text{ contains } w \text{ for each } q_i \text{ in Hist}\}$.

2.5   Forward Security

Informal speaking, forward security requires that the previous search tokens cannot be exploited to match the new update. That is, the data update operation should reveal no information about the keywords. Similar as [22], the definition of forward secure SSE is formalized as follows:

Definition 1. *(Forward Security). An $\mathcal{L}$-adaptively-secure searchable symmetric encryption scheme is forward secure if for an update query $q_i = (ind_i, w_i, op_i)$, the leakage function $\mathcal{L}_{\mathbf{Update}}(q_i) = (i, op_i, ind_i)$.*

3   Verifiable Forward Secure SSE Scheme

In this section, we firstly present the main idea of the proposed construction. Then, we present the proposed verifiable forward secure SSE scheme in detail.

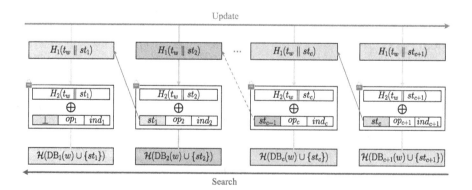

Fig. 1. Update and Search in our Scheme

3.1   Main Idea

In this paper, we propose an efficient verifiable forward secure SSE scheme, which can simultaneously achieve verifiability of search result and forward security property. Our proposed scheme is constructed with the state chain method adopted in Σοφος [2] and FAST [22]. As shown in Fig. 1, each keyword w corresponds to a state chain, and all identifiers matched w are stored in the locations derived from this chain. When the client wants to search on keyword w, he sends the last state st_{c+1} to the server. Starting from st_{c+1}, the server can get all the previous states $st_c, st_{c-1}, \cdots, st_1$. Hence, the server can walk through the state chain in reverse order and eventually get all the results. Note that the server cannot get the next state st_{c+2} from the current state st_{c+1}, which ensures the forward security property. To further improve the search and update efficiency, the states in our scheme are randomly generated, instead of using permutation functions as in Σοφος [2] and FAST [22].

3.2   The Concrete Construction

In this section, we present our proposed scheme which mainly consists of three protocols and one algorithm $\Pi = (\textbf{Setup}, \textbf{Search}, \textbf{Update}, \textbf{Verify})$. Suppose that $H_1 : \{0,1\}^* \rightarrow \{0,1\}^n$ and $H_2 : \{0,1\}^* \rightarrow \{0,1\}^{\lambda+l+1}$ are two hash functions, F_1 and F_2 are two pseudo random functions.

- **Setup**$(\lambda, \bot; \bot)$: With the security parameter λ, the client randomly chooses long-term keys k_s and k_r from $\{0,1\}^\lambda$, where k_s is used to generate the search token and k_r serves as the secret key of multiset hash functions. Then the client initializes an empty map Σ as the client storage and the server initializes T as the encrypted database.
- **Search**$(w, \Sigma; T)$: To perform a search query on w, the client firstly retrieves st_c from $\Sigma[w]$, where st_c is the latest state. If st_c is null, this protocol returns an empty set, indicating that no documents matches with w. Otherwise, the client calculates t_w and sends (t_w, st_c) to the server. Upon obtaining (t_w, st_c), the server firstly gets the *proof* from the last location. Then the server generates all the previous locations and retrieves corresponding search result. Note that the previous states can be obtained directly by decrypting the ciphertext without extra permutation functions like in Σοφος [2] and FAST [22], which improves the search efficiency.
- **Update**$(\Sigma, ind, w, op; T)$: To add or delete an entry (w, ind), both the client storage Σ and the server storage T need to be updated. For Σ, the client chooses a new state st_{c+1}, and then incrementally generates a new proof $hash'$ on the basis of $hash$. Finally, st_{c+1} and $hash'$ are stored in Σ. For T, the client encrypts the entry to e, and then calculates a new location u from st_{c+1}. Finally, $(u, e, hash')$ is sent to the server to update T.
- **Verify**$(w, \Sigma, \text{R}, proof)$: To verify the integrity of search result R, the client firstly guarantees the returned proof is the latest by comparing it with the one stored in Σ. Besides, the client recomputes multiset hash functions and

Algorithm 1. Verifiable Forward Secure SSE

Setup($\lambda, \perp; \perp$)

__Input:__ the security parameter λ

__Output:__ the initialized map Σ and T

    Client:

1: $k_s, k_r \xleftarrow{\$} \{0,1\}^\lambda$, $\Sigma \leftarrow$ empty map

    Server:

2: T $\leftarrow$ empty map

Search($k_s, w, \Sigma;$ T)

__Input:__ k_s, keyword w, map Σ and T

__Output:__ search result R and the corresponding *proof*

    Client:

1: $t_w \leftarrow F_1(k_s, w)$

2: $(st_c, hash) \leftarrow \Sigma[w]$

3: **if** $(st_c, hash) = \perp$

4:    **return** ϕ

5: **end if**

6: send (t_w, st_c) to the server

    Server:

7: R, $\Delta \leftarrow \phi$

8: get the *proof* from T[$H_1(t_w \parallel st_c)$]

9: **while** $st_c \neq \perp$ **do**

10:    $u \leftarrow H_1(t_w \parallel st_c)$

11:    $(e, proof_t) \leftarrow T[u]$

12:    delete $proof_t$ to release storage

13:    $(st_c, ind, op) \leftarrow H_2(t_w \parallel st_c) \oplus e$

14:    **if** $op = del$ **then**

15:       $\Delta \leftarrow \Delta \cup \{ind\}$

16:    **else if** $op = add$ **then**

17:       **if** $ind \in \Delta$ **then**

18:          $\Delta \leftarrow \Delta \setminus \{ind\}$

19:       **else**

20:          R $\leftarrow$ R $\cup \{ind\}$

21:       **end if**

22:    **end if**

23: **end while**

24: send (R, *proof*) to the client

Update($k_s, k_r, ind, w, op, \Sigma;$ T)

__Input:__ k_s, k_r, w, ind, op, Σ, T

__Output:__ possible updated map Σ and T

    Client:

1: $t_w \leftarrow F_1(k_s, w)$, $r_w \leftarrow F_2(k_r, w)$

2: $(st_c, hash) \leftarrow \Sigma[w]$

3: **if** $(st_c, hash) = \perp$ **then**

4:    $st_1 \xleftarrow{\$} \{0,1\}^\lambda$

5:    $e \leftarrow H_2(t_w \parallel st_1) \oplus (\perp \parallel op \parallel ind)$

6:    $hash' \leftarrow \mathcal{H}(r_w, \{t_w \parallel ind\}) +_\mathcal{H}$
             $\mathcal{H}(r_w, \{st_1\})$

7: **else**

8:    $st_{c+1} \xleftarrow{\$} \{0,1\}^\lambda$

9:    $e \leftarrow H_2(t_w \parallel st_{c+1}) \oplus (st_c \parallel op \parallel ind)$

10:    $hash' \leftarrow hash +_\mathcal{H} \mathcal{H}(r_w, \{t_w \parallel ind\}) -_\mathcal{H}$
             $\mathcal{H}(r_w, \{st_c\}) +_\mathcal{H} \mathcal{H}(r_w, \{st_{c+1}\})$

11: **end if**

12: $\Sigma[w] \leftarrow (st_{c+1}, hash')$

13: $u \leftarrow H_1(t_w \parallel st_{c+1})$

14: send $(u, e, hash')$ to the server

    Server:

15: T[u] $\leftarrow (e, hash')$

Verify($k_r, w, \Sigma,$ R, *proof*)

__Input:__ k_r, w, Σ, R and *proof* returned from server

__Output:__ *Accept* or *Reject*

    Client:

1: $(st_c, hash) \leftarrow \Sigma[w]$, $r_w \leftarrow F_2(k_r, w)$

2: $hash' \leftarrow \mathcal{H}(r_w, \{st_c\})$

3: **for all** $ind \in$ R **do**

4:    $hash' \leftarrow hash' +_\mathcal{H} \mathcal{H}(r_w, \{t_w \parallel ind\})$

5: **end for**

6: **if** ($proof \equiv_\mathcal{H} hash$) **and** ($proof \equiv_\mathcal{H} hash'$)

7:    **return** *Accept*

8: **else**

9:    **return** *Reject*

---

compares the output with the returned proof to verify the correctness and completeness of R. If both the two tests above pass, the query integrity can be ensured.

4 Security and Efficiency Analysis

In this section, we first present the security analysis of our work with the simulation-based approach. Then we provide a detailed analysis between our proposed scheme and the state-of-the-art solutions.

4.1   Security Analysis

We introduce the search pattern $\mathbf{sp}(w)$ and update history $\mathbf{uh}(w)$. The search pattern is defined as $\mathbf{sp}(w) = \{i \mid \text{for each}(i, w) \text{ in } Q\}$ which reveals all search queries on w, and the update history $\mathbf{uh}(w) = \{(i, op_i, ind_i) \mid \text{for each}(i, ind_i, w, op_i) \text{ in Hist}\}$. It is clear that $\mathbf{sp}(w)$ and $\mathbf{uh}(w)$ can be obtained from $(\mathbf{ap}(), \mathbf{qp}())$. Differ from [2, 22], our scheme extra leaks the proof history $\mathbf{ph}(w) = \{(i, proof_i) \mid \text{for each } (i, ind_i, w_i, op_i) \text{ in Hist}\}$ in the update protocol, which reveals all the proofs corresponding to each update query q_i.

Theorem 1. *Define leakage* $\mathcal{L} = \{\mathcal{L}_{\mathsf{Setup}}, \mathcal{L}_{\mathsf{Search}}, \mathcal{L}_{\mathsf{Update}}, \mathcal{L}_{\mathsf{Verify}}\}$ *as*

$$\begin{cases} \mathcal{L}_{\mathsf{Setup}} =\perp \\ \mathcal{L}_{\mathsf{Search}} = (\mathbf{sp}(w), \mathbf{uh}(w)) \\ \mathcal{L}_{\mathsf{Update}} = (\mathbf{ph}(w)) \\ \mathcal{L}_{\mathsf{Verify}} = (\mathbf{sp}(w), proof) \end{cases}$$

Then the proposed scheme is a $\mathcal{L}$*-adaptively-secure dynamic SSE with forward security.*

Proof. The proof of Theorem 1 works by a sequence of indistinguishable hybrids. The first hybrid is the real-world game and the last hybrid is the idea-world game. In the second hybrid, we replace the two PRF F_1 and F_2 by table **Key** and **Rw** respectively. In the third hybrid, H_1 is modeled as a random oracle. We replace the hash function H_1 by randomly chosen strings from $\{0, 1\}^n$ in the update protocol. The game will then program the random oracle during the search protocol so that we can produce the right results. Similarly, H_2 is modeled as a random oracle in the fourth hybrid. Note that the multiset hash functions $\mathcal{H}$ is also based on the standard hash function. Hence, the fifth hybrid can model it as a random oracle. The last hybrid only use the predefined leakage functions, which means that we have a simulator which is indistinguishable from the real-world game.

Game G_1: G_1 is the same as $\mathbf{Real}_{\mathcal{A}}^{\Pi}(\lambda)$ except that instead of generating t_w using F, the game maintains a mapping **Key** to store (w, t_w) pairs. Similarly, the game also maintains another mapping **Rw** to store (w, r_w) pairs. In the search protocol, when t_w is needed, the experiment first checks whether there is an entry in **Key** for w. If yes, returns the entry; otherwise randomly picks a t_w in $\{0, 1\}^l$ and stores the (w, t_w) pair in **Key**. The operations of **Rw** is the same as **Key**. It's trivial to see that G_1 and $\mathbf{Real}_{\mathcal{A}}^{\Pi}(\lambda)$ are indistinguishable, otherwise we can distinguish a pseudo random function and a truly random function.

$$Pr\left[\mathbf{Real}_{\mathcal{A}, \mathcal{S}}^{\Pi}(\lambda) = 1\right] - Pr(G_1 = 1) \leq \mathrm{Adv}_{F_1, F_2, B_1}^{\mathrm{prf}}(\lambda)$$

Game G_2: Instead of calling hash function H_1 to generate u, G_2 randomly picks a string from $\{0, 1\}^n$ and store it in the table **L** in the update protocol.

Algorithm 2. Game G_2

Setup$(\lambda, \perp; \perp)$
1: $\Sigma, T \leftarrow$ empty map
Update$(k_s, k_r, ind, w, op, \Sigma; T)$
    Client:
2: $t_w \leftarrow \mathbf{Key}[w], r_w \leftarrow \mathbf{Rw}[w]$
3: $(st_1, \ldots, st_c, hash) \leftarrow \Sigma[w]$
4: **if** $(st_1, \ldots, st_c, hash) = \perp$ **then**
5:     $st_1 \xleftarrow{\$} \{0,1\}^\lambda$
6:     $\mathbf{L}[t_w \parallel st_1] \xleftarrow{\$} \{0,1\}^n$
7:     $e \leftarrow H_2(t_w \parallel st_1) \oplus (\perp \parallel op \parallel ind)$
8:     $hash' \leftarrow \mathcal{H}(r_w, \{t_w \parallel ind\})$
           $+_\mathcal{H} \mathcal{H}(r_w, \{st_1\})$
9: **else**
10:    $st_{c+1} \xleftarrow{\$} \{0,1\}^\lambda$
11:    $\mathbf{L}[t_w \parallel st_{c+1}] \xleftarrow{\$} \{0,1\}^n$
12:    $e \leftarrow H_2(t_w \parallel st_{c+1})$
         $\oplus (st_c \parallel op \parallel ind)$
13:    $hash' \leftarrow hash +_\mathcal{H} \mathcal{H}(r_w, \{t_w \parallel ind\})$
         $-_\mathcal{H} \mathcal{H}(r_w, \{st_c\}) +_\mathcal{H} \mathcal{H}(r_w, \{st_{c+1}\})$
14: **end if**
15: $\Sigma[w] = (st_1, \ldots, st_c, st_{c+1}, hash')$
16: send $(\mathbf{L}[t_w \parallel st_{c+1}], e, hash')$ to server
    Server:
17: $T[\mathbf{L}[t_w \parallel st_{c+1}]] = (e, hash')$

Search$(k_s, \Sigma, w; T)$
    Client:
18: $t_w \leftarrow \mathbf{Key}[w]$
19: $(st_1, \ldots, st_c, hash) \leftarrow \Sigma[w]$
20: **if** $(st_1, \ldots, st_c, hash) = \perp$ **then**
21:     return ϕ
22: **end if**
23: **for** $i = 1$ **to** c **do**
24:     $\mathbf{H_1}(t_w \parallel st_i) = \mathbf{L}[t_w \parallel st_i]$
25: **end for**
26: send (t_w, st_c) to server
    Server:
27: perform search and return $(\mathbf{R}, proof)$

Verify$(w, \Sigma, \mathbf{R}, proof)$
    Client:
28: $(st_1, \ldots, st_c, hash) \leftarrow \Sigma[w]$
29: $r_w \leftarrow \mathbf{R}[w]$
30: $hash' \leftarrow \mathcal{H}(r_w, \{st_c\})$
31: **for** all $ind \in \mathbf{R}$ **do**
32:     $hash' = hash' +_\mathcal{H} \mathcal{H}(r_w, \{t_w \parallel ind\})$
33: **if** $(proof \equiv_\mathcal{H} hash)$ **and** $(proof \equiv_\mathcal{H} hash')$
34:     return *Accept*
35: **else**
36:     return *Reject*
37: **endif**

The random oracle is programmed in the search protocol, and we use table $\mathbf{H_1}$ to keep the track of the transcripts. G_2 keeps all st in $\Sigma[w]$ instead of only st_c for the reason that the process of programming $\mathbf{H_1}$ needs the information of all historical state of keyword w. The game is showed in Algorithm 2, note here that we get rid of the server's part in the update protocol.

G_1 and G_2 is indistinguishable except that the query result of random oracle can be inconsistent. Specifically, $\mathbf{L}[t_w \parallel st_{c+1}]$ is generated in the update protocol, but it is lazily programmed to $\mathbf{H_1}$ in the search protocol. Assume that the adversary does not perform any search queries after the update with $t_w \parallel st_{c+1}$, then it queries $\mathbf{H_1}$ with $t_w \parallel st_{c+1}$. Now with an overwhelming probability $\mathbf{L}[t_w \parallel st_{c+1}] \neq \mathbf{H_1}[t_w \parallel st_{c+1}]$. After the next search query, the adversary queries $\mathbf{H_1}$ again with $t_w \parallel st_{c+1}$, now he will get $\mathbf{L}[t_w \parallel st_{c+1}]$. In this case, the inconsistency in the random oracle is observed (we denote this event by **Bad**), hence the adversary knows it is in G_2 instead of the real world game. Thus, we have:

$$\Pr[G_2 = 1] - \Pr[G_1 = 1] \leq \Pr[\mathbf{Bad}]$$

Note that **Bad** happens when the adversary queries the oracle with $t_w \parallel st_{c+1}$. The adversary knows t_w but it has no knowledge about st_{c+1}. The probability for the adversary to choose st_{c+1} is $2^{-\lambda} + negl(\lambda)$. A PPT adversary

---

Algorithm 3. Simulator S

Setup()

1: $v \leftarrow 0$
2: $\mathbf{L}, \mathbf{E}, \mathbf{ST}, \mathbf{P} \leftarrow$ empty map
3: $\mathbf{Key}, \mathbf{Rw}, \Sigma, \mathbf{T} \leftarrow$ empty map
Update($\mathbf{ph}(w)$)
   Client:
4: parse $\mathbf{ph}(w)$ as $[(v_1, proof_1)$
       $, \ldots, (v_c, proof_c)]$
5: $\mathbf{L}[v] \xleftarrow{\$} \{0,1\}^n$
6: $\mathbf{E}[v] \xleftarrow{\$} \{0,1\}^{\lambda+l+1}$
7: $\mathbf{ST}[v] \xleftarrow{\$} \{0,1\}^\lambda$
8: if $v \in [v_1, \ldots, v_c]$
9:     $\mathbf{P}[v] \leftarrow proof_v$
10: else
11:     $\mathbf{P}[v] \xleftarrow{\$} \{0,1\}^m$
12: send $(\mathbf{L}[v], \mathbf{E}[v], \mathbf{P}[v])$ to server
13: $v \leftarrow v + 1$
Verify($\mathbf{sp}(w), proof$)
   Client:
14: $\overline{w} \leftarrow min\ \mathbf{sp}(w)$
15: $(st_c, hash) \leftarrow \Sigma[\overline{w}]$
16: $t_w \leftarrow \mathbf{Key}[\overline{w}], r_w \leftarrow \mathbf{Rw}[\overline{w}]$
17: $hash' = \mathbf{H_3}(0, r_w) \oplus \mathbf{H_3}(1, st_c)$
18: for all $ind \in \mathbf{R}$ do
19:     $hash' = hash' \oplus \mathbf{H_3}(1, t_w \parallel ind)$
20: if $proof = hash$ and $proof = hash'$
21:     return $Accept$
22: else
23:     return $Reject$

Search($\mathbf{sp}(w), \mathbf{uh}(w)$)
   Client:
24: $\overline{w} \leftarrow min\ \mathbf{sp}(w)$
25: $t_w \leftarrow \mathbf{Key}[\overline{w}]$
26: $r_w \leftarrow \mathbf{Rw}[\overline{w}]$
27: if $\mathbf{H_3}(0, r_w) = \perp$
28:     $\mathbf{H_3}(0, r_w) \xleftarrow{\$} \{0,1\}^m$
29: end if
30: parse $\mathbf{uh}[w]$ as $[(v_1, op_1, ind_1)$
       $, \ldots, (v_c, op_c, ind_c)]$
31: $c \leftarrow |\mathbf{uh}[w]|$
32: if $c = 0$
33:     return ϕ
34: end if
35: $\mathbf{P}[v_0] \leftarrow \mathbf{H_3}(0, r_w), st_0 \leftarrow \perp$
36: $\mathbf{H_3}(1, st_0) \leftarrow 0^m$
37: for $i = 1$ to c do
38:     $st_i \leftarrow \mathbf{ST}[v_i], st_{i-1} \leftarrow \mathbf{ST}[v_{i-1}]$
39:     $\mathbf{H_3}(1, st_i) \xleftarrow{\$} \{0,1\}^m$
40:     program $\mathbf{H_1}: \mathbf{H_1}(t_w \parallel st_i) = \mathbf{L}[v_i]$
41:     program $\mathbf{H_2}: \mathbf{H_2}(t_w \parallel st_i) = \mathbf{E}[v_i] \oplus$
             $(st_{i-1} \parallel op_i \parallel ind_i)$
42:     program $\mathbf{H_3}: \mathbf{H_3}(1, t_w \parallel ind_i) = \mathbf{P}[v_i] \oplus$
             $\mathbf{H_3}(1, st_i) \oplus \mathbf{P}[v_{i-1}] \oplus \mathbf{H_3}(1, st_{i-1})$
43: end for
44: $\Sigma[\overline{w}] = (\mathbf{ST}[v_c], \mathbf{P}[v_c])$
45: send $(t_w, \mathbf{ST}[v_c])$ to server
   Server:
46: perform search and returns $(\mathbf{R}, proof)$

---

can make at most $\mathbf{poly}(\lambda)$ guesses, then $\Pr[\mathbf{Bad}] \leq \mathbf{poly}(\lambda) \cdot (2^{-\lambda} + negl(\lambda))$. The probability $\Pr[\mathbf{Bad}]$ is negligible so that G_1 and G_2 are indistinguishable.

Game G_3: G_3 does exactly what G_2 did for H_1, but for H_2. We can prove that G_3 and G_2 are perfectly indistinguishable by the same reduction.

$$Pr(G_3 = 1) - Pr(G_2 = 1) \leq negl(\lambda)$$

Game G_4: In G_3, $hash'$ is calculated by multiset hash functions with the knowledge of ind and st_{c+1}. While in G_4, the client randomly chooses a string from $\{0,1\}^m$ as $hash'$ and records it to the table $\mathbf{P}$. G_4 and G_3 behave exactly the same in the adversary's perspective. In the update protocol, both the two games output three uniformly random strings. In the verify algorithm, the client can recalculate the output of $\mathcal{H}(\mathbf{R})$ to get the correct verify result.

$$Pr(G_4 = 1) - Pr(G_3 = 1) = 0$$

Game G_5: In G_5, we introduce a global counter v to record the number of updates operations. v is initialized in the setup protocol and increases in the update protocol. We will show that G_5 and G_4 are indistinguishable. In the update phase, the client generates st, e and $proof$ randomly and sends them to the server in both games. The adversary cannot distinguish the two games for the reason that for every update operation, there are always three new strings sent from the client to server. For the search phase, the client sends two strings st_c and t_w to the server and the server will do the exact same thing.

$$Pr(G_5 = 1) - Pr(G_4 = 1) = 0$$

The Simulator: The simulator, as shown in Algorithm 3, is the same as G_5, except those two places. Firstly, the simulator gets the update history of keyword w from leakage function $\mathbf{uh}(w)$. Secondly, the simulator uniquely maps from keyword w to $\overline{w} = \min \mathbf{sp}(w)$.

$$Pr\left[\mathbf{Ideal}^{\Pi}_{\mathcal{A},\mathcal{S}}(\lambda) = 1\right] - Pr(G_5 = 1) = 0$$

4.2   Comparison

We compare our scheme with FAST [22], $\Sigma o \phi o \varsigma$ [2], $\Sigma o \phi o \varsigma$-$\epsilon$ [2], Janus [4] and Janus++ [24] in this section. All of those schemes can achieve forward security. Janus and Janus++ mainly focus on backward security, but they can achieve forward security as well. Only our scheme and $\Sigma o \phi o \varsigma$-$\epsilon$ can ensure verifiability of search result. Our scheme can be viewed as an extension of FAST to improve the search efficiency and to support verifiability of search result.

Table 2. Performance comparison

Schemes	FS	BS	Update	Search	Verify
$\Sigma o \phi o \varsigma$ [2]	✓	✗	$t_{TP} + 2t_H$	$\lvert U_w \rvert \cdot (t_{TP} + 2t_H)$	✗
$\Sigma o \phi o \varsigma$-$\epsilon$ [2]	✓	✗	$t_{TP} + t_{\mathcal{H}} + 2t_H$	$\lvert U_w \rvert \cdot (t_{TP} + 2t_H)$	$t_{\mathcal{H}} + t_{VHT}$
FAST [22]	✓	✗	$t_P + 2t_H$	$\lvert U_w \rvert \cdot (t_P + 2t_H)$	✗
Our Scheme	✓	✗	$t_{\mathcal{H}} + 2t_H$	$\lvert U_w \rvert \cdot (2t_H)$	$t_{\mathcal{H}}$
Janus [4]	✓	✓	t_{PPE}	$(\lvert U_w \rvert - \lvert D_w \rvert) \cdot t_{PPE}$	✗
Janus++ [24]	✓	✓	t_{SPE}	$(\lvert U_w \rvert - \lvert D_w \rvert) \cdot t_{SPE}$	✗

We denote by TP a trapdoor permutation, t_{TP} the time cost of TP, P a standard permutation, t_P the time cost of P. The public puncturable encryption scheme is denoted as PPE and the time cost of its operations (encrypt, puncture and decrypt included) is denoted as t_{PPE}. The symmetric puncturable encryption scheme is denoted as SPE and the time cost of its operations (encrypt, puncture and decrypt included) is denoted as t_{SPE}. t_H stands for the time cost of standard hash function and $t_{\mathcal{H}}$ for the multiset hash functions. t_{VHT} is the time cost of reconstructing the verifiable hash table. U_w is the number of update operations about keyword w, i.e., the number of times that keyword w was historically added and deleted in the database. D_w is the number of delete operations about keyword w. FS (resp. BS) stands for forward (resp. backward) security. Table 2 gives the performance comparison of the four schemes above.

5 Performance Evaluation

In this section, we present a thorough performance evaluation of our proposed scheme. We implement our scheme in C/C++ and use crypto++ [9] library to instantiate the cryptographic operations: AES in CTR model for the PRF F_1 and F_2, SHA256 for the hash function H_1 and H_2. We evaluate the proposed scheme by comparing it with Σοφος [2], Σοφος-ε [2] and FAST [22]. For all those schemes, we use Rocksdb [10] to store the data in the client and the server, and gRPC [14] to implement the communication between them. The length of symmetric keys are set to 128 bits in all schemes.

We evaluate our scheme using two LINUX machines, one is service node and the other is client node. Both of them have 4 cores with 8 threads (Intel Xeon E5-1620 v3, 3.50 GHz), 16 GB RAM and 1 TB disk, running on Ubuntu 14.04 LTS. We adopt the open-source C++ implementation of Σοφος and FAST from GitHub for the comparison. The implementation of our scheme is also an open source project in GitHub [28].

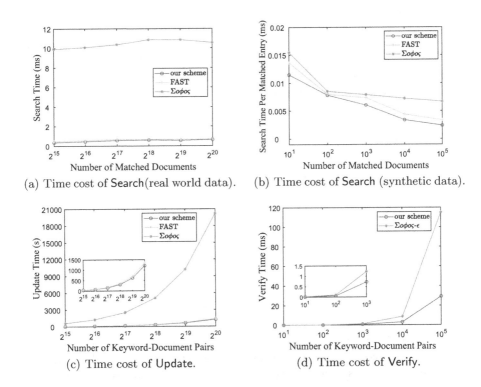

(a) Time cost of Search(real world data).   (b) Time cost of Search (synthetic data).

(c) Time cost of Update.   (d) Time cost of Verify.

Fig. 2. The performance comparison.

Firstly, we consider the real-world dataset from Wikimedia Download [11] to drive our evaluations. The dataset is preprocessed into a Rocksdb file from which the update algorithm reads out keyword-document pairs. There are 786,629 documents and 4,006,619 distinct keywords in the dataset. We perform our evaluation with different database of the size ranging from 2^{15} to 2^{20}. When evaluating the search efficiency, we choose randomly a keyword and search it using three schemes.

To evaluate the efficiency of search and verification in the case a single keyword is included by a large number of documents, we also use 5 synthetic datasets of increasing size. The number of matched documents ranges from 10 to 10^5. When evaluating the search efficiency, we repeat the search process 10 times and take the average, then divided it by the number of matched documents to get the search time per matched entry.

Search Efficiency. Figure 2(a) shows the evaluation results of the search protocol on real-world dataset. As we can see, the search efficiency of $\Sigma o \phi o \varsigma$ is obviously inferior to FAST and our scheme. The reason is that $\Sigma o \phi o \varsigma$ needs to perform a trapdoor permutation, a public key primitive, to get the previous state from the current state. Both our scheme and FAST use only symmetric key operations, but an extra trapdoor permutation operation needs to be performed in FAST. Hence, our scheme performs better than $\Sigma o \phi o \varsigma$ and FAST.

Figure 2(b) shows the evaluation results of the search protocol on synthetic data. As we can see, when the number of matched documents increases, the search time of per matched entry decreases. The reason is that all of those schemes have some initializing operations in search protocol, such as reading out the current state from Σ and generating the search token. Actually, the search complexity of all the three schemes depends only on the number of matched documents. Those one-time costly operations are amortized into every entry in the search result. The search time of per matched entry of $\Sigma o \phi o \varsigma$ is larger than both of our scheme and FAST for the reason mentioned above.

Table 3. Update efficiency

Schemes	$\Sigma o \phi o \varsigma$	FAST	Our scheme
Throughput (ops/s)	3997	43764	78125
Single update time (ms)	0.25	0.023	0.013

Update Efficiency. Figure 2(c) shows the performance of update protocol on real-world dataset. Note that the latencies caused by RPC communication and disk access are included in our evaluations. For example, the update algorithm needs to read out keyword-document from Rocksdb files and the update requests need to be sent to the server. Intuitively, the bottleneck of update protocol is the computation of the new update token. The update time of $\Sigma o \phi o \varsigma$ is the largest for the reason that it needs to perform a trapdoor permutation in the update protocol. For FAST, the update protocol consists of a permutation and two hash functions. For our scheme, the update protocol includes an update operation of multiset hash functions and two hash functions. Note that the update operation of multiset hash functions is some hash function operations in our scheme, which is much more efficient than permutation functions. Hence, our scheme performs better than FAST on update efficiency. The difference of their efficiency has become more and more obvious as the number of keyword-document pairs increases.

To further evaluate the update efficiency, we calculate the throughput of update operation and the update time of single keyword-document pair of the three schemes. As shown in Table 3, the throughput of our scheme is about 1.7 times that of FAST and about 19 times that of $\Sigma o\phi o\varsigma$. The experimental results confirm that the proposed scheme has a better performance in terms of update efficiency.

Verify Efficiency. Figure 2(d) shows the performance of verify operation. Our scheme performs better than $\Sigma o\phi o\varsigma\text{-}\epsilon$ since an extra reconstruction of verifiable hash table is involved in it. As we can see, the difference increases dramatically with the increasing of the number of keyword-document pairs. The reason is that the time cost of reconstructing a hash table is proportional to the number of elements of it.

6 Conclusion

In this paper, we study the problem of forward secure SSE in the malicious setting. A new efficient verifiable forward secure SSE is proposed based on the primitive of multiset hash functions, which can ensure query integrity and forward security. Additionally, we provide a formal security proof to prove that our scheme can achieve the desired security goals. The proposed scheme is implemented and the experiment result shows that it can provide a more efficient performance in search and update processes.

Acknowledgement. This work is supported by National Key Research and Development Program of China (No. 2017YFB0802202), National Natural Science Foundation of China (Nos. 61702401 and 61572382), the Fundamental Research Funds for the Central Universities (XJS17053), National Cryptography Development Fund (No. MMJJ20180110) and China 111 Project (No. B16037).

References

1. Azraoui, M., Elkhiyaoui, K., Önen, M., Molva, R.: Publicly verifiable conjunctive keyword search in outsourced databases. In: Proceedings of 2015 IEEE Conference on Communications and Network Security, CNS 2015, pp. 619–627. IEEE (2015)

2. Bost, R.: Σοφος: forward secure searchable encryption. In: Proceedings of the 2016 ACM Conference on Computer and Communications Security, CCS 2016, pp. 1143–1154. ACM (2016)

3. Bost, R., Fouque, P., Pointcheval, D.: Verifiable dynamic symmetric searchable encryption: optimality and forward security. IACR Cryptology ePrint Archive 2016, p. 62 (2016). http://eprint.iacr.org/2016/062

4. Bost, R., Minaud, B., Ohrimenko, O.: Forward and backward private searchable encryption from constrained cryptographic primitives. In: Proceedings of the 2017 ACM SIGSAC Conference on Computer and Communications Security, CCS 2017, pp. 1465–1482. ACM (2017)

5. Cash, D., Jarecki, S., Jutla, C., Krawczyk, H., Roşu, M.-C., Steiner, M.: Highly-scalable searchable symmetric encryption with support for Boolean queries. In: Canetti, R., Garay, J.A. (eds.) CRYPTO 2013. LNCS, vol. 8042, pp. 353–373. Springer, Heidelberg (2013). https://doi.org/10.1007/978-3-642-40041-4_20

6. Chai, Q., Gong, G.: Verifiable symmetric searchable encryption for semi-honest-but-curious cloud servers. In: Proceedings of 2012 IEEE International Conference on Communications, ICC 2012, pp. 917–922. IEEE (2012)

7. Clarke, D., Devadas, S., van Dijk, M., Gassend, B., Suh, G.E.: Incremental multiset hash functions and their application to memory integrity checking. In: Laih, C.-S. (ed.) ASIACRYPT 2003. LNCS, vol. 2894, pp. 188–207. Springer, Heidelberg (2003). https://doi.org/10.1007/978-3-540-40061-5_12

8. Curtmola, R., Garay, J.A., Kamara, S., Ostrovsky, R.: Searchable symmetric encryption: improved definitions and efficient constructions. J. Comput. Secur. **19**(5), 895–934 (2011)

9. Dai, W.: Crypto++: A free C++ class library of cryptographic schemes (2019). https://cryptopp.com/. Accessed 10 June 2019

10. Facebook Inc.: Rocksdb: a persistent key-value store for flash and ram storage (2019). http://rocksdb.org Accessed 10 June 2019

11. Foundation, W.: Wikimedia downloads (2019). https://dumps.wikimedia.org. Accessed 10 June 2019

12. Giraud, M., Anzala-Yamajako, A., Bernard, O., Lafourcade, P.: Practical passive leakage-abuse attacks against symmetric searchable encryption. In: Proceedings of the 14th International Joint Conference on e-Business and Telecommunications, pp. 200–211. IEEE (2017)

13. Goh, E.: Secure indexes. IACR Cryptology ePrint Archive 2003, p. 216 (2003). http://eprint.iacr.org/2003/216

14. Google, Inc.: GRPC: a high performance, open-source universal RPC framework (2019). http://www.grpc.io/. Accessed 10 June 2019

15. Hashim, A.: Latest facebook data breach totals over 540 million records found unsecured. https://latesthackingnews.com/2019/04/04/latest-facebook-data-breach-totals-over-540-million-records-found-unsecured/. Accessed 29 Apr 2019

16. Islam, M.S., Kuzu, M., Kantarcioglu, M.: Access pattern disclosure on searchable encryption: ramification, attack and mitigation. In: Proceedings of the 19th Annual Network and Distributed System Security Symposium. NDSS (2012)

17. Kamara, S., Papamanthou, C., Roeder, T.: Dynamic searchable symmetric encryption. In: Proceedings of the 19th ACM Conference on Computer and Communications Security, CCS 2012, pp. 965–976. ACM (2012)

18. Kurosawa, K., Ohtaki, Y.: UC-secure searchable symmetric encryption. In: Proceedings of the 16th International Conference on Financial Cryptography and Data Security, FC 2012, pp. 285–298. IEEE (2012)

19. Kurosawa, K., Sasaki, K., Ohta, K., Yoneyama, K.: UC-secure dynamic searchable symmetric encryption scheme. In: Proceedings of the 11th International Workshop on Security Advances in Information and Computer Security, IWSEC 2016, pp. 73–90. IEEE (2016)
20. Ogata, W., Kurosawa, K.: Efficient no-dictionary verifiable searchable symmetric encryption. In: Proceedings of the 21st International Conference on Financial Cryptography and Data Security, FC 2017, pp. 498–516. IEEE (2017)
21. Song, D.X., Wagner, D.A., Perrig, A.: Practical techniques for searches on encrypted data. In: Proceedings of 2000 IEEE Symposium on Security and Privacy, S&P 2000, pp. 44–55. IEEE (2000)
22. Song, X., Dong, C., Yuan, D., Xu, Q., Zhao, M.: Forward private searchable symmetric encryption with optimized I/O efficiency. IEEE Trans. Dependable Secur. Comput. (2018). https://doi.org/10.1109/TDSC.2018.2822294
23. Stefanov, E., Papamanthou, C., Shi, E.: Practical dynamic searchable encryption with small leakage. In: Proceedings of the 21st Annual Network and Distributed System Security Symposium, NDSS (2014)
24. Sun, S., et al.: Practical backward-secure searchable encryption from symmetric puncturable encryption. In: Proceedings of the 2018 ACM SIGSAC Conference on Computer and Communications Security, CCS 2018, pp. 763–780 (2018)
25. Sun, W., Liu, X., Lou, W., Hou, Y.T., Li, H.: Catch you if you lie to me: efficient verifiable conjunctive keyword search over large dynamic encrypted cloud data. In: Proceedings of 2015 IEEE Conference on Computer Communications, INFOCOM 2015, pp. 2110–2118. IEEE (2015)
26. Wang, J., Chen, X., Sun, S.-F., Liu, J.K., Au, M.H., Zhan, Z.-H.: Towards efficient verifiable conjunctive keyword search for large encrypted database. In: Lopez, J., Zhou, J., Soriano, M. (eds.) ESORICS 2018. LNCS, vol. 11099, pp. 83–100. Springer, Cham (2018). https://doi.org/10.1007/978-3-319-98989-1_5
27. Zhang, Y., Katz, J., Papamanthou, C.: All your queries are belong to us: the power of file-injection attacks on searchable encryption. In: Proceedings of the 25th Security Symposium, USENIX 2016, pp. 707–720. IEEE (2016)
28. Zhang, Z.: Implementation of our scheme (2019). https://github.com/zhangzhongjun/VFSSSE. Accessed 10 June 2019

Generic Multi-keyword Ranked Search on Encrypted Cloud Data

Shabnam Kasra Kermanshahi[1,2](✉), Joseph K. Liu[1](✉), Ron Steinfeld[1](✉), and Surya Nepal[2](✉)

[1] Monash University, Melbourne, VIC 3800, Australia
{shabnam.kasra,joseph.liu,ron.steinfeld}@monash.edu
[2] CSIRO Data 61, Melbourne, VIC 3008, Australia
Surya.Nepal@data61.csiro.au

Abstract. Although searchable encryption schemes allow secure search over the encrypted data, they mostly support conventional Boolean keyword search, without capturing any relevance of the search results. This leads to a large amount of post-processing overhead to find the most matching documents and causes an unnecessary communication cost between the servers and end-users. Such problems can be addressed efficiently using a ranked search system that retrieves the most relevant documents. However, existing state-of-the-art solutions in the context of Searchable Symmetric Encryption (SSE) suffer from either (a) security and privacy breaches due to the use of Order Preserving Encryption (OPE) or (b) non-practical solutions like using the two non-colluding servers. In this paper, we present a generic solution for multi-keyword ranked search over the encrypted cloud data. The proposed solution can be applied over different symmetric searchable encryption schemes. To demonstrate the practicality of our technique, in this paper we leverage the Oblivious Cross Tags (OXT) protocol of Cash et al. (2013) due to its scalability and remarkable flexibility to support different settings. Our proposed scheme supports the multi-keyword search on Boolean, ranked and limited range queries while keeping all of the OXT's properties intact. The key contribution of this paper is that our scheme is resilience against all common attacks that take advantage of OPE leakage while only a single cloud server is used. Moreover, the results indicate that using the proposed solution the communication overhead decreases drastically when the number of matching results is large.

Keywords: SSE · Multi keywords · Ranked search

1 Introduction

In contrast to Boolean queries, which rely on appearance of the queried keywords in the database and return the matching documents, the ranked search captures the most relevant documents for a query. In the potentially huge result space, ranked search systems minimize the post processing of data for end-users.

© Springer Nature Switzerland AG 2019
K. Sako et al. (Eds.): ESORICS 2019, LNCS 11736, pp. 322–343, 2019.
https://doi.org/10.1007/978-3-030-29962-0_16

Moreover, it has a great impact on the system usability and performance when dealing with the massive amounts of data stored in the cloud. Ranked search has been widely studied by Information Retrieval (IR) and database communities. Top-$\mathscr{K}$ query processing techniques such as TA [13] and FA [12] are well-known examples of such systems.

However, such techniques do not preserve the privacy of the data stored on the database. That is, they require direct access to the relevance scores as well as various modes of access to data which makes them inapplicable in the context of encrypted data search.

Related Works. The first multi-keyword ranked search scheme was proposed by Cao et al. [6], where both documents and queries are represented as vectors of dictionary size. This scheme sorts documents using the score based on Inner Product Similarity (IPS), where a document score is simply the number of matches of queried keywords in each document, which is not accurate [3]. In general, for ranked search the following techniques are proposed in the literature.

- **Fully Homomorphic Encryption (FHE)**: Although FHE [14] supports arbitrary computations over the encrypted data, due to the high performance overheads its not suitable for practical database queries [21].
- **ORAM**: Similar to FHE, ORAM (Oblivious Random-Access Machine) [16] is computationally expensive to be used in practice [21]. Although some works tried to improve ORAM efficiency [4,10,17,27], its application in symmetric encryption for execution of top-$\mathscr{K}$ queries is limited [24].
- **OPE**: Order Preserving Encryption (OPE) [1] allows efficient range queries over the encrypted data. However, OPE reveals the relative order of elements in the database, and therefore does not meet the data owner's data privacy.
- **Using two (or more) non-colluding servers**: The authors of [3] justified the assumption of non-colluding servers; these parties are usually supplied by different companies hence have also commercial interests not to collude. This model would be a solution to avoid multiple rounds of user-to-server interactions. However, it requires the server-to-server interactions instead. Moreover, this assumption is less appealing in practice compared to the traditional single-server model [25].

Motivations. Among different methods to support ranked query for searchable encryption, OPE is the most popular one due to its efficiency. However, the leakage associated with OPE makes it vulnerable to several attacks. Naveed et al. [22] presented two attacks against OPE as follows:

Sorting Attack: This attack decrypts the OPE-encrypted columns. That is, adversary sorts the ciphertext and the message space, and outputs a function that maps each ciphertext to the element of message space with the same rank.

Cumulative Attack: OPE reveals the frequency of the data and its relative order at the same time which helps an adversary to find out what fraction of encrypted data is smaller than each ciphertext. This is known as cumulative attack. This attack recovers plaintext from OPE with high probability using auxiliary information[1].

Table 1. Summary of comparison

Protocol	Encryption method	Single/twin server	No OPE leakage
Meng et al. [21]	Encrypted hash list using Paillier	Twin server	?
Shen et al. [23]	OPE	Single server	×
Baldimtsi and Ohrimenko [3]	Paillier	Twin server	?
Jiang et al. [18]	Paillier	Twin server	?
Wang et al. [26]	One-to-many OPE	Single server	×
Our MRSSE	SWHE	Single server	✓

Durak et al. [11] showed that the above attacks did not take advantage of the additional leakage that is present in OPE constructions. They discussed additional two types of attacks *Inter-column correlation-based attacks* and *Inter+Intra-column correlation-based attack*. The former takes the advantage of correlation between OPE columns where the adversary knows a bounding box for the plaintext. That is, the columns of data in a table are usually correlated because a row of a table usually corresponds to an individual record. The latter attack uses both inter and intra column correlations.

Table 1 provides a summary of some related works that support ranked search over an encrypted database. They either used OPE or cryptographic primitives over two servers. The former suffers from serious leakages and the latter from usability (i.e., issues to use in practice). Shen et al. [23] built an OPE on the top of Oblivious Cross Tags (OXT) protocol of [7]. Although their scheme is efficient, it is vulnerable against aforementioned attacks due to the OPE leakage. To avoid revealing the distribution of scores in OPE, Wang et al. [26] proposed one-to-many OPE. Their construction conceals the distribution of scores using a probabilistic encryption. However, Li et al. [19] presented a differential attack over one-to-many OPE which reveals the leakage of distribution by exploiting the difference between ciphertexts. It is assumed that the attacker has some background information which helps him to infer the encrypted keywords using differential attacks. On the other hand, if two servers are located in the same place, this contradicts with the assumption that they do not collude. There would be server-to-server communication overhead if they are located in different places. This cancels out the major advantage of ranked query, minimizing the

---

[1] Auxiliary information are publicly-available information such as application details, public statistics, and prior versions of the database (possibly achieved by a prior data breach).

unnecessary network traffics. Therefore, an effective solution to support ranked query over symmetric searchable encryption schemes is still a challenge. Our proposed approach in this paper aims to address this challenge.

Our Contributions. The key contribution of this paper is a generic solution for supporting effective multi-keyword ranked search over an encrypted database. We demonstrate the application of this solution through the proposed Multi-keyword Ranked Searchable Symmetric Encryption scheme (MRSSE). MRSSE is secure against all of the attacks related to OPE without relying on a two server assumption, and hence overcomes the limitations of existing approaches. More precisely, MRSSE uses somewhat homomorphic encryption within our proposed filtering techniques instead of OPE to provide a ranked search. In terms of functionality, MRSSE supports the multi-keyword search over Boolean, ranked and limited range queries without adding any extra leakage. It reduces the communication overhead when the number of search results is large (we give examples in Sect. 5.2) while the security is guaranteed. The effectiveness of MRSEE is proven via security and efficiency analyses. It is important to note that though our approach is generic, in this paper we leverage OXT protocol[2] as an example to demonstrate the applicability of the proposed approach.

It is worth to note that when performing rank search, the server learns a set of ciphertexts which are satisfying the ranking condition, this is an inherent leakage in ranked search. Moreover, in the most of the current solutions for ranked-search the relative order of the importance of the document (ranking) is also leaked to the server. However, the proposed solution in this paper avoids this leakage as the server returns always a fixed size of unsorted results (the actual results are padded with the encryption of 0s) and the client performs sorting locally.

Our Technique. We used various homomorphic encryption tools and techniques to efficiently filter the search results. We considered using BGV-type homomorphic encryption but it resulted in high depth for equality check on integers (j and P)[3]. Hence, we reduced this depth by using unary encoding (we also have document scores encoded in unary which are small). However, the conditional increment of the pointer "P" involves a multiplication. Therefore, we switched to Ring-GSW homomorphic encryption which allows us to do the repeated multiplications with low noise growth (refer to Sect. 3.1 for details).

2 Preliminaries

In this section, we present notations and definitions needed in our construction.

Cryptographic Primitives. The utilized cryptographic primitives in this paper are presented in details in the appendix.

Notations. Notations frequently used in this paper are listed in Table 2.

---

[2] For detailed explanations of OXT refer to the appendix.

[3] ($f_j(.)$) in line 18 and line 19 of Algorithm 1 where j is the counter for candidate list and P is the pointer of the output buffer.

Table 2. Notations and Terminologies

Notation	Description
id_i	The document identifier of the i-th document
W_{id_i}	A list of keywords contained in the i-th document
$DB = (id_i, W_{id_i})_{i=1}^{\mathscr{D}}$	A database consisting of a list of document identifier and keyword-set pairs
$DB[w] = \{id : w \in W_{id}\}$	The set of identifiers of documents that contain keyword w
$W = \bigcup_{i=1}^{\mathscr{D}} W_{id_i}$	The keyword set of the database
EDB	The encrypted database
SEDB	The scored encrypted database
sterm	The least frequent term among queried terms (or keywords) in a search query
xterm	Other queried terms in a search query (i.e., the queried terms excluding sterm)
TSet	An array that presents equal sized lists for each keyword in the database
XSet	A lookup table that contains elements computed from each keyword-document pair
P	Pointer to the output buffer
j	Counter for the candidate list
t	Threshold
$\hat{t}$	Encrypted threshold
N	Size of the output buffer
L	Number of search keyword
l	Bit length of the score
n	Number of search results
z	A bit showing whether the threshold condition holds
s	Score
$\hat{s}$	Encrypted score
λ	Security parameter
n_b	Breaking point

Scoring Approach. We use a common method of evaluating a relevance score, called $TF \times IDF$ (term frequency times inverse document frequency) [28]. However, it should not be regarded as the name suggest. It is defined as $Score(w_j, id_i) = \frac{1}{|id_i|} . (ln(1 + \frac{N}{f_{w_j}})) . (1 + ln(f_{id_i, w_j}))$. This score consists of two main components; term weight $tw = (ln(1 + \frac{N}{f_{w_j}}))$ and relative term frequency

$r_{d,t} = (ln(1 + \frac{N}{f_{w_j}}))$. Here, f_{w_j} is the number of documents that contain the keyword/term w_j, N is total number of documents in the collection, f_{id_i,w_j} is the frequency of w_j in the document id_i and, $|id_i|$ is a normalization factor to discount the contribution of long documents and obtained by counting the number of indexed terms in a document. Note that $Score(w_j, id_i)$ is set to zero if the keyword w_j does not appear in document with identifier id_i. Finally, the similarity measure is the sum of the products of the weights of query terms (Q) and the corresponding document terms [28]: $Score(Q, id_i) = \sum_{w_j \in Q} Score(w_j, id_i)$.

3 Our Threshold-Based Filtering Approach

We solve the problem of multi-keyword ranked search by introducing threshold-based filtering on the ciphertexts. This generic approach can be applied on symmetric searchable encryption schemes. Assume that the database DB is going to be outsourced to a honest-but-curious cloud server. The first step for the data owner is to generate the scored encrypted database. In this phase the data owner can apply any desired scoring technique (such as $TF \times IDF$). Whenever, the data owner wants to search through the scored encrypted database, he need to generate a search token and choose a threshold value. Thus, the server would be able to find the matching results, then using homomorphic operations aggregate the scores and filter them according to the threshold and return the most relevant results (with the scores higher or equivalent to the threshold). Since the size of output buffer, N, is independent of total number of search results, n, we can achieve a homomorphic computation and communication independent of n.

3.1 Homomorphic Operations

We define the following homomorphic operations which are used in the homomorphic search and homomorphic filter presented in Sects. 3.2 and 3.3, respectively.

- **Component-wise homomorphic Operations:** We represent the encryption of a ℓ-bit integer such as $s = s_{\ell-1}s_{\ell-2}...s_0$ using Ring-GSW (see appendix) as $\hat{s} = Enc(s_{\ell-1}) Enc(s_{\ell-2})...Enc(s_0)$, where the plaintext space of encryption is $(\mathbb{Z}_2, (+, .))$. We denote addition and multiplication over ciphertext with $\boxplus$ and $\boxdot$, respectively. It extends to vectors of encrypted bits by just doing $\boxplus$ and $\boxdot$ operations component-wise. Thus, the multiplication of an encryption of a bit z with a vector of the encryption of bits like $\hat{s} = Enc(s_{\ell-1})Enc(s_{\ell-2})...Enc(s_0)$, is defined to be $(Enc(z) \boxdot Enc(s_{\ell-1}))(Enc(z) \boxdot Enc(s_{\ell-2}))...(Enc(z) \boxdot Enc(s_0))$.
  Remark. All of the following algorithms are applying the same operation component-wise to each bit ciphertext of the score except $Convert_{GSW,RLWE}(.)$.
- **Greater-Than Comparison ($\boxgeq$):** For two encrypted unsigned ℓ-bit integers $\hat{s}_i$ and $\hat{t}$, the operation $(\hat{s}_i \boxgeq \hat{t})$ outputs 1 if $s_i \geq t$ and 0 otherwise. We

adapt the greater-than comparison circuit of Cheon et al. [8] by defining a NOT operation. That is, $NOT(b)$ outputs 1 if $b = 1$ and 0 otherwise. This operation can be defined as $NOT(b) = 1 - b$. Thus, $\boxdot$ operation can be defined as $\hat{z}_i = \hat{s}_i \boxdot \hat{t}$ for $\hat{z}_i = 1 \boxplus (1 \boxplus \hat{s}_{i,\ell-1}) \boxdot \hat{t}_{\ell-1} \boxplus \sum_{j=0}^{\ell-2} (1 \boxplus \hat{s}_{i,j}) \boxdot \hat{t}_j \boxdot d_{j+1}, ..., d_{\ell-1}$.

Here, $d_j = (1 \boxplus \hat{s}_{i,j} \boxplus \hat{t}_j)$. The depth of this circuit is $log(\ell+1)$ and, to evaluate this circuit, $2\ell - 2$ homomorphic multiplication is required.

- **Integer Addition** ($\dotplus$): We use $\dotplus$ to denote the homomorphic integer addition operation. For addition of two ν-bit integer, x and y, first we make them ℓ-bit by padding with zeros on the left (here, $\ell > \nu$). Then, the sum $\hat{s}_i = \hat{x} \dotplus \hat{y}$ can be computed efficiently using SIMD operations as introduce in [8]. For $i \in [1, \ell-1]$ with initial values $\hat{s}_0 = \hat{x}_0 \boxplus \hat{y}_0$ and $Carry_0 = \hat{x}_0 \boxdot \hat{y}_0$, where the $\hat{s}_i$s are written as $\hat{s}_i = \hat{x} \boxplus \hat{y} \boxplus \sum_{j=0}^{i-1} t_{ij}$ where, $t_{ij} = (\hat{x}_i \boxdot \hat{y}_i) \Pi_{j+1 \leqslant k \leqslant i-1} (\hat{x}_k \boxplus \hat{y}_k)$ for $j < i - 1$ and $t_{i,i-1} = \hat{x}_{i-1} \boxdot \hat{y}_{i-1}$. The circuit has $log(\ell-2) + 1$ depth and using SIMD and parallelism, it can be evaluated just by $3\ell - 5$ homomorphic multiplications.

- **Unary encoding:** We represent the unary encoding of a number such as $p \in [0, N)$ (we assume $N < d - 1$, where d is the ring dimension) as $p(x) = 0x^0 + 0x^1 + ... + 1x^p + ... + 0x^{N-1}$. The RLWE encryption of $\hat{p}(x)$ is in the form of $(c = \psi_0 u + tg + p(x), c' = \psi_1 u + tf)$ where (ψ_0, ψ_1) is the public key, u, f, g are small random noises and t is the plaintext space (here $\{0, 1\}$). Note that, $\psi_0 = (\psi_1.s + te)$ where s is the secret. We may represent n-dimension encryption of p using matrices as follows:

$$
\begin{bmatrix} c_0 \\ \vdots \\ c_{n-1} \end{bmatrix} = \begin{bmatrix} \psi_{0,0} & -\psi_{0,n-1} & \cdots & -\psi_{0,1} \\ \psi_{0,1} & \psi_{0,0} & \cdots & \vdots \\ \vdots & \vdots & \ddots & \vdots \\ \psi_{0,n-1} & \psi_{0,n-2} & \cdots & \psi_{0,0} \end{bmatrix} \begin{bmatrix} u_0 \\ \vdots \\ u_{n-1} \end{bmatrix} + t \begin{bmatrix} g_0 \\ \vdots \\ g_{n-1} \end{bmatrix} + \begin{bmatrix} \psi_0 \\ \vdots \\ \psi_{n-1} \end{bmatrix}
$$

$$
\begin{bmatrix} c'_0 \\ \vdots \\ c'_{n-1} \end{bmatrix} = \begin{bmatrix} \psi_{0,0} & -\psi_{0,n-1} & \cdots & -\psi_{0,1} \\ \psi_{0,1} & \psi_{0,0} & \cdots & \vdots \\ \vdots & \vdots & \ddots & \vdots \\ \psi_{0,n-1} & \psi_{0,n-2} & \cdots & \psi_{0,0} \end{bmatrix} \begin{bmatrix} u_0 \\ \vdots \\ u_{n-1} \end{bmatrix} + t \begin{bmatrix} f_0 \\ \vdots \\ f_{n-1} \end{bmatrix}
$$

- **Increment by 1:** The operation $Inc(\hat{p})$ increases the value of $p \in [0, N)$ by 1, unconditionally: $Inc(\hat{p}) = x.\hat{p}(x)$ Here, $\hat{p}(x)$ is the unary encryption of p.
- **Conditional Increment by 1:** The operation $Inc(\hat{p}, \hat{z}_i)$ increases the value of $\hat{p}(x)$ (which is the unary encoding of $p \in [0, N)$) by 1 if $\hat{z}_i = 1$. This function can be defined as $Inc(\hat{p}, \hat{z}_i) = \hat{z}_i(x).(x.\hat{p}(x)) + (1 - \hat{z}_i(x)).\hat{p}(x)$. Here,

$$\hat{z}_i = \begin{cases} 0 \\ 1 \end{cases}$$

is a constant polynomial. This point to the line 10 of Filter in Algorithm 1. To efficiently compute the iterated homomorphic multiplications of the increment function in the loop (line 10 of algorithm 1), we applied GSW encryption based on ring-LWE. More precisely, for $i = 0, ..., n - 1$, we can rewrite the increment as $\hat{P}_{i+1} = \hat{z}_i.x\hat{P}_i + (1 - \hat{z}_i).\hat{P}_i = (x - 1)\hat{z}_i\hat{P}_i + \hat{P}_i$ which can be simplified to $\hat{P}_{i+1} = [(x - 1)\hat{z}_i + 1]\hat{P}_i$. Then, if we expand this down to $i = 0$:

$$\hat{P}_{i+1} = \prod_{j=1}^{i} \hat{z}'_j \hat{P}_0$$

where $\hat{z}'_j = (x - 1)\hat{z}_i + 1$. Note that there is no multiplicative depth in these computations due to the use of GSW encryption. One of the advantages of using GSW is the additive noise growth for iterative homomorphic multiplications [15]. Thus, the noise growth for $\hat{z}_i$ and $\hat{z}'_j$ is equivalent to i additions.

- **Equality $(f_j(.))$:** To evaluate the equality of j and p in **Filter(S, t)** (line 18/19 of Algorithm 1), we define a function $f_j(p) = Enc_{LWE}(\langle p, j \rangle)$. Here, $f_j(p)$ is equal to "$\hat{1}$" if $j = p$, and "$\hat{0}$" otherwise. Note that both p and j are unary encoded. Therefore, $f_j(p) = j^T p$. Given the RLWE ciphertext $\hat{p} = (c, c')$ for unary encoded p and the plaintext j, we implement $f_j(p)$ operation homomorphically as follows, which outputs LWE ciphertext of $f_j(p)$:

$$c_{LWE} = j^T c = j^T rot(\psi_0)u + t.j^T g + j^T p$$
$$c'_{LWE} = \hat{c}'^T = j^T rot(c') = j^T rot(\psi_0)rot(u) + tj^T rot(f)$$

By substituting the $rot(\psi_0)$ for $rot(\psi_1)rot(s) + trot(e)$, we can rewrite this operation in terms of the secret as follows:

$$c_{LWE} = (j^T rot(\psi_1)rot(u))s + t.(j^T(rot(e)u + g)) + j^T p$$
$$c'_{LWE} = j^T(rot(\psi_1)rot(u))s + t.(j^T(rot(e)rot(u) + rot(f)))$$

To do the decryption using the secret s, we proceed as follows:

$$\hat{c}'^T s = (j^T rot(\psi_1)rot(u))s + j^T rot(f)s$$
$$j^T c - \hat{c}'^T s = tj^T(rot(e)u + g - rot(f)s) + j^T p$$

By reducing this result modulo t, the message which is $j^T p$ can be obtained.

- **Convert GSW to RLWE:** We define $Convert_{GSW,RLWE}(.)$ function to convert a GSW ciphertext of kth bit $s_{i,k}$ of score into RLWE ciphertext of $s_{i,k}$ with message multiplied by $\frac{q}{2^{k+1}}$ for $k = 0, ..., 6$. We define the convert function as $Convert_{GSW,RLWE}(C_{GSW}, i)$ which picks the row $\ell - (r - i)$ of C_{GSW} and outputs the RLWE ciphertext of form $c_0 = a.t + e + \frac{q}{2^r}.2^i.s_i$, $c_1 = a$ which is an encryption of the plaintext $2^i.s_i$ with plaintext space modulo 2^r. For the bits $s_0, ..., s_{r-1}$ that at the end we want to pack into one ciphertext of the integer $s = \sum 2^i.s_i$, we use $Convert_{GSW,RLWE}(C_{GSW}, i)$ for the bit s_i to encode s_i as $2^i.s_i$ and at the end we add the ciphertext i to get the ciphertext for $\sum 2^i.s_i = s$.

- **Convert RLWE to LWE:** We define $Convert_{RLWE,LWE}(.)$ function to convert a RLWE ciphertext of a bit to the LWE ciphertext. More precisely, in Algorithm 1 line 11, the generated value y_i is a GSW ciphertext, however, the homomorphic operation in the line 18 is done using LWE (similarly for y_i'). Therefore, we define the convert function as follows over the plaintext:

$$Convert_{RLWE,LWE}(y_i) = < \begin{bmatrix} 1,0,\ldots,0 \end{bmatrix}, \begin{bmatrix} y_i \\ 0 \\ \vdots \\ 0 \end{bmatrix} >= y_i$$

Here, $y_i(x) = y_i x^0 + 0x^1 + \ldots + 0x^{n-1}$. Similarly, for the ciphertext for $\hat{y}_i = (c,c')$, the conversion function $Convert_{RLWE,LWE}(\hat{y}_i)$ operates as follows:

$$c_{LWE} =< \begin{bmatrix} 1,0,\ldots,0 \end{bmatrix}, rot(c') >$$
$$c'_{LWE} =< \begin{bmatrix} 1,0,\ldots,0 \end{bmatrix}, c >$$

3.2 Homomorphic Search Algorithm

The search algorithm only requires one homomorphic operation, an integer addition when the overall score using the aggregation function is computed. For instance, homomorphic aggregation of the scores in **Server Search**(Tok_q, SEDB) of Algorithm2 can be written as follows:

```
function Score − Cipher((XSet))
    for i = 1, ..., L do
        Ŝ(GSW) ← Ŝ(GSW) + cscorexᵢ and Ŝ(GSW) ← Ŝ(GSW) + cscores
    end for
```

Here, $cs\hat{c}ore_s$ and $cs\hat{c}ore_{x_i}$ are the ciphertexts of the scores of sterm and xterms, respectively. $\hat{S}^{(GSW)}$ denotes the GSW ciphertext of the aggregated score. The details of this homomorphic integer addition operation is given in Sect. 3.1.

3.3 Homomorphic Filter Algorithm

Algorithm 1 shows how the filtrating is performed on the ciphertexts. This algorithm reflects **Filter**(S,t) while the homomorphic computations are used. Figure 1 demonstrates the functionality of the Algorithm 1 (which is also used in the plaintext form in Filter of Algorithm 2). First, it compares the overall scores (output of the monotone aggregation function in the search algorithm) with the considered threshold value received from the user to set z_is. Whenever, $s_i \geq t$ it sets $z_i = 1$; otherwise it is set to zero. Whenever $z_i = 1$, it copies the corresponding score to the buffer. Finally, it returns the scores stored in the buffer which are in fact equal or greater than the threshold value.

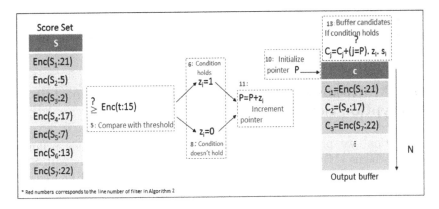

Fig. 1. Example of filter algorithm

Algorithm 1 Filter-ciphertext

Input: Score set $\hat{S} = \{(\hat{s}_1^{(GSW)}, e_1), ..., (\hat{s}_n^{(GSW)}, e_n)\}$, Threshold $\hat{t}^{(2)}$
Output: two lists of score-ciphertext where the scores are higher than the threshold; $\hat{C}_f$ and $\hat{C}'_f$

```
1: function Filter(Ŝ, t̂)
2:    i ← 1
3:    j ← 1
4:    Initialize pointer P̂ = 0 (beginning of output)
5:    Ĉ_f ← Enc^(LWE)(0)
6:    Ĉ'_f ← Enc^(LWE)(0)
7:    for i = 1, ..., n do
8:        ê_i^(GSW) = Enc^(GSW)(e_i)
9:        ẑ_i^(GSW) = ŝ_i^(GSW) ⊡ t̂^(GSW)
10:       P̂^(GSW) = Inc(P̂^(GSW), ẑ_i^(GSW))
11:       ŷ_i^(GSW) = ẑ_i^(GSW) ⊡ ŝ_i^(GSW)
12:       ŷ'_i^(GSW) = ẑ_i^(GSW) ⊡ ê_i^(GSW)
13:       ŷ_i^(RLWE) = Convert_{GSW,RLWE}(ŷ_i^(GSW))
14:       ŷ'_i^(RLWE) = Convert_{GSW,RLWE}(ŷ'_i^(GSW))
15:       ŷ_i^(LWE) = Convert_{RLWE,LWE}(ŷ_i^(RLWE))
16:       ŷ'_i^(LWE) = Convert_{RLWE,LWE}(ŷ'_i^(RLWE))
17:       for j = 1, ..., N do
18:           ĉ_j^(LWE) = ĉ_j^(LWE) ⊞ (f_j(P̂)) ⊡ ŷ_i^(LWE)
19:           ĉ'_j^(LWE) = ĉ'_j^(LWE) ⊞ (f_j(P̂)) ⊡ ŷ'_i^(LWE)
20:       end for
21:    end for
22:    Ĉ_f = ĉ_1^(LWE), ..., ĉ_N^(LWE)
23:    Ĉ'_f = ĉ'_1^(LWE), ..., ĉ'_N^(LWE)
24:    return Ĉ_f and Ĉ'_f
25: end function=0
```

In Algorithm 1, we start homomorphic computations with GSW with the modulus q, where we have s as the secret key (line 9 to 11). Then we do the conversion to LWE with the modulus q using the secret key s. The last multiplication (in line 18/19) involves three steps as defined in [5]; Mult, Scale, and SwitchKey. After the first step, in the LWE with modulus q, the secret key becomes s''. Then, we do the modulus switching in the second step. We do the conversion to LWE with modulus q' using the secret key s''. In the last step, we switch the key back to s while the modulus is still q'. Note that to support the above mentioned chain, we need to publish the public key of GSW as well as the key switching public key of LWE which is $\tau_{s'' \to s}$.

4   Our Multi-keyword Ranked Searchable Symmetric Encryption Scheme

In this section, we present our multi-keyword ranked searchable symmetric encryption scheme (MRSSE). By leveraging OXT [7] in a novel way, MRSSE can support multi-keyword ranked search as well as conjunctive and limited range queries. Let us consider the database DB consists of $\mathscr{D}$ documents where each keyword-document pair has a score which shows their relevance. MRSSE first encrypts the scored database using SEDB **Setup** algorithm. In order to perform a ranked search over the encrypted database, the **Search** protocol must be run between the client and the server. Then, the server performs **Filter** algorithm to narrow down the results by comparing them with the given threshold in order to return the most relevant documents to the client. Afterwards, the client can sort the received results using **Sort** algorithm. Finally, the client retrieves the top-$\mathscr{K}$ most relevant documents using **Retrieve** algorithm.

Our construction given in Algorithm 2 consists of the following algorithms.

- SEDB **Setup**(λ, DB): This algorithm is similar to the one in OXT [7] except that here the scores of keywords are also encrypted and inserted to XSet (the differences are highlighted in red). The score of each keyword-document pairs is computed using the scoring approach introduced in Sect. 2.
- **Search**: This protocol consists of two algorithms:
    - **Client Search**(K , $q(\bar{w} = (w_1, ..., w_L))$): This algorithm inputs the PRF's keys K and the search keywords $(w_1, ..., w_L)$ then generates the search token and outputs it alongside of the chosen threshold.
    - **Server Search**(Tok_q, SEDB): This algorithm inputs the search token Tok_q and the scored database SEDB. Next, finds the match for the least frequent keyword in TSet and then tests the membership of corresponding document Ids in XSet for the other searched keywords. Moreover, in parallel this algorithm computes the aggregation function over the collected scores homomorphically. It is worth to note that when we perform ranking, we might not want to ignore the documents that do not contain sterm with the intersection of all of xterms. That is, there might be some documents which contains a few of xterms with high scores. Thus, if we want to return only documents matching all queried keyword, we keep the XSet as it is in the **Server Search**(Tok_q, SEDB) algorithm; otherwise we can simply remove it.

Algorithm 2 Our MRSSE

SEDB **Setup**(λ, DB)

Input Security parameter λ, Database DB, *Data owner's public key* PK

output *Encrypted scored database* SEDB

1: Initialize $\mathcal{T} \leftarrow \emptyset$ indexed by keywords W.
2: Select key K_S for PRF F. Select keys K_X, K_I, K_Z for PRF F_p with range $\mathbb{Z}_p^*$. XSet $\leftarrow \emptyset$
3: SEDB$\leftarrow \{\}$
4: **for** $w \in$ W **do**
5:     Initialize $\vartheta \leftarrow \{\}$
       $K_e \leftarrow F(K_S, w)$
6:     **for** id $\in$ DB(w) **do**
7:         Set a counter $\mathscr{C} \leftarrow 1$
8:         Compute xid $\leftarrow F_p(K_I, \text{id})$,
9:         $z \leftarrow F_p(K_Z, w || \mathscr{C})$; $y \leftarrow \text{xid} z^{-1}$,
10:        $e \leftarrow \text{Enc}(K_e, \text{id})$
11:        *Compute* $s_w = Score(w, \text{id})$
12:        Set xtag $\leftarrow g^{F_p(K_X, w) \cdot \text{xid}}$
13:        *Compute* $cscore = Enc(\text{PK}, s_w)$
14:        *Set* XSet $\leftarrow$ XSet $\cup$ (xtag, $cscore$)
15:        *Append* $(y, e, cscore)$ to ϑ
16:        $\mathscr{C} \leftarrow \mathscr{C} + 1$
17:     **end for**
18:     $\mathcal{T}[w] \leftarrow \vartheta$
19: **end for**
20: Set (TSet, K_T) $\leftarrow$ TSet.Setup$(\mathcal{T})$ and let SEDB = (TSet, XSet).
21: **return** SEDB, $K = (K_S, K_X, K_I, K_Z)$

Search

Client **Search**$(K, q(\bar{w} = (w_1, ..., w_L)))$:

Input $K, q(\bar{w} = (w_1, ..., w_L))$

Output Tok_q, t

1: Client's input is K and query q.
2: Computes stag $\leftarrow$ TSet.GetTag(K_T, w_1).
3: Client sends stag to the server.
4: **for** $\mathscr{C} = 1, 2, ...$ until the server stops **do**
5:     **for** $i = 2, ..., L$ **do**
6:         xtoken$[\mathscr{C}, i] \leftarrow g^{F_p(K_Z, w_1 || \mathscr{C}) \cdot F_p(K_X, w_i)}$
7:     **end for**
8:     xtoken$[\mathscr{C}] \leftarrow$ (xtoken$[\mathscr{C}, 2], ...,$ xtoken$[\mathscr{C}, L])$
9: **end for**
10: $Tok_q \leftarrow$ (stag, xtoken$[\mathscr{C}]$)
11: Client chooses a threshold t
12: **return** Tok_q, t

Server **Search**(Tok_q, SEDB):

Input Tok_q, SEDB

Output S

1: S $\leftarrow \{\}$
2: $\vartheta \leftarrow$ TSetRetrieve(TSet, stag)
3: **for** $\mathscr{C} = 1 : |\vartheta|$ **do**
4:     Retrieve $(e_{\mathscr{C}}, y_{\mathscr{C}}, cscore_{s, \mathscr{C}})$ from the $\mathscr{C}$-th tuple in ϑ
5:     **if** XSet contains (xtoken$[\mathscr{C}, i]^{y_{\mathscr{C}}}, cscore_{x_i})$ for some $cscore_{x_i}$ for all $i = 1, ..., L$ **then**

6:         $s_{\mathscr{C}} \leftarrow$ Score − Cipher(XSet)
           // that is $s_{\mathscr{C}} = \sum_{i=1}^{L} cscore_{x_i} + cscore_{s, \mathscr{C}}$ in the plaintext form
7:         $S \leftarrow S \cup \{(s_{\mathscr{C}}, e_{\mathscr{C}})\}$
8:     **end if**
9: **end for**
10: **return** S

Filter$(\hat{S}, \hat{t})$

Input Score set S, Threshold t

Output two lists of score-ciphertext where the scores are higher than the threshold; $\hat{C}_f$ and $\hat{C}'_f$

1: $(\hat{C}_f, \hat{C}'_f) \leftarrow Filter(\hat{S}, \hat{t})$
   // the following demonstrate the filter in plaintext form
2: $i \leftarrow 1$
3: $j \leftarrow 1$
4: **for** $i = 1, ..., n$ **do**
5:     **if** $s_i \geq t$ **then**
6:         Set $z_i = 1$
7:     **else**
8:         Set $z_i = 0$
9:     **end if**
10:    Initialize pointer $P = 0$ to the output buffer
11:    $P = P + z_i$
12:    **for** $j = 1, ..., N$ **do**
13:        $c_j = c_j + (j \stackrel{?}{=} P).z_i.s_i$
14:        $c'_j = c'_j + (j \stackrel{?}{=} P).z_i.e_i$
15:    **end for**
16: **end for**
17: $C_f = (c_1, ..., c_N)$
18: $C'_f = (c'_1, ..., c'_N)$
19: **return** C_f, C'_f

Sort$(\hat{C}_f, \hat{C}'_f)$

Input $\hat{C}_f, \hat{C}'_f$

Output C_s

1: **for** $j = 1, 2, ... N$ **do**
2:     $s \leftarrow Dec(\text{sk}, c_j)$
3:     $e \leftarrow Dec(\text{sk}, c'_j)$
4:     $C \leftarrow C \cup \{(s, e)\}$
5:     $C_s \leftarrow Sort(C)$ // sort the set using any well-known sorting algorithm
6: **end for**
7: **return** C_s

Retrieve$(C_s, \mathscr{K})$

Input

Sorted encrypted results C_s and the number $\mathscr{K}$ of top documents to be retrieved

Output Result id

1: *Client computes* $k_e \leftarrow PRF(k_s, w_1)$
2: **for** $\mathscr{P} = 1, ..., \mathscr{K}$ **do**
3:     compute id $\leftarrow Dec(k_e, e_{\mathscr{P}})$
4:     **return** id
5: **end for**

- **Filter**(S, t): Given the score set S and the threshold t, this algorithm compares the overall scores (output of the monotone aggregation function in **Server Search**(Tok_q, SEDB)) with the threshold value. It returns the scores which are equal or greater than the considered threshold and the corresponding ciphertext[4].
- **Sort**(C_f, C_f'): This algorithm inputs two list with corresponding elements (score/ciphertext). First, decrypts the score list and then uses any well-known sorting algorithm to sort the received list of candidates. Finally, it outputs the ordered set of the score-ciphertext pairs.
- **Retrieve**$(C_s, \mathscr{K})$: To retrieve the top-$\mathscr{K}$ documents, this algorithm first computes the decryption key and then decrypts the first $\mathscr{K}$ documents from the ordered set of the score-ciphertext pairs C_s.

For the sake of readability, in this section, the homomorphic computations are not considered in **Search** protocol and **Filter**(S, t) algorithm. That is, we show only operations performed on plaintext values. Section 3 presented the actual algorithms with the required homomorphic computations on ciphertexts.

4.1 Modes of Operation

To minimize the communication overhead, we define two modes for our scheme: trivial and filtered. The former refers to the condition where the number of results in **Search** is smaller than the breaking point[5]. In this mode, both **Filter**(S, t) and **Sort**(C_f, C_f') algorithms are not required. Otherwise, the server performs in the filtered mode by running the **Filter**(S, t) algorithm to narrow down the results to the most relevant ones. This leads to the lower communication overhead and network traffic. These two modes are illustrated in Fig. 2 where we discus the communication overhead of our scheme. That is, the communication overhead in trivial mode (black line) is linear to the number of matching result whereas it is constant in the filtered mode (red line). Note that the communication cost in the filtered mode is independent of number of matching results.

5   Evaluation

In this section we discuss the cost evaluation of MRSSE from computation and communication complexity viewpoints (refer to the full version for the security analysis).

---

[4] We are assuming the size of output buffer (here, N) is big enough to contain all of the results which has equal/higher score than the considered threshold. If not, our protocol returns last N results higher than the threshold since the pointer P is incremented modulo N.

[5] breaking point is the point that the number of filtered results is the same as unfiltered results- refer to Sect. 5.2.

5.1 Computation Complexity

The costs that our design added on the top of OXT to support ranked queries are related to the homomorphic computations in **Server Search**(Tok_q, SEDB) and **Filter**(S, t) algorithm. In **Server Search**(Tok_q, SEDB), we need to compute the score aggregation function using the integer addition operation $(\dot{+})$ in a loop that costs $L \times \dot{+}$. The evaluation of this circuit in the loop has multiplicative depth of $logL(log(\ell - 2) + 1)$. **Filter**(S, t) algorithm requires more homomorphic computations which are performed over $(\mathbb{Z}_N, (+, .))$ as follows:

- $n \times \boxdot$ for the loop in line 9 of Algorithm 1,
- $2 \times n \times \boxdot$ for the loop in line 11 of Algorithm 1,
- $2 \times n \times N \times (\ell \boxplus + f_j(\hat{P}) + (\ell + 1)\boxdot)$ for line 18 and line 19 of Algorithm 1,

where the computation cost of $f_j(\hat{P})$ is negligible. Finally, the overall multiplicative depth of **Filter**(S, t) would be $Depth(Filter) = 2 + (log\ell + 1)$. Therefore, the overall multiplicative depth would be:

$$Depth(Search) + Depth(Filter) = logL(log(\ell - 2) + 1) + (2 + (log\ell + 1))$$

5.2 Communication Complexity

In order to determine the communication complexity, we should set the parameters in such way that the following conditions hold. We denote as $\|.\|_\infty$ standard norm for scalars and vectors.

- *Aggregation noise growth.* Let D_{Agg} be the depth of the aggregation function in $Search_{mr}$ algorithm. The noise growth of this function is at most $(\eta d + 1)^{\frac{1}{2}D_{Agg}} . \sigma(CScore)$ where $\sigma(CScore) = \sqrt{m.d}\sigma(e)$ is the noise for the fresh ciphertext from GSW encryption. By assuming $\sigma(e) = 2$, the noise growth of aggregation function is at most $(\eta d + 1)^{\frac{1}{2}D_{Agg}} . 2\sqrt{m.d}$.
- NAND *gate homomorphic noise growth.* We use NAND operation to restrict the message space to $\{0, 1\}$ in order to avoid blowup of error. The noise of NAND of ciphertexts C_1, C_2 for the message $\mu \in \{0, 1\}$ is:

$$|noise(\mathsf{NAND}(C_1, C_2))| = \mu.noise(C_1) + \|C_1.noise(C_2)\|_\infty$$
$$|noise(\mathsf{NAND}(C_1, C_2))| \le \|noise(C_1)\|_\infty + \|C_1.noise(C_2)\|_\infty$$
$$|noise(\mathsf{NAND}(C_1, C_2))| \le (\eta.d + 1) \times max(\|noise(C_1)\|_\infty, \|noise(C_2)\|_\infty)$$

We analyze the standard deviation growth using independence heuristic assumption (that indicates the coordinates of noise vector are independent of Gaussian samples), for each coordinates of noise (similar to the assumption in [9]):
$Var(noise(\mathsf{NAND}(C_1, C_2)) \le (\eta.d + 1) \times max(Var(noise(C_1)) \, Var(noise(C_2))$
$\sigma = sd(noise(\mathsf{NAND}(C_1, C_2)) \le \sqrt{(\eta.d + 1)} \times max(sd(noise(C_1)), sd(noise$
$(C_2)) \, \sigma_{\mathsf{NAND}}(out) \le \sqrt{(\eta.d + 1)}\sigma_{\mathsf{NAND}}(in)$.
Therefore, for the depth $D - D'$, the noise growth is $\sigma_{\mathsf{NAND}}(out) \le (\eta.d + 1)^{\frac{D-D'}{2}} \sigma_{\mathsf{NAND}}(in)$.

- *Homomorphic noise growth for conditional increment.* The conditional increment of the encrypted pointer $\hat{P}$ can be implemented using Mult operation: $\hat{P}_{i+1} = \hat{P}_i \hat{z}'_i = \mathsf{Mult}(\hat{P}_i, \hat{z}'_i) = \mathsf{Flatten}(\hat{P}_i \hat{z}'_i)$. Here, $\hat{z}'_i = \mathsf{Flatten}((x-1).I.\hat{z}_i + I)$, which has the noise $\|noise(\hat{z}'_i)\| = noise(\hat{z}_i).\|(x-1)\|$
$sd(\hat{z}'_i) = \|(x-1)\|.sd(\hat{z}_i)$
Therefore, the conditional increment has the noise growth as follows:
$noise(\hat{P}_{i+1}) = \hat{z}'_i.noise(\hat{P}_i) + \hat{P}_i.noise(\hat{z}'_i)$
$Var(\hat{P}_{i+1}) \leq \|\hat{z}'_i\|^2. Var(\hat{P}_i) + \eta d\, Var(\hat{z}'_i)$
Here, $\|\hat{z}'_i\| = 1$ because $\hat{z}'_i \in \{x^0, x'\}$, and $Var(\hat{z}'_i) \leq 2 \times Var(\hat{z}_i)$. Therefore,
$Var(\hat{P}_{i+1}) \leq Var(\hat{P}_i) + 2\eta d\, Var(\hat{z}_i)$
$\forall i = 0, ..., n-1$
$Var(\hat{P}_i) \leq Var(\hat{P}_n) \leq Var(\hat{P}_0) + (n-1) \times 2Nd(max\, Var(\hat{z}_i))$
$\forall i\ sd(\hat{P}_i) \leq \sqrt{2n\eta d} \times max\, sd(\hat{z}_i)$
- *Overall noise growth condition.* We denote the depth of $\boxdot$ homomorphic operation by $D_{\boxdot}$. The overall noise noise growth condition for Ring-GSW is
$$\sigma_{out} \leq \sigma_{in} \times (\eta d + 1)^{\frac{1}{2}D_{\boxdot}} . \sqrt{2n\eta d}.\sqrt{\eta d + 1}$$ where σ_{in} indicates the input noise to the **Filter**(S, t) algorithm. This noise is generated by the aggregation function in **Server Search**(Tok_q, SEDB). Note that here, $s(\eta d + 1)^{\frac{1}{2}D_{\boxdot}}$, $\sqrt{2n\eta d}$, and $\sqrt{\eta d + 1}$ correspond to lines 9, 10, and 11 of Algorithm 1, respectively. More accurately, the noise for $\hat{P}_i$ is at most $\sigma_{\hat{P}_i} = 2\sqrt{md}(\eta d+1)^{\frac{1}{2}(D_{\boxdot} + D_{agg})}.\sqrt{2n\eta d}$
whereas, the noise for $\hat{y}_i$ is at most $\sigma_{\hat{y}_i} = 2\sqrt{md}(\eta d+1)^{\frac{1}{2}(D_{\boxdot} + D_{agg})}.\sqrt{\eta d + 1}$.
When we perform $f_j(\hat{P})$, $\hat{P}$ will be converted to LWE. Hence, we switch from modulus q to q'. Therefore, for the last multiplication in **Filter**(S, t) algorithm $\sigma^{(LWE),q'}_{f_j(\hat{P}) \boxdot \hat{y}_i}$ is at most $\sigma^{(LWE),q}_{f_j(\hat{P})}$ if the condition: $2 \times (\sigma^{(LWE),q}_{\hat{P}})\gamma_{\mathbb{Z}} \leq \Delta$ is satisfied. Here, $\Delta = \frac{q}{q'}$ is the ratio between q and q'. The noise in each $\hat{c}_j$ (with modulus q') would be at most $\sqrt{n} \times \sigma^{(LWE),q'}_{f_j(\hat{P})}$. That is, each $\hat{c}_j$ is computed as a sum of n intermediate ciphertexts thus, the standard deviation gets multiplied by $\sqrt{n}$.
The BGV-type LWE multiplication consists of three steps; Mult, Scale, and SwitchKey [5]. After the first step, the noise has length at most $\gamma_{\mathbb{Z}} B^2$ (here B is a bound on the noise length). Then, we apply the Scale function (as defined in Lemma 4 in [5]), after which the noise length is at most $(q'/q)\gamma_{\mathbb{Z}} B^2 + \eta_{Scale}$ where $\eta_{Scale} \leq (\tau/2)\sqrt{d}\gamma_{\mathbb{Z}} h$. After the last step (the SwitchKey is defined in Lemma 9 in [5]), the noise become at most $(q'/q)\gamma_{\mathbb{Z}} B^2 + \eta_{Scale} + \eta_{SwitchKey}$ where $\eta_{SwitchKey} \leq 2\gamma_{\mathbb{Z}}\binom{d+1}{2}(logq')^2$. At the end, we want the noise to be smaller than $\frac{1}{2}(q'/\tau)$ to decrypt correctly. Note that, in BGV-type LWE, the actual bound on the noise length is used, whereas, in our case, we use the standard deviation but the relation is similar. In fact, the last multiplication has the standard deviation of the noise of input $\sigma_{\hat{P}_i}$ and $\sigma_{\hat{y}_i}$. We are assuming these are heuristically independent of Gaussian noises. Therefore, if the ratio between the threshold q'/τ and the standard deviation is more than $\sqrt{2ln(2/\epsilon)} \leq \frac{q'}{2\tau}$, then the probability, that the noise crosses this threshold, is less than ϵ.

- *Decryption correctness condition.* For the correctness of decryption, at the end the condition: $\frac{\sigma_{\hat{P}_i} \cdot \sigma_{\hat{y}_i}}{\Delta} + \eta_{Scale} + \eta_{SwitchKey} \leq \frac{q'}{\tau\sqrt{2ln(2/\epsilon)}}$ must hold. Here, $\epsilon = 2^{-20}$.
  For the security, the hardness of RLWE 2^{λ} security for GSW keys must be hold.
  Thus, we need to show that the RLWE with noise $\sigma(e) = 2$, dimension d and modulus q is hard. The condition $\alpha = 2/q$ ensures this assumption.

Parameter Setting: We can determine the parameters based on the above mentioned conditions and the security of RLWE. To determine d, we need to choose it based on the complexity of best lattice attack against underlying Ring-LWE problem in dimension d with modulus q and noise σ. Once we determined α, q and d, we can find the security against lattice attack, T_{attack}. That is, we set the security parameter λ so that $T_{attack} \geq 2^{\lambda}$. Table 4 provides a few examples of parameter setting on the security parameter $\lambda = 80$. We used an attack estimator for the Learning with Errors Problem [2,20]. The output of **Filter**(S, t) algorithm are LWE ciphertexts encrypted with the modulus, q'. For kth bit of each score s_i, its LWE ciphertext is in the form of $(a_{i,k}, b_{i,k} = a_{i,k}.s + e + \frac{q'}{2^i}.s_{i,k})$. Each ciphertext is $(d+1) \times logq'$ bits, for 7 bits score and 64 bits document identifier, we would have $71 \times N \times (d+1) \times logq'$ bits of N filtered results to be delivered to the client. This can be reduced by packing each $log \tau$ bits ciphertext into one ciphertext by homomorphic addition of the ciphertexts.
This results the following overall communication cost:

$$Communication\ cost = \frac{71N}{log\ \tau} \times (d+1) \times (logq')$$

Although the length of ciphertext in symmetric cipher of OXT is relatively small, the overall communication overhead is directly related to the number of matching results. This is evident in the case of cloud storage where the result space is potentially huge. The following example clarifies the significance of this issue. Let us assume that the scores are 7 bits and document Ids are 64 bits, which results in about 200 bits of ciphertext in OXT assuming AES CBC mode is used. Thus, the communication cost would be $CC_{OXT} = 200n$ (where n is the number of matching results for all queried keywords). Let us assume the total number of matching results $n = 10^6$, then the communication cost of OXT would be 25MB. However, this can be reduced to just about 6.5MB by performing our scheme in the filtered mode. More precisely, the server can compute the breaking point $n_b = \frac{\frac{71N}{log\ \tau} \times (d+1) \times (logq')}{200}$ which in this case is about 263055 matching results (for $N = 2^6$, $d = 4750$, $log\ \tau = 32$), and then compares it with the total results $n = 10^6$. Since the breaking point is smaller than n, the server runs filtered mode which has the communication cost of $CC_{our} = \frac{71N}{log\ \tau} \times (d+1) \times (logq') = 6.55MB$. Table 3 shows the communication cost improvement when the filtration approach is used versus the trivial mode that returns all of the matching documents. It is apparent from this table that the proposed approach has a significant impact on the communication cost.

Table 3. Communication cost improvement

Number of matching results	400000	600000	800000	1000000
Communication cost of Trivial mode	8×10^7 Bits	12×10^7 Bits	16×10^7 Bits	2×10^8 Bits
Communication cost of Filter mode	52611×10^3 Bits	52611×10^3 Bits	52611×10^3 Bits	52611×10^3 Bits
Communication cost improvement	34.23%	56.15%	67.11%	73.69%

Table 4. Parameter settings

Parameters									T_{attack}			Breaking point (n_b)
L	ℓ	N	d	D	α	q	q'	$\log \tau$	usvp	dec	dual	
4	7	2^6	4750	8	$2^{(-216)}$	2^{217}	2^{78}	32	$2^{80.8}$	$2^{81.4}$	$2^{82.2}$	263055

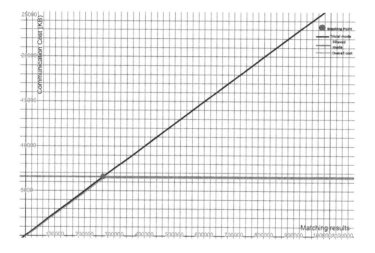

Fig. 2. Overall communication cost (Color figure online)

Figure 2 illustrates the overall communication cost of our scheme. Note that the trivial mode introduced in Sect. 4.1 acts the same way as OXT. It is apparent from this figure that our scheme (the green line) reduces the communication cost significantly by filtering the results to the most relevant ones.

6   Conclusion

We have presented a generic solution for efficient multi-keyword ranked searchable symmetric encryption. The proposed threshold-based filtering solution enables the honest-but-curious server to refine the encrypted search results and returns only the most relevant ones to the user. The proposed scheme supports multi-keyword ranked search as well as Boolean and limited range queries. Our scheme resists all attacks associated with OPE leakage. In comparison with the conventional searchable symmetric encryption schemes, our solution decreases the communication overhead between the client and server significantly without adding any additional leakage to the server.

Acknowledgement. The work of Ron Steinfeld and Joseph K. Liu were also supported in part by ARC Discovery Project grant DP180102199.

A   Review of OXT

As discussed earlier, our scheme MRSSE leverages the protocol by Cash et al. [7] called Oblivious Cross Tags (OXT) to demonstrate its applicability in Searchable Symmetric Encryption (SSE). In this section, we provide a brief review of OXT to explain how it works. OXT is the first SSE scheme that goes beyond a single-keyword search. This scalable scheme supports boolean queries over the encrypted database in sublinear time. OXT consists of an algorithm EDBSetup and a protocol Search as follows.

EDBSetup(λ, DB): Given a security parameter λ and a DB $= (id_i, W_i)_{i=1}^{\mathscr{D}}$, this algorithm generates the encrypted database EDB which is given to the server and a secret key for the user[6].

Note that EDB consists of two data structures TSet and XSet. The former allows one to associate a list of fixed-sized data tuples with each keyword in the database, and later issues the keyword-related tokens to retrieve these lists [7]. The latter contains elements computed from each keyword-document pair, called Xtag.

The protocol Search running between the user and server consists of following algorithms;

TokenGeneration($(q(\bar{w}) = (w_1, \ldots, w_n)$, EDB)): If a user wants to make a query $q(\bar{w})$ over EDB, the search tokens are required. This algorithm generates the search tokens Tok_q based on the given query.

Search(Tok_q, EDB): The algorithm gets the inputs the search token $Tok_q = $ (stag, xtoken[1], xtoken[2], $\cdots$) and outputs the encrypted search result(s) $ERes$.

DecResult ($ERes$, K): This algorithm takes the encrypted search result $ERes$ and the utilized secret key as inputs and outputs the corresponding document identifier(s) $id(s)$.

---

[6] In single-writer/single-reader setting like OXT and our scheme, data owner and the client/user are the same entity.

B   Cryptographic Primitives

Pseudorandom Function (PRF): $F : \{0,1\}^\lambda \times X \to Y$ is a pseudorandom function where X and Y are sets and for all efficient adversaries A, $Adv^{prf}_{F,A}(\lambda)$ is negligible [7];

$$Adv^{prf}_{F,A}(\lambda) = Pr[A^{F(K,.)}(1^\lambda) = 1] - Pr[A^{f(.)}(1^k) = 1]$$

Here, the probability is over the randomness of A, $K \xleftarrow{\$} \{0,1\}^\lambda$, and $f \xleftarrow{\$} Fun(X,Y)$.

Homomorphic Encryption from Ring Learning with Errors (RLWE): Ring-LWE encryption scheme is associated with a number of parameters [8]:

- λ: Security parameter
- $R = \mathbb{Z}[X]/(x^d + 1)$: polynomial ring of degree d
- $R_q := R/qR$: ring mod q for an integer q (ciphertexts are pairs of R_q elements)
- $R_\tau := R/\tau R$: message space for $\tau = 2$, R_τ can be represented by polynomials $p(x) = \sum_{i<mu} p_i x^i$ for $p_i \in \mathbb{Z}_\tau$.
- χ: a distribution of polynomials over R_q with 'small' coefficients (with standard deviation σ).

Ring-LWE encryption can be described by the following algorithms:

KeyGen(): This algorithm samples $t \leftarrow \chi$, $e \leftarrow \chi$ and defines the secret key $sk = s \leftarrow (1, -t)$ and computes the public key $pk = (a, b)$. Here, $a \xleftarrow{\$} R_q$ and $b = at + e$.

Enc():Given the public key and a message $m \in R_\tau$, the encryption algorithm chooses a small polynomial $v \leftarrow \chi$ and two polynomials e_0 and e_1 and computes the ciphertext $c = (c_0, c_1)$ where $(c_0, c_1) = (m.q/\tau, 0) + (bv + e_0, av + e_1)$ (note that $c_0 = a't + (e_0 + ev) + m.q/\tau$ and $c_1 = a' + e_1$, where $a' = av$).

Dec(): Given a ciphertext $c = (c_0, c_1)$, this algorithm outputs $m' = c \cdot s$ and round m' coefficient to nearest multiple of q/τ.

Eval(): Given two ciphertexts, this algorithm outputs the ciphertext obtained through the considered operation over the given ciphertexts (for detailed operations refer to Sect. 3).

Homomorphic Encryption from Learning with Errors (LWE). We also use LWE-based Regev's encryption scheme rather than Ring-LWE, denoted by Enc_{LWE}. In Regev's encryption, the public key consists of a matrix $\mathbb{A} \xleftarrow{\$} \mathbb{Z}^{n \times m}_q$ and an LWE sample $a \in \mathbb{Z}^m_q$ ($q, m,$ and n are integers). Let $a = \mathbb{A}^T s + e$ where $s \xleftarrow{\$} \mathbb{Z}^n_q$ is the secret and $e \in \mathbb{Z}^m$ is the error. For the encryption, one chooses uniformly random vectors $y \in \{0,1\}^m$ and computes $c = \mathbb{A}y \mod q$, $c' = <a, y> + m.\lfloor q/2 \rfloor \mod q$. For the decryption, $c' - s^T c \mod q$ must be computed to remove the common part and recover the message by rounding the "error" to nearest multiple of $\lfloor q/2 \rfloor$.

Homomorphic Encryption from Ring-GSW: Let $\mathbf{G} = [\mathbf{I}, 2\mathbf{I}, 4\mathbf{I}...2^{l-1}\mathbf{I}]^t \in R_q^{2l \times 2}$ be the gadget matrix. Homomorphic Encryption from Ring-GSW can be described by the following algorithms:

KeyGen(): This algorithm samples $t \leftarrow \mathbb{Z}_q$ and defines the secret key $sk = \mathbf{s} \leftarrow (1, -t)$ and set $\mathbf{v} = \mathbf{Gs}$. To define public key $pk = A$, this algorithm first generates a $m \times 1$ matrix $B \xleftarrow{\$} R_q^{m \times i}$ (where $R_q = \mathbb{Z}_q(x)/(x^d + 1)$) and a vector $e \leftarrow \chi^m$; it sets $\mathbf{b} = B.\mathbf{t} + e$, and A to be the 2-column matrix consisting of $\mathbf{b}$ followed by the n columns of B ($A.\mathbf{s} = e$).

Enc(): To encrypt the message $\mu \in \{0, 1\}$, this algorithm computes a ciphertext in the form of $C = \mathsf{Flatten}(C')$ where $C' = \mu.I_\eta + \mathsf{BitDecomp}(RA)$. Here, $\eta = 2 \times l$ and $\mathsf{BitDecomp}(a) = (a_0, ..., a_{l-1}) \in R_q^l$ where each a_i is an element of R that when represented as a polynomial of degree $d - 1$ has coefficients that are all in $\{0, 1\}$.

Let $C'' = \mathsf{BitDecomp}^{-1}(C')$, thus $C = \mathsf{Flatten}(C') = \mathsf{BitDecomp}(C'')$. Flatten ensures that the coefficients of C are small; therefore C has the proper form of a ciphertext that permits our homomorphic operations [15].

Dec(): This algorithm computes $C.\mathbf{v} = \mu.\mathbf{v} + \mathsf{BitDecomp}(C'').\mathbf{v} = \mu.\mathbf{v} + C''.\mathbf{s} = \mu.\mathbf{v} + e'$ where e' is a small noise of C.

The other utilised homomorphic operations are NAND and Mult as follows.

$$\mathsf{NAND}(C_1, C_2) = \mathsf{Flatten}(I_N - C_1.C_2)$$

$$\mathsf{Mult}(C_1, C_2) = \mathsf{Flatten}(C_1.C_2)$$

References

1. Agrawal, R., Kiernan, J., Srikant, R., Xu, Y.: Order preserving encryption for numeric data. In: Proceedings of the 2004 ACM SIGMOD, pp. 563–574. ACM (2004)
2. Albrecht, M.R., Player, R., Scott, S.: On the concrete hardness of learning with errors. J. Math. Cryptol. **9**(3), 169–203 (2015)
3. Baldimtsi, F., Ohrimenko, O.: Sorting and searching behind the curtain. In: Böhme, R., Okamoto, T. (eds.) FC 2015. LNCS, vol. 8975, pp. 127–146. Springer, Heidelberg (2015). https://doi.org/10.1007/978-3-662-47854-7_8
4. Boneh, D., Mazieres, D., Popa, R.A.: Remote oblivious storage: making oblivious ram practical (2011)
5. Brakerski, Z., Gentry, C., Vaikuntanathan, V.: (Leveled) fully homomorphic encryption without bootstrapping. ACM Trans. Comput. Theor. (TOCT) **6**(3), 13 (2014)
6. Cao, N., Wang, C., Li, M., Ren, K., Lou, W.: Privacy-preserving multi-keyword ranked search over encrypted cloud data. In: INFOCOM, 2011 Proceedings IEEE, pp. 829–837. IEEE (2011)
7. Cash, D., Jarecki, S., Jutla, C., Krawczyk, H., Roşu, M.-C., Steiner, M.: Highly-scalable searchable symmetric encryption with support for Boolean queries. In: Canetti, R., Garay, J.A. (eds.) CRYPTO 2013. LNCS, vol. 8042, pp. 353–373. Springer, Heidelberg (2013). https://doi.org/10.1007/978-3-642-40041-4_20

8. Cheon, J.H., Kim, M., Kim, M.: Optimized search-and-compute circuits and their application to query evaluation on encrypted data. IEEE Trans. Inf. Forensics Secur. **11**(1), 188–199 (2016)

9. Chillotti, I., Gama, N., Georgieva, M., Izabachène, M.: TFHE: fast fully homomorphic encryption over the torus. J. Cryptol., 1–58 (2018)

10. Damgård, I., Meldgaard, S., Nielsen, J.B.: Perfectly secure oblivious RAM without random oracles. In: Ishai, Y. (ed.) TCC 2011. LNCS, vol. 6597, pp. 144–163. Springer, Heidelberg (2011). https://doi.org/10.1007/978-3-642-19571-6_10

11. Durak, F.B., DuBuisson, T.M., Cash, D.: What else is revealed by order-revealing encryption? In: Proceedings of the 2016 ACM SIGSAC Conference on Computer and Communications Security, pp. 1155–1166. ACM (2016)

12. Fagin, R.: Combining fuzzy information from multiple systems. J. Comput. Syst. Sci. **58**(1), 83–99 (1999)

13. Fagin, R., Lotem, A., Naor, M.: Optimal aggregation algorithms for middleware. J. Comput. Syst. Sci. **66**(4), 614–656 (2003)

14. Gentry, C.: A fully homomorphic encryption scheme. Stanford University (2009)

15. Gentry, C., Sahai, A., Waters, B.: Homomorphic encryption from learning with errors: conceptually-simpler, asymptotically-faster, attribute-based. In: Canetti, R., Garay, J.A. (eds.) CRYPTO 2013. LNCS, vol. 8042, pp. 75–92. Springer, Heidelberg (2013). https://doi.org/10.1007/978-3-642-40041-4_5

16. Goldreich, O., Ostrovsky, R.: Software protection and simulation on oblivious RAMs. J. ACM (JACM) **43**(3), 431–473 (1996)

17. Goodrich, M.T., Mitzenmacher, M.: Privacy-preserving access of outsourced data via oblivious RAM simulation. In: Aceto, L., Henzinger, M., Sgall, J. (eds.) ICALP 2011. LNCS, vol. 6756, pp. 576–587. Springer, Heidelberg (2011). https://doi.org/10.1007/978-3-642-22012-8_46

18. Jiang, X., Yu, J., Yan, J., Hao, R.: Enabling efficient and verifiable multi-keyword ranked search over encrypted cloud data. Inf. Sci. **403**, 22–41 (2017)

19. Li, K., Zhang, W., Yang, C., Yu, N.: Security analysis on one-to-many order preserving encryption-based cloud data search. IEEE Trans. Inf. Forensics Secur. **10**(9), 1918–1926 (2015)

20. Albrecht, M.R., Player, R., Scott, S.: Security estimates for the learning with errors problem (2015). https://bitbucket.org/malb/lwe-estimator

21. Meng, X., Zhu, H., Kollios, G.: Top-k query processing on encrypted databases with strong security guarantees. arXiv preprint arXiv:1510.05175 (2015)

22. Naveed, M., Kamara, S., Wright, C.V.: Inference attacks on property-preserving encrypted databases. In: Proceedings of the 22nd ACM SIGSAC Conference on Computer and Communications Security, pp. 644–655. ACM (2015)

23. Shen, Y., Zhang, P.: Ranked searchable symmetric encryption supporting conjunctive queries. In: Liu, J.K., Samarati, P. (eds.) ISPEC 2017. LNCS, vol. 10701, pp. 350–360. Springer, Cham (2017). https://doi.org/10.1007/978-3-319-72359-4_20

24. Vaidya, J., Clifton, C.: Privacy-preserving top-k queries. In: 21st International Conference on Data Engineering, ICDE 2005, Proceedings, pp. 545–546. IEEE (2005)

25. Wang, B., Li, M., Wang, H.: Geometric range search on encrypted spatial data. IEEE Trans. Inf. Forensics Secur. **11**(4), 704–719 (2016)

26. Wang, C., Cao, N., Ren, K., Lou, W.: Enabling secure and efficient ranked keyword search over outsourced cloud data. IEEE Trans. Parallel Distrib. Syst. **23**(8), 1467–1479 (2012)
27. Williams, P., Sion, R.: Single round access privacy on outsourced storage. In: Proceedings of the 2012 ACM conference on Computer and Communications Security, pp. 293–304. ACM (2012)
28. Witten, I.H., Moffat, A., Bell, T.C.: Managing Gigabytes: Compressing and Indexing Documents and Images. Morgan Kaufmann, Burlington (1999)

An Efficiently Searchable Encrypted Data Structure for Range Queries

Florian Kerschbaum[1]([✉]) and Anselme Tueno[2]

[1] University of Waterloo, Waterloo, Canada
fkerschb@uwaterloo.ca
[2] SAP, Karlsruhe, Germany

Abstract. At CCS 2015 Naveed et al. presented first attacks on efficiently searchable encryption, such as deterministic and order-preserving encryption. These plaintext guessing attacks have been further improved in subsequent work, e.g. by Grubbs et al. in 2016. Such cryptanalysis is crucially important to sharpen our understanding of the implications of security models. In this paper we present an order-preserving encryption scheme in the form of an efficiently searchable, encrypted data structure that is provably secure against these and even more powerful chosen plaintext attacks. Our data structure supports logarithmic-time search with linear space complexity. The indices of our data structure can be used to search by standard comparisons and hence allow easy retrofitting to existing database management systems. We implemented our scheme and show that its search time overhead is only 10 ms compared to non-secure search on a database with 1 million entries.

1 Introduction

At CCS 2015 Naveed et al. [27] presented attacks on order-preserving encryption. Later Grubbs et al. [16] improved the precision of these attacks. Further attacks on searchable encryption have been presented [7, 12, 14, 18, 20, 23, 29, 32]. Such cryptanalysis is crucially important to sharpen our understanding of the implications of security models, since many of the attacked encryption schemes are proven secure in their specific security models. In this paper we formalize security against these attacks and show a connection to chosen plaintext attacks. We also demonstrate that there exists an encrypted data structure that supports efficient range queries by regular comparisons and that provably prevents these attacks.

Comparison using regular, unmodified comparison operators, e.g., greater-than, as enabled by our scheme and order-preserving encryption has many practical benefits. These encryption schemes can be retrofitted to existing database management systems making them extra-ordinarily fast, flexible and easy-to-deploy. We preserve this property as our implementation demonstrates, but some minor modifications to the search procedure are necessary.

© Springer Nature Switzerland AG 2019
K. Sako et al. (Eds.): ESORICS 2019, LNCS 11736, pp. 344–364, 2019.
https://doi.org/10.1007/978-3-030-29962-0_17

Table 1. Comparison of efficiency and security of schemes for range queries over encrypted data

Scheme	Search time $O(\log n)$	Space $O(n)$	IND-CPA-DS-secure[a]
Partial order preserving encoding [30]	Yes	Yes	Only before queries
Searchable encryption with replicated index [10]	Yes	No	Yes
Searchable encryption with dynamic index [17]	Only amortized	Yes	Only before queries
Searchable encryption with index replacement [2]	Yes	Yes	No
Order-revealing encryption [24]	No	Yes	Yes
This paper	Yes	Yes	Yes

[a]IND-CPA-DS is defined in Sect. 3.2.

Efficiency – logarithmic time and linear space complexity – is also an important property of search over encrypted data. In Table 1 we provide a comparison of our scheme to the most secure and efficient order-preserving schemes [30], order-revealing encryption [24] and range-searchable encryption [2,10,17] schemes. No searchable encryption scheme – including ours – offers perfect security and efficiency for all functions (equality and range search, insertions, deletions, etc.). It is a research challenge to balance the trade-off between the two objectives, even for a restricted set of functions. We aim at provable security against the recently publicized plaintext guessing attacks while still enabling efficient range search. In this respect, we achieve a novel and preferable trade-off between security and efficiency.

The construction of our scheme combines the benefits of previous order-preserving encryption schemes: modular order-preserving encryption by Boldyreva et al. [4], ideal secure order-preserving encoding by Popa et al. [28] and frequency-hiding order-preserving encryption by Kerschbaum [21]. We assign a distinct ciphertext for each – even repeated – plaintext as Kerschbaum does, but his scheme statically leaks the partial insertion order. So, we compress the randomized ciphertexts to the minimal ciphertext space using Popa et al.'s interactive protocol. Then we rotate around a modulus as Boldyreva et al., but on the ciphertexts and not on the plaintexts.

As a result we achieve *structural independence* between the ciphertexts and plaintexts which is a prerequisite for security against chosen plaintext attacks and plaintext guessing attacks – particularly, if the adversary has perfect background knowledge on the distribution of plaintexts. We formalize this insight as a novel security model (IND-CPA-DS-security) for efficiently searchable, encrypted data structures and we prove our scheme secure in this model. Our security model encompasses a number of recently publicized attacks where attackers broke into cloud system and stole the stored data. Such an attack will reveal no additional information when data is encrypted with our scheme. This will also thwart the attacks by Naveed et al. [27] and Grubbs et al. [16] mentioned at the beginning of the introduction.

As a scientific contribution we falsify two hypotheses commonly assumed to be true in the database security community. The first hypothesis is that all order-preserving encryption schemes are susceptible to ciphertext-only attacks – as those demonstrated by Naveed et al. and Grubbs et al. We do this by carefully defining security against such attacks and then constructing a provably secure scheme. The second hypothesis is that in order to securely store values in a database it suffices to encrypt them using a probabilistic encryption scheme (e.g. AES in CBC or GCM mode). The fallacy is ignoring that in order to store the data it has to have an address in the storage medium. If this address correlates with the data, probabilistic encryption is insufficient. Oblivious RAM (ORAM) randomizes this address under dynamic accesses and our security definition does the same for static data.

2   Efficiently Searchable Encrypted Data Structures

First, we define what we mean by an efficiently searchable encrypted data structure (ESEDS). We start by defining what we mean by a data structure. We use the fundamental representation of a data structure in random-access memory, i.e. an array. Each cell of the array consists of a structured element. We do not impose any restriction on the structure of the element, but usually this element contains two parts: the data to be searched over and further structural information, such as indices of further entries. Note that structural information may be *implicit*, i.e. the index where an element is stored itself is structural information albeit not explicitly stored. This implicit structural information may also not be encrypted, but only randomized. An example of *explicit* structural information are the indices of the cells of the two children in a binary search tree which would be stored in a cell's structure in addition to the data of a tree node. Explicit structural information can be encrypted. We write $\mathbb{C}[j]$ for the j-th element and if it is clear from the context, we assume it consists only of a ciphertext of the data element (with j being the implicit structural information).

Definition 1 (DS). *A data structure* DS *consists of an array of elements* $\mathbb{C}[j]$ *($0 \le j < n$).*

For an encrypted data structure there are a number of options on the type of encryption. First, we can choose symmetric or public-key encryption. We can instantiate our encrypted data structure with either one. Let PSE be a probabilistic symmetric encryption scheme consisting of three – possibly probabilistic – polynomial-time algorithms $\mathsf{PSE} = \mathsf{KGen}(1^\lambda), \mathsf{Enc}(\mathsf{k}, m), \mathsf{Dec}(\mathsf{k}, c)$. Let PPKE be a probabilistic public-key encryption scheme consisting of three – possibly probabilistic – polynomial-time algorithms $\mathsf{PPKE} = \mathsf{KGen}(1^\lambda), \mathsf{Enc}(\mathsf{pk}, m), \mathsf{Dec}(\mathsf{sk}, c)$.

Let $\mathsf{pk} \leftarrow \mathsf{KDer}(\mathsf{sk})$ be a deterministic algorithm that derives the public key from the private key in a public-key encryption scheme. For symmetric key encryption let KDer be the identity function. Let $\mathsf{PE} \in \{\mathsf{PSE}, \mathsf{PPKE}\}$ and we use PE when we leave the choice of encryption scheme open.

Second, we can either encrypt the data structure as a whole or parts of the data structure – ideally each cell. Our requirement of efficient search rules out the first option. Since in this case each search operation would require decrypting the data structure which is at least linear in the ciphertext size, sublinear search is impossible. Hence, we require each cell to be encrypted as a separate ciphertext.[1]

Third, for data security it may only be necessary to encrypt the data elements of a cell and not the structural information. In fact, our own proposed ESEDS is an instance of such a case where the structural information is implicit from the array structure and unencrypted. Hence, we only require the data element of each cell to be encrypted.

Definition 2 (EDS). *An encrypted data structure* $\mathsf{EDS_{PE}}$ *consists of an array of elements* $\mathbb{C}[j]$ *where at least the data part has been encrypted with* PE.

We can now define the operations on a searchable encrypted data structure $\mathsf{SEDS_{PE}}$. We write SEDS when the choice encryption scheme is clear from the context. Furthermore we sometimes denote the version h (after h insertions) of a data structure as SEDS^h. Our definition is for range-searchable encrypted data structures, but this implies a definition for keyword searchable data structure as well (where the range parameters are equal: $a = b$). Furthermore, we do not define how operations on our SEDS are to be implemented. These operations can be implemented as algorithms running on a single machine or protocols distributed over a client and server (hiding the secret key from the server). Both choices are covered by our definition.

Definition 3 (SEDS). *A searchable encrypted data structure* $\mathsf{SEDS_{PE}}$ *offers the following operations.*

- $\mathsf{k} \leftarrow \mathsf{KGen}(1^\lambda)$: *Generates a – either secret or private – key* k *from the encryption scheme* PE *according to the security parameter* λ.
- $\mathbb{C}^{h+1} \leftarrow \mathsf{Enc}(\mathsf{k}, \mathbb{C}^h, m)$: *Encrypts the plaintext* m *using* $\mathsf{PE.Enc}(\mathsf{KDer}(\mathsf{k}), m)$ *and inserts it into the data structure* $\mathbb{C}^h$ *resulting in data structure* $\mathbb{C}^{h+1}$.[2]
- $m := \mathsf{Dec}(\mathsf{k}, \mathbb{C}[j])$: *Computes the plaintext* m *for the data part of encrypted cell* $\mathbb{C}[j]$ *using key* k.
- $\{j_0, \ldots, j_{\ell-1}\} := \mathsf{Search}(\mathsf{k}, \mathbb{C}, a, b)$: *Computes the set of indices* $\{j_0, \ldots, j_{\ell-1}\}$ *for the range* $[a, b]$ *on the encrypted data structure* $\mathbb{C}$ *using key* k.

---

[1] In case several cells of a simple data structure are encrypted as a whole, we call this combination a cell of another data structure.

[2] Note that in case of public key encryption our definition does not imply that the entire operation can be completed using only the public key.

For the correctness of encryption we expect in a sequence of operations

$$\mathsf{Enc}(\mathsf{k}, \mathbb{C}^0, m_0), \ldots, \mathsf{Enc}(\mathsf{k}, \mathbb{C}^{n-1}, m_{n-1})$$

resulting in data structure $\mathbb{C}^n$ that

$$\forall i \, \exists j \, m_i = \mathsf{Dec}(\mathsf{k}, \mathbb{C}^n[j]).$$

For the correctness of search we expect that for any

$$\{j_0, \ldots, j_{\ell-1}\} := \mathsf{Search}(\mathsf{k}, \mathbb{C}, a, b)$$

it holds that

$$\forall j \in \{j_0, \ldots, j_{\ell-1}\} \implies \mathsf{Dec}(\mathsf{k}, \mathbb{C}[j]) \in [a, b]$$

and

$$\forall j \in \{j | \mathsf{Dec}(\mathsf{k}, \mathbb{C}[j]) \in [a, b]\} \implies j \in \{j_0, \ldots, j_{\ell-1}\}.$$

We can now finally define an efficiently searchable encrypted data structure.

Definition 4 (ESEDS). *An efficiently searchable encrypted data structure ESEDS is a searchable encrypted data structure where the running time τ of Search is poly-logarithmic in n (plus the size of the returned set of matching ciphertext indices) and the space σ of ESEDS is linear in n:*

$$\tau(\mathsf{Search}) \leq \mathcal{O}(\mathrm{polylog}(n) + \ell)$$
$$\sigma(\mathsf{ESEDS}) = \mathcal{O}(n)$$

It is now clear that efficient search prevents encrypting the entire data structure and thereby achieving semantic (IND-CPA) security. Next, we give our definition of security that implies that each cell's data is encrypted with a semantically secure encryption scheme. Our security definition also prevents all plaintext guessing attacks of the type of Naveed et al. and Grubbs et al. Furthermore, we show that even when the data structure consists of only one semantically secure ciphertext in each cell, this does not guarantee security against these plaintext guessing attacks.

3   Security of **ESEDS**

Before we define the security of an **ESEDS** we will review recent attacks on cloud infrastructures and searchable encryption scheme to motivate our security model. Particular we review in depth plaintext guessing attacks that only need a (multi-)set of ciphertexts as input (and do not perform active attacks during encryption or search operations). We try to generalize these attacks and show that even if all elements in an **ESEDS** are semantically secure encrypted, this does not imply that these attacks are infeasible.

3.1   Motivation

Our model is motivated by recent attacks on cloud infrastructures and order-preserving or deterministic encryption. Not only the theoretic demonstrations, but also real world incidents show the risks of deterministic – not even order-preserving – encryption. In at least one case passwords were encrypted using a deterministic algorithm and many subsequently broken [11]. The cryptanalysis was performed on stolen ciphertexts only (using additional plaintext hints). Many other hacking incidents have been recently publicized, e.g. [13,26], that resulted in leakage of sensitive information – not necessarily ciphertexts.

All these attacks share a common "anatomy". The hackers are capable to break in, access and copy sensitive information. They used the opportunity of access to gain as much data as possible in a short time, i.e. the adversary obtains a *static* snapshot. Note that this does not rule out the revelation of more sophisticated, longitudinal attacks in the future, but underpins the pressure to secure our current systems.

In this respect our model achieves the following: An attacker gaining access to all ciphertexts stored in an encrypted database does not gain additional information without making any assumption about his background knowledge. We can even assume perfect background knowledge, i.e. the adversary has chosen all plaintexts. This may sound contradictory at first – why would someone break into a database which he entirely created. However, if we are able to show security against such strong adversaries, security holds even if the adversary has less, e.g. imperfect, background knowledge.

3.2   Security Definition

We give our security definition as an adaptation of semantic security to data structures. We show that our adaptation implies that each data value is semantically secure encrypted. However, we also show that even if all cells consist of only one semantically secure ciphertext, our adaptation is not necessarily fulfilled.

First, recall the definition of semantic security.

Definition 5 (IND-CPA Security). *A public-key encryption scheme* PPKE *has* indistinguishable encryptions under a chosen-plaintext attack, *or is* IND-CPA-secure, *if for all PPT adversaries* $\mathcal{A}$ *there is a negligible function* $\mathsf{negl}(\lambda)$ *such that*

$$\mathsf{Adv}^{\text{IND-CPA}}_{\mathcal{A},\mathsf{PPKE}}(\lambda) := \left| \Pr\left[\mathsf{Exp}^{\text{IND-CPA}}_{\mathcal{A},\mathsf{PPKE}}(\lambda) = 1\right] - \frac{1}{2} \right|$$
$$\leq \mathsf{negl}(\lambda)$$

$$\underline{\mathrm{Exp}_{\mathcal{A},\mathsf{PPKE}}^{\mathrm{IND\text{-}CPA}}(\lambda)}$$

$\langle \mathsf{pk}, \mathsf{sk} \rangle \leftarrow \mathsf{PPKE.KGen}(1^{\lambda})$

$\langle m_0, m_1, \mathsf{st} \rangle \leftarrow \mathcal{A}(1^{\lambda}, \mathsf{pk})$

$b \leftarrow_{\$} \{0, 1\}$

$c \leftarrow \mathsf{PPKE.Enc}(\mathsf{pk}, m_b)$

$b' \leftarrow \mathcal{A}(1^{\lambda}, \mathsf{pk}, c, \mathsf{st})$

return $b = b'$

We note that IND-CPA-security only considers a single ciphertext whereas a data structure consists of multiple ciphertexts and hence some structural information. Exactly this structural information can be used in plaintext guessing attacks and we need to adapt semantic security to all ciphertexts. We call our adaptation *indistinguishability under chosen-plaintext attacks for data structures* or IND-CPA-DS-security for short. Loosely speaking, our security model ensures that an adversary who has chosen all plaintexts encrypted in a data structure cannot guess the plaintext of *any* ciphertext better than a random guess. We denote the size of multi-set $\mathbb{M}$ as $|\mathbb{M}|$ and the number of occurrences of element m in multi-set $\mathbb{M}$ as $\#_{\mathbb{M}} m$.

Definition 6 (IND-CPA-DS Security). *An efficiently searchable encrypted data structure* ESEDS *is indistinguishable under a chosen-plaintext attack, or is* IND-CPA-DS-*secure, if for all PPT adversaries* $\mathcal{A}$ *there is a negligible function* $\mathsf{negl}(\lambda)$ *such that*

$$\mathsf{Adv}_{\mathcal{A},\mathsf{ESEDS}}^{\mathrm{IND\text{-}CPA\text{-}DS}}(\lambda) := \left| \Pr\left[\mathrm{Exp}_{\mathcal{A},\mathsf{ESEDS}}^{\mathrm{IND\text{-}CPA\text{-}DS}}(\lambda) = \langle 1, p \rangle \right] - p \right|$$
$$\leq \mathsf{negl}(\lambda)$$

$$\underline{\mathrm{Exp}_{\mathcal{A},\mathsf{ESEDS}}^{\mathrm{IND\text{-}CPA\text{-}DS}}(\lambda)}$$

$\langle \mathsf{pk}, \mathsf{sk} \rangle \leftarrow \mathsf{ESEDS.KGen}(1^{\lambda})$

$\langle \mathbb{M}_0, \mathbb{M}_1, \mathsf{st} \rangle \leftarrow \mathcal{A}(1^{\lambda}, \mathsf{pk})$

if $|\mathbb{M}_0| \neq |\mathbb{M}_1|$ **then return** $\bot$

$b \leftarrow_{\$} \{0, 1\}$

$\mathbb{C} := \varepsilon$

foreach $m \in \mathbb{M}_b$ **do**

$\quad \mathbb{C} \leftarrow \mathsf{ESEDS.Enc}(\mathsf{sk}, m, \mathbb{C})$

endforeach

$\langle j', m' \rangle \leftarrow \mathcal{A}(1^{\lambda}, \mathsf{pk}, \mathbb{C}, \mathsf{st})$

return $\left\langle \mathsf{ESEDS.Dec}(\mathsf{sk}, \mathbb{C}[j']) = m', \dfrac{\#_{\mathbb{M}_0 \cup \mathbb{M}_1} m'}{|\mathbb{M}_0 \cup \mathbb{M}_1|} \right\rangle$

There are two differences between IND-CPA-security and IND-CPA-DS-security. First, the adversary chooses two multi-sets of plaintexts as input to the challenge instead of two single plaintexts. This enables the adversary to create different situations to distinguish. Assume the adversary returns two disjoint multi-sets as $\mathbb{M}_0$ and $\mathbb{M}_1$, e.g. $\mathbb{M}_0 = \{0,0\}$ and $\mathbb{M}_1 = \{1,1\}$. Then it can attempt to distinguish which of the two plaintext multi-sets have been encrypted by guessing any plaintext in the data structure. Assume the adversary returns the same multi-set as $\mathbb{M}_0$ and $\mathbb{M}_1$, but with distinct plaintexts in the (identical) multi-set, e.g. $\mathbb{M}_0 = \mathbb{M}_1 = \{0,1\}$. This is admissible in the definition of IND-CPA-DS-security, since the only requirement is that the two multi-sets are of the same size. The adversary can then attempt to distinguish at which position in the data structure each plaintext has been encrypted.

In order to enable the adversary to win the game when the position in the data structure is not indistinguishable, we made a second change to IND-CPA-security: The adversary's guess is the plaintext of a single ciphertext at any position in the data structure. Hence, the adversary does not necessarily have to distinguish between the two plaintext multi-sets, it is sufficient, if it guesses correctly within the choice of sets (which may be equal). However, even if the position in the ciphertext is indistinguishable, in order to win the adversary only has to guess correctly with a probability non-negligibly better than the frequency of the plaintext in the *union of the multi-sets*. Hence, if the two multi-sets are not equal and the adversary can guess the chosen multi-set, it can win the game.

We next explain the implications of IND-CPA-DS-security and first prove that IND-CPA-DS-security implies IND-CPA-security. Our proof assumes the use of public-key encryption, but the proof for symmetric encryption is analogous using an encryption oracle. We prove this by turning an adversary $\mathcal{B}$ that has advantage ϵ in experiment $\mathrm{Exp}_{\mathcal{B},\mathsf{PPKE}}^{\mathrm{IND\text{-}CPA}}$ into an adversary $\mathcal{A}$ that has advantage ϵ in experiment $\mathrm{Exp}_{\mathcal{A},\mathsf{ESEDS}_{\mathsf{PPKE}}}^{\mathrm{IND\text{-}CPA\text{-}DS}}$.

Theorem 1. *If* $\mathsf{ESEDS}_{\mathsf{PPKE}}$ *is* IND-CPA-DS-*secure, then each ciphertext of the data element in* $\mathbb{C}[j]$ $(0 \leq j < n)$ *must be from a* IND-CPA-*secure encryption scheme.*

Proof. Let $\mathcal{B}$ be an adversary that has advantage ϵ in experiment $\mathrm{Exp}_{\mathcal{B},\mathsf{PPKE}}^{\mathrm{IND\text{-}CPA}}$. We construct an adversary $\mathcal{A}$ for experiment $\mathrm{Exp}_{\mathcal{A},\mathsf{ESEDS}_{\mathsf{PPKE}}}^{\mathrm{IND\text{-}CPA\text{-}DS}}$ as follows.

$\mathcal{A}(1^\lambda, \mathsf{pk})$	$\mathcal{A}(1^\lambda, \mathsf{pk}, \mathbb{C}, \mathsf{st})$
$\langle m_0, m_1, \mathsf{st}' \rangle \leftarrow \mathcal{B}(1^\lambda, \mathsf{pk})$	$\mathsf{st}' \Vert \{\mathbb{M}_0, \mathbb{M}_1\} := \mathsf{st}$
$\mathbb{M}_0 := \{m_0\}$	$b' \leftarrow \mathcal{B}(1^\lambda, \mathsf{pk}, \mathbb{C}[0], \mathsf{st}')$
$\mathbb{M}_1 := \{m_1\}$	**return** $\langle 0, \mathbb{M}_{b'}[0] \rangle$
$\mathsf{st} := \mathsf{st}' \Vert \{\mathbb{M}_0, \mathbb{M}_1\}$	
return $\langle \mathbb{M}_0, \mathbb{M}_1, \mathsf{st} \rangle$	

The adversary $\mathcal{B}$'s view is indistinguishable from experiment $\mathrm{Exp}_{\mathcal{B},\mathsf{PPKE}}^{\mathrm{IND\text{-}CPA}}$ If adversary $\mathcal{B}$ guesses correctly, then $\mathcal{A}$'s output is also correct. Hence, if $\mathcal{B}$'s advantage is ϵ, then $\mathcal{A}$'s advantage is ϵ.

However, we also prove that even if each cell in $\mathbb{C}$ consists of a single cipher-text from a IND-CPA-secure, public-key encryption scheme PPKE, then this does not imply IND-CPA-DS-security. We prove by giving a data structure that consists of a single ciphertext from PPKE, but that is not IND-CPA-DS-secure. Again, the proof for symmetric encryption is analogous.

Theorem 2. *If each ciphertext in an efficiently searchable, encrypted data structure* $\mathsf{ESEDS}_{\mathsf{PPKE}}$ $\mathbb{C}[j]$ $(0 \leq j < n)$ *is from a IND-CPA-secure encryption scheme* PPKE*, then* $\mathsf{ESEDS}_{\mathsf{PPKE}}$ *is not necessarily IND-CPA-DS-secure.*

Proof. Given a multi-set of plaintexts $\mathbb{M}$ and a IND-CPA-secure, public-key encryption scheme PPKE, we construct a data structure as follows. Let rand-order(m_i) be the randomized order of each plaintext $m_i \in \mathbb{M}$. Recall that in a randomized order of a multi-set, elements are sorted, but ties are broken based on the outcome of a coin flip.

$$\mathbb{C}[\text{rand-order}(m_i)] \leftarrow \mathsf{PPKE.Enc}(\mathsf{pk}, m_i)$$

This data structure has equivalent leakage to frequency-hiding order-preserving encryption (FH-OPE) by Kerschbaum [21]. It is easy to see that each cell of the data structure consists of only one semantically secure cipher-text. However, we construct an adversary that succeeds with probability 1 for $p = \dfrac{1}{2}$ in our experiment $\mathsf{Exp}_{\mathcal{A},\mathsf{ESEDS}_{\mathsf{PPKE}}}^{\mathsf{IND\text{-}CPA\text{-}DS}}$.

$\mathcal{A}(1^\lambda, \mathsf{pk})$	$\mathcal{A}(1^\lambda, \mathsf{pk}, \mathbb{C}, \mathsf{st})$
$\mathbb{M} := \{0, 1\}$	**return** $\langle 0, 0 \rangle$
return $\langle \mathbb{M}, \mathbb{M}, \varepsilon \rangle$	

The adversary always wins the game, since in the given encryption scheme plaintext 0 will always be encrypted at position 0. Grubbs et al. showed in [16] the practicality of the attack by constructing a plaintext guessing attack on FH-OPE. In their experiments it succeeds with probability 30% where the base line guessing probability is only 4%.

Relation to Other Security Definitions. In searchable encryption a secu-rity definition of indistinguishability under chosen-keyword attack (IND-CKA-security) has been defined in [9] and used in many subsequent works. Loosely speaking, this security definition states that the data structure is IND-CKA-secure, if it is indistinguishable from a simulator given (a set of) leakage func-tion(s) $\mathcal{L}$. However, this can be misleading, since the leakage function does not necessarily clearly state the impact on plaintext guessing attacks. We first state the following corollary:

Corollary 1. *If a public-key encryption scheme* PPKE *is IND-CPA-secure, then there exists a simulator* $\mathsf{Sim}_{\mathsf{PPKE}}(1^\lambda, \mathsf{pk})$, *such that for all PPT adversaries* $\mathcal{A}$ *and all PPT distinguishers* Dist

$$\mathsf{Adv}_{\mathcal{A},\mathsf{Dist},\mathsf{PPKE}}^{\text{IND-CPA}}(\lambda) :=$$

$$\Big| \Pr\Big[\mathsf{Dist}(c,\mathsf{pk}) = 1 : \langle c,\mathsf{pk}\rangle \leftarrow \mathrm{RealExp}_{\mathcal{A},\mathsf{PPKE}}^{\text{IND-CPA}}(\lambda)\Big] -$$
$$\Pr\Big[\mathsf{Dist}(c,\mathsf{pk}) = 1 : \langle c,\mathsf{pk}\rangle \leftarrow \mathrm{SimExp}_{\mathsf{Sim}_{\mathsf{PPKE}},\mathsf{PPKE}}^{\text{IND-CPA}}(\lambda)\Big] \Big|$$

$$\leq \mathsf{negl}(\lambda)$$

$\mathrm{RealExp}_{\mathcal{A},\mathsf{PPKE}}^{\text{IND-CPA}}(\lambda)$	$\mathrm{SimExp}_{\mathsf{Sim}_{\mathsf{PPKE}},\mathsf{PPKE}}^{\text{IND-CPA}}(\lambda)$
$\langle \mathsf{pk},\mathsf{sk}\rangle \leftarrow \mathsf{PPKE.KGen}(1^\lambda)$	$\langle \mathsf{pk},\mathsf{sk}\rangle \leftarrow \mathsf{PPKE.KGen}(1^\lambda)$
$\langle m_0, m_1, \mathsf{st}\rangle \leftarrow \mathcal{A}(1^\lambda, \mathsf{pk})$	$c \leftarrow \mathsf{Sim}_{\mathsf{PPKE}}(1^\lambda, \mathsf{pk})$
$b \leftarrow_\$ \{0,1\}$	**return** c, pk
$c \leftarrow \mathsf{PPKE.Enc}(\mathsf{pk}, m_b)$	
return c, pk	

It follows that there exists a simulator for an encrypted data structure whose cells consists only of semantically secure ciphertexts which requires a leakage function of only the length n of the data structure and the public key pk. However, as we have shown in Theorem 2 such a data structure may not be IND-CPA-DS-secure and susceptible to plaintext guessing attacks.

Theorem 3. *An efficiently searchable, encrypted data structure* $\mathsf{ESEDS}_{\mathsf{PPKE}}$ *may be indistinguishably simulated with a leakage function* $\mathcal{L} = \{\mathsf{pk}, n\}$ *and be susceptible to plaintext guessing attacks.*

Proof. Consider the data structure from the proof of Theorem 2. It is indistinguishable from $n = |\mathbb{M}|$ ciphertexts produced using public key pk and successful plaintext guessing attacks have been shown by Grubbs et al. in [16].

Hence, leaking the number of plaintexts may be sufficient for a successful plaintext guessing attack in a simulation-based security proof. Our IND-CPA-DS-security model prevents this by introducing a *structural independence* constraint. While Curtmola et al. have been careful not to make this mistake in [9] and their ESEDS is IND-CPA-DS-secure, subsequent work was not as careful. Boelter et al.'s data structure [2] has a (correct) simulation-based proof and is not IND-CPA-DS-secure and susceptible to plaintext guessing attacks.[3]

Impact on Plaintext Guessing Attacks. We can now revisit the plaintext guessing attacks on deterministic and order-preserving encryption. First, our security model fully captures the attack setup. The adversary is given full ciphertext information and can chose the plaintexts such that it has perfect

---

[3] This is easy to see, since they do not encrypt the structural information in their data structure, i.e. the pointers to leaf nodes in the tree, and hence the ciphertexts can be ordered.

background knowledge[4], i.e. the adversary in our model has at least the same information as was used in those attacks. Second, our security definition implies that if the adversary is then able to infer even one plaintext better than with negligible probability over guessing our scheme is broken. Hence security in the IND-CPA-DS model implies security against all (passive, ciphertext-only) plaintext guessing attacks.

4   An IND-CPA-DS-Secure **ESEDS** for Range Queries

We next present our efficiently searchable, encrypted data structure for range queries that is IND-CPA-DS-secure. We emphasize that using the result from the data structure we can perform range queries in any commodity database management system without modifications. Hence, our data structure is as easy to integrate as order-preserving encryption, yet it is secure against chosen-plaintext attacks. We begin by describing the system architecture and give the intuition of our construction.

In our setup we assume a client holding the secret key $k \leftarrow$ ESEDS.KGen(1^λ) and a server that holds the data structure $\mathbb{C}$. The server may hold several data structures managed independently for each database column, but needs to take care of correlation attacks as in [12]. A database table then contains the rows linking the entries by their index in the data structure. After encrypting the plaintexts, the client and the server can interactively perform a search query, e.g. a range query, on the server's data structure which results in two indices j, j'. Then these two indices j, j' can be used in subsequent range queries on the database management system. We assume that the server is *semi-honest*, i.e. only performs *passive* attacks. This model is commonly assumed in the scientific literature on database security.

4.1   Intuition

Our data structure combines the ideas of three previous order-preserving encryption schemes: First, the scheme by Popa et al. [28] provides the basis for managing the order of ciphertexts in a stateful, interactive manner. Of course, this scheme is not secure against the attacks by Naveed et al., since it is deterministic and ordered. Second, we add the frequency-hiding aspect of the scheme by Kerschbaum [21]. The scheme itself cannot be used as the basis of an IND-CPA-DS-secure data structure, since it partially leaks the insertion order. Therefore the frequency-hiding idea needs to be fit into Popa et al.'s scheme. We do this by encrypting the plaintext using a probabilistic algorithm (similar to the stOPE scheme in [28]) and also inserting a ciphertext for each plaintext using Kerschbaum's random tree traversal. This combined construction would still not be IND-CPA-DS secure. Third, we apply Boldyreva et al.'s modular order-preserving encryption idea [4]. This idea rotates the plaintexts around a modulus

---

[4] Recall that the adversary is allowed to submit the same plaintext multi-sets in the IND-CPA-DS-security experiment.

statically hiding the order. However, modular order-preserving encryption has been developed for *deterministic* order-preserving encryption. In our probabilistic encryption – as introduced by Kerschbaum – we need to apply the modulus on the ciphertexts. This can be done by updating the modulus after encryption.

In summary, intuitively our encryption scheme works as follows: We maintain a list of ciphertexts for each plaintext (including duplicates) sorted by the plaintexts on the server. However, the list is rotated around a random offset (chosen uniformly from the range between 1 and the number of ciphertexts). We then encrypt and search using binary search. However, due to the rotation which can divide a set of identical plaintexts adjacent in the list into a lower and upper part, the search and encryption algorithms become significantly more complex which is apparent in their detailed description below.

5 Encryption Algorithm

Let PE be a standard, probabilistic encryption scheme supporting the following three – possibly probabilistic – polynomial-time algorithms: KGen, Enc and Dec. We use symmetric encryption, e.g. AES in CBC or GCM mode, for speed, but assume an encryption oracle in the definition of semantic security. Let $\mathbb{D}$ be the domain of plaintexts and $N = |\mathbb{D}|$ its size. We now describe the algorithms and protocols of our efficiently searchable, encrypted data structure:

- $k \leftarrow \mathsf{KGen}(1^\lambda)$: Execute $k \leftarrow \mathsf{PSE.KGen}(1^\lambda)$.
- $\mathbb{C}^{h+1} \leftarrow \mathsf{Enc}(k, m, \mathbb{C}^h)$: We denote $\mathbb{C}^h$ as $\mathbb{C}$ for brevity, if it is clear from the context. First the client and server identify the index j_m where m is to be inserted (before). Then the client sends the ciphertext of m to the server which inserts it at position j_m. Finally the server rotates the data structure by a random offset.
  1. The client sets $l := 0$ and $u := n - 1$.
  2. If $n = 0$ then go to step 5.
  3. The client requests $\mathbb{C}[0]$ and sets $r := \mathsf{Dec}(k, \mathbb{C}[0])$.
  4. Set $j := \lfloor l + \frac{u-l}{2} \rfloor$. The client requests $\mathbb{C}[j]$ and executes $m' := \mathsf{Dec}(k, \mathbb{C}[j])$. If $m' - r \bmod N > m - r \bmod N$, then the client sets $l := j + 1$. If $m' - r \bmod N < m - r \bmod N$, then the client sets $u := j$. If $m' = m \bmod N$, then the client flips a random coin and sets either $l := j + 1$ or $u := j$ depending on the outcome of the coin flip. The client repeats this step until $l = u$.
  5. The client sends $c \leftarrow \mathsf{PSE.Enc}(k, m)$ to the server.
  6. The server sets

$$\mathbb{C}[n] := \mathbb{C}[n - 1]$$
$$\mathbb{C}[n - 1] := \mathbb{C}[n - 2]$$
$$\cdots$$
$$\mathbb{C}[l + 1] := \mathbb{C}[l]$$
$$\mathbb{C}[l] := c$$

The server sets $n := n + 1$.

7. The server chooses a random number $s \leftarrow_\$ \mathbb{Z}_{n-1}$. The server sets the new encrypted data structure to $\mathbb{C}^{h+1}[j] := \mathbb{C}[j + s \bmod n]$ for $0 \leq j < n$ as a result of the encryption operation. This data structure $\mathbb{C}^{h+1}$ will be used as input to the next encryption operation.

- $\langle j, j' \rangle := \mathsf{Search}(\mathsf{k}, \mathbb{C}, a, b)$: Wlog. we assume that $a \leq b$ in the further exposition. In case $a > b$ the query is rewritten as to match all x, such that $0 \leq x < b \lor a \leq x < N$.

Let $j_{\min}(v)$ be the minimal index of plaintext v and $j_{\max}(v)$ be the maximal index of plaintext v.

$$j_{\min}(v) := \min(j | \mathsf{Dec}(\mathsf{k}, \mathbb{C}[j]) = v)$$

$$j_{\max}(v) := \max(j | \mathsf{Dec}(\mathsf{k}, \mathbb{C}[j]) = v)$$

If $j_{\min}(v) = 0$ and $j_{\max}(v) = n - 1$ and there are two distinct plaintexts in the data structure, then we redefine as

$$j_{\min}(v) := j + 1 | \mathsf{Dec}(\mathsf{k}, \mathbb{C}[j]) < v \land \mathsf{Dec}(\mathsf{k}, \mathbb{C}[j + 1]) = v$$

$$j_{\max}(v) := j - 1 | \mathsf{Dec}(\mathsf{k}, \mathbb{C}[j]) > v \land \mathsf{Dec}(\mathsf{k}, \mathbb{C}[j - 1]) = v$$

If a and b do not span the modulus, i.e. $j_{\min}(a) < j_{\max}(b)$, then a query for $x \in [a, b]$ is rewritten to $j_{\min}(a) \leq x \leq j_{\max}(b)$. Else, it is rewritten to $0 \leq x < j_{\max}(b) \lor j_{\min}(a) \leq x < n'$.

Both $j_{\min}(a)$ and $j_{\max}(b)$ are found using a separately run, interactive binary search. We next present this protocol.

1. The client sets $l := 0$ and $u := n - 1$.
2. The client requests $\mathbb{C}[0]$, $\mathbb{C}[n - 1]$ and sets $r := \mathsf{Dec}(\mathsf{k}, \mathbb{C}[0])$. If $\mathsf{Dec}(\mathsf{k}, \mathbb{C}[0]) = \mathsf{Dec}(\mathsf{k}, \mathbb{C}[n-1])$ and searching for $j_{\min}(a)$, it sets $r := r+1$.
3. Set $j := \lfloor l + \frac{u-l}{2} \rfloor$. The client requests $\mathbb{C}[j]$ and executes $m := \mathsf{Dec}(\mathsf{k}, \mathbb{C}[j])$. If $m - r \bmod N < a - r \bmod N$ (or $m - r \bmod N \leq b - r \bmod N$, respectively) then the client sets $l := j + 1$. Else the client sets $u := j$. The client repeats this step until $l = u$.
4. The client returns $j_{\min}(a) := l$ (or $j_{\max}(b) := u$, respectively).

- $m := \mathsf{Dec}(\mathsf{k}, \mathbb{C}[j])$: Set $m := \mathsf{PSE.Dec}(\mathsf{k}, \mathbb{C}[j])$.

5.1 Security

Theorem 4. *Our efficiently searchable, encrypted data structure* $\mathsf{ESEDS_{PSE}}$ *is IND-CPA-DS-secure.*

Proof. Since all cells of the data structure consists only of ciphertexts from a IND-CPA-secure encryption scheme, we can replace the encrypted data structure by a simulator. Let the simulator $\mathsf{Sim}_{\mathsf{ESEDS}}^{E_k}(1^\lambda, n)$ output n ciphertexts $c \leftarrow E_k(0)$. The adversary $\mathcal{A}$ cannot distinguish the following experiment $\mathsf{Exp}_{\mathcal{A}, \mathsf{Sim_{ESEDS}}, \mathsf{ESEDS_{PSE}}}^{\mathrm{IND\text{-}CPA\text{-}DS}}$ from experiment $\mathsf{Exp}_{\mathcal{A}, \mathsf{ESEDS_{PSE}}}^{\mathrm{IND\text{-}CPA\text{-}DS}}$ except with negligible probability.

$$\underline{\mathrm{Exp}^{\mathrm{IND\text{-}CPA\text{-}DS}}_{\mathcal{A},\mathsf{Sim}_{\mathsf{ESEDS}},\mathsf{ESEDS}_{\mathsf{PSE}}}(\lambda)} \qquad\qquad\qquad \underline{\mathrm{E}_{\mathsf{k}}(m)}$$

$\langle \mathsf{k}, \mathbb{C} \rangle \leftarrow \mathsf{ESEDS.KGen}(1^\lambda)$ $\qquad\qquad\qquad\qquad c \leftarrow \mathsf{PSE.Enc}(\mathsf{k}, m)$

$\langle \mathbb{M}_0, \mathbb{M}_1, \mathsf{st} \rangle \leftarrow \mathcal{A}^{\mathrm{E}_\mathsf{k}}(1^\lambda)$ $\qquad\qquad\qquad\qquad$ **return** c

if $|\mathbb{M}_0| \neq |\mathbb{M}_1|$ **then return** $\bot$

$\mathbb{C} \leftarrow \mathsf{Sim}^{\mathrm{E}_\mathsf{k}}_{\mathsf{ESEDS}}(1^\lambda, |\mathbb{M}_0|)$

$\langle j', m' \rangle \leftarrow \mathcal{A}^{\mathrm{E}_\mathsf{k}}(1^\lambda, \mathbb{C}, \mathsf{st})$

return $\left\langle \mathsf{ESEDS.Dec}(\mathbb{C}[j']) = m', \dfrac{\#_{\mathbb{M}_0 \cup \mathbb{M}_1} m'}{|\mathbb{M}_0 \cup \mathbb{M}_1|} \right\rangle$

The adversary $\mathcal{A}$ in $\mathrm{Exp}^{\mathrm{IND\text{-}CPA\text{-}DS}}_{\mathcal{A},\mathsf{Sim}_{\mathsf{ESEDS}},\mathsf{ESEDS}_{\mathsf{PSE}}}$ clearly has no information which plaintext multi-set has been encrypted or about the plaintexts' positions in the data structure. Since in our $\mathsf{ESEDS}_{\mathsf{PSE}}$ each plaintext has equal probability of being at any index within the data structure, the adversary can at best guess the index j' for any $m' \in \mathbb{M}$. However, the probability of a successful guess is bounded by $\dfrac{\#_{\mathbb{M}_0 \cup \mathbb{M}_1} m'}{|\mathbb{M}_0 \cup \mathbb{M}_1|}$.

6 Performance Evaluation

We prototypically implemented and in a number of experiments evaluated the performance our IND-CPA-DS-secure ESEDS. In this section we report the results of our experiments measuring the run-time of range searching over encrypted data.

6.1 Implementation

We used Java for our implementation and evaluation, since many multi-tier applications are implemented in Java. Although a native cryptographic library, such as Intel's AES-NI, promises further performance improvements, programming languages such as C or C++ are more commonly used for systems software (such as database management systems) rather than for database applications (which only issue database queries). However, in our setup encryption and decryption is performed in the database application. We used Oracle's Java 1.8 and all experiments were run on the Java SE 64-Bit Server virtual machine. The database backend was the MySQL replacement MariaDB in version 10.1. When using a database, such as MariaDB, that was not specifically developed for operation on encrypted data, one needs to configure it to prevent the attacks on configuration described by Grubbs et al. [15]. All experiments were run on a single machine with a 4-core Intel i7 CPU at 2.9 GHz and 16 GB of RAM on Windows 10 Enterprise.

6.2 Experimental Setup

We measure the run-time of a typical, simply structured (i.e. a single search term and no conjunctions or disjunctions) database query on a single ordered database column, e.g. a range query or a top-k query. We use synthetic data and queries. However, we adapt our choice of parameters to the data from the DBLP data set [1]. In the spirit of Grubbs et al. [16] we considered author names. At the time of our experiments there were about 1.500.000 million distinct author names in DBLP, the most frequent of which appears roughly 80 times.

We implement the client interface as it would be used in an application using a database. The application supplies the parameters, e.g. the start a and end b of a range or the k in top-k, and receives the results in plaintext. Thus, our measured run-time includes the Search algorithm, the standard query by the database management system and the decryption of the result. We emphasize that in more complex queries, e.g. including multiple search terms combined by conjunction and disjunctions, the relative time for executing the query on the database management system would be proportionally higher. Hence, our experiments put an upper bound on the worst case of the relative overhead, since our queries are of the simplest form.

Our target quantity in our measurements is the absolute run-time in milliseconds. For range queries we measure the dependence of the run-time on different parameters.

- *Size of the database*: We vary the database size from 100.000 to 1.000.000 plaintexts in steps of 100.000, i.e. data items before encryption.
- *Size of the queried range*: We vary the range size and consequently the result set size in the query from 10 to 100 in steps of 10.

For top-k queries we measure the dependence of the run-time of the following parameter.

- k: We vary the limit k from 10 to 100 in steps of 10.

We compare the run-time on encrypted data to the run-time on plaintext data. Note that queries on plaintext only need to execute the query on the database management system, i.e. the time for the Search algorithm and decryption of results is 0.

We use synthetically generated data and queries. We uniformly choose distinct plaintexts and we uniformly choose a begin of the range query and then compute the end using the fixed size parameter of the experiment.

We repeat each experiment 30 times discarding the first 10 experiments in order to allow to adjust the Java JIT compiler. We report the mean and 95% confidence interval for each parameter setting.

6.3   Results

Database Size: Figure 1 shows the running time over the database size. We use a query range size of 10. The database size increases from 100.000 to 1.000.000 plaintexts in steps of 100.000. The running time is measured in milliseconds. The error bars show the 95% confidence interval. Since our search algorithms run in sub-linear time only a very slight increase (20%) in running time is measurable compared to the increase in database size (900%). The overhead of our encryption is roughly 9 ms.

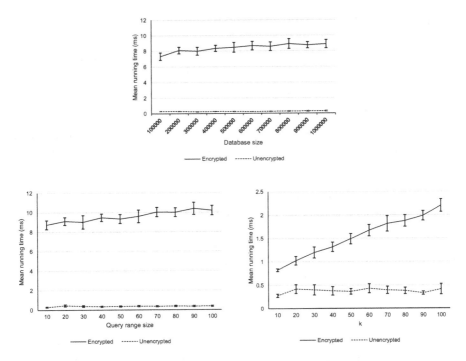

Fig. 1. (top) Performance over different database sizes (left) Performance over query range size (right) Performance over k for top-k queries

Query Range Size: Figure 1 shows the running time over the query range size. We use a database size of 1.000.000 plaintexts. The query range size and hence the expected result set size increases from 10 to 100 in steps of 10. The running time is measured in milliseconds. The error bars show the 95% confidence interval. The running time increase is slight and approximately linear in the query range size and there is a constant baseline. We attribute the constant cost to our binary search algorithm which as shown in Fig. 1 behaves almost constant for these database sizes. We attribute this increase to the cost of decryption which is dominated by the cryptographic operations.

Top-k Queries: Figure 1 shows the running time for top-k queries over k. We use a database size of 1.000.000 plaintexts. The value of k increases from 10 to 100 in steps of 10. The running time is measured in milliseconds. The error bars show the 95% confidence interval. The constant baseline is lower, since top-k queries can be executed without a search algorithm, when the minimum ciphertext (the rotation value) is stored as part of the key. The linear increase due to decryption of results is now clearly visible.

7   Related Work

Our work is related to other searchable encryption schemes – particularly for range queries –, order-revealing encryption and leakage-abuse attacks.

7.1   Searchable Encryption

Searchable encryption allows the comparison of a token (corresponding to a plaintext) to a ciphertext. The ciphertext (without any token) is IND-CPA-secure. The token can match plaintexts for equality or the plaintext to a range. Only the secret key holder can create tokens.

Tackling range queries with searchable encryption is complex. The first proposal by Boneh and Waters in [6] had ciphertext size linear in the size of the domain of the plaintext. The first poly-logarithmic sized ciphertexts scheme was proposed by Shi et al. in [31]. However, their security model is somewhat weaker than standard searchable encryption. The construction is based on inner-product predicate encryption which has been made fully secure by Katz et al. in [19]. All schemes follow the construction by Song et al. (without inverted indices) and require linear search time. The first attempt to build range-searchable encryption into an index (an ESEDS) has been made by Lu in [25]. However, the inverted index tree reveals the pointers and is hence no more secure than order-preserving encryption. Demertzis et al. [10] map a range query to keyword queries by providing tradeoffs between storing replicated values in each of its ranges and enumerating all values within range query. The search can then be easily performed using the data structure of Curtmola et al. [9]. While the scheme is range searchable, its queries are very revealing and it has high storage cost (at least $O(n \log n)$). Boelter et al. [2] use garbled circuits to implement the search within a node of the index. They do not encrypt the pointers in the index and are hence susceptible to the attacks by Naveed et al. and are not IND-CPA-DS secure. The scheme by Hahn and Kerschbaum [17] creates an index using the access pattern of the range queries. No other information is leaked, however, this provides amortized poly-logarithmic search time. The scheme is only IND-CPA-DS-secure as long as no queries have been performed (and the index has been partially built). Their scheme is based on inner-product predicate encryption which is too slow for practical use.

7.2   Order-Revealing Encryption

Order-revealing encryption [5,8,24] is an alternative to order-preserving encryption. Instead of preserving the order there is a public function that reveals the order of two plaintexts using the ciphertexts only. At first, it may seem paradoxical to combine the disadvantages of order-preserving and searchable encryption: order revelation and modified comparison function. However, order-revealing encryption has also advantages. It allows an IND-OCPA secure (as defined in [3]) encryption with constant-size ciphertexts, constant size client storage and without mutation circumventing impossibility results in [3] and [28]. However, the first construction was not only impractical due to its disadvantages, but also due to its performance. A different construction with slightly more leakage, but significantly better performance was presented by Chenette et al. in [8]. This construction was further improved by Lewi and Wu in [24]. They allow comparison only between a token and an IND-CPA-secure ciphertext as in searchable encryption, i.e. the scheme has no leakage when no token is revealed. Their search procedure requires a linear search over all ciphertext and no indexing is possible. Hence, compared to our scheme which has logarithmic search time, order-revealing encryption currently remains impractical.

7.3   Leakage-Abuse Attacks

We discussed many leakage-abuse attacks on search over encrypted data. There are static attacks on order-preserving encryption [12,16,27,29] and attacks using dynamic information that also work on searchable encryption [7,14,18,20,23,32].

Kellaris et al. [20] have presented generic inference attacks on encrypted data using range queries. Their attacks work in a setup where the adversary has compromised the database server and can observe all queries, i.e. they work for dynamic leakage during the execution of queries and are not ciphertext-only attacks. They do not assume a specific cryptographic protection mechanism, but work only on its dynamic leakage profile, such as the access pattern or the result size, i.e. they also apply to ORAM-protected databases. The prerequisite assumption for Kellaris et al.'s attack to work is that the distribution of queries and the distribution of plaintexts differ. Specifically, they assume that each possible query will be executed, but not each possible plaintext is in the database. We note that Kellaris et al. performed all their attacks on synthetic data and queries whereas static ciphertext-only attacks on real data have been publicized [11].

There are also some more specific inference attacks. Islam et al. [18] and Cash et al. [7] have performed inference attacks by observing the queries on encrypted data. Islam et al. assume that the distribution of query keywords is approximately known and then can recover the query keywords using frequency analysis. Cash et al. improve the accuracy of this attack even under slightly weaker assumptions about the knowledge of query distribution, but then also use the information to recover plaintexts from the access pattern. Lacharite et al. [23] improve the accuracy of plaintext guessing by incorporating information from observed queries.

Next to the ones already discussed plaintext guessing attacks Pouliot and Wright show that adding deterministic encryption to Bloom filters – not surprisingly – does not prevent cryptanalysis [29]. Zhang et al. assume that the adversary can actively insert plaintexts and can then recover query plaintexts from the access pattern [32]. Grubbs et al. [14] also attacked an implementation of multi-user searchable encryption which allows inferences between users leading to a complete breakdown of the security guarantee of encrypted web applications.

Kolesnikov and Shikfa proposed to limit the querier's abilities to increase the security of order-preserving encryption [22]. In this paper we extend this idea and formally show that if we exclude queries, the static leakage from order-preserving ciphertexts (an ESEDS) can be negligible.

8   Conclusions

We give a new definition of security against plaintext guessing attacks by a snapshot adversary and show that it is insufficient to prove that all data items have been probabilistically encrypted in order to be secure against these attacks. Then we prove by construction that the new definition can be fulfilled by an encrypted data structure, i.e. one secure against plaintext guessing attacks.

References

1. http://dblp.l3s.de/dblp++.php
2. Boelter, T., Poddar, R., Popa, R.A.: A secure one-roundtrip index for range queries. Technical report 568, IACR Cryptology ePrint Archive (2016)
3. Boldyreva, A., Chenette, N., Lee, Y., O'Neill, A.: Order-preserving symmetric encryption. In: Joux, A. (ed.) EUROCRYPT 2009. LNCS, vol. 5479, pp. 224–241. Springer, Heidelberg (2009). https://doi.org/10.1007/978-3-642-01001-9_13
4. Boldyreva, A., Chenette, N., O'Neill, A.: Order-preserving encryption revisited: improved security analysis and alternative solutions. In: Rogaway, P. (ed.) CRYPTO 2011. LNCS, vol. 6841, pp. 578–595. Springer, Heidelberg (2011). https://doi.org/10.1007/978-3-642-22792-9_33
5. Boneh, D., Lewi, K., Raykova, M., Sahai, A., Zhandry, M., Zimmerman, J.: Semantically secure order-revealing encryption: multi-input functional encryption without obfuscation. In: Oswald, E., Fischlin, M. (eds.) EUROCRYPT 2015. LNCS, vol. 9057, pp. 563–594. Springer, Heidelberg (2015). https://doi.org/10.1007/978-3-662-46803-6_19
6. Boneh, D., Waters, B.: Conjunctive, subset, and range queries on encrypted data. In: Vadhan, S.P. (ed.) TCC 2007. LNCS, vol. 4392, pp. 535–554. Springer, Heidelberg (2007). https://doi.org/10.1007/978-3-540-70936-7_29
7. Cash, D., Grubbs, P., Perry, J., Ristenpart, T.: Leakage-abuse attacks against searchable encryption. In: Proceedings of the 22nd ACM Conference on Computer and Communications Security, CCS (2015)
8. Chenette, N., Lewi, K., Weis, S.A., Wu, D.J.: Practical order-revealing encryption with limited leakage. In: Peyrin, T. (ed.) FSE 2016. LNCS, vol. 9783, pp. 474–493. Springer, Heidelberg (2016). https://doi.org/10.1007/978-3-662-52993-5_24
9. Curtmola, R., Garay, J., Kamara, S., Ostrovsky, R.: Searchable symmetric encryption: improved definitions and efficient constructions. J. Comput. Secur. 19(5), 895–934 (2011)
10. Demertzis, I., Papadopoulos, S., Papapetrou, O., Deligiannakis, A., Garofalakis, M.: Practical private range search revisited. In: Proceedings of the ACM International Conference on Management of Data, SIGMOD (2016)
11. Ducklin, P.: Anatomy of a password disaster - adobe's giant-sized cryptographic blunder (2013). https://nakedsecurity.sophos.com/2013/11/04/anatomy-of-a-password-disaster-adobes-giant-sized-cryptographic-blunder/

12. Durak, B., DuBuisson, T., Cash, D.: What else is revealed by order-revealing encryption? In: Proceedings of the 23rd ACM Conference on Computer and Communications Security, CCS (2016)
13. Fitzpatrick, A.: Apple says systems weren't hacked in nude pics grab (2014). http://time.com/3257945/apple-icloud-brute-force-jennifer-lawrence/
14. Grubbs, P., McPherson, R., Naveed, M., Ristenpart, T., Shmatikov, V.: Breaking web applications built on top of encrypted data. In: Proceedings of the 23rd ACM Conference on Computer and Communications Security, CCS (2016)
15. Grubbs, P., Ristenpart, T., Shmatikov, V.: Why your encrypted database is not secure. Technical report 468, IACR Cryptology ePrint Archive (2017)
16. Grubbs, P., Sekniqi, K., Bindschaedler, V., Naveed, M., Ristenpart, T.: Leakage-abuse attacks against order-revealing encryption. Technical report 895, IACR Cryptology ePrint Archive (2016)
17. Hahn, F., Kerschbaum, F.: Poly-logarithmic range queries on encrypted data with small leakage. In: Proceedings of the ACM Workshop on Cloud Computing Security Workshop, CCSW (2016)
18. Islam, M., Kuzu, M., Kantarcioglu, M.: Access pattern disclosure on searchable encryption: ramification, attack and mitigation. In: Proceedings of the 19th Network and Distributed System Security Symposium, NDSS (2012)
19. Katz, J., Sahai, A., Waters, B.: Predicate encryption supporting disjunctions, polynomial equations, and inner products. In: Smart, N. (ed.) EUROCRYPT 2008. LNCS, vol. 4965, pp. 146–162. Springer, Heidelberg (2008). https://doi.org/10.1007/978-3-540-78967-3_9
20. Kellaris, G., Kollios, G., Nissim, K., O'Neill, A.: Generic attacks on secure outsourced databases. In: Proceedings of the 23rd ACM Conference on Computer and Communications Security, CCS (2016)
21. Kerschbaum, F.: Frequency-hiding order-preserving encryption. In: Proceedings of the 22nd ACM Conference on Computer and Communications Security, CCS (2015)
22. Kolesnikov, V., Shikfa, A.: On the limits of privacy provided byorder-preserving encryption. Bell Labs Tech. J. **17**(3), 135–146 (2012)
23. Lacharité, M.S., Minaud, B., Paterson, K.: Improved reconstruction attacks on encrypted data using range query leakage. Technical report 701, IACR Cryptology ePrint Archive (2017)
24. Lewi, K., Wu, D.: Order-revealing encryption: new constructions, applications, and lower bounds. In: Proceedings of the 23rd ACM Conference on Computer and Communications Security, CCS (2016)
25. Lu, Y.: Privacy-preserving logarithmic-time search on encrypted data in cloud. In: Proceedings of the 19th Network and Distributed System Security Symposium, NDSS (2012)
26. McCarthy, K.: Panama papers hack: unpatched wordpress, drupal bugs to blame? (2016). http://www.theregister.co.uk/2016/04/07/panama_papers_unpatched_wordpress_drupal/
27. Naveed, M., Kamara, S., Wright, C.V.: Inference attacks on property-preserving encrypted databases. In: Proceedings of the 22nd ACM Conference on Computer and Communications Security, CCS (2015)
28. Popa, R.A., Li, F.H., Zeldovich, N.: An ideal-security protocol for order-preserving encoding. In: 34th IEEE Symposium on Security and Privacy, S&P (2013)
29. Pouliot, D., Wright, C.: The shadow nemesis: inference attacks on efficiently deployable, efficiently searchable encryption. In: Proceedings of the 23rd ACM Conference on Computer and Communications Security, CCS (2016)

30. Roche, D., Apon, D., Choi, S., Yerukhimovich, A.: Pope: partial order preserving encoding. In: Proceedings of the 23rd ACM Conference on Computer and Communications Security, CCS (2016)
31. Shi, E., Bethencourt, J., Chan, H.T.H., Song, D.X., Perrig, A.: Multi-dimensional range query over encrypted data. In: Proceedings of the 2007 Symposium on Security and Privacy, S&P (2007)
32. Zhang, Y., Katz, J., Papamanthou, C.: All your queries are belong to us: the power of file-injection attacks on searchable encryption. In: Proceedings of the 25th USENIX Security Symposium, USENIX SECURITY (2016)

Privacy

GDPiRated – Stealing Personal Information On- and Offline

Matteo Cagnazzo[1(✉)], Thorsten Holz[2], and Norbert Pohlmann[1]

[1] Institute for Internet-Security, University of Applied Sciences Gelsenkirchen,
Gelsenkirchen, Germany
{cagnazzo,pohlmann}@internet-sicherheit.de

[2] Horst Görtz Institute (HGI), Ruhr-Universität Bochum, Bochum, Germany
thorsten.holz@rub.de

Abstract. The European *General Data Protection Regulation* (GDPR) went into effect in May 2018. As part of this regulation, the *right to access* was extended, it grants a user the right to request access to all personal data collected by a company about this user. In this paper, we present the results of an empirical study on data exfiltration attacks that are enabled by abusing these so called *subject access requests*. More specifically, our *GDPiRate attack* is performed by sending subject access requests (as demanded by the GDPR) with spoofed recipient addresses either in the on- or offline realm. Our experimental results show that entities accepting and processing offline requests (e.g., letters) perform worse in terms of ensuring that the requesting entity is the correct data subject. The worrying finding is that affected organizations send personal data to unverified requests and therefore leak personal user data. Our research demonstrates a novel attack on privacy by abusing a right the GDPR tries to protect.

Keywords: GDPR · Privacy · Offensive security

1 Introduction

On May 25, 2018, the General Data Protection Regulation (GDPR) went into effect in the European Union. Its major goal is to harmonize privacy protection mechanisms across the European Union (EU) and enable users to exercise their rights, whenever and wherever data of them is processed. On- and offline services provided to European citizens are affected by these changes and required to adopt this regulation. An important aspect of the GDPR is the *right to access*, which grants a user the right to request access to all personal data collected by a company about this user via a so called *subject access request* (SAR).

While these changes are generally considered positive in terms of privacy and transparency for users, little research has been done on how these new mechanisms could be exploited by an adversary trying to gather personal information. In this paper, we describe an empirical case study we conducted in the year

© Springer Nature Switzerland AG 2019
K. Sako et al. (Eds.): ESORICS 2019, LNCS 11736, pp. 367–386, 2019.
https://doi.org/10.1007/978-3-030-29962-0_18

2018 using rather simple techniques to exfiltrate personal data out of municipal, healthcare, and other providers that process sensitive data. Broadly speaking, we send SARs to a company and request access to data belonging to a victim user, an attack we call *GDPiRate attack*. Due to the private nature of the data we exfiltrated and the fact that most of the services we examined are identity- and location-based in terms of who uses the platforms, we decided to conduct only a small case study with data from the authors to not harm any person. We also took special measures to limit the potential impact of our analysis and to perform the attack in a responsible way. The exfiltrated data could especially be misused by attackers who are trying to *dox* other users or want to conduct targeted (spear)phishing attacks in an advanced persistent threat (APT) or a fraud scheme. Our experiments hence required special handling of sensitive data.

Our experimental results show that despite all the positive effects that the GDPR had on privacy in Europe, a new attack surface is made available due to SARs and the fines that organizations face if they do not respond within one month. We show that a lot of organizations do not seem to have proper protection and authentication mechanisms in place to verify if a subject access request indeed belongs to a legitimate and authorized user. More specifically, 10 out of 14 spoofed SARs were successful and we were able to obtain access to sensitive information. Whenever services or organizations provide a mix of online and offline data and do not have a dedicated process dealing with SARs, it appears that these services are susceptible to our GDPiRate attack. The short timeframe which is given to companies to react to SARs is a positive effect to transparency of users, but also facilitates our attack. It seems that only a small number of companies have proper authentication processes for SARs in place to determine if a legitimate user or an attacker contacts them via mail, fax, or email.

In summary, our paper makes the following contributions:

- In a case study, we introduce a new attack on how the GDPR might help identity thefts, doxers, and fraudsters to gain access to personal information. Our empirical results indicate that spoofed subject access requests are often successful in practice (10 out of 14 cases) given that companies to not perform enough checks to verify the identify of the source of a SAR.
- We analyze the collected data and categorize the impact using the Common Vulnerability Scoring System (CVSS) based on the accessible data.
- We discuss both operational and strategic mitigations for the vulnerabilities we found. We hope that our research raises awareness of this problem and that more companies start to implement proper mechanisms to verify the identity and source of SARs.

2   Related Work

According to a study by the Ponemon Institute [31], 52 % of companies said they are GDPR-ready before the deadline in May 2018. The same study found that 50% of companies in the health sector and 47.2% in the public sector expected to be GDPR compliant before this date. Contrary to this study, we found that major flaws exist in the operational section of privacy implementations, especially in terms of subject access request handling.

There have been many studies on privacy policies, presumably because they are the primary factor in terms of transparency [2,21,23,28,40]. There is much work on how privacy policies are perceived by users, what they disclose, and how accessible the information is to users. For example, Degeling et al. examined popular websites in the European union and their implementation of the GDPR [8]. Linden et al. reviewed privacy policies pre- and post-GDPR and found overall positive improvements to privacy rights of citizens in the EU [30].

Another important factor are cookies and web tracking in general [11,12,44]. For example, Urban et al. showed that cookie providers generally comply with GDPR, but not within an appropriate timeframe [51].

Our GDPiRate attack is a general attack not exploiting a technical flaw, but rather an organizational and human protocol flaw. A technical analogy would be to visit a website and by changing the user agent string of the web browser, an attacker would gain access to personal data on this website. A similar approach has been taken by Gruss et al. [22], where the technical use-after-free vulnerability of memory unsafe languages like C/C++ was generalized to "any environment and situation where resources can be silently exchanged". While Gruss et al. wait for resources to be freed or released, GDPiRate uses the information while it is still in use of the legitimate user.

Concurrently and independently, Di Martino et al. [32] performed a similar study in Belgium and showed that the attack is not only feasible in Germany but also in Belgium. This highlights the fact that our attack seems to be a bigger European problem which needs to be solved, so the privacy of individuals is better protected.

3   Background

In this section, we provide a brief overview and introduction to the GDPR and its history. Furthermore, we cover attack techniques such as social engineering, phishing, and doxing.

3.1   General Data Protection Regulation (GDPR)

The need to protect the privacy of individuals and still be able to share data across the EU has been an European effort for more than twenty years. In 1995, the Data Protection Directive 95/46/EC was created to regulate the processing of personal data and harmonize European data processing. Directives are not directly applicable to members of the European Union. Each state has to adopt an individual implementing act. Therefore, the harmonization of European privacy laws failed. Recital 9 of the GDPR explicitly points out that implementations differed widely, which resulted in a complex privacy law landscape across Europe.

In 2016, the European Parliament and Council came to an agreement on a new data protection law following a four year proposal and trilogue period. The Council and Parliament decided that the General Data Protection Regulation (GDPR) will be fully enforceable throughout the EU after a two year post-adoption grace period. The aim of the GDPR is to protect citizens of the EU from privacy violations and data breaches. The GDPR's integral goal is to harmonize privacy laws all over Europe. In addition to the GDPR, the ePrivacy regulation is currently passing the EU's legislative process to complement the GDPR.

One of the key changes of the GDPR in accordance to harmonizing the law landscape on privacy is an increased territorial scope (Art. 3 GDPR). It applies to all entities processing personal data of subjects residing within the EU. It is not important where the processing entity is located. Furthermore penalties can be fines up to 4% of annual global turnover or 20 million euro. This fine is applicable if user consent is not sufficient or other core privacy principles are violated. User consent is another key change of the GDPR because the conditions became stronger. Data processors must provide the request for consent in an easily accessible form with purpose of processing directly attached to this form. Withdrawal of consent must be as easy as it is to give consent (Art. 7 GDPR).

Data must be protected by design and default. Article 25 of the GDPR states that entities need to *implement appropriate technical and organizational measures [...] designed to implement data protection principles[...] in an effective manner [...] taking into account the state of art* [16]. This means that processing entities must ensure that private data is not publicly available without the user's consent. Higher protection standards must be implemented for sensitive categories of data like religious or health data (Art. 9 GDPR) [17].

Another integral change for data processors is the *right of access*. Every user has the right to access their personal data which is collected and processed, according to Article 15 [15]. If they are requesting this in an electronic form, the answer must be provided in an electronic manner as well. First access to their personal data is to be provided free of charge by the person responsible with a copy of the data subjects available data. If the request is made via postal mail, the response should also be sent via mail. Recital 74 states that the identity of the applicant must be verified so that only the person whose data is processed has access to the data [15]. According to Article 12 [18], a processor can request additional information to confirm the identity of the data subject requesting the information. The GDPR states companies "should use all reasonable measures to verify the identity of a data subject who requests access", to make sure they do not disclose data to the wrong person. This identification process is supposed to add a layer of security. If a data processor is not complying to such a request in a reasonable timespan, he can be fined according to the fines mentioned above.

According to Art. 9 of the GDPR, the following types of data are in a special category and processing of this data is always prohibited unless explicit consent is given by the data subject [17]:

- racial or ethnic origin
- political opinions

- religious beliefs or other beliefs of a similar nature
- trade union membership
- physical or mental health or condition
- sex life and sexual orientation
- genetic data and biometric data

We use healthcare data to describe special categories in detail, the other categories follow a similar scheme. According to Art. 4 of the GDPR, healthcare data is defined as *personal data related to the physical or mental health of a natural person, including the provision of health care services, which reveal information about his or her health status;* [14]. This data is sensitive and needs specific protection from unlawful processing and data leaks. A report by the EC confirms that respondents from the EU are concerned about applications tracking their activities and vital data [13].

Even though the data is sensitive and needs more protection, a study by the compliance analytics company Protenus [42] found that in 2017 there were 477 data breaches reported to the United States Department of Health and Human Services, which is a slight increase from previous monitoring periods. The main reasons for these breaches are hackings and insider threats [42]. According to Fuentes [19], attackers found multiple ways to profit from stolen medical health records for example by misusing data to get medical prescriptions or perform identity theft.

Apart from official medical institutions being targeted, there is a large number of healthcare online platforms and applications which closely monitor users' vital parameters. The applications range from weight tracking to suicide prevention, from online platforms where types of donors are managed. They all have in common that they hold and process sensitive data which is related to (mental) health of users. Papageorgiou et al. [38] found that mobile health applications do not follow well-known best practices and guidelines, or comply to legal restrictions. Rasthofer et al. [43] analyzed multiple mutual agreement tracking applications and found that the state of security in these applications is worrisome.

Alongside badly coded applications and adversaries, some companies that track data share anonymized datasets. For example, fitness trackers that track heartrate and geolocation offer publicly available data, which can be deanonymized because too much private information is embedded in the anonymized data [24]. This data is very specific for individual users, causing more pretext information for (spear)phishing attacks [5].

Starting our research of GDPiRate with healthcare services, we realized that there are more entities which are vulnerable to our attack. Especially credit bureaus, address dealers, tenant information services, and transport services could be vulnerable. Hence we decided to include such companies into our study, even though they are not connected to the medical landscape. Nevertheless, they also handle sensitive and private data which is categorized as data with increased protection requirements.

3.2 Social Engineering

In the information security context, social engineering is an attack technique with the goal of influencing potential victims to disclose information or perform a specific action. Attackers do not exclusively use technical means; social manipulation is at the forefront of social engineering. Criminals often make use of social, established behavior. Holding open an access-restricted door for another person would be such an exploitable behaviour. The information or actions received are often just a means to an end, and in most cases are used to enter an information processing system or to gain access to an asset within a company. The manipulation can affect trustworthiness, integrity, or availability. Deception and manipulation are the basics of social engineering-based attacks. Against private individuals, social engineering campaigns are usually conducted to impersonate identity theft. For example, the user is directed to fake web portals to enter credentials, such as username, password, or banking details. Individuals also become victims of social engineering to steal access to company information.

Current technical countermeasures are usually ineffective against these attacks. Companies have little information about what data employees share on the Internet. In addition, many victims of social engineering attacks feel that they are good at detecting these attacks, but in practice they are not. An increased risk comes from *Unintentional Insider Threats* (UIT). The CERT Insider Threat Team defines a UIT as follows: "An Unintentional Insider Threat is (1) a current or former employee, contractor or business partner (2) who has or has authorized access to an organization's network, system or data Action or omission without malicious intent (4) will cause harm or substantially increase the likelihood of future serious damage to the confidentiality, integrity or availability of the organization's information or information system." These insider threats, whether intended or not, are considered to be one of the greatest risks to operational and organizational security. The two threats are different in motivation, indication, and other differences. Therefore, it is important to study and understand these threats in detail.

A common route of infection is phishing which is explained in the following section. Another emerging trend in social engineering is the exploitation of machine-learning-based insights to target users individually with phishing links.

3.3 Phishing

Phishing is a neologism of "fishing" and an act of deception. For the first time, the term was used in 1996 in the context of a theft of America Online (AOL) accounts [36]. Previously, swindlers used classic scams to help people to save their data or belongings. False messages promising money go back to the nineteenth century. Suspected Spanish prisoners wrote letters to wealthy US citizens. The author is always in prison as a political prisoner, but has a large amount of money to dispose of as soon as he is released. To obtain the dismissal, the attacker only needs some money. It is unclear how much damage has actually been done, because even then the prosecution was a problem [49].

In phishing, an attacker uses a fake e-mail, short message, or website to trick a victim into revealing non-public information. Often, passwords or bank details are stolen, but personal information can also be lost. One of the most common problems with phishing attacks is one that is prevalent in any deception: the victim often does not realize that he has been the victim of fraud. Only the abuse of information often leads to the victim noticing that they were deceived. For example, an American study shows that more than 1 million children in the US have already been the victims of identity theft. The resulting economic damage amounts to $ 2.6 billion in damage, which is transferred directly to the families [39].

Phishing scales very well because there are hardly any costs for sending an e-mail. An attacker needs an e-mail account and an Internet connection, then they can start attacking. In its specification, the SMTP protocol offers no possibility to authenticate a sender [29]. Although e-mail is the primary means of phishing, phishing is also available by phone (*vishing*), SMS (*smishing*), and social networks (*Snishing*) [53]. Especially in social networks, it is more complex for an attacker to scale, because there is trust among users. Attackers often resort to creating false customer support accounts and then phishing links in the comment columns. This procedure is called "angler phishing": a study by Proofpoint shows that about 30% of all known market accounts are a form of fraud and security risk [41]. These fraudulent acts are different. From the theft of account data to click fraud to the distribution of pornographic material. This means that customers of the affected brands lose data, while it also leads to a reputation loss for the brand.

The phishing link is distributed by an attacker in an arbitrary way, for example in social networks or via an e-mail. It should be noted that there is no prevailing modus operandi for phishing, but an adversary can choose from a variety of possible procedures. An attack, however, usually consists of three steps: (1) setting up the attack, (2) carrying out the attack, and (3) monetizing the information. In the first phase of the attack, the phishing emails are created and the page on which the users submit their information is set up. In addition, the circle of victims must be defined, for example, by collecting e-mail addresses. In this phase, spear phishing differentiates itself from phishing [3]. Spear phishing often contains *pretexting*, which represents the "phisher" as a trusted third party and tailored to individual preferences of individual victims. Information from the private or professional environment of the victim is the key to success for this type of manipulation. Using this information enormously increases the probability of success of an attack, even when users are trained and have increased awareness [6]. Advanced Persistent Threats (APTs) can include spear phishing as an initial compromise vector, such as Operation Pawn Storm or TG-4127 [46,50].

3.4 Doxing

Doxing is an attack where private information of a victim is released online [48]. This attack is technically unsophisticated, but it can cause serious harm to its victims not just online but also offline, as quantitative [48] and qualitative research [10] shows. Hacking technologies or services, on the other hand, involves a certain skillset of an attacker to cause social harm to a victim. Doxing is, technically speaking, an unsophisticated release of documents. Prior to releasing information, the adversary must somehow access sensitive data about the victim.

An interesting case study is for example the release of e-mails of the Democratic Party during the 2016 US elections. The Mueller report [35] states that "a Russian intelligence service conducted computer -intrusion operations against entities, employees, and volunteers working on the Clinton Campaign and then released stolen documents". A sophisticated hacking effort took place before the emails and other materials were released by the two personas "Guccifer2.0" and "DCLeaks" (and later on Wikileaks).

Especially in Germany, doxing gained attention and awareness during 2019 due to mass doxing of German politicians [4], where a twenty year old suspect was accused and arrested for collecting and releasing partly public information of German politicians and celebrities. This leak was also partly politically motivated even though no state actor was involved. The suspect said he was "angry over politicians" [27].

Note that doxing is not always hostile. As Chen et al. [7] find, there are two main categories of doxing: hostile and social doxing. About half of the people studied by Chen et al. said they perform social doxing to fulfil social needs, for example obtaining social data or relationship statuses. In contrast, the other half of the respondents of this study used doxing in a hostile way.

4   Approach

Our study on potential ways to abuse subject access requests builds on simple techniques, no cryptography or technical concept was broken to achieve private data exfiltration from organizations and municipal administrative authorities. In the following, we describe our approach in more detail.

4.1   Ethical Considerations and Responsible Disclosure

Given the sensitive nature of this study, we first discuss both ethical considerations and the way we handled responsible disclosure. Neither Ruhr-Universität Bochum nor the Westphalian University for Applied Sciences have an Institutional Review Board (IRB) for computer science. Our work was conducted according to ethical best practices [1,9,33] and privacy laws. We used synthetic information wherever possible and handled the required data securely in terms of access control and storage. If data was sent to us via normal postal mail, the letters were stored in a locked container inside a locked office. Only researchers participating in this paper had access to this container and if non-synthetic data was used, it was personal data belonging to one of the authors. If data was sent to us electronically, it was sent to private or synthetic mailboxes.

We stored electronically received data on encrypted systems only. All private data was sent to spoofed mailboxes. Only the owner of the requested data had

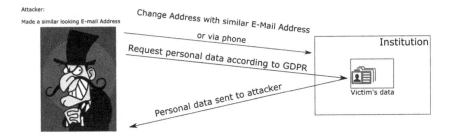

Fig. 1. High-level attack overview for *GDPiRate*

access to these mailboxes. Furthermore, we did not report any of the vulnerable organizations to a third party (e.g., a data protection authority). We anonymized the identity of the vulnerable organizations in this paper to minimize fraudulent activities based on our research. In addition, we modified individual proofs of identities before sending the SAR to an organization, therefore it should be mentioned that no official government documents were altered for this research. By the time of publication, we have contacted the affected organizations and informed them about the outcomes of our research. We gave each affected organization individual advice on how to improve their handling of SARs. In this paper, no information about the identity of affected organizations is included to minimize potential harm and damage related to the reputation of the affected organizations.

4.2   Attacker Model and Approach

We use an active adversary to interact with institutions and companies such that we can study how these entities react to spoofed SARs. The general goal of our attack is to gather personal information that is potentially sensitive.

A high-level overview of the attack flow is shown in Fig. 1, we call it the *GDPi-Rate attack*. The attacker needs to know with which e-mail address or real-world address a victim is registered at a certain service or organization. For example, she can figure this out with open-source intelligence. If she knows the e-mail address, she registers a similar-looking address (e.g., if the victim's e-mail address is `example@example.com`, the attacker would register `exmple@example.com` or another perturbation of the e-mail address). She then contacts the institutions support via e-mail to change her residing address. If they reject this change, she will call them with a spoofed number either of the victim or the city the victim is residing in, depending on the level of open-source intelligence she has acquired. After she initiated the address change, she waits a few days until she requests "her" data according to Art. 15 of the GDPR. In return, she will either receive the data directly to her spoofed e-mail address or via postal services to her spoofed street address. If she only knows the name of the victim, she can try to request data from the services or organizations just using a spoofed address. If she knows the street address of her victim, she can use offline channels and a similar strategy over which a SAR can be made. All an attacker needs to know is the last place of residence. She can say she moved and requests her data now to the new address. This will lead to data sent out to the attacker and the integrity of the data being changed. For both types of this attack, she needs to put up a sign on her mailbox.

To evaluate how effective the GDPiRate attacks is in practice, we performed an empirical study in which the authors registered an account with synthetic data. In the evaluation phase, we spoofed our own identity as an attacker to request this data over another channel. The text we used is available in the Appendix of this paper, one version in German and one in English. As part of this experiment, we also requested data with correct identity information.

5   Results

We contacted 14 services and evaluated how they react to our spoofed SARs, basically to test whether they implement proper mechanisms that only entitled and correctly identified users can gain access to private information. We focused on Germany since municipal data can only be requested for a real person and not synthetic data. We evaluated whether these 14 parties have a privacy policy and send out personal data to a spoofed recipient. To perform our SARs, we mainly sent out e-mails or used a fax machine as described in Sect. 4.2. Table 1 provides a detailed overview of our findings.

We verified our results in a control phase by requesting data about the same "victim" to the correct address and analyzed whether different data was sent. This was done to prevent an assumption that the requested entity will look up the victim at the spoofed address and if he is not registered at this address, they will just send out that a response that states that no data is stored.

Our study shows that all the requests we made were answered during the required time period. In our control phase, the requests were answered in the appropriate time frame as well. One vendor needed further clarification on which data we wanted to access in both time periods. All services we tested had a privacy policy in place and it was possible to interact with them via e-mail or telephone. Of our fourteen tested services, only two services reacted to the spoofed address by sending us a letter back requesting verification of our spoofed address. The other two services that are stated as "no" in Table 1 stated they do not process personal data.

All other companies sent out personal information, without asking for additional verification of the spoofed address and identity. During the control phase, we were able to verify if companies had other "identification processes" in place, for example verifying the identity via postal address. No company we tested sent out other data to the real address. We believe no verification of the identity is in place, therefore all these services violate the GDPR since they send out personal information to spoofed recipients and are therefore vulnerable to the GDPiRate attack. An overview of our results can be seen in Fig. 2.

We found that an attacker can possibly steal private and sensitive information with a success of approximately 71% (10 out of 14 cases). In half of the cases,

Table 1. Overview of results

Service	Purpose	Location	Has Privacy Policy	Sent Out Personal Data to spoofed recipient	Particularly sensitive data	Responded in time
Medical Institution 1	Donation service	Germany	Yes	Yes	Yes	Yes
Medical Institution 2	Donation service	Germany	Yes	Yes	Yes	Yes
Broadcasting Service 1	Broadcasting media	Germany	Yes	Yes	Yes	Yes
Postal Service 1	Postal Services	Germany	Yes	Yes	No	Yes
Travel Service 1	Transportation Services	Germany	Yes	Yes	Yes	Yes
Financial Service 1	Credit Bureaue	Germany	Yes	Yes	Yes	Yes
Financial Service 2	Creditbureau	Germany	Yes	Yes	Yes	Yes
Financial Service 3	Credit Bureau	Germany	Yes	Yes	No	Yes
Financial Service 4	Credit Bureaeu	Germany	Yes	Yes	Yes	Yes
Financial Service 5	Credit Bureau	Germany	Yes	No	No	Yes
Financial Service 6	Credit Bureau	Germany	Yes	No	No	Yes
Financial Service 7	Credit Bureau	Germany	Yes	No	No	Yes
Adress Service 1	Adress Broker	Germany	Yes	Yes	No	Yes
Government Service	Federal Bureau	Germany	Yes	No	No	Yes

an attacker obtains sensitive data like financial or healthcare information. For example, it is possible to obtain access to health data like blood type, HIV status, or if blood has been donated and where. This is critical private data and should never be handed out to a spoofed request. Our study shows that it is easily possible to steal data from various services to do so with a spoofed mail or postal address according to our attack scheme shown in Fig. 1. Here is an exemplary list of data we were able to obtain:

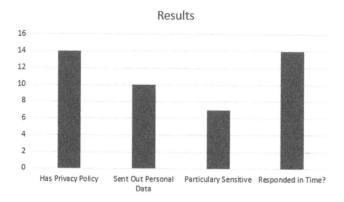

Fig. 2. Results of empirical study of GDPiRate attack.

- Health data
- Complete bank details (IBAN/BIC)
- Credit scores
- Business registration history
- Debt collection information
- Complete train travel history of the last 12 months
- Date of birth

In two cases, we were able to observe that the integrity of the data changed. Our request to the spoofed address changed or added the spoofed address in the control SAR response.

Especially health and financial data is critical since they clarify as special data category according to the GDPR. We also obtained other types of data that can be used for fraudulent activities by criminals and should therefore be mitigated. Every bit of analog information is valuable for an attacker because it can be referenced forever. For example, if a person has a heart condition this is unlikely to change and if a person lived at a certain address paying with a certain bank account, this data will likely not change either. Digitally generated data can be used and deleted later, but every data point that has its source in the real world cannot be deleted electronically.

We were able to access the whole train travel history including payment details, real address and more metadata like mobile numbers, employment information, and profession of one of the authors. The travel data we were able to send to a spoofed address is depicted in Fig. 3. Some data is redacted due to privacy reasons. This data was sent to the spoofed address. This is especially critical in doxing scenarios and a starting point for every information-based attack such as (spear)phishing.

We used the CVSS framework to rate our vulnerability. Of course, CVSS is normally used to describe software vulnerabilities, but we describe our attack using this framework as well [34]. We get a score of 8.2 (High) for GDPiRate. The CVSS string is:

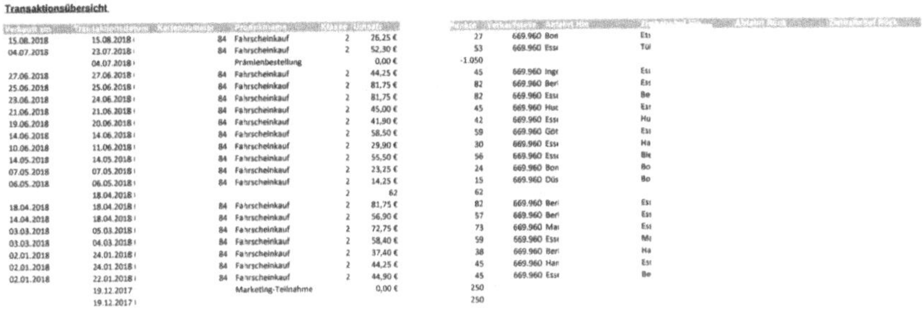

Transaktionsübersicht

15.08.2018	15.08.2018	84	Fahrscheinkauf	2	26,25 €	27	669.960	Bon	Es
04.07.2018	23.07.2018	84	Fahrscheinkauf	2	52,30 €	53	669.960	Ess	Tü
	04.07.2018		Prämienbestellung		0,00 €	-1.050			
27.06.2018	27.06.2018	84	Fahrscheinkauf	2	44,25 €	45	669.960	Ing	Es
25.06.2018	25.06.2018	84	Fahrscheinkauf	2	81,75 €	82	669.960	Ber	Es
23.06.2018	24.06.2018	84	Fahrscheinkauf	2	81,75 €	82	669.960	Ess	Be
21.06.2018	21.06.2018	84	Fahrscheinkauf	2	45,00 €	45	669.960	Huc	Es
19.06.2018	20.06.2018	84	Fahrscheinkauf	2	41,90 €	42	669.960	Ess	Hu
14.06.2018	14.06.2018	84	Fahrscheinkauf	2	58,50 €	59	669.960	Göt	Es
10.06.2018	11.06.2018	84	Fahrscheinkauf	2	29,90 €	30	669.960	Ess	Ha
14.05.2018	14.05.2018	84	Fahrscheinkauf	2	55,50 €	56	669.960	Ess	Bi
07.05.2018	07.05.2018	84	Fahrscheinkauf	2	23,25 €	24	669.960	Bon	Bo
06.05.2018	06.05.2018	84	Fahrscheinkauf	2	14,25 €	15	669.960	Düs	Bo
	18.04.2018			2	62	62			
18.04.2018	18.04.2018	84	Fahrscheinkauf	2	81,75 €	82	669.960	Ber	Es
14.04.2018	18.04.2018	84	Fahrscheinkauf	2	56,90 €	57	669.960	Ber	Es
03.03.2018	05.03.2018	84	Fahrscheinkauf	2	72,75 €	73	669.960	Ma	Es
03.03.2018	04.03.2018	84	Fahrscheinkauf	2	58,40 €	59	669.960	Ess	M
02.01.2018	24.01.2018	84	Fahrscheinkauf	2	37,40 €	38	669.960	Ber	Ha
02.01.2018	24.01.2018	84	Fahrscheinkauf	2	44,25 €	45	669.960	Han	Es
02.01.2018	22.01.2018	84	Fahrscheinkauf	2	44,90 €	45	669.960	Ess	Be
	19.12.2017		Marketing-Teilnahme		0,00 €	250			
	19.12.2017					250			

Fig. 3. Travel history sent to spoofed mailbox

CVSS:3.0/AV:N/AC:L/PR:N/UI:R/S:C/C:H/I:L/A:N/E:F/RL:W/RC:C/CR:H/IR:H/AR:M.

We defined the attack vector as *network* because we can trigger the attack via mail, letter, or fax from anywhere in the world. This is not OSI layer 3 as defined by CVSS, but it is the option that is closest to our attack. All we need is an endpoint to send our SAR to and it is possible to trigger the attack from anywhere in the world as long as the spoofed mailbox is located in the country of the victim. In terms of attack complexity, we rank the vulnerability with *low* because an attacker just needs a name and can send spoofed SARs to the entities. With a success probability of 71% in our study, it is likely that the attack is successful and an adversary can collect personal information in a spoofed mailbox either on- or offline. The attacker needs no privileges to trigger the attack. She can just start the attack and does not need any specific privileges. If an entity is unsure about the identity of the attacker, they will likely request additional verification. A successful attack is dependent on the operator processing the SAR. Therefore we assume that we need user interaction for our attack to be successful in the wild. Our attack strategy does not verify whether a real user interacts with the SAR or everything is automated. The scope changes because we are requesting victim information and data over a third party which processes the spoofed SAR. If we want to request information on victim A, we ask organization B impersonating victim A.

The GDPiRate attack breaks confidentiality of the user data which is especially critical if health, financial, or other personal data is obtained, which is the case in every second spoofed SAR response we obtained. Figure 4 shows a credit score we were able to obtain to a spoofed mailbox.

The integrity of the data can be altered if we can change addresses beforehand, which was the case in two cases. Figure 5 shows a response we received where the spoofed address was used instead of the real author's address. The figure is redacted for privacy reasons. We could not monitor a change of the availability of data.

Ihr aktueller Wahrscheinlichkeitswert (Score):

Zum heutigen Zeitpunkt würden wir folgenden Scorewert zu Ihrer Person ermitteln: **501**

Es handelt sich bei dem Scorewert um den „Basic-Score". Der niedrigste erreichbare Scorewert beträgt 275, der höchste erreichbare Scorewert beträgt 641. Die Erfüllungswahrscheinlichkeit liegt in Ihrem Scoresegment bei 95%. Im Durchschnitt liegt sie bei 91,5%.
In die Berechnung des Scorewertes fließen -in der nachstehenden Reihenfolge und mit absteigender Gewichtung- folgende Daten(arten) ein:

- Adressbezogene Daten (Bekanntsein des Namens bzw. des Haushalts an der Adresse, Anzahl bekannter Personen im Haushalt (Haushaltsstruktur), Bekanntsein der Adresse)
- Anschriftendaten (Informationen zu vertragswidrigem Zahlungsverhalten in Ihrem Wohnumfeld (Straße/Haus))
- Personenbezogene Daten (Ihr Geschlecht, Ihr Alter)

Fig. 4. Credit score sent to spoofed mailbox

Personendaten:

Unser Unternehmen hat zu Ihrer Person folgende Daten gespeichert:
Vor- und Nachname:
Straße und Hausnummer: Changed Spoofed Address
PLZ und Ort:
Geburtsdatum:

Fig. 5. Integrity of data is altered

The data we gathered during our case study is very valuable to an attacker that wants to phish, spear phish, social engineer, or dox a victim. An attacker could use the data she obtains through the GDPiRate attack to attack a user in a private or business context. The attack is very targeted but can have devastating effects on single users and organizations. Note that our attack gives away very specific information about single targets, while being totally unsophisticated. All an attacker needs to do is set up a spoofed mailbox electronically or in the real world. Reconnaissance and information gathering is an important step in successful social engineering attacks. Especially individual, non-generic information like the information we gather with GDPiRrate can provide valuable information to an attacker because she has correct information about her victims.

6 Mitigation

Mitigating our attack is not trivial given that the underlying problem is not on the technical level. We combine off- and online identities with on- and offline communication channels and it turns out that these cannot be easily verified in the same system apparently. In most cases, a holistic approach to the connection and verification of on- and offline identities is needed, but there is unfortunately no out-of-the-box solution for this at the moment. Another facet is that the detection of spoofing is a hard problem even in the digital realm. A recent study [26] finds that for example most mail providers offer spoofing detection, but still deliver some spoofed mails to inboxes. If an email is from an unverified sender, only nine out of 35 mail providers provide visual clues for the end user.

The main problem is that real-world information can be referenced forever and is therefore valuable for all kinds of attackers and attacks. This is not a new insight, but with the informative duty that organizations now have under GDPR, it is important that users and organizations realize that everything that is not a *cryptographic secret* cannot be used as an authorization factor because one cannot expect it to be secret. If cryptographic secrets are not used, but rather something public such as a name and address is used, this can be abused by an adversary as the entry point to a variety of personal information as shown with GDPiRate. As we discussed in the previous section, the attack is easy to exploit and since spoofed emails are a common threat, we cannot rule out that this attack has not been exploited so far in the wild.

Currently there are several projects that try to map an offline identity to an online user or application, e.g., in ecommerce [20] or municipal data [25]. If these research projects are successful, this could be one way to map municipal data to an off- and online persona at least. This could be applied by private data brokers and SAR respondents as well to be sure that an offline entity requesting information can be verified as the digital identity to which the data belongs.

Companies should review their implementation and processes of how user data is accessed and forwarded under a SAR. These processes seem to be implemented incorrectly in many cases. To implement these processes correctly requires organizations to look past the border of securing data online, but also verify the security and privacy of processes and non-digital communication channels in organizations. In the short term, companies should implement precautions and extra steps to avoid sending out private data to any attacker.

The attack can be mitigated if SARs are made within a dedicated web portal or application function. The user identifies via a username/password/2FA combination and is authenticated. The user requests his data using a dedicated function in the application. This prevents the GDPiRate attack most efficiently, because there is a fixed process to gain access to personal data according to the GDPR. If organizations do not have a web portal or application they need to make sure that they provide a robust mechanism to verify the identity of the requester.

One way to mitigate the attack could be to ask for additional information if a data point that is used to identify a user is wrong, for example the recipient address does not conform with the data an organization has. During our case study, one of the companies performed such as check when we requested data with a fake address and persona. In particular, this company obtains data directly from banks where it is required to open a bank account with an identity card. They have a verified data point to which they can fall back if a spoofed SAR is sent to them and request additional information before they send out private data. Such processes could be implemented in other companies as well.

GDPiRate can generally be mitigated by making staff more aware of how privacy can be broken in the analogous world. If staff sees a wrong data point submitted in a SAR, they should request additional data to identify the requesting entity. For example voice recognition on the phone or a holistic identity and verification framework could be used. If voice recognition techniques are used, it should be mentioned that there are ways to break them too as an authentication mechanism, but it would significantly increase the attack complexity for a successful attack [47].

7   Conclusion and Future Work

Mitigating and avoiding GDPiRate is essential for organizations that process personal data, otherwise they could send out private data to a false requestor or get fined according to GDPR guidelines because they did not implement countermeasures to false requests. Even with the GDPR in place and demanding quick response times to SARs, just sending out personal information of a user to an attacker who only uses a spoofed address and another communication channel is clearly problematic. Especially in times where politically-motivated doxing and targeted attacks against organizations and governments using (spear)phishing attacks are on the rise.

Our work has limitations due to the relatively small sample size of fourteen data processors where we requested data with a SAR. We had to make sure that GDPiRate works, while providing integrity of the data we used, since in most cases we were not able to use synthetic data beforehand and used real-world data of one of the authors. Doxing as a service and the commercialization of doxing made it easier to conduct harassment online. An attacker can use a dox-for-hire service to conduct research and compile information about potential victims from as low as $50 [52]. A dox is more valuable the more private, previously undisclosed data it contains. Therefore organizations need to make sure that they do not provide anyone else than the real owner personal data access to the data (as also stated by the GDPR).

Further research should focus on preventing these attacks and to bridge the gap between online and offline identity, while preserving as much privacy as possible for each individual. This work is not intended to pave the road for laws like a planned Austrian law ("Bundesgesetz über Sorgfalt und Verantwortung im Netz - SVN-G"), where users are required to register before they can connect and interact with the Internet and therefore abandoning online privacy completely [37].

In conclusion, it becomes more apparent that a vast research field emerges at the intersection of digital and analog processes and the transformation between an analog process to a digital process is complex in terms of security and privacy. Private data that is stored in an organization needs to be stay private and must be accessible only to the authorized data owner. If the organization offers a digital authentication, it should use this mechanism to provide data only to authenticated users. This would prevent an unauthenticated, spoofed attack like GDPiRate is.

Acknowledgements. This work is partly funded by the Federal Ministry of Education and Research in Germany (Grant. Nr: 16SV7775 and Grant. Nr: 16KIS1016).

Appendix

SAR Text in German

Betreff: Auskunft nach Artikel 15 DSGVO

Sehr geehrte Damen und Herren,
auf der Grundlage von Artikel 15 der Datenschutz-Grundverordnung (DSGVO) verlange ich hiermit Auskunft darüber, ob bei Ihnen personenbezogene Daten über mich gespeichert sind. Falls dies der Fall ist, verlange ich Auskunft über die Informationen nach Artikel 15, Absätze 1 und 2 DSGVO. Bitte stellen Sie mir die gewünschten Informationen gemäßß Artikel 12 Absatz 3 DSGVO innerhalb eines Monats nach Eingang dieses Antrags zur Verfügung. Bei Nichtbeachtung meiner Forderung werde ich mich an eine Datenschutzbehörde wenden. Zudem behalte ich mir weitere rechtliche Schritte vor, die auch die Geltendmachung von Schadenersatzansprüchen nach Artikel 82 DSGVO umfassen.

Mein Name: NAME
Mein Geburtsdatum: GEBURTSDATUM
Meine gegenwärtige Anschrift:
ADRESSE

Mit freundlichen Grüßen
NAME
SIGNATURE

SAR Text translated to English

Subject: Information according to Article 15 GDPR

Dear Sir and Madam,
I hereby request, on the basis of Article 15 of the General Data Protection Regulation (GDPR), information about whether personal data about myself are stored by your company. If this is the case, I request information about the stored information based on Article 15, paragraphs 1 and 2 GDPR. Please provide me with the requested information in accordance with Article 12 paragraph 3 GDPR within one month after receipt of this subject access request. In case of failure to comply with my request, I will contact a data protection authority. I also reserve the right to take further legal action, including the assertion of claims for damages under Article 82 GDPR.

My name: NAME
My date of birth: DATE OF BIRTH
My current address:
ADDRESS

Yours sincerely,
SURNAME
SIGNATURE

References

1. Bailey, M., Dittrich, D., Kenneally, E., Maughan, D.: The menlo report. IEEE Secur. Priv. **10**(2), 71–75 (2012)
2. Bélanger, F., Crossler, R.E.: Privacy in the digital age: a review of information privacy research in information systems. MIS Q. **35**(4), 1017–1042 (2011)
3. Benenson, Z., Gassmann, F., Landwirth, R.: Unpacking spear phishing susceptibility. In: Brenner, M., et al. (eds.) FC 2017. LNCS, vol. 10323, pp. 610–627. Springer, Cham (2017). https://doi.org/10.1007/978-3-319-70278-0_39
4. Bundeskriminalamt: Festnahme eines Tatverdächtigen im Ermittlungsverfahren wegen des Verdachts des Ausspähens und der unberechtigten Veröffentlichung personenbezogener Daten, January 2019. https://www.bka.de/DE/Presse/Listenseite_Pressemitteilungen/2019/Presse2019/190108_FestnahmeDatenausspaehung.html
5. Cagnazzo, M., Pohlmann, N.: Using geolocation data as a threat enlargener for social engineering attacks. In: DACH Security (2019)
6. Caputo, D.D., Pfleeger, S.L., Freeman, J.D., Johnson, M.E.: Going spear phishing: exploring embedded training and awareness. IEEE Secur. Priv. **12**(1), 28–38 (2013)
7. Chen, M., Cheung, A.S.Y., Chan, K.L.: Doxing: what adolescents look for and their intentions. Int. J. Environ. Res. Public Health **16**(2), 218 (2019)
8. Degeling, M., Utz, C., Lentzsch, C., Hosseini, H., Schaub, F., Holz, T.: We value your privacy... now take some cookies: measuring the GDPR's impact on web privacy. In: Network and Distributed Systems Security (NDSS) (2018)
9. Dittrich, D., Kenneally, E.: The menlo report: ethical principles guiding information and communication technology research. Technical report, US Department of Homeland Security (2012)
10. Douglas, D.M.: Doxing: a conceptual analysis. Ethics Inf. Technol. **18**(3), 199–210 (2016)
11. Englehardt, S., Narayanan, A.: Online tracking: a 1-million-site measurement and analysis. In: ACM SIGSAC Conference on Computer and Communications Security, CCS 2016, pp. 1388–1401 (2016)
12. Englehardt, S., et al.: Cookies that give you away: the surveillance implications of web tracking. In: International Conference on World Wide Web, WWW 2015, pp. 289–299 (2015)
13. European Commission: Special eurobarometer 431: Data protection, July 2015. http://data.europa.eu/euodp/en/data/dataset/S2075_83_1_431_ENG
14. European Union: Council regulation art. 12 regulation (eu) 2016/679 (2016)
15. European Union: Council regulation art. 15 regulation (eu) 2016/679 (2016)
16. European Union: Council regulation art. 25 regulation (eu) 2016/679 (2016)
17. European Union: Council regulation art. 4 regulation (eu) 2016/679 (2016)
18. European Union: Council regulation art. 9 regulation (eu) 2016/679 (2016)
19. Fuentes, M.R.: Cybercrime and other threats faced by the healthcare industry. Trend Micro (2017)
20. Geodakyan, G.S., Yen, Y.J.S., Foss, R.A., Hardy, J., Broen, W.D., Born, N.M.: Method and system for combining offline and online identities with associated purchasing intention indicators in view of a geographic location, US Patent App. 15/712,036, 18 September 2018
21. Gluck, J., et al.: How short is too short? Implications of length and framing on the effectiveness of privacy notices. In: Symposium on Usable Privacy and Security (SOUPS), pp. 321–340 (2016)

22. Gruss, D., et al.: Use-after-freemail: generalizing the use-after-free problem and applying it to email services. In: Proceedings of the 2018 on Asia Conference on Computer and Communications Security, pp. 297–311. ACM (2018)
23. Harkous, H., Fawaz, K., Lebret, R., Schaub, F., Shin, K.G., Aberer, K.: Polisis: automated analysis and presentation of privacy policies using deep learning. In: 27th USENIX Security Symposium (USENIX Security 18), pp. 531–548 (2018)
24. Hern, A.: Fitness tracking app Strava gives away location of secret US armybases. Guardian, **28** (2018)
25. Hertlein, M.: Digitale identitäten erfolgreich schützen, April 2019. https://www.security-insider.de/digitale-identitaeten-erfolgreich-schuetzen-a-821563/
26. Hu, H., Wang, G.: End-to-end measurements of email spoofing attacks. In: 27th USENIX Security Symposium, pp. 1095–1112 (2018)
27. Jansen, F.: Verdächtiger nennt Ärger über Politiker als Motiv für Datenklau, January 2019. https://m.tagesspiegel.de/politik/datendiebstahl-verdaechtiger-nennt-aerger-ueber-politiker-als-motiv-fuer-datenklau/23838452.html
28. Jensen, C., Potts, C.: Privacy policies as decision-making tools: an evaluation of online privacy notices. In: Proceedings of the SIGCHI Conference on Human Factors in Computing Systems, CHI 2004, pp. 471–478 (2004)
29. Klensin, J., Freed, N., Rose, M., Stefferud, E., Crocker, D.: SMTP service extensions. Technical report, RFC 2846, November 1995
30. Linden, T., Harkous, H., Fawaz, K.: The privacy policy landscape after the GDPR. arXiv preprint arXiv:1809.08396 (2018)
31. Ponemon Institute, LLC: The race to GDPR: a study of companies in the United States & Europe. Technical report, McDermott Will & Emery LLP (2018)
32. Martino, M.D., Robyns, P., Weyts, W., Quax, P., Lamotte, W., Andries, K.: Personal information leakage by abusing the GDPR right of access. In: Symposium on Usable Privacy and Security (SOUPS) (2019)
33. Matwyshyn, A.M., Cui, A., Keromytis, A.D., Stolfo, S.J.: Ethics in security vulnerability research. IEEE Secur. Priv. **8**(2), 67–72 (2010)
34. Mell, P., Scarfone, K., Romanosky, S.: Common vulnerability scoring system. IEEE Secur. Priv. **4**(6), 85–89 (2006)
35. Mueller, R.: Report on the investigation into Russian interference in the 2016 presidential election. US Dept. of Justice. Washington, DC (2019)
36. Ollmann, G.: The phishing guide-understanding & preventing phishing attacks. NGS Software Insight Security Research (2004)
37. Österreich, N.: Entwurf bundesgesetz über sorgfalt und verantwortung im netz (2019). https://cdn.netzpolitik.org/wp-upload/2019/04/Digitales-Vermummungsverbot-Gesetzesentwurf.pdf
38. Papageorgiou, A., Strikos, M., Politou, E., Alepis, E., Solanas, A., Patsakis, C.: Security and privacy analysis of mobile health applications: the alarming state of practice. IEEE Access **6**, 9390–9403 (2018)
39. Pascual, A., Marchini, K.: 2018 child identity fraud study, April 2018. https://www.javelinstrategy.com/coverage-area/2018-child-identity-fraud-study
40. Pollach, I.: What's wrong with online privacy policies? Commun. ACM **50**(9), 103–108 (2007)
41. Proofpoint: Social media brand protection fraud (2017). https://www.proofpoint.com/sites/default/files/pfpt-en-social-media-protection-brand-fraud-report.pdf
42. Protenus: 2017 breach barometer annual report (2017). https://www.protenus.com/2017-breach-barometer-annual-report
43. Rasthofer, S., Huber, S., Arzt, S.: All your family secrets belong to us - worrisome security issues in tracker apps. In: DEF CON 26 (2018)

44. Roesner, F., Kohno, T., Wetherall, D.: Detecting and defending against third-party tracking on the web. In: Presented as part of the 9th USENIX Symposium on Networked Systems Design and Implementation (NSDI), pp. 155–168 (2012)
45. Schneier, B.: Doxing as an attack, January 2015. https://www.schneier.com/blog/archives/2015/01/doxing_as_an_at.html
46. Secureworks Counter Threat Unit Threat Intelligence: Threat Group 4127 Targets Hillary Clinton Presidential Campaign, June 2016. https://www.secureworks.com/research/threat-group-4127-targets-hillary-clinton-presidential-campaign
47. Seymour, J., Aqil, A.: Your voice is my passport. In: DEF Con 26 (2018)
48. Snyder, P., Doerfler, P., Kanich, C., McCoy, D.: Fifteen minutes of unwanted fame: detecting and characterizing doxing. In: Internet Measurement Conference, IMC 2017, pp. 432–444 (2017)
49. New York Times: An old swindle revived, March 1898. https://www.nytimes.com/1898/03/20/archives/an-old-swindle-revived-the-spanish-prisoner-and-buried-treasure.html
50. TrendLabs Security Intelligence: Operation Pawn Storm Ramps Up its Activities. Targets NATO, White House (2015)
51. Urban, T., Tatang, D., Degeling, M., Holz, T., Pohlmann, N.: The unwanted sharing economy: an analysis of cookie syncing and user transparency under GDPR. arXiv preprint arXiv:1811.08660 (2018)
52. Web Investigations: Investigation and Doxing Prices, July 2019. https://doxanybody.wordpress.com/category/investigation-and-doxing-prices/
53. Yeboah-Boateng, E.O., Amanor, P.M.: Phishing, smishing & vishing: an assessment of threats against mobile devices. J. Emerg. Trends Comput. Inf. Sci. 5(4), 297–307 (2014)

Location Privacy-Preserving Mobile Crowd Sensing with Anonymous Reputation

Xun Yi[1]([⊠]), Kwok-Yan Lam[2], Elisa Bertino[3], and Fang-Yu Rao[3]

[1] RMIT University, Melbourne, Australia
xun.yi@rmit.edu.au
[2] Nanyang Technological University, Jurong West, Singapore
kwokyan.lam@ntu.edu.sg
[3] Purdue University, West Lafayette, USA
bertino@purdue.edu

Abstract. In this paper, we give a location privacy-preserving solution for the mobile crowd sensing (MCS) system. The solution makes use of the blind signature technique for anonymous authentication and allows a mobile user to participate in the MCS for certain times set in the registration. Furthermore, we introduce a concept of anonymous reputation for mobile users on the basis of the blind signature technique as well. An anonymous reputation can be referred by the MCS platform when assigning tasks to a mobile user and can be upgraded or downgraded by the MCS platform, depending on the quality of reports submitted by the mobile user. For the security analysis, we provide security proofs for our solution on the basis of our formal definitions for anonymity, unlinkability and unforgeability for MCS. The performance analysis and experiments have shown that our solution is more efficient than existing solutions for MCS based on the blind signature technique.

Keywords: Mobile crowd sensing · Location privacy protection · Anonymity · Blind signature · Reputation

1 Introduction

An emerging category of devices at the edge of the Internet are consumer-centric mobile sensing and computing devices, such as smartphones, music players, and in-vehicle sensors. These devices will fuel the evolution of the Internet of Things as they feed sensor data to the Internet at a societal scale [14]. Mobile crowd sensing (MCS) has been gaining popularity, with several systems and applications being proposed to leverage users' mobile devices to measure environmental context. The building blocks of an MCS are the central authority that provides the application (the platform) and the participants (the users) that contribute their collected data. Applications of MCS include monitoring city noise, city climate, people density, emergency behavior, traffic anomalies and even detecting earthquakes [15,16].

© Springer Nature Switzerland AG 2019
K. Sako et al. (Eds.): ESORICS 2019, LNCS 11736, pp. 387–411, 2019.
https://doi.org/10.1007/978-3-030-29962-0_19

One of the most significant advantages of these MCS applications is that given the large number of existing cellular users, they have the potential to collect data like never before and from places not economically feasible before, and in a fast, easy, and cost-effective manner. For example, traffic congestion applications with MCS have the potential to collect real-time data not only from main interstate roads but also from secondary and even tertiary roads, something that is very costly using current technologies. Deploying static sensors over all roads will be economically expensive in terms of capital, installation and maintenance costs.

The MCS data is usually tagged with locations of mobile users. Mobile users' locations are vulnerable to malicious attacks. Even if mobile users are protected by fake identities like pseudonym, an adversary can utilize their locations to infer the private information, such as political affiliations, alternative lifestyles, or medical problems. Therefore, it is especially essential to achieve location privacy protection.

Location privacy has been vastly studied in Location Based Service (LBS) and crowd sensing system, where the servers or platforms are often regarded untrusted. To preserve location privacy, various methods were proposed to prevent the servers or platforms inferring users' exact locations. Some surveys on location privacy-preserving mechanisms for MCS have been done in [10,31]. In terms of the underlying techniques for building MCS with location privacy protection, current solutions can be classified into: k-anonymity based, blind signature based, and group signature based.

In the existing solutions for location privacy protection in MCS, there are some problems, summarized as follows:

- Trusted third party problem: k-anonymity based solutions [30,32] assume the existence of a trusted third party (TTP) between mobile users and the platform. The TTP knows the exact locations of mobile users and performs location data perturbation before forwarding it to the platform. It is hard to ensure the TTP security against hackers.
- Linkability problem: Blind signature based solution [21] allows the platform to trace mobile users with the same certified pseudonym. In some applications, it may not be acceptable for privacy concern. The problem can be overcome by using multiple blind signatures, each of them can be used once only. But a mobile user has to keep many blind signatures. Ramzan and Ruhl [26] suggested a method to reduce the number of blind signatures.
- Secret sharing problem: In the solutions [20,28] based on group signature, a mobile user is issued by the platform a kind of secret to prove to the platform the eligibility for participation in MCS. A dishonest mobile user may share the secret with others. Although this problem also exists in blind signature based solutions, it is not serious because a blind signature can be used once only.

The above problems are interdependent. It is a challenge to provide a solution for MCS to overcome all the problems.

Besides the location privacy issue, recent research in MCS finds another important challenge: the need to understand user intentions and to quantify their reputation. A user might simply think that an MCS application is not good for the community and protest it by contributing incorrect data intentionally or might have a faulty mobile device that takes imprecise or wrong measurements. Trustworthiness of the collected data is a primary concern for both the platform and the end users who request sensed data as a service [2].

Current research on the reputation of mobile user has not considered the location privacy for mobile users. To protect the location privacy of mobile users in MCS, the mobile users have to perform anonymous authentication with the MCS platform. Due to the anonymity requirement, it is difficult for the MCS platform to score user reputation. It is a challenge to make use of user reputation in MCS with user location privacy and unlinkability.

Our Contribution. In this paper, we propose a new solution to protect location privacy for mobile users in MCS. Our solution is built on the blind signature technique.

The basic idea for anonymous authentication is as follows: At first, the platform issues a mobile user a blind signature on the times that the user can participate in MCS, so called anonymous certificate. When the mobile user wishes to participate in MCS, he submits the anonymous certificate to the platform for authentication and then the platform returns him a new anonymous certificate, a blind signature on the remaining times that the user can participate in MCS. During the authentication, the platform and the user agree on a secret key to protect information exchanged later, such tasks, reports, etc. After the user submits the reports, the platform rewards the user with e-cash. The user can spend the e-cash anonymously.

In addition, we introduce a new concept of anonymous reputation to improve MCS performance. The basic idea for anonymous reputation is similar to the basic idea for anonymous authentication. Each time when the mobile user submits the report, the platform issues a blind signature on the level of the user reputation, so-called anonymous reputation, on the basis of the quality of the report. Next, when the user wishes to participate in MCS, he submits his anonymous reputation to the platform for reference. The platform usually assigns a task to the user with the highest level of anonymous reputation.

Our solution has the following security properties:

- Anonymity. The MCS platform cannot determine any mobile user's identity when the user participates in MCS.
- Unlinkability. The MCS platform cannot determine whether two anonymous certificates belong to the same mobile user.
- Unforgeability. A mobile user cannot forge any anonymous certificate or any anonymous reputation to obtain more than the specified number of MCS accesses or a reputation higher than the specified level. Even if several mobile users collude (by sharing their anonymous certificates and anonymous reputation) they cannot obtain more MCS accesses than they are paid for as a group or higher level of reputation than they are awarded for as a group.

In addition, our solution has the following system properties:

- Limited Access: The number of MCS accesses is limited. That is, the mobile user is allowed to access the MCS system only a specified number of times. After that his access privileges (implicitly, i.e. without any communication among the platform and users) terminate.
- Unshareable: It is impossible to share a single anonymous certificate or a single anonymous reputation among two or more mobile users.

Our basic idea for anonymous authentication is motivated by [26], where two solutions were proposed. In the first solution, a user needs to keep a number of blind signatures, which is the bit length of the times that the user can access the system, and the user keeps track of the remaining subscription length, and shows only part of that information to the supplier when accessing the service. The second solution adopts signatures of knowledge [6] that enable a user to prove to the server that user is in possession of a valid RSA blind signature of the server on the user's public key. Although a user only has to keep a constant number secrets, i.e., his secret key as well as the blind signature, the invocation of the protocol proving the knowledge of both his secret key and the blind signature incurs a lot of computational overhead. However, in our solution, a user needs to keep one blind signature only and submits one blind signature to the platform for authentication. Therefore, in terms of anonymous authentication, our solution is more efficient than [26].

In addition, in our solution, for authentication, a mobile user submits an anonymous certificate to the platform and obtains a new anonymous certificate from the platform. This idea is similar to [3]. But [3] requires to run the zero-knowledge proof between the user and the server for authentication, while our solution needs to verify a blind signature only. Thus, in terms of anonymous authentication, our solution is also more efficient than [3].

Organization. The rest of our paper is organized as follows. We survey the related works in Sect. 2. Then we give the security definitions in Sect. 3, describe the proposed solution in Sect. 4, and analyze the security and performance for the proposed protocols in Sect. 5. Conclusions are drawn in the last section.

2   Related Works

A popular approach to preserving privacy of user's data is anonymization [29], which removes any identifying information from the sensor data before sharing it with a third party. k-anonymity is a property possessed by certain anonymized data. A release of data is said to have the k-anonymity property if the information for each person contained in the release cannot be distinguished from at least $k-1$ individuals whose information also appear in the release. Regarding k-anonymity of location privacy, at least k users' locations are mixed into a group, in which an adversary cannot distinguish one user's location from the rest of others'. In the scenario of MCS system, the MCS server may be malicious, thus directly exposing users' raw locations is harmful to the location privacy. A trusted third party, which is a cellular service provider, is supposed to protect the location privacy and process the sensory data.

In 2014, To et al. [30] proposed a framework for protecting privacy of worker locations in MCS. In their framework, every worker subscribes to a cellular service provider (CSP) that has access to the worker locations. The CSP sanitizes the worker locations dataset using the powerful differential privacy model [13]. First, workers send their locations to the trusted CSP which builds and releases a Private Spatial Decomposition (PSD) according to a privacy budget ϵ mutually agreed upon with the workers. A PSD [11] is a spatial index transformed according to differential privacy, where each index node is obtained by releasing a noisy count of the data points enclosed by that node's extent. When the MCS server has a task t, it queries the PSD to determine a geocast region (GR) that encloses with high probability workers in relative proximity to t. Next, the MCS server initiates a geocast communication [23] process to disseminate t to all workers within the GR.

In 2017, Wang et al. [32] considered how to incentivize mobile users to participate in MCS while preserving their location privacy. To reduce the risk of location privacy disclosure, they utilized k-anonymity. Their basic idea is: (1) Users report their locations to a trusted third party for location privacy protection. Along with those locations, the users will also claim costs for taking the sensing tasks; (2) The trusted third party is supposed to perform aggregation on the locations and interact with an untrusted crowd sensing platform. In view of k-anonymity privacy, the trusted third party constructs groups with each group size no less than k. Based on the group aggregation results, group values and group costs will be computed; (3) According to group values and costs, the crowd sensing platform selects the winning groups and calculate corresponding group payments; (4) The users in winning groups are winning users, and their payments will be computed based on group payments; (5) Winning users will undertake the sensing tasks, and the trusted third party will process the sensory results within the same groups, such as computing the mean values; (6) The processed sensory data tagged with groups centroids will be uploaded to the crowd sensing platform; (7) The crowd sensing platform pays the winning users the determined values through the trusted third party according to (3) and (4). k-anonymity based MCS is efficient, however, it assumes the existence of a trusted third party which knows the exact locations of mobile users. It may be hard to ensure a trusted third party security against hackers.

The second approach to preserving lcation privacy in MCS is based on blind signature [8]. A blind signature is a form of digital signature in which the content of a message is disguised (blinded) before it is signed. The resulting blind signature can be publicly verified against the original, unblinded message in the manner of a regular digital signature.

In 2013, Konidala et al. [21] proposed the anonymous authentication of visitors protocol to authenticate the information reported by a visitor inside a thematic park without divulging the visitor's identity. The protocol protects the visitors' location privacy with the partially blind signature [1]. A partially blind signature here has two portions: one portion consists of the message that is hidden by the user (e.g., demographic details, such as age, gender, nationality, height, dietary restrictions and other health issues, as well as preferences for rides; must go and must skip attractions and etc.) and in the other portion, the signer can explicitly embed necessary information such as issuing date, expiry date, signer's identity and etc.). The protocol is executed in two phases: (1) certified pseudonym issuing phase, and (2) subsequent interaction phase. In the first phase, the visitor generates a pseudonym P and utilizes a partially blind signature to hide P in a blinded message B, which is sent to the park operator. The operator inputs an expiry date while digitally signing B. In the end of this phase, the visitor derives a certified pseudonym (i.e., blind signature). In the second phase, before the expiry date, the visitor can send the certified pseudonym to the operator repeatedly to receive the optimal route, and the dynamically calibrated personalized time slots for various attractions in the park, as well as rewards.

Because the operator has no clue about visitor's pseudonym in the first phase, he cannot link the pseudonym to the visitor in the second phase. But the operator is able to trace the visitor with the same pseudonym. For some applications, the linkability may not be allowed.

The third approach for location privacy protection in MCS is based on group signature. A group signature scheme is a method for allowing a member of a group to anonymously sign a message on behalf of the group. The concept was first introduced by David Chaum and Eugene van Heyst in 1991 [9]. For example, a group signature scheme could be used by an employee of a large company where it is sufficient for a verifier to know a message was signed by an employee, but not which particular employee signed it.

AnonySense [20, 28] is an MCS system based on group signature. The system periodically posts the tasking campaign and when the participants are in public locations, locations considered by the participant as nonsensitive ones, they download all available tasks from a tasking service. For each connection, the participant performs an anonymous authentication, based on a group signature defined by direct anonymous attestation [5], in order to prove to the system that it is a valid participant, but without revealing its identity. Therefore, the system only learns that some participants are in public locations but nothing else, which is the main advantage of this system. However, its main drawback is that, since the system only learns that some users are in public locations, the system cannot predict how many users are likely to visit a particular region and guarantee a good inference and data analysis. In addition, some users may share their secret key with others, which results that unauthorized users can also participate in MCS without registration.

On the reputation of mobile users in MCS, Kantarci et al. [18] proposed data trustworthiness assurance in user incentivization using statistical-based and recommendation - based user reputation-awareness methods, and a Social Network-Assisted Trustworthiness Assurance (SONATA) [19], which is a recommendation-based approach to identify malicious users who manipulate sensor readings to spread disinformation. SONATA adopts a vote-based trust-worthiness analysis to minimize the manipulation probability in an MCS framework. Pouryazdan et al. [24] introduced anchor nodes, which are deployed as trusted entities in an MCS system in order to improve the platform and user utility by eliminating adversaries at the end of a recommendation-based user recruitment process. Pouryazdan et al. [25] also introduce a new metric - collaborative reputation scores. Ren et al. [27] proposed a participant selection method to choose well-suited users for assigning tasks as well as to consider a reputation management scheme to evaluate the trustworthiness of the contributed data. These works on the reputation of mobile user have not considered the location privacy.

3   Security Model

In this section, we define the security of location privacy-preserving (LPP) protocol for MCS with anonymous reputation as follows.

Participants, Initialization, Registration. An LPP protocol involves two kinds of protocol participants: (1) An MCS platform P, which provides MCS service, authenticates mobile users, assigns tasks to mobile users on the basis of their reputation, receives reports from the mobile users, and pays the mobile users for their reports and scores their reputation. (2) A group of mobile users $U_1, U_2, \cdots, U_n$, who participates in MCS, receives tasks from the platform, submits reports to the the platforms, and receives payment from the platform.

Prior to any execution of the protocol, we assume that an initialization phase occurs. During initialization, the platform generates public parameters for the protocol, which are available to all participants.

We assume that each mobile user U_i, runs a registration protocol, with the MCS platform P. During registration, the MCS platform issues an anonymous certificate (i.e., a blind signature) and an anonymous reputation (i.e., a blind signature) at level 1 to the user.

Execution of the Protocol. After registration, a mobile user U_i can run the LPP protocol with the MCS platform P. The protocol includes three phases as follows.

- Authentication: When a mobile user wishes to participate in MCS, he submits his anonymous certificate and location to the MCS platform for authentication. The platform checks if the anonymous certificate has been used before. If not, the mobile user and the MCS platform agree on a secret key to protect information exchanged later.
  Remark: Like a blind signature, each anonymous certificate can be used once only. We assume that the MCS platform keeps all used anonymous certificates in its database.
- Task assignment: The platform sends a list of tasks (near the location of the user) with costs to the mobile user. The user chooses a task and submits his anonymous reputation to the platform if any. The platform check

if the anonymous reputation has been used before. If there are several users to compete for one task, the platform assigns the task to the user with the highest level of reputation. The information exchanged in this phase is protected with a secret key agreed on in the authentication phase.

Remark: Like an anonymous certificate, each anonymous reputation can be used once only. We assume that the MCS platform keeps all used anonymous reputation in its database.

– Report and Reward: The mobile user performs the task at the specified location and sends a report back to the MCS platform. The report is protected with a secret key agreed on in the authentication phase. After checking the report, the MCS platform rewards the mobile user with bitcoins. In addition, the platform upgrades or downgrades the reputation of the user accordingly.

Now we define the anonymity for mobile users. To define the anonymity for mobile users, we assume that the MCS platform is malicious and attempts to reveal the identity of a mobile user in the protocol.

We use a game to formally define the anonymity. In the game, suppose that the adversary $\mathcal{A}$ (i.e., the MCS platform) chooses two mobile users U_0 and U_1 from all users, and the challenger $\mathcal{C}$ randomly chooses a bit b and runs the LPP protocol with the adversary $\mathcal{A}$ on behalf of the mobile user U_b. As defined in the LPP protocol, the adversary $\mathcal{A}$ is able to view all messages exchanged with the mobile user U_b, including authentication, task assignment, report and reward messages from the mobile user U_b. In the end, the adversary outputs a bit b' (i.e., his guess about the bit b chosen by the challenger).

The adversary $\mathcal{A}$ wins the game if $b' = b$. The probability of the adversary $\mathcal{A}$ winning the game is called the advantage of the adversary $\mathcal{A}$ in attacking the anonymity of the LPP protocol, denoted as $\mathsf{AnonymityAdv}_{\mathcal{A}}^{LPP}(k)$, where k is a security parameter.

Definition 1. An LPP protocol has anonymity for mobile users if for any Probabilistic Polynomial Time (PPT) adversary $\mathcal{A}$, there is a negligible function $\epsilon(\cdot)$, such that $|\mathsf{AnonymityAdv}_{\mathcal{A}}^{LPP}(k) - 1/2| < \epsilon(k)$, where k is a security parameter.

Next we define the unlinkability for the mobile user. We also assume that the MCS platform is malicious and attempts to link two accesses from the same mobile user.

We use a game to formally define the unlinkability. In the game, suppose that the adversary $\mathcal{A}$ (i.e., the MCS platform) chooses two mobile users U_0 and U_1 from all users, and the challenger $\mathcal{C}$ runs the LPP protocol with the adversary $\mathcal{A}$ on behalf of the mobile user U_0 and U_1, respectively, and also discloses the corresponding identities of the mobile users communicating with the adversary $\mathcal{A}$. Next, the challenger $\mathcal{C}$ randomly chooses a bit b and runs the LPP protocol with the adversary $\mathcal{A}$ on behalf of the mobile user U_b without telling b to the adversary. As defined in the LPP protocol, the adversary $\mathcal{A}$ is able to view all messages exchanged with the mobile user U_b. In the end, the adversary outputs a bit b' (i.e., his guess about the bit b chosen by the challenger).

The adversary $\mathcal{A}$ wins the game if $b' = b$. The probability of the adversary $\mathcal{A}$ winning the game is called the advantage of the adversary $\mathcal{A}$ in attacking the unlinkability of the LPP protocol, denoted as $\mathsf{UnlinkabilityAdv}_{\mathcal{A}}^{LPP}(k)$, where k is a security parameter.

Definition 2. An LPP protocol has unlinkability for mobile users if for any PPT adversary $\mathcal{A}$, there is a negligible function $\epsilon(\cdot)$, such that $|\mathsf{UnlinkabilityAdv}_{\mathcal{A}}^{LPP}(k) - 1/2| < \epsilon(k)$, where k is a security parameter.

At last, we define the unforgeability for the MCS platform. To define the unforgeability, we assume that a group of mobile users are malicious and attempt to forge an anonymous certificate or an anonymous reputation to obtain more than the specified number of MCS accesses or a reputation higher than the specified level.

We also use a game to formally define the unforgeability. In the game, suppose that the adversary $\mathcal{A}$ (i.e., the group of malicious mobile users) is provided with t anonymous certificates or anonymous reputations. If the adversary $\mathcal{A}$ can forge any new anonymous certificate or anonymous reputation, the adversary wins the game. The probability of the adversary $\mathcal{A}$ winning the game is called the advantage of the adversary $\mathcal{A}$ attacking the unforgeability of the LPP protocol, denoted as $\mathsf{UnforgeabilityAdv}_{\mathcal{A}}^{LPP}(k)$.

Definition 3. An LPP protocol has unforgeability for the MCS platform if for any PPT adversary $\mathcal{A}$, there is negligible function $\epsilon(\cdot)$, such that $\mathsf{UnforgeabilityAdv}_{\mathcal{A}}^{LPP} < \epsilon(k)$, where k is a security parameter.

4 Location Privacy-Preserving Protocol for MCS with Anonymous Reputations

In this section, we describe the initialization (parameter generation) and registration of the LPP protocol at first and then three phases (authentication, task assignment, report and reward) of the protocol.

4.1 Initialization

The initialization performs parameter generation as follows: Given a security parameter $k \in Z$, the MCS platform chooses two large primes $p = 2p' + 1$ and $q = 2q' + 1$, where $p, q > \sqrt{k}$ and (p', q') are primes as well, and computes $N = pq$ and $\phi(N) = (p-1)(q-1) = 4p'q'$. The MCS platform chooses a public key e_a for anonymous certificate and a public key e_r for anonymous reputation, and computes the corresponding private keys d_a and d_r, such that $gcd(e_a, \phi(N)) = 1, gcd(e_r, \phi(N)) = 1$, $e_a d_a = 1(mod\ \phi(N)), e_r d_r = 1(mod\ \phi(N))$. The MCS platform publishes the public key e_a, e_r and N, but keeps the private keys d_a, d_r and p, q secret. In addition, the MCS platform publishes a secure hash function $H : Z \rightarrow Z_N$.

4.2   Registration

Suppose that the mobile user U_i wants to access the MCS system for n times by registration, the user randomly chooses integers r, m, R, M from Z_N^* and computes

$$A_a = r^{(2n+1)e_a} \cdot H(MCS, m)(mod\ N) \tag{1}$$
$$A_r = R^{3e_r} \cdot H(MCS, M)(mod\ N) \tag{2}$$

Then the user sends a registration request including $\{(n, A_a), (1, A_r)\}$ to the MCS platform.

After receiving the registration request, the MCS platform signs the blinded message by computing

$$B_a = A_a^{(2n+1)^{-1}d_a}(mod\ N) = r \cdot H(MCS, m)^{(2n+1)^{-1}d_a}(mod\ N) \tag{3}$$
$$B_r = A_r^{3^{-1}d_r}(mod\ N) = R \cdot H(MCS, M)^{3^{-1}d_r}(mod\ N) \tag{4}$$

and returns B_a, B_r to the mobile user. Note the probability of $gcd(2n + 1, \phi(N)) \neq 1$ or $gcd(3, \phi(N)) \neq 1$ can be ignored because $\phi(N) = 4p'q'$ and p', q' are large primes, and therefore the MCS platform can compute $(2n + 1)^{-1}(mod\ \phi(N))$ and $3^{-1}(mod\ \phi(N))$.

Finally, the user removes the blindness by computing

$$C_a = r^{-1}B_a(mod\ N) = H(MCS, m)^{(2n+1)^{-1}d_a}(mod\ N) \tag{5}$$
$$C_r = R^{-1}B_r(mod\ N) = H(MCS, M)^{3^{-1}d_r}(mod\ N) \tag{6}$$

In the end of registration, the mobile user obtains an anonymous certificate, $\{n, m, C_a\}$, by which the mobile user can participate in MCS for n times, and an anonymous reputation at level 1, $\{1, M, C_r\}$.

Remark. Unless otherwise specified, the user will always verify the blind signature produced by the MCS platform in our protocol.

4.3   Protocol Execution

When a mobile user U_i wishes to participate in MCS to perform any tasks near his location, he initializes a request to run the LPP protocol with the MCS platform and the protocol runs in three phases as follows:

Authentication. Assume that the mobile user U_i has an anonymous certificate $\{\ell, m, C_a\}$, by which the user can participate in MCS for ℓ times, where $\ell \geq 1$.

The mobile user U_i randomly chooses integers r', m', s from Z_N^* and computes

$$D = s^{e_a}(mod\ N) \tag{7}$$
$$k = H(s) \tag{8}$$
$$A_a' = r'^{(2\ell-1)(2\ell+1)e_a}H(MCS, m')(mod\ N) \tag{9}$$

Next, the mobile user encrypts $\{MCS, (\ell, m, C_a), A'_a\}$ with a secret key encryption algorithm, e.g., AES [12], by the secret key k. The encryption result is denoted as $E_k(MCS, (\ell, m, C_a), A'_a)$.

Then, the user submits an authentication request $\{MCS, D, E_k(MCS, (\ell, m, C_a), A'_a)\}$ to a nearby base station for mobile communication. The base station forwards the authentication request together with the location L of the base station to the MCS platform.

Remark. We assume that the mobile user is able to submit his authentication request to the base station anonymously. For example, the mobile user may use a dual SIM smart phone[1]. One SIM is for normal use and another SIM is specially developed for the purpose of MCS. The MCS SIM submits the authentication request to the base station without any additional information by which the base station can identify the mobile user.

After receiving the message $\{MCS, D, E_k(MCS, (\ell, m, C_a), A'_a), L\}$, the MCS platform computes

$$s = D^{d_a} (mod\ N) \tag{10}$$

and $k = H(s)$ and decrypt $E_k(MCS, (\ell, m, C_a), A'_a)$ with the secret key k to obtain $\{\ell, m, C_a\}$. Then the MCS platform checks if $\{\ell, m, C_a\}$ appears in the used anonymous certificate database and if

$$C_a^{(2\ell+1)e_a} = H(MCS, m)(mod\ N). \tag{11}$$

If $\{\ell, m, C_a\}$ does not appear in the used anonymous certificate database and the Eq. (11) holds, the mobile user is authentic and the MCS platform adds $\{\ell, m, C_a\}$ into the used anonymous certificate database. In addition, the MCS platform also keeps $\{D, k, (\ell, m, C_a), A'_a, L\}$ for next two phases of communication with the user U_i. The protocol continues.

If $\{\ell, m, C_a\}$ appears in the used anonymous certificate database or the Eq. (11) does not hold, the protocol terminates.

Task Assignment. After anonymous authentication, the MCS platform returns to the mobile user U_i a list of tasks near the location L and the corresponding costs for the user to choose. This information should be encrypted and decrypted with the secret key k agreed on in the authentication phase if the tasks are confidential.

Without loss of generality, we consider one task assignment to the mobile user U_i. But it is easy to extend it to multiple tasks assignment. There are two cases when the MCS platform assigns a task to the mobile user U_i.

- If there is no task near the user, or the user is not interested in taking any task in the list, the MCS platform computes

$$B'_a = A'_a{}^{(2\ell+1)^{-1}d_a}(mod\ N) = r'^{(2\ell-1)} \cdot H(MCS, m')^{(2\ell+1)^{-1}d_a} \tag{12}$$

---

[1] https://en.wikipedia.org/wiki/Dual_SIM.

and returns B'_a to the mobile user U_i.

The user removes blindness by computing

$$C'_a = r'^{-(2\ell-1)}B'_a(mod\ N) = H(MCS, m')^{(2\ell+1)^{-1}d_a}(mod\ N) \qquad (13)$$

In the end, the user obtains a new anonymous certificate $\{\ell, m', C'_a\}$, by which the user can still participate in MCS for ℓ times. The protocol terminates.

– Assume that the user has an anonymous reputation at the level λ, $\{\lambda, M, C_r\}$, where $\lambda \geq 1$, and wishes to get an assignment to perform a task T, from the list of tasks near his location L, the user randomly chooses integers R', M' from Z_N^* and computes

$$A'_r = R'^{(2\lambda-1)(2\lambda+1)(2\lambda+3)e_r}H(MCS, M') \qquad (14)$$

Then the user sends to the MCS platform a task request including $\{MCS, D, E_k(MCS, (\lambda, M, C_r), A'_r, T)\}$.

Based on D in the task request, the MCS platform uses the corresponding secret key k to decrypt the request to obtain $(\lambda, M, C_r), A'_r, T$. Then the platform checks if the anonymous reputation $\{\lambda, M, C_r\}$ appears in the used anonymous reputation database and if

$$C_r^{(2\lambda+1)e_r} = H(MCS, M)(mod\ N). \qquad (15)$$

(i) If $\{\lambda, M, C_r\}$ does not appear in the used anonymous reputation database, the Eq. (15) holds, and the level of the reputation of any other user requesting the same task T is lower than λ, the platform assigns the task T to the mobile user U_i as follows.

The platform computes

$$B'_a = A'^{(2\ell-1)^{-1}d_a}_a(mod\ N) = r'^{(2\ell+1)} \cdot H(MCS, m')^{(2\ell-1)^{-1}d_a} \qquad (16)$$

and generates a signature δ on $\{MCS, (\ell, m, C_a), A'_a, (\lambda, M, C_r), A'_r, T\}$, that is,

$$\delta = H(MCS, (\ell, m, C_a), A'_a, (\lambda, M, C_r), A'_r, T)^{d_r} \qquad (17)$$

Then the platform returns $\{(\ell - 1, B'_a), \delta\}$ to the user U_i and appends $(\lambda, M, C_r), A'_r$ to $\{D, k, (\ell, m, C_a), A'_a, L\}$ for next phase of communication with the user U_i.

The user removes blindness by computing

$$C'_a = r'^{-(2\ell+1)}B'_a(mod\ N) = H(MCS, m')^{(2\ell-1)^{-1}d_a}(mod\ N) \qquad (18)$$

The user then obtains a new anonymous certificate $\{\ell - 1, m', C'_a\}$, by which the user can only participate in MCS for $\ell - 1$ times.

In addition, the user checks if

$$\delta^{e_r} = H(MCS, (\ell, m, C_a), A'_a, (\lambda, M, C_r), A'_r, T) \qquad (19)$$

If the Eq. (19) holds, the task assignment for T is confirmed and the user then performs the task T. The protocol continues.

(ii) If $\{\lambda, M, C_r\}$ does not appear in the used anonymous reputation database and the Eq. (15) holds, but the level of the reputation of some user requesting the task T is higher than λ, the platform computes B'_a as the Eq. (12) and

$$B'_r = A'^{(2\lambda+1)^{-1}d_r}_r (mod\ N) = R'^{(2\lambda-1)(2\lambda+3)} \cdot H(MCS, M')^{(2\lambda+1)^{-1}d_r} \quad (20)$$

Then the platform informs the user that no task is available and returns (ℓ, B'_a) and (λ, B'_r). With (ℓ, B'_a), the user can compute C'_a as the Eq. (13), and with (λ, B'_r), the user can compute

$$C'_r = R'^{-(2\lambda-1)(2\lambda+3)} B'_r (mod\ N) = H(MCS, M')^{(2\lambda+1)^{-1}d_r} (mod\ N) \quad (21)$$

In the end, the user obtains a new anonymous certificate $\{\ell, m', C'_a\}$, by which the user can still participate in MCS for ℓ times, and a new anonymous reputation still at the level λ, $\{\lambda, M', C'_r\}$. The protocol terminates.

(iii) If $\{\lambda, M, C_r\}$ appears in the used anonymous reputation database or the Eq. (15) does not hold, the protocol terminates.

Report and Reward. After the mobile user U_i performs the task T, he writes a task report (e.g., the photos taken at an accident scene near the location L), encrypts it with the secret key k (agreed on in the authentication phase), and submits the encrypted report to the platform.

After receiving the encrypted report, the platform decrypts it with the secret key k to obtain the task report.

The MCS platform may assign the task T to multiple mobile users and compare the quality of their task reports. Based on the report from the mobile user U_i, the MCS platform rewards the mobile user with bitcoins. In this way, the MCS platform cannot even reveal the identity of the user when the user spends the bitcoin later.

Next, the MCS platform generates a new anonymous reputation for the mobile user in three cases as follows:

– If the MCS platform thinks that the reputation of the mobile user should be upgraded, the MCS platform computes

$$B'_r = A'^{(2\lambda+3)^{-1}d_r}_r (mod\ N) = R'^{(2\lambda-1)(2\lambda+1)} H(MCS, M')^{(2\lambda+3)^{-1}d_r} \quad (22)$$

and returns $(\lambda + 1, B'_r)$ to the mobile user. The mobile user removes the blindness by computing

$$C'_r = R'^{-(2\lambda-1)(2\lambda+1)} B'_r (mod\ N) = H(MCS, M')^{(2\lambda+3)^{-1}d_r} \quad (23)$$

and obtains a new anonymous reputation at level $\lambda+1$, $\{\lambda+1, M', C'_r\}$. The protocol terminates.

- If the MCS platform thinks that the reputation of the mobile user should be kept without change, the MCS platform computes B'_r as the Eq. (20) and returns (λ, B'_r) to the users. Then the user removes the blindness by computing C'_r as the Eq. (21). In the end, the user obtains a new anonymous reputation still at level λ, $\{\lambda, M', C'_r\}$. The protocol terminates.
- If the MCS platform thinks that the reputation of the mobile user should be downgraded, the MCS platform computes

$$B'_r = A'^{(2\lambda-1)^{-1}d_r}_r (mod\ N) = R'^{(2\lambda+1)(2\lambda+3)} H(MCS, M')^{(2\lambda-1)^{-1}d_r} \quad (24)$$

and returns $(\lambda - 1, B'_r)$ to the mobile user. The mobile user removes the blindness by computing

$$C'_r = R'^{-(2\lambda+1)(2\lambda+3)} B'_r (mod\ N) = H(MCS, M')^{(2\lambda-1)^{-1}d_r} \quad (25)$$

and obtains a new anonymous reputation at level $\lambda - 1$, $\{\lambda - 1, M', C'_r\}$. The protocol terminates.

Link. After a mobile user has been authenticated anonymously by the MCS platform, if the mobile user does not care about linking his previous location with his current location for the purpose of efficiency, in particular when the user has not been assigned any task yet, the mobile user may choose to link his current location with his previous location with the secret key k agreed with the MCS platform in the authentication phase.

To do so, the mobile user computes

$$h = H(MCS, D, (\ell, m, C_a), A'_a, (\lambda, M, C_r), A'_r, t, k) \quad (26)$$

where t is a time stamp, and submits a re-authentication request $\{MCS, D, t, h\}$ to the MCS platform, through nearby base station for mobile communication. The base station forwards the request together with the location L to the MCS platform.

After receiving the link request, the MCS platform searches for D in its records and retrieves the corresponding secret key k, and then checks if the Eq. (26) holds. If so, the mobile user is re-authenticated. Note that the MCS platform keeps $\{D, k, (\ell, m, C_a), A'_a, L\}$ in the authentication phase.

5   Security and Performance Analysis

Due to the page limit, we provide security analysis in Appendix. In this section, we analyze the computation and communication overhead for our solution.

5.1   Performance of Our Scheme

The proposed LPP protocol consists of two main components that involve expensive operations on the participating parties: (1) Registration and (2) Protocol Execution. Within the second component, after a successful authentication of a mobile user U_i, two sub-components including (i) Task Assignment, and (ii) Report and Reward, may be executed, depending on whether or not U_i is assigned a task. In what follows, we focus on analyzing those expensive operations and the bandwidth consumption in each component.

Registration. During the registration for a mobile user U_i, after determining the number of times n this user is willing to participate in the protocol, U_i creates a random mask by raising a random element r to the power of $(2n+1)e_a$ modulo N, which is then multiplied by $H(MCS, m)$ to construct a blinded message A_a that will be forwarded as part of the registration request to the MCS platform P. Another blinded message A_r is created using a random element R and then sent to P likewise. After receiving the request, P creates two blind signatures B_a and B_r via raising A_a and A_r to the power of $(2n + 1)^{-1}d_a$ and $3^{-1}d_r$ modulo N, respectively. Knowing r and R, the mobile user U_i removes those previously attached random masks to create two signatures from the MCS platform. Two additional exponentiations modulo N are also needed to make sure the signatures are valid. In total, the number of exponentiations in Z_N^* performed by the MCS platform is 2, whereas it is 4 for U_i. On the other hand, at most $(4|Z_N| + |n|)$ bits are transmitted, where $|Z_N|$ and $|n|$ denote the bit-lengths of an element in Z_N^* and n, respectively.

Protocol Execution. A mobile user U_i participates in the LPP protocol by first authenticating himself with the MCS platform. Depending on the results of authentication and the ensuing task assignment, various computational and communicational costs will be incurred. To provide an upper bound on the overhead resulting from our protocol execution, in the following, we consider the case when U_i: (i) successfully passes the authentication; (ii) receives and accomplishes a task assignment from the MCS platform, and then (iii) updates his anonymous certificate and reputation for the next participation.

During the first stage, U_i encrypts a valid signature on (MCS, m) received from the MCS platform using a key k derived from raising a random element s in Z_N^* to the power of e_a. A blinded message A'_a for the next authentication is prepared by U_i as well, which costs 1 exponentiation. Both the encrypted signature and blinded message are sent to the MCS platform, which in turn computes the decryption key k via raising the concealed key to its d_a-th power to retrieve the anonymous certificate C_a. The MCS platform then verifies the validity of C_a by raising it to the power of $(2\ell + 1)e_a$. To sum up, both the MCS platform and U_i carry out 2 exponentiations in Z_N^*, and at most $(4|Z_N| + |L| + |\ell| + 2|MCS|)$ bits are transmitted, where $|L|$, $|\ell|$, and $|MCS|$ denote the respective bit-lengths of L, ℓ, and MCS.

Once the verification succeeds, U_i sends to the MCS platform a task request, which consists of U_i's reputation λ along with its signature C_r encrypted by the same key k in the previous stage. A blinded message A'_r that incurs 1 exponentiation on U_i for updating the reputation in the next task assignment is sent with C_r as well. After obtaining λ and C_r using k, the MCS platform verifies the validity of the signature, which takes 1 exponentiation. When C_r is valid and the reputation submitted by U_i is the highest one, the MCS platform generates and sends to U_i the signature σ on the assigned task T as well as the blinded signature B'_a on (MCS, m') for U_i's next authentication, each costs 1 exponentiation, respectively. Other than checking the validity of σ, U_i also makes sure the anonymous certificate C'_a is valid after removing the corresponding random mask $r'^{(2\ell+1)}$ from B'_a. Three additional exponentiations are thus performed by U_i. In total, the MCS platform performs 3 exponentiations and U_i performs 4 exponentiations. The number of bits exchanged is at most $(6|Z_N|+2|MCS|+|\ell|+|\lambda|+|T|)$, where $|\lambda|$, and $|T|$ correspond to the bit-lengths of λ, and T.

After the assigned task T is finished, depending on the submitted task report from U_i, the MCS platform computes the blind signature B'_r on U_i's updated reputation $\lambda' \in \{\lambda-1, \lambda, \lambda+1\}$, which takes 1 exponentiation. To create an updated anonymous reputation C'_r, U_i first produces $R'^{(2\lambda-1)(2\lambda+1)}$, $R'^{(2\lambda-1)(2\lambda+3)}$, or $R'^{(2\lambda+1)(2\lambda+3)}$ modulo N to remove the random mask from C'_r, when the MCS platform decides to upgrade, maintain, or downgrade the reputation of U_i. The verification of the updated reputation is performed by U_i as usual, which costs 1 exponentiation. Overall, the MCS platform carries out 1 exponentiation and U_i performs 2 exponentiations. At most $(|Z_N| + |\lambda'| + |T_R|)$ bits are transmitted in this phase, where $|\lambda'|$ and $|T_R|$ represent the bit-lengths of the updated reputation λ' and task report T_R, respectively.

5.2   Comparison

Let us theoretically compare the computation and communication complexities of the registration and authentication phases in our protocol with some existing protocols, e.g., Ramzan et al.'s protocol [26], and Blanton's protocol [3], both of which support anonymous authentication. The protocol in [26] allows each user access to the service for a fixed number of times, whereas a user in the latter protocol [3] is able to obtain the service before the specified expiration time. Since our protocol also incurs costs stemming from reputation updates and task assignments that do not exist in the other two schemes, for the sake of comparison, we exclude those costs when comparing our protocol with the other two, i.e., we only consider operations directly related to registration and authentication in the following comparisons.

Moreover, both Ramzan et al.'s and Blanton's protocols invoke zero-knowledge protocols as building blocks and thus the related security parameters have to be specified when necessary. In what follows, we use κ_1, κ_2, κ_3 to denote the security parameters associated with the soundness, completeness, and statistical zero-knowledge of a protocol, respectively. Alternatively, κ_4 is used to represent the bit-length of a user authentication key, when it is explicitly specified in a protocol. We also use n' and n'' to denote the maximum number of accesses allowed and the maximum expiration time in a system, respectively, and let $|n'|$ and $|n''|$ denote their corresponding bit-lengths.

To compare the computational complexities of different protocols, for each protocol, we count the expensive operations, e.g., exponentiations or pairing operations in the corresponding groups. We will use the name of a group to denote the exponentiations under this group. For instance, our scheme requires exponentiations in Z_N^*, which are also necessary to construct and verify range proofs [7] in Ramzan et al.'s protocol. Additionally, based on an RSA modulus N, a large prime $P' = jN+1$ for some integer j has to be generated to enable the creation and verification of signatures of knowledge [6] in a cyclic multiplicative subgroup of $Z_{P'}^*$ for Ramzan et al.'s scheme. In Blanton's protocol, two cyclic groups G_1 and G_T of prime order Q equipped with an efficient bilinear pairing are needed instead to create blind signatures and the corresponding proofs of knowledge. A bilinear pairing is a map $e : G_1 \times G_1 \rightarrow G_T$ such that for all g, $h \in G_1$, a, $b \in Z$, it holds that $e(g^a, h^b) = e(g, h)^{ab}$. The term Pp will be used to denote such an operation. Moreover, a term nG^x indicates n multi-exponentiations in the group G with x bases.

On the other hand, when comparing the communication complexities, $|G|$ is used to signify the size of a group element in the group G. We will also use $|X|$ to denote the bit-length to represent a variable X when it is clear from the context. For instance, we use $|MCS|$ to denote the bit-length of MCS.

We first compare these protocols in terms of computational complexities in the registration stage. Table 1 lists the expensive operations performed in each protocol on the server and user sides, respectively[2].

Table 1. Computation comparison (registration)

Protocol	Server	User	Communication cost
Ours	$2Z_N$	$4Z_N$	$\|n'\| + 4\|Z_N\|$
Ramzan et al. [26]	$(\kappa_1 + 4)Z_N + (\kappa_1 + 1)Z_{P'}$	$(\kappa_1 + 7)Z_N + (\kappa_1 + 2)Z_{P'}$	$(\kappa_1 + 3)\|Z_N\| + 2\|Z_{P'}\| + 4\kappa_1 + 2\kappa_2 + \kappa_3 + 2\kappa_4 + 1$
Blanton [3]	$9G_1 + G_1^2 + G_1^3$	$G_1 + 2G_1^2 + G_T + G_T^3 + 20Pp$	$11\|G_1\| + 3\|Z_Q\| + \kappa_1$

It can be seen that our scheme is much more efficient than Ramzan et al.'s because the number of exponentiations carried out in the zero-knowledge protocols they adopt depends on κ_1, the soundness of the zero-knowledge protocols. To be exact, this security parameter guarantees that a cheating prover can only succeed in constructing a valid zero-knowledge proof with probability at most $1/2^{\kappa_1}$. In practice, κ_1 should be at least 40 to thwart a cheating prover. The computational complexity of Blanton's protocol does not depend on κ_1 as described above even though they also adopt zero-knowledge proofs as building blocks. However, our scheme still requires much less computation in terms of the number of exponentiations. It shall be clear in Sect. 5.3 that our scheme is much more efficient empirically.

As for the communication complexities, we provide the information in Table 1 as well. Our scheme is the most efficient one among these three. Ramzan et al.'s

---

[2] Note that we will use Server to denote our MCS platform when focusing our comparisons on registration and authentication.

protocol consumes the highest bandwidth resulting from the invocation of zero-knowledge protocols. Although Blanton's protocol does not incur such a high communication cost, it still requires exchanging at least 11 group elements in G_1, each of which is of similar bit-length to an element in Z_N^* if we adopt the parameter setting described at the beginning of Sect. 5.3.

In Table 2, we provide a comparison of these three schemes based on the computational costs incurred in the authentication phase. Again, our protocol requires the lowest number of exponentiations during authentication on both the server and user sides. As seen previously, Ramzan's scheme incurs a much higher computational cost, which grows linear in κ_1. The number of exponentiations performed in Blanton's protocol, on the other hand, depends on $|n''|$, the bit-length used to represent the maximum expiration time in a system. This is mainly because this scheme has to invoke a zero-knowledge protocol that proves a committed number lies within a range in a bitwise manner. We can see that even when $|n''|$ is set to a small integer, e.g., 10, this protocol still needs much more exponentiations than ours does.

Table 2. Computation comparison (authentication)

Protocol	Server	User	Communication cost
Ours	$3Z_N$	$4Z_N$	$4|Z_N| + 2|MCS| + |n'|$
Ramzan et al. [26]	$\kappa_1 Z_N + (\kappa_1 + 11)Z_{P'}$	$\kappa_1 Z_N + (\kappa_1 + 13)Z_{P'}$	$2|Z_{P'}| + (\kappa_1 + 5)|Z_N| + 3\kappa_1$
Blanton [3]	$8G_1 + 2G_1^3 + (2|n''| + 1)G_1^2 + G_T + G_T^2 + G_T^3 + 6Pp$	$(|n''|+11)G_1 + (|n''| + 2)G_1^2 + G_T + 2G_T^2 + 2G_T^3 + 26Pp$	$(2|n''| + 21)|G_1| + |G_T| + (4|n''| + 7)|Z_Q| + (|n''| + 2)\kappa_1$

Lastly, we compare the communication costs in Table 2. Our protocol consumes the lowest bandwidth because its bandwidth consumption is affected by neither κ_1 nor $|n''|$.

5.3 Experiments

To assess the efficiency of various schemes, we implement our and Ramzan et al.'s protocols using the GNU MP library[3]. The RSA modulus N needed in our and Ramzan et al.'s protocol is of 1,024-bit long, a product of two safe primes $p = 2p' + 1$ and $q = 2q' + 1$ of equal bit-length, where p' and q' are both primes. As for the prime P' that will be additionally required in Ramzan et al.'s protocol, we set $P' = 2N + 1$ to estimate the lower bound on the computational complexity of exponentiations in $Z_{P'}^*$. On the other hand, for Blanton's protocol, we use the Pairing-Based Cryptography Library (PBC) [22] to instantiate an

---

[3] https://gmplib.org/.

A512 group of order Q, a 160-bit prime. In our experiments, we set those four security parameters as $\kappa_1 = 80$, $\kappa_2 = \kappa_3 = 40$, and $\kappa_4 = 160$, when necessary[4]. The bit-length $|n'|$ to represent the maximum number of accesses allowed in a system is set to 80 and the bit-length $|n''|$ to represent the maximum expiration time in Blanton's protocol is set to 10.

The machine we use has an Intel i7-4770HQ with 16 GBytes of RAM and the operating system installed is an Ubuntu 14.04 LTS. All the source code for the prototype of server and user is implemented in C.

Table 3. Registration and authentication time comparison of user (in ms)

Protocol	Registration	Authentication
Ours	0.822	1.302
Ramzan et al. [26]	48.598	51.378
Blanton [3]	13.312	62.836

The computational cost incurred on the MCS platform and a mobile user in each stage that involves expensive operations, i.e., exponentiations in Z_N^*, are 0.822 ms and 1.64 ms, respectively, in registration stage, and 2.466 ms and 2.604 ms, respectively, in protocol execution stage. We can see that our protocol incurs very little cost on both the server and user in each phase involving expensive operations. On average, the time spent in a single stage on either party is below 2.7 ms. It will also be clearer that our scheme is much more efficient when it is empirically compared with the other two.

Let us now compare our protocol with the other two in terms of the computational overhead on the user in the registration and authentication phases. The detailed information is given in Table 3, according to which we can see that our scheme requires a minimum amount of computation on the user in both phases. Specifically, each invocation of our registration or authentication protocol takes less than 1.4 ms to finish on average. On the other hand, as analyzed in Sect. 5.2, Ramzan et al.'s protocol incurs the highest overhead during registration. We also find out that even when the maximum expiration time is as small as $2^{|n''|} = 2^{10}$, a user in Blanton's scheme still has to spend at least 62.8 ms to complete the authentication, which is at least 44 times higher than ours.

We have also conducted experiments to measure the computational costs imposed on the server by varying the number of users it needs to process during registration and authentication. The results are given in Figs. 1 and 2, respectively. In all of these protocols, the computational cost grows linearly in the number of users served. However, Ramzan et al.'s and Blanton's schemes grow much faster than ours due to their dependence on either the soundness security parameter κ_1 or the bit-length of maximum expiration time $|n''|$. To be precise, when there are 10,000 users waiting to be authenticated, the other two protocols

---

[4] We adopt the suggested setting of κ_1, κ_2, and κ_3 in [4] and [6].

require at least 8 min to accomplish the task, whereas it only takes our protocol less than 13 s, which clearly indicates that our scheme is much more scalable.

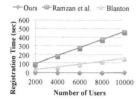

Fig. 1. Registration time comparison of server when varying number of users

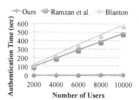

Fig. 2. Authentication time comparison of server when varying number of users

6   Conclusions

In this paper, we have described a location privacy-preserving (LPP) protocol for MCS. The proposed protocol overcomes the trusted third party, linkability and key sharing problems of the existing solutions for location privacy protection in MCS. In addition, we introduce a new concept of anonymous reputation. The MCS platform can refer to the anonymous reputation of a mobile user when assigning tasks to the user. Based on the report submitted by the user, the MCS platform can upgrade or downgrade the reputation of the user.

Acknowledgements. This research is supported by the National Research Foundation, Prime Minister's Office, Singapore under its Strategic Capability Research Centres Funding Initiative, and Australian Research Council (ARC) Discovery Projects DP160100913 & DP180103251.

Appendix: Security Analysis

The proposed LPP protocol is based on the blind signature scheme. According to [17], a blind digital signature scheme is secure if for all probabilistic polynomial-time (PPT) algorithms $\mathcal{A}$, the following two considerations hold.

Blindness Property: Let b is a random bit which is kept secret from $\mathcal{A}$. $\mathcal{A}$ executes the following experiment (where $\mathcal{A}$ controls the signer, but not the user, and tries to predict b):

Step 1: $(pk, sk) \leftarrow \mathsf{Gen}(1^k)$

Step 2: $(m_0, m_1) \leftarrow \mathcal{A}(1^k, pk, sk)$ (i.e. $\mathcal{A}$ produces two documents, where (m_0, m_1) are by convention lexicographically ordered and may even depend on pk and sk).

Step 3: We denote by (m_b, m_{1-b}) the same two documents (m_0, m_1), ordered according to the value of bit b, where the value of b is hidden from $\mathcal{A}$. $\mathcal{A}(1^k, pk, sk, m_0, m_1)$ engages in two parallel (and arbitrarily interleaved) interactive protocols, the first with $User(pk, m_b)$ and the second with $User(pk, m_{1-b})$.

Step 4: If the first user outputs on his private tape $\sigma(m_b)$ (i.e., does not output fail) and the second user outputs on his private tape $\sigma(m_{1-b})$ (i.e., also does not output fail) then $\mathcal{A}$ is given as an additional input $(\sigma(m_b), \sigma(m_{1-b}))$ ordered according to the corresponding (m_0, m_1) order. (We remark that we do not insist that this happens, and either one or both users may output fail).

Step 5: $\mathcal{A}$ outputs a bit b' (given his view of steps 1 through 3, and if conditions are satisfied, of step 4 as well).

Then the probability, taken over the choice of b, over coin-flips of key-generation algorithm, the coin-flips of $\mathcal{A}$, and (private) coin-flips of both users (from step 3), $b' = b$ is negligibly close to $1/2$.

Unforgeability Property: $\mathcal{A}$ executes the following experiment (where $\mathcal{A}$ controls the user, but not the signer, and tries to get one more signature):

Step 1: $(pk, sk) \leftarrow \mathsf{Gen}(1^k)$

Step 2: $\mathcal{A}(pk)$ engages in polynomially many (in k) adaptive, parallel and arbitrarily interleaved interactive protocols with polynomially many copies of $\mathsf{Signer}(pk, sk)$, where $\mathcal{A}$ decides in an adaptive fashion when to stop. Let ℓ denote the number of executions, where the signer outputted completed in the end of Step 2.

Step 3: $\mathcal{A}$ outputs a collection $\{(m_1, \sigma(m_1)), (m_2, \sigma(m_2)), \cdots, (m_j, \sigma(m_j))\}$ subject to the constraint the all $(m_i, \sigma(m_i))$ for $1 \leq i \leq j$ are all accepted by $\mathsf{Verify}(pk, m_i, \sigma(m_i))$.

Then the probability, taken over coin-flips of key - generation algorithm, the coin flips of $\mathcal{A}$, and over the (private) coin-flips of the $Signer$, that $j > \ell$ is negligible.

For the following security analysis, we make an assumption, which can reasonably be expected to hold in practice. We assume that on average the users have the same total access times (i.e., during the registration, n is the same for every user), and access the MCS system with the same frequency. This implies that at every given point in time, there will be a similar number of users that have each possible remaining access times (i.e., ℓ). In other words, the number of remaining access times for a user is equally likely to be any number between 1 and n (i.e., $1 \leq \ell \leq n$).

In addition, we assume the Chaum's blind signature scheme [8] is secure in terms of blindness and forgeablility.

During MCS, the platform learns one thing. He sees the anonymous certificates and anonymous reputations, i.e., the blind signatures, used in MCS. We claim that the MCS platform learns nothing from the blind signatures themselves, and only the number of the participation of the mobile user and the reputation level of the mobile user in MCS.

At first, let us analyse the anonymity of the proposed protocol with a game according to Definition 1 in Sect. 2. For this security analysis, we assume that the MCS platform is malicious and tries to identify the mobile user.

Given two mobile users U_0 and U_1, assume that the MCS platform runs the registration protocol with them, respectively, to issue blind signatures to them for anonymous authentication.

Let us choose a bit b randomly.

In the authentication phase, the mobile user U_b submits the authentication request $\{MCS, D_b, E_{k_b}(MCS, (\ell_b, m_b, C_{a,b}), A'_{a,b})\}$ to the platform. The platform can derive the secret key k_b from D_b with its private key d_a and perform decryption to obtain the anonymous certificate $\{\ell_b, m_b, C_{a,b}\}$. Due to the blindness property of the Chaum's blind signature, the platform cannot tell if the blind signature is from the mobile user U_0 or U_1.

In the task assignment phase, the mobile user U_b submits to the MCS platform a task request $\{MCS, D_b, E_{k_b}(MCS, (\lambda_b, M_b, C_{r,b}), A'_{r,b}, T_b)\}$. With k_b corresponding to D_b, the platform performs decryption to obtain the anonymous reputation $\{\lambda_b, M_b, C_{r,b}\}$. Due to the blindness property of the Chaum's blind signature, the MCS platform cannot tell if the blind signature is from the mobile user U_0 or U_1.

In the report and reward phase, the mobile user does not submit any blind signature to the MCS platform. The MCS platform has no way to distinguish the mobile users in this phase.

Based on the above security analysis, according to Definition 1 for anonymity, we conclude that

Theorem 1. The proposed LPP protocol has anonymity if the Chaum's blind signature has blindness.

Next, let us analyse the unlinkability of the proposed protocol with a game.

Given two mobile users U_0 and U_1, assume that the platform runs the protocol with U_0 and U_1, respectively, and keeps two anonymous certificates and two anonymous reputations: $\{\ell_0, m_0, C_{a,0}\}$ and $\{\ell_0, M_0, C_{a,0}\}$ from U_0, $\{\ell_1, m_1, C_{a,1}\}$ and $\{\ell_1, M_1, C_{a,1}\}$ from U_1.

Next, let us choose a bit b randomly. User U_b runs the protocol with the MCS platform again and provides the MCS platform with anonymous certificate and anonymous reputation: $\{\ell'_b, m'_b, C'_{a,b}\}$ and $\{\ell'_b, M'_b, C'_{a,b}\}$.

Due to the blindness property of the Chaum's blind signature, the MCS platform cannot tell if the blind signatures $\{\ell'_b, m'_b, C'_{a,b}\}$ and $\{\ell'_b, M'_b, C'_{a,b}\}$ are from the mobile user U_0 or U_1. Based on the above analysis, according to Definition 2 for unlinkability, we conclude that

Theorem 2. The proposed LPP protocol has unlinkability if the Chaum's blind signature has blindness.

At last, let us analyse the unforgeability of the proposed protocol with a game.

For this analysis, we assume a group of mobile users are malicious. For simplicity, we consider anonymous certificates only at first and then we can easily extend the security analysis for anonymous reputation, because both of them are blind signatures anyway.

In the proposed LPP protocol, a valid anonymous certificate takes the form of $\{\ell, m, C = H(MCS, m)^{(2\ell+1)^{-1}d_a}\}$ for $\ell = 1, 2, \cdots$. Assume that the adversary is given t valid anonymous certificates $\{\ell_i, m_i, C_i\}$ for $i = 1, 2, \cdots, t$, if the adversary can generate a new anonymous certificate, which is different from the given t anonymous certificates, he wins the game.

In the given t valid anonymous certificates, if $\ell_1 = \ell_2 = \cdots = \ell_t = \ell$, the adversary cannot forge any more new anonymous certificate because the Chaum's blind signature for the public key $(2\ell + 1)e_a$ has unforgeability.

In the given t valid anonymous certificates, if we group certificates on the basis of the public key $(2\ell + 1)e_a$, the adversary cannot forge any more new certificate in any group with the same public key because the Chaum's blind signature for the public key $(2\ell + 1)e_a$ has unforgeability.

Now let us consider the possibility of forging a new anonymous certificate across the groups, i.e., how to forge a new anonymous certificate $\{\ell', m', C' = H(MCS, m')^{(2\ell'+1)^{-1}d_a}\}$ with two anonymous certificates $\{\ell_1, m_1, C_1\}$ such that $C_1 = H(MCS, m_1)^{(2\ell_1+1)^{-1}d_a} (mod\ N)$ and $\{\ell_2, m_2, C_2\}$ such that $C_2 = H(MCS, m_2)^{(2\ell_2+1)^{-1}d_a} (mod\ N)$, where $\ell_1 \neq \ell_2$.

Because the hash function H is collision-resistant, from $H(MCS, m_1)^{(2\ell_1+1)^{-1}d}$ and $H(MCS, m_2)^{(2\ell_2+1)^{-1}d}$, it is hard to forge a new anonymous certificate (ℓ', m', C') as follows.

- $C' = H(MCS, m_1)^{(2\ell'+1)^{-1}d_a} (mod\ N)$ for some ℓ', such that $\ell' \neq \ell_1$.
- $C' = H(MCS, m_2)^{(2\ell'+1)^{-1}d_a} (mod\ N)$ for some ℓ', such that $\ell' \neq \ell_2$.
- $C' = H(MCS, m')^{(2\ell'+1)^{-1}d_a} (mod\ N)$ for some ℓ', such that $m' \neq m_1$ and $m' \neq m_2$.

In view of this, we conclude that

Theorem 3. The proposed LPP protocol has unforgeability if the Chaum's blind signature has unforgeability and the hash function H is collision-resistant.

References

1. Abe, M., Fujisaki, E.: How to date blind signatures. In: Kim, K., Matsumoto, T. (eds.) ASIACRYPT 1996. LNCS, vol. 1163, pp. 244–251. Springer, Heidelberg (1996). https://doi.org/10.1007/BFb0034851
2. Bellavista, P., Corradi, A., Foschini, L., Ianniello, R.: Scalable and cost-effective assignment of mobile crowdsensing tasks based on profiling trends and prediction: the participact living lab experience. Sensors **15**(8), 18613–18640 (2015)
3. Blanton, M.: Online subscriptions with anonymous access. In: Proceedings of ASI-ACCS 2008, pp. 217–227 (2008)

4. Boudot, F.: Efficient proofs that a committed number lies in an interval. In: Preneel, B. (ed.) EUROCRYPT 2000. LNCS, vol. 1807, pp. 431–444. Springer, Heidelberg (2000). https://doi.org/10.1007/3-540-45539-6_31
5. Brickell, E., Camenisch, J., Chen, L.: Direct anonymous attestation. In: Proceedings of 11th ACM Conference on Computer and Communication Security, pp. 132–145 (2004)
6. Camenisch, J., Stadler, M.: Efficient group signature schemes for large groups. In: Kaliski, B.S. (ed.) CRYPTO 1997. LNCS, vol. 1294, pp. 410–424. Springer, Heidelberg (1997). https://doi.org/10.1007/BFb0052252
7. Chan, A., Frankel, Y., Tsiounis, Y.: Easy come — easy go divisible cash. In: Nyberg, K. (ed.) EUROCRYPT 1998. LNCS, vol. 1403, pp. 561–575. Springer, Heidelberg (1998). https://doi.org/10.1007/BFb0054154
8. Chaum, D.: Blind signatures for untraceable payments. In: Chaum, D., Rivest, R.L., Sherman, A.T. (eds.) Advances in Cryptology, pp. 199–203. Springer, Boston, MA (1983). https://doi.org/10.1007/978-1-4757-0602-4_18
9. Chaum, D., van Heyst, E.: Group signatures. In: Davies, D.W. (ed.) EUROCRYPT 1991. LNCS, vol. 547, pp. 257–265. Springer, Heidelberg (1991). https://doi.org/10.1007/3-540-46416-6_22
10. Christin, D.: Privacy in mobile participatory sensing: current trends and future challenges. J. Syst. Softw. **116**, 57–68 (2016)
11. Cormode, G., Procopiuc, C., Srivastava, D., Shen, E., Yu, T.: Differentially private spatial decompositions. In: Proceedings of ICDE 2012, pp. 20–31 (2012)
12. Daemen, J., Rijmen, V.: The Design of Rijndael: AES - The Advanced Encryption Standard. Springer, Berlin (2002). https://doi.org/10.1007/978-3-662-04722-4
13. Dwork, C.: Differential privacy. In: Bugliesi, M., Preneel, B., Sassone, V., Wegener, I. (eds.) ICALP 2006. LNCS, vol. 4052, pp. 1–12. Springer, Heidelberg (2006). https://doi.org/10.1007/11787006_1
14. Ganti, R.K., Ye, F., Lei, H.: Mobile crowdsensing: current state and future challenges. IEEE Commun. Mag. **49**(11), 32–39 (2011)
15. Guo, B., Calabrese, F., Miluzzo, E., Musolesi, M.: Mobile crowd sensing: part 1. IEEE Commun. Mag. **52**(8), 20–21 (2014)
16. Guo, B., Calabrese, F., Miluzzo, E., Musolesi, M.: Mobile crowd sensing: part 2. IEEE Commun. Mag. **52**(10), 76–77 (2014)
17. Juels, A., Luby, M., Ostrovsky, R.: Security of blind digital signatures. In: Kaliski, B.S. (ed.) CRYPTO 1997. LNCS, vol. 1294, pp. 150–164. Springer, Heidelberg (1997). https://doi.org/10.1007/BFb0052233
18. Kantarci, B., Glasser, P.M., Foschini, L.: Crowdsensing with social network-aided collaborative trust scores. In: Proceedings of IEEE Global Communication Conference (GLOBECOM), pp. 1–6 (2015)
19. Kantarci, B., Carr, K.G., Pearsall, C.D.: SONATA: social network assisted trustworthiness assurance in smart city crowdsensing. Int. J. Distrib. Syst. Technol. **7**(1), 59–78 (2016)
20. Kapadia, A., Triandopoulos, N., Cornelius, C., Peebles, D., Kotz, D.: AnonySense: opportunistic and privacy-preserving context collection. In: Proceedings of 6th International Conference on Mobile System, Applications and Services (MobiSys), pp. 280–297 (2008)
21. Konidala, D.M., Deng, R.H., Li, Y., Lau, H.C., Fienberg, S.E.: Anonymous authentication of visitors for mobile crowd sensing at amusement parks. In: Deng, R.H., Feng, T. (eds.) ISPEC 2013. LNCS, vol. 7863, pp. 174–188. Springer, Heidelberg (2013). https://doi.org/10.1007/978-3-642-38033-4_13

22. Lynn, B.: On the implementation of pairing-based cryptosystems. Stanford University (2007)
23. Navas, J.C., Imielinski, T.: GeoCast - geographic addressing and routing. In: Proceedings of ACM International Conference on Mobile Computing and Networking, pp. 66–76 (1997)
24. Pouryazdan, M., Kantarci, B., Soyata, T., Song, H.: Anchor-assisted and vote-based trustworthiness assurance in smart city crowdsensing. IEEE Access **4**, 529–541 (2016)
25. Pouryazdan, M., Kantarci, B., Soyata, T., Foschini, L., Song, H.: Quantifying user reputation scores, data trustworthiness, and user incentives in mobile crowdsensing. IEEE Access **5**, 1382–1397 (2017)
26. Ramzan, Z., Ruhl, M.: Protocols for anonymous subscription services (2000). (Unpublished Manuscript)
27. Ren, J., Zhang, Y., Zhang, K., Shen, X.S.: SACRM: social aware crowdsourcing with reputation management in mobile sensing. Comput. Commun. **65**, 55–65 (2015)
28. Shina, M., Cornelius, C., Peebles, D., Kapadia, A., Kotz, D., Triandopoulos, N.: AnonySense: a system for anonymous opportunistic sensing. Pervasive Mobile Comput. **7**, 16–30 (2011)
29. Sweeney, L.: k-anonymity: a model for protecting privacy. Int. J. Uncertainty Fuzziness Knowl.-Based Syst. **10**, 557–570 (2002)
30. To, H., Ghinita, G., Shahabi, C.: A framework for protecting worker location privacy in spatial crowdsourcing. In: Proceedings of VLDB 2014, pp. 919–930 (2014)
31. Vergara-Laurens, I.J., Jaimes, L.G., Labrador, M.A.: Privacy-preserving mechanisms for crowdsensing: survey and research challenges. IEEE IoT J. **4**(4), 855–869 (2017)
32. Wang, X., Liu, Z., Tian, X., Gan, X., Guan, Y., Wang, X.: Incentivizing crowdsensing with location-privacy preserving. IEEE Trans. Wirel. Commun. **16**(10), 6940–6952 (2017)

OCRAM-Assisted Sensitive Data Protection on ARM-Based Platform

Dawei Chu[1,2,3], Yuewu Wang[1,2,3], Lingguang Lei[1,2,3($\boxtimes$)], Yanchu Li[1,2,3], Jiwu Jing[4], and Kun Sun[5]

[1] State Key Laboratory of Information Security,
Institute of Information Engineering,
Chinese Academy of Sciences, Beijing, China
`leilingguang@iie.ac.cn`
[2] Data Assurance and Communication Security Research Center,
Chinese Academy of Sciences, Beijing, China
[3] School of Cyber Security, University of Chinese Academy of Sciences,
Beijing, China
[4] School of Computer Science and Technology,
University of Chinese Academy of Sciences, Beijing, China
[5] Center for Secure Information Systems, George Mason University,
Fairfax, USA

Abstract. On mobile devices, security-sensitive tasks (e.g., mobile payment, one-time password) involve not only sensitive data such as cryptographic keying material, but also sensitive I/O operations such as inputting PIN code via touchscreen and showing the authentication verification code on the display. Therefore, a comprehensive protection of these services should enforce a Trusted User Interface (TUI) to protect the sensitive user inputs and system outputs, in addition to preventing both software attacks and physical memory disclosure attacks. In this paper, we present an On-Chip RAM (OCRAM) assisted sensitive data protection mechanism named Oath on ARM-based platform to protect the sensitive data, particularly, sensitive I/O data, against both software attacks and physical memory disclosure attacks. The basic idea is to store and process the sensitive data in the OCRAM that is only accessible to the TrustZone secure world. After figuring out how to enable TrustZone protection for iRAM, we develop a trusted user interface with an OCRAM allocation mechanism to efficiently share the OCRAM between the secure OS and the rich OS. A prototype implemented on the OP-TEE system shows that Oath works well and has a small system overhead.

Keywords: OCRAM(iRAM) · TrustZone · Cold boot attacks · Trusted User Interface

1 Introduction

To facilitate security-sensitive tasks such as mobile payment, mobile wallet, etc., mobile terminal vendors have integrated hardware-assisted Trusted Execution

© Springer Nature Switzerland AG 2019
K. Sako et al. (Eds.): ESORICS 2019, LNCS 11736, pp. 412–438, 2019.
https://doi.org/10.1007/978-3-030-29962-0_20

Environment (TEE) [3] features in their devices. For instance, SAMSUNG utilizes ARM TrustZone technology [12] to secure SAMSUNG PAY [8], FIDO relies on TEE technology to protect the authentication procedure [20], and Google adopts TEE to implement a secure cryptographic service for Android apps [2]. TEE takes advantage of hardware isolation mechanism to defeat various software attacks. As one hardware TEE solution, the ARM TrustZone security extension [12] can isolate the system resources including CPU, memory, and peripherals between two execution environments, namely, the *secure world* and the *normal world* (or *non-secure world*). Thus, the TEE-based solutions [23,31,34,36,38,47,50,51,57] can effectively protect various secure software running in the secure world from the untrusted rich OS running in the normal world.

Though the TEE-based solutions can effectively defeat software attacks, they suffer from physical memory disclosure attacks such as cold boot attacks [32,43] and bus snooping attacks [28], since the sensitive data are stored in DRAM as plaintext. Therefore, with physical access to the stolen or lost mobile devices, the adversary may have opportunity to obtain sensitive data such as credit card numbers and user passwords from the system DRAM. To mitigate these attacks, several solutions have been proposed by constraining the storing and processing of sensitive data within the on-chip storage, such as CPU registers [44,48], CPU cache [19,30,56], and on-chip RAM (OCRAM, also known as internal RAM (iRAM)) [19]. The on-chip storage is naturally immune to the bus snooping attacks, since the data needs not to be transmitted from the CPU to the DRAM. Also, due to a smaller data remanence rate than DRAM [19], the on-chip storage can provide a better protection against cold boot attacks. However, it remains as a challenge to provide a comprehensive protection on both sensitive data such as cryptographic keys and sensitive I/O operations such as inputting PIN code via touchscreen or showing the authentication verification code on the display. Most on-chip storage based solutions do not resolve the software attacks [19,19,30,44,48] or are not able to protect the I/O operations [56].

In this paper, we provide an on-chip storage based security solution that could protect the sensitive data including sensitive I/O data against both software attacks and physical memory disclosure attacks. We develop an OCRAM assisted mechanism named Oath, whose basic idea is to protect the sensitive data by processing it in the TrustZone secure world and further locking the sensitive data in the OCRAM (i.e., iRAM). Because the sensitive data is only processed in the secure world, it can prevent the software attacks from the normal world. Moreover, since the secure sensitive data only resides in OCRAM, it can prevent physical memory disclosure attacks.

We choose to use OCRAM for two major reasons. First, different from cache, OCRAM can be addressed the same manner as DRAM. Thus, it can be used to support the TUI operations that rely heavily on DMA mechanism to directly access the I/O devices. For instance, it is difficult for the Image Processing Unit (IPU) to address and read the display framebuffer in cache and then send it to the external display device [56]. Second, OCRAM has been widely used in

ARM processors, and the size of OCRAM is usually larger than the available number of registers that are basically too small to accommodate the associated sensitive data. For example, modern high-end processors typically have from 128 KB to 2 MB OCRAM memory [1,4,9,10,25,46,52,56]. In the following, we use OCRAM and iRAM interchangeably.

We solve three major challenges on developing Oath. First, to defeat the software attacks from malicious rich OS, the iRAM region containing sensitive data should be isolated from the normal world. However, iRAM is by default used by rich OS and set as non-secure, and there lacks available public documentations on enabling the TrustZone protection for iRAM. We have to figure it out by trial and error on a real hardware platform. Second, we observe that iRAM has been used by rich OS in situations such as system sleeping/resuming, video playing, etc., and it may impose negative function and performance impacts on rich OS when we use iRAM to store sensitive data. To minimize the impacts on rich OS, we develop a dynamic iRAM allocation mechanism to adjust the size of the secure iRAM region on demand and return the unused iRAM memory to rich OS. Third, due to the small size of available iRAM (e.g., the Cortex A9 ARM processors usually accommodate 256 KB iRAM [4,10,46]), it is difficult to store multiple secure applications into iRAM. To solve this problem, we develop a memory splitting mechanism that can partition the application's data into sensitive part and nonsensitive part, and only store the sensitive data in the secure iRAM. In addition, current mobile phones are usually equipped with high-resolution screen, which can easily demand more than 1 MB memory for displaying an image with minimum pixel format. We solve it by enabling the dual display mode and displaying the sensitive data as an size-adjustable foreground image on a portion of the screen.

We implement a system prototype of Oath on the i.MX6Quad platform, with an OP-TEE OS 2.2.0 [6] ported to the secure world and an Android OS 6.0.1 (Linux kernel 4.1.15) ported as rich OS in the normal world. The experimental results show that our defense mechanism incurs a small overhead over both OP-TEE OS and Android OS.

In summary, we make the following contributions in this paper.

– We develop an iRAM-assisted sensitive data protection solution that can effectively defeat both software attacks and physical memory disclosure attacks. It also provides a trusted path to protect the user's I/O interactions with the mobile devices.
– We develop a memory splitting mechanism and a dynamic iRAM allocation mechanism to improve the usage efficiency of the small-capacity iRAM, so that it can better serve both the secure OS and the rich OS. We provide detail guidance on how to use TrustZone to protect iRAM, which can promote the usage of iRAM in the TrustZone.
– We develop a system prototype on the OP-TEE OS system, which is compliant with the GlobalPlatform TEE specifications [3] and is compatible with many other hardware platforms.

The remaining of the paper is organized as follows. Section 2 introduces necessary background knowledge. Section 3 describes the threat model and assumptions. Section 4 presents an overview of system design. A prototype implementation is detailed in Sect. 5. Section 6 discusses the evaluation of our work. Discussion and future work are illustrated in Sect. 7. We describe related works in Sect. 8. Finally, we conclude the paper in Sect. 9.

2   Background

We first introduce the ARM TrustZone hardware security extension. Then we discuss the internal Random Access Memory (iRAM) in ARM processors and the protection of iRAM with TrustZone technology. Next, We introduce the Open Portable Trusted Execution Environment (OP-TEE) system.

2.1   ARM TrustZone

TrustZone is a hardware security extension since ARMv6 architecture to provide a complete isolation environment for secure code execution. The security is achieved by partitioning the resources of the ARM System-on-a-Chip (SoC) including processor, memory, and peripherals, so that they can exist in one of two worlds - the *secure world* and the *normal world.* The normal world cannot access the secure world's resources such as memory, I/O devices etc., while the secure world can access the resources of both worlds. The normal world is usually used to run a commodity OS (also referred to as rich OS), while the secure world is used to run an isolated secure OS. Switching of the two worlds is supervised by a *Secure Monitor* running in monitor mode. The entry to monitor mode can be triggered by software executing a dedicated instruction, i.e., the Secure Monitor Call (SMC) instruction, or by emitting a secure interrupt request. Normally, Interrupt Request (IRQ) is configured as a normal world interrupt and Fast Interrupt Request (FIQ) is configured as a secure world interrupt. When a secure interrupt arrives, TrustZone switches the processor core to the monitor mode in order to handle it.

2.2   iRAM in ARM Processors

iRAM is an On-Chip Random Access Memory (OCRAM) constructed with a fast and expensive Static Random Access Memory (SRAM). iRAM is a common component on the ARM processors usually used in two situations. First, it is used to store the information such as system suspend/resume codes, DDR frequency modification codes etc. Second, it could be used to accelerate the multimedia processing, such as video playing. Modern high-end processors typically have 128 KB to 2 MB iRAM memory [1,4,9,10,25,46,52,56], for example, the Cortex A8 and A9 ARM processors usually have 128 KB and 256 KB iRAM, respectively [4,10,25,46,56].

iRAM can be protected through two on-SoC components, i.e., *TrustZone Memory Adapter (TZMA)* and *TrustZone Protection Controller (TZPC)* [13]. The TZMA is designed to secure a region within an on-SoC static memory such as a SRAM, and it only supports the partition of one secure region. The TZPC is a configurable signal control block to dynamically control the security states of on-SoC components, such as iRAM, TZMA etc. Theoretically, protection of iRAM could be achieved in two steps. In the first step, we can utilize TZMA to enable TrustZone protection on iRAM and partition it into two regions, i.e., secure region and non-secure region. For convenience, we refer to the secure region as secure iRAM and to the non-secure region as non-secure iRAM. However, normal world codes can still have the access to the secure iRAM. In the second step, we can set the permission of iRAM as *secure access only* through TZPC. In addition, TZPC can be used to dynamically change the size of secure iRAM at run-time by sending signals to TZMA.

2.3   OP-TEE System

GlobalPlatform TEE specification [3] has been proposed to facilitate the adaptation of TrustZone security features by providing common APIs to be called in mobile apps. OP-TEE is an open source TEE system that is compliant with the GlobalPlatform TEE specification and compatible with many hardware platforms [7].

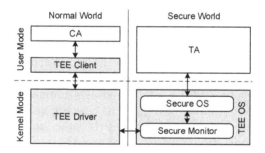

Fig. 1. Architecture of OP-TEE

OP-TEE is a typical TEE implementation based on the ARM TrustZone technology. Figure 1 shows the architecture of OP-TEE, which consists of three components, i.e., *TEE Client, TEE Driver*, and *TEE OS*. The TEE client and the TEE driver are executed in the normal world, and the TEE OS is executed in the secure world. The TEE client executes in the user mode and provides APIs for Client Apps (CAs) in the normal world, and it communicates with the TEE driver running in the kernel mode. The TEE driver is in charge of the communication between TEE client and TEE OS, e.g., by executing the SMC privileged instruction. The TEE OS is composed of a Secure Monitor and a Secure OS. The secure monitor is responsible for context switching between the normal world and the secure world, and the secure OS communicates with Trusted Apps (TAs) according to the requests from the TEE client. OP-TEE supports two types of TAs, i.e., the static TA and the dynamic TA. The former is statically compiled and loaded along with TEE OS image when the secure OS boots up, while the later could be dynamically loaded from file system at run-time.

3   Threat Model and Assumptions

We assume the attackers can launch sophisticated multi-vector attacks, including software attacks and physical memory disclosure attacks. For software attacks, the attackers can compromise the rich OS, thus gaining unrestricted access to not only DRAM but also on-chip memory (e.g., CPU cache, registers, OCRAM etc.) in the normal world. However, the attackers cannot access DRAM and on-chip memory in the secure world due to the protection of TrustZone. The attackers may also launch physical memory disclosure attacks, such as cold boot attacks [32,43], to steal the sensitive code and data in DRAM. The attackers can also snoop the data transferred on the bus between CPU and DRAM [28]. However, we assume the attackers could not physically access the data on the on-chip memory. Side-channel attacks such as timing-based and power-based analysis are out of the scope of this paper.

We assume the ARM-based platform supports the TrustZone security extension, and the hardware implementations of TrustZone are correct and can be trustworthy. We also assume the TEE OS including the secure OS and the secure monitor in the secure world is trusted and it can boot up securely via the *secure boot* technology of TrustZone. In this work, we focus on protecting the confidentiality and integrity of the sensitive data, such as the cryptographic key used to perform encryption and decryption, the authentication verification code shown on the display devices, and the PIN code input by the user via touchscreen. We assume the TA running in the secure world can be trusted and will not leak sensitive data deliberately to the rich OS. Moreover, since the TA image is stored in the file system of normal world without encryption, we assume no sensitive data is statically stored in the TA binary image.

4   System Design

Our goal is to construct a TEE system that can ensure sensitive data (including sensitive I/O data) against both software attacks and physical memory disclosure attacks. The basic idea of Oath is to ensure that the sensitive data is only stored in the secure iRAM and processed by the secure CPU cores, so that it can protect sensitive data against software attacks from the rich OS and the physical memory disclosure attacks. Our design is based on the OP-TEE system to be compliant with the GlobalPlatform TEE specifications [3]. In general, Oath is composed of four modules implemented in the secure OS of OP-TEE, as shown in Fig. 2. One module is implemented by modifying the *TA Loader* of the secure OS, and the other three modules, i.e., *TUI Driver*, *iRAM Manager*, and *iRAM Controller*, are newly added into the secure OS. In the following, we provide a description of each module and present how they work together to achieve the design goals.

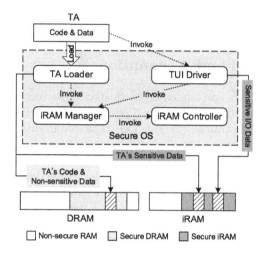

Fig. 2. Architecture of Oath

TA Loader. In the OP-TEE system, the TA loader is responsible to load a TA into memory and allocate the dynamic memory like stack and heap for it. Normally, the memory will be allocated from secure DRAM. To defend against the physical memory disclosure attacks, we modify the TA loader to store the TA in the secure iRAM. However, the small-capacity iRAM memory makes it difficult to support the simultaneous execution of multiple TAs, so we develop a memory splitting mechanism in the TA loader. Specifically, the TA's memory is split into an sensitive part (i.e., memory containing sensitive data) and a nonsensitive part, and only sensitive part is stored in secure iRAM. The splitting mechanism is achieved based on the observation that the TA image is originally stored in the unprotected file system, so it becomes a nature choice for the developers to store nonsensitive data in the constant parts of the TA image, e.g., the .text and .rodata sections of the ELF file. As such, Oath counts the memory containing the constant data as nonsensitive. To further optimize the utilization efficiency of iRAM, we enable the TA loader to selectively load sensitive data of specific TAs into the secure iRAM.

TUI Driver. The TUI driver is responsible for supporting trusted user interactions, e.g., trusted display and trusted input. To ensure security, the TUI driver stores the sensitive I/O data only in the secure iRAM. However, the sensitive data is sometimes too large to be stored in the small-capacity iRAM memory, such as the large-sized sensitive image to be securely displayed on the screen. The TUI driver enables trusted display based on the observation that most platforms support dual display mode, i.e., blending a foreground image and background image to form the final image. Although displaying an image on the entire screen needs a large memory, the size of foreground image is adjustable and could be smaller. Therefore, when receiving a trusted display request, the TUI driver enables the dual display mode and displays the sensitive data as a foreground image on only a portion of the screen.

iRAM Manager. The iRAM manager module manages the secure iRAM for multiple TAs by allocating and freeing memory spaces from the secure iRAM. It is invoked by the TA loader when loading/unloading a TA and by the TUI driver when performing trusted user interactions.

iRAM Controller. The function of the iRAM controller is two-fold. First, it enables the TrustZone protection for iRAM when the TEE OS boots up. Second, to reduce the impacts on the performance and function of rich OS, it contains a dynamic iRAM allocation mechanism to minimize the size of secure iRAM at run time. Originally, most iRAM memory is set as non-secure. During system execution, the iRAM controller will be invoked by the iRAM manager to enlarge or shrink the secure iRAM region. The sensitive data on the secure iRAM region will be wiped out before it is set as non-secure and accessed by the rich OS.

5   Implementation

We implement an Oath prototype on the FreeScale i.MX6Quad platform with an OP-TEE 2.2.0 OS system in the secure world and an Android 6.0.1 system deployed in normal world. The Android OS with Linux kernel 4.1.15 is ported from the secure world to the normal world.

5.1   iRAM Controller

In general, the iRAM controller performs two tasks, namely, enabling the TrustZone protection for iRAM and dynamically adjusting the size of secure iRAM. In Sect. 2.2, we briefly describe how to control the TrustZone protection on iRAM through two on-SoC components, i.e., TZMA and TZPC. On the i.MX6Quad platform, the function of TZMA is integrated into an on-SoC multiplex controller called I/O Multiplexer Control (IOMUXC), which is shared by multiple I/O devices. The function of TZPC is implemented through an on-SoC component called Central Security Unit (CSU). CSU can only be set by the secure world, which sets individual security access privileges on each of the peripherals. In the following, we present the implementation details of the iRAM controller.

Enabling TrustZone Protection for iRAM. The IOMUXC controller on the i.MX6Quad platform consists of a few registers, and the TrustZone protection for iRAM is controlled through the General Purpose Register 10 (GPR10). Specifically, OCRAM_TZ_ADDR and OCRAM_TZ_EN fields on GPR10 define the start address of the secure iRAM and if TrustZone protection on iRAM is enabled, respectively. The end address of secure iRAM is not configurable, and its value is the highest address of the iRAM. By default, IOMUXC is a non-secure peripheral that could be read/written by rich OS in the normal world. Therefore, two other fields are provided in GPR10, i.e., LOCK_OCRAM_TZ_ADDR and LOCK_OCRAM_TZ_EN, which ensure the values of OCRAM_TZ_ADDR and OCRAM_TZ_EN fields cannot be modified until reset.

Besides the above configuration through IOMUXC, we need to set the access privilege of the iRAM as secure through the central security unit (CSU). In total, there are 40 Config Security Level (CSL) registers on CSU. Each CSL consists of two fields that determine the access permissions for two peripherals. For example, the first field of CSL6 and CSL27 corresponds to IOMUXC and HDMI, respectively. When the permission of a peripheral is set as secure, it could only be accessed when the CPU works in the secure mode.

Since the reference manual of i.MX6 families does not provide clear instructions on what CSL controls the access permission of the iRAM, we perform experiments to figure it out. First, we set the access permissions of all peripherals as secure, except the Universal Asynchronous Receiver/Transmitter (UART1) used to print the log in the normal world. Next we access the secure iRAM from the normal world, and find the secure iRAM could not be read or written. It means iRAM is indeed protected by one of the 40 CSLs. Then we identify the corresponding CSL using a binary search algorithm to narrow down the protected peripherals in half each time. Finally, we find that the second field of CSL26 corresponds to iRAM, while it is marked as reserved in the reference manual for i.MX6 families.

Adjusting the Size of Secure iRAM. Since we can lock the OCRAM_TZ_ADDR and OCRAM_TZ_EN fields, the sensitive data in secure iRAM could not be attacked by the rich OS at run time via either disabling TrustZone protection on iRAM or shrinking the size of secure iRAM. However, it also constrains the dynamic adjustment on the size of secure iRAM, and it may affect efficient utilization of the small-capacity iRAM. When allocating a fixed large size of secure iRAM, it will affect the rich OS on running some operations such as multimedia processing; when allocating a fixed small size of secure iRAM, it will affect the execution of multiple TAs and the trusted display. Therefore, it is necessary for Oath to be able to dynamically adjust the size of secure iRAM. To accomplish this, we achieve security through setting the access permission of IOMUXC as secure, rather than locking the start address of secure iRAM. Thus, the size of secure iRAM can be dynamically adjusted by the secure OS only.

However, since setting IOMUXC as secure peripheral will fail the reading and writing of IOMUXC in rich OS. we must port these operations from the normal world to the secure world. It is not an easy task, since IOMUXC is a multiplexer controller shared by multiple I/O devices, such as HDMI, ENET, USB, UART, SD, etc. The codes to read or write IOMUXC scatter among the rich OS, such as initializing the devices during system boots up. After analyzing the source code, we port the related codes as follows. In general, the registers of IOMUXC could be divided into two types, i.e., device dedicated registers vs. general purpose registers. Access of the former ones is concentrated through the device tree mechanism, so they could be ported uniformly. Though the operations

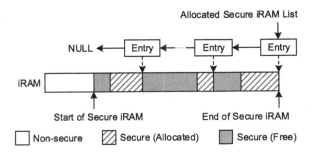

Fig. 3. Management of the secure iRAM

on the later ones are scattered, we can identify them via keyword searching such as GPR, MUX, etc.

In total, 102 IOMUXC operations are ported. Specifically, we substitute the reading and writing of IOMUXC in rich OS with two methods *secure_readl* and *secure_writel*, whose pseudo codes are depicted in Listing 1.1. When being invoked, they first switch to the secure world, perform the read/write operations, and then switch back to the normal world. Since these two methods may be abused by the attackers as a springboard into the secure world, we must check the input *regAddr* parameter to ensure that they can only be used to read or write portions of the IOMUXC registers that are not sensitive-critical. For example, writing to the OCRAM_TZ_ADDR and OCRAM_TZ_EN fields in GRP10 register will be blocked.

Listing 1.1. Secure Read And Write Methods

```
//return value of the register "regAddr"
secure_readl(regAddr);
//write register "regAddr" with value "val"
secure_writel(val, regAddr);
```

5.2   iRAM Manager

The iRAM manager is responsible to manage the secure iRAM. The detailed implementation is illustrated in Fig. 3. The memory range between *Start of Secure iRAM* and *End of Secure iRAM* is the secure iRAM, while the address lower than *Start of Secure iRAM* is non-secure iRAM. The allocated memory is managed with a list named *Allocated Secure iRAM List*, and each entry in the list specifies an allocated memory slot, marked with slash in Fig. 3. Free memory slots are marked gray. The allocation and release of memory is achieved by inserting and deleting an entry to and from the list, respectively. Basically, we adopt the simple but efficient first-fit algorithm [17] to search a free space for allocation. The searching starts from *End of Secure iRAM*, traverses the *Allocated Secure iRAM List*, and stops until finding the first free space whose size is equal or larger than the required size.

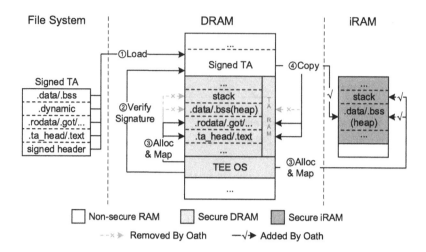

Fig. 4. Procedure to load a TA

The iRAM manager is also responsible for invoking iRAM controller to dynamically adjust the size of secure iRAM region. To enhance the efficient usage of iRAM for both secure OS and rich OS, we need to first figure out the exact utilization of iRAM in rich OS. After investigating the i.MX6 application processor's reference manual [26] and the rich OS source codes, we identify that iRAM is used by rich OS in two main scenarios. First, the lowest 20 KB iRAM memory is statically allocated when rich OS boots up, to store the information such as system suspend/resume codes, DDR frequency modification codes, etc. Second, another 204 KB iRAM is allocated at run time when playing the videos via hardware decoder. The remaining 32 KB iRAM has not been used by rich OS. To make full use of the iRAM memory, the iRAM manager reserves the lowest 20 KB for rich OS and highest 32 KB for secure OS. To minimize the impacts on rich OS, the remaining 204 KB will be set as non-secure when the system boots up. When receiving a TA loading or trusted user interaction request, iRAM controller will set them as secure temporarily, and restore them as non-secure once the sensitive operations are done. In addition, before restoring the iRAM region as non-secure, the iRAM manager erases the iRAM data to prevent potential data leakage.

5.3 Memory Splitting in TA Loader

To support multi-TA execution, we develop a memory splitting mechanism to reduce the secure iRAM usage of each TA. The basic idea is to split the data of a TA into sensitive part and nonsensitive part, and allocate secure iRAM to store and process the sensitive data only. Before implementing the memory splitting mechanism, we first present the normal working flow of the TA loader.

Normal Working Flow of TA Loader. A dynamic TA will be loaded into memory through four steps, as depicted in Fig. 4. Originally, the TA image is stored in the file system of rich OS, consisting of a signed header and an ELF file. When receiving a loading request, the entire image is firstly loaded to the non-secure memory by the TEE client, as shown in Fig. 1. Then the TA loader reads the signed header and verifies the signature of the ELF file. If the verification passes, the TA loader allocates a stack memory from the TA RAM (a secure DRAM region dedicated for TAs) to store the segments in the ELF file marked as PT_LOAD, and then constructs the virtual to physical memory mapping for them. The size of the stack memory is specified in the .ta_head section of ELF file. Finally, the PT_LOAD segments are copied from the non-secure memory to the allocated TA RAM.

Memory Splitting in TA Loader. We first identify the sensitive memory that may contain sensitive data via two following analysis. First, we investigate the TA loading procedure of popular TEE systems including QSEE and OP-TEE, and find that the TA images are stored without encryption in the rich OS's file system. Due to the concerns on data confidentiality, the developers should not store sensitive data directly in the read-only segments, such as .text, .rodata, etc. Otherwise, iRAM or TrustZone can hardly protect them, since the attackers can directly analyze the static images. Second, this work is done cooperatively with a real smartphone vendor. With the access to its commercial TEE platform, we also discover the same sensitive data characteristics by analyzing their TAs, including the TAs used for trusted payment, social interaction, etc. Due to the concern of business confidentiality, related results are excluded from the paper.

In this paper, we assume the sensitive data will only appear in the writable memory, including the initialized or uninitialized global/static variables and the dynamically created stack and heap variables. Therefore, the sensitive sections including the .bss section storing heap variables and the uninitialized global and static variables, the .data section storing the initialized global and static variables, and the stack section are allocated from the secure iRAM memory. We implement a memory splitting mechanism by modifying the last two steps of the TA loader in Fig. 4. Specifically, the TA loader allocates secure iRAM for the sensitive sections including .bss, .data, and stack, with the help of the iRAM manager. The remaining sections are still allocated from the TA RAM. Accordingly, the virtual to physical memory mappings for the .bss, .data, and stack sections are modified. Moreover, the initialized data in the .data and .bss sections are copied to the allocated secure iRAM, while other sections remain unchanged.

5.4   TUI Driver

TUI operations should protect user interactions against the software attacks from compromised rich OS. In addition, we enhance the security of TUI operations to defend against the physical memory disclosure attacks. Basically, the TUI driver stores the sensitive data input and output in the secure iRAM. The current implementation includes two typical user interaction operations, i.e., trusted input and trusted display. The implementation of trusted input is straightforward, as the size of input data is usually small and could be easily stored in the secure iRAM. However, there are two challenges for implementing trusted display. The first one is on the contradiction between the large-size image and the small-capacity iRAM memory, and the other one is on enabling the access of secure iRAM from DMA controller that is needed for displaying. In the following, we introduce the detailed implementation of trusted input and trusted display.

Trusted Input. We illustrate the implementation of trusted input with a simple PIN code input application. Generally, it is achieved through the cooperation of a TA and the TUI driver in the secure world. The TA is responsible to provide a software PIN pad with numbers 0–9 on the touchscreen and derive the input number from the touch event. The TUI driver takes charge to collect the touch events securely and pass them to the TA. First, the trusted input operation is initiated by the user through an app (i.e., CA) in the normal world. Next, after the execution context is switched to the secure world, the TA displays the PIN pad. As such, once the screen is touched, an X-Y coordinate pair representing the position touched is stored into the Analog-to-Digital Converter (ADC) register. Then, the TUI driver can read the coordinate value through the Inter-Integrated Circuit (IIC) bus and store it in the secure iRAM. Finally, the parsing procedure in the TA can derive the corresponding number based on the coordinate value and location of each number. To ensure security, the TUI driver sets the touchscreen's interrupt as secure once the software PIN pad is displayed. When there is a touch on the screen, an interrupt arises in the secure domain and the coordinate value could be obtained in the interrupt handler. When the PIN pad is closed, the interrupt will be restored to non-secure, so that rich OS can use the touchscreen. Moreover, we utilize an on-board LED light (set as a secure peripheral) as an indicator when the TA's PIN pad is displayed, to prevent the malicious rich OS from displaying a fake PIN pad and launching phishing attacks [50].

Trusted Display. We resolve the two challenges for trusted display with two mechanisms. First, we enable dual display and display the sensitive data as a size-adjustable foreground image. Second, during a trusted display, we temporarily set the iRAM memory containing sensitive framebuffer as non-secure and pause the non-secure cores and non-related DMA operations. We resume them when the trusted display is done.

(a) **Configuring IPU for Trusted Display.** The on-SoC Image Processing Unit (IPU) works as part of the video and graphics subsystem on most of i.MX products including i.MX6Quad. It reads the framebuffer data in memory, processes the data, and presents the final image on the display devices such as LCD. In our implementation, we first figure out how data is processed and displayed through IPU. As shown in Fig. 5, IPU can work in single display mode and dual display mode, where the former displays only the background image while the later merges both the foreground and background images. In general, five components of IPU are involved to perform image display, including *Image DMA Controller (IDMAC)*, *Display Multi FIFO Controller (DMFC)*, *Display Processor (DP)*, *Display Controller (DC)*, and *Display Interface (DI)*.

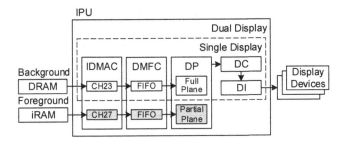

Fig. 5. Image displaying through IPU

As shown in Fig. 5, IDMAC is in charge of controlling the memory port and transferring data from system memory. There are total 64 IDMAC channels for each IPU, in which channel 23 (CH23) and channel 27 (CH27) are responsible to transfer the background and foreground data, respectively. DMFC controls multiple FIFOs for the IDMAC channels related to the display system, which relays the data from IDMAC channels to DP. DP performs the processing required for data sent to a display, such as combining 2 graphics planes and adjusting the brightness, contrast, color saturation, etc. DP has two input FIFOs holding the data of full plane and partial plane, where the former one corresponds to a fixed size background, while the later one corresponds to the foreground whose size is adjustable. DC controls the display ports and thereby specifies the interface to display the image. DI converts the data from the DC to a format suitable for the specific display interface.

Normally, the IPU works in the single display mode. Therefore, in the TUI driver, we switch the IPU to dual display mode, and display the sensitive data as a foreground image. As shown in Fig. 5, three components, i.e., IDMAC, DMFC, and DP, need to be configured to enable dual display, and DC and DI can remain unchanged. To reduce the run-time computations and minimize the memory requirement, we utilize the Look-Up Table (LUT) [5] for the image displaying. With LUT, the Bits Per Pixel (BPP) could be reduced to 4 on our i.MX6Quad platform. It means we can display the sensitive data as a foreground image on the sharpness screen with resolution up to 1920 * 1080 pixels, and it can cover 1/6 screen with only 168.75 KB memory required.

The details on configuring the IPU for sensitive data displaying is illustrated in Listing 1.2. Originally, the rich OS is displaying the User Interface (UI) through IPU. When receiving a trusted display request, the TUI driver first saves the context of IPU and creates the LUT. Then, the IDMAC, DMFC, and DP are configured to display the sensitive data as a foreground image. Specifically, the IDMAC is configured through the `Fg_IDMAC_Config()` method. The parameter `FrameBufAddr` points to the address of foreground framebuffer in secure iRAM, `width` and `height` set the size of the foreground image, `LUTMode` tells the system to adopt LUT mode for displaying. DMFC is then configured to relay the foreground data from CH27 to the DP through the method `DMFC_Config()`.

DP_Config() method configures the position of the foreground on the screen and the transparency. Now the foreground will display the sensitive data stored in the iRAM, while the background is unaffectedly displaying the UI in rich OS. The TUI driver keeps the trusted display until receiving a stop signal from user and then restores the context of IPU.

Listing 1.2. Configuring IPU for Trusted Display

```
//width, height: foreground width and height
//xp, yp: x and y position of foreground
//trans: transparency of foreground
ConfigIPUForTrustedDisplay(width,height,xp,yp,trans) {
    //Preparation
    OriginalIPUContextSave();
    LookUpTableCreate();
    //Configuration
    Fg_IDMAC_Config(FrameBufAddr, width, height, LUTMode)
        ;
    DMFC_Config(FgCH27);
    DP_Config(xp, yp, trans);
    WaitForStop();
    //Restoration
    OriginalIPUContextRestore();
}
```

The configuration in Listing 1.2 also works well when the IPU is origi- nally running in the dual display mode. In this situation, the OriginalIPU ContextSave() and OriginalIPUContextRestore() methods will save and restore the IPU context for both foreground and background. When displaying the sensitive data, the background image will not be affected, while the original foreground will be temporarily interrupted.

(b) **Enabling the Access of Secure iRAM from IPU.** Generally, there are two ways to enable the access of secure iRAM from DMA devices like IPU. First, we can set the IPU as a secure master peripheral, so that it can access the secure memory. Second, we can temporarily set the iRAM containing the sensi- tive foreground framebuffer as non-secure. The first solution can be achieved by configuring the assess policy of IPU as *secure access* through setting the secure access register in CSU. However, the same register also controls the other 5 DMA devices including *VDOA*, *VPU*, *GPU2D*, *GPU3D* and *OPENVG*. Thereby, the configuration enlarges the Trusted Computing Base (TCB) size by allowing the access of secure memory (including secure iRAM and DRAM) to 6 DMA devices. The second solution can be achieved by shrinking the size of secure iRAM through the iRAM controller. However, i.MX6Quad has a quad-core pro- cessor, temporarily setting the sensitive iRAM as non-secure might cause data disclosure to the compromised rich OS. To ensure security, the non-secure cores and non-related DMA operations should be temporarily paused before setting the sensitive iRAM as non-secure, which will thence affect the performance. After considering the trade-off between performance and security, we mainly implement the second solution in this work, i.e., temporarily pausing the execution of rich OS and setting the iRAM containing the sensitive foreground framebuffer as non-secure before conducting the configuration operations in Listing 1.2 and restoring them once the trusted display ends.

As described in Sect. 2.1, one processor core enters the monitor mode when receiving a secure interrupt. Thereby, pausing of non-secure cores could be achieved by sending an inter-processor or inter-core secure interrupt from the secure core. Specifically, the TUI driver first configures the interrupts numbered 8–15 as secure FIQs for each core when the TEE OS boots up. Then, it can pause the non-secure cores by sending an FIQ numbered between 8 and 15. In order to resume the non-secure cores in time, the TUI driver stores a global $flag$ valued 0 in secure DRAM before sending the FIQ, and sets it to 1 once trusted display ends. The corresponding interrupt handler polls the value of $flag$ and switches the cores to the normal world once $flag$ is not set to 0.

There are two types of DMA controllers on our i.MX6Quad platform. One is the controller shared by peripherals, i.e., Smart Direct Memory Access (SDMA). The other one is internal controller associated with dedicated peripheral, e.g., IDMAC of IPU. Both types of DMA controllers could be paused and resumed by writing corresponding registers. For example, the SDMA could be paused and resumed by writing the SDMAARM_STOP_STAT and SDMAARM_HSTART registers, respectively. And each channel of IDMAC could be closed and opened by writing the corresponding IPUx_IDMAC_CH_EN_1 and IPUx_IDMAC_CH_EN_2 registers. The TUI driver saves the original states of these DMA controllers in secure DRAM before pausing them, and restores them once trusted display ends.

6   Evaluation

We evaluate Oath by conducting extensive experiments on the prototype implemented on the FreeScale i.MX6Quad sabre development board. The board is equipped with a quad-core ARM Cortex-A9 processor running at 1.2 GHz with 1GB DDR3 SDRAM and 256 KB onboard internal RAM. The secure world is deployed with the OP-TEE OS 2.2.0, and the normal world is installed with a FreeScale Android 6.0.1 system with a 4.1.15 Linux kernel. The board is also connected with a screen whose resolution is 1024 * 768 pixels. To minimize the noise involved during our experiment, we run each test with 1,000 iterations and take the average values as our measurement results.

6.1   Function Impacts

This section explores the function impacts of Oath upon the rich OS and OP-TEE systems.

Impacts on OP-TEE. Oath is implemented in the secure OS using the OP-TEE system, so we first evaluate if functions of OP-TEE system are affected with the modification introduced by Oath. A test suite named *xtest* (optee_test)

[11,35] is shipped with the OP-TEE source codes as a standard test tool for a complete test on the TEE-solution. The test suite includes test cases for both performance test and function test. Here, we utilize only the function-related test cases, whose number is 22647 in total. Among them, 28 test cases fail on the original OP-TEE system, since they need to invoke the static TAs or hardware components that are missing on our platform. Finally, 22619 test cases are used for evaluation. Generally, the tests are carried out by invoking 12 TAs included in the test suite. The original OP-TEE system loads these TAs in the secure DRAM, and Oath loads .bss, stack, and .data sections of the TAs in the secure iRAM and other parts in the secure DRAM.

Table 1. Function Impacts on OP-TEE

Category	Original	Oath
Main functions (8815)	$\checkmark$	$\checkmark$
TEE internal API (12894)	$\checkmark$	$\checkmark$
TA storage (268)	$\checkmark$	$\checkmark$
Shared memory (125)	$\checkmark$	$\checkmark$
Key derivation (225)	$\checkmark$	$\checkmark$
Sanity test (292)	$\checkmark$	$\checkmark$

To give a clear comparison, we divide the test cases into six categories according to the functions involved. As shown in Table 1, Oath passes all tests that succeed on the original system, which means Oath introduces no negative impacts on the functions of the OP-TEE system. One thing needs to be mentioned here is that 2 among the 12 TAs have a .bss section whose size exceeds 256 KB (the size of iRAM on our i.MX6Quad platform), and therefore they could not be loaded in iRAM successfully. After a detailed analysis, we find these two TAs are set with a huge .bss section to test the concurrent processing capability of the system, e.g., how many TA instances could execute concurrently. It is not a normal requirement for a usual TA. Our investigation on a commercial TEE vendor also shows the .bss sections of real TAs are commonly no more than 32 KB. Therefore, in our experiments, we modify the .bss size of these two TAs to 32 KB. This causes a smaller concurrent number being output in the results, but does not affect the tests of other functions.

Though Oath does not affect the basic functions of the OP-TEE, it does indeed enforce a limitation on the number of the TAs that could be executed concurrently and the size of image that could be securely displayed on the screen, mainly due to the small capacity of the iRAM memory. Table 2 lists the total memory demands and iRAM memory demands of the 12 TAs after deploying Oath. Except two TAs whose iRAM memory demands exceed 256 KB for the requirement of concurrency tests, the average demand of iRAM memory for each TA is 50.52 KB. Therefore, it is able to execute 4 TAs concurrently with the

Table 2. Memory Demands of TAs

TA name	Total(T) (KB)	iRAM(I) (KB)	Ratio (1-I/T)
aes_perf	111.04	47.04	57.64%
concurrent	110.95	46.95	57.68%
* concurrent_large	2126.95	2062.95	3.01%
create_fail_test	89.95	45.95	48.92%
crypt	135.52	47.52	64.94%
* os_test	1122.69	926.69	17.46%
rpc_test	96.96	48.96	49.50%
sha_perf	110.95	46.95	57.68%
sims	128.98	80.98	37.21%
storage	114.95	46.95	59.16%
storage2	114.95	46.95	59.16%
storage_benchmark	98.97	46.97	52.54%

* iRAM memory demand exceeds 256 KB.

maximum secure iRAM of 236 KB. The *Ratio* column illustrates the effectiveness of the memory splitting mechanism introduced in Oath, which reduces 56.49% iRAM memory demand on average. As for the trusted display, our platform is equipped with a screen whose resolution is 1024 * 768 pixels, therefore it needs only 96 KB to display an image covering 1/4 screen.

Impacts on Rich OS. Oath introduces two function impacts on rich OS. The first one is to introduce a transient suspension of the rich OS during trusted display. Generally, 6 actions are performed for an image to be displayed securely. The request is first initiated by user from the normal world, which causes a world context switching. Then, the TUI driver suspends non-secure cores and non-related DMA operations, shrinks secure iRAM to exclude the sensitive frame-buffer, saves the IPU context, and configures IPU for trusted display. As such, the image will be displayed on the screen through IPU. We measure the time consumed for each action with the Performance Monitoring Unit (PMU) in Cortex-A9 processor. The time breakdown is illustrated in Table 3. Totally, it takes 17293.04 μs for the sensitive data to be displayed on the screen. The duration of rich OS suspension is 2884.44 μs, which includes the actions marked with *.

The rich OS continues to be suspended until the user requests to end trusted display. When receiving a stop request, 5 actions are involved to restore the system. First, the TUI driver will enlarge the secure iRAM to include the sensitive framebuffer, restore the IPU context for normal world, and resume the execution of the DMA operations and non-secure cores. Then, the context will be switched to normal world. Totally, it takes 84.63 μs and the duration of rich OS suspension is 50.17 μs. Therefore, the necessary suspension time for each trusted display operation is 2934.61 μs plus the time to wait for the stop request from user.

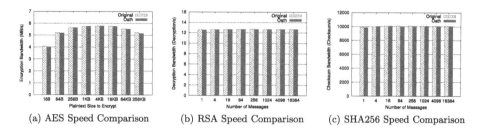

(a) AES Speed Comparison   (b) RSA Speed Comparison   (c) SHA256 Speed Comparison

Fig. 6. Speed comparisons on cryptographic algorithms

Table 3. Time breakdown of trusted display

Action	Display (μs)	Restore (μs)
World switching	14408.60	34.46
* Core suspending/resuming	3.47	42.24
* DMA suspending/resuming	3.24	3.02
* Secure iRAM adjusting	0.08	0.20
* IPU context saving/restoring	1.44	4.71
* IPU configuring	2876.21	–
Total	17293.04	84.63

* Rich OS is suspended.

The second functional impact on the rich OS is due to the occupation of the iRAM memory. As discussed in Sect. 5.2, the lowest 20 KB of iRAM will always be reserved for rich OS. Therefore, the only impact introduced by occupying iRAM is the hardware-based video playing. The experiment results show that the hardware video decoder on our platform utilizes 204 KB iRAM, which means the hardware-based video playing will fail when the available non-secure iRAM is less than 204 KB. However, this problem could be compensated for the following two reasons. First, most video players support two types of decoder, i.e., the hardware decoder and the software decoder. Software video decoder usually does not utilize the iRAM memory. Therefore, it is able to continue video playing through software decoder when TAs or trusted user interactions are executed in the secure OS. On our platform, the videos with resolution not exceeding 1280 * 720 pixels could be played normally through software decoder. Second, in the normal Android OS, video playing would be suspended once the user shifts focus to another application. Therefore, temporarily suspending video playing can hardly impair user experience when another app is performing TUI operations, since the user interface is commonly multiplexed in a time-sharing fashion among different apps.

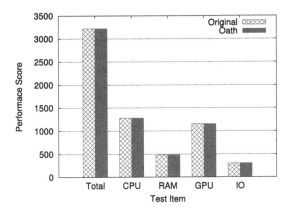

Fig. 7. Comparison of Rich OS Performance

6.2 Performance Impacts

We also study the performance impacts of Oath on the original OP-TEE and rich OS systems. We treat the performance observed from native OP-TEE and Android systems as our baseline and compare it with that observed from Oath.

Impacts on OP-TEE. Generally, the impacts on the OP-TEE system are in two aspects. The first one is the time to load a TA, caused by modifying the TA loading procedure. We test the average loading time for the 10 normal TAs in Table 2 with the help of PMU. The result shows that the time to load a TA with and without Oath is 111.27 ms and 109.77 ms, respectively. In other words, Oath introduces an 1.37% overhead.

The second one is the TA execution performance, as the sensitive TA data is now read from or written to iRAM rather than DRAM. We figure it out by implementing the AES, RSA, and SHA 256 algorithms in three TAs, respectively, and comparing their execution performance on the systems with and without Oath deployed. Figure 6 illustrates the speed comparisons on the three cryptographic algorithms, which shows Oath imposes a small overhead on the TA execution. For example, the highest overhead is introduced when making AES encryption with the plaintext size of 256 KB, and the overhead is 1.8%.

Impacts on Rich OS. Oath introduces two differences in rich OS, i.e., porting the IOMUXC operations into the secure world and occupying part of the iRAM memory. As discussed in Sect. 6.1, the later one is more likely to have function impacts on rich OS rather than performance impacts. However, since the porting introduces two additional world context switching between the secure world and the normal world for each IOMUXC operation, it indeed imposes some overhead on rich OS. First, we compare the system booting time with and without Oath. This is achieved by enabling the *CONFIG_PRINTK_TIME* configuration in Android OS, and obtaining the booting time from the output logs. The result shows that Oath imposes 0.16% overhead in rich OS booting.

Second, we study the overall performance of rich OS through a comprehensive benchmark suite, i.e., AnTuTu 2.9.4. It measures the performance in integer computation, float point operation, 2D and 3D graphic rendering, etc. The results are illustrated in Fig. 7, which shows Oath introduces negligible overhead (less than 0.5%) on the execution of rich OS. There is no changes on the computation overhead when we increase the size of secure iRAM in 32 KB increments.

6.3   Security Analysis

Our system targets at protecting the secure sensitive data, including the user input and output data, against both software attacks and physical memory disclosure attacks. In most case, the sensitive data is only stored in secure iRAM and processed by the secure CPU core, so it is immune against both attacks. However, there are two exceptions.

First, when performing the trusted display operations, the iRAM region containing sensitive framebuffer needs to be accessed by the IPU and thus temporarily set as non-secure. However, the data will remain secure. IPU is also an on-SoC component and all data processed by IPU is stored in the internal buffers that are not accessible from outside. Therefore, the data on IPU could resist both attacks. Moreover, the rich OS is suspended when the sensitive iRAM region is temporarily set as non-secure, thereby it cannot carry out software attacks.

Second, during the trusted input process, since the rich OS is not suspended, the coordinate value in ADC register might be leaked if the rich OS polls the register with a small interval. However, since the ADC register is not writable and will be zeroed once it is read, if the attacker gets the value first, the interrupt handler in the secure world can detect it since the register has been zeroed and stop the trusted input operation. If the value is obtained by the normal secure interrupt handler, the attacker can only obtain value 0.

Both code and data integrity protection depend on the TCB of the Oath system, which is protected by the ARM TrustZone technique. Oath introduces four small modules into the secure OS. In total, Oath adds 764 source line of code (SLOC), where 637 SLOC is on implementing the TUI driver.

7   Discussion and Future Work

Transient Suspension During Trusted Display. During the trusted display procedure, Oath temporarily suspends the execution of rich OS for a few seconds to prevent rich OS from stealing the sensitive display data. Two options could be adopted to optimize the user experience during trusted display. First, we can interleave two mutually exclusive activities, running rich OS and displaying trusted output, with a short time interval, instead of totally pausing the rich OS when waiting until the user finishes. A similar solution has been proposed in TrustOTP to shorten the suspension time [50]. Second, the TZ-RKP solution [14] could be adopted to not affect the availability of rich OS for trusted display. The basic idea is to monitor the memory operations, and block the ones accessing the sensitive iRAM memory region. The optimized solution will cause only transient performance degradation during trusted display rather than entire suspend. We leave these optimization solutions as future work.

Portability on Other Hardware Platforms. We design Oath according to the specification of TrustZone architecture. When manufacturers have different implementations based on TrustZone specification, our detailed implementation may need to be changed accordingly. The dual display technology adopted by Oath to achieve trusted display is not dedicated to i.MX6Quad, which has been supported in many platforms, e.g., NXP i.MX 6Quad/7Dual/8DualXPlus/8QuadXPlus, TI DRA71x/DRA72x, and HiSilicon Kirin 960, etc.

Size Limitation of iRAM. Oath shares the same size-limitation problem as other on-chip storage based solutions. We mitigate the size-limitation problem by introducing a memory splitting mechanism, i.e., locking only the sensitive data rather than entire TA in iRAM. In practice, it works well on most of TAs. Furthermore, we can extend Oath to support TAs with a larger size by introducing another level of virtual memory, i.e., utilizing DRAM as a backup storage for encrypted iRAM pages. A similar work has been proposed in CaSE [56] (a cache-based solution) to support larger sensitive applications.

8   Related Work

One research effort focuses on constructing a trusted execution environment through a high privileged entity, such as hypervisor [18,33,40,53–55] or System Management Mode (SMM) [15]. For example, [18,33] encrypt address space for an application through a hypervisor, so that a hostile OS can only view the address space of the application in ciphertext. However, hypervisor-based solution can not provide the best performance for the resource-constrained mobile platforms. In addition, the hypervisor is already struggling with its own security problems due to increasing TCB size [21,22]. In this work, Oath utilizes the TrustZone technology to shield applications from potentially compromised OS, which eliminates complex, error-prone resource allocation in a hypervisor.

Hardware-assisted protection is also widely explored to shield the applications from untrusted OSes. Flicker [41] takes advantage of Intel Trusted Execution Technology (TXT) and AMD Secure Virtual machine (SVM) to construct a secure isolated execution environment for protecting security sensitive applications. Haven [16] safeguards applications through Intel Software Guard eXtension (SGX) [42], which provides an efficient secure enclave for isolating sensitive applications and automatically encrypts the data stored outside of enclave. For the mobile devices running on ARM processors, TrustZone technology is widely utilized for shielding applications [23,31,34,36,38,47,50,51,57]. While these works take advantage of TrustZone, they require modifications to applications, and could not tackle the physical memory leakage attacks [28,32,39,43]. CaSE [56] realized similar security goal as this paper, by constructing an isolated environment in the L2 cache of the processor. However, occupation of the cache downgrades the performance of normal OS. According to their evaluation, the system becomes unavailable when more than 60% L2 cache (153.6 KB) is used for CaSE applications. Moreover, as cache is not addressable, CaSE hinders the support of TUI operations as many I/O devices work through DMA mechanisms which could only access the addressable memory. Oath tackles these problems by shielding the application on the on-SoC iRAM memory, which is rarely utilized by the rich OS and can be addressed as normal DRAM.

To defend against the physical memory disclosure attacks, several research works [19,27,29,30,44,48,49,56] are proposed, which protect the sensitive application in the on-SoC memory, such as register, cache and OCRAM. For example, Sentry [19] and CaSE [56] use cache locking function for CPU-bound execution. Solutions such as ARMORED [27,29,44,48,49] store the sensitive data in the register. Most of the SoC-bound execution solutions are based on the assumption that the mobile OS is trusted, while Oath assumes the OS could be compromised.

A number of research works [36,37,45,50] devote to provide TUI support in the isolated execution environment. For example, Pawel et al. [45] provide trusted input and output functions through a customized PANTA display processor [24]. It can ensure a strong I/O isolation between two execution environments, however it may have compatible issues and increase the cost, as it depends on a dedicated co-processor. TrustOTP [50] enables trusted display and input, however the sensitive data displayed or input is stored in the DRAM rather than OCRAM as done by our Oath, therefore it may suffer physical memory disclosure attacks. Li et al. [37] propose a trusted path design named TrustUI for mobile devices, which enables secure interaction between end users and services against the software attacks. Based on TrustUI, AdAttester [36] detects and prevents well-known ad frauds by providing unforgeable clicks and verifiable display with the help of TrustZone. AdAttester focuses on remote attestation of the UI operations, while Oath focuses on confidentiality and integrity of the sensitive data (including I/O data).

9   Conclusion

To facilitate the security-critical tasks, vendors have integrated TEE systems on their mobile devices. However, the existing TEE systems mainly focus on defending against the software attacks with the help of the TrustZone mechanism. In this paper, we construct an iRAM-based TEE system named Oath that can protect sensitive data against both software attacks and physical memory disclosure attacks. To be compliant with the GlobalPlatform TEE specifications, we implement a prototype of Oath based on the OP-TEE system. Our experimental results show that Oath introduces negligible function and performance overhead on the OP-TEE and Android systems running in the secure world and the normal world, respectively.

Acknowledgment. This work is supported by the National Key Research and Development Program of China under Grant No. 2016YFB0800102 and No.

2017YFB0802401, the National Natural Science Foundation of China under Grant No. 61802398, the National Cryptography Development Fund under Award No. MMJJ20180222 and MMJJ20170215, the U.S. ONR grants N00014-16-1-3214 and N00014-16-1-3216, and the NSF grants CNS-1815650.

References

1. Quad-core Cortex-A15 SoC features 6MB on-chip RAM (2014). http://linuxgizmos.com/quad-core-cortex-a15-soc-features-6mb-on-chip-ram/
2. Android KeyStore System (2017). https://developer.android.com/training/articles/keystore.html
3. GlobalPlatform made simple guide: Trusted Execution Environment (TEE) Guide (2017). https://www.globalplatform.org/mediaguidetee.asp
4. i.MX 6Dual/6Quad Applications Processors Reference Manual (2017). http://www.nxp.com/products/microcontrollers-and-processors/arm-based-processors-and-mcus/i.mx-applications-processors/i.mx-6-processors
5. Lookup Table (2017). https://en.wikipedia.org/wiki/Lookup_table#Lookup_tables_in_image_processing
6. optee-os (2017). https://github.com/OP-TEE
7. Platforms Supported by OP-TEE (2017). https://github.com/OP-TEE/optee_os#3-platforms-supported
8. Press Guidance Samsung Pay (2017). http://security.samsungmobile.com/doc/Press_Guidance_Samsung_Pay.pdf
9. ARM1176JZF Development Chip On-Chip Memory (2018). http://infocenter.arm.com/help/index.jsp?topic=/com.arm.doc.ddi0375a/Cegegajh.html
10. Arria 10 SoC Hard Processor System (2018). https://www.altera.com/products/soc/portfolio/arria-10-soc/arria10-soc-hps.html
11. OP-TEE sanity testsuite (2018). https://github.com/OP-TEE/optee_test
12. Alves, T., Felton, D.: TrustZone: Integrated hardware and software security. ARM White Paper **3**(4) (2004)
13. ARM.: TrustZone Secure White Paper (2005). http://infocenter.arm.com/help/topic/com.arm.doc.prd29-genc-009492c/PRD29-GENC-009492C_trustzone-security_whitepaper.pdf
14. Azab, A.M., et al.: Hypervision across worlds: real-time Kernel protection from the arm TrustZone secure world, pp. 90–102 (2014)
15. Azab, A.M., Ning, P., Zhang, X.: SICE: a hardware-level strongly isolated computing environment for x86 multi-core platforms. In: ACM Conference on Computer and Communications Security, pp. 375–388 (2011)
16. Baumann, A., Peinado, M., Hunt, G.C.: Shielding applications from an untrusted cloud with haven. ACM Trans. Comput. Syst. **33**(3), 8:1–8:26 (2015). https://doi.org/10.1145/2799647
17. Bays, C.: A comparison of next-fit, first-fit, and best-fit. Commun. ACM **20**(3), 191–192 (1977)
18. Chen, X., et al.: Overshadow: a virtualization-based approach to retrofitting protection in commodity operating systems, pp. 2–13 (2008)
19. Colp, P., et al.: Protecting data on smartphones and tablets from memory attacks. In: Architectural Support for Programming Languages and Operating Systems, vol. 50, no. 4, pp. 177–189 (2015)

20. Coombs, R.: FIDO&TEE: Simpler, Stronger, Authentication (2017). http://www.armtechforum.com.cn/2014/sz/A-8_FIDOandTEE-SimplerStrongerAuthentication.pdf
21. CVEdetails.com.: VMware: Vulnerability statistics (2018). http://www.cvedetails.com/vendor/252/Vmware.html
22. CVEdetails.com.: XEN: Vulnerability statistics (2018). http://www.cvedetails.com/vendor/6276/XEN.html
23. Samsung Electronics: Samsung KNOX (2018). http://www.samsung.com/global/business/mobile/solution/security/samsung-knox
24. Evatronix: Evatronix Launches Display Processor based on Latest ARM Security Technology (2012). http://www.electronicsweekly.com/noticeboard/general/evatronix-launches-display-processor-based-on-latest-arm-security-techno-logy-2012-05/
25. Freescale: Hardware Reference Manual for i.MX53 Quick Start (2011). https://www.nxp.com/docs/en/reference-manual/IMX53QSBRM.pdf
26. Freescale: i.MX 6Solo/6DualLite Applications Processor Reference Manual (2015). http://cache.freescale.com/files/32bit/doc/ref_manual/IMX6SDLRM.pdf
27. Garmany, B., Müller, T.: PRIME: private RSA infrastructure for memory-less encryption. In: Annual Computer Security Applications Conference, ACSAC 2013, New Orleans, LA, USA, 9–13 December 2013, pp. 149–158 (2013). https://doi.org/10.1145/2523649.2523656
28. Gogniat, G., Wolf, T., Burleson, W., Diguet, J., Bossuet, L., Vaslin, R.: Reconfigurable hardware for high-security/ high-performance embedded systems: the SAFES perspective. IEEE Trans. Very Large Scale Integr. Syst. **16**(2), 144–155 (2008)
29. Götzfried, J., Müller, T.: ARMORED: CPU-bound encryption for android-driven ARM devices. In: 2013 International Conference on Availability, Reliability and Security, ARES 2013, Regensburg, Germany, 2–6 September 2013, pp. 161–168 (2013). https://doi.org/10.1109/ARES.2013.23
30. Guan, L., Lin, J., Luo, B., Jing, J.: Copker: computing with private keys without RAM. In: Network and Distributed System Security Symposium (2014)
31. Guan, L., Liu, P., Xing, X., Ge, X., Zhang, S., Yu, M., Jaeger, T.: TrustShadow: secure execution of unmodified applications with ARM TrustZone. In: Proceedings of the 15th Annual International Conference on Mobile Systems, Applications, and Services, MobiSys 2017, Niagara Falls, NY, USA, 19–22 June 2017, pp. 488–501 (2017). https://doi.org/10.1145/3081333.3081349
32. Halderman, J.A., et al.: Lest we remember: cold-boot attacks on encryption keys. Commun. ACM **52**(5), 91–98 (2009)
33. Hofmann, O.S., Kim, S., Dunn, A.M., Lee, M.Z., Witchel, E.: InkTag: secure applications on an untrusted operating system. In: ASPLOS, pp. 265–278 (2013)
34. Jang, J.S., Kong, S., Kim, M., Kim, D., Kang, B.B.: SeCReT: secure channel between rich execution environment and trusted execution environment. In: 22nd Annual Network and Distributed System Security Symposium, NDSS 2015, San Diego, California, USA, 8–11 February 2015 (2015). https://www.ndss-symposium.org/ndss2015/secret-secure-channel-between-rich-execution-environment-and-trusted-execution-environment
35. Bech, J.: Testing a Trusted Execution Environment (2016). https://www.linaro.org/blog/testing-a-trusted-execution-environment/

36. Li, W., Li, H., Chen, H., Xia, Y.: AdAttester: secure online mobile advertisement attestation using TrustZone. In: Proceedings of the 13th Annual International Conference on Mobile Systems, Applications, and Services, MobiSys 2015, Florence, Italy, 19–22 May 2015, pp. 75–88 (2015). https://doi.org/10.1145/2742647.2742676

37. Li, W., et al.: Building trusted path on untrusted device drivers for mobile devices. In: Proceedings of 5th Asia-Pacific Workshop on Systems, p. 8. ACM (2014)

38. Marforio, C., Karapanos, N., Soriente, C., Kostiainen, K., Capkun, S.: Smartphones as practical and secure location verification tokens for payments. In: 21st Annual Network and Distributed System Security Symposium, NDSS 2014, San Diego, California, USA, 23–26 February 2014 (2014). https://www.ndss-symposium.org/ndss2014/smartphones-practical-and-secure-location-verification-tokens-payments

39. Markuze, A., Morrison, A., Tsafrir, D.: True IOMMU protection from DMA attacks: when copy is faster than zero copy. In: Architectural Support for Programming Languages and Operating Systems, vol. 50, no. 2, pp. 249–262 (2016)

40. McCune, J.M., et al.: TrustVisor: efficient TCB reduction and attestation. In: IEEE Symposium on Security and Privacy, pp. 143–158 (2010)

41. McCune, J.M., Parno, B., Perrig, A., Reiter, M.K., Isozaki, H.: Flicker: an execution infrastructure for TCB minimization. In: EuroSys, pp. 315–328 (2008)

42. McKeen, F., et al.: Innovative instructions and software model for isolated execution. In: HASP 2013, The Second Workshop on Hardware and Architectural Support for Security and Privacy, Tel-Aviv, Israel, 23–24 June 2013, p. 10 (2013). https://doi.org/10.1145/2487726.2488368

43. Muller, T., Spreitzenbarth, M.: FROST: forensic recovery of scrambled telephones. In: Applied Cryptography and Network Security, pp. 373–388 (2013)

44. Muller, T., Freiling, F.C., Dewald, A.: TRESOR runs encryption securely outside RAM. In: Usenix Security Symposium (2011)

45. Pawel Duc: Secure Mobile Payments - Protecting display data in TrustZone-enabled SoCs with the Evatronix PANTA Family of Display Processors (2013). http://www.design-reuse.com/articles/30675

46. Samsung: Samsung Exynos 4412 (2017). http://linux-exynos.org/wiki/Samsung_Exynos_4412

47. Santos, N., Raj, H., Saroiu, S., Wolman, A.: Using ARM TrustZone to build a trusted language runtime for mobile applications. In: Architectural Support for Programming Languages and Operating Systems, ASPLOS 2014, Salt Lake City, UT, USA, 1–5 March 2014, pp. 67–80 (2014). https://doi.org/10.1145/2541940.2541949

48. Simmons, P.: Security through amnesia: a software-based solution to the cold boot attack on disk encryption. In: Annual Computer Security Applications Conference, pp. 73–82 (2011)

49. Simmons, P.: Security through amnesia: a software-based solution to the cold boot attack on disk encryption. In: Twenty-Seventh Annual Computer Security Applications Conference, ACSAC 2011, Orlando, FL, USA, 5–9 December 2011, pp. 73–82 (2011). https://doi.org/10.1145/2076732.2076743

50. Sun, H., Sun, K., Wang, Y., Jing, J.: TrustOTP: transforming smartphones into secure one-time password tokens. In: Proceedings of the 22nd ACM SIGSAC Conference on Computer and Communications Security, Denver, CO, USA, 12–16 October 2015, pp. 976–988 (2015). https://doi.org/10.1145/2810103.2813692

51. Sun, H., Sun, K., Wang, Y., Jing, J., Wang, H.: TrustICE: hardware-assisted isolated computing environments on mobile devices, pp. 367–378 (2015)

52. TEXAS INSTRUMENTS: AM5K2E0x Multicore ARM KeyStone II System-on-Chip (SoC) DataSheet (2015). http://www.ti.com/lit/ds/symlink/am5k2e04.pdf
53. Vasudevan, Amit, Parno, Bryan, Qu, Ning, Gligor, Virgil D., Perrig, Adrian: Lockdown: towards a safe and practical architecture for security applications on commodity platforms. In: Katzenbeisser, Stefan, Weippl, Edgar, Camp, L.Jean, Volkamer, Melanie, Reiter, Mike, Zhang, Xinwen (eds.) Trust 2012. LNCS, vol. 7344, pp. 34–54. Springer, Heidelberg (2012). https://doi.org/10.1007/978-3-642-30921-2_3
54. Wang, Z., Jiang, X.: HyperSafe: a lightweight approach to provide lifetime hypervisor control-flow integrity. In: IEEE Symposium on Security and Privacy, pp. 380–395 (2010)
55. Yang, J., Shin, K.G.: Using hypervisor to provide data secrecy for user applications on a per-page basis, pp. 71–80 (2008)
56. Zhang, N., Sun, K., Lou, W., Hou, Y.T.: Case: cache-assisted secure execution on arm processors. In: IEEE Symposium on Security and Privacy, pp. 72–90 (2016)
57. Zhou, Y., Wang, X., Chen, Y., Wang, Z.: ARMlock: hardware-based fault isolation for ARM. In: Proceedings of the 2014 ACM SIGSAC Conference on Computer and Communications Security, Scottsdale, AZ, USA, 3–7 November 2014, pp. 558–569 (2014). https://doi.org/10.1145/2660267.2660344

Privacy-Preserving Collaborative Medical Time Series Analysis Based on Dynamic Time Warping

Xiaoning Liu and Xun Yi[✉]

RMIT University, Melbourne, Australia
{maggie.liu,xun.yi}@rmit.edu.au

Abstract. Evaluating medical time series (e.g., physiological sequences) under dynamic time warping (DTW) derives insights assisting biomedical research and clinical decision making. Due to the natural distribution of medical data, a collaboration among multiple healthcare institutes is required to carry out a reliable and quality medical judgment. Yet sharing medical data cross the boundaries of multiple institutions faces widespread privacy threats, along with increasingly stringent laws and privacy regulations nowadays. Addressing such demands, we propose a privacy-preserving system tailored for the DTW-based analysis over the decentralized medical time series sequences. Our system constructs a secure and scalable architecture to deliver comprehensive results from a joint data analytic task with privacy preservation. To accelerate complicated DTW query processing, our system adapts the advancement in secure multi-party computation (MPC) framework to realize encrypted DTW computation, decomposing complicated and iterative operations into atomic functions under suitable MPC primitives and optimized for DTW. Moreover, our system introduces a secure hybrid pruning strategy that diminishes the volume of time series sequences that are submitted before and processed within the encrypted DTW query. We implement a prototype and evaluate its performance on Amazon Cloud. The empirical evaluation demonstrates the feasibility of our system in practice.

Keywords: Privacy-preserving time series analysis ·
Dynamic time warping · Secure medical application ·
Multi-party computation

1 Introduction

Medical time series analysis produces comprehensive knowledge for modern medical research, driven by the ubiquity of medical data continuously captured by electrical sensors over time. A typical use case comes for a joint disease screening for public health, where researchers, hospitals, and healthcare institutes wish to collaboratively find patients who display similar medical characteristics to the sample of interest. To derive a reliable and quality conclusion, such an analytic

© Springer Nature Switzerland AG 2019
K. Sako et al. (Eds.): ESORICS 2019, LNCS 11736, pp. 439–460, 2019.
https://doi.org/10.1007/978-3-030-29962-0_21

task often requires specific matching algorithms over time series. As a well-known distance metric, dynamic time warping (DTW) is ascendant in answering medical time series mining, such as detecting Premature Ventricular Contraction (PVC) with Electrocardiography (ECG) data [29], and Cardiac Tamponade with Photoplethysmogram (PPG) data [10]. It is effective to handle time shifting that two time series with similar shapes will be matched even they are not synchronized in the time axis.

Advancement in the DTW-based medical analysis system makes it plausible. However, a consensus in practice has emerged that the adoption of the above system will be heavily stumbled due to the privacy issues. Unauthorized exposure of the confidential patient records inflicts severe commercial damages and putting the individuals' privacy in danger [8,12,25]. Atop protecting data confidentiality, underpinning medical analysis to be practical requires the collaboration of multiple institutions. For most medical practices, the data volume and diversity accumulated in a single hospital cannot provide sufficient disease information due to the intrinsic distribution of medical data [12,37]. This is challenging since privacy regulations and laws (e.g., HIPAA in USA [3] and GDPR in Europe [21]) prevent sensitive medical data from ever being shared or pooled together.

One promising approach to deal with joint medical research is leveraging the secure multi-party computation (MPC) techniques [12,19,33]. While the latest studies [20,27] display the ability of MPC to handle large-scale data, how to adapt it to private time series evaluation is unclear. Meanwhile, applying MPC techniques to DTW faces with cumbersome computational overhead. DTW, as a dynamic programming algorithm, the rationale behind is to compute the all-pair underlying distance between elemental vectors of time series. Afterwards, it iteratively finds the minimum cumulative distance of a slightly larger portion of time series until reaching the entire time series. Plenty of iterations of vectorized operations introduce heavy computational costs, which may result in long processing time. As seen, the plaintext algorithm of DTW between only two time series already involves a bunch of complicated operations that are quadratic to the sequence length. Therefore, how to efficiently compute DTW in the encrypted domain, and how to build a secure architecture to facilitate healthcare institutes to jointly and scalably perform encrypted DTW over decentralized medical time series become particularly challenging.

Contributions: In this paper, we propose a system tailored for privacy-preserving collaborative medical time series data analysis based on dynamic time warping. Our system suffices for capturing the above demands: embracing the large volume medical time series sequences that are naturally decentralized, conducting secure DTW queries with practical performance, and delivering quality analytic results benefited from joint mining. The contributions of our proposed system are summarized as follows:

- We construct an architecture allowing multiple healthcare institutes to carry out a joint analytic task over encrypted medical time series sequences supplied by geographically separated parties. This architecture is amiable for a real-world medical analysis scenario. It provides a scalable and dedicated computation service to serve for multiple participants, and releases each party from heavy computation and communication workload.

- We devise a mixed protocol which modularly composes a bunch of customized atomic functions under MPC primitives. Each function in the protocol is carefully devised for the DTW algorithm. This synergy enriches the expressive power of our medical system while providing guaranteed security for the sensitive data sequences.

- Our system elaborates a hybrid pruning strategy to accelerate the secure DTW-query processing on two aspects. Globally, it employs a two-phase scheme to diminish the volume of sequences that will be submitted to the secure protocol. In the first phase, the query is compared only with cluster centers which are precomputed on local, so as to find out candidate clusters whose records are similar to the query. Afterward, in the second phase, the secure DTW query is conducted only within the resulting clusters of the first phase. From the aspect of distance algorithm, resorting to a highly parallel lower bounding technique, our system prunes off the sequences that are not possible to be the best match before submitting to heavyweight secure DTW computation.

- We implement a Java prototype of our system from FlexSC [34], and provide empirical evidence to confirm the practicality of our system using realistic public physiological sequences (ECG data) [1]. We conduct a comprehensive set of evaluations on each component and each phase of our protocol in terms of time and communication costs. Theoretically, each call of comparing two data sequences under the DTW distance function requires 1920 calculations of underlying distance and comparisons to find the minimum distance. Our results show that it takes about 2×10^4 s to process a secure DTW query over 15,000 sequences (each contains 128 vectors), achieving a $100\times$ saving compared with naive sequential scan.

The rest of the paper is organized as follows. Section 2 discusses related literature. Section 3 introduces the preliminaries used in this paper. Section 4 presents our architecture, and detailed system and protocol designs. We give implementation and evaluation in Sect. 5, and conclude the paper in Sect. 6.

2   Related Works

We organize this section as prior arts of privacy-preserving medical data analysis, MPC frameworks and applications, and works of DTW in database domain.

Privacy-Preserving Analysis over Medical Data: Privacy-preserving analysis over human genome sequences is a long-studied problem in secure medical data mining domain, such as evaluating similarity via private set intersection [7] and distance calculation [31], and obtaining statistics via secure genome-wide association studies [19,32]. Recent design [33] proposed by Wang *et al.* embraces million-scale genomic data evaluated under private Edit Distance (ED). Their design preprocesses the data into sets and compares the plaintext values with a public reference genome to find the variances. Then by leveraging the certain pattern of human genome sequences, it approximates the ED computation as *set different size* protocols. Their secure computation is performed over the variances sets, thus achieving high scalability. Zheng *et al.* enable a private medical image (Chest X-ray images) denoising framework based on Deep Neural Network [38]. Their framework securely delivers high-quality content assuring the reliability of image-centric applications, such as cloud side diagnosing. Privacy-aware evaluation over physiological data brings new insights to the secure medical data mining, such as ECG data classification via branching program and neural network [8]. Recently, Zhu *et al.* propose two privacy-preserving protocols to evaluate Paillier-encrypted time series data under DTW and Discrete Frechet Distance (DFD), respectively, in the client-server setting [40]. Their protocols introduce considerable amount of crypto-operations and several rounds of data transfer. Thus, the design is not suitable for the real-world collaborative mining scenario, where multiple parties are involved and the communication cost dominates the overall efficiency. This limitation enlightens us to devise a more scalable and efficient time series evaluation system for encrypted medical data.

Secure Multi-party Computation Framework: Recent years have witnessed a paradigm shift in MPC frameworks, introducing an approach that is mixed with various MPC primitives to achieve efficient secure computation. Kerschbaum *et al.* [24] design a framework combining Yao's Garbled Circuits (GC) and homomorphic encryption (HE). Sharemind [14] develops a high-level language SecreC for Arithmetic sharing, and later is extended to a mixed protocol in [13]. A very recent framework ABY [20] provides automated generation of mixed protocols supporting efficient conversions between Arithmetic sharing, Boolean sharing and Yao's GC. Due to scalability, the mixed-protocols have been applied to many applications [15,22,27,28,39]. Following the same philosophy, we tailor a mixed protocol, one of the key components in our system, to process secure DTW queries for distributed medical data. In the meantime, Blanton *et al.* devise a general distributed platform enabling private medical data analysis [12]. They take the parents assignment problem as an example to show how their platform provides guaranteed security under different settings of the problem and the roles played by the participants. Besides, threshold HE can be used for MPC applications, such as coopetitive learning against a malicious adversary [37] and user profile matching in social networks [36].

Dynamic Time Warping for Time Series Data: DTW is a prevalent distance measure in time series data related mining domains, such as medicine, image/speech processing, and astronomy. It is firstly introduced by Berndt *et al.* in [11]. To accelerate DTW, Keogh proposes an indexing method [23] to perform similarity search on archived data. Atop this index, they design a suite of optimization techniques [29] to search on trillions of streaming data. Beyond search, DTW can also be applied to time series classification [18] and clustering [10].

3   Background

Dynamic Time Warping: Dynamic time warping [23] is a distance metric which measures the dissimilarity over time series data. It is effective to handle time shifting, whereby two time series with similar wavelets are matched even if they are "shrank" or "stretched" in the time axis.

Let $X = (\mathbf{x}_1, ..., \mathbf{x}_{|X|})$ and $Y = (\mathbf{y}_1, ..., \mathbf{y}_{|Y|})$ be two time series sequences consisting with $|X|$ and $|Y|$ numbers of dim-dimensional vectors $\mathbf{x}_i$ and $\mathbf{y}_j$, respectively. Let X_i be the subsequence of X starting from the first vector $\mathbf{x}_1$ to the i-th vector $\mathbf{x}_i$; likewise, Y_j is the subsequence of Y from $\mathbf{y}_1$ to $\mathbf{y}_j$. In our paper, we consider only the data points in X and Y being integers. Without loss of generality, we compare equal-length sequences, that is $|X| = |Y|$. We further denote a dataset contains n-sequences as $\mathbf{Y} = \{Y^1, ..., Y^n\}$.

To align X and Y, we define an *optimal warping path* indicating the minimum warping cost. It is a monotonic and non-overlapped warping path $W = w_1, ..., w_K$, and has to use every index of each time series. W can be evaluated via a dynamic programming approach, i.e., recursively finding the minimum cumulative distance $D(X_i, Y_j)$ of slightly larger portions of subsequences until reaching the entire sequences. $D(X_i, Y_j)$ is declared as the underlying distance $dist(\mathbf{x}_i, \mathbf{y}_j)$ (i.e., the Euclidean distance (ED)) plus the minimum of cumulative distances of adjacent cells. We formulate it as follows:

$$D(X_i, Y_j) = dist(\mathbf{x}_i, \mathbf{y}_j) + min\{D(X_{i-1}, Y_{j-1}), D(X_{i-1}, Y_j), D(X_i, Y_{j-1})\}. \quad (1)$$

The $DTW(X, Y)$ is equal to $D(X_{|X|}, Y_{|Y|})$, and the optimal W is found in the reverse order by a greedy search.

DTW normally applies a global constraint to avoid pathological warping, where a relatively small portion of one sequence would not be warped to map a considerably large portion of another. The constraint introduces a cr-width sliding window that only the elements within the window can be compared; that is for $w_k = (i, j)_k$, i, j should be $j - cr \leq i \leq j + cr$. Both the time and space complexity of DTW is $O(|X||Y|)$. In our design, we expect the proposed protocol to output DTW yet hiding the optimal path since it is the intermediate result. Hence, only the cumulative distances of the adjacent cells are required to be maintained in each iteration. As a result, a linear space complexity can be achieved by only maintaining $\{D(X_i, Y_j)\}_{j=1}^{|Y|}$ and $\{D(X_{i-1}, Y_j)\}_{j=1}^{|Y|}$ in memory.

Keogh's Lower Bound of DTW: Since calculating DTW is very time-demanding, we use the linear-time lower bounding LB_{Keogh} algorithm [23] to prune off sequences that are not possible to be the best match. Given a query X, LB_{Keogh} defines an upperbound U and a lowerbound L surrounding it as $\mathbf{u}_i = max(\mathbf{x}_{i-cr} : \mathbf{x}_{i+cr})$ and $\mathbf{l}_i = min(\mathbf{x}_{i-cr} : \mathbf{x}_{i+cr})$ that $\forall_i, \mathbf{u}_i \geq \mathbf{x}_i \geq \mathbf{l}_i$. Given candidate Y, the distance $LB_{Keogh}(X, Y)$ is formulated as follows:

$$LB_{Keogh}(X, Y) = \sqrt{\sum_{i=1}^{|X|} \begin{cases} (\mathbf{y}_i - \mathbf{u}_i)^2 & \text{if } \mathbf{y}_i > \mathbf{u}_i \\ (\mathbf{y}_i - \mathbf{l}_i)^2 & \text{if } \mathbf{y}_i < \mathbf{l}_i \\ 0 & \text{otherwise} \end{cases}} \quad (2)$$

It is provably tight that $LB_{Keogh}(X, Y) \leq DTW(X, Y)$ and holds linear time complexity. LB_{Keogh} can be deemed as the ED between Y and the closer one of $\{U, L\}$. Since the function of ED is monotonic and concave, we *omit the step of square root* for the ease of deploying to secure computation.

Density Peaks Clustering: Density Peaks (DP) algorithm [30] is a density-based clustering algorithm that is amiable for time series with various shapes (unlike R-tree based DBSCAN and k-means). Given a dataset **Y** and a matrix containing all-pair DTW distances, the DP elects k cluster centers $\{\mathfrak{C}^1, ..., \mathfrak{C}^k\}$, where each $\mathfrak{C}$ is surrounded by lower local density neighbors and is relatively far from any points with higher local densities.

Arithmetic Sharing: On input an ℓ-bit value x, Arithmetic Sharing [6,20] generates shares $\langle x \rangle_0^A, \langle x \rangle_1^A$ in the ring $\mathbb{Z}_{2^\ell}$ uniformly at random, where $\langle x \rangle_0^A + \langle x \rangle_1^A \equiv x \pmod{2^\ell}$. Unless an explicit claim, *all operations performed under* $\pmod{2^\ell}$. For our shared dim-dimensional vectors, P_i calculates the addition non-interactively as $\langle \mathbf{z} \rangle_i^A = \langle \mathbf{x} \rangle_i^A + \langle \mathbf{y} \rangle_i^A$. Multiplication relies on a pre-computed Beaver's Multiplication Triple [9] (denote as MT) of the form $\langle \mathbf{c} \rangle^A = \langle \mathbf{a} \rangle^A \cdot \langle \mathbf{b} \rangle^A$. P_i computes $\langle \mathbf{e} \rangle_i^A = \langle \mathbf{x} \rangle_i^A - \langle \mathbf{a} \rangle_i^A$ and $\langle \mathbf{f} \rangle_i^A = \langle \mathbf{y} \rangle_i^A - \langle \mathbf{b} \rangle_i^A$, and recover $\mathbf{e}$ and $\mathbf{f}$ by sending to the counter-party, and let $\mathsf{Mul}(\langle \mathbf{x} \rangle_i^A, \langle \mathbf{y} \rangle_i^A) = i \cdot \mathbf{e} \times \mathbf{f} + \langle \mathbf{a} \rangle_i^A \times \mathbf{f} + \langle \mathbf{b} \rangle_i^A \times \mathbf{e} + \mathbf{c}$. The MTs can be generated offline and shared obliviously via correlated oblivious transfer extension (COT)[1] [5,20]. Details of generating MTs are given in the full version.

Yao's Garbled Circuits: Yao's protocol (aka garbled circuits (GC)) [35] empowers two secret owners evaluating an arbitrary function $\mathsf{f}(\cdot, \cdot)$ over their inputs x_0, x_1 and obtaining no more than the function's outputs z. Let $GI(z) \leftarrow \mathsf{GC}(x_0; x_1, \mathsf{f})$ denote the above procedure, where $GI(z)$ is the garbled label associated with z. The secret owners can learn the output by communicating the truth table. The point-and-permute [26] optimization allows to reuse the circuit for the same f with different inputs. Given a random in $\mathbb{Z}_{2^\ell}$, Yao's share $\langle x \rangle^Y$ and Arithmetic share $\langle x \rangle^A$ can be converted via modulo subtraction/addition inside the circuits.

4   Our Proposed Design

4.1   Architecture and Assumptions

Figure 1 depicts our architecture overview. It comprises three entities: the owners of medical time series data (aka *"hospitals"* for brevity), the *querier*, and the computational services (aka *"services"*). In our setting, the hospitals gather and archive their medical datasets independently, and a querier holds a patient's data (i.e., the query). Both of them require guaranteed privacy, while all entities perform in a *semi-honest* manner. Everyone will not deviate from the protocol but aiming to deduce the private inputs supplied by other entities. The DTW

---

[1] [20] suggests that the OT-based Multiplication Triples generation is faster than the Homomorphic encryption-based protocol by up to three orders of magnitude.

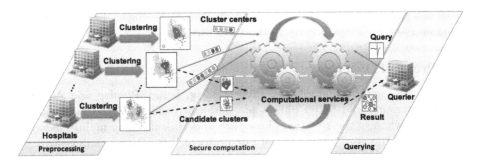

Fig. 1. System architecture

query[2] is issued by the querier who can learn and recover the encrypted results that match the query at the end. We do not constrain the roles of the querier; an individual (medical researcher) or a healthcare stakeholder (hospital) is entitled to extract knowledge about a specific disease. In a typical scenario of medical data analysis, some hospital with insufficient volume of data wishes to act as the querier and seeks assistance from other hospitals to draw a robust conclusion that is only available to herself. Considering the privacy protection, we emphasize two requirements: (1) the querier has to be distinct from the computational services, and (2) each hospital should archive the dataset independently and distributes data directly to the services. In this setting, even the querier conspires with a hospital; they cannot learn private data supplied by the others.

Our security guarantee hinges on the primary requirement that the services learn nothing about the private data they are evaluating. For this reason, it is essential to expatiate on the trust assumption of the services. They are two semi-honest but *non-colluding* services and each consists of a bunch of servers dedicating to the computation over encrypted data. In practice, they can be viewed as the full-fledged cloud services, and follow the prescribed protocols faithfully. It is reasonable since cheating would ruin their reputations. Besides, they should not be simultaneously corrupt or connive with each other. This requirement can be realized by setting up a service agreement that restricts the collusion when signing the business contracts with the two services.

Remark: The above server-aided computational model follows the rationales of prior works [27,28]. Delegating our secure computation on two services relaxes the other parties from involving in all through. Yet it is distinct from the server-aided storage model [4] with regard to the consequences when the trust assumptions are broken. In the server-aided storage model, a logically single data owner partitions the data into shares and outsources each share in different untrusted storage services who cannot communicate mutually. Collusion leads to recover the entire dataset and incurs catastrophic consequence as the whole system is compromised directly. Whereas in our setting, collusion affects the privacy of

---

[2] The DTW query is the process to find the sequences similar to the query based on the DTW distance within a given threshold.

query and query related data, since they are only data engaged in the computation and are deployed directly to the services.

4.2   Protocol Overview

Our protocol includes four phases: Preprocessing, Setup, Pruning and Analysis. The Preprocessing and Setup phases are performed offline at the local side of each party, whereas the rest two phases are undertaken online mainly between two services. The core innovation of our protocol is a secure pruning strategy via two treatments: (1) the Pruning phase for securely comparing the query with the preprocessed cluster centers to prune away the unpromising clusters whose centers are dissimilar to the query, and (2) a secure lower bounding function (the SLB function) to ensures the sequences that are not possible to be the best match being eliminated from the quadratic-time DTW computation (the SDTW function).

To support the pruning strategy, in the Preprocessing phase, each hospital clusters its local sequences into clusters, electing the centers on behalf of the corresponding clusters based on the DP algorithm. Meanwhile, the querier synthesizes an upperbound (U) and a lowerbound (L) binding the range of query based on the LB_{Keogh} algorithm. The synthesized bounds will join the SLB computation in online phases. The intuition of preprocessing is to minimize the portion of secure computation on protected sequences, which always induces higher overheads than an equivalent calculation over the local plaintext values. Afterward, in the Setup phase, both the hospitals and the querier generate secrets of their private sequences under MPC primitives.

To realize the first treatment, the Pruning phase securely compares the query with the cluster centers only. If a center is not similar to the query, none of the sequences in the cluster it represents for would be into the querier's interest. Thus, all sequences in the cluster will be eliminated from further consideration. And if none of the centers of a hospital is similar to the query, it will be considered as an unpromising hospital, then the services will revoke the communications between them. Thereafter, the promising hospitals will be notified to supply the secrets of only candidate clusters into the Analysis phase. This treatment accelerates the overall efficiency by avoiding a considerable amount of sequences from the sequential scan in the Analysis phase. Besides, involving only the promising hospitals in the secure computation can relax other data owners, thus benefiting the case that whose medical devices possessing the data sources cannot always stay online, such as the wearable health-monitor devices and network-enabled implantable medical devices [16].

The second treatment is integrated throughout the online phases. Upon receiving the query, U, and L, whenever in the phase of comparing query with cluster centers (the Pruning phase) or scanning through all sequences in candidate clusters (the Analysis phase), the services always run the SLB function at first to abandon the unpromising sequences as early as possible. Afterward, the SDTW function is carried out between the query and eligible sequences which are closer enough according to the output of the SLB function. This treatment is

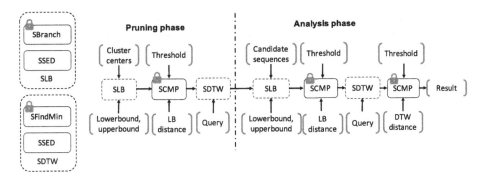

Fig. 2. Online phases overview

economical since SLB involves fewer operations and can be smoothly proceeded in parallel, unlike the must-be-sequential SDTW computation. At the end of the Analysis phase, the services send the result back to the querier. Upon receiving the result, the querier locally reconstructs it yet knowing nothing else.

4.3 Design Rationale

As described above, our secure DTW-based medical analysis protocol is conducted via a hybrid approach that any time series sequences are tested by the LB distance ahead of calculating the DTW distance, defined in Eq. 2 and Eq. 1, respectively. We observe that both equations are performed in an iterative way comprising a series of aggregations. Each aggregation can be divided into two subtasks: (1) computing the secure squared Euclidean distance (SED), and (2) comparison among two items (for LB distance) or three items (for DTW distance). The former consists of only additions and multiplications, and the latter can be achieved by boolean operations. To tackle the above subtasks in a privacy-preserving manner, we choose Arithmetic Sharing for computing secure SED distance and Yao's GC for comparison regarding the reasons below.

(1) Using Yao's GC for all aggregations requires a monolithic circuit solving a linear system as follows. On inputs dim-dimensional vectors $\mathbf{x}_i$ of query X and $\mathbf{y}_j$ of candidate Y, the circuit sequentially computes $(\mathbf{x}_i - \mathbf{y}_j)^2$ along with a comparison, and sums up the result of each iteration as the input of the next iteration. The size of the circuit relies on both dim and the sequence lengths. Putting aside the design difficulty in practice, evaluation on such a large circuit is quit time-consuming. Meanwhile, the circuit cannot be reused on different queries with various lengths due to the dependence between the circuit size and the sequence lengths. We further observe that dim is relatively small in real applications and the comparison involves few items. Thus, we apply GC only for comparison. With optimization [26], we can build the circuit once at the setup phase and used in several epochs. Note that prior work [20] shows that for an atomic comparison circuit on

an integer (i.e., 32-bit values) with long-term security parameter, Yao's GC introduces less query time and bandwidth because of its constant round of interaction.

(2) To avoid the overhead from crypto-operations and considerable data transfer, we choose Arithmetic Sharing to protect the data as random shares in $\mathbb{Z}_{2^\ell}$. For $\ell = 32$-bit operands, it depicts the asymptotic communication [20]. As a result, the online phase is much faster as only a few data (less than 1MB for 10^4 data points) are transferred beyond the private shares, particularly in our cross-institute scenario.

Given the rationale, the Setup phase performs offline to generate the shares of private data, and prepare MTs assisting Arithmetic multiplication. As depicted in Fig. 2, the online phases involves three distance functions SSED, SLB and SDTW, and three GC-based gadgets SBranch, SFindMin, and SCMP. The Pruning phase securely measures the LB and DTW distances between the centers and query via the SLB and the SDTW functions, respectively. Similarly, the Analysis phase computes LB and DTW between candidate sequences and query. All distances are compared with threshold via the SCMP gadget. Both the SLB and SDTW functions resort the SSED function to compute the SED distance. While the SLB resorts the SBranch gadget to determine the LB distance between sequence and U, L based on their rank, the SDTW uses SFindMin to find the minimum cumulative distance.

Gadget SBranch($\langle \mathbf{m_1} \rangle^A, \langle \mathbf{m_2} \rangle^A, \langle c_1 \rangle^A, \langle c_2 \rangle^A, \omega$):
- $S_1 \rightarrow S_0$ sends a pre-built circuit of function f along with its truth table.
- S_0 evaluates $GI(z) \leftarrow$ Y2A(A2Y(GC($\omega, \langle \mathbf{m_1} \rangle^A_1, \langle \mathbf{m_2} \rangle^A_1, \langle c_1 \rangle^A_1, \langle c_2 \rangle^A_1; \langle \mathbf{m_1} \rangle^A_0,$ $\langle \mathbf{m_2} \rangle^A_0, \langle c_1 \rangle^A_0, \langle c_2 \rangle^A_0,$ f))), where f performs the following:
  1. switches $\langle \mathbf{m_1} \rangle^A, \langle \mathbf{m_2} \rangle^A, \langle c_1 \rangle^A, \langle c_2 \rangle^A$ to $\mathbf{m_1}, \mathbf{m_2}, c_1, c_2$ via modular additions;
  2. compares $\mathbf{m_1}$ and $\mathbf{m_2}$, then sets a bit b that $b = 0$ indicates $\|\mathbf{m_1}\| < \|\mathbf{m_2}\|$ and $b = 1$ indicates $\|\mathbf{m_1}\| \geq \|\mathbf{m_2}\|$;
  3. if $b = 0$, sets $z = \langle dist \rangle^A_0 = (c_1 - \omega) \bmod 2^\ell$ so that $\langle dist \rangle^A_1 = \omega$;
  4. if $b = 1$, sets $z = \langle dist \rangle^A_0 = (c_2 - \omega) \bmod 2^\ell$ so that $\langle dist \rangle^A_1 = \omega$;
  5. outputs $GI(z)$ to the evaluator S_0.
- S_0 decodes according to the truth table to get his share as $\langle dist \rangle^A_0 = z$.
- S_1 sets his share as $\langle dist \rangle^A_1 = \omega$

Fig. 3. SBranch gadget.

4.4   Cryptographic Gadgets

Secure Branching Gadget: A branching function is that one of the two values c_1 or c_2 could be assigned to the output c depending on the rank of input messages m_1 and m_2; that is, if $(m_1 > m_2)$ then $c \leftarrow c_1$ else $c \leftarrow c_2$. Let c_1 denote $(\mathbf{y} - \mathbf{u})^2$ and c_2 denote $(\mathbf{l} - \mathbf{y})^2$. Equation 2 ($LB_{Keogh}$) can be viewed as two branching functions running in parallel, and formulated as: (1) if $(\mathbf{y} > \mathbf{u})$ then $dist \leftarrow c_1$ else $dist \leftarrow 0$; and (2) if $(\mathbf{l} > \mathbf{y})$ then $dist \leftarrow c_2$ else $dist \leftarrow 0$. Along with the implicit condition, i.e., $\forall \mathbf{l}, \mathbf{u}$ that $(\mathbf{l} < \mathbf{u})$, this variant is correct as it suggests three conditions $(\mathbf{y} > \mathbf{u} \&\& \mathbf{y} > \mathbf{l})$, $(\mathbf{y} < \mathbf{u} \&\& \mathbf{y} > \mathbf{l})$, and $(\mathbf{y} < \mathbf{u} \&\& \mathbf{y} < \mathbf{l})$ corresponding to the result that $dist$ could be c_1, 0, or c_2, respectively. A naive approach solving this branching function is to determine the rank of $\mathbf{y}$ and $\mathbf{u}$ (or $\mathbf{l}$) via GC, which compares its inputs, and outputs a bit indicating their rank, so that S_0 and S_1 can choose the result from c_1 and c_2. However, leaking the rank of every vector in Y and $\{U, L\}$ allows an adversary to estimate a tight range of query X through adaptive testings with a set of evenly incremented Y. Thus, it is desired to devise a secure branching scheme solving two branching functions at the same time, and obliviously assigns the shares of distance to S_0 and S_1 according to the rank of two inputs.[3] In addition, the outputs of the scheme should be well masked. Even after S_0 and S_1 adding the two outputs up, they cannot deduce the conditions based on the shares they have received. We now describe our proposed secure branching gadget SBranch. Given S_1 as the *generator* and S_0 as the *evaluator*, the shared messages $\mathbf{m_1}$, $\mathbf{m_2}$, the shares of the values to be selected c_1, c_2, a pre-build circuit, and $\omega \in \mathbb{Z}_{2^\ell}$. The SBranch gadget is detailed in Fig. 3. It hides the rank of $\mathbf{m_1}$ and $\mathbf{m_2}$ because S_* always obtains his share as a randomly generated value distributed in $\mathbb{Z}_{2^\ell}$.

Remark: Prior work [27] constructs a branching scheme via GC to test if the input lies in a constant interval. Their scheme cannot directly apply to solve our branching assignments in LB_{Keogh}, where the conditions rely on the values of variables $\mathbf{u}$ and $\mathbf{l}$. Another work [8] represents a linear branching program as a decision tree, where each input is encrypted by homomorphic cryptosystem and comparison is performed via GC, thus introducing heavy crypto-operations.

Secure Find Minimum Gadget: Gadget SFindMin is used to find the minimum value among three given shares, and generate new shares of the minimum value. In our protocol, SFindMin is invoked by the SDTW function. It chooses the minimum cumulative distance $\langle D_{min} \rangle^A$ and re-generates new shares. This operation hides the index of the D_{min}, because revealing the index can leak the optimal warping path of X and Y, and further let the adversary estimate the range of X (or Y). Given S_1 as the *generator* and S_0 as the *evaluator*, a pre-built circuit, the SFindMin gadget is detailed in Fig. 4. Let S_1 generate a random $r \in \mathbb{Z}_{2^\ell}$ as his share $\langle D_{min} \rangle_1^A$, gadget SFindMin outputs $\langle D_{min} \rangle_0^A$ to S_0.

Secure Comparison Gadget: Gadget SCMP is used to compare two given shares and outputs a bit indicating their rank via GC. In our protocol, it determines whether a specific distance is within a matching threshold. Given S_1 as the *generator* and S_0 as the *evaluator*, a pre-build circuit, the gadget SCMP compares its two inputs and output a bit indicating the rank. The SCMP gadget is

---

[3] Another way is building a monolithic circuit to solve a decision tree. This is not under our consideration, since it leads higher latency.

Gadget SFindMin($\langle a \rangle^A$, $\langle b \rangle^A$, $\langle c \rangle^A$):
- S_1 generates $r \in_R \mathbb{Z}_{2^\ell}$ at random.
- $S_1 \rightarrow S_0$ sends a pre-built circuit of function $f(\cdot)$ along with its truth table.
- S_0 evaluates $GI(z) \leftarrow \text{Y2A}(\text{A2Y}(\text{GC}(r, \langle a \rangle_1^A, \langle b \rangle_1^A, \langle c \rangle_1^A; \langle a \rangle_0^A, \langle b \rangle_0^A, \langle c \rangle_0^A, f)))$,
  where f performs the followings:
  1. switches $\langle a \rangle^A$, $\langle b \rangle^A$ and $\langle c \rangle^A$ to a, b and c via modular additions;
  2. compares a, b and c to find the minimum value D_{min};
  3. switches D_{min} back to $\langle D_{min} \rangle^A$ by performing modular subtraction,
     where $\langle D_{min} \rangle_1^A = r$ and $z = \langle D_{min} \rangle_0^A = (D_{min} - r) \bmod 2^\ell$;
  4. outputs $GI(z)$ to the evaluator S_0.
- S_0 decodes according to the truth table to get his share $\langle D_{min} \rangle_0^A = z$.
- S_1 sets his share $\langle D_{min} \rangle_1^A = r$.

Fig. 4. SFindMin gadget.

Gadget SCMP($\langle a \rangle^A$, $\langle b \rangle^A$):
- S_1 generates $r \in_R \mathbb{Z}_{2^\ell}$ at random.
- $S_1 \rightarrow S_0$ sends a pre-built circuit of function f along with its truth table.
- S_0 evaluates $GI(z) \leftarrow \text{Y2A}(\text{A2Y}(\text{GC}(\langle a \rangle_1^A, \langle b \rangle_1^A; \langle a \rangle_0^A, \langle b \rangle_0^A, f)))$, where f
  switches $\langle a \rangle^A$ and $\langle b \rangle^A$ to a and b via modular additions, and compares a
  and b. Then sets a bit z that if $z = 0, a < b$ and if $z = 1, a \geq b$. Then sets
  $z = (a - r) \bmod 2^\ell$ if $a < b$, and $z = (b - r) \bmod 2^\ell$ if $a \geq b$.
- S_0 decodes $GI(z)$ according to the truth table to obtain z.

Fig. 5. SCMP gadget. (Color figure online)

detailed in Fig. 5. It can be realized in two versions achieving different security strengths and performance. Version 1 reveals the rank of LB/DTW distances and threshold when comparing the cluster centers, since this information is not directly related to the private inputs and protocol results. Version 2 in color compares DTW distances of candidate sequences and threshold, and outputs the shares of rank securely.

Function SSED($\langle \mathbf{x} \rangle^A$, $\langle \mathbf{y} \rangle^A$, $\langle \mathbf{x}^2 \rangle^A$, $\langle \mathbf{y}^2 \rangle^A$, MT):
- S_* sets $\langle dist \rangle_*^A = \langle \mathbf{x}^2 \rangle_*^A + \langle \mathbf{y}^2 \rangle_*^A - 2(\text{Mul}^A(\langle \mathbf{x} \rangle_*^A, \langle \mathbf{y} \rangle_*^A))$, where $* \in \{0, 1\}$.

Fig. 6. SSED function.

4.5   Distance Functions

Secure Squared Euclidean Distance Function: Suppose that S_0 and S_1 already obtain the shared vectors of query X and the candidate sequence Y, and the shares of their squared values, denoted as $\langle \mathbf{x} \rangle^A$ and $\langle \mathbf{y} \rangle^A$, and $\langle \mathbf{x}^2 \rangle^A$ and $\langle \mathbf{y}^2 \rangle^A$. They also have a bunch of pre-generated MTs. S_0 and S_1 run function SSED to attain $\langle dist \rangle_0^A$ and $\langle dist \rangle_1^A$ as shown in Fig. 6.

Algorithm 1. Secure LB_{Keogh} function

1: **function** SLB($\langle U \rangle^A, \langle U^2 \rangle^A, \langle L \rangle^A, \langle L^2 \rangle^A, \langle Y \rangle^A, \langle Y^2 \rangle^A, MTs$)
2:     S_* initializes $\langle LB \rangle_*^A$ and $r \leftarrow 0$ for $* \in \{0, 1\}$.
3:     **for** $i \in [1, |X|]$ **do**
4:         S_* initializes $\langle dist_1 \rangle_*^A$, $\langle dist_2 \rangle_*^A$, $\langle c_1 \rangle_*^A$ and $\langle c_2 \rangle_*^A$.
5:         S_1 generates $\omega_i^1, \omega_i^2 \in \mathbb{Z}_{2^\ell}$ at random.
6:         S_* runs to get $\langle c_1 \rangle_*^A \leftarrow$ SSED($\langle \mathbf{u}_i \rangle^A, \langle \mathbf{y}_i \rangle^A, \langle \mathbf{y}_i^2 \rangle^A, \langle \mathbf{u}_i^2 \rangle^A, MT$)
7:         S_* runs to get $\langle c_2 \rangle_*^A \leftarrow$ SSED($\langle \mathbf{l}_i \rangle^A, \langle \mathbf{y}_i \rangle^A, \langle \mathbf{y}_i^2 \rangle^A, \langle \mathbf{l}_i^2 \rangle^A, MT$).
8:         S_* runs to get $\langle dist_1 \rangle_*^A \leftarrow$ SBranch($\langle \mathbf{u} \rangle^A, \langle \mathbf{y} \rangle^A, \langle c_1 \rangle^A, r, \omega_i^1$).
9:         S_* runs to get $\langle dist_2 \rangle_*^A \leftarrow$ SBranch($\langle \mathbf{y} \rangle^A, \langle \mathbf{l} \rangle^A, \langle c_2 \rangle^A, r, \omega_i^2$).
10:         S_* sets $\langle dist \rangle_*^A = \langle dist_1 \rangle_*^A + \langle dist_2 \rangle_*^A$, and $\langle LB \rangle_*^A = \langle LB \rangle_*^A + \langle dist \rangle_*^A$.
11:     **end for**
12:     S_* gets $\langle LB \rangle_*^A$.
13: **end function**

Secure LB_{Keogh} Function: Algorithm 1 shows the SLB function running between sequence Y and two synthesized sequences U and L. It iteratively sums up $|X|$ numbers of secure SED distances indicating how far Y falls out of the range of X bound by U and L. Let $\langle Y \rangle^A$, $\langle Y^2 \rangle^A$, $\langle U \rangle^A$, $\langle U^2 \rangle^A$, $\langle L \rangle^A$, $\langle L^2 \rangle^A$ denote the shares of Y, U, and L, and the shares of their squared values, respectively. On inputs these shares, and MTs, the SLB function outputs $\langle LB \rangle_*^A$ in private. In detail, once it is launched, S_* initialize variable $r = 0$ as one of the distances awaiting to be selected by the SBranch gadget, where $* \in \{0, 1\}$. In each iteration, S_1 generates randomnesses $\omega_i^1, \omega_i^2 \in \mathbb{Z}_{2^\ell}$. Afterwards, S_* invoke the SSED function to compute the shares of $dist(\langle \mathbf{y}_i \rangle^A, \langle \mathbf{u}_i \rangle^A)$ as $\langle c_1 \rangle_*^A$, and the shares of $dist(\langle \mathbf{y}_i \rangle^A, \langle \mathbf{l}_i \rangle^A)$ as $\langle c_2 \rangle_*^A$. They then invoke SBranch to assign one of the values $\langle c_1 \rangle_*^A$ (or $\langle c_2 \rangle_*^A$) and r to $\langle dist_1 \rangle_*^A$ (or $\langle dist_2 \rangle_*^A$), according to the rank of $\mathbf{y}$ and $\mathbf{u}$ (or $\mathbf{l}$). The output distance is masked with ω_i^1 (or ω_i^2). In other words, the value of $\langle dist_1 \rangle^A$ could be c_1 or 0, while the value of $\langle dist_2 \rangle^A$ could be c_2 or 0. This treatment is correct, since after S_0 and S_1 adding them up, the value of $\langle dist \rangle^A$ could be c_1, c_2 or 0, yet not $c_1 + c_2$, because of the implicit condition $\mathbf{u} > \mathbf{l}$ excludes this case. At the end of each iteration, S_* add $\langle dist \rangle_*^A$ on the $\langle LB \rangle_*^A$ attained in the previous iteration. Ultimately, they get the final result of secure LB distance between Y and $\{U, L\}$.

Secure DTW Function: The SDTW function, as Algorithm 2 illustrates, is the core building block as it measures whether a sequence Y matches the given query X based on DTW. On inputs $\langle Y \rangle^A, \langle Y^2 \rangle^A, \langle X \rangle^A, \langle X^2 \rangle^A$ and MTs, it returns $\langle DTW \rangle^A$. Because the parameter cr of global constraint is a data-independent constant, we assume it is known by S_0 and S_1 as a system parameter. We briefly sketch the philosophy of realizing the SDTW function. We maintain a pair of

---

Algorithm 2. Secure DTW function:

1: **function** SDTW($\langle X \rangle^A, \langle X^2 \rangle^A, \langle Y \rangle^A, \langle Y^2 \rangle^A, MTs$)

2:     S_* initializes $\langle DTW \rangle_*^A$ and two arrays $cost_*$ and $cost_{prev,*}$ with numeric infinity (INF), that each has $(2cr + 1)$ numbers of cells for $* \in \{0, 1\}$.

3:     **for** $i \in [0, |X| - 1]$ **do**

4:         S_* initializes $k \leftarrow max(0, cr - i)$.

5:         **for** $j \in [\, max(0, i - cr), min(|X| - 1, i + cr)]$ **do**

6:             S_* initializes $\langle a \rangle_*^A, \langle b \rangle_*^A, \langle c \rangle_*^A$ with INF, $\langle dist \rangle_*^A$, and $\langle D \rangle_*^A$.

7:             If $i = 0$ && $j = 0$, S_* jointly run to get $\langle dist \rangle_*^A \leftarrow$ SSED($\langle \mathbf{x_0} \rangle^A, \langle \mathbf{y_0} \rangle^A$, $\langle \mathbf{x_0^2} \rangle^A, \langle \mathbf{y_0^2} \rangle^A, MT$), and stores each share at $cost_*[k]$. S_* sets $k ++$, and continues to next iteration.

8:             If $j \geq 1$ && $k \geq 1$, S_* sets $\langle b \rangle_*^A \leftarrow cost_*[k-1]$; else INF.

9:             If $i \geq 1$ && $k + 1 \leq 2 * cr$, S_* sets $\langle a \rangle_*^A \leftarrow cost_{perv,*}[k+1]$; else INF.

10:             If $i \geq 1$ && $j \geq 1$, S_* sets $\langle c \rangle_*^A \leftarrow cost_{prev,*}[k]$; else INF.

11:             S_* run $\langle D \rangle_*^A \leftarrow$ SSED($\langle \mathbf{x}_i \rangle^A, \langle \mathbf{y}_j \rangle^A, \langle \mathbf{x}_i^2 \rangle^A, \langle \mathbf{y}_j^2 \rangle^A, MT$) + SFindMin ($\langle a \rangle^A, \langle b \rangle^A, \langle c \rangle^A$), and stores each share at $cost_*[k]$, and then sets $k ++$.

12:         **end for**

13:         S_* copies $cost_*$ to $cost_{prev,*}$, and cleans $cost_*$.

14:     **end for**

15:     S_* gets $\langle DTW \rangle_*^A \leftarrow cost_{prev,*}[cr]$.

16: **end function**

---

arrays $cost$ and $cost_{prev}$ with $2cr + 1$ cells to record the cumulative distances between X_i, X_{i+1} and Y. For each i, the arrays act as vertical bars moving from left to right and bottom-up one cell each iteration. Let us consider how to calculate one distance $D(X_i, Y_j)$ only. Assume cell $cost[k]$ store $D(X_i, Y_j)$, where $k \in [max(0, cr-i), 2cr+1]$. We first calculate $dist(\mathbf{x_i}, \mathbf{y_j})$. We then check whether the awaiting calculated $D(X_i, Y_j)$ is located at the edge of the sliding window formed by the global constraint, i.e., at $cost_*[0]$ or $cost_*[2cr + 1]$. If not, we find the minimum value among its adjacent cumulative distances, i.e., $D(X_i, Y_{j-1})$, $D(X_{i-1}, Y_j)$ and $D(X_{i-1}, Y_{j-1})$ located at cells $cost[k - 1]$, $cost_{prev}[k + 1]$ and $cost_{prev}[k]$. Otherwise, we retrieve the minimum among the existences of the above three values. We add the above results up as $D(X_i, Y_j)$, and store into cell $cost[k]$. At the end, the DTW is located at $cost_{prev}[cr]$. Following the above methodology, S_0 and S_1 iteratively calculate $\langle dist \rangle^A$ via the SSED function, find the minimum $\langle D_{min} \rangle_*^A$ among $\langle a \rangle_*^A$, $\langle b \rangle_*^A$ and $\langle c \rangle_*^A$ via the SFindMin gadget, and sum them up as $\langle D \rangle_*^A$. Ultimately, S_0 and S_1 obtain $\langle DTW \rangle_*^A$ at $cost_{prev,*}^A[cr]$.

4.6   Secure DTW-based Medical Analysis Protocol

Figure 7 describes our protocol Φ that modularly composes the above crypto-gadgets and atomic functions.

Setup Phase: Consider each hospital $H_\alpha \in \{H_1, ..., H_m\}$ holds an n-sequences dataset $\mathbf{Y}^\alpha = \{Y^1, ..., Y^n\}$. Each hospital pre-partitions the local dataset as k clusters $\mathbf{C}_1 = \{C^1, ..., C^k\}$ represented by centers $\mathfrak{C}^1, ..., \mathfrak{C}^k$. Given pre-computed

Protocol Φ:

Setup$(X, U, L, \{\mathbf{C}_1, ..., \mathbf{C}_m\}, \Delta)$:

1: S_0 and S_1 interactively generate M sets of MTs. S_1 generates three circuits for the SBranch, SFindMin and SCMP gadgets.

2: Q locally generates the shares $\langle \Delta \rangle^A$, $\langle X \rangle^A$, $\langle X^2 \rangle^A$, $\langle U \rangle^A$, $\langle U^2 \rangle^A$, $\langle L \rangle^A$, $\langle L^2 \rangle^A$, and distributes them to S_0 and S_1.

3: Each H_α locally generates the shares $\langle Y \rangle^A$ and $\langle Y^2 \rangle^A$ of $Y \in \mathbf{Y}_\alpha$, $\langle \mathfrak{C}^\beta \rangle^A$ and $\langle (\mathfrak{C}^\beta)^2 \rangle^A$ of $\mathfrak{C}^\beta$, and dummy indices $r_\beta \in \{r_1, ..., r_k\}$ randomly for each cluster, where $\beta \in [1, k]$, and distributes them to S_0 and S_1.

Pruning$(\langle U \rangle^A, \langle U^2 \rangle^A, \langle L \rangle^A, \langle L^2 \rangle^A, \langle X \rangle^A, \langle X^2 \rangle^A, \langle \mathfrak{C}^\beta \rangle^A, \langle (\mathfrak{C}^\beta)^2 \rangle^A, \langle \Delta \rangle^A)$:

1: S_0 initializes an array $\mathbf{Arr}_\alpha^C$.

2: **for** each cluster center $\mathfrak{C}^\beta \in \mathbf{C}_\alpha$ in each H_α **do**

3:     S_* run $\langle LB_{\mathfrak{C}} \rangle_*^A \leftarrow$ SLB$(\langle U \rangle^A, \langle U^2 \rangle^A, \langle L \rangle^A, \langle L^2 \rangle^A, \langle \mathfrak{C}^\beta \rangle^A, \langle (\mathfrak{C}^\beta)^2 \rangle^A, MTs)$ for $* \in \{0, 1\}$.

4:     If SCMP$(\langle LB_{\mathfrak{C}} \rangle^A, \langle \Delta \rangle^A) == 0$, S_* run $\langle DTW_{\mathfrak{C}} \rangle_*^A \leftarrow$ SDTW$(\langle X \rangle^A, \langle X^2 \rangle^A,$ $\langle \mathfrak{C}^\beta \rangle^A, \langle (\mathfrak{C}^\beta)^2 \rangle^A, MTs)$. Else, continue to next.

5:     If SCMP$(\langle DTW_{\mathfrak{C}} \rangle^A, \langle \Delta \rangle^A) == 0$, S_0 adds index r_β of cluster C^β to $\mathbf{Arr}_\alpha^C$. Else, continue to next.

6: **end for**

7: If $\mathbf{Arr}_\alpha^C = \perp$, S_* close the connections with H_α. Else, S_0 sends $\mathbf{Arr}_\alpha^C$ to H_α.

8: H_α distributes $\langle \bar{Y} \rangle^A$ of each $\bar{Y}$ in all candidate clusters $\bar{C}^\beta$ to S_0 and S_1.

Analysis$(\langle U \rangle^A, \langle U^2 \rangle^A, \langle L \rangle^A, \langle L^2 \rangle^A, \langle X \rangle^A, \langle X^2 \rangle^A, \langle \bar{Y} \rangle^A, \langle \bar{Y}^2 \rangle^A, \langle \Delta \rangle^A)$:

1: S_* initialize arrays $\mathbf{Arr}_{\alpha,*}$.

2: **for** each sequence $\bar{Y}$ in all candidate clusters $\bar{C}^\beta$ **do**

3:     S_* run $\langle LB \rangle_*^A \leftarrow$ SLB$(\langle U \rangle^A, \langle U^2 \rangle^A, \langle L \rangle^A, \langle L^2 \rangle^A, \langle \bar{Y} \rangle^A, \langle \bar{Y}^2 \rangle^A, MTs)$.

4:     If SCMP$(\langle LB \rangle^A, \langle \Delta \rangle^A) == 0$, S_* run $\langle DTW \rangle_*^A \leftarrow$ SDTW$(\langle X \rangle^A, \langle X^2 \rangle^A,$ $\langle \bar{Y} \rangle^A, \langle \bar{Y}^2 \rangle^A, MTs)$. Else, continue to next.

5:     S_* tun to get $\langle res \rangle_*^A \leftarrow$ SCMP$(\langle DTW \rangle^A, \langle \Delta \rangle^A)$ and store to $\mathbf{Arr}_{\alpha,*}$.

6: **end for**

7: S_* sends $\mathbf{Arr}_{\alpha,*}$ to Q.

8: Q runs reconstruction Rec$^A(res)$ and remove 0 to get each DTW in $\mathbf{Arr}_\alpha$.

Fig. 7. Secure DTW-based medical time series analysis protocol

synthesized U and L binding the query X, and the matching threshold Δ held by querier Q. Once the Setup phase begins, the querier and all hospitals run in parallel to generate the Arithmetic shares of their private data, and distribute the shares to S_0 and S_1. To assist multiplication over shares, S_0 and S_1 interactively derive dim-dimensional MT. $(\langle \mathbf{c} \rangle^A, \langle \mathbf{a} \rangle^A, \langle \mathbf{b} \rangle^A)$ that $\mathbf{c} = \mathbf{a} \times \mathbf{b}$. Note that single multiplication operation requires one MT. Apart from MTs, S_1 generates three circuits for the SBranch, SFindMin and SCMP gadgets, respectively.

Secure Pruning Phase: The Pruning phase runs in parallel between each pair of instances of S_0 and S_1 connecting with each H_α. Without loss of generality, we discuss one pair of instances with H_α as an example. S_0 initializes a dynamic array $\mathbf{Arr}_\alpha^C$ used to store the dummy index r_β of the potential clusters C^β. S_0 and S_1 jointly run the SLB function to get $\langle LB_{\mathfrak{C}} \rangle_*^A$ between $\mathfrak{C}^\beta$ and $\{U, L\}$, where $* \in \{0,1\}$. They then invoke the SCMP gadget to check if the resulted $\langle LB_{\mathfrak{C}} \rangle_*^A$ is less than $\langle \Delta \rangle^A$. If so, they run the SDTW function to get $\langle DTW_{\mathfrak{C}} \rangle_*^A$ and check whether it is less than $\langle \Delta \rangle^A$. If it is, S_0 adds the dummy index r_β of the currently processed $\mathfrak{C}^\beta$ to $\mathbf{Arr}_\alpha^C$. After checking all $\mathfrak{C}^\beta$, if $\mathbf{Arr}_\alpha^C$ is not empty, S_0 sends it to H_α, and H_α sends back the shares of each sequence $\bar{Y}$ in candidate clusters $\bar{C}^\beta$ corresponding to r_β. Otherwise, S_0 and S_1 revoke the connection with H_α who does not need to stay online anymore.

Secure DTW-Based Analysis Phase: The Anaysis phase runs in parallel between S_0 and S_1 with each candidate hospital $\bar{H}_\alpha$. S_* initializes dynamic array $\mathbf{Arr}_{\alpha,*}$ to store the shares of resulting secure DTW distances, where $* \in \{0,1\}$. For each candidate sequence $\bar{Y}$ (i.e., the results of previous phase), S_* runs the SLB function to get the shares of LB distance between $\bar{Y}$ and X, denoted as $\langle LB \rangle_*^A$. S_* then calls the SCMP gadget to compare $\langle LB \rangle^A$ and $\langle \Delta \rangle^A$. If $\langle LB \rangle_*^A$ is within the threshold, they run SDTW to get $\langle DTW \rangle_*^A$. Services then input $\langle DTW \rangle^A$ and $\langle \Delta \rangle^A$ to the SCMP gadget which outputs the shares of the smaller one, and store to $\mathbf{Arr}_{\alpha,*}$. Ultimately, S_0 and S_1 send $\mathbf{Arr}_{\alpha,*}$ to Q who then reconstructs the results, excludes the values identical to threshold, and get DTWs indicating how likely an individual will have a specific disease.

Remark of Complexity: Suppose sequence length $|X|$, global constraint cr, pruning ratio σ of the SLB function, and pruning ratio μ of the Pruning phase. Given all cluster centers $\mathfrak{C}^{\alpha,\beta}$, all dataset $\mathbf{Y}^\alpha$ with n sequences, where $\alpha \in [1,m], \beta \in [1,k]$. Computing one SLB function requires $2|X|$ calls of the SSED function and the SBranch gadget. Computing one SDTW function runs $|X| \cdot (2cr + 1) - cr \cdot (cr + 1)$ (denoted as θ_{sdtw}) times the SSED function and the SFindMin gadget. The number of calls of atomic functions is summarized in Table 1.

Table 1. Number of calls of atomic functions

	#SBranch	#SFindMin	#SCMP	#SSED	#SLB	#SDTW
Pruning phase	$2\|X\|mk$	$\theta_{sdtw}\sigma mk$	$(1+\sigma)mk$	$(\theta_{sdtw}\sigma + 2\|X\|)mk$	mk	σmk
Analysis phase	$2\|X\|\mu mn$	$\theta_{sdtw}\mu\sigma mn$	$(1+\sigma)\mu mn$	$(\theta_{sdtw}\sigma + 2\|X\|)\mu mn$	μmk	$\mu\sigma mn$

4.7   Security Guarantee

For our multi-instance and concurrent-execution protocol Φ, we define security following the *Universally Composable* (UC) security framework [17], where under a general protocol composition operation (*universal composition*), the security of our protocol is preserved. Consider engaged parties a querier Q, hospitals $H_1, ..., H_m$ and two non-colluding services S_0, S_1. Suppose a semi-honest *admissible adversary* $\mathcal{A}$ who can corrupt the querier, any subset of hospitals, as well as one of the two non-colluding services at most, i.e., if S_0 is compromised by $\mathcal{A}$, S_1 acts honestly; vice versa. Yet we do not restrict the collusions among the rest parties. Since our protocol directly follows the security of the Arithmetic sharing [6] and GC [35], and all medical sequences, MTs, and intermediate results are well protected as randomly generated shares in the ring $\mathbb{Z}_{2^\ell}$, we argue that Φ UC-realizes an ideal functionality $\mathcal{F}$ against $\mathcal{A}$. The security captures the property that the only pertinent data learned by any corrupted parties are their inputs and outputs from the protocol yet nothing about the data of the remaining honest parties. Due to space constraints, formal security proof is given in the full version of this paper.

5   Performance Evaluation

5.1   Implementation and Setup

We implement a prototype of our secure DTW-based medical analysis system in Java. For the choice of OT and GC, we utilize FlexSC [34], i.e., a Java-based toolkit implementing extended OTs [5] and optimizations of GC. Regarding Arithmetic Sharing, we set the size of the ring as 2^{31} to fit in the Java primitive type int rather than BigInteger, resulting in acceleration on modulo addition and multiplication. We deploy this prototype on 4 Amazon EC2 c5.4xlarge instances running Ubuntu 16.04 LTS with 3.0 GHz Intel Xeon Platinum processor (16 vCPUs), 32 GB RAM, and 10 Gpbs virtual NIC each; performing two services, a hospital and a querier. The reported measurements make use of a 256 Hz ECG dataset, derived from UCR Time Series Datasets at [2] (a real-world dataset from PhysioBank [1]). Our dataset contains 15K sequences and queries with length 128, formed with single dimensional vectors. The dataset is stored at in-memory Redis(v3.0.6) database as key-value pairs. We apply global constraint $cr = 0.05 * 128 = 7$ to LB and DTW [29].

To improve runtime performance, we use the in-memory Redis database to catch the intermediate results, such as the all-pair distance matrix used for DP clustering. Besides, we store a bunch of randomly generated MTs in files (300 triples each file). Once required, the services will randomly select files to retrieve a set of MTs upon the demand of computation, and then delete the files to ensure the randomization of MTs. Besides, we modify FlexSC slightly to enable concurrent processing of the SLB function.

5.2   Evaluation

Cryptographic Gadgets: The performance of crypto-gadgets is summarized in Table 7 regarding the running time on the local network, the bandwidth and the number of AND gates. All three measures are increased linearly to the number of inputs, while the time fluctuates slightly. Besides, the empirical cumulative distribution function (CDF), as shown in Fig. 11, sheds light on the distribution of the time on running individual gadget. We grab 1K executions and all of four gadgets can be done within 0.4 s.

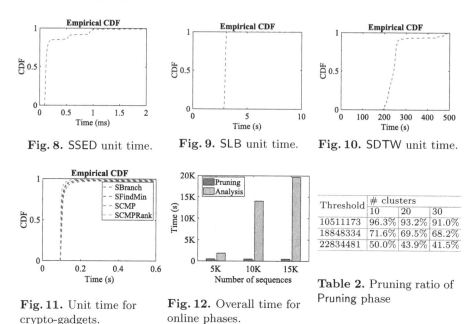

Fig. 8. SSED unit time.   **Fig. 9.** SLB unit time.   **Fig. 10.** SDTW unit time.

Fig. 11. Unit time for crypto-gadgets.   **Fig. 12.** Overall time for online phases.

Threshold	# clusters		
	10	20	30
10511173	96.3%	93.2%	91.0%
18848334	71.6%	69.5%	68.2%
22834481	50.0%	43.9%	41.5%

Table 2. Pruning ratio of Pruning phase

Distance Functions: We benchmark the execution of distance functions SSED, SLB, and SDTW. The time and bandwidth ascend linearly for all of them in line with the number of calls as Table 3 illustrates. In addition, we grasp 5K unit execution times of SSED, SLB, and SDTW to form their distributions by empirical CDF. As exhibited in Fig. 8, the unit call of SSED can be finished within 1.5 ms. Likewise, Fig. 9 depicts the unit time of SLB, where 4 s is sufficient to a single execution. We further estimate the theoretical unit time of SLB, combining 128*2 calls of SSED and SBranch. Given the unit time of SBranch as 0.055 s and SSED as 1.5 ms, the theoretical unit time is 15 s. The retrenchment of time consumed in practice is contributed by the concurrent implementation, where every distance between each two data vectors can be calculated by independent thread in parallel. Similarly, Fig. 10 illustrates the unit time of SDTW, which is larger than 200 s. This confirms the reasonableness of our pruning strategy.

Table 3. Performance of distance functions

	SSED		SLB		SDTW	
# calls	Time	Comm.	Time	Comm.	Time	Comm.
10000	1.88 s	0.30 MB	18462.5 s	108.7 GB	2167591.4 s	731.9 GB
20000	3.30 s	0.61 MB	44609.6 s	217.3 GB	5221399.3 s	1463.9 GB
30000	4.59 s	0.91 MB	79900.5 s	325.9 GB	7551764.1 s	2195.8 GB

Yet we remark this experiment result does not beyond our expectation, because running SDTW function over 10K sequences involves $1.92 * 10^7$ calls of SSED and SFindMin.

Online Phases: We then turn our attention from runtime overhead of atomic operations to the workload of each party in each phase of our protocol. The overall time of online phases is evaluated in chunks of 5K sequences with threshold 22834481. Each set of data is randomly selected from our dataset and partitioned in 10 clusters. We report the number of sequences similar to the query as 8 for 5K data, 59 for 10K data, and 87 for 15K data. As Fig. 12 depicts, followed by the growth of dataset, the run-time of Pruning phase remains a flat trend as its computational overhead depends on the number of clusters. In contrast, the time of Analysis phase ascends sharply yet does not form linear increase, since its workload depends on two aspects: (1) the sequential test under the SLB function over all candidate sequences submitted to Analysis phase, and (2) the quadratic time SDTW computation over resulting sequences from the SLB function.

The effectiveness of applying Pruning phase is confirmed via pruning ratios with 15K sequences classified in 10, 20 and 30 clusters and a group of thresholds randomly extracted from DTW distances. The ratio is qualitative as the number of excluded sequences divides the size of dataset. As Table 2 exhibits, the ratio drops down with the increasing amount of clusters and values of threshold, yet avoiding at least 6K sequences from the sequential scan.

# MTs	Time	Comm.
10^5	610.4s	2.9GB
10^7	60885.1s	292.6GB
10^9	6052449.5s	29263.2GB

Table 4. Setup phase performance of services

# queries	Time (LB/UB)	Time (sharing)
1	2.0ms	1.3ms
100	10.6ms	10.5ms
1000	51.5ms	38.5ms

Table 5. Preprocess and setup phases performance of querier

# sequences	Time (DP)	Time (sharing)
5000	5467.6s	0.2s
10000	55558.2s	0.3s
15000	421895.4s	0.6s

Table 6. Preprocess and setup phases performance of hospital

Preprocess and Setup Phases: Table 4 shows the time and bandwidth costs of two services in the Setup phase. Both of them rise linearly with the amount

Table 7. Performance of gadgets.

# inputs	Time	Comm	Gates	# inputs	Time	Comm	Gates
SBranch				SFindMin			
10^5	605.1 s	3.0 GB	$859*10^5$	10^6	5533.2 s	26.9 GB	$764*10^6$
10^6	6190.5 s	30.2 GB	$859*10^6$	10^7	58915.2 s	268.9 GB	$764*10^7$
10^7	69387.3 s	301.5 GB	$859*10^7$	10^8	576590.7 s	2689.6 GB	$764*10^8$
SCMP				SCMP (leak rank)			
10^4	46.5 s	0.2 GB	$541*10^4$	10^4	39.5 s	0.17 GB	$350*10^4$
10^5	455.1 s	2.1 GB	$541*10^5$	10^5	389.3 s	1.68 GB	$350*10^5$
10^6	4652.6 s	21.3 GB	$541*10^6$	10^6	3846.5 s	16.8 GB	$350*10^6$

of MTs. Table 5 shows the light workload of the querier, encompassing synthesizing U and L in Preprocessing phase and generating shares of queries in Setup phase. Table 6 shows the time cost of the hospital. Despite the intensive workload brought by DP [30] clustering in Preprocessing phase, the Setup phase does not aggravate its workload, as generating shares of 15K sequences can be completed within 1 s.

6   Conclusion

In this paper, we propose a privacy-preserving DTW-based analysis system over distributed medical time series data. Our system constructs a scalable architecture providing dedicate computational services that allow multiple healthcare institutes to carry out secure joint medical data computation. Atop this architecture, our system enables a mixed protocol with tailored atomic functions under MPC primitives. The composed protocol empowers rich expressive power to support various functionality and strong security guarantee. To descend the query latency, together with preprocessing, we devise a two-layer pruning strategy which reduces the portion of secure computation and excludes the unpromising sequences from a sequential scan under DTW. Comprehensive empirical validation shows the potential of our system to be deployed in practice.

Acknowledgment. This work was supported by Australian Research Council Discovery and Linkage Projects (DP180103251 and LP160101766).

References

1. PhysioBank ATM. http://physionet.org/cgi-bin/atm/ATM
2. UCR time series classification archive. https://www.cs.ucr.edu/~eamonn/time_series_data_2018/
3. 104th United States Congress: Health Insurance Portability and Accountability Act of 1996 (HIPPA) (1996). https://www.hhs.gov/hipaa/index.html
4. Aggarwal, G., et al.: Two can keep a secret: a distributed architecture for secure database services. In: Proceedings of CIDR (2005)
5. Asharov, G., Lindell, Y., Schneider, T., Zohner, M.: More efficient oblivious transfer and extensions for faster secure computation. In: Proceedings of ACM CCS (2013)
6. Atallah, M., Bykova, M., Li, J., Frikken, K., Topkara, M.: Private collaborative forecasting and benchmarking. In: Proceedings of WPES (2004)
7. Baldi, P., Baronio, R., De Cristofaro, E., Gasti, P., Tsudik, G.: Countering Gattaca: efficient and secure testing of fully-sequenced human genomes. In: Proceedings of ACM CCS (2011)
8. Barni, M., Failla, P., Lazzeretti, R., Sadeghi, A.R., Schneider, T.: Privacy-preserving ECG classification with branching programs and neural networks. IEEE TIFS **6**, 452–468 (2011)
9. Beaver, D.: Efficient multiparty protocols using circuit randomization. In: Proceedings of Crypto (1991)

10. Begum, N., Ulanova, L., Wang, J., Keogh, E.: Accelerating dynamic time warping clustering with a novel admissible pruning strategy. In: Proceedings of ACM SIGKDD (2015)
11. Berndt, D.J., Clifford, J.: Using dynamic time warping to find patterns in time series. In: Proceedings of KDD Workshop (1994)
12. Blanton, M., Kang, A.R., Karan, S., Zola, J.: Privacy preserving analytics on distributed medical data. CoRR abs/1806.06477 (2018). http://arxiv.org/abs/1806.06477
13. Bogdanov, D., Laud, P., Randmets, J.: Domain-polymorphic language for privacy-preserving applications. In: Proceedings of the ACM Workshop on Language Support for Privacy-Enhancing Technologies (2013)
14. Bogdanov, D., Laur, S., Willemson, J.: Sharemind: a framework for fast privacy-preserving computations. In: Proceedings of ESORICS (2008)
15. Brickell, J., Porter, D.E., Shmatikov, V., Witchel, E.: Privacy-preserving remote diagnostics. In: Proceedings of ACM CCS (2007)
16. Camara, C., Peris-Lopez, P., Tapiador, J.E.: Security and privacy issues in implantable medical devices: a comprehensive survey. J. Biomed. Inform. **55**, 272–289 (2015)
17. Canetti, R.: Universally composable security: a new paradigm for cryptographic protocols. Cryptology ePrint Archive, Report 2000/067 (2000)
18. Chen, Y., Hu, B., Keogh, E., Batista, G.E.: DTW-D: time series semi-supervised learning from a single example. In: Proceedings of ACM SIGKDD (2013)
19. Cho, H., Wu, D.J., Berger, B.: Secure genome-wide association analysis using multiparty computation. Nat. Biotechnol. **36**(6), 547–551 (2018)
20. Demmler, D., Schneider, T., Zohner, M.: ABY-a framework for efficient mixed-protocol secure two-party computation. In: Proceedings of NDSS (2015)
21. European Parliament and of the Council: The General Data Protection Regulation (GDPR) (2016). http://data.europa.eu/eli/reg/2016/679/2016-05-04
22. Huang, Y., Malka, L., Evans, D., Katz, J.: Efficient privacy-preserving biometric identification. In: Proceedings of NDSS (2011)
23. Keogh, E.: Exact indexing of dynamic time warping. In: Proceedings of VLDB (2002)
24. Kerschbaum, F., Schneider, T., Schröpfer, A.: Automatic protocol selection in secure two-party computations. In: Boureanu, I., Owesarski, P., Vaudenay, S. (eds.) ACNS 2014. LNCS, vol. 8479, pp. 566–584. Springer, Cham (2014). https://doi.org/10.1007/978-3-319-07536-5_33
25. Lindell, Y., Pinkas, B.: Privacy preserving data mining. J. Cryptol. **15**(3), 177–206 (2002)
26. Malkhi, D., Nisan, N., Pinkas, B., Sella, Y., et al.: Fairplay-secure two-party computation system. In: Proceedings of USENIX Security (2004)
27. Mohassel, P., Zhang, Y.: SecureML: a system for scalable privacy-preserving machine learning. In: Proceedings of IEEE S&P (2017)
28. Nikolaenko, V., Weinsberg, U., Ioannidis, S., Joye, M., Boneh, D., Taft, N.: Privacy-preserving ridge regression on hundreds of millions of records. In: Proceedings of IEEE S&P (2013)
29. Rakthanmanon, T., et al.: Searching and mining trillions of time series subsequences under dynamic time warping. In: Proceedings of ACM SIGKDD (2012)
30. Rodriguez, A., Laio, A.: Clustering by fast search and find of density peaks. Science **344**(6191), 1492–1496 (2014)
31. Salem, A., Berrang, P., Humbert, M., Backes, M.: Privacy-preserving similar patient queries for combined biomedical data. Proc. PETS **2019**, 47–67 (2019)

32. Tkachenko, O., Weinert, C., Schneider, T., Hamacher, K.: Large-scale privacy-preserving statistical computations for distributed genome-wide association studies. In: Proceedings of ACM AsiaCCS (2018)
33. Wang, X.S., Huang, Y., Zhao, Y., Tang, H., Wang, X., Bu, D.: Efficient genome-wide, privacy-preserving similar patient query based on private edit distance. In: Proceedings of ACM CCS (2015)
34. Wang, X.: FlexSC (2018). https://github.com/wangxiao1254/FlexSC
35. Yao, A.C.C.: How to generate and exchange secrets. In: Proceedings of IEEE FOCS (1986)
36. Yi, X., Bertino, E., Rao, F.Y., Bouguettaya, A.: Practical privacy-preserving user profile matching in social networks. In: Proceedings of IEEE ICDE (2016)
37. Zheng, W., Popa, R., Gonzalez, J.E., Stoica, I.: Helen: Maliciously secure coopetitive learning for linear models. In: Proceedings of IEEE S&P (2019)
38. Zheng, Y., Duan, H., Tang, X., Wang, C., Zhou, J.: Denoising in the dark: privacy-preserving deep neural network based image denoising. IEEE TDSC (2019)
39. Zheng, Y., Duan, H., Wang, C.: Learning the truth privately and confidently: encrypted confidence-aware truth discovery in mobile crowdsensing. IEEE TIFS **13**(10), 2475–2489 (2018)
40. Zhu, H., Meng, X., Kollios, G.: Privacy preserving similarity evaluation of time series data. In: Proceedings of EDBT (2014)

Key Exchange Protocols

IoT-Friendly AKE: Forward Secrecy and Session Resumption Meet Symmetric-Key Cryptography

Gildas Avoine[1,2], Sébastien Canard[3], and Loïc Ferreira[1,3(✉)]

[1] Univ Rennes, INSA Rennes, CNRS, IRISA, Rennes, France
`gildas.avoine@irisa.fr`
[2] Institut Universitaire de France, Paris, France
[3] Orange Labs, Applied Crypto Group, Caen, France
{`sebastien.canard,loic.ferreira`}`@orange.com`

Abstract. With the rise of the Internet of Things and the growing popularity of constrained end-devices, several security protocols are widely deployed or strongly promoted (e.g., Sigfox, LoRaWAN, NB-IoT). Based on symmetric-key functions, these protocols lack in providing security properties usually ensured by asymmetric schemes, in particular forward secrecy. We describe a 3-party authenticated key exchange protocol solely based on symmetric-key functions (regarding the computations done between the end-device and the back-end network) which guarantees forward secrecy. Our protocol enables session resumption (without impairing security). This allows saving communication and computation cost, and is particularly advantageous for low-resources end-devices. Our 3-party protocol can be applied in a real-case IoT deployment (i.e., involving numerous end-devices and servers) such that the latter inherits from the security properties of the protocol. We give a concrete instantiation of our key exchange protocol, and formally prove its security.

Keywords: Security protocols · Authenticated key exchange · Symmetric-key cryptography · Session resumption · Forward secrecy · Security model · Internet of Things

1 Introduction

1.1 Context

The arising of the Internet of Things (IoT) gives birth to different types of use cases and environments (smart home, smart cities, eHealth, Industrial IoT, etc.). According to several reports, *"the Industrial Internet of Things [IIoT] is the biggest and most important part of the Internet of Things"* [12]. The IIoT covers sensitive applications since it aims at managing networks that provide valuable resources (e.g., energy, water, etc.). Contrary to the smart home case, where a network is localised to the house perimeter and implies merely a domestic

© Springer Nature Switzerland AG 2019
K. Sako et al. (Eds.): ESORICS 2019, LNCS 11736, pp. 463–483, 2019.
https://doi.org/10.1007/978-3-030-29962-0_22

management of the network, the IIoT context may require a large coverage zone where connected objects (e.g., sensors, actuators, etc.) are widespread all over an urban area. This implies the involvement of, at least, two players: the application provider (which exploits the connected objects to get some valuable data and provide some service), and the communication provider whose network is used by the application provider to communicate with its connected objects (see Fig. 1).

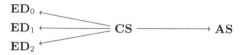

Fig. 1. Connection between end-devices (ED) and an application server (AS) through a communication server (CS)

Cryptographic Separation of the Layers. The (Industrial) IoT involves low-resources end-devices which are not able to apply heavy computations implied by asymmetric schemes. Consequently, security protocols used on currently deployed IoT networks usually implement symmetric-key functions only, and are based on a unique (per end-device) symmetric root key. Using the same root key implies that the communication layer and the application layer are entangled. The communication provider must guarantee that only legitimate parties can send data through its network, but does not need to get the application data. The application provider must keep full control over its connected objects, but must not be able to interfere with the management of the communication network. Therefore, the communication and the application layers must be cryptographically distinct.

Forward Secrecy. The (Industrial) IoT protocols based on symmetric-key functions do not provide strong security properties usually ensured by asymmetric schemes, in particular *forward secrecy*. The disclosure of the root key compromises all the past sessions established with that key, not to mention the consequences of an intrusion into the back-end server that centralises all the root keys. The current symmetric-key based IoT protocols lack in providing this fundamental security property.

Session Resumption. A session resumption scheme allows establishing a new session at a reduced cost: once two parties has performed a first key exchange, they can use some shared key material to execute subsequent runs faster. This means less data exchanged during the key agreement, and reduced time and energy, which is particularly convenient and advantageous for low-resources end-devices. Yet, the symmetric-key based IoT protocols always execute the same full key exchange.

1.2 Related Work

Several protocols for the (Industrial) IoT have been proposed. Among these, the following are widely deployed or strongly promoted. They all build their security on symmetric-key functions, and make use of a static and unique (per end-device) root key shared between the end-device and the back-end network.

Sigfox [20, 21] corresponds to a centric model: one entity (the Sigfox company or one of its partners) manages a proprietary network. The application data (sent by the end-devices) is managed by the central entity (Sigfox) and then delivered to the different Sigfox's customers. The latter are compelled to have confidence in Sigfox, and, in a way, to let the company disintermediate them.

LoRaWAN 1.0 [23] provides more flexibility: any company can deploy a LoRa network. Two session keys are derived from the end-device's root key to protect the communication and the application layers. Hence, this root key gives access to both (cryptographic) layers. Moreover, several weaknesses in LoRaWAN 1.0 have been identified which lead to likely practical attacks [2].

In LoRaWAN 1.1 [22], a "Join Server" is added to the architecture (compared to version 1.0). It is in charge of doing the key exchange with the end-device [24]. Two distinct static symmetric root keys are used. Each yields a session key. This allows to cryptographically separate the communication and the application layers. Then each session key is respectively sent to the communication server, and to the application server. In such a context, the Join Server is always solicited during the key exchange, including when the end-device makes a new run with the *same* server. Furthermore, only the end-device can initiate a key exchange (as in version 1.0).

Contrary to the previous technologies, Narrowband IoT (NB-IoT), enhanced Machine-Type Communication (eMTC), Extended Coverage GSM IoT (EC-GSM-IoT) are cellular technologies. eMTC provides enhancements to the Long Term Evolution (LTE/4G) technology for machine type communications. NB-IoT is also based on LTE, whereas EC-GSM-IoT is based on GSM/EDGE technologies and dedicated to low-cost end-devices. The security of all these systems relies on the underlying technology (GSM, EDGE, LTE), hence on a static symmetric root key known to a central authority, likely the telecom operator. They inherit the intrinsic security limitations of the schemes they are built on.

Furthermore, *none* of the aforementioned protocols provide forward secrecy.

To the best of our knowledge, no IoT protocol proposes a session resumption scheme. Such schemes exist in other contexts. In TLS 1.2 [10], the server can encrypt the "master secret" and store that "Session Ticket" [17] at the client. In TLS 1.3 [15], the server encrypts a "resumption master secret" (RMS) output by the previous key exchange, and stores it at the client. In IKEv2 [14], a similar approach is used [19].

From the *same* secret value, used as symmetric master key, successive runs can be executed with these (TLS, IKE) procedures. Hence disclosure of the reused secret may compromise several past sessions: this breaks forward secrecy. In TLS 1.3, a fresh secret can be added, but this implies applying the Diffie-Hellman scheme. Moreover, in TLS, the same Session Ticket Encryption Key

(STEK) is used by the server to encrypt several RMS values (corresponding to different clients). Hence a STEK may be persistent in the server's memory and its disclosure compromises past sessions. Therefore these solutions are not satisfactory with respect to forward secrecy.

Aviram, Gellert, and Jager [1] propose a resumption scheme aiming at guaranteeing forward secrecy and non-replayability when 0-RTT is used in TLS 1.3. They describe two concrete instantiations. One is based on RSA, the other is a tree-based scheme. As all the aforementioned session resumption schemes, Aviram et al.'s proposal implies to store a ticket at the client. Therefore the number of tickets to store grows with the number of servers it can resume a session with. Hence, low-resources end-devices with constrained memory cannot apply these schemes.

Reversing the roles taken by the client and the server (i.e., the client computes and the server stores the ticket) is not sufficient. First, the Aviram et al.'s RSA based scheme is excluded, despite its elegance, for low-cost IoT end-devices that can only implement symmetric-key functions. Moreover, their tree-based scheme implies that the decryption key grows (up to some point) each time a ticket is used, which is prohibitive for the end-device (client). They also propose an alternative that trades decryption key size for ticket size. However sending (and retrieving) big tickets is an issue for a low-resources end-device. As noticed by Aviram et al., each transmitted bit costs energy, which limits the battery lifetime of self-powered end-devices.

1.3   Our Approach

The basis of our approach is the need for an authenticated key exchange protocol guaranteeing better security properties than that of existing IoT protocols (including widely deployed ones), and being at the same time suitable for low-resources end-devices. Consequently, we consider the symmetric-key setting. In order to cryptographically separate the communication and the application layers, we consider a LoRaWAN-like architecture with a trusted third party behaving as a key server. But we use the latter in a more efficient way. We describe an authenticated key exchange protocol that involves three parties: an end-device, a (communication or application) server, and a trusted third party (the key server). This protocol is solely based on symmetric-key functions (regarding the computations done by the end-device), and yet it provides forward secrecy.

Our 3-party protocol allows resuming sessions. A full run implies the involvement of the trusted third party in order to establish a session between an end-device and a (communication or application) server. The resumption procedure allows executing the subsequent runs between the end-device and the same server without the trusted third party being involved. That is, all the messages exchanged with the latter are saved. This means a faster session establishment with reduced time and energy (in particular for the low-resources end-device). Our resumption scheme implies a small and fixed size storage in the end-device's memory independently of the number of sessions that can be resumed. Finally, our protocol allows resuming sessions without impairing security: it combines session resumption and forward secrecy.

An IoT network involves many entities and not only a pair of end-device and server. Our 3-party key exchange protocol can be used to deploy an arbitrary number of end-devices and (communication or application) servers within the same network (i.e., affiliated to the same trusted third party). This allows in particular a (mobile) end-device to switch from one communication server to another one, or to be used by two different application servers without compromising sessions established with other servers.

1.4   Contribution

In this paper, we present a 3-party authenticated key exchange (3-AKE) protocol executed between an end-device, a server, and a trusted third party, which matches *at the same time* the following properties:

– The protocol is solely based on symmetric-key functions (regarding the computations done by the end-device).
– Application and communication security layers are separated.
– The protocol enables session resumption.
– The protocol provides forward secrecy.

In addition, we describe a security model in order to formally prove the security of our protocol, and give a concrete instantiation of the latter.

2   Description of the 3-Party AKE

2.1   The Different Roles

The real-case IoT deployment we consider involves four *roles*: the trusted third party that we name *(Authentication and) Key Server* (KS), the *(Application) End-device* (ED), the *Communication Server* (CS), and the *Application Server* (AS). The purpose of AS is to provide some service (e.g., telemetry, asset tracking, equipment automation, etc.). The AS exploits ED (e.g., a sensor, an actuator, etc.) to ensure that service. In order to exchange data, ED and AS use a communication network. The entry point is CS, which grants ED access to that network. Typically CS is managed by a telecom operator.

One KS can manage several EDs. An ED can be either static or mobile, hence may have to connect one or several CS. An AS can use several EDs in order to provide its service. The kind of ED we consider is a (low-resource) wireless end-device whereas we assume that KS, CS, and AS use high-speed (wired) connections with each other, and have heavier (computational) capabilities.

As said, the architecture we consider involves four types of entities: KS, ED, CS, and AS. However, from a cryptographic perspective, CS and AS behave the same way with respect to KS and ED. The main goal to reach is to allow ED to share a session key with a server $XS \in \{CS, AS\}$ which ensures some functionality (communication or application in our case). This is achieved with our 3-AKE protocol: executed between KS, ED, and XS, the protocol outputs key material that allows ED and XS to establish a secure channel. In the remainder of the paper, we will mention for simplicity only the two *types* of CS and AS servers. Nonetheless, recall that they represent in fact the several servers which are actually involved in the IoT architecture we consider.

2.2 Key Computation and Distribution

Our 3-AKE protocol is based on a pre-shared symmetric key mk known only to two parties: ED, and KS which ED is affiliated to. Each ED owns a distinct master key mk. A 3-AKE run is split in two main phases. Each phase appeals to a 2-party authenticated key exchange (2-AKE) protocol, whose security properties will be made explicit in Sect. 2.3. During the first phase, ED and KS perform a 2-AKE run with the shared master key mk. During the second phase, ED and XS $\in \{$CS, AS$\}$ use the output of the first key exchange to perform an additional 2-AKE run. This yields a session key used to establish a secure channel between ED and XS. In practice, since our architecture involves two types of XS servers, a 3-AKE run is done first between KS, ED, and CS, and then between KS, ED, and AS. This yields two distinct secure channels: ED-CS and ED-AS.

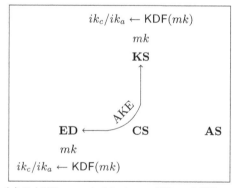
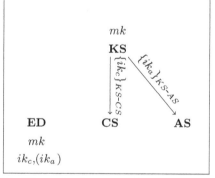

(a) 2-AKE executed between ED and KS (relayed by CS) with mk

(b) KS sends the intermediary keys ik_c (to CS) and ik_a (to AS) respectively through the secure channels $\{\cdot\}_{KS\text{-}CS}$ and $\{\cdot\}_{KS\text{-}AS}$, established between KS and CS, and KS and AS.

Fig. 2. 2-AKE done between ED and KS with mk, and distribution of ik_c, ik_a

More precisely, the following steps are executed between KS, ED, CS, and AS (see Figs. 2 and 3).

1. Based on the shared master key mk, KS and ED perform an AKE, relayed by CS (Fig. 2a). This first AKE outputs a *communication intermediary key* ik_c.

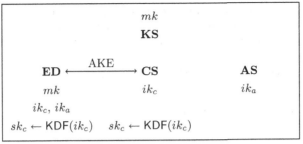

(a) 2-AKE executed between ED and CS with ik_c

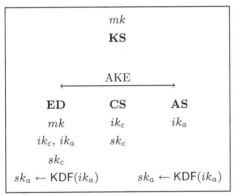

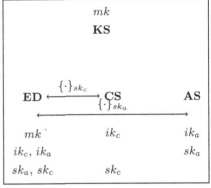

(b) 2-AKE executed between ED and AS (relayed by CS) with ik_a

(c) Secure channels established: communication channel $\{\cdot\}_{sk_c}$ between ED and CS, and application channel $\{\cdot\}_{sk_a}$ between ED and AS

Fig. 3. 2-AKE executed between ED and AS (resp. CS) with ik_a (resp. ik_c), and subsequent secure channels

2. The previous step (2-AKE) is repeated between KS and ED. It outputs an *application intermediary key* ik_a.
3. KS sends ik_c to CS, and ik_a to AS through two distinct pre-existing secure channels (Fig. 2b). Then, to guarantee the security of the subsequent phases of the protocol, KS deletes its copy of the intermediary keys ik_c and ik_a (we elaborate more on this in Sect. 2.4).
4. Using ik_c, ED and CS perform an AKE which outputs a *communication session key* sk_c (Fig. 3a).
5. Using ik_a, ED and AS perform an AKE which outputs an *application session key* sk_a (Fig. 3b).
6. Using the application session key sk_a, ED and AS can now establish an *application secure channel*. Likewise, with the communication session key sk_c, ED and CS can establish a distinct *communication secure channel* (Fig. 3c).

We call P the protocol that involves ED, and is used to perform the 2-AKE runs between ED and KS (steps 1–2), ED and CS (step 4), and ED and AS (step 5). We call P' the 2-AKE protocol used on the back-end side between KS and AS (resp. CS). Let Enc be the function used to set up the secure channel between KS and AS (resp. CS) with the session key output by P' (step 3).

2.3   The Building Blocks P, P', and Enc

Our 3-AKE protocol depends crucially on the 2-party protocols P and P', and function Enc. We list below the main features we require these three building blocks to have.

Protocol P. We require protocol P to fulfill the following properties.

- The scheme is a 2-party AKE that provides mutual authentication.
- The scheme is based on symmetric-key functions solely.
- The scheme guarantees forward secrecy.

Although it is not related to the main security issue we tackle, we add the following requirement in order to improve the flexibility of the 3-AKE protocol:

- Any of the two parties can initiate a run of protocol P.

Combining symmetric-key cryptography and forward secrecy may appear counterintuitive. Therefore, we informally recall what such a property means in that context. Once a 2-AKE run of P is complete, *past* output secrets must remain private even if the current symmetric root key is revealed.

   More precisely, in a 2-AKE run done between ED and KS, the disclosure of the current master key mk (used as root key) must not compromise past intermediary keys ik computed by these two parties. Likewise, in a 2-AKE run done between ED and some XS, the disclosure of the current intermediary key ik (used as root key in that case) must not compromise past session keys sk computed by ED and XS (a concrete instantiation of P is given in Sect. 4).

Protocol P' and Function Enc. We demand P' to be a secure 2-AKE that provides mutual authentication, and forward secrecy. Since P' is applied between KS and XS, asymmetric functions may be used.

   We demand Enc to provide data confidentiality and data authenticity. In the latter we include non-replayability of messages.

2.4   Main Features of the 3-AKE Protocol

Management of the Security. The key hierarchy (between mk, ik, and sk), allows ED and KS to manage the overall security of the system. The key exchange done between KS and ED (steps 1–2, Sect. 2.2) can be initiated by any but *only* these two entities. Each 2-AKE done between ED and KS creates a new intermediary key ik. This obsoletes the current intermediary key shared by ED and XS, and "disconnects" ED from XS by resetting ik at ED. Hence, KS and ED can defend against a dishonest or corrupted XS.

Cryptographic Separation of the Layers. The use of two distinct intermediary keys ik_c and ik_a allows separating the communication layer (ED-CS) and the application layer (ED-AS). The mutual authentication between KS and, respectively, CS and AS, guarantees that the intermediary keys are sent to and received from legitimate parties only.

Secure Connection to Any Server. The 3-AKE protocol allows ED to share an intermediary key ik with *any* server. Moreover, ED can connect any such server without impairing the security with another server. First, each 2-AKE run done between ED and KS yields a different intermediary key ik. Hence each partnered ED and XS use a distinct key ik. Next, KS deletes its copy of ik as soon as received by XS. Finally, P provides forward secrecy. The disclosure of the current master key mk (stored at ED and KS) does not compromise a past output key ik. The forward secrecy ensured by P' and the security of the channel established with Enc participate also in the privacy of ik. Likewise, due to the forward secrecy of P, past session keys sk (computed between ED and XS) remain private, even if the current key ik (stored at ED and XS) is exposed.

Quick Session Establishment. Once a first intermediary key ik is shared between ED and XS, these two parties can perform as many 2-AKE runs (hence set up as many successive secure channels) as wished *without* soliciting KS anymore (i.e., ED and XS repeats several times step 4 or 5, Sect. 2.2). This avoids overloading KS (which has to manage many ED and XS). At the same time this hides to KS the number and the frequency of the connections established between ED and XS.

3   Session Resumption Procedure

3.1   Rationale for a Session Resumption Procedure

As explained in Sect. 2.4, after a first 2-AKE run with KS, ED shares an intermediary key ik with XS. Then, ED and XS can execute, from ik, subsequent 2-AKE runs without soliciting KS anymore. Consequently, as soon as ED shares (distinct) intermediary keys with several servers, it can quickly switch from one server to another back and forth without the help of KS. Likewise, this allows ED to connect several AS servers, hence to be securely used by different application providers. Moreover, since P guarantees forward secrecy, the disclosure of (the current value of) ik does not compromise past session keys sk. We call this faster mode (without KS) a *session resumption* procedure.

Due to the intrinsic properties of the 2-AKE scheme P (see Sect. 2.3), *both* peers (ED or XS) can initiate the session resumption procedure.

This mode is particularly advantageous and convenient for a mobile ED which must connect different CS. Avoiding the involvement of KS (i.e., a whole 2-AKE run between ED and KS), allows to save time, computation cost and communication cost for KS but mainly for ED. The ED we consider are low-resource, self-powered devices. The energy cost to transmit and to receive data usually exceeds the cost of cryptographic processing [18].

Another limitation of a constrained ED is its memory space. Being able to resume a session with several servers implies to store simultaneously as many intermediary keys. This is prohibitive for such kind of ED. Section 3.2 presents a session resumption scheme that solves this issue.

3.2   Session Resumption Procedure for Low-Resources ED

Overview of the Procedure. The session resumption procedure for a low-resources ED with XS is made of two phases:

(a) The *storage phase.* ED and XS have an ongoing secure channel set up with a session key sk (output by P). Both share an intermediary key ik. First, ED encrypts ik under a key known only to itself. Next, ED sends this "ticket" to XS through the ongoing secure channel. Upon reception of the ticket by XS, ED deletes ik. Then ED can close the channel any time.
(b) The *retrieval phase.* ED starts a new 2-AKE run with a known XS. First, ED gets, in the continuity of the run, the ticket it has sent previously. Next, ED decrypts the ticket and gets the corresponding key ik. Then, ED and XS complete the run with ik, and compute a new session key sk.

This procedure is reminiscent of existing schemes (e.g., [15,17,19]). However none of the latter succeeds in combining session resumption and forward secrecy without asymmetric cryptography or prohibitive requirements (for a constrained ED) regarding memory, or the amount of transmitted data [1,15]. In contrast, our 3-AKE protocol provides a nifty solution to this issue, as explained below.

Computing the Ticket. The intermediary key ik that is stored at the server and later retrieved by ED is encrypted. Only ED needs to decrypt ik since the server stores its own copy of the key. Using the same encryption key k to protect different intermediary keys (sent to different servers) obviously breaks forward secrecy: revealing k allows decrypting *past* intermediary keys, hence compromising the session keys sk computed with the latter. Therefore each ik must be encrypted with a different key k. But replacing in ED's memory each intermediary key ik with another key k yields the same memory issue and is pointless. Therefore, we compute the keys k as elements of a one-way key chain.

From an initial random key k_0, each ticket is computed as $ticket_{i+1} = \mathsf{KW}(k_{i+1}, ik)$ with $k_{i+1} = \mathsf{H}(k_i)$, $i \geq 0$. KW is a key-wrap function [16], and H a one-way function. ED keeps only one key k_j. This key is the child of the key that has decrypted the last used ticket. When ED wants to consume $ticket_i$, it first computes the decryption key k_i from the current key k_j, $i \geq j$: $k_i = \mathsf{H}^{i-j}(k_j)$. Then k_j is replaced by $k_{i+1} = \mathsf{H}(k_i)$, and $ticket_i$ *cannot* be decrypted anymore.

This *unique* encryption key gives ED the ability to compute multiple tickets, therefore to resume as many sessions.

Two Chains of Keys. When $ticket_i$ is used, the current decryption key is replaced with $k_{i+1} = \mathsf{H}(k_i)$. Hence any previous $ticket_j$, $j \leq i$, is obsoleted. Let us consider the following scenario. A mobile low-resources ED is managed by one AS, and switches back and forth between two other servers CS_a and CS_b. ED stores fresh $ticket_i$, $ticket_j$, and $ticket_k$, $i < j < k$, respectively at AS, CS_a, and CS_b. ED keeps the decryption key k_i. When ED makes a new key exchange with CS_a, it retrieves $ticket_j$ and decrypts it with $k_j = \mathsf{H}^{j-i}(k_i)$. Then, ED replaces the current key k_i with $k_{j+1} = \mathsf{H}(k_j)$. Whenever ED alternates between CS_a and CS_b, the ticket decryption key is updated. Consequently, ED cannot use $ticket_i$. This makes the session resumption procedure unusable with AS. Therefore, we advocate the use of two chains of decryption keys corresponding to the *two types* of CS and AS servers (see Fig. 4). Note that, if the tickets are used in the same order they are computed, all can be (legitimately) decrypted.

Figure 4a depicts the case where a CS ticket ($ticket_i$) is used. The corresponding decryption key k_i is deleted, and ED keeps only k_{i+1}. This obsoletes all previous CS tickets. Figure 4b depicts the case where an AS ticket ($ticket_0'$) is used. The decryption key k_0' is deleted, and ED keeps only k_1'. All AS $ticket_j'$, $j \geq 1$, are still usable.

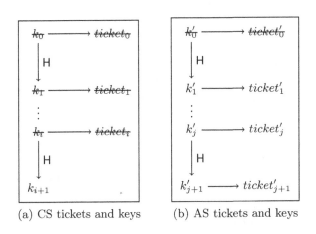

(a) CS tickets and keys   (b) AS tickets and keys

Fig. 4. Chains of keys used to compute a ticket

Maintaining Forward Secrecy. When $ticket_i$ is used, the current encryption key k_j, $j \leq i$, stored at ED, is replaced with the next encryption key $k_{i+1} = \mathsf{H}(k_i)$. This forbids any old ticket from being decrypted. All the remaining tickets that can be decrypted (from the now current key k_{i+1}) have not been used yet. Moreover, the protocol P provides forward secrecy. Hence, the disclosure of the intermediary key ik protected into a (not used yet) ticket does *not* compromise past session keys sk. In a way, the session resumption procedure inherits forward secrecy from P.

4   Instantiation of the 3-AKE Protocol

In this section we present a concrete instantiation of our 3-AKE protocol described in Sect. 2. We have to choose a 2-AKE protocol P, a 2-AKE protocol P', and an encryption function Enc. Recall that the protocol P must fulfill the properties listed in Sect. 2.3, which includes the essential *forward secrecy*.

We describe an instantiation of P with (Sect. 4.3) and without (Sect. 4.2) the session resumption procedure for low-resources ED.

4.1   Protocol P' and Function Enc

We instantiate the 2-AKE protocol P' with TLS 1.3. In order not to impair the security, we enforce (EC)DHE and forbid 0-RTT mode. We define the Enc function to be the record layer of TLS 1.3.

4.2   Forward Secret 2-AKE Protocol P

We instantiate the 2-AKE protocol P with the SAKE protocol [4]. SAKE fulfills all the properties listed in Sect. 2.3.[1]

SAKE uses a key-evolving scheme, based on a one-way function, to update the symmetric root key shared by the two peers. The root key is made of two main components: a derivation key K, and an independent integrity key K'. K is used in the session key derivation. K' allows authenticating the messages, tracking the root key evolution (i.e., its successive updates), and, if necessary, resynchronising in the *continuity* of the protocol run. After a complete and correct run of SAKE, both peers have the guarantee that their root key is updated and synchronised. That is, SAKE is *self-synchronising*. When *any* of the two peers deems the session key can be safely used, it has the guarantee that its partner is synchronised (in particular, it is not late). Hence, SAKE guarantees forward secrecy.

Thus, applying SAKE, ED and KS compute an intermediary ik with their shared master key mk (used as SAKE root key). The current master key is then updated with the one-way function update: $mk^{i+1} \leftarrow \mathsf{update}(mk^i)$. Likewise, applying SAKE, ED and XS compute a session key sk with the key ik they share (used as SAKE root key in that case). Eventually, the SAKE root key used in that case is updated: $ik^{t+1} \leftarrow \mathsf{update}(ik^t)$.

Figure 5 depicts the evolution of the three types of keys over time: the master key mk, the intermediary key ik, and the session key sk. The computation of ik^0 and mk^1 from mk^0 corresponds to a 2-AKE run executed between ED and KS as depicted by Fig. 2a. The computation of sk^2 and ik^3 from ik^2 corresponds to a 2-AKE run executed between ED and CS (resp. AS) with $ik = ik_c$ (resp. $ik = ik_a$) as depicted by Fig. 3a (resp. Figure 3b). Note that the keys ik_c and ik_a are computed from two different values mk (i.e., yielded by two different 2-AKE runs between ED and KS). In Fig. 5, the branch $mk^0 \rightarrow mk^1 \rightarrow \cdots$

---

[1] Any other 2-AKE protocol can be used, as long as it provides the same properties as SAKE, but we are not aware of other such protocols.

corresponds to the evolution of mk throughout successive key exchange runs executed between ED and KS. Each of these runs yields a new intermediary key $ik = ik^0$. The branch $ik^0 \rightarrow ik^1 \rightarrow \cdots$ corresponds to the evolution of ik throughout successive key exchange runs (each one outputting a session key sk^i) executed between ED and XS *without* the involvement of KS.

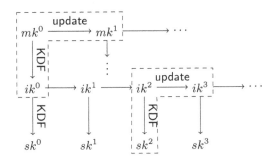

Fig. 5. Key chains in SAKE

4.3   Protocol P with Session Resumption Scheme for Low-Resources ED

The session resumption scheme dedicated to low-resources ED presented in this section fulfills the features listed in Sect. 3.2. It is a variant of the SAKE protocol adapted to include the use of the ticket. We call this variant *SAKE-R*.

Session Resumption Procedure with SAKE-R. During the *storage phase*, ED merely sends the ticket through the ongoing secure channel established with XS (see Sect. 3.2). When ED initiates the *retrieval phase* with SAKE-R (see Fig. 6), XS sends back the ticket. ED decrypts the ticket and gets ik, and the subsequent messages are essentially the same as the original SAKE protocol.[2] SAKE (hence SAKE-R) uses two main keys: an integrity key K' and a derivation key K. Therefore, ik corresponds to $K\|K'$. Figure 7 depicts the two phases of the procedure regarding the evolution of the master and intermediary keys mk and ik.

   kdf corresponds to: $sk \leftarrow \mathsf{KDF}(K, r_A, r_B)$. KDF is the session key derivation function used in SAKE (and SAKE-R). upd corresponds to (i) $K \leftarrow \mathsf{update}(K)$, followed by (ii) $K' \leftarrow \mathsf{update}(K')$. update is the one-way function used to update the root key (i.e., the intermediary key ik in that case). $\mathsf{verif}(k, m, \tau)$ denotes the MAC verification function.

   Once ED gets ik, the ticket decryption key k_j currently kept by ED is replaced with $k_{i+1} = \mathsf{H}(k_i)$, where k_i is the key used to decrypt the retrieved ticket. Therefore ED rejects any replay of an already consumed ticket.

---

[2] The case where XS is the initiator is very similar.

ED [A]	XS ∈ {CS, AS} [B]
(k_j, id_{ticket})	$(K, K', id_{ticket}, ticket)$

$r_A \xleftarrow{\$} \{0,1\}^\lambda$
$m_A \leftarrow A\|r_A\|id_{ticket}$ $\xrightarrow{\quad m_A \quad}$ if (id_{ticket} not found) then
                                                                      abort

                                                    $r_B \xleftarrow{\$} \{0,1\}^\lambda$
                                                    $\tau_B \leftarrow \mathsf{MAC}(K', B\|A\|r_B\|r_A\|id_{ticket}\|ticket)$
$\xleftarrow{\quad m_B \quad}$ $m_B \leftarrow r_B\|ticket\|\tau_B$

$k_i \leftarrow \mathsf{H}^{i-j}(k_j)$
$ik \leftarrow \mathsf{KW}^{-1}(k_i, ticket)$
if ($ik = \bot$) then
    abort
// $ik = K\|K'$
if ($\mathsf{verif}(K', B\|A\|r_B\|r_A\|id_{ticket}\|ticket, \tau_B) = \mathtt{false}$) then
    abort

$k_{i+1} \leftarrow \mathsf{H}(k_i)$
delete k_j, k_i

$\tau_A \leftarrow \mathsf{MAC}(K', A\|r_A\|r_B)$
$sk \leftarrow \mathsf{kdf}$
$K, K' \leftarrow \mathsf{upd}$ $\xrightarrow{\quad \tau_A \quad}$ if ($\mathsf{verif}(K', A\|r_A\|r_B, \tau_A) = \mathtt{false}$) then
                                                                      abort

                                                    $sk \leftarrow \mathsf{kdf}$
                                                    $K, K' \leftarrow \mathsf{upd}$
                                                    $\tau'_B \leftarrow \mathsf{MAC}(K', r_B\|r_A)$
$\xleftarrow{\quad \tau'_B \quad}$ delete $ticket$
if ($\mathsf{verif}(K', r_B\|r_A, \tau'_B) = \mathtt{false}$) then
    abort

Fig. 6. Session resumption with SAKE-R, initiated by ED

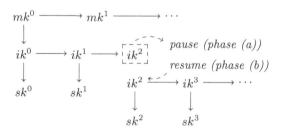

Fig. 7. Resuming a chain of intermediary keys (from ik^2)

5   Security of the 3-AKE Protocol

5.1   Main Theorem

Security of a 3-AKE protocol Π is defined in terms of two properties: *entity authentication* and *key indistinguishability*. Informally, the first property guarantees that any party that accepts (i.e., deems the session key can be safely used) has a unique partner. The second property guarantees that an adversary can do no better than guess the session key negotiated by the two partnered parties. The advantage of an adversary $\mathcal{A}$ of breaking these properties is respectively defined as $\mathsf{adv}_\Pi^{\mathsf{ent\text{-}auth}}(\mathcal{A})$ and $\mathsf{adv}_\Pi^{\mathsf{key\text{-}ind}}(\mathcal{A})$.

Definition 1 (3-AKE Security). *A protocol Π is 3-AKE-secure if Π satisfies correctness, and for all probabilistic polynomial time adversary $\mathcal{A}$, $\mathsf{adv}_\Pi^{\mathsf{ent\text{-}auth}}(\mathcal{A})$ and $\mathsf{adv}_\Pi^{\mathsf{key\text{-}ind}}(\mathcal{A})$ are a negligible function of the security parameter.*

We use the security model described in Sects. A.1 and A.2 to prove the security of the generic 3-AKE protocol Π depicted in Sect. 2. The protocol Π is based on: (i) the 2-AKE protocol P executed between ED and KS, ED and XS, (ii) the 2-AKE protocol P' executed between KS and XS, and (iii) the function Enc used to set up a secure channel between KS and XS with a session key output by P'. The security of Π relies on the 2-AKE-security [9] of P and P', and on the sAE-security [6] of the function Enc.

Theorem 1. *The protocol Π is a secure 3-AKE protocol under the assumption that P is a secure 2-AKE protocol, P' is a secure 2-AKE protocol, and Enc is a secure sAE function, and for any probabilistic polynomial time adversary $\mathcal{A}$ in the 3-AKE security experiment against Π*

$$\mathsf{adv}_\Pi^{\mathsf{ent\text{-}auth}}(\mathcal{A}) = n_K \cdot n_E \cdot n_X \left[2\mathsf{adv}_P^{\mathsf{ent\text{-}auth}} + \mathsf{adv}_{P'}^{\mathsf{ent\text{-}auth}} + \mathsf{adv}_{P'}^{\mathsf{key\text{-}ind}} + 2\mathsf{adv}_{\mathsf{Enc}}^{\mathsf{sAE}} \right]$$

$$\mathsf{adv}_\Pi^{\mathsf{key\text{-}ind}}(\mathcal{A}) = \mathsf{adv}_\Pi^{\mathsf{ent\text{-}auth}}(\mathcal{A}) + n_K \cdot n_E \cdot n_X \left[2\mathsf{adv}_P^{\mathsf{key\text{-}ind}} + \mathsf{adv}_{P'}^{\mathsf{key\text{-}ind}} + \mathsf{adv}_{\mathsf{Enc}}^{\mathsf{sAE}} \right]$$

where n_K, n_E, n_X are respectively the number of KS, ED, and XS parties.

Sketch of Proof. In order to win the entity authentication (EA) experiment, the adversary can try to break the EA-security of the 2-AKE protocol P executed between ED and KS, and ED and XS ($2\mathsf{adv}_P^{\mathsf{ent\text{-}auth}}$), or P' executed between KS and XS ($\mathsf{adv}_{P'}^{\mathsf{ent\text{-}auth}}$). Another possibility is to decrypt ik (or forge an equivalent message) sent by KS to XS ($2\mathsf{adv}_{\mathsf{Enc}}^{\mathsf{sAE}}$). Resistance to the latter relies on the fact that the encryption key (output by P') used to key Enc be indistinguishable from random ($\mathsf{adv}_{P'}^{\mathsf{key\text{-}ind}}$).

The key indistinguishablity security of Π relies on the corresponding property for P and P' ($2\mathsf{adv}_P^{\mathsf{key\text{-}ind}} + \mathsf{adv}_{P'}^{\mathsf{key\text{-}ind}}$). The adversary can also try to get ik (sent by KS to XS) in order to compute the session key sk output by P when executed between ED and XS ($\mathsf{adv}_{\mathsf{Enc}}^{\mathsf{sAE}}$).[3]

---

[3] The detailed proof is given in the extended version of the paper [3].

5.2 Achieving 3-AKE Security

P = SAKE is proved to be a secure 2-AKE protocol [4] in the Brzuska, Jacobsen and Stebila security model (which captures forward secrecy) [9]. P = SAKE-R is a 2-AKE-secure protocol.[4] P' = TLS 1.3 is proved to be a secure 2-AKE protocol [11]. Although this result applies to an earlier draft of the protocol, we may reasonably assume that the final version also guarantees 2-AKE-security. Enc defined as the record layer of TLS 1.3 is proved to be AE-secure [5]. In addition, in TLS 1.3, a per-record nonce derived from a sequence number aims at guaranteeing non-replayability of the records (the sequence number being maintained independently at both sides). Hence we assume the sAE-security of Enc.

Hence, from Theorem 1, our instantiation (with and without the session resumption scheme for low-resources ED) is a 3-AKE-secure protocol according to Definition 1.

6 Conclusion

We have described a generic 3-party authenticated key exchange (3-AKE) protocol dedicated to IoT. Solely based on symmetric-key functions (regarding the computations done between the end-device and the back-end network), our 3-AKE protocol guarantees forward secrecy, in contrast to widely deployed symmetric-key based IoT protocols. It also enables session resumption without impairing security (in particular, forward secrecy is maintained). This allows saving communication and computation cost, and is advantageous for low-resources end-devices.

In addition, we have described a concrete instantiation of our 3-AKE protocol, and presented a security model used to formally prove the security of our 3-AKE protocol and its concrete instantiation.

Our 3-AKE protocol can be applied in a real-case IoT deployment (i.e., involving numerous end-devices and servers) such that the latter inherits from the security properties of the protocol. This results in the ability for the (mobile) end-device to securely switch from one server to another back and forth at a reduced (communication and computation) cost, without compromising the sessions established with other servers.

A 3-AKE Security Model

Taking inspiration from the 3(S)ACCE model of Bhargavan, Boureanu, Fouque, Onete, and Richard [8], we extend the 2-AKE model of Brzuska et al. [9] in order to incorporate the three parties of our 3-AKE protocol, and their interleaved operations.

---

[4] The proof of SAKE-R is similar to that of SAKE and is given in the extended version of the paper.

In our 3-AKE security model, the adversary has full control over the communication network. It can forward, alter, drop any message exchanged by honest parties, or insert new messages. Our 3-AKE model captures also *forward secrecy*.

A.1   Execution Environment

Protocol Entities. Our model considers three sets of parties: a set $\mathcal{K}$ of KS servers, a set $\mathcal{E}$ of ED parties, and a set $\mathcal{X}$ of XS $\in \{\mathrm{CS}, \mathrm{AS}\}$ servers. Each party is given a long term key ltk.

P is a symmetric-key based protocol, and P' can implement asymmetric schemes. We define the long term key ltk of each party to be ltk $=$ (pubk, prvk, rootk) where (i) pubk is a certified public key, (ii) prvk is the corresponding private key, and (iii) rootk is a symmetric root key. For any party in $\mathcal{K}$, the three components of ltk are defined. For any party in $\mathcal{X}$, ltk is fully defined *after* the first 3-AKE run (before that, rootk $=\perp$). For any party in $\mathcal{E}$, ltk $= (\perp, \perp, \mathrm{rootk})$.

Session Instances. Each party P_i maintains a set of instances $\{\pi_i^0, \pi_i^1, \ldots\}$ modeling several (sequential or parallel) executions of the 3-party protocol Π. Each instance π_i^n has access to the long term key ltk of its party parent P_i. Moreover, each instance π_i^n maintains the following internal state:

- The *instance parent* π_i^n.parent $\in \mathcal{K} \cup \mathcal{E} \cup \mathcal{X}$ indicating the party owning that instance.
- The *partner-party* π_i^n.pid $\in \mathcal{K} \cup \mathcal{E} \cup \mathcal{X}$ indicating the intended party partner.
- The *role* $\pi_i^n.\rho \in \{\mathsf{ed}, \mathsf{ks}, \mathsf{cs}, \mathsf{as}\}$ of $P_i = \pi_i^n$.parent. If $P_i \in \mathcal{E}$, then $\pi_i^n.\rho = \mathsf{ed}$. If $P_i \in \mathcal{K}$, then $\pi_i^n.\rho = \mathsf{ks}$. If $P_i \in \mathcal{X}$, then $\pi_i^n.\rho \in \{\mathsf{as}, \mathsf{cs}\}$.
- The *session identifier* π_i^n.sid of an instance.
- The *acceptance flag* $\pi_i^n.\alpha \in \{\perp, \mathtt{running}, \mathtt{accepted}, \mathtt{rejected}\}$.
- The *session key* π_i^n.ck set to $\perp$ at the beginning of the session, and set to a non-null bitstring once π_i^n computes the session key.
- The *key material* π_i^n.km. If π_i^n.parent $\in \mathcal{K}$ (resp. π_i^n.parent $\in \mathcal{X}$) and π_i^n.pid $\in \mathcal{X}$ (resp. π_i^n.pid $\in \mathcal{K}$), then π_i^n.km is set to $\perp$ at the beginning of the session, and set to a non-null bitstring once π_i^n ends in accepting state. Otherwise π_i^n.km is always set to $\perp$.
- The *status* $\pi_i^n.\kappa \in \{\perp, \mathtt{revealed}\}$ of the session key π_i^n.ck.
- The *transcript* π_i^n.trscrpt of the messages sent and received by π_i^n.
- The *security bit* π_i^n.b sampled at random at the beginning of the security experiments.
- The *partner-instances set* π_i^n.ISet stores the *instances* that are involved in the same protocol run as π_i^n (including π_i^n).
- The *partner-parties set* π_i^n.PSet stores the *parties* parent of the instances in π_i^n.ISet (including π_i^n.parent).

Adversarial Queries. The adversary $\mathcal{A}$ is assumed to control the network, and interacts with the instances by issuing the following queries to them.

- NewSession(P_i, ρ, pid): this query creates a new instance π_i^n at party P_i, having role ρ, and intended partner pid.
- Send(π_i^n, M): this query allows the adversary to send any message M to π_i^n. If $\pi_i^n.\alpha \neq \texttt{running}$, it returns $\bot$. Otherwise π_i^n responds according to the protocol specification.
- Corrupt(P_i): this query returns the long-term key $P_i.\mathsf{ltk}$.
- Reveal(π_i^n): this query returns the session key $\pi_i^n.\mathsf{ck}$, and $\pi_i^n.\kappa$ is set to $\texttt{revealed}$.
- Test(π_i^n): this query may be asked only once per pairwise partnered instances throughout the game. If $\pi_i^n.\alpha \neq \texttt{accepted}$, then it returns $\bot$. Otherwise it samples an independent key $k_0 \xleftarrow{\$} \mathcal{KEY}$, and returns k_b, where $k_1 = \pi_i^n.\mathsf{ck}$. The key k_b is called the Test-*challenge*. In order to preclude trivial attacks, we forbid the adversary from issuing a Test-query, and answering a Test-challenge as soon as the corresponding key $\pi_i^n.\mathsf{ck}$ is used during the session. Moreover, the adversary is stateless with respect to this query (it does not keep track of k_b).

A.2   Security Definitions

Partnership. In order to define the partnership between two instances involved in a 2-AKE run, we use the definition of matching conversations initially proposed by Bellare and Rogaway [7], and modified by Jager, Kohlar, Schäge and Schwenk [13]. Consequently, we define sid to be the transcript, in chronological order, of all the (valid) messages sent and received by an instance during a 2-AKE run, but, possibly, the last message. We say that two instances π_i^n and π_j^u are pairwise partnered if $\pi_i^n.\mathsf{sid} = \pi_j^u.\mathsf{sid}$. Then, we define the 3-AKE partnering with the sets ISet and PSet. $\pi_i^n.\mathsf{ISet}$ stores instances partnered with π_i^n, and $\pi_i^n.\mathsf{PSet}$ stores parties partnered with π_i^n.

Definition 2 (Correctness). *We define the* correctness *of a 3-AKE protocol as follows. We demand that, for any instance π ending in an accepting state, the following conditions hold:*

- $|\pi.\mathsf{ISet}| = 6$. *Let $\pi.\mathsf{ISet}$ be* $\{\pi_i^n, \pi_i^m, \pi_k^\ell, \pi_k^s, \pi_j^u, \pi_j^v\}$.
- $\pi_i^n.\mathsf{parent} = \pi_i^m.\mathsf{parent} = P_i \in \mathcal{E}$
- $\pi_k^\ell.\mathsf{parent} = \pi_k^s.\mathsf{parent} = P_k \in \mathcal{K}$
- $\pi_j^u.\mathsf{parent} = \pi_j^v.\mathsf{parent} = P_j \in \mathcal{X}$
- $\pi.\mathsf{PSet} = \{P_i, P_j, P_k\}$
- $\pi_i^m.\mathsf{sid} = \pi_k^\ell.\mathsf{sid} \neq \bot$ *and* $\pi_i^m.\mathsf{ck} = \pi_k^\ell.\mathsf{ck} \neq \bot$
- $\pi_i^n.\mathsf{sid} = \pi_j^u.\mathsf{sid} \neq \bot$ *and* $\pi_i^n.\mathsf{ck} = \pi_j^u.\mathsf{ck} \neq \bot$
- $\pi_k^s.\mathsf{sid} = \pi_j^v.\mathsf{sid} \neq \bot$ *and* $\pi_k^s.\mathsf{ck} = \pi_j^v.\mathsf{ck} \neq \bot$
- $\pi_j^v.\mathsf{km} = \pi_k^s.\mathsf{km} = \pi_i^m.\mathsf{ck} = \pi_k^\ell.\mathsf{ck}$
- $\exists f \mid f(\pi_i^m.\mathsf{ck}, \pi_i^n.\mathsf{trscrpt}) = \pi_i^n.\mathsf{ck} = \pi_j^u.\mathsf{ck} = f(\pi_j^v.\mathsf{km}, \pi_j^u.\mathsf{trscrpt})$

The last two conditions aim at "binding" the six instances involved in a 3-AKE run. Function f corresponds typically to the session key derivation function used by P_i (ED) and P_j (XS) together.

More concretely, ck corresponds either to ik output by the 2-AKE run between ED and KS, or to sk output by the 2-AKE run between ED and XS (both with protocol P), or to the session key output by the 2-AKE run between KS and XS (with protocol P'). km denotes the intermediary key ik sent by KS to XS.

Security of a 3-AKE protocol is defined in terms of an experiment played between a challenger and an adversary. This experiment uses the execution environment described in Sect. A.1. The adversary can win the 3-AKE experiment in one of two ways: (i) by making an instance accept maliciously, or (ii) by guessing the secret bit of the Test-instance. In both, the adversary can query all oracles NewSession, Send, Reveal, Corrupt, and Test.

Entity Authentication (EA). This security property must guarantee that (i) any instance $\pi \in \{\pi_i^n, \pi_i^m, \pi_k^\ell, \pi_k^s, \pi_j^u, \pi_j^v\}$ ending in accepting state is pairwise partnered with a *unique* instance, and (ii) the output of a 2-AKE run between P_k and P_i is *used as root key* in a 2-AKE run between P_i and P_j.

Definition 3 (Entity Authentication (EA)). *An instance π of a protocol Π is said to* maliciously accept *in the 3-AKE security experiment with intended partner $\tilde{P}$, if*

(a) $\pi.\alpha = $ accepted and $\pi.\mathsf{pid} = \tilde{P}$ when $\mathcal{A}$ issues its ν_0-th query.
(b) Any party in $\pi.\mathsf{PSet}$ is ν-corrupted with $\nu > \nu_0$.
(c) Any instance in $\pi.\mathsf{ISet}$ is ν'-revealed with $\nu' > \nu_0$.
(d) There is no unique instance $\tilde{\pi}$ such that $\pi.\mathsf{sid} = \tilde{\pi}.\mathsf{sid}$,
   or there is no instances $\pi_i^m, \pi_i^n, \pi_j^u, \pi_j^v \in \pi.\mathsf{ISet}$ such that
   – $\pi_i^m.\mathsf{pid} = \pi_j^v.\mathsf{pid} \in \mathcal{K}$,
   – $\pi_i^n.\mathsf{parent} = \pi_i^m.\mathsf{parent} \in \mathcal{E}$,
   – $\pi_j^u.\mathsf{parent} = \pi_j^v.\mathsf{parent} \in \mathcal{X}$, and
   – $f(\pi_i^m.\mathsf{ck}, \pi_i^n.\mathsf{trscrpt}) = \pi_i^n.\mathsf{ck} = \pi_j^u.\mathsf{ck} = f(\pi_j^v.\mathsf{km}, \pi_j^u.\mathsf{trscrpt})$.

The adversary's advantage is defined as its winning probability:

$$\mathsf{adv}_\Pi^{\mathsf{ent\text{-}auth}}(\mathcal{A}) = \Pr[\mathcal{A} \text{ wins the EA game}].$$

Definition 4 (Key Indistinguishability). *An adversary $\mathcal{A}$ against a protocol Π, that issues its Test-query to instance π during the 3-AKE security experiment, answers the Test-challenge correctly if it terminates with output b', such that*

(a) $\pi.\alpha = $ accepted
(b) Let π' be the last instance in $\pi.\mathsf{ISet}$ to end in accepting state: $\pi'.\alpha = $ accepted when $\mathcal{A}$ issues its ν_0-th query.
(c) Any party in $\pi.\mathsf{PSet}$ is ν-corrupted with $\nu > \nu_0$.
(d) No instance in $\pi.\mathsf{ISet}$ has been queried in Reveal queries.
(e) $\pi.b = b'$

The adversary's advantage is defined as $\mathsf{adv}_\Pi^{\mathsf{key\text{-}ind}}(\mathcal{A}) = \left| \Pr[\pi.b = b'] - \frac{1}{2} \right|$.

References

1. Aviram, N., Gellert, K., Jager, T.: Session resumption protocols and efficient forward security for TLS 1.3 0-RTT. In: Ishai, Y., Rijmen, V. (eds.) EUROCRYPT 2019. LNCS, vol. 11477, pp. 117–150. Springer, Cham (2019). https://doi.org/10.1007/978-3-030-17656-3_5. (Cryptology ePrint Archive, Report 2019/228)
2. Avoine, G., Ferreira, L.: Rescuing LoRaWAN 1.0. In: Tsudik, G. (ed.) FC 2018. LNCS, vol. 10957. Springer, Heidelberg (2018)
3. Avoine, G., Canard, S., Ferreira, L.: IoT-friendly AKE: forward secrecy and session resumption meet symmetric-key cryptography. Cryptology ePrint Archive, Report 2019 (2019)
4. Avoine, G., Canard, S., Ferreira, L.: Symmetric-key authenticated key exchange (SAKE) with perfect forward secrecy. Cryptology ePrint Archive, Report 2019/444 (2019)
5. Badertscher, C., Matt, C., Maurer, U., Rogaway, P., Tackmann, B.: Augmented secure channels and the goal of the TLS 1.3 record layer. In: Au, M.-H., Miyaji, A. (eds.) ProvSec 2015. LNCS, vol. 9451, pp. 85–104. Springer, Cham (2015). https://doi.org/10.1007/978-3-319-26059-4_5
6. Bellare, M., Kohno, T., Namprempre, C.: Authenticated encryption in SSH: provably fixing the SSH binary packet protocol. In: Atluri, V. (ed.) ACM CCS 02, pp. 1–11. ACM Press, New York (2002)
7. Bellare, M., Rogaway, P.: Entity authentication and key distribution. In: Stinson, D.R. (ed.) CRYPTO 1993. LNCS, vol. 773, pp. 232–249. Springer, Heidelberg (1994). https://doi.org/10.1007/3-540-48329-2_21
8. Bhargavan, K., Boureanu, I., Fouque, P.A., Onete, C., Richard, B.: Content delivery over TLS: a cryptographic analysis of keyless SSL. In: 2017 IEEE European Symposium on Security and Privacy (EuroS&P), pp. 1–16. IEEE, April 2017
9. Brzuska, C., Jacobsen, H., Stebila, D.: Safely exporting keys from secure channels. In: Fischlin, M., Coron, J.-S. (eds.) EUROCRYPT 2016. LNCS, vol. 9665, pp. 670–698. Springer, Heidelberg (2016). https://doi.org/10.1007/978-3-662-49890-3_26
10. Dierks, T., Rescorla, E.: The Transport Layer Security (TLS) Protocol - Version 1.2 (2008)
11. Dowling, B., Fischlin, M., Günther, F., Stebila, D.: A cryptographic analysis of the TLS 1.3 draft-10 full and pre-shared key handshake protocol. Cryptology ePrint Archive, Report 2016/081 (2016)
12. i-scoop: The Industrial Internet of Things (IIoT): the business guide to Industrial IoT (2018). https://www.i-scoop.eu/internet-of-things-guide/industrial-internet-things-iiot-saving-costs-innovation/
13. Jager, T., Kohlar, F., Schäge, S., Schwenk, J.: On the security of TLS-DHE in the standard model. Cryptology ePrint Archive, Report 2011/219 (2011)
14. Kaufman, C., Hoffman, P., Nir, Y., Eronen, P., Kiviner, T.: Internet Key Exchange Protocol Version 2 (IKEv2), October 2014
15. Rescorla, E.: The Transport Layer Security (TLS) Protocol Version 1.3 (2018)
16. Rogaway, P., Shrimpton, T.: A provable-security treatment of the key-wrap problem. In: Vaudenay, S. (ed.) EUROCRYPT 2006. LNCS, vol. 4004, pp. 373–390. Springer, Heidelberg (2006). https://doi.org/10.1007/11761679_23
17. Salowey, J., Zhou, H., Eronen, P., Tschofenig, H.: Transport Layer Security (TLS) Session Resumption without Server-Side State, January 2008

18. Seys, S., Preneel, B.: Power consumption evaluation of efficient digital signature schemes for low power devices. In: IEEE International Conference on Wireless And Mobile Computing, Networking And Communications. WiMob 2005, vol. 1, pp. 79–86. IEEE, August 2005
19. Sheffer, Y., Tschofenig, H.: Internet Key Exchange Protocol Version 2 (IKEv2) - Session Resumption, January 2010
20. Sigfox: Secure SigFox Ready devices - Recommendation guide (2017)
21. Sigfox: SigFox Technical Overview, May 2017
22. Sornin, N.: LoRaWAN 1.1 Specification. LoRa Alliance (2017)
23. Sornin, N., Luis, M., Eirich, T., Kramp, T.: LoRaWAN Specification. LoRa Alliance, v1.0 (2016)
24. Yegin, A.: LoRaWAN Backend Interfaces 1.0 Specification. LoRa Alliance (2017)

Strongly Secure Identity-Based Key Exchange with Single Pairing Operation

Junichi Tomida[1]($\boxtimes$), Atsushi Fujioka[2], Akira Nagai[1], and Koutarou Suzuki[3]

[1] NTT Secure Platform Laboratories, Tokyo, Japan
{junichi.tomida.vw, akira.nagai.td}@hco.ntt.co.jp
[2] Kanagawa University, Yokohama, Japan
fujioka@kanagawa-u.ac.jp
[3] Toyohashi University of Technology, Toyohashi, Japan
suzuki@cs.tut.ac.jp

Abstract. This paper proposes an id-eCK secure identity-based authenticated key exchange (ID-AKE) scheme, where the id-eCK security implies that a scheme resists against leakage of all combinations of master, static, and ephemeral secret keys except ones trivially break the security. Most existing id-eCK secure ID-AKE schemes require two symmetric pairing operations or a greater number of asymmetric pairing, which is faster than symmetric one, operations to establish a session key. However, our scheme is realized with a single asymmetric pairing operation for each party, and this is an advantage in efficiency.

The proposed scheme is based on the ID-AKE scheme by McCullagh and Barreto, which is vulnerable to an active attack. To achieve id-eCK security, we apply the HMQV construction and the NAXOS technique to the McCullagh–Barreto scheme. The id-eCK security is proved under the external Diffie–Hellman for target group assumption and the q-gap-bilinear collision attack assumption.

Keywords: Identity-based authenticated group key exchange ·
id-eCK security · Asymmetric pairing ·
External Diffie–Hellman for target group assumption ·
q-gap-bilinear collision attack assumption · HMQV construction ·
NAXOS technique

1 Introduction

Recently, Internet of Things (IoT) devices have been increasing rapidly, and the number of them will reach 25 billion by 2021 [19]. At the same time, an impact of cyberattacks against IoT devices on the real world has become more significant. Whereas authentication is one of fundamental technologies against the cyberattacks, the best way to authenticate IoT devices has still been unclear. Public key infrastructure (PKI)-based authentication is re-emerging as a proper candidate to address the issue.

© Springer Nature Switzerland AG 2019
K. Sako et al. (Eds.): ESORICS 2019, LNCS 11736, pp. 484–503, 2019.
https://doi.org/10.1007/978-3-030-29962-0_23

We explore the potential of another candidate to realize an authentication system for IoT devices via using identity-based cryptography formulated by Shamir [26]. It yields encryption and authentication mechanisms without certificates and thus is suitable to manage a huge number of devices. In particular, identity-based authenticated key exchange (ID-AKE) protocols allow two parties in an open network to securely compute a session key based on their identities. In this paper, we construct a strongly secure ID-AKE protocol that works on resource-constrained devices.

For ID-AKE, several security models have been investigated, and they are influenced by the security models of PKI-based AKE. For PKI-AKE, the Canetti–Krawczyk (CK) security [7] and the extended Canetti-Krawczyk (eCK) security [23] followed the Bellare–Rogaway (BR) security [4]. Based on these security models, the id-BR [5,9], id-CK [6], and id-eCK [20] security models were defined. The CK security and the eCK security are stronger than the BR security [7,11,23], however, the CK security and the eCK security are incompatible [12,13]. These relations hold in the security definitions of ID-AKE, i.e., the id-CK and id-eCK security models, also. We adopt the id-eCK security, which is one of the strongest security notions that capture all combinations of leakage of master, static, and ephemeral secret keys except ones trivially break the security, where both static and ephemeral secret key of the initiator or the responder are leaked.

Most ID-AKE protocols [9,15,16,20,24] are realized by using pairing as an important element. Pairing is a function, e, from two groups, G_1 and G_2, to another group, G_T, and pairing functions are classified into two types: symmetric pairing where $G_1 = G_2$ and asymmetric pairing where $G_1 \neq G_2$. Optimal-ate pairing [27] on BN curves [2] increases advantage of asymmetric pairing comparing with symmetric pairing, i.e., computing of asymmetric pairing is faster than that of symmetric pairing.

However, the existing id-eCK secure ID-AKE schemes require two symmetric pairing operations or more times of faster asymmetric ones as in Table 1. The table shows the comparison of existing ID-AKE schemes and the proposed scheme, in terms of the number of pairings for each party, the type of pairing that can be used, and the security model. Notice that there exists remarkable ID-AKE scheme [14], that does not require pairing so is very efficient, but requires pre-key-issue, i.e., secret key needs to be issued by KGC *before* parties start a session.

1.1 Proposed Protocol

In this paper, we propose the first id-eCK secure ID-based authenticated key exchange scheme that requires single asymmetric pairing operation for each party. Our protocol can be seen as an extension of the protocol by McCullagh and Barreto [24], which only satisfies a very weak security requirement.

To achieve the id-eCK security, we enhance their protocol by two steps. In the first step, we modify their scheme so that we can conduct a security proof similarly to HMQV [22]. Roughly speaking, the modification is necessary

Table 1. Comparison with existing schemes.

Scheme	# of pairings	Type of pairing	Security model	Assumption
MB05 [24]	1	sym, asym	id-BR	BIDH
CCS07 [9]	2	sym, asym	id-BR	BDH
HC09 [20]	2	sym	id-eCK	BDH
FG10 [14]	0	–	id-CK, pre-key-issue	strong-DH
FSU10 [16]	2	sym	id-eCK	Gap-BDH
FSU13 [15]	4	asym	id-eCK	Gap-BDH
Proposed	1	asym	id-eCK	XDTH, q-Gap-BCA

to maintain the security against active attacks. Technically, the modification adds a term to a session key that an adversary cannot set as it desires. Such a term can be generated by hashing a ephemeral public key that is used to generate the session key, thanks to the one-wayness of the hash function. Thus, the adversary cannot control the session key even if it generates a ephemeral public key maliciously.

The second step is to maintain the security against ephemeral secret key leakage. We can achieve this by the technique used in the NAXOS protocol [23]. Their simple and elegant technique is to hash static and ephemeral secret keys to generate the exponent of a ephemeral public key. Then, even if the ephemeral secret key is revealed, the exponent of the ephemeral public key is still hidden without the knowledge of the static secret key. By these modifications, we can achieve the id-eCK security.

1.2   Implementation and Experiments

In order to check the efficiency of our new proposed protocol, we implemented it on the ARM Cortex-M processors. The ARM Cortex-M processors are well used in a wide range of IoT applications, e.g., Smart Home, Smart Farming, etc. In our computation environment with Arm Cortex-M7 processor, our program achieves about 1.5 seconds to compute a session key. This means that our authentication method is practical and useful for IoT devices. Section 6 contains remarks on the implementation of the proposed protocol in C language and computational time comparing it to the (asymmetric pairing based) FSU [15] protocol with the 128-bit security parameter. The benchmark example and specific parameters of an elliptic curve which we used for the timings are listed, also.

2   Preliminary

2.1   Notation

For prime p, $\mathbb{Z}_p$ denotes field $\mathbb{Z}/p\mathbb{Z}$. For set S, $s \xleftarrow{\mathsf{U}} S$ denotes that s is uniformly chosen from S. For natural number n, $[n]$ denotes set $\{1, 2, , \ldots, n\}$. Function $f : \mathbb{N} \to \mathbb{R}$ is called negligible if $f(\lambda) = \lambda^{-\omega(1)}$.

2.2   Bilinear Groups and Assumptions

Definition 2.1 (Bilinear   Groups).   *Bilinear   groups* $\mathbb{G}:=(p, G_1, G_2, G_T, g_1, g_2, e)$ *consist of a prime, p, cyclic groups, G_1, G_2, G_T, of order p, generators, g_1 and g_2, of G_1 and G_2, respectively, and a bilinear map, $e : G_1 \times G_2 \rightarrow G_T$, which has two properties.*

- *(Bilinearity):* $\forall h_1 \in G_1$, $\forall h_2 \in G_2$, *and* $\forall a, b \in \mathbb{Z}_p$, $e(h_1^a, h_2^b) = e(h_1, h_2)^{ab}$ *holds.*
- *(Non-degeneracy): For generators g_1 and g_2, $e(g_1, g_2)$ is a generator of G_T.*

A bilinear group generator, $\mathcal{G}_{\mathsf{BG}}(1^\lambda)$, takes security parameter 1^λ and outputs bilinear groups $\mathbb{G}$ with a $t(\lambda)$-bit prime, p, for some polynomial t. We denote $e(g_1, g_2)$ by g_T.

Throughout the paper, we only consider asymmetric bilinear groups where no efficient isomorphisms exist between G_1 and G_2.

Definition 2.2 (XDHT   Assumption).   *The eXternal Diffie–Hellman for Target group (XDHT) assumption says that all probabilistic polynomial-time bounded (PPT) adversaries cannot compute T given P with non-negligible probability. T and P are defined as follows:*

$$\mathbb{G} \leftarrow \mathcal{G}_{\mathsf{BG}}(1^\lambda), \quad a, b \xleftarrow{\mathsf{U}} \mathbb{Z}_p, \quad P = (\mathbb{G}, g_1^a, g_1^b), \quad and \quad T = g_T^{ab}.$$

The XDHT assumption is implied by the standard XDH assumption, which says the difficulty of distinguishing g_1^{ab} from random given g_1^a and g_1^b.

Definition 2.3 (q-Gap-BCA Assumption [10]).   *The q-Gap-Bilinear Collision Attack (q-Gap-BCA) assumption says that all PPT adversaries cannot compute T given P and an oracle, $\mathcal{O}$, with non-negligible probability. Here, T and P are defined as follows:*

$$\mathbb{G} \leftarrow \mathcal{G}_{\mathsf{BG}}(1^\lambda), \quad h_0, h_1, \ldots, h_q, w \xleftarrow{\mathsf{U}} \mathbb{Z}_p,$$

$$P = \left(\mathbb{G}, g_1^w, h_0, \left(h_1, g_2^{\frac{1}{w+h_1}}\right), \ldots, \left(h_q, g_2^{\frac{1}{w+h_q}}\right)\right), \quad and \quad T = g_T^{\frac{1}{w+h_0}}.$$

The oracle, $\mathcal{O}$, takes three inputs (X, Y, Z) and outputs the truth value that $\frac{\log_{g_1} X}{\log_{g_1} Y} = \log_{g_T} Z \mod p$ holds where $X \in G_1$, $Y \in G_1$, and $Z \in G_T$.

It is known that the q-BCA assumption, which is the same as the q-Gap-BCA assumption except that the oracle $\mathcal{O}$ is not given to the adversary, is implied by the well-known $(q+1)$-BDHI assumption for asymmetric bilinear groups, which says the difficulty of computing $g_T^{1/x}$ given $(g_1^x, \ldots, g_1^{x^{q+1}}, g_2^x, \ldots, g_2^{x^{q+1}})$ [8]. Thus, this q-Gap-BCA assumption is implied by the gap-variant [25] of the $(q+1)$-BDHI assumption.

3   Security Model for ID-Based AKE

We recall the id-eCK security model for ID-AKE by Huang and Cao [20] that is the ID-based version of the eCK security model by LaMacchia, Lauter and Mityagin [23].

We denote a party by U_i and the identifier of U_i by ID_i. We outline our model for two-pass ID-AKE protocol, where parties U_A and U_B exchange ephemeral public keys, X_A and X_B, i.e., U_A sends X_A to U_B and U_B sends X_B to U_A, and thereafter compute a session key. The session key depends on the exchanged ephemeral keys, identities of the parties, the static keys corresponding to these identities and the protocol instance that is used.

In the model, each party is a PPT machine in security parameter λ and obtains a static secret key corresponding to its identity string from a key generation center (KGC) via a secure and authenticated channel. The KGC uses a master secret key together with public parameters to generate individual static secret keys.

Session. An invocation of a protocol is called a *session*. For a party U_A, a session is activated via an incoming message of the forms $(\mathcal{I}, ID_A, ID_B)$ or $(\mathcal{R}, ID_B, ID_A, X_B)$. If U_A is activated with $(\mathcal{I}, ID_A, ID_B)$, then U_A is the session *initiator*, otherwise the session *responder*. After activation, U_A switches the first element (or role) of the incoming massage and appends an ephemeral public key X_A to it, then sends it as an outgoing response. If U_A is the responder, U_A computes a session key. If U_A is the initiator, U_A that has been successfully activated via $(\mathcal{I}, ID_A, ID_B)$ can be further activated via $(\mathcal{I}, ID_A, ID_B, X_A, X_B)$ to compute a session key.

A session initiator U_A identifies the session via $(\mathcal{I}, ID_A, ID_B, X_A, \times)$ or $(\mathcal{I}, ID_A, ID_B, X_A, X_B)$. If U_A is the responder, the session is identified via $(\mathcal{R}, ID_B, ID_A, X_B, X_A)$. For the session $(\mathcal{I}, ID_A, ID_B, X_A, X_B)$, the *matching session* has the identifier $(\mathcal{R}, ID_A, ID_B, X_A, X_B)$ and vice versa. We refer to the party as the *owner* of session sid that is identified by the second element of initiator's sid or the third element of responder's sid. Similarly, we refer to the party as the *peer* of sid that is identified by the third element of initiator's sid or the second element of responder's sid. We say that a session is *completed* if its owner computes a session key.

Adversary. The adversary, $\mathcal{A}$, is modeled as a probabilistic Turing machine that controls all communications between parties including session activation, performed via a Send(message) query. The message has one of the following forms: $(\mathcal{I}, ID_A, ID_B)$, $(\mathcal{R}, ID_A, ID_B, X_A)$, or $(\mathcal{I}, ID_A, ID_B, X_A, X_B)$. Each party submits its responses to the adversary, who decides the global delivery order. Note that the adversary does not control the communication between each party and the KGC.

A party's private information is not accessible to the adversary, however, leakage of private information is captured via the following adversary queries.

- SessionKeyReveal(sid) The adversary obtains the session key for session sid, provided that the session holds a session key.

- EphemeralKeyReveal(sid) The adversary obtains the ephemeral secret key associated with session sid.
- StaticKeyReveal(ID_i) The adversary learns the static secret key of a party U_i.
- MasterKeyReveal() The adversary learns the master secret key of the KGC.
- EstablishParty(ID_i) This query allows the adversary to register a legal party U_i on behalf of the identity ID_i, and the adversary totally controls that party. If a party is established by an EstablishParty(ID_i) query, then we call the party *dishonest*, and if not, we call the party *honest*. This query models malicious insiders.

Freshness. Our security definition requires the notion of "freshness".

Definition 3.1 (Freshness). *Let* sid* *be the session identifier of a completed session, owned by an honest party U_A with a peer U_B, who is also honest. If the matching session exists, then let* $\overline{\text{sid}^*}$ *be the session identifier of the matching session of* sid*. *Define* sid* *to be fresh if none of the following conditions hold:*

1. *$\mathcal{A}$ issues* SessionKeyReveal(sid*) *or* SessionKeyReveal($\overline{\text{sid}^*}$) *(if* $\overline{\text{sid}^*}$ *exists).*
2. $\overline{\text{sid}^*}$ *exists and $\mathcal{A}$ makes either of the following queries*
   - *both* StaticKeyReveal(ID_A) *and* EphemeralKeyReveal(sid*), *or*
   - *both* StaticKeyReveal(ID_B) *and* EphemeralKeyReveal($\overline{\text{sid}^*}$).
3. $\overline{\text{sid}^*}$ *does not exist and $\mathcal{A}$ makes either of the following queries*
   - *both* StaticKeyReveal(ID_A) *and* EphemeralKeyReveal(sid*), *or*
   - StaticKeyReveal(ID_B).

Note that if $\mathcal{A}$ issues MasterKeyReveal(), *we regard $\mathcal{A}$ as having issued both* StaticKeyReveal(ID_A) *and* StaticKeyReveal(ID_B).

Security Experiment. The adversary, $\mathcal{A}$, starts with a set of honest parties, for whom $\mathcal{A}$ adaptively selects identifiers. The adversary makes an arbitrary sequence of the queries described above. During the experiment, $\mathcal{A}$ makes a special query, Test(sid*), and is given with equal probability either the session key held by sid* or a random key. The experiment continues until $\mathcal{A}$ makes a guess whether the key is random or not. The adversary *wins* the game if the test session, sid*, is fresh at the end of $\mathcal{A}$'s execution and if $\mathcal{A}$'s guess was correct.

Definition 3.2 (security). *The advantage of the adversary, $\mathcal{A}$, in the experiment with ID-AKE protocol Π is defined as*

$$\text{Adv}_{\Pi,\mathcal{A}}^{\text{ID-AKE}}(1^\lambda) = \Pr[\mathcal{A} \ wins] - \frac{1}{2}.$$

We say that Π is secure ID-AKE protocols in the id-eCK model if, for any PPT adversary, $\mathcal{A}$, $\text{Adv}_{\Pi,\mathcal{A}}^{\text{ID-AKE}}(1^\lambda)$ is negligible in security parameter λ.

$U_A \ (ID_A)$		$U_B \ (ID_B)$
	$msk = w \xleftarrow{U} \mathbb{Z}_p$	
$i_A = H_1(ID_A)$	$pp = W = g_1^w$	$i_B = H_1(ID_B)$
$sk_A = K_A = g_2^{\frac{1}{w+i_A}}$		$sk_B = K_B = g_2^{\frac{1}{w+i_B}}$
$esk_A = r_A \xleftarrow{U} \{0,1\}^\lambda$	$\xrightarrow{\quad X_A \quad}$	$esk_B = r_B \xleftarrow{U} \{0,1\}^\lambda$
$x_A = H_2(K_A, r_A)$		$x_B = H_2(K_B, r_B)$
$X_A = (Wg_1^{i_B})^{x_A}$	$\xleftarrow{\quad X_B \quad}$	$X_B = (Wg_1^{i_A})^{x_B}$
$d_A = H_3(X_A, ID_A, ID_B)$		$d_A = H_3(X_A, ID_A, ID_B)$
$d_B = H_3(X_B, ID_A, ID_B)$		$d_B = H_3(X_B, ID_A, ID_B)$
$\sigma = e((X_B(Wg_1^{i_A})^{d_B})^{x_A+d_A}, K_A)$		$\sigma = e((X_A(Wg_1^{i_B})^{d_A})^{x_B+d_B}, K_B)$
$K = H_4(\sigma, ID_A, ID_B, X_A, X_B)$		$K = H_4(\sigma, ID_A, ID_B, X_A, X_B)$

Fig. 1. Informal description of our protocol

4   Our ID-Based AKE Protocol

In our protocol, we assume that the description of bilinear groups $\mathbb{G}$ is public. Let $H_1, H_2, H_3 : \{0,1\}^* \to \mathbb{Z}_p$ and $H_4 : \{0,1\}^* \to \{0,1\}^\lambda$ be hash functions modeled as random oracles. Let Π be the protocol identifier of our protocol. We denote $H_1(ID_j)$ by i_j. We present an informal description in Fig. 1.

KGC

1. It randomly selects a master secret key as $w \xleftarrow{U} \mathbb{Z}_p$ and publishes a public parameter $W = g_1^w$.
2. When it generates a static secret key K_j for a party U_j with ID_j, it sets $K_j = g_2^{\frac{1}{w+i_j}}$ where $i_j = H_1(ID_j)$.

Parties. In the following, let U_A be a session initiator and U_B be a session responder.

1. Upon receiving $(\mathcal{I}, ID_A, ID_B)$, U_A selects a random ephemeral secret key, $r_A \xleftarrow{U} \{0,1\}^\lambda$, computes $x_A = H_2(K_A, r_A)$, and sets the ephemeral public key, $X_A = (Wg_1^{i_B})^{x_A} = g_1^{(w+i_B)x_A}$. It destroys x_A and sends $(\mathcal{R}, ID_A, ID_B, X_A)$ to U_B.
2. Upon receiving $(\mathcal{R}, ID_A, ID_B, X_A)$, U_B selects a random ephemeral secret key, $r_B \xleftarrow{U} \{0,1\}^\lambda$, computes $x_B = H_2(K_B, r_B)$, and sets the ephemeral public key, $X_B = (Wg_1^{i_A})^{x_B} = g_1^{(w+i_A)x_B}$. It sends $(\mathcal{I}, ID_A, ID_B, X_A, X_B)$ to U_A.
   U_B computes the session key, K, as
   $$d_A = H_3(X_A, ID_A, ID_B), \quad d_B = H_3(X_B, ID_A, ID_B),$$
   $$\sigma = e((X_A(Wg_1^{i_B})^{d_A})^{x_B+d_B}, K_B), \text{ and}$$
   $$K = H_4(\sigma, ID_A, ID_B, X_A, X_B).$$

Then, it destroys the session state and completes the session.

3. Upon receiving $(\mathcal{I}, ID_A, ID_B, X_A, X_B)$, U_A checks whether U_A has sent $(\mathcal{R}, ID_A, ID_B, X_A)$ to U_B and aborts the session if not.
U_A computes $x_A = H_2(K_A, r_A)$ again and the session key, K, as

$$d_A = H_3(X_A, ID_A, ID_B), \quad d_B = H_3(X_B, ID_A, ID_B),$$
$$\sigma = e((X_B(Wg_1^{i_A})^{d_B})^{x_A+d_A}, K_A), \text{ and}$$
$$K = H_4(\sigma, ID_A, ID_B, X_A, X_B).$$

Then, it destroys the session state and completes the session.

Correctness. If both parties run the protocol honestly, we have

$$\sigma = g_T^{(x_A+d_A)(x_B+d_B)},$$

and they compute the same session key.

5   Security

Theorem 5.1. *Our protocol is id-eCK secure in the random oracle model under the XDHT and q-GAP-BCA assumptions. That is, for all PPT adversary $\mathcal{A}$, $\mathrm{Adv}_{\Pi,\mathcal{A}}^{\mathrm{ID\text{-}AKE}}(1^\lambda)$ is negligible in λ.*

Let the test session be $\mathtt{sid}^* = (\mathcal{I}, ID_A, ID_B, X_A, X_B)$ or $(\mathcal{R}, ID_A, ID_B, X_A, X_B)$, which is a completed session between honest parties U_A and U_B. That is, the session key, K^*, of the test session equals to $H_4(\sigma, X_A, X_B, ID_A, ID_B)$ where $\sigma = g_T^{(\log_{g_1} X_A^{\frac{1}{w+iB}}+d_A)(\log_{g_1} X_B^{\frac{1}{w+iA}}+d_B)}$. Let Q be the event where the adversary $\mathcal{A}$ queries H_4 on $(\sigma, X_A, X_B, ID_A, ID_B)$. If $\mathcal{A}$ does not query H_4 on $(\sigma, X_A, X_B, ID_A, ID_B)$ throughout the experiment, the session key K^* is distributed randomly in the key space from the viewpoint of $\mathcal{A}$ in the random oracle model. Thus, we have

$$\begin{aligned}\Pr[\mathcal{A} \ wins] &= \Pr[Q]\Pr[\mathcal{A} \ wins|Q] + (1 - \Pr[Q])\Pr[\mathcal{A} \ wins|\neg Q]\\ &\leq \Pr[Q](\Pr[\mathcal{A} \ wins|Q] - 1/2) + 1/2.\end{aligned} \tag{5.1}$$

Next, we consider the three events in the experiment.

- E_1: There exists an honest party U_C such that $\mathcal{A}$ queries H_2 on $(K_C, *)$ before issuing StaticKeyReveal(ID_C) or MasterKeyReveal(), where K_C is the static secret key of U_C.
- E_2: E_1 does not occur, and the test session has a matching session.
- E_3: E_1 does not occur, and the test session does not have a matching session.

Clearly, they are exclusive and $\Pr[E_1] + \Pr[E_2] + \Pr[E_3] = 1$. Thanks to Lemmas 5.1 to 5.3, we can say that $\Pr[Q] = \sum_{i=1}^{3} \Pr[Q \wedge E_i]$ is negligible and thus $\mathrm{Adv}_{\Pi,\mathcal{A}}^{\mathrm{ID\text{-}AKE}}(1^\lambda)$ is also negligible from Eq. (5.1). $\square$

Lemma 5.1. *Let n be the maximum number of honest parties involved in the experiment and q be the maximum number of queries to H_1. For any PPT adversary, $\mathcal{A}$, against our protocol, there exists a PPT adversary, $\mathcal{B}$, that solves the q-Gap-BCA problem with probability P_1, and we have*

$$nP_1 \geq \Pr[Q \wedge E_1].$$

Proof. We describe $\mathcal{B}$'s behavior in the following. $\mathcal{B}$ obtains an instance of the q-Gap-BCA problem,

$$P = \left(\mathbb{G}, g_1^w, h_0, \left(h_1, g_2^{\frac{1}{w+h_1}} \right), \ldots, \left(h_q, g_2^{\frac{1}{w+h_q}} \right) \right),$$

and sets a public parameter as $W = g_1^w$. Note that $\mathcal{B}$ can utilize the oracle $\mathcal{O}$ given in Definition 2.3. $\mathcal{B}$ instantiates n honest parties, $U_1, \ldots, U_n$, and selects one party at random, say U_C. $\mathcal{B}$ records the queries to the random oracle, H_1, as $i_C = H_1(ID_C) = h_0$ and $i_j = H_1(ID_j) = h_j$ for $j \in [n] \backslash C$. By the definition, $\mathcal{B}$ possesses static secret keys of all honest parties except party U_C. Then, $\mathcal{B}$ responds to queries as follows.

1. $\mathsf{Send}(\mathcal{I}, ID_j, ID_\ell)$: $\mathcal{B}$ executes the protocol honestly. That is, it computes $X_j = (Wg_1^{i_j})^{x_j}$ following the protocol and returns $(\mathcal{R}, ID_j, ID_\ell, X_j)$ to $\mathcal{A}$.
2. $\mathsf{Send}(\mathcal{R}, ID_j, ID_\ell, X_j)$: $\mathcal{B}$ executes the protocol honestly. That is, it computes $X_\ell = (Wg_1^{i_j})^{x_\ell}$ following the protocol and returns $(\mathcal{I}, ID_j, ID_\ell, X_j, X_\ell)$ to $\mathcal{A}$. After that, if $\ell \neq C$, $\mathcal{B}$ computes the session key, K, honestly. Otherwise, it sets K as follows. First, $\mathcal{B}$ looks up query records of form $H_4(\sigma', ID_j, ID_\ell, X_j, X_\ell)$ that satisfies relation

$$1 \leftarrow \mathcal{O}\left(X_j^{x_\ell + d_\ell}, Wg_1^{i_\ell}, \sigma' g_T^{-d_j(x_\ell + d_\ell)} \right),$$

   where $d_j = H_3(X_j, ID_j, ID_\ell)$ and $d_\ell = H_3(X_\ell, ID_j, ID_\ell)$. If such a record is found, $\mathcal{B}$ sets $K = H_4(\sigma', ID_j, ID_\ell, X_j, X_\ell)$. Otherwise, it sets $K \xleftarrow{\mathsf{U}} \{0,1\}^\lambda$.
3. $\mathsf{Send}(\mathcal{I}, ID_j, ID_\ell, X_j, X_\ell)$: If the same query has already been made before or $\mathcal{B}$ has never returned the message, $(\mathcal{R}, ID_j, ID_\ell, X_j)$, in item 1, $\mathcal{B}$ does nothing in this query. Otherwise, $\mathcal{B}$ computes K as follows. If $j \neq C$, $\mathcal{B}$ computes the session key, K, honestly. If $j = C$, $\mathcal{B}$ picks x_j that is used to compute $X_j = (Wg_1^{i_\ell})^{x_j}$ in item 1. Then, it looks up query records of form $H_4(\sigma', ID_j, ID_\ell, X_j, X_\ell)$ that satisfies relation

$$1 \leftarrow \mathcal{O}\left(X_\ell^{x_j + d_j}, Wg_1^{i_j}, \sigma' g_T^{-d_\ell(x_j + d_j)} \right).$$

   If such a record is found, $\mathcal{B}$ sets $K = H_4(\sigma', ID_j, ID_\ell, X_j, X_\ell)$. Otherwise, it sets $K \xleftarrow{\mathsf{U}} \{0,1\}^\lambda$.
4. $H_1(ID_j)$: If the query, $H_1(ID_j)$, has been made before, $\mathcal{B}$ returns the same value. Otherwise, it returns h_ℓ, chosen from the instance, that has not been used yet for the reply.

5. $H_2(K_j, r_j)$: If the query, $H_2(K_j, r_j)$, has been made before, $\mathcal{B}$ returns the same value. Otherwise, it checks whether $e(Wg_1^{ic}, K_j) = g_T$ or not. If so, $\mathcal{B}$ outputs $e(g_1, K_j)$ and finish the experiment. Otherwise, it returns a random value, $x_j \xleftarrow{\mathsf{U}} \mathbb{Z}_p$.

6. $H_3(X, ID_j, ID_\ell)$: $\mathcal{B}$ simulates the random oracle in the normal way.

7. $H_4(\sigma, ID_j, ID_\ell, X_j, X_\ell)$: If the query, $H_4(\sigma, ID_j, ID_\ell, X_j, X_\ell)$, has been made before, it returns the same value. Otherwise, it computes the return value as follows. $\mathcal{B}$ looks up query records of $\mathsf{Send}(\mathcal{R}, ID_j, ID_\ell, X_j)$ in which the returned message is $(\mathcal{I}, ID_j, ID_\ell, X_j, X_\ell)$ or $\mathsf{Send}(\mathcal{I}, ID_j, ID_\ell, X_j, X_\ell)$.
    - If such a record, $\mathsf{Send}(\mathcal{R}, ID_j, ID_\ell, X_j)$, is found, $\mathcal{B}$ picks x_ℓ that is used to compute X_ℓ. Then, it checks whether the following relationship holds;
    $$ 1 \leftarrow \mathcal{O}\left(X_j^{x_\ell + d_\ell}, Wg_1^{i_\ell}, \sigma g_T^{-d_j(x_\ell + d_\ell)}\right). $$
    If so, $\mathcal{B}$ returns K that has been set in item 2. Otherwise, it returns a random value, $K \xleftarrow{\mathsf{U}} \{0, 1\}^\lambda$.
    - If such a record, $\mathsf{Send}(\mathcal{I}, ID_j, ID_\ell, X_j, X_\ell)$, is found, $\mathcal{B}$ picks x_j that is used to compute X_j. Then it checks whether the following relationship holds;
    $$ 1 \leftarrow \mathcal{O}\left(X_\ell^{x_j + d_j}, Wg_1^{i_j}, \sigma' g_T^{-d_\ell(x_j + d_j)}\right). $$
    If so, $\mathcal{B}$ returns K that has been set item 3. Otherwise, it returns a random value, $K \xleftarrow{\mathsf{U}} \{0, 1\}^\lambda$.
    - Otherwise, $\mathcal{B}$ returns a random value, $K \xleftarrow{\mathsf{U}} \{0, 1\}^\lambda$.

8. $\mathsf{SessionKeyReveal}((\mathcal{I}, ID_j, ID_\ell, X_j, X_\ell)$ or $(\mathcal{R}, ID_j, ID_\ell, X_j, X_\ell))$:
    - $(\mathcal{I}, ID_j, ID_\ell, X_j, X_\ell)$: $\mathcal{B}$ looks up query records of $\mathsf{Send}(\mathcal{I}, ID_j, ID_\ell, X_j, X_\ell)$. If such a record is found, $\mathcal{B}$ returns K computed in the Send query. Otherwise, it returns $\perp$.
    - $(\mathcal{R}, ID_j, ID_\ell, X_j, X_\ell)$: $\mathcal{B}$ looks up query records of $\mathsf{Send}(\mathcal{R}, ID_j, ID_\ell, X_j)$ in which $\mathcal{B}$ returned the message, $(\mathcal{I}, ID_j, ID_\ell, X_j, X_\ell)$. If such a record is found, $\mathcal{B}$ returns K computed in the Send query. Otherwise, it returns $\perp$.

9. $\mathsf{EphemeralKeyReveal}(\mathsf{sid})$: $\mathcal{B}$ returns the corresponding ephemeral secret key r_j or r_ℓ that is used in item 1 or item 2, respectively.

10. $\mathsf{StaticKeyReveal}(ID_j)$: If $j = C$, $\mathcal{B}$ aborts the experiment. Otherwise, it returns the static secret key for U_j.

11. $\mathsf{MasterKeyReveal}()$: $\mathcal{B}$ aborts the experiment.

12. $\mathsf{Test}(\mathsf{sid})$: $\mathcal{B}$ returns the corresponding static secret key or a random key following the definition of the experiment.

13. $\mathsf{EstablishParty}(ID_j)$: $\mathcal{B}$ returns the static secret key for U_j honestly.

Analysis. In the above description, $\mathcal{B}$ correctly simulates the experiment to $\mathcal{A}$ until $\mathsf{StaticKeyReveal}(ID_C)$ or $\mathsf{MasterKeyReveal}()$ is made in item 10 or item 11. However, if event E_1 occurs and the choice of U_C is correct, $\mathcal{B}$ never aborts in them because these events imply that $\mathcal{B}$ returns a correct output in item 5 before those queries are made. Note that the probability that the choice of U_C is correct is $1/n$ because U_C is uniformly selected from n parties. Thus, we have $P_1 \geq \frac{1}{n} \Pr[E_1] \geq \frac{1}{n} \Pr[Q \wedge E_1]$. $\qquad\qquad\square$

Lemma 5.2. *Let s_I be the maximum number of sessions owned by honest session initiators, s_R be the maximum number of sessions owned by honest session responders, and q_H be the maximum number of queries to H_4. For any PPT adversary, $\mathcal{A}$, against our protocol, there exists a PPT adversary, $\mathcal{B}$, that solves the XDHT problem with probability P_2, and we have*

$$q_H s_I s_R P_2 + 2^{-\Omega(\lambda)} \geq \Pr[Q \wedge E_2].$$

Proof. We describe $\mathcal{B}$'s behavior in the following. $\mathcal{B}$ obtains an instance of the XDHT problem, $P = (\mathbb{G}, g_1^a, g_1^b)$. $\mathcal{B}$ generates a master secret key and a public parameter as $w \xleftarrow{\mathsf{U}} \mathbb{Z}_p$ and $W = g_1^w$, respectively. Note that $\mathcal{B}$ can generate any static secret key because it has the master secret key. $\mathcal{B}$ instantiates n honest parties, $U_1, \ldots, U_n$, and randomly selects two numbers, $s_1 \xleftarrow{\mathsf{U}} [s_I], s_2 \xleftarrow{\mathsf{U}} [s_R]$. Let sid' and sid'' be the sessions that is generated in the s_1-th Send query of item 1 (and possibly completed in item 3) and the s_2-th Send query of item 2, respectively. Let U_C and U_D be the owners of sid' and sid'', respectively. $\mathcal{B}$ responds to queries as follows.

1. $\mathsf{Send}(\mathcal{I}, ID_j, ID_\ell)$: If this is the s_1-th query of the form, $\mathsf{Send}(\mathcal{I}, ID_j, ID_\ell)$, $\mathcal{B}$ selects (but does not use) an ephemeral secret key, r_C^*, and sets $X_C = (g_1^a)^{w+i_\ell}$. Note that r_C^* is prepared for $\mathsf{EphemeralKeyReveal}$ query. Otherwise, $\mathcal{B}$ computes $X_j = (Wg_1^{i_\ell})^{x_j}$ following the protocol. Then, $\mathcal{B}$ returns $(\mathcal{R}, ID_j, ID_\ell, X_j)$ to $\mathcal{A}$.

2. $\mathsf{Send}(\mathcal{R}, ID_j, ID_\ell, X_j)$: If this is the s_2-th query of the form, $\mathsf{Send}(\mathcal{R}, ID_j, ID_\ell, X_j)$, $\mathcal{B}$ selects (but does not use) an ephemeral secret key, r_D^*, and sets $X_D = (g_1^b)^{w+i_j}$. Otherwise, $\mathcal{B}$ computes $X_\ell = (Wg_1^{i_j})^{x_\ell}$ following the protocol. Then, $\mathcal{B}$ returns $(\mathcal{I}, ID_j, ID_\ell, X_j, X_\ell)$ to $\mathcal{A}$. Except the s_2-th query, it also computes the session key, K, honestly utilizing the static secret key of U_ℓ.

3. $\mathsf{Send}(\mathcal{I}, ID_j, ID_\ell, X_j, X_\ell)$: $\mathcal{B}$ checks whether it has returned message, $(\mathcal{R}, ID_j, ID_\ell, X_j)$, in item 1 and $X_j \neq (g_1^a)^{w+i_\ell}$. If so, $\mathcal{B}$ picks x_j used in item 1 and computes the session key, K, honestly. Otherwise, $\mathcal{B}$ does nothing.

4. $H_1(ID_j)$: $\mathcal{B}$ simulates the random oracle in the normal way.

5. $H_2(K_j, r_j)$: If $H_2(K_C, r_C^*)$ or $H_2(K_D, r_D^*)$ is queried, $\mathcal{B}$ aborts the experiment, where r_C^* and r_D^* are the ephemeral secret keys associated with $X_C = (g_1^a)^{w+i_\ell}$ and $X_D = (g_1^b)^{w+i_j}$, respectively. Otherwise, it simulates the random oracle in the normal way.

6. $H_3(X, ID_j, ID_\ell)$: $\mathcal{B}$ simulates the random oracle in the normal way.

7. $H_4(\sigma, ID_j, ID_\ell, X_j, X_\ell)$: $\mathcal{B}$ simulates the random oracle in the normal way.

8. $\mathsf{SessionKeyReveal}((\mathcal{I}, ID_j, ID_\ell, X_j, X_\ell)$ or $(\mathcal{R}, ID_j, ID_\ell, X_j, X_\ell))$:
   - $(\mathcal{I}, ID_j, ID_\ell, X_j, X_\ell)$: $\mathcal{B}$ looks up query records of $\mathsf{Send}(\mathcal{I}, ID_j, ID_\ell, X_j, X_\ell)$. If such a record is not found, $\mathcal{B}$ returns $\bot$. If found and $X_j = (g_1^a)^{w+i_\ell}$, $\mathcal{B}$ aborts the experiment. Otherwise, it returns K computed in the Send query.

- $(\mathcal{R}, ID_j, ID_\ell, X_j, X_\ell)$: $\mathcal{B}$ looks up query records of $\mathsf{Send}(\mathcal{R}, ID_j, ID_\ell, X_j)$ in which $\mathcal{B}$ returned the message, $(\mathcal{I}, ID_j, ID_\ell, X_j, X_\ell)$. If such a record is not found, $\mathcal{B}$ returns $\perp$. If found and $X_\ell = (g_1^b)^{w+i_j}$, $\mathcal{B}$ aborts the experiment. Otherwise, it returns K computed in the Send query.

9. $\mathsf{EphemeralKeyReveal}(\mathtt{sid})$: $\mathcal{B}$ returns the corresponding ephemeral secret key, r_j or r_ℓ, that is used in item 1 or item 2, respectively.
10. $\mathsf{StaticKeyReveal}(ID_j)$: $\mathcal{B}$ returns the static secret key of U_j.
11. $\mathsf{MasterKeyReveal}()$: $\mathcal{B}$ returns the master secret key, w.
12. $\mathsf{Test}(\mathtt{sid})$: $\mathcal{B}$ returns a random key, $K \xleftarrow{\mathsf{U}} \{0,1\}^\lambda$.
13. $\mathsf{EstablishParty}(ID_j)$: $\mathcal{B}$ returns the static secret key for U_j honestly.
14. $\mathsf{Finalize}(b')$: When $\mathcal{A}$ outputs the answer b', $\mathcal{B}$ uniformly selects one query record of form $H_4(\sigma, ID_j, ID_\ell, X_j, X_\ell)$ and outputs $\sigma g_T^{-ad_\ell - bd_j - d_j d_\ell}$.

Analysis. In the above description, $\mathcal{B}$ correctly simulates the experiment to $\mathcal{A}$ until $\mathcal{B}$ aborts the experiment in item 5 or item 8. However, if event E_2 occurs and $\mathcal{B}$ has correctly guessed the test session and its matching session, i.e., $(\mathtt{sid}^*, \overline{\mathtt{sid}^*}) = (\mathtt{sid}', \mathtt{sid}'')$, it never aborts in those queries except the negligible probability. This follows from the two observations.

- E_2 says that $\mathcal{A}$ can make a query, $H_2(K_C, r_C^*)$ (resp. $H_2(K_D, r_D^*)$), only after making a query, $\mathsf{StaticKeyReveal}(ID_C)$ (resp. $\mathsf{StaticKeyReveal}(ID_D)$) or $\mathsf{MasterKeyReveal}()$. This means that $\mathcal{A}$ cannot query $\mathsf{EphemeralKeyReveal}$ on $\mathtt{sid}'$ (resp. $\mathtt{sid}''$) before the query, $H_2(K_C, r_C^*)$ (resp. $H_2(K_D, r_D^*)$). Thus, the probability that $\mathcal{A}$ makes the query, $H_2(K_C, r_C^*)$ or $H_2(K_D, r_D^*)$, in item 5 is $2^{-\Omega(\lambda)}$, because r_C^* or r_D^* is completely hidden from $\mathcal{A}$.
- $\mathcal{B}$ never aborts in item 8 from the definition of the id-eCK security, which prohibits $\mathsf{SessionKeyReveal}$ on $\mathtt{sid}^*$ and $\overline{\mathtt{sid}^*}$.

Furthermore, if event Q also occurs, $\mathcal{A}$ makes a query, $H_4(\sigma, ID_C, ID_D, X_C^*, X_D^*)$, before $\mathcal{A}$ outputs the answer, where X_C^* and X_D^* are ephemeral public keys in the test session and $\sigma = g_T^{ab + ad_D + bd_C + d_C d_D}$. Thus, $\mathcal{B}$ outputs g_T^{ab} at least with probability $1/q_H$ in item 14. In conclusion, we have

$$P_2 + 2^{-\Omega(\lambda)} \geq \frac{1}{q_H} \Pr[(\mathtt{sid}^*, \overline{\mathtt{sid}^*}) = (\mathtt{sid}', \mathtt{sid}'') \wedge Q \wedge E_2] = \frac{1}{q_H s_\mathcal{I} s_\mathcal{R}} \Pr[Q \wedge E_2].$$

$\square$

Lemma 5.3. *Let n be the maximum number of honest parties, s be the maximum number of sessions owned by honest parties, q be the maximum number of queries to H_1, q_F be the maximum number of queries to H_3, and q_H be the maximum number of queries to H_4. For any PPT adversary, $\mathcal{A}$, against our protocol, there exist a PPT adversary, $\mathcal{B}$, that solves the q-Gap-BCA problem with probability P_3, and we have*

$$nsq_H \sqrt{q_F P_3} + 2^{-\Omega(\lambda)} \geq \Pr[Q \wedge E_3].$$

Proof. We describe $\mathcal{B}$'s behavior in the following. $\mathcal{B}$ obtains the instance of q-Gap-BCA problem,

$$P = \left(\mathbb{G}, g_1^w, h_0, \left(h_1, g_2^{\frac{1}{w+h_1}} \right), \ldots, \left(h_q, g_2^{\frac{1}{w+h_q}} \right) \right),$$

and sets a public parameter as $W = g_1^w$. Note that $\mathcal{B}$ can utilize the oracle, $\mathcal{O}$, given in Definition 2.3. $\mathcal{B}$ instantiates n honest parties, $U_1, \ldots, U_n$, and selects one party at random, say U_C. $\mathcal{B}$ records the queries to the random oracle, H_1, as $i_C = H_1(ID_C) = h_0$ and $i_j = H_1(ID_j) = h_j$ for $j \in [n] \backslash C$. By the definition, $\mathcal{B}$ possesses static secret keys of all honest parties except party U_C. $\mathcal{B}$ also randomly selects a number, $s' \xleftarrow{\mathsf{U}} [s]$, and let the session be $\mathtt{sid}'$ that is generated by the s'-th Send query of item 1 and item 2 in total. Let U_D and U_E be the owner and the peer of $\mathtt{sid}'$, respectively. Then, $\mathcal{B}$ responds to queries made by $\mathcal{A}$ as follows.

1. $\mathsf{Send}(\mathcal{I}, ID_j, ID_\ell)$:
   - If this is the s'-th Send query (i.e., $j = D$) and $D = C$, $\mathcal{B}$ aborts the experiment.
   - If this is the s'-th Send query (i.e., $j = D$) and $D \neq C$, $\mathcal{B}$ selects a random value, $y \xleftarrow{\mathsf{U}} \mathbb{Z}_p$, and sets $X_D = g_1^y$. It also selects an ephemeral secret key, r_D^*.
   - Otherwise, $\mathcal{B}$ computes $X_j = (Wg_1^{i_\ell})^{x_j}$ following the protocol.
   Then, $\mathcal{B}$ returns $(\mathcal{R}, ID_j, ID_\ell, X_j)$.
2. $\mathsf{Send}(\mathcal{R}, ID_j, ID_\ell, X_j)$: If this is the s'-th Send query (i.e., $\ell = D$) and
   - $D = C$, then $\mathcal{B}$ aborts the experiment.
   - $D \neq C$, then $\mathcal{B}$ selects a random value, $y \xleftarrow{\mathsf{U}} \mathbb{Z}_p$, and sets $X_D = g_1^y$. $\mathcal{B}$ also selects an ephemeral secret key, r_D^*. Then, it returns $(\mathcal{I}, ID_E, ID_D, X_E, X_D)$ and finish the procedure without setting the session key, K.
   If this is not the s'-th Send query, $\mathcal{B}$ computes $X_\ell = (Wg_1^{i_j})^{x_\ell}$ following the protocol and returns $(\mathcal{I}, ID_j, ID_\ell, X_j, X_\ell)$. After that,
   - if $\ell \neq C$, $\mathcal{B}$ computes the session key, K, honestly.
   - if $\ell = C$, $\mathcal{B}$ looks up query records of form $H_4(\sigma', ID_j, ID_\ell, X_j, X_\ell)$ that satisfies relation

$$1 \leftarrow \mathcal{O}\left(X_j^{x_\ell + d_\ell}, Wg_1^{i_\ell}, \sigma' g_T^{-d_j(x_\ell + d_\ell)} \right),$$

   where d_j and d_ℓ are computed from X_j and X_ℓ following the protocol, respectively. If such a record is found, $\mathcal{B}$ sets $K = H_4(\sigma', ID_j, ID_\ell, X_j, X_\ell)$. Otherwise, it randomly selects $K \xleftarrow{\mathsf{U}} \{0,1\}^\lambda$.
3. $\mathsf{Send}(\mathcal{I}, ID_j, ID_\ell, X_j, X_\ell)$: In the following cases, $\mathcal{B}$ does nothing in this query.
   - The same query has already been made before.
   - $\mathcal{B}$ has never returned the message, $(\mathcal{R}, ID_j, ID_\ell, X_j)$ in item 1.
   - $\mathcal{B}$ has returned the message, $(\mathcal{R}, ID_j, ID_\ell, X_j)$ in item 1 and $X_j = g_1^y$.

Otherwise, it computes K as follows.

- If $j \neq C$, $\mathcal{B}$ computes the session key, K, honestly.
- If $j = C$, $\mathcal{B}$ picks x_j that is used to compute $X_j = (Wg_1^{i_\ell})^{x_j}$ in item 1. Then, $\mathcal{B}$ looks up query records of form $H_4(\sigma', ID_j, ID_\ell, X_j, X_\ell)$ that satisfies relation

$$1 \leftarrow \mathcal{O}\left(X_\ell^{x_j+d_j}, Wg_1^{i_j}, \sigma' g_T^{-d_\ell(x_j+d_j)}\right).$$

If such a record is found, $\mathcal{B}$ sets $K = H_4(\sigma', ID_j, ID_\ell, X_j, X_\ell)$. Otherwise, it sets $K \xleftarrow{\mathsf{U}} \{0,1\}^\lambda$.

4. $H_1(ID_j)$: If the query, $H_1(ID_j)$, has been made before, $\mathcal{B}$ returns the same value. Otherwise, it returns h_ℓ, chosen from the instance, that has not been used yet for the reply.

5. $H_2(K_j, r_j)$: If $H_2(K_D, r_D^*)$, which corresponds to $\frac{y}{w+i_E}$, is queried, $\mathcal{B}$ aborts the experiment. Otherwise, it simulates the random oracle in the normal way.

6. $H_3(X, ID_j, ID_\ell)$: $\mathcal{B}$ simulates the random oracle in the normal way.

7. $H_4(\sigma, ID_j, ID_\ell, X_j, X_\ell)$: If the query, $H_4(\sigma, ID_j, ID_\ell, X_j, X_\ell)$, has been made before, $\mathcal{B}$ returns the same value. Otherwise, $\mathcal{B}$ computes the return value as follows. $\mathcal{B}$ looks up query records of $\mathsf{Send}(\mathcal{R}, ID_j, ID_\ell, X_j)$ in which it has returned the message, $(\mathcal{I}, ID_j, ID_\ell, X_j, X_\ell)$ or $\mathsf{Send}(\mathcal{I}, ID_j, ID_\ell, X_j, X_\ell)$.

- If such a record, $\mathsf{Send}(\mathcal{R}, ID_j, ID_\ell, X_j)$, is found, $\mathcal{B}$ picks x_ℓ that is used to compute X_ℓ. Then $\mathcal{B}$ checks whether the following relationship holds;

$$1 \leftarrow \mathcal{O}\left(X_j^{x_\ell+d_\ell}, Wg_1^{i_\ell}, \sigma g_T^{-d_j(x_\ell+d_\ell)}\right).$$

If so, $\mathcal{B}$ returns K that has been set in item 2. Otherwise, it returns a random value, $K \xleftarrow{\mathsf{U}} \{0,1\}^\lambda$.

- If such a record, $\mathsf{Send}(\mathcal{I}, ID_j, ID_\ell, X_j, X_\ell)$, is found, $\mathcal{B}$ picks x_j that is used to compute X_j. Then $\mathcal{B}$ checks whether the following relationship holds;

$$1 \leftarrow \mathcal{O}\left(X_\ell^{x_j+d_j}, Wg_1^{i_j}, \sigma' g_T^{-d_\ell(x_j+d_j)}\right).$$

If so, $\mathcal{B}$ returns K that has been set item 3. Otherwise, it returns a random value, $K \xleftarrow{\mathsf{U}} \{0,1\}^\lambda$.

- Otherwise, $\mathcal{B}$ returns a random value, $K \xleftarrow{\mathsf{U}} \{0,1\}^\lambda$.

8. $\mathsf{SessionKeyReveal}((\mathcal{I}, ID_j, ID_\ell, X_j, X_\ell)$ or $(\mathcal{R}, ID_j, ID_\ell, X_j, X_\ell))$:

- $(\mathcal{I}, ID_j, ID_\ell, X_j, X_\ell)$: $\mathcal{B}$ looks up query records of $\mathsf{Send}(\mathcal{I}, ID_j, ID_\ell, X_j, X_\ell)$. If such a record is not found, $\mathcal{B}$ returns $\perp$. If found and $X_j = g_1^y$, $\mathcal{B}$ aborts the experiment. Otherwise, it returns K computed in the Send query.

- $(\mathcal{R}, ID_j, ID_\ell, X_j, X_\ell)$: $\mathcal{B}$ looks up query records of $\mathsf{Send}(\mathcal{R}, ID_j, ID_\ell, X_j)$ in which $\mathcal{B}$ returned the message, $(\mathcal{I}, ID_j, ID_\ell, X_j, X_\ell)$. If such a record is not found, $\mathcal{B}$ returns $\perp$. If found and $X_\ell = g_1^y$, $\mathcal{B}$ aborts the experiment. Otherwise, it returns K computed in the Send query.

9. EphemeralKeyReveal(sid): $\mathcal{B}$ returns the corresponding ephemeral secret key, r_j or r_ℓ, that is used in item 1 to item 2, respectively.
10. StaticKeyReveal(ID_j): If $j = C$, $\mathcal{B}$ aborts the experiment. Otherwise, $\mathcal{B}$ returns the static secret key for U_j.
11. MasterKeyReveal(): $\mathcal{B}$ aborts the experiment.
12. Test(sid): $\mathcal{B}$ returns a random key, $K \xleftarrow{\mathsf{U}} \{0,1\}^\lambda$.
13. EstablishParty(ID_j): $\mathcal{B}$ returns the static secret key for U_j honestly.
14. Finalize(b'): When $\mathcal{A}$ outputs the answer b', $\mathcal{B}$ uniformly selects one query record of the form $H_4(\sigma, ID_j, ID_\ell, X_j, X_\ell)$. Then, it outputs

$$S = \begin{cases} \left(\sigma e(X_\ell, K_j)^{-d_j} g_T^{-d_j d_\ell} \right)^{\frac{1}{y}} & \text{if } \mathtt{sid}^* = (\mathcal{I}, \ldots) \\ \left(\sigma e(X_j, K_\ell)^{-d_\ell} g_T^{-d_j d_\ell} \right)^{\frac{1}{y}} & \text{if } \mathtt{sid}^* = (\mathcal{R}, \ldots) \end{cases}.$$

Analysis. In the above description, $\mathcal{B}$ correctly simulates the experiment to $\mathcal{A}$ until $\mathcal{B}$ aborts the experiment in one of items 1, 2, 5, 8, 10 and 11. However, if event E_3 occurs, $\mathtt{sid}^* = \mathtt{sid}'$, and $C = E$, then $\mathcal{B}$ never aborts in those queries except the negligible probability. This follows from the following observations.

- $D \neq C$ because $C = E$. Thus, $\mathcal{B}$ does not abort in item 1 or item 2.
- Event E_3 says that $\mathcal{A}$ can make a query, $H_2(K_D, r_D^*)$, only after making a query, StaticKeyReveal(ID_D) or MasterKeyReveal(). This means that $\mathcal{A}$ cannot query EphemeralKeyReveal on $\mathtt{sid}'$ before the query $H_2(K_D, r_D^*)$. Thus, the probability that $\mathcal{A}$ makes the query, $H_2(K_D, r_D^*)$, in item 5 is $2^{-\Omega(\lambda)}$, because r_D^* is completely hidden from $\mathcal{A}$.
- $\mathcal{B}$ never aborts in item 8 from the definition of the id-eCK security, which prohibits SessionKeyReveal on $\mathtt{sid}^*$.
- $\mathcal{B}$ never aborts in item 10 or item 11 from the definition of the id-eCK security, which prohibits StaticKeyReveal on the peer of $\mathtt{sid}^*$.

Furthermore, if event Q also occurs, $\mathcal{A}$ makes a query, $H_4(\sigma, ID_C, ID_D, X_C^*, X_D^*)$ (the order of C and D may be in reverse), before $\mathcal{A}$ outputs the answer, where X_C^* and X_D^* are ephemeral public keys in the test session, $\sigma = g_T^{(\frac{z}{w+i_D} + d_C)(\frac{y}{w+i_C} + d_D)}$, and $z = \log_{g_1} X_C^*$. Thus, $\mathcal{B}$ outputs $S^* = g_T^{\frac{1}{w+i_C}(\frac{z}{w+i_D} + d_C)}$ at least with probability $1/q_H$ in item 14. In conclusion, we have

$$\Pr[S^* \leftarrow \mathcal{B}] \geq \frac{1}{q_H} \Pr[\mathtt{sid}^* = \mathtt{sid}' \wedge C = E \wedge Q \wedge E_3] + 2^{-\Omega(\lambda)}$$

$$= \frac{1}{nsq_H} \Pr[Q \wedge E_3] + 2^{-\Omega(\lambda)}.$$

At this point, we use the forking lemma [3]. That is, we consider the following experiment. Suppose $\mathcal{A}$ has correctly output the answer in item 14 after all events listed above occurred. Then, $\mathcal{B}$ rewinds $\mathcal{A}$ until the point where $\mathcal{A}$ makes a query $H_3(X_C^*, ID_C, ID_D)$ and reruns $\mathcal{A}$ by randomly selecting all outputs of H_3

independently of those in the first run. All other randomnesses are not changed. Let d_C be the output of $H_3(X_C^*, ID_C, ID_D)$ in the first run and d_C' be that in the second run. Clearly, $d_C \neq d_C'$ holds with overwhelming probability. The forking lemma says that $\mathcal{B}$ can extract $S^* = g_T^{\frac{1}{w+i_C}(\frac{z}{w+i_D}+d_C)}$ in the first run and $S^{**} = g_T^{\frac{1}{w+i_C}(\frac{z}{w+i_D}+d_C')}$ in the second run from H_4 with probability

$$P_3 \geq \frac{1}{q_F}\left(\frac{1}{nsq_H}\Pr[Q \wedge E_3]\right)^2 - 2^{-\Omega(\lambda)}.$$

Finally, $\mathcal{B}$ outputs $(S^*/S^{**})^{\frac{1}{d_C-d_C'}}$, which corresponds to $g_T^{\frac{1}{w+h_0}}$. $\square$

6   Implementation and Experiments

6.1   Experimental Evaluation

In this section, we show the efficiency of our new proposed protocol through our implementation. We implemented the proposed protocol by using our cryptographic library and compared its performance against the implementation of [15]. Our software cryptographic library is written in C, using OpenSSL C library for operations of a multiple precision integer. We used the Gallant–Lambert–Vanstone (GLV) [18] and Galbraith–Lin–Scott (GLS) [17] techniques for the scalar multiplication. We also applied the optimal ate pairing on BN curve to the pairing operation.

Table 2. Execution environment

CPU	Cortex-M7
Clock	216 MHz
RAM	512 KB
ROM	2 MB
Development Board	STM32 Nucleo-144
MCU	STM32F767ZI
Compiler system	IAR C Compiler for ARM 8.32

Table 3. Experimental results (msec)

Proposed	1421
FSU [15]	4759
Scalar Mult. in G_1	128
Scalar Mult. in G_2	237
Pairing	737

We summarize our execution environment for our experiment in Table 2. In Table 3, we show the total computation time of the ephemeral public key X and the session key K in our proposed one and FSU. Table 3 contains average time (in milliseconds) of 100 iterations, and also includes the timing of computing pairing and scalar multiplication in G_1, G_2. In IoT applications, real-time computing is not always necessary but about 10 seconds for mutual authentication is not realistic. Even though our program couldn't achieve real-time computing, our result enables an enough practical authentication. We put specific parameters of BN curve and a snapshot of the computation of the session key in the rest of this section.

6.2   Parameters

Based on the security analysis by Kim and Barbulescu [21], we generated the following 128-bit security parameters by referring to [1].

Base Field

1. Fp462
    - Prime number p:
        0x240480360120023ffffffffffff6ff0cf6b7d9bfca00000000
        00d812908f41c8020ffffffffffff6ff66fc6ff687f640000000
        002401b00840138013
    - Bit-length of the group order: 462 bits

Extension Field

1. Fp462n2
    - Irreducible polynomial: $u^2 + 1$
    - Bit-length of the group order: 923 bits
2. Fp462n12
    - Irreducible polynomial: $w^2 - v$, $v^3 - u - 2$ and $u^2 + 1$
    - Bit-length of the group order: 5535 bits

BN Curve

1. Fp462BN
    - Field: Fp462
    - Elliptic curve: $y^2 = x^3 + 5$
    - Torsion number:
        0x240480360120023ffffffffffff6ff0cf6b7d9bfca00000000
        00d812908ee1c201f7ffffffffffff6ff66fc7bf717f7c0000000
        002401b007e010800d
    - Cofactor: 1
    - Base point(x, y):
        0x21a6d67ef250191fadba34a0a30160b9ac9264b6f95f63b3
        edbec3cf4b2e689db1bbb4e69a416a0b1e79239c0372e5cd70
        113c98d91f36b6980d, 0x0118ea0460f7f7abb82b33676a74
        32a490eeda842cccfa7d788c659650426e6af77df11b8ae40e
        b80f475432c66600622ecaa8a5734d36fb03de
2. Fp462n2BN
    - Field: Fp462n2
    - Elliptic curve: $y^2 = x^3 - u + 2$
    - Torsion number:
        0x240480360120023ffffffffffff6ff0cf6b7d9bfca00000000
        00d812908ee1c201f7ffffffffffff6ff66fc7bf717f7c0000000
        002401b007e010800d

- Cofactor:

      0x240480360120023ffffffffff6ff0cf6b7d9bfca00000000
      00d812908fa1ce0227ffffffffff6ff66fc63f5f7f4c0000000
      002401b008a0168019

- Base point(x, y):

      0x1d2e4343e8599102af8edca849566ba3c98e2a354730cbed
      9176884058b18134dd86bae555b783718f50af8b59bf7e850e
      9b73108ba6aa8cd283*u + 0x0257ccc85b58dda0dfb38e3a8
      cbdc5482e0337e7c1cd96ed61c913820408208f9ad2699bad9
      2e0032ae1f0aa6a8b48807695468e3d934ae1e4df, 0x073ef
      0cbd438cbe0172c8ae37306324d44d5e6b0c69ac57b393f1ab
      370fd725cc647692444a04ef87387aa68d53743493b9eba14c
      c552ca2a93a*u + 0x0a0650439da22c1979517427a20809ec
      a035634706e23c3fa7a6bb42fe810f1399a1f41c9ddae32e03
      695a140e7b11d7c3376e5b68df0db7154e

6.3   Benchmark Example

```
master secret key:
06bf77eb1d54f38a7fa7ec0b69641f75a6f30165d6c8e537fbe543a76ca4f60d
030e973d2076acb55464778cf18f3f0e4a8fcdf7b121fccd338e

master public key:
04091d3b07de2ca91874b06296ab8b9439a6802c48f2a22391548f94ca958758
3895c57d4b2f4b0f8e540762164af5c34b9700cc669815432d101e1784b906a0
d4447a48dc4290df70c46060119906ee048579d93ef643a04da745c8aadd6fef
de581f1f0699e18eadc642f8a0a4f545a709dcfa01

Generate a ephemeral public key for sender:272 msec
Generate a ephemeral public key for receiver:270 msec
Generate a session key for sender:1149 msec
Generate a session key for receiver:1151 msec
session key K:
0f6932471500267c8e09ea75a52767e57862c2f76b97e3af821eb9791ae8e971

sender's session key ?= receiver's one: True
```

7   Conclusion

We proposed an id-eCK secure ID-AKE scheme, where the id-eCK security implies that a scheme resists against leakage of all combinations of master, static, and ephemeral secret keys except ones trivially break the security. Most existing id-eCK secure ID-AKE schemes require two symmetric pairing operations or a greater number of asymmetric pairing, which is faster than symmetric one, operations to establish a session key. However, our scheme is realized with a single asymmetric pairing operation for each party, and this is an advantage in efficiency.

The proposed scheme is based on the ID-AKE scheme by McCullagh and Barreto, which is vulnerable to an active attack. To achieve id-eCK security, we applied the HMQV construction and the NAXOS technique to the McCullagh–Barreto scheme. The id-eCK security is proved under the external Diffie–Hellman for target group assumption and the q-gap-bilinear collision attack assumption.

References

1. Barbulescu, R., Duquesne, S.: Updating key size estimations for pairings. Cryptology ePrint Archive, Report 2017/334 (2017)
2. Barreto, P.S.L.M., Naehrig, M.: Pairing-friendly elliptic curves of prime order. In: Preneel, B., Tavares, S. (eds.) SAC 2005. LNCS, vol. 3897, pp. 319–331. Springer, Heidelberg (2006). https://doi.org/10.1007/11693383_22
3. Bellare, M., Neven, G.: Multi-signatures in the plain public-key model and a general forking lemma. In: ACM CCS 2006, pp. 390–399. ACM Press (2006)
4. Bellare, M., Rogaway, P.: Entity authentication and key distribution. In: Stinson, D.R. (ed.) CRYPTO 1993. LNCS, vol. 773, pp. 232–249. Springer, Heidelberg (1994). https://doi.org/10.1007/3-540-48329-2_21
5. Boyd, C., Choo, K.-K.R.: Security of two-party identity-based key agreement. In: Dawson, E., Vaudenay, S. (eds.) Mycrypt 2005. LNCS, vol. 3715, pp. 229–243. Springer, Heidelberg (2005). https://doi.org/10.1007/11554868_17
6. Boyd, C., Cliff, Y., Gonzalez Nieto, J., Paterson, K.G.: Efficient one-round key exchange in the standard model. In: Mu, Y., Susilo, W., Seberry, J. (eds.) ACISP 2008. LNCS, vol. 5107, pp. 69–83. Springer, Heidelberg (2008). https://doi.org/10.1007/978-3-540-70500-0_6
7. Canetti, R., Krawczyk, H.: Analysis of key-exchange protocols and their use for building secure channels. In: Pfitzmann, B. (ed.) EUROCRYPT 2001. LNCS, vol. 2045, pp. 453–474. Springer, Heidelberg (2001). https://doi.org/10.1007/3-540-44987-6_28
8. Chen, L., Cheng, Z.: Security proof of Sakai-Kasahara's identity-based encryption scheme. Cryptology ePrint Archive, Report 2005/226 (2005)
9. Chen, L., Cheng, Z., Smart, N.P.: Identity-based key agreement protocols from pairings. Int. J. Inf. Secur. **6**(4), 213–241 (2007)
10. Cheng, Z., Chen, L.: On security proof of McCullagh-Barreto's key agreement protocol and its variants. Cryptology ePrint Archive, Report 2005/201 (2005)
11. Choo, K.-K.R., Boyd, C., Hitchcock, Y.: Examining indistinguishability-based proof models for key establishment protocols. In: Roy, B. (ed.) ASIACRYPT 2005. LNCS, vol. 3788, pp. 585–604. Springer, Heidelberg (2005). https://doi.org/10.1007/11593447_32
12. Cremers, C.J.F.: Session-state Reveal is stronger than Ephemeral Key Reveal: attacking the NAXOS authenticated key exchange protocol. In: Abdalla, M., Pointcheval, D., Fouque, P.-A., Vergnaud, D. (eds.) ACNS 2009. LNCS, vol. 5536, pp. 20–33. Springer, Heidelberg (2009). https://doi.org/10.1007/978-3-642-01957-9_2
13. Cremers, C.J.F.: Examining indistinguishability-based security models for key exchange protocols: the case of CK, CK-HMQV, and eCK. In: ACM CCS 2011, pp. 80–91. ACM (2011)

14. Fiore, D., Gennaro, R.: Making the Diffie-Hellman protocol identity-based. In: Pieprzyk, J. (ed.) CT-RSA 2010. LNCS, vol. 5985, pp. 165–178. Springer, Heidelberg (2010). https://doi.org/10.1007/978-3-642-11925-5_12

15. Fujioka, A., Hoshino, F., Kobayashi, T., Suzuki, K., Ustaŏglu, B., Yoneyama, K.: id-eCK secure ID-based authenticated key exchange on symmetric and asymmetric pairing. IEICE Trans. Fundam. **E96–A**(6), 1139–1155 (2013)

16. Fujioka, A., Suzuki, K., Ustaoğlu, B.: Ephemeral key leakage resilient and efficient ID-AKEs that can share identities, private and master keys. In: Joye, M., Miyaji, A., Otsuka, A. (eds.) Pairing 2010. LNCS, vol. 6487, pp. 187–205. Springer, Heidelberg (2010). https://doi.org/10.1007/978-3-642-17455-1_12

17. Galbraith, S.D., Lin, X., Scott, M.: Endomorphisms for faster elliptic curve cryptography on a large class of curves. J. Cryptol. **24**(3), 446–469 (2011)

18. Gallant, R.P., Lambert, R.J., Vanstone, S.A.: Faster point multiplication on elliptic curves with efficient endomorphisms. In: Kilian, J. (ed.) CRYPTO 2001. LNCS, vol. 2139, pp. 190–200. Springer, Heidelberg (2001). https://doi.org/10.1007/3-540-44647-8_11

19. Gartner Inc., Newsroom: Gartner Identifies Top 10 Strategic IoT Technologies and Trends. https://www.gartner.com/en/newsroom/press-releases/2018-11-07-gartner-identifies-top-10-strategic-iot-technologies-and-trends

20. Huang, H., Cao, Z.: An ID-based authenticated key exchange protocol based on bilinear Diffie-Hellman problem. In: ASIACCS 2009, pp. 333–342. ACM Press (2009)

21. Kim, T., Barbulescu, R.: Extended tower number field sieve: a new complexity for the medium prime case. In: Robshaw, M., Katz, J. (eds.) CRYPTO 2016. LNCS, vol. 9814, pp. 543–571. Springer, Heidelberg (2016). https://doi.org/10.1007/978-3-662-53018-4_20

22. Krawczyk, H.: HMQV: a high-performance secure Diffie-Hellman protocol. In: Shoup, V. (ed.) CRYPTO 2005. LNCS, vol. 3621, pp. 546–566. Springer, Heidelberg (2005). https://doi.org/10.1007/11535218_33

23. LaMacchia, B., Lauter, K., Mityagin, A.: Stronger security of authenticated key exchange. In: Susilo, W., Liu, J.K., Mu, Y. (eds.) ProvSec 2007. LNCS, vol. 4784, pp. 1–16. Springer, Heidelberg (2007). https://doi.org/10.1007/978-3-540-75670-5_1

24. McCullagh, N., Barreto, P.S.L.M.: A new two-party identity-based authenticated key agreement. In: Menezes, A. (ed.) CT-RSA 2005. LNCS, vol. 3376, pp. 262–274. Springer, Heidelberg (2005). https://doi.org/10.1007/978-3-540-30574-3_18

25. Okamoto, T., Pointcheval, D.: The gap-problems: a new class of problems for the security of cryptographic schemes. In: Kim, K. (ed.) PKC 2001. LNCS, vol. 1992, pp. 104–118. Springer, Heidelberg (2001). https://doi.org/10.1007/3-540-44586-2_8

26. Shamir, A.: Identity-based cryptosystems and signature schemes. In: Blakley, G.R., Chaum, D. (eds.) CRYPTO 1984. LNCS, vol. 196, pp. 47–53. Springer, Heidelberg (1985). https://doi.org/10.1007/3-540-39568-7_5

27. Vercauteren, F.: Optimal pairings. IEEE Trans. Inf. Theory **56**, 455–461 (2010)

A Complete and Optimized Key Mismatch Attack on NIST Candidate NewHope

Yue Qin[1], Chi Cheng[1($\boxtimes$)], and Jintai Ding[2]

[1] China University of Geosciences, Wuhan 430074, China
{qy52hz,chengchi}@cug.edu.cn
[2] University of Cincinnati, Cincinnati 45219, USA
jintai.ding@gmail.com

Abstract. In CT-RSA 2019, Bauer et al. have analyzed the case when the public key is reused for the NewHope key encapsulation mechanism (KEM), a second-round candidate in the NIST Post-quantum Standard process. They proposed an elegant method to recover coefficients ranging from -6 to 4 in the secret key. We repeat their experiments but there are two fundamental problems. First, even for coefficients in $[-6, 4]$ we cannot recover at least 262 of them in each secret key with 1024 coefficients. Second, for the coefficient outside $[-6, 4]$, they suggested an exhaustive search. But for each secret key on average there are 10 coefficients that need to be exhaustively searched, and each of them has 6 possibilities. This makes Bauer et al.'s method highly inefficient. We propose an improved method, which with 99.22% probability recovers all the coefficients ranging from -6 to 4 in the secret key. Then, inspired by Ding et al.'s key mismatch attack, we propose an efficient strategy which with a probability of 96.88% succeeds in recovering all the coefficients in the secret key. Experiments show that our proposed method is very efficient, which completes the attack in about 137.56 ms using the NewHope parameters.

Keywords: Post-quantum cryptography · Key exchange ·
Ring learning with errors · Key mismatch attack

1 Introduction

Currently, the standardization process of post-quantum cryptography algorithms run by the NIST has completed the first round and the second round workshop is scheduled to be held on August, 2019 [1]. As one of the most promising candidates for future post-quantum cryptography standard, the ring learning with errors (Ring-LWE) based approaches have attracted a lot of attention due to the provable security and high efficiency [13,15,17].

To construct DH-like key exchange schemes whose hardness are based on the Ring-LWE problem, the key breakthrough is to use the error reconciliation

© Springer Nature Switzerland AG 2019
K. Sako et al. (Eds.): ESORICS 2019, LNCS 11736, pp. 504–520, 2019.
https://doi.org/10.1007/978-3-030-29962-0_24

mechanism, which means that one party needs to send additional information to help the other party agree on an exactly same key. The first paper proposing this idea was attributed to Ding, Xie, and Lin [10]. Then, an authenticated key exchange variant was proposed by Zhang et al. [19]. Peikert proposed a key encapsulation mechanism (KEM) using a tweaked error correction mechanism in [16], which is then reformulated by Bos et al. as a key exchange scheme and inserted into the Transport Layer Security (TLS) protocol [6]. Later, a further tweaked Ring-LWE based key exchange scheme, the NewHope-Usenix [4], also attracts significant attention since Google has tested it in its browser Chrome to get real-world experiences about the deployment of the post-quantum cryptography. But the error reconciliation mechanism in the original NewHope-Usenix was so complex that later Alkim et al. proposed a simplified variant called the NewHope-simple [3], where the authors use the encryption-based approach to transfer the keys. In the submission to the competition of NIST's post-quantum cryptography, the submitted NewHope [2] was based on NewHope-simple, and in this paper we only consider the NewHope scheme with the encryption-based approach.

Note that in the widely used Internet standards, the key reuse mode is commonly used. For example, in the recently released TLS 1.3 [18], there exists a pre-shared key (PSK) mode in which the key can be reused. But the key reuse in lattice-based key exchange could cause the key reuse attacks. Generally, the key reuse attacks can be further divided into signal leakage attack and the key mismatch attack. The main cause of the signal leakage attack is that if the key is reused, the corresponding signal information used for exact key recovery reveals information about the secret key. On the other side, the key mismatch attack tries to recover the secret by querying a number of times whether the shared keys generated by the two parties match or not.

Recently, a series of key reuse attacks on the reconciliation based approaches have been proposed. Fluhrer first proposed the idea to exploit the leakage of secret keys of Ring-LWE based key exchange when one participant's public key is reused [11]. Later, Ding et al. has developed a key leakage attack on [10], where the reused keys leak information about the secret key [7]. In [9], a key mismatch attack was proposed on the one pass case of [10], without using the information leaked by the signal function. To thwart the proposed key leakage attack in case the public key is required to be reused, in [12] a randomized method has been proposed. Another related work is [14], in which Liu et al. proposed a signal leakage attack against the reconciliation-based NewHope-Usenix key exchange protocol [4].

Unlike the DH-like key exchange protocols, the NewHope KEM submitted to the NIST [3] is based on the encryption rather than the reconciliation mechanism, and newly designed Encode and Compress functions are used. Therefore, these attacks proposed by Fluhrer [11], Ding et al. [7–9], or Liu et al. [14] cannot be directly applied to the encryption-based NewHope key exchange protocol [2]. The main challenge for launching a key mismatch attack is that the Encode and Decode functions in NewHope deal with four coefficients together, which makes it hard to recover the secret key using the previous methods.

In CT-RSA 2019, Bauer et al. have proposed a key mismatch attack on NewHope [5]. As we know, the coefficients of the secret key in NewHope belong to $[-8, 8]$ due to the fact that they are selected from the centered binomial distribution ψ_8^n. The key observation of Bauer et al. is that in a secret key with 1024 coefficients, 99.22% of them lie in $[-6, 4]$. From this observation, they have proposed an elegant method, which is claimed to recover all the coefficients belonging to $[-6, 4]$ in the key.

However, their recovery is first incomplete. Through our experiments, for each secret key with 1024 coefficients there are at least 262 coefficients in $[-6, 4]$ but cannot be recovered using their method. Second, for the coefficients outside $[-6, 4]$, i.e. those selected from $\{-8, -7, 5, 6, 7, 8\}$, they suggested an exhaustive search. But for each secret key on average there are 10 coefficients that need to be exhaustively searched, and each of them has 6 possibilities. The resulted $6^{10} \approx 6 \times 10^7$ possibilities make Bauer et al.'s method highly inefficient.

After analyzing the cause of the incomplete recovery, we propose an improved method, which with 99.22% probability can recover all the coefficients ranging from -6 to 4 in the secret key. Then, inspired by Ding et al.'s key mismatch attack, we propose an efficient strategy which with a probability of 96.88% succeeds in recovering all the coefficients belonging to $[-8, 8]$ in the secret key. Recall that in NewHope four coefficients are encoded at a time. Through in-depth analysis of the properties of the Decode function, we notice that it can help us find the sum of the 4 coefficients. Since in a targeted quadruplet, there is a 96.88% probability that only one coefficient belongs to $\{-8, -7, 5, 6, 7, 8\}$, and the other 3 coefficients belong to $[-6, 4]$. The key idea of our strategy is that we can first recover the 3 coefficients using our improved method, then recover the remaining coefficient since the sum of the 4 coefficients is known. Experiments show that our proposed method is very efficient, which completes the attack in about 137.56 ms using the NewHope parameters.

2   The Ring-LWE Problem and NewHope KEM

Set $\mathbb{Z}_q$ the ring with all coefficients are integers modulo q, then $\mathbb{Z}_q[x]$ represents a polynomial ring, where all the polynomials in $\mathbb{Z}_q[x]$ are with coefficients selected from $\mathbb{Z}_q$. Then, we can define the polynomial ring $\mathcal{R}_q = \mathbb{Z}_q[x]/(x^n + 1)$, in which for every polynomial $f(x) = a_0 + a_1 x + \cdots + a_{n-1} x^{n-1} \in \mathcal{R}_q$, each coefficient $a_i \in \mathbb{Z}_q$ ($0 \leq i \leq n-1$) and the polynomial additions and multiplications are operated modulo $x^n + 1$. All polynomials are in bold, and we treat a polynomial $\mathbf{c} \in \mathcal{R}_q$ the same with its vector form $(\mathbf{c}[0], \cdots, \mathbf{c}[n-1])$, here $\mathbf{c}[i]$ ($0 \leq i \leq n-1$) represents the ith coefficient of the polynomial $\mathbf{c}$. The operation $\lfloor x \rfloor$ represents the maximum integer not exceeding x, and $\lfloor x \rceil = \lfloor x + \frac{1}{2} \rfloor$.

The schemes based on Ring-LWE enjoy certain advantages due to the fact that there exists a quantum reduction which solves a hard problem in ideal lattices in the worst-case to solving a Ring-LWE problem in the average-case, as well as high efficiency even in resource-limited devices. Similar to the DH problems, there exist two versions of the Ring-LWE problem. The decision Ring-LWE is to distinguish the pair $(\mathbf{a}, \mathbf{as} + \mathbf{e})$ from randomly selected pair $(\mathbf{x}, \mathbf{y})$, where $\mathbf{a}$ is randomly sampled from $\mathcal{R}_q$ and $\mathbf{s}, \mathbf{e}$ are randomly selected according to a error distribution. Similarly, the search Ring-LWE is to recover $\mathbf{s}$ with the above pair $(\mathbf{a}, \mathbf{as} + \mathbf{e})$.

Since in the submission to the competition of NIST's post-quantum cryptography, the submitted NewHope KEM was based on NewHope-simple, in the remaining of this paper we refer to the encryption based approach when we use NewHope. In NewHope, the polynomial ring $\mathcal{R}_q = \mathbb{Z}_q[x]/(x^n + 1)$ is set with $q = 12289$ and $n = 1024$ or $n = 512$. The selected error distribution in NewHope is ψ_8^n, which is a centered binomial distribution with parameter 8, and can be easily sampled from computing $\sum_{i=1}^{8}(b_i - b_i')$. Here b_i and b_i' is randomly selected from $\{0, 1\}$. The most important functions in the NewHope KEM are defined as follows.

Definition 1. *The Encode function can map each bit in $\nu'_\mathbf{B} \in \{0,1\}^{256}$ to four bits in $\mathbf{k}$, which is for $i = 0, 1, \ldots, 255$,*

$$\mathbf{k}[i] = \mathbf{k}[i + 256] = \mathbf{k}[i + 512] = \mathbf{k}[i + 768] = \left\lfloor \frac{q}{2} \right\rfloor \nu'_B[i]. \tag{1}$$

Definition 2. *The Decode function is designed to recover one bit of $\nu'_A \in \{0,1\}^{256}$ from four bits in $\mathbf{k}'$, i.e., $\nu'_A = Decode(\mathbf{k}')$ and*

$$\nu'_A[i] = \begin{cases} 1 & \text{if } m[i] < q, \\ 0 & \text{otherwise,} \end{cases} \tag{2}$$

where $m[i] = \sum_{j=0}^{3} |\mathbf{k}'[i + 256j] - \lfloor \frac{q}{2} \rfloor|$ for $i = 0, 1, \ldots, 255$.

Definition 3. *The Compression function Compress: $\mathbb{Z}_q \to \mathbb{Z}_8$ is defined as $\bar{\mathbf{c}} = Compress(\mathbf{c})$ and for $i = 0, 1, \ldots, 1023$,*

$$\bar{\mathbf{c}}[i] = \lfloor (\mathbf{c}[i] \cdot 8)/q \rceil \pmod{8}. \tag{3}$$

Definition 4. *The Decompression function Decompress: $\mathbb{Z}_8 \to \mathbb{Z}_q$ is defined as $\mathbf{c}' = Decompress(\bar{\mathbf{c}})$, which is for $i = 0, 1, \ldots, 1023$,*

$$\mathbf{c}'[i] = \lfloor (\bar{\mathbf{c}}[i] \cdot q)/8 \rceil. \tag{4}$$

In Table 1, we describe the details of the NewHope KEM. Since in NewHope, the number-theoretic transform (NTT) is used to speed up the polynomial multiplication, which has nothing to do with security. To simplify the security analysis of NewHope, in Table 1 we use ordinary multiplication instead of NTT. To share a same key, the two participants Alice and Bob should share a common $\mathbf{a}$ in advance, which is randomly selected from $\mathcal{R}_q$. The NewHope key exchange protocol consists of three parts:

Table 1. The NewHope KEM

Common parameter: $\mathbf{a} \leftarrow \mathcal{R}_q$	
Alice	**Bob**
$\mathbf{s}_A, \mathbf{e}_A \overset{\$}{\leftarrow} \psi_8^n$	
$\mathbf{P}_A \leftarrow \mathbf{as}_A + \mathbf{e}_A \qquad \xrightarrow{\quad \mathbf{P}_A \quad}$	$\mathbf{s}_B, \mathbf{e}_B, \mathbf{e}'_B \overset{\$}{\leftarrow} \psi_8^n$
	$\mathbf{P}_B \leftarrow \mathbf{as}_B + \mathbf{e}_B$
	$\nu_B \overset{\$}{\leftarrow} \{0,1\}^{256}$
	$\nu'_B \leftarrow \text{SHA3-256}(\nu_B)$
	$\mathbf{k} \leftarrow \text{Encode}(\nu'_B)$
	$\mathbf{c} \leftarrow \mathbf{P}_A \mathbf{s}_B + \mathbf{e}'_B + \mathbf{k}$
$\mathbf{c}' \leftarrow \text{Decompress}(\bar{\mathbf{c}}) \qquad \xleftarrow{(\mathbf{P}_B, \bar{\mathbf{c}})}$	$\bar{\mathbf{c}} \leftarrow \text{Compress}(\mathbf{c})$
$\mathbf{k}' = \mathbf{c}' - \mathbf{P}_B \mathbf{s}_A$	$S_{k_B} \leftarrow \text{SHA3-256}(\nu'_B)$
$\nu'_A \leftarrow \text{Decode}(\mathbf{k}')$	
$S_{k_A} \leftarrow \text{SHA3-256}(\nu'_A)$	

(1) Alice selects $\mathbf{s}_A$ and $\mathbf{e}_A$ uniformly at random from ψ_8^n, and computes a public key $\mathbf{P}_A = \mathbf{as}_A + \mathbf{e}_A$. Then Alice will send $\mathbf{P}_A$ to Bob.

(2) After receiving $\mathbf{P}_A$ sent by Alice, Bob will select $\mathbf{s}_B$, $\mathbf{e}_B$ and $\mathbf{e}'_B$ uniformly at random from ψ_8^n, and compute a public key $\mathbf{P}_B = \mathbf{as}_B + \mathbf{e}_B$. Then Bob will choose ν_B randomly from $\{0,1\}^{256}$ and compute $\nu'_B \leftarrow \text{SHA3-256}(\nu_B)$, $\mathbf{k} \leftarrow \text{Encode}(\nu'_B)$, $\mathbf{c} \leftarrow \mathbf{P}_A \mathbf{s}_B + \mathbf{e}'_B + \mathbf{k}$ and $\bar{\mathbf{c}} \leftarrow \text{Compress}(\mathbf{c})$. Subsequently, Bob will send $\mathbf{P}_B$ and $\bar{\mathbf{c}}$ to Alice, and compute the shared key $S_{k_B} \leftarrow \text{SHA3-}256(\nu'_B)$.

(3) When Alice receives the $\mathbf{P}_B$ and $\bar{\mathbf{c}}$ sent by Bob, she will calculate $\mathbf{c}' \leftarrow \text{Decompress}(\bar{\mathbf{c}})$, $\mathbf{k}' = \mathbf{c}' - \mathbf{P}_B \mathbf{s}_A$, $\nu'_A \leftarrow \text{Decode}(\mathbf{k}')$ and her shared key $S_{k_A} \leftarrow \text{SHA3-256}(\nu'_A)$.

3   The Proposed Key Mismatch Attack

In this section, we will use the key mismatch method to assess the security of the NewHope KEM when the public key is reused.

In a key mismatch attack, the adversary $\mathcal{A}$ is an active adversary who plays the role of Bob, and we build an oracle $\mathcal{O}$ that simulates Alice in Table 1. We assume that Alice's public key $\mathbf{P}_A$ is reused and $\mathcal{A}$ can query the oracle a number of times. In Algorithm 1 we describe how the oracle works. To be specific, $\mathcal{A}$ calculates $\mathbf{P}_B$, as well as $\bar{\mathbf{c}}$ and S_{k_B} generated by using a selected ν'_B. By receiving the input $(\mathbf{P}_B, \bar{\mathbf{c}}, S_{k_B})$, the oracle will use $\mathbf{P}_B$ and $\bar{\mathbf{c}}$ to calculate $\mathbf{c}'$, $\mathbf{k}'$, ν'_A, S_{k_A} and checks whether $S_{K_A} = S_{K_B}$ holds, if yes the oracle $\mathcal{O}$ will output 1 and 0 otherwise. Specifically, if $\mathcal{O}$ outputs 1, S_{k_A} and S_{k_B} match and $\nu'_A = \nu'_B$. If $\mathcal{O}$ outputs 0, S_{k_A} and S_{k_B} mismatch and $\nu'_A \neq \nu'_B$. We can see that the adversary can get useful information from the oracle by knowing whether the two keys S_{k_A} and S_{k_B} match or not, and further recover $\mathbf{s}_A$ using these information.

Algorithm 1. Oracle

Input: $\mathbf{P}_B, \bar{\mathbf{c}}, S_{k_B}$
Output: 1 or 0
1 $\mathbf{c}' = \text{Decompress}(\bar{\mathbf{c}})$;
2 $\mathbf{k}' = \mathbf{c}' - \mathbf{P}_B \mathbf{s}_A$;
3 $\nu'_A \leftarrow \text{Decode}(\mathbf{k}')$;
4 $S_{k_A} \leftarrow \text{SHA3-256}(\nu'_A)$;
5 **if** $S_{k_A} = S_{k_B}$ **then**
6   **Return** 1;
7 **else**
8   **Return** 0;

The main challenge in launching a key mismatch attack against the NewHope KEM is that, 4 coefficients of $\mathbf{s}_A$, for example $\mathbf{s}_A[i]$, $\mathbf{s}_A[i+256]$, $\mathbf{s}_A[i+512]$, and $\mathbf{s}_A[i+768]$ are encoded and decoded together, which makes it hard to decide each of them.

3.1 Bauer et al.'s Method

In this subsection, we briefly introduce Bauer et al.'s method in [5]. They used the key mismatch attack to recover Alice's private key $\mathbf{s}_A$ if Alice's public key $\mathbf{P}_A$ is reused. Set $S_1 = \{-8, -7, \ldots, -1, 0, 1, \ldots, 7, 8\}$ and $S_2 = \{-6, -5, \ldots, 2, 3, 4\}$. Their basic idea is to recover all the coefficients in S_2. First of all, the adversary $\mathcal{A}$ directly chooses $\nu'_B = (1, 0, \cdots, 0)$. If $\mathcal{A}$ wants to recover the quadruplet $(\mathbf{s}_A[i], \mathbf{s}_A[i+256], \mathbf{s}_A[i+512], \mathbf{s}_A[i+768])$, he will set his public key $\mathbf{P}_B = \lfloor \frac{q}{8} \rfloor x^{-i}$ and $\bar{\mathbf{c}} = \sum_{j=0}^{3} ((l_j + 4) \bmod 8) x^{256j}$, here each l_j ranges from -4 to 3. Then he will send $(\mathbf{P}_B, \bar{\mathbf{c}}, S_{k_B})$ to the oracle $\mathcal{O}$. When $\mathcal{O}$ receives $(\mathbf{P}_B, \bar{\mathbf{c}}, S_{k_B})$, he will honestly calculate $\mathbf{c}', \mathbf{k}', \nu'_A$ and S_{k_A}. If $S_{k_A} = S_{k_B}$ he will return 1 and 0 otherwise. Finally, $\mathcal{A}$ will calculate the private key according to $\mathcal{O}$'s output. Since each quadruplet (l_0, l_1, l_2, l_3) corresponds to an output of $\mathcal{O}$, the adversary $\mathcal{A}$ can recover the coefficients of the private key if he can find outputs in a form like $1, \cdots, 1, 0, \cdots, 0, 1, \cdots, 1$ as (l_0, l_1, l_2, l_3) changes. Here this kind of form is called a favorable case.

Specifically, if $\mathcal{A}$ wants to recover $\mathbf{s}_A[i]$ in $\mathbf{s}_A$, he can first set each l_j ($j = 1, 2, 3$) be randomly selected from -4 to 3, and then by letting $l_0 = -4$, the resulted output is a bit b_0. Next $\mathcal{A}$ can increase l_0 to -3, with the same l_j ($j = 1, 2, 3$) the resulted output is another bit b_1. Repeating the above processes until l_0 becomes 3, there will be 8 bits b_j ($j = 0, 1, \cdots, 7$). The above processes will be repeated with different l_j ($j = 1, 2, 3$) until $\mathcal{A}$ finds a favorable case. Then the adversary $\mathcal{A}$ can recover the coefficients in S_2 by recording the positions where 1 changes to 0 and 0 goes to 1 in the favorable case. $\mathcal{A}$ will repeat the above processes until he recovers all the coefficients of $\mathbf{s}_A$ that belongs to S_2.

We have generated $1,000$ secret keys and repeated the experiments using Bauer et al.'s method. Unfortunately, even for coefficients in $[-6, 4]$ we cannot recover at least 262 of them in each secret key with 1024 coefficients. What makes the situation worse is that in some cases the recovered coefficients are wrong and we cannot detect these cases using Bauer et al.'s method. Another problem is that, for the coefficients outside $[-6, 4]$, they suggested an exhaustive search. But for each secret key on average there are 10 coefficients that need to be exhaustively searched, and each of them has 6 possibilities. This makes Bauer et al.'s method highly inefficient.

3.2   Our Improved Method

In this subsection, we propose an improved method to recover the coefficients in S_2.

First in Algorithm 2 we propose how to calculate τ_1 and τ_2, which play an important role in our following recovery. We can also determine whether $\mathbf{b} = (b_0, \ldots, b_7)$ is a favorable case or not through the calculated τ_1 and τ_2. In Bauer et al.'s method, there is only one kind of favorable case in the form $1, \cdots, 1, 0, \cdots, 0, 1, \cdots, 1$. In this case, we use Bauer et al.'s method to calculate τ_1 and τ_2, which records the positions where 1 goes to 0 and 0 changes to 1, respectively. Through experiments, we find that there is another favorable case in the form $0, 0, \cdots, 0, 1, \cdots, 1, 0, \cdots, 0$. In this case, we use τ_1 and τ_2 to record the positions where 0 goes to 1 and 1 changes to 0, respectively. The precise definition of τ_1 and τ_2 can be found in Algorithm 2. If the output of Algorithm 2 is NULL, there is no favorable case, otherwise we can find a favorable case.

In Bauer et al.'s method, they assume that the value of $\tau = \tau_1 + \tau_2$ is either always even or always odd. But our experiments show that the value of τ can be either even or odd, and this is also the reason why Bauer et al.'s method cannot recover the coefficients completely. In order to find the relationship between τ and each coefficient $\mathbf{s}_A[i] \in [-6, 4]$, we generate 1000 secret keys, and record the possible values of τ with different $\mathbf{s}_A[i]$. The results of the experiments are listed in Table 2.

Then, in Algorithm 3 we propose how to recover all the coefficients in S_2. The main idea is that we repeat the processes in Algorithm 2 until we find enough favorable cases. Of course if we can find more favorable cases, then the recovery of coefficients can be more exact, but this needs more time and more queries. To take a balance, in Algorithm 3, we try to get 50 favorable cases. Next, we can use the data collected in these 50 favorable cases to recover the coefficients in S_2.

We use odd-number and even-number to record the times the odd and even τ occurs, and the corresponding values of τ are stored in odd_τ and even_τ, respectively. We can see from Table 2 that if the coefficient $\mathbf{s}_A[i]$ is odd, then odd-number is larger than the even-number, and vice versa. Therefore, if even-number is larger than the odd-number, the corresponding

---

Algorithm 2. Find-τ

Input: b
Output: τ

1 set $\tau = $ NULL, $\tau_1 = $ NULL, $\tau_2 = $ NULL ;
2 **if** $b[0] = 1$ **then**
3 | **for** $i := 1$ to 6 **do**
4 | | **if** $(b[i-1] = 1)$ and $(b[i] = 0)$ **then**
5 | | $\tau_1 = i - 4$;
6 | | **if** $(b[i] = 0)$ and $(b[i+1] = 1)$ **then**
7 | | $\tau_2 = i - 4$;
8 | **end**
9 **else if** $b[0] = 0$ **then**
10 | **for** $i := 1$ to 6 **do**
11 | | **if** $(b[i-1] = 0)$ and $(b[i] = 1)$ **then**
12 | | $\tau_1 = i - 4$;
13 | | **if** $(b[i] = 1)$ and $(b[i+1] = 0)$ **then**
14 | | $\tau_2 = i - 4$;
15 | **end**
16 $\tau = \tau_1 + \tau_2$;
17 **if** $\tau > 0$ and $b[0] = 1$ **then**
18 | $\tau = \tau - 8$;
19 **else if** $\tau <= 0$ and $b[0] = 1$ **then**
20 | $\tau = \tau + 8$;
21 **if** τ is odd and $\tau_1 \neq$ NULL and $\tau_2 \neq$ NULL **then**
22 | odd_number = odd_number +1;
23 | odd_$\tau = \tau$;
24 **else if** τ is even and $\tau_1 \neq$ NULL and $\tau_2 \neq$ NULL **then**
25 | even_number = even_number +1;
26 | even_$\tau = \tau$;
27 **else**
28 | $\tau = $ NULL;
29 **end**
30 **Return** τ;

---

coefficient $s_A[i]$ is calculated as $s_A[i] = $ even_τ. Otherwise, we calculate it as $s_A[i] = $ odd_τ.

Since we only get 50 favorable cases, there may exist the case one coefficient is recovered to be another coefficient. For example when $s_A[i] = 3$, the corresponding odd-number and even-number are close. So if the recovered coefficient is 3, we need to eliminate the case that we recover 4 to be 3. In order to solve this problem, in our experiments we also record the possible values of τ for each coefficient between -6 and 4. As shown in Table 3, the corresponding τs can help us decide which one is correct. For example, when $s_A[i] = 4$, the possible values of τ are 3 and 4, but if $s_A[i] = 3$, the corresponding values of τ are 2 and 3. Since 3 is odd, the recovered 3 must be calculated by odd_τ. We can know that odd_$\tau = 3$, and odd-number must be bigger than the even-number. We can

Table 2. The relationship between τ and $s_A[i] \in [-6, 4]$

$s_A[i]$	Odd τ	Even τ	Favorable cases	$s_A[i]$	Odd τ	Even τ	Favorable cases	$s_A[i]$	Odd τ	Even τ	Favorable cases
−6	0	2048	2048	−5	1408	0	1408	−4	0	1952	1952
	136	1784	1920		1160	296	1456		152	1792	1944
−3	1408	0	1408	−2	0	2080	2080	−1	2176	0	2176
	1312	232	1544		240	1824	2064		1808	320	2128
0	0	2080	2080	1	1472	0	1472	2	0	2048	2048
	400	1656	2056		1344	512	1856		504	1328	1832
3	1408	0	1408	4	0	2048	2048				
	848	808	1656		520	1264	1784				

Algorithm 3. Find-s-in-S_2

Output: s (the coefficients in S_2)

```
1  for k := 0 to 255 do
2      Set P_B = ⌊9/8⌋x^{-k};
3      for j := 0 to 3 do
4          Set odd_number = 0, even_number = 0, count = 0;
5          while count < 50 do
6              (l_0, l_1, l_2, l_3) ← [-4, 3]^4; b[8] ← 0;
7              for i := -4 to 3 do
8                  l_j = i; c̄ = Σ_{h=0}^{3}((l_h + 4) mod 8)x^{256*h};
                    b[i] = Oracle(P_B, c̄, S_{k_B});
9              end
10             t = Find-τ(b);
11             if t ≠ NULL then
12                 count = count + 1
13         end
14         if odd_number >= even_number then
15             temp_s = odd_τ;
16             test(temp_s);
17         else if even_number > odd_number then
18             temp_s = even_τ;
19             test(temp_s);
20         end
21     end
22 end
23 s[k + j * 256] = temp_s;
24 Return s
```

---

see that in the two cases the odd_τs are the same, but the even_τs are different, so we can distinguish them according to the value of even_τ. Specifically, if even_$\tau = 2$ we can determine that the recovered coefficient is correct. But if even_$\tau = 4$, we make sure that the recovered coefficient is wrong, which should be 4. Similarly we can correct most of the errors using this method, and finally with a high probability we can recover all the coefficients in S_2.

Table 3. $s_A[i]$ and the possible τs

$s_A[i]$	4		3		2		1		0		-1		-2		-3		-4		-5		-6	
τ	3	4	2	3	1	2	0	1	0	1	-2	-1	-3	-2	-4	-3	-5	-4	-6	-5	-7	-6

Table 4. The distribution of the coefficients in a quadruplet

$S_1 = \{-8, -7, \ldots, -1, 0, 1, \ldots, 7, 8\}$	
$S_2 = \{-6, -5, \ldots, 2, 3, 4\}$ $S_1-S_2 = \{-8, -7, 5, 6, 7, 8\}$	
4 coefficients in S_1	
100%	
4 coefficients in S_2	Others
95.84%	4.16%
	3 coefficients in S_2 / 2 coefficients in S_2
	1 coefficient in S_1-S_2 / 2 coefficients in S_1-S_2
	98.50% / 1.47%
	1 coefficient in S_2 / 0 coefficient in S_2
	3 coefficients in S_1-S_2 / 4 coefficients in S_1-S_2
	0.03% / 0%

3.3   The Complete Attack

After recovering all the coefficients that belongs to S_2, the remaining problem is how to recover the coefficients in S_1-S_2. In Table 4, we have analyzed and listed the distribution of the coefficients in a quadruplet through our experiments. We have generated 10^6 keys following the centered binomial distribution, and then taken an average. We can see that all the coefficients are in set S_1, and the probability that all the coefficients of the quadruplet are in S_2 is 95.84%. In the remaining 4.16% quadruplets, there is at least 1 coefficient that belongs to S_1-S_2. Our key observation is that, with 98.50% probability there is only 1 coefficient that belongs to S_1-S_2, while the other 3 coefficients are in S_2 in the remaining quadruplets.

Without loss of generality, we assume that $s_A[i+256]$, $s_A[i+512]$ and $s_A[i+768]$ are in S_2 and $s_A[i]$ is in S_1-S_2. Using our improved method in Algorithms 2 and 3, we can recover $s_A[i+256]$, $s_A[i+512]$ and $s_A[i+768]$. Then, our strategy is that if we can compute the sum of these four coefficients, we can recover $s_A[i]$ by eliminating $s_A[i+256]$, $s_A[i+512]$ and $s_A[i+768]$ from the sum. In the following, we describe the complete attack.

To launch the attack, the adversary $\mathcal{A}$ will deliberately select the parameters s_B and e_B to calculate the public key $\mathbf{P}_B$, as well as the parameter ν'_B to calculate $\bar{c}$. For each integer i in $0, 1, \cdots, 255$, if $\mathcal{A}$ wants to recover $s_A[i], s_A[i+256], s_A[i+512], s_A[i+768]$, he will choose s_B and e'_B to be $\mathbf{0}$ in R_q, and an e_B

of which coefficients are all zero, except that $\mathbf{e}_B[512] = h_1$. Here h_1 increases from 0 to $q - 1$. Instead of randomly selecting ν_B to calculate ν'_B, the adversary $\mathcal{A}$ will directly set all coefficients of ν'_B as 0 except that $\nu'_B[i] = 1$.

As $\mathcal{A}$ sets $\mathbf{s}_B = \mathbf{0}$, correspondingly now the public key is $\mathbf{P}_B = \mathbf{as}_B + \mathbf{e}_B = \mathbf{e}_B$. According to the definition of the Encode function, we have

$$\mathbf{k} = \mathbf{Encode}(\nu'_B) = \left\lfloor \frac{q}{2} \right\rfloor x^i + \left\lfloor \frac{q}{2} \right\rfloor x^{i+256} + \left\lfloor \frac{q}{2} \right\rfloor x^{i+512} + \left\lfloor \frac{q}{2} \right\rfloor x^{i+768},$$

and the resulted $\mathbf{c} = \mathbf{P}_A \mathbf{s}_B + \mathbf{e}'_B + \mathbf{k} = \mathbf{k}$.

Then, since $\bar{\mathbf{c}}[i] = \lfloor (\mathbf{c}[i] \cdot q)/8 \rfloor \bmod 8$, if $\mathbf{c}[i] = \lfloor \frac{q}{2} \rfloor$, then $\bar{\mathbf{c}}[i] = 4$, according to the above analysis and the definition of the Compress function

$$\bar{\mathbf{c}} = \mathbf{Compress}(\mathbf{c}) = \mathbf{Compress}(\mathbf{k}) = 4x^i + 4x^{i+256} + 4x^{i+512} + 4x^{i+768}.$$

After that $\mathcal{A}$ will send $(\mathbf{P}_B, \bar{\mathbf{c}}, S_{k_B})$ to $\mathcal{O}$, who will then calculate

$$\mathbf{c}' = Decompress(\bar{\mathbf{c}}) = \left\lfloor \frac{q}{2} \right\rfloor x^i + \left\lfloor \frac{q}{2} \right\rfloor x^{i+256} + \left\lfloor \frac{q}{2} \right\rfloor x^{i+512} + \left\lfloor \frac{q}{2} \right\rfloor x^{i+768}, \quad (5)$$

as well as

$$\mathbf{k}' = \mathbf{c}' - \mathbf{P}_B \mathbf{s}_A = \mathbf{c}' - \mathbf{e}_B \mathbf{s}_A. \quad (6)$$

Finally $S_{k_A} = \text{SHA3} - 256(\text{Decode}(\mathbf{k}'))$.

In the following, we propose our method to recover the exact value of $\mathbf{s}_A[i]$ in an efficient way.

The adversary $\mathcal{A}$ chooses the parameters as described above, and the complete attack consists of four steps.

Step 1: In this step, the adversary $\mathcal{A}$ uses our improved method in Algorithm 2 to recover all the coefficients belonging to S_2.

Step 2: In this step, the adversary $\mathcal{A}$ wants to decide $m_1 = |\mathbf{s}_A[i]| + |\mathbf{s}_A[i + 256]| + |\mathbf{s}_A[i + 512]| + |\mathbf{s}_A[i + 768]|$. First, $\mathcal{A}$ sets all the coefficients of $\mathbf{e}_B$ as $\mathbf{0}$, except $\mathbf{e}_B[512] = h_1$. From Eqs. 5, 6 and $\lfloor \frac{q}{2} \rfloor = 6145$, we have

$$\begin{aligned}
\mathbf{k}' &= \mathbf{c}' - \mathbf{e}_B \mathbf{s}_A \\
&= [6145 - (-\mathbf{s}_A[i + 512]\mathbf{e}_B[512])]x^i + [6145 - (-\mathbf{s}_A[i + 768]\mathbf{e}_B[512])]x^{i+256} \\
&\quad + (6145 - \mathbf{s}_A[i]\mathbf{e}_B[512])x^{i+512} + (6145 - \mathbf{s}_A[i + 256]\mathbf{e}_B[512])x^{i+768} \\
&= [6145 - (-\mathbf{s}_A[i + 512]h_1)]x^i + [6145 - (-\mathbf{s}_A[i + 768]h_1)]x^{i+256} \\
&\quad + (6145 - \mathbf{s}_A[i]h_1)x^{i+512} + (6145 - \mathbf{s}_A[i + 256]h_1)x^{i+768}.
\end{aligned}$$

The last equation holds since $x^{1024} = -1$ in R_q. So, for $i = 0, 1, \ldots, 255$, according to the Decode function we have

$$\begin{aligned}
m &= \sum_{j=0}^{3} |\mathbf{k}'[i + 256j] - 6145| \\
&= |1 + \mathbf{s}_A[i + 512]h_1| + |1 + \mathbf{s}_A[i + 768]h_1| + |1 - \mathbf{s}_A[i]h_1| + |1 - \mathbf{s}_A[i + 256]h_1| \\
&= 1 + \mathbf{s}_A[i + 512]h_1 + 1 + \mathbf{s}_A[i + 768]h_1 + \mathbf{s}_A[i]h_1 - 1 + \mathbf{s}_A[i + 256]h_1 - 1 \\
&= (\mathbf{s}_A[i] + \mathbf{s}_A[i + 256] + \mathbf{s}_A[i + 512] + \mathbf{s}_A[i + 768])h_1.
\end{aligned}$$

Algorithm 4. Find-m_1

Input: i
Output: m_1
1 **for** $h_1 := 0$ *to* $q - 1$ **do**
2 | $\mathbf{e}_B = \mathbf{0}$, set $\mathbf{e}_B[512] = h_1$; $\mathbf{P}_B = \mathbf{e}_B$;
3 | $\nu'_B = \mathbf{0}$, set $\nu'_B[i] = 1$;
4 | $\mathbf{k} \leftarrow$ Encode(ν'_B); $\bar{\mathbf{c}} =$ Compress$(\mathbf{k})$;
5 | $S_{k_B} \leftarrow$ SHA3-256(ν'_B); $v =$ Oracle$(\mathbf{P}_B, \bar{\mathbf{c}}, S_{k_B})$;
6 | **if** $v = 1$ **then**
7 | | $m_1 = \lfloor (q+2)/h_1 \rfloor$;
8 | | break;
9 | **else**
10 | | continue;
11 **end**
12 **Return** m_1

Algorithm 5. Full-recovery

Output: s' (All the coefficients in S_1)
1 $\mathbf{s}' \leftarrow$ Find-s-in-S$_2$();
2 **for** $i := 0$ *to* 255 **do**
3 | **for** $j := 0$ *to* 3 **do**
4 | | **if** $\mathbf{s}'[i + 256 * j] < -6$ or $\mathbf{s}'[i + 256 * j] > 4$ **then**
5 | | | break;
6 | **end**
7 | $m_1 =$ Find-m_1(i);
8 | **for** $k := 0$ *to* 3 **do**
9 | | **if** $k \neq j$ **then**
10 | | | $m_1 = m_1$ - $|\mathbf{s}'[i + 256 * k]|$;
11 | **end**
12 | **if** $\mathbf{s}'[i + 256 * j] < 0$ **then**
13 | | $\mathbf{s}'[i + 256 * j] = -m_1$;
14 | **else**
15 | | $\mathbf{s}'[i + 256 * j] = m_1$;
16 **end**
17 **Return** $\mathbf{s}'$

Then the adversary let h_1 change from 1 to q, at the beginning $m < q$, $Decode(\mathbf{k}'[i]) = 1$ and the oracle $\mathcal{O}$ will output 1. As h_1 increases, correspondingly m also increases until it reach the point that $m \geq q$. Now the output of $\mathcal{O}$ becomes 0. By recording the value of h_1 when the output of $\mathcal{O}$ changes, we can know that here m roughly equals q, and $\mathcal{A}$ can calculate $m_1 = \lfloor \frac{q}{h_1} \rceil$ by setting $m = m_1 h_1 = q$.

It should be noted that with $m_1 = |\mathbf{s}_A[i + 256]| + |\mathbf{s}_A[i + 512]| + |\mathbf{s}_A[i + 768]|$, if $\mathcal{A}$ can determine that $\mathbf{s}_A[i] = 0$, then $\mathcal{A}$ will skip Step 3.

The main processes of Step 2 is shown in Algorithm 4.

Step 3: In this step, the adversary $\mathcal{A}$ tries to determine the sign of $s_A[i]$. In Step 1, if $s_A[i]$ is outside $[-6, 4]$, then $s_A[i]$ will be recovered to an incorrect value, but its sign is correct. So, we can directly determine the sign of $s_A[i]$ according to this. There are only two special cases when $s_A[i] = 8$ or $s_A[i] = -8$ then the correct sign of $s_A[i]$ is opposite to that recovered in Step 1.

Step 4: The adversary $\mathcal{A}$ verifies whether the private key he recovered is correct by calculating the distribution of $P_A - as_A$. Since a and P_A are public, if $\mathcal{A}$ gets the correct private key, then the distribution is the same as that of e_A, which should follow the centered binomial distribution.

4   Experiments

In this section, we show the efficiency of our proposed attack. All our implementations are done on a MacBook Air, which is equipped with an Intel Core i7 processor at 2.7 GHz and an 8 GB RAM.

First of all, we want to show the advantage of our proposed Algorithm 2 in recovering coefficients belonging to $S_2 = \{-6, -5, \ldots, 2, 3, 4\}$. To make our experiment more convincing, we use the code the designers of NewHope submitting to the NIST [2] to generate 1000 secret keys. Then we implement Bauer et al.'s method to recover the coefficients belonging to S_2. Unfortunately, using Bauer et al.'s method we cannot even recover all the coefficients belonging to S_2 in every secret key. In other words, in every secret key with 1024 coefficients, there are at least 262 coefficients in S_2 that cannot be recovered.

On the other side, when we use our method as shown in Algorithm 2, in 992 keys we can recover all the coefficients belonging to S_2, and in the remaining 8 keys there are at most 2 coefficients that cannot be recovered. Then, by using Algorithms 2 and 4 together we can recover all the coefficients belong to $S_1 = \{-8, -7, \ldots, 6, 7, 8\}$. In our experiment, we also generate 1,000 secret keys. The result is, in 969 keys we recover all the coefficients in S_1. Thus the probability of successfully recovering the whole secret key is 96.9%.

In our proposed method, first we implement our proposed Algorithms 2 and 3 to recover the coefficients belonging to S_2. Then we will use Algorithm 4 to calculate $m_1 = |s_A[i]| + |s_A[i + 256]| + |s_A[i + 512]| + |s_A[i + 768]|$, and get the absolute value of the coefficient that belonging to S_1-S_2. For example, if we do not know $s_A[i]$, we can have $|s_A[i]| = m_1 - |s_A[i+256]| - |s_A[i+512]| - |s_A[i+768]|$. Finally, we will follow the Step 3 to decide the sign of $s_A[i]$ and verify whether the recovered is correct using the method in Step 4.

From the above experiments, we also find that in each secret key with 1024 coefficients, the most possible number of coefficients that belongs S_1-S_2 is between 7 and 15. In the following, we set T the number of coefficients in S_1-S_2.

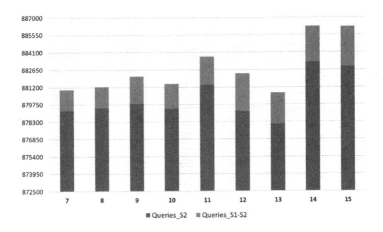

Fig. 1. Comparison of queries between different T

Table 5. Queries needed in recovering coefficients in S_2 and S_1–S_2

T	7	8	9	10	11	12	13	14	15
Queries_S_2	879,246	879,458	879,829	879,396	881,418	879,181	878,118	883,281	882,896
Queries_S_1–S_2	1,764	1,795	2,269	2,094	2,319	3,167	2,583	2,988	3,346
Total queries	881,010	881,254	882,098	881,490	883,738	882,348	880,701	886,269	886,242

In Fig. 1, we report the average number of queries for recovering coefficients in S_2 and S_1–S_2 when T ranges from 7 to 15. The specific queries is given in Table 5. We can see that the number of queries used in recovering coefficients in S_2 is almost 365 times more than the number of queries required to recover the coefficients in S_1–S_2. The reason is when recovering a coefficient in S_2, we need to find 50 favorable cases, which need a large number of queries. We can also observe that as T increases from 7 to 15, the average number of queries for recovering coefficients in S_2 is between $878,118$ and $883,281$. It does not increase a lot as T increases. This is because when we recover coefficients in S_2, we need to randomly generate (l_0, l_1, l_2, l_3) to get the favorable cases. Since the number of favorable cases is fixed at 50, the number of queries is almost the same. On average the number of needed queries is $879,725$. On the other side, as T increases, the number of queries for recovering coefficients in S_1–S_2 will increase. When we recover a coefficient in S_1–S_2, we need to use the Algorithm 4. Larger T means that there are more coefficients that cannot be recovered by Algorithm 2, and more queries are needed.

When T increases from 7 to 15, the average time for recovering coefficients in S_2 and S_1–S_2 is shown in Fig. 2, and the specific data is given in Table 6. We can see that the time required to recover coefficients in S_2 occupies 99% of the total time, since a lot of time is spent on looking for the 50 favorable cases when we recover the coefficient in S_2. We can also observe that as T increases,

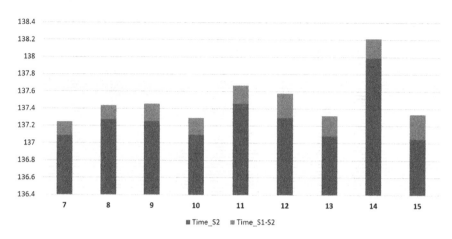

Fig. 2. The average time (ms) between different T

Table 6. Average time (ms) needed in recovering coefficients in S_2 and S_1–S_2

T	7	8	9	10	11	12	13	14	15
Time_S_2	137.08	137.27	137.25	137.09	137.45	137.29	137.08	137.99	137.04
Time_S_1–S_2	0.16	0.16	0.20	0.19	0.20	0.28	0.23	0.22	0.28
Total Time	137.24	137.43	137.45	137.29	137.66	137.58	137.31	138.21	137.33

the average time for recovering coefficients in S_2 is between 136 ms and 138 ms, which is almost the same due to our above analysis.

Compared with using an exhaustive research to find coefficients in S_1–S_2, our proposed method is much more efficient. In the exhaustive search experiment the best strategy is to search each element in the order $\{5, 6, 7, -7, 8, -8\}$. Then, we can verify whether the recovered private key is correct by calculating the distribution of $\mathbf{e}'_A = \mathbf{P}_A - \mathbf{as}_A$. If we get a correct private key, then the distribution of $\mathbf{e}'_A$ is the same as that of $\mathbf{e}_A$, which follows the centered binomial distribution. As an example, when $T = 12$, if we use an exhaustive search the required time is about 1.91 h. From this perspective, our proposed attack is very efficient.

5   Conclusion

In this paper, we have analyzed the security of NewHope when the public key is reused. We developed Bauer et al.'s method and proposed a complete and efficient key mismatch attack on NewHope. Since these kinds of lattice-based key exchange schemes are widely believed to replace the DH key exchange in the quantum age, their resistance to misuse situations are of high importance. It is worth noting that the NewHope KEM submitted to NIST is CPA secure, which is then transformed into CCA-secure using Fujisaki-Okamoto transformation. Therefore, the proposed key mismatch attack does not harm the NewHope designers' security goals. But our results show that when designers who b ase their approaches on the lattice-based key exchange should be careful to avoid the public key reuse, which is common in the design with DH key exchange approaches.

Acknowledgments. The work presented in this paper was supported in part by the National Natural Science Foundation of China under Grant no. 61672029. Jintai Ding would like to thank the partial support of USA Air Force and NSF.

References

1. Alagic, G., et al.: Status report on the first round of the NIST post-quantum cryptography standardization process. US Department of Commerce, National Institute of Standards and Technology (2019). https://nvlpubs.nist.gov/nistpubs/ir/2019/NIST.IR.8240.pdf. Accessed 26 Feb 2019
2. Alkim, E., et al.: Newhope: algorithm specification and supporting documentation. Submission to the NIST post-quantum cryptography standardization project (2017). https://newhopecrypto.org/data/NewHope_2018_12_02.pdf. Accessed 27 Feb 2019
3. Alkim, E., Ducas, L., Pöppelmann, T., Schwabe, P.: Newhope without reconciliation. IACR Cryptology ePrint Archive **2016**, 1157 (2016). https://www.cryptojedi.org/papers/newhopesimple-20161217.pdf. Accessed 17 Feb 2019
4. Alkim, E., Ducas, L., Pöppelmann, T., Schwabe, P.: Post-quantum key exchangea new hope. In: 25th USENIX Security Symposium (USENIX Security 2016), pp. 327–343 (2016)
5. Bauer, A., Gilbert, H., Renault, G., Rossi, M.: Assessment of the key-reuse resilience of NewHope. In: Matsui, M. (ed.) CT-RSA 2019. LNCS, vol. 11405, pp. 272–292. Springer, Cham (2019). https://doi.org/10.1007/978-3-030-12612-4_14
6. Bos, J.W., Costello, C., Naehrig, M., Stebila, D.: Post-quantum key exchange for the TLS protocol from the ring learning with errors problem. In: 2015 IEEE Symposium on Security and Privacy, pp. 553–570. IEEE (2015)
7. Ding, J., Alsayigh, S., Saraswathy, R., Fluhrer, S., Lin, X.: Leakage of signal function with reused keys in RLWE key exchange. In: 2017 IEEE International Conference on Communications (ICC), pp. 1–6. IEEE (2017)
8. Ding, J., Cheng, C., Qin, Y.: A simple key reuse attack on LWE and ring LWE encryption schemes as key encapsulation mechanisms (KEMS). Cryptology ePrint Archive, Report 2019/271 (2019). https://eprint.iacr.org/2019/271. Accessed 21 Apr 2019
9. Ding, J., Fluhrer, S., Rv, S.: Complete attack on RLWE key exchange with reused keys, without signal leakage. In: Susilo, W., Yang, G. (eds.) ACISP 2018. LNCS, vol. 10946, pp. 467–486. Springer, Cham (2018). https://doi.org/10.1007/978-3-319-93638-3_27
10. Ding, J., Xie, X., Lin, X.: A simple provably secure key exchange scheme based on the learning with errors problem. IACR Cryptology EPrint Archive **2012**, 688 (2012). https://eprint.iacr.org/2012/688.pdf. Accessed 26 Feb 2019

11. Fluhrer, S.R.: Cryptanalysis of ring-LWE based key exchange with key share reuse. IACR Cryptology ePrint Archive **2016**, 85 (2016). http://eprint.iacr.org/2016/085. Accessed 18 Feb 2019

12. Gao, X., Ding, J., Li, L., Liu, J.: Practical randomized rlwe-based key exchange against signal leakage attack. IEEE Trans. Comput. **67**(11), 1584–1593 (2018)

13. Lindner, R., Peikert, C.: Better key sizes (and attacks) for LWE-based encryption. In: Kiayias, A. (ed.) CT-RSA 2011. LNCS, vol. 6558, pp. 319–339. Springer, Heidelberg (2011). https://doi.org/10.1007/978-3-642-19074-2_21

14. Liu, C., Zheng, Z., Zou, G.: Key reuse attack on newhope key exchange protocol. In: Lee, K. (ed.) ICISC 2018. LNCS, vol. 11396, pp. 163–176. Springer, Cham (2019). https://doi.org/10.1007/978-3-030-12146-4_11

15. Lyubashevsky, V., Peikert, C., Regev, O.: On ideal lattices and learning with errors over rings. In: Gilbert, H. (ed.) EUROCRYPT 2010. LNCS, vol. 6110, pp. 1–23. Springer, Heidelberg (2010). https://doi.org/10.1007/978-3-642-13190-5_1

16. Peikert, C.: Lattice cryptography for the internet. In: Mosca, M. (ed.) PQCrypto 2014. LNCS, vol. 8772, pp. 197–219. Springer, Cham (2014). https://doi.org/10.1007/978-3-319-11659-4_12

17. Regev, O.: On lattices, learning with errors, random linear codes, and cryptography. J. ACM (JACM) **56**(6), 34:1–40 (2009)

18. Rescorla, E.: The transport layer security (TLS) protocol version 1.3. Technical report (2018). http://www.rfc-editor.org/info/rfc8446. Accessed 26 Feb 2019

19. Zhang, J., Zhang, Z., Ding, J., Snook, M., Dagdelen, Ö.: Authenticated key exchange from ideal lattices. In: Oswald, E., Fischlin, M. (eds.) EUROCRYPT 2015. LNCS, vol. 9057, pp. 719–751. Springer, Heidelberg (2015). https://doi.org/10.1007/978-3-662-46803-6_24

Breakdown Resilience
of Key Exchange Protocols:
NewHope, TLS 1.3, and Hybrids

Jacqueline Brendel[1]([⊠]), Marc Fischlin[1], and Felix Günther[2]

[1] Cryptoplexity, Technische Universität Darmstadt, Darmstadt, Germany
{jacqueline.brendel,marc.fischlin}@cryptoplexity.de
[2] Department of Computer Science and Engineering,
University of California San Diego, La Jolla, USA
mail@felixguenther.info

Abstract. Broken cryptographic algorithms and hardness assumptions are a constant threat to real-world protocols. Prominent examples are hash functions for which collisions become known, or number-theoretic assumptions which are threatened by advances in quantum computing. Especially when it comes to key exchange protocols, the switch to quantum-resistant primitives has begun and aims to protect today's secrets against future developments, moving from common Diffie–Hellman-based solutions to Learning-With-Errors-based approaches, often via intermediate hybrid designs.

To this date there exists no security notion for key exchange protocols that could capture the scenario of breakdowns of arbitrary cryptographic primitives to argue security of prior or even ongoing and future sessions. In this work we extend the common Bellare–Rogaway model to capture *breakdown resilience* of key exchange protocols. Our extended model allows us to study security of a protocol even in case of unexpected failure of employed primitives, may it be number-theoretic assumptions, hash functions, signature schemes, key derivation functions, etc. We then apply our security model to analyze two real-world protocols, showing that breakdown resilience for certain primitives is achieved by both an authenticated variant of the post-quantum secure key encapsulation mechanism NEWHOPE (Alkim et al.) which is a second round candidate in the Post Quantum Cryptography standardization process by NIST, as well as by TLS 1.3, which has recently been standardized as RFC 8446 by the Internet Engineering Task Force.

1 Introduction

Modern designs of cryptographic protocols are accompanied by a security proof which reduces the security of the protocol to the security of the employed cryptographic primitives. The security guarantees for the protocol are ultimately tied to the security of each individual primitive: with only one of the primitives

© Springer Nature Switzerland AG 2019
K. Sako et al. (Eds.): ESORICS 2019, LNCS 11736, pp. 521–541, 2019.
https://doi.org/10.1007/978-3-030-29962-0_25

being broken, all bets are usually off. However, the actual security guarantees that remain may vary with the protocol under consideration.

Key exchange protocols in particular often rely on a significant number of cryptographic primitives and hardness assumptions (e.g., collision resistant hash functions, unforgeable signature schemes, Diffie–Hellman-type assumptions, etc.). Yet, not all of them may contribute equally to the protocol's overall security at every point in time. While in general it is indeed expected that future sessions are vulnerable once the security of a component in a key exchange is broken, the question is: what can we say about the secrecy of sessions established prior to that breakdown? For special protocol designs with built-in resilience to component failures, we may even be asking for security of ongoing and future sessions if a subset of components breaks down. The notions of forward secrecy [18,23,32] and post-compromise security [19] answer these questions only partially, as we will see, for the usage of long-term secrets. A comprehensive notion of security against breakdowns of arbitrary (keyed and unkeyed) primitives as well as cryptographic hardness assumptions is however lacking.

1.1   Breakdowns and Mitigations in Real-World Key Exchange

The absence of a precise understanding of primitive breakdowns is despite such disruptions being an ever present threat, through failures or significant weakening of cryptographic algorithms and assumptions. With computational and cryptanalytic capabilities steadily evolving, examples of such incidences abound and range from weak ciphers like RC4 [2,33] over poor Diffie–Hellman parameter choices [1] to advances in breaking widely deployed hash functions like MD5 [22,45,47] or SHA-1 [42–44,46] enabling key-exchange-level attacks [9].

Moreover, the anticipated advent of quantum computers promises to render many of the currently used cryptographic algorithms and hardness assumptions obsolete. To remedy this situation, post-quantum secure schemes and in particular key exchange protocols are already developed (e.g., [5,11–13]) and have in parts been experimentally deployed (e.g., [14,37]). However, often only the most crucial cryptographic algorithms are replaced by post-quantum secure alternatives. Other components of the protocol, especially signature schemes, remain "classical" for the time being. The reasoning behind this is that exploits for these components would need to happen during the protocol execution to enable attacks on the key exchange, and not only once quantum computers reach maturity. Indeed, for example, the authors of the quantum-secure key-exchange protocol NEWHOPE argue that "[. . .] attacks on the [classical] signature will not compromise previous communication" [5]. While this intuition may be correct, there are no formal justifications for such statements at this point.

Until full confidence in the recently proposed post-quantum schemes and their parameter selection is established (see, e.g., the NIST post-quantum cryptography standardization effort [39]), so-called *hybrid* schemes are seen as a suitable way to guard today's communications from "record-today-then-break-later" adversaries, which are often referred to as future quantum adversaries. These key exchange schemes combine classical and post-quantum secure mechanisms such that the resulting session key remains secure as long as one of the two (or more) components remains secure. Academia has recently investigated how to build such hybrid schemes, e.g., from KEM combiners [10, 30]. While [30] solely treats the construction of KEM combiners, [10] additionally introduces security notions for hybrid authenticated key exchange with respect to quantum adversaries, but still focuses exclusively on KEM-based protocols.

1.2 Our Contributions

There is hence a need for a generic formal tool to assess the precise security of key exchange protocols in case (some) arbitrary underlying primitives or hardness assumptions break. Our contributions can be summarized as follows:

Security Model for Breakdown Resilience. To provide a formal ground for analyses concerning the effects primitive breakdowns have on key exchange protocols, we propose a formal security model in Sect. 3 capturing such breakdowns as an extension to the well-established model by Bellare and Rogaway [6]. The resulting security notion of *breakdown resilience* demands that keys established in sessions prior to the point of breakdown remain secure, i.e., indistinguishable from random. Our model can generically handle different choices for consequences of breakdowns. The conservative choice here is to consider strong break capabilities, such as being able to find arbitrary hash collisions, making the adversary more powerful and thus providing stronger security guarantees of resistant protocols. Later, in Sect. 6, we additionally consider a *strong* breakdown resilience variant which demands security even for ongoing and future sessions, and which we show is achievable by specifically designed protocols such as hybrid schemes.

Breakdown Resilience of NewHope and TLS 1.3. We then exercise our model in Sect. 4 on an authenticated variant of NEWHOPE-NIST, a post-quantum key encapsulation mechanism proposed by Alkim et al. [3] and a Round 2 candidate in the NIST Post Quantum Cryptography standardization effort [39]. Using our new formalism, we confirm the intuition that, in particular, a signature breakdown does not compromise the security of prior completed sessions.

As the second example, we assess in Sect. 5 the breakdown resilience of the key exchange of TLS 1.3, the latest version of the Transport Layer Security protocol [41]. To this end, we consider two major handshake modes, the full (elliptic-curve) ephemeral-Diffie–Hellman ((EC)DHE) handshake, as well as the resumption-style (PSK) handshake based on pre-shared keys. In contrast to the (EC)DHE mode, we establish that for the PSK(-only) handshake—perhaps surprisingly at first glance—no breakdown resilience at all is provided for technical reasons, even though both modes follow a similar structure.

1.3 Related Work and Delineation

Our work extends, and is inspired by, conceptual ideas of prior work on the security of both key exchange specifically and cryptographic protocols more broadly. Yet, our notion of breakdown resilience is novel and unmet by any (combination of) previously defined security goals, as we discuss in the following.

Forward Secrecy. While similar in spirit, breakdown resilience should not be confused with the concept of forward secrecy [18,23,32]. Forward secrecy as a security property of session keys derived in a key exchange protocol demands that even if an involved party's long-term secret is compromised, any key derived previously remains secure. While this property is closely related to our scenario, breakdown resilience takes a conceptually distinct approach to forward secrecy (and also stronger security models allowing ephemeral key reveal [18,36]): its focus is on the breakdown of complete primitives or hardness assumptions rather than on the exposure of specific protocol values like long-term keys. Furthermore, breakdown resilience also covers breaks of unkeyed cryptographic building blocks (e.g., breaking collision resistance of hash functions) and more generally cryptographic hardness assumptions such as the discrete logarithm problem.

Post-Compromise Security. With their notion of *post-compromise security*, Cohn-Gordon, Cremers, and Garratt [19] establish security guarantees for communication *after* participants have been compromised. (Strong) breakdown resilience differs from this notion in that it considers not the compromise of single parties but the global breakdown of cryptographic building blocks on a protocol level. Strong breakdown resilience may be seen as a generalization of the concept of post-compromise security while our standard notion is concerned with the security of sessions that were completed *before* a breakdown occurred.

Bitcoin Security in the Presence of Broken Primitives. Giechaskiel, Cremers, and Rasmussen [31] were the first to systematically explore how broken or weakened hash functions and/or signatures affect the security of Bitcoin. While their study focused on Bitcoin, we present a general framework that can be applied to analyze a whole class of cryptographic protocols, namely authenticated key exchange protocols, and may very well be transferable to other kinds of protocols.

Downgrade Resilience. A breakdown of a primitive or hardness assumption willingly employed by both parties conducting a key exchange is conceptually different from a downgrade of a connection to an insecure cipher suite during the negotiation phase. In the breakdown resilience setting we are concerned with the security of past sessions after a breakdown has occurred, while downgrade resilience, formally treated by Bhargavan et al. [8] and Dowling and Stebila [26], assures that weak cipher suites will never be successfully negotiated in case matching stronger suites are preferred by both participants.

Hybrid Key Exchange. The model for hybrid authenticated key exchange proposed by Bindel et al. [10] is a Bellare–Rogaway-style model adjusted to two-stage adversaries with different levels of quantumness. Their constructions focus on hybrid key encapsulation mechanisms (KEMs), where the breakdowns are caused exclusively by these quantum adversaries. Our model for (strong) breakdown resilience offers a more general, alternative approach. It is able to explicitly capture the breakdown of multiple arbitrary primitives or even hardness assumptions, irrespective of the cause, thus in particular avoiding the complexities of a two-stage adversary setting.

2   The Bellare–Rogaway Model

We begin by recapping key exchange security in the style of the model by Bellare and Rogaway [6] which forms the basis for our model of breakdown resilience. This model provides strong security guarantees for authenticated key exchange in the presence of an active adversary. As formalized in the following, the adversary interacts with protocol instances via oracle queries with the goal to distinguish the real session key established in a 'test' session of its choice from a randomly chosen one (via a Test oracle). The adversary is considered to have full control over the network (modeled via a Send oracle delivering messages to key exchange sessions). It is furthermore able to corrupt some of the parties' long-term secrets (via a Corrupt oracle) and to reveal some of the established session keys in honest sessions (via a Reveal oracle).

In this work we focus on the case of mutually authenticated key exchange protocols with pre-specified peer identities, but note that the model can be extended to capture unilaterally authenticated or anonymous key exchange as well as post-specified peers. We furthermore distinguish between protocols providing and not providing forward secrecy.

Notation and Overview. The participants in a key exchange protocol KE are given by elements U from the set of users $\mathcal{U}$, each of whom holds a long-term public key pk_U with corresponding secret key sk_U. Each participant can act as initiator or responder of a protocol execution and may run multiple instances, so-called *sessions*, of the key exchange protocol in parallel. To uniquely refer to the k-th session owned by user $U \in \mathcal{U}$ with intended communication partner $V \in \mathcal{U}$ on an administrative level, we use the notation $\pi_{U,V}^k$. Each such session is associated with the set of variables described in Table 1. To be able to refer to a specific entry for a session $\pi_{U,V}^k$, we use the notation $\pi_{U,V}^k$.entry. For example, $\pi_{U,V}^k$.role specifies the session owner U's role in session $\pi_{U,V}^k$. For simplicity, we sometimes simply write π and π' to refer to sessions in a general context where the specific indices do not matter.

Partnering of Sessions. The partnering of sessions is defined via the session identifiers. More precisely, we call the session $\pi_{U,V}^k$ owned by U *partnered* with the session $\pi_{V',U'}^{k'}$ owned by V' (and vice versa), if the sessions share the same session identifier, i.e., $\pi_{U,V}^k.\mathsf{sid} = \pi_{V',U'}^{k'}.\mathsf{sid} \neq \bot$. We require that any execution between honest instances is partnered.

Adversarial Queries. In order to break key secrecy, the goal of the adversary is to distinguish real from random session keys. Not all interactions of the adversary with the protocol are admissible at any point. In particular, there are conditions under which the adversary trivially loses the game, e.g., when both revealing and testing session keys of partnered sessions as mentioned before. To keep track if one of these cases has occurred, we leverage a flag lost initialized to false.

The adversary interacts with the protocol via the queries described in Table 2.

Table 1. Session variables.

- role $\in$ {initiator, responder} is the session owner's role in this session.
- $\mathsf{st_{exec}} \in$ {running, accepted, rejected} denotes the current state of execution (default: running).
- sid $\in \{0,1\}^* \cup \{\bot\}$ indicates the session identifier (default: $\bot$).
- $\mathsf{st_{key}} \in$ {fresh, revealed} indicates the state of the session key K (default: fresh).
- K $\in \{0,1\}^* \cup \{\bot\}$ indicates the established session key (default: $\bot$).
- tested $\in$ {true, false} indicates whether the session key K has been tested or not (default: false).

Table 2. Adversarial queries.

NewSession($U, V, role$): Establishes a new session $\pi_{U,V}^k$ for U (with k being a counter value for sessions of U with intended partner V), stores the given role value in $\pi_{U,V}^k$.role $\leftarrow role$, and returns the identifier $\pi_{U,V}^k$

Send($\pi_{U,V}^k, m$): Causes the message m to be sent to the session $\pi_{U,V}^k$. If there exists no session $\pi_{U,V}^k$, the query outputs $\bot$. Else the response of the session owner U upon receipt of message m is returned, and the state of execution $\mathsf{st_{exec}}$ is updated. If $\mathsf{st_{exec}}$ changes to accepted with an intended communication partner V that was previously corrupted, then set $\mathsf{st_{key}} \leftarrow$ revealed

Reveal($\pi_{U,V}^k$): Returns the session key K of session $\pi_{U,V}^k$. If there exists no session $\pi_{U,V}^k$ or if $\mathsf{st_{exec}} \neq$ accepted, then return $\bot$. Otherwise, set $\mathsf{st_{key}}$ to revealed and return K to the adversary

Corrupt(U): Returns the long-term secret key sk_U of U to the adversary. No further queries may be issued to sessions owned by U. In case of no forward secrecy, $\mathsf{st_{key}}$ is set to revealed in all sessions $\pi_{V,W}^k$ where $V = U$ or $W = U$

Test($\pi_{U,V}^k$): Tests the session key of session $\pi_{U,V}^k$. The oracle uses a test bit b_{test} chosen uniformly at random at the outset and then fixed during the game execution. For simplicity, we restrict the adversary to ask a single Test query only. If there exists no session $\pi_{U,V}^k$ or if $\pi_{U,V}^k.\mathsf{st_{exec}} \neq$ accepted, the query returns $\bot$. Otherwise, $\pi_{U,V}^k$.tested is set to true. If $b_{\mathsf{test}} = 0$, a key $\mathcal{K} \xleftarrow{\$} \mathcal{D}$ is sampled at random from the session key distribution $\mathcal{D}$. If $b_{\mathsf{test}} = 1$, $\mathcal{K}$ in contrast is set to the actual session key $\pi_{U,V}^k$.K. Return $\mathcal{K}$

Bellare–Rogaway AKE Security Games. We adopt the approach of Brzuska et al. [16,17] to separate the overall BR security properties into the notions of BR-Match security and BR key secrecy. The conditions of BR-Match security guarantee that the session identifiers sid ensure an appropriate identification of partnered sessions, that at most two sessions are partnered, and that partnered sessions hold the same key. BR key secrecy then ensures that a protocol establishes session keys that are indistinguishable from random strings and (implicitly) mutually authenticated. This, of course, excludes some trivial attacks like distinguishing revealed session keys from random keys.

In Sect. 3.3, we will give slightly changed versions of the definitions for BR-Match security and BR key secrecy when adjusting them to the breakdown resilience setting. Since the modifications to the definitions there are small and well-indicated, we defer for the definitions of the original BR setting to the full version [15].

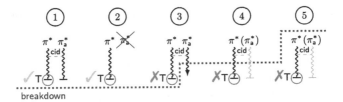

Fig. 1. Illustration of (non-)permissible Test queries wrt. a breakdown. The dotted purple line indicates the point in time of a breakdown with respect to the five scenarios of (completed, running, or future) test sessions. T denotes a test query on session π^*, π_a^* denotes a (potential, if gray) associated session (semi-)partnered with π^* holding the same contributive identifier (cid). A checkmark ✓ (resp. a cross ✗) indicates whether the test query is admissible or not. (Color figure online)

3   Modeling Breakdown Resilience

For integrating *breakdown resilience* into the generic (Bellare–Rogaway-style) security model for authenticated key exchange, we are interested in the security of completed sessions in the case that one or multiple cryptographic primitives or hardness assumptions underlying the key exchange protocol's security break. Note that for classical key exchange designs one cannot expect any security guarantees to remain for ongoing and future sessions, as they may crucially rely on the broken primitive's security. In Sect. 6, we will discuss the specific class of hybrid designs which achieve a *strong* variant of breakdown resilience we define there, capturing security also of ongoing and future sessions.

Figure 1 illustrates how different scenarios are treated in our model. For now, we are interested in the question of whether the expected security level is still achieved in *past* sessions (Scenarios 1 to 3 in Fig. 1) and thus exclude sessions that are still active at the time of breakdown or start after it (Scenarios 4 and 5). It is however not only the status of the test session which is crucial for the security guarantees, but also that of a potential (unfinished) communication partner, which we refer to as the associated session. A breakdown of a primitive in the middle of the communication may enable the adversary to interfere with the correct partnering of sessions, leading to trivial attacks on the session key in question, which we need to capture in our model. Consider, for example, a test session that has accepted and has output its last message, say, to authenticate itself, waiting to be delivered to its intended partner session. Such final-message authentication is indeed very common in key exchange protocols. An adversary with breakdown capabilities can now modify this last message, e.g., by forging a new signature, to cause the intended partner to accept with a different session identifier. Yet, the intended partner may still derive the same key as our test session as the relevant key material is already established. The adversary could hence safely learn the session key through a Reveal query on the now unpartnered session, trivially distinguishing the tested key from random. This situation is depicted in Scenario 3 of Fig. 1.

Hence, we need to exclude sessions from being tested that accepted prior to the breakdown but have a "semi-completed" partner session that, at the time, already holds all the relevant cryptographic material for the final key derivation (Scenario 3). We use a notion of contributive identifiers (cid) to identify such almost-partnered sessions. Identical contributive identifiers indicate that sessions may eventually derive the same key, despite not being partnered yet.

An alternative to using contributive identifiers would be to demand that only sessions that fully completed before breakdown with an honest partner would be considered valid test sessions (as in Scenario 1). This, however, would limit the adversary to purely passive attacks in the pre-breakdown phase. In contrast, our approach with contributive identifiers is less restrictive, as we still allow the adversary to test completed sessions without an honest partner (Scenario 2), e.g., where the adversary communicated with that party.

To capture resilience against breakdowns, we augment our model with a Break query that allows the adversary to break the security of cryptographic primitives or hardness assumptions contained in a dedicated, specified set $\mathcal{F}_{\mathsf{BDR}}$. More precisely, this set has the form $\mathcal{F}_{\mathsf{BDR}} = \{(f_1, \mathsf{sec\text{-}prop}_1), (f_2, \mathsf{sec\text{-}prop}_2), \ldots\}$, i.e., $\mathcal{F}_{\mathsf{BDR}}$ contains tuples $(f, \mathsf{sec\text{-}prop})$, determining all primitives/hardness assumptions f for which some security property $\mathsf{sec\text{-}prop}$ may break. As a result of the Break query, the adversary may—depending on the broken security property of the primitive or assumption—be given certain key material or access to additional oracles in the model. To capture that we expect only sessions to remain secure that completed before the breakdown occurred, we introduce a flag breakdown which is set when Break is called and checked within the (accordingly modified) Send query. These changes enable us to formalize a model for breakdown resilience in a generic way. As we will see, our notion of a Break query is versatile and can capture a wide variety of breakdowns. Primitives and assumptions for which we provide a concrete specification of a breakdown include, e.g., the unforgeability of signatures, CCA security of encryption schemes, collision resistance of hash functions, or the discrete logarithm problem. As it turns out, breakdown resilience (with/without forward secrecy) provides strictly stronger security than the notion of BR security given in the previous section.

3.1 Extensions to the Security Model

Breakdown Flag. We introduce a global flag breakdown (initialized to false) in the security game, indicating whether the adversary has issued a Break query.

Contributive Identifiers. We augment the model with the concept of contributive (session) identifiers.[1] Intuitively, contributive identifiers relate two sessions which exchanged the messages establishing the key material (e.g., values g^x and g^y in a Diffie–Hellman-style protocol), but are not yet partnered (e.g., because the authenticating signatures have not been sent yet). In the breakdown setting,

---

[1] We here use the formalization by Dowling et al. [24] from their analysis of TLS 1.3 candidate handshakes in the multi-stage key exchange setting.

contributive identifiers enable us to specify that we do not expect security of sessions that, at time of breakdown, had a "semi-partnered" session that shares the same key material. The reason is that the adversary could eventually make this "semi-partnered" party accept after the breakdown for the same session key but a different session identifier, e.g., by forging the final protocol signature after the breakdown; in this case achieving key indistinguishability would be impossible. We thus demand that the tested session accepted prior to the breakdown and does not share a contributive identifier with another session that was still running at the time of breakdown.

Formally, we add the following variables associated with each session $\pi_{U,V}^k$:

- cid $\in \{0,1\}^* \cup \{\bot\}$ indicates the contributive identifier (default: $\bot$).
- $\mathsf{st}_{\mathsf{exec}}^{\mathsf{bd}} \in \{\mathsf{running}, \mathsf{accepted}, \mathsf{rejected}, \bot\}$ denotes the state of execution at the time of breakdown, i.e., when the Break query was issued the first time (default prior to breakdown: $\bot$).

To avoid trivial choices and to relate the contributive identifiers (cid) to session identifiers (sid) we add two requirements for Match security: First, as in [24], same session identifiers must imply same contributive identifiers, capturing the intuition that partnered session should in particular be contributively partnered. Second, since we restrict the Test query based on common contributive identifiers, we demand that at most two sessions share the same cid to prevent that Test queries are excluded by trivial choices of colliding contributive identifiers.

Break Query. We add a Break query to the adversarial queries described in Sect. 2 which allows the adversary to schedule the timing of breakdowns. The query sets breakdown to true, records the current execution state of sessions, and provides the adversary with the capability to break the security of any $(f, \mathsf{sec\text{-}prop}) \in \mathcal{F}_{\mathsf{BDR}}$, where $\mathcal{F}_{\mathsf{BDR}}$ is a fixed parameter of the security game. Which capability the adversary is given when breaking the security sec-prop of a primitive or assumption f depends on the latter's type and may, e.g., be exposing all key material used within f to the adversary or granting it access to additional oracles. We discuss options for the common primitives below in Sect. 3.2 and specify the corresponding behavior of Break in Table 3. As we will see, additional primitives and assumptions can easily be added to capture further key exchange designs as the Break query itself is generic.

Break(): Causes for all $(f, \mathsf{sec\text{-}prop}) \in \mathcal{F}_{\mathsf{BDR}}$ the breakdown of the security property sec-prop of the cryptographic primitive or hardness assumption f.

   If breakdown = false, for all sessions π record the current state of execution as $\pi.\mathsf{st}_{\mathsf{exec}}^{\mathsf{bd}} \leftarrow \pi.\mathsf{st}_{\mathsf{exec}}$. Set breakdown $\leftarrow$ true. Depending on the entries in the set $\mathcal{F}_{\mathsf{BDR}}$, provide the adversary with the responses and/or oracle accesses specified in Table 3. The Break oracle may be queried repeatedly, which enables the adversary to obtain an updated response in order to, e.g., receive further key material used in an encryption scheme since the last call of Break.

Table 3. Potential Break oracle specifications.

Primitive/Hardness Assumption (f)	Algorithms	Security Assumption (sec-prop)	Break Response
Signatures $\mathcal{S}$	$\mathcal{S} = (\mathsf{SKG}, \mathsf{Sig}, \mathsf{SVf})$	EUF-CMA (existential unforgeability under chosen message attack)	return all previous pairs (pk, sk) for which $(pk, sk) \leftarrow \mathsf{SKG}$
MAC $\mathcal{M}$	$\mathcal{M} = (\mathsf{MKG}, \mathsf{MAC}, \mathsf{MVf})$	EUF-CMA (existential unforgeability under chosen message attack)	return all previous values sk for which $sk \leftarrow \mathsf{MKG}$
Hash Function $\mathcal{H}$	$\mathcal{H} = (\mathsf{HKG}, \mathsf{Hash})$	STD-Coll-Res (standard-model collision resistance)	programmable access to Hash: After breakdown, $\mathcal{A}$ sets output of Hash queries on previously unseen values
Key Derivation KDF	KDF	KDF-sec (output pseudorandomness)	return all previous values k for which $k \leftarrow \mathsf{KDF}$
PRF $\mathcal{P}$	$\mathcal{P} = (\mathsf{PKG}, \mathsf{PRF})$	PRF-sec (output pseudorandomness)	return all previous values k for which $k \leftarrow \mathsf{PKG}$
Discrete Log	$\mathsf{GroupExp}(h, x) = h^x$ in multiplicative cyclic group $\mathbb{G} = \langle g \rangle, h \in \mathbb{G}$	Discrete Logarithm Problem	return all previous pairs (x, h^x) for which $h^x \leftarrow \mathsf{GroupExp}(h, x)$

Modified Send *Query.* Once the breakdown flag is set to true, ongoing sessions and sessions that are initiated after the breakdown must be considered revealed as we expect their keys to be affected by the breakdown. To enforce this, we replace the Send query from Sect. 2 by the following slightly modified version that sets the session key state to revealed if breakdown = true; the change is underlined in the following description.

$\mathsf{Send}_{\mathsf{BDR}}(\pi_{U,V}^k, m)$: Causes the message m to be sent to the session $\pi_{U,V}^k$. If there exists no session $\pi_{U,V}^k$, the query outputs $\bot$. Else the response of the session owner U upon receipt of message m is returned, and the state of execution $\mathsf{st}_{\mathsf{exec}}$ is updated. If $\mathsf{st}_{\mathsf{exec}}$ changes to accepted with an intended communication partner V that was previously corrupted <u>or if breakdown = true</u>, then set $\mathsf{st}_{\mathsf{key}} \leftarrow$ revealed.

3.2 Breakdown of Primitives and Assumptions

We next specify the behavior of the Break query and capabilities the adversary is provided with for a number of common cryptographic primitives and hardness assumptions. Table 3 covers a range of standard primitives and assumptions underlying the security of most key exchange protocols (and in particular the NEWHOPE [5] and TLS 1.3 [41] protocols we analyze in Sects. 4 and 5); due to space restrictions, we defer for further examples to [15, Table 1].

For keyed primitives (both public-key and secret-key ones), the basic idea for the Break oracle is to hand to the adversary all secret keys which have been created in protocol executions so far. Since the adversary in our model can call the Break oracle multiple times it may also access subsequently generated keys. In order for Break to provide the necessary information, we make the key generation algorithm of a primitive explicit and have all honest parties invoke it when generating key material for this primitive. For example, any keys used for a MAC scheme $\mathcal{M} = (\mathsf{MKG}, \mathsf{MAC}, \mathsf{MVf})$ in honest sessions will be generated via the key generation algorithm MKG, with the challenger in the security game storing the output. This approach enables the challenger to return an exhaustive list of all secret keys of a primitive up to the point of breakdown when a Break query is asked.

In key exchange protocols it is common that keys for keyed primitives are not derived via an explicit key generation algorithm but, e.g., sampled at random or generated through a key derivation function. We implicitly treat such key derivations as a trivial key generation algorithm in our model, hence recording also such keys for exposure through a Break query.

For unkeyed primitives with a secret input, such as key derivation functions, we model a break of the output behavior by returning all outputs of evaluations so far. This means for example that the function is no longer unpredictable or pseudorandom. To capture this formally, we again assume that the challenger keeps a list of all function outputs generated by honest sessions, in order to provide the according list to the adversary in case of a Break query.

For public primitives like a hash function $\mathcal{H}$ and security properties like collision resistance we have to capture the increased capabilities of the adversary $\mathcal{A}$ after the breakdown differently. Here, regardless of whether $\mathcal{H}$ is modeled as a random oracle RO or considered in the standard model, the adversary $\mathcal{A}$ might be able to craft collisions after the break. We would model this by allowing $\mathcal{A}$ to program $\mathcal{H}$ globally on previously unseen inputs after the breakdown. More precisely, after the break, $\mathcal{A}$ answers all queries by honest sessions to the hash function $\mathcal{H}$ itself (but consistently with previous replies). If, on the other hand, we aim at modeling breakdown of the one-wayness of a random oracle, we instead hand the adversary all input-output pairs which honest parties have evaluated.

Finally, we can also treat the breakdown of interesting cryptographic assumptions for key exchange via the Break oracle. We illustrate this here by the discrete logarithm problem (DLP), which we treat similarly to public-key primitives. For the example of DLP, we mandate that honest sessions invoke a given algorithm GroupExp for group exponentiations, which then allows the challenger in the security game to provide the adversary with all secret exponents employed in honest sessions on a Break query. Note that for related cryptographic assumptions, the breakdown of one assumption can imply the breakdown of the other. For example, we can restrict our attention to DLP for Diffie–Hellman-style protocols, as (resilience against) a breakdown of DLP in particular implies (resilience against) the breakdown of other commonly used assumption like DDH and CDH.

Setup. The challenger generates long-term public/private-key pairs with certificates for each participant $U \in \mathcal{U}$.

Query. The adversary $\mathcal{A}$ receives the generated public keys and has access to the queries NewSession, Send$_{\mathsf{BDR}}$, Reveal, Corrupt, Test, and Break.

Stop. At some point, the adversary stops with no output.

Winning conditions:

1. There exist two distinct sessions π and π' with $\pi.\mathsf{sid} = \pi'.\mathsf{sid} \neq \perp$, and $\pi.\mathsf{st}_{\mathsf{exec}}, \pi'.\mathsf{st}_{\mathsf{exec}} \neq \mathsf{rejected}$, but $\pi.\mathsf{K} \neq \pi'.\mathsf{K}$. (Different session keys.)
2. There exist two distinct sessions π and π' such that $\pi.\mathsf{sid} = \pi'.\mathsf{sid} \neq \perp$, but $\pi.\mathsf{cid} \neq \pi'.\mathsf{cid}$ or $\pi.\mathsf{cid} = \pi'.\mathsf{cid} = \perp$. (Different/unset cids.)
3. There exist two sessions $\pi := \pi_{U,V}^k$ and $\pi' := \pi_{V',U'}^{k'}$ such that $\pi.\mathsf{sid} = \pi'.\mathsf{sid} \neq \perp$, $\pi.\mathsf{role} = $ initiator, and $\pi'.\mathsf{role} = $ responder, but $U \neq U'$ or $V \neq V'$. (Different intended partner.)
4. There exist at least three sessions π, π', and π'' such that π, π', π'' are pairwise distinct, but $\pi.\mathsf{sid} = \pi'.\mathsf{sid}' = \pi''.\mathsf{sid} \neq \perp$ or $\pi.\mathsf{cid} = \pi'.\mathsf{cid}' = \pi''.\mathsf{cid} \neq \perp$. (More than two sessions share the same sid or cid.)

Fig. 2. Game $G_{\mathsf{KE},\mathcal{A}}^{\mathsf{BDR\text{-}Match}(\mathcal{F}_{\mathsf{BDR}})}$ for BDR-Match security of key exchange protocol KE.

We stress that Table 3 only gives (conservative) recommendations on how the Break oracle can be implemented for some common primitives and hardness assumptions. Depending on the security properties required in a specific key-exchange setting, one may wish to specify different responses for the Break query. Likewise, weaker Break capabilities can be defined for demonstrating negative results, as we will do in our analysis of the TLS 1.3 PSK mode in Sect. 5.

3.3 Breakdown-Resilient AKE Security Games

We are now ready to define the security notion of *breakdown resilience* (BDR) for an authenticated key exchange protocol. Extending the Bellare–Rogaway-like model from Sect. 2, we similarly divide the security properties into BDR-Match security and BDR key secrecy. Both security notions differ from the original Bellare–Rogaway-like notions by including the set of primitive breakdowns $\mathcal{F}_{\mathsf{BDR}}$ under consideration and the novel Break query as well as replacing the original Send oracle by the modified Send$_{\mathsf{BDR}}$ version. The BDR-Match definition further-more reflects that contributive identifiers must coincide in matching sessions but be distinct otherwise, while BDR key secrecy leverages the introduced contributive identifiers to exclude test sessions with semi-completed partners at the time of breakdown.

Definition 1 (BDR-Match Security). *Let λ be the security parameter, KE a key exchange protocol, and $\mathcal{A}$ a PPT adversary interacting with KE via the queries NewSession, Send$_{\mathsf{BDR}}$, Reveal, Corrupt, and Break in the game $G_{\mathsf{KE},\mathcal{A}}^{\mathsf{BDR\text{-}Match}(\mathcal{F}_{\mathsf{BDR}})}$ depicted in Fig. 2.*

Setup. The challenger generates long-term public/private-key pairs for each participant $U \in \mathcal{U}$, chooses the test bit $b_{test} \xleftarrow{\$} \{0, 1\}$ at random and sets lost $\leftarrow$ false.

Query. The adversary $\mathcal{A}$ receives the generated public keys and has access to the queries NewSession, Send$_{BDR}$, Reveal, Test, and Break.

Guess. At some point, $\mathcal{A}$ stops and outputs a guess b_{guess}.

Finalize. The challenger sets the lost flag to lost $\leftarrow$ true if at least one of the following conditions hold:

1. There exist two (not necessarily distinct) sessions π, π' such that $\pi.\text{sid} = \pi'.\text{sid}$, $\pi.\text{st}_{key} = $ revealed, and $\pi'.\text{tested} = $ true. (Adversary has tested and revealed the key in a single session or in two partnered sessions.)

2. There exist two distinct sessions π, π' such that $\pi.\text{tested} = $ true, $\pi.\text{cid} = \pi'.\text{cid}$, and $\pi'.\text{st}_{exec}^{bd} = $ running. (Adversary has tested a session whose contributive partner session was running at the time of breakdown.)

Fig. 3. Game $G_{KE,\mathcal{A}}^{BDR(\mathcal{F}_{BDR}),\mathcal{D}}$ for BDR key secrecy of key exchange protocol KE.

Let $\mathcal{F}_{BDR}$ be a set of cryptographic primitives and hardness assumptions the adversary can break in the model. The adversary $\mathcal{A}$ wins the game, denoted by $G_{KE,\mathcal{A}}^{BDR\text{-}Match(\mathcal{F}_{BDR})}(\lambda) = 1$, if at least one of the winning conditions 1–4. holds. We say KE is BDR-Match-secure for $\mathcal{F}_{BDR}$ if for all PPT adversaries $\mathcal{A}$ the advantage function $\mathsf{Adv}_{KE,\mathcal{A}}^{BDR\text{-}Match(\mathcal{F}_{BDR})} := \Pr\left[G_{KE,\mathcal{A}}^{BDR\text{-}Match(\mathcal{F}_{BDR})}(\lambda) = 1 \right]$ is negligible in the security parameter λ.

Definition 2 (BDR Key Secrecy). *Let λ be the security parameter, KE a key exchange protocol with key distribution $\mathcal{D}$, and $\mathcal{A}$ a PPT adversary interacting with KE via the queries NewSession, Send$_{BDR}$, Reveal, Corrupt, Break, and Test in the game $G_{KE,\mathcal{A}}^{BDR(\mathcal{F}_{BDR}),\mathcal{D}}$ depicted in Fig. 3.*

Let $\mathcal{F}_{BDR}$ be a set of cryptographic primitives and hardness assumptions the adversary can break in the model. The adversary $\mathcal{A}$ wins the game, denoted by $G_{KE,\mathcal{A}}^{BDR(\mathcal{F}_{BDR}),\mathcal{D}}(\lambda) = 1$, if $b_{guess} = b_{test}$ and lost $=$ false.

We say that KE provides BDR key secrecy for $\mathcal{F}_{BDR}$ with/without forward secrecy if for all PPT adversaries $\mathcal{A}$ the advantage function $\mathsf{Adv}_{KE,\mathcal{A}}^{BDR(\mathcal{F}_{BDR}),\mathcal{D}}(\lambda) :=$ $\Pr\left[G_{KE,\mathcal{A}}^{BDR(\mathcal{F}_{BDR}),\mathcal{D}}(\lambda) = 1 \right] - \frac{1}{2}$ is negligible in the security parameter λ.

Definition 3 (Breakdown Resilience). *We say a key exchange protocol KE is breakdown resilient for $\mathcal{F}_{BDR}$ (with/without forward secrecy) if KE provides BDR-Match security and BDR key secrecy for $\mathcal{F}_{BDR}$ (with/without forward secrecy), according to Definitions 1 and 2.*

Note that the model for breakdown resilience is a proper extension of the Bellare–Rogaway model for AKE:

Proposition 1. *If a key exchange protocol KE achieves breakdown resilience for some $\mathcal{F}_{BDR}$ (incl. $\mathcal{F}_{BDR} = \emptyset$) with/without forward secrecy according to Definition 3, then KE is also BR-secure with/without forward secrecy.*

4   NewHope

As a first application of our new security model, we analyze the breakdown resilience of an authenticated variant of the NEWHOPE scheme. NEWHOPE is a post-quantum secure key exchange protocol originally introduced in 2016 by Alkim et al. [5]. It has gained widespread attention, not least because of its experimental deployment in Google Chrome Canary [14]. The same year, a simpler encryption-based version NEWHOPE-SIMPLE was introduced [4]. Contrary to the previous reconciliation-based design this variant is based on encryption of the shared key and constitutes the basis for the candidate key encapsulation schemes [3] that were submitted to the NIST Post-Quantum Cryptography standardization process [39] and have made it to the second round of the process. The post-quantum security of all NEWHOPE schemes is based on the ring learning with errors problem (RLWE), which states that $as + e$ for secret s, public a, and small error e is indistinguishable from random.

In our analysis, we consider an authenticated version of the passively secure KEM provided in the NIST candidate submission NEWHOPE-NIST [3]. For illustrative purposes, the description of AUTH-NEWHOPE in Fig. 4 in Appendix A has been divided according to the two phases of the unauthenticated NEWHOPE-NIST key encapsulation and the ensuing SIGMA-style authentication. One can, of course, condense the entire protocol in a three-move key exchange by having Alice send r_A in the first step and Bob attach B, r_B, σ_B, τ_b to its last message in the NEWHOPE step. This does not affect our security proof of breakdown resilience. For details on the key encapsulation mechanism and its IND-CPA security, we refer the interested reader to the original specification in [3, Sect. 1.2].

AUTH-NEWHOPE relies on the following cryptographic primitives and hardness assumptions: IND-CPA security of the key encapsulation scheme KEM, pseudorandomness of the key derivation function KDF, and existential unforgeability of the signature scheme $\mathcal{S}$ and MAC scheme $\mathcal{M}$. In the following, we show that AUTH-NEWHOPE achieves breakdown resilience for $\mathcal{F}_{\mathsf{BDR}} = \{(\mathcal{S}, \mathsf{EUF\text{-}CMA}), (\mathcal{M}, \mathsf{EUF\text{-}CMA})\}$. Note that $\mathcal{F}_{\mathsf{BDR}}$ neither contains the IND-CPA security of KEM nor the key derivation function KDF, as a break of any of these makes key secrecy impossible to achieve. Due to space restrictions, we only state the key secrecy theorem here; BDR-Match security and all proofs can be found in the full version [15].

Theorem 1 (BDR key secrecy of AUTH-NEWHOPE). *Let* $\mathcal{F}_{\mathsf{BDR}} = \{(\mathcal{S}, \mathsf{EUF\text{-}CMA}), (\mathcal{M}, \mathsf{EUF\text{-}CMA})\}$. *Then* AUTH-NEWHOPE *achieves breakdown-resilient key secrecy for* $\mathcal{F}_{\mathsf{BDR}}$ *with forward secrecy. More precisely, for any efficient, adversary* $\mathcal{A}$ *there exist efficient adversaries* $\mathcal{B}_1, \ldots, \mathcal{B}_4$ *such that*

$$
\mathsf{Adv}^{\mathsf{BDR}(\mathcal{F}_{\mathsf{BDR}}),\mathcal{D}}_{\mathsf{A\text{-}NH},\mathcal{A}} \leq n_s^2 \cdot 2^{-|\mathsf{nonce}|} + n_s \cdot \left(n_u \cdot \mathsf{Adv}^{\mathsf{EUF\text{-}CMA}}_{\mathcal{S},\mathcal{B}_1} \right.
$$
$$
\left. + n_s \cdot \left(\mathsf{Adv}^{\mathsf{IND\text{-}CPA}}_{\mathsf{KEM},\mathcal{B}_2} + \mathsf{Adv}^{\mathsf{KDF\text{-}sec}}_{\mathsf{KDF},\mathcal{B}_3} + \mathsf{Adv}^{\mathsf{EUF\text{-}CMA}}_{\mathcal{M},\mathcal{B}_4} \right) \right),
$$

where n_s is the maximum number of sessions, n_u is the maximum number of users, and |nonce| is the bit-length of the nonces.

5   TLS 1.3

We now turn towards the second protocol for our exemplary breakdown resilience analysis, the Transport Layer Security (TLS) protocol in its latest version 1.3 [41]. Although not designed with breakdown resilience as a security goal in mind, the TLS 1.3 key exchange (or "handshake") achieves resilience against the breakdown of some of its cryptographic components, as we will see.

TLS 1.3 specifies four different handshake modes: a full Diffie–Hellman-based handshake (referred to as (EC)DHE mode), a resumption-style pre-shared key mode (PSK), a PSK mode combined with a Diffie–Hellman exchange (PSK-(EC)DHE), and a low-latency, zero round-trip (0-RTT) mode based on the PSK modes. Providing a full key exchange security analysis of these modes is beyond the scope of this work; for this we refer to prior analyses [7,20,21,24,25,28,29,35, 38] and also to [40] for a review of the standardization process. In our analysis, we focus on the full/(EC)DHE and PSK(-only) handshake modes, which suffice to demonstrate some essential breakdown-resilience properties of TLS 1.3.

Interestingly, despite sharing the same structure, the (EC)DHE and PSK modes differ in the provided breakdown resilience. More precisely, the (EC)DHE mode offers resilience against breakdown of the signature, MAC, and hash collision resistance, consistent with the high-level expectations from the protocol design. The PSK-only handshake in contrast does not provide the same resilience against a hash function breakdown; here, our analysis exhibits how seemingly minor technical design choices impact breakdown resilience.

The Protocol. The TLS 1.3 [41] handshake protocol is given in Appendix A. In the following, we focus on the PSK mode for space restrictions. We refer to the full version [15] for the description of the (EC)DHE handshake and our analysis that it achieves breakdown-resilient key secrecy for $\mathcal{F}_{\mathsf{BDR}} = \{(\mathsf{Hash}, \mathsf{STD\text{-}Coll\text{-}Res}), (\mathcal{S}, \mathsf{EUF\text{-}CMA}), (\mathsf{HMAC}, \mathsf{EUF\text{-}CMA})\}$ with forward secrecy.

In the PSK mode, client and server agree on a previously established shared secret via the `PreSharedKey` messages. This pre-shared secret PSK enters the HKDF-based key derivation prior to deriving the handshake secret HS. Optionally, both sides can also send Diffie–Hellman shares (within `KeyShare` messages) to be included in the key derivation; this variant constitutes the PSK-(EC)DHE mode. Authentication relies on the pre-shared key only through the `Finished` messages, i.e., no certificates and signatures are exchanged.

Breakdown Resilience. The PSK(-only) handshake's security is based solely on hash collision resistance and pseudorandomness of HKDF. We cannot hope for breakdown resilience of the latter, as it immediately voids key secrecy. However, and in contrast to the (EC)DHE handshake, the PSK-only mode in general is also not resilient against certain collisions in the hash function Hash. This is due to the deterministic key derivation from PSK using *hashed* transcripts, where potentially the *same* pre-shared key PSK is used across multiple sessions.

Consider an adversary $\mathcal{A}$ that, after running an honest protocol for the test session, can find (suitable) collisions in Hash (modeled through the Break oracle). It can then run another session with an honest client, picking the server nonce in a way that the transcript of this session collides with that of the test session. To be precise, the adversary would target a collision in $H_1 = $ Hash(CH∥SH) which ensures that the deterministically derived keys and MACs are the same in the test session and the colliding client's session.[2]

As a consequence, the TLS 1.3 PSK-only handshake is not breakdown resilient wrt. any of its core cryptographic components, although the described hash collision is restricted through structure and the limited lifetime of pre-shared keys. Still, our model enables insights into such composed components' breakdown resilience and that including ephemeral Diffie–Hellman shares (in the PSK-(EC)DHE handshake) not only provides forward secrecy but also can recover breakdown resilience, as we discuss further in the full version [15].

6   Strong Breakdown Resilience and Hybrid Protocols

For hybrid constructions that specifically aim to withstand cryptographic breakdowns of individual components, we demand an even stronger version of resilience: In such protocols, not only past sessions, but also ongoing and future sessions should remain secure in case a subset of the protocol's components $\mathcal{F}_{BDR}$ breaks down. We term the resulting notion *strong* breakdown resilience. Note that in contrast to the regular notion of breakdown resilience from Sect. 3, $\mathcal{F}_{BDR}$ for strong breakdown resilience will necessarily be restricted to those cryptographic components for which the (hybrid) protocol ensures some redundancy in order to maintain ongoing security.

In order to extend the basic model from Sect. 3 to encompass security for future and ongoing sessions, a couple of minor changes are necessary. Going back to Fig. 1, this renders all depicted Test scenarios admissible for *strong* breakdown resilience (i.e., especially Scenarios 3, 4, and 5).

---

[2] In terms of our model, the Break oracle would on input a prefix b and hash value h provide the adversary with a random preimage d such that Hash($a||b||c||d||e$) = h, where a, c, e are fixed strings (in this case matching the CH and SH message structure). Note this exemplifies a restricted, weaker Break oracle than the conservatively strong collision oracle from Table 3 we used for proving (EC)DHE breakdown resilience.

Send *Query*. The previously introduced modified $\mathsf{Send}_{\mathsf{BDR}}$ made sure that ongoing and future sessions at the time of breakdown were set to revealed and could thus not be tested by the adversary. This is no longer true for strong breakdown resilience, so we employ the original, unmodified Send query (cf. Sect. 2).

Contributive Identifiers and State of Execution at Breakdown. Similarly, contributive identifiers (cid) that were needed to identify cases that are not testable (cf. Fig. 1) become superfluous and any mention of them in the security definitions of BDR-Match security and BDR key secrecy (Definitions 1 and 2) are omitted. Finally, we no longer need to record the execution state at breakdown $\mathsf{st}_{\mathsf{exec}}^{\mathsf{bd}}$.

Break *Oracle*. To model the Break oracle for hybrid protocols we introduce a $(\mathsf{KE}, \mathsf{BR})$ entry for breaking BR key secrecy (cf. [15, Table 1]). When calling the Break oracle, all the session keys of accepted sessions are disclosed to the adversary and the oracle proceeds as specified before in the model.

In the full version [15], we show how our notion of strong breakdown resilience can capture the combiner-type security of an arbitrary hybrid key exchange construction, going beyond previously considered KEM-based combiners [10,30].

7   Conclusion

We presented the first AKE security model that allows to the impact of breakdowns of arbitrary cryptographic building blocks or hardness assumptions, extending the widely used Bellare–Rogaway model [6]. Our general security notion of *breakdown resilience* considers already completed sessions and, as we show, is achieved to different extends by two established real-world protocols, AUTH-NEWHOPE and TLS 1.3. A stronger variant furthermore allows to analyze hybrid key exchange designs providing security even for ongoing and future sessions.

We are confident that the presented formalization of breakdown resilience can be integrated into other models for authenticated key exchange, e.g. [18,27, 34,36], and possibly transferred to other classes of cryptographic protocols.

Acknowledgments. Felix Günther is supported in part by Research Fellowship grant GU 1859/1-1 of the DFG and National Science Foundation (NSF) grants CNS-1526801 and CNS-1717640. This work has been co-funded by the DFG as part of project S4 within the CRC 1119 CROSSING and as part of project D.2 within the RTG 2050 "Privacy and Trust for Mobile Users."

A   Auth-NewHope Protocol and TLS 1.3 Handshake Flow

The authenticated version of NewHope-Nist and the handshake flow of TLS 1.3 (in full/(EC)DHE, PSK, and PSK-(EC)DHE mode) are depicted in Fig. 4.

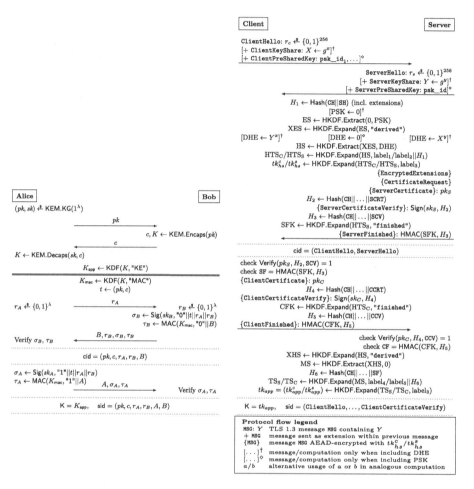

Fig. 4. The Auth-NewHope protocol with the IND-CPA-secure KEM KEM from NewHope-Nist above the double line and SIGMA-style authentication (left). The TLS 1.3 [41] handshake protocol in full/(EC)DHE, PSK, and PSK-(EC)DHE mode (right).

References

1. Adrian, D., et al.: Imperfect forward secrecy: how Diffie-Hellman fails in practice. In: ACM CCS 2015, pp. 5–17 (2015)
2. AlFardan, N.J., Bernstein, D.J., Paterson, K.G., Poettering, B., Schuldt, J.C.N.: On the security of RC4 in TLS. In: USENIX Security 2013, pp. 305–320 (2013)
3. Alkim, E., et al.: NewHope: algorithm specifications and supporting documentation (2019). https://csrc.nist.gov/CSRC/media/Projects/Post-Quantum-Cryptography/documents/round-2/submissions/NewHope-Round2.zip. Accessed 24 Apr 2019
4. Alkim, E., Ducas, L., Pöppelmann, T., Schwabe, P.: NewHope without reconciliation. Cryptology ePrint Archive, Report 2016/1157 (2016). http://eprint.iacr.org/2016/1157
5. Alkim, E., Ducas, L., Pöppelmann, T., Schwabe, P.: Post-quantum key exchange - a new hope. In: USENIX Security 2016, pp. 327–343 (2016)
6. Bellare, M., Rogaway, P.: Entity authentication and key distribution. In: Stinson, D.R. (ed.) CRYPTO 1993. LNCS, vol. 773, pp. 232–249. Springer, Heidelberg (1994). https://doi.org/10.1007/3-540-48329-2_21
7. Bhargavan, K., Blanchet, B., Kobeissi, N.: Verified models and reference implementations for the TLS 1.3 standard candidate. In: 2017 IEEE Symposium on Security and Privacy, pp. 483–502 (2017)
8. Bhargavan, K., Brzuska, C., Fournet, C., Green, M., Kohlweiss, M., Zanella-Béguelin, S.: Downgrade resilience in key-exchange protocols. In: 2016 IEEE Symposium on Security and Privacy, pp. 506–525 (2016)
9. Bhargavan, K., Leurent, G.: Transcript collision attacks: breaking authentication in TLS, IKE and SSH. In: NDSS 2016 (2016)
10. Bindel, N., Brendel, J., Fischlin, M., Goncalves, B., Stebila, D.: Hybrid key encapsulation mechanisms and authenticated key exchange. In: Ding, J., Steinwandt, R. (eds.) PQCrypto 2019. LNCS, vol. 11505, pp. 206–226. Springer, Cham (2019). https://doi.org/10.1007/978-3-030-25510-7_12
11. Bos, J.W., et al.: Frodo: take off the ring! Practical, quantum-secure key exchange from LWE. In: ACM CCS 2016, pp. 1006–1018 (2016)
12. Bos, J.W., Costello, C., Naehrig, M., Stebila, D.: Post-quantum key exchange for the TLS protocol from the ring learning with errors problem. In: 2015 IEEE Symposium on Security and Privacy, pp. 553–570 (2015)
13. Bos, J.W., et al.: CRYSTALS - Kyber: a CCA-secure module-lattice-based KEM. In: IEEE EuroS&P 2018, pp. 353–367 (2018)
14. Braithwaite, M.: Google security blog: experimenting with post-quantum cryptography (2016). https://security.googleblog.com/2016/07/experimenting-with-post-quantum.html. Accessed 24 Apr 2019
15. Brendel, J., Fischlin, M., Günther, F.: Breakdown resilience of key exchange protocols: NewHope, TLS 1.3, and hybrids. Cryptology ePrint Archive, Report 2017/1252 (2019). https://eprint.iacr.org/2017/1252
16. Brzuska, C.: On the foundations of key exchange. Ph.D. thesis, Technische Universität Darmstadt, Darmstadt, Germany (2013). http://tuprints.ulb.tu-darmstadt.de/3414/
17. Brzuska, C., Fischlin, M., Warinschi, B., Williams, S.C.: Composability of Bellare-Rogaway key exchange protocols. In: ACM CCS 2011, pp. 51–62 (2011)
18. Canetti, R., Krawczyk, H.: Analysis of key-exchange protocols and their use for building secure channels. In: Pfitzmann, B. (ed.) EUROCRYPT 2001. LNCS, vol.

2045, pp. 453–474. Springer, Heidelberg (2001). https://doi.org/10.1007/3-540-44987-6_28

19. Cohn-Gordon, K., Cremers, C.J.F., Garratt, L.: On post-compromise security. In: IEEE CSF 2016, pp. 164–178 (2016)

20. Cremers, C., Horvat, M., Hoyland, J., Scott, S., van der Merwe, T.: A comprehensive symbolic analysis of TLS 1.3. In: ACM CCS 2017, pp. 1773–1788 (2017)

21. Cremers, C., Horvat, M., Scott, S., van der Merwe, T.: Automated analysis and verification of TLS 1.3: 0-RTT, resumption and delayed authentication. In: 2016 IEEE Symposium on Security and Privacy, pp. 470–485 (2016)

22. den Boer, B., Bosselaers, A.: Collisions for the compression function of MD5. In: Helleseth, T. (ed.) EUROCRYPT 1993. LNCS, vol. 765, pp. 293–304. Springer, Heidelberg (1994). https://doi.org/10.1007/3-540-48285-7_26

23. Diffie, W., Van Oorschot, P.C., Wiener, M.J.: Authentication and authenticated key exchanges. Des. Codes Cryptogr. **2**(2), 107–125 (1992)

24. Dowling, B., Fischlin, M., Günther, F., Stebila, D.: A cryptographic analysis of the TLS 1.3 handshake protocol candidates. In: ACM CCS 2015, pp. 1197–1210 (2015)

25. Dowling, B., Fischlin, M., Günther, F., Stebila, D.: A cryptographic analysis of the TLS 1.3 draft-10 full and pre-shared key handshake protocol. Cryptology ePrint Archive, Report 2016/081 (2016). http://eprint.iacr.org/2016/081

26. Dowling, B., Stebila, D.: Modelling ciphersuite and version negotiation in the TLS protocol. In: Foo, E., Stebila, D. (eds.) ACISP 2015. LNCS, vol. 9144, pp. 270–288. Springer, Cham (2015). https://doi.org/10.1007/978-3-319-19962-7_16

27. Fischlin, M., Günther, F.: Multi-stage key exchange and the case of Google's QUIC protocol. In: ACM CCS 2014, pp. 1193–1204 (2014)

28. Fischlin, M., Günther, F.: Replay attacks on zero round-trip time: the case of the TLS 1.3 handshake candidates. In: IEEE EuroS&P 2017, pp. 60–75 (2017)

29. Fischlin, M., Günther, F., Schmidt, B., Warinschi, B.: Key confirmation in key exchange: a formal treatment and implications for TLS 1.3. In: 2016 IEEE Symposium on Security and Privacy, pp. 452–469 (2016)

30. Giacon, F., Heuer, F., Poettering, B.: KEM combiners. In: Abdalla, M., Dahab, R. (eds.) PKC 2018. LNCS, vol. 10769, pp. 190–218. Springer, Cham (2018). https://doi.org/10.1007/978-3-319-76578-5_7

31. Giechaskiel, I., Cremers, C., Rasmussen, K.B.: On bitcoin security in the presence of broken cryptographic primitives. In: Askoxylakis, I., Ioannidis, S., Katsikas, S., Meadows, C. (eds.) ESORICS 2016. LNCS, vol. 9879, pp. 201–222. Springer, Cham (2016). https://doi.org/10.1007/978-3-319-45741-3_11

32. Günther, C.G.: An identity-based key-exchange protocol. In: Quisquater, J.-J., Vandewalle, J. (eds.) EUROCRYPT 1989. LNCS, vol. 434, pp. 29–37. Springer, Heidelberg (1990). https://doi.org/10.1007/3-540-46885-4_5

33. Gupta, S.S., Maitra, S., Paul, G., Sarkar, S.: (Non-)random sequences from (non-)random permutations - analysis of RC4 stream cipher. J. Cryptol. **27**(1), 67–108 (2014)

34. Jager, T., Kohlar, F., Schäge, S., Schwenk, J.: On the security of TLS-DHE in the standard model. In: Safavi-Naini, R., Canetti, R. (eds.) CRYPTO 2012. LNCS, vol. 7417, pp. 273–293. Springer, Heidelberg (2012). https://doi.org/10.1007/978-3-642-32009-5_17

35. Krawczyk, H.: A unilateral-to-mutual authentication compiler for key exchange (with applications to client authentication in TLS 1.3). In: ACM CCS 2016, pp. 1438–1450 (2016)

36. LaMacchia, B., Lauter, K., Mityagin, A.: Stronger security of authenticated key exchange. In: Susilo, W., Liu, J.K., Mu, Y. (eds.) ProvSec 2007. LNCS, vol. 4784, pp. 1–16. Springer, Heidelberg (2007). https://doi.org/10.1007/978-3-540-75670-5_1

37. Langley, A.: ImperialViolet: CECPQ2 (2018). https://www.imperialviolet.org/2018/12/12/cecpq2.html. Accessed 24 Apr 2019

38. Li, X., Xu, J., Zhang, Z., Feng, D., Hu, H.: Multiple handshakes security of TLS 1.3 candidates. In: 2016 IEEE Symposium on Security and Privacy, pp. 486–505 (2016)

39. NIST: Post-quantum cryptography standardization (2017). https://csrc.nist.gov/Projects/Post-Quantum-Cryptography/Post-Quantum-Cryptography-Standardization. Accessed 24 Apr 2019

40. Paterson, K.G., van der Merwe, T.: Reactive and proactive standardisation of TLS. In: Chen, L., McGrew, D., Mitchell, C. (eds.) SSR 2016. LNCS, vol. 10074, pp. 160–186. Springer, Cham (2016). https://doi.org/10.1007/978-3-319-49100-4_7

41. Rescorla, E.: The Transport Layer Security (TLS) Protocol Version 1.3. RFC 8446 (2018)

42. Stevens, M.: New collision attacks on SHA-1 based on optimal joint local-collision analysis. In: Johansson, T., Nguyen, P.Q. (eds.) EUROCRYPT 2013. LNCS, vol. 7881, pp. 245–261. Springer, Heidelberg (2013). https://doi.org/10.1007/978-3-642-38348-9_15

43. Stevens, M., Bursztein, E., Karpman, P., Albertini, A., Markov, Y.: The first collision for full SHA-1. In: Katz, J., Shacham, H. (eds.) CRYPTO 2017. LNCS, vol. 10401, pp. 570–596. Springer, Cham (2017). https://doi.org/10.1007/978-3-319-63688-7_19

44. Stevens, M., Karpman, P., Peyrin, T.: Freestart collision for full SHA-1. In: Fischlin, M., Coron, J.-S. (eds.) EUROCRYPT 2016. LNCS, vol. 9665, pp. 459–483. Springer, Heidelberg (2016). https://doi.org/10.1007/978-3-662-49890-3_18

45. Stevens, M., Lenstra, A., de Weger, B.: Chosen-prefix collisions for MD5 and colliding X.509 certificates for different identities. In: Naor, M. (ed.) EUROCRYPT 2007. LNCS, vol. 4515, pp. 1–22. Springer, Heidelberg (2007). https://doi.org/10.1007/978-3-540-72540-4_1

46. Wang, X., Yin, Y.L., Yu, H.: Finding collisions in the full SHA-1. In: Shoup, V. (ed.) CRYPTO 2005. LNCS, vol. 3621, pp. 17–36. Springer, Heidelberg (2005). https://doi.org/10.1007/11535218_2

47. Wang, X., Yu, H.: How to break MD5 and other hash functions. In: Cramer, R. (ed.) EUROCRYPT 2005. LNCS, vol. 3494, pp. 19–35. Springer, Heidelberg (2005). https://doi.org/10.1007/11426639_2

Web Security

The Risks of WebGL: Analysis, Evaluation and Detection

Alex Belkin[1]([✉]), Nethanel Gelernter[2], and Israel Cidon[1]

[1] Technion University, Israel Institute of Technology, Haifa, Israel
abelkin@campus.technion.ac.il
[2] The College of Management Academic Studies, Rishon LeZion, Israel

Abstract. WebGL is a browser feature that enables JavaScript-based control of the graphics processing unit (GPU) to render interactive 3D and 2D graphics, without the use of plug-ins. Exploiting WebGL for attacks will affect billions of users since browsers serve as the main interaction mechanism with the world wide web. This paper explores the potential threats derived from the recent move by browsers from WebGL 1.0 to the more powerful WebGL 2.0. We focus on the possible abuses of this feature in the context of distributed cryptocurrency mining. Our evaluation of the attacks also includes the practical aspects of successful attacks, such as stealthiness and user-experience. Considering the danger of WebGL abuse, as observed in the experiments, we designed and evaluated a proactive defense. We implemented a Chrome extension that proved itself effective in detecting and blocking WebGL. We demonstrate the major improvements of WebGL 2.0 and our results show that it is possible to use WebGL 2.0 in distributed attacks under real-world conditions. Although WebGL 2.0 shows similar hash rates as CPU-based techniques, WebGL 2.0 proved to be significantly harder to detect and has a lesser effect on user experience.

Keywords: WebGL · Distributed-attack · Crypto-mining · Web-browser · Security

1 Introduction

The rapid evolution of web technologies has delivered new possibilities to billions of users, while at the same time exposing them to new security threats. Browsers are an excellent example of this phenomenon. Their new features are being abused by malicious hackers to create attack vectors and efficiently launch attacks not previously considered a risk.

Some recent examples are the Cache API [38] and the ServiceWorker [48] features, which allow the launch of sophisticated timing side-channel attacks [41,47]. Another example is the Quota API, which can be used to extract the exact size of cross-site requests [24].

Browsers serve users as the main interaction mechanism with the world wide web. Therefore, security vulnerabilities or browser features that can be exploited

© Springer Nature Switzerland AG 2019
K. Sako et al. (Eds.): ESORICS 2019, LNCS 11736, pp. 545–564, 2019.
https://doi.org/10.1007/978-3-030-29962-0_26

for attacks will affect billions of users and close to two billion websites that are being accessed. Previous works by both Van Goethem, Gerlernter [24,41,47], and many others [23,35] offer examples of methods that exploit browser features to attack users. Other browser features, such as web-workers or web-sockets, have been used to effectively launch distributed denial-of-service attacks on websites [21,34,43].

This paper explores the risks posed to web users by WebGL 2.0 [19]. Web Graphics Library (WebGL) is a JavaScript API that uses the graphics processing unit (GPU) to render interactive 3D and 2D graphics within any compatible web browser, without the use of plug-ins [40]. WebGL allows users to communicate directly with the graphics hardware. It comes with its own programming language called GLSL. GLSL allows anyone to control the computational power of the GPU, using it as they wish.

Initially, GPUs were designed to accelerate the creation of images intended for output to a display device. However, their highly parallel structure makes them more efficient than general-purpose CPUs for algorithms that process large blocks of data in parallel. This made GPUs rise to prominence in the fields of crypto-mining, deep-learning, and more.

Controlling the GPU via the browser has introduced several new opportunities for attackers. For example, GPUs are used to efficiently break hashes [10] or for Bitcoin mining [46]. The ability to abuse the previous version of this API has already been examined by researchers. Fortunately, WebGL 1.0 is quite limited and does not support 32-bit integers or bitwise operators [18]. This makes it difficult to implement algorithms that efficiently calculate MD5 hashes, and much harder to implement more complex hashing algorithms such as SHA-2. Marc Blanchou's presentation at Black Hat Europe [12] showed that these limitations make the abuse of WebGL 1.0 ineffective, even compared to more naive implementations in JavaScript that use the CPU.

WebGL 2.0 was recently integrated into the popular browsers Google Chrome and Mozilla Firefox. WebGL's new features (e.g., support for 32-bit integers) establish the need to reevaluate the risks posed by this API. Due to the expected danger, it was also essential to develop countermeasures that can detect malicious WebGL 2.0 code and block it. This is a challenge that has not been studied before.

A few months into the research, the crypto-currency market began its rapid growth, and our research on the abuse of browsers for hash cracking became a reality. Coinhive [2] and other similar companies made it easy for every website owner to mine crypto-currency such as Monero [9], on the browsers of people who visit their page. As a result, the browsers of hundreds of millions of web users were abused to mine crypto-currency. In most cases, it was done without the permission or the knowledge of the users [16]. This phenomenon encouraged researchers [26,32] to perform an in-depth investigation of the landscape and impact of in-browser crypto-currency mining.

Both Hong et al. [26] and Konoth et al. [32] show how prevalent and potentially profitable crypto-currency mining can be for attackers. They explored the distribution of the infected websites containing mining code and demonstrate that no type of website is safe. Both works emphasize the inadequacy of current defense mechanisms, which are based on blacklists, and each suggested their own innovative countermeasure. Konoth et al. [32] managed to identify as many as 20 different active crypto-currency mining campaigns in 0.18% of Alex's Top 1 Million websites.

Other researchers implemented a framework to allow persistent and stealthy bot operation through web browsers without the need to install any software on the client side called MarioNet [42]. The effectiveness of MarioNet is demonstrated by designing a large set of successful attack scenarios where the user's system resources are abused to perform malicious actions including DDoS attacks to remote targets, cryptojacking, malicious/illegal data hosting, and darknet deployment. At this point, we decided to research and examine the consequences of WebGL 2.0 abuse for distributed crypto-mining.

1.1 Contributions

The main contributions of this paper are the analysis and evaluation of the risks posed by WebGL 2.0 under real-world conditions, and a prevention method to WebGL 2.0 attacks. To the best of our knowledge this is the first work to analyze the risks associated with WebGL 2.0. We addressed both the computational and user experience aspects of such potential exploits. Specifically, our research studies the following questions:

1. Can WebGL 2.0 be used to launch practical attacks?
2. How effective is WebGL 2.0 for distributed crypto-currency mining compared to CPU-based techniques?
3. What can be done to detect and block WebGL 2.0 attacks?

Evaluating WebGL 2.0 only in terms of the theoretical attacker scenario benefit is not enough. It is also crucial to include different aspects that affect the effectiveness of distributed attacks under real-world conditions, such as user experience and stealthiness. Even if we manage to show a high performance attack under lab conditions, it isn't worth much to the attacker if the user can sense or even detect our attack. We implemented a distributed attack, which was used in several experiments on numerous users, to test all the necessary aspects of a distributed attack. Our results show that when it comes to performance, WebGL 2.0 and Coinhive show approximately the same hash rate as shown in Fig. 1. However, for distributed attack aspects, our results in Sect. 5 demonstrate that WebGL 2.0 is much harder to detect and has a lesser effect on user experience compared to CPU miner. Shown in Fig. 2 and the results of Experiment 3, this proves that WebGL 2.0 miner is more suited to cryptocurrency mining distributed attacks than CPU miner.

We further implemented and tested a means to detect such an attack. As shown in the Sect. 6, we implemented a Chrome extension to serve as a means for detecting and blocking the use of WebGL. We performed an experiment with numerous participants over an extended period of time to test the extension's efficiency and collect statistics about the use of WebGL in websites. Our results show that our extension is efficient in preventing WebGL abuse and that WebGL is relatively rare in websites.

Furthermore, we additionally explored [11] the issue of password cracking using WebGL 1.0 and WebGL 2.0, and introduced Litecoin cryptocurrency mining using WebGL 2.0, but omitted it here as of space limitations.

Our findings are important and relevant to the Web community, mainly because the attacks studied in this paper have already been launched in different ways in the wild.

1.2   Paper Organization

Section 2 offers relevant background material about hash cracking, browser-based attacks, and the difference between GPU and CPU implementations. Section 3 discusses related work. Section 4 analyzes the abuse of WebGL 2.0 for cryptocurrency mining. The analysis is done from the perspective of a single victim and compares similar implementations using CPU. Section 5 evaluates the abuse of WebGL 2.0 in a distributed attack under real-world conditions. Section 6 suggests and evaluates a means of defense and Sect. 7 concludes.

2   Background and Motivation

The following section briefly explains concepts that will help the reader acquire a deeper understanding of the issues addressed in this paper. The section reviews hash cracking, browser-based distributed attacks, and the key differences between hash cracking implementation in WebGL and CPU.

2.1   Hash Cracking

This work addresses the challenge of hash cracking in the scope of cryptocurrency mining. In cryptocurrency mining, hash cracking is needed to ensure the authenticity of the information and to update the blockchain with the transaction [13]. Each time a cryptocurrency transaction is made, the cryptocurrency miners must solve complicated mathematical problems using cryptographic hash functions; these functions are associated with a block containing the transaction data. The mining process validates the calculated hashes on incremental values, called nonce, which are added to the given block data. The hash output must match a certain criterion: it needs to be less than the cryptocurrency's current target value. The current target value is also represented by the cryptocurrency's difficulty. Cryptocurrency difficulty is a measure of how long would it take at a given hash rate to find a block that matches the current target. Higher difficulty means a lower target value. The difficulty increases over time and varies between cryptocurrencies. Mining also involves competing with other cryptocurrency miners. Only the first one to crack the hash is rewarded with small amounts of cryptocurrency.

Browser-based CPU hash crackers written in JavaScript are generally slower than native CPU hash crackers due to their implementation and the browser's overhead. However, in recent years, a new browser-based CPU hash cracker was introduced: WebAssembly hash cracker. WebAssembly (Wasm) is a binary instruction format for a stack-based virtual machine. Wasm is designed as a portable target for the compilation of high-level languages like C/C++/Rust, enabling deployment on the web for client and server applications [50]. Wasm is designed to be faster to parse than JavaScript, as well as faster to execute, enabling very compact code representation [8]. This led to the introduction of Coinhive [2], the first browser-based CPU cryptocurrency miner. Coinhive uses Wasm to increase the hash rate and reduce JavaScript overhead. As a result, the Coinhive Wasm miner outperforms JavaScript miners. Coinhive [2] even states that they are able to reach about 65% of the performance of a native miner.

At the time of writing, we found no efficient browser-based GPU hash crackers.

2.2 Browser-Based Distributed Attacks

Distributed computing takes complex computing tasks, such as breaking cryptographic hashes, and splits them up into smaller parts. It then sends them out to many different personal computers or servers to be processed in parallel and return with results. This parallel processing of many smaller parts serves to significantly reduce the time needed to compute each given task. In general, distributed computing uses abundant compute resources, including many CPUs, high network bandwidth, and a diverse set of IP addresses.

A browser-based distributed attack allows the attacker to exploit web users to perform distributed tasks at will. The attack starts when a victim enters a web page that is controlled by the attacker. Opening a web page causes the web browser to initiate a series of background communication messages to fetch and display the requested page. This requires the client's web browser to download and run code that is served from the website on the client's device. The code that gets executed in the client's browser is assumed to be related to the functionality of the site being browsed. Technically, however, there is nothing stopping a website from serving arbitrary code that is not related to the browsing experience. With the absence of any protection, the client's web browser will blindly execute whatever code it downloads from the website.

At this point, a malicious code can run and gain full access to the web browser's API, which presents an increasingly powerful set of web technologies. The code is transient and difficult to detect once the user has navigated away from the website. This gives the attacker access to the compute resources of all concurrent website visitors at any given time. This amount of compute power is especially significant on high-traffic websites. An attacker can take advantage of these opportunities to execute large-scale browser-based distributed attacks. For example, these attacks may exploit the victims' compute resources to perform in-browser distributed hash cracking.

In [14], Dorsey explains how easy it is to execute distributed attacks on the browsers of unsuspecting users. With small effort and funds (spending less than

100$), he managed to reach thousands of victims, using paid advertisements as a means of distribution. This allowed him to freely run the code of his choosing in the clients' browsers. He then demonstrated the feasibility of CPU mining bots, distributed denial of service bots, torrent bots, and more.

2.3 Differences Between WebGL and CPU Implementations

As stated in the introduction, WebGL is designed to provide graphics operations, so it is naturally more difficult to implement a GPU hash cracker than a CPU hash cracker. WebGL 1.0 has several limitations that create difficulties in implementing hash crackers. These include inability to return values other than pixel color, lack of dynamic access to arrays, no debugging abilities, lack of bitwise operators, and no 32-bit support. All of these are needed to implement any cryptographic function. WebGL 2.0 makes the browser more vulnerable, as it introduces an improvement in its capabilities and relaxes some of the implementation limitations. It adds support for 32-bit integers and provides implementation for the majority of bitwise operators (not all); however, the rest of the limitations are still present.

GPUs are massively parallel, with hundreds (if not thousands) of stream processors that can simultaneously calculate hashes. Although a CPU core is much faster than a GPU core, the CPU usually limited to only four to eight cores. Hash cracking is highly suited to parallel computing due to the need to execute the same cryptographic functions on independent data sets. This gives GPUs a tremendous edge in hash cracking over CPUs. The open question we address is whether overcoming WebGL limitations would inflict a heavy cost on performance and eliminate the GPU hardware advantage over the CPU.

3   Related Work

Recently, a new phenomenon known as cryptojacking was discovered. This involves the in-browser mining of crypto-currencies, sometimes even after the browser window is closed, [16,29,31,37,44], and more. Specifically, this entails the mining of Monero [9] using Coinhive [2,15] or similar JavaScript CPU mining tools. Several papers in the past year performed a comprehensive analysis and in-depth study of cryptojacking [26,28,32,45]. These papers examine and analyze the phenomenon and its prevalence, each in its own unique way. To overcome the naive detection methods, modern mining tools commonly use evasion techniques such as limiting CPU usage, code obfuscation, and hiding the malicious code in popular third-party libraries. Both Hong et al. [26] and Konoth et al. [32] introduce countermeasures that enable the user to detect the different in-browser CPU mining tools more efficiently than the existing naive methods. Some websites may use such mining tools as an alternative to ad-based financing or offer premium content in exchange for mining. Other websites unknowingly fall victim to attacks that cause them to unwittingly serve mining code that uses the computer resources of their visitors.

Both Hong et al. [26] and Konoth et al. [32] show that detecting miners by means of blacklists, string patterns, or CPU throttling alone is an ineffective strategy, because of both false positives and false negatives. They thoroughly explored the mining attack structure, miner communication, and distribution methods of current in-browser CPU mining tools and provided important insights that allowed them to implement more efficient defense mechanisms. They prove that it is more effective to use their suggested behavioral-based detection methods by using either static analysis [32] or runtime profilers [26].

Both Eskandari et al. [45] and Rüth et al. [28] tried to investigate how often cryptojacking occurs in websites using two straightforward approaches. Eskandari et al. [45] queried the top million sites indexed by Zmap.io and PublicWWW.com to determine which websites contained coinhive.min.js script in their body. Over 30,000 websites were found. Rüth et al. [28] inspected the .com/.net/.org and Alexa Top 1M domains for mining code, and found mining code in a relatively low percentage 0.08% of the probed sites; however, this still accounts for more than 100,000 websites.

Konoth et al. [32] crawled Alexa's Top 1 Million websites for a week. Using static analysis, they managed to detect 1,735 websites containing cryptojacking code out of 991,513 websites in total, meaning 0.18%. On the other hand, Hong et al. [26] used their CMTracker detector, which has two runtime behaviour-based profilers, to collect 2,770 cryptojacking samples from 853,936 popular web pages, including 868 among the top 100K in Alexa's list, meaning 0.32%. In addition, according to their findings, 53.9% of these identified samples would have not been identified with current widely used detectors that are based on blacklists.

The increase use of crypto-currency as an alternative means of payment and the rise in performance and compute resources provided by in-browser coding, specifically with the use of WebAssembly, have made cryptojacking very appealing to criminals as a continuous source of income.

We predict that cryptojacking has the potential to be very profitable in high traffic websites, but the potential harm to users introduces ethical problems that must be considered. Some of the problems include higher energy bills, accelerated device degradation, slower system performance, and poor web experience. This forecast led researchers [26,32] to address the magnitude of the potential harm and investigate potential defense mechanisms against this type of CPU-based in-browser cryptojacking. Some researchers state that the trust model of web, which considers web publishers as trusted and allows them to execute code on the client-side without any restrictions is flawed and needs reconsideration [42]. Furthermore, it is essential to explore other means of in-browser cryptojacking that may attract attackers, alongside effective defense mechanisms where necessary. This increases the importance of our WebGL research.

4 Cryptocurrency Mining Attack

The rising popularity of both purchasing and mining cryptocurrency, caused a significant growth of the mining community and the introduction of new cryptocurrencies. This section introduces the Monero [9] cryptocurrency which we experimented with. We evaluated the effectiveness of WebGL in distributed Monero cryptocurrency mining and compared it to the JavaScript CPU miner, Coinhive [2].

As noted in Sect. 5.1, we wanted to compare the miner part of the cryptocurrency mining attack. We do not address the performance of other aspects in distributed cryptocurrency mining, such as mining pools, server side, databases, and more. For these elements we used commercial tools to which we added our WebGL miner; we only measured the mining performance.

4.1   Monero

Recently, a new type of cryptocurrency mining was introduced: CPU mining using JavaScript-based miners [16]. These JavaScript mining tools can be injected into popular websites as a source of income, at the expense of users' resources. The most common cryptocurrency mined using these web browser mining tools was Monero [9]. Monero experienced rapid growth in market capitalization and transaction volume during the year 2016. This was partly due to its adoption by the major darknet market AlphaBay, which was later closed down in mid-2017 [20,30].

Monero's proof of work, the process that must be done to ensure a block is valid before it is added to the blockchain, is based on the underlying CryptoNote protocol [3], called CryptoNight [17]. Unlike other cryptocurrencies that are derivatives of Bitcoin, the CryptoNight proof-of-work hash algorithm is a memory-intense function. Monero's proof-of-work algorithm is designed to be inefficiently computable on GPU, FPGA, and ASIC architectures, which makes it ideal for mining on CPUs. Therefore, the two main features of the algorithm that challenge our WebGL implementation are:

- CryptoNight uses large fast memory to work on 2 MB (L2 cache size), which requires a lot of silicon. This is far more than what is needed by the SHA-256 circuitry used for Bitcoin, and other similar cryptocurrency mining algorithms.
- CryptoNight is based on AES (Advanced Encryption Standards, a cryptographic cipher applied by the majority of organizations) [22] and was designed to take advantage of the AES-NI instruction set [36], which uses existing hardware circuitry on modern x86_64 CPUs to speed up AES operations.

The following section describes the challenges presented in implementing the CryptoNight hashing algorithm in WebGL.

4.2   WebGL Monero Implementation Challenges

Implementing cryptocurrency mining on WebGL 1.0 has proven to be inefficient. The performance cost is too high since the use of bitwise operators and 32-bit variables (which we implemented ourselves) is significantly greater compared to the MD5 hashing algorithm. Therefore, we evaluated cryptocurrency mining experiments only with WebGL 2.0.

After the initialization of an AES key from the input using the Keccak hashing algorithm [4], the CryptoNight algorithm consists of three main steps: initializing a 2 MB scratch pad, executing a memory-hard loop, and finalizing the hash output. Each step presents different implementation challenges.

WebGL's Memory Limit. WebGL is unable to allocate a consecutive 2 MB memory array to be used as a scratch pad for the first step. We could split the array into smaller chunks, but it would significantly affect the algorithm's performance.

Potentially Long Runtime. After initializing the scratch pad, a memory-hard loop of 524288 iterations on non-consecutive array elements is performed; this can take a significant amount of time. WebGL calls are done in the main UI thread, so we want to minimize the time it takes for a WebGL call to return. Long periods would cause the users to feel the page was unresponsive or even lead to a context-lost event for WebGL.

Large Shader Code. For the CryptoNight output, a hash function is randomly chosen out of four possibilities and applied on the state resulting from the previous steps. The resulting hash is the output of CryptoNight's algorithm. This step presents us with the new challenge of implementing all four possible hash functions: Blake [33], Groestl [25], JH [27], and Skein [7]. This would result in a major increase of the shader code size.

Finally, as we stated before, GPUs are all about parallelism. We needed to make the CryptoNight algorithm parallel, despite the fact that there is no natural way to share data between shader threads.

The question remains whether overcoming the challenges in implementing the CryptoNight algorithm on WebGL would result in a severe cost in performance and make WebGL unusable for Monero mining.

4.3   Experiment 1: Cryptomining Performance and User Experience

We overcame the major challenges presented in each step of the CryptoNight algorithm by using data textures, dividing the data efficiently, and moving some of the large code but non-intensive calculations to the CPU side. After implementing Monero's algorithm in WebGL 2.0, we can proceed to evaluating the major aspects of the Monero mining attack.

In our experiment, we compared our WebGL 2.0 miner to the Coinhive browser-based CPU miner. The results compared the performance, user experience, and hardware load locally on our computer.

Evaluation Setup. Intel i5 6600K @3.5 GHz, 2X4 GB @2400 MHz, GeForce GTX1080, Chrome Canary 64.0.3282.

We tested different parameters to determine how the GPU and CPU load are affected. This allowed us to find the best trade-off values for a cryptocurrency mining attack. To evaluate the proposed implementation techniques, we devised an experiment to compare the results of WebGL 2.0 and CPU-based techniques. We tested several parameters for both WebGL 2.0 and Coinhive Monero miners. For the WebGL 2.0 miner our parameters were: number of threads and time between draws. Shorter times between draw calls means a higher hash rate, but it also leads to a higher GPU load. WebGL 2.0 did not allow us to choose more than 32 threads.

For the CPU miner, we controlled the number of HTML workers [39] in Coinhive. We ran each parameter combination of the GPU and CPU miners in turn for the duration of two minutes. During each of the combinations, we measured the hash rate and the load on the GPU or CPU, accordingly.

Goal: Find the best trade-off evaluation parameters and compare the effectiveness of Monero cryptocurrency mining using WebGL 2.0 and CPU techniques.

Process: We ran each of the proposed techniques and parameters in turn for a duration of two minutes while the user continued using the web-browser and other programs to simulate practical conditions. We then compared the hash rate achieved by each of the techniques and checked with the user when they felt any effect on their usual experience.

Results: The best trade-off parameters for the evaluation were the ones that gave us the highest hash rate, while still not affecting the user experience.

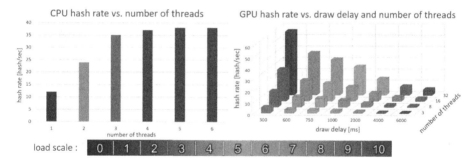

Fig. 1. Cryptomining - Experiment 1 Results. Each column in both graphs presents the hash rate achieved and it's corresponding parameter. Each column is colored according to the measured percentage load. (Color figure online)

We can see that the best trade-off results would be achieved if we limit Coinhive to using 2 threads, which leads to about 60% CPU usage. For the WebGL 2.0 miner, the best performance was achieved using 32 threads with a 1 s draw delay, resulting in 50% GPU usage. Using these best trade-off parameters, we reached a hash rate of 25 hashes/s in WebGL and 24 hashes/s in Coinhive. We observed that the WebGL miner is just as fast as the Coinhive miner. We did not detect any impact on the user experience when we evaluated performance on a single user's machine.

5   Evaluating the Distributed Attack

The previous section analyzed the exploit of WebGL 2.0 from the narrow perspective of single user. An attacker who aims to abuse WebGL for cryptocurrency mining, must launch the attack on many web users. This section analyzes the practical aspects of distributing these attacks.

In Sect. 5.1 we introduce cryptocurrency mining distributed attacks and our implementation. Section 5.2 discusses different aspects of distribution on a large scale and how we handled them.

In Sect. 5.4 the experiment evaluates the user experience of the attack using our WebGL miner and Coinhive with specific parameters. Section 5.5 describes our experiment to check the stealthiness of the attack. We wanted to examine whether users could locate the attack if they are aware it is running on their computer. Each of the experiments focuses on a different aspect of distributed cryptocurrency mining attacks, while providing additional data about the mining hash rate.

5.1   Implementing the Distributed Attack

Similar to what we introduced in Sect. 2, the goal of distributed attacks for cryptocurrency mining is to find input data for which, after applying the appropriate hashing function, the result matches the attacker's desired criterion: it needs to be less than the chosen cryptocurrency's current target value. This would give the mining reward to the attacker based on work done using the victims' resources. The attack is performed by dividing the data search among as many clients as possible.

The process of distributed hash cracking attacks on the victim's browser works as follows:

1. Malicious code reaches a victim as per the distribution methods described in Sect. 5.2
2. Attacker's code in the victim's browser sends a message to the attack server asking for a target and data range
3. The code calculates the appropriate hash function on the data range using the victim's resources
4. The code compares the crypto hash function's output to the desired target value
5. The results are posted from the victim's browser to the attack server
6. The server sends a new target and data range to run on the victim's browser
7. The process returns to Step 3 until there are no calculations to be done for the attacker

In addition to the attack process on the victims' side as described above, the cryptocurrency mining attack involves several additional elements that an attacker needs to address. Cryptocurrency mining starts by creating a new mining pool or joining an existing one. The mining pool is a group of cooperating miners who agree to share block rewards in proportion to the mining hash power they contribute. After the server has a working mining pool, it is ready to send mining tasks to its member clients.

Cryptocurrency mining is a race to find the corresponding hash, so time is of essence. Performance and speed play a vital part in the success of cryptocurrency mining. Even if we are behind the competitors by just a fraction from posting the correct hash, this will mean we miss out on the mining reward. In a distributed cryptocurrency mining attack, the server can divide the data range between its cooperating miners and increase the chances of finding a match to the transaction hash. The potential reward increases with the computational speed.

In the following experiments we evaluated Step 3 of the distributed hash cracking process (described above) using WebGL calculations. We show the effectiveness of WebGL in mining Monero cryptocurrency as compared to an equivalent CPU hasher. This should prove that WebGL can handle mining cryptocurrency that is of significant relevance today.

5.2   Large Scale Distribution Aspects

In this section we describe the different issues an attacker needs to consider before launching a large-scale distributed attack, and how we resolved them for our evaluations.

The browser's GPU can be abused by an attacker to conduct efficient distributed crypto-currency mining. To start spreading the attack, the attacker just needs to somehow inject their JavaScript code into a website that will reach as many users as possible. An attacker can achieve this through several methods, depending on her technical knowledge and resources:

- Come to an arrangement with websites to insert attacker code, for example, by sharing earnings
- Pay an ad company to pop ads containing attacker's code [14], this can be done with or without the ad company's knowledge
- Inject attacker code maliciously into websites
- Come to an arrangement with extension companies, such as AdBlock [1]
- Develop a popular website to lure victims

An attacker who wishes to launch such an attack on many web users for an extended period of time, must consider additional aspects of the attack:

1. *Stealthiness.* The attack must be conducted without arousing the user's suspicion. If the user feels any impact on his browsing experience, he may close the website or even contact the website's owner. This can lead to detection and prevent the attack from running for a prolonged period of time.
2. *Management.* Assuming thousands of browsers run the attack for different periods of time, it is necessary to manage them all to maximize the profit. Duplicate runs need to be avoided because they waste valuable computing power. Moreover, there is a need to keep track of users going offline to prevent computations from being skipped. To accomplish this, the attacker needs an efficient and synchronous control server.

5.3   Implementing Distributed Attack Experiments

In our experiments, we didn't need any of the distribution methods mentioned above because we had volunteers who knowingly entered websites that contained our attacking code.

In Sect. 4, for CPU mining experiments we used Coinhive, which handled the management of all the users. It also enabled some degree of stealthiness by setting the CPU usage limit to avoid detection and by the use of WASM, which makes it difficult to find the mining code.

For experimental purposes only, we implemented our own naive WebGL mining server to handle our user scale. Then we installed a NodeJS server [6] that served mining jobs to each of the clients. We used a MongoDB [5] to keep track of ongoing work and store the target hashes. To keep things simple and isolate our WebGL miner, we didn't connect it to any active Monero mining pools.

For the client side, we had an iframe with obfuscated code; this received the WebGL mining code from our server and contributed greatly to our miner's stealthiness. We also limited the WebGL performance, using the best trade-off parameters observed in Experiment 2 in Sect. 4.3 to prevent high GPU usage, with a minimal effect on the user experience.

As stated in Sect. 5.1, we only planned to evaluate the effectiveness and performance of Step 3 of the in-browser attack process. Consequently, we used commercial tools for the other steps to narrow our measurements to the achieved hash rate and user experience.

5.4   Experiment 2: Distributed Cryptocurrency Mining Performance and User Experience

The following distributed experiment extended the previous one described in Sect. 4.3 to test several chosen best trade-off parameters on a larger scale. Our GPU was relatively high end and to see how well we could perform on weaker GPUs, we also used some of the parameters that showed only 30% load on our GPU. This enabled us to show the relevance of our local results to a wider range of GPUs and CPUs. Similar to previous experiments, we ran each combination in turn for two minutes. During each of the combinations, the user was asked to state whether he felt any effect on his computer's performance.

Goal: Check whether the user notices the effect of a cryptocurrency mining process running in the background. Further compare the effectiveness of distributed cryptocurrency mining using WebGL 2.0 and CPU techniques.

Methodology and Ethics: The experiment was carried out with 100 volunteers. All the volunteers were paid to cover their expenses (primarily electricity), signed a consent form, and used their own computers to simulate a more realistic scenario. Mining can result in high electricity use and even lead to physical damage to less suitable devices (overheating cellphones for instance), so we only ran the experiment on personal computers. To avoid unintentional bias by participants and/or staff, the experiment was 'double blinded'. The users were assigned randomly to one of two sets, (*CPU mining* or *GPU mining*), without either the user of the staff being aware of the assignment. We didn't collect any statistics or personal information from the volunteers so there were no privacy issues.

Process: Users were asked to visit the website that contained our cryptocurrency mining logic and leave it open to run in the background. The users were then instructed to continue using the web-browser and other programs to simulate practical conditions for the duration of 10 min, and write down the times when they felt any influence on their browser's performance. There were three possible answers: (1) Significant effect. (2) Minor effect. (3) No effect. We then randomly assigned to each visitor one of the two mining options: *CPU mining* or *GPU mining*. For *CPU mining* users, we ran Coinhive Wasm miner in the background. For *GPU mining* users, we ran our WebGL miner in the background.

For each visitor, we saved the hash rate we managed to achieve with each parameter combination, and used it to compare between GPU and CPU mining hash rates.

Results: We observed that most of the users assigned to a CPU miner did notice some effect on their browsing experience.

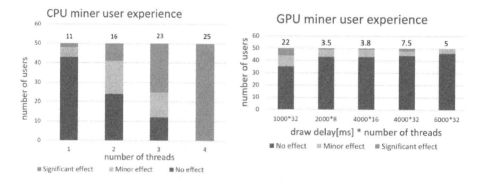

Fig. 2. Distributed Cryptomining - Experiment 2 Results. The results show the degree to which users felt their computer's performance was affected, if at all. Above each column is the average hash rate [hash/s].

A substantial number of users have CPU usage monitoring tools that allowed them to immediately notice the browser's high CPU use. Moreover, some of the users were simultaneously running CPU intensive tasks in the background, which resulted in a significant deterioration of their computer's performance.

On the other hand, only a few users out of the GPU mining group reported noticing any effect. The common ground for the users that did feel some deterioration in the GPU group was that it occurred during the period with a high number of threads and a low draw delay. Moreover, their computers were relatively old and weak, in particular their GPU (more than five years old) or integrated GPUs.

We can see that the best trade-off parameters from the previous experiment gave us a high average hash rate of 22 hashes/s. However, almost a third of the users did notice some effect on their performance when using this parameter combination of 32 threads with a 1 s draw delay. Perhaps this could have been avoided if we had added adaptation logic in our WebGL 2.0 miner to make it reduce its performance on weaker machines. Until we do, in our opinion, it is better to choose less demanding parameters for a wide range attack.

The best trade-off values for WebGL 2.0 that give us the highest hash rate while having a minimal effect on user experience (about 10%) are: 32 threads and a 4 s draw delay. This gave us the average hash rate of 7.5 hashes/s for the WebGL 2.0 miner, while the Coinhive miner's average hash rate reached 16 hashes/s with 2 threads. That said, if we had demanded the same degree of minimal effect on user experience from the CPU miner, we would need to limit Coinhive to using only 1 thread, giving us an average hash rate of 11 hashes/s. We concluded that, although we could reach a higher hash rate in WebGL 2.0, we should compromise on lower values until we optimize the miner with adaptation logic.

This experiment demonstrated that the CPU hash rate is faster than the GPU hash rate in typical home machines. The results also indicate that the user experience is affected much more during CPU attacks than GPU attacks, making the CPU attacks easier to notice and detect. Sixty percent of the CPU miner group reported degraded performance compared to only 15% on average in the GPU miner group. This corroborates our view that the GPU can be used for effective attacks.

The fact that users notice an intensive task happening in the background doesn't necessarily mean that they can find it. We therefore conducted Experiment 4 to evaluate how difficult it would be for them to discover the attack in each miner type (CPU or GPU).

5.5   Experiment 3: Cryptocurrency Mining Stealthiness

Goal: Using the best trade-off evaluation parameters from previous experiments, observe whether the user can locate our cryptocurrency mining code running in the background.

Methodology and Ethics: Similar to the previous experiment to measure the user experience during cryptocurrency mining, the experiment was carried out with 80 volunteers. The volunteers were paid to cover their expenses (primarily electricity), signed a consent form, and used their own computers to simulate a realistic scenario. Mining could lead to physical damage on less suitable devices (overheating cellphones for instance), so we only ran the experiment on their personal computers. To avoid unintentional bias by participants and/or staff, the experiment was 'double blinded.' The users were randomly assigned to one of two sets, *CPU mining* or *GPU mining*, without either the user or staff aware of the assignment. The users were told that we are going to try to steal money from them and they need to find out how. We didn't collect any statistics or personal information from the visitors so there were no privacy issues.

Process: Each user received a list of five different websites. One of them contained our mining logic from the previous experiment; the other websites were 'clean'. The users were instructed to open all of the websites and leave them open in the background. We then randomly assigned each visitor to one of the two mining options: *CPU mining* or *GPU mining*. For *CPU mining* users, we ran Coinhive miner in the background. For *GPU mining* users, we ran our WebGL miner in the background. The users had to detect how we were stealing money from them i.e., find our CPU miner or GPU miner (depending what they were assigned).

There were four possible outcomes to this experiment: (1) Found *CPU mining*, (2) Found *GPU mining*, (3) Didn't find *CPU mining*, (4) Didn't find *GPU mining*.

Results: We observed that when it comes to stealthiness, GPU-based miners are much more effective and harder to detect than CPU-based miners. In the CPU group, 22 out of 40 users were able to find the CPU mining code, representing 55% of the users. Out of 40 users in the GPU group, only 1 user with a high level of technical knowledge in web research was able to find the GPU mining code, representing only 2.5%. Clearly, an attacker who launches a GPU-based attack on a large scale can be less concerned about detection. This strengthens the advantages of GPU miners as compared to CPU miners.

6   Defenses

Today, WebGL is still not widely used by most of the common websites. Most do not harness the power of the GPU to perform any of the rendering on their pages. Apparently, WebGL is primarily being used in online web games or websites containing 3D imaging. Therefore, in our opinion, the most effective way to prevent WebGL attacks would be using an extension that can disable WebGL when it's not supposed to be used.

Similar to web notifications [49], which can send alerts to the user outside the context of a web page, it would be preferable to have WebGL disabled by default. The user would have the option to enable WebGL for each website individually, if it is required.

We considered looking into other directions for defense mechanisms to prevent the abuse of WebGL. For example, trying to detect when the canvas color is posted to a remote server, since it should only be used locally for further rendering. Another example might detect the increased use of bitwise operations inside shader code, which typically characterizes crypto calculations. However, we felt that this would be an overkill and we should consider a more simple solution.

Until a solution is addressed by browsers, our extension could operate as follows:

- Detect that the current website is using WebGL.
- Alert the user that the current website is using WebGL.
- Ask the user if the current website is supposed to use WebGL in any way, say for: online gaming, 3D imaging, augmented reality, complex geometric rendering, and more.
- Allow the user to easily disable WebGL for the current website if none of the above conditions are met.

We could also maintain a blacklist of websites for which WebGL should be disabled by default and reduce the need for user interaction. This extension would enable us to minimize or even entirely eliminate WebGL attacks.

The following experiment allowed us to evaluate how well our extension works and to test our assumption that most of the websites don't use WebGL.

6.1   Experiment 4: Extension Effectiveness

Goal: Collect statistics about the use of WebGL in websites and test the extension's efficiency.

Methodology and Ethics: The experiment was carried out with 50 volunteers who installed the extension on their personal computers for 3 weeks. They were instructed to keep their usual browsing habits and not try to test the extension intentionally. They were also asked to report if they noticed anything unusual: slow browsing, pages not loading, crashes, and so forth. The extension reported back statistics on how many websites the user visited, how many of them contained WebGL code, and how many users chose to disable WebGL. We didn't collect any personal information on the visitors so there were no privacy issues.

Process: Each volunteer installed our extension and continued using their personal computer as usual. After three weeks, we instructed them to uninstall the extension and we reviewed the statistics collected by the extension.

Results: None of the volunteers reported any issues regarding the extension.

During our evaluation, the extension encountered 1345 websites in total. Surprisingly, during the experiment period our extension came across very few websites containing WebGL. The extension encountered only 6 websites containing WebGL, and only one instance where the user chose to disable WebGL. We conjecture that some (if not all) of these WebGL website entries derive from the users wanting to challenge our extension, although they were instructed against this.

These results strengthen our assumption that WebGL websites are only a small fraction of existing sites and most websites don't use WebGL rendering. For the average user, disabling WebGL by default in their browsers, probably will not have any effect on their browsing experience and can only enhance their security.

7 Conclusions

Most of the popular web browsers today support WebGL 2.0 and it is enabled by default for all websites. WebGL is completely integrated into the web standards of these web browsers, allowing GPU-accelerated usage of image processing and 3D effects as part of the web page canvas. WebGL allows browsers to communicate directly with graphics hardware, enabling code to harness the GPU's power. Currently, web browsers have not implemented any countermeasures or detection mechanisms for malicious WebGL code or the misuse of WebGL.

Our experiments show that WebGL 2.0 has introduced major improvements over WebGL 1.0 both in performance and in convenience. We also show that WebGL 2.0 can be used in practical attacks, such as exploitation for cryptocurrency mining, where in some cases it even outperforms CPU-based attacks. We demonstrated how difficult it is for a user to detect attacks that use GPU-based techniques compared to similar CPU-based techniques. WebGL allows an attacker to benefit financially by abusing users' resources without their knowledge. Our work also suggests a practical defense mechanism.

We hope this paper will call attention to the problem and help tackle this vulnerability. It is our intention to raise awareness regarding the risk posed by WebGL, and the need for this risk to be addressed by web browsers.

Acknowledgements. This research was supported by a grant from the Ministry of Science and Technology, Israel.

References

1. AdBlock Extension. https://getadblock.com/
2. Coinhive – Monero JavaScript Mining. https://coinhive.com/
3. CryptoNote - the next generation cryptocurrency. https://cryptonote.org/
4. Keccak Team. https://keccak.team/keccak.html
5. MongoDB. https://www.mongodb.com/
6. Node.js. https://nodejs.org
7. The Skein Hash Function Family. http://www.skein-hash.info/
8. WebAssembly High-Level Goals. https://github.com/WebAssembly/design/blob/master/HighLevelGoals.md
9. Home—Monero - secure, private, untraceable (2014). https://getmonero.org/
10. Alcantara, D.A., et al.: Real-time parallel hashing on the GPU. ACM Trans. Grap. (TOG) **28**(5), 154 (2009)
11. Belkin, A., Gelernter, N., Cidon, I.: The risks of WebGL: analysis, evaluation and detection (2019). https://arxiv.org/abs/1904.13071
12. Blanchou, M.: Harnessing GPUs building better browser based botnets. Black Hat Europe (2013)
13. Blockgeeks: What Is Hashing? Under the Hood of Blockchain (2017). https://blockgeeks.com/guides/what-is-hashing/
14. Dorsey, B.: Browser as botnet, or the coming war on your web browser (2018). https://medium.com/@brannondorsey/browser-as-botnet-or-the-coming-war-on-your-web-browser-be920c4f718

15. Krebs, B.: Who and What Is Coinhive? (2018). https://krebsonsecurity.com/2018/03/who-and-what-is-coinhive/
16. Check Point Research Team: Crypto Miners - The Silent CPU Killer of 2017 (2017). https://blog.checkpoint.com/2017/10/23/crypto-miners-the-silent-cpu-killer-of-2017
17. CryptoNote: CryptoNight Hash Function (2013). https://cryptonote.org/cns/cns008.txt
18. Jackson, D.: WebGL 1.0 specification, October 2014. https://www.khronos.org/registry/webgl/specs/1.0/
19. Jackson, D., Gilbert, J.: WebGL 2.0 specification, November 2016. https://www.khronos.org/registry/webgl/specs/latest/2.0/
20. Gómez, E.: Monero (XMR) on the rise following its inclusion in the darknet market AlphaBay (2016). https://themerkle.com/monero-xmr-on-the-rise-following-its-inclusion-in-the-darknet-market-alphabay/
21. Erkkilä, J.P.: Websocket security analysis, pp. 2–3. Aalto University School of Science (2012)
22. Federal Information Processing Standards Publication 197, NIST: Announcing the Advanced Encryption Standard (2001). http://nvlpubs.nist.gov/nistpubs/FIPS/NIST.FIPS.197.pdf
23. Gelernter, N., Grinstein, Y., Herzberg, A.: Cross-site framing attacks. In: Proceedings of the 31st Annual Computer Security Applications Conference, pp. 161–170. ACM (2015)
24. Goethem, T.V., Vanhoef, M., Piessens, F., Joosen, W.: Request and conquer: exposing cross-origin resource size. In: 25th USENIX Security Symposium (USENIX Security 2016), Austin, TX, USA, pp. 447–462, August 2016
25. Groestl Team: Hash function Groestl - SHA-3 candidate. http://www.groestl.info/
26. Hong, G., et al.: How you get shot in the back: a systematical study about cryptojacking in the real world (2018)
27. Wu, H.: Hash Function JH. http://www3.ntu.edu.sg/home/wuhj/research/jh/index.html
28. Rüth, J., Zimmermann, T., Wolsing, K., Hohlfeld, O.: Digging into browser-based crypto mining (2018)
29. Grunzweig, J.: The rise of the cryptocurrency miners (2018). https://researchcenter.paloaltonetworks.com/2018/06/unit42-rise-cryptocurrency-miners/
30. JP Buntinx: The early history of Monero in 500 words (2017). https://themerkle.com/the-early-history-of-monero-in-500-words/
31. Segura, J.: Persistent drive-by cryptomining coming to a browser near you (2017). https://blog.malwarebytes.com/cybercrime/2017/11/persistent-drive-by-cryptomining-coming-to-a-browser-near-you/
32. Konoth, R.K., et al.: MineSweeper: an in-depth look into drive-by cryptocurrency mining and its defense (2018)
33. Kudelski Security: The BLAKE2 cryptographic hash and message authentication code (2015). https://tools.ietf.org/html/rfc7693
34. Lam, V., Antonatos, S., Akritidis, P., Anagnostakis, K.G.: Puppetnets: misusing web browsers as a distributed attack infrastructure. In: Proceedings of the 13th ACM Conference on Computer and Communications Security, pp. 221–234. ACM (2006)
35. Lee, S., Kim, H., Kim, J.: Identifying cross-origin resource status using application cache. In: 22nd Annual Network and Distributed System Security Symposium, NDSS 2015 (2015)

36. Xu, L., Intel Corporation: Securing the enterprise with Intel AES-NI (2010). https://www.intel.com/content/dam/doc/white-paper/enterprise-security-aes-ni-white-paper.pdf

37. Nadeau, M.: What is cryptojacking? How to prevent, detect, and recover from it. https://www.csoonline.com/article/3253572/internet/what-is-cryptojacking-how-to-prevent-detect-and-recover-from-it.html

38. Mozilla Developer Network: Cache API. https://developer.mozilla.org/en-US/docs/Web/API/Cache

39. Mozilla Developer Network: Using web workers. https://developer.mozilla.org/en-US/docs/Web/API/Web_Workers_API/Using_web_workers

40. Mozilla Developer Network: WebGL. https://developer.mozilla.org/en-US/docs/Web/API/WebGL_API

41. Gelernter, N.: Timing attacks have never been so practical: advanced cross-site search attacks. Black Hat USA (2016)

42. Papadopoulos, P., Ilia, P., Polychronakis, M., Markatos, E.P., Ioannidis, S., Vasiliadis, G.: Master of web puppets: abusing web browsers for persistent and stealthy computation (2018)

43. Pellegrino, G., Rossow, C., Ryba, F.J., Schmidt, T.C., Wählisch, M.: Cashing out the great cannon? On browser-based DDoS attacks and economics. In: 9th USENIX Workshop on Offensive Technologies (WOOT 2015) (2015)

44. Hackett, R.: Popular google chrome extension caught mining cryptocurrency on thousands of computers (2018). http://fortune.com/2018/01/02/google-chrome-extension-cryptocurrency-mining-monero/

45. Eskandari, S., Leoutsarakos, A., Mursch, T., Clark, J.: A first look at browser-based cryptojacking (2018)

46. Taylor, M.B.: Bitcoin and the age of bespoke silicon. In: Proceedings of the 2013 International Conference on Compilers, Architectures and Synthesis for Embedded Systems, p. 16. IEEE Press (2013)

47. Van Goethem, T., Joosen, W., Nikiforakis, N.: The clock is still ticking: timing attacks in the modern web. In: Proceedings of the 22nd ACM SIGSAC Conference on Computer and Communications Security, pp. 1382–1393. ACM (2015)

48. W3C: Service Workers, June 2015. https://www.w3.org/TR/service-workers/

49. W3C: Web Notifications, October 2015. https://www.w3.org/TR/notifications/

50. WASM: WebAssembly. https://webassembly.org/

Mime Artist: Bypassing Whitelisting for the Web with JavaScript Mimicry Attacks

Stefanos Chaliasos[1], George Metaxopoulos[1], George Argyros[2], and Dimitris Mitropoulos[1(✉)]

[1] Department of Management Science and Technology,
Athens University of Economics and Business, Athens, Greece
stefanoshaliassos@gmail.com, george.metaxopoulos@gmail.com,
dimitro@aueb.gr
[2] Department of Computer Science, Columbia University, New York, USA
argyros@cs.columbia.edu

Abstract. Despite numerous efforts to mitigate Cross-Site Scripting (XSS) attacks, XSS remains one of the most prevalent threats to modern web applications. Recently, a number of novel XSS patterns, based on code-reuse and obfuscated payloads, were introduced to bypass different protection mechanisms such as sanitization frameworks, web application firewalls, and the Content Security Policy (CSP). Nevertheless, a class of script-whitelisting defenses that perform their checks inside the JavaScript engine of the browser, remains effective against these new patterns. We have evaluated the effectiveness of whitelisting mechanisms for the web by introducing "JavaScript mimicry attacks". The concept behind such attacks is to use slight transformations (i.e. changing the leaf values of the abstract syntax tree) of an application's benign scripts as attack vectors, for malicious purposes. Our proof-of-concept exploitations indicate that JavaScript mimicry can bypass script-whitelisting mechanisms affecting either users (e.g. cookie stealing) or applications (e.g. cryptocurrency miner hijacking). Furthermore, we have examined the applicability of such attacks at scale by performing two studies: one based on popular application frameworks (e.g. WordPress) and the other focusing on scripts coming from Alexa's top 20 websites. Finally, we have developed an automated method to help researchers and practitioners discover mimicry scripts in the wild. To do so, our method employs symbolic analysis based on a lightweight weakest precondition calculation.

Keywords: Cross-site Scripting · JavaScript · Whitelisting · Mimicry attacks

1 Introduction

For more than 15 years, Cross-site Scripting (XSS) has been one of the top security problems on the web. Researchers and practitioners have been either introducing different XSS variations [1–7], or developing approaches to defend against

K. Sako et al. (Eds.): ESORICS 2019, LNCS 11736, pp. 565–585, 2019.
https://doi.org/10.1007/978-3-030-29962-0_27

such attacks [8–13]. In practice, XSS attacks are usually addressed through the utilization of XSS sanitization frameworks [14,15] which encode and transform the input before further processing by the application to remove any potentially dangerous parts of the input, Web Application Firewalls (WAFs) [16] which block potentially malicious requests and the Content Security Policy (CSP) [17] which enforces specific policies for all scripts in a website.

Recently, a number of novel attacks have been introduced to bypass the aforementioned defenses. Specifically, Lekies et al. [1] have introduced a novel form of code-reuse attacks on the web by employing "script gadgets". In such an attack, a malicious user injects HTML markup into a website with an XSS vulnerability. Initially, such content will not be identified as an executable script code. However, throughout the application's lifetime, the various script gadgets of the website will transform the injected content into a valid XSS attack, thus bypassing a variety of defense mechanisms including WAFs, sanitizers and CSP. In addition, Heiderich et al. [18] employed encryption techniques to turn malicious scripts into obfuscated payloads that can bypass a number of defenses including sanitization frameworks.

Given the impact of such attacks, it is important to evaluate the effectiveness of other defenses against these patterns. In particular, a class of proposed defenses based on script-whitelisting [13,19–22] remains effective against the aforementioned attacks. A whitelisting mechanism that protects web applications from XSS attacks operates in two modes: First, it creates unique identifiers for every valid script during a training phase, that takes place before the application goes on-line. These identifiers combine elements that are extracted from either the script, e.g. a part of its Abstract Syntax Tree (AST), or its execution environment, such as the URL that triggered the execution. All identifiers are stored into a whitelist. Then, during production, only scripts that generate identifiers that exist in the whitelist will be identified and approved for execution.

The most recent whitelisting mechanisms [13,19,22] perform such checks at runtime, in the JavaScript engine of the browser. Thus, they can examine all scripts that reach a browser from alternative routes and can deal with various attacks such as Document Object Model (DOM)-based XSS [3]. The reason why whitelisting defenses can hinder code-reuse attacks on the web is that the payload of a script gadget per se, is not a script coming from the application. When this script reaches the JavaScript engine of the browser and an identifier is generated, this identifier will not be in the whitelist (even if identifiers for the different script gadgets may exist), thus the attack will be prevented. In the case of an obfuscated payload, whitelisting mechanisms will prevent the attack after its decryption on the client-side when it reaches the engine. At this point, the mechanisms will prevent its execution because they will not find a corresponding identifier.

Given that whitelisting mechanisms can potentially thwart advanced XSS attacks such as the above, it is significant to assess the security guarantees they offer. A remaining avenue of attacking a whitelisting defense is through a *mimicry attack*. The concept behind a mimicry attack is to employ a rather benign functionality of the target system to achieve a different outcome, that in turn serves a malicious purpose. Different kinds of mimicry have been introduced to circumvent intrusion detection systems [23] and the anomaly detection mechanisms of UNIX [24].

The authors of some of the aforementioned whitelisting mechanisms point out that mimicry attacks could affect their defenses [13,19]. However, they argue that such attacks are not applicable on a large-scale and downplay their potential impacts. This is mainly because there has not been an in-depth investigation of *JavaScript mimicry attacks* in terms of practicality and severity. In this paper, our goal is to answer the following question:

What is the impact of JavaScript mimicry attacks against whitelisting defenses for the Web?

To answer this question, we present the first large-scale study on JavaScript mimicry attacks and how they can bypass whitelisting mechanisms. In the context of our study, adversaries can either employ the benign scripts of an application exactly as they are, or craft and use script variations, i.e. scripts with the same AST but with different leaf values. Such variations can be used because the mechanisms usually do not take into account the whole AST of a script, especially if the script is dynamic and its values change frequently.

Our contributions can be summarized as follows:

1. We introduce JavaScript mimicry attacks, a variation of XSS attacks. Based on a formal attack model, we identify different attack patterns and show that they can have a major impact to either users or websites, e.g. cookie stealing and token modification (Sect. 3).
2. Through JavaScript mimicry, we evaluate the effectiveness of whitelisting for the web. Specifically, we point out the weaknesses that may allow mimicry attacks to circumvent such mechanisms and highlight the features that help them prevent some of the attacks. To do so, we examine the applicability of JavaScript mimicry on a large scale by examining hundreds of scripts coming from vulnerable versions of widespread application frameworks (e.g. WordPress) and Alexa's top 20 popular websites (Sect. 4).
3. We introduce an automatic method that can analyze a set of given scripts to identify potential attack vectors. Our method employs symbolic analysis based on a lightweight weakest precondition calculation [25] to decide if a mimicry script can be generated from these vectors. Throughout our evaluations, our approach did not produce any false alarms and caused a minimum of false negatives (Sect. 5).
4. We provide a number of recommendations derived from our study. The recommendations can be of use to researchers who intend to develop new and more robust whitelisting mechanisms for the web (Sect. 6).

2 Whitelisting for the Web

Whitelisting is based on a number of ideas introduced in the original intrusion detection framework [26,27]. We analyze these concepts and identify the key characteristics of each mechanism that implements this approach.

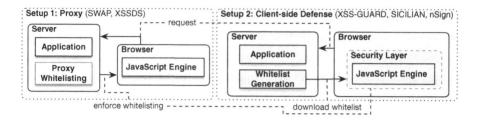

Fig. 1. The two different setups for performing whitelisting on the Web. Notably, setup 1 is vulnerable to DOM-based XSS attacks [3,27].

2.1   General Principles

To protect web applications from XSS attacks, a whitelisting mechanism operates in two phases. First, it "learns" all benign scripts, usually in the form of unique identifiers, during a training phase. This is done in different ways depending on the implementation. Then, only those scripts will be recognized and approved for execution during production.

The authors of whitelisting mechanisms for the web, follow two different setups illustrated in Fig. 1. In the first one, a server-side proxy is responsible for enforcing the whitelisting by examining the scripts included in the HTTP responses. XSSDS [21] and SWAP [20] are two typical mechanisms that follow this setup. The second setup involves a security layer that wraps the JavaScript engine of the browser. When a request is performed, this layer receives the identifiers from the server-side. Then, based on the identifiers it distinguishes benign scripts from malicious ones.

The major difference between the two setups is that the first one is vulnerable to DOM-based XSS attacks [3,27]. This is because in such an attack, the payload, hidden in a URL sent to the web user, never reaches the server. As a result, it is not contained in the HTTP response and the proxy will not prevent the attack. Note also that the first whitelisting mechanisms do not support dynamic scripts and only focus on the creation of identifiers for static ones. This significantly restricts the applicability of those mechanisms due to the dynamic nature of today's websites.

2.2   Recent Developments

The most recent whitelisting defenses follow setup 2 (see Fig. 1), are able to handle dynamic scripts, and can prevent a variety of XSS attacks including code-reuse attacks [1]. When they generate a script identifier, the mechanisms associate different elements that come either from the script or from its execution environment. There are three mechanisms that implement this method, namely: XSS-GUARD [22], SICILIAN [13], and nSign [19]. Table 1, illustrates the different elements that each mechanism takes into account.

XSS-GUARD [22] is not a recent approach per se, but it is the first that aimed to defend against XSS attacks on the client-side. During training, XSS-GUARD

Table 1. The different elements considered by whitelisting mechanisms that follow setup 2.

Mechanism	Script-related				Script-independent		
	AST parts	Literals	Static URL references	URLs assembled at runtime	URL triggering the execution	Script type	eval
XSS-GUARD [22]	✓	✗	✗	✗	✗	✗	✗
SICILIAN [13]	✓	✓*	✓	✗	✓	✗	✓
nSing [19]	✓	✗	✓	✓	✓	✓	✓

*SICILIAN includes literals (i.e. constant-strings and integer values) only for specific scripts that are specified by the developers. These scripts should not contain values that constantly change over time because that would lead to false positives.

extracts the AST of a script and associates it to the corresponding HTTP response. When in production, the mechanism examines again the AST of each script and prevents the ones that are not associated with a response. Apart from using the AST of a script, SICILIAN [13] looks for static URL references in the script to check for interactions with other websites. Furthermore, SICILIAN incorporates the URL that triggered the execution of the script as an element, and handles scripts that are passed as arguments to the **eval** function. nSign [19] considers similar elements with SICILIAN. However, it does not take into account the entire AST of a script, focusing more on specific keywords and their number of appearances. Also, it examines the type of the script (i.e. if it is inline or external) and the dynamic URLs that may be passed as arguments to the script at runtime.

As we will observe in the upcoming section, an attack vector arises because of the ways that the above mechanisms handle the AST of a script. Specifically, when XSS-GUARD compares ASTs during production mode, it also checks for an exact match of lexical entities. Nevertheless, constants are not compared literally. nSign does not consider such values too when it examines a script. On the other hand, SICILIAN includes constant strings and integer values as elements. However, in the case of dynamic scripts (that include frequently changing values), the mechanism lets developers exclude such elements.

3   JavaScript Mimicry Under Whitelisting

To evaluate whitelisting mechanisms we introduce JavaScript mimicry attacks. Specifically, we provide a formal model and present different attack patterns.

3.1   Attack Model

For any JavaScript expression, we consider the abstract syntax tree T of the expression and denote by literal any constant value in this expression, such as constant-strings or integer values. For an AST T_l, we denote by l the set of literals for T_l and we define $T_{l/\sigma}$ as the tree resulting by substituting the set of literals l with a set of literals σ. For example in Fig. 2 we display the AST for the expression

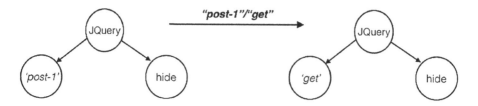

Fig. 2. (Left) AST for the expression `JQuery('post-1').hide()`. (Right) AST for the expression `JQuery('get').hide()` resulting by substituting the literal `post-1` with the literal `get`.

`JQuery('post-1').hide()`, with the corresponding literal "post-1" in the left subtree and the AST resulting by substituting the literal "post-1" with the literal "get".

The attacks we consider in this paper are constructed by replaying or manipulating valid scripts found in the context of vulnerable websites. More specifically, for a website, we consider the set $\mathcal{T}$ of ASTs for all expressions in the website. Specifically, this set contains ASTs coming from either inline and external scripts. Inline scripts refer to JavaScript code contained within HTML `<script>` `...</script>` tags, or code included in event handlers (e.g `onclick = "..."`). External scripts are typically referenced by a web page using the `src` attribute of the script tag and they are included in external documents. Then, we consider the set:

$$\mathcal{A} = \{T_{l/\sigma} : T_l \in \mathcal{T} \wedge \sigma \text{ is a substitution of literals for } l\}$$

The set $\mathcal{A}$ contains all ASTs of valid JavaScript expressions, which result by taking all expressions found in the target website and performing arbitrary changes in their literals. We call the set $\mathcal{A}$ to be the set of *mimicry expressions* for the target site. Notably, a script is included in $\mathcal{A}$ only if it is invoked by the application and thus, there is an identifier in the corresponding whitelist.

The goal of the attacker is to use the restricted set of statements in $\mathcal{A}$, in order to construct a target exploit program. The set of useful exploit programs can vary from application to application and is discussed in greater detail in the following section. Recall that our attack model is based on the fact that whitelisting mechanisms do not consider the entire AST of a script (see Subsect. 2.2) to deal with dynamic scripts that change frequently [13,21].

3.2 Attack Patterns

We have identified two basic attack patterns that can bypass whitelisting mechanisms: *script replay* and *tampering literals*. The concept behind script replay is to extract scripts from a website and inject them as they are into another potentially vulnerable part of the same site. When they run in the context of this part though, they will affect the functionality of the application in a different way. By tampering literals, attackers can exploit the fact that string-constants

```
$(document).ready(function(){
  $("button").click(function(){
    $.ajax( {
      url: "foo.com",
      success: function(result){
        // do something with the returned data.
    }});
  });
});
```

```
document.getElementById("example").innerHTML =

  "example_value"
```

```
ytcfg.set({

  'XSRF_TOKEN': 'token_value'
})
```

(a) Ajax request

(c) Setting a property

Fig. 3. Potential attack vectors.

and integer values are not considered as elements of the corresponding unique identifier generated by the defenses. Tampering literals may involve either (1) the simple modification of the web page's properties, or the utilization of (2) DOM elements and (3) Ajax requests.

In an *Ajax-based* mimicry attack we employ jQuery's `.ajax()` function to make asynchronous requests. A common example is presented in Fig. 3a where a script makes a request to a specific URL to retrieve some data. With a mimicry attack, we can execute this function with a different element and URL.

A DOM *manipulation* mimicry attack employs code constructs that manipulate the DOM elements of a page. As an example, consider an application that specifies the value of an HTML element named **example**, using the script of Fig. 3b. This allows us to modify the content of this element and display another element, by changing the **example_value**.

An attack that employs *property modification* targets scripts that explicitly define certain object properties, such as personalization specifications and tokens. For example, consider the script in Fig. 3c where the argument values of `ytcfg.set` are literals. Through mimicry, attackers can modify the value of XSRF_TOKEN thus changing the web page's CSRF token value.

4   Proof-of-Concept Exploitations

We searched for proof-of-concept exploitations in two different use cases. First, we analyzed vulnerable versions of well-known *application frameworks* and performed real-world exploitations. Then, we looked for potential attacks that can affect *Alexa's top 20 websites* assuming the existence of an arbitrary vulnerability (worst-case assumption).

In all cases, we assumed that the entity under attack employs one of the mechanisms discussed earlier (Subsect. 2.2). Our initial intention was to deploy the mechanisms and examine their effectiveness in practice. However, nsign was the only mechanism available [28] and consequently the only mechanism that we could install. The effectiveness of the other mechanisms was examined based on their design principles.

As we discovered, mimicry attacks can have different impacts. Table 2, illustrates the impact of each attack pattern on the aforementioned use cases. Key

Table 2. Attack patterns and their impacts in the different use cases.

Use case	Tampering literals			Replay scripts
	DOM manipulation	Ajax-based	Property modification	
Frameworks	HE, R, FL, MH	✗	CMH	HE, R, MH
Alexa top 20	HE, R, FL, AM	FL, CS, AM	TM, CD	CD, FL, R, HE

CS: Cookie Stealing, CD: Cookie Deletion, TM: Token Modification, AM: API Manipulation, R: Redirection, CMH: Cryptocurrency Miner Hijacking, HE: Hide Elements, MH: Message Handling, FL: Force Logout

impacts involve cookie stealing, cryptocurrency miner hijacking, API manipulation, message handling, token modification and cookie deletion. Notably, we did not manage to find valid Ajax-based attacks for any of the application frameworks that we examined. This is mainly because the applications mainly use submission forms instead of Ajax requests.

Below, we present one attack per pattern for brevity. We also present two additional exploitations in our Appendix A. Furthermore, we discuss how the attack can bypass these mechanisms and if it cannot, we highlight the design choices that led to the prevention. Table 3, summarizes which of the identified attack patterns can bypass each of the examined mechanisms. Note that the mechanisms that follow setup 1 can be easily bypassed because they cannot handle dynamic scripts (which we extensively use in our exploitations). Finally, notice that some of the mechanisms can be bypassed under certain circumstances. If this is the case, we describe these circumstances in detail.

4.1   Application Frameworks

We have examined popular frameworks such as WordPress, Joomla, and Moodle to highlight how mimicry attacks may affect multiple websites that are based on such frameworks. For instance, WordPress currently powers over 30% of the web [29] and Moodle is a prevalent CMS (Content Management System) framework for academic applications.

Methodology. Initially, we explored the lists of published XSS vulnerabilities for each framework (and their plug-ins), as reported by CVE [30]. In the case of WordPress we found more than 100 related reports (23 of them were reported since 2017). We also found 68 and 81 reports for Joomla and Moodle respectively.

Then we downloaded and installed different vulnerable versions of each framework. In addition, we examined vulnerable versions of popular WordPress plug-ins (e.g. the *Participants Database*, which is used in more than 320.000 installations).

Finally, we inspected all scripts used by each framework to identify potential attack vectors. Then, by using the selected scripts we performed real-world exploitations.

Table 3. Attacks that can bypass the mechanisms. In some cases the attacks are successful under specific circumstances, as we explain in our proof-of-concepts.

Approach	Mechanism	Mimicry attacks				DOM-XSS
		Tampering literals			Replay scripts	
		DOM manipulation	Ajax-based	Property modification		
Client-Side	XSS-GUARD [22]	✓	✓	✓	✓	✗
	SICILIAN [13]	✓	UC	✓	✓	✗
	nsing [19]	UC	UC	✓	✓	✗
Server-Side	XSSDS [21]	✓	✓	✓	✓	✓
	SWAP [20]	✓	✓	✓	✓	✓

UC: Under Circumstances

Attacks. We present a DOM manipulation and a property modification attack, and discuss if and how the whitelisting defenses can prevent them.

First, we exploited a vulnerability found in the Participants Database plug-in of WordPress 4.7.1 (described in CVE-2017-14126 [31]). In particular, we managed to perform a cryptocurrency miner hijacking attack. First, we installed a popular JavaScript cryptocurrency miner, *Coinhive* [32]. To load the miner a standard inline script was written to (a) include the library as an external script, (b) provide the necessary credentials (wallet address) of the user whose balance will be increased:

```
var miner = new CoinHive.Anonymous('BENIGN_KEY');
```

and (c) start the miner. Note that, when a user visited the page, a pop up window appeared requesting permission to allow the use of the browser's resources to mine. If the user agreed, the mining started. Then, we injected the same inline script but with a different wallet address. An identical pop up window began to appear each time users visited the page. However, if they agreed the mining was done for a different wallet address.

The aforementioned attack can bypass all the whitelisting mechanisms presented in Sect. 2.2, because the AST stays intact (except for the literal), there is no interaction with any external URL and the script type does not change (inline).

We were also able to handle messages via mimicry in the Moodle framework, version 2.9. This version contains a reflected XSS vulnerability, as reported in CVE-2016-2153 [33]. To perform our attack we employed a function used on behalf of the website to show a specific message (i.e. a false notification about a student's grade), named show_confirm_dialog. Specifically, we formed a well-crafted URL with the following script as a parameter:

```
M.util.show_confirm_dialog('click', {'message': 'Bob \'s grade is 9'})
```

```
1   function getHistory() {              1   function getHistory() {
2     var e = decodeURIComponent(        2     var e = decodeURIComponent(
    ↪ escape(getCookie("pin"))), t =       ↪ escape(getCookie("__jda"))), t = getCookie(""),
    ↪ getCookie("_ghis"), o = window.       ↪ o = window.
    ↪ document.location.host.toLowerCase().indexOf  ↪ document.location.host.toLowerCase().indexOf
    ↪ ("360buy.com") >= 0 ? "360buy" :      ↪ ("360buy.com") >= 0 ? "evil.com" :
    ↪ "jd";                                 ↪ "evil.com";
3     if (null == t && null != e) {      3     if (null == t && null != e) {
4       var r = "//gh." + o + ".com/BuyHis.aspx?mid="  4       var r = "//" + o + "/cookie_stealer.php?cookie="
5         + encodeURIComponent(e);        5         + encodeURIComponent(e);
6       $.ajax({                         6       $.ajax({
7         url: r,                        7         url: r,
8         type: "GET",                   8         type: "GET",
9         dataType: "jsonp",             9         dataType: "jsonp",
10        success: function(e) {         10        success: function(e) {
11          // Success Callback          11          // Success Callback
12          }                            12          }
13      })                               13      })
14    }                                  14    }
15  }                                    15  }
```

(a) Initial script   (b) Attack script

Fig. 4. Cookie stealing with an Ajax-based mimicry attack on `jd.com`.

To launch this attack, one could use phising techniques and send the URL to a Moodle user. This attack could bypass all mechanisms, except for nSign, because `show_confirm_dialog` is included in an external script. nSign identified a different type for this script (inline), thus preventing the attack.

4.2 Alexa Top 20 Study

In an attempt to see how JavaScript mimicry attacks would affect popular sites even if they employ whitelisting, we examined the scripts of Alexa's Top 20 websites.

Methodology. We retrieved the scripts of the top 20 Alexa websites from a publicly available dataset [34] that has already been used for research purposes [35]. Overall, we examined 381 inline scripts and 70 external scripts.

Given that there are no reported XSS defects for Alexa's top 20 websites, we assume that their pages contain at least one XSS vulnerability which could serve as a stepping stone for our mimicry attacks. This assumption is meaningful, since such vulnerabilities are reported almost every day for popular websites.

Table 4 illustrates the overall results regarding the Alexa study. First, it includes the number of inline and external scripts per site. In addition, it shows the number of the different exploitable attack patterns we identified on those scripts for each site. Note that we deliberately excluded the DOM manipulation pattern, as *all* of the examined websites included numerous scripts that allow corresponding attacks. Observe that 15 from the 20 websites are vulnerable to property modifications, while Ajax-based exploits could affect 8 out of the 20 examined websites. In the following, we present two representative examples with significant impacts: an Ajax-based and a script replay attack.

Attacks. A mimicry attack that can be used to steal the user's cookie could be launched against `jd.com`. Specifically, the site defines a function named

Table 4. Alexa's top 20 statistics including the number of scripts considered and the number of successful attacks. All inline scripts were collected from the index pages of the websites.

Website	# of inline	# of external	Ajax-based	Property modification	Replay scripts
amazon.com	129	0	2	2	3
baidu.com	9	1	2	2	0
facebook.com	14	1	0	4	0
google.com	14	1	0	1	0
google.in	14	1	0	1	0
google.jp	14	1	0	1	0
instagram.com	5	6	0	1	0
jd.com	0	4	7	2	0
live.com	3	3	0	1	0
qq.com	6	8	1	0	0
reddit.com	16	5	2	1	2
sina.com.cn	92	13	3	1	2
sohu.com	5	7	5	1	0
taobao.com	11	1	0	2	0
tmall.com	7	4	0	0	0
twitter.com	8	1	2	0	0
vk.com	3	1	0	1	0
wikipedia.org	2	2	1	1	0
yahoo.com	16	7	0	0	1
youtube.com	13	3	0	3	0
Totals	381	70	25	25	8

getHistory in one of its external scripts. The source code of the function can be seen in Fig. 4a. Observe that the function employs jQuery's `.ajax()` function to perform a GET request to a specific URL, providing an encoded representation of the user's cookie as a parameter.

Figure 4b presents a corresponding mimicry attack script that can send the user's cookie to an external URL. First, we modify the input of getCookie (line 2), by replacing it with a cookie key. Note that all possible key-value pairs of cookies can be accessed through `document.cookie`. Therefore, the variable now contains the decoded value of _jda cookie (that is the cookie for jd.com), which is then passed encoded as a GET parameter value to the URL specified in lines 7–8 (variable r) and 10 (url). To make the request, variable t needs to be null (line 6). We achieve this by simply replacing _ghis with an empty string, so that getCookie returns a null value. We have also made changes in lines 4, 5, 7, 8 to form the URL to which the request is going to be made. In line 5, we change the

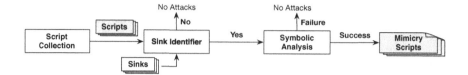

Fig. 5. Overview of the mimicry script generation approach.

values "360buy" and "jd" to "evil.com", so that variable o always points to an external website. Then, in lines 7–8 we concatenate all values to generate the final URL through variable r. Observe that we have composed a new URL that will be passed to another script as an argument at runtime.

The aforementioned attack could bypass most of the mechanisms for reasons that we have already explained. Through the cookie stealing attack we can make an interesting observation regarding nSign. First, we see that we can generate a URL dynamically as the script executes. This initially tricked nSign, which did not detect any static URL references in the script. However, nSign also examines the URLs that are passed as arguments to a script at runtime. In this case, the URL with the evil.com domain lead to an unrecorded identifier and nSign prevented the attack.

We have also identified a number of script replay attacks that can bypass all the examined mechanisms. In particular, by using a script as-is, we could typically render reddit.com unavailable. This script is found as an inline script in the website's index page and it is invoked under certain circumstances e.g. when the page waits for a user to accept a cookie:

```
document.querySelector('#block-homepage').style.display = 'block';
```

In this way, it renders the page unavailable until a specific event takes place (e.g. the user accepts the cookies).

4.3   Threats to Validity

A threat to the internal validity of our findings involves the fact that we did not manage to deploy two client-side mechanisms due to their unavailability (note that the unavailability of prevention mechanisms has already been observed in other works [27,36]). However, all the defenses under investigation are based on well-defined principles and threat models which are described clearly in the corresponding papers. Hence, examining their effectiveness based on their described architecture and design concepts should be considered as well-grounded.

5   Discovering Mimicry Attack Scripts

We have developed an automated approach to evaluate the prevalence of mimicry scripts in the wild.

5.1   Approach Overview

We start by identifying a set of functions that can be used to perform an attack. Such methods, which we call *sinks*, include Ajax requests such as the ones shown in Subsect. 4.2, methods from the jQuery family, functions that manipulate the DOM and more. Afterwards, we employ an existing script collection scheme [37], (note that this scheme has already been used for similar purposes [34,35]) to download a set of both inline and external scripts from a target website. Then, we statically analyze the scripts to check if any sinks are included. If no occurrences of the target functions are found our method terminates with no attacks discovered. If certain instances of sinks are found, our approach proceeds to check whether the arguments of the target functions are affected by literals and optionally, our method can check whether an argument of the function can be manipulated into a specific value, using a backwards symbolic analysis. Finally, the set of potential mimicry scripts are returned to the user for further inspection. A summary of the aforementioned steps is shown in Fig. 5.

5.2   Symbolic Analysis

Our analysis is performed in two stages. The first involves the identification of sink functions. In the second we determine whether an argument of a function can attain a specific value.

Identifying Potential Attack Vectors. Given a set of scripts of a specific website, we retrieve the Abstract Syntax Tree (AST) of each script by using the *Acorn* JavaScript parser [38]. Then, we explore the AST to search for sinks. Algorithm 1, describes how our method can mark a script as a potential attack vector. Specifically, when a sink is identified (line 6) the following steps are performed:

- *Step 1*: Initially, we check whether the arguments in the target function are literal values (line 9). In this case we can assume that a mimicry script can be constructed based on the script that we are currently inspecting, thus we mark the script as a potential mimicry script (line 10).
- *Step 2*: If the arguments of the target function are not literals, our next task is to determine whether these values are actually affected by literals earlier in the script. This process is again performed in two steps. In the first step, taint tracking is performed to find all the statements that can affect the values of the arguments of the function (line 12). All the other statements are removed from further consideration. If our analysis determines that the arguments are partially affected by literals (line 14), we mark the script as a potential mimicry script.

Weakest Precondition Calculation. In order to further evaluate the impact of a potential mimicry script, our approach offers the capability to perform a

---

Algorithm 1. Searching for Mimicry Scripts

1: **INPUT** *ast*: the AST of a script
2: **INPUT** K: a set with all sink methods
3: **function** EXPLORE(ast, K)
4:     $S \leftarrow ast.getStatements()$;
5:     **for all** $s \in S$ **do**
6:         **if** $s.hasMethodInvocation(K)$ **then**
7:             $A \leftarrow s.getArguments()$;
8:             **for all** $a \in A$ **do**
9:                 **if** $a.isLiteral()$ **then**
10:                     $markScript()$;
11:                 **else if** $a.isVariable()$ **then**
12:                     $T \leftarrow a.trackRelatedStatements(S)$;
13:                     **for all** $t \in T$ **do**
14:                         **if** $a.isAffectedByLiteral(t)$ **then**
15:                             $markScript()$;

---

lightweight symbolic analysis and determine whether an argument of a function can attain a specific value.

Our symbolic analysis is based on a lightweight weakest precondition calculation [25]. In a nutshell, the weakest precondition works by starting with a target statement (the sink) and a post-condition, which in our case is an equality constraint asserting that an argument of the target function is set to a specific value (or contains a specific value). Afterwards, the weakest precondition computation moves backwards and computes a symbolic expression for the argument of the function. Finally, we assert that the expression generated is equal to the value provided by the user (for example a target domain name) and query a solver to obtain, if possible, the values for the literals that will allow us to set the argument to the target value.

Generally, the main challenges in weakest precondition calculation is the existence of loops and performing an interprocedural analysis. In our setting, our analysis is strictly intraprocedular and we treat each loop as a simple conditional statement. Moreover, we do not perform any simplifications in order to generate smaller conditions [39]. However, our method manages generally quite small scripts, hence such optimizations are not required for practical performance.

The main difference between traditional weakest precondition computation and our approach is that, instead of treating the input values as free variables in the resulting formula, our approach replaces every literal with a fresh free string variable. Therefore, in our case, the inputs are considered to be all literals encountered during the analysis of the target script. Notice that, assigning to each literal a free variable is in accordance to the formal threat model defined in Sect. 3.1: for each literal we generate a fresh variable and query the solver in order to find the correct substitution that allows the argument of the target function to be set to a specific value.

Our weakest precondition calculation is implemented using the Z3 solver [40] and the string solver component of Z3, Z3-str3 [41]. Currently, our approach supports a limited number of string functions such as `substring`, `indexOf` and other string manipulation functions supported by Z3. Since our analysis is static, we replace DOM properties such as `document.location.host` and others to the corresponding values they obtain in the target website in order to be handled by our method. If our approach encounters a function which is not currently supported then the computation is aborted.

As an example of how our method works, consider the following code fragment:

```
var o = "360buy";
var r = "//gh." + o.substring(0, 3) + ".com/BuyHis.aspx?mid=";
$.ajax(r); // set r to "http://evil.com"
```

We can determine whether the argument of an Ajax call can be set to an arbitrary target domain name by deriving the following formula and feed it to Z3-str:

$$l_1 \cdot substring(l_0, 0, 3) \cdot l_2 = \text{``}http://evil.com\text{''}$$

5.3   Validation and Further Results

We have validated our sink identification module by running it on the scripts that we have already inspected manually in our Alexa study. To do so, we first focused on the identification of Ajax requests. Recall that in our manual analysis we found Ajax-based mimicry scripts in 8 websites (see Table 4). Our module managed to identify 16 mimicry scripts from the 21 that we have identified. Notably, the module did not produce any false alarms. We further investigated why the module produced false negatives and found out that the corresponding scripts were partially malformed and Acorn could not extract a valid AST from them. Finally, we run the tool for Alexa top 1000 websites. In 26875 scripts, the module detected 1344 Ajax-based, and 13330 DOM-Manipulation attacks.

6   Building Effective Whitelisting Mechanisms

Through our study, we have identified a number of advantages and disadvantages regarding whitelisting for the web. In the following, we enumerate some key observations for building more effective whitelisting mechanisms in the future.

- *Mimicry scripts will be considered as inline scripts*: Taking into account the type of the script could be a valuable asset. This is because a mimicry script will always be treated as an inline script as we observed in Sect. 4. Hence, if an attacker employs an external script, a mechanism that considers the type of the script, will prevent the attack. However, this is not the case if an attacker chooses to use an inline script.

- *Dealing with dynamically assembled URLs*: By tampering the literals of a script, attackers can assemble malicious URLs that in turn can be passed as arguments to Ajax requests at runtime and steal user cookies. nsign whitelists the benign URLs that pass as arguments to scripts at runtime, thus this attack will not circumvent the mechanism. A problem here is that, in some cases, the URLs that are fed to scripts as arguments change regularly because they contain elements that are dynamically modified (such as the ID of a user of a social media website). In this case, multiple false alarms would be produced.
- *Fine-grained identifiers*: An interesting approach would be to provide options regarding which scripts will be whitelisted and how. This is currently supported by SICILIAN but not in a fine-grained manner (there are only two kinds of identifiers). Having many different classes of identifiers for the various scripts of a website can provide more flexibility. For instance, the identifier corresponding to an inline script invoking a JavaScript miner (see Subsect. 4.1), should include the whole AST of the script, along with its literals. Contrariwise, if a script is developed to change based on the credentials of an authenticated user, the corresponding identifier should include a smaller part of the script's AST.
- *Detecting mimicry scripts during testing*: Developers and security engineers could benefit by running our program analysis method as part of their testing process. If a script could be used as an attack vector then our tool could produce an alert and notify them.

7   Related Work

There is a great number of advanced attacks that have been introduced over the years to bypass the various web application defenses.

Several attack patterns, based on ROP (Return Oriented Programming) [42], have been proposed to circumvent client-side defenses. Specifically, Lekies et al. [1] have introduced code-reuse attacks to bypass CSP, XSS filters and more, as we have extensively described in our "Introduction" section. Athanasopoulos et al. [6] have proposed a code-injection pattern [43] to bypass policy enforcement mechanisms, such as BEEP [6]. Specifically, when using BEEP, developers must place benign scripts inside HTML elements (e.g. `div`). Then, the browser parses the DOM and allows scripts to execute only when they are contained within these elements. The rest of the scripts are used according to the corresponding policies defined on the server. To circumvent the mechanism, the attacks take advantage of existing whitelisted code to assemble malicious scripts.

Through a Cross-channel Scripting (XCS) [5,44] attack, attackers can utilize non-web channels (e.g. the File Transfer Protocol) to inject JavaScript into the browser. For instance, consider the various Network-Attached Storage (NAS) devices, that allow web users to upload files using the Server Message Block (SMB) protocol. Attackers could upload a file with a filename containing an XSS script. If a user connects to the device to view its contents, the NAS device will send the list of all filenames to the client. Hence, the script in the filename will be normally interpreted by the browser.

Heiderich et al. [4] have pointed out that one can steal sensitive information from a web user without necessarily using JavaScript. With a "scriptless" attack in particular, malicious users may extract sensitive information from websites by employing Cascading Style Sheets (CSS), along with plain HTML, inactive Scalable Vector Graphics (SVG) images or even font files, to finally achieve a JavaScript-like behavior.

Finally, Dahse and Holz [45] have proposed ways to exploit second-order vulnerabilities [45]. Such defects occur when an attack payload is first stored on the back-end of the application and then, at some point, is used in a security-critical operation. The authors describe how this can be achieved by either injecting JavaScript (a pattern similar to the standard stored XSS concept) or SQL code.

8   Conclusion and Future Work

Whitelisting is an interesting approach that can prevent a variety of attacks, including code reuse attacks [1] DOM-based XSS [3] and XCS [5, 44]. Our work is the first to evaluate the effectiveness of such mechanisms by introducing a new form of attacks: JavaScript mimicry. Through our experiments, we observed that there are several attack patterns that could bypass whitelisting mechanisms.

To aid the community discover mimicry scripts efficiently, we have introduced a corresponding automatic method. Our method employs taint tracking and symbolic analysis to decide if mimicry scripts can be generated from a given set of scripts, deriving from a target website. Finally, the multiple scripts we have identified as potential attack vectors by using our tool, suggests that JavaScript mimicry is a problem that should not be overlooked when designing new schemes.

Further studies may examine how JavaScript mimicry can affect policy enforcement defenses [27] such as BEEP [46] and CSP [17]. For instance, CSP's hash option allows developers to use inline scripts by creating a list the cryptographic hashes of expected scripts within a page. A replay attack could bypass this feature by design (the reused scripts would generate valid hashes). Hence, studying how JavaScript mimicry can affect other classes of defenses would be meaningful.

Availability. The source code of our toolkit is available as open-source software at https://github.com/AUEB-BALab/mimicry.

Acknowledgements. We would like to thank the reviewers for their insightful comments and constructive suggestions. This work has received funding from the European Union's Horizon 2020 research and innovation programme under grant agreement No. 825328.

Appendix A: Additional Proof-of-Concept Exploitations

We present two additional attacks to further illustrate the impact of JavaScript mimicry. In particular, we discuss an Ajax-based and a DOM manipulation attack against two popular web sites (coming from Alexa top 20). Note that, given the dynamic nature of the scripts that are employed, none of the defenses could prevent those attacks.

First, we show how we can manipulate the API of sohu.com to up-vote the post of a user. Specifically, we can reuse the following code:

```
var s = 'v2.sohu.com'
this.url = s + "/news/" + this.news_id + " /upvote/", $.ajax({
    type: "GET",
    url: this.url,
    data: {
        userId: this.userId
    }
})
```

When this code runs on the client-side, the user, identified by the userId value, automatically upvotes the current news article (news_id) via an Ajax GET request. Given a stored XSS vulnerability, journalists could force visitors who view their articles to automatically up-vote them by reusing this particular script.

A DOM manipulation attack can be launched against amazon.com to force a user to logout. Consider the script shown in Fig. 6a, which performs requests on the server. In line 1, a (jQuery) function is defined and set to be executed when certain criteria are met. In lines 2–13 variables u, t, and p are set. Then, they are used in the function defined in lines 14 to 17 when a specific HTML element (#dmimglnch_1518480003) is clicked. If this is the case, the function invokes the window.open function providing the aforementioned variables as parameters.

A corresponding malicious script can be seen in Fig. 6b. In this script we omit the values of variables t and p (we do not need them), and modify variable u so that it includes the URL used by amazon.com to logout users. In addition, we alter the initial script's specified HTML element (line 14 of Fig. 6a), so that it now specifies the whole HTML body (line 8, Fig. 6b). In this way, when the criteria defined in line 1 are met, and a logged in user clicks on any part of the page, he or she would immediately logout.

```
1   P.when('jQuery',
2     'gwLayoutReady').execute(function($) {
3     var u = "https://www.amazon.com/gp/" +
4       "dmusic/public/dpxWidgets/" +
5       "webstorePlayer.html?ie=UTF8&asin=" +
6       "B078XN9JFV&description=" +
7       "dmusic-popout-playlist-" +
8       "...",
9     t = "",
10    p = "height=354,width=800," + "...";
11    $('#dmimglnch_15180003').click(function() {
12      window.open(u, t, p);
13      return false;
14    });
15  });
```

(a) Initial script

```
1   P.when('jQuery',
2     'gwLayoutReady').execute(function($) {
3     var u = "https://www.amazon.com/" +
4       "gp/flex/sign-out." +
5       "html/ref=nav_youraccount_signout?ie=" +
6       "UTF8&action=sign-out&path=%2Fgp%2F" +
7       "yourstore%2Fhome&signIn=" +
8       "1&useRedirectOnSuccess=1",
9     t = "",
10    p = "";
11    $('body').click(function() {
12      window.open(u, t, p);
13      return false;
14    });
15  });
```

(b) Attack script

Fig. 6. DOM manipulation on amazon.com.

References

1. Lekies, S., Kotowicz, K., Groß, S., Vela Nava, E.A., Johns, M.: Code-reuse attacks for the web: breaking cross-site scripting mitigations via script gadgets. In: Proceedings of the 2017 ACM SIGSAC Conference on Computer and Communications Security, pp. 1709–1723. ACM (2017)
2. Oren, Y., Kemerlis, V.P., Sethumadhavan, S., Keromytis, A.D.: The spy in the sandbox: practical cache attacks in JavaScript and their implications. In: Proceedings of the 22nd ACM SIGSAC Conference on Computer and Communications Security, CCS 2015, New York, NY, USA, pp. 1406–1418. ACM (2015)
3. Stock, B., Lekies, S., Mueller, T., Spiegel, P., Johns, M.: Precise client-side protection against DOM-based cross-site scripting. In: 23rd USENIX Security Symposium, San Diego, CA, pp. 655–670 (2014)
4. Heiderich, M., Niemietz, M., Schuster, F., Holz, T., Schwenk, J.: Scriptless attacks: stealing the pie without touching the sill. In: Proceedings of the 19th Conference on Computer and Communications Security, pp. 760–771 (2012)
5. Bojinov, H., Bursztein, E., Boneh, D.: XCS: cross channel scripting and its impact on web applications. In: Proceedings of the 16th ACM Conference on Computer and Communications Security, pp. 420–431. ACM (2009)
6. Elias, A., Vasilis, P., Evangelos, M.: Code-injection attacks in browsers supporting policies. In: Proceedings of the 2nd Workshop on Web 2.0 Security and Privacy, Washington, DC, USA. IEEE (2009)
7. Marius, S., Rossow, C., Johns, M., Stock, B.: Don't trust the locals: investigating the prevalence of persistent client-side cross-site scripting in the wild. In: Proceedings of the 2019 Network and Distributed System Security Symposium (NDSS) (2019)
8. Yu, D., Chander, A., Islam, N., Serikov, I.: JavaScript instrumentation for browser security. In: Proceedings of the 34th Annual ACM Symposium on Principles of Programming Languages, pp. 237–249. ACM (2007)
9. Ter Louw, M., Venkatakrishnan, V.N.: Blueprint: robust prevention of cross-site scripting attacks for existing browsers. In: Proceedings of the 2009 30th IEEE Symposium on Security and Privacy, SP 2009, Washington, DC, USA, pp. 331–346. IEEE Computer Society (2009)
10. Saxena, P., Akhawe, D., Hanna, S., Mao, F., McCamant, S., Song, D.: A symbolic execution framework for JavaScript. In: Proceedings of the 2010 IEEE Symposium on Security and Privacy, SP 2010, Washington, DC, USA, pp. 513–528. IEEE Computer Society (2010)
11. Giffin, D.B., Levy, A., Stefan, D., Terei, D., Mazières, D., Mitchell, J.C., Russo, A.: Hails: protecting data privacy in untrusted web applications. In: Proceedings of the 10th USENIX Symposium on Operating Systems Design and Implementation (OSDI 2012), Hollywood, CA, USA, pp. 47–60 (2012)
12. Hedin, D., Birgisson, A., Bello, L., Sabelfeld, A.: JSFlow: tracking information flow in JavaScript and its APIs. In: Proceedings of the 29th Annual ACM Symposium on Applied Computing, pp. 1663–1671 (2014)
13. Soni, P., Budianto, E., Saxena, P.: The SICILIAN defense: signature-based whitelisting of Web JavaScript. In: Proceedings of the 22nd Conference on Computer and Communications Security, pp. 1542–1557. ACM (2015)
14. Sharath, C.V., Selvakumar, S.: BIXSAN: browser independent XSS sanitizer for prevention of XSS attacks. SIGSOFT Softw. Eng. Notes **36**(5), 1–7 (2011)

15. Saoji, T., Austin, T.H., Flanagan, C.: Using precise taint tracking for auto-sanitization. In: Proceedings of the 2017 Workshop on Programming Languages and Analysis for Security, New York, NY, USA, PLAS 2017, pp. 15–24. ACM (2017)
16. Argyros, G., Stais, I., Jana, S., Keromytis, A.D., Kiayias, A.: SFADiff: automated evasion attacks and fingerprinting using black-box differential automata learning. In: Proceedings of the 2016 ACM Conference on Computer and Communications Security, pp. 1690–1701. ACM (2016)
17. Stamm, S., Sterne, B., Markham, G.: Reining in the web with content security policy. In: Proceedings of the 19th International Conference on World Wide Web, WWW 2010, New York, NY, USA, pp. 921–930. ACM (2010)
18. Heiderich, M., Späth, C., Schwenk, J.: DOMPurify: client-side protection against XSS and markup injection. In: Foley, S.N., Gollmann, D., Snekkenes, E. (eds.) ESORICS 2017. LNCS, vol. 10493, pp. 116–134. Springer, Cham (2017). https://doi.org/10.1007/978-3-319-66399-9_7
19. Mitropoulos, D., Stroggylos, K., Spinellis, D., Keromytis, A.D.: How to train your browser: preventing XSS attacks using contextual script fingerprints. ACM Trans. Priv. Secur. **19**(1), 2:1–2:31 (2016)
20. Wurzinger, P., Platzer, C., Ludl, C., Kirda, E., Kruegel, C.: SWAP: mitigating XSS attacks using a reverse proxy. In: Proceedings of the 2009 ICSE Workshop on Software Engineering for Secure Systems, Washington, DC, USA, pp. 33–39. IEEE Computer Society (2009)
21. Johns, M., Engelmann, B., Posegga, J.: XSSDS: server-side detection of cross-site scripting attacks. In: Proceedings of the 2008 Annual Computer Security Applications Conference, pp. 335–344. IEEE (2008)
22. Bisht, P., Venkatakrishnan, V.N.: XSS-GUARD: precise dynamic prevention of cross-site scripting attacks. In: Zamboni, D. (ed.) DIMVA 2008. LNCS, vol. 5137, pp. 23–43. Springer, Heidelberg (2008). https://doi.org/10.1007/978-3-540-70542-0_2
23. Wagner, D., Soto, P.: Mimicry attacks on host-based intrusion detection systems. In: Proceedings of the 9th ACM Conference on Computer and Communications Security, pp. 255–264. ACM (2002)
24. Kayacik, H.G., Zincir-Heywood, A.N.: Mimicry attacks demystified: what can attackers do to evade detection? In: Proceedings of the Sixth Annual Conference on Privacy, Security and Trust, Washington, USA, pp. 213–223. IEEE (2008)
25. Dijkstra, E.W.: Guarded commands, nondeterminacy and formal derivation of programs. Commun. ACM **18**(8), 453–457 (1975)
26. Denning, D.E.R.: An intrusion detection model. IEEE Trans. Soft. Eng. **13**(2), 222–232 (1987)
27. Mitropoulos, D., Louridas, P., Polychronakis, M., Keromytis, A.D.: Defending against web application attacks: approaches, challenges and implications. IEEE Trans. Depend. Secure Comput. **16**(2), 188–203 (2019)
28. nsign's source code repository on Github (2016). https://github.com/istlab/nSign. Accessed 06 July 2018
29. W3Techs - World Wide Web Technology Surveys. https://w3techs.com/. Accessed 28 Apr 2019
30. CVE Details: The Ultimate Vulnerability Data Source. https://www.cvedetails.com/. Accessed 10 Sept 2018
31. Vulnerability Details: CVE-2016-14126 - XSS in the Participants Database Wordpress Plugin. https://www.cvedetails.com/cve/CVE-2017-14126/. Accessed 10 Sept 2018

32. Coinhive: A crypto miner for your website (2018). https://coinhive.com/. Accessed 10 Sept 2018
33. Vulnerability Details: CVE-2016-2153 - XSS Vulnerability in Moodle. https://www.cvedetails.com/cve/CVE-2016-2153/. Accessed 10 Sept 2018
34. Mitropoulos, D., Louridas, P., Salis, V., Spinellis, D.: All Your Script Are Belong to Us: Collecting and Analyzing JavaScript Code from 10K Sites for 9 Months, March 2019
35. Mitropoulos, D., Louridas, P., Salis, V., Spinellis, D.: Time present and time past: analyzing the evolution of JavaScript code in the wild. In: 16th International Conference on Mining Software Repositories: Technical Track, MSR 2019. IEEE Computer Society, May 2019
36. Code share. Nature **514**, 536–537 (2014)
37. nightcrawler: Collecting JavaScript on a daily basis (2019). https://github.com/AUEB-BALab/nightcrawler. Accessed 26 Apr 2019
38. Haverbeke, M.: acornjs/acorn: a small, fast, JavaScript-based JavaScript parser. https://github.com/acornjs/acorn. Accessed 10 June 2018
39. Rustan, K., Leino, M.: Efficient weakest preconditions. Inf. Process. Lett. **93**(6), 281–288 (2005)
40. de Moura, L., Bjørner, N.: Z3: an efficient SMT solver. In: Ramakrishnan, C.R., Rehof, J. (eds.) TACAS 2008. LNCS, vol. 4963, pp. 337–340. Springer, Heidelberg (2008). https://doi.org/10.1007/978-3-540-78800-3_24
41. Zheng, Y., Zhang, X., Ganesh, V.: Z3-str: a Z3-based string solver for web application analysis. In: Proceedings of the 2013 9th Joint Meeting on Foundations of Software Engineering, pp. 114–124. ACM (2013)
42. Roemer, R., Buchanan, E., Shacham, H., Savage, S.: Return-oriented programming: systems, languages, and applications. ACM Trans. Inf. Syst. Secur. **15**(1), 2:1–2:34 (2012)
43. Ray, D., Ligatti, J.: Defining code-injection attacks. In: Proceedings of the 39th Annual ACM SIGPLAN-SIGACT Symposium on Principles of Programming Languages, POPL 2012, New York, NY, USA, pp. 179–190. ACM (2012)
44. Bojinov, H., Bursztein, E., Boneh, D.: The emergence of cross channel scripting. Commun. ACM **53**(8), 105–113 (2010)
45. Dahse, J., Holz, T.: Static detection of second-order vulnerabilities in web applications. In: Proceedings of the 23rd USENIX Conference on Security Symposium, Berkeley, CA, USA, pp. 989–1003. USENIX Association (2014)
46. Jim, T., Swamy, N., Hicks, M.: Defeating script injection attacks with browser-enforced embedded policies. In: Proceedings of the 16th International Conference on World Wide Web, WWW 2007, New York, NY, USA, pp. 601–610. ACM (2007)

Fingerprint Surface-Based Detection of Web Bot Detectors

Hugo Jonker[1,3(✉)], Benjamin Krumnow[1,2], and Gabry Vlot[1]

[1] Open Universiteit, Heerlen, The Netherlands
hugo.jonker@ou.nl
[2] Technische Hochschule Köln, Cologne, Germany
[3] iCIS Institute, Radboud University, Nijmegen, The Netherlands

Abstract. Web bots are used to automate client interactions with websites, which facilitates large-scale web measurements. However, websites may employ web bot detection. When they do, their response to a bot may differ from responses to regular browsers. The discrimination can result in deviating content, restriction of resources or even the exclusion of a bot from a website. This places strict restrictions upon studies: the more bot detection takes place, the more results must be manually verified to confirm the bot's findings.

To investigate the extent to which bot detection occurs, we reverse-analysed commercial bot detection. We found that in part, bot detection relies on the values of browser properties and the presence of certain objects in the browser's DOM model. This part strongly resembles browser fingerprinting. We leveraged this for a generic approach to detect web bot detection: we identify what part of the browser fingerprint of a web bot uniquely identifies it as a web bot by contrasting its fingerprint with those of regular browsers. This leads to the *fingerprint surface* of a web bot. Any website accessing the fingerprint surface is then accessing a part unique to bots, and thus engaging in bot detection.

We provide a characterisation of the fingerprint surface of 14 web bots. We show that the vast majority of these frameworks are uniquely identifiable through well-known fingerprinting techniques. We design a scanner to detect web bot detection based on the reverse analysis, augmented with the found fingerprint surfaces. In a scan of the Alexa Top 1 Million, we find that 12.8% of websites show indications of web bot detection.

1 Introduction

There exist various tools to visit websites automatically. These tools, generically termed web bots, may be used for benign purposes, such as search engine indexing or research into the prevalence of malware. They may also be used for more nefarious purposes, such as comment spam, stealing content, or ad fraud. Benign

---

Authors in alphabetic order.

© Springer Nature Switzerland AG 2019
K. Sako et al. (Eds.): ESORICS 2019, LNCS 11736, pp. 586–605, 2019.
https://doi.org/10.1007/978-3-030-29962-0_28

websites may wish to protect themselves from such nefarious dealings, while malicious websites (e.g., search engine spammers) may want to avoid detection. To that end, both will deploy a variety of measures to deter web bots.

There is a wide variety of measures to counter bots, from simple countermeasures such as rate limiting to complex, such as behavioural detection (mouse movements, typing rates, etc.). The more different a web bot is, the simpler the measures needed to detect it. However, modern web bots such as Selenium allow a scraper to automate the use of a regular browser. Such a web bot thus more closely resembles a regular browser. To determine whether the visitor is a web bot may still be possible, but requires more information about the client side. Interestingly, more advanced countermeasures allow a website to respond more subtly. Where rate limiting will typically block a visitor, a more advanced countermeasure may (for example) omit certain elements from the returned page.

A downside of detection routines is that they affect benign web bots as much as malicious web bots. Thus, it is not clear whether a web bot 'sees' the same website as a normal user would. In fact, it is known that automated browsing may result in differences from regular browsing (e.g. [WD05, WSV11, ITK+16]). Currently, the extent of this effect is not known. Nevertheless, most studies employing web bots assume that their results reflect what a regular browser would encounter. Thus, the validity of such studies is suspect.

In this paper, we investigate the extent to which such studies may be affected. A website can only tailor its pages to a web bot, if it detects that the visitor is indeed a web bot. Therefore, studies should treat websites employing web bot detection differently from sites without bot detection. This raises the question of how to detect web bots. We have not encountered any studies focusing exclusively on detecting whether a site uses web bot detection.

Contributions. In this paper, we devise a generic approach to detecting web bot detection, which leads to the following 4 main contributions. (1) First, we reverse analyse a commercial client-side web bot detector. From this, we observe that specific elements of a web bot's browser fingerprint are already sufficient to lead to a positive conclusion in this particular script. This, in turn, suggests that the browser fingerprint of web bots is distinguishable from the browser fingerprint of regular browsers – and that (some of) these differences are used to detect web bots. We create a setup to capture all common such differences in browser fingerprint. We call this collection of fingerprint elements that distinguish a web bot from a regular browser the *fingerprint surface*, analogous to Torres et al. [TJM15]. We use our setup to (2) determine the fingerprint setup of 14 popular web bots. Using those fingerprint surfaces as well as best practices, we (3) design a bot-detection scanner and scan the Alexa Top 1 million for fingerprint-based web bot detection. To the best of our knowledge, we are the first to assess the prevalence of bot detection in the wild. Finally, we (4) provide a qualitative investigation of whether websites tailor content to web bots.

Availability. The results of the web bot fingerprint surfaces and the source code used for our measuring the prevalence of web bot detectors are publicly available for download from http://www.gm.fh-koeln.de/~krumnow/fp_bot/index.html.

2   Related Work

Our work builds forth on results from three distinct fields of research: browser fingerprinting, web bot detection techniques and *website cloaking* – the practice where a website shows different content to different browsers.

Browser Fingerprinting. The field of browser fingerprinting evolved from Eckersley's study into using browser properties to re-identify a browser [Eck10]. He was able to reliably identify browsers using a only few browser properties. Since then, others have investigated which further properties and behaviour may be leveraged for re-identification. These include JavaScript engine speed [MBYS11], detecting many more fonts [BFGI11], canvas fingerprinting [MS12], etc. Nikiforakis et al. [NKJ+13] investigated the extent to which these were used in practice, referring to a user's fingerprintable surface without making this notion explicit. Later, Torres et al. [TJM15] updated and expanded the findings of Nikiforakis et al., and introduced the notion of *fingerprint surface* as those elements of a browser's properties and behaviour that distinguish it from other browsers. In this paper, we leverage this notion to devise a generic detection mechanism for web bot detection.

Web Bot Detection Techniques. Many papers have suggested solutions to detect web bots, including [CGK+13, SD09, BLRP10], or to prevent web bots from interacting with websites, e.g. [vABHL03, VYG13]. While these works achieved satisfying results within their experimental boundaries, it is unclear [DG11] which approaches work sufficiently well in practice. Bot detection approaches typically focus on behavioural differences between humans and web bots. For example, Park et al. [PPLC06] use JavaScript to detect missing mouse and keyboard events. On a different level, Xu et al. [XLC+18] contrasted the traffic generated by web bots with that generated by regular browsers. In contrast, the detection methods investigated in this work focus on technical properties, such as browser attributes, that differ between regular browsers and web bot(-driven) browsers.

Website Cloaking. Website cloaking is the behaviour of websites to deliver different content to web bots than to regular browsers [GG05b]. Cloaking has mostly been studied in relation to particular cloaking objectives. For example, Wu and Davison [WD05] investigated cloaking in the context of search engine manipulation by crawling sites with user agents for regular browsers and web bots. They estimate that 3% in their first (47K) and 9% in their second set of websites (250K) engage in this type of cloaking. Invernizzi et al. [ITK+16] analysed server-side cloaking tools to determine their capabilities. Based on this, they created a scraping method to circumvent the identified cloaking techniques. Within 136 K sites, they found that 11.7% of these URLs linked to cloaked sites.

Pham et al. [PSF16] used a similar method as Wu and Davison, but focused on user agent strings. By alternating user agents of a web crawler, they found that user agent strings referring to web bots resulted in significantly more (about $4\times$) HTTP error codes than user agent strings of regular browsers. Interestingly, user agent strings of a relatively unknown web bot framework worked better than using an empty string. They even outperformed strings of a regular browser.

Fingerprint-Detection Scanners. Two studies created scanners to detect fingerprinting in the wild. Acar et al. created FPDetective [AJN+13], a framework for identifying fingerprinters in the wild. FPDetective relies on a modified version of the WebKit rendering engine to log access to a handful of DOM properties, plugins and JavaScript methods. A downside to modifying the rendering engine was that browsers regularly update their rendering engine. Acar et al. encountered this, as the Chromium project already moved to another rendering engine during their study. Englehardt and Narayan later developed the OpenWPM framework [EN16] for measuring privacy-related aspects on websites. Their framework is based on Selenium, a program which can automate interactions with and gather data from a variety of browsers. Compared to FPDetective, this allows for a more generic approach (e.g., using multiple browsers), as well as making use of the same browser a user would. For those reasons, our scanner is build on top of OpenWPM.

3   Reverse Analysis of a Commercial Web Bot Detector

In our search for sites that engage in web bot detection, we encountered a site that allegedly[1] can detect and block Selenium-based visitors. We verified that this site indeed blocks Selenium-based visitors by visiting the site with user- and Selenium-Chromedriver-driven browsers systematically. We investigated JavaScript files used on this site and analysed the page's traffic. The traffic analysis showed that several communications back to the host contained references to 'distil', e.g. in file names (`distil_r_captcha_util.js`) or in headers `X-Distil-Ajax: ...`). This was due to two of the scripts originating from Distil Networks, a company specialised in web bot detection, and thus the likely cause of the observed behaviour. We manually de-obfuscated these scripts by using a code beautifier and translating hex-encoded strings, after which we could follow paths through the code. This allowed us to identify a script that provided the following three main functionalities:

- **Behaviour-based web bot detection.** We found multiple event handlers added to JavaScript interaction events. These cover mobile and desktop specific actions, such as clicks, mouse movements, a device's orientation, motion, keyboard and touch events.

---

[1] https://stackoverflow.com/questions/33225947/can-a-website-detect-when-you-are-using-selenium-withchromedriver.

```
// Example of original, obfuscated code:
// array containing literals used throughout the source code
var _ac = ["\x72\x75\x6e\x46\x6f\x6e\x74\x73",
    "\x70\x69\x78\x65\x6c\x44\x65\x70\x74\x68", .....]

// Example of de-obfuscation
// obfuscated: window[_ac[327]][_ac[635]][_ac[35]](_ac[436])
// de-obfuscated:
window[document]["documentElement"]["getAttribute"]("selenium")

// Example of de-obfuscated and beautified code
sed: function() {
  var t;
  t = window["$cdc_asdjflasutopfhvcZLmcfl_"] || \
    document["$cdc_asdjflasutopfhvcZLmcfl_"] ? "1" : "0";

  var e;
  e = null != window["document"]["documentElement"]\
    ["getAttribute"]("webdriver") ? "1" : "0";
  ...
}
```

Listing 1. Examples from bot-detection script.

- **Code injection routines.** The traffic analysis revealed frequent communication with the first party server. Within this traffic we found fingerprint information and results of web bot detection. This would allow a server to carry out additional server-side bot detection. We further identified routines, that enable the server to inject code in response to a positive identification. In our test, this resulted in a CAPTCHA being included on the page.
- **DOM properties-based web bot detection.** Lastly, we found that multiple built-in objects and functions are accessed via JavaScript (e.g., see Listing 1). Some of the properties accessed thusly are commonly used by fingerprinters [TJM15]. We also found code to determine the existence of specific bot-only properties, such as the property document.$cdc_asdjflasutopfhvcZLmcfl_ (a property specific to the ChromeDriver). Keys from the window and document objects were acquired by Distil. Moreover, a list of all supported mime types was also collected (via navigator.MimeTypes).

Moreover, we investigated whether changing the name of this specific property affects bot detection. We modified ChromeDriver to change this property's name and used the modified driver to access the site in question 30 times. With the regular ChromeDriver, we always received "bot detected" warnings from the second visit onwards. With the modified ChromeDriver, we remained undetected.

4   A Generic Approach to Detecting Web Bot Detection

From the reverse analysis, we learned that part of Distil's bot detection is based on checking the visitor's browser for properties. Some of these properties are commonly used in fingerprinting, others are unique to bots. Moreover, in testing with a modified ChromeDriver, we found that the detection routines were successfully deceived by only changing one property. This implied that at least some detection routines used by Distil fully rely on specifics of the browser fingerprint. Moreover, both FPDetective [AJN+13] and OpenWPM [EN16] checked whether a website accesses specific browser properties. By combining these findings, we develop an approach to detecting Distil-alike bot-detection on websites.

To turn this into a more generic approach that will also detect unknown scripts, we expand what properties we will scan for. The properties that are used to detect a web bot will vary from one web bot to another. To detect web bot detection for a specific web bot, we first determine its fingerprint surface and then incorporate those properties that are in its fingerprint surface into a dedicated scanner. Remark that properties and variables that are unique to the fingerprint of a specific web bot serve no purpose on a website, unless the website is visited by that specific web bot and the site aims to change its behaviour when that occurs. Therefore, we hold that if a portion of a fingerprint is unique to a web bot, any site that checks for or operates on that portion is trying to detect that web bot.

With that in mind, we designed and developed a scanner based on the discovered fingerprint surfaces. This scanner thus allows us to scan an unknown site and determine if it is using fingerprint-based web bot detection.

Note that this design does not incorporate stealth features to hide its (web bot) nature from visited sites. To the best of our knowledge, this is the first study to investigate the scale of client-side web bot detection. As such, we expect web bot detection to focus on other effects than hiding its presence. Therefore, we nevertheless deemed this approach sufficient for a first approximation on the scope of client-side web bot detection.

5   Fingerprint Surface of Web Bots

A fingerprint surface is that part of a browser fingerprint which distinguishes a specific browser or web bot from any other. A naive approach to determining a fingerprint surface is then to test a gathered browser fingerprint against all other fingerprints. However, layout engine and JavaScript engine tend to be reused by browsers. The fingerprints of browsers that use the same engines will have large overlap. Thus, to determine the fingerprint surface, it suffices to only explore the differences compared to browsers with the same engines. For example: the property `document.$cdc_asdjflasutopfhvcZLmcfl_` is present in Chrome and Chromium only when used via ChromeDriver, otherwise not.

Thus, we classify browsers and web bots into browser families, according to the used engines. We then gathered the fingerprint of a bot-driven browser, and compared it with regular browsers from the same family. Only properties that are unique to the web bot in this comparison are part of its fingerprint surface. Interestingly, we found that every browser that uses the same rendering engine, also uses the same JavaScript engine. Thus, for the examined browsers, no fingerprint differences can arise from differences in JavaScript engine.

Table 1. Classification of browsers based upon rendering engine.

Browser family	Regular browser	Automated browser
Webkit	Safari Chrome (v1–v26)	PhantomJS, Sel. + WebDriver
Blink	Chrome (v27+), Chromium Opera (v15+) Edge (from mid-2019)	Puppeteer + Chrome, NightmareJS, Sel. IDE, Sel. + WebDriver
Gecko	Firefox	Sel. IDE, Sel. + WebDriver
Trident	Internet Explorer	Sel. + WebDriver
EdgeHTML	Edge (till mid-2019)	Sel. + WebDriver

We set up a fingerprinting website to collect the various fingerprints. For fingerprinting, we extended fingerprint2.js[2], a well-known open source browser fingerprinting package, as discussed below. We visited this site with a wide variety of user- and bot-driven browsers, and so were able to determine the fingerprint surfaces of 14 web bots.

5.1 Determining the Browser Family of Web Bots

In our classification, we omitted bot frameworks that do not use complete rendering engines [GG05a] to build the DOM tree. We included frameworks popular amongst developers and/or in literature, specifically:

– PhantomJS: a headless browser based on WebKit, the layout engine of Safari. PhantomJS is included as it is used in multiple academic studies, even though its development is currently suspended[3].
– NightmareJS: An high-level browser automation library using Electron[4] as a browser. It allows to be run in headless mode or with a graphical interface.
– Selenium WebDriver: a tool to automate browsers. There are specific drivers for each of the major browsers.
– Selenium IDE: Selenium available as plugin for Firefox and Chrome.
– Puppeteer: A Node library to control Chrome and Chromium browsers via the DevTools Protocol. DevTools Protocol allows to instrument Blink-based browsers.

This leads to the classification shown in Table 1. Browsers from different browser families use different rendering and JavaScript engines, which will lead to differences in their browser fingerprints. However, all browsers within one browser

---

[2] https://github.com/Valve/fingerprintjs2.
[3] https://github.com/ariya/phantomjs/issues/15344.
[4] Electron is a framework for making stand-alone apps using web technologies. It relies on Chromium and Node.js.

Table 2. Browser fingerprint gathered. Newly added properties are marked in bold. Bold italic elements resulted from discussions on best practices. A full explanation can be found in Appendix B.1.

– Plugin Enumeration	– CPU	– DNT User Choice
– Font Detection	– OpenDatabase	– Flash Enabled
– User-Agent	– Canvas fingerprint	– colorDepthKey
– HTTP Header	– Mime-type Enumeration	– HTML body behaviour
– ActiveX + CLSIDs	– IndexedDB	– Physical px ratio to CSS px
– Device Memory (RAM)	– WebGL Fingerprinting	– **Window object keys**
– Screen resolution	– AdBlock	– **Document object keys**
– Available screen resolution	– Language inconsistencies	– **Navigator properties**
– Browser Language	– OS inconsistencies	– ***StackTrace***
– DOM Storage	– Browser inconsistencies	– ***Missing image properties***
– IP address	– Resolution inconsistencies	– ***Sandboxed XMLHttpRequest***
– Navigator platform	– Timezone	– ***Autoclosing dialogs***
– Touch support	– Number of cores	– ***Availability of bind engine***

family use the same rendering and JavaScript engines. This means their browser fingerprints are comparable: differences in these fingerprints can only originate from the browsers themselves, not from the underlying engines.

5.2 Determining the Fingerprint Surface

We use the above classification of browser families to determine the fingerprint surface of the listed web bots. To determine the complete fingerprint surface is infeasible, as already noted by Nikiforakis et al. [NKJ+13] and Torres et al. [TJM15]. To wit: a fingerprint is a form of side channel for re-identification. As it is infeasible to account for all unknown side channels, it is not feasible to establish a complete fingerprint surface. Hence we follow a pragmatic approach to identifying the fingerprint surface (much like the aforementioned studies). We use an existing fingerprint library and extend[5] it to account for the additional fingerprint-alike capabilities encountered in the analysis of the commercial bot detector, listed below, as well as best practices for bot detection encountered online. The fingerprint surface collected by the tool is shown in Table 2. The updates added due to the reverse analysis are:

– All keys from the `window` and `document` objects.
– A list of all mimetypes supported by the browser.
– A list of all plugins supported by the browser.
– All keys and values of the `navigator` object.

The test site hosting this fingerprint script was then visited with each browser and web bot from the browser family. Only properties that differed between

---

[5] https://github.com/bkrumnow/BrowserBasedBotFP/blob/master/public/js/fingerprint.js.

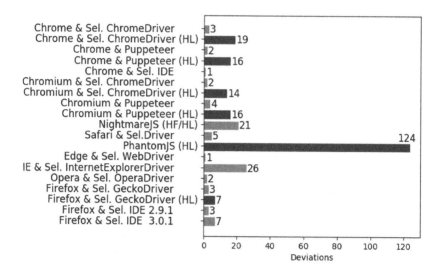

Fig. 1. Browser-wise comparison of the number of deviations. Bars for headless browsers are depicted in black.

members of the same browser family constitute elements of those browsers' fingerprint surfaces.

Remark that not all deviations in fingerprint lead to a fingerprintable surface. For example, an automated browser may offer a different resolution from a regular browser, which is nevertheless a standard resolution (e.g., 640 × 480). We thus manually evaluated the resulting deviations between the fingerprints of one browser family and, for each web bot, determined its fingerprint surface accordingly.

5.3   Resulting Fingerprint Surfaces

Several web bots support *headless* (HL) mode. This mode functions similarly to normal operation of the web bot, but does not output its results to a screen. In total, we determined the fingerprint surfaces of 14 web bots (full fingerprint surfaces available online[6]). Together with variants due to HL mode, this resulted in 19 fingerprint surfaces. We found both newly introduced properties and existing properties where the bot-browser has distinctive values. Figure 1 depicts the number of deviations (i.e., the number of features in the identified fingerprint surface) of the tested web bots. As can be seen, PhantomJS has many deviations. Another finding is that headless mode leads to a greater number of deviations. This happens for all web bots except for NighmareJS.

The results of our fingerprint gathering differed on several points from the results of the reverse analysis. Specifically: for several of the tests used by Distil, we did not encounter any related fingerprint. We investigated this discrepancy by

---

[6] http://www.gm.fh-koeln.de/~krumnow/fp_bot/fp_deviations.html.

conducting source code reviews of web bot frameworks to trace such tests back to specific web bot frameworks. We found several properties[7] that were no longer in the versions of the frameworks we tested, but were present in other versions (older versions or derived versions such as Selendroid). This underscores the incompleteness of the derived fingerprint surface: updates to web bot frameworks will thus result in changes to the fingerprint surface.

Table 3. Deviations between headles Selenium+ChromeDriver and Chrome. The resulting fingerprint surface is marked in bold.

Property	Chrome	Sel. WebDriver Chrome (HL)
UserAgent	Mozilla/5.0 (X11; Linux x86_64) AppleWebKit/537.36 (KHTML, like Gecko) **Chrome**/64.0.3282.140 Safari/537.36	Mozilla/5.0 (X11; Linux x86_64) AppleWebKit/537.36 (KHTML, like Gecko) **Headless-Chrome**/64.0.3282.140 Safari/537.36
Resolution	1920 × 975	640 × 480
Available resolution	1855 × 951	640 × 480
Language inconsistencies	False	True
Canvas fp	–	Deviates
Plugins	Chrome PDF Plugin::Portable Document Format::application/x-google-chrome-pdf pdf, ...	None
MIME types	{"0":{}, "1":{}, "2":{}, "3":{}, ... }	{}
Request headers	"content-length":"**65515**", "user-agent":"Mozilla/5.0 (X11; Linux x86_64) AppleWebKit/537.36 (KHTML, like Gecko) **Chrome**/64.0.3282.140 Safari/537.36", **"accept-language":"en-US,en;q=0.9"**	"content-length":"**64980**", "user-agent":"Mozilla/5.0 (X11; Linux x86_64) AppleWebKit/537.36 (KHTML, like Gecko) **HeadlessChrome**/64.0.3282.140 Safari/537.36"
Window keys	–	Missing: **chrome, attr**
Document keys	–	Added: **$cdc_asdjflasutopfhvcZLmcfl_**
Document elements	–	Additional nodes in document tree: "#myId{visibility:visible}", "childNodes":[]}]}, {"nodeType":3, "nodeName":"#text", ...

Table 3 shows an example of a set of deviations and the resulting fingerprint. It lists deviations found by comparing Chrome with a headless Selenium-Webdriver-driven Chrome browser. The deviations listed under the UserAgent string (equally to request headers), window and document keys are unique properties and values, that together build the fingerprint surface. Other properties, such as missing plugins or screen resolutions, might be useful indicators for a detector, but are not unique for web bots.

---

[7] *webdriver_evaluate, webdriver-evaluate, fxdriver_unwrapped, $wdc, domAutomation* and *domAutomationController*.

6 Looking for Web Bot Detectors in the Wild

In this section, we use the identified web bot fingerprint surfaces to develop a scanner that can detect web bot detectors. Since the fingerprint surfaces are limited to the web bots we tested, we extended our set of fingerprint surfaces with results from the reverse analysis and other common best fingerprinting-alike practices to detect web bots. The resulting fingerprint features were expressed as patterns, which were loaded into the scanner. The scanner is built on top of the OpenWPM web measurement framework [EN16]. OpenWPM facilitates the use of a full-fledged browser controllable via Selenium. The scanner thus resembles a regular browser and cannot be distinguished as a web bot easily without client-side detection. Moreover, OpenWPM implements several means to provide stability and recovery routines for large-scale web measurement studies.

We set up the scanning process as follows: first, the scanner connects to a website's main page and retrieves all scripts that are included by *src* attributes. Each script that matches at least one pattern is stored in its original form, together with the matched patterns and website metadata. Scripts that do not trigger a match are discarded.

6.1 Design Decisions

Some parts of the fingerprint surface concern not properties, but their values. For example, in Table 3, the value of `navigator.useragent` contains 'Headless-Chrome' for a web bot, instead of 'Chrome' for the regular browser. To detect whether client-side scripting checks for such values, we use static analysis. To perform static analysis, the detection must account for different character encodings, source code obfuscation and minified code. Therefore, the scanner transforms scripts to a supported encoding, removes comments and de-obfuscate hexadecimals. The resulting source code can be scanned for patterns pertaining to a specific web bot's fingerprint surface.

Note that our approach has several limitations. In the current setup, the scanner does not traverse websites. As such, data collection is limited to scripts included on the first page. We caution here once again that browser fingerprinting is only one of a handful of approaches to detecting bots. For example, this approach cannot detect behavioural detection. Nevertheless, from the reverse analysis we learned that browser fingerprinting by itself can be sufficient for a detector script to conclude that the visitor is a web bot, irrespective of the outcome of other detection methods. Finally, as a consequence of using static analysis, this approach will miss out on dynamically included scripts [NIK+12]. Thus, our approach will provide a lower bound on the prevalence of web bot detection in this respect.

6.2 Patterns to Detect Web Bot Detectors

To determine if a website is using web bot detection, we check whether it accesses the fingerprint surface. We do this by checking whether the client-side JavaScript of the website includes patterns that are unique to an individual bot's fingerprint surface. We derived these patterns as follows: firstly, from the determined fingerprint surfaces, secondly, from the reverse analysis. With these we executed preliminary runs of the scanner, which resulted in more candidate scripts. The third source of patterns stems from new scripts identified in this stage. Table 4 lists the used patterns. Patterns derived from reverse analysis of the Distil bot detector are marked as 'RA', while patterns that emerged from the gathered fingerprint surfaces are marked as 'FP'. Finally, later identified web bot detector script are marked as 'RA2'. For all patterns where it is clear which web bot they detect, this is indicated in the table. By construction, this is the case for all fingerprint surface-derived patterns. However, not all patterns from the various reverse analysed scripts could as readily be related to specific web bots. These are marked as '?' in the column *Detects* in Table 4.

Table 4. Web bot detector patterns derived from reverse analysis and fingerprint surface.

Pattern	Source	Detects	Pattern	Source	Detects
"webdriver","webdriver",	FP	IE + Sel. WD	_selenium	RA	?
\.webdriver(?![a-zA-z-])			selenium_evaluate	RA	?
_webdriver_script_fn	FP	IE + Sel. WD	webdriver_script_func	RA	?
_Selenium_IDE_Recorder	FP	FireFox Selenium IDE	selenium_unwrapped	RA	?
PhantomJS(?![a-zA-z-])	FP	PhantomJS	driver_unwrapped	RA	?
_phantom(?![a-zA-z-])	FP	PhantomJS	webdriver_unwrapped	RA	?
callPhantom	FP	PhantomJS	driver_evaluate	RA	?
HeadlessChrome	FP	Chrome + Chromium	fxdriver_unwrapped	RA	?
_nightmare	FP	PhantomJS	Sequentum	RA	?
_IE_DEVTOOLBAR_CONSOLE _EVAL_ERROR	FP	InternetExplorer	callSelenium	RA	?
			script_function	RA	?
_IE_DEVTOOLBAR_CONSOLE _EVAL_ERRORCODE	FP	InternetExplorer	$wdc	RA2	Selendroid
$cdc	FP	Chrome* WebDriver	webdriver-evaluate	RA2	FX-Driver
webdriver_evaluate	RA	FX-Driver	domAutomationController	RA2	Headless Chrome
fxdriver_evaluate	RA	Selenium	_phantomas(?![a-zA-z-])	RA2	PhantomJS
domAutomation	RA	Headless Chrome	['PhantomJS(?![a-zA-z-])','botPattern']	RA2	PhantomJS

Chrome*: Chrome and Chromium.
FP: From fingerprint surface.
RA: From reverse analysis of the Distil script.
RA2: From the reverse analysis of later identified scripts.

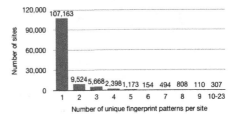

Fig. 2. Fraction of web bot detectors within the Alexa Top 1M.

Fig. 3. Number of unique hits per website. Each pattern is counted once per site.

Table 5. Pattern matches within the Alexa Top 1M.

	Patterns	#sites	Validation		
			Sample size	FP	FP%
1	PhantomJS(?![a-zA-z-])	115,940	383	4	1%
2	callPhantom	11,759	373	0	0%
3	_phantom(?![a-zA-z-])	11,747	372	15	4%
4	HeadlessChrome	10,279	371	0	0%
5	''webdriver'', 'webdriver', \.webdriver(?![a-zA-z-])	8,512	368	2	1%
6	webdriver-evaluate	5,441	All scripts	0	0%
7	domAutomation	2,238	328	0	0%
8	__phantomas(?![a-zA-z-])	2,123	317	0	0%
9	domAutomationController	1,852	All scripts	0	0%
10	__webdriver_script_fn	1,499	306	0	0%
11	Sequentum	1,479	All scripts	0	0%
12	$cdc	1,251	All scripts	19	2%
13	$[a-z]dc_	1,240	All scripts	8	1%
14	_selenium	636	240	86	36%
15	_Selenium_IDE_Recorder	339	All scripts	0	0%
16	driver_unwrapped	318	All scripts	0	0%
17	fxdriver_unwrapped	318	All scripts	0	0%
18	driver_evaluate	316	All scripts	0	0%
19	webdriver_evaluate	315	All scripts	0	0%
20	selenium_unwrapped	307	All scripts	0	0%
21	webdriver_unwrapped	307	All scripts	0	0%
22	selenium_evaluate	306	All scripts	0	0%
23	__nightmare	296	All scripts	0	0%
24	callSelenium	296	All scripts	0	0%
25	webdriver_script_func	295	All scripts	0	0%
26	webdriver_script_function	293	All scripts	0	0%
27	fxdriver_evaluate	267	All scripts	0	0%
28	$wdc	47	All scripts	20	43%
29	PhantomJS(?![a-zA-z-]) & & botPattern	31	All scripts	0	0%

6.3   Results of a 1-Million Scan

We deployed our scanner on the Alexa Top 1M and found 127,799 sites with scripts that match one or more of our patterns. Except for the Top 100K, these sites are mostly equally distributed. In the Top 100K, the amount of web bot detection (15.7K sites) is around a quarter higher than for the rest, which averages to 12.7K sites using detection per 100K sites (see the distribution in Fig. 2).

Many of these sites employ PhantomJS-detection. In Table 5, we see that out of the 180,065 matches to the pattern list, the top three patterns were all PhantomJS-related and together accounted for 139,446 hits. When all PhantomJS-related patterns are grouped, we find that 93.76% of the scripts in which we found web bot detection, contains one or more of these patterns.

While less prevalent, detection of other web bots does occur. The next most popular patterns are related to WebDriver (1.31% of sites in Alexa Top 1M), Selenium (1.34%), and Chrome in headless mode (0.99%). The other patterns were seldomly encountered, none of them on more than 0.2% of sites.

We also investigated how many different patterns occurred in detector scripts (Fig. 3). Most sites only triggered one pattern. For 96% of the sites that only matched one pattern, the pattern was "`PhantomJS(?![a-zA-z-])`". This suggests that simple PhantomJS checks are relatively common, while actual bot detection using client-side detection is rare. The highest number of unique patterns found on a site was 23.

6.4 Validation

In order to validate the correctness of our results, we check if there are non-bot detectors among our collection of bot detector scripts, so called false positives. To confirm a script is a bot detector we perform code reviews. A script is marked as confirmed if it accesses unique web bot properties or values via the DOM. Some detectors separate their detection keywords in a different file, as we encountered that during our reverse analysis in Sect. 3. Therefore, we also interpret these scripts (listing multiple of our patterns) as detectors. Note, our validation is limited to false positives. We do not investigate false negatives (scripts that do perform bot detection, but were not detected): such scripts were not collected.

In a preliminary validation run, we observed that some patterns are more likely to produce false positives than others. Therefore, we assessed false positive rates for the patterns individually by building sets containing all scripts that triggered a specific pattern.

Table 5 depicts the results of our validation by showing the set size of validated scripts, number of false positives (FP) and the percentage of false positives per set. For 20 out of 29 patterns, many sites used the exact same script. In these cases, we validated the entire set by reviewing all unique scripts in the set. Any found false positives were weighted accordingly.

For the remaining patterns, the sets of scripts was too diverse to allow full manual validation. We used random sampling with a sample size that provides 95% confidence to validate these patterns. In Table 5, we list these patterns together with the sample size.

Our validation shows that the patterns $wdc and _selenium raise a non-negligible number of false positives, though scripts matching these patterns only constitute a tiny portion of our dataset. The other patterns are good indicators of web bot detection.

7 Cloaking: Are Some Browsers More Equal Than Others?

Finally, we studied whether sites we identified as engaging in bot detection respond differently to web bot visitors. That is: do these websites tailor their response to specific web bots? Note that we manually examine the response to generic web bots, which differs from previous work that investigated cloaking in the context of search engine manipulation [ITK+16, WD05, WSV11].

We first assess the range of visible variations by visiting 20 sites that triggered a high number of patterns. To do so, we visited websites and took screenshots with a manual driven Chrome browser and an automated PhantomJS browser – the most detected and most detectable automation framework in our study. This was repeated 5 times to exclude other causes, such as content updates. We found four types of deviating responses: CAPTCHAs (3 sites), error responses of being blocked (1 site), connection cancellation or content not displayed (1 site) and different content (12 sites).

The differences in content concerned page layout (2 sites), videos that do not load (3 sites), missing ads (9 sites) and missing elements (1 site). We found that these deviations are highly likely to be caused by bot detection, e.g. one site in our set does not display login elements to web bots (see Fig. 6 in Appendix A). In contrast, deviations such as malformed page layouts may be a result of PhantomJS' rendering engine.

We found that sites with missing videos use scripts to serve the videos by wistia.com. These scripts include code to detect PhantomJS. We therefore believe the lack of video to be due to web bot detection, though we cannot be certain without reverse engineering these scripts fully.

Lastly, we explored how often deviations due to bot detection occur. In addition to PhantomJS, we add a Selenium-driven Chrome browser. We randomly selected 108 sites out of our set of detectors. Each site was visited once manually and 5 times with each bot, using different machines and IPs. By comparing the resulting screenshots we found deviations on 50 sites. From these deviations, we removed every observation (e.g. deformed layouts and inconsistent results over multiple visits) that we could not clearly relate to web bot detection. This results in 29 websites where we interpret deviations as a cause of web bot detection (see Appendix A).

We found 10 websites that do not display the main page or show error messages to web bots. CAPTCHAs were shown on 2 sites. We further encountered missing elements on 2 sites and videos failed to load on 4 sites. Lastly, 15 sites served less ads. Overall, deviations appeared more often in PhantomJS (24) than in Selenium-driven Chrome browsers (14).

8   Conclusions

The detection of web bots is crucial to protect websites against malicious bots. At the same time, it affects automated measurements of the web. This raises the question of how reliable such measurements are. Determining how many websites use web bot detection puts an upper bound on how many websites may respond differently to web bots than to regular browsers.

This study explored how prevalent client-side web bot detection is. We reverse engineered a commercial client-side web bot detection script, and found that it partially relied on browser fingerprinting. Leveraging this finding, we set out to determine the unique parts of the browser fingerprint of various web bots: their *fingerprint surface*. To this end, we grouped browsers into families as determined by their layout and rendering engines. Differences between members of the same family then constituted the fingerprint surface. We determined the fingerprint surface of 14 web bots. We found PhantomJS in particular to stand out: it has many features by which it can be detected.

We translated the fingerprint surfaces into patterns to look for in JavaScript source code, and added additional patterns from the reverse analysis and common best practices. We then developed a scanner built upon OpenWPM to scan the JavaScript source of the main page of all websites in the Alexa Top 1M. We found that over 12% of websites detect PhantomJS. Other web bots are detected less frequently, but browser automation frameworks Selenium, WebDriver and Chrome Headless are each detected on about 1% of the sites.

Lastly, we performed a qualitative investigation whether web bot detection leads to a different web page. We found that indeed, some browsers are more equal than others: CAPTCHAs, blocked responses different content occur. In a further experiment, we attribute at least 29 out of 108 encountered differences.

Future Work. We plan to investigate advanced fingerprint techniques to reveal further unique properties in web bots fingerprint surfaces. Further, expanding our current measurement technique with dynamic approaches can contribute to deliver more accurate measurements of the occurrence of web bot detection. Finally, we plan to develop a stealth scanner, whose browser fingerprint is as close as possible to that of a regular browser. This can be used for future studies, as well as experiments repeating previous studies to determine the effect of web bot detection on those studies.

A   Screenshots from Effects of Web Bot Detection

Comparing websites requested from web bots with websites requested from human controlled browsers can lead to various deviations. On sites that perform bot detection, we found websites that do not display login elements for visitors using PhantomJS or do not load videos (c.f. Figs. 6 and 7) (Figs. 4 and 5).

Fig. 4. Missing login fields on kiyu.tw.

Fig. 5. Missing video on hummingbird drones.ca.

Pardon Our Interruption

As you were browsing, something about your browser made us think you were a
bot. There are a few reasons why this might happen:

- You're using a **browser plugin** that is preventing JavaScript from running
- You're using a VPN or privacy software often used by attackers
- You're a power user moving through this website with super-human speed

After completing the CAPTCHA below, you will immediately regain access

Loading Captcha ...
You reached this page when attempting to access http://frankmotorsinc.com/ from 81.173.226.63 on 2018-11-11
15:16:15 UTC.
Trace: 3d5a7aae-7f31-42d4-be59-6834234a5bc0 via 60c20ce9-25f9-404c-90f0-115de631f853

Fig. 6. Blockage and loading of a CAPTCHA on frankmotorsinc.com.

Fig. 7. Missing ads on cordcutters news.com.

B   Advanced Notes to Determining the Fingerprint Surface

The following subsections provide further insights into our process to derive a fingerprint surface for web bots. We begin with the description of our modification to fingerprintjs2, in order to cover more web bot specific characteristics. Then, we give an overview of our used setup during to make this process repeatable.

B.1   Extra Elements Used in Determining the Fingerprint

There are several discussions on best practices for identifying web bots available online. From this, we included the following extra elements to include in the browser fingerprint:

- Lack of "bind" JavaScript engine feature[8].
  Certain older web bots make use of outdated JavaScript engines that do not support this feature, which allows them to be distinguished from full JavaScript engines.
- StackTrace[9].
  When throwing an error in PhantomJS, the resulting StackTrace includes the string 'phantomjs'.
- Properties of missing images[10].
  The width and height of a missing image is zero in headless Chrome, while being non-zero in full Chrome.
- Sandboxed `XMLHttpRequest` (See footnote 8).
  PhantomJS allows turning off "web-security", which permits a website to execute a cross-domain `XMLHttpRequest()`.
- Autoclosing dialog windows (See footnote 8).
  PhantomJS auto-closes dialog windows.

---

[8] https://blog.shapesecurity.com/2015/01/22/detecting-phantomjs-based-visitors/.

[9] https://www.slideshare.net/SergeyShekyan/shekyan-zhang-owasp.

[10] https://antoinevastel.com/bot%20detection/2017/08/05/detect-chrome-headless.html.

B.2   Setup for Determining the Fingerprint Surface

The resulting fingerprint surface of a web bot framework depends on used versions of the framework and corresponding browser. The versions and setup that were used during our experiment are listed in Table 6. Human-controlled browsers are marked as bold.

Table 6. Configurations used to determine fingerprint surfaces.

OS	Browser	Version
Ubuntu 16.04	**Chrome**	64.0.3282.140
	Chrome & Chromium + Selenium ChromeDriver	Sel: 4.0.0; WD: 2.35
	Chrome + Selenium IDE	C: 62.0.3202.94; IDE: 3.0.1
	NightmareJS	2.10
	Chrome & Chromium Puppeteer	1.1.0
	Firefox	54.0.1
	Firefox + Selenium GeckoDriver	Sel: 4.0.0; WD: 0.19.1
	Firefox + Selenium IDE	2.9.1 & 3.0.1
	Opera	53
	Opera + Selenium OperaDriver	Sel: 4.0.0; WD: 2.36
Windows 10	**Microsoft Edge**	41.16.299.15.0
	Microsoft Edge + Selenium Edge Driver	Sel: 4.0.1; WD: 10.0.16299.15
	Internet Explorer	11.0.50
	IE + Selenium InternetExplorerWebDriver	Sel: 4.0.1; WD: 3.9.0
OS X 10.13.5	**Safari**	12.0
	SafariDriver	Sel: 3.6.0; WD: N/A
	PhantomJS	2.1.0

References

[AJN+13] Acar, G., et al.: FPDetective: dusting the web for fingerprinters. In Proceedings of the 2013 ACM SIGSAC conference on Computer and Communications Security, pp. 1129–1140. ACM (2013)

[BFGI11] Boda, K., Földes, Á.M., Gulyás, G.G., Imre, S.: User tracking on the web via cross-browser fingerprinting. In: Laud, P. (ed.) NordSec 2011. LNCS, vol. 7161, pp. 31–46. Springer, Heidelberg (2012). https://doi.org/10.1007/978-3-642-29615-4_4

604   H. Jonker et al.

[BLRP10] Brewer, D., Li, K., Ramaswamy, L., Pu, C.: A link obfuscation service to detect webbots. In: 2010 IEEE International Conference on Services Computing, SCC 2010, Miami, Florida, USA, 5–10 July 2010, pp. 433–440 (2010)

[CGK+13] Chu, Z., Gianvecchio, S., Koehl, A., Wang, H., Jajodia, S.: Blog or block: detecting blog bots through behavioral biometrics. Comput. Netw. **57**(3), 634–646 (2013)

[DG11] Doran, D., Gokhale, S.S.: Web robot detection techniques: overview and limitations. Data Min. Knowl. Discov. **22**(1–2), 183–210 (2011)

[Eck10] Eckersley, P.: How unique is your web browser? In: Atallah, M.J., Hopper, N.J. (eds.) PETS 2010. LNCS, vol. 6205, pp. 1–18. Springer, Heidelberg (2010). https://doi.org/10.1007/978-3-642-14527-8_1

[EN16] Englehardt, S., Narayanan, A.: Online tracking: a 1-million-site measurement and analysis. In: Proceedings of the 2016 ACM SIGSAC Conference on Computer and Communications Security, pp. 1388–1401. ACM (2016)

[GG05a] Grosskurth, A., Godfrey, M.W.: A reference architecture for web browsers. In: 21st IEEE International Conference on Software Maintenance (ICSM 2005), Budapest, Hungary, 25–30 September 2005, pp. 661–664 (2005)

[GG05b] Gyöngyi, Z., Garcia-Molina, H.: Web spam taxonomy. In: First International Workshop on Adversarial Information Retrieval on the Web, AIRWeb 2005, Co-located with the WWW Conference, Chiba, Japan, May 2005, pp. 39–47 (2005)

[ITK+16] Invernizzi, L., Thomas, K., Kapravelos, A., Comanescu, O., Picod, J.M., Bursztein, E.: Cloak of visibility: detecting when machines browse a different web. In: Proceedings of the 37th IEEE Symposium on Security and Privacy, SP 2016, San Jose, CA, USA, 22–26 May 2016, pp. 743–758 (2016)

[MBYS11] Mowery, K., Bogenreif, D., Yilek, S., Shacham, H.: Fingerprinting information in JavaScript implementations. In: Proceedings of Web 2.0 Security and Privacy (W2SP 2011), vol. 2. IEEE Computer Society (2011)

[MS12] Mowery, K., Shacham, H.: Pixel perfect: fingerprinting canvas in HTML5. In: Proceedings of Web 2.0 Security and Privacy (W2SP 2012). IEEE Computer Society (2012)

[NIK+12] Nikiforakis, N., et al.: You are what you include: large-scale evaluation of remote javascript inclusions. In: Proceedings of the 19th ACM Conference on Computer and Communications Security, CCS 2012, Raleigh, NC, USA, 16–18 October 2012, pp. 736–747 (2012)

[NKJ+13] Nikiforakis, N., Kapravelos, A., Joosen, W., Kruegel, C., Piessens, F., Vigna, G.: Cookieless monster: exploring the ecosystem of web-based device fingerprinting. In: Proceedings of 34th IEEE Symposium on Security and Privacy (SP 2013), pp. 541–555. IEEE Computer Society (2013)

[PPLC06] Park, K.S., Pai, V.S., Lee, K.-W., Calo, S.B.: Securing web service by automatic robot detection. In: Proceedings of the 2006 USENIX Annual Technical Conference, Boston, MA, USA, 30 May–3 June 2006, pp. 255–260 (2006)

[PSF16] Pham, K., Santos, A.S.R., Freire, J.: Understanding website behavior based on user agent. In: Proceedings of the 39th International ACM SIGIR Conference on Research and Development in Information Retrieval, SIGIR 2016, Pisa, Italy, 17–21 July 2016, pp. 1053–1056 (2016)

[SD09] Stassopoulou, A., Dikaiakos, M.D.: Web robot detection: a probabilistic reasoning approach. Comput. Netw. **53**(3), 265–278 (2009)

[TJM15]   Torres, C.F., Jonker, H., Mauw, S.: *FP-Block*: usable web privacy by controlling browser fingerprinting. In: Pernul, G., Ryan, P.Y.A., Weippl, E. (eds.) ESORICS 2015. LNCS, vol. 9327, pp. 3–19. Springer, Cham (2015). https://doi.org/10.1007/978-3-319-24177-7_1

[vABHL03] von Ahn, L., Blum, M., Hopper, N.J., Langford, J.: CAPTCHA: using hard AI problems for security. In: Biham, E. (ed.) EUROCRYPT 2003. LNCS, vol. 2656, pp. 294–311. Springer, Heidelberg (2003). https://doi.org/10.1007/3-540-39200-9_18

[VYG13]   Vikram, S., Yang, C., Gu, G.: NOMAD: towards non-intrusive moving-target defense against web bots. In: IEEE Conference on Communications and Network Security, CNS 2013, National Harbor, MD, USA, 14–16 October 2013, pp. 55–63 (2013)

[WD05]   Wu, B., Davison, B.D.: Cloaking and redirection: a preliminary study. In: First International Workshop on Adversarial Information Retrieval on the Web, AIRWeb 2005, Co-located with the WWW Conference, Chiba, Japan, May 2005, pp. 7–16 (2005)

[WSV11]   Wang, D.Y., Savage, S., Voelker, G.M.: Cloak and dagger: dynamics of web search cloaking. In: Proceedings of the 18th ACM Conference on Computer and Communications Security, CCS 2011, Chicago, Illinois, USA, 17–21 October 2011, pp. 477–490 (2011)

[XLC+18] Xu, H., et al.: Detecting and characterizing web bot traffic in a large e-commerce marketplace. In: Lopez, J., Zhou, J., Soriano, M. (eds.) ESORICS 2018. LNCS, vol. 11099, pp. 143–163. Springer, Cham (2018). https://doi.org/10.1007/978-3-319-98989-1_8

Testing for Integrity Flaws
in Web Sessions

Stefano Calzavara$^{(\boxtimes)}$, Alvise Rabitti, Alessio Ragazzo, and Michele Bugliesi

Università Ca' Foscari Venezia, Venice, Italy
stefano.calzavara@unive.it

Abstract. Web sessions are fragile and can be attacked at many different levels. Classic attacks like session hijacking, session fixation and cross-site request forgery are particularly dangerous for web session security, because they allow the attacker to breach the integrity of honest users' sessions by forging requests which get authenticated on the victim's behalf. In this paper, we systematize current countermeasures against these attacks and the shortcomings thereof, which may completely void protection under specific assumptions on the attacker's capabilities. We then build on our security analysis to introduce black-box testing strategies to discover insecure session implementation practices on existing websites, which we implement in a browser extension called Dredd. Finally, we use Dredd to assess the security of 20 popular websites from Alexa, exposing a number of session integrity flaws.

Keywords: Web sessions · Session hijacking · Session fixation · CSRF

1 Introduction

Since the HTTP protocol is stateless, web applications treat each HTTP request independently from all the others by default. However, online services often need to track state information across multiple HTTP requests to provide controlled access to private data and authorize security-sensitive operations for authenticated users. HTTP *cookies* are the most common mechanism to maintain state information across HTTP requests [2], thus enabling the implementation of *authenticated web sessions*. Unfortunately, web session security is hard to get right, as shown by the huge number of attacks and defenses presented in the literature [13]. As a result, although it is possible to ensure the security of web sessions using existing technologies, web session implementations in the wild still suffer from severe security flaws [8,29,30,35].

Security testing is a very popular solution to detect vulnerabilities in web applications [5]. The Open Web Application Security Project (OWASP) has long recognized the importance of testing for web application security and maintains a guide with recommendations about it - the OWASP Testing Guide [25] - which also includes a section about *session management*. Although this guide provides useful advice to improve web session security, it is not systematic and does not

© Springer Nature Switzerland AG 2019
K. Sako et al. (Eds.): ESORICS 2019, LNCS 11736, pp. 606–624, 2019.
https://doi.org/10.1007/978-3-030-29962-0_29

provide a comprehensive coverage of realistic attack vectors based on a rigorous threat model. For instance, the proposed testing strategy for cross-site request forgery vulnerabilities is insufficient to assess security against network attackers who have control of the HTTP traffic, because it does not consider their ability to compromise cookie integrity [4]. Moreover, a number of recommendations in the OWASP Testing Guide are rather generic or overly conservative, making them hard to follow for web developers. For instance, the proposed testing strategy for session hijacking recommends the use of an intercepting proxy to check that all cookies containing session identifiers are marked with the `Secure` attribute to prevent their leakage over HTTP. However, this can be hard to do in practice, because it presupposes that security testers know the role of all cookies, and it might even be unnecessary, because when multiple cookies are used for session management it might suffice to protect just one of them [15,23].

Our main goal in the present work is to make security testing for web sessions more principled and systematic by building on precise security properties and threat models. At the same time, we advocate the adoption of testing strategies which *semantically* capture attacks, thus detecting exploitable vulnerabilities, as opposed to testing strategies based on syntactic conditions, such as the aforementioned use of the `Secure` attribute, which instead can just identify room for *potential* attacks. Our approach makes security testing more effective by eliminating false positives and enables a more precise security assessment.

Contributions. Concretely, we make the following contributions:

1. we provide an in-depth, up-to-date security analysis of web sessions that reviews attacks, current countermeasures and the shortcomings thereof. While several of such considerations have been piecemeal reported in the literature, we are not aware of any previous attempt to organize them within a comprehensive, uniform framework. In particular, our analysis is based on a clear notion of *session integrity* and a rich threat model which includes web attackers, related-domain attackers and network attackers (Sect. 3);
2. we design black-box testing strategies to systematically detect integrity flaws in existing web session implementations. Each testing strategy is parametric with respect to the choice of an arbitrary attacker from our threat model and targeted at detecting *exploitable* vulnerabilities, without requiring deep understanding of the web application logic (Sect. 4);
3. we implement our testing strategies in a browser extension, called Dredd[1], which we make available upon request. We use Dredd to assess the security of 20 popular websites from the Alexa ranking, exposing a number of session integrity flaws exploitable by different attackers (Sect. 5).

---

[1] The browser extension is named after Judge Joseph Dredd, a law enforcement and judicial officer in the dystopian future created by some popular British comic books.

2   Background

2.1   Same-Origin Policy

The same-origin policy (SOP) is a security policy implemented by all browsers, which enforces a strict separation between contents provided by unrelated websites [22]. SOP allows scripts running in a page to access data of another page only if the pages have the same *origin*, i.e., the same protocol, host and port [3].

SOP mediates several operations in the browser, including DOM and cookie accesses. For instance, if a page at `https://www.example.com` embeds an iframe from `http://www.evil.com`, malicious scripts running in the iframe cannot read or write the DOM of the embedding page, because they come from a different origin. However, a few important browser operations are not subject to same-origin checks, e.g., the inclusions of scripts and the submissions of forms. This leaves room for attacks like cross-site request forgery, which is extensively discussed in the next sections.

2.2   HTTP Cookies

Roughly, a cookie is a key-value pair, which is set by the server into the browser and then automatically attached by the browser to all the subsequent requests to the server, using the `Cookie` header. Cookies can be set using the `Set-Cookie` header or by means of JavaScript through the `document.cookie` property.

Cookies rely on a relaxed definition of origin, since they are normally shared across all protocols and ports of the host setting them. For instance, scripts at `https://www.example.com` can read the cookies of `http://www.example.com`, although these two origins do not match. By default, cookies are only attached to requests sent to the same host which set them (*host-only cookies*). However, a host may also set cookies for a parent domain by means of the `Domain` attribute, as long as the parent domain does not occur in a list of public suffixes[2]: these cookies are shared across all the sub-domains of such domain (*domain cookies*).

It is sometimes desirable to improve the confidentiality guarantees of cookies. For instance, scripts at `http://www.example.com` can normally access cookies set by `https://www.example.com`, although these scripts were not sent over a secure channel. The `Secure` attribute can be used to mark cookies which must only be accessed from HTTPS pages and sent over HTTPS channels.

2.3   HTTP Strict Transport Security

HTTP Strict Transport Security (HSTS) is a security policy implemented in all modern web browsers, which allows hosts to require browsers to communicate with them only over HTTPS [18]. Specifically, HTTP requests to HSTS hosts are automatically upgraded to HTTPS by the browser before they are sent.

HSTS can be activated over HTTPS using the `Strict-Transport-Security` header, where it is possible to specify for how long HSTS should be active and

---

[2] Available at https://publicsuffix.org/.

whether its protection should additionally be extended to sub-domains. Alternatively, hosts may request to be included in the HSTS preload list of major web browsers, so that HSTS is activated on them by default. We refer to *full* HSTS adoption when a host activates HSTS for itself and all its sub-domains, and to *partial* HSTS adoption when a host activates HSTS just for itself. We discuss a few shortcomings of the partial HSTS adoption in the next sections.

3   Integrity Analysis of Web Sessions

We describe the typical set-up of a web session. Browser B, operated by user Alice, submits a login form including valid access credentials to website W, which replies by sending back a cookie *sid* storing a session identifier which uniquely identifies Alice; we refer to *sid* as the *session cookie*[3]. Browser B then automatically attaches *sid* to all the subsequent requests sent to W, so that W has a way to authenticate Alice and authorize operations on her behalf.

3.1   Web Session Integrity

We say that Alice's session has *integrity* when a malicious user Mallory cannot forge requests which get authenticated under Alice's identity. There are three ways available to Mallory to break session integrity:

1. *session hijacking*: if Mallory is able to steal Alice's *sid*, she can authenticate as Alice at W directly from her browser (Sect. 3.3);
2. *session fixation*: if Mallory can force Alice's *sid* to a known value, she can authenticate as Alice at W directly from her browser (Sect. 3.4);
3. *cross-site request forgery*: if Mallory cannot steal or force the choice of Alice's *sid*, she can still forge security-sensitive requests from Alice's browser B, so as to fool W into processing such requests on Alice's behalf (Sect. 3.5).

We only cover attacks where Mallory intrudes on Alice's session. Attacks where Alice is forced into Mallory's session, e.g., login CSRF and cookie forcing [13], are considered out of scope. The reason is that such threats are specific to a relatively narrow class of web applications and use cases.

3.2   Threat Model

The goal of Mallory is to break the integrity of sessions established between Alice and the target website $W = $ www.target.com. We consider three different attackers. The weakest one is the *web attacker*, who is the owner of a malicious website [1]. This attacker can reply to HTTP requests to her website with arbitrary contents and can obtain a valid HTTPS certificate for her website

---

[3] Real services often use multiple session cookies, but the discussion abstracts from this point for simplicity. Session cookies have also been called *authentication cookies* in related work [15].

from a trusted certification authority. To simplify the exposition, we stipulate that the web attacker operates `https://www.attacker.com`. We assume that the user accesses this malicious website from her browser, either deliberately or because she is fooled into doing it. However, we assume that the web attacker has no scripting capabilities at the target: she has no control of active contents included by the target itself and she cannot exploit cross-site scripting vulnerabilities (XSS) therein. This is a standard assumption, motivated by the fact that most web defenses are voided when the attacker can script in the target's origin.

The *related-domain* attacker is a stronger variant of the web attacker, who can host her website on a related domain of the target website [6]. Two domains are related when they share a sufficiently long suffix, e.g., `accounts.example.com` and `mail.example.com`; any non-public suffix will work in current browsers. The related-domain attacker is traditionally considered in the web session security literature, due to her extended ability to compromise cookie confidentiality and integrity compared to the web attacker. Though most websites do not lease subdomains to untrusted organizations, a recent study highlighted the threats of the related-domain attacker due to the common use of a large number of subdomains, many of which at low security [12]. To improve readability, we stipulate that the related-domain attacker is hosted at `https://attacker.target.com`.

Finally, the *network attacker* extends the capabilities of the web attacker with the ability to read, modify and block the contents of all the HTTP traffic. However, we assume that this attacker cannot sniff or corrupt the HTTPS traffic, due to the adoption of trusted certificates at the target website. When reasoning about session integrity against the network attacker, we always assume that the target website is deployed on HTTPS, otherwise the website is trivially insecure.

Observe that the web attacker is weaker than both the related-domain attacker and the network attacker by definition, while the related-domain attacker and the network attacker are incomparable. In particular, although the network attacker can masquerade as any HTTP website, she cannot host any HTTPS website on a related domain of the target website.

3.3   Session Hijacking

Session hijacking happens when the attacker is able to steal the session cookies of the victim and uses them to impersonate her at the target website. Different attackers have different ways to steal session cookies: although the web attacker has no access to such cookies in absence of XSS (thanks to SOP), the related-domain attacker and the network attacker are more powerful. In particular, the related-domain attacker can potentially access all the domain cookies of the target website and intrude on the victim's session by reusing them.

The picture is more complex for the network attacker. If HSTS is not enabled at the target website, any cookie without the `Secure` attribute can be disclosed. This is true even if the target website is entirely deployed on HTTPS, because the network attacker can still force the victim's browser into trying to contact the target website over HTTP [8]. If instead HSTS is partially adopted, host-only cookies cannot be disclosed irrespective of the use of the `Secure` attribute,

Table 1. Conditions for cookie leakage under different attackers

Attacker	Condition for cookie leakage
Web attacker	No leakage is possible (in absence of XSS)
Related-domain attacker	The `Domain` attribute is set to a parent domain
Network attacker	Either of the following conditions holds true: 1. No HSTS adoption and the `Secure` attribute is not set; 2. Partial HSTS adoption, the `Secure` attribute is not set and the `Domain` attribute is set to a parent domain

because the victim's browser will never contact the target website over HTTP; however, domain cookies must still be marked with the `Secure` attribute to prevent their disclosure [21]. Finally, in the case of a full HSTS adoption, the network attacker is no more powerful than the web attacker for session hijacking and the use of the `Secure` attribute is redundant.

Table 1 summarizes the conditions under which the confidentiality of cookies can be violated. To ensure protection against session hijacking, it is critical to ensure the confidentiality of the session cookies.

3.4   Session Fixation

Session fixation is enabled by the insecure practice of preserving the same value of the session cookies before and after authentication. This typically happens when session cookies are used to store state information even before login, e.g., to add items to a shopping cart. In this case, the attacker can obtain a set of session cookies from the target website without authenticating and force them into the victim's browser, using different techniques; if the victim later authenticates at the target, she will be identified by the session cookies chosen by the attacker, who will then become able to impersonate the victim [19].

Different attackers have different ways to force session cookies into the victim's browser. Again, the web attacker lacks this capability in absence of XSS, because SOP prevents her from setting cookies for the target website, but the related-domain attacker and the network attacker are more powerful. Specifically, the related-domain attacker can set domain cookies for the target website, which are indistinguishable from host-only cookies to it [6]. Though the related-domain attacker cannot overwrite host-only cookies previously set by the target website due to SOP, she can still issue domain cookies before the host-only cookies are set, which often suffices to prevent the host-only cookies from ever being issued. Moreover, the related-domain attacker can set domain cookies with the same name of host-only cookies, which may fool the target website into choosing the domain cookies over the host-only cookies [35]. The only effective way

Table 2. Conditions for cookie compromise under different attackers

Attacker	Condition for cookie compromise
Web attacker	No compromise is possible (in absence of XSS)
Related-domain attacker	Lack of __Host- prefix in the cookie name
Network attacker	Both the following conditions hold true: 1. Lack of full HSTS adoption; 2. Lack of __Host- and __Secure- prefixes in the cookie name

to prevent these attacks is extending the name of the session cookies with the __Host- prefix, which requires cookies to be set as host-only [32]. The __Host-prefix also has the benefit of requiring cookies to be set over HTTPS with the Secure attribute, which is useful against the network attacker.

As to the network attacker, she can abuse the lack of HSTS to set cookies for the target website by forging HTTP traffic. Notice that a full HSTS adoption is needed to prevent this attack, otherwise the network attacker could still make the victim's browser contact a sub-domain of the target website over HTTP and then forge domain cookies from there. If full HSTS is not an option for some reason, an alternative protection mechanism is based on the use of the __Secure-prefix in the cookie name, which requires cookies to be set over HTTPS with the Secure attribute [32]. Notice that the Secure attribute alone does not suffice to provide cookie integrity, because modern browsers prevent cookies with the Secure attribute from being set or overwritten over HTTP, yet cookies with the same name but without the Secure attribute can still be forged over HTTP before the legitimate cookies are actually issued [33].

Table 2 provides a summary of the conditions under which the integrity of cookies can be violated. To prevent session fixation, it is important to guarantee the integrity of the session cookies which are not freshly issued upon login.

3.5 Cross-Site Request Forgery

Cross-site request forgery (CSRF) is enabled by the standard behavior of web browsers to attach cookies to all HTTP requests by default, irrespective of the origin of the page which fired the request [4]. A CSRF attack typically works as follows: the victim first logs into the target website and gets a set of session cookies which authenticates her; the victim then visits the attacker's website, which sends a *cross-site* request to the target, e.g., using HTML or JavaScript. Since the request includes the victim's cookies, it is authenticated as coming from the victim, hence it may be abused to trigger security-sensitive operations at the victim's account. There are different defenses against CSRF.

Custom Headers. JavaScript can set HTTP headers with custom names, for instance X-Requested-With, to be attached to outgoing HTTP requests. Since

Table 3. Examples of dangerous Referer/Origin headers

Attacker		Spoofed Referer/Origin
Web attacker		`https://www.target.com.attacker.com`
Related-domain attacker		`https://attacker.target.com`
Network attacker	No HSTS	`http://www.target.com`
	Partial HSTS	`http://attacker.target.com`
	Full HSTS	`https://www.target.com.attacker.com`

SOP prevents the setting of custom headers for cross-origin requests, the mere presence of such headers can be used to stop CSRF attempts. Given that none of the attackers we consider controls the exact origin of the target website, custom headers are an effective protection mechanism against all the attackers. Unfortunately, custom headers can only be used by websites which implement all their security-sensitive operations via JavaScript.

Referer/Origin Header. Browsers normally attach to each outgoing request at least one between two standard HTTP headers, called `Referer` and `Origin`, which contain the URI and the origin of the page which triggered the request respectively. This can be used to filter out cross-site requests, but some care is needed to implement this check correctly. We discuss just the case of the `Referer` header, because the same reasoning applies to the `Origin` header.

Though the web attacker is hosted at `https://www.attacker.com`, she could try to fool the target via the sub-domain `www.target.com.attacker.com`, so that the `Referer` header of requests coming from this sub-domain will start with the substring `https://www.target.com`. This would be enough to fool a `Referer` check based on a liberal regular expression. The related-domain attacker, instead, could send requests from `https://attacker.target.com`, which would bypass lenient `Referer` checks allowing requests from any sub-domain. Finally, the network attacker could abuse the lack of HSTS to send requests from `http://www.target.com`, which would escape `Referer` checks that are intended to filter out cross-site requests, but do not enforce the use of the HTTPS protocol. Observe that, if HSTS is only partially adopted, the network attacker could attempt a variant of the attack from `http://attacker.target.com`. This would fool `Referer` checks which are intended to only accept requests from sub-domains, but do not check for the adoption of the HTTPS protocol. In the case of a full HSTS adoption, the network attacker loses these capabilities and becomes no more powerful than the web attacker.

Table 3 shows "canonical" examples of `Referer` values which could be abused by the different attackers based on the previous discussion. Recall that both the related-domain attacker and the network attacker subsume the web attacker, so the first choice in the table is also available to them.

Anti-CSRF Tokens. Another common approach to CSRF prevention is based on the use of random tokens to be included in legitimate authenticated requests: requests lacking a valid token do not get processed. Tokens are normally embedded in DOM elements which fire requests for security-sensitive operations, e.g., as a hidden field of payment forms. If tokens cannot be predicted or disclosed, the attacker cannot craft cross-site requests which get successfully processed by the target website. There are two traditional ways to implement tokens.

The first approach is based on *stateful tokens*. Stateful tokens are stored at the server side, typically bound to users' sessions. For example, the server could store in Alice's session the information that authenticated requests from Alice must include the token `Xf12gh68g`. The second approach is based on *stateless tokens*, which do not require such server-side state, but are harder to implement securely. Stateless tokens are stored at the browser side, often inside a cookie. For example, the server could set a cookie containing the token `G9jp3mNt` in Alice's browser and require authenticated requests to include such token inside a parameter: this pattern is called *double submit*. Variants of this approach rely on the encryption or other transformations of the token set in the cookie.

Stateless tokens can be attacked at different levels. If the confidentiality of the cookie storing the token is not guaranteed, no protection against CSRF is granted when the token validation process is performed via a parameter value which can be computed from the token alone: we refer to Table 1 for a summary of the conditions which can lead to cookie leakage. If instead the attacker can compromise the integrity of the cookie storing the token, she can acquire a valid token from the server and force it in the victim's browser, so that the session is still protected with a token known by the attacker. To avoid this issue, stateless tokens must be *session-dependent*, so that the attacker's tokens cannot be used in the victim's session [4]. We refer to Table 2 for a summary of the conditions which enable cookie compromise.

Same-Site Cookies. Cookies can be marked with the `SameSite` attribute to signal to the browser that they should not be attached to cross-site requests, thus preventing CSRF attempts directly at the client side. This approach is effective, since it fixes one of the root causes of CSRF, i.e., browsers attaching session cookies by default. Strict or lax protection can be given by the `SameSite` attribute, with the latter mode relaxing the mentioned security restriction in the case of top-level navigations with a "safe" HTTP method [34].

4   Integrity Testing of Web Sessions

We now build on our security analysis to design precise black-box testing strategies which allow human experts to detect session integrity flaws. Our main goal is finding *exploitable* vulnerabilities without requiring an in-depth understanding of the web application logic. All the testing strategies presuppose the availability of two test accounts at the website under scrutiny, called Alice and Mallory. Alice acts as the victim, while Mallory acts as the attacker; each strategy is parametric with respect to the choice of an attacker from our threat model, which defines Mallory's capabilities (see Sect. 3.2). If Mallory's actions affect Alice's session, we have a session integrity problem.

4.1 Testing for Session Hijacking

The intuition behind the testing strategy for session hijacking is to simulate a scenario where Mallory steals all Alice's cookies she might be exposed to (cf. Table 1). Mallory may then use these cookies to access Alice's account: if they are enough to act on Alice's behalf, session hijacking is possible. Even when this is not possible, however, security might still be at risk, because it might be that not all the cookies were disclosed to Mallory and the attempted operation failed because just a subset of the expected cookies was sent to the website. To account for this case, we also perform a fresh login to the website as Mallory to get a full set of cookies and then restore the cookies stolen from Alice before reattempting the operation, so that all the website cookies (though mixed from two different accounts) are sent as part of a new operation attempt: if the operation succeeds in Alice's account, session hijacking is possible. Specifically, the testing strategy proceeds as follows:

1. Login to `www.target.com` as Alice and reach the page under test;
2. Find the cookies which satisfy the cookie leakage conditions in Table 1 based on Mallory's capabilities and clear all the other cookies from the browser;
3. Perform the operation under test;
4. Check: has the operation been performed? If yes, report as insecure;
5. Clear the cookies from the browser;
6. Login to `www.target.com` as Mallory and reach the page under test;
7. Restore in the browser the cookies previously kept at step 2;
8. Perform again the operation under test;
9. Clear the cookies from the browser and login to `www.target.com` as Alice;
10. Check: has the operation been performed? If yes, report as insecure.

4.2 Testing for Session Fixation

To test for session fixation, we simulate a scenario where Mallory forces in Alice's browser all the cookies which are not freshly issued after login and do not have integrity against her (cf. Table 2). After Alice's login, Mallory presents the forced cookies to access Alice's account: if they are enough to act on Alice's behalf, session fixation is possible. The testing strategy for session fixation thus follows the same pattern of the testing strategy for session hijacking, with the only exception of step 2. More precisely, we replace step 2 as follows:

2. Find the cookies which satisfy the cookie compromise conditions in Table 2 based on Mallory's capabilities and were not freshly issued after the login process, then clear all the other cookies from the browser;

The testing strategy still has two exit conditions for the reasons explained above.

4.3   Testing for Cross-Site Request Forgery

The proposed testing strategy for CSRF is a variant of the one presented in [30], extended to consider related-domain attackers and network attackers, as well as to cover a few additional subtleties emerged in our security analysis. The idea is to trigger the operation under test as Mallory and intercept the corresponding HTTP request to transform it into a variant which can be forged from Alice's browser from a cross-site position. The forged request lacks both custom headers and same-site cookies, yet includes a potentially dangerous value in the `Referer` and `Origin` headers, based on Mallory's capabilities (cf. Table 3). If the request is successfully processed by the website, a CSRF attack is possible. More precisely, the testing strategy proceeds as follows:

1. Login to `www.target.com` as Mallory and reach the page under test;
2. Perform the operation under test and intercept the corresponding HTTP request before it is sent;
3. Clear the cookies from the browser;
4. Login to `www.target.com` as Alice;
5. Forge a copy of the HTTP request intercepted at step 2 from a cross-site position and let the browser attach the HTTP headers (including the `Cookie` header containing Alice's cookies, with the exception of same-site cookies);
6. Set the `Referer` and `Origin` headers of the forged request to the values in Table 3 based on Mallory's capabilities, e.g., using an intercepting proxy;
7. Check: has the operation been performed? If yes, report as insecure.

If the operation has not been performed, we can conclude security against web attackers, but the picture is more complicated in case of stronger attackers, who can break the confidentiality and the integrity of stateless anti-CSRF tokens. We identify potentially vulnerable implementations of the double submit pattern by inspecting the HTTP request intercepted at step 2. If the request contains a cookie c and a parameter p such that the value of c matches the value of p, we reason about the confidentiality and the integrity of c (cf. Tables 1 and 2 respectively) and we revise the original testing strategy accordingly.

If c has low confidentiality, the anti-CSRF token stored in c becomes useless, because its value might be known to the attacker. However, this does not necessarily mean that it is possible to run a CSRF attack, because the tested website might implement multiple defenses against CSRF, e.g., it might also check for the presence of custom headers. To confirm the potential attack, we thus revise the original testing strategy as follows: after step 4 we read the value of the cookie c from Alice's session and at step 6 we modify the forged HTTP request so that the parameter p matches such value. This simulates a scenario where Mallory stole Alice's token and used it to forge the malicious request.

If c has low integrity, CSRF protection can be bypassed if the token stored in c is not session-dependent. To detect this, we have to test whether Mallory's token can successfully be used in Alice's session. We can do this by revising the original testing strategy as follows: after step 1 we read the value of the cookie c from Mallory's session and at step 6 we modify the forged HTTP request so that the cookie c matches such value. This simulates a scenario where Mallory's forced her own token into Alice's browser before forging the malicious request.

4.4 Discussion

Testing is a powerful tool to unveil security breaches, but clearly it is of no use in establishing security proofs. Irrespective of how carefully a testing strategy might have been designed, there is no way that black-box testing can be made complete in general: for instance, it is not possible to know whether a stateless anti-CSRF token is cryptographically bound to the value of a request parameter without having access to the web application code. A further important remark concerns *coverage*. In our testing strategies we assume that the security tester knows the security-sensitive operations to scrutinize. However, identifying all such operations in real websites might be complex: we refer to [10] for a recent research work on the topic. Having said that, the testing strategies we have just described turned out to be rather effective and useful in practice (see below).

5 Dredd: Implementation and Experiments

5.1 Security Testing with Dredd

We developed Dredd, a browser extension for Mozilla Firefox which implements and semi-automates the testing strategies presented in the previous section. The configuration of Dredd requires the specification of the access credentials of two test accounts (Alice and Mallory) for the website under test. When activated on a website, Dredd asks for the vulnerability to test for (session hijacking, session fixation or CSRF) and the attacker of interest (web attacker, related-domain attacker or network attacker). Dredd then instructs the security tester to login using one of the test accounts and perform the operation under test. Once the tester confirms that this has been done, Dredd runs the corresponding testing strategy up to completion and asks the security tester to confirm its outcome, i.e., to flag whether Mallory successfully managed to attack Alice or not. This is trivial to do for the security tester by visually checking the website, yet generally hard to automate given the variegate nature of existing web applications.

The Mozilla Firefox extension APIs support a natural and direct implementation of Dredd, because the `webRequest` API provides the ability to intercept and modify HTTP requests and responses, and extensions can ask for the `cookies` permission to access the cookie jar of all web origins. Porting Dredd to Google Chrome would be straightforward, given that Mozilla Firefox and Google Chrome essentially implement the same extension architecture.

5.2 Experimental Evaluation

We tested Dredd on 20 randomly sampled websites from the Alexa Top 1,000. We only considered websites in English or in Italian, since we were required to

Table 4. Overview of the vulnerabilities identified with Dredd

Website	Session hijacking		Session fixation		CSRF		
	Related	Network	Related	Network	Web	Related	Network
www.adobe.com	x	x					
www.airbnb.it	x						
www.aol.com	x						
www.bitdefender.net							
www.coursera.org	x						
www.expedia.com	x						
www.geeksforgeeks.org	x						
www.genius.com	x						
www.glassdoor.com		x					
www.groupon.com	x						
www.imgur.com	x	x				x	x
www.immobiliare.it	x	x	x	x			
www.instacart.com	x						
www.kijiji.it							
www.medium.com	x						
www.mondadoristore.it	x	x	x	x	x	x	x
www.prezi.com						x	x
www.quora.com	x	x	x	x	x	x	x
www.scoop.it		x					
www.yandex.com	x						

understand the website user interface and potential error messages. Moreover, we only considered websites which allow single sign-on access with a major identity provider (Google or Facebook), so as to avoid the manual account creation process. Finally, we only considered websites served over HTTPS, because the network attacker is part of our threat model.

For each website, we chose a single security-sensitive operation to test, based on our understanding of the web application semantics, and ran all our testing strategies under all the attackers of our threat model. Occasionally, we managed to avoid a few redundant tests: for instance, if a website is already vulnerable to CSRF attacks against the web attacker, then it also suffers from the same flaw against the related-domain attacker and the network attacker.

Table 4 provides the full breakdown of the identified vulnerabilities on the tested websites. We present the details in the rest of this section and discuss the security impact of our findings in Sect. 5.3.

Session Hijacking. The first observation we make is that the related-domain attacker is significantly more powerful than the network attacker when it comes to session hijacking. In particular, we found that the related-domain attacker can hijack the sessions of 15 websites, which is motivated by the fact that large websites often span multiple sub-domains, hence the use of domain cookies for session management is widespread. The proposed testing strategy completed 13 times at step 4 and twice at step 10, which shows that having two exit conditions there is sometimes useful in practice.

The network attacker can perform session hijacking on 7 websites, all of which were deemed as vulnerable at step 4 of the testing strategy. These websites do not implement full HSTS, yet make an insufficient use of the Secure attribute to protect their session cookies; 5 of them do not activate HSTS at all, while the other 2 websites do it only partially, i.e., without protecting their sub-domains. As to the 13 secure cases, 9 websites adopt full HSTS and 4 websites do not, but still manage to protect their sessions thanks to an appropriate use of the Secure attribute and/or the adoption of host-only cookies (in case of partial HSTS).

Session Fixation. We identified room for session fixation in 3 websites. All these websites are vulnerable against both the related-domain attacker and the network attacker. None of the websites uses cookies prefixes, 2 of them do not activate HSTS at all, while the last website does it only partially, hence cookie integrity is not guaranteed against the aforementioned attackers. The proposed testing strategy completed twice at step 4 and once at step 10, hence handling two exit conditions is occasionally useful to catch real-world vulnerabilities.

Cross-Site Request Forgery. The web attacker is able to exploit CSRF vulnerabilities just in 2 websites. This suggests that the large majority of the developers of the websites we tested are aware of the dangers of CSRF, which is reassuring considered their popularity. Remarkably, however, both the related-domain attacker and the network attacker are able to exploit 2 additional CSRF vulnerabilities on the tested websites, due to incorrect implementations of the double submit pattern. We discuss these two cases in detail.

The website www.imgur.com performs the double submit using a domain cookie which is not marked as Secure, hence both the related-domain attacker and the network attacker can breach its confidentiality and circumvent the CSRF protection. The website www.prezi.com implements the double submit pattern by using a cookie which is not session-dependent, without deploying HSTS or cookie prefixes to protect its integrity, hence both the related-domain attacker and the network attacker can bypass the CSRF protection mechanism. Moreover, this cookie is shared with the sub-domains and lacks the Secure attribute, hence its confidentiality is not guaranteed against the aforementioned attackers, which enables an additional vector for CSRF.

5.3   Security Impact

Web Attacker. The web attacker is the baseline attacker to consider on the Web, since the owner of any untrusted website can potentially act as the web attacker against a high-profile service. Luckily, we only found two websites which suffer from significant security flaws exploitable by the web attacker. It is worth discussing here the case of www.mondadoristore.it. This e-commerce website does not implement any form of protection against CSRF, hence all the security-sensitive functionality typical of such services, e.g., shopping cart management, is left vulnerable. Even worse, the password change functionality can be abused to change the account password to a new value chosen by the attacker, which enables account takeover. This provides illegitimate access to confidential information like shipping addresses and credit card numbers.

Network Attacker. The network attacker is now a common web security threat to deal with, due to the widespread adoption of WiFi networks. Observe that all the attacks we discussed are effective even under the (optimistic) assumption that users navigate just low-profile websites over untrusted WiFi. The network attacker can perform session hijacking on 7 websites and session fixation on 3 websites, thus taking full control of the victim's session. Moreover, the network attacker can exploit CSRF vulnerabilities on 4 websites: 3 of them already suffer from a more serious security flaw like session hijacking, while www.prezi.com can only be targeted by means of CSRF. It is worth noticing that the network attacker can entirely bypass CSRF protection there and abuse all the website functionality, since the implementation of the defense mechanism itself is flawed.

Related-Domain Attacker. The related-domain attacker is the strongest attacker in our pool on the 20 tested websites, in particular due to her ability of performing session hijacking on 15 websites. One might argue that this was expected, given the common practice of building sessions on top of domain cookies, and that the related-domain attacker is not a realistic threat, given that most websites are not leasing sub-domains to untrusted users and organizations. Although we acknowledge that we cannot tell for sure whether the related-domain attacker is part of the threat model of the tested websites, we point out that recent work highlighted the dangers of related domains for session security [12]. In particular, the authors showed that the high number of sub-domains in popular websites amplifies the attack surface against web sessions, because it is common to identify TLS vulnerabilities in at least one of these hosts.

In our work, we further substantiate the threats posed by the related-domain attacker. By crawling the Certificate Transparency logs, we observed that 6 out of the 20 tested websites have more than 100 sub-domains and that the median number of sub-domains is 26, i.e., the attack surface coming from related domains is large. Notice that these numbers represent a lower bound of the number of existing sub-domains and that 18 out of the 20 websites use a wildcard HTTPS certificate, which means that the number of their sub-domains can grow arbitrarily large. Most importantly, we analyzed all the 20 websites with the tool developed in [12] to identify TLS vulnerabilities in any of their sub-domains, exposing 5 vulnerable websites: www.adobe.com, www.aol.com, www.expedia.com, www.groupon.com and www.yandex.com. Since the detected TLS vulnerabilities affect the confidentiality of domain cookies, we note that at least these 5 websites are at concrete risk of session hijacking (see Table 4).

5.4 Responsible Disclosure

We responsibly disclosed all the identified vulnerabilities exploitable by the web attacker and the network attacker to the respective website owners or security teams. We also reported all the sub-domains suffering from TLS vulnerabilities according to the tool developed in [12], which may allow an attacker with control of the network traffic to play the role of the related-domain attacker.

We also collected a few responses to our responsible disclosure. In particular, www.imgur.com and www.quora.com acknowledged the reported vulnerabilities as valid through their bug bounty programs. Though none of our reports was deemed invalid, which confirms the effectiveness of Dredd, we unfortunately noticed that developers are not always aware of the security implications of the reported vulnerabilities or do not consider security as a priority. For example, we observed that several bug bounty programs consider out of scope the following security issues: lack of cookie security attributes, CSRF, misconfiguration of TLS. However, these vulnerabilities have already been exploited multiple times, often with severe security consequences: for example, CSRF has recently been proved exploitable for purchase hijacking, payment hijacking and account takeover on existing websites [10]. We hope that the security awareness of web developers will increase in the next future as a result of recent security analyses of existing websites, including the present one.

6 Related Work

Web session security is a popular research area, which received extensive attention from the security community: we refer to [13] for a recent survey.

Session hijacking is a major threat for web sessions, yet no rigorous testing strategy for it has been proposed so far. However, several protection mechanisms have been designed, including one-time cookies [16], origin-bound certificates [17] and a variety of browser extensions which protect session cookies [8,24,31]. A variant of the attack called *sub-session hijacking* has also been studied [14].

Session fixation has been thoroughly studied in previous work, which also proposed a methodology to identify room for potential attacks [19]. Unfortunately, the proposed approach assumes the knowledge of the full set of the session cookies and might produce false positives, since it is based on manual code inspection and does not take cookie integrity into account.

Robust defenses against CSRF have been first presented in [4]. Although the security analysis therein is thorough and exhaustive, it is also quite outdated: when the paper was published, HSTS, cookie prefixes and same-site cookies were not available yet, and the threats posed by related-domain attackers were still unknown [6]. A testing strategy for CSRF vulnerabilities has been first proposed in [30]. Our strategy extends this work to cover related-domain attackers and network attackers, which requires one to reason about their ability to circumvent the protection granted by stateless anti-CSRF tokens.

Deemon [26] is a dynamic analysis tool which can be used to identify CSRF vulnerabilities in PHP code. Deemon is a language-based tool, which only works on PHP and requires access to the web application code, while our testing strategies are language-independent and black-box. Mitch [10] is a black-box analysis tool for CSRF vulnerabilities based on machine learning and syntactic heuristics on HTTP responses, but its threat model only considers the web attacker.

Different flavours of web session integrity have been already discussed and formalized in the literature [1,9,11,20]. Notable practical papers on web session integrity include [29] and [35], which showed the dangers posed by the lack of cookie confidentiality and integrity on existing popular websites.

Finally, it is worth noticing that *model-based* testing has been proposed for web application security in a number of papers [7,27,28]. This approach operates on a formal model of the web application, rather than on its implementation. As such, it can leverage tools like model-checkers to perform a systematic exploration of the web application state space, but it requires the creation of formal web application models. This is typically a time-consuming and complex task, which does not match the expertise of most web developers.

7   Conclusion

We discussed session integrity as a necessary property for web session security, which is violated by classic attacks like session hijacking, session fixation and cross-site request forgery. We then proposed black-box testing strategies to detect session integrity flaws and we implemented these strategies in a browser extension called Dredd to semi-automate the testing process. Finally, we used Dredd to expose a significant number of vulnerabilities in popular websites from the Alexa ranking. Our work provides yet another proof of the security challenges of web session implementations: though all the attacks we considered are well-known, the complexity of the web platform and its threat model makes subtle security issues hard to detect. We showed that Dredd is a useful tool to support web developers in a systematic security assessment, which identifies exploitable vulnerabilities without requiring a deep understanding of the web application.

As future work, we plan to further automatize the security testing process to extend its coverage and enlarge the scope of our analysis to a larger number of websites, so as to get a better understanding of session security on the current Web. Moreover, we also would like to devise new testing strategies to cover more attacks, like login CSRF and cookie forcing [13].

Acknowledgements. We would like to thank Alessandro Busatto for contributing to an early stage of the project.

References

1. Akhawe, D., Barth, A., Lam, P.E., Mitchell, J.C., Song, D.: Towards a formal foundation of web security. In: Proceedings of the 23rd IEEE Computer Security Foundations Symposium, CSF 2010, pp. 290–304 (2010)

2. Barth, A.: HTTP state management mechanism (2011). http://tools.ietf.org/html/rfc6265
3. Barth, A.: The web origin concept (2011). http://tools.ietf.org/html/rfc6454
4. Barth, A., Jackson, C., Mitchell, J.C.: Robust defenses for cross-site request forgery. In: Proceedings of the 15th ACM Conference on Computer and Communications Security, CCS 2008, pp. 75–88 (2008)
5. Bau, J., Bursztein, E., Gupta, D., Mitchell, J.C.: State of the art: automated black-box web application vulnerability testing. In: 31st IEEE Symposium on Security and Privacy, S&P 2010, Berleley/Oakland, California, USA, 16–19 May 2010, pp. 332–345 (2010)
6. Bortz, A., Barth, A., Czeskis, A.: Origin cookies: session integrity for web applications. In: Web 2.0 Security and Privacy Workshop (W2SP 2011) (2011)
7. Büchler, M., Oudinet, J., Pretschner, A.: SPaCiTE - web application testing engine. In: Fifth IEEE International Conference on Software Testing, Verification and Validation, ICST 2012, Montreal, QC, Canada, 17–21 April 2012, pp. 858–859 (2012)
8. Bugliesi, M., Calzavara, S., Focardi, R., Khan, W.: CookiExt: patching the browser against session hijacking attacks. J. Comput. Secur. **23**(4), 509–537 (2015)
9. Bugliesi, M., Calzavara, S., Focardi, R., Khan, W., Tempesta, M.: Provably sound browser-based enforcement of web session integrity. In: Proceedings of the IEEE 27th Computer Security Foundations Symposium, CSF 2014, pp. 366–380 (2014)
10. Calzavara, S., Conti, M., Focardi, R., Rabitti, A., Tolomei, G.: Mitch: a machine learning approach to the black-box detection of CSRF vulnerabilities. In: IEEE European Symposium on Security and Privacy (2019)
11. Calzavara, S., Focardi, R., Grimm, N., Maffei, M.: Micro-policies for web session security. In: IEEE 29th Computer Security Foundations Symposium, CSF 2016, Lisbon, Portugal, 27 June–1 July 2016, pp. 179–193 (2016)
12. Calzavara, S., Focardi, R., Nemec, M., Rabitti, A., Squarcina, M.: Postcards from the post-HTTP world: amplification of HTTPS vulnerabilities in the web ecosystem. In: IEEE Symposium on Security and Privacy (2019)
13. Calzavara, S., Focardi, R., Squarcina, M., Tempesta, M.: Surviving the web: a journey into web session security. ACM Comput. Surv. **50**, 13 (2017)
14. Calzavara, S., Rabitti, A., Bugliesi, M.: Sub-session hijacking on the web: root causes and prevention. J. Comput. Secur. **27**(2), 233–257 (2019)
15. Calzavara, S., Tolomei, G., Casini, A., Bugliesi, M., Orlando, S.: A supervised learning approach to protect client authentication on the web. TWEB **9**(3), 15:1–15:30 (2015)
16. Dacosta, I., Chakradeo, S., Ahamad, M., Traynor, P.: One-time cookies: preventing session hijacking attacks with stateless authentication tokens. ACM Trans. Internet Technol. **12**(1), 1–24 (2012)
17. Dietz, M., Czeskis, A., Balfanz, D., Wallach, D.S.: Origin-bound certificates: a fresh approach to strong client authentication for the web. In: Proceedings of the 21th USENIX Security Symposium, USENIX 2012, pp. 317–331 (2012)
18. Hodges, J., Jackson, C., Barth, A.: HTTP Strict Transport Security (HSTS) (2012). http://tools.ietf.org/html/rfc6797
19. Johns, M., Braun, B., Schrank, M., Posegga, J.: Reliable protection against session fixation attacks. In: Proceedings of the 26th ACM Symposium on Applied Computing, SAC 2011, pp. 1531–1537 (2011)
20. Khan, W., Calzavara, S., Bugliesi, M., De Groef, W., Piessens, F.: Client side web session integrity as a non-interference property. In: Prakash, A., Shyamasundar, R. (eds.) ICISS 2014. LNCS, vol. 8880, pp. 89–108. Springer, Cham (2014). https://doi.org/10.1007/978-3-319-13841-1_6

21. Kranch, M., Bonneau, J.: Upgrading HTTPS in mid-air: an empirical study of strict transport security and key pinning. In: 22nd Annual Network and Distributed System Security Symposium, NDSS 2015, San Diego, California, USA, 8–11 February 2015 (2015)

22. Mozilla: Same-Origin Policy (2015). http://developer.mozilla.org/en-US/docs/Web/Security/Same-origin_policy

23. Mundada, Y., Feamster, N., Krishnamurthy, B.: Half-baked cookies: hardening cookie-based authentication for the modern web. In: Proceedings of the 11th ACM on Asia Conference on Computer and Communications Security, AsiaCCS 2016, Xi'an, China, 30 May–3 June 2016, pp. 675–685 (2016)

24. Nikiforakis, N., Meert, W., Younan, Y., Johns, M., Joosen, W.: SessionShield: lightweight protection against session hijacking. In: Erlingsson, Ú., Wieringa, R., Zannone, N. (eds.) ESSoS 2011. LNCS, vol. 6542, pp. 87–100. Springer, Heidelberg (2011). https://doi.org/10.1007/978-3-642-19125-1_7

25. OWASP: OWASP Testing Guide (2016). https://www.owasp.org/index.php/OWASP_Testing_Guide_v4_Table_of_Contents

26. Pellegrino, G., Johns, M., Koch, S., Backes, M., Rossow, C.: Deemon: detecting CSRF with dynamic analysis and property graphs. In: Proceedings of the 2017 ACM SIGSAC Conference on Computer and Communications Security, CCS 2017, Dallas, TX, USA, 30 October–03 November 2017, pp. 1757–1771 (2017)

27. Peroli, M., Meo, F.D., Viganò, L., Guardini, D.: MobSTer: a model-based security testing framework for web applications. Softw. Test. Verif. Reliab. **28**(8), e1685 (2018)

28. Rocchetto, M., Ochoa, M., Torabi Dashti, M.: Model-based detection of CSRF. In: Cuppens-Boulahia, N., Cuppens, F., Jajodia, S., Abou El Kalam, A., Sans, T. (eds.) SEC 2014. IAICT, vol. 428, pp. 30–43. Springer, Heidelberg (2014). https://doi.org/10.1007/978-3-642-55415-5_3

29. Sivakorn, S., Polakis, I., Keromytis, A.D.: The cracked cookie jar: HTTP cookie hijacking and the exposure of private information. In: IEEE Symposium on Security and Privacy, SP 2016, San Jose, CA, USA, 22–26 May 2016, pp. 724–742 (2016)

30. Sudhodanan, A., Carbone, R., Compagna, L., Dolgin, N., Armando, A., Morelli, U.: Large-scale analysis & detection of authentication cross-site request forgeries. In: 2017 IEEE European Symposium on Security and Privacy, EuroS&P 2017, Paris, France, 26–28 April 2017, pp. 350–365 (2017)

31. Tang, S., Dautenhahn, N., King, S.T.: Fortifying web-based applications automatically. In: Proceedings of the 18th ACM Conference on Computer and Communications Security, CCS 2011, pp. 615–626 (2011)

32. West, M.: Cookie prefixes (2016). https://tools.ietf.org/html/draft-ietf-httpbis-cookie-prefixes-00

33. West, M.: Strict secure cookies (2016). https://tools.ietf.org/html/draft-ietf-httpbis-cookie-alone-01

34. West, M., Goodwin, M.: Same-site cookies (2016). https://tools.ietf.org/id/draft-ietf-httpbis-cookie-same-site-00.txt

35. Zheng, X., et al.: Cookies lack integrity: real-world implications. In: Proceedings of the 24th USENIX Security Symposium, USENIX 2015, pp. 707–721 (2015)

Author Index

Albrecht, Martin R. II-151
Alcaraz, Cristina II-263
Alrabaee, Saed II-47
Arfelt, Emma I-681
Argyros, George II-565
Avoine, Gildas II-463

Barthe, Gilles I-300
Basin, David I-681
Belaïd, Sonia I-300
Belkin, Alex II-545
Bertino, Elisa I-619, II-387
Bizjak, Manca I-3
Boldyreva, Alexandra I-404
Böttinger, Konstantin I-259
Brendel, Jacqueline II-521
Bugliesi, Michele II-606
Bursuc, Sergiu I-361
Buser, Maxime I-194

Cagnazzo, Matteo II-367
Calzavara, Stefano II-606
Canard, Sébastien II-463
Cassel, Darion II-26
Cassiers, Gaëtan I-300
Chaliasos, Stefanos II-565
Chang, Ee-Chien I-790
Chen, Keke I-41
Chen, Shan I-404
Chen, Xiaofeng II-134, II-304
Cheng, Chi II-504
Choo, Kim-Kwang Raymond I-493
Chu, Dawei II-412
Cidon, Israel II-545
Curran, Max I-556

Dang, Hung I-790
Das, Samir R. I-556
Davidsson, Nicolai II-88
de Guzman, Jaybie A. I-149
Debant, Alexandre I-383
Debbabi, Mourad I-658, II-47, II-239
Debois, Søren I-681

Delaune, Stéphanie I-383
Deng, Robert H. I-619
Ding, Jintai II-504
Duan, Huayi I-22

Emura, Keita II-113

Fang, Chengfang I-66
Ferreira, Loïc II-463
Filimonov, Ihor I-577
Fischlin, Marc II-521
Fleischhacker, Nils II-172
Fong, Philip W. L. II-195
Fouque, Pierre-Alain I-300
Fujioka, Atsushi II-484

Gabert, Stephan I-429
Garmany, Behrad II-68
Gawlik, Robert II-68
Gelernter, Nethanel II-545
Giechaskiel, Ilias I-512
Gondron, Sébastien I-535
Grassi, Lorenzo II-151
Grégoire, Benjamin I-300
Gruss, Daniel I-279
Guarnizo, Juan I-767
Günther, Felix II-521
Guo, Hui I-234
Gupta, Himanshu I-556

Hartman, Jan I-3
Haupert, Vincent I-429
Holz, Thorsten II-68, II-88, II-367
Horne, Ross I-577
Hu, Haibo I-66
Hu, Xuexian II-134
Huang, Yan II-26

Jagielski, Matthew I-404
Jarraya, Yosr I-658, II-239
Jero, Samuel I-404
Jha, Sanjay I-619
Jia, Limin II-26

Jia, Yan   I-638
Jiang, Lijun   I-493
Jing, Jiwu   II-412
Jonker, Hugo   II-586

Kamiya, Norifumi   I-595
Karbab, ElMouatez Billah   II-47
Kasra Kermanshahi, Shabnam   II-322
Kate, Aniket   I-173
Katsumata, Shuichi   II-113
Kawamoto, Yusuke   I-128
Kelkar, Mahimna   I-173
Kerschbaum, Florian   II-344
Kim, Jongkil   I-215
Kinder, Johannes   I-341
Kirchner, Matthias   I-450
Kremer, Steve   I-361
Krumnow, Benjamin   II-586
Kuchta, Veronika   I-703

Lam, Kwok-Yan   II-387
Le Tien, Dat   I-790
Le, Duc V.   I-173
Leach, Kevin   II-217
Lei, Lingguang   II-412
Li, Juanru   I-619
Li, Wenjuan   I-493
Li, Yanchu   II-412
Liang, Xiao   I-556
Lipp, Moritz   I-279
Liu, Dongxi   I-215
Liu, Joseph K.   I-194, II-283, II-322
Liu, Peng   I-638
Liu, Xiaoning   II-439
Liu, Zhen   I-726
Lopez, Javier   II-263
Lovisotto, Giulio   I-471
Lu, Kangjie   II-3

Ma, Jianfeng   II-134
Ma, Siqi   I-619
Majumdar, Suryadipta   II-239
Malavolta, Giulio   II-172
Manulis, Mark   II-263
Marc, Tilen   I-3
Martin, Jason   I-87
Martinovic, Ivan   I-471
Masters, Jon   I-279
Mauw, Sjouke   I-577
Meng, Weizhi   I-493

Metaxopoulos, George   II-565
Miller, Loïc   I-107
Minematsu, Kazuhiko   I-595
Mitchell, Duncan   I-341
Mitropoulos, Dimitris   II-565
Mödersheim, Sebastian   I-535
Modic, Jolanda   I-3
Mohammady, Meisam   II-239
Murakami, Takao   I-128

Nagai, Akira   II-484
Nepal, Surya   I-619, II-322
Nguyen, Khoa   I-726
Nita-Rotaru, Cristina   I-404
Novakovic, Chris   I-319

Okhravi, Hamed   I-87
Oqaily, Alaa   II-239
Oqaily, Momen   I-658
Ostry, Diethelm   I-619

Pakki, Aditya   II-3
Pandey, Omkant   I-556
Parker, David   I-319
Pawlowski, Andre   II-88
Pelsser, Cristel   I-107
Pereira, Henrique G. G.   II-195
Perrin, Léo   II-151
Phuong, Tran Viet Xuan   I-215
Pieprzyk, Josef   II-283
Pohlmann, Norbert   II-367
Pourzandi, Makan   I-658, II-239

Qin, Yue   II-504
Quiring, Erwin   I-450

Rabitti, Alvise   II-606
Ragazzo, Alessio   II-606
Ramacher, Sebastian   II-151
Rao, Fang-Yu   II-387
Rasmussen, Kasper B.   I-512
Rechberger, Christian   II-151
Rieck, Konrad   I-450
Rotaru, Dragos   II-151
Roy, Arnab   II-151
Rubio, Juan E.   II-263

Sakzad, Amin   I-194
Schofnegger, Markus   II-151

Schröder, Dominique   II-172
Schütte, Julian   I-747
Schwarz, Michael   I-279
Schwarzl, Martin   I-279
Seneviratne, Aruna   I-149
Shao, Jun   II-283
Sharma, Sagar   I-41
Shi, Jie   I-66
Skowyra, Richard   I-87
Smith, Zach   I-577
Spensky, Chad   I-87
Sperl, Philip   I-259
Standaert, Francois-Xavier   I-300
Steinfeld, Ron   I-194, II-322
Stoffel, Martin   II-68
Stopar, Miha   I-3
Su, Chunhua   I-493
Su, Yaping   II-304
Sun, Kun   II-412
Sun, Shi-Feng   I-194, II-283
Susilo, Willy   I-215
Suzuki, Koutarou   II-484
Szalachowski, Pawel   I-767

Tabiban, Azadeh   II-239
Thilakarathna, Kanchana   I-149
Tomida, Junichi   II-484
Tueno, Anselme   II-344
Turner, Henry   I-471

Vlot, Gabry   II-586

Wang, Cong   I-22
Wang, Guojun   II-217
Wang, Huaxiong   I-726

Wang, Jianfeng   II-134, II-304
Wang, Lingyu   I-658, II-47, II-239
Wang, Yuewu   II-412
Wang, Yunling   II-304
Ward, Bryan C.   I-87
Watanabe, Yohei   II-113
Wei, Jianghong   II-134
Weimer, Westley   II-217
Weiss, Konrad   I-747
Wiedling, Cyrille   I-383
Wong, Duncan S.   I-726
Wu, Qiushi   II-3

Xia, Mingyuan   I-234
Xiao, Jidong   II-217
Xu, Jing   I-234

Yang, Guomin   I-215, I-726
Yao, Yao   I-638
Ye, Qingqing   I-66
Yi, Xun   II-387, II-439

Zhang, Fengwei   II-217
Zhang, Mengyuan   I-658
Zhang, Youqian   I-512
Zhang, Yuqing   I-638
Zhang, Zhenfeng   I-234
Zhang, Zhongjun   II-304
Zheng, Huadi   I-66
Zheng, Yifeng   I-22
Zhou, Lei   II-217
Zhou, Wei   I-638
Zhu, Lipeng   I-638
Zolotavkin, Yevhen   I-703
Zuo, Cong   II-283

Printed in the United States
By Bookmasters